T0180772

Lecture Notes of the Institute for Computer Sciences, Social Informatics and Telecommunications Engineering 369

More information about this series at http://www.springer.com/series/8197

Houbing Song · Dingde Jiang (Eds.)

Simulation Tools and Techniques

12th EAI International Conference, SIMUtools 2020
Guiyang, China, August 28–29, 2020
Proceedings, Part I

 Springer

Editors
Houbing Song (iD)
Embry-Riddle Aeronautical University
Daytona Beach, FL, USA

Dingde Jiang (iD)
School of Astronautics and Aeronautic
UESTC
Chengdu, China

ISSN 1867-8211   ISSN 1867-822X (electronic)
Lecture Notes of the Institute for Computer Sciences, Social Informatics
and Telecommunications Engineering
ISBN 978-3-030-72791-8   ISBN 978-3-030-72792-5 (eBook)
https://doi.org/10.1007/978-3-030-72792-5

This Springer imprint is published by the registered company Springer Nature Switzerland AG
The registered company address is: Gewerbestrasse 11, 6330 Cham, Switzerland

Preface

We are delighted to introduce the proceedings of the twelfth edition of the European Alliance for Innovation (EAI) International Conference on Simulation Tools and Techniques (SIMUTools). The conference focuses on a broad range of research challenges in the field of simulation, modeling and analysis, addressing current and future trends in simulation techniques, models, practices and software. The conference is dedicated to fostering interdisciplinary collaborative research in these areas and across a wide spectrum of application domains.

The technical program of SIMUTools 2020 consisted of 125 full papers. Coordination with the steering chair, Imrich Chlamtac, was essential for the success of the conference. We sincerely appreciate his constant support and guidance. It was also a great pleasure to work with such an excellent organizing committee team for their hard work in organizing and supporting the conference. In particular, the Technical Program Committee completed the peer-review process of technical papers and made a high-quality technical program. We are also grateful to the Conference Manager, Karolína Marcinová, for her support and to all the authors who submitted their papers to the SIMUTools 2020 conference.

We strongly believe that the SIMUTools conference provides a good forum for all researchers, developers and practitioners to discuss all scientific and technological aspects that are relevant to simulation tools and techniques. We also expect that future SIMUTools conferences will be as successful and stimulating, as indicated by the contributions presented in this volume.

March 2021

Houbing Song
Dingde Jiang

Organization

Steering Committee

Chair

Imrich Chlamtac   Bruno Kessler Professor, University of Trento, Italy

Organizing Committee

General Chair

Dingde Jiang   University of Electronic Science and Technology
of China, China

General Co-chair

Houbing Song   Embry-Riddle Aeronautical University, USA

Technical Program Committee Co-chairs

Lei Shi   Institute of Technology Carlow, Ireland
Sheng Qi   University of Electronic Science and Technology
of China, China
Binbing Hou   Louisiana State University, USA
Chenggang Li   Guizhou University of Finance and Economics, China
Bangtao Zhou   University of Electronic Science and Technology
of China, China

Publicity and Social Media Co-chairs

Litao Zhang   Zhengzhou Institute of Aeronautical Industry
Management, China
Zhihao Wang   University of Electronic Science and Technology
of China, China
Jingyang Zhang   University of Electronic Science and Technology
of China, China

Workshops Co-chairs

Zhi Zhu   National University of Defense Technology, China
Yihang Zhang   University of Electronic Science and Technology
of China, China
Zhibo Zhang   University of Electronic Science and Technology
of China, China
Wenbo Yan   University of Electronic Science and Technology
of China, China

Sponsorship and Exhibits Co-chairs

Changsheng Zhang   Northeastern University, China
Yuwen Wang   University of Electronic Science and Technology
                          of China, China

Publications Co-chairs

Qingshan Wang   Hefei University of Technology, China
Feng Wang   University of Electronic Science and Technology
                          of China, China

Panels Chairs

Lei Miao   Middle Tennessee State University, Murfreesboro,
                          USA
Feilong He   University of Electronic Science and Technology
                          of China, China

Tutorials Chairs

Peiying Zhang   China University of Petroleum, China
Li Xue   University of Electronic Science and Technology
                          of China, China

Demos Chairs

Minhong Sun   Hangzhou Dianzi University, China
Lisha Cheng   University of Electronic Science and Technology
                          of China, China

Posters and PhD Track Co-chairs

Lei Chen   Xuzhou University of Technology, China
JunYang Zhang   University of Electronic Science and Technology
                          of China, China

Web Chairs

Xiongzi Ge   NetApp, Advanced Technology Group, USA
Liuwei Huo   Northeastern University, China
Jian Jin   University of Electronic Science and Technology
                          of China, China

Local Co-chairs

Mingsen Deng   Guizhou University of Finance and Economics, China
Zhihao Wang   University of Electronic Science and Technology
                          of China, China
Hujun Shen   Guizhou Education University, China

Technical Program Committee

Dingde Jiang	University of Electronic Science and Technology of China, China
Litao Zhang	Zhengzhou University of Aeronautics, China
Lei Shi	Institute of Technology Carlow, Ireland
Sheng Qi	University of Electronic Science and Technology of China, China
Lei Chen	Xuzhou University of Technology, China
Bangtao Zhou	University of Electronic Science and Technology of China, China
Giovanni Stea	University of Pisa, Italy
Lorenzo Donatiello	University of Bologna, Italy
Andrea D'Ambrogio	University of Rome Tor Vergata, Italy
Christian Engelmann	Oak Ridge National Laboratory, USA
Kevin Jin	Illinois Institute of Technology, USA
Gary Tan	National University of Singapore, Singapore
Jiaqi Yan	Microsoft, USA
James Byrne	Dublin City University, Ireland
Jan Himmelspach	Nordakademie University of Applied Sciences, Germany
Johannes Lüthi	University of Applied Sciences Kufstein, Austria
Linbo Luo	Xidian University, China
Stephan Eidenbenz	Los Alamos National Laboratory, USA
Yiping Yao	National University of Defense Technology, China
Francesco Quaglia	University of Rome Tor Vergata, Italy
Zongwei Luo	Southern University of Science and Technology, China

Technical Program Committee

Contents – Part I

Contents – Part II

A Secure and Trustable Access Method of Power Business in 5G Networks

Huan Li[1]([✉]), Fanbo Meng[2], Dongdong Wang[2], and Zhibin Yang[1]

[1] Electric Power Research Institute of State Grid Liaoning Electric Power Supply Co., Ltd., Shenyang 110006, China
lihuan213@sina.com
[2] State Grid Liaoning Electric Power Supply Co., Ltd, Shenyang 110004, China

Abstract. The 5G power network has gradually adopted mobile terminal access to access the network to manage business. With the continuous expansion of access terminal scale, if the attacker impersonates the terminal or hijack the terminal to attack the master server, it will cause serious consequences. Therefore, this paper proposes a lightweight and efficient terminal secure and trustable access method in 5G power business network. Considering the core idea of security stratification and network special, we design a three-layer security access architecture to ensure the security of terminals in the access process and data protection process. Then, we propose a lightweight secure certification method for large-scale terminal accessing power network. The simulation results show that the proposed method can reduce the communication overhead and provide good security when massive terminals accessing.

Keywords: 5G network · Power business · Secure and trustable access · Communication overhead

1 Introduction

With the construction of smart grid, the information confidentiality, integrity and availability of power grid enterprise have higher requirements [1–3]. At present, the main businesses of power grid, like production, marketing, materials, emergency command, mobile office, have gradually adopted mobile terminals with wireless accessing. The data exchange is conducted through 5G wireless access technology and internal and external networks, and the number of access terminals has continued rapid growth. Based on above, how to ensure that all kinds of decentralized mobile terminals can be safely connected to the smart grid network, and how to monitor and audit the access terminals to realize the confidentiality and controllability in the process of information transmission, has become the urgent problem to be considered and solved with information construction [4–6]. In the future network, with the continuous expansion of access terminal scale, the complexity of access environment and the diversification of access methods, the security, confidentiality and controllability of all kinds of information transmission process will face more severe challenges. The security risks of power grid mainly exist

© ICST Institute for Computer Sciences, Social Informatics and Telecommunications Engineering 2021
Published by Springer Nature Switzerland AG 2021. All Rights Reserved
H. Song and D. Jiang (Eds.): SIMUtools 2020, LNICST 369, pp. 1–11, 2021.
https://doi.org/10.1007/978-3-030-72792-5_1

in terminal, transmission channel and application system. Among them, terminal risks mainly include physical security and data storage security, system vulnerabilities, illegal software installation, equipment non-security management, illegal use risks, etc. The risk of transmission channel includes illegal information interception and tampering and illegal terminal access through private network channel [7–10]. Application system risks mainly include unauthorized access, sensitive data leakage and illegal attacks on the system.

The complete business access process is shown in Fig. 1. Specifically, large-scale power terminal access under 5G wireless communication has the following security access problems:

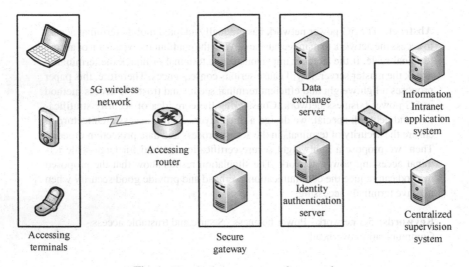

Fig. 1. Terminal secure access framework.

1) **Illegal terminal access.** The power communication network has more and more intelligent terminals accessing. The network security protection boundaries is expended, so that the terminal access requirements for various business are flexible, which has security risks of illegal access [11, 12]. An attacker can counterfeit illegal terminal or taking control terminal, making it a springboard to attack main servers and issue fault information. Once entering the network system, it will be seen as credible user access to the main resources for illegal operation [13, 14], thus causing a wider range of security threats.

2) **Fake master server control.** The main server of power communication network mainly carry out the application functions such as data acquisition and monitoring and analysis in real time. As the core component of intelligent power business network, it will send the control instruction to the intelligent terminals for production operations, dispatching operation and accident repair work to provide business support and direct service [15, 16]. If an attacker impersonates a master server and sends

malicious control instructions to intelligent terminals, causing them to make erroneous actions, there will be incalculable consequences for the entire power system and national infrastructure.

3) **Communication data breach.** Real-time data and operations between the whole system of smart power network and external users are becoming more and more intensive. Data acquisition, storage, communication and processing operation mode has been different from the past distribution network. As the boundaries of data communication networks expand, the risk of data being broken increases greatly. In power communication system, wireless data transmission is used between master server and terminals, including control data and real-time monitoring data. Once the data is tampered, resulting in the destruction of integrity, the intelligent distribution network terminal may make wrong actions, and the intelligent distribution network server may make wrong decisions [16, 17].

4) **Multiple cyber-attacks.** The communication system of intelligent power network has a mixture of communication modes, which can be divided into wireless communication and wired communication. The mixed communication mode makes the power communication system vulnerable to all kinds of communication attacks, such as denial of service attack, replay attack, data injection attack, man-in-the-middle attack and so on [18–20]. For example, a denial-of-service attack on the accessing terminals may make it impossible to get control instructions from the master server in a timely manner, triggering abnormal control instruction settings or business failures, thus greatly reducing the reliability and security of power supply.

Considering the above risks in the 5G power business network, this paper proposes a mobile terminal security access architecture according to the security requirements of the network. The core idea is security stratification and network exclusive utilization. We analyze the mobile applications of power networks and the safety risks of mobile terminals, and design a secure access method according to the proposed architecture to realize terminal access security. Then, considering limitation of the calculation capacity and the communication resources, we propose a lightweight safe access method MTS for 5G power business network.

The rest of this paper is arranged as follows. Section II analyze the access risks of terminals and presents the secure access architecture. Section III propose a lightweight safe access method MTS for 5G power business network. Section IV displays the simulation results and analysis. We then conclude our work in Section V.

2 System Architecture

In order to ensure the access security of power business network, we proposes an intelligent terminal security access architecture, which takes security stratification and network exclusive utilization as the core idea, as shown in Fig. 2. Security stratification refers to the mobile terminal access security protection. The whole process is divided into security terminal layer, security access and transmission layer and application interface layer. Network exclusive utilization refers to the network involved is divided into mobile private network, border security access network and internal business private network, each network to implement strict access control. The proposed architecture will meet the requirements of data closed-loop secure transmission, prevent information leakage and illegal access. The purpose of the architecture is to protect the integrity of information and fine-grained access control, so as to ensure the secure access of the wireless mobile terminals.

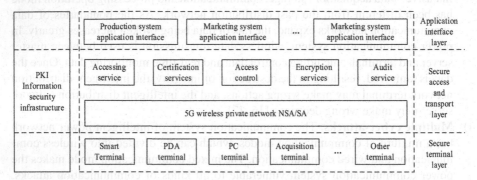

Fig. 2. Secure accessing architecture of power business networks.

As shown in the figure, the whole terminal security access architecture for power business network is divided into three layers:

Terminal Access Layer: According to the application of mobile terminals in power business networks, the terminal access layer mainly includes computer, PDA, smart phone and wireless collection terminal, etc. For these terminals, secure SIM/UIM card, security control software, security inspection module and security communication module are used to ensure the terminal security, improve the reliability of authentication, ensure data transmission security, and prevent the terminal from being counterfeits and data leakage. At the same time, the corresponding management software is installed to standardize the terminal operation to avoid malicious software applications, prevent illegal mobile terminal access.

Secure Transport Layer: The secure transport layer mainly provides the secure access service for all kinds of terminals, including the security of wireless channel transmission and the secure data exchange. Among them, the wireless transmission channel adopts the wireless private network to ensure the integrity and security of data in the transmission process. Between the power business network and the wireless transmission channel, it can set up a secure access area for security isolation and access. Secure transport layer, as the core part of terminal secure access, achieve secure access, identity authentication, data filtering and centralized supervision and other functions. The transport layer transmits various access control data efficiently through the high-speed channels. What's more, it provides access, authentication, access control, encryption, proxy, exchange, filtering, supervision and other security services through various functional components. It coordinates the whole process of secure access of various terminals, and makes all functional components of the system cooperate and work together to form a unified power business network.

Application Interface Layer: The application interface layer is mainly used to realize the application data interface between the security access layer and the production management, marketing management, material management and other systems. t can manage the security data transmitted between the terminal and the master server system. Application services customize security policies through the application interface layer, authorize specific terminal access, and conduct two-way security data interaction.

The above architecture determines each security authentication process in the terminal access process from the system level. Next, we propose a lightweight terminal security access method MTS, suitable for large-scale wireless terminal access in power business network.

3 Secure Access Method

In order to achieve large-scale and lightweight terminal secure access, it is necessary to improve the traditional asymmetric encryption method and reduce the algorithm complexity. At the same time, considering the mobility of the power grid terminal, the primary server and terminal need to maintain a unique identity of mutual authentication [21, 22]. The primary server does not need to re-register the newly accessed terminal if it has been securely registered, thus reducing the overall algorithm complexity. Specifically, the process of the proposed MTS method is as follows.

The initialization algorithm is implemented by the mains server platform. By inputting security parameters of λ bit length, the algorithm outputs the common parameter PB, which is shared among all participating entities in the scheme, specifically including the following steps:

(1) The registry of main server platform selects cyclic group G and large integer group Z_q^* of order q through the security parameters of λ bit length, and the generation element of the group is g. Different Hash functions are selected:

$$H_0 : G \times G \to Z_q^* \tag{1}$$

(2) Two safety parameters n and k are randomly selected. Calculate and generate two prime numbers p and m with length of n/k bits from the group, which satisfy the following requirements:

$$\gcd((p-1), (m-1)) = 2 \tag{2}$$

Then, calculate $N = p^{(k-1)} \times m$. In the power business network, each terminal equipment TU and server MS has its unique identification information ID_{TU} and ID_{MS}, and the terminal equipment sends access request to the server by virtue of its unique identification information ID_{TU}.

(3) The cloud platform first generates a set of pseudo-random numbers $a_1, a_2, \ldots a_z, \in Z_p^*$ randomly through the pseudo-random function generator. Then it generates public key information $MK_{TU} = \{MK_{TU,1}, MK_{TU,i} \cdots, MK_{TU,z}\}$ according to the personal information ID_{TU} provided by the terminal, where $MK_{TU,i} = g^{a_i}$. Further, it generates anonymous identifying data $PID_{TU} = \{PID_{TU,1}, PID_{TU,i}, \ldots, PID_{TU,z}\}$,

where $PID_{TU,i} = H_0((ID_{TU}||ID_{MS}) \oplus MK_{TU,i})$. In this way, the real identity information of the terminal device is hidden in the anonymous identity.

(4) Formula (3) is used to calculate and generate two secret values K_{TU} and K_{MS}. Then find the integer d by traversal, and $d = K_{TU}$ mod $(p-1) = K_{MS}$ mod $(m-1)$. Then, calculate $e = d^{-1}$ mod $(\phi(N))$. The registry of the main server returns $<MK_{TU}, PID_{TU}, K_{TU}>$ to the terminal device over the secure channel.

$$\begin{cases} \gcd(K_{EU}, (p-1)) = 1 \\ \gcd(K_{ES}, (m-1)) = 1 \\ K_{EU} = K_{ES} \text{ mod } (2) \end{cases} \tag{3}$$

(5) The cloud platform generates the anonymous identity polynomial $acc(x)$ of the terminal device:

$$acc(x) = g^{\prod\limits_{x \in PID_{TU}} (x - PID_{TU,j})} \tag{4}$$

The coefficients of the polynomial can be represented by the set $\left\{ g^1, g^s, g^{s^2}, \ldots, g^z \right\}$. The anonymous information set $\langle Set\_PID, K_{MS} \rangle$ of registered terminal devices is signed with the private key of the main server:

$$\text{Sign}_{K_{priv}}\left(\text{Enc}_{PK_{MS}}(Set\_PID, K_{MS})\right) \tag{5}$$

When the terminal accesses, the private key is used to decrypt and the identity information of the registered terminal device is stored locally.

The authentication phase begins when the registered terminal device TU accesses the master server MS. When the terminal device TU needs to access the master server node MS in that location, generally, the terminal device does not know the identity information of the master server node, but only sends a request to the specific master server [23, 24]. The process is divided into the following 4 steps:

(1) $TU \rightarrow MS$: The terminal device randomly selects $(PK_{TU,i}, PID_{TU,i}, SK_{TU,i})$ from $\{PK_{TU}, PID_{TU}, SK_{TU}\}$. Then, it broadcasts message $<$HelloMS, $PID_{TU}, T_i>$, where T_i is the current time stamp.

(2) $MS \rightarrow TU$: After the master server receives the access request, it verifies whether the time stamp T_i is expired and whether the terminal device has been registered through Formula (6):

$$\begin{cases} acc(PID_{TU,i}) = \prod\limits_{j=1}^{z} g^{s^j \cdot PD_{TU,i}^j} = 1 \\ \text{verify}(T - T_i) \leq \Delta T \end{cases} \tag{6}$$

If the verification is passed, it returns $\{ID_{MS}, PID_{TU,i}, T_i\}$ to the terminal device.

(3) $TU \rightarrow MS$: The terminal device first verifies whether the time stamp T_i is expired, then verifies the identification correctness of the primary server through formula (7).

$$\begin{cases} \text{Verify}\left(H_0((ID_{TU}||ID_{MS}) \oplus MK_{TU,i}) = PID_{TU,i}\right) \\ cha = (c + T_i + ID_{MS})^e \text{ mod } (N) \end{cases} \tag{7}$$

Then, randomly selects $c \in Z_p^*$ to generate cha of challenge report, and then sends $<cha, T_i>$ to the main server.

(4) $MS \rightarrow TU$: After the master server receives the challenge message, it first verifies whether the time stamp T_i is expired, then recovers the challenge value c' sent by the terminal device by calculating $cha^{K_{ES}}$ mod (q), and finally calculates the reply message:

$$res = \left(c' + T_i + PID_{TU,i}\right)^e \bmod (N) \tag{8}$$

Then, send $<res, T_i>$ to the terminal device.

Finally, the terminal verifies that the challenge value obtained is correct. If the verification is successful, the challenge value can be used as the data encryption key for subsequent communication to ensure the security phase and integrity of communication.

In the proposed method, the identity information of terminals stored in the primary server is shared. Therefore, when the terminal connects to different servers and conducts authentication, the two-way authentication between the terminal and the server can still be completed by repeating the above steps, and the same authentication result can be obtained.

4 Simulation Analysis

In this section, the MTS security access scheme designed in the previous chapter is verified through analysis and experiment in terms of availability and security. In terms of availability, simulation experiments are carried out on communication overhead and network connectivity to verify whether the scheme has lower communication overhead and good network connectivity, and the results are analyzed. Then the storage requirements and computing costs are analyzed. Three attack methods are constructed to verify and analyze the security of the scheme [25, 26]. Under two common attack modes, replay attack and node forgery attack, it is proved to have the ability to resist replay attack and node forgery attack through analysis [27]. Simulation experiments show that the scheme can maintain certain network connectivity under denial of service attacks.

4.1 Simulation Environment

This simulation platform is based on the 5G virtual wireless sensor networks environment. The specific environment is one PC with 2.3 GHz CPU and 8 MB RAM. The software environment is 64-bit windows 10 operating system. We use MATLAB software for experiments. We set the area of the wireless sensor network as a 100×100 square, and deployed 100–300 wireless sensor terminals in this area. The characteristics of nodes are the same, such as physical structure unit, communication capability and energy. In the experiment, the communication flow of the nodes is used as the energy factor to measure the nodes, and the nodes all have the function of data fusion. The experimental results are as follows:

4.2 Communication Overhead Evaluation

The study in this paper is not limited to specific power terminals, so the energy consumption model of terminals cannot be obtained. Therefore, this section chooses the consumption of communication traffic and node access time to complete the estimation of communication overhead. The communication overhead is evaluated from the communication traffic consumption, taking Byte as the unit. When the communication traffic is higher, the corresponding terminal energy consumption is higher.

In order to verify the performance of the proposed method, three other terminal access authentication schemes are simulated, namely RCA scheme based on RSA cryptosystem, ECA scheme based on ECC cryptosystem and traditional CA scheme. Under the four schemes, the unified setting node is successfully authenticated for 2 to 14 times. After each successful authentication, the terminal leaves the network and re-initiates the authentication with a delay of 200 ms. The communication traffic consumption under each scheme was recorded respectively, and the simulation results were shown in Fig. 3.

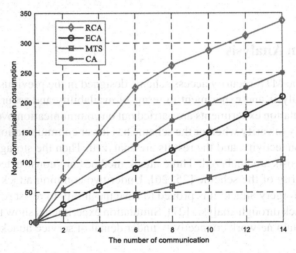

Fig. 3. The comparison of communication consumption of node access.

According to the analysis of simulation results in Fig. 3, the method proposed in this paper has a great advantage in communication consumption because, compared with other schemes, the key of terminal and master server is uniquely stored. In the second access, if the authorized terminal can directly obtain the security access permissions, there is no need to recertification, thus greatly reducing the communication overhead.

Next, we evaluate the communication cost from the access authentication time. The longer the access time is, the higher the corresponding terminal energy consumption will be. Under the four schemes, the unified set node is successfully authenticated for 2 to 14 times. After each successful authentication, the node leaves the network and re-initiates the authentication with a delay of 200 ms. The average access time of each scheme was recorded, and the simulation results were shown in Fig. 4.

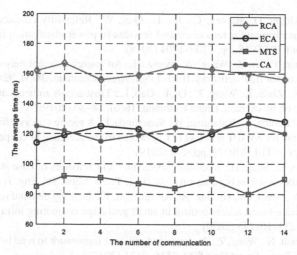

Fig. 4. The comparison of average time of node access.

According to the analysis of simulation results in Fig. 4, the improved MTS in this paper has a great advantage in average access time, because the improved access authentication scheme has a certain advantage in terms of fewer authentication exchange times and the minimum computation required for authentication. To sum up, the MTS method proposed in this paper has some improvements in communication traffic consumption and access time of nodes, which proves that the scheme has a more lightweight improvement in communication overhead.

From the analysis above, we can find that the proposed terminal access scheme can not only realize better secure access efficiency, but also have better performance in communication overhead. This is of great help to large-scale terminal security access under 5G power business network. Therefore, the method presented in this paper is lightweight and effective.

5 Conclusion

This paper proposes a lightweight and efficient terminal secure and reliable access method in 5G power service network. Considering the core idea of security stratification and network special, we design a three-layer terminal security access framework to ensure the security of terminals in the access process and data protection process. Then, we propose a lightweight terminal security access scheme to adapt to large-scale terminal access power network scenario. The simulation results show that the proposed method can reduce the communication overhead and provide good security.

References

1. Wang, Y., Yang, W., Shang, X., Hu, J., Huang, Y., Cai, Y.: Energy-efficient secure transmission for wireless powered internet of things with multiple power beacons. IEEE Access **6**, 75086–75098 (2018)

2. Liming, C., Xuzhu, D., Baoren, C., Jin, L., Qiqi, W.: Reliability enhancement of public wireless communication for remote control services in power distribution in smart grid. In: Proceedings of CICED'18, pp. 1700–1704 (2018)
3. Jiang, D., Wang, Y., Lv, Z., Wang, W., Wang, H.: An energy-efficient networking approach in cloud services for IIoT networks. IEEE J. Sel. Areas Commun. **38**(5), 928–941 (2020)
4. Guo, S., Hu, X., Zhou, Z., Wang, X., Qi, F., Gao, L.: Trust access authentication in vehicular network based on blockchain. China Commun. **16**(6), 18–30 (2019)
5. Lubega, P., Ssettumba, T., Nabuuma, H., Serugunda,J.: A secure energy efficient multi-user selection scheme for SWIPT wireless IoT networks in the presence of cooperative jamming. In: Proceedings of TELFOR'19, pp. 1–4 (2019)
6. Jiang, D., Huo, L., Song, H.: Rethinking behaviors and activities of base stations in mobile cellular networks based on big data analysis. IEEE Trans. Netw. Sci. Eng. **7**(1), 80–90 (2020)
7. Chaudhry, S.A., Alhakami, H., Baz, A., Al-Turjman, F.: Securing demand response management: a certificate-based access control in smart grid edge computing infra-structure. IEEE Access **8**, 101235–101243 (2020)
8. Sha, K., Alatrash, N., Wang, Z.: A secure and efficient framework to read isolated smart grid devices. IEEE Trans. Smart Grid **8**(6), 2519–2531 (2017)
9. Jiang, D., Wang, W., Shi, L., Song, H.: A compressive sensing-based approach to end-to-end network traffic reconstruction. IEEE Trans. Netw. Sci. Eng. **7**(1), 507–519 (2020)
10. Navya, M., Sanjay, H.A., Deepika, K.: Securing smart grid data under key exposure and revocation in cloud computing. In: Proceedings of I4C'18, pp. 1–4 (2018)
11. Chekired, D., Khoukhi, L., Mouftah, H.: Decentralized cloud-SDN architecture in smart grid: A dynamic pricing model. IEEE Trans. Industr. Inf. **14**(3), 1220–1231 (2018)
12. W. Chen, B. Liu, H. Huang, et al. When UAV swarm meets edge-cloud computing: The QoS perspective, IEEE Network, 2019, 36–43
13. Liu, B., Jia, D., Wang, J., et al.: Cloud-assisted safety message dissemination in VANET–cellular heterogeneous wireless network. IEEE Syst. J. **11**(1), 128–139 (2017)
14. Jiang, D., Huo, L., Li, Y.: Fine-granularity inference and estimations to network traffic for SDN. PLoS One **13**(5), 1–23 (2018)
15. Zhou, Y., Zhu, X.: Analysis of vehicle network architecture and performance optimization based on soft definition of integration of cloud and fog. IEEE Access **7**(2019), 101171–101177 (2019)
16. El-sayed, H., Sankar, S., Prasad, M., et al.: Edge of things: the big picture on the integration of edge, IoT and the cloud in a distributed computing environment. IEEE Access **6**, 1–12 (2018)
17. Jiang, D., Li, W., Lv, H.: An energy-efficient cooperative multicast routing in multi-hop wireless networks for smart medical applications. Neurocomputing **2017**(220), 160–169 (2017)
18. Zhang, K., Mao, Y., Leng, S., et al.: Mobile-edge computing for vehicular networks. IEEE Veh. Technol. Mag. **12**, 36–44 (2017)
19. Pu, L., Chen, X., Mao, G., et al.: Chimera: an energy-efficient and deadline-aware hybrid edge computing framework for vehicular crowdsensing applications. IEEE Internet of Things J. **6**(1), 84–99 (2019)
20. Jiang, D., Wang, Y., Lv, Z., Qi, S., Singh, S.: Big data analysis based network behavior insight of cellular networks for industry 4.0 applications. IEEE Trans. Ind. Inf. **16**(2), 1310–1320 (2020)
21. Eldjali, C., Lyes, K.: Optimal priority-queuing for EV charging-discharging service based on cloud computing. In: Proceedings of the ICC'17, pp. 1–6 (2017)
22. Xie, R., Tang, Q., Wang, Q., et al.: Collaborative vehicular edge computing networks: architecture design and research challenges. IEEE Access **7**(2019), 178942–178952 (2019)

23. Jiang, D., Huo, L., Lv, Z., Song, H., Qin, W.: A joint multi-criteria utility-based network selection approach for vehicle-to-infrastructure networking. IEEE Trans. Intell. Transp. Syst. **19**(10), 3305–3319 (2018)
24. Yang, Y., Niu, X., Li, L., et al.: A secure and efficient transmission method in connected vehicular cloud computing. IEEE Netw. **32**, 14–19 (2018)
25. Jiang, D., Zhang, P., Lv, Z., et al.: Energy-efficient multi-constraint routing algorithm with load balancing for smart city applications. IEEE Internet of Things J. **3**(6), 1437–1447 (2016)
26. Kaur, K., Garg, S., Kaddoum, G., et al.: Demand-response management using a fleet of electric vehicles: an opportunistic-SDN-based edge-cloud framework for smart grids. IEEE Netw. **33**, 46–53 (2019)
27. Guo, H., Zhang, J., Liu, J.: FiWi-enhanced vehicular edge computing networks. IEEE Veh. Technol. Mag. **14**, 45–53 (2019)

A 5G Network Slice Based Edge Access Approach with Communication Quality Assurance

Fanbo Meng[1]([⊠]), Huan Li[2], Bin Lu[1], Shuai Ren[2], and Dongdong Wang[1]

[1] State Grid Liaoning Electric Power Supply Co., Ltd., Shenyang 110004, China
mengfanbo221@sina.com
[2] Electric Power Research Institute of State Grid Liaoning Electric Power Supply Co., Ltd., Shenyang 110006, China

Abstract. With the development of various vertical industry services such as autonomous driving, energy Internet, and smart cities, mobile communication networks need to provide users with ubiquitous high-speed access while using limited network resources to provide differentiated and customized services, the 5G network satisfies the requirement of the future . However, for the access network, there are many types services accessing the network. In order to provide users with diverse personalized services, network slicing scheme is introduced into 5G network. Network slicing is based on the technology of network function virtualization, which can establish multiple virtual private networks in the device according to the needs of users. Each slice is a private network, and different virtual networks are kept isolated from each other. This article studies the access network of the 5G network, in order to ensure the quality of user access, we study the mapping scheme of network slices and NFV to ensure the communication quality of access networks of different user types. Finally, we perform some simulations to verify the proposed method, and the result shows that our proposed can ensure the communication quality for the users which connect into the 5G network.

Keywords: Network slicing · 5G · NFV

1 Introduction

With the widespread use of various new mobile terminals such as smart terminals and the rapid development of Internet technologies, the number of smart terminal devices connected to the network will explode, this poses a huge challenge to the existing network architecture and network capacity. Obviously, due to the inherent defects of the traditional network, such as the network architecture cannot be flexibly configured and adjusted, so it cannot cope with the future needs of users for mobile networks [1–3]. At the same time, new applications such as augmented reality, smart homes, and intelligent transportation enable people to experience new lifestyles. However, these applications place higher demands on system throughput, end-to-end delay and network reliability.

H. Song and D. Jiang (Eds.): SIMUtools 2020, LNICST 369, pp. 12–23, 2021.
https://doi.org/10.1007/978-3-030-72792-5_2

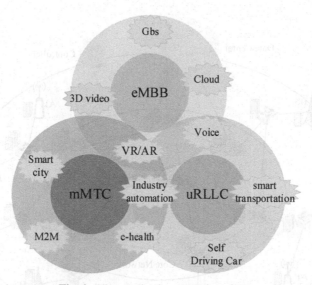

Fig. 1. The application scenarios of 5G.

At the same time, the emergence of new technologies such as autonomous driving and virtual reality has made the types of communication services more complicated [4–6]. Increasing data traffic, network device connections, and increasingly complex service scenarios make the 4G network face huge challenges [7–9]. Due to the limitations of network architecture, spectrum resources, and energy consumption, existing 4G networks cannot meet users' needs in terms of system capacity, data transmission rate, transmission delay, and resource utilization. In order to meet the data growth demand for users to access the network, the wireless communication group of International Telecommunication Union (ITU) propose the fifth generation mobile communication technology (5G) [10–12]. The 5G network meet the goal of connection between humans and things in the industry, agriculture, medical, education, transportation, etc. Compared with 4G network, 5G network has a big improvement in performance and function. It can provide greater throughput, ultra-high link density, lower latency and more secure and reliable communication [13–15]. At the same time, network energy consumption and network deployment costs are more low. The ITU has determined that the three major application scenarios of 5G, namely: enhanced mobile broadband (eMBB), mass machine communication (mMTC), low latency and highly reliable communication (uRLLC). The application scenarios as Fig. 1 shows.

(1) eMBB: Compared with 4G networks, the transmission rate and network coverage of users are greatly improved, and the user's communication is further improved in the existing broadband scenario Experience

(2) mMTC: The mMTC is the basic of large-scale IoT, it mainly oriented to the communication between objects, suitable for the scenarios of Internet of Things communication. The main advantage lies in supporting higher peak rate of uplink and downlink on the basis of ensuring coverage and power consumption; supporting

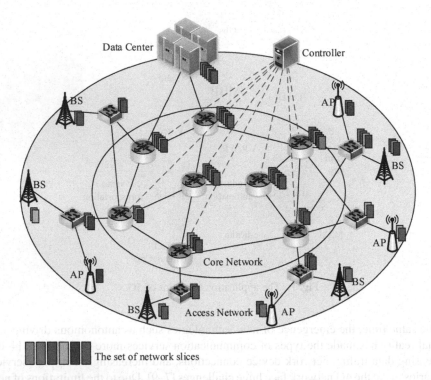

The set of network slices

Fig. 2. The Network slicing service in 5G.

the mobility of the connected state to improve the performance of handover and improve the user experience;

(3) uRLLC: The uRLLC mainly used for Internet of Vehicles, precise positioning and virtual reality services. Such services have high reliability and latency requirements and need to provide millisecond end-to-end latency and extremely high availability for users.

Due to the diverse application scenarios and business requirements of 5G, the traditional unified network deployment method cannot flexibly provide users with multiple business services [16, 17]. The network slicing technology shown in Fig. 2 is introduced into 5G networks, it has the following advantages:

(1) Sharing resources, reducing costs, and improving efficiency: multiple network slices operating simultaneously on a unified infrastructure can significantly reduce network construction and operating costs, and improve the resource utilization of general infrastructure;
(2) Logical isolation, safe and reliable: each slice has its own independent virtual resources and life cycle, the creation and destruction of network slices will not affect other slices;

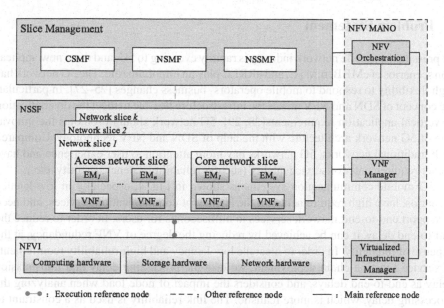

Fig. 3. The architecture of network slicing.

(3) Customized on demand, flexible expansion: the cloud-based network slicing native architecture provides services for different businesses, and infrastructure-as-a-service (IaaS) resources can be customized according to different business scenarios; cloud monitoring can achieve network Real-time monitoring of resource utilization provides high reliability and flexible expansion;

(4) End-to-end to meet differentiated needs: Different business needs determine the performance of network slicing. Through end-to-end deployment, the core network, transmission network and access network are divided to fully meet the needs of 5G diversified services.

The diversification of business and application requirements in the 5G network requires the network to allocate resources more flexibly according to different business characteristics [19–21]. Therefore, 5G networks require a completely innovative network architecture to achieve flexible and alternative networking methods, then the network slicing become as one of the best alternative technologies. Network slicing is an on-demand networking method that allows operators to separate multiple virtual end-to-end networks on a unified infrastructure. Each network slice is logical from the wireless access network bearer network to the core network [22–24]. Isolation to suit various types of applications. The network slicing as Fig. 2 shows.

The architecture of network slicing is shown in Fig. 3, which mainly includes four parts: Network Functions Virtualization Infrastructure (NFVI), NFV Management and Orchestration (MANO), Network Slice Selection Function (NSSF), and Slice management function. There are three functions of network slice management, namely communication service management function (CSMF), network slicing management function (NSMF), and network slicing subnet management function (NSSMF).

2 Problem Statement

At present, the mobile network industry is rapidly evolving to 5G, and three new application scenarios of eMBB, mMTC, and uRRLC play an important role. The 5G network has high flexibility to respond to mobile operators' business changes [25–27]. In particular, the concept of SDN and NFV makes the infrastructure flexible to meet the diversification of vertical application requirements[28, 29]. 5G network slicing promotes the innovation of 5G network architecture with the help of SDN and NFV technology. Compared with traditional networks, 5G networks pay more attention to user experience and have higher requirements for service quality (such as reliability, latency, security, etc.).

5G mobile communication systems as shown in Fig. 4, especially in low-latency scenarios, have high requirements for the latency of communication services, and need to support end-to-end network services in milliseconds for users. In order to reduce the end-to-end delay, it can be achieved by reducing the degree of VNF redundancy, at the expense of reliability. In order to meet the low-latency and high-reliability requirements of service function chain deployment, we take the processing delay and transmission delay as end-to-end delays, and considers the impact of node load when analyzing the processing delay, which is more realistic. The link reliability is used as a constraint to establish a model, and a service function chain deployment algorithm based on QoS guarantee is proposed. The algorithm includes two stages: a virtual network function deployment algorithm based on node invulnerability and a link mapping algorithm based on reliability [30, 31]. We consider the link's resource capacity and reliability conditions during the VNF deployment phase, and realizes two-phase collaborative deployment, which reduces the complexity of the algorithm and improves the utilization of resources while achieving the overall goal of optimizing delay and reliability. In order to more effectively achieve load balancing and protect the underlying nodes and link failures. The continuous iterations of the system obtain a smooth distribution of scores, and the final result can more reasonably reflect the importance of the node in the entire network. Then select the node with the highest score to deploy VNF, effectively balance the node load, reduce processing delay, and at the same time improve the reliability of service function request deployment without reserving resources. Finally, the reliability-based link mapping algorithm is used to select the shortest delay path that meets the reliability requirements to further optimize the performance of the deployment. The proposed algorithm effectively achieves load balancing, maximizes the resource utilization of the underlying network, and guarantees QoS.

Considering the low latency and high reliability requirements of 5G network slicing, we study the deployment of service function chains based on QoS guarantees in the access network of 5G [32, 33]. The bottom layer of the 5G slicing network is a network composed of OpenFlow-based switches, and we use the undirected graph $G^s = (N^s, L^s)$ to represent it, where N^s is the node set of switches, each switch can deploy one or more NFV functions; L^s represents the link set of the network.

$$LS(j) = \sum_{i=1}^{n} r_i LR(i) \qquad (1)$$

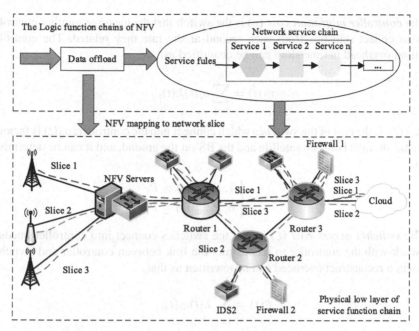

Fig. 4. Mapping of access network and service chain based on network slice.

where $LS(j)$ is the total overload of the SWITCH j, n represent the number of overload factor, r_i represent the coefficient of the weight, $LR(i)$ represent the usage state of the controller overload factor i. Assuming that the load of the controller close value of the threshold is $MAX(j)$, there are two situations about the controller migration:

In the process of controller migration, we set the signal strength from BS to the Switch as one of the triggering conditions, the signal strength from BS to the satellite can be written as

$$P_{mean}(t) = \frac{\sum_{k=1}^{K} \alpha_k P(t - k\Delta T)}{K} \qquad (2)$$

where K is the window duration of the signal sampling; ΔT is the sampling period; α_k is the weight when sampling the signal. When the signal strength $P_{mean}(t)$ is smaller than the threshold P_T, therefore, signal strength is a necessary condition for controller migration in the 5G network.

The controller migration cost based on dynamic feedback adopted in this paper not only considers dynamic load information but also static load information when considering migration cost. When calculating the comprehensive cost value and selecting the target controller and switch, the corresponding main influencing factors are mainly considered.

The *controller migration cost* (η) is the switch that the message number controller needs to collect statistics from each second at the rate they related. The controller migration overhead in time slot t can be quantified as:

$$\eta_1(t) = \sum_{i=1}^{N} a_i(t)\lambda(t)_i \tag{3}$$

where $\lambda(t)_i$ is the cost of the switches which connect into the controller; $a_{ij}(t)$ is factor of the signal strength between satellite and the BS on the ground, and it can be determined as that

$$a_{ij}(t) = \begin{cases} 1, P_{mean}(t) > P_T \\ 0, P_{mean}(t) \le P_T \end{cases} \tag{4}$$

The *switches access cost* (ξ) is that the switches connect into controller needs to handwork with the controller to reconstruct the link between controller and switches. The switch reconstruct overhead can be rewritten as that

$$\xi(t) = \sum_{i=1}^{N} \lambda(t)_i x(t)_i \tag{5}$$

where $\lambda(t)_i$ is the cost of the switches which connect into the controller; $x(t)_i$ is the view duration that the switch access cost when connect into the controller in the SWITCH network.

The migration cost of the controller is the issue that we should pay attention to at present. When the controller is migrated from one Switch into another satellite, switches on the transmission path needs to be re-connected to the new controller periodically to adjust the control plane of the network. The goal of the controller migration in 5G network is to minimize the response time and switching time of the controller, while keeping control flow overhead low [34, 35]. Therefore, we apply the weighting factor to the response time in the objective function.

$$\min \eta_1(t) + \xi(t)$$
$$s.t.$$
$$C1 : a_i(t) \in \{0, 1\}$$
$$C2 : \lambda(t) \in \{0, 1\}$$
$$C3 : P_{mean}(t) < P_T$$
$$C4 : \alpha_k \in [0, 1] \tag{6}$$

where the condition $C1$, $C2$ and $C3$ ensure that the BS on the ground can be connected into the satellite or not. Constraint $C3$ is the necessary condition of the BS which can be connected into the satellite in the 5G network. Then, the controller migration step can be written as

Step 1 The measurement configuration information delivered by the source satellite through the BS includes the neighbor measurement trigger threshold P_T.

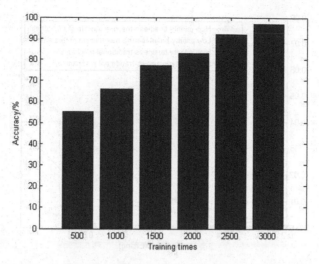

Fig. 5. Relationship between business perception accuracy and training times

Step 2 The BS measures the signal strength of the serving satellite.

Step 3 When the signal strength of the serving satellite is lower than the neighboring satellite measurement trigger threshold, the BS calculates the service satellite sub-satellite point according to the ephemeris information, predicts the handover trigger time handover, and further calculates the neighbor satellites list at the handover trigger time.

Step 4 The BS simultaneously measures the signal of the neighboring satellite and the serving satellite.

Step 5 When the signal strength of the serving satellite is lower than the handover trigger threshold, the handover trigger is determined. The BS calculates the link duration of all neighbor satellites in the neighbor satellite list, filters out the neighbor satellites whose link duration is too long, and then calculates the switching weight of each neighbor satellite.

Step 6 If the link duration with the largest switching weight in the neighbor list is still the current service satellite, and it is determined that the result of switching to the current service satellite, the switching is aborted, and the switching trigger process is interrupted; otherwise, migrating the controller to the target satellite.

Step 7 Return Step 2.

3 Simulation Result and Analysis

In order to verify the proposed mechanism, this paper builds a simulation system on the edge of the network based on the NS2 simulation software. The simulation system consists of 32 network elements mounted on a terminal, designing an SDN network, adding edge nodes, and verifying the proposed service perception technology at the edge of the network can achieve satisfactory results. Through simulation, we compare the network edge with service awareness mechanism and the network edge without service awareness [21, 36]. In the simulation, the service types are divided into two types: packet loss rate sensitive service and delay sensitive service.

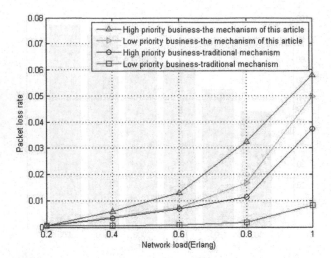

Fig. 6. Comparison of packet loss rate

Figure 5 is a diagram of the relationship between the accuracy of service perception and the number of trainings. It can be seen that as the number of trainings increases, the accuracy of business perception also increases. The fully trained echo state network algorithm can ensure the accuracy of business classification.

At the edge network, this method (service-aware) and the traditional non-service-aware mechanism are used for simulation. Figure 6 and Fig. 7 are the results of comparison. Combining the simulation results of Fig. 6 and Fig. 7, with the increase of the network service load, the packet loss rate and real-time performance of our constructed system show a tendency to deteriorate. Under high load, the network edge system adopting the mechanism of this paper is superior to the traditional EPON system in two important indicators of high-priority service, such as packet loss rate and transmission delay. On the other hand, low-priority services have low requirements on transmission delay and packet loss rate, the mechanism of this paper will reduce the performance of services to a certain extent. In exchange for overall business service quality, especially high priority QoS requirements for high-level services.

The comparison of packet loss rate and delay shows that the business-aware method proposed in this paper can ensure that different types and different priorities of services at the edge of the network can be matched with the lower computational complexity, and ensure the overall service quality of the business.

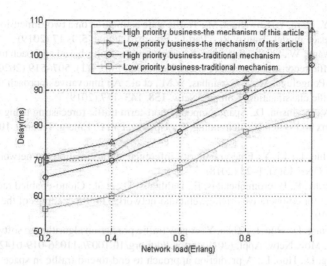

Fig. 7. Delay comparison

4 Conclusions

In this paper, we study the 5G network slice based edge access approach with the communication quality insurance. In response to the requirements of 5G network low-latency and high-reliability scenarios and the deficiencies of traditional service function chain deployment methods, we take into account the invulnerability of nodes and the reliability of links while studying latency issues, ensuring the reliability of service function chain deployment. The feasibility and effectiveness of the method are verified. This method evaluates the node through comprehensive factors such as node invulnerability and link reliability, and then selects the node for service function chain deployment to achieve load balancing and reduce processing delay. At the same time, the shortest path that meets the reliability constraints is found to reduce the shortest path. Transmission delay reflects the overall performance of optimizing delay and reliability. The simulation results show that the algorithm in this chapter significantly improves the service function chain request acceptance rate, end-to-end delay, node and link utilization, and node and link reliability performance.

References

1. Guo, Y., Wang, Z., Yin, X., et al.: Traffic engineering in hybrid SDN networks with multiple traffic matrices. Comput. Netw. **126**, 187–199 (2017)
2. Liu, G., Guo, S., Zhao, Q., et al.: Tomogravity space based traffic matrix estimation in data center networks. Transp. Res. Part C: Emerg. Technol. **86**, 39–50 (2018)
3. Jiang, D., Wang, Y., Lv, Z., Wang, W., Wang, H.: An energy-efficient networking approach in cloud services for IIoT networks. IEEE J. Sel. Areas Commun. **38**(5), 928–941 (2020)
4. Hashemi, H., Abdelghany, K.F., et al.: Real-time traffic network state estimation and prediction with decision support capabilities: Application to integrated corridor management. Transp. Res. Part C: Emerg. Technol. **73**, 128–146 (2016)

5. Kawasaki, Y., Hara, Y., Kuwahara, M.: Traffic state estimation on a two-dimensional network by a state-space model. Transp. Res. Part C: Emerg. Technol. **5**, 1–17 (2019)
6. Jiang, D., Wang, W., Shi, L., Song, H.: A compressive sensing-based approach to end-to-end network traffic reconstruction. IEEE Trans. Netw. Sci. Eng. **7**(1), 507–519 (2020)
7. Dias, K.L., Pongelupe, M.A., Caminhas, W.M., et al.: An innovative approach for real-time network traffic classification. Comput. Netw. **158**, 143–157 (2019)
8. Ermagun, A., Levinson, D.: Spatiotemporal short-term traffic forecasting using the network weight matrix and systematic detrending. Transp. Res. Part C: Emerg. Technol. **104**(5), 38–52 (2019)
9. Jiang, D., Huo, L., Li, Y.: Fine-granularity inference and estimations to network traffic for SDN. PLoS ONE **13**(5), 1–23 (2018)
10. Keshavamurthy, P., Pateromichelakis, E., Dahlhaus, D., et al.: Cloud-enabled radio resource management for co-operative driving vehicular networks. In: Proceedings of the WCNC'19, pp. 1–6 (2019)
11. Wang, Y., Jiang, D., Huo, L., Zhao, Y.: A new traffic prediction algorithm to software defined networking. Mob. Netw. Appl. (2019). https://doi.org/10.1007/s11036-019-01423-3
12. Qi, S., Jiang, D., Huo, L.: A prediction approach to end-to-end traffic in space information networks. Mob. Netw. Appl. (2019). https://doi.org/10.1007/s11036-019-01424-2
13. Jiang, D., Zhang, P., Lv, Z., et al.: Energy-efficient multi-constraint routing algorithm with load balancing for smart city applications. IEEE Internet of Things J. **3**(6), 1437–1447 (2016)
14. Li, J., Shen, X., Chen, L., et al.: Service migration in fog computing enabled cellular networks to support real-time vehicular communications. IEEE Access **7**(2019), 13704–13714 (2019)
15. Wang, F., Jiang, D., Qi, S., et al.: A dynamic resource scheduling scheme in edge computing satellite networks. Mob. Netw. Appl. (2019). https://doi.org/10.1007/s11036-019-01421-5
16. El-sayed, H., Sankar, S., Prasad, M., et al.: Edge of things: the big picture on the integration of edge, IoT and the cloud in a distributed computing environment. IEEE Access **6**, 1–12 (2018)
17. Jiang, D., Huo, L., Song, H.: Rethinking behaviors and activities of base stations in mobile cellular networks based on big data analysis. IEEE Trans. Netw. Sci. Eng. **7**(1), 80–90 (2020)
18. Zhang, K., Mao, Y., Leng, S., et al.: Mobile-edge computing for vehicular networks. IEEE Veh. Technol. Mag. **12**, 36–44 (2017)
19. Pu, L., Chen, X., Mao, G., et al.: Chimera: an energy-efficient and deadline-aware hybrid edge computing framework for vehicular crowdsensing applications. IEEE Internet of Things J. **6**(1), 84–99 (2019)
20. Jiang, D., Wang, Y., Lv, Z., Qi, S., Singh, S.: Big data analysis based network behavior insight of cellular networks for industry 4.0 applications. IEEE Trans. Ind. Inf. **16**(2), 1310–1320 (2020)
21. Eldjali, C., Lyes, K.: Optimal priority-queuing for EV charging-discharging service based on cloud computing. In: Proceedings of the ICC'17, pp. 1–6 (2017)
22. Jiang, D., Huo, L., Lv, Z., Song, H., Qin, W.: A joint multi-criteria utility-based network selection approach for vehicle-to-infrastructure networking. IEEE Trans. Intell. Transp. Syst. **19**(10), 3305–3319 (2018)
23. Xie, R., Tang, Q., Wang, Q., et al.: Collaborative vehicular edge computing networks: architecture design and research challenges. IEEE Access **7**(2019), 178942–178952 (2019)
24. Yang, Y., Niu, X., Li, L., et al.: A secure and efficient transmission method in connected vehicular cloud computing. IEEE Netw. **32**, 14–19 (2018)
25. Jiang, D., Li, W., Lv, H.: An energy-efficient cooperative multicast routing in multi-hop wireless networks for smart medical applications. Neurocomputing **2017**(220), 160–169 (2017)

26. Kaur, K., Garg, S., Kaddoum, G., et al.: Demand-response management using a fleet of electric vehicles: an opportunistic-SDN-based edge-cloud framework for smart grids. IEEE Netw. **33**, 46–53 (2019)
27. Guo, H., Zhang, J., Liu, J.: FiWi-enhanced vehicular edge computing networks. IEEE Veh. Technol. Mag. **14**, 45–53 (2019)
28. Liu, H., Zhang, Y., Yang, T.: Blockchain-enabled security in electric vehicles cloud and edge computing. IEEE Netw. **32**(3), 78–83 (2018)
29. Wang, F., Jiang, D., Qi, S.: An adaptive routing algorithm for integrated information networks. China Commun. **7**(1), 196–207 (2019)
30. Wang, J., He, B., Wang, J., et al.: Intelligent VNFs selection based on traffic identification in vehicular cloud networks. IEEE Trans. Veh. Technol. **68**(5), 4140–4147 (2019)
31. Huo, L., Jiang, D., Qi, S., et al.: An AI-based adaptive cognitive modeling and measurement method of network traffic for EIS. Mob. Netw. Appl. (2019). https://doi.org/10.1007/s11036-019-01419-z
32. Li, M., Si, P., Zhang, Y.: Delay-tolerant data traffic to software-defined vehicular networks with mobile edge computing in smart city. IEEE Trans. Veh. Technol. **67**(10), 9073–9086 (2018)
33. Garg, S., Kaur, K., Ahmed, S., et al.: MobQoS: mobility-aware and QoS-driven SDN framework for autonomous vehicles. IEEE Wirel. Commun. **26**, 12–20 (2019)
34. Huo, L., Jiang, D., Lv, Z., et al.: An intelligent optimization-based traffic information acquirement approach to software-defined networking. Comput. Intell. **36**, 1–21 (2019)
35. Lin, C., Deng, D., Yao, C.: Resource allocation in vehicular cloud computing systems with heterogeneous vehicles and roadside units. IEEE Internet of Things J. **5**(5), 3692–3700 (2018)
36. Garg, S., Singh, A., Batra, S., et al.: UAV-empowered edge computing environment for cyber-threat detection in smart vehicles. IEEE Netw. **32**, 42–51 (2018)

A Lightweight Network Edge Service-Aware Method for Edge Networks

Guochun Li[1], Chuan Liu[2,3(✉)], Yan Chen[4], Rui Ma[1], Xiaolu Chen[4], and Gang Sun[5]

[1] State Grid Information and Telecommunication Branch, Beijing 100761, China
[2] Global Energy Interconnection Research Institute Co., Ltd., Nanjing 210003, China
[3] State Grid Laboratory of Electric Power Communication Network Technology, Nanjing 210003, China
[4] State Grid Shanghai Municipal Electric Power Company, Shanghai 200122, China
[5] State Grid Zhejiang Electric Power Co., Ltd., Hangzhou 310007, China

Abstract. Edge computing is one of the main components of 5 g technology. It is used to adapt to the rapid development of the Internet of things and improve the service quality of the network. The combination of SDN and NFV can improve the flexibility of network service deployment. But at the edge of the network, the change of service will affect the quality of service. Therefore, we need a real-time business change perception system to provide differentiated services to improve the quality of different services. This paper proposes a lightweight service awareness technology based on network edge. This technology is based on the perception of mobile service flow in hierarchical echo state network (ESN). Traffic flow is sensed by discrete echo state network algorithm, and mobile resource scheduling and allocation ability are improved. Finally, the experimental results show that the proposed method can sense the services at the edge of the network, improve the capacity and bandwidth of the network, meet the differentiation of multiple services and QoS.

Keywords: Service-aware · Network edge · QoS · ESN

1 Introduction

With the development of Internet of Things, more and more services (such as vehicle communication, virtual reality, increased reality) and human interaction continue to arise, humans and environment, humans and machines have also gone through changes to the at the same time, more and more mobile devices and applications are used the fim to improve the user experience and ensure the quality of the network service, the edge computing scheme is proposed. This is also an important part of the fifth-generation network [1, 2]. NFV and SDN, as the key technologies of the 5 g network are more and more attention. Note that the NFV virtualization technology can be used simultaneously to provide flexible network services for all SDN network topologies and information e. Cross you are from the combination of the NFV and SDN commission, a new medium is provided all. Serving network connections. O number of users and devices accessing the

© ICST Institute for Computer Sciences, Social Informatics and Telecommunications Engineering 2021
Published by Springer Nature Switzerland AG 2021. All Rights Reserved
H. Song and D. Jiang (Eds.): SIMUtools 2020, LNICST 369, pp. 24–33, 2021.
https://doi.org/10.1007/978-3-030-72792-5_3

network. If the broad server cannot provide matching network resources, the quality of network services will be reduced. In computing edges, users different types of network services for video transmission, virtual reality, increased reality, reality, e mail and online games, online medical training network service tem different requirements of network resources [3, 4]. Video transmission requires high speed and low delay data transmission, and virtual reality needs high-speed computing performance. How provide it on the net? Changing the characteristics of the real-time business on the network edge [4, 5], adjusting parameters to meet different business needs, and providing differentiated services became a theme.

Sensing technology is environmental conditions, customer behavior and movement of the object. This document is a method to explain the concept and context mechanism. Suggested. Wait. if the 5 g network satisfies the quality of service (QoS) in scenarios different. The reference [6] proposes a dynamic network system of wave resources, supporting services sensitive to a 5 g front delay end. The experimental results show that the system can effectively reduce delay in border [7]. This article proposes the dynamic composition of virtual services. According to the types of network services, summarize the types of different network services, define the characteristics of the use of network resources, and users need services to redevelop service types and propose corresponding solutions. The reference [8] proposed the network-based media framework. In order to achieve the traditional industrial hybrid router (using the OSPF protocol, etc.) And the switching network, it proposed the active control of network resources and the cooperation of multiple clients based on the flow of regenerative experience based on http [9], based on the SDN support (opening protocol, this paper proposes a smart transmission strategy based on QoS, a unique minimum price correction algorithm and a k-path targeting algorithm in industrial applications transmission system has improved.

Based on the way the change in service characteristics under the network edge can be felt in real time, this paper proposes a light network edge service sensing method before. This Method based on the echo state (ESN) mobile radio service influenza awareness mechanism. It uses discrete echo state network algorithm, to identify and perceive traffic flow in order to efficiently match network edge services to Research and development in the field of Top sensor technology. this basis will be the mobile resource allocation and allocation optimized. The fully utilizing the capacity and bandwidth of the technology also improves the ability to distinguish and support QoS from different services.

2   Hierarchical Echo State Network Classification Algorithm

2.1   Principles of Echo State Network

ESN algorithm is a new network algorithm Neural Recognition Model. It's a simplified form of recurring neural network (RNN). Compared to the traditional predictive algorithm of the coupling structure, HE HAS THE MOST FORTUNATIVE ABILITY NOT linear. Has Best non-linear dynamic performance simulation. ESN algorithm of the system is currently studying the most extensive and extensive neural network predictive algorithm, which is widely used in artificial intelligence field.

ESN uses a storage sphere composed of neurons randomly connected as a hidden layer and enters in a highly dimensional way and not linear. This It has nothing to do with the process of forming the Ecological State [10, 11]. It is a network, just one method linear. Practice the Reserve Bar Weight at the beginning ratio. East Method Simplifies the process of networking formation and ensures overall optimization determined. it has good generalization capacity and prevents the problems of the traditional neural network training algorithm from being complex and extremely local small. These advantages from autumn onwards there is great possibility of application in the state network Echo, control. Traffic. The typical structure of Echo State network is shown in Fig. 1. It consists of an input layer, core layer, and output layer.

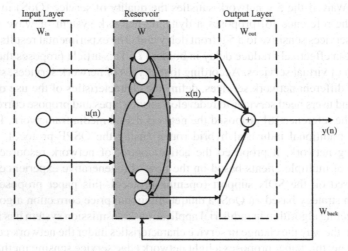

Fig. 1. Echo state network structure diagram

It is assumed that the echo state network consists of K input units, N standby pool processing units and N output units the basic equations of the echo state network are (1) and (2), where (1) is the status update equation of the internal neuron node, and (2) is the output forecast equation.

$$x(n+1) = f(W^{in}u(n+1) + Wx(n) + W^{back}y(n)) \tag{1}$$

$$y(n+1) = f^{out}(W^{out}u(n+1) + Wx(n+1) + W^{back}y(n)) \tag{2}$$

Where $u(n) = (u_1(n), \cdots, u_K(n))^T$ is the input variable of ESN, $x(n) = (x_1(n), \cdots, x_N(n))^T$ is the internal state variable, and $y(n) = (y_1(n), \cdots, y_L(n))^T$ is the output variable. The main parameters are: input connection weight W^{in}, N, x, K; intermediate weight connection matrix $W, N, x, (K+N)$; output weight connection matrix $W^{out}, L, x, (K+N+L)$; feedback weight connection matrix W^{back}, N, x, L; input is represented by u, DR dynamic pool is represented by x, output is used y said. In addition, f and f^{out} in the ESN model can be considered as stimulating functions of the processing unit and the output unit. It is usually a sigmoid function, expressed as follows:

$$f(x) = \frac{e^x - e^{-x}}{e^x + e^{-x}} \tag{3}$$

The echo state refers to the internal state of the ESN, which is a limited function of the historical data input, i.e. "echo" of the historical Data entry. To ensure that ESN has echo status characteristics; when initializing structure W, the spectral radius of W should be less than 1 be. The main advantage of the neural ESN network is, the training method is simple and the dynamic pool structure is a simple random connection In the ESN training, the sample data stimulate the processing unit of the core layer by randomly generated weight matrix W^{in} and W^{back}. After each training round, the internal parameters of the ESN can be changed by linear regression to change the mean square error. The Input variables are connected to the processing unit from ESN to W^{in}, W^{back} is the connecting weight between the starting layer and the core layer, and W^{out} is the connecting weight between the core and the starting layer. In the training process the internal state weight matrix of the dynamic pool remains unchanged, only the connecting weight matrix W^{out} from dynamic pool to output is updated and the minimum mean square error nrmse calculated. In addition, W^{in}, W and W^{back} is generally set as a constant, and W^{out} can be achieved by certain training.

The mathematical expression of mean square error NRMSE is shown in (4):

$$MSE_{min} = \frac{1}{T - T_c} \sqrt{\sum_{n=T_c}^{T} (d(n) - y(n))^2} \tag{4}$$

when NRMSE is minimum, use the offline generalized inverse matrix to calculate W^{out}, i.e. $W^{out} = M^{-1}T$, where $M = (x(n))$, $T = (d(n))$. When the W^{out} calculation is complete, you can start predicting the data.

2.2 Echo State Network Classification Algorithm

The basic principle of the classification of the acoustic state is represented in Eq. (5) in which $(n + 1)$ represents only different samples, not time. In the classification must remain unchanged until the value of the status variable of the reserve pool is stable; so that the difference between the results of the two iterations is minimal.

$$\begin{cases} x(n+1)^{(i)} = W^{in}u(n+1) + Wx(n+1)^{i-1} \\ x(n+1)^{(0)} = 0 \end{cases} \tag{5}$$

The advantage of the algorithm is that it stabilizes the status variables only by the activation function of the reserve building processing unit prior to processing and preserves the simple characteristics of the echo state network training [10], reduces complexity and ensures the overall optimal performance of operating results.

3 Business Perception Based on Hierarchical Echo State Network Algorithm

3.1 Principle of Business Classification Perception Based on Hierarchical ESN

In order to further improve service awareness, this paper proposes a service awareness algorithm, based on a hierarchical echo state network based. Service Perception Based on the hierarchical ESN algorithm is essentially the assignment of business properties to business types [12, 13], and its essence is the process the classification of decision-making fees (business types) based on conditional attributes (business characteristics).

According to the architecture of the network border system, a hierarchical ESN model The Commission hierarchical ESN model is divided into control layer, control layer and agent layer (as shown in Fig. 2).

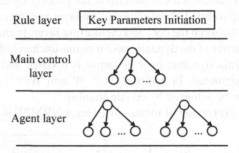

Fig. 2. Structure diagram of hierarchical ESN model

The main control consists of the ESN main control module and the Training module. The main control module introduces a large number of sample sets from the training module for a uniform ESN training up to the formation of a complete ESN classification. The training method used by ESN is the same as for the existing ESN- Training methods. the formation of the ESN Classifier, the main control module distributes the parameter information of the ESN Classifier to all.

The service perception process based on the hierarchical echo state network algorithm is divided into three parts: service feature parameter extraction, ESN training and ESN decision making [14]. The main characteristic parameters of the received two-way traffic flow, including frame length, service throughput time and service package flow interval, are considered traffic characteristics $u = \{u_1, u_2, \ldots, u_k, \ldots\}$. The auxiliary u of the traffic flow is entered into the trained echo state network model and the type of classification of the service is determined by calculating W^{out}.

3.2 Extraction and Preprocessing of Business Flow Feature Parameters

Both the main layer and the agent layer must have the characteristic parameters of the business process pre-processing [14, 15]. Before the main control must normalize the function parameters in the sample set and the agent layer must also normalize the function parameters extracted from the incoming traffic flow The Pre-treatment is presented in formula (6).

$$
\begin{cases}
U(i) = (x_{i,1}, x_{i,2}, x_{i,3}, x_{i,4}) \\[2mm]
x_{i,1} = \dfrac{P_{SIZE}(i)}{P_{SIZE\_MAX}} \quad x_{i,2} = \dfrac{P_{INTERVAL}(i)}{P_{INTERVAL\_MAX}} \\[4mm]
x_{i,3} = \dfrac{P_{DUR}(i)}{P_{DUR\_MAX}} \quad x_{i,4} = \dfrac{P_{LOAD}(i)}{P_{LOAD\_MAX}}
\end{cases}
\tag{6}
$$

where P_{SIZE_MAX} is the maximum packet length of statistics, $P_{INTERVAL\_MAX}$ is the maximum arrival interval, P_{DUR_MAX} is he maximum service duration, and P_{LOAD_MAX} is the maximum load rate of network cell nodes.

Before the training, the main control layer produces the traffic flow characteristics are provided for in the training sample according to formula (6). In the agent layer processes each Bayesian agent module the extracted traffic flow characteristic data according to formula (6) prior to the ESN classification operation, so that the ESN classification can calculate priority type of traffic flow.

3.3 Implementation of Business Awareness Mechanism

With a view to implementing the service awareness mechanism, this paper establishes a service awareness implementation system compatible with the network edge system architecture. The commission the master slave service awareness mechanism consists mainly of the master ESN module and each ESN module. The most important ESN module is for the first configuration of the ESN and training of the complex ESN responsible and transmits the parameter information of the trained ESN classification to each network unit. Each network unit configures the parameters of the ESN classifier and is independently responsible for the local service awareness function. The network unit extracts the parameters for the service flow.

In the main control layer, the ESN master module can use existing ESN training methods to form an ESN classifier. The ESN training shall be undefined to the terminal to ensure that all network elements of the system use the same ESN classifier, the consistency of service perception from a global perspective. In addition, the network node counts the records (including own values and classification results) of the traffic flow classification identification and periodically returns the records to the main control layer; to continuously add new training samples sets. The terminal Bayes main control module regularly trains the ESN after the test set to form a new ESN classification.

The function of the agent layer is realized by ESN proxy module, which running in the network unit device. The business flow perception can be divided into three processes: business flow feature extraction, ESN classification operation, and priority queue scheduling. Save Implement the information parameters of the ESN classifier emitted by the terminal and consolidate the ESN classifier internally via the Hardware. The "ESN agent module" extracts the characteristic parameters for each traffic flow and normalizes in order to avoid over-adaptation, so that the feature set describing the traffic flow receives and then enters the ESN classification to obtain the classification result, namely the priority of the traffic flow.

4   Simulation Result and Analysis

In order to check the proposed mechanism, a simulation system based on NS2 simulation software will be installed at the edge of the network. The simulation system consists of 32-network elements installed on the terminal. The SDN network is designed and the edge nodes are added. It shall be examined: whether the proposed service awareness technology achieves satisfactory results at the edge of the network can. By the simulation becomes the network edge with service award mechanism without service awareness with the network edge compared. In the simulation will turn traffic types into package-loss-rate-sensitive service and time-delay-sensitive Service divided.

Figure 3 shows the relationship between the accuracy of service delivery and training time, which can see that with the increase in training time also the accuracy of the company's performance improves is. Full permanently trained echo state network algorithm can ensure the accuracy of the service classification.

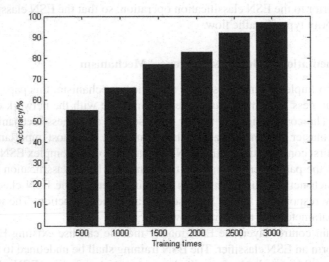

Fig. 3. Relationship between business perception ac-curacy and training times

In the edge network, this method (Service Awareness) and the traditional non-service-conscious mechanism for simulation used. Figure 4 and Fig. 5 are the results of Comparison. In Link to the simulation results of Fig. 4 and Fig. 5, with the increase in the net transport burden, the package loss rate and the real-time performance of the system we have designed tend to deteriorate. In the high load exceeds the traditional EPON system based on this mechanism in package losses and transmission processes Rounded. On the other hand, low priority services have lower requirements for transmission delays and package losses. The mechanism proposed in this paper will, to a certain extent, make the provision of services. In the exchange for the general quality of service, especially the QoS requirements of high quality services.

Comparison of package losses and delays shows that the proposed service sensing method can ensure the reconciliation of the different types and priorities of services on

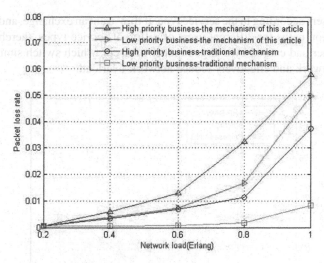

Fig. 4. Comparison of packet loss rate

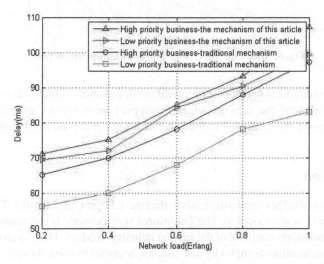

Fig. 5. Delay comparison

the periphery of the network with low computational complexity and ensure the overall quality of the service.

Figure 6 shows how the network block rate is changed when using different vertical transmission algorithms with different arrival rates changes. In Fig. 6, the arrival rate of users is very low and the network resources are sufficient to meet the needs of users, so that the lock rate is almost zero. With the continuous increase in the rate of arrival, however, increases the blocking rate, we can see that the lock rate of the algorithm proposed in this chapter is lower than that of the AHP-SAW and TOPSIS algorithms under the same rate of arrival of the users. This depends on that the algorithm in this chapter sorts users according to the service type, if they want an exchange, and constructs different decision paths for different users of different service types, thereby avoiding the network overload caused by a large number of users, which switch simultaneously to the same network and effectively reduce network overload.

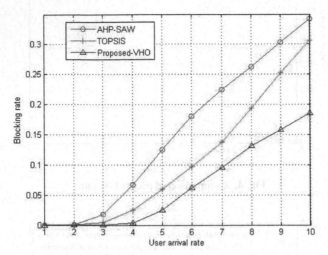

Fig. 6. Blocking rate change graph with user arrival rate

Finally, I would like to say that the proposed service awareness method can effectively improve the ability of the network edges to support multi-service differentiation, in particular to ensure the quality of the service with high real-time availability and high reliability.

5 Conclusion

The introduction of Edge Computing leads to the rise of High-end networks. The diversity and complexity of new services to. The Traditional service mode is increasingly difficult to adapt to the development trend of the service industry to adapt. There is an urgent need for more precise, medium complexity and simpler A sensor to solve these problems, this paper proposes a mobile service Influenza awareness mechanism, which will operate on a hierarchical echo-state network Based. Discrete Echo State Network algorithm is used to identify traffic flow and flush On the base Mobile Resource Mining and Allocation Options will be optimized and research on network edge technology Based on the planning and allocation functions of mobile resources will be based on an easy network edge service award process optimized. The Simulation results show, that this method also improves the ability to distinguish different services and support QoS.

Acknowledgements. This work was supported in part by the Science and technology program of State Grid "Research on Key Technologies of New Generation Power Data Communication Network Based on SDN/NFV" (No. 5700-201952237A-0-0-00). The authors wish to thank the reviewers for their helpful comments.

References

1. Hairuman, A., Zahra, A., Kusuma, G.P., Murad, D.F.: MEC deployment with distributed cloud in 4G network for 5G success. In: 2019 6th International Conference on Information Technology, Computer and Electrical Engineering (ICITACEE), pp. 1–6 (2019)
2. Jiang, D., Wang, Y., Lv, Z., Wang, W., Wang, H.: An energy-efficient networking approach in cloud services for IIoT networks. IEEE J. Sel. Areas Commun. 38(5), 928–941 (2020)
3. Guerzoni, R., et al.: Network functions virtualisation: an introduction benefits enablers challenges and call for action introductory white paper. SDN and OpenFlow World Congress 1, 5–7 (2012)
4. He, K., Fisher, A., Wang, L., Gember, A., Akella, A., Ristenpart, T.: Next stop the cloud: understanding modern web service deployment in ec2 and azure. In: Conference on Internet Measurement Conference, pp. 177–190 (2013)
5. Jiang, D., Wang, W., Shi, L., Song, H.: A compressive sensing-based approach to end-to-end network traffic reconstruction. IEEE Trans. Netw. Sci. Eng. 7(1), 507–519 (2020)
6. Han, S., Li, J., Ma, Y.X., Dong, Q., et al.: A dynamic energy-saving deployment algorithm for virtual data centers. In: Conference on Smart Cloud, pp. 92–97 (2019)
7. Jiang, D., Huo, L., Song, H.: Rethinking behaviors and activities of base stations in mobile cellular networks based on big data analysis. IEEE Trans. Netw. Sci. Eng. 7(1), 80–90 (2020)
8. Wang, S., Zhang, X., Zhang, Y., et al.: A survey on mobile edge networks: convergence of computing caching and communications. IEEE Access 99, 1 (2017)
9. Zhao, X., Yongchareon, S., Cho, N., Shen, J., Dewan, S.: Enabling intelligent business processes with context awareness. In: 2018 IEEE International Conference on Services Computing (SCC), pp. 153–160 (2018)
10. Jiang, D., Wang, Y., Lv, Z., Qi, S., Singh, S.: Big data analysis based network behavior insight of cellular networks for industry 4.0 applications. IEEE Trans. Ind. Inf. 16(2), 1310–1320 (2020)
11. Zhang, L., et al.: Service-aware network slicing supporting delay-sensitive services for 5G fronthaul. In: 2018 23rd Opto-Electronics and Communications Conference (OECC), Jeju Island, Korea (South), pp. 1–2 (2018)
12. Han, S., Li, J., Dong, Q., Ma, Y., Song, L.: Service-aware based virtual network functions deployment scheme in edge computing. In: International Conference on Advanced Communication Technology (ICACT), pp. 562–565 (2020)
13. Jiang, D., Huo, L., Lv, Z., Song, H., Qin, W.: A joint multi-criteria utility-based network selection approach for vehicle-to-infrastructure networking. IEEE Trans. Intell. Transp. Syst. 19(10), 3305–3319 (2018)
14. Yan, Z., Zhao, M., Westphal, C., Chen, C.W.: Toward guaranteed video experience: service-aware downlink resource allocation in mobile edge networks. IEEE Trans. Circ. Syst. Video Technol. 29(6), 1819–1831 (2019)
15. Bi, Y., Han, G., Lin, C., et al.: Intelligent quality of service aware traffic forwarding for software-defined networking/open shortest path first hybrid industrial internet. IEEE Trans. Industr. Inf. 16(2), 1395–1405 (2020)

A Load Balancing-Based Real-Time Traffic Redirection Method for Edge Networks

Chuan Liu[1,2](✉), Shidong Liu[1,2], Ningzhe Xing[3], Shen Jin[3], Yutong Ji[3], Ning Zhang[4], and Jia Tang[4]

[1] Global Energy Interconnection Research Institute Co., Ltd., Nanjing 210003, China
[2] State Grid Laboratory of Electric Power Communication Network Technology, Nanjing 210003, China
[3] State Grid Jibei Electric Power Company Limited, Beijing, China
[4] State Grid Information and Telecommunication Branch, Beijing 100761, China

Abstract. Abundant application services make the scale of data centers continue to expand. The complex data processing business and the communication mode based on cluster communication have brought great challenges to the processing capabilities and network transmission capabilities of the internal servers of the data center. Edge computing extends cloud computing service resources to the edge of the network, and solves the problems of poor cloud computing mobility, weak geographic information perception, and high latency. Traditional edge computing networks still have certain limitations. The SDN network provides a new solution for network innovation research. This article proposes a new real-time traffic redirection method for edge network based on load balancing. It monitors the link resource usage status of the edge network through the OpenFlow controller, and dynamically adjusts the flow path through the redirection algorithm to achieve load balancing on the edge network. Simulation results confirmed the feasibility of the algorithm.

Keywords: Load balancing · Edge computing · OpenFlow · Redirection

1 Introduction

As an important infrastructure of the Internet network, the data center undertakes important tasks such as data storage, calculation and transmission. Various key business systems are centrally placed in the data center, such as search services, distributed databases, and network services. Abundant application services make the scale of the data center continue to expand. The complex data processing business and the use of communication-based communication modes have brought great challenges to the processing capabilities and network transmission capabilities of the internal server of the data center. The traditional cloud computing network architecture can provide resource-centric remote services, but when the amount of data services increases dramatically, it cannot meet the requirements for separate, low-latency, and intensive network access and services.

H. Song and D. Jiang (Eds.): SIMUtools 2020, LNICST 369, pp. 34–43, 2021.
https://doi.org/10.1007/978-3-030-72792-5_4

Therefore, how to effectively use dispersed computing resources and perform data processing tasks at the edge of the network will become a key challenge for the development of the Internet of Things. Edge computing is proposed to meet this computing demand [1], which effectively reduces the network bandwidth and computing load of cloud data centers. The edge computing model has attracted the attention of academia and industry.

In order to solve the load balancing problem in the edge computing network, M. Li et al. [2] proposed a hybrid load balancing (HLB) scheme based on the improved cournot game model. The HLB algorithm combines mobile load balancing and unit scaling functions, and performs better in terms of edge throughput and system blocking rate. S. Ningning et al. [3] studied the framework of fog computing and used cloud fog technology to transform physical nodes of different levels into virtual machine nodes. On this basis, they proposed the use of graph partition theory, based on the dynamic graph partition to build a load balancing algorithm for fog computing. The simulation results show that the cloud computing framework after cloud atomization can flexibly build a system network [4], and the dynamic load balancing mechanism can effectively configure system resources and reduce node migration consumption caused by system changes. R. Beraldi et al. [5] proposed CooLoad, which is a cooperative solution between nearby data centers to improve the service quality of the edge computing infrastructure. CooLoad is a collaborative load balancing solution that can minimize the congestion state of each data center and reduce the execution delay of tasks. Y. Moon et al. [6] proposed a load distribution scheme based on sand piles. This scheme is confident to ensure that the entire edge resources [7] will naturally develop to the most stable state in a natural way. K. Addali et al. [8] proposed a mobility load balancing algorithm for 5G small cellular networks. The results show that, compared with the algorithm in the literature [9], the algorithm minimizes the standard deviation and increases the network throughput. Y. Dong et al. [10] used the deployment model of the joint cloud model, on this basis, proposed a deployment strategy HEELS based on heuristic task clustering method and analysis [11] of firefly swarm optimization algorithm. M. Li et al. [12] proposed an edge network-based LBPC (edge-based load balancing algorithm based on popularity and concentration) and implemented the deployment of computing units at edge nodes. Experimental results show that LBPC can effectively reduce communication delay and balance network load.

However, problems such as the wide variety of network protocols, complex network architecture, and difficulty in maintaining are still the limitations of traditional networks. In response to these shortcomings, SDN, as a next-generation network research and innovation platform, has improved the overall response speed of the network and significantly increased the point-to-point forwarding speed. The SDN network allows developers to control the network flow through network programming methods. Through a controller, the entire network parameters can be adjusted in real time and globally, and the resource status of network devices can be monitored. When the state changes in the network, the underlying network equipment will notify the controller of the changes. The controller will calculate the optimal result according to the built-in algorithm, and then feed back to the network bottom equipment.

This paper proposes a new real-time traffic redirection algorithm to balance the load in the edge network. It can integrate and utilize the information of the entire edge network very well, monitor the link resource usage status of the edge network through the OpenFlow controller, and dynamically adjust the flow path through the redirection algorithm to achieve load balancing of the edge network. It not only strengthens the network data processing capability, but also improves the flexibility and availability of the network.

2 Mathematical Model

Edge computing is a service and application built on the edge server between the user layer and the data center. It migrates some functions from the user layer and data center, and provides limited distributed computing, storage, and network services. Existing research generally divides the architecture of edge computing from the center of the network to the edge of the network into three layers [13, 14]: the cloud computing layer, the edge computing layer, and the terminal layer, as shown in Fig. 1. Different layers are generally divided according to their computing and storage capabilities. The computing and storage capabilities of the terminal layer, edge computing layer, and cloud computing layer increase in sequence.

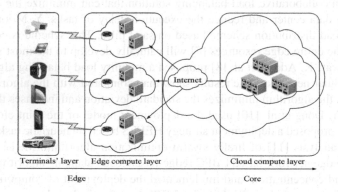

Fig. 1. The edge network architecture.

On this basis, we propose an edge computing network model based on OpenFlow controller, as shown in Fig. 1. We mainly consider the edge network composed of Open-Flow controller and edge computing layer, including an OpenFlow controller and a certain number of OpenFlow switches. OpenFlow is a new type of architecture that separates control and forwarding. It is a specific example of SDN network The device provides control and management of the overall network, and the OpenFlow switch is responsible for data forwarding through the matching flow table.

Many traditional data center network topologies have a hierarchical tree structure. Servers are connected to the network using inexpensive edge switches. Such networks are generally connected in two to three layers to overcome the shortcomings of the limited port density of single commercial switches. Faced with the pressure to build a large data center containing tens of thousands of servers, current researchers have proposed a horizontal expansion method to replace the original vertical expansion. When constructing a network, a large number of parallel paths will be used instead of using expensive large switches with high speed and high port density.

(1) Basic control layer. The main function of the basic control layer is to provide basic management and control services to the SDN network, ensure the normal operation of the network and provide the necessary support for the upper layer services. This layer mainly includes device management module, topology management module, statistics management module and core management module. The specific functions of each module are as follows. Device management module: manages switches and terminal devices connected in the SDN network. Maintain the instance of the switch and related state information (switch type, port, working mode, bandwidth, etc.) on the controller and maintain the synchronization of the corresponding state of the switch instance and the physical switch, and respond to changes in the state of the switch and network events in a timely manner.

(2) Traffic redirection strategy layer. Route calculation module: determine the end-to-end specific information according to the source address and destination address pair of each flow, and use the routing algorithm to calculate the shortest path and all feasible paths of the flow in the network [15]. In the calculation of routes, it is necessary to make full use of the advantages of the network topology to calculate feasible multiple paths, including not only the shortest path, but also multiple feasible paths that satisfy the conditions. Link state collection: Responsible for collecting the status information of each switch and link from the network, calculating the link utilization and the bandwidth usage of the flow.

This article combines the sFlow network measurement technology, because the main job is to communicate with the sFlow collector to read the corresponding status information. Traffic classification module: The main function of traffic classification is to distinguish the traffic in the network, identify different types of traffic in the network, and then use different routing strategies for different flows. Traffic redirection decision module: After identifying the flow in the link, the flow is processed according to different routing strategies, the path is reasonably selected, the global optimal traffic distribution is found, and the flow is assigned to other paths to avoid congestion and improve network utilization.

Edge computing is a service and application built on the edge server between the user layer and the data center. It migrates some functions of the user layer and the data center, and provides limited distributed computing, storage, and network services. Existing research generally divides the architecture of edge computing from the center of the network to the edge of the network into three layers: cloud computing layer, edge computing layer and terminal layer, as shown in Fig. 1 [5–7]. Different layers are generally divided according to their computing and storage capabilities. The computing and storage capabilities of the terminal layer, edge computing layer, and cloud computing layer increase in sequence.

On this basis, we mainly consider the edge network composed of the controller and the edge computing layer, including a controller and a certain number of OpenFlow switches. OpenFlow is a new type of architecture that separates control and forwarding. In a specific example, the controller provides control and management of the overall network, and the OpenFlow switch is responsible for data forwarding through matching flow tables.

The existing edge network resource management key technologies mainly include edge cache technology, edge computing technology.

1. Edge Cache Technology. With the explosive growth of wireless access network equipment and the increase in demand for video services, mobile data traffic has increased significantly to approximately 60% of total network traffic. Although various key technologies can be used to increase the transmission rate, the density of the network infrastructure can be increased by deploying various base stations to improve the performance of the mobile communication system. However, with the proliferation of transmission rates and the number of base stations, the backhaul link congestion in wireless networks is becoming increasingly prominent. In order to alleviate this situation, the researchers proposed edge caching technology, that is, by storing popular content at the edge network infrastructure to reduce backhaul link load and avoid redundancy.

2. Edge computing technology. With the increasing popularity of mobile devices, the demand for running various applications on mobile devices has also increased. However, many emerging applications, such as interactive games, virtual reality, and natural language processing, require high computing power and strict delay constraints, thus placing higher demands on the computing power of mobile devices. Due to the small physical size of mobile devices, their data processing capacity, battery and storage capacity are subject to strict restrictions, resulting in the inability to directly support such applications on mobile devices.

In the entire system, the switch is connected to multiple servers and communicates with the controller through OpenFlow messages, receives instructions from the controller, and processes matching data packets according to the corresponding instructions. Different services or virtual machines are running on the server, and a lot of communication work is performed with other servers, thereby generating traffic across multiple Pods. The sFlow agent installed in the switch is responsible for measuring the status information of the network and reporting to the collector. The controller can obtain the current operating status of the network by periodically querying the information in the collector. When the traffic in the network reaches the access switch for the first time, because there is no relevant flow entry in the flow table of the switch, the query will fail, and the switch uses PacketIn messages to report to the controller. The controller uses the default routing algorithm based on the shortest path to generate routing decisions, and then generates flow table entries to deliver to the switch. The switch forwards the data packet according to the flow entry delivered by the controller.

The system continuously collects the status of the network through the SNMP. The main parameters are two parameters, which are the link utilization and the type of traffic in the network. Identify the flow, and then reroute the flow according to the link utilization based on the identified flow information. In the process of rerouting, both the utilization rate of the link on the current path and the bandwidth usage on the target link must be considered. In the selection of multiple equivalent paths, try to choose non-congested paths as much as possible while avoiding the mutual influence of multiple flows, so this paper models the distribution of flows based on the multi-commodity flow problem and uses particle swarm The algorithm solves the global optimal value so that the flow can choose the path, as Fig. 2 shows.

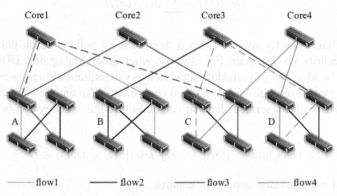

Fig. 2. The flow redirection in the edge network

Network topology diagram can be expressed as $G(V; E)$, where E is the set of edges connected to the switch, S is the set of switches, H is the set of hosts, D is Virtual security device collection (security resource pool), then the security resource pool is as follows:

(1) There are multiple types of security devices in the security resource pool, which can provide a variety of different security capabilities. A security resource pool with p types of security devices is $D = \{D_1, D_2, D_3, \ldots, D_p\}$, where p is a positive integer.

(2) There can be multiple security devices of the same type VSA instance, where q is a positive integer, which refers to the number of instances. And the idle degree of memory utilization and CPU utilization of any instance object are

$$idel_m(d_{pq}) = (thr_{m(d_{pq})} - util_{m(d_{pq})})/thr_{m(d_{pq})} \tag{1}$$

$$idel_m(d_{pq}) = (thr_{m(d_{pq})} - util_{m(d_{pq})})/thr_{m(d_{pq})} \tag{2}$$

where $util$ and thr respectively represent the current utilization and utilization threshold, the threshold is determined by VSA.

(3) If the CPU or memory utilization of a VSA instance is less than zero, the instance is considered to be overloaded, and a new instance needs to be initialized and connected to the network.

Security service chain pulls network flows through security service nodes in a specific order, and the impact of link transmission delay on data transmission performance needs to be considered. The delay in the security service chain is divided into two categories: chain Road transmission delay, service node processing delay. The service node processing delay is the sum of the delays of the security service node, which means that after the data packet enters the virtual security device, the data packet is subjected to corresponding detection and analysis. Due to the same service chain The order and type of internal virtual security equipment are fixed, and the delay difference is not large, which is ignored in this article. Yes, the delay is randomly measured t times and the average value is taken, the link delay can be expressed as

$$Delay(e) = \sum_{i=1}^{t} delay(e)/t \tag{3}$$

Service chain security service chain is described by policies, each policy can be parsed as a security service chain. For example, when defending against DDoS attacks, users need to build a policy to schedule network flows in sequence Fine-grained security protection is formed through Web protection equipment WAF and flow cleaning equipment ADS. The security service chain corresponding to this strategy can be expressed as

$$ServiceChain = \{(Src, D_1, D_2, Dst)\}, D_1 \in D, D_2 \in D \tag{4}$$

It can be further divided into three subunits.

$$Path = [Path_{Src,D1}, Path_{D1,D2}, \ldots, Path_{Dn,Dst}] \tag{5}$$

where routes are scheduled for the security device type of the current security service chain, and routes are generated in order of VSA priority from large to small, and there are scheduled routes between adjacent virtual security devices. The network flow scheduling node will resolve $policy_n$ to the corresponding security service chain, select the appropriate VSA instance to be stored in the network flow scheduling algorithm and update the policy executor as the network flow scheduling node, and then send the security service chain policy to the SDN controller. The SDN controller receives and analyze the strategy to generate the corresponding network flow scheduling route, and decompose it into several subunits, generate flow instructions in turn and issue the switch to complete the traffic redirection, and the network flow matching domain is the policy attribute domain information.

In order to ensure that all security service chain policies are correctly implemented, so that the network flow is correctly protected by the VSA sequence corresponding to the security service chain policy, a complete policy conflict decision mechanism needs to be established. To this end, priority is applied to the VSA in the security service chain policy. The sequence is arranged dynamically and reasonably to resolve the conflict of strategies.

Due to the differences in access networks and the diversification of user business needs, different user association and content placement strategies will have a greater impact on the overall performance of the network. For edge networks that use edge caching technology, designing a reasonable joint resource management strategy is an important issue to improve network resource utilization and ensure user QoS. This chapter proposes a joint user association and cache content placement algorithm based on network cost optimization for edge networks, comprehensively considering the characteristics of user business needs and network resources, and determining an optimization strategy for joint user association and cache content placement to achieve network optimization.

3 Simulation Analysis

3.1 Simulation Environment

This section evaluates the performance of the proposed joint user association and cache content placement algorithm, and compares the performance of the algorithm with the previously proposed algorithm through simulation.

3.2 Network Performance Evaluation

Figure 3 plots the network throughput change. Figure 4 shows the relationship between the network cost and the number of iterations in the algorithm proposed in this chapter. The number of users is set to 5, and the algorithm performance of different sub-channel bandwidths is simulated and compared. It can be seen from the figure that the algorithm converges within a small number of iterations, which proves the effectiveness of the proposed algorithm. Comparing the results obtained with different subchannel bandwidths, it can be concluded that the network cost decreases as the subchannel bandwidth increases.

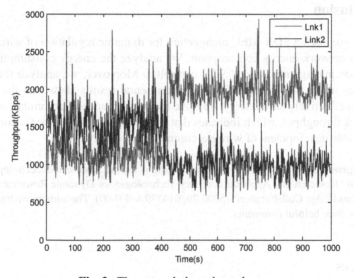

Fig. 3. The network throughput change.

Moreover, Fig. 4 also shows the relationship between network cost and sub-channel bandwidth under different weights and the number of users. The number of users is set to 5 and 6, respectively. In this section, the system performance of the algorithm proposed in this paper and the algorithm proposed in is obtained. It can be seen from the figure that for a given weighted value, the network cost decreases as the sub-channel bandwidth.

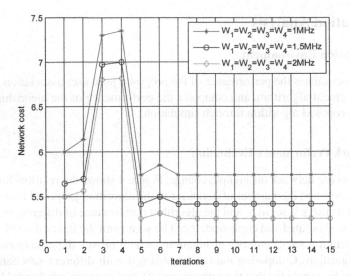

Fig. 4. The network cost over iterations.

4 Conclusion

This paper proposes a SDN-MEC architecture for dynamic regulation of wireless communication network energy consumption. We analyze the energy consumption model and the node management under SDN controller. Moreover, we analyze the network performance under this framework. The experimental results show that the proposed method can effectively save energy, improve the performance of communication delay and network throughput, which indicates that the research of this paper is conducive to the sustainable development of wireless communication network.

Acknowledgements. This work was supported in part by the the Science and technology program of State Grid "Research and Application of Key Technologies of Dynamic Resource Allocation Based on Cloud-Edge Collaboration" (5700-202014179A-0-0-00). The authors wish to thank the reviewers for their helpful comments.

References

1. Baburao, D., Pavankumar, T., Prabhu, C.: Survey on service migration, load optimization and load balancing in fog computing environment. In: Proceedings of the I2CT'19, pp. 1–5 (2019l)
2. Li, M., Xu, X., Wang, Y., et al.: Game theory based load balancing in small cell heterogeneous networks. In: Proceedings of the ICCVE'15, pp. 26–31 (2015)
3. Ningning, S., Chao, G., Xingshuo, A., et al.: Fog computing dynamic load balancing mechanism based on graph repartitioning. China Commun. **13**(3), 156–164 (2016)
4. Jiang, D., Wang, Z., Huo, L., et al.: A performance measurement and analysis method for software-defined networking of IoV. IEEE Trans. Intell. Transp. Syst. (2020). https://doi.org/10.1109/TITS.2020.3029076

5. Beraldi, R., Mtibaa, A., Alnuweiri, H.: Cooperative load balancing scheme for edge computing resources. In: Proceedings of the FMEC'17, pp. 94–100 (2017)
6. Moon, Y., Lee, Y.: A sandpile based load distribution over edges. In: Proceedings of the ICTC'18, pp. 979–981 (2018)
7. Jiang, D., Huo, L., Zhang, P., et al.: Energy-efficient heterogeneous networking for electric vehicles networks in smart future cities. IEEE Trans. Intell. Transp. Syst. (2020). https://doi.org/10.1109/TITS.2020.3029015
8. Addali, K., Kadoch, M.: Enhanced mobility load balancing algorithm for 5G small cell networks. In: Proceedings CCECE'19, pp. 1–5 (2019)
9. Jiang, D., Wang, W., Shi, L., Song, H.: A compressive sensing-based approach to end-to-end network traffic reconstruction. IEEE Trans. Netw. Sci. Eng. 7(1), 507–519 (2020)
10. Dong, Y., Xu, G., Ding, Y., et al.: A 'joint-me' task deployment strategy for load balancing in edge computing. IEEE Access 7, 99658–99669 (2019)
11. Jiang, D., Wang, Y., Lv, Z., Wang, W., Wang, H.: An energy-efficient networking approach in cloud services for IIoT networks. IEEE J. Sel. Areas Commun. 38(5), 928–941 (2020)
12. Li, M., Rui, L., Qiu, X., et al.: Design of a service caching and task offloading mechanism in smart grid edge network. In: Proceedings of IWCMC'19, pp. 249–254 (2019)
13. Jiang, D., Huo, L., Song, H.: Rethinking behaviors and activities of base stations in mobile cellular networks based on big data analysis. IEEE Trans. Netw. Sci. Eng. 7(1), 80–90 (2020)
14. Kiran, N., Pan, C., Wang, S., et al.: Joint resource allocation and computation offloading in mobile edge computing for SDN based wireless networks. J. Commun. Netw. 22(1), 1–11 (2020)
15. Lin, F.P., Tsai, Z.: Hierarchical edge-cloud SDN controller system with optimal adaptive resource allocation for load-balancing. IEEE Syst. J. 14(1), 265–276 (2020)

A Network Energy Efficiency Measurement Method for Cloud-Edge Communication Networks

Ningzhe Xing[1], Chuan Liu[2,3]($\boxtimes$), Rui Ma[4], Jing Tao[2,3], Shidong Liu[2,3], and Yutong Ji[1]

[1] State Grid Jibei Electric Power Company Limited, Beijing, China
[2] Global Energy Interconnection Research Institute Co., Ltd., Nanjing 210003, China
[3] State Grid Laboratory of Electric Power Communication Network Technology, Nanjing 210003, China
[4] State Grid Information and Telecommunication Branch, Beijing 100761, China

Abstract. In the process of network consumption management of traditional wireless communication network, it is impossible to timely adjust according to the network energy efficiency, and the communication effect between nodes is not ideal. Therefore, this paper proposes a dynamic edge-cloud architecture of wireless communication network based on Software defined networking (SDN) architecture. According to the proposed model, the energy consumption of wireless communication network is analyzed. From the point of view of node communication distance, the model of energy consumption regulating is constructed. The experimental results show that the proposed SDN-based edge-cloud model can improve the delay and throughput performance of the network, which indicates that the research of this paper is conducive to the sustainable development of wireless communication network.

Keywords: Software defined networking · Wireless communication network · Edge computing · Network energy consumption

1 Introduction

Recently, cloud computing technology has been greatly developed and applied. Due to its high efficiency and flexibility, cloud computing realizes the functions of computing, storage and network management in a centralized way, and provides services for users in the way of on-demand deployment. But with the development of mobile Internet, such as AR, VR, HD video, the rise of Live services, the centralized cloud computing architecture faces greatly challenge [1, 2]. Because the cloud server is often deployed far away from the end user, and with the increase of the number of users, the cloud computing network bandwidth will be seriously insufficient, and the robustness is poor. Therefore, the cloud computing network architecture is difficult to meet the needs of users for low latency and high reliability services [3, 4]. The mobile end devices access to the backbone network and connect to remote cloud server to obtain services.

H. Song and D. Jiang (Eds.): SIMUtools 2020, LNICST 369, pp. 44–53, 2021.
https://doi.org/10.1007/978-3-030-72792-5_5

For cloud computing, how to overcome the problems of high delay and low energy efficiency in traditional cloud computing architecture is the main challenge. The edge cloud framework enables collaboration between cloud and edge devices to make intelligent decisions related to charging and discharging of electric vehicles [1]. In addition to stable supply and demand, use software to define network convergence to achieve traffic balance. In [3], the author designs a software defined IOT management framework, which is based on a software defined network awareness architecture for edge computing multi domain wireless sensor networks. In [5], the author studies the scalability and resource allocation of wireless MEC, aiming to minimize the battery delay in the user equipment and the delay at the same time [6]. In [7], a new framework for joint optimization of energy consumption and computation of M2M communication in virtual cellular network based on MEC is proposed. In order to improve the computing capacity [8], MEC is introduced into M2M communication network. In [9], a SDN architecture for energy efficiency optimization in 5G Ethernet Passive Optical Network is studied. An open control layer framework based on SDN is proposed, which can prepare EPON backhaul to handle 5G applications and services. In [7], mobile edge computing is introduced into the virtual cellular network of M2M communication to reduce energy consumption, optimize the allocation of computing resources and improve the computing capacity [10]. The random-access process of MTCDs is expressed as partially observable Markov process [11].

In order to solve the problems of high delay, network load and network energy consumption when traditional cloud computing architecture deals with large amount of data business, we analyze the problems existing in cloud computing architecture, proposes a SDN-based cloud-edge integration network architecture [12]. Mobile edge computing (MEC) offloads the business requirements and computing storage resources of traditional cloud computing data center to the edge of the network close to users, while devices on the edge side and cloud computing devices are used for collaborative energy efficiency optimization. [13, 14] MEC technology migrates the computing power to the mobile edge server close to the user. Compared with the cloud server's architecture far away from the user, mobile edge computing can significantly reduce the user's delay in communication and improve the service ability of cloud computing [15, 16]. MEC technology provides it and cloud computing capabilities for wireless access network (RAN) close to mobile users by deploying servers with computing and storage capabilities on the edge of the network.

2 Mathematical Model

SDN is an encouraging solution to the above problems, with the following advantages: 1) Cloud technology provides utilities with high computing power. In addition, the huge amount of data stored in the cloud can help users improve the demand side management services and participation, so as to realize efficient electricity consumption. 2) Through so-called cloud computing, the decentralization of cloud networks can be used to manage and control each microgrid in a distributed manner. 3) SDN technology adopts standards and introduces abstractions to centralize control and management of various types of common network equipment and multiple suppliers. 4) The hardware of SDN solves the problem of managing different networks and reduces the energy consumption of network equipment. 5) Programmability of operators, enterprises, independent software vendors, and users using a common programming environment.

The SDN-MEC architecture of wireless communication network is shown in Fig. 1. As can be seen from Fig. 1, the SDN architecture is composed of three layers, namely the application layer, the communication layer and the node layer. The communication layer and the node layer are connected by a plane interface, and the communication adopts the OpenFlow protocol, with unified communication identification. Figure 1 shows the SDN architecture of wireless communication network.

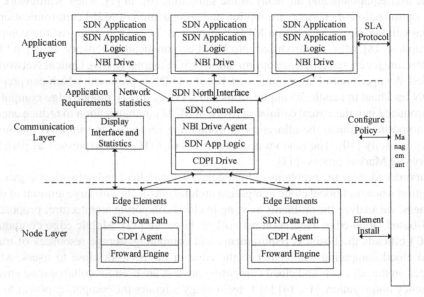

Fig. 1. SDN-MEC architecture of wireless communication network

As can be seen from Fig. 2, the SDN architecture consists of three layers: the application layer, the communication layer and the node layer. The communication layer and the node layer are connected through a plane interface. The communication adopts the OpenFlow protocol and the unified communication ID.

In the wireless communication network, cloud computing architecture is considered to be able to efficiently handle a large number of businesses. In the wireless communication network, the basic architecture of MEC is shown in Fig. 2.

As shown in Fig. 1, the edge cloud framework in the wireless communication network is mainly composed of MEC devices, mobile intelligent terminals and cloud data centers. The deployment of MEC devices is one of the major differences between edge cloud architectures and traditional cloud computing architectures.

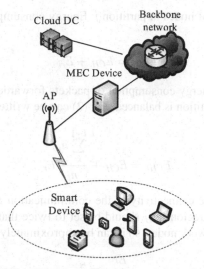

Fig. 2. MEC architecture in wireless communication network

2.1 Node Division and Dynamic Adjustment of Energy Consumption

Under the support of SDN architecture, network nodes can be divided to reduce the energy consumption of nodes. According to the SDN architecture, the wireless network can be divided into n regions, as shown in Fig. 3.

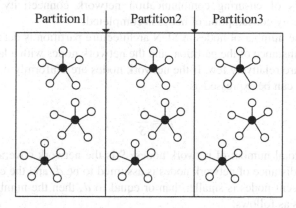

Fig. 3. Network node partition

Since the forwarding energy consumption between the first area and the tail area changes with the partition change, the regulation process is a dynamic regulation. Then, the forwarding energy consumption of the partition node i can be represented by E_r, and the energy consumption of the region node is equal to the energy consumed by all the packets fused in the partition as follows:

$$E_{ri} = \sum_{j}^{i-1} n_j E_r \tag{1}$$

where n_j is the number of nodes in partition j. Energy consumption E_{CH} in partition i can be expressed as:

$$E_{CHI} = E_{CH} + E_{ri} \tag{2}$$

Assuming that the energy consumption of packets forwarded by the first region in the SDN architecture partition is balanced, Eq. (2) can be written as follows:

$$E_{CHI} = E_{CH} + \frac{\sum\limits_{k}^{i-1} n_j}{n_i} E_r \tag{3}$$

In order to ensure the connectivity of the communication network, the communication radius of the first region R_{CH} should be set to twice that of the communication radius R_{node} of other network nodes, so it can be approximately considered as follows:

$$\frac{Er}{E_{node}} = 2 \tag{4}$$

Substitute Eq. (4) into Eq. (3) and then we get as follows:

$$E_{CHI} = E_{CH} + 2\frac{\sum\limits_{k}^{i-1} n_j}{n_i} E_{node} \tag{5}$$

On the basis of ensuring communication network connectivity, the dynamic regulation of energy consumption of nodes is completed.

Moreover, the number of nodes in SDN architecture partition is determined by the communication distance of the partition, and the network nodes with a large communication distance are relatively few. If the network nodes are uniformly distributed, then the node density can be expressed as

$$\rho = \frac{N}{S} \tag{6}$$

where N is the total number of network nodes; S is the network coverage area. If the communication distance of network nodes is assumed to be d, and the communication distance of adjacent nodes is smaller than or equal to d, then the number of adjacent member nodes is as follows:

$$n_{nei} = \rho \times d^2 \tag{7}$$

Each wireless communication node in the network has a communication distance identifier, and all nodes in the network have a communication distance identifier of 0. After a network node collects the broadcast message from the base station, the communication distance identifier of the wireless communication network node is 1.

The dynamic regulation model of wireless communication energy consumption is as follows: it is assumed that node b far away from node d sends a data packet, whose data packet byte is l, and is the associative property of sending data, then the communication data energy consumption is as follows:

$$E(l, d) = \begin{cases} n_{nei}(lE + l\varepsilon_{fs}) \ d \leq d_0 \\ n_{nei}(lE + l\varepsilon_{mp}) \ d > d_0 \end{cases} \tag{8}$$

where E is the energy consumption per bit of data sent or received; ε_{fs} and ε_{mp} are the amplification coefficients of sending and receiving respectively. When the energy consumption is high, the communication path will be redeployed, and when the receiving node is fixed, the sending node will choose a shorter path to realize the communication, thus completing the dynamic adjustment of the energy consumption of the partition communication distance.

2.2 The Network Performance Analysis

The SDN-MEC architecture is proposed above, and the scheme of node division and dynamic regulation of energy consumption is also proposed. This subsection analyzes the performance of business responses between nodes under the proposed architecture. In the SDN-MEC network architecture, in order to reduce the delay of business response, MEC technology is introduced to process the computation-intensive operations at the edge of the network. At the same time, SDN technology is introduced to realize the centralized control network and collect the global information of the network. In the real scenario, we consider a software-defined-cloud-edge computing architecture, composed of k MEC devices, and its network topology is denoted by graph $G = (V, E)$, V is the node set and E is the edge set. So $V = \{v_1, v_2, \ldots, v_k, S, C\}$, where v_i is the MEC device, k is the number of device, S is the SDN controller, and C is the cloud platform. The computing capacity of each device v_i is denoted by c_{v_i}. The computing capacity of the cloud server is denoted by c_c. The edge set can be denoted by $E = \{e_{v_1v_2}, \ldots, e_{v_iv_j}, \ldots, e_{v_iv_c}, e_{v_jv_c}, \ldots, e_{v_{k-1}v_k}\}$. $e_{v_iv_j}$ expresses the communication link between node v_i and v_j. $W_{v_iv_j}$ denotes the delay of node v_l and v_j.

In the process of business execution, the business $Task$ received by the MEC devices is first divided into many sub-tasks $Task_i$, and meets $Task_i = \delta_i Task$, where δ_i is the proportion of the sub-tasks in the total Task, and then the sub-tasks are unloaded to each MEC device for parallel preprocessing. Finally, the pre-processed result $Task_{pre}$ is sent to the cloud computing platform for decision making. Since the business response delay in distributed computing is equal to the maximum processing delay for all subtasks, the total business response delay in the SDN-MEC network architecture is represented as follows:

$$t = \max\left\{ \frac{\delta_i Task}{c_{v_i}} + W_{v_i,v_j}m_{v_i,v_j} \right\} + \frac{Task_{pre}}{c_c} + W_{v_i,c} \tag{9}$$

where $\frac{\delta_i Task}{c_{v_i}}$ is the computing time of subtask $Task_i$ in MEC device v_i, W_{v_i,v_j} denote the delay of node v_i and v_j, m_{v_i,v_j} denote the subtask assignment relationship of node v_i and v_j. When $m = 1$, subtask allocation relationship exists, and when $m = 0$, subtask allocation relationship does not exist. $\frac{Task_{pre}}{c_c}$ represents the delay in matching and identifying the pre-processed result on the cloud. $W_{v_i,c}$ represents the communication delay when the pre-processed result is sent to the cloud server.

In order to optimize the delay of business response and achieve the goal of minimizing the delay of business response, an optimal set of task assignment coefficient δ_i is needed, so that the delay t in Eq. (9) is minimized. Therefore, the business response delay based on SDN-MEC network architecture can be expressed as follows:

$$\min \max \left\{ \frac{\delta_i Tusk}{c_{v_i}} + W_{v_i,v_j} m_{v_i,v_j} \right\} + \frac{Tusk_{pre}}{c_c} + W_{v_i,c} \quad i,j = 1,2,\cdots k$$

$$s.t. \quad m_{v_i,v_j} = \begin{cases} 1, & \delta_i \neq 0 \\ 0, & \delta_i = 0 \end{cases}$$

$$\sum_{i=1}^{k} \delta_i = 1 \tag{10}$$

In the SDN-MEC architecture, the edge nodes are used to preprocess the business data, and the carrying capacity and transmission efficiency of the network are improved through the above analysis, which is conducive to the sustainable development of wireless communication network.

3 Simulation Analysis

3.1 Simulation Environment

This simulation platform is based on the SDN virtual environment composed by floodlight and mininet. The specific environment is one PC with 2.6 GHz CPU and 8 MB RAM. The software environment is 64-bit ubuntu 16.04 operating system with Floodlight, Mininet, and Iperf simulation tools. Floodlight is the current mainstream SDN controller, which is stable and easy to control SDN network flexibly.

3.2 Network Performance Evaluation

Then, we simulates and compares the time delay performance of SDN-MEC model, traditional cloud computing model, and single MEC device model. In the simulation, the MEC device v1 is selected as the single MEC device. The simulation results are shown in Fig. 4. When the number of user requests is less than 10, the time delay of SDN-MEC model is smaller than that of cloud computing model and single MEC device model, but the delay difference of the three scheme is not large.

Because the link bandwidth directly affects the data transmission delay, it will affect the business response delay. In addition, in the actual environment, the link bandwidth between the MEC device and the cloud server also changes in real time. Therefore, we study the impact of the uplink bandwidth of the cloud server on the SDN-MEC model's business response delay performance. When the number of user requests is 35, the uplink bandwidth of the cloud server varies between 5 Mbps and 45 Mbps. The simulation results are shown in Fig. 5. It shows that with the increase of link bandwidth, the business

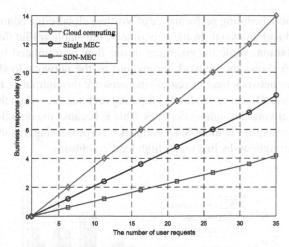

Fig. 4. The comparison of delay performance.

response delay of cloud computing model and single MEC model are gradually reduced, but the business response delay of SDN-MEC architecture is only slightly reduced. In cloud computing and single MEC model, the increase of link bandwidth will lead to the significant reduction of data transmission delay, so the business response delay will decrease with the increase of bandwidth. However, in the SDN-MEC architecture, the amount of pre-processed data is small. When the uplink bandwidth of the cloud server increases, the transmission of a small amount of data to the cloud server will not cause significant time delay reduction. Therefore, as the bandwidth of the cloud server link increases, the delay performance of the SDN-MEC architecture only decreases slightly. To sum up, when the uplink bandwidth of the cloud server is limited, the SDN-MEC architecture has more obvious advantages in reducing the delay of business response.

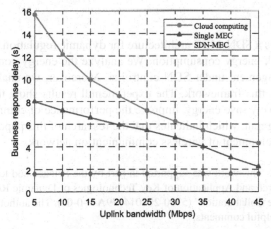

Fig. 5. The impact of uplink bandwidth on delay performance.

Next, the traffic scheduling performance of wireless cloud-edge communication network is simulated and analyzed. In the experiment, the stable traffic flow is simulated by Poisson distribution, while the emergent traffic flow is simulated by Random distribution. Figure 6 shows the network throughput as the network load increases. We can see that, as the network load increases, the network throughput of the three model continues to increase. However, in cloud computing architecture, when the network load exceeds 0.7, the network throughput declines. This is because the data flows are all preempting network resources without SDN controller co-processing, resulting in network congestion and throughput decline under high load conditions.

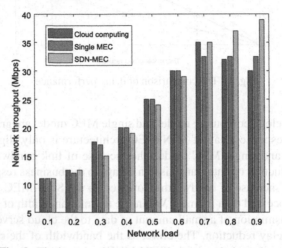

Fig. 6. The impact of network load on network throughput.

4   Conclusion

This paper proposes a SDN-MEC architecture for dynamic regulation of wireless communication network energy consumption. We analyze the energy consumption model and the node management under SDN controller. Moreover, we analyze the network performance under this framework. The experimental results show that the proposed method can effectively save energy, improve the performance of communication delay and network throughput, which indicates that the research of this paper is conducive to the sustainable development of wireless communication network.

Acknowledgements. This work was supported in part by the Science and technology program of State Grid "Research and Application of Key Technologies of Dynamic Resource Allocation Based on Cloud-Edge Collaboration" (5700-202014179A-0-0-00). The authors wish to thank the reviewers for their helpful comments.

References

1. Kaur, K., Garg, S., Kaddoum, G., et al.: Demand-response management using a fleet of electric vehicles: an opportunistic-SDN-based edge-cloud framework for smart grids. IEEE Network **33**(5), 46–53 (2019)
2. Jiang, D., Wang, Z., Huo, L., et al.: A performance measurement and analysis method for software-defined networking of IoV. IEEE Trans. Intell. Transp. Syst. (2020). https://doi.org/10.1109/TITS.2020.3029076
3. Mavromatis, A., Colman-Meixner, C., Silva, A.P., et al.: A software-defined IoT device management framework for edge and cloud computing. IEEE Internet Things J. **7**(3), 1718–1735 (2020)
4. Jiang, D., Huo, L., Zhang, P., et al.: Energy-efficient heterogeneous networking for electric vehicles networks in smart future cities. IEEE Trans. Intell. Transp. Syst. **22**, 1868–1880 (2020). https://doi.org/10.1109/TITS.2020.3029015
5. Kiran, N., Pan, C., Wang, S., et al.: Joint resource allocation and computation offloading in mobile edge computing for SDN based wireless networks. J. Commun. Netw. **22**(1), 1–11 (2020)
6. Jiang, D., Wang, Y., Lv, Z., Wang, W., Wang, H.: An energy-efficient networking approach in cloud services for IIoT networks. IEEE J. Sel. Areas Commun. **38**(5), 928–941 (2020)
7. Li, M., Yu, F.R., Si, P., Zhang, Y.: Energy-efficient Machine-to-Machine (M2M) communications in virtualized cellular networks with Mobile Edge Computing (MEC). In: IEEE Transactions on Mobile Computing, pp. 1541–1555 (2019)
8. Jiang, D., Wang, W., Shi, L., Song, H.: A compressive sensing-based approach to end-to-end network traffic reconstruction. IEEE Trans. Netw. Sci. Eng. **7**(1), 507–519 (2020)
9. Khalili, H., Khodashenas, P.S., Rincon, D., Siddiqui, S., Piney, J.R., Sallent, S.: Design considerations for an energy-aware SDN-based architecture in 5G EPON nodes. In: Proceedings of ICTON, Bucharest, pp. 1–4 (2018)
10. Jiang, D., Huo, L., Song, H.: Rethinking behaviors and activities of base stations in mobile cellular networks based on big data analysis. IEEE Trans. Netw. Sci. Eng. **7**(1), 80–90 (2020)
11. Jiang, D., Wang, Y., Lv, Z., Qi, S., Singh, S.: Big data analysis based network behavior insight of cellular networks for industry 4.0 applications. IEEE Trans. Ind. Inform. **16**(2), 1310–1320 (2020)
12. Moreno, R., Huedo, E., Montero, R.S., et al.: A disaggregated cloud architecture for edge computing. IEEE Internet Comput. **23**(3), 31–36 (2019)
13. Nguyen, D.M., Pham, C., Nguyen, K.K., et al.: Placement and chaining for run-time IoT service deployment in edge-cloud. IEEE Trans. Network Serv. Manage. **17**(3), 214–562 (2019)
14. Sun, H., Yu, H., Fan, G., et al.: Energy and time efficient task offloading and resource allocation on the generic IoT-fog-cloud architecture. Peer-to-Peer Networking Appl. **13**(2), 548–563 (2020)
15. Jiang, D., Huo, L., Lv, Z., Song, H., Qin, W.: A joint multi-criteria utility-based network selection approach for vehicle-to-infrastructure networking. IEEE Trans. Intell. Transp. Syst. **19**(10), 3305–3319 (2018)
16. Li, C., Sun, H., Tang, H., et al.: Adaptive resource allocation based on the billing granularity in edge-cloud architecture. Comput. Commun. **145**, 29–42 (2019)

A Traffic Prediction Algorithm Based on Converged Networks of LTE and Low Power Wide Area Networks

Huan Li[1]([✉]), Feng Sun[1], Yang Liu[1], Shuai Ren[1], Yang Nan[2], and Chao Chen[2]

[1] Electric Power Research Institute of State Grid Liaoning Electric Power Supply Co., Ltd., Shenyang 110006, China
[2] BaoDing HaoYuan Electric Technology Co., Ltd., Baoding 071000, Hebei, China

Abstract. Network traffic plays an important role in network management and network activities. It has an important impact on traffic engineering and network performance. However, we have larger difficulties in capturing and estimating them. This paper proposes a new estimating algorithm to forecast and model network traffic in time-frequency synchronization applications. Our approach is based on the normal regression theory. Firstly, normal regression theory is used to characterize and model network traffic. Secondly, the corresponding normal regression model is created to describe network traffic by finding the model parameters using the samples about network traffic. Finally, the estimation algorithm is proposed to predict network traffic in time-frequency synchronization applications. Simulation results indicate that our approach is effective.

Keywords: Network traffic · Traffic estimation · Traffic modeling · Normal regression model · Dynamic changes

1 Introduction

Within the transmission network, network services have a significant impact on network management, transmission technology and optimization of improvements, reception of network messages, and transmission of activities, in particular with regard to deadlines [1, 2]; network services are one of the specific communications energy terminal services Form. The article describes the behavior, characteristics, and working methods and procedures of network users; The Network (OD) between source and destination shall be provided as a network service [3, 4]. Network transfer assessment is always a burning issue in the area of network research, which has attracted the attention of others. Okay, They are difficult to estimate and predict, different. Actually, To improve the expected accuracy of intelligent network traffic, a two-dimensional method of forecasting is based on analysis: Li Wei and other characteristics are recommended [5, 6]. The phone suggested a new traffic forecast to predict the Bay space network. Unlike existing methods, this method integrates all available waste information into the transport network in order to predict the current flow of local traffic [7, 8].

H. Song and D. Jiang (Eds.): SIMUtools 2020, LNICST 369, pp. 54–63, 2021.
https://doi.org/10.1007/978-3-030-72792-5_6

Zhi, et al. analyzed the characteristics of network traffic data of power grid industrial control system, built a global security monitoring and early warning platform for power grid industrial control system and proposed a suitable platform architecture and detection method of network traffic anomaly detection security monitoring and early warning of power grid industrial control system [9–11]. W. Chen proposed a dynamic baseline Traffic detection Method which is based on the historical traffic data for the Power data network [12–14]. Zhao, et al. expounded the electric power communication network traffic prediction research present situation, summarized the characteristics of the forecast and the influencing factors, put forward to the return of the electric power communication network traffic based on libsvm prediction method and the PSO (Particle Swarm Optimization) algorithm is adopted to model parameters optimization [15–18]. Tang, et al. presented an analytical study of the traffic in power distribution communication network and proposed a new feature matching model. Simulation results show that the proposed model can not only capture the distribution probability faithfully but also depict the self-similarity and multi-fractal characteristics of the traffic [19, 20]. Li, et al. analyzed business traffic according to business characteristics of electric power communication network and proposed an algorithm for uniform business optimization based on entropy [21–23]. Others are very sensitive about this. Summer, yeah. Since the accuracy and accuracy of the network traffic forecasting model are low, they should be further described.

Figure 1 shows the integrated network architecture of LTE wireless and low power wide area network. The network mainly includes User Equipment (UE), Evolved UMTS Terrestrial Radio Access Network (E-UTRAN), Evolved Node B (eNB), Packet Core Evolution (EPC), and Low Power Wide Area Network (LPWAN). Evolved packets the core network communicates with packet data networks such as the Internet, private enterprise networks, or IP multimedia subsystems. Different from these algorithms, this paper proposes a new method for LTE low power wide area fusion communication network traffic estimation based on Principal Component Analysis (PCA) and linear regression model. First, the principal component analysis method is used to decompose the network traffic into a principal component and a non principal component. Second, the main components were analyzed using a linear regression model and the third noise model was used to perform unnecessary component analysis, which included: closure. network traffic samples shall be used to determine model parameters and calculate the next network traffic. The samples are given below. At this point, our model can effectively and accurately reflect the dynamic characteristics of network traffic. Fergus. NGN. The algorithm can effectively stop low-voltage bush regular traffic. The simulations show that the TEMUNE method offers good prospects for implementation. This algorithm can effectively estimate the network traffic in the LTE low-power wide-area converged communication network. Simulation results show that this method has a good application prospect.

The rest of this article is organized as follows. The second part is the problem statement and prediction method. The third part is the simulation results and analysis. The fourth part summarizes the work of this paper.

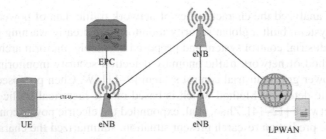

Fig. 1. The integrated network architecture of LTE wireless and low power wide area network.

2 Problem Statement

The principal component analysis is used to divide the network traffic $x(t)$ into the main component and a non-principal component. In order to systematically analyze the problem, the forecast network traffic analysis must take into account several factors [24, 25]. Due to the auto-correlation of network traffic, each piece of traffic data reflects to some extent certain information about network traffic at the next moment, and the traffic data has a certain correlation with each other. According to the characteristics of the automatic correction of network traffic, it must be possible to follow up direct traffic data to some extent association data. Therefore, because the variables in the quantitative analysis are small, the information is large so that the main method of analysis DOS components are used for separate network traffic. First, the raw data is standardized as follows:

$$x_{ij} = \frac{x_{ij} - x_{\bar{i}}}{s_i} (i = 1, 2, \ldots, n; j = 1, 2, \ldots, p) \tag{1}$$

where x_{ij} is the original data, and $x_{\bar{i}}$ s_i are the sample mean and standard deviation of the i–th and j–th flow vectors, respectively. Then we can get the normalization matrix X [26–29].

Find the correlation coefficient matrix for the normalization matrix X:

$$R = \left[r_{ij}\right]_p xp = \frac{X^T X}{n - 1} \tag{2}$$

where $r_{ij} = \frac{\sum z_{kj} z_{kj}}{n-1}, i, j = 1, 2, \ldots, p$. Solve the characteristic equation of Eq. 2:

$$|R - \lambda I_p| = 0 \tag{3}$$

Get p characteristic roots, and Then identify the key elements.

Determine the value of m according to

$$\frac{\sum_{j=1}^m \lambda_j}{\sum_{j=1}^p \lambda_j} \geq 0.85 \tag{4}$$

so that the utilization rate of the data reaches more than 85%. For each $\lambda_j, j = 1, 2, \ldots, m$, solve the system of equations $Rb = \lambda_j b$ to obtain the unit eigenvector b_j^O.

Convert the standardized indicator variable into a main component:

$$U_{ij} = z_i^T b_j^o, j = 1, 2, \ldots, m \tag{5}$$

For the obtained m principal component components,

$$U = (U_1, U_2, \cdots, U_M) \tag{6}$$

The main elements shall be modelled and analysed using the linear regression equation. We perform linear regression modeling:

$$f(u_i) = \omega^T u_i(t) + \varepsilon_i \tag{7}$$

Parameters ω and ε_i are determined using the least square method. It is assumed that the error ε_i follows a Gaussian distribution [30–33].

$$p(\varepsilon_i) = \frac{1}{\sqrt{2\pi}\sigma} \exp\left(-\frac{\varepsilon_i^2}{2\sigma^2}\right) \tag{8}$$

The objective function of less squared method is as follows:

$$J(\omega) = \frac{1}{2}\sum_{i=1}^{m}(y_i - \omega^T u_i)^2 = \frac{1}{2}\left\|y - \omega^T X\right\|^2$$
$$= \frac{1}{2}(y - \omega^T x)^T(y - \omega^T x) \tag{9}$$

The objective function finds the main derivative of inflated surface, finds position 0 and finds the best solution. The solution process is as follows:

$$\frac{\partial J(\omega)}{\partial \omega} = \frac{1}{2}\frac{\partial}{\partial \omega}\left((y - \omega^T x)^T(y - \omega^T x)\right)$$
$$= X^T X \omega - Xy \tag{10}$$

$$\frac{\partial J(\omega)}{\partial \omega} = 0 \tag{11}$$

$$\omega^* = X^T X^{-1} X^T y \tag{12}$$

Using a linear regression model, you can see the speed of movement below at the moment. However, the value is closer to the actual value [34–36], we model the noise of the sub-components 3 times as follows:

$$g(t) = a_3(x(t))^3 + a_2(x(t))^2 + a_1 x(t) + a_0 + \delta(t) \tag{13}$$

By building a model, the final network traffic can be expressed as:

$$y(t) = u(t) + g(t)$$
$$= \omega u(t) + b_0 + a_3(x(t))^3 + a_2(x(t))^2 + a_1 x(t) + a_0 + \delta(t) \tag{14}$$

The modeling algorithm proposed in this paper is as follows:

Step 1: Use principal component analysis to divide network traffic into principal and non-principal components.

Step 2: For the principal component, according to Eq. (7), use a linear regression model to model it.

Step 3: According to Eq. (9), use the least squares method to find the parameters of the linear regression model.

Step 4: For the non-principal component, according to Eq. (13), use the third-order noise model to model and analyze it.

Step 5: According to Eq. (14), use the established network traffic prediction model to perform network traffic prediction.

The algorithm flowchart is shown in Fig. 2.

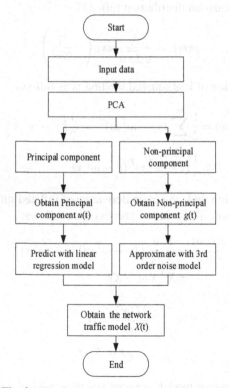

Fig. 2. The flow chart of the flow traffic model.

3 Simulation Results and Analysis

Now we perform many experiments to validate our algorithm NRTA. Using the acronym to simulate the mainframe's current Keyboard. STKCS [7], WABR [12], PCA [15], and TomoG [19] are reported as good estimation approaches for network traffic. Here, we use real traffic data to compare NRTA with them [37, 38]. Accordingly, their estimation performance is analyzed in detail.

Figures 3 and 4 illustrate the estimation results of four algorithms for ODs 23, 68, 83, and 123, respectively, where Real denotes the real network traffic in the real network. From Fig. 3, These four algorithms show that you get better results for pets. Compared with the other three algorithms, NRTA has exhibited the best estimation value of network traffic for ODs 23 and 68. In contrast, TomoG indicates larger estimation errors than the other two algorithms. Figure 4 illustrates that four algorithms can also better estimate the traffic of ODs 83 and 123. Although network traffic changes significantly over time, these four algorithms can change which way to go. This will also enable the Committee to assess more accurately the EM network movements. TomoG holds better estimation ability, while STKCS and WABR indicate the larger estimation errors for network traffic. WABR products the larger under-estimation for OD 123. This shows that NRTA holds a better prediction performance for network traffic.

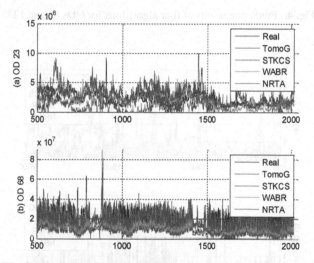

Fig. 3. Prediction results of four algorithms for ODs 23 and 68.

Figures 5 and 6 describe the relative estimation errors of four algorithms for ODs 23, 68, 83, and 123, relative to the real network traffic. Figure 5 demonstrates that NRTA shows the lowest relative prediction errors in four algorithms for network traffic of ODs 23 and 68. TomoG has the largest estimation errors, but STKCS and WABR illustrate the lower estimation errors. WABR shows much lower estimation errors than STKCS. This demonstrates that NRTA holds the best estimation ability for network traffic. Figure 6 shows that for OD 83, STKCS and WABR hold similar errors, and they are the largest. TomoG and NRTA hold lower errors and NRTA is much lower than TomoG. For OD 123, we can see that NRTA has the lowest error. This further indicates that NRTA exhibits a better estimation ability for network traffic.

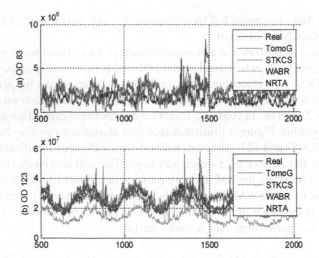

Fig. 4. Prediction results of four algorithms for ODs 83 and 123.

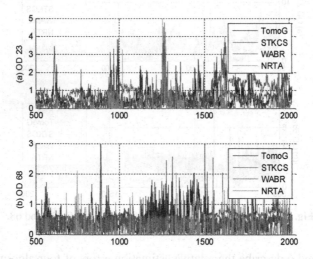

Fig. 5. Relative prediction errors of four algorithms for ODs 23 and 68.

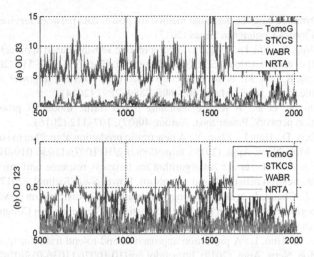

Fig. 6. Relative prediction errors of four algorithms for ODs 83 and 123.

4 Conclusions

This paper uses the normal regression theory to model network traffic in time-frequency synchronization applications in power communications. Using the theory of normal regression, the dynamic properties over time can be accurately measured. Network traffic is converted into the normal regression process to capture dynamic features of network traffic. Then the normal regression theory-based estimation model is created to estimate network traffic. Finally, we propose the corresponding estimation algorithm to estimate network traffic accurately. Simulation results shows that the proposed approach in this paper is feasible.

References

1. Akgul, T., Baykut, S., Kantarci, M., Oktug, S.: Periodicity-based anomalies in self-similar network traffic flow measurements. In: Proceedings of TIM 2011, vol. 60, no. 4, pp. 1358–1366 (2011)
2. Wei, L., Ma, L., Ju, X., et al.: Research on combination traffic forecasting method based on power grid IMS platform framework. Electric Power Inf. Commun. Technol. 93(442), 557–576 (2018)
3. Jiang, D., Wang, Y., Lv, Z., Wang, W., Wang, H.: An energy-efficient networking approach in cloud services for IIoT networks. IEEE J. Sel. Areas Commun. 38(5), 928–941 (2020)
4. Sun, S., Zhang, C., Zhang, Y.: Traffic flow forecasting using a spatio-temporal Bayesian network predictor. In: Duch, W., Kacprzyk, J., Oja, E., Zadrożny, S. (eds.) ICANN 2005. LNCS, vol. 3697, pp. 273–278. Springer, Heidelberg (2005). https://doi.org/10.1007/115509 07_43
5. Jiang, D., Huo, L., Song, H.: Rethinking behaviors and activities of base stations in mobile cellular networks based on big data analysis. IEEE Trans. Netw. Sci. Eng. 7(1), 80–90 (2020)
6. Zhichen, Z.: Security monitoring technology of power grid industrial control system based on network traffic anomaly detection. Electric Power Inf. Commun. Technol. 93(442), 557–576 (2017)

7. Chen, W.: Dynamic baseline detection method for power data network service. In: American Institute of Physics Conference Series (2017)
8. Jiang, D., Wang, W., Shi, L., Song, H.: A compressive sensing-based approach to end-to-end network traffic reconstruction. IEEE Trans. Netw. Sci. Eng. **7**(1), 507–519 (2020)
9. Zhao, Z., Xiao, R., Pei, M., et al.: Prediction based on PSO-SVM in power communication network traffic. Appl. Mech. Mater. **602–605**, 2889–2892 (2014)
10. Tang, L., Du, S., et al.: A feature matching based traffic model of power distribution communication network. Power Syst. Autom. **40**(07), 107–112 (2016)
11. Wang, Y., Jiang, D., Huo, L., Zhao, Y.: A new traffic prediction algorithm to software defined networking. Mob. Netw. Appl. (2019). https://doi.org/10.1007/s11036-019-01423-3
12. Li, C., Jing, S., Sha, L., et al.: An algorithm for business resource uniform distribution in power communication network based on entropy. Power Syst. Technol. (2017)
13. Luo, Z., Yu, J., Chang, J., et al.: Modeling and simulation of distribution power communication traffic engineering based on PTN. In: International Conference on Computer Science & Network Technology. IEEE (2012)
14. Qi, S., Jiang, D., Huo, L.: A prediction approach to end-to-end traffic in space information networks. Mob. Netw. Appl. (2019). https://doi.org/10.1007/s11036-019-01424-2
15. Kuchu, G., Kharchenko, V., Kovalenko, A., et al.: Approaches to selection of combinatorial algorithm for optimization in network traffic control of safety-critical systems. In: 2016 IEEE East-West Design & Test Symposium (EWDTS). IEEE (2016)
16. Xiong, L., Fan, Y., Liu, Y., et al.: Reliability analysis of service routing for a power system communication network based on MCS-RBD: reliability analysis of service routing based on MCS-RBD. IEEJ Trans. Electr. Electron. Eng. **13**(1), 127–135 (2018)
17. Jiang, D., Li, W., Lv, H.: An energy-efficient cooperative multicast routing in multi-hop wireless networks for smart medical applications. Neurocomputing **2017**(220), 160–169 (2017)
18. Yang, Y., Niu, X., Li, L., et al.: A secure and efficient transmission method in connected vehicular cloud computing. IEEE Network **32**, 14–19 (2018)
19. Kaur, K., Garg, S., Kaddoum, G., et al.: Demand-response management using a fleet of electric vehicles: an opportunistic-SDN-based edge-cloud framework for smart grids. IEEE Network **32**, 46–53 (2019)
20. Jiang, D., Huo, L., Lv, Z., Song, H., Qin, W.: A joint multi-criteria utility-based network selection approach for vehicle-to-infrastructure networking. IEEE Trans. Intell. Transp. Syst. **19**(10), 3305–3319 (2018)
21. Guo, H., Zhang, J., Liu, J.: FiWi-enhanced vehicular edge computing networks. IEEE Veh. Technol. Mag. **14**, 45–53 (2019)
22. Huo, L., Jiang, D., Lv, Z., et al.: An intelligent optimization-based traffic information acquirement approach to software-defined networking. Comput. Intell. **36**, 1–21 (2019)
23. Liu, H., Zhang, Y., Yang, T.: Blockchain-enabled security in electric vehicles cloud and edge computing. IEEE Network **32**, 78–83 (2018)
24. Wang, F., Jiang, D., Qi, S.: An adaptive routing algorithm for integrated information networks. China Commun. **7**(1), 196–207 (2019)
25. Huo, L., Jiang, D., Zhu, X., et al.: An SDN-based fine-grained measurement and modeling approach to vehicular communication network traffic. Int. J. Commun. Syst. 1–12 (2019). Online available
26. Wang, J., He, B., Wang, J., et al.: Intelligent VNFs selection based on traffic identification in vehicular cloud networks. IEEE Trans. Veh. Technol. **68**(5), 4140–4147 (2019)
27. Wang, F., Jiang, D., Qi, S., et al.: A dynamic resource scheduling scheme in edge computing satellite networks. Mob. Netw. Appl. (2019). https://doi.org/10.1007/s11036-019-01421-5

28. Li, M., Si, P., Zhang, Y.: Delay-tolerant data traffic to software-defined vehicular networks with mobile edge computing in smart city. IEEE Trans. Veh. Technol. **67**(10), 9073–9086 (2018)
29. Jiang, D., Zhang, P., Lv, Z., et al.: Energy-efficient multi-constraint routing algorithm with load balancing for smart city applications. IEEE Internet Things J. **3**(6), 1437–1447 (2016)
30. Garg, S., Kaur, K., Ahmed, S., et al.: MobQoS: Mobility-aware and QoS-driven SDN framework for autonomous vehicles. IEEE Wireless Commun. **26**, 12–20 (2019)
31. Lin, C., Deng, D., Yao, C.: Resource allocation in vehicular cloud computing systems with heterogeneous vehicles and roadside units. IEEE Internet Things J. **5**(5), 3692–3700 (2018)
32. Jiang, D., Huo, L., Li, Y.: Fine-granularity inference and estimations to network traffic for SDN. PLoS ONE **13**(5), 1–23 (2018)
33. Garg, S., Singh, A., Batra, S., et al.: UAV-empowered edge computing environment for cyber-threat detection in smart vehicles. IEEE Network **32**, 42–51 (2018)
34. Huo, L., Jiang, D., Qi, S., et al.: An AI-based adaptive cognitive modeling and measurement method of network traffic for EIS. Mob. Netw. Appl. (2019). https://doi.org/10.1007/s11036-019-01419-z
35. Keshavamurthy, P., Pateromichelakis, E., Dahlhaus, D., et al.: Cloud-enabled radio resource management for co-operative driving vehicular networks. In: Proceedings of WCNC 2019, pp. 1–6 (2019)
36. Jiang, D., Wang, Y., Lv, Z., Qi, S., Singh, S.: Big data analysis based network behavior insight of cellular networks for industry 4.0 applications. IEEE Trans. Ind. Inform. **16**(2), 1310–1320 (2020)
37. Li, J., Shen, X., Chen, L., et al.: Service migration in fog computing enabled cellular networks to support real-time vehicular communications. IEEE Access **7**(2019), 13704–13714 (2019)
38. Das, D.: Improving throughput and energy efficiency in vehicular Ad-Hoc networks using Internet of vehicles and mobile femto access points. In: Proceedings of TENCON 2019, pp. 1–5 (2019)

Analysis on the Current Situation of Network Media Literacy of the Post-90s University Students

Wen Zhou[1(✉)] and Xiannu Wei[2]

[1] South China Business College of Guangdong, University of Foreign Studies,
Guangzhou 510545, Guangdong, China
[2] Shaoyang University, Shaoyang 422000, Hunan, China

Abstract. At present, the post-90s undergraduates are the main group to use new media, and their network media literacy is highly concerned by academic circles. The paper analyzes the current situation of the undergraduates' network literacy from several universities in Guangzhou in three aspects including channel of network contact, media literacy awareness, and understanding and critical ability for information sources of the post-90s university students, and finds out that the post-90s university students have a certain judgement for the media resources, but they lack critical thinking and critical abilities for media resources from the multiple perspectives.

Keywords: Post-90s · University students · Media literacy · Literacy education · Critical ability

1 Foreword

Media literacy has always been an important topic in the field of Journalism and communication, In the era of network communication, there are more and more problems of media literacy, and more and more people pay attention to media literacy. Nowadays China's post-90s quickly become the main force to use new media [1]. In the endless social public events, the post-90s college students are the main concern, direct participants and promoters, and become the main driver and backbone of public events. Therefore, it has become an urgent problem to understand the network media literacy of post-90s college students, analyze the existing problems, and seek effective ways to improve.

At the National Conference on network security and informatization in April 20, 2018, general secretary Xi Jinping put forward the strategy of "network power", put forward the idea of building a network power, talent is the key, we need to gather talent resources, put forward the work of strengthening personnel training, and cultivate high-quality information talents who understand strategy and management in network technology [2]. General secretary Xi Jinping pointed out that to vigorously promote the development of China's network power strategy, we must attach great importance

H. Song and D. Jiang (Eds.): SIMUtools 2020, LNICST 369, pp. 64–77, 2021.
https://doi.org/10.1007/978-3-030-72792-5_7

to providing strong talent support for the construction of the network power [3]. As the main force of the strategic development of network power, college students should assume the responsibility and mission of practicing the network power.

With the continuous economic globalization, in the context of China's strategy of building a network power, strengthening China's network security and improving citizens' network media is the premise of media ecological improvement and benign operation. Especially for contemporary college students, the media has brought them unprecedented huge impact, but there are also some drawbacks, network information is mixed, college students are faced with complex network information, and their cognition of media is fuzzy or lost in it. How to use the network reasonably, maintain the network security, improve the media literacy, and promote the steady realization of the network power is the contemporary college students need to solve the topic of the times.

2 Literature Review

2.1 Theoretical Analysis of Network Media Literacy Research

It is the premise and basis for the research to analyze the related concepts of network media literacy, sort out the research status at home and abroad, and accurately define the meaning and components of post-90s university students network media literacy.

"Media literacy" is an imported word, which was first put forward by European scholars. In 1933, scholars Levis and Thompson published the pioneering work of media literacy education culture and environment: the cultivation of critical consciousness. For the first time, they made a systematic exposition on the introduction of media literacy education in schools, put forward a complete set of suggestions, and designed a wealth of classroom exercises [4]. From the definition of media literacy, it includes four skills: access to information, analysis of information, evaluation of information, production of information [5]. Canadian education expert Joan Talim interprets media literacy from the perspective of audience's independent criticism, emphasizing the subjectivity of the audience. He believes that "media literacy is the ability of the audience to choose and analyze the information they receive every day, and it is to deal with the media with critical skills." [6]. Bill Walsh, an American scholar, explains media literacy from the perspective of traditional literacy. He regards it as an integral part of public life. As a necessary ability in life, he puts forward that "media literacy is an expansion or extension of traditional literacy, not a substitute for it. It is to make each of us more happy, more critical, and more familiar with various communication methods." [7]. Walliborn defined media literacy as the embodiment of civil rights, emphasizing the audience's active participation in media information. He advocated that "media literacy is to seek citizens' independent rights, and change the passive relationship between the audience and the media into an active and critical agreement" [8]. Rubin believes that there are three levels of media literacy, "capability model", "knowledge model" and "understanding model" [9]. Potter W.J. believes that the media literacy refers to the ability that people obtain, analyze, evaluate and spread a variety of media information and use them to serve the work and life of individuals [10].

In 1992, the American Media Literacy Research Center defined media literacy as "the ability of people to choose, question, understand, evaluate, create, produce and respond intelligently to information in different media" [11]. According to the American media literacy research center, media literacy is an educational method in the 21st century. It enables people to contact, analyze, evaluate and create various spatial forms of information, from printing to images to the internet. Media literacy is the basic inquiry skills, necessary self-expression and the ability to understand social media of citizens in a democratic society. The concept of media literacy in China was gradually accepted after the 1990s. In 1997, Bu Wei, researcher of Chinese Academy of Sciences, published the first article on the research of media literacy. Since then, his "on the significance, content and method of media education" has opened the door of media literacy research in China [12]. In "Media Literacy Education Proceedings", Chinese scholar named Qiu Peihuang pointed out: "the network media literacy refers to people's ability to choose, understand, question, evaluate, create and make, and the reaction ability of critical thinking to information." [13]. At present, domestic and foreign academic circles have not formed a unified understanding on the definition and meaning of "media literacy". Based on the above interpretations of media literacy, the media literacy in this paper refers to the individuals's ability to recognize and use the network media, which is embodied in the motivation of using media, ways and means and attitudes for media resources, validity of using media resources, and critical thinking and critical ability for the media resources.

With the rapid development of the network, the network has penetrated into every aspect of the society. The influence of the network has exceeded the traditional media such as newspapers, radio and television. It has also attracted the attention of the academic circles at home and abroad. The network media literacy has been brought into the theory and practice of media literacy education. In the article "media literacy in an interactive age", its author, Art Silverblatt, Professor of communication and Journalism at the University of Webster, pointed out that the internet has emerged as an important research field of media literacy, and put forward a unique research perspective of "network literacy" and "information literacy" [14]. At present, there are 1367 articles about "network media literacy" in CNKI. In the existing literature, many excellent master's and doctoral dissertations have made a comprehensive and systematic research on "network media literacy". Zhou Fangfang, a graduate student of East China Normal University, believes that network media literacy refers to users' correct use and effective use of the network, creation and dissemination of information on the basis of certain network knowledge, so as to achieve the purpose of serving personal development [15]. Qiao shuaiqi, a graduate student of ideological and political education in Henan Normal University, has made "Research on the media literacy education of teenagers in the perspective of network culture" from the perspective of cultural construction and school moral education; Huang Xiaowei, a graduate student of higher education of Southwest University, has made a "Research on the media literacy problems and Educational Countermeasures of college students" from the perspective of media literacy education of college students, and the communication research of Southwest University of political science and law from the perspective of media communication [16]. Han Yongqing, a graduate student of educational technology of East China Normal University, made a research on the current situation and promotion strategies of College Students' network media literacy from the perspective of educational informatization [17].

2.2 Literature Summary

The existing research has made a certain theoretical contribution to the media literacy education of college students and the network media literacy of college students. Most of these studies are conducted from the perspective of communication, journalism and education. The western theory is introduced into the domestic theoretical field, combined with the actual situation of China's national conditions and the actual situation of college students. These theories concern the practice of theoretical exploration and sublimation, and basically formed a feasible research method to explore the media literacy and network media literacy of college students, which provides thinking reference for subsequent researchers. However, compared with other fields, the research in this field started late, and its quantity and quality are weaker than those in other fields. The high-quality literature mainly focuses on the theoretical analysis of Western media quality education. The quantitative research on the media literacy of local college students is less, and the research on the network media literacy of post-90s college students is even rarer. The network media literacy discussed in this paper is the network media literacy, which refers to the media literacy under the network environment. The main factors include the cognition and use ability of the network media, the acceptance and discrimination of the network media, the ethics and values of the network media, and the social activities of the network media. In the definition of connotation, this paper mainly focuses on the quantitative research of localization, and puts forward countermeasures on the basis of mastering rich and accurate data.

3 Survey and Analysis on the Status of Post-90s College Students' Network Media Literacy

Under the context of the WEB 2.0 new media, the new media network mixing with good and bad information has become an important immersing carrier for constructing the social ecology, in the acceptance and acquisition of imbued information, some post-90s university students lack a certain cognition and screening literacy when using online media; Due to the lack of network moral literacy, they are easily deceived by false information on the Internet or utilized by unscrupulous public opinion environment to become the producers or communicators of rumors. So the media literacy of post-90s university students and the arising problems cannot be underestimated.

The author selects the on-site questionnaire samples from Sun Yat-sen University, Guangdong University of Finance and Economics, South China Agricultural University and Guangdong University of Foreign Studies, comprehensively considers the factors such as the levels of universities, majors, grades, etc. to strive for the universality and representation of the selected samples. The questionnaire involves the university students' contact and motivation for media, university students' cognitive degree on the media literacy, university students' critical ability on media and so on. 300 paper questionnaires were issued, and 299 questionnaires were recovered on site, with a recovery rate of 99.67%. Among them, there are 283 valid questionnaires with a recovery rate of 94.3%.

The author further explores and analyzes the current situation of the network media literacy of the post-90s university students, which will be beneficial for cultivating the university students to have a certain critical ability on media and become the participants and builders of a good public opinion environment. Finally, experimental results that the post-90s university students have a certain judgement for the media resources, but they lack critical thinking and critical abilities for media resources from the multiple perspectives.

Provided that the reliability of the questionnaires is real, through the statistics and analysis for questionnaires, the media literacy of "post-90s" university students is as follows:

3.1 Types of Media

In 2019, the 43rd China Internet Development Statistics Report showed that as of December 2018, China's internet population was 829 million, of which 8.7% had college-level education, 9.9% had undergraduate-level education or above [18]. Obviously, the university student is the new media important audience group. As the core audiences of new media, the post-90s university students have an active thinking, and have a relatively high acceptability for the fourth media and the fifth media represented by network and mobile phone, while having a relatively low acceptability for the traditional media represented by newspapers, radios and television. Among the 283 effective questionnaires, 88.96% of the "post-90s" college students use mobile phones, 79.26% of them use the internet, and 51.5% of them are both internet and mobile phone users. At the same time, only 6.02% of post-90s use the traditional media newspaper, and only 7.02% of university students receive information by radio. Many university students think mobile phone use is so necessary that it has become a part of the life. Once they do not contact mobile phone, they will feel psychological anxiety. And the new media of network is closely related to life, the post-90s university students' network expense keeps strong a month and becomes the main monthly expense.

The fast consumption culture of fragmentation reading is also reflected in the media contact content of post-90s university students. From 283 valid questionnaires, 88.3% of the university students mainly receive the images and videos in the daily information reception. The respondents admitted that "reading images or watching videos takes a shorter time, and is more suitable for the larger daily information demand". For the written report that requires more than three minutes for reading, 78.9% of post-90s choose to give up the reading because it costs a longer time and requires for in-depth thinking. It can be found in the results of survey that post-90s university students have changed to the reading of videos and images via television, mobile phone and network from the reading of literature information in the traditional magazine and newspapers (Fig. 1).

3.2 Media Use Behavior

The length of media use time to a certain extent can reflect the importance of the media to the user and the user's dependence on the media. Therefore, the use of media time is also an important index to examine the media literacy of the post-90s college students. For media contacting time, the post-90s university students interviewed express that they spend most of their spare time on using mobile phone and network. According to

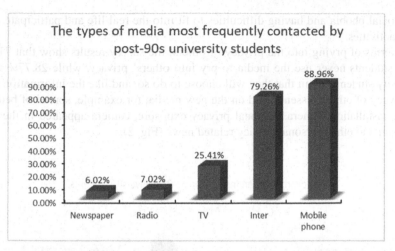

Fig. 1. The types of media most frequently contacted by post-90s university students

the survey, more than half of the university students use the mobile phone and network media for more than three hours within 24 h, accounting for 62.96%. 101 university students use the new media for 0.5–3 h per day, accounting for 34%. And only nine university students fill in 0.5 h or below for using media in the questionnaire. Due to the lack of supervision of parents and teachers in the spare time, the management and self-discipline awareness on using media and the self-management ability of university students are very weak. Some university students said that mobile phones and network have occupied the entire spare time, and the mobile phone and network have become a best means of time consuming.

During the use of new media, most of interviewed post-90s university students said that since payment, learning, social contact and literature search are mostly completed on line, thus most of their time using mobile phones is for the above activities. According to the results of survey, those who use the new media for study account for 30%, those who read news for keeping relations with society account for 20%, and those who aim at social contact account for 49.2%, while 41.2% of university students use it for fragmentation entertainment. Those who do not use it for data collection account for 30.76%, those who make less use of it for information acquisition account for 40.08%, and those who are limited to the learning and reading and make less use of it for social contact account for 8.9%. It can be seen that university students mainly use the new media for completing three functions including information acquisition, social contact and learning. However, during the on-site questionnaire distribution and interview, the author finds that the social abilities of post-90s university students have fallen obviously because they rely much on the social contact functions of new media. Many respondents admit that they prefer to communicate with real classmates and friends via text messages and voice in the online virtual social environment provided by mobile phone rather than communicating frankly face to face. Then, they usually stay in dormitory in their spare time, rarely communicate with classmates and teachers, indulge in the network and mobile phone, thus suffering from social phobia and having difficulties to fit into the real life and participate in the social activities.

In terms of prying into the privacy of others, the survey results show that 71.23% of the students never use the media to pry into others' privacy, while 28.77% of the university students admit that they will choose to do so, and like the information about the privacy of others disseminated on the new media, for example, spread of bedroom remote installation camera, personal privacy exposure, camera appeared in the girls' bathroom and other personal privacy related news (Fig. 2).

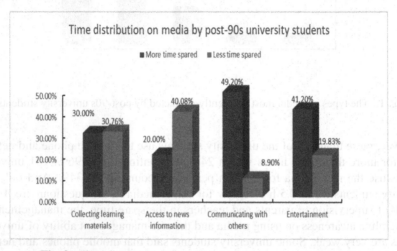

Fig. 2. Time distribution on media by post-90s university students

3.3 Attitudes to the Media Literacy

The awareness of media literacy is weak. In 1947, American social psychologist and one of the four founders of communication science Kurt Lewin proposed the concept of "gatekeeper" in the Channels of Group Life [19]. Lewin believes, in his study of the group communication, that the information flows in the channels with "door area", in which there are some gatekeepers, and only the information which meets the group norms or gatekeeper's value standards can enter the channels of dissemination. As the gatekeeper, the professional media organizations control the discourse power through agenda setting. In the We-Media era, anyone can give opinions on the common topic as long as you possess a mobile phone or computer, and the traditional gatekeeper is transferred to the civil public opinion field. In the one-way communication of traditional media receiving and releasing information, media organizations assume the responsibility and role of gatekeepers. In the context of we media, individuals become the gatekeeper of news information screening. Therefore, the media literacy of college students is particularly important. In the context of we media, the media literacy of college students is particularly important. But they have little idea about the "media literacy". Over half of the post-90s university students said that they have never heard about the concept, accounting for

53.89%. And 43.72% of them know the connotation of media literacy through lectures and courses. It can be seen that the post-90s media literacy education has not attracted the attention of relevant departments of universities (Fig. 3).

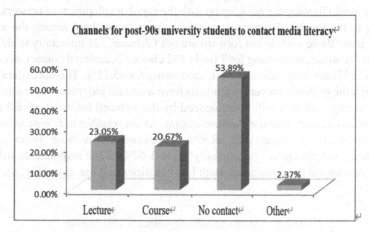

Fig. 3. Channels for post-90s university students to contact media literacy

3.4 The Interpretation Ability of Media Information

When the media reflects reality, it is not a "mirror-like" reflection of the objective world, but a screening and rewriting of reality information according to certain frames, values and ideologies, thus presents one kind of media construction "reality". The audience with media literacy must be able to distinguish the authenticity of the media information, understand the hidden intention of the media, distinguish the facts and viewpoints in the information, and understand the difference between the reality of media construction and the objective reality. In other words, the audience has the ability to interpret and criticize the media information is an important media literacy. "Media Literacy" means to let people know that mass communication, as the information system of society, is the product of organizations, has its own interests and demands, and there is a gap between the world constructed by media and the real world.

The survey shows that "post-90s" college students have a certain ability of interpretation, and can make judgments on the authenticity of media information in line with their knowledge framework and thinking ability. Such as "one movement a day keeps the cancer away", "seaweed is actually made of plastic", "a pupil who is infected with rabies barks like a dog during outbreak", "property can be stolen via WeChat payment code screenshots" and so on, "Post-90s" college students can use common sense to falsify. For the complex information that needs to be checked to judge whether it is true or not, the vast majority of "post-90s" college students can also maintain a certain degree of vigilance, and can rationally carry out the next step of action. 57.57% of them will check the authenticity of the information, but will not forward it; 36.3% of the people will only forward it after confirming the authenticity of the information; only 6.06% of the "post-90s" college students will forward it without thinking. They can keep a certain of vigilance generally and know to judge the truth of the information through the inquiry of information sources.

Due to the young and irrational psychological characteristics of post-90s college students, their media literacy can not keep up with the rapid development of network media. According to the results of survey, as for the rumors transmitted among the acquaintances, such as "those who do not forward are not Chinese", 21 university students will choose active contact, accounting for 7.04%; 142 choose occasional contact, accounting for 47.49%; 135 choose no active contact, accounting for 45.15%. This set of data reflects that although the post-90s university students have a certain judgment, their self-control is still not strong, and they will be influenced by the induced information and become the intermediary carrier of rumor communication. As for whether to release information about bad emotions and vulgar tastes, 68.89% of the respondents chose "never", 29.43% of the college students chose "occasionally", and 1.67% of the respondents still chose to publish or forward the information with bad emotions and low taste (Fig. 4).

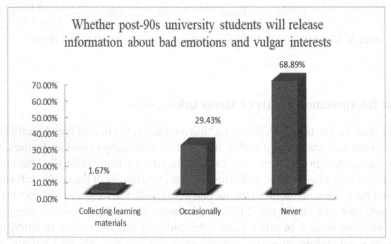

Fig. 4. Whether post-90s university students will release information about bad emotions and vulgar interests

The mass media is a material carrier for dissemination of all kinds of information to a wide audience. Traditionally, it refers to six media of books, newspapers, magazines, radio, television and movies with a wide range of dissemination. Nowadays, the development of new media depends on the rapid development of information technology. Lasswell summarized the basic functions of mass media as environmental monitoring, social coordination and inheritance of society heritage in 《The Structure and Function of Communication in Society》 published in 1948 [20]. In 1959, based on the views of Lasswell, Charles Wright supplemented the statement of "entertainment" function and expended the social functions of mass communication to "four-function theory" including environmental monitoring, interpretations and regulations, social functions and provision of entertainment in the Mass Communication: Discuss on Functions [21].

The survey shows that the post-90s university students have stronger personality and purpose, which is reflected in the use of new media. The post-90s university students use smart phones and networks with a strong purpose to satisfy their own learning, information, and social contact functions, which reflects the relative rationality of this group for the use of new media. But obtaining and transmitting information and providing entertainment are the basic functions of mass media, the post-90s university students under-utilize the social functions of mass media. Mass communication plays a key role in the dissemination of knowledge, values and code of conduct. The audiences are cultivated in the social composition factors such as family, school, etc., namely, the specific mass communication environment. The interviewed post-90s university students are mostly in the level of passive acceptance of information, and they selectively read, understand and absorb the major news with a certain orientation for public opinion, prefer to the entertaining and relaxing soft news with one-way thinking and rarely select the hard news such as the current political news, and they have insufficient sensitivity to news and lack universal humanistic care. In other words, the post-90s college students' use of the social coordination function, interpretation function and heritage function of mass media is inefficient.

The post-90s university students possess a certain critical thinking but lack critical ability for media resources. The critical ability of network public opinion refers to the ability to treat network information critically and to select, select and process information according to certain position, policy and value standard. The critical ability of network media can be further divided into media information processing ability, which can be divided into deep reading ability, critical questioning ability and independent thinking ability. The interactivity and quickness of new media bring convenience to the post-90s university students, while its complexity, grassroots and diversity are also weakening the university students' ability to interpret and criticize the information. For the phenomenon of "human flesh search" and "network tyranny" emerging in an endless stream on the Internet, 47.12% of the post-90s college students interviewed "know", 50.23% of them "don't care", and 2.65% of them "don't know". In "do not care about" 50.23% of the students said "do not want to know, do not care, no interest". On the choice of how to view this social phenomenon, 34.45% of the students thought it was "immoral", 53.78% of the students thought "netizens have the right to express their own opinions, it is a need to vent their emotions", and the remaining 11.77% students thought that "it doesn't matter, it's none of my business". From the perspective of the attitude towards bad information and the phenomenon of "network tyranny", the survey results show that some students can distinguish between the media reality and the objective reality, have certain thinking about the pseudo environment, and have a certain shallow ability to deal with the complex media content, but lack of in-depth thinking and questioning of the media content.

Based on the above data, a total of 93.87% of college students will make various judgments on the authenticity of information sources. However, "having certain judgment" is only a shallow level to judge whether the information is true. 62.23% of post-90s college students lack the ability to analyze media information in depth, and to think and criticize media resources from multiple perspectives.

4 Conclusions and Recommendations

4.1 The Main Conclusion

This paper focus on study the current situation of network media literacy of the post-90s university students in Guangzhou city. This paper analyzes the current situation of the undergraduates' network literacy from several universities in Guangzhou in four aspects including channel of network contact, media literacy awareness, and understanding and critical ability for information sources of the post-90s university students. From the above analysis, we can see that for the use of new media resources, post-90s university students not only show their psychological dependence on media resources and their certain discrimination ability for information source, but also shows their media literacy acquired in long-term information infiltration. The study found that the post-90s university students have a certain judgement for the media resources, but they lack the awareness of critical view of media information and lack critical thinking and critical abilities for media resources from the multiple perspectives.

4.2 Countermeasures and Suggestions on Improving the Network Media Literacy of Post-90s College Students

A sample survey of several universities in Guangzhou shows that media literacy is becoming more and more important to the post-1990s college students and has become a quality they must possess. However, although some "post-90s" college students have certain media literacy, it is still not enough to cope with the endless variety of media and complex media information, and their media literacy needs to be improved.

With the development of the media and the emergence of new media, the impact of the media, especially the new media represented by the mobile phone and the internet, on the "post-90s" college students is more and more extensive and profound, they live in the media, the media production information constructs the media ecology. In contrast, the post-90s college students rely more and more on the media, mobile phones, the internet and other new media have become their study, social and even leisure are inseparable partners, tools. However, when the new media represented by the mobile phone and the internet become more and more close to the post-90s college students, some negative or even negative influences also appear. It can be seen that the interactivity, quickness and intelligentization of the new media are really convenient for the post-90s college students, but the interactivity, quickness and intelligentization are based on the correct use of the new media and media information. In other words, only with a certain degree of media literacy, post-90s college students can effectively use a variety of media while trying to avoid their negative effects. Therefore, the media literacy for the post-90s of the importance of college students more and more prominent.

The media literacy of post-90s college students needs to be improved. The survey shows that the post-90s college students have certain media literacy. However, their media literacy still has obvious weak links and bias. Most students have not studied the relevant courses, lack of systematic media literacy knowledge and theory. Some post-90s college students spend a lot of time using the new media such as mobile phones and internet for social intercourse and entertainment, which not only affects their study and life, but also weakens their social ability. Even some students have a psychological dependence on mobile phones, internet and other new media, a little long time without contact with mobile phones, internet and other new media will feel abnormal anxiety.

Because of the lack of media literacy and breeding, the evolution of a variety of problems, the consequences can not be underestimated. Some post-90s college students are relatively weak in resisting the bad media information, will contact the bad media information on their own initiative, and are easily affected by the bad information. Some college students also release or forward the information with bad mood and low-level interest, and become the disseminator and intermediary of the bad information. Therefore, as soon as possible to improve post-90s college students of the media literacy has become the school, the community is facing an urgent need to solve the problem.

Needless to say, there are many ways to improve the media literacy of post-90s college students. From the UK, the United States and other countries, media education is the main way of school education, social education and media publicity. Yu Guoming, Professor of Communication University of China, once pointed out that the choice and use of media is a kind of accomplishment. Its cultivation requires not only knowledge, experience and accumulation, but also wisdom, understanding and renewal. Although it belongs to the category of lifelong learning in essence, the school education of media literacy is one of the most important links. The surveys show that, the knowledge and ability of post-90s college students about media literacy are not acquired through systematic education. However, formal school education is the most direct and effective way to improve their media literacy. Because of this, media literacy has become a general course for all students in many colleges and universities in many developed countries. At present, China has carried out media literacy education for decades, but the importance of media literacy has not risen to the functional level of local government or national government departments. The implementation of media literacy education proposed by local governments or official institutions has been blank, and few universities have incorporated media literacy education into general compulsory courses. In view of this, it is suggested that media education should be included in the curriculum system of primary and secondary schools and universities, and clear teaching objectives, teaching methods and other teaching standards should be determined, so as to make it the same compulsory course as ideological and moral education, physical education and painting, and become a part of the teaching system of cultivating students' minds. In the stage of higher education, the media literacy of post-90s college students can be improved by setting up media literacy compulsory courses or elective courses. Media education is not only a kind of professional education, but also an important part of general education for college students. From the perspective of school education, the general course of media literacy promotion is widely carried out in universities. It is an effective way to promote media literacy in universities.

It can be seen that the media literacy education for the post-90s college students is not only a realistic need, but also a general trend in the era of globalization. Compared with the media literacy education in developed countries, the media literacy education for university students in our country starts relatively late, we must arouse the attention of relevant universities and administrative departments. China's universities should take the initiative to deal with the current situation of media development, realize the necessity and urgency of developing media literacy education, and carry out media literacy education for post-90s college students as soon as possible.

From the perspective of self-education approach, the media literacy of the post-90s college students is mainly embodied by self-identification, self-study, self-restraint and self-cultivation. In the aspect of strengthening self-study, the post-90s college students can acquire positive media information actively, and form their own recognition symbols of media information through their own decoding, coding and sorting, so as to understand and accept them selectively, turn the symbol into self-cognition and complete self-education. This self-screening of media information and the acquisition of self-learning ability are rooted in school media literacy, so the path of self-education is inseparable from the premise of establishing stable and effective school education.

Secondly, the self-discipline and self-cultivation of the post-90s college students is the media ability, which is the ability to use and deal with the media information. At present, most universities have set up information retrieval, web page production, short video production, public number operation and other basic courses using new media. The survey found that the post-90s college students have a certain ability to operate the media, can produce and publish information through multimedia materials, participate in the discussion of topics on the Internet, in constant practice and learning to improve their own ability to operate the media. But faced with a variety of news information in a changing process, the post-90s college students lack a certain ability to identify and process it, which requires a great deal of contact and comparison of information in order to identify the true and false, this ability is the self-cultivation process of post-90s college students, is an important reflection of self-cultivation. And this kind of self-cultivation needs to be formed through reflection and self-denial. The post-90s college students need to resist the temptation of all kinds of vulgar information, form their own self-restraint system, keep their alertness on the ideological level at all times, and comply with social norms. Especially in the virtual environment where morality and law are difficult to restrain, strong moral consciousness can restrain self. Post-90s college students must cultivate self-restraint media character and form their own unique media self-cultivation.

Therefore, it is urgent and necessary to construct an efficient and reasonable media literacy education system. Only in this way can post-90s university students obtain the personal recognition on new media and the comprehensive ability for rational use of media resources.

Acknowledgement. This paper is the result of South China Business College of Guangdong University of Foreign Studies' research project "Study on the current status of post-90s university students' media literacy and the guidance" (16-009B).

References

1. Yuan, J.: The World Vision of Media Literacy Education and the Chinese Model. International Press **5**(1), 34–42 (2011)
2. Xi, J.P.: Speech at the symposium on network security and information technology. http://www.cac.gov.cn. Accessed 25 April 2016

3. Xi, J.P.: Xi Jinping Talk About Governing the Country (second volume), 3rd edn. Foreign Language Press, Beijing (2018)
4. Chen, Z.Y.: Ideological and Political Education of College Students in the New Media Era, 2nd edn. China Literature and History Press, Beijing (2014)
5. Lu, Y.: Media Literacy: Concept, Cognition and Participation, 7th edn. Economic Science Press, Beijing (2010)
6. Gong, ShH, Zhang, J.: Theory and Practice of Media Literacy Education, 5th edn. Shandong People's Publishing House, Shandong (2010)
7. Chen, L.W., Influence of mass communication on Ideological and political education of college students and countermeasures. Central China Normal University (2008)
8. Le Pen, G.: A Motley Crew (Mobile, Translated by Yu Xian), 7th edn. Yuanyuan publishing house, Inner Mongolia (2016)
9. Cai, G.F., Liu, X.Y.: Media Literacy, 2nd edn. Communication University of China Press, Beijing (2014)
10. Liang, Q.T.: Research on the Ideological and Political Education Function of Mass Media. University of Electronic Science and Technology Press, Chengdu (2012)
11. Qi, H.Q.: The new direction of communication education: from media study to media literacy. Modern Commun. **6**(1), 21–42 (2013)
12. Lu, Q.P: Media Survival: A Study on the Media Quality of Chinese Youth, 7th edn. Communication University of China Press, Beijing (2007)
13. Guo, F.P., Wang, Sh: Y: An empirical analysis of the development of media literacy education research in China. Res. Audio-Vis. Educ. **7**(5), 12–23 (2019)
14. Xie, Y.G.: New Media and Society (Volume 1), 1st edn. Shanghai Jiaotong University Press, Shanghai (2011)
15. Lu, F.: Localization of media literacy education. Nanjing Normal University (2011)
16. Huang, X.X.: Research on media literacy and education strategies of college students. Southwest University (2010)
17. Fan, J.J.: Research on media literacy cultivation of college students in the new media era. Beijing University of Posts and Telecommunications (2014)
18. The 43rd Statistical Report on the development of Internet in China. http://www.cnnic.cn/hlwfzyj. Accessed 28 Feb 2019
19. Peng, Sh.J.: Research Report on Chinese Media Literacy, 1st edn. China Radio and Television Press, Beijing (2014)
20. Wang, X.H.: Media Agenda and Public Cognition: An Empirical Study on the Impact of Communication on People, 6th edn. People's Publishing House, Beijing (2012)
21. Lee, N.M.: Fake news, phishing, and fraud: a call for research on digital media literacy education beyond the classroom. Commun. Educ. **18**(09), 88–99 (2018)

Fast Preconditioned Iterative Method for the Space Fractional Complex Ginzburg-Landau Equation

Lu Zhang[1]($\boxtimes$), Lei Chen[2], and Wenyu Zhou[1]

[1] School of Mathematics and Statistics,
Xuzhou University of Technology, Xuzhou 221018, Jiangsu, China
yulu7517@126.com
[2] School of Information Engineering, Xuzhou University of Technology,
Xuzhou 221018, Jiangsu, China
chenlei@xzit.edu.cn

Abstract. In this work, we give an effective preconditioned numerical method to solve the discreted linear system, which is obtained from the space fractional complex Ginzburg-Landau equation. The coefficient matrix of the linear system is the sum of a symmetric tridiagonal matrix and a complex Toeplitz matrix. The preconditioned iteration method has computational superiority since we can use the fast Fourier transform (FFT) and the circulant preconditioner to solve the discreted linear system. Numerical examples are tested to illustrate the advantage of the proposed preconditioned numerical method.

Keywords: Space fractional Ginzburg-Landau equation · Toeplitz matrix · Preconditioned numerical method

1   Introduction

In this paper, we solve the space fractional complex Ginzburg-Landau equation as follows [39]

$$\frac{\partial v}{\partial t} + (\nu_1 + \mathbf{i}\eta_1)(-\Delta)^{\frac{\beta}{2}}v + (\kappa_1 + \mathbf{i}\zeta_1)|v|^2 v - \gamma_1 v = 0, \tag{1}$$

$$v(x,0) = v_0(x), \tag{2}$$

where $x \in \mathbb{R}$, $1 < \beta \leqslant 2$, $\mathbf{i}$ is the imaginary unit, $0 < t \leqslant T_1$, $v(x,t)$ is a complex-value function, $\nu_1 > 0$, $\kappa_1 > 0$, η_1, ζ_1, and γ_1 are real constants, and $v_0(x)$ is an initial function. Furthermore, the operator $(-\Delta)^{\frac{\beta}{2}}v(x,t)$ $(1 < \beta \leqslant 2)$ in (1) is defined [9] as follows

Supported by the "Peiyu" Project from Xuzhou University of Technology (Grant Number XKY2019104).

H. Song and D. Jiang (Eds.): SIMUtools 2020, LNICST 369, pp. 78–89, 2021.
https://doi.org/10.1007/978-3-030-72792-5_8

$$-(-\Delta)^{\frac{\beta}{2}}v(x,t) = -\frac{\frac{\partial^2}{\partial x^2}\int_{-\infty}^{\infty}|x-\xi|^{1-\beta}v(\xi,t)\mathrm{d}\xi}{2\cos(\frac{\beta\pi}{2})\Gamma(2-\beta)}. \tag{3}$$

The operator $(-\Delta)^{\frac{\beta}{2}}$ is equivalent to

$$-(-\Delta)^{\frac{\beta}{2}}v(x,t) = -\frac{-\infty\hat{D}_x^\beta v(x,t) +_x \hat{D}_{+\infty}^\beta v(x,t)}{2\cos(\frac{\beta\pi}{2})},$$

where the two operators $_{-\infty}\hat{D}_x^\beta$ and $_x\hat{D}_{+\infty}^\beta$ are defined in [32].

The fractional Ginzburg-Landau equation has been used to describe a lot of physical phenomena; see [29,30,35]. However, there are few works on the numerical methods for the fractional complex Eq. (1)–(2) [10,13,33,38,39]. Based on the extensive application background of this equation, it is interesting to study the numerical methods for solving the fractional complex Eq. (1)–(2).

Recently, some new approaches are proposed to improve network routing and measurement [14,37,41]. Based on effective user behavior and traffic analysis methods [4,5,17,19], new scheduling strategies are designed to raise resources utilization [6,18,20,36] and energy-efficiency [21,22]. To test these new scheduling strategies, traffic Reconstruction is important [15,16,23,24,27,40]. Fluid model is effective model to reconstruct the bursty data traffic. Moreover, fractional differential equation can be used to build the fluid model. In our paper, we develop an effective preconditioned numerical method to solve the linear system, which is discreted from the fractional complex Eq. (1)–(2). Compared to the direct method, the complex linear systems can be fast solved by the circulant matrix and the FFT at each step due to the Toeplitz structure of coefficient matrices.

2   A Finite Difference Scheme

In this part, we exploit the fourth-order finite difference scheme [39] to discretize the fractional complex Eq. (1)–(2). For the two operators $_{-\infty}\hat{D}_x^\beta$ and $_x\hat{D}_{+\infty}^\beta$, the WSGD method [12] is used to approximate them. The shifted Grunwald formulae [28] is defined as

$$_L\tilde{\mathcal{A}}_{\hat{h},p_1}^\beta v(x) = \frac{\sum_{i=0}^{+\infty} d_i^{(\beta)} v(x-(i-p_1)\hat{h})}{\hat{h}^\beta},$$

$$_R\tilde{\mathcal{A}}_{\hat{h},q_1}^\beta v(x) = \frac{\sum_{i=0}^{+\infty} d_i^{(\beta)} v(x+(i-q_1)\hat{h})}{\hat{h}^\beta},$$

where p_1, q_1 are positive integers and the coefficients $d_i^{(\beta)}$ are computed as follows

$$d_0^{(\beta)} = 1, \quad d_i^{(\beta)} = \frac{i-\beta-1}{i}d_{i-1}^{(\beta)}, \quad i \in \mathbb{Z}^+.$$

According to the reference [12] and using the shifted Grunwald formulae, the WSGD operator is of the following form:

$$_L\tilde{D}_h^\beta v(x) = \frac{\sum_{i=0}^{+\infty} z_i^{(\beta)} v(x - (i-1)\hat{h})}{\hat{h}^\beta},$$

$$_R\tilde{D}_h^\beta v(x) = \frac{\sum_{i=0}^{+\infty} z_i^{(\beta)} v(x + (i-1)\hat{h})}{\hat{h}^\beta},$$

where

$$\begin{cases} z_0^{(\beta)} = \tilde{\lambda}_1 d_0^{(\beta)}, \ z_1^{(\beta)} = \tilde{\lambda}_1 d_1^{(\beta)} + \tilde{\lambda}_0 d_0^{(\beta)}, \\ z_i^{(\beta)} = \tilde{\lambda}_1 d_i^{(\beta)} + \tilde{\lambda}_0 d_{i-1}^{(\beta)} + \tilde{\lambda}_{-1} d_{i-2}^{(\beta)}, \ i \geqslant 2, \end{cases} \tag{4}$$

and

$$\tilde{\lambda}_1 = \frac{\beta^2}{12} + \frac{\beta}{4} + \frac{1}{6}, \ \tilde{\lambda}_0 = \frac{2}{3} - \frac{\beta^2}{6}, \ \tilde{\lambda}_{-1} = \frac{\beta^2}{12} - \frac{\beta}{4} + \frac{1}{6}.$$

Let the operator $\mathcal{B}$ be

$$\mathcal{B}v(x) = c^\beta v(x - \hat{h}) + (1 - 2c^\beta)v(x) + c^\beta v(x + \hat{h}),$$

where $c^\beta = -\frac{\beta^2}{24} + \frac{\beta}{24} + \frac{1}{6}$. Therefore, the fourth-order approximation to the operator $(-\Delta)^{\frac{\beta}{2}}$ can be obtained by

$$\Delta_h^\beta v(x) = \frac{_L\tilde{D}_h^\beta v(x) +_R \tilde{D}_h^\beta v(x)}{2\cos(\frac{\beta\pi}{2})} \tag{5}$$

$$= \mathcal{B}(-\Delta)^{\frac{\beta}{2}} v(x) + \mathcal{O}(\hat{h}^4). \tag{6}$$

In the following, we will give the numerical discretization of (1)–(2) in the domain $\Pi = [a_1, b_1]$. Let $\hat{\tau} = \frac{T_1}{N_1}$ and denote $t_i = i\hat{\tau}$, where N_1 is a positive integer, $0 \leqslant i \leqslant N_1$. Given a grid function $u = \{u^i | 0 \leqslant i \leqslant N_1\}$, denote

$$\tilde{D}_t u^{i+1} = \frac{3u^{i+1} - 4u^i + u^{i-1}}{2\hat{\tau}},$$

$$\tilde{u}^{i+1} = 2u^i - u^{i-1}.$$

Let $\hat{h} = \frac{b_1 - a_1}{M_1}$ and $x_i = a_1 + i\hat{h}$, where M_1 is a positive integer, $0 \leqslant i \leqslant M_1$. Moreover, we denote $\mathfrak{F}_{M_1} = \{i | i = 1, 2, \ldots, M_1 - 1\}$. According to the method of [39], we can obtain the following finite difference scheme for the fractional complex Eq. (1) and (2):

$$\mathcal{B}\tilde{D}_t v_j^{i+1} + (\nu_1 + \mathrm{i}\eta_1)\Delta_h^\beta v_j^{i+1} + (\kappa_1 + \mathrm{i}\zeta_1)\mathcal{B}|\tilde{v}_j^{i+1}|^2 \tilde{v}_j^{i+1} - \gamma_1 \mathcal{B}\tilde{v}_j^{i+1} = 0,$$

$$j \in \mathfrak{F}_{M_1}, \ 1 \leqslant i \leqslant N_1 - 1, \tag{7}$$

$$v_j^0 = v_0(x_j), j \in \mathbb{Z}, \tag{8}$$

$$v_j^i = 0, j \in \mathbb{Z} \setminus \mathfrak{F}_{M_1}, \ 0 \leqslant i \leqslant N_1. \tag{9}$$

In the practical computation, we can calculate u^1 as follows [39]

$$\begin{cases} \mathcal{B}(\frac{v_j^1 - v_{0j}}{\hat{\tau}}) + (\nu_1 + i\eta_1)\Delta_{\hat{h}}^{\beta}\frac{v_j^1 + v_{0j}}{2} + (\kappa_1 + i\zeta_1)\mathcal{B}|v_j^{(1)}|^2 v_j^{(1)} = \gamma_1 \mathcal{B}v_j^{(1)}, \\ \mathcal{B}(\frac{v_j^{(1)} - v_{0j}}{\hat{\tau}/2}) + (\nu_1 + i\eta_1)\Delta_{\hat{h}}^{\beta}v_{0j} + (\kappa_1 + i\zeta_1)\mathcal{B}|v_{0j}|^2 v_{0j} = \gamma_1 \mathcal{B}v_{0j}, j \in \mathfrak{F}_{M_1}. \end{cases} \tag{10}$$

Let

$$v^{i+1} = [v_1^{i+1}, \ldots, v_{M_1-1}^{i+1}]^T,$$

$$D_1 = \hat{\tau}(\kappa_1 + i\zeta_1)\begin{bmatrix} |v_{01}|^2 & 0 & \cdots & 0 \\ 0 & |v_{02}|^2 & \cdots & 0 \\ \vdots & \vdots & \ddots & \vdots \\ 0 & 0 & \cdots & |v_{0,M_1-1}|^2 \end{bmatrix} - (2 + \gamma_1\hat{\tau})I,$$

$$D_2 = (\kappa_1 + i\zeta_1)\begin{bmatrix} |v_1^{(1)}|^2 & 0 & \cdots & 0 \\ 0 & |v_2^{(1)}|^2 & \cdots & 0 \\ \vdots & \vdots & \ddots & \vdots \\ 0 & 0 & \cdots & |v_{M_1-1}^{(1)}|^2 \end{bmatrix} - \gamma_1 I,$$

$$D_3 = (\kappa_1 + i\zeta_1)\begin{bmatrix} |\tilde{v}_1^{i+1}|^2 & 0 & \cdots & 0 \\ 0 & |\tilde{v}_2^{i+1}|^2 & \cdots & 0 \\ \vdots & \vdots & \ddots & \vdots \\ 0 & 0 & \cdots & |\tilde{v}_{M_1-1}^{i+1}|^2 \end{bmatrix} - \gamma_1 I,$$

$$Z = \begin{bmatrix} z_1^{(\beta)} & z_0^{(\beta)} & 0 & \cdots & 0 & 0 \\ z_2^{(\beta)} & z_1^{(\beta)} & z_0^{(\beta)} & 0 & \cdots & 0 \\ \vdots & \ddots & \ddots & \ddots & \ddots & \vdots \\ \vdots & & \ddots & \ddots & \ddots & 0 \\ z_{M_1-2}^{(\beta)} & \ddots & & \ddots & z_1^{(\beta)} & z_0^{(\beta)} \\ z_{M_1-1}^{(\beta)} & z_{M_1-2}^{(\beta)} & \cdots & \cdots & z_2^{(\beta)} & z_1^{(\beta)} \end{bmatrix}, \tag{11}$$

and

$$A_\beta = \text{tridiag}\left(c^\beta, 1 - 2^\beta, c^\beta\right),$$

then the fourth-order finite difference scheme (7)–(10) has the following form

$$2A_\beta v^{(1)} = -A_\beta D_1 v^0 - \omega C v^0, \tag{12}$$

$$(A_\beta + \frac{\omega_1}{2}C)v^1 = (A_\beta - \frac{\omega_1}{2}C)v^0 - \hat{\tau}A_\beta D_2 v^{(1)}, \tag{13}$$

$$(\frac{3}{2}A_\beta + \omega_1 C)v^{i+1} = A_\beta(2v^i - \frac{1}{2}v^{i-1} - \hat{\tau}D_3\tilde{v}^{i+1}), 1 \leqslant i \leqslant N_1 - 1. \tag{14}$$

where $C = Z + Z^T$ and $\omega_1 = \frac{(\nu_1 + i\eta_1)\hat{\tau}}{2\hat{h}^\beta \cos(\frac{\beta\pi}{2})}$.

3   A Fast Preconditioned Numerical Method

In this part, we give an effective preconditioned generalized minimum residual (PGMRES) method [34] to solve the discreted linear system of the finite difference scheme (7)–(10), in which the preconditioned matrix is Strang's circulant preconditioner proposed in [2].

3.1   Toeplitz Matrix and GMRES Method

The Toeplitz linear system is as follows

$$B_{n_1} u = \tilde{b},$$

where B_{n_1} is a Toeplitz matrix, $\tilde{b}$ is a given vector. Toeplitz systems are widely used in various fields; see [1,3,7,11,25,26,31]. The elements of an $n_1 \times n_1$ Toeplitz matrix B_{n_1} satisfy $(B_{n_1})_{ij} = b_{i-j}$ for $i,j = 1,2,\ldots,n_1$. The elements of a circulant matrix C_{n_1} satisfy $c_{-i} = c_{n_1-i}$ for $1 \leqslant i \leqslant n_1 - 1$ [2].

It is well-known that [8] the computation cost will be $\mathcal{O}(n_1 \log n_1)$ operations if one wants to compute the matrix-vector products $C_{n_1} u$ and $C_{n_1}^{-1} u$ by the fast Fourier transform. In addition, we can calculate the matrix-vector product $B_{n_1} u$ in $\mathcal{O}(2n_1 \log(2n_1))$ by the FFT [2]. These important properties can be exploited to fast solve the discreted linear system in the form (12)–(14).

Consider the following non-Hermitian linear systems

$$Bu = \tilde{b},$$

where B is a non-Hermitian matrix. As we know, the GMRES method [34] is a very effective iterative method for solving these linear systems. Under normal circumstances, the convergent rate of the this method is very slow because of the very large condition number of the matrix B. To deal with this drawback, we could exploit the preconditioned matrix to speed up the convergent rate of the GMRES method. Please refer to [34] for the PGMRES method.

3.2   A Preconditioner for the Implicit-Explicit Difference Scheme

It can be seen that A_β and C are Toeplitz matrices in the matrix-vector form (12)–(14). According to Sect. 3.1, we can store an $M_1 \times M_1$ Toeplitz matrix B_{M_1} in $\mathcal{O}(M_1)$ of memory, and we can compute the matrix-vector product $B_{M_1} u$ in $\mathcal{O}(M_1 \log M_1)$ by the FFT. Moreover, the coefficient matrices of the complex linear systems (13) and (14) are non-Hermitian.

In this section, we exploit Strang's circulant matrix as a preconditioner to speed up the GMRES method. For the matrix A_β in (12), the preconditioned matrix is

$$S_1 = s(A_\beta),$$

where $s(A_\beta)$ is the Strang circulant matrix for the matrix A_β. For the matrix $A_\beta + \frac{\omega_1}{2} C$ in (13), the preconditioned matrix is

$$S_2 = s(A_\beta) + \frac{\omega_1}{2} s(C).$$

For the matrix $\frac{3}{2}A_\beta + \omega_1 C$ in (14), the preconditioned matrix is

$$S_3 = \frac{3}{2}s(A_\beta) + \omega_1 s(C).$$

It easily knows that S_1, S_2 and S_3 are circulant matrices. In the following, we will see that the proposed preconditioners are very efficient to speed up the GMRES method.

4 Numerical Experiments

In this part, we show the computational advantage of the PGMRES algorithm by two numerical examples for the fractional complex equation. We denote "GaE" by the direct method, which is implemented by left divide in MATLAB. For the PGMRES method with Strang's circulant preconditioner, we denote by "cPGM-RES". We stop the cPGMRES method if the condition satisfies

$$\frac{\|\mathrm{res1}^k\|_2}{\|\mathrm{res1}^0\|_2} < 10^{-7},$$

where $\mathrm{res1}^k$ denotes the k-th residual vector for the cPGMRES method. In all tables, "Icpu" denotes the computational time in seconds for GaE and cPGM-RES, and "Ite" is the iteration numbers for cPGMRES.

Example 1. In this example, the parameters in the fractional complex Eq. (1) and (2) are same as these in [39].

Furthermore, according to [39], the numerical exact solution v is calculated with $\hat{\tau} = 10^{-4}$ and $\hat{h} = 1.25 \times 10^{-2}$. Let $v_{\hat{h}}$ be the numerical solution. We compute the error $\mathrm{ERR} = v - v_{\hat{h}}$ as the numerical accuracy at $T_1 = 2$ with the $l_{\hat{h}}^\infty$ norm.

We report the numerical results in Table 1. In this table, ERR_1 and ERR_2 denote the errors for the cPGMRES method and the GaE method, respectively. We can see that there is little difference between numerical errors of the two methods. But, if the size of the matrix in the complex linear systems (12)–(13) is large, the computational times of GaE are much more than the computational times of cPGMRES. Furthermore, Figs. 1, 2 and 3 show the distribution of the eigenvalues for the matrix $\frac{3}{2}A_\beta + \omega_1 C$ and $S_3^{-1}(\frac{3}{2}A_\beta + \omega_1 C)$ at $T_1 = 2$, respectively, when the size of the matrix is 320, and $\beta = 1.3$, 1.6, 1.9. In the figures, the blue points indicate that most of the eigenvalues of the matrix $S_3^{-1}(\frac{3}{2}A_\beta + \omega_1 C)$ approach to 1, while the eigenvalues of the matrix $\frac{3}{2}A_\beta + \omega_1 C$ do not approach to 1. Therefore, the figures show that our new preconditioner is very effective for solving the linear systems (12)–(14).

Table 1. Numerical results for Example 1

β	$(\hat{\tau}, \hat{h})$	cPGMRES			GaE	
		ERR$_1$	Ite	Icpu	ERR$_2$	Icpu
1.3	$(2^{-4}, 0.4)$	3.7500e − 2	3.1	0.0470	3.7500e − 2	0.0160
	$(2^{-6}, 0.2)$	2.4074e − 3	3.0	0.1090	2.4074e − 3	0.1870
	$(2^{-8}, 0.1)$	1.6404e − 4	2.9	0.4070	1.6405e − 4	3.1100
1.6	$(2^{-4}, 0.4)$	2.1789e − 2	3.0	0.0320	2.1789e − 2	0.0150
	$(2^{-6}, 0.2)$	1.3764e − 3	2.8	0.0780	1.3764e − 3	0.1570
	$(2^{-8}, 0.1)$	8.8752e − 5	2.0	0.3120	8.8693e − 5	3.0000
1.9	$(2^{-4}, 0.4)$	1.4653e − 2	2.1	0.0160	1.4653e − 2	0.0150
	$(2^{-6}, 0.2)$	9.1163e − 4	2.0	0.0620	9.1163e − 4	0.1570
	$(2^{-8}, 0.1)$	5.7246e − 5	2.0	0.2970	5.7246e − 5	3.1250

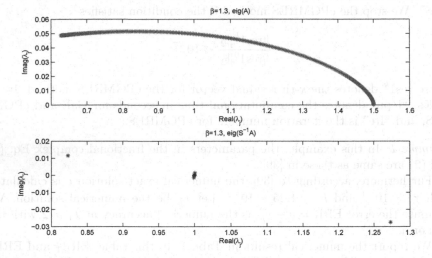

Fig. 1. Example 1: Spectrum of $\frac{3}{2}A_\beta + \omega_1 C$ (upper) and $S_3^{-1}(\frac{3}{2}A_\beta + \omega_1 C)$ (lower), when $\beta = 1.3$.

Example 2. In this example, we take the parameters which are same as these in [39]. Moreover, we compute the exact solution v with $\hat{\tau} = 10^{-4}$ and $\hat{h} = 1.25 \times 10^{-2}$.

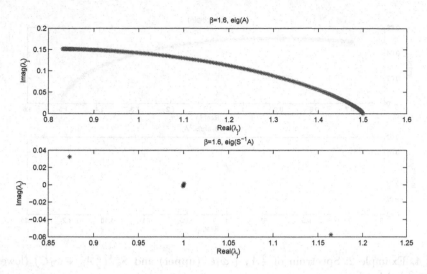

Fig. 2. Example 1: Spectrum of $\frac{3}{2}A_\beta + \omega_1 C$ (upper) and $S_3^{-1}(\frac{3}{2}A_\beta + \omega_1 C)$ (lower), when $\beta = 1.6$.

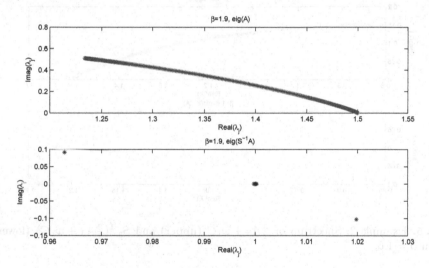

Fig. 3. Example 1: Spectrum of $\frac{3}{2}A_\beta + \omega_1 C$ (upper) and $S_3^{-1}(\frac{3}{2}A_\beta + \omega_1 C)$ (lower), when $\beta = 1.9$.

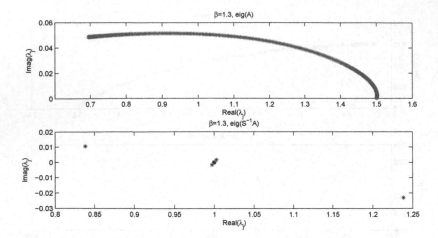

Fig. 4. Example 2: Spectrum of $\frac{3}{2}A_\beta + \omega_1 C$ (upper) and $S_3^{-1}(\frac{3}{2}A_\beta + \omega_1 C)$ (lower), when $\beta = 1.3$

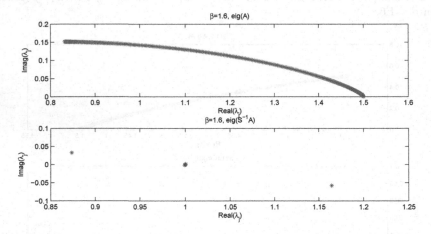

Fig. 5. Example 2: Spectrum of $\frac{3}{2}A_\beta + \omega_1 C$ (upper) and $S_3^{-1}(\frac{3}{2}A_\beta + \omega_1 C)$ (lower), when $\beta = 1.6$.

Table 2 gives the numerical results and Figs. 4, 5 and 6 show the distribution of the eigenvalues for the matrices $\frac{3}{2}A_\beta + \omega_1 C$ and $S_3^{-1}(\frac{3}{2}A_\beta + \omega_1 C)$ at $T_1 = 2$, respectively, when the size of the matrix is 320, and $\beta = 1.3$, 1.6, 1.9. Similar to Example 1, the computational results and figures indicate the superiority of the preconditioned numerical method.

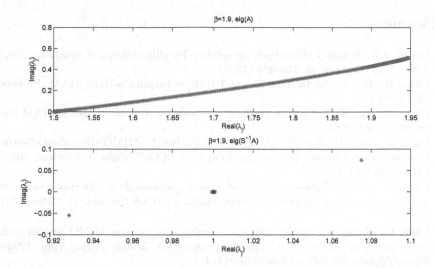

Fig. 6. Example 2: Spectrum of $\frac{3}{2}A_\beta + \omega_1 C$ (upper) and $S_3^{-1}(\frac{3}{2}A_\beta + \omega_1 C)$ (lower), when $\beta = 1.9$.

Table 2. Numerical results for Example 2

β	$(\hat{\tau}, \hat{h})$	cPGMRES			GaE	
		ERR$_1$	Ite	Icpu	ERR$_2$	Icpu
1.3	$(2^{-4}, 0.4)$	$1.6529e-4$	3.9	0.0250	$1.6529e-4$	0.0160
	$(2^{-6}, 0.2)$	$1.1880e-5$	3.7	0.1160	$1.1879e-5$	0.1870
	$(2^{-8}, 0.1)$	$7.5537e-7$	3.0	0.4440	$7.5333e-7$	3.2500
1.6	$(2^{-4}, 0.4)$	$2.1495e-4$	3.4	0.0250	$2.1495e-4$	0.0160
	$(2^{-6}, 0.2)$	$1.6276e-5$	2.8	0.1010	$1.6276e-5$	0.1400
	$(2^{-8}, 0.1)$	$1.0397e-6$	2.6	0.3470	$1.0396e-6$	3.0790
1.9	$(2^{-4}, 0.4)$	$3.3256e-4$	2.9	0.0250	$3.3256e-4$	0.0160
	$(2^{-6}, 0.2)$	$2.5996e-5$	2.6	0.0960	$2.5996e-5$	0.1560
	$(2^{-8}, 0.1)$	$1.6857e-6$	2.2	0.3000	$1.6857e-6$	2.9380

5   Conclusion and Future Work

In this work, we have given a fast preconditioned numerical method to solve the linear system, which is discreted from the space fractional complex Ginzburg-Landau equation. We propose a circulant preconditioner due to the Toeplitz structure of the coefficient matrix of the linear system. Numerical examples show that the preconditioned numerical method is very efficient.

References

1. Bunch, J.R.: Stability of methods for solving Toeplitz systems of equations. SIAM J. Sci. Stat. Comput. **6**, 349–364 (1985)
2. Chan, R., Jin, X.: An Introduction to Iterative Toeplitz Solvers. SIAM, Philadelphia (2007)
3. Chan, R., Ng, M.: Conjugate gradient methods for Toeplitz systems. SIAM Rev. **38**, 427–482 (1996)
4. Chen, L., Jiang, D., Bao, R., Xiong, J., Liu, F., Bei, L.: MIMO scheduling effectiveness analysis for bursty data service from view of QoE. Chin. J. Electron. **26**(5), 1079–1085 (2017)
5. Chen, L., et al.: A lightweight end-side user experience data collection system for quality evaluation of multimedia communications. IEEE Access **6**(1), 15408–15419 (2018)
6. Chen, L., Zhang, L.: Spectral efficiency analysis for massive MIMO system under QoS constraint: an effective capacity perspective. Mobile Netw. Appl. (2020). https://doi.org/10.1007/s11036-019-01414-4
7. Ching, W.-K.: Iterative Methods for Queuing and Manufacturing Systems. Springer, London (2001)
8. Davis, P.: Circulant Matrices, 2nd edn. AMS Chelsea, Providence, RI (1994)
9. Gorenflo, R., Mainardi, F.: Random walk models for space-fractional diffusion processes. Fractional Calc. Appl. Anal. **1**(2), 167–191 (1998)
10. Guo, B.-L., Huo, Z.-H.: Well-posedness for the nonlinear fractional Schrödinger equation and inviscid limit behavior of solution for the fractional Ginzburg-Landau equation. Fract. Calc. Appl. Anal. **16**(1), 226–242 (2012)
11. Hansen, P.C., Nagy, J.G., O'Leary, D.P.: Deblurring Images: Matrices, Spectra, and Filtering. SIAM, Philadelphia (2006)
12. Hao, Z.-P., Sun, Z.-Z., Cao, W.-R.: A fourth-order approximation of fractional derivatives with its applications. J. Comput. Phys. **281**, 787–805 (2015)
13. He, D., Pan, K.: An unconditionally stable linearized difference scheme for the fractional Ginzburg-Landau equation. Numer. Algor. **79**, 899–925 (2018)
14. Huo, L., Jiang, D., Lv, Z., et al.: An intelligent optimization-based traffic information acquirement approach to software-defined networking. Comput. Intell. **36**(1), 1–21 (2019)
15. Huo, L., Jiang, D., Qi, S., Song, H., Miao, L.: An AI-based adaptive cognitive modeling and measurement method of network traffic for EIS. Mob. Netw. Appl. 1–11 (2019). https://doi.org/10.1007/s11036-019-01419-z
16. Huo, L., Jiang, D., Zhu, X., et al.: An SDN-based fine-grained measurement and modeling approach to vehicular communication network traffic. Int. J. Commun. Syst. **2019**(9), 1–19 (2019)
17. Jiang, D., Huo, L., Song, H.: Rethinking behaviors and activities of base stations in mobile cellular networks based on big data analysis. IEEE Trans. Netw. Sci. Eng. **1**(1), 1–12 (2018)
18. Jiang, D., Huo, L., Lv, Z., et al.: A joint multi-criteria utility-based network selection approach for vehicle-to-infrastructure networking. IEEE Trans. Intell. Transp. Syst. **19**(10), 3305–3319 (2018)
19. Jiang, D., Wang, Y., Lv, Z., et al.: Big data analysis-based network behavior insight of cellular networks for industry 4.0 applications. IEEE Trans. Ind. Inf. **16**(2), 1310–1320 (2020)

20. Jiang, D., Zhang, P., Lv, Z., et al.: Energy-efficient multi-constraint routing algorithm with load balancing for smart city applications. IEEE Int. Things J. **3**(6), 1437–1447 (2016)
21. Jiang, D., Li, W., Lv, H.: An energy-efficient cooperative multicast routing in multi-hop wireless networks for smart medical applications. Neurocomputing **220**, 160–169 (2017)
22. Jiang, D., Wang, Y., Lv, Z., et al.: Intelligent optimization-based reliable energy-efficient networking in cloud services for IIoT networks. IEEE J. Sel. Areas Commun. **38**(5), 928–941 (2019)
23. Jiang, D., Wang, W., Shi, L., et al.: A compressive sensing-based approach to end-to-end network traffic reconstruction. IEEE Trans. Netw. Sci. Eng. **5**(3), 1–12 (2018)
24. Jiang, D., Huo, L., Li, Y.: Fine-granularity inference and estimations to network traffic for SDN. Plos One **13**(5), 1–23 (2018)
25. Jin, X.-Q.: Developments and Applications of Block Toeplitz Iterative Solvers. The Netherlands, and Science Press, Beijing, China, Kluwer Academic Publishers, Dordrecht (2002)
26. Kailath, T., Sayed, A.H. (eds.): Fast Reliable Algorithms for Matrices with Structure. SIAM, Philadelphia (1999)
27. Qi, S., Jiang, D., Huo, L.: A prediction approach to end-to-end traffic in space information networks. Mob. Netw. Appl. 1–10 (2019). https://doi.org/10.1007/s11036-019-01424-2
28. Meerschaert, M.-M., Tadjeran, C.: Finite difference approximations for fractional advection-dispersion flow equations. J. Comput. Appl. Math. **172**, 65–77 (2004)
29. Milovanov, A., Rasmussen, J.: Fractional generalization of the Ginzburg-Landau equation: an unconventional approach to critical phenomena in complex media. Phys. Lett. A **337**, 75–80 (2005)
30. Mvogo, A., Tambue, A., Ben-Bolie, G., Kofane, T.: Localized numerical impulse solutions in diffuse neural networks modeled by the complex fractional Ginzburg-Landau equation. Commun. Nonlinear Sci. **39**, 396–410 (2016)
31. Ng, M.K.: Iterative Methods for Toeplitz Systems. Oxford University Press, Oxford (2004)
32. Podlubny, I.: Fractional Differential Equations. Academic Press, New York (1999)
33. Pu, X., Guo, B.: Well-posedness and dynamics for the fractional Ginzburg-Landau equation. Appl. Anal. **92**, 318–334 (2013)
34. Saad, Y.: Iterative Methods for Sparse Linear Systems. SIAM, Philadelphia (2003)
35. Tarasov, V., Zaslavsky, G.: Fractional Ginzburg-Landau equation for fractal media. Physica A **354**, 249–261 (2005)
36. Wang, F., Jiang, D., Qi, S., Qiao, C., Shi, L.: A dynamic resource scheduling scheme in edge computing satellite networks. Mob. Netw. Appl. 1–12 (2020). https://doi.org/10.1007/s11036-019-01421-5
37. Wang, F., Jiang, D., Qi, S.: An adaptive routing algorithm for integrated information networks. China Commun. **7**(1), 196–207 (2019)
38. Wang, P., Huang, C.: An implicit midpoint difference scheme for the fractional Ginzburg-Landau equation. J. Comput. Phys. **312**, 31–49 (2016)
39. Wang, P., Huang, C.: An efficient fourth-order in space difference scheme for the nonlinear fractional Ginzburg-Landau equation. BIT **58**, 783–805 (2018)
40. Wang, Y., Jiang, D., Huo, L., Zhao, Y.: A new traffic prediction algorithm to software defined networking. Mob. Netw. Appl. 1–10 (2019). https://doi.org/10.1007/s11036-019-01423-3
41. Zhang, K., Chen, L., An, Y., et al.: A QoE test system for vehicular voice cloud services. Mob. Netw. Appl. (2019). https://doi.org/10.1007/s11036-019-01415-3

The Mechanism and Case Analysis of Restriction on the Diffusion Effect of "Development Pole" in Gelao Ethnic Group Areas in Northern Guizhou

Hongyan Zeng[✉]

Guizhou Minzu University, Guiyang 550025, Guizhou, China

Abstract. In the context of Guizhou's rapid economic growth, the county's economy of the whole province has shown an increasingly unbalanced economic development pattern. This phenomenon is more prominent in the province's minority autonomous counties, and has been in a "Two-Tiered Lag" development state for a long time. Based on this background, this article focuses on the Gelao ethnic's settlements in northern Guizhou Province, and uses the theory of development poles to analyze its causes and formation mechanisms. The conclusion is that the essence of "two-tier lag" is that the diffusion effect of "development pole" has not been brought into full play effectively, which is due to the priority policy of lagging behind in transportation, less and later, and finally evolved into a vicious circle of low finance, insufficient transportation and weak economy. The article selects Wuchuan district's economic and transportation data from 2003 to 2014, and uses factor analysis and comprehensive evaluation to quantify the matching degree of the economic and transportation development of Wuchuan district. The results are the average matching degree of economic and transportation development in Wu-chuan district was poor, the development of transportation has been unable to keep up with the demands of economic growth. And development has entered a well-matched low-level development model, strengthening the vicious circle path.

Keywords: Qianbei Gelao nationality · Developmental pole theory · Diffusion effect · Compatibility

1 Introduction

In the 70s century, China's economy began to develop. The strategy was adopted: priority policies such as material resources, financial resources, and manpower were tilted to the east first and then transferred to the west. With its construction of different levels of "development poles", the nation achieved common prosperity. The ultimate goal. Therefore, in the process of China's economic development, the Pearl River Delta, the Yangtze River Delta and other places have taken the lead in becoming the "development poles" of urbanization and the fastest-growing regions in China's economy. In order to

© ICST Institute for Computer Sciences, Social Informatics and Telecommunications Engineering 2021
Published by Springer Nature Switzerland AG 2021. All Rights Reserved
H. Song and D. Jiang (Eds.): SIMUtools 2020, LNICST 369, pp. 90–104, 2021.
https://doi.org/10.1007/978-3-030-72792-5_9

promote the spreading effect of the "development poles" of eastern urbanization, the state implemented the strategy of western development in 2000, and constructed the "development poles" with 12 provincial capitals and some prefecture-level cities in the western regions. The preferential policies of various regions have fostered the necessary conditions for maximizing acceptance of the diffusion effect of the "development pole" of eastern urbanization, thereby accelerating the economic growth of the "development pole" of urbanization in the western region. The "development poles for making the urbanization of the western region bigger and stronger" drive the economic development of the western region through the radiation effect. Under this background, the economic development of the Guizhou Qianbei Gelao populated area is observed vertically (See Fig. 1), but from a horizontal perspective, the indicators of the two counties have lagged behind the average level of the entire Zunyi region for a long time. To further compare the economic structure, the total rural economic volume and growth rate of the region lag behind the average development level of the county. It is a "two-layer lagging" (see Figs. 2 and 3).

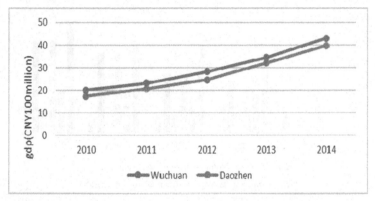

Fig. 1. GDP of chuan Wuchuan County and Daozhen County, 2010–2014 Unit: 100 million yuan. Data source: research materials

The Realistic economic development is far from the "unbalanced-balanced" economic development pattern predicted in the theory. This topic attracts academics and political circles to actively discuss it. The scope of discussion is global, national, and regional. The research perspective includes natural conditions, history, human capital, Finance, etc., research methods are qualitative and quantitative [1–5]. The research conclusions show that: due to the different endowments of economic entities and different stages of economic development, the main factors that cause the imbalance in the local economy are various. Not the same, but for the main cause of the more unbalanced development of the economy in the initial development, scholars believe that the transportation factor is the main explanatory variable, because transportation facilities have a guiding, supporting and guaranteeing role in regional development, and reflect the advantages and disadvantages of regional development conditions Important indicators. A convenient network of transportation facilities is a prerequisite for strengthening regional economic ties and enhancing regional comparative advantage [6, 7]. Scholars

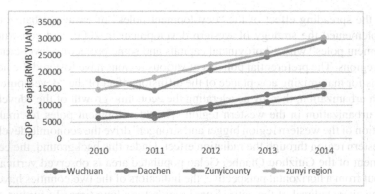

Fig. 2. GDP per capita from 2010 to 2014 Unit: RMB Yuan. Data source: Website of Zunyi Municipal Government of Guizhou Province

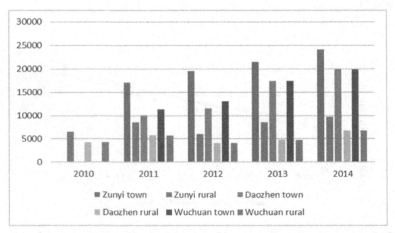

Fig. 3. Per capita income of urban and rural in Daozhen County and Wuchuan County from 2011 to 2013 Unit: Yuan. Data source: Website of Zunyi Municipal Government of Guizhou Province.

have further analyzed the development and evolution mechanism of regional economic development and transportation development that are based on each other, are mutually dependent, and are interdependent and mutually reinforcing [8–13].

Based on the research on the relationship between transportation and regional economy, and based on the development pole theory, the formation mechanism of the "two-tier lagging" economic phenomenon in the northern Qianbei Gelao community is clarified in three steps, and combined with the current country marked by the rural revitalization plan. The "balanced" economic development strategy focuses on the purpose of maximizing the "development pole" diffusion effect and cracking its formation mechanism as a breakthrough point. The article proposes to increase the financial support of the Gelao ethnic community in northern Guizhou as the first driving force to make up for short traffic. Suggestions and countermeasures such as infrastructure and cultivation industry to expand the effects of fiscal policy as a channel, with a view to promoting the local economy from exogenous growth to endogenous growth.

2 Economic Development Status and Transportation Situation of Gelao Ethnic Community in Northern Guizhou

2.1 Economic Development Status of Gelao Nationality Community in Northern Guizhou

The Gelao nationalities are mainly distributed in Guizhou, and they mainly live in the three counties of Wuchuan, Daozhen and Zheng'an in the northern Guizhou area. The development history shows that the Zunyi area is not only culturally developed, but also has been at the forefront of economic development in Guizhou Province, but it is measured by the county and measured by the GDP growth rate in 2011. Among the 88 counties in Guizhou, Daozhen and Wuchuan are two the autonomous counties are ranked in the bottom 10, and after struggling to catch up during the 12th Five-Year Plan period, in 2014, Daozhen County and Wuchuan County ranked 25th and 32nd in the province's 57 non-economically strong counties, respectively. When the overall ranking has improved, the gap between the rural economy of the two counties and the average level of the entire county is getting wider. See the following data.

2.1.1 The Level of Economic Development Generally Over the Years

Longitudinal observation, from 2010 to 2014, Wuchuan and Daozhen counties achieved certain economic growth: the regional GDP of Wuchuan County was 2.18 billion yuan, 2.366 billion yuan, 2.828 billion yuan, 3.449 billion yuan, and 4.299 billion yuan in that order. The regional GDP of Daozhen Autonomous Region was 1.674 billion yuan, 2.04 billion yuan, 2.458 billion yuan, 3.203 billion yuan, and 3.965 billion yuan in turn (see Fig. 1). From the horizontal observation, from 2010 to 2014, the development level of Wuchuan and Daozhen counties lags behind Zunyi City and other counties in Zunyi area (such as Zunyi County), and there is no sign of the gap narrowing (see Fig. 2). From a structural perspective, from 2010 to 2014, there was a large gap between urban income and rural per capita income in Wuchuan and Daozhen counties, and the gap tended to widen significantly (see Fig. 3).

Longitudinal observation shows that from 2010 to 2014, the economy of both Wuchuan and Daozhen counties has achieved certain growth: the regional GDP of Wuchuan county is RMB 2.180 billion, RMB 2.366 billion, RMB 2.828 billion, RMB 3.449 billion and RMB 4.299 billion respectively; the regional GDP of Daozhen Autonomous County is RMB 1.674 billion, RMB 2.04 billion, RMB 2.458 billion, RMB 3.203 billion and RMB 3.965 billion respectively (see Fig. 1). According to the horizontal observation, the development level of Wuchuan and Daozhen counties from 2010 to 2013 lagged behind that of Zunyi City and other counties in Zunyi region (such as Zunyi County), and the gap did not narrow (see Fig. 2). From the perspective of structure, there is a large gap between urban income and rural per capita income in Wuchuan and Daozhen counties from 2010 to 2013, and the gap has a significant trend of expansion (see Fig. 3).

2.1.2   Transportation Status of Gelao Ethnic Community in Northern Guizhou

The investigation data and data show that the transportation infrastructure construction in the area inhabited by the Qibei Gelao nationality is seriously backward (see Fig. 4). The length of highway in the two counties is far less than that of other counties in Zunyi (such as Zunyi). There is no railway, no water transport in the county, county and township roads for a long-time overload operation, serious damage, traffic conditions are extremely bad. Among them: Wuchuan county is the only county in Zunyi region and one of the few counties in the province that does not have the highway above grade 2 (including national highway). Although Daozhen has the geographical advantage of being close to Chongqing, the lagging traffic blocks the radiation of Chongqing's economy. There is no interconnection between the two counties, and the construction of roads to villages is even weaker. By the end of 2013, 14 villages in Wuchuan county had not opened asphalt (cement) roads. At the end of 2014, seven villages in Daozhen county still had no asphalt (cement) roads.

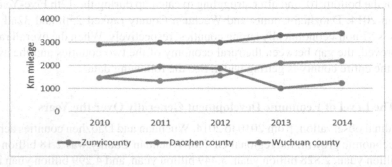

Fig. 4. Road mileage of Zunyi County, Daozhen County and Wuchuan County, 2010–2012 Unit: km. Data source: Website of Zunyi Municipal Government of Guizhou Province

In a word, in terms of economic development and traffic conditions, Daozhen and Wuchuan counties lag behind the average level of development in Zunyi area, and the urban and rural development of the two counties also presents a more unbalanced pattern, and the imbalance of these two levels tends to expand.

3   An Analysis of the Restrictive Mechanism of the Development Effect of the "Development Pole" of the Gelao Community in Northern Guizhou

3.1   Theoretical Basis-Development Pole Theory

The theory of development poles was formed in the 1940s and 1950s, and the viewpoint was: Priority policy to build "development poles", through the diffusion effect of "development poles", to radiate the economic development of the surrounding areas and achieve an "unbalanced-balanced" economic development. However, the actual economic phenomenon shows a siphon effect, the production factors in the surrounding areas are further lacking, and they fall into a lower level of economic development. The gap between the "development pole" and the surrounding areas is widening. This phenomenon is explained by scholars: Because the "development pole" not only has a diffusion effect, but also an echo effect, when the "development pole" has a diffusion effect greater than the echo effect, the region will present an "unbalanced-balanced" economic state on the contrary, there will be another economic state of "imbalance-more imbalance". Considering the fact that the market operating mechanism of developing economies is not sound, the economic growth benefits cannot be automatically and naturally radiated to the peripheral areas, but the fact that the echo effect is more likely to be exerted. It is recommended that the government participate in ensuring that the development potential of the peripheral areas is not destroyed, which is a reversal. The best way to "Matthew Effect".

3.2 The Causal Mechanism Restricting the Development Effect of the "Development Pole"

Based on the economic facts obtained from the research, and according to the development pole theory, the article further clarifies the mechanism of the "development pole" diffusion effect that the Qianbei Gelao community has failed to play effectively:
—Traffic lag—Limited funding for road construction—low fiscal revenue—relative lag in economic development—the diffusion effect of the "development pole" did not play well. Vicious circle (see Fig. 5). According to this, the formation of "two-layer lag" can be decomposed into three layers of causal mechanism: 1) The "two-tiered lag" economic development pattern stems from the fact that the "development pole" diffusion effect has not been effectively exerted; 2) the "development pole" diffusion effect has not played well due to the lagging traffic; 3) the lagging traffic originates from local government repair Road matching funds are limited.

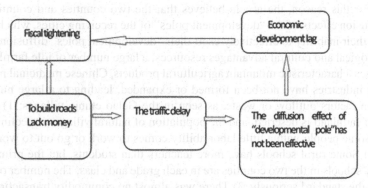

Fig. 5. Intrinsic Determining Mechanism of the "Two-tiered Lag" Economic Phenomenon in the Gelao Community in Northern Guizhou

3.2.1 The First Causal Mechanism: The "Two-Tiered Lag" Economic Development Pattern is Due to the Two-Tiered "Development Pole's" Diffusion Effect not Being Effectively Exerted

With the implementation of the western strategy, Zunyi City has become the "development pole" of urbanization in northern Guizhou. The policy promotes the accumulation of factors, Zunyi City's economy has achieved rapid growth and its development potential has been enhanced. The regional economies have been radiated through the diffusion effect, and the regional economy as a whole has achieved relatively high growth. The average level of economic development in Zunyi. Investigate the reason: The article believes that the conditions for the diffusion effect of Wuchuan and Daozhen counties receiving the "development pole" of Zunyi City have not been formed, and there is a large gap compared with other counties. Just like investigating the economic facts, the population flow between the two counties and the surrounding counties has shown over the years-the two counties are a net outflow of population, and the surrounding counties are a net inflow of population. The surrounding counties of the two counties have gradually formed a crowd of people, especially talents, and an industrial cluster of a certain size. The economic vitality of the surrounding counties has been rapidly improved, and transportation and other infrastructure have been further improved, which has increasingly attracted people from the two counties to the surrounding areas. The outflow of production factors such as county home ownership, population and other factors has weakened the two counties ability or conditions to accept the "development pole" diffusion effect in Zunyi City, increasing the economic development level of the two counties and their surrounding counties.

Moves from urbanization to the stage of urbanization, the county seat plays the role of "development pole" of the county economy. Its purpose is to make the county economy bigger and stronger, and to use the "development pole" of the county seat to promote the growth of the county economy. However, the towns and rural areas of the two counties, Daozhen and Wuchuan, are showing an increasingly uneven economic development pattern. For this reason, the article believes that the two counties and counties have weak diffusion effects of the "development poles" of the receiving cities, which further results in their inability to effectively exert their "development poles" diffusion effects. Rich ecological and cultural advantages resources, a large number of idle farmland and farm houses, characteristic mountain agricultural products, Chinese medicinal materials and other industries have not been formed or expanded, leading to a large number of production factors outflow or waste, as seen in the Gelao ethnic villages: 1) A large amount of farmland is deserted, and the population of natural villages is declining year by year. Some people with a little labor ability comes to work or go out to work in the county. 2) Some rural schools have more teachers than students, but the primary and secondary schools in the two counties are in each grade and class. The number of people exceeded the standard seriously. 3) There was almost no commodity transaction in the countryside, and they were self-sufficient or bought in the county seat. Therefore, the "development pole" of urbanization exerts more of an echo effect, further reducing the economic development potential of the two counties. Therefore, the "development pole" of urbanization exerts more of an echo effect, further reducing the economic development potential of the two counties.

3.2.2   The Second Causal Mechanism: The "Development Pole" Diffusion Effect Does not Play Well Due to Lagging Traffic

According to the related research on the mechanism of the role of transportation and economic development and the facts of the investigation, the article believes that the main factor restricting the diffusion effect of the "development poles" in the two counties is the lagging transportation. Because the transmission mechanism of the "development pole" diffusion effect is [15]: The continuous expansion of the "development pole" production scale will cause a tight supply of production factors, increase production costs, favorable investment opportunities will gradually decrease, the scale effect will disappear, and capital will necessarily find a way out in other regions. At this time, capital and technology will appear. The phenomenon of spreading to the "development pole" surrounding areas, the surrounding areas obtain economic development factors (capital, technology, etc.), and enhance the economic development potential of the surrounding areas; at the same time, the slowdown of the "development pole" economic growth leads to the decline in prices of production factors The scale effect of the "development pole" is gradually disappearing, which will further stimulate the concentration of production factors and commodity flows in the periphery of the "development pole" and promote economic growth in the periphery. The theory is also the reason why China's countryside revitalization strategy is launched at this stage: the implementation of the imbalanced economic development strategy has formed large and small "development poles" in China, and the "development poles" represented by cities have experienced excessive production factors. Clusters, low production efficiency, and the surrounding areas represented by countryside areas are seriously lacking in production factors, the production potential has been severely damaged for a long time, widening the gap between urban and countryside development, and the introduction of countryside revitalization plans, which aim to guide production factors to flow to less developed areas through national policies to achieve the current "harmonious" goal of improving the efficiency of production factors and balanced development.

But, the flow of various production factors and commodities from scope, category and speed must be effectively expanded and improved, and convenient transportation is a key leading factor. However, the current transportation situation in Wuchuan and Daozhen districts: Th traffic between the County town and the outside world is behind and the transportation in the County is slowing down. The full flow of production factors and commodities between the "development poles" of Zunyi City and the two counties and counties, and between the two counties and the county countryside area was severely restricted, and the regional production function could not be optimized. Therefore, just as the Daozhen and Wuchuan counties have rich Gelao national culture and a good ecological environment, they have entered the era of leisure, health, and greenness in the country's economic development. The products and services of rural tourism and ecological leisure should have comparative advantages and can form a certain scale of industry, but the facts of the investigation are not the case. Investigation facts show that due to the inconvenience of transportation, 1) higher logistics costs weaken the relative advantage of the product; 2) most rural tourist spots are difficult to enter the 1–1.5-h journey circle; 3) the ecological leisure network is difficult to synchronize the surrounding county attractions. In short, lagging transportation makes the advantages of resource endowment unable to be reflected, the factors are difficult to agglomerate, the industry cannot be formed and upgraded, resulting in the inability to optimize the local production function and fail to form the ideal mechanism shown in Fig. 6.

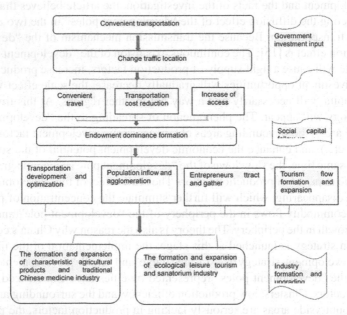

Fig. 6. Optimized mechanism for facilitating transportation optimization in Wuchuan and Daozhen counties

3.2.3 The Third Causal Mechanism: The Lagging Traffic Is Due to the Limited Funding for Road Construction by the Local Government

The inconvenient transportation in the two counties is the lack of investment in transportation infrastructure. According to survey materials, there are two reasons for the lack of investment: 1) the current policy on exempting road construction support funds from ethnic minority areas has not been implemented. Economic facts show that for each road construction, the governments at the county and township levels need to bear about 50–60% of supporting funds, and the proportion of supporting funds for local roads in rural areas is higher. 2) Local governments at all levels have limited financial resources, as shown in Fig. 7. Fiscal expenditures are far greater than fiscal revenues. This is partly due to China's tax-sharing system, which has greatly reduced the fiscal revenue of local governments. In 2006, the state introduced a policy of exempting agricultural taxes. In this context, the two counties of Wuchuan and Daozhen, which are mainly agricultural economies, in terms of finances, fiscal revenues are more and more inadequate. Over the years, total expenditures are about 10 times the general budget revenue. Therefore, as a result, by step-by-step exhaustion of the reasons behind the long-term "two-tier lagging" in the economic development of the northern Qiang Gelao populated area, the conclusion is: the reason is that the layers are superimposed, and its backward relationship "the development pole diffusion effect has not been effectively played Lagging traffic priority policies are less and late", which eventually evolved into a vicious circle of low finances, poor transportation, and weak economy, presented as a "two-tiered lagging" economic phenomenon.

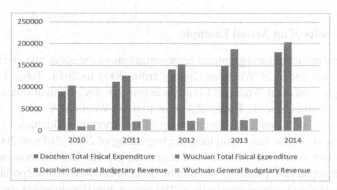

Fig. 7. Total fiscal expenditure and general budget revenue of Daozhen and Wuchuan, 2010–2013. Unit: 10,000 yuan

4 Case Study on the Matching Degree Between Traffic and Economic Development in Wuchuan Gelao Autonomous County

4.1 Indicator Construction and Sample Period

According to the availability of data, Wuchuan County was selected as the research sample for the study period from 2003 to 2014. The variables that characterize the state of economic development are: GDP, GDP per capita, GDP growth rate, tertiary value added, general fiscal budget revenue, fixed asset investment, and per capita income. The variables that characterize traffic are: infrastructure, highway mileage, and freight Volume, cargo turnover. The data are from the official websites of Zunyi and Wuchuan Government of Guizhou.

4.2 Analysis Methods and Reasoning

The article uses factors analysis, comprehensive analysis, elastic coefficient analysis and other methods to quantify the matching degree of economic development and transportation facilities in Wuchuan County over the years, The idea is: the first concept, Construction of regional economic indicator system and transportation facility indicator system, The scores of the respective systems were calculated by factor analysis and recorded as the comprehensive development index of the region's economy and transportation system. In the second concept, based on the comprehensive development index of the two, the elasticity coefficient is used to describe the matching degree all of the two, The specific implementation steps are: the first case use factor analysis to extract economic factors and traffic factors, and get factor scores; second, based on factor scores, use the comprehensive evaluation method to calculate the economic development index and transportation development index; the third, use the elastic coefficient method to calculate the degree of matching between the two.

4.3 Case Results of an Actual Example

Table 1 present numerical and graphical representations of the economic and transportation development index of Wuchuan County from 2003 to 2014. Table 2 shows the matching degree between Wuchuan County's economic development index and transportation development index. The results show that: 1) Wuchuan County's economy is in a long-term growth trend; the development of transportation fluctuates greatly, and the trend of rapid decline has begun from the beginning of 2012. 2) From 2003 to 2010, the transportation-first model favored local economic growth. In 2010, economic growth changed from negative to positive. At the same time, in early 2010, transportation development lagged behind economic growth, and transportation development could not keep up with economic development needs. 3) There are 7 "poor" and 4 "good" matches, with an average of −3.83036. The overall match between the two is "poor", of which 2003–2008 consists of three "poor" to "good" cycles Explain that the transportation-first model greatly improves the local economic situation. The spiral growth of economic growth is matched with the development of transportation, showing the state of the economic system being pushed up. During 2009–2013, 4 consecutive "poor", with 1 A "better" end, explaining the role of transportation in boosting the economy, began to turn into a restrictive effect in 2009, and finally in 2013, the economy and transportation entered a low-level development state with a matching degree of "better". In summary, the results of the case analysis show that the previous mode of transportation advancement is beneficial to promote the economic growth of Wuchuan County, but since the beginning of 2009, transportation development has not kept up with the needs of economic development, restricting the development of the "development pole" diffusion effect. Step into a vicious circle of low finance, lack of transportation and weak economy.

5 Suggestions and Countermeasures for Maximizing the Diffusion Effect of the "Development Pole" in the Gelao Ethnic Community in Northern Guizhou

In the context of China's realization of common prosperity through the construction of large and small "development poles", the "development poles" diffusion effect has not been effectively exerted, leading to a long-term economic phenomenon of "two-tiered lag" in the Gelao ethnic settlements At the same time, the national economic development strategy has shifted—to give way to "equilibrium", and it is proposed to increase efforts to promote the return of production factors to less developed regions to achieve harmonious development. Combining the strategy of revitalizing the countryside led by the prosperity of the industry, the article puts forward suggestions to

Table 1. Comprehensive development index of regional economic and transportation system in Wuchuan County from 2003 to 2014.

Time	Economic	Transportation
2003	−10.468	5.274
2004	−8.679	−0.530
2005	−7.594	−0.462
2006	−10.222	−3.676
2007	−4.100	−2.123
2008	−3.896	5.217
2009	−1.828	3.045
2010	0.966	4.523
2011	4.222	3.409
2012	10.153	4.810
2013	13.163	−8.331
2014	18.282	−11.154

Table 2. Analysis of the matching degree between the traffic system and regional economy in Wuchuan from 2003 to 2013.

Time	Elasticity	Compatibility
2003	13.100	Poor
2004	1.024	Relatively good
2005	5.263	Poor
2006	0.626	Relatively good
2007	−92.799	Poor
2008	0.727	Relatively good
2009	−0.060	Poor
2010	−0.223	Poor
2011	0.413	Poor
2012	28.906	Poor
2013	0.889	Relatively good

alleviate the local "two-tiered lagging" economic phenomenon: the theme of expanding the "development pole" diffusion effect and cracking its formation mechanism (low finances-poor transportation-weak economy- Low down finance) as the starting point, increasing financial investment as the first driving force, and developing industries as a channel to improve the effect of fiscal policy, prompting the local transition to an endogenous economic growth model as soon as possible. Therefore, it is suggested to improve the circular path of the region's economy from the perspective of ethnic support, improve transportation infrastructure, support and cultivate industries, and increase economic development potential, development opportunities and development levels.

5.1 Improve National Policy Support

It is recommended to implement the "zero matching" policy for infrastructure construction projects in ethnic areas in the laws and regulations of ethnic minority areas, cancel the county-level supporting funds for public welfare construction projects in ethnic areas and concentrated and particularly poor areas, and exempt the northern Qiang Gelao ethnic communities from the county level. The supporting funds for public welfare projects are included in the year-end assessment of relevant departments and bureaus, and the "zero matching" is effectively implemented. The state should pay more attention to the objects that are neither in the category of large ethnic groups nor in the very small ethnic groups (based on the total number of ethnic populations). For a long time, the state has invested a lot in both ends, but the ethnic minorities in the middle of the total population have not been the same for a long time. Degree of financial support, it is recommended to implement equivalent economic support policies.

5.2 Improve Transportation and Information Convenience

The state needs to increase the construction of transportation and other infrastructure facilities in the Gelao community in northern Guizhou, and improve and build the transportation infrastructure in order to: 1) Optimize the structure of the highway network and strengthen the accessibility of county-to-district, county-level counties, county-to-township, and town-to-town highway; 2) Reconstruct and upgrade some potential highways, increase the proportion of high-grade highways and highways, and increase transportation capacity; 3) Expand and optimize the construction of information networks to improve rural 4G coverage. Specifically: as soon as possible, the county roads in the northern Guilin Gelao community can be upgraded to provincial roads, second-level highways in tourist attractions, second-level highways in towns and villages, third-level highways in administrative villages, and fourth-level highways in natural villages Oil road, fully realize the last mile project of transportation, fast logistics and e-commerce services.

5.3 Establish a Government-Led Industry Fund

This local government has rich Gelao Ethnic's culture and good ecological resources. Through fund support, it can reduce risks and guide social capital to enter. First, it can cultivate and expand local characteristic agricultural products and traditional Chinese medicine industry to realize the integrated development of the first industry and the second industry. Second, it can develop healthy, leisure and other tourism products in combination with the local minority culture and good natural environment to expand the cooperation with the local government Optimize the products and services of the tertiary industry; finally, rely on good ecology to promote the integration of agriculture, processing industry, tourism and other primary, secondary and tertiary industries.

5.4 Increase Ecological Compensation

In the industrialization era, due to geographical and location reasons, the Qianbei Gelao community has not been able to participate in it, and has saved a lot of mountains and rivers. The country has entered the post-industrialization era and proposed green economic development goals. The ecological economic development model is reflecting local resources. Given the endowment advantages, it is recommended to increase the details of detailed compensation for reducing CO_2 in forests, etc., which is more conducive to the local green and economic harmonious development, and is also a blueprint for implementing the country's rural revitalization.

5.5 Improving the Reform Policy of Peasants' Idle Fields and Farm Houses

A large amount of idle farmland and farmhouse resources require capital and entrepreneurs to activate. Therefore, it is recommended that the "three rights separation" reform be promoted and detailed rules be issued to promote the flow of more production factors to the local area and cultivate and expand local specialty agricultural products, Chinese medicinal materials and leisure tourism. And other industries, expanding the effects of fiscal policy and shifting towards an endogenous economy.

Acknowledgements. Supported by the project: Study on the Optimal Financial Structure construction of Green Economy in Guizhou (Guizhou Science and Technology Co., LTD. LH [2015]7222).

References

1. Xu, Y., Su, B., et al.: Comprehensive evaluation and adaptability study of regional economy and transportation system development in Shaanxi province. Ecol. Econ. (3), 108–112 (2016)
2. Yan, P., Shao, Q.: Research on the theory of economic growth pole. Financ. Theory Prac. (3), 2–6 (2001)
3. Fen, R.: Empirical research on the relationship between transportation and regional economic growth, pp. 8–12. Tianjin University, Tianjin (2013)
4. Liang, L., Zhang, H.: Convergence of unbalanced regional economic development in China – from the perspective of three industries. Res. Econ. Issues (1), 37–42 (2011)
5. Zhao, W., Ma, R.: Convergence, causes and policy suggestions of regional financial development in China. China Soft Sci. (2), 94–101 (2006)
6. Meng, D., Lu, Y., et al.: Evaluation of the coordination between transportation and economy in Henan counties based on projection tracing model. Geogr. Res. (11), 2092–2106 (2013)
7. Xie, J., Zhang, Y.: Correlation analysis of highway traffic and economic development in northern Shaanxi during the economic transformation period. Hum. Geogr. (5), 103–107 (2010)
8. Li, J., Wang, Q.: Theory of regional economic development stage and analysis of the status quo of regional economic development stage in China. Econ. Geogr. (4) 6–9, 25 (2010)
9. Cheng, M., Ge, Q., Shi, Q.: Income inequality of Chinese farmers and its determinants. Economics (quarterly) (4), 1253–1272 (2016)
10. Furhudi, M.: Transportation infrastructure and long-run economic growth in OECD countries. Transp. Res. Part A **74**, 73–90 (2015)

11. Diaz, R., Behr, J.G., Wong, Q.: Quantifying the economic and demographic impact of transportation infrastructure investments: Trans. Soc. Model. Simul. Int. **92**(4), 377–397 (2016)
12. Sousa, C., Roseta-Palma, C., Martin, L.F.: Economic growth and transport: on the road to sustainability. Nat. Resour. Forum **39**, 3–14 (2015)
13. Xin, L., Xiao, L., Tiyan, S., Martin, S.: Comparing China's city transportation and economic network. Cities **53**, 43–50 (2016)
14. Wan, L., Liu, Y.: Theoretical research and empirical analysis on the appropriateness of China's transportation infrastructure investment. Econ. Res. (5), 34–40 (2014)
15. Yi, W., Ou, Y.: Path selection of new rural construction in underdeveloped areas - from the perspective of urban-rural relationship. J. Jiangxi Inst. Governance (3), 38–42 (2011)

Debt Risk Research on PPP Model Based on VAR (Value at Risk) Model

GuangLi Yang[1(✉)], Chao Wang[2], and Wenmin Kuang[3]

[1] School of Accountancy, Xinhua College of Sun Yat-Sen University, Dongguan, China
491082948@qq.com
[2] Zibo Local Financial Supervision Bureau of Shandong Province, Zibo, China
[3] Beijing Global Industrial Safety Technology Co., Ltd., Beijing, China

Abstract. The report of the 19th national congress points out that from now on to 2020 is the decisive period for building a moderately prosperous society in an all-round way, while PPP project investment involves 19 industries, such as transportation, comprehensive development of cities and towns, education, health care, pension, etc., providing more convenience and services for people's life. At present, the amount of investment in PPP projects in China is relatively large, and the cumulative investment is more than 13 trillion yuan. China's PPP projects have formed the largest PPP market in the world. The promotion of PPP model is conducive to solving the problem of funds shortage of local governments, but the poor application of PPP model will lead to debt risk, even financial risk. This paper first analyzes the current situation of PPP model in China, then uses VAR model to quantify the debt risk loss caused by PPP projects, and local governments should prepare corresponding reserve funds to prevent the loss. Finally, in view of the debt risk, it puts forward some policy suggestions, such as the establishment of PPP project feasibility analysis, implementation process supervision, performance evaluation, and risk prevention mechanism.

Keywords: PPP model · Value at risk · VAR model · Risk prevention

1 Introduction

PPP (public-private partnership) mode refers to the government's cooperation with social capital, which is mainly used in municipal engineering, transportation and other public infrastructure construction projects. It is also an important financing mode. In this mode, the government can not only solve the problem of finance shortage in infrastructure construction, but also reduce the cost and improve the efficiency of the project through private capital financing [1]. In recent years, with the increase of PPP project investment and the amount of investment, in order to standardize PPP projects, the government set up a PPP project management library in 2018. At the same time, PPP projects need the government and enterprises to sign project contracts or agreements, respectively regulating the rights and obligations of both parties [2].

© ICST Institute for Computer Sciences, Social Informatics and Telecommunications Engineering 2021
Published by Springer Nature Switzerland AG 2021. All Rights Reserved
H. Song and D. Jiang (Eds.): SIMUtools 2020, LNICST 369, pp. 105–116, 2021.
https://doi.org/10.1007/978-3-030-72792-5_10

Local government debt can be divided into explicit debt and implicit debt, direct debt and contingent debt, while under PPP mode, the government mainly faces implicit debt. According to the investment reporting mechanism, PPP projects can be divided into user paid projects, feasibility gap subsidy projects and government paid projects. User - paid items do not constitute government debt. Feasibility gap subsidy projects and government paid projects can adopt government budget expenditure according to PPP contract to form government direct debt, explicit debt and contingent debt. From the perspective of PPP project financing, it can be roughly divided into self-financing by enterprises through banks, bonds, funds, etc. and guaranteed financing by the government. The latter is the contingent liability that the government needs to bear when the enterprise cannot repay normally. The government does not reflect the debt in the budget. Once it occurs, it will form the government's implicit debt. In addition, many enterprises will turn projects that do not conform to the PPP model into PPP projects through packaging. If such PPP projects cannot be implemented normally or problems arise in the implementation process are eliminated, the government will bear corresponding debts, which also form the implicit debts of the government. Therefore, under the PPP model, the government mainly faces implicit debt risk.

Chinese experts and scholars have a lot of research on the debt risk of local governments under the PPP model: Ou Chunzhi and Jia Kang pointed out that PPP should fully consider its adaptability, value for money and financial tolerance in the process of promotion, so as to prevent inducing new financial risks [3]. Zhang Ping pointed out that the promotion of PPP model is indeed conducive to alleviating the finance shortage of local governments and controlling the debt increase of local governments, but at the same time, attention should be paid to the prevention and control of project risks [4]. Han Jun and others clearly pointed out that not all projects are suitable for PPP mode, and blindly use PPP may damage public interests and increase government debt burden [5]. Darrin and Mervyn also believe that although PPP mode financing has many advantages, it involves a series of complex implementation and supervision processes. Therefore, due to different national conditions, its implementation in different countries may lead to different consequences [6]. Bai Dequan pointed out that PPP has a double impact on local government debt risk. PPP is likely to induce local government financial risk in the short term, chain hidden debt risk in the medium term, and systemic financial risk in the long term [7]. Zhang Tong pointed out that in the PPP mode, the financing mode guaranteed by the government is the contingent responsibility that the government only assumes when the enterprises cannot repay the financing funds to the financial institutions in the PPP project, which will not be reflected in the financial budget and the balance sheet of the government, and will constitute the implicit debt of the government [8]. From the above expert's point of view, it can be concluded that the promotion of PPP model is conducive to solving the problem of funds shortage of local governments, but the poor application of PPP model will generate debt risk, even financial risk.

The government debt of PPP model in China has four important characteristics: universality, complexity, concealment and separation of rights and responsibilities [9]. At present, the amount of investment in PPP projects in China is relatively large, with a total investment of more than 13 trillion yuan, has formed the largest PPP market in the world. However, there are still many problems in the operation of PPP projects.

According to the latest data released by the Ministry of finance, as to April 23, 2018, there are 1695 projects that have been cleaned up and returned to the treasury, involving an investment of 1.8 trillion yuan; there are 2005 projects that need to be rectified, involving an investment of 3.1 trillion yuan [10].

Table 1. Statistics of items returned from management warehouse, rectification and withdrawal of reserve list

Items to be withdrawn from the management warehouse, rectification and reserve list	Numbers
PPP mode is not suitable	397
Early preparation not in place	506
Failure to carry out "two arguments" as required	217
No more PPP implementation	1120
No compliance with standard operation requirements	277
Suspected illegal debt guarantee	14
Failure to disclose information as required	488
Removed or rectified for other reasons	1354
Total	4373

From the above statistical table, it can be seen that the number of PPP projects which will no longer continue to adopt PPP mode and other reasons is as high as 56%, and the number of projects which are not in place in the early stage and have not made information disclosure as required is 22%. From the above Table 1, it can be seen that PPP project operation is not standardized, and there is no effective supervision in the operation process. At present, there are still some problems in PPP projects in China, such as the local government's illegal borrowing, the irregular financing mode which has large scale, the disguised borrowing through the financing platform, the inadequate competition, the inadequate supervision, the lack of legal constraints on PPP projects and so on. If the PPP project is not well operated, it will bring debt risk to the government. The following content of this paper uses VAR (value-at-risk) model to quantify the investment risk of PPP project in China, and provides suggestions for preventing the debt risk of PPP.

2 Empirical Study on VAR Model

Value at risk refers to the maximum possible loss of a certain investment portfolio in a given confidence level in a certain period in the future under normal fluctuation. Value at risk is the amount of a loss. VaR is a tool for measuring risk, which applies statistics and technology to risk management and quantify risk. In this paper, VAR model is used to analyse the amount of investment and the quantity of investment under PPP mode in China, and quantify the debt risk generated by PPP project through VAR model, and then propose the debt risk response measures.

2.1 Data and Analysis

As of the end of the first quarter of 2019, the investment of PPP management base projects in China is shown in Table 2, mainly involving 19 industries such as transportation, municipal engineering and tourism, with a total cumulative investment of 13421.1 billion yuan and 8843 investment projects. The top three cumulative investment are transportation, municipal engineering and urban comprehensive development, accounting for 29.9%, 29.8% and 13.8% of the amount of total investment respectively, and the project investment accounts for 14.4%, 39.3% and 9.6% of the quantity of total investment respectively. Therefore, municipal engineering accounts for a large proportion in the amount of investment and the quantity of total investment of the project, which is an important management project in PPP project management.

Table 2. Investment of PPP management base project at the end of the first quarter of 2019

Project	Cumulative investment (100 million yuan)	Cumulative number of investment projects
Transportation	40122	1269
Municipal engineering	40034	3474
Urban comprehensive development	18584	561
Ecological construction and environmental protection	9395	849
Tourism	4763	334
Water conservancy construction	3053	374
Affordable housing project	2822	158
Education	2471	425
Others	2103	140
Government infrastructure	2101	205
Health care	1957	256
Culture	1788	193
Forestry	978	41
Sports	956	113
Technology	908	132
Agriculture	769	72
Pension	724	107
Energy	562	107
Social secure	121	33
Total	**134211**	**8843**

Correlation Analysis. According to the data in Table 2, the correlation analysis is carried out on the accumulated investment amount and the accumulated investment quantity of PPP projects at the end of the first quarter of 2019. The analysis results are shown in Table 3.

It can be seen from Table 3 that there is a large correlation between the accumulated investment quantity of PPP projects and accumulated investment amount of PPP projects.

Table 3. Correlation Analysis of investment amount and investment quantity of PPP project at the end of the first quarter of 2019

	Cumulative investment (100 million yuan)	Number of projects
Cumulative investment (100 million yuan)	1	
Number of projects	0.861862522	1

Sample t-test. The results of t-test on the selected samples are shown in Table 4. Through this table, it is known that the p value is less than 0.05, and the average value of the two groups of data is statistically different, that is, there is a significant difference between the quantity of cumulative investment and the number of cumulative investment projects of the selected sample PPP project, and the data is valid.

Table 4. t-test: two sample equal variance hypothesis.

	Variable 1	Variable 2
Average	7063.736842	465.4211
Variance	153565386	626739.8
Observed value	19	19
Combined variance	77096062.9	
Hypothetical mean deviation	0	
df	36	
t Stat	2.316214623	
P(T ≤ t) single tail	0.013176648	
t single tail criticality	1.688297714	
P(T ≤ t) double tails	0.026353295	
t double tails criticality	2.028094001	

Regression Analysis. On the basis of correlation analysis and sample t test, it is, there is a large correlation between the cumulative investment quantity and cumulative investment amount of PPP project and the selected data is valid. Then, regression analysis is conducted on the cumulative investment quantity and the cumulative investment amount of PPP projects. The analysis results are shown in Table 5.

Table 5. Regression Analysis of accumulated investment quantity and accumulated investment amount of PPP project at the end of the first quarter of 2019

	Intercept	Project amount
Coefficients	784.7865	13.4909
Standard error	1733.205	1.925343
t Stat	0.452795	7.007012
P-value	0.656422	2.11E−06
Lower 95%	−2871.96	9.428784
Upper 95%	4441.529	17.55302
Lower limit 95.0%	−2871.96	9.428784
Upper limit 95.0%	4441.529	17.55302

From Table 5, it can be concluded that there is a linear relationship between the quantity of cumulative investment and the amount of investment of PPP projects. Assuming y is the quantity of cumulative investment of PPP projects and X is the amount of investment projects, it can be concluded that the relationship between the quantity of cumulative investment and the amount of investment projects is as follows:

$$Y = 784.79 + 13.49X \tag{1}$$

At the same time, according to the regression analysis of the data in Table 2, Fig. 1 is obtained. It can be seen from the analysis that there is a linear relationship between the quantity of cumulative investment of PPP projects and the amount of cumulative investment, with a slope of 784.79. The quantity of accumulated investment of PPP project can be predicted through Fig. 1. By the end of the first quarter of 2019, the total amount of PPP projects is 8843. When the total amount of PPP projects is predicted to reach 10000 in the future, the total quantity of investment will reach 13568.479 billion yuan. At the same time, through the linear regression analysis of the quantity of cumulative investment and the amount of investment in PPP projects, it is found that the quantity of cumulative investment of PPP projects is distributed in discrete form. When the VAR model is used to analyze the debt risk of PPP, the calculation formula of discrete distribution should be used.

2.2 VAR Model Analysis

VAR refers to the value at risk, that is, the maximum possible loss faced by a portfolio under a given confidence level in a certain probability level and a certain period in the

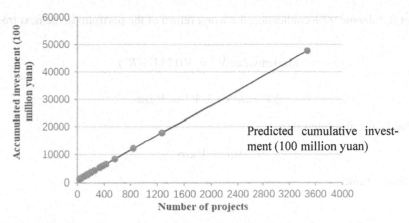

Fig. 1. The relationship diagram between the accumulative invest amount and the accumulative investment amount of PPP projects.

future under normal fluctuation. In this paper, the VAR model is used to quantify the debt risk of PPP project, and then we can know the maximum possible debt loss of PPP project.

According to the investment reporting mechanism, PPP projects can be divided into user paid projects, feasibility gap subsidy projects and government paid projects. Among them, feasibility gap subsidy projects and government paid projects need government subsidies or payments, which may form government debts in the future. By the end of the first quarter of 2019, there were 4892 feasibility gap subsidy projects and 324 government paid projects respectively, with an investment quantity of 8.7 trillion and 3.5 trillion respectively, accounting for 64.9% and 25.7% of the total quantity of investment of PPP projects. It can be seen that the feasibility gap subsidy projects and government paid projects account for a large proportion of the quantity of investment in PPP projects. Because the government bears the expenses of this part, if the PPP projects in this part are not well operated, or they cannot generate the expected income, or the expected income is greatly reduced, it will bring serious losses to the government. In this paper, VAR model is used to quantify the loss, so as to prevent the loss caused by local debt risk in advance.

There are two kinds of VAR calculation, one is based on continuous distribution and the other is based on discrete distribution. According to the regression analysis of the above data, it is found that the quantity of cumulative investment of PPP projects is distributed in a discrete form. Therefore, this paper calculates the possible losses of PPPP projects through the discrete VAR model.

VAR calculation based on continuous distribution. Let V0 represent the current market price of an investment exposure, whose return follows the normal distribution R ~ n $(\mu, \sigma 2)$ at any future point, and the market value of the exposure is:

$$VT = V0^* (1 + RT) \tag{2}$$

$$\text{Expected value } E(V) = V0^* (1 + \mu) \tag{3}$$

Let R * denote 99% confidence, the worst return of the portfolio in the next trading day,

$$\text{Market value } V^* = V0^* (1 + R^*) \qquad (4)$$

$$\Delta V = E(V) - V^* = V_0 \alpha \sigma \qquad (5)$$

That is, the absolute value

$$Var = V_0 \alpha \sigma \qquad (6)$$

Relative value

$$Var = \alpha \sigma \qquad (7)$$

In the above formula, V0 represents the cumulative investment of PPP projects, Vt represents the market value of PPP projects at any point in the future, RT represents the return on investment, μ represents the mean value, $\sigma 2$ represents the variance of random variables, and V0 represents the current market price of an investment exposure.

VAR Calculation Based on Discrete Distribution. For population X and given C (0 < C < 1), if x exists, the formula is:

$$F(x) = P(X \le x) = \int f(u)du = C \qquad (8)$$

Then x is called the C quantile of X (or the probability distribution of x). In the value at risk (VAR), we can use the cut-off point to explain the probability of occurrence, which will not be greater than the loss of a certain probability. Because in discrete distribution, C represents the probability of integration.

$$C = \int_{-\infty}^{x} \frac{1}{b-a} dx \qquad (9)$$

Where C represents the probability of loss, X represents the maximum loss amount under the condition of probability C (that is, VAR of discrete distribution), b represents the maximum income of the investment project, and a represents the maximum loss amount of the investment project.

According to the regression analysis of the quantity of cumulative investment and the amount of investment projects, it is found that the investment amount of PPP projects is discrete distribution, and the discrete distribution method is used in the calculation of VAR. By the end of the first quarter of 2019, the total quantity of investment of PPP project is 13421.1 billion yuan, assuming a return on investment is 6.56%. According to the formula of one-year compound interest final value:

$$F = P \times (F/P, i, n) \qquad (10)$$

It is calculated that when the total quantity of investment of PPP project is 13421.1 billion yuan and the return on investment is 6.56%, the return on investment in one year is 143015.5 billion yuan. VAR is calculated based on the amount of return on investment.

Among the assumptions: (1) the probability of cumulative investment loss of PPP project is 1%; (2) the outlook period is 1 year; (3) the confidence degree is 99%; then the VAR is calculated as follows:

$$1\% = \int_{-\infty}^{x} \frac{1}{b-a} dx = \int_{-143015}^{x} \frac{1}{b-a} dx \qquad (11)$$

Among them, b is the maximum income of the PPP projects investment and a is the maximum loss of the PPP projects investment.

It is calculated that

$$x = 14015.5 \; billion \; yuan \qquad (12)$$

That is to say, the total quantity of investment of PPP project is 13421.1 billion yuan. In the case of one year's outlook and 99% confidence, there are 1% possible to generate 14015.5 billion yuan of investment loss. Therefore, local governments in China should do a good job in debt loss in order to prevent of PPP projects in advance, that is to say, 140.155 billion (14015.5 × 1% = 140.155 billion yuan) of reserve funds should be prepared to prevent the debt risk of PPP projects.

3 Conclusions and Suggestions

3.1 Conclusions

Based on the above analysis, it can be concluded that the project investment of PPP management base in China mainly involves 19 industries, such as transportation, municipal engineering, tourism, etc. There is a linear relationship between the quantity of accumulated project investment and the amount of accumulated project investment. The future investment can be predicted according to the linear regression line. As of the first quarter of 2019, the total investment of PPP project is 13421.1 billion yuan. In the prospect period of one year, under the condition of 99% confidence, when the return on investment is 6.56%, the maximum loss will be 14015.5 billion yuan, that is, there are 1% possible to generate 14015.5 billion yuan of investment loss. Local governments in China should do a good job in debt loss prevention of PPP projects in advance, that is to say, 140.155 billion yuan of reserve funds should be prepared to prevent the debt risk of PPP projects. At the same time, we found that the larger the investment quantity of PPP project, the greater the debt risk faced by the government, and the greater the possibility of investment loss. Therefore, the government should control the investment scale of PPP projects and carry out strict supervision.

3.2 Suggestions

Improve the Risk Prevention Mechanism of PPP Project. PPP project is an agreement or contract signed by the government and the enterprise department. Although PPP project is a debt risk shared by the government and the enterprise, when the enterprise is in crisis or bankruptcy, the government will bear all risks for the debt. Therefore, the government should establish a risk prevention mechanism for PPP projects. The specific contents include the following aspects: firstly, the government should conduct a comprehensive investigation on the cooperative enterprises to ensure that the enterprises have certain economic strength and credit conditions; secondly, the government can stipulate in the agreement or contract that the cooperative enterprises should reserve certain working capital as the guarantee fund for the PPP projects when the PPP projects In case of problems, this part of funds can be used; secondly, it is clear that the government and the cooperative enterprises bear the responsibility in proportion, which can reduce the debt risk borne by the government when there is debt risk in the PPP project; finally, during the implementation of the PPP project, the government should assign special personnel to supervise and manage, to ensure the effective implementation of the PPP project, to avoid uncompleted projects, which will lead to the debt risk borne by the government.

Establish Double Warning Lines for Debt Risk Assessment Indicators of PPP Projects. In the process of PPP project operation in China, financing often plays an important role, because PPP project involves amount Large, most enterprises finance through banks, trusts, funds, etc. as an important participant in PPP projects, financial institutions often provide more than 70% of the total amount of projects [8]. Some PPP projects are government guaranteed financing, once there is a problem in PPP projects, it will bring serious losses to the government, which forms the government's implicit debt. At present, China's PPP project has set a financial capacity warning line of 10%, but has not yet established a PPP project financing warning line. Therefore, in order to prevent the debt risk of PPP project, we should establish a dual warning line of PPP project financing and financial capacity. The compliant PPP project should not only meet the financial capacity, but also the financing scale should not be too large, otherwise it will bring implicit debt to the PPP project and the government.

Establishment of PPP Project Life Cycle Supervision System. PPP project life cycle includes identification, preparation, procurement, implementation and handover. PPP projects should be strictly reviewed in the identification stage. For example, some projects that do not conform to the PPP model are transformed into PPP projects through packaging. Such PPP projects should be strictly reviewed. At the same time, government funded representatives should be prohibited from signing any supporting documents. If such PPP projects occur, they should be stopped immediately. In addition, in the process of PPP project implementation (i.e. preparation, procurement, implementation and other stages), real-time monitoring shall be carried out at each stage, mainly to comprehensively monitor whether the cost amount and cost of the project are reasonable, the implementation progress and the specific implementation process [11]. Problems in the implementation of PPP project shall be found and solved in time to avoid the interruption of PPP project and failure to continue the implementation, and the debts incurred by this part shall be borne by the government. At the same time, we should be careful to carry out government paid projects to prevent the rapid growth of the government's financial expenditure on the project, so as to exceed the financial tolerance.

Establish Performance Appraisal System of PPP Project. The performance appraisal system of PPP project is to carry out comprehensive evaluation in the whole PPP project, i.e. according to the PPP project. All stages of the life cycle. In the identification stage of PPP project, it is necessary to assess the debt risk of PPP project, whether it is within the financial tolerance range, i.e. no more than 10% of the warning line. PPP projects beyond the warning line will not be passed, and the financing scale will also be considered. In the implementation process of PPP projects, success factor analysis, data envelopment analysis and balanced scorecard can also be used to assess the performance of PPP projects [12]. After the PPP project is completed, it also needs to be assessed, that is, whether the completion of each indicator of the PPP project is consistent with the budget. For the inconsistent PPP projects, the reasons should be found and analyzed, so that the subsequent PPP project implementation can learn from the experience and lessons. In addition, for the PPP projects that are not completed as required, corresponding countermeasures shall be given to avoid the failure of the PPP project, and the government will incur large debts. Meanwhile, the Department and person in charge of the project shall bear corresponding responsibilities. As for the PPP project completed according to the regulations, and the completion effect is good, it can be vigorously publicized and promoted, so that other PPP projects can learn from the experience of the successful project.

Acknowledgements. This work was supported in part by the Characteristic key discipline project of Guangdong Province, Public Management (No. F2017STSZD01), The Department of Finance of Guangdong Province, Research on social Welfare Effect of Tax Reduction and Fee Reduction (No. Z2020121), Research on the Long-term Mechanism and implementation of Vocational education to consolidate the achievements of poverty alleviation (No. 412/31512000106). The authors wish to thank the reviewers for their helpful comments.

References

1. Qi, X., Ke, Y., Wang, S.: Analysis of main risk factors of China's PPP project based on case. China Soft Sci. **05**, 107–113 (2009)
2. Yang, W.: Characteristics of contractual relationship between government and social capital under PPP mode. China Government Procurement News, 10 May 2019 (003)
3. Ou, C., Jia, K.: Solving the financing constraints of basic public services with PPP innovation. Econ. Manag. Res. **4**, 85–94 (2017)
4. Zhang, P.: A study on the repayment pressure of various debts in China during the 13th Five Year Plan period. Econ. Syst. Reform **1**, 5–10 (2017)
5. Han, J., Lv, Y., Xu, Y.: Study on the cooperation mode of government and social capital. Shanghai Econ. Res. **2**, 106–110 (2017)
6. Grimsey, D., Lewis, M.K.: The Worldwide Revolution in Infrastructure Provision and Project Finance. China Renmin University Press, Beijing (2016)
7. Bai, D.: Regulating PPP development, preventing and resolving local government debt risk. Theor. Discuss. **03**, 88–94 (2018)
8. Zhang, T.: Analysis of financial institutions to prevent the hidden debt risk of PPP government – based on the interpretation of Caijin 2019 No. 10. J. Financ. Account. (17), 172–176 (2019)

9. Dong, Z.: Analysis of types and characteristics of government debt in PPP mode in China. Local Financ. Res. (09), 61–66+87 (2016)
10. Luo, Y.: On the normalization of PPP project mode. Archit. Budg. **12**, 16–21 (2018)
11. Jiang, D., Huo, L., Lv, Z., Song, H., Qin, W.: A joint multi-criteria utility-based network selection approach for vehicle-to-infrastructure networking. IEEE Trans. Intell. Transp. Syst. **19**(10), 3305–3319 (2018)
12. Mu, Z., Zheng, L., Cheng, Y.: Study on performance appraisal system of PPP project. J. Eng. Manag.

A Space-Air-Ground Integrated Networking Method for Air Mobile Targets

Yuwen Wang[1], Lei Wang[2], WeiJiong Zhang[2], and Dingde Jiang[1](✉)

[1] School of Astronautics and Aeronautic, University of Electronic Science and Technology of China, Chengdu 611731, China
jiangdd@uestc.edu.cn

[2] Shanghai Electro-Mechanical Engineering Institute, Shanghai 201109, China

Abstract. With the development of communication technology, the integration of space and space information network has become a research hotspot. This network can be used for data transmission and sharing on the ground, in the air and in outer space, which can greatly enhance the coverage and speed of the network. However, the air space integration information network is composed of a large number of mobile nodes, which makes it highly dynamic. Based on the time-varying graph, this paper proposes a dynamic networking method to connect the aircraft in the atmosphere to the space-based satellite network, which transforms the problem into the shortest path solution at a certain time and avoids a lot of calculation. At the same time, according to the established scene, the joint simulation platform is built. And the simulation architecture with MATLAB as the core and STK and NS-3 as the auxiliary is completed. On this platform, the simulation test of air space integration information network can be carried out. Through the test of the algorithm on the built simulation platform, the results show that this networking method has good performance in the dynamic network networking.

Keywords: Space-air-ground integrated network · Graph · Shortest path algorithm

1 Introduction

The space network technology based on satellite is now developing rapidly, gradually realizing the satellite broadband access, satellite mobile data and other services [1, 2]. Because the satellite network can form a good complementary relationship with the network on the ground in terms of coverage and mobile access, the combination of the two is the best solution to the problem that the current network cannot cover the world. Therefore, it is an inevitable trend that the air space integrated network is composed of ground network, UAV network and satellite network system [3, 4].

Satellite networks are different from fixed networks and mobile networks on the ground because satellites move in high-speed periodic motion in orbit outside the earth, which will cause the topological structure of satellite networks to change. So that the inter satellite link will be periodically established and interrupted due to the selection of the

© ICST Institute for Computer Sciences, Social Informatics and Telecommunications Engineering 2021
Published by Springer Nature Switzerland AG 2021. All Rights Reserved
H. Song and D. Jiang (Eds.): SIMUtools 2020, LNICST 369, pp. 117–126, 2021.
https://doi.org/10.1007/978-3-030-72792-5_11

optimal link [5, 6]. When providing services to a certain place on the ground, the current satellite may be not the best access point due to the change of topology. So it is necessary to switch services to other satellite nodes which have good access conditions. In this way, satellite can provide services to the ground. At present, there are a lot of researches. W. Zhang et al. studies the topological control problem in spatial information network (SIN) by using the method of hierarchical autonomous system (AS) [7]. An AS-TC algorithm is proposed to minimize the delay in sin; J. Spencer et al. proposed using software to define the network application in the integrated network to improve the flexibility and traffic management ability of the network [8]; F. Wang et al. studied the satellite network routing algorithm based on software defined network, which can find the shortest path [9]. F. D. Kronewitter propose a real-time tactical mobile network optimization agent (TNOA) based on real-time simulation is proposed. The near real-time modeling of wired and wireless links is carried out by using a large-scale parallel and high-performance network simulator, QUALNET, to simulate the air space integrated information network [10, 11].

2 Problem Statement and System Model

Since the network nodes on the ground do not have the characteristics of high-speed movement, it is considered that the topological shape of the ground network is unchanged in the study. We only study the connection between the satellite network and the air network of the aircraft in the atmosphere. The flying speed of the air vehicle is slow, and the optimal access point is no longer the optimal access point after a period of operation. This high-speed moving characteristic causes the complexity of the topology structure, which leads to the communication link need to be established and switched from time to time. For the general satellite topology structure, it can be represented by the graph $G(V, E)$, where E is the connection relationship between the satellites. It can be described as fallowed:

$$V = \{s_1, s_2, \ldots, s_n\} \tag{1}$$

where n is the number of satellites in the satellite network topology. Each vertex in the graph represents a satellite. And the relationship between each satellite can be described by the edge set E, which is recorded as:

$$E = \{s_1 s_2, s_1 s_3, \ldots, s_i s_j\}, i \neq j, i \in n, j \in n \tag{2}$$

where i, j are the number of satellite, $s_i s_j$ indicates that there is a link between nodes s_i and s_j. Through the mathematical description of nodes and edges, the mathematical model of the whole satellite network is established based on this.

In order to solve the problem that the traditional graph theory cannot accurately describe, the time-varying graph theory used in the delay tolerant network (DTN) is applied to this problem. In reference, Fraire transformed the shortest delay path problem in the delay tolerant network into the shortest path problem in the time-varying graph [12–14]; S. Qi et al. Using software defined network to analyze network traffic of satellite network [15]. Huang et al. studied the link scheduling method in the sensor network [16].

Based on the theory of time-varying graph, it can guarantee the link connectivity in a given period of time, but it considers the reliability in a fixed time interval T, which is not realistic for the integrated information network of Space-Air-Ground. The static topological graph of network in discrete time is used to describe the change of network topology. However, this method is to superimpose the fast photos at different times in the network to form a graph, which will greatly increase the complexity of calculation when the path of large time span needs to be calculated [17]. Therefore, it is only suitable for satellite networks with fewer satellite nodes. P. Yuan et al. the method of event driven graph is used to record the operation of satellite nodes sending and receiving data at different times as events [18]. The vertex set in the event driven graph is composed of all events, and link arcs are used to connect the events of the same link. The continuous events of the same node are connected by storage arcs [19, 20]. Although this method reduces the redundancy of the graph, it is mainly used to describe the data transmission in the network, and the link planning is too complex [21, 22].

Different from the above method, this paper studies the networking mode of satellite network and air target in the atmosphere. The proposed method based on time-graph does not consider complex data transmission. It directly introduces time parameters into general network topology to carve the changing network, so as to solve the problem of rapid change of network topology. Because there is time parameter t in the graph. The exact network topology can be obtained by taking different T and the satellites' orbit motion constraints. Given the starting time and time span, the satellite network topology can be obtained at any time [23–25]. The optimal link switching decision condition can be obtained by this method. This method avoids a lot of mathematical calculation and has no too many constraints. The optimal link path and link switching time can be obtained by simple calculation.

3 A Method of Space-Air-Ground Integrated Network for Air Mobile Target

The network includes:

a) $S = \{s_1, s_2, \ldots, s_m\}$ is the aggregate of m near earth satellites in the space. Each satellite near the earth can establish communication with the ground launch station or other satellites.

b) $A = (a_1, a_2, \ldots, a_j)$ is the aggregate of j aircrafts in the air, which are detected and guided by satellite.

After the satellite detects the air moving vehicle target, the missile is launched from the ground launch station. At this time, the communication among the missile, the satellite network and the air vehicle are established. The satellite network is responsible for the guidance of the missile and the detection of the air vehicle. In this scenario, the main problem to be solved is the movement of missile, satellite and air target vehicle, which results in the connection and switching of satellite network to the other two.

In order to solve the problem of topological dynamic change of satellite network, the time parameter t is introduced to describe the topological map of satellite network, and the time-varying map of satellite network can be recorded as the time-varying map of time t as:

$$G(V, E(t)) \tag{3}$$

Among them, V is the vertex set composed of all communication nodes such as ground station, air target and LEO satellite. $E(t)$ represents the edge set in graph $G(t)$, which represents the link connection relationship and the optimal connection mode. Considered scene is composed of multiple satellites, according to the same or not satellite orbit, the satellites can be divided as:

$$\begin{cases} S_1 = \{s_{11}, s_{12}, \ldots s_{1i}\} \\ S_2 = \{s_{21}, s_{22}, \ldots s_{2i}\} \\ \ldots \\ S_n = \{s_{n1}, s_{n2}, \ldots s_{ni}\} \end{cases} \tag{4}$$

where S_n represents the set of all satellites in n orbit, and i represents the number of different satellites in the same orbit. At a certain time t_0, consider that all the vertices in the network are stationary, and all the edges in the graph $G(V, E(t_0))$ will not change any more. At the same time, according to the parameters of satellite orbit, all the information of satellite motion can be calculated to obtain the longitude lo_s and latitude la_s of the satellite. And then the satellite and the target can be connected by these. Suppose that the longitude lo_a and latitude la_a of the air moving target are known. Now it is necessary to connect the target to the satellite network. In the past, all the satellites were divided into n different longitudes through the orbit of the satellite. Now, the lo_a longitude of the target aircraft is known, and the absolute value of the difference between the longitude of n orbits and the longitude of the target aircraft is calculated by the following formula:

$$D_i = \left| lo_{s_i} - lo_a \right|, i = 1, 2, 3 \ldots n \tag{5}$$

where D_i represents the difference between the longitude of the ith orbit and the target aircraft. Through the calculation of the above formula, n sets D_i can be recorded as:

$$D = \{D_1, D_2, \ldots, D_n\} \tag{6}$$

All elements in D are sorted, and the minimum value is recorded as D_m, m is the orbit of the satellite closest to the air target. When the minimum two values in D are the same, the satellite orbit with small label is taken. The next step is to calculate the distance. Obtain the longitude and latitude of all the satellites on the m orbit, and calculate the distance from the target aircraft according to the following formula:

$$\begin{cases} L = 2 \arcsin \sqrt{\sin^2 \frac{a}{2} + \cos(la_a) \cdot \cos(la_s) \cdot \sin^2 \frac{b}{2}} \cdot R \\ a = la_a - la_s \\ b = lo_a - lo_s \end{cases} \tag{7}$$

where L is the distance between the satellite in m orbit and the target flying object, R is the radius of the earth. Through calculation, the nearest three satellites are obtained. The best communication satellite node is obtained, the communication link between the selected satellite and the air target is established. And the shortest path at the current time has been established too. We get the link connection mode at a specific time. However, due to the motion of the satellite and the target aircraft, we need to predict the position of the next time. Set the next link transformation time t, at this time, the satellite and the aircraft have moved. According to the speed of the satellite and the aircraft, calculate the longitude and latitude of them after t. And then implement the above steps again. Repeat this process until the end of the scenario. Because the missile strikes the air target in this scenario, the missile, as the air target after launch, uses the same method to connect another satellite node to enter the network. At the same time, it is necessary to establish a connection between the satellite nodes connected with the flight target. Because the same satellite network, the topology of the network is fixed at a certain time. Therefore, Djsktra algorithm can find the shortest path with the smallest number. According to this path, satellites, missiles and air targets are networked. If the topology changes, the new topology is input to complete the path finding again. The reasoning process of the whole networking method is given above, and the main steps of this method are given in Algorithm 1.

4 Simulation and Analysis

STK (Satellite Tool Kit) developed by analytical graphics company is used to build the simulation environment. We also need another simulation platform to realize the whole algorithm and establish a connection with STK and send control instructions to control STK. MATLAB has an interface with STK, as shown in Fig. 1. The data exchange between them can be carried out better. By calling the STK function in MATLAB, we can control the satellite and other targets, so as to complete the whole algorithm process. A network simulation system is required to simulate the network in operation. NS-3 (Network Simulator-3) network simulation tool is used for network simulation. MATLAB sends out instructions to control STK and sends calculated parameters to NS-3, which establishes the corresponding network topology to obtain the network simulation parameters. Therefore, in order to complete the whole simulation process, it needs to be completed through the combination of three platforms.

Algorithm 1. Networking algorithm	
Input:	Satellite adjacency matrix M ,The number of Satellite orbit n
	The longitude Lo_a and the latitude La_a of missile,
	The number of satellites per orbit m
Output:	Nearest access satellite. The j th satellite in the k th orbit
1	**function** SATELLITECLASSIFICATION(n)
2	**for** $i = 1$ **to** n
3	$Table [i] = n \rightarrow longitude$
4	**end for**
5	**return** $Table$
6	**end function**
7	
8	**function** FINDORBIT($Table$, Lo_a)
9	**for** $i = 1$ **to** n
10	$d[i] = |Lo_a - Table[i]|$
11	$min = 1$
12	**if** ($i > 1$ and $d[min] > d[i]$) **then**
13	$min = i$
14	**end if**
15	**end for**
16	**return** min
17	**end function**
18	
19	**function** FINDSATELLITE ($Table$, Lo_a , La_a , n , m)
20	$Table$ = SATELLITECLASSIFICATION(n)
21	k = FINDORBIT($Table$, Lo_a)
22	$j = 1$
23	**for** $i = 1$ **to** m
24	$Lo_a = M[k][i] \rightarrow longitude$
25	$La_a = M[k][i] \rightarrow latitide$
26	$L[i]$ = GETDISTANCE(Lo_a , La_a , Lo_s , La_s) // Equ(7).
27	**if** ($i > 1$ and $d[j] > d[i]$) **then**
28	$j = i$
29	**end if**
30	**end for**
31	**return** j , k
32	**end function**

Figure 2 shows the data relationship between the simulation platforms. In this scenario, 132 low earth orbit satellites are used, which are distributed over 6 different orbits. Each orbit is evenly distributed with 12 satellites, with height of 758.14 km from ground and operation cycle of 6027.15 s. Three ground launch stations, missile everywhere and a target flying object are established. Because NS-3 is on the Linux and the former two simulation tools are on Windows operating system. It is necessary to interconnect the two platforms to transfer the data from MATLAB running algorithm to NS-3 in real time to complete network simulation. MySQL database is used to solve this problem. Because NS-3 bases C++ to program to call internal functions to complete the establishment of simulation scenarios. It is easy to read the data in MySQL which generated by MATLAB in the Windows. And the shell script of Linux is used to control the data receive and the working way of NS-3. According to the above operation scenario, the algorithm completes the animation scenario of missile attacking the UAV. Although the movement of the satellite at this time is the optimal access node, there is a link between the missile, the satellite and the target flying object. As the operation time progresses.

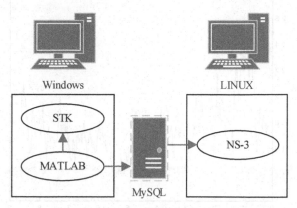

Fig. 1. Simulation platform

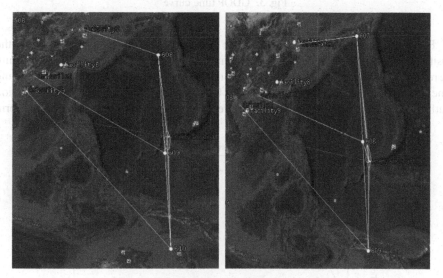

Fig. 2. Experiment result.

Figure 3 shows the link switching which is calculated by MATLAB. The distance between the satellite and the target flying object at the current time is not the shortest distance, so the link will automatically switch to the satellite with the shortest distance. Through the processing of this algorithm, it can be seen that the target flying object can be well connected to the satellite network, and the link can be switched when the satellite topology changes. The Djsktra algorithm is used to calculate the shortest path adjacency matrix which obtained according to the current topology. The detailed information of the system can be obtained by the simulation platform.

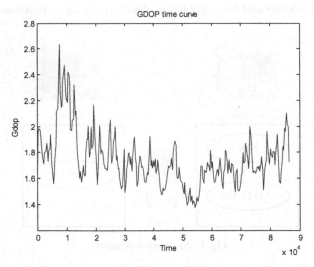

Fig. 3. GDOP time curve

Figure 4 shows the GDOP (Geometric Dilution Precision) which represents the positioning accuracy of the satellite system. In order to show the validity of the algorithm, we record calculation time in Fig. 4. If we do not use this model to calculate the switching time which is based distance, we will use a lot of time in calculation. For a simulation platform, it will waste a lot of computing resources. Because the simulation platform

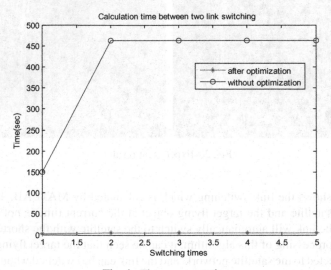

Fig. 4. Time consumption

is composed of many software, the large amount of computation overhead will lead to the incompatibility between the simulation software. The simulation model in this paper can simplify the solution of link switching problem and greatly improve the efficiency of operation. With the proposed simulation platform, the simulation task of air space integrated information network can be completed well. According to the results of the above scenario operation, it can be seen that the algorithm completed the animation scene of missile attacking the target flying object. The link in the scenario can be smoothly switched, and the target flying object and other air flying ground objects can be connected to the satellite network. Compared with the previous method, only the network topology map with equal time interval is calculated.

5 Conclusion

This paper studies the networking problem in the air space integrated information network. Using MATLAB, STK and NS-3 to stimulate. Although the simulation platform built in this paper can simulate most of the problems in the research of air space integrated information network, it includes a large number of programming parts, which need to cross platform and involve the use of a variety of simulation tools. It also requires higher requirements for different programming languages. And simulation has become a big difficulty in the research. Therefore, in the future research, the new model construction of dynamic topology and the construction of network simulation platform will be considered.

Acknowledgements. This work was supported in part by the National Natural Science Foundation of China (No. 61571104), the Sichuan Science and Technology Program (No. 2018JY0539), the Key projects of the Sichuan Provincial Education Department (No. 18ZA0219), the Fundamental Research Funds for the Central Universities (No. ZYGX2017KYQD170), the CERNET Innovation Project (No. NGII20190111), the Fund Project (Nos. 61403110405, 315075802), and the Innovation Funding (No. 2018510007000134). The authors wish to thank the reviewers for their helpful comments.

References

1. Jiang, D., Huo, L., Li, Y.: Fine-granularity inference and estimations to network traffic for SDN. PLoS One **13**(5), 1–23 (2018)
2. Jiang, F., Zhang, Q., Yang, Z., Yuan, P.: A space-time graph based multipath routing in disruption-tolerant earth-observing satellite networks. IEEE Trans. Aero-Space Electron. Syst. **55**(5), 2592–2603 (2019)
3. Jiang, D., Huo, L., Song, H.: Rethinking behaviors and activities of base stations in mobile cellular networks based on big data analysis. IEEE Trans. Netw. Sci. Eng. **7**(1), 80–90 (2020)
4. Wang, Y., Sheng, M., Li, J., Wang, X., Liu, R., Zhou, D.: Dynamic contact plan design in broadband satellite networks with varying contact capacity. IEEE Commun. Lett. **20**(12), 2410–2413 (2016)
5. Jiang, D., Li, W., Lv, H.: An energy-efficient cooperative multicast routing in multi-hop wireless networks for smart medical applications. Neurocomputing **2017**(220), 160–169 (2017)

6. Yuan, P., Yang, Z., Zhang, Q., Wang, Y.: A minimum task-based end-to-end delivery delay routing strategy with updated discrete graph for satellite disruption-tolerant net-works. In: 2018 IEEE/CIC International Conference on Communications in China (ICCC), Beijing, China, pp. 293–297 (2018)

7. Zhang, W., Zhang, G., Gou, L., et al.: A hierarchical autonomous system based topology control algorithm in space information network. KSII Trans. Internet Inf. Syst. 9(9), 3572–3593 (2015)

8. Spencer, J., Taylor, R., Hancock, R.: Evaluation of software-defined networking control plane performance in deployed military communications systems. In: Proceedings of CROWN, pp. 1–7 (2017)

9. Wang, F., Jiang, D., Qi, S.: An adaptive routing algorithm for integrated information networks. China Commun. 7(1), 196–207 (2019)

10. Kronewitter, F.D.: A tactical network optimization engine using simulation. In: Proceedings of MILCOM, pp. 1093–1098 (2015)

11. Jiang, D., Wang, W., Shi, L., Song, H.: A compressive sensing-based approach to end-to-end network traffic reconstruction. IEEE Trans. Netw. Sci. Eng. 7(1), 507–519 (2020)

12. Fraire, J., Finochietto, J.: Design challenges in contact plans for disruption-tolerant satellite networks. IEEE Commun. Mag. 53(5), 163–169 (2015)

13. Wang, Y., Jiang, D., Huo, L., Zhao, Y.: A new traffic prediction algorithm to software defined networking. Mob. Netw. Appl. (2019)

14. Fraire, J., Finochietto, J.: Routing-aware fair contact plan design for predictable delay tolerant networks. Ad Hoc Netw. 25(Part B), 303–313 (2015)

15. Qi, S., Jiang, D., Huo, L.: A prediction approach to end-to-end traffic in space information networks. Mob. Netw. Appl. (2019)

16. Li, F., Chen, S., Huang, M., et al.: Reliable topology design in time-evolving delay-tolerant networks with unreliable links. IEEE Trans. Mob. Comput. 14(6), 1301–1314 (2015)

17. Jiang, D., Huo, L., Lv, Z., Song, H., Qin, W.: A joint multi-criteria utility-based network selection approach for vehicle-to-infrastructure networking. IEEE Trans. Intell. Transp. Syst. 19(10), 3305–3319 (2018)

18. Yuan, P., Yang, Z., Li, Y., et al.: An event-driven graph-based min-cost delivery algorithm in earth observation DTN networks. In: International Conference on Wireless Communications Signal (2015)

19. Jiang, D., Zhang, P., Lv, Z., et al.: Energy-efficient multi-constraint routing algorithm with load balancing for smart city applications. IEEE Internet Things J. 3(6), 1437–1447 (2016)

20. Wu, G., Pedrycz, W., Li, H., et al.: Coordinated planning of heterogeneous earth observation resources. IEEE Trans. Syst. Cybern. Syst. 46(1), 109–112 (2016)

21. Jiang, D., Wang, Y., Lv, Z., Qi, S., Singh, S.: Big data analysis based network behavior insight of cellular networks for industry 4.0 applications. IEEE Trans. Ind. Inform. 16(2), 1310–1320 (2020)

22. Liu, R., Sheng, M., Lui, K.-S., et al.: Capacity analysis of two-layered LEO/MEO satellite networks. In: Proceedings of IEEE VTC, pp. 1–5 (2015)

23. Jiang, D., Wang, Y., Lv, Z., Wang, W., Wang, H.: An energy-efficient networking approach in cloud services for IIoT networks. IEEE J. Sel. Areas Commun. 38(5), 928–941 (2020)

24. Shi, C., Shi, C., Yuan, P., Yang, Z.: A space-time graph based minimum cost routing algorithm for the random traffic in the satellite network. In: 2018 10th International Conference on Wireless Communications and Signal Processing (WCSP), Hangzhou, pp. 1–6 (2018)

25. Huo, L., Jiang, D., Qi, S., et al.: An AI-based adaptive cognitive modeling and measurement method of network traffic for EIS. Mob. Netw. Appl. (2019)

An Adaptive Algorithm Based on Adaboost for Mimicry Multimode Decisions

Feng Wang[1], Dingde Jiang[1]([✉]), Zhihao Wang[1], and Yingchun Chen[2]

[1] School of Astronautics and Aeronautic, University of Electronic Science
and Technology of China, Chengdu 611731, China
jiangdd@uestc.edu.cn
[2] No. 30 Research Institute, CETC, Beijing, China

Abstract. The traditional information security protection cannot prevent the malicious and directed intrusion of the network. To discover potential risks comprehensively, accurately, and timely, the polymorphic heterogeneous executor is constructed to confuse the attacker, called mimicry multimode decision. However, heterogeneous executors are composed of complex hardware, systems and applications, so how to select the optimal combination to face the potential risks becomes a problem. This paper proposes a mimicry multimode decision scheme based on Adaboost machine learning algorithm. The administrator can utilize Adaboost classifier to adaptively select the combination of the most defensible executor, so as to realize mimicry multimode defense and improve the security of applications. Simulation results demonstrate that the adaptive mimicry multimode decision method is promising.

Keywords: Information security · Mimicry multimode decision · Heterogeneous executor · Adaboost

1 Introduction

While the improvement of information technology and the increasing coverage of information system [1–3], the information disclosure is no longer only the loss of economic interests to the society, enterprises and individuals [4]. The importance of information security has gradually risen. To effectively cope with the increasingly complex information threats and attacks, Technologies like Intrusion Detection system (IDS), vulnerability scanning system, firewall, are widely used [5]. However, these traditional security protection systems still have insufficiencies. IDS can only detect the attack, with high non-response rates and the rate of false positives. The existing firewall technology cannot solve the malicious intrusion behavior of the internal network [6]. In addition, these defense techniques are passive, often focusing on localized threat information. At the same time, considering the polymorphic and heterogeneous service system, these self-directed working mechanisms are unable to find potential risks comprehensively, accurately and timely [7]. As a result, the detection results of existing technologies are

H. Song and D. Jiang (Eds.): SIMUtools 2020, LNICST 369, pp. 127–136, 2021.
https://doi.org/10.1007/978-3-030-72792-5_12

greatly deviated, which is not conducive to helping administrators to formulate security defense strategies. At present, the architecture of information system is polymorphic and heterogeneous, which not only includes the heterogeneity of hardware such as CPU, but also exists the heterogeneity of operating system [8, 9]. Therefore, the storage, transfer and elimination of all kinds of services on heterogeneous platforms may be targeted at any time. Backdoor, virus, and Trojans are emerging in endlessly [10]. The traditional information system defense methods can no longer meet the needs of existing information system [11–13]. The lack of security perception ability now is the biggest threat to the security protection of key services.

Aiming at the above problems, many researchers are studying the mimicry defense system. The current information network is a huge and time-varying system, different kinds of network behaviors have different hidden dangers [14–17]. Aiming at the protection of execution applications, the heterogeneous executors are constructed to confuse the attacker. This kind of protection is called mimicry multimode decision. It will turn the vulnerability backdoor of the specific applications into the uncertain attack effect at the system level. As shown in Fig. 1, Different platforms are combined into a heterogeneous executor set. The administrator selects the currently most secure executor to load the application and extend it to all executors to confuse the attacker. This mechanism can make the target system from the attacker's perspective and present an "uncertainty" effect, so as to effectively improve the level of protection system. Among them, how to efficiently select heterogeneous executor and the adaptive transformation is the key to realize intelligent multimode decision. There have been several research about mimicry multimode decision. Zheng et al. [18] analyzed two background mimicry defense method: the semantic modeling method and the semantic consistency analysis method. They proposed a novel software defined networking (SDN) mimic server defense method, which could effectively modify the active defense efficiency of malicious attacks on Web servers. Authors in [19] proposed a random seed scheduling method considering historical confidence for maximum heterogeneity and QoS. The proposed method could achieve a good dynamic balance between security, dynamics, and QoS. Although some mimicry defense methods were proposed in the above studies, they were complex and lack of adaptability. These methods were difficult to be effective in environments where the best heterogeneous implementations need to be updated at all times.

Machine learning algorithm can keep the continuous learning of decision and improve the accuracy. Consider the above defects, we propose a mimicry multimode decision scheme based on Adaboost machine learning algorithm in this paper. Under the management of the controller, the heterogeneous actuator can use Adaboost model to adaptively select the combination of the currently most defensible executors to face the potential attack threat, so as to realize mimicry multimode defense and improve the security of the important applications.

The following is organized as follows. Section 2 constructs the mathematical model of Adaboost algorithm and then proposes the mimicry multimode decision scheme. The simulation results and analysis are expressed in Sect. 3. We then conclude our work in Sect. 4.

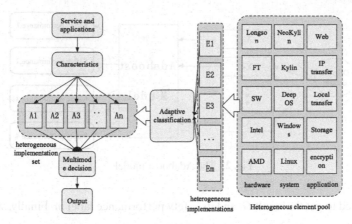

Fig. 1. The mimicry multimode decision architecture.

2 Adaboost Model

In this section, we mainly consider how to carry out mimicry multimode decision using Adaboost classifiers. First, we analyze the classification indicators needed. Subsequently, we established the Adaboost classification model.

As shown in Fig. 1, the heterogeneous element pool includes heterogeneous hardware such as Longson, Intel, AMD, etc. It also includes heterogeneous systems such as Kirin system, Deep OS system, Windows system, Linux system and so on. It also includes heterogeneous applications such as Web services, IP transport services, Local transport services, Storage services, Encryption services and so on. The combination of different platforms has different capabilities of risk resistance. We can evaluate the capabilities of different combinations and set a label based on specific requirements. For example, we can divide all the combinations into four levels: Safety performance 1, 2, 3, and 4. The higher the value, the higher the resistance capabilities. So the problem is how to quickly and efficiently select the most appropriate combination to implement mimicry multimodal decision. The traditional approach, which considers only a limited number of combinations, is weak in the face of endless risks. Therefore, we need to use machine learning algorithms, like Adaboost model, to help administrators adaptively choose the best combination.

AdaBoost is an adaptive classification algorithm, as Fig. 2 shows. A fleet of weak classifiers is trained then combined to form a strong classifier to complete the training framework. The adaptability is that the weight of the data from the samples wrongly classified by the former weak classifier will increase. The weight of properly classified samples will be reduced. These are utilized to build the next weak classifier. The final classifier will only be determined in the following cases: if the error coefficient is small enough or reaches the maximum number of iterations.

Firstly, we obtain a collection of $N + P$ heterogeneous combinations. Then we get the result $R_1, R_2, \cdots, R_N, \cdots, R_{N+P}$. Each R_i has n items that can be represented by $R_i = [v_1, v_2, \cdots, v_n]^T$, where v_i is the code name of the platform. Each result R_i is then

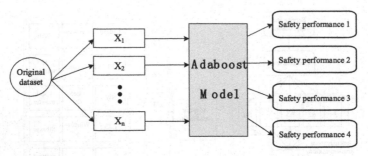

Fig. 2. The Adaboost model.

pre-processed to get the result G_i and its safety performance label m. Finally, we get the dataset D:

$$D = \{(G_1, m_1), (G_2, m_2), \cdots, (G_{N+P}, m_{N+P})\} \tag{1}$$

where $G_i \in \chi \subseteq N^n$, $m_i \in \{1, 2, 3, 4\}$. We divide the former N data into the training dataset D_N. We set the other P data as the testing dataset D_P. Now the training dataset D_N is utilized for model training. We divide D_N into two datasets, where class I is $m = 1, m = 2$ and class II is $m = 3, m = 4$. Then dataset $D_N^{(1)}$ with current classification label is shown as:

$$D_N^{(1)} = \{(G_1, m_1^{(1)}), (G_2, m_2^{(1)}), \cdots, (G_N, m_N^{(1)})\} \tag{2}$$

where the classification features are:

$$m_i^{(1)} = \begin{cases} 1, & m \in \{1, 2\}; \\ 0, & m \in \{3, 4\}; \end{cases} \tag{3}$$

Then, we configure the weight value of each G_i in $D_N^{(1)}$. The initial weight value of each training item is uniform. We can calculate that the initial weight value $W_1(i)$ of the training data set $D_N^{(1)}$ is:

$$W_1(i) = (w_1, w_2, \cdots w_N), \ w_i = 1/N \tag{4}$$

Then, the fleet of weak classifiers begin to be trained in t times iterative. The training steps are shown as follows:

Step 1: Initialing the weight value W_t of $D_N^{(1)}$. Then, design the t weak classifier:

$$H_t(x) : G \to \{1, 0\} \tag{5}$$

Step 2: Using the current weak classifier to divide the training dataset $D_N^{(1)}$. The classification error is calculated:

$$e_t = P(H_t(G_i) \neq m_i) = \sum_{i=1}^{N} w_{ti} I(H_t(G_i) \neq m_i) \tag{6}$$

Step 3: The weight value v of current weak classifier in the final strong classifier is calculated as follows:

$$v_t = \frac{1}{2} \ln(\frac{1 - e_t}{e_t}) \tag{7}$$

Then the t weak classifier is obtained:

$$f_t(x) = v_t H_t(x) \tag{8}$$

Step 4: Update the weight value of the training dataset $D_N^{(1)}$:

$$W_{t+1} = \frac{W_t(i) \exp(-v_t m_i H_t(x_i))}{Z_t} \tag{9}$$

where Z_t is the normalization constant:

$$Z_t = 2\sqrt{e_t(1 - e_t)} \tag{10}$$

Assemble existing weak classifiers:

$$f(x) = \sum_{t=1}^{T} v_t H_t(x) \tag{11}$$

Then we evaluate the current strong classifier. If the classification error is below the threshold, the iteration is over, and the final strong classifier is obtained as:

$$H_{strong} = sign(f(x)) = sign\left(\sum_{t=1}^{T} v_t H_t(x)\right) \tag{12}$$

Otherwise, enter the $t + 1$ iteration until the classification error reaches the threshold.

After obtaining the first strong classifier, we make all the data $D_N^{(1)}$ pass through the strong classifier, and pick out the data with $H_{strong}(X_i) > 0$, which represent the data classified into safety performance 1 and safety performance 2. The remaining data is safety performance 3 and safety performance 4. Analogously, the classification feature for safety performance 1 and safety performance 3 is labeled as 1, the classification feature for safety performance 2 and safety performance 4 is labeled as 0. Repeat the training process once again and the 2nd and 3rd layer strong classifiers will be obtained:

$$H_{strong}^{(2)} = sign(f^{(2)}(x)) = sign\left(\sum_{t=1}^{T} v_t H_t^{(2)}(x)\right)$$

$$H_{strong}^{(3)} = sign(f^{(3)}(x)) = sign\left(\sum_{t=1}^{T} v_t H_t^{(3)}(x)\right) \tag{13}$$

Then, the first time of Adaboost classifier training is complete and the classifier will be tested later. According to the above, process of classifying the safety performance is shown in Fig. 3. The detailed steps are expressed in Algorithm 1.

Algorithm 1 Adaboost based mimicry multimode decision

Input: Table O of original items.

Input: Adaboost classifier $H_1(x)$, $H_2(x)$, $H_3(x)$.

Output: Safety performance vector: SP[N]

1: **for** j= 1 to n **do**
2:     SP [j] = 0 ;
3:     **if** sign(H_1 (O[j] > 0) **then**
4:         **if** sign(H_2 (O[j] > 0) **then**
5:             SP[j] = 1;
6:         **else**
7:             SP[j] = 2;
8:     **else if** sign(H_1 (O[j]< 0) **then**
9:         **if** sign(H_3 (O[j] > 0) **then**
10:            SP[j] = 3;
11:        **else**
12:            SP[j] = 4;
13: **end for**
14: **return** SP[N]

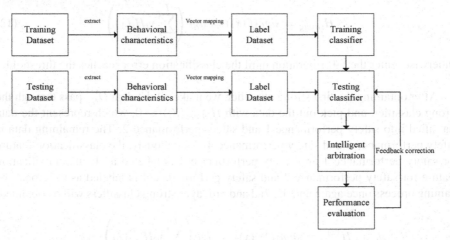

Fig. 3. The Adaboost-based mimicry multimode decision architecture.

3 Simulation Results

Next, we verify the proposed Adaboost classification model for mimicry multimode decision. We mark different types of hardware, systems and applications to values 1–6. Meantime, we make a high defense level environment configuration table and added security performance 1–4 labels for different combinations according to this table. All the preprocessed items are divided into the training dataset and the test dataset of the Adaboost model, and the label are considered as the output result of the model and the reference of the security performance. We first evaluated the model training accuracy under different training samples. Then, we compared the model training complexity of Adaboost algorithm and other common machine learning algorithms. We implement all the algorithms in Matlab 2017b and on the Window10 platform of 3.6 GHz CPU and 32.00 GB RAM. The simulation results are as follows.

We first examined the training results of adaboost model under 100 items. We randomly divided 70 items into a training set, 30 items into a test set, and set the number of weak classifiers to 20. Figure 4 shows the model training results, taking the average value after several experiments. As can be seen from Fig. 4, with the increase of the number of weak classifiers, the training error decreases gradually, and it drops to 0 when the number of weak classifiers reaches 20. At the same time, the test error decreases with the increase of weak classifier, and the final test error is 6%. This shows that Adaboost model can better identify the security performance of different platforms and help realize mimicry multimode decision.

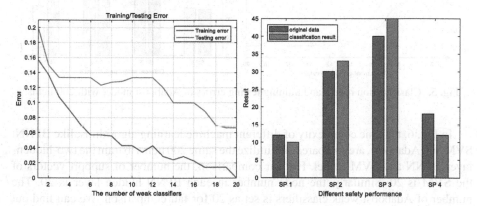

Fig. 4. Classification results and training/testing errors of Adaboost model with 100 items.

Then, we made these 100 items as input to detect the performance of mimicry multimode decision, and the results are shown in the right of Fig. 4. It can be seen that the model can well distinguish the platform combinations with different security performance, and the classification error is 10%. These results show that the training model performs well under 100 items.

In order to verify the adaptability of the proposed model, we randomly selected 200 test items to verify the model classification accuracy at different scales. We randomly divided 150 items into a training set, 50 items into a test set, and set the number of weak classifiers to 20. Figure 5 shows the model training results, taking the average value after several experiments. As can be seen from Fig. 5, with the increase of the number of weak classifiers, the training error decreases gradually, and it drops to 3% when the number of weak classifiers reaches 20. At the same time, the test error decreases with the increase of weak classifier, and the final test error is 4%. These results show that the training accuracy of the model increases with the increase of training samples. Although the error is larger when the number of weak classifiers is less, the model training error decreases rapidly with the increase of the number of weak classifiers. It shows that the model has a better classification performance under 200 items. Then, we made these 200 items as input to detect the performance of mimicry multimode decision, and the results are shown in the right of Fig. 5. It can be seen that the model can well distinguish the platform combinations with different security performance, and the classification error is 7%. These results show that the proposed mimicry multi-mode decision model has good learning-ability and self-adaptability under the complex and changeable environment.

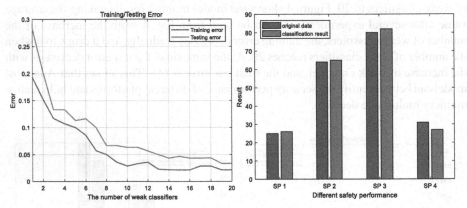

Fig. 5. Classification results and training/testing errors of Adaboost model with 200 items.

In Fig. 6, the time complexity of different machine learning algorithms, like BPNN, SVM and Adaboost, are compared. We utilize the same 200 items to train the two-hidden-layer BPNN and SVM model. For fair comparison, the number of support vectors of the SVM is 20. Similarly, the node number in each BPNN hidden layer is 20. The number of Adaboost weak classifiers is set as 20 for fair comparison. We can find out that as the number of training items increasing, the training time of both BPNN and SVM algorithm are higher than that of Adaboost. The time complexity of upper bound SVM method is a few magnitude orders higher than other three methods. Considering the mimicry multimode decision model needs to keep learning and adaptability in a changing environment, the lightweight Adaboost model that has better performance on time complexity is the optimal machine learning algorithm for mimicry multimode decision.

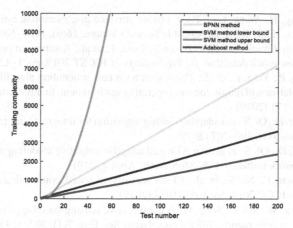

Fig. 6. The comparison of training complexity.

4 Conclusion

The performance of mimicry multimode decision directly affects the intrusion tolerance ability and operation efficiency of the executive system. This paper proposes a mimicry multimode decision scheme based on Adaboost machine learning algorithm. The heterogeneous actuator pool can adaptively select the combination of the most defensible executor using Adaboost classifiers to realize mimicry multimode defense and improve the security of the applications. Simulation results show that the proposed lightweight method can keep good self-learning and adaptability.

Acknowledgements. This work was supported in part by the National Natural Science Foundation of China (No. 61571104), the Sichuan Science and Technology Program (No. 2018JY0539), the Key projects of the Sichuan Provincial Education Department (No. 18ZA0219), the Fundamental Research Funds for the Central Universities (No. ZYGX2017KYQD170), the CERNET Innovation Project (No. NGII20190111), the Fund Project (Nos. 61403110405, 315075802), and the Innovation Funding (No. 2018510007000134). The authors wish to thank the reviewers for their helpful comments.

References

1. Jiang, D., Wang, Y., Lv, Z., Wang, W., Wang, H.: An energy-efficient networking approach in cloud services for IIoT networks. IEEE J. Sel. Areas Commun. **38**(5), 928–941 (2020)
2. Jiang, D., Wang, Y., Lv, Z., Qi, S., Singh, S.: Big data analysis based network behavior insight of cellular networks for industry 4.0 applications. IEEE Trans. Ind. Inform. **16**(2), 1310–1320 (2020)
3. Qi, S., Jiang, D., Huo, L.: A prediction approach to end-to-end traffic in space information networks. Mob. Netw. Appl. (2020)
4. Rassouli, B., Rosas, F.E., Gündüz, D.: Data disclosure under perfect sample privacy. IEEE Trans. Inf. Forensics Secur. **15**, 2012–2025 (2020)

5. Han, X., Huang, H., Wang, L.: F-PAD: private attribute disclosure risk estimation in online social networks. IEEE Trans. Dependable Secure Comput. **16**(6), 1054–1069 (2019)
6. Husseis, A., Liu-Jimenez, J., Goicoechea-Telleria, I., et al.: A survey in presentation attack and presentation attack detection. In: Proceedings of ICCST 2019, pp. 1–13 (2019)
7. Huo, L., Shao, P., Ying, F., et al.: The research on task scheduling algorithm for the cloud management platform of mimic common operating environment. In: Proceedings of DCABES 2019, pp. 167–171 (2019)
8. Wang, F., Jiang, D., Qi, S.: An adaptive routing algorithm for integrated information networks. China Commun. **7**(1), 196–207 (2019)
9. Huo, L., Jiang, D., Qi, S., et al.: An AI-based adaptive cognitive modeling and measurement method of network traffic for EIS. Mob. Netw. Appl. (2019)
10. Liang, H., Chen, F., Ni, S., et al.: Cloud security in space communication network. In: Proceedings of ICCC 2019, pp. 1053–1057 (2019)
11. Jiang, D., Wang, W., Shi, L., Song, H.: A compressive sensing-based approach to end-to-end network traffic reconstruction. IEEE Trans. Netw. Sci. Eng. **7**(1), 507–519 (2020)
12. Jiang, D., Huo, L., Lv, Z., Song, H., Qin, W.: A joint multi-criteria utility-based network selection approach for vehicle-to-infrastructure networking. IEEE Trans. Intell. Transp. Syst. **19**(10), 3305–3319 (2018)
13. Wang, Y., Jiang, D., Huo, L., Zhao, Y.: A new traffic prediction algorithm to software defined networking. Mob. Netw. Appl. (2020)
14. Jiang, D., Huo, L., Song, H.: Rethinking behaviors and activities of base stations in mobile cellular networks based on big data analysis. IEEE Trans. Netw. Sci. Eng. **7**(1), 80–90 (2020)
15. Jiang, D., Huo, L., Li, Y.: Fine-granularity inference and estimations to network traffic for SDN. PLoS ONE **13**(5), 1–23 (2018)
16. Jiang, D., Zhang, P., Lv, Z., et al.: Energy-efficient multi-constraint routing algorithm with load balancing for smart city applications. IEEE Internet Things J. **3**(6), 1437–1447 (2016)
17. Jiang, D., Li, W., Lv, H.: An energy-efficient cooperative multicast routing in multi-hop wireless networks for smart medical applications. Neurocomputing **220**(2017), 160–169 (2017)
18. Zheng, J., Wu, G., Wen, B., et al.: Research on SDN-based mimic server defense technology. In: Proceedings of ICAICS 2019, pp. 163–169 (2019)
19. Wu, Z., Wei, J.: Heterogeneous executors scheduling algorithm for mimic defense systems. In: Proceedings of CCET 2019, pp. 279–284 (2019)

A Modified Gauss-Seidel Iteration Method for Solving Absolute Value Equations

Peng Guo[1(✉)] and Shi-liang Wu[1,2]

[1] School of Mathematics and Statistics, Anyang Normal University, Anyang 455000, People's Republic of China
[2] School of Mathematics, Yunnan Normal University, Kunming, Yunnan 650500, People's Republic of China

Abstract. The iterative Gauss-Seidel method is an effective and practical method for solving the absolute value equations. However, the solution efficiency of this method usually decreases, and even the equation cannot be solved even when the problem reaches a certain large scale. To improve the efficiency of the Gauss-Seidel method for solving absolute value equations, a modified Gauss-Seidel (MGS) iteration method is presented in this paper. In the our method, we create a diagonal matrix Ω with nonnegative diagonal elements in the Gauss-Seidel matrix splitting. Under the given constraints the convergence theory of the MGS method have been studied. The numerical results show that the method is effective. It can be noted that with the increase in the scale of the problem, the setting effect of the matrix Ω is more obvious.

Keywords: Absolute value equation · Gauss-Seidel splitting · MGS iteration method · Convergence theory

1 Introduction

Let matrix $A = (a_{ij}) \in \mathbb{R}^{n \times n}$, $b \in \mathbb{R}^n$, we consider the absolute value equation with the following form

$$Ax - |x| = b, \tag{1.1}$$

where $|x|$ denotes the absolute value of the vector x.

Absolute value equalization is a special, non-differentiable optimization problem proposed by O.L. Mangasarian in 2006 [1]. Absolute value equalization is widely distributed in the optimization field There are many optimization problems that can be transformed into Eqs. (1.1), such as linear programming

---

Supported by NSFC(11961082) and 17HASTIT012.

H. Song and D. Jiang (Eds.): SIMUtools 2020, LNICST 369, pp. 137–148, 2021.
https://doi.org/10.1007/978-3-030-72792-5_13

problems, convex quadratic optimization problems and general linear complementarity problems [2–6]. Formally, the Eq. (1.1) is relatively simple, but in fact the equation is NP-hard in general [1].

Since the absolute equation has been proposed, there are many different methods to solve the Eq. (1.1) from different perspectives have been proposed. In recent years we have found that there are many iterative methods to solve the Eq. (1.1). In [7], D.K. Salkuyeh proposed the iterative method picard-HSS, which is used, to the formula $Ax - |x| = b$, where $A \in \mathbb{C}^{n \times n}$ and $b \in \mathbb{C}^n$. In [8], by the Gauss-Seidel matrix splitting, Edalatpour et al. established the generalized Gauss-Seidel (GGS) iteration method for solving the Eq. (1.1). The Eq. (1.1) is used on the SOR-like iterative method in two non-linear equations with two blocks in both [9] and [10] block converted, Ke et al. and Guo et al. presented the SOR-like iteration methods to solve the Eq. (1.1) respectively.

It is worth mentioning that Edalatpour et al. establishes an iterative Gauss-Seidel method based on the Gauss-Seidel splitting, and analyses its convergence from a specific angle in [8]. However, we find that the GGS method cannot solve the equation when the problem size n becomes larger. Therefore this paper improves the GGS method to improve the efficiency of theGauss-Seidel method in solving the Eq. (1.1). Inspired by the work of Edalatpour et al. in [8], by introducing a diagonal matrix Ω whose diagonal elements are all nonnegative in the splitting of the matrix A, we propose a modified iterative modified Gauss-Seide (MGS) to solve the Eq. (1.1). Some convergence theories of the method are maintained and given limitations proven. In the last phase we give some examples to illustrate the effectiveness of the iterative MGS method.

In this article the rest of the organization is as follows. In the Second section, we list some necessary results in the form of symbols, definitions and frames. The third section, the MGS method for solving the Eq. (1.1) is determined and its convergence under given conditions has been proven. In fourth section numerical examples are given to illustrate the effectiveness of the MGS method and the results of the comparison between the MGS method and the GGS method are given.

2   Preliminaries

For the sake of the subsequent convergence discussions, we list some summary results in this section.

For the given matrices $A = (a_{ij}) \in \mathbb{R}^{m \times n}$ and $B = (b_{ij}) \in \mathbb{R}^{m \times n}$, then $A \geq B(A > B)$ if $A - B \geq 0(A - B > 0)$. The absolute value of the matrix A is denoted by $|A| = (|a_{ij}|)$. The infinity norm of the matrix A is defined as

$$\|A\|_\infty = \max_{1 \leq i \leq m} \sum_{j=1}^{n} |a_{ij}|.$$

Moreover, the definitions of the absolute value and infinity norm of the matrices can be applied to the vectors.

Suppose $A = (a_{ij}) \in \mathbb{R}^{n \times n}$, then the comparison matrix of A is defined as $\langle A \rangle = (\langle a_{ij} \rangle)$, where

$$\langle a_{ij} \rangle = \begin{cases} |a_{ij}|, & for \quad i = j, \\ -|a_{ij}|, & for \quad i \neq j, \end{cases} \quad i, j = 1, 2, \cdots, n.$$

The above results can be seen in [11].

Next, we will list some special matrices for the sequel discussions. Assume that the matrix $A = (a_{ij}) \in \mathbb{R}^{n \times n}$, then A is said to be [12]

(1) a Z-matrix if $a_{ij} \leq 0$ holds for all $i \neq j$.
(2) an M-matrix if $A^{-1} \geq 0$ and A is a Z-matrix.
(3) an H-matrix if $\langle A \rangle$ is an M-matrix;
(4) an H_+-matrix if A is an H-matrix and $a_{ij} > 0$ holds for all $i = j$.

Lemma 1. *[13] If $A = (a_{ij}) \in \mathbb{R}^{n \times n}$ and $B = (b_{ij}) \in \mathbb{R}^{n \times n}$ be two matrices which satisfy $B \geq A$ and $b_{ij} \leq 0$ for any $i \neq j$. Then the matrix B is an M-matrix if A is an M-matrix.*

Lemma 2. *[14] If A be an H-matrix. Then $\langle A \rangle^{-1} \geq |A^{-1}|$.*

Lemma 3. *[11] If A be a $n \times n$ matrix and $A = M - N$ be a regular splitting of the matrix A. Then A is nonsingular with $A^{-1} \geq 0$ if and only if $\rho(M^{-1}N) < 1$* .

Lemma 4. *[11] If A be a $n \times n$ nonnegative matrix. Then $I - A$ is nonsingular with $(I - A)^{-1} \geq 0$ if and only if $\rho(A) < 1$.*

Lemma 5. *[11] Let x, y be two vectors $\in \mathbb{R}^n$. Then $\|x - y\|_\infty \geq \|\,|x| - |y|\,\|_\infty$.*

3 The MGS Method

For the Eq. (1.1), we make the following matrix splitting

$$A = D - L - U = (\Omega + D - L) - (\Omega + U),$$

where D, L and U, respectively, are the diagonal, the strictly lower-triangular and the strictly upper-triangular matrices of A, and Ω is a $n \times n$ nonnegative diagonal matrix.

Based on the above splitting, we can convert the Eq. (1.1) to the fixed-point equation with the form

$$(\Omega + D - L)x - |x| = (\Omega + U)x + b. \tag{3.1}$$

Then, we present a modified Gauss-Seidel (MGS) iteration method to solve the Eq. (1.1) which has the iterative scheme as follows

$$(\Omega + D - L)x^{(k+1)} - |x^{(k+1)}| = (\Omega + U)x^{(k)} + b, k = 0, 1, 2, \ldots, \qquad (3.2)$$

where the initial vector $x^{(0)}$ is given in advance by the experimenter.

By adjusting the matrix Ω, we expect to be able to improve the solving efficiency of the Gauss-Seidel method for the Eq. (1.1). It is easy to see that the MGS method just reduces to the GGS method when $\Omega = 0$.

In the following, we will discuss the convergence properties for the MGS method.

Theorem 1. *Assume that the Eq. (1.1) is solvable. Suppose the diagonal entries of the matrix A are all greater than 1, the matrix Ω is a $n \times n$ nonnegative diagonal matrix, the matrix I is the $n \times n$ identity matrix and the matrix $\Omega + D - L - I$ be strictly row diagonally dominant. If*

$$\|(\Omega + D - L)^{-1}(\Omega + U)\|_\infty < 1 - \|(\Omega + D - L)^{-1}\|_\infty, \qquad (3.3)$$

then the iteration sequence $\{x^{(k)}\}_{k=0}^{\infty}$ generated by (3.2) converges to the unique solution x^* of the Eq. (1.1) for any initial vector $x^{(0)} \in \mathbb{R}^n$.

Proof. By the conditions of the theorem, we can obtain that the diagonal entries of the matrix D are all greater than 1.

Firstly, we will prove that $\|(\Omega + D - L)^{-1}\|_\infty < 1$.

For $L = 0$, because Ω is a nonnegative diagonal matrix and the diagonal entries of D are all greater than 1, it can be shown that

$$\|(\Omega + D - L)^{-1}\|_\infty = \|(\Omega + D)^{-1}\|_\infty < 1.$$

We assume that $L \neq 0$ in the following. By the assumption of the theory, one can get

$$0 \le |L|e < (\Omega + D - I)e,$$

or equivalently,

$$(\Omega + D)^{-1}e < (I - |F|)e, \qquad (3.4)$$

where $e = (1, 1, \cdots, 1)^T$ and $F = (\Omega + D)^{-1}L$. In addition, we have

$$0 \le |(I - F)^{-1}| = |I + F + F^2 + \cdots + F^{n-1}|$$
$$\le (I + |F| + |F|^2 + \cdots + |F|^{n-1}) = (I - |F|^{-1}). \qquad (3.5)$$

Hence, from (3.4) and (3.5), we obtain

$$|(\Omega + D - L)^{-1}|e = |(I - F)^{-1}(\Omega + D)^{-1}|e$$
$$\le |(I - F)^{-1}||(\Omega + D)^{-1}|e$$
$$< |(I - |F|)^{-1}||I - |F||e = e.$$

Therefore,

$$\|(\Omega + D - L)^{-1}\|_\infty < 1. \qquad (3.6)$$

Next, we are going to show that the Eq. (1.1) has an unique solution. Assume that x^* and y^* are two different solutions of the Eq. (1.1). From the Eq. (3.1), we have

$$x^* = (\Omega + D - L)^{-1}|x^*| + (\Omega + D - L)^{-1}[(\Omega + U)x^* + b], \qquad (3.7)$$

$$y^* = (\Omega + D - L)^{-1}|y^*| + (\Omega + D - L)^{-1}[(\Omega + U)y^* + b],$$

then

$$x^* - y^* = (\Omega + D - L)^{-1}(|x^*| - |y^*|) + (\Omega + D - L)^{-1}(\Omega + U)(x^* - y^*).$$

By taking infinity norm on both sides of the latter equation, it holds from Lemma 5 and the Eq. (3.3) that

$$\begin{aligned}
\|x^* - y^*\|_\infty &\leq \|(\Omega + D - L)^{-1}\|_\infty \||x^*| - |y^*|\|_\infty \\
&\quad + \|(\Omega + D - L)^{-1}(\Omega + U)\|_\infty \|x^* - y^*\|_\infty \\
&< \|(\Omega + D - L)^{-1}\|_\infty \|x^* - y^*\|_\infty \\
&\quad + (1 - \|(\Omega + D - L)^{-1}\|_\infty)\|x^* - y^*\|_\infty \\
&= \|x^* - y^*\|_\infty,
\end{aligned}$$

which is a contradiction. Thus, $x^* = y^*$.

Finally, we will prove that the iteration sequence $\{x^{(k)}\}_{k=0}^\infty$ generated by (3.2) converges to the unique solution x^* of the Eq. (1.1). From (3.2), we get

$$x^{(k+1)} = (\Omega + D - L)^{-1}|x^{(k+1)}| + (\Omega + D - L)^{-1}[(\Omega + U)x^{(k)} + b]. \qquad (3.8)$$

From (3.7) and (3.8), it holds that

$$x^{(k+1)} - x^* = (\Omega + D - L)^{-1}(|x^{(k+1)}| - |x^*|) + (\Omega + D - L)^{-1}(\Omega + U)(x^{(k)} - x^*).$$

Taking infinity norm on both sides of the latter equation. By similarly calculations, we get the following results

$$\begin{aligned}
\|x^{(k+1)} - x^*\|_\infty &= \|(\Omega + D - L)^{-1}(|x^{(k+1)}| - |x^*|) \\
&\quad + (\Omega + D - L)^{-1}(\Omega + U)(x^{(k)} - x^*)\|_\infty \\
&\leq \|(\Omega + D - L)^{-1}(|x^{(k+1)}| - |x^*|)\|_\infty \\
&\quad + \|(\Omega + D - L)^{-1}(\Omega + U)(x^{(k)} - x^*)\|_\infty \\
&\leq \|(\Omega + D - L)^{-1}\|_\infty \||x^{(k+1)}| - |x^*|\|_\infty \\
&\quad + \|(\Omega + D - L)^{-1}(\Omega + U)\|_\infty \|x^{(k)} - x^*\|_\infty,
\end{aligned}$$

which equivalent to

$$\begin{aligned}
\|x^{(k+1)} - x^*\|_\infty &- \|(\Omega + D - L)^{-1}\|_\infty \||x^{(k+1)}| - |x^*|\|_\infty \\
&\leq \|(\Omega + D - L)^{-1}(\Omega + U)\|_\infty \|x^{(k)} - x^*\|_\infty.
\end{aligned}$$

By Lemma 5, we obtain the following formula

$$\|x^{(k+1)} - x^*\|_\infty - \|(\Omega + D - L)^{-1}\|_\infty \|x^{(k+1)} - x^*\|_\infty$$
$$\leq \|(\Omega + D - L)^{-1}(\Omega + U)\|_\infty \|x^{(k)} - x^*\|_\infty.$$

By a simple calculation, one can see that the above formula is equivalent to

$$(1 - \|(\Omega + D - L)^{-1}\|_\infty)\|x^{(k+1)} - x^*\|_\infty \leq \|(\Omega + D - L)^{-1}(\Omega + U)\|_\infty \|x^{(k)} - x^*\|_\infty.$$

Since $\|(\Omega + D - L)^{-1}\|_\infty < 1$, then

$$\|x^{(k+1)} - x^*\|_\infty \leq \frac{\|(\Omega + D - L)^{-1}(\Omega + U)\|_\infty}{1 - \|(\Omega + D - L)^{-1}\|_\infty}\|x^{(k)} - x^*\|_\infty.$$

By the above inequality, we can find that the sequence $\{x^{(k)}\}_{k=0}^\infty$ converges to the unique solution x^* when the condition (3.3) is fulfilled.

The convergence theory of the MGS method to solve the Eq. (1.1) is proved.

By the Theorem 1, one can obtain the following corollary easily.

Corollary 1. *Assume that the Eq. (1.1) is solvable. Suppose the matrix $A - I$ is a strictly row diagonally dominant matrix with positive diagonal entries and the matrix Ω is a nonnegative diagonal matrix. If*

$$\|(\Omega + D - L)^{-1}(\Omega + U)\|_\infty < 1 - \|(\Omega + D - L)^{-1}\|_\infty, \tag{3.9}$$

then the iteration sequence $\{x^{(k)}\}_{k=0}^\infty$ generated by (3.2) converges to the unique solution x^* of the Eq. (1.1) for any initial vector $x^{(0)} \in \mathbb{R}^n$.

Following, we will demonstrate the convergence property of the MGS method when the matrix A is an H-matrix.

Theorem 2. *Assume that the Eq. (1.1) is solvable. Suppose the matrix $A - I$ is an H_+-matrix and the matrix Ω is a nonnegative diagonal matrix. Then the iteration sequence $\{x^{(k)}\}_{k=0}^\infty$ obtained from (3.2) converges to the unique solution x^* for any initial vector $x^{(0)}$.*

Proof. From the mentioned splitting in this section

$$A = (\Omega + D - L) - (\Omega + U),$$

by the definition of the comparison matrix, we can get

$$\langle A \rangle = \langle \Omega + D - L \rangle - |\Omega + U|.$$

Then, we obtain

$$\langle A - I \rangle \leq \langle A \rangle \leq \langle \Omega + D - L \rangle \leq \text{diag}(\Omega + D - L) = \Omega + D.$$

Therefore, by Lemma 1, it can be easy to know that $\Omega + D - L$ is an H-matrix. With that, we get the following formula by Lemma 2

$$|(\Omega + D - L)^{-1}| \leq \langle \Omega + D - L \rangle^{-1}. \tag{3.10}$$

Since x^* is the solution of the Eq. (1.1), from (3.2) and (3.7) we obtain

$$x^{(k+1)} - x^* = (\Omega + D - L)^{-1}(|x^{(k+1)}| - |x^*|) + (\Omega + D - L)^{-1}(\Omega + U)(x^{(k)} - x^*).$$

By the inequality (3.10), by taking absolute values on both sides of the latter equation, we get

$$\begin{aligned} |x^{(k+1)} - x^*| &\leq |(\Omega + D - L)^{-1}||x^{(k+1)} - x^*| + |(\Omega + D - L)^{-1}||\Omega + U||x^{(k)} - x^*| \\ &\leq \langle \Omega + D - L \rangle^{-1}|x^{(k+1)} - x^*| + \langle \Omega + D - L \rangle^{-1}|\Omega + U||x^{(k)} - x^*|. \end{aligned} \tag{3.11}$$

Let $G = \langle \Omega + D - L \rangle^{-1}$. Because of the matrix $\Omega + D - L$ is an H-matrix, we can know that the matrix $\langle \Omega + D - L \rangle$ is an M-matrix with $\langle \Omega + D - L \rangle^{-1} \geq 0$. In addition, it is obviously shown that $\rho(G) < 1$ because $A - I$ is an H_+-matrix. By Lemma 4, one can derive that $I - G$ is nonsingular and $(I - G)^{-1} \geq 0$. Therefore, it follows from the Eq. (3.11) that

$$\begin{aligned} |x^{(k+1)} - x^*| &\leq (I - \langle \Omega + D - L \rangle^{-1})^{-1} \langle \Omega + D - L \rangle^{-1}|\Omega + U||x^{(k)} - x^*| \\ &\leq (\langle \Omega + D - L \rangle - I)^{-1}|\Omega + U||x^{(k)} - x^*|. \end{aligned}$$

Let $\widetilde{M} = \langle \Omega + D - L \rangle - I$ and $\widetilde{N} = |\Omega + U|$. Assume that $\widetilde{A} = \widetilde{M} - \widetilde{N}$, it just be a matrix splitting of $\widetilde{A}$, then $\widetilde{G} = \widetilde{M}^{-1}\widetilde{N}$ is the iteration matrix corresponding to the splitting. As we all know that the sequence $\{x^{(k)}\}_{k=0}^{\infty}$ converges to x^* if $\rho(\widetilde{G}) < 1$. Since the matrix $A - I$ is an H_+-matrix, the diagonal entries of A are all greater than one. It is obviously that $\widetilde{A} = \langle A \rangle - I = \langle A - I \rangle$ and $\widetilde{M} = \langle \Omega + D - L - I \rangle$. Hence, by Lemma 1, we know that $\widetilde{A}$ is an M-matrix and then $\widetilde{M}$ is also an M-matrix because of $\widetilde{M} > \widetilde{A}$. Moreover, the matrix splitting $\widetilde{A} = \widetilde{M} - \widetilde{N}$ is a regular splitting because of $\widetilde{N} \geq 0$. Then, by Lemma 3, it holds true that

$$\rho(\widetilde{G}) = \rho(\widetilde{M}^{-1}\widetilde{N}) < 1.$$

The conclusion is obtained.

4 Numerical Examples

In this section, three examples are used to verify the efficiency of the MGS method to solve the Eq. (1.1). We compare the MGS method with the GGS method in the iteration steps (IT), CPU time in seconds (CPU).

In the examples, the right-hand-side vector b is uniquely determined by substituting the vector $x^* = (x_1, x_2, ..., x_n)^T (x_i = (-1)^i, i = 1, 2, ..., n)$ into the Eq. (1.1). Let $\Omega = \alpha I$ with $\alpha \geq 0$, the values of α is obtained by the experiments. For the sake of clarity, we denote the experimental optimum parameter as α_{exp}

in the following examples. All of the runs terminated if the current iteration satisfies $IT \geq 500$ or $ERR < 10^{-9}$, where

$$ERR = \frac{\|Ax^{(k)} - |x^{(k)}| - b\|_2}{\|b\|_2}.$$

Example 1. [15] Let $m \in \mathbb{N}^+$ and $n = m^2$, we consider the Eq. (1.1) in which $A = M + \mu I \in \mathbb{R}^{n \times n}$, where

$$M = tridiag(-I, S, -I) \in \mathbb{R}^{n \times n},$$

with

$$S = tridiag(-1, 4, -1)$$

$$= \begin{pmatrix} 4 & -1 & 0 & \cdots & 0 & 0 \\ -1 & 4 & -1 & \cdots & 0 & 0 \\ 0 & -1 & 4 & \cdots & 0 & 0 \\ \vdots & \vdots & \vdots & \ddots & \vdots & \vdots \\ 0 & 0 & 0 & \cdots & 4 & -1 \\ 0 & 0 & 0 & \cdots & -1 & 4 \end{pmatrix} \in \mathbb{R}^{m \times m},$$

and I being the m order identity matrix. $b = Ax^* - |x^*| \in \mathbb{R}^n$, here $x^* = (-1, 1, ..., (-1)^n)^T$.

Table 1. Numerical results for Example 1

M	Method	$\mu = 0$			$\mu = -0.5$		
		α_{exp}	IT	CPU	α_{exp}	IT	CPU
20	GGS	–	112	0.1875	–	68	0.1719
	MGS	0.10	111	0.1563	0	68	0.1719
40	GGS	–	112	3.8125	–	73	4.4063
	MGS	0.20	102	3.4688	0	73	4.4063
60	GGS	–	115	22.0469	–	75	25.7813
	MGS	0.20	100	19.1406	0	75	25.7813
80	GGS	–	119	121.5781	–	76	81.2188
	MGS	0.20	98	125.5938	0.10	75	47.2188
100	GGS	–	122	315.4375	–	77	133.1875
	MGS	0.20	97	321.0781	0.10	75	127.8438

We use the methods GGS and MGS to use the Eq. (1.1) of Example 1 separately. Table 1 lists the calculation results of the CPU time of the above two methods for different problem sizes of n are listed when $\mu = 0$ and $\mu = -0.5$.

For $\mu = 0$, we found that the MGS method is smaller than the GGS method when the parameter α_{exp} is correctly specified. In other words, the matrix $\Omega = \alpha I$ plays an important role in our method, and with the magnification of the problem the adaptation effect of the matrix Ω is more obvious. For $\mu = -0.5$, we can see that the parameter $\alpha_{exp} = 0$ when the scale of the problem is small ($m = 20, 40, 60$), and the MGS method is reduced exactly to GGS. It is not difficult to see that the MGS method is also superior to the GGS method when we choose $\alpha_{exp} = 0.1$ with the larger problem size ($m = 80, 100$).

Example 2. [15] Let $m \in \mathbb{N}^+$ and $n = m^2$, we consider the Eq. (1.1) in which $A = M + \mu I \in \mathbb{R}^{n \times n}$, where

$$M = tridiag(-1.5I, S, -0.5I) \in \mathbb{R}^{n \times n},$$

with
$$S = tridiag(-1.5, 4, -0.5)$$

$$= \begin{pmatrix} 4 & -0.5 & 0 & \cdots & 0 & 0 \\ -1.5 & 4 & -0.5 & \cdots & 0 & 0 \\ 0 & -1.5 & 4 & \cdots & 0 & 0 \\ \vdots & \vdots & \ddots & \ddots & \vdots & \vdots \\ 0 & 0 & \ddots & \ddots & 4 & -0.5 \\ 0 & 0 & \ddots & \ddots & -1.5 & 4 \end{pmatrix} \in \mathbb{R}^{m \times m},$$

and I being the m order identity matrix. $b = Ax^* - |x^*| \in \mathbb{R}^n$, here $x^* = (-1, 1, ..., (-1)^n)^T$.

Table 2. Numerical results for Example 2

M	Method	$\mu = 0$			$\mu = -0.5$		
		α_{exp}	IT	CPU	α_{exp}	IT	CPU
20	GGS	–	143	0.6563	–	Fail	–
	MGS	0	143	0.6563	0.20	263	1.1719
40	GGS	–	Fail	–	–	Fail	–
	MGS	0.075	284	12.8594	0.29	263	12.0156
60	GGS	–	Fail	–	–	Fail	–
	MGS	0.19	444	91.1875	0.30	255	55.9375
80	GGS	–	Fail	–	–	Fail	–
	MGS	–	Fail	–	0.30	249	157.1563
100	GGS	–	Fail	–	–	Fail	–
	MGS	–	Fail	–	0.30	244	366.7656

For Example 2, we also list the calculation data related to the Example 2 for different problem sizes of n when $\mu = 0$ and $\mu = -0.5$ in Table 2. The table shows $'Fail'$ that the method cannot find a solution if the abortion condition is met, such as Example 4.2.

Table 2 shows that the GGS method can solve the problem of $\mu = 0$ when $m = 20$ and and the GGS method is $'Fail'$ when $m > 20$. Compared with the GGS method, the MGS method can solve the problem when $m \leq 60$. For $\mu = -0.5$, it is obvious that the GGS method cannot find the solution for all the given m in Table 2. Nevertheless, the MGS method can solve the problems for all the given m when the the parameters α_{exp} are suitable choice. That is to say, the regulating role of the matrix $\Omega = \alpha I$ becomes more obvious as the problem size has increased.

Example 3. Let $m \in \mathbb{N}^+$ and $n = m^2$, we consider the Eq. (1.1) in which $A = M + \mu I \in \mathbb{R}^{n \times n}$, where

$$M = tridiag(-0.5I, S, -1.5I) \in \mathbb{R}^{n \times n},$$

with

$$S = tridiag(-0.5, 4, -1.5)$$

$$= \begin{pmatrix} 4 & -1.5 & 0 & \cdots & 0 & 0 \\ -0.5 & 4 & -1.5 & \cdots & 0 & 0 \\ 0 & -0.5 & 4 & \cdots & 0 & 0 \\ \vdots & \vdots & \ddots & \ddots & \vdots & \vdots \\ 0 & 0 & \ddots & \ddots & 4 & -1.5 \\ 0 & 0 & \ddots & \ddots & -0.5 & 4 \end{pmatrix} \in \mathbb{R}^{m \times m},$$

and I being the m order identity matrix. $b = Ax^* - |x^*| \in \mathbb{R}^n$, here $x^* = (-1, 1, ..., (-1)^n)^T$.

Table 3. Numerical results for Example 3

M	Method	$\mu = 0$			$\mu = -0.5$		
		α_{exp}	IT	CPU	α_{exp}	IT	CPU
20	GGS	–	143	0.7344	–	Fail	–
	MGS	0	143	0.7344	0.20	263	1.2344
40	GGS	–	Fail	–	–	Fail	–
	MGS	0.075	284	13.8438	0.29	263	11.0469
60	GGS	–	Fail	–	–	Fail	–
	MGS	0.19	444	90.2563	0.30	255	45.4688
80	GGS	–	Fail	–	–	Fail	–
	MGS	0.20	462	220.3634	0.30	249	154.3366
100	GGS	–	Fail	–	–	Fail	–
	MGS	–	Fail	–	0.30	243	328.6675

To better observe the adaptation effect of the matrix $\Omega = \alpha I$ in MGS method, we construct Example 3. Similar to the Example 1 and Example 2, we also list the calculation data for different problem sizes of n when $\mu = 0$ and $\mu = -0.5$ in Table 3. In the table, $'Fail'$ still denotes that the method cannot find the solution for Example 3 when the termination conditions are satisfied.

As shown in Table 3, if the parameter α_{exp} is the right choice, the MGS method can solve more problems than the GGS method. The results also show that Matrix Ω plays an important role in the solution.

5 Conclusion

In this paper, by introducing a non-negative diagonal matrix Ω, a new split of the matrix A in the absolute Eq. (1.1) is given firstly. And then, based on the new splitting, we have presented the MGS method for solving the Eq. (1.1) and discussed the convergence theory of the method. The numerical results show that the MGS method is better than the GGS method if the matrix Ω is appropriate. In general, the matrix Ω plays an important role in our method. It can effectively improve not only the convergence rate, but also the iterative Gauss-Seidel method for solving Eqs. (1.1). It creates some uncertainty that the parameter α in the matrix $\Omega = \alpha I$ is acquired by the experiments. This affects the efficiency of the algorithm to some extent. In the following research, we will try to determine the optimal parameters α through the theoretical derivation and further improve the efficiency of the method.

References

1. Mangasarian, O.L., Meyer, R.R.: Absolute value equations. Linear Algebra Appl. **419**(2), 359–367 (2006)
2. Murty, K.G.: Linear Complementarity. Linear and Nonlinear Programming. Heldermann, Berlin (1988)
3. Bai, Z.Z.: Modulus-based matrix splitting iteration methods for linear complementarity problems. Numer. Linear Algebr. **17**(6), 917 933 (2010)
4. Chung, S.J.: NP-completeness of the linear complementarity problem. J. Optimiz Theory APP. **60**(3), 393–400 (1989)
5. Cottle, R.W., Dantzig, G.: Complementary pivot theory of mathematical programming. Linear Algebra Appl. **1**(1), 103–125 (1968)
6. Rohn, J.: A theorem of the alternatives for the equation $|Ax| - |B : x| = b$. Linear Multilinear A. **6**(3), 585–591 (2012)
7. Salkuyeh, D.K.: The picard-HSS iteration method for absolute value equations. Optim. Lett. **8**, 2191–2202 (2014)
8. Edalatpour, V., Hezari, D., Salkuyeh, D.K.: A generalization of the GaussCSeidel iteration method for solving absolute value equations. Appl. Math. Comput. **293**, 156–167 (2017)
9. Ke, Y.F., Ma, C.F.: SOR-like iteration method for solving absolute value equations. Appl. Math. Comput. **311**, 195–202 (2017)
10. Guo, P., Wu, S.L., Li, C.X.: On the SOR-like iteration method for solving absolute value equations. Appl. Math. Lett. **97**, 107–113 (2019)
11. Varga, R.S.: Matrix Iterative Analysis, 2nd edn. Springer, Berlin (2000)

12. Berman, A., Plemmons, R.J.: Nonnegative Matrix in the Mathematical Sciences. Academic Press, NewYork (1979)
13. Saad, Y.: Iterative Methods for Sparse Linear Systems, 2nd edn. SIAM, Philadelphia (2003)
14. Axelsson, O.: Iterative Solution Methods. Cambridge University Press, New York (1994)
15. Bai, Z.Z., Zhang, L.L.: Modulus-based synchronous multisplitting iteration methods for linear complementarity problems. Numer. Linear Algebra Appl. **20**(3), 425–439 (2013)

Modified LPMHSS Method for a Class of Complex Symmetric Linear Systems

Shi-Liang Wu$^{(\boxtimes)}$ and Cui-Xia Li

School of Mathematics, Yunnan Normal University, Kunming 650500, Yunnan,
People's Republic of China

Abstract. In this paper, a modified LPMHSS (MLPMHSS) method is proposed to solve the problem of a class of complex symmetric linear systems with strong Hermitian parts. Theoretical analysis shows that the MLPMHSS method can converge to the unique solution of linear equations under appropriate conditions. Numerical experiments show that the method is effective.

Keywords: Complex symmetric linear system · Modified LPMHSS method · Convergence

1 Introduction

Consider the numerical solution of the linear system of the form

$$Ax = b, A \in \mathbb{C}^{n \times n}, x, b \in \mathbb{C}^n, \tag{1.1}$$

where

$$A = W + iT, \tag{1.2}$$

$i = \sqrt{-1}$ is the imaginary unit, and $W \in \mathbb{R}^{n \times n}$ is symmetric positive definite, and $T \in \mathbb{R}^{n \times n}$ is symmetric positive semidefinite. In the fields of structural dynamics, diffuse reflectance optical tomography, lattice quantum chromodynamics, eddy current problems, molecular dynamics, fluid dynamics and quantum chemistry, this form of complex symmetric linear system can be used to model these problems. You can view and reference [1–10] for more specific examples.

In order to solve the large-scale sparse complex symmetric linear system (1.1)–(1.2), based on the HSS method [11] and MHSS method [2], the preprocessing MHSS (PMHSS) method was ingeniously designed by Bai *et al.* [3] and the following work was done.

The PMHSS Method. Assum that $\alpha > 0$ and $x^{(0)} \in \mathbb{C}^n$ is a given arbitrary initial vector. For $k = 0, 1, 2, \ldots$ until the iterative sequences $\{x^{(k)}\}_{k=0}^{\infty}$ are convergent, calculate $x^{(k+1)}$ by

$$\begin{cases} (\alpha V + W)x^{(k+\frac{1}{2})} = (\alpha V - iT)x^{(k)} + b, \\ (\alpha V + T)x^{(k+1)} = (\alpha V + iW)x^{(k+\frac{1}{2})} - ib, \end{cases} \tag{1.3}$$

This research was supported by NSFC (No.11961082).

H. Song and D. Jiang (Eds.): SIMUtools 2020, LNICST 369, pp. 149–163, 2021.
https://doi.org/10.1007/978-3-030-72792-5_14

where $V \in \mathbb{R}^{n \times n}$ is a given symmetric positive definite matrix.

Under suitable conditions, the convergence of PMHSS method is given by Bai *et al.* [3]. Numerical experiments which is solving complex symmetric linear system (1.1)–(1.2) show that PMHSS method has better performance than MHSS method.

In order to further enhance the effect of this iterative method, a lopsided PMHSS (LPMHSS) method is introduced to solve the problem of complex symmetric linear system (1.1)–(1.2) in [12] and described as follows.

The LPMHSS Method. Assum that $\alpha > 0$ and $x^{(0)} \in \mathbb{C}^n$ is a given arbitrary initial vector. For $k = 0, 1, 2, \ldots$ until the iterative sequences $\{x^{(k)}\}_{k=0}^{\infty}$ are convergent, calculate $x^{(k+1)}$ by

$$\begin{cases} Wx^{(k+\frac{1}{2})} = -iTx^{(k)} + b, \\ (\alpha V + T)x^{(k+1)} = (\alpha V + iW)x^{(k+\frac{1}{2})} - ib, \end{cases} \tag{1.4}$$

where $V \in \mathbb{R}^{n \times n}$ is a given symmetric positive definite matrix.

The convergence theory of LPMHSS method is proposed in [12] by Li *et al.* and the theoretical optimal parameter with the minimum upper bound of spectral radius of LPMHSS iterative matrix is also derived. The numerical experiments in [12] show that the LPMHSS method is more efficient than the PMHSS method when it is used to solve complex symmetric linear systems with strong Hermitian parts (1.1)–(1.2).

In this paper, the iterative method for solving the complex symmetric linear system with strong Hermitian part (1.1)–(1.2) is further studied, in which the strong Hermitian part represents $\|W\| \gg \|T\|$ in (1.2) of a matrix norm. Based on the previous work in [13], a modified LPMHSS (MLPMHSS) method for a class of complex symmetric linear systems with strong Hermitian parts is proposed. Based on the upper bound of the spectral radius of MLPHSS iterative matrix, the convergence conditions of MLPHSS method are given, and the optimal parameters of MLPHSS method are given theoretically. The MLPHSS method is compared with LPMHSS method. Numerical experiments verify the effectiveness of the proposed method.

This paper is organized below. In Sect. 2, the MLPMHSS method is established and its convergence condition is discussed. Numerical examples are provided to verify the efficiency of the proposed method in Sect. 3. Finally, in Sect. 4, some conclusions are drawn to end this paper.

2   The MLPMHSS Method

To establish the MLPMHSS iteration method, the complex symmetric linear system (1.1)–(1.2) can be equivalently expressed as

$$Wx = -iTx + b \tag{2.1}$$

and

$$(\alpha V + W)x = (\alpha V - iT)x + b, \tag{2.2}$$

where $V \in \mathbb{R}^{n \times n}$ is a given symmetric positive definite matrix. Based on Eqs. (2.1) and (2.2), we can establish the following alternating splitting method for the complex symmetric linear system (1.1)–(1.2). Since the following alternating splitting method is similar to the LPMHSS method, which is called the MLPMHSS method.

The MLPMHSS Method. Assum that $\alpha > 0$ and $x^{(0)} \in \mathbb{C}^n$ is a given arbitrary initial vector. For $k = 0, 1, 2, \ldots$ until the iterative sequences $\{x^{(k)}\}_{k=0}^{\infty}$ are convergent, calculate $x^{(k+1)}$ by

$$\begin{cases} Wx^{(k+\frac{1}{2})} = -iTx^{(k)} + b, \\ (\alpha V + W)x^{(k+1)} = (\alpha V - iT)x^{(k+\frac{1}{2})} + b, \end{cases} \tag{2.3}$$

where $V \in \mathbb{R}^{n \times n}$ is a given symmetric positive definite matrix.

To gain the convergence condition of the MLPMHSS method, we require Lemma 2.1.

Lemma 2.1 [11]. *Let $A = M_i - N_i$ $(i = 1, 2)$ be two splittings of $A \in \mathbb{C}^{n \times n}$, and let $x^{(0)} \in \mathbb{C}^n$ be a given initial vector. If the two-step iteration sequence $\{x^{(k)}\}$ is defined by*

$$\begin{cases} M_1 x^{(k+\frac{1}{2})} = N_1 x^{(k)} + b, \\ M_2 x^{(k+1)} = N_2 x^{(k+\frac{1}{2})} + b, \end{cases}$$

then

$$x^{(k+1)} = M_2^{-1} N_2 M_1^{-1} N_1 x^{(k)} + M_2^{-1}(I + N_2 M_1^{-1})b, \quad k = 0, 1, \ldots.$$

When $\rho(M_2^{-1} N_2 M_1^{-1} N_1) < 1$, for all initial vectors $x^{(0)} \in \mathbb{C}^n$, the iteration sequence $\{x^{(k)}\}$ converges to the unique solution $x_* \in \mathbb{C}^n$ of the linear system (1.1).

Based on Lemma 2.1, from (2.3) we have

$$x^{(k+1)} = M_\alpha x^{(k)} + N_\alpha b, k = 0, 1, 2, \ldots, \tag{2.4}$$

where

$$M_\alpha = -i(\alpha V + W)^{-1}(\alpha V - iT)W^{-1}T$$

and

$$N_\alpha = (\alpha V + W)^{-1}(\alpha V + W - iT)W^{-1}b.$$

Theorem 2.1. *Let $A = W + iT \in \mathbb{C}^{n \times n}$ in (1.2) be normal, $V \in \mathbb{R}^{n \times n}$ be a symmetric positive definite and $\alpha > 0$. Then the iteration matrix M_α of MLPMHSS method is*

$$M_\alpha = -i(\alpha V + W)^{-1}(\alpha V - iT)W^{-1}T \tag{2.5}$$

and

$$\rho(M_\alpha) \leq \delta(\alpha) = \frac{\mu_{\max}\sqrt{\alpha^2 + \mu_{\max}^2}}{\lambda_{\min}(\alpha + \lambda_{\min})}, \tag{2.6}$$

where $\mu_{\max}$ is the largest eigenvalue of $V^{-1}T$ and $\lambda_{\min}$ is the smallest eigenvalue of $V^{-1}W$. Moreover, if

$$\mu_{\max} \leq \lambda_{\min},$$

then $\delta(\alpha) < 1$, i.e., the MLPMHSS method (2.3) is convergent.

Proof. Let

$$M_1 = W, N_1 = -iT, M_2 = \alpha V + W \text{ and } N_2 = \alpha V - iT.$$

Then the matrices W and $\alpha V + W$ are nonsingular on the base of the above assumptions, so (2.5) is valid.

Since matrix $A = W + iT$ is normal matrix, by simple computations, we obtain $WT = TW$. Further, $W^{-1}T = TW^{-1}$. Based on (2.5), the matrix M_α is equal to

$$M_\alpha = -i(\alpha V + W)^{-1}(\alpha V - iT)TW^{-1}.$$

Noting that V is symmetric positive definite, the matrices

$$\bar{W} = V^{-\frac{1}{2}}WV^{-\frac{1}{2}} \text{ and } \bar{T} = V^{-\frac{1}{2}}TV^{-\frac{1}{2}}$$

are well-defined. It follows that M_α is similar to

$$\bar{M}_\alpha = -i(\alpha I - i\bar{T})\bar{T}\bar{W}^{-1}(\alpha I + \bar{W})^{-1}.$$

Because $\bar{W}$ and $\bar{T}$, respectively, are symmetric positive definite and symmetric positive semidefinite, there exist unitary matrices V_1 and V_2 such that

$$\bar{W} = V_1\Lambda_1V_1^*, \ \bar{T} = V_2\Lambda_2V_2^*,$$

where $\Lambda_1 = \text{diag}(\lambda_1, \lambda_1, \ldots, \lambda_n)$ and $\Lambda_2 = \text{diag}(\mu_1, \mu_2, \ldots, \mu_n)$ with λ_j and μ_j $(j = 1, 2, \ldots, n)$ being the eigenvalues of matrices $\bar{W}$ and $\bar{T}$, respectively.

Further, we obtain

$$
\begin{aligned}
\rho(M_\alpha) =&\rho(\bar{M}_\alpha)\\
=&\rho(-i(\alpha I - i\bar{T})\bar{T}\bar{W}^{-1}(\alpha I + \bar{W})^{-1})\\
=&\rho((\alpha I - i\bar{T})\bar{T}\bar{W}^{-1}(\alpha I + \bar{W})^{-1})\\
\leq&\|(\alpha I - i\bar{T})\bar{T}\bar{W}^{-1}(\alpha I + \bar{W})^{-1}\|_2\\
=&\|V_2(\alpha I - i\Lambda_2)\Lambda_2V_2^*V_1\Lambda_1^{-1}(\alpha I + \Lambda_1)^{-1}V_1^*\|_2\\
\leq&\|(\alpha I - i\Lambda_2)\Lambda_2\|_2\|(\alpha I + \Lambda_1)^{-1}\Lambda_1^{-1}\|_2.
\end{aligned}
$$

Since $\bar{W}$ is similar to $V^{-1}W$ and $\bar{T}$ is similar to $V^{-1}T$,

$$\|(\alpha I + \Lambda_1)^{-1}\Lambda_1^{-1}\|_2 = \max_{\lambda_j \in \lambda(V^{-1}W)} \frac{1}{\lambda_j(\alpha + \lambda_j)} = \frac{1}{\lambda_{\min}(\alpha + \lambda_{\min})} \qquad (2.7)$$

and

$$\|(\alpha I - i\Lambda_2)\Lambda_2\|_2 = \max_{\mu_j \in \mu(V^{-1}T)} \mu_j \sqrt{\alpha^2 + \mu_j^2} = \mu_{\max}\sqrt{\alpha^2 + \mu_{\max}^2}, \qquad (2.8)$$

where $\lambda(V^{-1}W)$ and $\mu(V^{-1}T)$ the spectrum of matrices $V^{-1}W$ and $V^{-1}T$, respectively.

Combining (2.7) with (2.8), the bound $\delta(\alpha)$ in (2.6) for $\rho(M_\alpha)$ can be obtained. If $\mu_{\max} \leq \lambda_{\min}$, then $\rho(M_\alpha) \leq \delta(\alpha) < 1$. $\qquad\square$

Theorem 2.1 tells us that the rate of convergence of the MLPMHSS method is limited by $\delta(\alpha)$, which depends on the largest eigenvalue of $V^{-1}T$ and the smallest eigenvalue of $V^{-1}W$. If the largest eigenvalue of $V^{-1}T$ and the smallest eigenvalue of $V^{-1}W$ are obtained, then the specifical upper bound of $\rho(M_\alpha)$ can be provided. In the meantime, we gain the theoretical optimal parameter to minimize this upper bound, see Corollary 2.1.

Corollary 2.1. *Let the conditions of Theorem 2.1 be satisfied. Then the optimal value of the parameter α is $\alpha^* = \frac{\mu_{\max}^2}{\lambda_{\min}}$ and the minimum bound for $\rho(M_\alpha)$ is*

$$\delta(\alpha^*) = \frac{\mu_{\max}^2}{\lambda_{\min}\sqrt{\mu_{\max}^2 + \lambda_{\min}^2}}. \tag{2.9}$$

Proof. Differentiating the bound $\delta(\alpha)$ leads to

$$\delta'(\alpha) = \frac{\mu_{\max}}{\lambda_{\min}} \cdot \frac{\lambda_{\min}\alpha - \mu_{\max}^2}{\sqrt{\alpha^2 + \mu_{\max}^2}(\alpha + \lambda_{\min})^2}.$$

Setting $\delta'(\alpha) = 0$, we have

$$\alpha^* = \frac{\mu_{\max}^2}{\lambda_{\min}}, \tag{2.10}$$

Substituting (2.10) into (2.6) leads to (2.9). $\qquad\square$

It is emphasized that in Corollary 2.1, the upper bound $\delta(\alpha)$ of $\rho(M_\alpha)$ achieves the minimum under the optimal parameter α^*, but this optimal parameter α^* does not minimize $\rho(M_\alpha)$ of M_α. Even so, based on Corollary 2.1, we can choose an effective parameter α for the MLPMHSS method. If we can choose the precondition matrix V such that $\mu_{\max} = \lambda_{\min}$, then $\rho(M_{\alpha^*}) \leq \delta(\alpha^*) = \frac{\sqrt{2}}{2}$.

For the convergence condition of the LPMHSS method, the following result was obtained in [12].

Theorem 2.2. *Let $A = W + iT \in \mathbb{C}^{n\times n}$ be defined in (1.2), $V \in \mathbb{R}^{n\times n}$ be symmetric positive definite and $\alpha > 0$. Let $\mu_{\max}$ and $\lambda_{\min}$ be defined in Theorem 2.1. Then the iteration matrix L_α of the LPMHSS method is*

$$L_\alpha = -i(\alpha V + T)^{-1}(\alpha V + iW)W^{-1}T$$

and $\rho(L_\alpha) \leq \sigma(\alpha)$, where

$$\sigma(\alpha) = \frac{\mu_{\max}\sqrt{\alpha^2 + \lambda_{\max}^2}}{\lambda_{\min}(\alpha + \mu_{\max})}.$$

Moreover, it holds that

(i) If $\lambda_{\min} \geq \mu_{\max}$, then $\sigma(\alpha) < 1$ for any $\alpha > 0$;
(ii) If $\lambda_{\min} < \mu_{\max}$, then $\sigma(\alpha) < 1$ if and only if

$$\alpha < \frac{2\mu_{\max}^2 \lambda_{\min}}{\mu_{\max}^2 - \lambda_{\min}^2}.$$

Further, the optimal parameter α is $\alpha^* = \frac{\lambda_{\min}^2}{\mu_{\max}}$ and

$$\sigma(\alpha^*) = \frac{\mu_{\max}}{\sqrt{\mu_{\max}^2 + \lambda_{\min}^2}}.$$

Based on Corollary 2.1 and Theorem 2.2, Theorem 2.3 gives a comparison between the MLPMHSS method and the LPMHSS method.

Theorem 2.3. *Let $A = W + iT \in \mathbb{C}^{n \times n}$ in (1.2) be normal, $V \in \mathbb{R}^{n \times n}$ be symmetric positive definite and $\alpha > 0$, and let $\mu_{\max}$ and $\lambda_{\min}$ be defined in Theorem 2.1. Then the optimal upper bound $\delta(\alpha^*)$ of the spectral radius of the MLPMHSS iteration matrix and the optimal upper bound $\sigma(\alpha^*)$ of the spectral radius of the LPMHSS iteration matrix satisfy*

$$\delta(\alpha^*) \leq \sigma(\alpha^*) \text{ for } \mu_{\max} \leq \lambda_{\min}.$$

Proof. By calculation, we have

$$\frac{\mu_{\max}}{\sqrt{\mu_{\max}^2 + \lambda_{\min}^2}} \geq \frac{\mu_{\max}^2}{\lambda_{\min}\sqrt{\mu_{\max}^2 + \lambda_{\min}^2}}.$$

This completes the proof.   □

Theorem 2.3 tells us that when both of them are optimal parameters, the optimal upper bound of MLPMHSS is less than or equal to the optimal upper bound of MLPMHSS, and the maximum eigenvalue of $V^{-1}T$ is less than or equal to the minimum eigenvalue $V^{-1}W$. It is worth noting that the result of Theorem 2.3 gives the comparison of the upper bounds of spectral radius of MLPMHSS and MLPMHSS iterative matrices, but does not give the comparison of spectral radii of MLPMHSS and MLPMHSS iterative matrices. Even so, Theorem 2.3 may imply that the convergence rate of LPMHSS is less than that of MLPMHSS when the complex symmetric linear system (1.1)–(1.2) takes their respective optimal parameters. The numerical results are confirmed in the next section.

3   Numerical Experiments

In this section, we test three problems to demonstrate the effectiveness of the MLPMHSS method for solving the complex symmetric linear system (1.1)–(1.2). In the implementations, $x^{(0)} = 0$ is chosen as the initial guess and

$$\frac{\|b - Ax^{(k)}\|_2}{\|b\|_2} \leq 10^{-6}$$

is chosen as the stopping criteria. All tests are performed in MATLAB 7.0 with machine precision 10^{-16}.

In order to verify the effectiveness of MLPMHSS, LPMHSS in [12] is better than PMHSS and MHSS, while PMHSS in [2,3] is better than MHSS and HSS. Based on the above characteristics, we compare MLPMHSS with LPMHSS.

In our calculation, based on the choice of V in LPMHSS [12], the precondition V used in LMPHSS and MLPMHSS methods is set to $V = W$. Since the coefficient matrices of all linear subsystems are symmetric and positive definite in each iteration step of LMPHSS and MLPMHSS methods, we use sparse Cholesky factorization to obtain the inverse of the corresponding matrix. Based on two aspects, we compare MLPMHSS method with LPMHSS method: one is iteration step (expressed by "IT") and the other is CPU running time in seconds (represented by "CPU").

3.1   Results for MLPMHSS Iteration

Example 3.1 ([7,12,14]). Let σ_1, σ_2 be two real coefficient functions. Then we consider the Helmholtz equation

$$-\Delta u + \sigma_1 u + i\sigma_2 u = f,$$

where u satisfies Dirichlet boundary conditions in $D = [0,1] \times [0,1]$. Using the five-point centered difference technique for the negative Laplacian operator on an uniform mesh with mesh-size $h = \frac{1}{m+1}$, we can obtain the complex symmetric linear system (1.1)–(1.2) of the form

$$[(H + \sigma_1 I) + i\sigma_2 I]x = b,$$

where $H = B_m \otimes I + I \otimes B_m$ with $B_m = h^{-2} \cdot \text{tridiag}(-1, 2, -1) \in \mathbb{R}^{m \times m}$. Clearly, H is an $n \times n$ block-tridiagonal matrix with $n = m^2$. In addition, we set $\sigma_1 = 100$ and $b = (1+i)Ae$, with $e = (1, 1, \ldots, 1)^T$. Further, by multiplying both sides by h^2, we can normalize the corresponding system.

To compare the MLPMHSS method with the LPMHSS method under the same conditions, based on Theorem 2.3, some values of the real coefficient function σ_2 are necessary to be selected. In this case, Table 1 lists some values of the real coefficient function σ_2.

Next, the spectral radius of MLPMHSS and LPMHSS iterative matrix is considered, because the spectral radius of iterative matrix largely determines

Table 1. The optimal parameters and the least upper bounds of MLPMHSS and LPMHSS for Example 3.1.

		σ_2	20	40	60	80	100
$n = 16384$	MLPMHSS	α^*	0.0279	0.1116	0.2511	0.4464	0.6975
		$\sigma(\alpha^*)$	0.0275	0.1059	0.2245	0.3712	0.5353
	LPMHSS	$\alpha^\star$	5.9869	2.9935	1.9956	1.4967	1.1974
		$\sigma(\alpha^\star)$	0.1647	0.3168	0.4480	0.5555	0.6410
$n = 65536$	MLPMHSS	α^*	0.0279	0.1116	0.2511	0.4464	0.6975
		$\sigma(\alpha^*)$	0.0275	0.1059	0.2245	0.3712	0.5353
	LPMHSS	$\alpha^\star$	5.9869	2.9935	1.9956	1.4967	1.1974
		$\sigma(\alpha^\star)$	0.1647	0.3168	0.4480	0.5555	0.6410

the convergence speed of iterative method. The comparison of spectral radii of two different iterative matrices obtained by MLPMHSS and LPMHSS is shown in Table 1. When the optimal parameter α^* of MLPMHSS method is selected by inference 2.1, and the optimal parameter $\alpha^\star$ of LPMHSS method is selected by Theorem 2.2. See Table 1 for details. The numerical results in Table 1 show that the theoretical results in Theorem 2.3 are valid.

From the numerical results in Table 1, fixing the mesh size m with σ_2 increasing, it is easy to see that the optimal parameter α^* and the upper bound $\sigma(\alpha^*)$ of the MLPMHSS method are increased, the optimal parameter $\alpha^\star$ of the LPMHSS method are decreased but the upper bound $\sigma(\alpha^\star)$ are increased. Fixing σ_2 with the mesh size m increasing, we find that the optimal parameter α^* and the upper bound $\sigma(\alpha^*)$ of the MLPMHSS method are decreased, the optimal parameter $\alpha^\star$ of the LPMHSS method are increased but the upper bound $\sigma(\alpha^\star)$ are decreased.

The numerical results of MLPMHSS and LPMHSS are given in Table 2 using the best parameters in Table 1. It can be seen from the numerical results in Table 2 that the iteration steps and CPU time of MLPMHSS and LPMHSS methods increase with the increase of σ_2. With the increase of mesh size m,

Table 2. IT and CPU of MLPMHSS and LPMHSS for Example 3.1.

		σ_2	20	40	60	80	100
$n = 16384$	MLPMHSS	IT	3	5	8	11	18
		CPU	0.609	0.984	1.578	2.187	3.547
	LPMHSS	IT	6	10	14	19	24
		CPU	1.235	2.063	2.875	3.828	4.875
$n = 65536$	MLPMHSS	IT	3	5	7	10	16
		CPU	4.109	6.765	9.454	13.609	21.719
	LPMHSS	IT	6	9	12	17	22
		CPU	8.203	12.516	16.656	23.516	29.672

the iteration steps of MLPMHSS and LPMHSS methods decrease after fixed σ_2. Not surprisingly, the CPU time of all methods increases with the grid size of m. It can be seen from the numerical results in Table 2 that the MLPMHSS method is superior to the LPMHSS method in iterative step size and CPU time in solving complex symmetric linear systems (1.1)–(1.2). Under certain conditions, MLPMHSS is more effective than LPMHSS for solving complex symmetric linear systems (1.1)–(1.2).

Example 3.2 ([2,3,9,15,16]). Consider the complex symmetric linear system

$$[(-\omega^2 M + K) + i(\omega C_V + C_H)]x = b,$$

where ω is the driving circular frequency, K and M are the stiffness and inertia matrices, C_H and C_V are the hysteretic damping and viscous matrices, respectively. In our numerical computations, we take $\omega = 1$, $M = I$, $C_V = 10I$, $C_H = \mu K$ with μ being a damping coefficient, where $K = I \otimes V_m + V_m \otimes I$ with $V_m = h^{-2}\text{tridiag}(-1, 2, -1)$ and the mesh-size $h = \frac{1}{m+1}$. In addition, we take $b = (1 + i)Ae$ with $e = (1, 1, \ldots, 1)^T$.

Table 3. The optimal parameters and the least upper bounds of MLPMHSS and LPMHSS for Example 3.2.

		μ	0.1	0.01	0.001
$n = 16384$	MLPMHSS	α^*	0.4083	0.2962	0.2859
		$\sigma(\alpha^*)$	0.3441	0.2602	0.2521
	LPMHSS	α^*	1.5649	1.8376	1.8701
		$\sigma(\alpha^*)$	0.5385	0.4780	0.4715
$n = 65536$	MLPMHSS	α^*	0.4083	0.2961	0.2859
		$\sigma(\alpha^*)$	0.3441	0.2601	0.2521
	LPMHSS	α^*	1.5650	1.8376	1.8702
		$\sigma(\alpha^*)$	0.5384	0.4780	0.4715

Analogously to Example 3.1, we select some values of μ to satisfy Theorem 2.3 such that we can compare the MLPMHSS method with the LPMHSS method under the same conditions. Specifically, see Table 3. Numerical results in Table 3 further confirm that the theoretical results in Theorem 2.3 are right.

From these numerical results in Table 3, fixing the mesh size m with μ decreasing, we find that the optimal parameter α^* and the upper bound $\sigma(\alpha^*)$ of the MLPMHSS method are decreased, the optimal parameter α^* of the MLPMHSS method are increased but the upper bound $\sigma(\alpha^*)$ are decreased. When $n = 256, 1024$ and 4096, fixing μ with the mesh size m increasing, the optimal parameter α^* and the upper bound $\sigma(\alpha^*)$ of the MLPMHSS method are decreased, and the optimal parameter α^* of the LPMHSS method are increased but the upper bound $\sigma(\alpha^\star)$ are decreased. When $n = 16384$ and 65536, the optimal parameters and the upper bounds of both are almost unchanged, see Table 3.

Table 4. IT and CPU of MLPMHSS and LPMHSS for Example 3.2.

		μ	0.1	0.01	0.001
$n = 16384$	MLPMHSS	IT	9	7	7
		CPU	1.75	1.36	1.359
	LPMHSS	IT	15	12	12
		CPU	2.969	2.391	2.375
$n = 65536$	MLPMHSS	IT	8	6	6
		CPU	10.469	7.828	7.828
	LPMHSS	IT	13	11	11
		CPU	17.172	14.547	14.453

Table 4 lists the numerical results of the MLPMHSS and LPMHSS methods for Example 3.2 when the optimal parameters in Table 3 are employed. From Table 4, fixing the mesh size m with μ decreasing, the number of iteration steps and CPU times of the MLPMHSS and LPMHSS methods decrease. Fixing μ with the mesh size m increasing, the number of iteration steps of the MLPMHSS and LPMHSS methods are decreased. It is no surprise that CPU times for all methods grow with the mesh size m. Based on the numerical results in Table 4, from the view of iteration step and CPU time, the MLPMHSS method is superior to the LPMHSS method. That is to say, the MLPMHSS method is more efficient than the LPMHSS method when both are used to solve the complex symmetric linear system (1.1)–(1.2).

In all, by our numerical experiments, the MLPMHSS method is superior to the LPMHSS method under certain conditions when both are employed to solve the complex symmetric linear system (1.1)–(1.2).

3.2   Results of the Related Preconditioner

In this subsection, we consider the related preconditioner for the complex symmetric linear system (1.1)–(1.2). When $V = W$, the preconditioner $P_2 = \alpha W + T$ was considered in [12]. In the same way, we take the preconditioner $P_1 = \alpha W + W = (1 + \alpha)W$. It is noted that the multiplicative factor $1 + \alpha$ in the preconditioner P_1 has no influence on the preconditioned system and thus it can be dropped. Whereas, for convenient comparison, in our numerical experiment, the multiplicative factor $1 + \alpha$ in the preconditioner P_1 is not deleted.

For Example 3.1, in Tables 5, 6, 7, 8 and 9, we present some numerical results of GMRES(20) with P_1 and P_2 for solving the complex symmetric linear system (1.1)–(1.2).

Table 5. IT and CPU of P_1 and P_2 for $\sigma_2 = 20$.

		α	0.01	0.05	0.1	0.5
$n = 16384$	P_1	IT	2	2	2	2
		CPU	0.437	0.453	0.453	0.453
	P_2	IT	16	8	6	3
		CPU	1.9061	1.047	0.844	0.531
$n = 65536$	P_1	IT	2	2	2	2
		CPU	2.765	2.719	2.765	2.75
	P_2	IT	15	7	5	3
		CPU	11.89	6.093	4.719	3.344

Table 6. IT and CPU of P_1 and P_2 for $\sigma_2 = 40$.

		α	0.01	0.05	0.1	0.5
$n = 16384$	P_1	IT	3	3	3	3
		CPU	0.547	0.547	0.547	0.563
	P_2	IT	21	10	7	4
		CPU	2.594	1.25	0.937	0.625
$n = 65536$	P_1	IT	2	2	2	2
		CPU	2.719	2.719	2.719	2.672
	P_2	IT	19	9	6	3
		CPU	14.969	7.578	5.406	3.297

Table 7. IT and CPU of P_1 and P_2 for $\sigma_2 = 60$.

		α	0.01	0.05	0.1	0.5
$n = 16384$	P_1	IT	3	3	3	3
		CPU	0.531	0.531	0.531	0.531
	P_2	IT	26	11	8	4
		CPU	3	1.328	1.016	0.594
$n = 65536$	P_1	IT	3	3	3	3
		CPU	3.344	3.328	3.328	3.28
	P_2	IT	24	10	7	4
		CPU	18.75	8.157	6	3.985

For Example 3.2, Tables 10, 11 and 12 present some numerical results of GMRES(20) with P_1 and P_2 for solving the complex symmetric linear system (1.1)–(1.2).

To easily compare the precondtioner P_1 with the precondtioner P_2, the same iteration parameter α is employed. With respect to the choice of α, one can

Table 8. IT and CPU of P_1 and P_2 for $\sigma_2 = 80$.

		α	0.01	0.05	0.1	0.5
$n = 16384$	P_1	IT	4	4	3	3
		CPU	0.656	0.641	0.531	0.531
	P_2	IT	29	12	9	5
		CPU	3.36	1.437	1.109	0.703
$n = 65536$	P_1	IT	3	3	3	3
		CPU	3.328	3.328	3.328	3.328
	P_2	IT	26	11	8	4
		CPU	20.015	8.781	6.75	4.016

Table 9. IT and CPU of P_1 and P_2 for $\sigma_2 = 100$.

		α	0.01	0.05	0.1	0.5
$n = 16384$	P_1	IT	4	4	4	4
		CPU	0.625	0.641	0.641	0.625
	P_2	IT	32	13	10	5
		CPU	3.625	1.531	1.219	0.687
$n = 65536$	P_1	IT	3	3	3	3
		CPU	3.391	3.328	3.343	3.344
	P_2	IT	28	12	9	4
		CPU	21.391	9.5	7.437	3.969

Table 10. IT and CPU of P_1 and P_2 for $\mu = 0.1$.

		α	0.01	0.05	0.1	0.5
$n = 16384$	P_1	IT	3	3	3	3
		CPU	0.532	0.531	0.515	0.516
	P_2	IT	6	5	5	3
		CPU	0.812	0.703	0.703	0.531
$n = 65536$	P_1	IT	3	3	3	2
		CPU	3.359	3.359	3.344	2.672
	P_2	IT	5	5	4	3
		CPU	4.719	4.625	3.953	3.281

see [17] for more details. In this case, some numerical results are presented in Tables 5, 6, 7, 8, 9, 10, 11 and 12 to illustrate the convergence behaviors of two preconditioners P_1 and P_2.

From Tables 5, 6, 7, 8, 9, 10, 11 and 12, it is easy to see that the iteration steps and CPU times of the preconditioner P_1 are less than the preconditioner

Table 11. IT and CPU of P_1 and P_2 for $\mu = 0.01$.

		α	0.01	0.05	0.1	0.5
$n = 16384$	P_1	IT	3	3	3	3
		CPU	0.531	0.531	0.531	0.531
	P_2	IT	12	8	6	4
		CPU	1.422	1.047	0.797	0.61
$n = 65536$	P_1	IT	3	3	3	2
		CPU	3.391	3.344	3.344	2.703
	P_2	IT	11	7	5	3
		CPU	8.828	6.063	4.64	3.13

Table 12. IT and CPU of P_1 and P_2 for $\mu = 0.001$.

		α	0.01	0.05	0.1	0.5
$n = 16384$	P_1	IT	3	3	3	3
		CPU	0.531	0.531	0.531	0.531
	P_2	IT	16	8	6	4
		CPU	1.875	1.016	0.812	0.609
$n = 65536$	P_1	IT	3	3	3	2
		CPU	3.344	3.36	3.359	2.688
	P_2	IT	15	7	6	3
		CPU	11.703	6.031	5.328	3.296

P_2 in [12]. When used as a preconditioner, the computational efficiency of P_1 performs much better than P_2. Based on these numerical results, we can draw a conclusion that the preconditioner P_1 has considerable competition.

Finally, the following complex symmetric linear system is considered.

Example 3.3 [2]. Consider the complex symmetric linear system of the form

$$(W + iT)x = b,$$

with

$$K = I \otimes V + V \otimes I \text{ and } W = 10(I \otimes V_c + V_c \otimes I) + 9(e_1 e_m^T + e_m e_1^T) \otimes I,$$

where $V = \text{tridiag}(-1, 2, -1) \in \mathbb{R}^{m \times m}$, $V_c = V - e_1 e_m^T - e_m e_1^T \in \mathbb{R}^{m \times m}$, and e_1 and e_m are the first and the last unit vectors in $\mathbb{R}^m$, respectively. We take $b = (1 + i)Ae$ with $e = (1, 1, \ldots, 1)^T$. Specifically, see Example 4.3 in [2].

From the numerical results in Tables 2, 4, 5, 6, 7, 8, 9, 10, 11 and 12, we find that the MLPMHSS method outperforms the LPMHSS method, the preconditioner P_1 also outperforms the preconditioner P_2. Further, we can find that the related preconditioner $P_1(P_2)$ with GMRES(20) is more efficiency than the MLPMHSS(LPMHSS) method. Based on this case, we only consider the efficiency of the preconditioners P_1 and P_2.

Table 13 reports the numerical results for GMRES(20) with P_1 and P_2 for Example 3.3.

Table 13. IT and CPU of P_1 and P_2 for Example 3.3.

		α	0.01	0.05	0.1	0.5
$n = 16384$	P_1	IT	8	8	8	8
		CPU	1.609	1.578	1.578	1.547
	P_2	IT	19	16	14	9
		CPU	3.437	2.86	2.562	1.719
$n = 65536$	P_1	IT	10	10	10	10
		CPU	15.171	15.094	15.125	15.188
	P_2	IT	25	19	17	11
		CPU	36.359	27.296	24.672	16.641

Compared with the preconditioner P_2, Table 13 further confirms that the preconditioner P_1 has considerable competition.

4 Conclusion

In this paper, a modified LPMHSS (MLPMHSS) method is proposed for a class of complex symmetric linear systems with strong Hermitian parts, and its convergence conditions are given. It is proved that the MLPMHSS method converges unconditionally under suitable conditions. The effectiveness of MLPMHSS is verified by three examples.

References

1. Arridge, S.R.: Optical tomography in medical imaging. Inverse Prob. **15**, R41–R93 (1999)
2. Bai, Z.-Z., Benzi, M., Chen, F.: Modified HSS iteration methods for a class of complex symmetric linear systems. Computing **87**, 93–111 (2010)
3. Bai, Z.-Z., Benzi, M., Chen, F.: On preconditioned MHSS iteration methods for complex symmetric linear systems. Numer. Algor. **56**, 297–317 (2011)
4. Bai, Z.-Z.: Block alternating splitting implicit iteration methods for saddle-point problems from time-harmonic eddy current models. Numer. Linear Algebra Appl. **19**, 914–936 (2012)
5. Bai, Z.-Z.: Structured preconditioners for nonsingular matrices of block two-by-two structures. Math. Comput. **75**, 791–815 (2006)

6. Benzi, M., Bertaccini, D.: Block preconditioning of real-valued iterative algorithms for complex linear systems. IMA J. Numer. Anal. **28**, 598–618 (2008)
7. Bertaccini, D.: Efficient solvers for sequences of complex symmetric linear systems. Electron. Trans. Numer. Anal. **18**, 49–64 (2004)
8. Day, D.D., Heroux, M.A.: Solving complex-valued linear systems via equivalent real formulations. SIAM J. Sci. Comput. **23**, 480–498 (2001)
9. Feriani, A., Perotti, F., Simoncini, V.: Iterative system solvers for the frequency analysis of linear mechanical systems. Comput. Methods Appl. Mech. Eng. **190**, 1719–1739 (2000)
10. Bai, Z.-Z.: On preconditioned iteration methods for complex linear systems. J. Eng. Math. **93**(1), 41–60 (2014). https://doi.org/10.1007/s10665-013-9670-5
11. Bai, Z.-Z., Golub, G.H., Ng, M.K.: Hermitian and skew-Hermitian splitting methods for non-Hermitian positive definite linear systems. SIAM J. Matrix Anal. Appl. **24**, 603–626 (2003)
12. Li, X., Yang, A.-L., Wu, Y.-J.: Lopsided PMHSS iteration method for a class of complex symmetric linear systems. Numer. Algorithms **66**(3), 555–568 (2013). https://doi.org/10.1007/s11075-013-9748-1
13. Noormohammadi Pour, H., Sadeghi Goughery, H.: New Hermitian and skew-Hermitian splitting methods for non-Hermitian positive-definite linear systems. Numer. Algorithms **69**(1), 207–225 (2014). https://doi.org/10.1007/s11075-014-9890-4
14. Wu, S.-L., Huang, T.-Z., Li, L., Xiong, L.-L.: Positive stable preconditioners for symmetric indefinite linear systems arising from Helmholtz equations. Phys. Lett. A **373**, 2401–2407 (2009)
15. Wu, S.-L.: Several variants of the HSS method for a class of complex symmetric linear systems. Numer. Linear Algebra Appl. **22**, 338–356 (2015)
16. Wu, S.-L., Li, C.-X.: A splitting iterative method for the discrete dynamic linear systems. J. Comput. Appl. Math. **267**, 49–60 (2014)
17. Benzi, M.: A generalization of the Hermitian and skew-Hermitian splitting iteration. SIAM J. Matrix Anal. Appl. **31**, 360–374 (2009)

Fast Rational Lanczos Method for the Toeplitz Symmetric Positive Semidefinite Matrix Functions

Lei Chen[1], Lu Zhang[2(✉)], Mengjia Wu[2], and Jianqiang Zhao[2]

[1] School of Information Engineering, Xuzhou University of Technology,
Xuzhou 221018, Jiangsu, China
chenlei@xzit.edu.cn

[2] School of Mathematics and Statistics, Xuzhou University of Technology,
Xuzhou 221018, Jiangsu, China

Abstract. In this paper, we use the rational Lanczos method to approximate Toeplitz matrix functions, in which the matrices are symmetric positive semidefinite (SPSD). In order to reduce the computational cost, we use the inverse of the Toeplitz matrix and the fast Fourier transform (FFT). Then, we apply this method to solve a heat equation. Numerical examples are given to show the effectiveness of the rational Lanczos method.

Keywords: Toeplitz · Matrix function · Rational lanczos method · Gohberg-Semencul formula

1 Introduction

Recently, many authors have been interested in exponential integrators which are widely used in various fields [15,16,27,32]. In the exponential integrators, one needs to compute some products of φ_i matrix functions and vectors:

$$y_i(t) = \varphi_i(-tA_m)\mathrm{v}, \quad i = 0, 1, 2, \ldots, s_1, \tag{1}$$

where A_m is an $m \times m$ matrix, s_1, t are given parameters, and v is a vector. And φ_i-functions are of the following form

$$\varphi_0(x) = \exp(x), \varphi_i(x) = \int_0^1 \frac{\exp\big((1-\xi)x\big)\xi^{i-1}}{(i-1)!} d\xi, i \in \mathbb{Z}^+. \tag{2}$$

Furthermore, the φ_i-functions satisfy the following relations

$$\varphi_i(x) = x\varphi_{i+1}(x) + \frac{1}{i}, \quad i \in \mathbb{Z}^+. \tag{3}$$

Supported by the "Peiyu" Project from Xuzhou University of Technology (Grant Number XKY2019104).

H. Song and D. Jiang (Eds.): SIMUtools 2020, LNICST 369, pp. 164–172, 2021.
https://doi.org/10.1007/978-3-030-72792-5_15

Toeplitz matrices have various applications [5,6]. Based on the importance of Toeplitz matrices, we want to approximate the products of the φ_i matrix functions and vectors (TMF), in which the matrices are the SPSD Toeplitz matrix. That is, in (1), the matrix A_m is the SPSD Toeplitz matrix. TMF can be applied to practical calculation problems; see [12,36] for example. Recently, some new techniques are proposed to improve network routing and performance measurement [17,39]. Based on effective user behavior and traffic analysis approaches [19,20], we can design more effective scheduling strategies to raise resources utilization [22,26] and energy-efficiency [23,24]. To test new scheduling strategies, traffic must be reconstructed in test bed [18,21,25,34,38]. Fluid model is effective model to reconstruct the bursty data traffic. In this situation, TMF can also be used to build the fluid model.

Classical methods for solving φ_i matrix functions require very high complexity [2]. Recently, Krylov subspace method has been widely studied in large-scale sparse matrix due to its high efficiency [1,3,4,7–9,29,30,40]. In this method, we only need to compute the smaller matrix functions instead of computing the large matrix functions. Moreover, rational technique could be exploited to speed up Krylov subspace method [10,11].

It is known that we can calculate Toeplitz matrix-vector products by the fast Fourier transform [5,6], and one can calculate the explicit inverse of the Toeplitz matrix by the Gohberg-Semencul formula (GS) [13,14]. These important properties can be used to accelerate the rate of convergence of the computation of TMF. In this work, we use the rational Lanczos method to compute the TMF and reduce the computational cost by using the GS.

2   Toeplitz Matrix

An $m \times m$ Toeplitz matrix T_m satisfies $(T_m)_{i,j} = t_{i-j}$ for $1 \leq i, j \leq m$. A circulant matrix $C_m((C_m)_{i,j} = c_{i-j})$ satisfies $c_i = c_{i-m}$, $1 \leq i \leq m - 1$. According to [5], we know that the complexity is $\mathcal{O}(m \log m)$, if one computes the products $C_m u$ and $C_m^{-1} u$ for a given vector u by the FFT.

A skew-circulant matrix $S_m((S_m)_{i,j} = s_{i-j})$ satisfies $s_i = -s_{i-m}$ for $1 \leq i \leq m - 1$. Similarly, the computational complexity of the products of $S_m u$ and $S_m^{-1} u$ is also $\mathcal{O}(m \log m)$ by the FFT.

In addition, by constructing a proper circulant matrix, we can compute $T_m u$ in $\mathcal{O}(2m \log(2m))$ complexity by the FFT; see [5,6].

The GS for the inverse of a Toeplitz matrix T_m which is SPD is as follows [13]

$$T_m^{-1} = \frac{1}{a_1}(A_m A_m^{\mathsf{T}} - \hat{A}_m \hat{A}_m^{\mathsf{T}}), \qquad (4)$$

where the matrices A_m and $\hat{A}_m$ are of the following forms

$$A_m = \begin{bmatrix} a_1 & 0 & \cdots & 0 \\ a_2 & a_1 & \ddots & \vdots \\ \vdots & \ddots & \ddots & 0 \\ a_m & \cdots & a_2 & a_1 \end{bmatrix}$$

and

$$\hat{A}_m = \begin{bmatrix} 0 & 0 & \cdots & 0 \\ a_m & 0 & \ddots & \vdots \\ \vdots & \ddots & \ddots & 0 \\ a_2 & \cdots & a_m & 0 \end{bmatrix}.$$

Denote $\mathbf{a} = [a_1, a_2, \ldots, a_m]^\mathsf{T}$, then we can get $\mathbf{a}$ by solving the following linear system

$$T_m \mathbf{a} = \mathbf{e}_1 = [1, 0, \ldots, 0]^\mathsf{T}. \tag{5}$$

According to [31, 33], by using (4), one can obtain

$$T_m^{-1} \mathbf{u} = Re(\mathbf{p}) + \hat{J} Im(\mathbf{p}) \tag{6}$$

and

$$\mathbf{p} = \frac{1}{2a_1} \left[(A_m + \hat{A}_m^\mathsf{T})(A_m^\mathsf{T} - \hat{A}_m) \right] (\mathbf{u} + \mathbf{i}\hat{J}\mathbf{u}), \tag{7}$$

where $\mathbf{i}$ is the imaginary unit and $\hat{J}$ is the anti-identity matrix, and $Re(\mathbf{p})$ is the real part of $\mathbf{p}$ and $Im(\mathbf{p})$ is the imaginary part of $\mathbf{p}$. Thus, we can compute $T_m^{-1}\mathbf{u}$ in $\mathcal{O}(m \log m)$ operations. To construct T_m^{-1} by the GS, we need to solve the Toeplitz linear system (5). We use the PCG with Strang's preconditioner to solve (5) in this paper.

3   Rational Lanczos Method

In this section, we first introduce the Lanczos method for solving $y_i(t) = \varphi_i(-tT_m)\mathbf{v}$. By using the Lanczos algorithm for a symmetric matrix T_m, we can get a basis of a Krylov subspace

$$\mathcal{K}_n(T_m, \mathbf{v}) = \text{span}\{\mathbf{v}, T_m\mathbf{v}, T_m^2\mathbf{v}, \ldots, T_m^{n-1}\mathbf{v}\}.$$

Please see [35] for the details of this algorithm.

The following formulation can be obtained by the Lanczos algorithm [35]

$$T_m U_n = U_n H_n + h_{n+1,n}\mathbf{v}_{n+1}\mathbf{e}_n^\mathsf{T}, \tag{8}$$

where $U_n = [\mathbf{u}_1, \mathbf{u}_2, \ldots, \mathbf{u}_n]$ is an $m \times n$ matrix. H_n is an $n \times n$ symmetric tridiagonal matrix, and $\mathbf{e}_n$ is the n-th column of the identity matrix. Therefore, we can give the following approximation

$$\varphi_i(-tT_m)\mathbf{v} \approx \hat{\beta} U_n \varphi_i(-tH_n)\mathbf{e}_1, \quad \hat{\beta} = \|\mathbf{v}\|_2.$$

Therefore, the computation of large matrix functions $\varphi_i(-tT_m)$ are replaced by the computation of the small matrix functions $\varphi_i(-tH_n)$. In addition, $\varphi_i(-tH_n)$ can be effectively calculated by the function "phipade" in the software package EXPINT [2].

According to [35], we note that, for approximating $\varphi_i(-tT_m)\mathbf{v}$, the rate of convergence of the Lanczos algorithm is very slow when the 2-norm of tT_m gets larger. In order to overcome this drawback, the rational Krylov subspace method is proposed [10,11,30,40].

Let I_m be the identity matrix and $\hat{\sigma}$ is a parameter. We give the rational Lanczos algorithm as follows:

Algorithm 1: Rational Lanczos algorithm

1. Calculate $\mathbf{u}_1 = \frac{\mathbf{v}}{\|\mathbf{v}\|_2}$
2. For $i = 1, 2, \ldots, n$
3. $\quad h_{i,i} = \mathbf{u}_i^\mathsf{T}(I_m + \hat{\sigma}T_m)^{-1}\mathbf{u}_i$
4. $\quad \hat{\mathbf{u}}_{i+1} = (I_m + \hat{\sigma}T_m)^{-1}\mathbf{u}_i - h_{i,i}\mathbf{u}_i - h_{i-1,i}\mathbf{u}_{i-1}$
5. $\quad h_{i+1,i} = \|\hat{\mathbf{u}}_{i+1}\|_2$
6. $\quad h_{i,i+1} = h_{i+1,i}$
7. $\quad \mathbf{u}_{i+1} = \frac{\hat{\mathbf{u}}_{i+1}}{h_{i+1,i}}$
8. End

Similar to (8), we have the following formulation

$$(I_m + \hat{\sigma}T_m)^{-1}U_n = U_nH_n + h_{n+1,n}\mathbf{u}_{n+1}\mathbf{e}_n^\mathsf{T}, \quad U_n^\mathsf{T}U_n = I_n. \qquad (9)$$

Therefore, we can approximate $\varphi_i(-tT_m)\mathbf{v}$ by

$$\varphi_i(-tT_m)\mathbf{v} \approx \hat{\beta}U_n\varphi_i(-tB_n)\mathbf{e}_1, \quad \hat{\beta} = \|\mathbf{v}\|_2, \qquad (10)$$

where

$$B_n = \frac{1}{\hat{\sigma}}(H_n^{-1} - I_n) + h_{n+1,n}^2\left(\frac{1}{\hat{\sigma}} + \mathbf{u}_{n+1}^\mathsf{T}T_m\mathbf{u}_{n+1}\right)H_n^{-1}\mathbf{e}_n\mathbf{e}_n^\mathsf{T}H_n^{-1} = U_n^\mathsf{T}T_mU_n.$$

In [11], the following error bound for approximating (10) is given.

Theorem 1. *Let $A_m = P_m^\mathsf{T}T_mP_m$, where P_m is the projection operator of T_m on the subspace $\mathcal{K}_n((I_m + \sigma T_m)^{-1}, \mathbf{v})$, then the approximation of $\varphi_i(-tT_m)\mathbf{v}$ on the subspace $\mathcal{K}_n((I_m + \hat{\sigma}T_m)^{-1}, \mathbf{v})$ has the following error bound*

$$\|\varphi_i(-tT_m)\mathbf{v} - \varphi_i(-tA_m)\mathbf{v}\| \le \frac{D}{m^{i/2}}\|\mathbf{v}\|, \qquad (11)$$

where D is a constant which depends on $\hat{\sigma}$ and i.

For the rational Lanczos algorithm, $P_m = U_nU_n^\mathsf{T}$, and

$$\varphi_i(-tA_m)\mathbf{v} = \varphi_i(-tP_mT_mP_m)\mathbf{v}$$

$$= U_n\varphi_i(-tU_n^\mathsf{T}T_mU_n)U_n^\mathsf{T}\mathbf{v}$$

$$= \hat{\beta}U_n\varphi_i(-tB_n)\mathbf{e}_1.$$

The error bound of Theorem 1 shows: Firstly, the error bound of the rational Lanczos method (11) does not depend on the 2-norm of the matrix tT_n. Secondly, if the i increases, the rate of convergence of the approximation $\varphi_i(-tT_m)\mathbf{v}$ will increase.

3.1 Implementation for the TMF Algorithm

In this section, we give the implementation of the algorithm for approximating the TMF. We note that if a Toeplitz matrix T_m is a SPSD, then $I_m + \hat{\sigma}T_m$ ($\hat{\sigma} > 0$) is a SPD Toeplitz matrix. Therefore, the GS can be used to solve the inverse of the Toeplitz matrix $I_m + \hat{\sigma}T_m$. For the computation of the TMF, the rational Lanczos algorithm using the GS is as follows:

Algorithm 2: Rational Lanczos algorithm for the TMF
1. Solve $(I_m + \hat{\sigma}T_m)\mathbf{a} = e_1$
2. Run Algorithm 1, where $(I_m + \hat{\sigma}T_m)^{-1}u_j$ is computed by (6) and (7)
3. Calculate $\tilde{y}_i(t) = \hat{\beta}U_n\varphi_i(-tB_n)e_1$

   In step 1 of Algorithm 2, the cost of solving $(I_m + \hat{\sigma}T_m)\mathbf{a} = e_1$ is $\mathcal{O}(m\log m)$ [5,6]. Then, the matrix-vector products $(I_m + \hat{\sigma}T_m)^{-1}u_j$ in step 2 of Algorithm 2 can be computed by using (6) and (7), and the cost of computation is $\mathcal{O}(m\log m)$. In step 3 of Algorithm 2, we need to approximate $\varphi_i(-tB_n)e_1$. From [37], we know that $n \ll m$ in general. Therefore, $\varphi_i(-tB_n)e_1$ can be fast approximated by the function "phipade" in the software package EXPINT [2], the computation amount is $\mathcal{O}(n^3)$. As a consequence, the computation amount of Algorithm 2 is $\mathcal{O}(nm\log m)$.

4 Numerical Examples

In this section, we show the effectiveness of the rational Lanczos algorithm to approximate $\varphi_i(-tT_m)v$ by two numerical examples. In Example 1, we use MATLAB command "phipade" to calculate the exact solution $\hat{y}(t)$. In the tables of numerical examples, "m" is the size of the matrix T_m, and "$Itol$" is the accuracy of the error

$$\frac{\|\hat{y}(t) - \hat{y}_n(t)\|_2}{\|\hat{y}(t)\|_2} < Itol,$$

where $\hat{y}_n(t)$ is the approximation of $\hat{y}(t)$. "IStand" and "IRL" denote the Lanczos method and rational Lanczos method, respectively. The parameter $\hat{\sigma}$ in Algorithm 2 is $\hat{\sigma} = \frac{t}{10}$ [28].

Example 1. In the first example, we study the SPD Toeplitz matrix. The elements of the SPD Toeplitz matrix are as follows [6].

$$t_i = \frac{1}{2\pi}\int_{-\pi}^{\pi} x^4 \exp(-\mathbf{i}ix)dx, i = 0, \pm1, \pm2, \dots, \pm(m-1).$$

The elements of the vector v are all 1. We approximate $\varphi_i(-tT_m)v$ ($i = 1, 2, 3$). In this example, the order of the matrix T_m is 2^{10} and the value of t changes.

   It can be seen from Tables 1, 2 and 3 that the numbers of iterations of the IRL are much less than these of the IStand, especially when the 2-norm of tT_m gets larger. In addition, for the IRL, the numbers of iterations do not change. This indicates that the rate of convergence of the IRL does not depend on the 2-norm of tT_m compared with the IStand.

Table 1. Numerical results for Example 1 ($i = 1$)

$m = 2^{10}$	t	$Itol = 10^{-4}$		$Itol = 10^{-7}$	
		IStand	IRL	IStand	IRL
	1	17	6	30	10
	10	56	6	91	11
	10^2	177	6	286	13
	10^3	562	6	880	13

Table 2. Numerical results for Example 1 ($i = 2$)

$m = 2^{10}$	t	$Itol = 10^{-4}$		$Itol = 10^{-7}$	
		IStand	IRL	IStand	IRL
	1	15	5	27	9
	10	48	5	83	10
	10^2	155	5	261	10
	10^3	493	6	807	12

To compare the computational time of the IStand and the IRL, we give the results of the numbers of iterations and computational time in seconds of the IStand and the IRL in Table 4, where $Itol = 10^{-9}$ and $m = 2^{10}$. It can be seen from Table 4: Firstly, the computational times and the numbers of iterations of the IRL are much less than these of the IStand. Furthermore, if the size of the matrix T_m gets larger, the superiority of the IRL will become more obvious. Secondly, if t is fixed, as i increases, the iteration numbers of the IRL decreases, which also validates the result of (11) in Theorem 1.

Example 2. In the second example, we study a heat equation [12]. Please refer to [12] for the detailed equation. Numerically solving the heat equation leads to a matrix function problem

$$\hat{v}(t) = (-tT_m)\varphi_1(-tT_m)v_0 + v_0,$$

Table 3. Numerical results for Example 1 ($i = 3$)

$m = 2^{10}$	t	$Itol = 10^{-4}$		$Itol = 10^{-7}$	
		IStand	IRL	IStand	IRL
	1	13	4	25	9
	10	43	5	77	9
	10^2	139	5	242	10
	10^3	444	5	752	10

Table 4. Numerical results of the IRL and the IStand for Example 1

	$i = 1$		$i = 2$		$i = 3$	
t	IStand	IRL	IStand	IRL	IStand	IRL
1	36(0.0107)	14(0.0030)	33(0.0113)	13(0.0042)	31(0.0073)	12(0.0014)
10	110(0.0261)	17(0.0041)	102(0.0246)	14(0.0012)	95(0.1597)	13(0.0056)
10^2	343(0.0524)	17(0.0043)	319(2.6682)	14(0.0019)	300(1.5130)	14(0.0063)
10^3	1050(59.1512)	17(0.0050)	980(77.9534)	16(0.1218)	915(85.0608)	14(0.0071)

where
$$\hat{v}(t) = [\hat{v}_1(t), \hat{v}_2(t), \dots, \hat{v}_m(t)]^\mathsf{T}$$

is an approximation solution, T_m is a SPD Toeplitz matrix, and v_0 is an initial vector. We solve $\hat{v}(t)$ by the IStand and the IRL, respectively. Table 5 lists the numbers of iterations and computational times of the IStand and the IRL for different m and t.

Table 5. Numerical results for Example 2

	$t = 60$			$t = 300$		
m	Ier	IRL	IStand	Ier	IRL	IStand
2^7	7.88×10^{-5}	12(0.0020)	60(0.0192)	6.71×10^{-5}	12(0.0011)	64(0.0231)
2^8	1.97×10^{-5}	14(0.0022)	142(0.0753)	1.68×10^{-5}	12(0.0011)	128(0.1570)
2^9	4.92×10^{-6}	14(0.0076)	270(0.9505)	4.19×10^{-6}	12(0.0069)	256(1.0489)
2^{10}	1.23×10^{-6}	14(0.0080)	510(8.0049)	1.05×10^{-6}	12(0.0241)	512(9.4987)
2^{11}	3.08×10^{-7}	14(0.0110)	1020(56.4147)	2.62×10^{-7}	12(0.0739)	1024(65.0765)
2^{12}	7.70×10^{-8}	14(0.0231)	2039(384.2013)	6.55×10^{-8}	12(0.2682)	2048(450.0337)
2^{13}	1.92×10^{-8}	14(0.0501)	> 3600	1.66×10^{-8}	12(0.3201)	> 3600

According to Table 5, it is seen that the IRL needs fewer numbers of iterations and calculation times to reach the final accuracies than these of the IStand. In addition, for the large matrix size, the IStand becomes unacceptable due to a lot of iteration numbers, while the IRL still works well.

5   Conclusion and Future Work

In this work, we use the rational Lanczos algorithm to approximate the TMF, and this method is applied to the numerical calculation. Using the GS, we can avoid the use of internal iterations to implement the rational Lanczos algorithm. In addition, due to the Toeplitz matrix, the amount of computation can be reduced. Numerical results show the advantage of the new method.

References

1. Al-Mohy, A., Higham, N.J.: Computing the action of matrix exponential, with an application to exponential integrators. SIAM J. Sci. Comput. **33**, 488–511 (2011)
2. Berland, H., Skaflestad, B., Wright, W.: Expint-A matlab package for exponential integrators. ACM Tran. Math. Soft. **33**(4), 4-es (2007)
3. Botchev, M., Grimm, V., Hochbruck, M.: Residual, restarting and Richardson iteration for the matrix exponential. SIAM J. Sci. Comput. **35**, A1376–A1397 (2013)
4. Caliari, M., Kandolf, P., Zivcovich, F.: Backward error analysis of polynomial approximations for computing the action of the matrix exponential. BIT Numer. Math. **58**, 907–935 (2018)
5. Chan, R., Jin, X.: An Introduction to Iterative Toeplitz Solvers. SIAM, Philadelphia (2007)
6. Chan, R., Ng, M.: Conjugate gradient methods for Toeplitz systems. SIAM Rev. **38**, 427–482 (1996)
7. Eiermann, M., Ernst, O.: A restarted Krylov subspace method for the evaluation of matrix functions. SIAM J. Numer. Anal. **44**, 2481–2504 (2006)
8. Frommer, A., Gttel, S., Schweitzer, M.: Efficient and stable Arnoldi restarts for matrix functions based on quadrature. SIAM J. Matrix Anal. Appl. **35**, 661–683 (2014)
9. Frommer, A., Simoncini, V.: Stopping criteria for rational matrix functions of hermitian and symmetric matrices. SIAM J. Sci. Comput. **30**, 1387–1412 (2008)
10. Gckler, T., Grimm, V.: Uniform approximation of φ functions in exponential integerators by a rational Krylov subspace method with simple poles. SIAM J. Matrix Anal. Appl. **35**, 1467–1489 (2014)
11. Grimm, V.: Resolvent Krylov subspace approximation to operator functions. BIT Numer. Math. **52**, 639–659 (2012)
12. Gockenbach, M.: Partial Differential Equations-Analytical and Numerical Methods. SIAM, Philadelphia (2002)
13. Gohberg, I., Semencul, A.: On the inversion of finite Toeplitz matrices and their continuous analogs. Matem. Issled. **2**, 201–233 (1972)
14. Heinig, G., Rost, L.: Algebraic Methods for Toeplitz-like Matrices and Operators. Birkhäuser, Basel (1984). https://doi.org/10.1007/978-3-0348-6241-7
15. Higham, N.J., Kandolf, P.: Computing the action of trigonometric and hyperbolic matrix functions. SIAM J. Sci. Comput. **36**, A613–A627 (2017)
16. Hochbruck, M., Ostermann, A.: Exponential integrators. Acta Numer. **19**, 209–286 (2010)
17. Huo, L., Jiang, D., Lv, Z., et al.: An intelligent optimization-based traffic information acquirement approach to software-defined networking. Comput. Intell. **36**, 1–21 (2019)
18. Huo, L., Jiang, D., Qi, S., Song, H., Miao, L.: An AI-based adaptive cognitive modeling and measurement method of network traffic for EIS. Mob. Net. Appl., 1–11 (2019). https://doi.org/10.1007/s11036-019-01419-z
19. Jiang, D., Huo, L., Song, H.: Rethinking behaviors and activities of base stations in mobile cellular networks based on big data analysis. IEEE Trans. Netw. Sci. Eng. **1**(1), 1–12 (2018)
20. Jiang, D., Wang, Y., Lv, Z., et al.: Big data analysis-based network behavior insight of cellular networks for industry 4.0 applications. IEEE Trans. Ind. Inf. **16**(2), 1310–1320 (2020)

21. Jiang, D., Huo, L., Li, Y.: Fine-granularity inference and estimations to network traffic for SDN. PLoS One **13**(5), 1–23 (2018)
22. Jiang, D., Huo, L., Lv, Z., et al.: A joint multi-criteria utility-based network selection approach for vehicle-to-infrastructure networking. IEEE Trans. Intell. Transp. Syst. **19**(10), 3305–3319 (2018)
23. Jiang, D., Li, W., Lv, H.: An energy-efficient cooperative multicast routing in multi-hop wireless networks for smart medical applications. Neurocomputing **220**, 160–169 (2017)
24. Jiang, D., Wang, Y., Lv, Z., et al.: Intelligent Optimization-based reliable energy-efficient networking in cloud services for IIoT networks. IEEE J. Sel. Areas Commun. Online available (2019)
25. Jiang, D., Wang, W., Shi, L., et al.: A compressive sensing-based approach to end-to-end network traffic reconstruction. IEEE Trans. Netw. Sci. Eng. **5**(3), 1–12 (2018)
26. Jiang, D., Zhang, P., Lv, Z., et al.: Energy-efficient multi-constraint routing algorithm with load balancing for smart city applications. IEEE Internet Things J. **3**(6), 1437–1447 (2016)
27. Kooij, G.L., Botchev, M.A., Geurts, B.J.: An exponential time integrator for the incompressible Navier-stokes equation. SIAM J. Sci. Comput. **40**, B684–B705 (2018)
28. Lee, S., Pang, H., Sun, H.: Shift-invert Arnoldi approximation to the Toeplitz matrix exponential. SIAM J. Sci. Comput. **32**, 774–792 (2010)
29. Lopez, L., Simoncini, V.: Analysis of projection methods for rational function approximation to the matrix exponential. SIAM J. Numer. Anal. **44**, 613–635 (2006)
30. Moret, I.: On RD-rational Krylov approximations to the core-functions of exponential integrators. Numer. Linear Algebra Appl. **14**, 445–457 (2007)
31. Ng, M., Sun, H., Jin, X.: Recursive-based PCG methods for Toeplitz systems with nonnegative generating functions. SIAM J. Sci. Comput. **24**, 1507–1529 (2003)
32. Noferini, V.: A formula for the Fréchet derivative of a generalized matrix function. SIAM J. Matrix Anal. Appl. **38**, 434–457 (2017)
33. Pang, H., Sun, H.: Shift-invert Lanczos method for the symmetric positive semidefinite Toeplitz matrix exponential. Numer. Linear Algebra Appl. **18**, 603–614 (2011)
34. Qi S., Jiang, D., Huo, L.: A prediction approach to end-to-end traffic in space information networks. Mob. Netw. Appl. Online available (2019)
35. Saad, Y.: Analysis of some Krylov subspace approximations to the matrix exponential operator. SIAM J. Numer. Anal. **29**, 209–228 (1992)
36. Tangman, D.Y., Gopaul, A., Bhuruth, M.: Exponential time integration and Chebychev discretisation schemes for fast pricing of options. Appl. Numer. Math. **58**, 1309–1319 (2008)
37. Van Den Eshof, J., Hochbruck, M.: Preconditioning Lanczos approximations to the matrix exponential. SIAM J. Sci. Comput. **27**, 1438–1457 (2006)
38. Wang, Y., Jiang, D., Huo, L., et al.: A new traffic prediction algorithm to software defined networking. Mob. Netw. Appl. Online available (2019)
39. Wang, F., Jiang, D., Qi, S.: An adaptive routing algorithm for integrated information networks. China Commun. **7**(1), 196–207 (2019)
40. Wu, G., Feng, T., Wei, Y.: An inexact shift-and-invert Arnoldi algorithm for Toeplitz matrix exponential. Numer. Linear Algebra Appl. **22**, 777–792 (2015)

A Bi-directional Residual Network for Image Expression Recognition

Daihong Jiang[1], Sanyou Zhang[2(⊠)], Cheng Yu[1], and Chuangeng Tian[1]

[1] Xuzhou University of Technology, Xuzhou 221000, Jiangsu, China
[2] China University of Mining and Technology, Xuzhou 221000, Jiangsu, China

Abstract. In this paper, an improved model based on the combination of residual and inverted residual blocks is proposed for image expression recognition, named as bi-directional residual network. The main objective of the proposed method is to alleviate the problem of feature dispersion due to the deep network level in traditional expression recognition research. In this case, residual block is a good solution. However, residual network with small scale of training data can easily lead to over-fitting, which is often the case for image expression recognition. To improve the robustness of the network during training, inverted residual blocks are therefore adopted. Depending on the organization sequence of residual blocks and inverted residual blocks, three network structures are proposed and studied. Fer2013 and CK+ datasets in facial field are adopted for experiment. The experimental results show that the optimized algorithm improves the accuracy by 2.79% on Fer2013 dataset compared with ResNet-50 models.

Keywords: Residual network · Deep learning · Image recognition · Feature expression

1 Introduction

Image expression recognition plays an important role in social life. It has also become an important research topic in the field of artificial intelligence. For example, according to some previous study [14], there are six basic expressions, including happy, angry, surprise, fear, disgust, and sad. Therefore, the goal of image expression recognition is to design algorithms [21] for machines to recognize image expressions, especially the six basic expressions.

So far, image expression recognition has been widely studied over the past several decades. The recent work mainly adopts deep learning to address the task. Liu et al. [17] proposed an expression recognition network based on deep belief network. With Convolutional Neural Networks (CNN) achieving great performance improvement in image recognition tasks, Yu and Zhang [26] proposed an expression recognition network based on deep convolutional network integration and came up with two different network integration strategies. Based on their work, Mollahosseini et al. [15] further proposed a deeper network by introducing the inception layer to the network structure. Recently,

© ICST Institute for Computer Sciences, Social Informatics and Telecommunications Engineering 2021
Published by Springer Nature Switzerland AG 2021. All Rights Reserved
H. Song and D. Jiang (Eds.): SIMUtools 2020, LNICST 369, pp. 173–182, 2021.
https://doi.org/10.1007/978-3-030-72792-5_16

Yang et al. [25] proposed to generate an expressionless face image through conditional generative adversarial network. Since the expression information is recorded in the middle layer of the network in this process, the article proposed a method of performing expression recognition based on residues in the middle layer of the network. Specifically, during the training process, the gradient of a derivative close to 0 will continue to decrease after multiple successive products (in a back propagation process), which makes the networks' training ability poor. However, according to some previous research, the deeper the network, the stronger the fitting ability. Therefore, there is a problem of how to make the deep network easy to train. Additionally, according to Orhan and Pitkow [16], the degradation of the weight matrix causes much worse problem, that is to say, only a small number of hidden units can output valid activation values. As the network growing deeper, this effect becomes worse. The deep residual network (ResNet) [11] can solve these problems. The residual unit used by ResNet is to add a shortcut outside the ordinary multi-layer convolutional layer. In this way, the gradient can be effectively transmitted back to the shallow layers.

However, directly using ResNet for image expression recognition may result in slow calculation speed and poor recognition performance, due to its deep network structure and strong fitting ability. When only relatively small dataset is available, it may become easily overfitting, leading to degraded performance. To address these problems, this paper proposes a bi-directional residual network (Bi-ResNet) which combines the inverted residual blocks [19] and residual blocks. Inverted residual block was proposed in MobileNetV2 [19], whose main idea is to replace the ordinary convolution of the residual block with DepthWise (DW) convolution and PointWise (PW) convolution. In DW convolution, a convolution kernel is responsible for the convolution of a channel, that is, convolution in a two-dimensional plane. DW convolution is followed by PW convolution, which combines the weights of the individual channels of the DW convolution into one new feature. These calculations effectively improve the calculation speed. In this paper, the network structure combining residual block and inverted residual block is studied. Specifically, three kinds of network structures, alternated residual connection, IR residual connection and RI residual connection, are proposed. Compared with traditional residual network structures, it is verified that the network structure of this paper performs better in expression recognition.

The main contributions of the paper are as follows:

In the proposed Bi-directional residual and the inverted residual network, alternated residual connection, IR residual connection and RI residual connection are proposed respectively in terms of the network structure design, with RI residual network finally chosen as the best proposal.

Through the results of multiple sets of experiments, the proposed algorithm is more advantageous than the traditional methods (baseline models). Specifically, RI achieves the best results on the tested two datasets.

2 Related Work

2.1 Traditional Feature Based Methods

Traditional expression recognition methods relies heavily on manual feature extraction. At the same time, it requires designing appropriate classifiers. There are many traditional feature based methods. Some famous manual feature have been applied to expression recognition, including Gabor wavelet transform [8, 23], Histogram of Oriented Gradient (HOG) [23], local binary patterns (LBP) [20], feature extraction based on manifold learning [1, 2, 5, 10, 22, 24]. For classifiers, in [6, 9], support vector machine is used as a classifier. Since the recognition algorithm directly depends on the features extracted manually, and the expression recognition is affected by many factors such as imaging posture, object occlusion, illumination change, etc., the robustness and recognition accuracy of traditional feature based methods still have much room for improvement.

2.2 Deep Learning Based Methods

Liu et al. [17] proposed an expression recognition network based on deep belief network. With Convolutional Neural Networks (CNN) presenting growing prominent advantages in image recognition, Yu and Zhang, in [18, 26], proposed an expression recognition network based on deep convolutional network integration and came up with two different network integration strategies. Based on this, Mollahosseini et al. [15] probed further and deeper by introducing the Inception layer in the network structure. Based on Generative Adversarial Networks (GANs), Yang et al. [25] proposed to generate an expressionless face image through cGAN. Since the expression information is recorded in the middle layer of the network in this process, the article proposed a method of performing expression recognition based on residuals in a network middle layer.

3 Facial Expression Recognition Model

3.1 The Overall Network Structure

The overall structure of the proposed model is shown in Fig. 1. First, the face image is aligned by a pre-processing module and we get normalized face images as input. Before training, the images are augmented by data augmentation methods, such as, rotation, cropping and so on. Then it will be input into one of the three networks proposed in this paper. Finally, a fully connected layer is used. Classification results are obtained by the Sigmoid classification layer. Categorical cross entropy is chosen as the loss function. In the following, the residual block unit structure and the inverted residual block unit structure will be introduced first. Then the three network structures proposed in this paper will be presented.

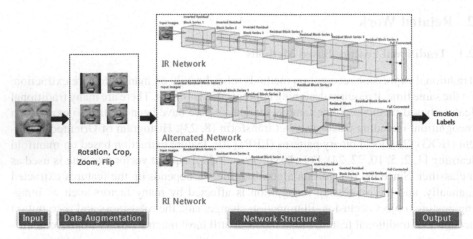

Fig. 1. Framework of the proposed method. With a normalized face input, data augmentation is firstly performed. The augmented training data will be input into one of the three proposed network structures for training. The final output is given by a sigmoid layer for all the three network structures.

3.2 Residual Block Unit

The residual network is a breakthrough of CNN network. It significantly improves the back-propagation ability of network, alleviating problems of gradient dispersion and gradient explosion. Also, it accelerates convergence and effectively improves deep learning ability. The basic unit of the residual network is the residual block [7, 11]. Each residual block contains a short-circuited parameter transfer path. This unique parameter transfer method can transmit information across layers, thereby improving the effect of back-propagation. A residual block is defined by the following function:

$$y = F(x, W_i) + x \tag{1}$$

Where x is the input vector, y is the output vector, and $F(x, W_i)$ represents the residual map to be learned. $F(x, W_i)$ consists of multiple convolutional layers, where x is a shortcut.

For the residual block unit in the above figure, if the x and F dimensions are different and the shortcut changes, the linear projection $h(x_l) = W_l'x$ is used to correspond to the dimension. The function of the residual block unit at this time is as follows:

$$x_{l+1} = h(x_l) + \mathcal{F}(x_l, W_l) \tag{2}$$

In the case where the residual block is stacked multiple times and the input dimension is maintained, the recursive expression can be obtained as follows:

$$x_L = x_l + \sum_{i=1}^{L-1} \mathcal{F}(x_i, W_i) \tag{3}$$

The gradient of the partial differential of a residual block can be obtained by the chain rule:

$$\frac{\partial \varepsilon}{\partial x_l} = \frac{\partial \varepsilon}{\partial x_L} \frac{\partial x_L}{\partial x_l} = \frac{\partial \varepsilon}{\partial x_L} \left(1 + \frac{\partial}{\partial x_l} \sum_{i=1}^{L-1} \mathcal{F}(x_i, W_i)\right) = \frac{\partial \varepsilon}{\partial x_L} + \frac{\partial \varepsilon}{\partial x_L} \frac{\partial}{\partial x_l} \sum_{i=1}^{L-1} \mathcal{F}(x_i, W_i) \qquad (4)$$

In the above formula, $\left(1 + \frac{\partial}{\partial x_l} \sum_{i=1}^{L-1} \mathcal{F}(x_i, W_i)\right)$ is never going to be 0, which means the gradient does not disappear, and it can be reversely inferred from the process of backpropagation that any shallower layers can receive the influence of the previous layer.

3.3 Inverted Residual Block Unit

The inverted residual block unit is proposed in MobileNetV2 [19] with the aim to reduce computational cost. To fulfil this objective, it adopts the DepthWise (DW) separable convolution and linear bottlenecks. Bottleneck and the DW separation convolution is used to raise and decrease dimensions respectively. Its operation consists of three steps: $F(x) = [A \circ N \circ B]x$. Among them, A and B are linear transformations, and N is a nonlinear layer-by-layer transformation. In actual use, $N = ReLU\ 6 \circ DW \circ ReLU\ 6$. Details can be found in [19].

With such a design to replace the convolutional operations, the inverted residual block can largely reduce the computational cost. However, we found that when combined with residual blocks, it can also improve the facial recognition performances under many cases.

3.4 Bi-directional Residual Block Network

Based on the above introduction of residual block and inverted residual block and considering that deep network close to the pyramid shape can improve accuracy, this paper introduces to combine residual and inverted residual blocks to form new network structures. Based on how we organize the sequence of residual and inverted residual blocks, three kinds of network structures are proposed and studied, which are as follows [4, 12].

(1) *Alternated residual and inverted residual network:* The alternated residual and inverted residual network first passes the data through the inverted residual block, then flows it through the residual block. Looping back and forth over multiple such connected inverted residual and residual blocks. Finally Relu(6) is used to activate and fully connected layer is used to produce output. Details of this network structure is shown in Fig. 1.

(2) *RI residual and inverted residual network:* The RI residual and inverted residual network first passes data through multiple consecutive residual blocks, then flows it through multiple consecutive inverted residual blocks.
Finally same structure as the alternated residual and inverted residual network is used to produce output. Details given in Fig. 1. Among all the proposed three networks, in RI network structure, since the residual block is first compressed and then expanded, and the inverted residual block is first expanded and then compressed, the shape of the RI residual and inverted residual network is closer to the shape of a

pyramid, which makes it performs best. The main reason may be because for structures of inverted pyramid shape, it is hard for network to complement information when expanding the network. In experiments, we verified RI network performs best among all the three network structures and it is also better compared with ResNet, MobileNet and MobileNet V2.

(3) IR residual and inverted residual network: The IR residual and inverted residual network adopts an inverse structure of the second network. Data flows through multiple consecutive inverted residual blocks first, then flows through multiple consecutive residual blocks. Details are given in Fig. 2.

Fig. 2. Example images from Fer2013+

3.5 Network Training Loss and Training Details

The fully connected layer adopts the Dense (2048)-BN-Dense (1024)-BN-Dense (10) structure. All networks in this paper use the classification categorical cross entropy as the loss function.

4 Experiment and Analysis

4.1 Dataset

The size of the facial expression dataset is mostly small. Most of the datasets only label smiling and not smiling. This paper uses the Fer2013 dataset. The Fer2013 dataset contains 35,886 images, including 28,708 images in the training set. There are 3,589 images in the validation set and 3,589 images in the test set. The FER+ [3] tag is used for multi-classification learning. Fer2013+ dataset tags consist of neutral, happiness, surprise, sadness, anger, disgust, fear, contempt, unknown, and NF, of which NF means the image is not human face. The image resolution of the Fer2013 dataset is 48 48 1. The images are collected in the wild with various variations than other facial expression datasets. Example images are given in Fig. 2

On the other hand, this paper also uses the CK+ dataset [13] to further verify the effectiveness of the three models introduced. The CK+ dataset has 593 sequences of images, of which 327 have expression tags, and the expression tags consist of anger, contempt, disgust, fear, happiness, sadness, and surprise.

4.2 Experimental Environment and Parameter Settings

The experiment is run on a computer with CPU of Intel(R) Xeon(R) E5-2698 v4 @ 2.20 GHz. The graphics card is Tesla V100 32G, the graphics card driver version is NVIDIA-SMI 384.125, and the total memory is 528275840 kB. The environment is Ubuntu 16.04.4 with Python version 2.7.12, Keras version 2.2.4, and tensorflow-gpu version 1.8.0.

The batch size is set to 64, the optimization function uses Adam (0.001, 0.5), and the learning rate is set as 0.0001. This paper uses two dropouts, one being Dropout (0.5) and the other being Dropout (0.3)-BN layer - Dropout (0.3). The residual and inverted residual block parameters adopt are embedded in ResNet-50 and MobileNetV2 models.

4.3 Comparison of the Proposed Method and State-of-the-Art Methods on FER2013

In the following, we mainly compare our three versions of methods with the current state-of-the-art methods. Details of the accuracy and loss are summarized in Table 1. We mainly compared our method with ResNet-50, MobileNet and MobileNet V2. Besides, to fully study the state-of-the- art methods, we also combine them with transfer learning, leading to six methods for comparison.

Table 1. Comparison of accuracy and loss of different networks on the FER2013 test set

Network	Accuracy	Loss
ResNet-50	79.19	1.0435
Migration Learning ResNet-50	78.76	1.0395
MobileNet	61.54	1.3921
Migration Learning MobileNet	81.12	1.0004
MobileNetV2	66.68	1.342
Migration Learning MobileNetV2	79.9	1.0209
Interspersed residual and inverted residual network	79.36	1.0313
MR residual and inverted residual network	75.72	1.1
RM residual and inverted residual network	**81.98**	**0.9803**

(1) ResNet-50 is the baseline model in this paper. ResNet-50, MobileNetV1, and MobileNetV2 that used transfer learning were upgraded by - 0.43%, 19.58%, and 13.22% respectively on the Fer2013 dataset compared with results without using transfer learning. Due to the serious over-fitting of ResNet-50, the accuracy is reduced.

(2) Transfer learning adopted by MobileNet and MobileNetV2 witness a 2.36% and 1.14% improvement respectively compared with ResNet-50 in recognition accuracy, which proves that series network like MobileNet has great demand for transfer

learning. MobileNet based network has the advantage of smaller scale hashes and faster convergence.

(3) In the absence of transfer learning, the accuracy of the alternated residual and inverted residual network is 0.17%, 17.82%, and 12.68% higher than that of ResNet-50, MobileNetV1, and MobileNetV2. Compared to MobileNet based network, its demand for transfer learning is significantly reduced, and its over-fitting problem is well suppressed compared to the ResNet-50 network.

(4) The accuracy of the proposed alternated network compared with the transfer learning based MobileNet and MoblineNetV2 is a little lower. However, the stability of our method is far better than that of MobileNet and MoblineNetV2. As the proposed method does not adopt transfer learning, it still got quite comparable result.

(5) Another finding is that, for the IR and RI residual and inverted residual networks, the accuracy of IR is reduced by 3.64% compared with the alternated type, while the RI network takes a leading position. RI network requires smaller number of iterations for fitting, indicating wonderful stability and lowest loss. Besides, it got the best accuracy with a nearly 82% accuracy. The accuracy is improved by 2.62% compared with the alternated network. Also, it compensates for the problem of overfitting which is severe for ResNet.

4.4 Results on CK+ Dataset

In order to further verify the effectiveness of the proposed residual and inverted residual network, the three residual and inverted residual block networks are further verified on the CK+ dataset. The following data is the test results of the validation optimal network after 1200 epoch training, given in Table 2.

Table 2. Comparison of accuracy and loss of different networks on CK+ test set.

Network	test_acc	test_loss
Interspersed residual and inverted residual network	96.70%	0.13781
RM residual and inverted residual network	**97.41%**	**0.09756**
MR residual and inverted residual network	95.92%	0.15331

In a laboratory environment where the image is clearer, the RI residual and inverted residual network still achieves the highest accuracy and lowest loss. Since the residual block is first compressed and then expanded, and the inverted residual block is first expanded and then compressed, the shape of the RI residual and inverted residual network is closer to the shape of a pyramid. When the number of layers being observed increases, the collected features by CNN network change from a lower level to a higher level. By using as many parameters as possible on a high level fitting, better expression recognition performance and fitting ability can be obtained, which also explains why the RI residual and inverted residual network can achieve better results.

5   Conclusion

In this paper, the residual and inverted residual blocks are combined and applied to the research of facial expression recognition. It adopts the two kinds of residual blocks iteratively in the designed network structure, which jointly promotes the feature representation ability of the neural network and alleviates the problem of feature dispersion caused by deep network shown in the traditional facial expression recognition research. The experimental results show that the RI residual network has achieved the best results in the three Bi-directional residual networks proposed in this paper, whose accuracy has increased by 2.62% compared with the alternated bi-directional residual network. It also compensates for the problem of over-fitting of ResNet. Meanwhile, the algorithm inherits the excellent features of ResNet and MobileNetV2 with high accuracy, robust to over-fitting, and impressive recognition performance. The next step of this research is to take a step further and accomplish the study on network confusion matrix data based on the transfer of the RI residual and inverted residual network. Considering that the network structure should be further optimized, it is also possible to try to improve and fine-tune the network structure.

Acknowledgement. The study was supported by the Major Project of Natural Science Research of the Jiangsu Higher Education Institutions of China (18KJA520012), and the Xuzhou Science and Technology Plan Project (KC19197).

References

1. Akiba, T., Suzuki, S., Fukuda, K.: Extremely large minibatch SGD: training ResNet-50 on ImageNet in 15 minutes (2017)
2. Balduzzi, D., Frean, M., Leary, L., Lewis, J.P., Mcwilliams, B.: The shattered gradients problem: if ResNets are the answer, then what is the question? (2017)
3. Barsoum, E., Zhang, C., Ferrer, C.C., Zhang, Z.: Training deep networks for facial expression recognition with crowd-sourced label distribution. In: ACM International Conference on Multimodal Interaction (2016)
4. Bengio, Y.: Knowledge matters: importance of prior information for optimization (2016)
5. Chen, Y., Li, J., Xiao, H., Jin, X., Yan, S., Feng, J.: Dual path networks (2017)
6. Chollet, F.: Xception: deep learning with depthwise separable convolutions. In: IEEE Conference on Computer Vision Pattern Recognition (2017)
7. Glorot, X., Bengio, Y.: Understanding the difficulty of training deep feedforward neural networks, pp. 249–256 (2010)
8. Gu, W., Xiang, C., Venkatesh, Y.V., Huang, D., Lin, H.: Facial expression recognition using radial encoding of local Gabor features and classifier synthesis. Pattern Recogn. 45(1), 80–91 (2012)
9. Guan-Ming, L.U., Guo, M., Xiao-Nan, L.I., Hai-Bo, L.I.: Recognition for expression of pain in neonate using support vector machine. J. Nanjing Univ. Posts Telecommun. 25(3), 582–587 (2008)
10. Guan-Ming, L.U., Zuo, J.K.: Feature extraction based on two-dimensional locality preserving discriminant analysis. J. Nanjing Univ. Posts Telecommun. (2014)
11. He, K., Zhang, X., Ren, S., Sun, J.: Deep residual learning for image recognition (2015)

12. Ioffe, S., Szegedy, C.: Batch normalization: accelerating deep network training by reducing internal covariate shift (2015)
13. Lucey, P., Cohn, J.F., Kanade, T., Saragih, J., Matthews, I.: The extended Cohn-Kanade dataset (CK+): a complete dataset for action unit and emotion-specified expression. In: Computer Vision Pattern Recognition Workshops (2010)
14. Mehrabian, A.: Communication without words. Commun. Theory **6**, 193–200 (2008)
15. Mollahosseini, A., Chan, D., Mahoor, M.H.: Going deeper in facial expression recognition using deep neural networks. In: IEEE Winter Conference on Applications of Computer Vision (2016)
16. Orhan, A.E., Pitkow, X.: Skip connections eliminate singularities (2017)
17. Ping, L., Han, S., Meng, Z., Yan, T.: Facial expression recognition via a boosted deep belief network. In: IEEE Conference on Computer Vision Pattern Recognition (2014)
18. Rusiecki, A.: Trimmed categorical cross-entropy for deep learning with label noise. Electron. Lett. **55**(6), 319–320 (2019)
19. Sandler, M., Howard, A., Zhu, M., Zhmoginov, A., Chen, L.C.: MobileNetV2: inverted residuals and linear bottlenecks (2018)
20. Shan, C., Gong, S., Mcowan, P.W.: Facial expression recognition based on local binary patterns: a comprehensive study. Image Vis. Comput. **27**(6), 803–816 (2009)
21. Shan, L., Deng, W.: Deep facial expression recognition: a survey (2018)
22. Szegedy, C., Ioffe, S., Vanhoucke, V.: Inception-v4, inception-ResNet and the impact of residual connections on learning (2016)
23. Wang, X., Chao, J., Wei, L., Min, H., Ren, F.: Feature fusion of HOG and WLD for facial expression recognition. In: IEEE/SICE International Symposium on System Integration (2013)
24. Wu, Z., Shen, C., Van Den Hengel, A.: Wider or deeper: revisiting the ResNet model for visual recognition, vol. 90 (2016)
25. Yang, H., Ciftci, U., Yin, L.: Facial expression recognition by de-expression residue learning. Int. J. Comput. Sci. Eng. (2018)
26. Yu, Z., Zhang, C.: Image based static facial expression recognition with multiple deep network learning. In: ACM on International Conference on Multimodal Interaction (2015)

A Traffic Feature Analysis Approach for Converged Networks of LTE and Broadband Carrier Wireless Communications

Huan Li[1(✉)], Yang Liu[1], Fanbo Meng[2], Zhibin Yang[1], Dongdong Wang[2], and Yang Nan[3]

[1] Electric Power Research Institute of State Grid Liaoning Electric Power Supply Co., Ltd., Shenyang 110006, China
[2] State Grid Liaoning Electric Power Supply Co., Ltd., Shenyang 110004, China
[3] BaoDing HaoYuan Electric Technology Co., Ltd., Baoding 071000, Hebei, China

Abstract. With the emergence of new requirements for the application of network access network, network traffic presents new characteristics, and network management faces new challenges. The main contribution of this paper is to propose a new network traffic model and prediction method based on generalized linear regression model. Firstly, the network traffic is modeled and generalized linear regression model is used to model it. Then, using the generalized linear regression theory, we can calculate the modified parameters and determine the appropriate model, so that we can accurately predict the network traffic. The simulation results show that the method is feasible.

Keywords: Network traffic · Generalized linear regression · Traffic modeling · Parameter estimation · Traffic prediction

1 Introduction

With the rise of smart grid related research, due to its unique characteristics, power line communication plays an increasingly important role in the power network. In the communication from the user terminal to the service switching point, wireless communication technology occupies a place and occupies a dominant position. As a kind of connection communication mode [1, 2], wireless communication can save cost, provide voice, data, video and other comprehensive services, and can meet the bandwidth, speed, waiting time and other QoS requirements. However, with the combination of intelligent devices and the rapid development of new intelligent network applications, the traditional intelligent network technology has brought great pressure to the traditional intelligent network. How to solve this problem is an important research direction, and there is no feasible solution to solve this problem.

In the network of wireless communication LTE and broadband providers, the network traffic has the update and unknown characteristics compared with the traditional network structure [5, 6]. How to effectively analyze and evaluate the transmission characteristics

© ICST Institute for Computer Sciences, Social Informatics and Telecommunications Engineering 2021
Published by Springer Nature Switzerland AG 2021. All Rights Reserved
H. Song and D. Jiang (Eds.): SIMUtools 2020, LNICST 369, pp. 183–193, 2021.
https://doi.org/10.1007/978-3-030-72792-5_17

of the network is a difficult problem to be solved; many algorithms can be used for network feature modeling and analysis, which is a new method to extract network traffic characteristics [7, 8]. Principal component analysis (PCA), RBM model and decision tree based model can predict network traffic in aggregation network [9, 10].

Deep learning model can also be used for network traffic analysis. Specific transmission modes can be classified by monitoring machine learning [11, 12]. At the same time, time-frequency analysis can be combined with network feature analysis to analyze the characteristics of traffic flow [15, 16]; the combination of recurrent neural network (RNN) and convolutional neural network (CNN) can also be used to construct intelligent, network traffic classifier with high recognition rate [17, 18].

The above methods can be used for network traffic modeling and analysis, but in the converged network, the network feature types are more complex. Compared with the traditional methods, the advantage of this method is that the traditional transmission analysis method is difficult to apply to this situation.

Figure 1 shows the converged communication network architecture based on LTE mobile and broadband operators. LTE wireless base station can not only transmit IP signal through IP network, but also use broadband carrier as support carrier of data transmission, and use licensed frequency band as main carrier [19, 20]. At present, the free and unauthorized frequency resources are determined by the cognition of related professions [21, 22]. It is an accurate and effective method to model and predict network traffic based on AR model and Taylor series. Generally speaking, terminals and base stations can control wireless resources within the approved frequency band. Because of the high temporal variability of network traffic, it is difficult to describe it in mathematical terms, so it is difficult to establish a model to simulate network traffic. In this paper, we use AR model for static parts and Taylor model for inactive parts. This defines model parameters based on network data, and then. Then we propose a new prediction algorithm to accurately evaluate network traffic and the simulation results show the effectiveness and application prospect of this method.

The rest of this paper is structured as follows. In Sect. 2, we build a mathematical model and describe the method. In Sect. 3, the experimental simulation is carried out, and the analysis of the results is given. Finally, we summarize our work in Sect. 4.

2 Problem Statement

Network traffic divides into stable and unstable parts. The stable component is the most important Energy in the transmission. The unstable component changes greatly with the passage of time, and network traffic details will also change. We use $x_S(t)$ to represent stable components $x_{NS}(t)$, and show the Components prompt in it. To better simulate flow, two methods are used in [24].

Firstly, $x(t)$ can be divided into stable and unstable parts by STFT, and $x(t) \in L^2(R)$ (the STFT with the window function $g(t)$) is assumed to be the following STFT.

$$WX_g(\omega, b) = \int_{-\infty}^{\infty} x(t)g(t-b)e^{-j\omega t}dt \tag{1}$$

In the above equation, b is the time domain migration parameter, ω is the frequency domain migration parameter, and $WX_g(\omega, b)$ is the spectral characteristics near the $t = b$.

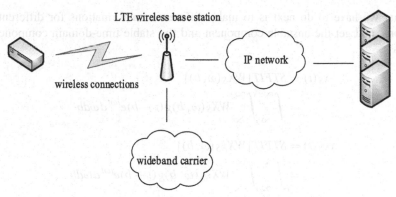

Fig. 1. The integrated network architecture of LTE wireless and broadband carrier communications.

Then, we can set $g(t)$ that meets this condition.

$$g_{\omega,b}(t) = g(t-b)e^{-j\omega t} \tag{2}$$

The Eq. (1) then is equal to:

$$WX_g(\omega, b) = \int_{-\infty}^{\infty} x(t)\overline{g}_{\omega,b}(t)dt = <x(t), g_{\omega,b}(t)> \tag{3}$$

When and only if the effective window width of $g(t)$ is D_t, $WX_g(\omega, b)$ can get the spectrum information of $x(t)$ in $[b - D_t/2, b + D_t/2]$ time interval.

Owing to the main Energy Sources of the Rivers are concentrated in the stable Components, the details are reflected in the unstable Components, it is only necessary to segment the Band signals in the frequency range.

Obviously, low pass filter and high pass filter are selected to filter the transformed time series $WX_g(\omega, b)$ [27, 28]. For low-pass filter, we can choose exponential low-pass filter, the formula is as follows.

$$H_L(u, v) = e^{-\left[\frac{\sqrt{u^2+v^2}}{D_0}\right]^{2n}} \tag{4}$$

Due to the filtering of low-pass filter, the stable part of the original signal can be obtained as follows:

$$WX_S(\omega, b) = WX_g(\omega, b) \circ H_L(\omega, b) \tag{5}$$

For high pass filter, since Butterworth high pass filter is selected, its formula will be as follows:

$$H_H(u, v) = 1\Big/(1 + (D_0\Big/\sqrt{u^2+v^2})^{2n}) \tag{6}$$

The unstable components of $WX_g(\omega, b)$ can be obtained by high pass filter [29, 30].

$$WX_{NS}(\omega, b) = WX_g(\omega, b) \circ H_H(\omega, b) \tag{7}$$

What we have to do next is to make different transformations for different distributions, and get the unstable component and the stable time-domain component as follows

$$x_S(t) = STFIT[WX_S(\omega, b)]$$
$$= \int_{-\infty}^{\infty} \int_{-\infty}^{\infty} WX_S(\omega, b)g(t-b)e^{j\omega t}d\omega db \qquad (8)$$

$$x_{NS}(t) = STFIT[WX_{NS}(\omega, b)]$$
$$= \int_{-\infty}^{\infty} \int_{-\infty}^{\infty} WX_{NS}(\omega, b)g(t-b)e^{j\omega t}d\omega db \qquad (9)$$

The stable component $x_S = \{x_S(t), t = 1, 2, 3, ...\}$ changes slowly and become a strong short correlation term. The author's AR model is widely used in linear forecasting, which can extract data from the model. The AR model is better than the interpolation method [31, 32], which is the representation of historical data Random. The process of this model may be as follows.

$$\begin{cases} x_S(t) = \varphi_1 x_S(t-1) + \cdots + \varphi_p x_S(t-p) + \theta(t) \\ E(\theta(t)) = 0 \\ E(\theta(s)\theta(t)) = \begin{cases} \sigma^2, s = t \\ 0, s \neq t \end{cases} \\ E(\theta(s)X_L(t)) = 0, s \neq t \end{cases} \qquad (10)$$

where φ_i is the auto-regressive coefficient that affects the other parameters, $\theta(t)$ is the disturbance term at the time t, p is the order of the AR model.

Then, we establish a queue model to describe the disturbance term of the network traffic, so as to obtain a model which obeys Poisson distribution and probability distribution [33, 34]. Finally, we express the mathematical description of the stable component as follows.

$$\theta(t) = \alpha\theta_p(t) + \beta\theta_e(t) \qquad (11)$$

In the above formula, the parameters $\theta_p(t) \sim P(\lambda_1)$ and $\theta_e(t) \sim e(\lambda_2)$, λ_1 and λ_2 are the relevant parameters of the model distribution respectively. In addition, α and β are traffic interference coefficients. The probability function of our model can be written as

$$P(\theta_p(t)) = \lambda_1^k \exp(-\lambda_1/\theta_p(t)!) \qquad (12)$$

$$P(X < \theta_e(t)) = \begin{cases} 1 - \exp(-\theta_e(t)/\lambda_2), \theta_e(t) > 0 \\ 0, \qquad \theta_e(t) \leq 0 \end{cases} \qquad (13)$$

Since we need to estimate the AR model parameters, there are three methods that can be considered. Moment. According to the characteristics of the model, we choose the moment estimation method [35, 36]. In this way, the coefficients of the model can be described by mathematical formulas, as shown below.

$$
\begin{bmatrix} \varphi_1 \\ \varphi_2 \\ \cdots \\ \varphi_p \end{bmatrix} = \begin{bmatrix} \rho_0 & \rho_1 & \cdots & \rho_{p-1} \\ \rho_1 & \rho_0 & \cdots & \rho_{p-2} \\ \vdots & \vdots & \ddots & \vdots \\ \rho_{p-1} & \rho_{p-2} & \cdots & \rho_0 \end{bmatrix}^{-1} \begin{bmatrix} \rho_1 \\ \rho_2 \\ \cdots \\ \rho_p \end{bmatrix}
$$

(14)

In the above formula, $\hat{\rho}_k = \gamma_k/\gamma_0 = \sum_{t=k+1}^{N} X_t X_{t-k} / \sum_{t=1}^{N} X_t^2$ is the autocorrelation function of the model. Furthermore, we can get the stable component of network traffic according to the above conclusions and expressions.

$$
\hat{x}_S(t) = \begin{cases} \sum_{i=1}^{p} \varphi_i x_S(t-i), t = 1 \\ \sum_{t=1}^{s-1} \varphi_i \hat{x}_S(t-i) + \sum_{t=1}^{p} \varphi_i x_S(t-i), 1 < t \leq p \\ \sum_{i=1}^{p} \varphi_t \hat{x}_S(t-i), t > p \end{cases}
$$

(15)

Naturally, the stable part $x_S(t)$ can be predicted by known conditions.

The unstable part includes more detailed information on network traffic and fluctuations. A general function can be approximated to a finite number of dates in the Taylor series. Theoretical Taylor gives a quantitative estimate of the error produced using this approach. It is the polynomial that records several initial conditions of Taylor's sequence. It's Taylor polynomial. This model extracts two concepts from the Taylor series of unstable components.

Therefore, we use the classical theory of Taylor series to express the unstable component.

$$
x_{NS}(t) = \sum_{n=0}^{\infty} \frac{x_{NS}^{(n)}(t_0)}{n!} (t - t_0)^n
$$

(16)

In the allowable range of error, the redundant terms of Taylor series of unstable components are removed.

$$
\hat{x}_{NS}(t) = \frac{x'_{NS}(t_0)}{n!} (t - t_0) + \frac{x''_{NS}(t_0)}{n!} (t - t_0)^2
$$

(17)

The final expression of the flow is as follows.

$$
\hat{x}(t) = \hat{x}_S(t) + \hat{x}_{NS}(t)
$$

(18)

Combined with the above mathematical derivation, we can design such an algorithm.

Step 1: According to formula (8), (9), the network is classified into two categories: steady state and unsteady state;

Step 2: According to formula (10), for Part 1, the method in (10) can be used for parameter setting;

Step 3: The selected probability method be used for parameter estimation;

Step 4: According to formula (17), the mathematical description of Part 2 is carried out and the approximate expression is established;

Step 5: Combine part one and part two to get the whole estimation model and calculate the result;

The final algorithm flow chart is shown in Fig. 2.

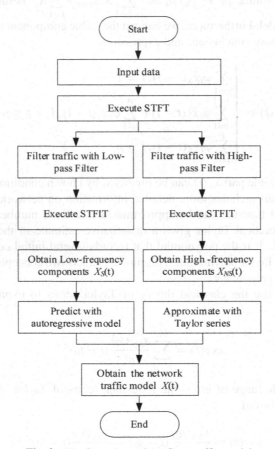

Fig. 2. The flow chart of the flow traffic model.

3 Simulation Results and Analysis

In this part, we conducted many tests to demonstrate our algorithm GLMTMA. We verify GLMTMA using real data from the U.S. real Abilene backbone. In order to highlight the performance of our algorithm, we compare our method with the best method today. All the experimental data are true and reliable. First of all, we carried out several groups of experiments on different methods. After the experiment, we analyze the network traffic prediction results of GLMTMA algorithm, and compare GLMTMA with other methods, and give the average relative error of network traffic of four algorithms. Moreover, in order to better highlight the performance ratio of the algorithm, we discuss the performance improvement of GLMTMA on PCA, WABR and HMPA. In our simulation, the data of the first 500 slots are used to train the models, while the other data are used to verify the performance of all algorithms.

Figure 3 shows the prediction results of network traffic 53 and 96, in which network traffic 53 and 96 are randomly selected from 144 end-to-end service pairs (or flows) in the Abilene backbone network. In our experiments, the results are basically in a stable range. The experiment only selected the most classic network traffic 53 and 96. Network traffic is also known as an origin destination (OD) pair. Figure 1(a) shows that GLMTMA can detect the dynamic changes of network flow 53 very quickly. For different time slots, the network traffic in the experiment also has a significant change law with time.

Obviously, we can draw the following conclusion from Fig. 3(a). Our algorithm can well detect the change trend of network traffic. In addition, as shown in Fig. 3(b), the change trend of network flow 96 is in winter. Although our method has a large prediction error for network traffic 96 under experimental conditions, it can still capture its changing trend. We also show a method that can effectively predict the change in network traffic over time.

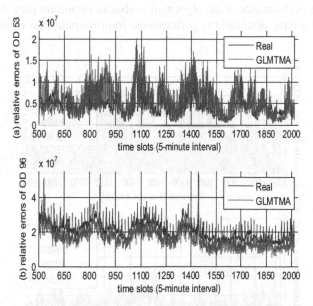

Fig. 3. Prediction results of network traffic flows 53 and 96.

From the above we can see that our method has good performance. In view of the limitation that traditional methods are difficult to detect the dynamic trend of network traffic, we can effectively solve this limitation. In order to further verify our method, we conducted a number of grouping experiments, each of which had more than 500 repetitions. The average relative prediction error is calculated.

The expression of average relative prediction error is as follow:

$$d(t) = \frac{1}{N} \sum_{i=1}^{N} \frac{||\hat{y}_i(t) - y_i(t)||_2}{||y_i(t)||_2} \tag{19}$$

In the above formula, $i = 1, 2, ..., N$ and N are the running times of the experimental algorithm, $||.||_2$ is the norm of L_2, and $\hat{y}_i(t)$ is the traffic prediction value of i running in time slot t.

Figure 4 shows the average relative prediction error of four algorithms for network level traffic 53 and 96. It can be seen from the figure that the relative errors of three methods (WABR, HMPA and GLMTMA) are relatively small for the two classic traffic 53 and 96, while the prediction error of PCA is relatively large. In addition, we can also see that the relative error of GLMTMA is the smallest. Based on this, we can conclude that GLMTMA has better network traffic prediction ability than the other three methods. More importantly, considering the comparison of repeated experiments, we can see the stability of the algorithm from the fluctuation of the average value of the experiment. Compared with the other three algorithms, GLMTMA has better stability, especially in detecting the dynamic trend of network traffic, which makes it more suitable for network traffic prediction and network analysis modeling. Based on the above conclusion, GLMTMA can predict network traffic more effectively than previous methods.

Finally, the performance of the algorithm is also an important part. Through many experiments, we have obtained the performance improvement rate of network traffic

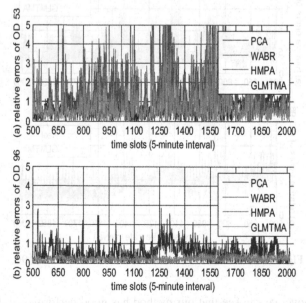

Fig. 4. Average relative errors for network traffic flows 53 and 96.

53 and 96, as shown in Fig. 5. For network traffic 53, GLMTMA is 23.1%, 20.3% and 1.33% higher than PCA, WABR and HMPA, respectively. In addition to the first time, for another network traffic, our method improves by 13.6%, 26.2% and 4.77% respectively compared with PCA, WABR and HMPA. The performance improvement of our method for other methods is at least 1.33%, and the maximum performance improvement is 23.1%. Moreover, this is the performance improvement under the condition of ensuring the prediction effect. This shows that our method has a comprehensive improvement over other methods in terms of performance. This is of great significance for the implementation of the algorithm. Because the efficiency and performance of the algorithm are closely related, the less the performance consumption and the faster the speed, the better the overall energy efficiency ratio. Based on this, we can see that our method has relative advantages in specific implementation, and can be better used as a tool for network traffic prediction.

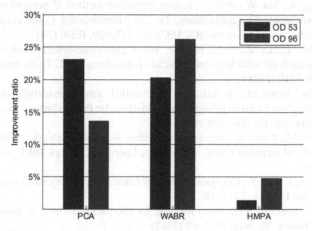

Fig. 5. Improvement ratio of network traffic flows 53 and 96.

4 Conclusions

A network traffic modeling and prediction method proposed in this paper, which is based on generalized linear regression theory. Different from the traditional methods, the generalized linear regression model with good robustness is selected to forecast the network flow. Firstly, we model the model in the way of probability, and express the parameters of the model with probability formula. Secondly, according to the regression characteristics of the model, the parameters of the model are iterated by the algorithm. Finally, through repeated iterations and calculations, we get the appropriate model parameters, so as to get a model that can effectively describe the network traffic. The simulation results show that the method is effective.

References

1. Zhang, Y., Liu, F., Pang, H., et al.: Research on smart grid power line broadband communication system. IOP Conf. Ser. Mater. Sci. Eng. **466**(1), 012075 (2018)
2. Sharma, K., Saini, L.M.: Power-line communications for smart grid: progress, challenges, opportunities and status. Renew. Sustain. Energ. Rev. **67**, 704–751 (2017)
3. Jiang, D., Wang, Y., Lv, Z., Qi, S., Singh, S.: Big data analysis based network behavior insight of cellular networks for industry 4.0 applications. IEEE Trans. Ind. Inform. **16**(2), 1310–1320 (2020)
4. Wang, D.: Bandwidth prediction for business requirement of electric power communication network with deep-learning. In: 2018 3rd International Workshop on Materials Engineering and Computer Sciences (IWMECS 2018). Atlantis Press (2018)
5. Casas, P., D'Alconzo, A., Wamser, F., et al.: Predicting QoE in cellular networks using machine learning and in-smartphone measurements. In: 2017 Ninth International Conference on Quality of Multimedia Experience (QoMEX), pp. 1–6. IEEE (2017)
6. Wu, F., Jiang, X., Ma, W., et al.: A feature extraction method of network traffic for time-frequency synchronization applications. In: 2017 International Conference on Computer Systems, Electronics and Control (ICCSEC), pp. 537–539. IEEE (2017)
7. Jiang, D., Huo, L., Lv, Z., Song, H., Qin, W.: A joint multi-criteria utility-based network selection approach for vehicle-to-infrastructure networking. IEEE Trans. Intel. Transp. Syst. **19**(10), 3305–3319 (2018)
8. Meidan, Y., Bohadana, M., Shabtai, A., et al.: ProfilIoT: a machine learning approach for IoT device identification based on network traffic analysis. In: Proceedings of the Symposium on Applied Computing, pp. 506–509. ACM (2017)
9. Lopez-Martin, M., Carro, B., Sanchez-Esguevillas, A., et al.: Network traffic classifier with convolutional and recurrent neural networks for Internet of Things. IEEE Access **5**, 18042–18050 (2017)
10. Jiang, D., Huo, L., Li, Y.: Fine-granularity inference and estimations to network traffic for SDN. PloS One **13**(5), 1–23 (2018)
11. Polson, N.G., Sokolov, V.O.: Deep learning for short-term traffic flow prediction. Transp. Res. Part C: Emerg. Technol. **79**, 1–17 (2017)
12. Saeed, A.T., Esmailpour, A.: Quality of service class mapping and scheduling scheme for converged LTE-WiFi in the next generation networks. Int. J. Commun. Netw. Distrib. Syst. **23**(3), 352–379 (2019)
13. Jiang, D., Wang, W., Shi, L., Song, H.: A compressive sensing-based approach to end-to-end network traffic reconstruction. IEEE Trans. Netw. Sci. Eng. **7**(1), 507–519 (2020)
14. Vaton, S., Bedo, J.: Network traffic matrix: how can one learn the prior distributions from the link counts only. In: Proceedings of ICC 2004, pp. 2138–2142 (2004)
15. Lad, M., Oliveira, R., Massey, D., et al.: Inferring the origin of routing changes using link weights. In: Proceedings of ICNP, pp. 93–102 (2007)
16. Tune, P., Veitch, D.: Sampling vs sketching: an information theoretic comparison. In: Proceedings of INFOCOM, pp. 2105–2113 (2011)
17. Huo, L., Jiang, D., Lv, Z., et al.: An intelligent optimization-based traffic information acquirement approach to software-defined networking. Comput. Intell. **36**, 151–171 (2020)
18. Wang, F., Jiang, D., Qi, S., et al.: A dynamic resource scheduling scheme in edge computing satellite networks. Mob. Netw. Appl. (2019). https://doi.org/10.1007/s11036-019-01421-5
19. Chekired, D., Khoukhi, L., Mouftah, H.: Decentralized cloud-SDN architecture in smart grid: a dynamic pricing model. IEEE Trans. Ind. Inform. **14**(3), 1220–1231 (2018)
20. Jiang, D., Wang, Y., Lv, Z., Wang, W., Wang, H.: An energy-efficient networking approach in cloud services for IIoT networks. IEEE J. Sel. Areas Commun. **38**(5), 928–941 (2020)

21. Wang, Y., Jiang, D., Huo, L., Zhao, Y.: A new traffic prediction algorithm to software defined networking. Mob. Netw. Appl. (2019). https://doi.org/10.1007/s11036-019-01423-3

22. Chen, W., Liu, B., Huang, H., et al.: When UAV swarm meets edge-cloud computing: the QoS perspective. IEEE Netw. **33**, 36–43 (2019)

23. Jiang, D., Li, W., Lv, H.: An energy-efficient cooperative multicast routing in multi-hop wireless networks for smart medical applications. Neurocomputing **2017**(220), 160–169 (2017)

24. Liu, B., Jia, D., Wang, J., et al.: Cloud-assisted safety message dissemination in VANET–cellular heterogeneous wireless network. IEEE Syst. J. **11**(1), 128–139 (2017)

25. Zhou, Y., Zhu, X.: Analysis of vehicle network architecture and performance optimization based on soft definition of integration of cloud and fog. IEEE Access **7**(2019), 101171–101177 (2019)

26. El-sayed, H., Sankar, S., Prasad, M., et al.: Edge of things: the big picture on the integration of edge, IoT and the cloud in a distributed computing environment. IEEE Access **6**, 1706–1717 (2018)

27. Jiang, D., Huo, L., Song, H.: Rethinking behaviors and activities of base stations in mobile cellular networks based on big data analysis. IEEE Trans. Netw. Sci. Eng. **7**(1), 80–90 (2020)

28. Zhang, K., Mao, Y., Leng, S., et al.: Mobile-edge computing for vehicular networks. IEEE Veh. Technol. Mag. **12**, 36–44 (2017)

29. Pu, L., Chen, X., Mao, G., et al.: Chimera: an energy-efficient and deadline-aware hybrid edge computing framework for vehicular crowdsensing applications. IEEE Internet Things J. **6**(1), 84–99 (2019)

30. Eldjali, C., Lyes, K.: Optimal priority-queuing for EV charging-discharging service based on cloud computing. In: Proceedings of ICC 2017, pp. 1–6 (2017)

31. Jiang, D., Zhang, P., Lv, Z., et al.: Energy-efficient multi-constraint routing algorithm with load balancing for smart city applications. IEEE Internet Things J. **3**(6), 1437–1447 (2016)

32. Xie, R., Tang, Q., Wang, Q., et al.: Collaborative vehicular edge computing networks: architecture design and research challenges. IEEE Access **7**(2019), 178942–178952 (2019)

33. Qi, S., Jiang, D., Huo, L.: A prediction approach to end-to-end traffic in space information networks. Mob. Netw. Appl. (2019). https://doi.org/10.1007/s11036-019-01424-2

34. Yang, Y., Niu, X., Li, L., et al.: A secure and efficient transmission method in connected vehicular cloud computing. IEEE Netw. **32**, 14–19 (2018)

35. Kaur, K., Garg, S., Kaddoum, G., et al.: Demand-response management using a fleet of electric vehicles: an opportunistic-SDN-based edge-cloud framework for smart grids. IEEE Netw. **33**, 46–53 (2019)

36. Guo, H., Zhang, J., Liu, J.: FiWi-enhanced vehicular edge computing networks. IEEE Veh. Technol. Mag. **14**, 45–53 (2019)

37. Liu, H., Zhang, Y., Yang, T.: Blockchain-enabled security in electric vehicles cloud and edge computing. IEEE Netw. **32**, 78–83 (2018)

38. Wang, J., He, B., Wang, J., et al.: Intelligent VNFs selection based on traffic identification in vehicular cloud networks. IEEE Trans. Veh. Technol. **68**(5), 4140–4147 (2019)

39. Li, M., Si, P., Zhang, Y.: Delay-tolerant data traffic to software-defined vehicular networks with mobile edge computing in smart city. IEEE Trans. Veh. Technol. **67**(10), 9073–9086 (2018)

An IoV Route Planning Service Based on LEO Constellation Satellites

Jingyang Zhang[1], Bo Liu[2], WeiJiong Zhang[2], and Dingde Jiang[1(✉)]

[1] School of Astronautics and Aeronautic, University of Electronic Science and Technology of China, Chengdu 611731, China
jiangdd@uestc.edu.cn

[2] Shanghai Electro-Mechanical Engineering Institute, Shanghai 201109, China

Abstract. With the arrival of Internet of Things, the Internet of Vehicles (IoV) is also developing rapidly. However, the construction of ground network in remote areas is difficult and expensive. Additionally, for urban areas, the traffic situations are sudden, the load pressure of the ground network is too high in this period. This paper introduces a method of IoV path planning based on LEO constellation satellite. The satellite first conducts global situational awareness, the control center makes the initial route and then obtains the optimal path according to Dijkstra algorithm and the Ant Colony Optimization (DiAC). It makes up for the defects of ground communication. Simulation results show that the vehicle network path planning based on STK+MATLAB designed in this paper is feasible and can relieve the ground traffic pressure and network load pressure.

Keywords: LEO constellation · Satellite communications · Internet of vehicles · Route planning · Smart optimization

1 Introduction

With the remarkable development of the Internet of Things (IoT) in recent years, our society has taken another step towards ubiquitous communication [1]. In the smart city scenario, as a smart object with its own processor, computing power and communication capabilities, the vehicle will become indispensable smart device in the future human life due to its rapid growth and high mobility [2–5]. However, the construction of ground network in remote areas such as the central and western regions is difficult and expensive. Additionally, for urban areas, traffic conditions are sudden, during the situation similar to the morning peak, the load pressure of the ground network is too high in this period [6]. Therefore, it is very important to study a path planning for IoV based on LEO constellation satellites.

Internet of Vehicles (IoV) can be seen as the convergence of the mobile Internet and the traditional IoT. As a huge interactive network, IoV technology refers to vehicle-to-vehicle (V2V), vehicle-to-roadside unit (V2R), vehicle-to-infrastructure (V2I), vehicle-to-human (V2H) and vehicle-to-grid (V2G) [7–13]. In addition to safety applications

H. Song and D. Jiang (Eds.): SIMUtools 2020, LNICST 369, pp. 194–203, 2021.
https://doi.org/10.1007/978-3-030-72792-5_18

in terms of collision avoidance and dissemination of accident data, there is a large amount of research for development that can help the Traffic Information Center (TIC) handle effective route management, route planning, and diversions [14, 15]. Zhang et al. proposed a route planning method based on vehicles and driving environment [16]. Jiang et al. proposed an effective method to cooperative routing [17]. J. Yang et al. proposed to assign multiple TICs to smaller networks in a larger map [18]. Satellite communication is a powerful and achievable supplement to terrestrial communication [19]. Compared with the traditional GEO, LEO has the advantages of low loss, low delay, wide coverage and large order of magnitude [20]. The introduction of 5G satellite communications provides more possibilities for future IoT applications [21, 22]. Therefore, LEO satellite coverage can be used to access the network. It can be seen that the future network is based on LEO satellites.

Based on the above analysis, the research problem is the IoV route planning service based on LEO constellation satellites under complex traffic flow [23–27]. We calculate the current coverage satellite in real time according to the change of time, add the sensor. The satellite realizes the perception of global road conditions through wide coverage, and hands it to the ground control center to formulate a global route planning scheme. Then the UAV, as a mobile communication auxiliary node and an edge network access node, flew to complex traffic areas (such as intersections) to further plan the latest route. In this paper, we proposed a specific algorithm for IoV route planning service based on LEO constellation satellites. Dijkstra algorithm and ant colony algorithm (DiAC) is used to plan the path, which makes the vehicle travel faster and relieves the pressure of ground transportation and network load.

The rest of this paper is organized as follows. Section 2 establishes the mathematical model of the network. The algorithm of route planning is described in Sect. 3. Section 4 illustrates the simulation analysis. We then conclude our work in Sect. 5.

2   Network Model

To cover certain area on the ground in some period of future time, and provide communication services for path planning under the IoV, we calculate the current coverage satellite in real time according to the change of time and add the sensor. We can obtain the satellite orbit parameters required at time t to cover the area of the sub-satellite point center to get the satellites currently covered. First calculate the latitude of the sub-satellite point. The geo-centric geodetic coordinates (L, B, H) of the sub-satellite point can be obtained from the digital earth. The geocentric coordinates (r, φ, L) are calculated as follows:

$$
\begin{cases}
\phi = \arctan\left[\dfrac{N\left(1 - e_E^2\right) + H}{N + H} \tan B\right] \\
r = (N + H)\dfrac{\cos B}{\cos \phi}
\end{cases}
\tag{1}
$$

$$
\begin{cases}
N = a_E / \sqrt{1 - e_E^2 \sin^2 B} \\
e_E^2 = 0.00669437999013 \\
a_E = 6378137\text{m}
\end{cases}
\tag{2}
$$

where B is earth latitude, north latitude is positive, south latitude is negative; L is longitude, east longitude is positive, and west longitude is negative.

When the sub-satellite point is (L, B, H), the satellite's flying height H_S, the satellite's geocentric radial direction $r_s = r + H_s$; the satellite's geocentric spatial rectangular coordinates (x_D, y_D, z_D) are calculated according to Eq. (3):

$$\begin{cases} x_D = r_S \cos\phi \cos L \\ y_D = r_S \cos\phi \sin L \\ z_D = r_S \sin\phi \end{cases} \tag{3}$$

The calculation of the hemispherical coordinates of the satellite at the future t at the center of the hotspot area is the conversion of the above-mentioned rectangular coordinates (x_D, y_D, z_D) of the geocentric space of the satellite into J2000.0.

Using the parameters of the elliptical orbit of the orbiting satellite and the flying height, by solving the system of equations, the velocity components (v_x, v_y, v_z) of the satellite in the hemispherical coordinate system are calculated when the latitude and longitude of the satellite's sub-satellite point at time t are L and B, respectively. The satellite operating speed v at time t can be calculated by Eq. (4):

$$v = \sqrt{\mu\left(\frac{2}{r_s} - \frac{1}{a}\right)} \tag{4}$$

where $\mu = 3.986004418 \times 10^{14} \ m^3/s^2$.

The satellite moves in elliptical orbit, and gets:

$$\begin{cases} \tan i = \frac{\sqrt{(yv_z - zv_y)^2 + (zv_x - xv_z)^2}}{xv_y - yv_x} \\ e = \sqrt{\frac{(xv_x + yv_y + zv_z)^2}{a\mu} + \left(1 - \frac{r_S}{a}\right)^2} \\ v^2 = v_x^2 + v_y^2 + v_z^2 \end{cases} \tag{5}$$

Among them, the semi-major axis a of the elliptical orbit of the orbiting satellite $a = 7177864.881 \ m$, the eccentricity $e = 0.0020$, the orbit inclination angle $i = 98.40°$, x, y, z is the satellite's flat sphere coordinate in epoch J2000.0.

Iterative method is used to obtain (v_x, v_y, v_z). Using mature software, the satellite's orbital parameters $a, e, i, \Omega, \varpi, M$ are obtained from the calculation of the satellite's position and velocity in the hemispherical coordinate system, and input the orbital parameters into the STK for simulation, we can calculate real-time coverage satellite.

3   Route Planning Algorithm

The route planning algorithm DiAC is divided into two parts: initial path planning and path optimization. Our IoV route planning strategy based on LEO constellation satellites is shown in Fig. 1.

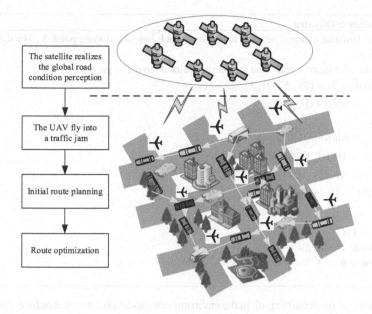

Fig. 1. Route planning strategy.

We model the intersection mathematically as a weight map. The congestion of the intersection will be detected by the UAV, based on the detected traffic flow of the current intersection, and the feedback of the current intersection congestion of the vehicle will be fed back to the vehicle to update the intersection weight. Carry out vehicle scheduling and plan vehicle travel paths. Therefore, our task is to quickly find an effective path that can be driven in the route planning of satellite car networking based on the LEO constellation, and to ensure the shortest path length while driving effectively. Therefore, we propose to use Dijkstra algorithm and ant colony optimization (ACO) algorithm (DiAC) to plan the path. Suppose the starting point is S, the destination node is T, and the objective function can be expressed as:

$$L(S, T) = \min[L(N_c, m)] \tag{6}$$

where $L(S, T)$ represents the path length, N_c stands for the number of iterations, $L(N_c, m)$ denotes the path length of the $m\text{-}th$ ant moving in the second iteration in the path planning process.

Dijkstra algorithm: Dijkstra algorithm has high reliability and robustness. It is often used to solve the shortest path problem in path planning. Therefore, we use the Dijkstra algorithm in the initial path planning as shown in Algorithm.

Algorithm 1: Dijkstra

Input: Distance matrix L between the nodes of each link, the starting point S, The destination node T.

Output: The shortest path from the starting point S to the target node T.

1: **Initialize** $M = \{S\}$, $N = \{V_1, V_2, ..., V_n, T\}$,

2:     $dist[V_i] = c[V_i][V_j]$

3: **do**

4:     $V_k = \min\{dist[V_i][V_j] \mid V_i \in N\}$

5:     $M = M \cup \{V_k\}$, $N = N - \{V_k\}$

6:     For vertex V_k in N

7:     **if** ($dist[V_k] + L[V_k][V_j] < dist[V_k] + L[V_k][V_j]$)

8:         $dist[V_i] = dist[V_k] + L[V_k][V_j]$

9:     **end if**

10: **While** $N = \varnothing$

11: **return** $dist$

12: **end**

According to the feasible path in the environment model constructed before, construct the distance matrix L between the nodes of each link. The construction rule of the distance between adjacent nodes is obtained by Eq. (7), and the distance between non-adjacent nodes is set as ∞.

$$L(v_i, v_j) = ||v_i, v_j|| \tag{7}$$

Where v_i and v_j are the $i-th$ and $j-th$ points, respectively.

Set two sets M and N, the role of M is to record the vertices of the shortest path and the corresponding length. The role of N is to record the vertices that have not found the shortest path and the distance between the vertices and the starting node S. According to the shortest path of Dijkstra algorithm, the initial path is planned. The Dijkstra algorithm is as Algorithm 1 shows.

According to the Dijkstra algorithm, the path can be initialized, but the path is not optimal. Next, use the ACO to optimize the path. The new optimal path can be obtained by using ACO algorithm. The goal is to solve some optimal parameters $(\lambda_1, \lambda_2, \ldots, \lambda_n)$ on the link that the initial path traverses, so that the coordinates of each node satisfy Eq. (8).

$$Q_i(\lambda_i) = Q_i^0 + (Q_i^1 - Q_i^0) \times \lambda_i \quad \lambda_i \in [0, 1], i = 1, 2, \ldots, n \tag{8}$$

Among them, Q_i^0 and Q_i^1 are the coordinates of the two endpoints of the i-th link, and λ_i is the scale parameter of the link.

Ant colony optimization (ACO): The basic principle of ant colony algorithm is that during the foraging process of ants, the probability of the next path selection is determined by the pheromone concentration and the heuristic information on the path between the ants. Path selection is determined by this probability. The path transition probability formula is as follows:

$$P_{ij}^k = \begin{cases} \dfrac{[\tau_{ij}(t)]^\alpha [\eta_{ij}(t)]^\beta}{\displaystyle\sum_{s \in allowed_k} [\tau_{ir}(t)]^\alpha [\eta_{ir}(t)]^\beta} & s \in allowed_k \\ \\ 0 & otherwise \end{cases} \tag{9}$$

$$\eta_{ij}(t) = \frac{1}{d_{ij}} \tag{10}$$

where $allowed_k$ is the node set that the k-th ant can choose next. $\tau_{ij}(t)$ is the pheromone concentration on the path from the current node to the next node at time t. α is the pheromone heuristic factor, and β is the expected heuristic factor. $\eta_{ij}(t)$ is the heuristic function on the path from the current node to the next node at time t.d_{ij} is the distance from the i-th node to the j-th node.

In order to avoid the influence of pheromone changes on node selection, all ants need to update and adjust the pheromone according to formula (12) after completing a detailed search.

$$\tau_{ij}(t+1) = (1-\rho)\tau_{ij}(t) + \rho\Delta\tau_{ij}(t, t+1) \tag{11}$$

$$\Delta\tau_{ij}(t, t+1) = \begin{cases} \dfrac{Q}{L_k} & ij \in L_k \\ \\ 0 & otherwise \end{cases} \tag{12}$$

where ρ is the volatilization rate of pheromone. $\Delta\tau_{ij}(t, t+1)$ is the pheromone concentration increment. Q is the pheromone intensity, which is a constant greater than zero. L_k is the path length of the k-th ant in this search. So, the ant colony algorithm is used to optimize the initial path. The process is as follows:

Step 1: Initialize the parameters of the ant colony algorithm;
Step 2: Start the path search, select the next node according to the current node information and the next node selection principle;
Step 3: After selecting the next node, update the local pheromone on the path that the ant has just passed;
Step 4: Judge whether the ant reaches the target node, if true, jump to the next step, otherwise repeat step 2;
Step 5: Search the optimal path for the current search, update the global pheromone;
Step 6: Judge the number of iterations and end the search if true, otherwise repeat step 2.

4 Simulation Analysis

The whole scenery is first built in the STK, including the low-orbit constellation satellite network and the ground scenery. Choose the ground scenery as Beijing in the STK. In the ground scenery, we select nine intersections to create a total of 74 cars, and a uniform UAV with sensors near each intersection as shown in Fig. 2.

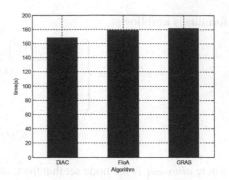

Fig. 2. Path planning results.

Fig. 3. Comparison of the same scale same congestion of intersection.

Taking the path planning of a car as an example, Fig. 2 shows the result of the path planning of the car from junction 1 to junction 9. Based on the DiAC algorithm, the optimum path from intersection 1 to intersection 9 is obtained, which is $1 \rightarrow 4 \rightarrow 5 \rightarrow 6 \rightarrow 9$. Ground traffic pressure and network load pressure are alleviated by vehicle network path planning algorithm based on low-orbit constellation satellite.

In order to evaluate the effect of the proposed DiAC algorithm, the Floyd-Warshall algorithm (FloA) and a method for calculating shortest path by using graphshortestpath (GRAS) are also built in MATLAB for comparison. In order to ensure that the evaluation results are reasonable, we take the average value after several times of each experiment. Firstly, evaluate the time required for the planned route at the same scale intersection (take 9 intersections as an example) and the congestion degree of the same intersection with the three methods.

As can be seen from Fig. 3, the time required by the car to plan the path according to the three methods is similar, and the proposed algorithm DiAC is slightly better than the other two algorithms. This is because in the DiAC method, when the car judges the next target intersection at any intersection, it can find the best next intersection. However, since the number of intersections is 9, the traffic situation is not very complicated at this time, so the results of the three algorithms are similar.

In order to evaluate the continuity of the algorithm, we considered the time required for the car to travel according to the path planning algorithm at the number of intersections of different sizes. The time obtained by the three algorithms at intersections of different sizes is shown in Fig. 4. It can be seen that the time under the three algorithms increases with the number of intersections. This is because the more complicated the intersection, the longer the car will travel, which is in line with our common sense of life. Among the three algorithms, the path planned by the DiAC algorithm requires less time. Since the DiAC algorithm is in the process of pathfinding, not only the shortest path but also the optimal path is considered, so when there are more intersections, the selected path can make the car travel faster.

Then, we compared the travel time of cars with different road congestion levels at the same intersection scale. The degree of road congestion can be expressed by the weight of each edge. The specific results are shown in Fig. 5. Here, nine intersections are used

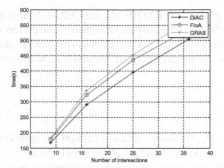
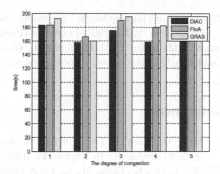

Fig. 4. Comparison of the different number of intersections.

Fig. 5. Comparison of the different congestion of intersection.

as examples to illustrate the problem. It can be seen that the car travel time is different under different congestion levels.

Among them, the travel time of the car obtained by the proposed DiAC method is lower than the other two. Shows the universality of the algorithm. When the degree of congestion changes, the proposed algorithm performs better than the other two methods. This is because the calculation speed and accuracy of the proposed DiAC algorithm path search are considered. As the degree of congestion changes, the importance of these two indicators becomes more and more prominent, thereby achieving a relatively uniform time change.

5 Conclusion

The LEO constellation satellite-based IoV is a supplement and extension to ground vehicle networking, which can greatly expand the coverage of ground IoV. Especially at the intersection, due to the complex road conditions, large traffic flow, the realization of intelligent traffic control requires a large number of concurrent connections and data calculations, intersection base stations are likely to overload, so there is an urgency to get the help from satellites and UVAs. Satellites and UAVs can cooperate with each other to achieve real-time control of vehicles within the coverage area and help base stations to relieve traffic pressure at the intersection. This paper introduces a method of IoV route planning based on low-orbit constellation satellite to provide the service of vehicle route planning. For providing path planning services, the satellite first carries out global situational awareness, and the control center formulates the initial route according to the Dijkstra algorithm, and then obtains the optimal path according to the Dijkstra algorithm and the ant colony algorithm (DiAC). Simulation results show that the design of STK+MATLAB IoV route planning based on LEO constellation satellite can be realized, which can efficiently relieve ground traffic pressure and network load pressure.

Acknowledgments. This work was supported in part by the National Natural Science Foundation of China (No. 61571104), the Sichuan Science and Technology Program (No. 2018JY0539), the Key projects of the Sichuan Provincial Education Department (No. 18ZA0219), the Fundamental

Research Funds for the Central Universities (No. ZYGX2017KYQD170), the CERNET Innovation Project (No. NGII20190111), the Fund Project (Nos. 61403110405, 315075802), and the Innovation Funding (No. 2018510007000134). The authors wish to thank the reviewers for their helpful comments. Dr. Dingde Jiang is corresponding author of this paper (email: jiangdd@uestc.edu.cn).

References

1. Jiang, D., Wang, Y., Lv, Z., Wang, W., Wang, H.: An energy-efficient networking approach in cloud services for IIoT networks. IEEE J. Sel. Areas Commun. **38**, 928–941 (2020)
2. Wu, J., Ota, K., Dong, M., Li, C.: A hierarchical security framework for defending against sophisticated attacks on wireless sensor networks in smart cities. IEEE Access **4**, 416–424 (2016)
3. Jiang, D., Zhang, P., Lv, Z., Song, H.: Energy-efficient multi-constraint routing algorithm with load balancing for smart city applications. IEEE Internet Things J. **3**(6), 1437–1447 (2016)
4. Ang, L., Seng, K.P., Ijemaru, G.K., Zungeru, A.M.: Deployment of IoV for smart cities: applications, architecture, and challenges. IEEE Access **7**, 6473–6492 (2019)
5. Jiang, D., Huo, L., Lv, Z., Song, H., Qin, W.: A joint multi-criteria utility-based network selection approach for vehicle-to-infrastructure networking. IEEE Trans. Intell. Transp. Syst. **19**(10), 3305–3319 (2018)
6. Jiang, D., Wang, W., Shi, L., Song, H.: A compressive sensing-based approach to end-to-end network traffic reconstruction. IEEE Trans. Netw. Sci. Eng. **7**(1), 507–519 (2020)
7. Hossain, M., Hasan, R., Zawoad, S.: Trust-IoV: a trustworthy forensic investigation framework for the internet of vehicles (IoV). In: 2017 IEEE International Congress on Internet of Things (ICIOT), Honolulu, HI, pp. 25–32 (2017)
8. Huo, L., Jiang, D., Qi, S., et al.: An AI-based adaptive cognitive modeling and measurement method of network traffic for EIS. Mobile Netw. Appl. https://doi.org/10.1007/s11036-019-01419-z (2019)
9. Wazid, M., Bagga, P., Das, A.K., Shetty, S., Rodrigues, J.J.P.C., Park, Y.: AKM-IoV: authenticated key management protocol in fog computing-based internet of vehicles deployment. IEEE Internet Things J. **6**(5), 8804–8817 (2019)
10. Cheng, J., et al.: Accessibility analysis and modeling for IoV in an urban scene. IEEE Trans. Veh. Technol. **69**(4), 4246–4256 (2020)
11. Benomarat, I., Madini, Z., Zouine, Y., Chaoub, A.: Enhancing internet of vehicles (IOVs) performances using intelligent cognitive radio principles. In: 2018 International Conference on Electronics, Control, Optimization and Computer Science (ICECOCS), Kenitra, pp. 1–4 (2018)
12. Taljegard, M.: Impact of vehicle-to-grid on the European electricity system - the electric vehicle battery as a storage option. In: 2019 IEEE Transportation Electrification Conference and Expo (ITEC), Detroit, MI, USA, pp. 1–5 (2019)
13. Zhou, Z., Sun, C., Shi, R., Chang, Z., Zhou, S., Li, Y.: Robust energy scheduling in vehicle-to-grid networks. IEEE Netw. **31**(2), 30–37 (2017)
14. Wang, F., Jiang, D., Qi, S.: An adaptive routing algorithm for integrated information networks. China Commun. **16**(7), 195–206 (2019)
15. Saif, A.-S., et al.: A comprehensive survey on vehicular Ad Hoc network. J. Netw. Comput. Appl. **37**, 380–392 (2014)
16. Zhang, J., et al.: Vehicle routing in urban areas based on the oil consumption weight -dijkstra algorithm. IET Intell. Transp. Syst. **10**(7), 495–502 (2016)
17. Jiang, D., Li, W., Lv, H.: An energy-efficient cooperative multicast routing in multi-hop wireless networks for smart medical applications. Neurocomputing **220**, 160–169 (2017)

18. Yang, J.Y., et al.: Autonomic navigation system based on predicted traffic and VANETs. Wireless Pers. Commun. **92**(2), 515–546 (2017)
19. Qi, S., Jiang, D., Huo, L.: A prediction approach to end-to-end traffic in space information networks. In: 2019 IEEE International Conference on Industrial Internet (ICII), Orlando, FL, USA, pp. 115–119 (2019)
20. Jin, C., He, X., Ding, X.: Traffic analysis of LEO satellite internet of things. In: 2019 15th International Wireless Communications & Mobile Computing Conference (IWCMC), Tangier, Morocco, pp. 67–71 (2019)
21. Guidotti, A., et al.: Architectures and key technical challenges for 5G systems incorporating satellites. IEEE Trans. Veh. Technol. **68**(3), 2624–2639 (2019)
22. Jiang, D., Huo, L., Song, H.: Rethinking behaviors and activities of base stations in mobile cellular networks based on big data analysis. IEEE Trans. Netw. Sci. Eng. **7**(1), 80–90 (2020)
23. Li, J., Deng, G., Luo, C., Lin, Q., Yan, Q., Ming, Z.: A hybrid path planning method in unmanned air/ground vehicle (UAV/UGV) cooperative systems. IEEE Trans. Veh. Technol. **65**(12), 9585–9596 (2016)
24. Jiang, D., Huo, L., Li, Y.: Fine-granularity inference and estimations to network traffic for SDN. PLoS ONE **13**(5), 1–23 (2018)
25. Yu, H., Meier, K., Argyle, M., Beard, R.W.: Cooperative path planning for target tracking in urban environments using unmanned air and ground vehicles. IEEE/ASME Trans. Mechatron. **20**(2), 541–552 (2015)
26. Jiang, D., Wang, Y., Lv, Z., Qi, S., Singh, S.: Big data analysis based network behavior insight of cellular networks for industry 4.0 applications. IEEE Trans. Industr. Inf. **16**(2), 1310–1320 (2020)
27. Wang, Y., Jiang, D., Huo, L., Zhao, Y.: On reconstruction and prediction of network traffic in software defined networking. In: 2019 IEEE International Conference on Industrial Internet (ICII), Orlando, FL, USA, pp. 98–102 (2019)

A Network Traffic Measurement Approach in Cloud-Edge SDN Networks

Liuwei Huo[1], Dingde Jiang[2(✉)], and Lisha Cheng[2]

[1] School of Computer Science and Engineering, Northeastern University,
Shenyang 110819, China
[2] School of Astronautics and Aeronautic, University of Electronic Science
and Technology of China, Chengdu 611731, China
jiangdd@uestc.edu.cn

Abstract. Edge computing is a supplement to cloud computing. It is deployed at the edge of the access network and is closer to where data is generated and used. In 5G and future networks, a large number of devices dynamically access the network and integrate them into cloud computing for deep processing and have high requirements for transfer rates and response time. However, network performance is the bottleneck of the collaboration between cloud computing and edge computing. Network traffic measurement is the core of network traffic management. In order to solve the problems of low utilization of network resources and high difficulty in network management, we study the problem of network traffic measurement in cloud edge computing networks based on software-defined networking (SDN). We propose a new cloud edge network traffic measurement method based on SDN. In this method, we extract statistical records coarse-grained from OpenFlow switches and use them to train an autoregressive moving average (ARMA) model. Use the ARMA model to make fine-grained predictions of network traffic. In order to reduce the estimation error, we propose to use optimization methods to optimize the estimation results. However, we found that the objective function is a very difficult NP-difficult problem, so we use a heuristic algorithm to quickly find the optimal solution. Finally, we repeat some simulations to evaluate the proposed method.

Keywords: Network traffic measurement · Software defined networking · Cloud-edge networks

1 Introduction

In the 5G and future networks, large capacity, low latency, and high dynamic will become the basic requirement of applications to the network. Improve network service capabilities by deploying cloud computing, edge computing, network slicing and network function virtualization (NFV), software-defined networking (SDN) and other new technologies in the access network and core network [1]. In the future, hundreds of millions of devices will need to connect to the network anytime and anywhere, which requires

H. Song and D. Jiang (Eds.): SIMUtools 2020, LNICST 369, pp. 204–214, 2021.
https://doi.org/10.1007/978-3-030-72792-5_19

high-performance cloud computing services to calculate and store massive amounts of data. However, as the number of access devices continues to increase, and in order to ensure that devices can access the network anytime and anywhere, a large number of access points must be deployed and corresponding access networks must be constructed. In this way, the network scale will be very large, and the access network will aggregate and process massive amounts of real-time data. The core networks will transmit and exchange a huge amount of data, which will be dozens of times the data volume of 4G/5G networks. The transmission network has become the bottleneck of data from service to cloud computing. For many delay-sensitive applications, the transmission from the terminal to cloud computing is intolerable. Edge computing is deployed in the network access network, and only one virtual resource pool contains multiple servers. In various terminal equipment, such as medical, industrial, and Internet of vehicles, many terminals and sensors are connected to the edge platform through the edge side. The pressure of resource shortage of edge computing is relatively high. Therefore, edge-cloud collaboration can effectively solve these problems.

Cloud-edge collaboration computing includes collaboration in computing resources, security policies, application management, and business management. To exchange the data between cloud computing and edge computing, the network must be flexibility and operability [2]. NFV utilizes IT (information technology) virtualization technology to perform network services on unified industrial standards, high-performance, large-capacity servers, or programmable switches to accelerate the development and update of new services. So, the network architecture must be changed for adopting these new applications. SDN decouples the control plane and forwarding plane in the traditional switch and centralizes the logical control plane to the SDN controller, so it enables the network to have functions such as flexibility, scalability, and programmability [3]. Network management has always been an important issue faced by operators and equipment vendors [4].

The volume of network traffic is the foundation of network management and often used for making decisions such as load balance, failure recovery, and anomaly detection [5]. Flow is the unit that is dispatched by switches and controllers in SDN. Flow that enters OpenFlow switch will match the flow entries in the flow table, and perform the corresponding actions [6]. In order to manage the cloud edge computing network and consider link load, quality of service (QoS) and network structure, the SDN controller needs to accurately understand the flow and link traffic.

Many measurement methods support flow-based measurement tasks such as sFlow, NetFlow, and SNMP (Simple Network Management Protocol) [7, 8]. sFlow and NetFlow are based on traffic sampling and packets of statistical methods, respectively. They are required the hardware supporting or the software that remote monitoring agent which runs in the network management server [7]. SNMP is a network management protocol that measures the network by sending probe packets. It has been widely used not only in a traditional network but also in the SDN network [8]. However, the SNMP protocol uses the polling method to collect the information of each switch in the network. The transmission of switch status information will consume a lot of bandwidth, and frequently reading switch information can cause network congestion.

In the SDN-based cloud edge computing network, we use pull-based methods for active network traffic measurement. This solution can not only measure flow flexibly and efficiently but can also be customized according to needs. Based on this, we extracted coarse-grained network traffic statistics from OpenFlow switches and used it to train the network traffic prediction model and infer other flows, and use optimization methods to estimate fine-grained network traffic optimization. The structure of this article is as follows. Section 1 is the summary. In Sect. 2, we describe a novel measurement architecture in the SDN-based cloud edge computing network, and use a traffic matrix to describe and analyze the scheme. In Sect. 3, we repeat the simulation to simulate the performance of the proposed scheme and compare the simulation results. The Sect. 4 is the conclusion.

2 Problem Statement

Cloud-edge computing networks are used for exchanging data between cloud computing and edge computing. Cloud computing will transmit applications to the edge computing platform, and edge computing transmits the raw data to the cloud computing platform for deep processing or storage. Then, the traffic between cloud computing and edge computing will have new characteristics. To this end, we study the cloud edge computing network traffic measurement under the SDN framework.

2.1 System Model

Network traffic measurement refers to selecting a representative grouping subset from the original traffic and tracking the characteristics of original traffic data through the grouping subset. With the increase of link capacity and the diversification of applications, huge network traffic measurement results are used for traffic recognition, transmission, storage, and analysis have brought huge pressure. To solve the problem of passive measurement of high-speed networks in SDN, we use the pull-based method and actively collect the statistics of Openflow-based switches for the high-speed cloud-edge computing network traffic measurement, which can reduce the use of measurement, storage, and processing under the condition of meeting the statistical accuracy of the problem.

In high-speed cloud-edge computing network traffic measurement, the implementation of active measurement is limited by technology and resources, and often requires a compromise between sampling rate and estimation accuracy. Coarse-grained traffic sampling can greatly reduce the processing load of the system and has better scalability, and can reflect the original flow characteristic parameters from the sample characteristic parameters, with certain measurement accuracy. In addition to the analysis of the flow characteristics, the sampling data is also widely used in the fields of traffic accounting, performance characteristic measurement, and abnormal detection. For flows in SDN, sampling methods are mainly used the flow sampling.

2.2 Traffic Matrix Construction

The network traffic matrix reflects the amount of traffic from the source to destination network nodes in the SDN-based cloud-edge computing network. Network engineering and network management projects (such as congestion control, load balancing, network security, etc.) are based on the traffic matrix. Therefore, the flow matrix has very great practical significance. However, in the current actual network, due to the different support for the flow measurement function of the equipment produced by different network equipment manufacturers, it is very time-consuming and costly to obtain an accurate flow matrix through direct measurement. In contrast, the method of estimating the flow matrix by combining mathematical methods has become more feasible.

The network traffic from the origin host to the destination host at the time slot t is x_{ij}, where i is the origin host and j is the destination host. So, the traffic matrix can be written as

$$X = [x_{11}, x_{12}, \ldots, x_{1N}, x_{21}, x_{22}, \ldots, x_{2N}, \ldots, x_{N1}, \ldots, x_{NN}]^T \tag{1}$$

However, the transmission of flows in the network are aggregated on links, so the link load can reflect some features of the flows. With the routing matrix, we know the relationship between flows and links, so the relationship among traffic matrix, link load, and routing matrix can be described as:

$$Y = AX \tag{2}$$

where Y represent the traffic matrix of links, $\tilde{X}$ means the traffic matrix of flows, and A represents the relationship of routing in the cloud-edge computing network.

Estimating the cloud-edge computing network traffic is a typical inversion problem. As we all know, there is at least one stream between the source host and the destination host in the network, and there is a link that transmits multiple data streams. In the cloud edge network, a large number of applications are deployed on the cloud computing platform. When real-time sensitive applications request services, cloud computing will offload the applications to the edge computing platform. Since the number of flows in the cloud edge computing network is far greater than the number of links in the network, this means that there are unlimited solutions for traffic solutions. Then, we need to find some ways to search the optimized network traffic in the SDN-based cloud edge computing network.

In order to reduce the measurement overhead of the SDN-based cloud edge computing network, we perform coarse-grained sampling on the SDN-based cloud edge computing network traffic, forecast the fine-grained network traffic and estimate other network traffic, and then predicted network traffic through optimization.

2.3 ARMA Model

Edge computing and cloud computing exchange data through networks and the traffic can be described as a time sequence. The ARMA model (Auto-Regressive and Moving Average Model) is a method that is widely used for predicting the time sequence, it includes an autoregressive model (AR) and a moving average model (MA). ARMA can collectively reflect the characteristics of variance changes and has been widely used in long-term time series analysis and forecasting.

The traffic of flow can be formed as a random sequence over time. The dependence of the random sequence reflects the continuity of the original data in time. The AR model can reflect the correlation of traffic in several adjacent time slots, so the traffic sequence $x_1, x_2, \ldots, x_t$ is

$$x_t = \sum_{i=1}^{p} \phi_i x_{t-i} + Z_t \tag{3}$$

where x_t represents the predicted value of the next time slot service sequence; Z_t represents the estimation error; $\phi_i(i = 1, \ldots, p)$ represents the autoregressive coefficient; p is the correlation order. The error Z_t is caused by white noise and can be expressed as a random sequence. Therefore, the MA model with random error is

$$Z_t = \gamma_t + \alpha_1 \gamma_{t-1} + \cdots + \alpha_i \gamma_{t-i} + \cdots + \alpha_q \gamma_{t-q} \tag{4}$$

where γ_t represents the Gaussian noise in the transmission links, the mean and variance of γ_t can be calculated as $E(\gamma_t) = 0$ and $E(\gamma_t^2) = \sigma^2$, respectively; The variable q is the moving average order; Variables $\alpha_j(j = 1, 2, \ldots, q)$ are the moving average coefficients. With the analysis above, the ARMA(p, q) is as follows:

$$\begin{aligned} x_t &= \phi_1 x_{t-1} + \cdots + \phi_j x_{t-j} + \cdots + \phi_p x_{t-p} \\ &+ \gamma_t + \alpha_1 \gamma_{t-1} + \cdots + \alpha_i \gamma_{t-i} + \cdots + \alpha_q \gamma_{t-q} \end{aligned} \tag{5}$$

The ARMA(p, q) model can predict the flow traffic accurately by determining the order p and q accurately.

Use the pull scheme to extract statistics from the OpenFlow-based switch flow table. The ARMA model is trained on the front end of the measurement data and uses it to fill and reference the fine-grained traffic in the cloud edge computing network.

$$\hat{X} = \text{ARMA}(X) \tag{6}$$

With the fine-grained network traffic that predicts by the ARMA model, we refer to the other flows with the constraints of link load. The fine-grained network traffic obtained by forecasting has an error with the actual network traffic, then we should optimize the forecasting result by utilizing the optimization method. In this process, we should measure the link load Y in SDN-based cloud-edge computing networks firstly. The objective of the flow traffic optimization is

$$f = \left\| Y - A\hat{X} \right\|_2 + \left\| \hat{X} \right\|_2 \tag{7}$$

where A means a routing matrix that can be obtained from the controller directly. Therefore, we use function (7) to construct a constrained target and use it to optimize the SDN-based cloud edge network traffic estimate. However, we find that the objective function is an NP-hard problem However, we find that the objective function is an NP-hard problem which cannot solve. To quickly approximate the optimal solution, we use a heuristic method to search for optimization results.

2.4 Artificial Fish Swarm Algorithm

The artificial fish swarm algorithm (AFSA) is a biomimetic optimization algorithm based on the intelligent behavior research of animal groups. It simulates the foraging behavior of fish swarm as they move toward nutritious areas in the waters. By simulating the behavior of a single fish, a global optimal value in the swarm is achieved through the local optimization of each fish. Artificial fish (AF) is an entity that abstracts and virtualizes real fish. It is composed of some characteristic data and a series of executable actions and can adjust its activities according to the information of the external environment. Each state of AF is located in the solution space and other AF solutions are the current environment. The next action of an AF will be affected by the solution space and its environment and will have a certain impact on other AF activities. The AF model uses the following methods to realize its virtual vision:

$$X_v = X + d_{visual} * Rand() \qquad (8)$$

$$X_{next} = X + \frac{X_v - X}{\|X_v - \bar{X}\|} * S * Rand() \qquad (9)$$

where X indicates the current state of AF; d_{visual} represents the visual distance of AF; $Rand()$ is a random function that randomly produces a number in the range [0,1], with S being the step size.

A. *Foraging Behavior*

This mimics the foraging activity of fish. The AF considers the next swimming direction by sensing the amount or concentration of food within the sensing range of the water. By setting the current state of AF, and randomly selecting other states to swim within its sensing range. If the new state objective function of AF is greater than its current state, the state updated based on the new selection is closer to one step. Otherwise, please randomly select a new state to determine whether it is satisfied. AF X_i selects the new state X_j in its field of vision to update:

$$X_j = X_i + d_{Visual} * Rand() \qquad (10)$$

Otherwise, X_i repeatedly calculate a new state X_j in its field of vision and determine whether the forward condition is satisfied. After repeatedly trying numbers, the forward condition is still not satisfied, and random behavior is performed.

B. *Cluster Behavior*

A large number of fish gathered together for food is a way of life in the evolution of fish. Each one will explore the current number of its adjacent individuals and calculate the center position of the fish cluster, and then compare the newly acquired center position target function with the current position target function. If the center position of the fish cluster is more crowded than the current position, the fish will from the current position swim towards the center position; otherwise, the fish will perform random foraging behavior.

AF X_i searches for the number of adjacent individuals n_f and the center position of the fish cluster X_c in its current visual field $d \leq d_{visual}$. If $X_c/n_f < \delta X_i$ is satisfied, fish will be performed in the foraging process. We write the clustering behavior as

$$X_i^{t+1} = X_i^t + \frac{X_c - X_{it}^t}{\|X_c - X_i\|} * S * Rand() \tag{11}$$

where X_c represents the center position of the AF cluster.

C. Rear-ending Behavior

When some find food, other fish will follow them to swim, causing fish to gather the food. The AF swim towards the optimal position of nearby fish. If a large number of fish gather together, it will cause AF to be overcrowded at the optimization point. Therefore, we introduce a threshold variable to prevent the AF from over clustering. If the optimization point is not very crowded, the AF will swim from the current position towards the optimal AF one step, otherwise, the AF swims a step randomly.

AF X_i looking for the optimal individual X_j in the partner of the current field of vision ($d_{ij} < d_{Visual}$). If $X_j/n_f > \delta X_i$ means that the optimal individual is not too crowded nearby, then X_i moves towards the partner, otherwise foraging behavior.

$$X_i^{t+1} = X_i^t + \frac{X_j - X_{it}^t}{\|X_j - X_i\|} * S * Rand() \tag{12}$$

D. Random Behavior

It is the foraging behavior of fish, which means that AF moves randomly within the visual field. When a fish find the food, it moves quickly in the direction of increasing food. The algorithm describes that the AF X_i moves towards the food a step and updates the current state:

$$X_i^{t+1} = X_i^t + Visual * Rand() \tag{13}$$

E. Bulletin board

The bulletin board records the best place to update the status of the fish cluster. After each iteration, each AF compares its current state with the best state recorded on the bulletin board. If the objective function value of the current state of the fish is higher than the objective function value of the bulletin board state, the state of the bulletin board update as its status; otherwise, the state of the bulletin board will remain unchanged. When the iterative process of the algorithm ends, the value recorded on the bulletin board is the best solution for the entire cluster of fish . The traffic in the SDN-based cloud edge computing network is AF, and the behavior evaluation reflects the autonomous behavior of AF.on the bulletin board is the best solution for the entire cluster of fish.

3 Analysis of Simulation Result

3.1 Simulation Environment

We evaluate the proposed network traffic measure and prediction method by implementing some simulations with the Ryu, Mininet, and Docker. We use python programming to implement functional modules and install them into the Ryu controller. Then, we use the Mininet to create the network topology and use the Open vSwitch to simulate the OpenFlow switches and create some hosts in the Mininet topology, and also use the docker to create the hosts and mount them on to the OpenFlow switch. Iperf is a software that can generate traffic and fill them into the access switches from the origin host and catching them at the destination host, then we send data from the origin host to the destination host. We used docker to create hosts H5, H8, H10 and H11, and transmit big packaged data from them to other hosts. The network traffic between two hosts is Fig. 1 shows.

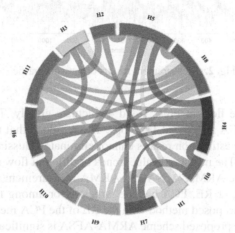

Fig. 1. Flows between two hosts in the SDN-based cloud-edge computing network.

To intuitively display and analyze the performance of the proposed scheme, we have introduced absolute error (AE) and relative error (RE) indicators. The AE and RE can be expressed as

$$AE_i = \left| x_i - \hat{x}_i \right| \tag{14}$$

$$RE_i = \left| x_i - \hat{x}_i \right| / \hat{x}_i \tag{15}$$

3.2 Simulation Evaluation

In this article, we choose two flows f1 and f2 as examples for discussion, as shown in Fig. 2. Therefore, in this scheme, we use ARMA and AFSA models to estimate and optimize the traffic in the cloud-side network. In the figure, we use ARMA-ASFA stands for the scheme proposed in this article. Then, compare and analyze with ARMA and Principal Component Analysis (PCA) methods.

Figures 3 and 4 respectively show the AE and RE of the measured results under different measurement methods. It can be seen from Fig. 3 that the AE of the ARMA-AFSA mentioned in this article is smaller than the AE of the measurement results of

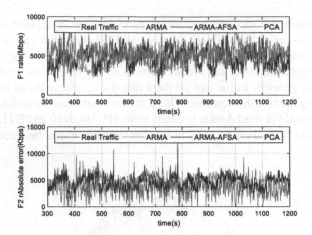

Fig. 2. Measurement results of network traffic.

ARMA and PCA. The flow in Figs. 3 and 4 fluctuate greatly. The AEs of ARMA-AFSA, ARMA and PCA all exceed 1000 bps. The reason is that the flow has random characteristics and the estimation results cannot eliminate Gaussian white noise in the transmission channel. The measured value trends of different flow rates are similar, and the relative error of the ARMA-AFSA and ARMA measurement methods is less than 0.3. Regardless of AE or RE, PCA has the largest error among these three methods. We also compare the proposed method with the RE of the PCA method and the ARMA method. The RE of the proposed scheme ARMA-AFSA is significantly smaller than the PCA and ARMA methods in Fig. 4.

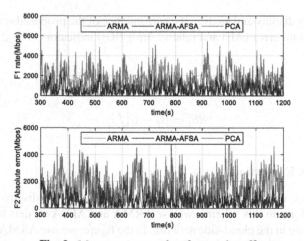

Fig. 3. Measurement results of network traffic.

In Fig. 5, we compare the CDF of RE of three network traffic estimation and measurement schemes. We have noticed that the RE of the proposed measurement scheme is

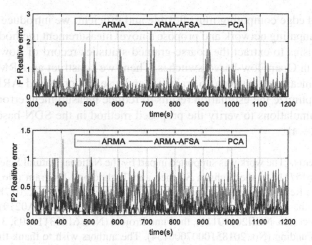

Fig. 4. The RE of different methods.

better than the CDF of the PCA method and the ARMA method. This is mainly because we use coarse-grained measurement results to help the ARMA model obtain the fine-grained measurement result, and use the AFSA method to reduce estimation errors. The optimization for network traffic estimation results is effective as shown in Fig. 5 directly.

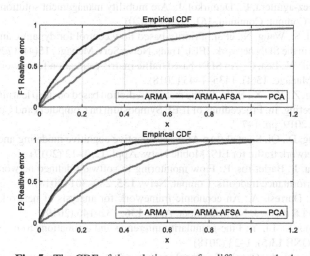

Fig. 5. The CDF of the relative error for different methods.

4 Conclusions

In the SDN-based cloud-edge computing network, the fine-grained network traffic measurement result is significant for network management. Since the network between cloud computing and edge computing must flexible and efficient, we introduce SDN into the cloud-edge computing network and propose a novel measurement method. We use pull-based mechanisms to extract the coarse-grained statistics record of flows and links in the flow table in OpenFlow-based switches. Then, we construct an ARMA model and use the front measurement data to train it , and use the proposed ARMA model to forecast and optimize the estimation results to reduce measurement errors. Finally, we repeat some simulations to verify the proposed method in the SDN-based cloud-edge computing network.

Acknowledgments. The work was supported in part by the National Natural Science Foundation of China (No. 61571104), the Sichuan Science and Technology Program (No. 2018JY0539), the Fundamental Research Funds for the Central Universities (No. ZYGX2017KYQD170), the Key projects of the Sichuan Provincial Education Department (No. 18ZA0219), the CERNET Innovation Project (No. NGII20190111), the Fund Project (Nos. 61403110405, 315075802), and the Innovation Funding (No. 2018510007000134). The authors wish to thank the reviewers for their helpful comments.

References

1. Long, Q., Chen, Y., Zhang, H., et al.: Software defined 5G and 6G networks: a survey. Mobile Netw. Appl. (5), 1–21 (2019)
2. Jain, A., Lopez-aguilera, E., Demirkol, I.: Are mobility management solutions ready for 5G and beyond? Comput. Commun. **161**, 50–75 (2020)
3. Oh, B., Vural, S., Wang, N., et al.: Priority-based flow control for dynamic and reliable flow management in the SDN network. IEEE Trans. Netw. Serv. Manage. **15**(4), 1720–1732 (2018)
4. Tian, Y., Chen, W., Lea, C.: An SDN-based traffic matrix estimation framework. IEEE Trans. Netw. Serv. Manage. **15**(4), 1435–1445 (2018)
5. Liu, Z., Wang, Z., Yin, X., et al.: Traffic matrix prediction based on deep learning for dynamic traffic engineering. In: Proceedings of IEEE Symposium on Computers and Communications (ISCC), July 2019, pp. 1–7
6. Huo, L., Jiang, D., Qi, S., et al.: An AI-based adaptive cognitive modeling and measurement method of network traffic for EIS. Mobile Netw. Appl. **12**, 1–12 (2019)
7. Suarez-varela, J., Barlet-ros, P.: Flow monitoring in software-defined networks: finding the accuracy/ performance tradeoffs. Comput. Netw. **135**, 289–301 (2018)
8. Karakus, M., Durresi, A.: An economic framework for analysis of network architectures: SDN and MPLS cases. J. Netw. Comput. Appl. **136**, 132–146 (2019)
9. Jiang, D., Huo, L., Li, Y.: Fine-granularity inference and estimations to network traffic for SDN. PLoS ONE **13**(5), 1–23 (2018)
10. Liu, C., Malboubi, A., Chuah, C.: OpenMeasure: adaptive flow measurement and inference with online learning in SDN. In: Proceedings of INFOCOM'16, pp. 47–52 (2016)
11. Shu, Z., Wan, J., Wang, S., et al.: Traffic engineering in software-defined networking: measurement and management. IEEE Access **4**, 3246–3256 (2016)

A Performance Analysis Approach for Network Intrusion Detection Algorithms

Zhihao Wang, Dingde Jiang[✉], Yuqing Wang, and Junyang Zhang

School of Astronautics and Aeronautic, University of Electronic Science
and Technology of China, Chengdu 611731, China
jiangdd@uestc.edu.cn

Abstract. With the development of mobile Internet and cloud computing, the amount of network traffic has been significantly increased. Security problems have drawn a lot of attention, while traditional methods are becoming increasingly unsuitable for it. In this paper, three machine learning algorithms are employed to detect network intrusion, including KNN, Random Forest, and Multilayer Perceptron. Performance evaluation and comparison between them are conducted, in terms of precision, recall, training time, etc. Simulation results on the NSL-KDD, a benchmark data set of network intrusion detection, show that the Random Forest algorithm exhibits higher detection accuracy and remarkably shorter training time.

Keywords: Network intrusion detection · Machine learning · Random forest · Multilayer Perceptron · Performance analysis

1 Introduction

With the development of the mobile Internet, many business systems are deployed on distributed cloud computing platforms. A large number of user groups generate massive amounts of network traffic. Much of network traffic is generated by malicious attacks carried out by attackers against certain servers or hosts. Some attackers act like normal users, generating data, and hiding their malicious activities under TB or even PB-level data. Due to a large amount of data or lack of network intrusion detection capabilities, hackers can invade enterprise computer systems through Trojans, backdoors, and even complex APT and "0-day" vulnerabilities, threatening the information security of the companies. When the Trojan communicates with the attacker, the generated network traffic showing obvious communication features, which can be effectively captured by intrusion detection technology [1]. However, the anomaly detection algorithms behave differently in different environments, and there is diversity between accuracy, recall, precision. Therefore, it is especially important to compare and evaluate the performance of different intrusion techniques.

Z. Li et al. propose a network intrusion detection method based on Recurrent Neural Networks and Broad Learning System to detect various known network attacks [2].

© ICST Institute for Computer Sciences, Social Informatics and Telecommunications Engineering 2021
Published by Springer Nature Switzerland AG 2021. All Rights Reserved
H. Song and D. Jiang (Eds.): SIMUtools 2020, LNICST 369, pp. 215–224, 2021.
https://doi.org/10.1007/978-3-030-72792-5_20

Authors study the prediction approach to end-to-end traffic in space information networks [3, 4]. I. Ahmad et al. compare the performance of support vector machine, random forest and extreme learning machine algorithm [5]. Some studies also focus on estimations to network traffic [6]. M. C. et al. study the IDS built by Snort and Suricata based on Raspberry Pi, and its performance comparison [7]. D. Jiang et al. research the behaviors and activities [8]. SAMIRA et al. designed an anomaly-based detection called Mutation Cuckoo Fuzzy for feature selection and Evolutionary Neural Network for classification [9]. Compressive sensing-based approach also can be used in [10]. Authors propose to optimize a soft computing tool widely used for intrusion detection namely Back Propagation Neural Network using a novel hybrid Framework based on improved Genetic Algorithm and Simulated Annealing Algorithm [11]. Wireless network is studied in [12–14]. The scholars use the proposed State Preserving Extreme Learning Machine algorithm [15]. Intrusion Detection for IoT network is studied in [16–18]. And industry application is studied in [19–22]. An improved convolutional neural network model is proposed in [23]. Large-Scale cyber networks are studied in [24, 25]. From the review above, we can see that the performance of the network intrusion detection algorithms still attracts a lot of attention in academia and industry.

In this paper, we study the performance comparison of three network intrusion detection algorithms. First, the general architecture of IDS (Intrusion Detection System) is illustrated. And three network intrusion algorithms are introduced, including KNN (K Nearest Neighbor), RF (Random Forest), and MLP (Multilayer Perceptron). To evaluate the performance of three network intrusion algorithms, the network intrusion dataset NSL-KDD is employed, which has been preprocessed to input to the algorithms. Besides, we present several performance comparison metrics. Evaluating simulations are carried out, which show that the Random Forest intrusion detection algorithm has better performance than the other two algorithms.

2   System Model

In this section, we will briefly introduce three intrusion detection algorithms compared in this paper, including KNN, RF, and MLP classifiers.

1. KNN

    The basic rule of the KNN algorithm is to find the k nearest neighbors in all the N samples. When $k = 1$, KNN becomes the nearest neighbor problem. The first step of KNN is to calculate the distance between the input sample and all samples. The distance between the n-dimension vector $a(x_{11}, x_{12}, \ldots, x_{1n})$ and $b(x_{21}, x_{22}, \ldots, x_{2n})$ is calculated as (1), which is called the Euclidean Distance.

    $$d_{12} = \sqrt{\sum_{k=1}^{n} (x_{1k} - x_{2k})^2} \tag{1}$$

    Then choose k nearest neighbors which have the shortest distance between the input sample. Based on the main class of these k neighbors, the classification of the input sample can be achieved.

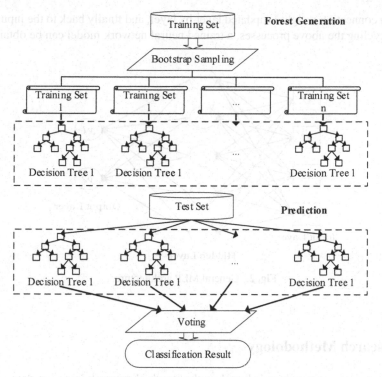

Fig. 1. Basic Architecture of Random Forest.

2. Random Forest

Random forest algorithm is an ensemble learning algorithm with decision tree as base learner. The forest is constructed by many decision trees. There is no correlation between each decision tree of random forest. After the forest constructed, when a new input sample enters, each decision tree in the forest judges separately and gets the classification result of the sample. Finally, through the voting mechanism, combine the results of all decision trees. The one with the most classification votes belongs to this category. The basic architecture of RF is shown in Fig. 1. Figure 1 Basic architecture of random forest.

3. MLP

MLP is also called artificial neural network (ANN). In addition to the input and output layer, there can be multiple hidden layers between the input layer and the output layer. The general MLP contains only one hidden layer, which is shown in Fig. 2. The cells of each layer are connected with all the cells of the adjacent layer. And there is no connection between the cells of the same layer. When a training sample is input to the network, the activation value of the neuron propagates from the input layer to the output layer through each middle layer. Each neuron in the output layer obtains the input response of the network. Next, according to the direction of reducing the target output and the actual error, from the output layer through the middle layer, each connection weight is updated layer by layer, and finally back to the input layer. By cycling the above processes, a trained neural network model can be obtained.

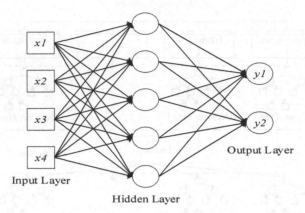

Fig. 2. General MLP architecture.

3   Research Methodology

The performance comparison is based on the standard network intrusion dataset NSL-KDD, which is the improved version of KDD-99. The data preprocessing is conducted to make the dataset more suitable for classifiers to handle. The metrics to evaluate the performance of different detection algorithms are presented in this section.

3.1   Data Preprocessing

NSL-KDD includes 39 common types of network attacks, 22 of them in the training set, and 17 in the test. There are several columns in text form. Therefore, it is necessary to convert them into the form which can be inputted into the classifier.

The raw data of the NSL-KDD dataset has some useless features and some of the features are in text form. And all of 39 types of attacks are in the data, causing it cannot be handled directly. Therefore, we carry out data preprocessing. The main steps of data preprocessing of NSL-KDD are data cleaning, data encoding, data normalization and label binarization.

1. Data Cleaning.
   The 43rd column attribute in the dataset indicates whether the sample is easy to classify, which is not essential for this paper. Thereby, it is necessary to eliminate the influence of useless features.
2. Data Encoding.
   There are three character-type features, including protocol type, service and flag. The detection algorithms based on machine learning are not capable of dealing with

characters. We conduct data encoding for the character-type features. For example, for the protocol type, there are three types, TCP, UDP and ICMP. We encode the TCP as 1, UDP as 2, and ICMP as 3. The remaining columns are also encoded in this way.

3. Data Normalization.

When the scales of features in different dimensions of the original data are inconsistent, normalization steps are needed to preprocess the data. The normalization method we conduct to deal with NSL-KDD is the Z-Score normalization method. Z-score standardization is to scale the data to a specific range, ensuring the $\sigma = 1$, $\mu = 1$. The σ is the standard deviation of samples, and the μ is the mean value of samples. The standard deviation is defined as

$$\sigma = \sqrt{\frac{1}{N} \sum_{i=1}^{N} (x_i - \mu)^2} \tag{2}$$

where N represents the total number of tested samples, x_i is the value of sample i. Z-Score transformation formula is:

$$z = \frac{x - \mu}{\sigma} \tag{3}$$

where x is the sample before Z-Score normalization and z is the converted value.

4. Label Binarization.

In some application scenarios, it is not necessary to distinguish different types of network attacks in detail. It only needs to detect normal and abnormal traffic. Therefore, in the data preprocessing, we encode the abnormal traffic type including Dos, Probe, R2L, U2R to 1 and the normal traffic to 0. The label binarization could effectively improve the performance of some classifiers.

3.2 Performance Comparison Metrics

The confusion matrix is a common evaluation method used to evaluate the classification performance of the intrusion detection binary classification problem. The confusion matrix used to determine the detection performance of the three systems in this paper is shown in Table 1.

Common performance metrics used to evaluate IDS performance are as follows:

- Precision
  The precision rate is an indicator of accuracy, which indicates the proportion of the number of positive cases correctly classified by the classifier to the number of positive cases. It can be expressed as

$$Precision = \frac{TP}{TP + FP} \tag{4}$$

where TP represents the number of abnormalities correctly detected, and the FP represents the false positive prediction of negative class.

Table 1. Confusion matrix.

	Predicted value	
Observed value	TP (True Positive)	FN (False Negative)
	FP (False Positive)	TN (True Negative)

- True Positive Rate (TPR)/Recall

  The *TPR* is defined as the ratio of the number of correctly predicted network anomalies and the total number of network anomalies. *TPR* is also called Recall or sensitivity. *TPR* can be represented as

$$TPR = \frac{TP}{TP + FN} = Recall = Sensitivity \tag{5}$$

  where FN represents the number of normal conditions that are erroneously detected.

- False Positive Rate (FPR)

  The false positive rate is defined as the proportion of normal conditions incorrectly classified as a intrusion and all normal conditions, which can be represented as

$$FPR = \frac{FP}{FP + TN} \tag{6}$$

  where TN represents the number of correctly detected normal conditions.

- F1-Score

  F-measure is the weighted harmonic average of precision and recall, which is quite effective for the imbalanced classification problem. We use the F1-Score in this paper, which can be expressed as:

$$F_1 = 2 \cdot \frac{precision \cdot recall}{precision + recall} = \frac{2TP}{2TP + FP + FN} \tag{7}$$

4 Simulation and Result Analysis

4.1 Evaluation Strategy

The simulation experiment in this paper is based on the NSL-KDD intrusion detection data set. 80% of the dataset is taken as training set and 20% is taken as the testing set. The officially provided test set is used as the validation set. We compared the training results of the classifiers with the original data, the normalized and binary data, as well as the training time and performance on the validation set. The metrics in 3.3 are used to evaluate the performance of the KNN, RF, and MLP classifier. And the ROC Curve is drawn to compare the performance of the two-class classification algorithm.

4.2 Simulation Results

Comparison on precision, recall, F1-Score and training time between KNN, RF and MLP is shown in Table 2. RF has better performance when processing the raw data of NSL-KDD dataset. The precision, recall and F1-Score are higher than the other two classifiers, while the training time is significantly shorter than them. As KNN is based on the distance calculation between the samples, the training time is much longer than the other classifiers, which will be even higher when the samples are normalized.

Table 2. Classification result on raw dataset.

	Precision	Recall	F1-Score	Time
KNN	0.71627	0.72529	0.67444	9.49819
RF	0.80297	0.73771	0.68995	0.83753
MLP	0.64075	0.70232	0.65793	4.54791

The detection precision on each attack type is shown in Fig. 3. If the detection accuracy is less than 50%, the classifier is almost unavailable, because the accuracy is less than that of the random guess classifier. Therefore, in the comparing experiment, we only illustrate the detection result higher than 50%. The detection precision of the three algorithms on the training data is higher than 95%. However, MLP cannot detect the R2L and U2R attacks effectively. There is not much difference in the detection precision between KNN and RF on the train data. As detecting on the test data, because there are unknown attack types, detection precision decrease obviously. And the Random Forest classifier has the best performance.

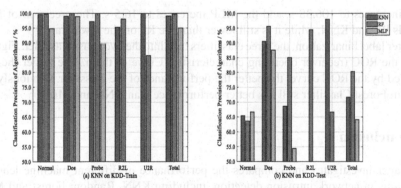

Fig. 3. Precision comparison on NSL-KDD.

The detection results after data normalization are shown in Fig. 4. After normalization, the detection precision of KNN and MLP increases, while the Random Forest decrease than before. Because KNN is based on the distance calculation of the samples, and MLP can converge better and faster after standardization. But the training time of

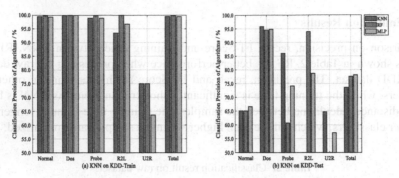

Fig. 4. Precision comparison on normalized NSL-KDD.

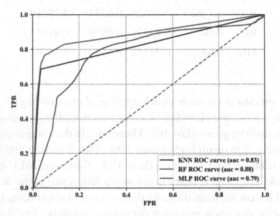

Fig. 5. ROC curve of two-class classifier.

KNN increases to 106.38 s, and the MLP increases to 16.5 s. The precision of MLP exceeds RF and KNN, while it is still lower than the RF on the raw data.

After label binarization, the three classifiers turn into the two-class classifier. Figure 5 shows the ROC (receiver operating characteristic) Curve of them. The larger the area occupied by the ROC curve, the better the performance of the classifier. Obviously, the Random Forest Classifier still has better performance than KNN and MLP.

5   Conclusion

This paper investigates and compares the performance of different machine learning algorithms in network intrusion detection, including KNN, Random Forest and MLP. The NSL-KDD data is employed in the comparison, with data preprocessing. Speaking of detecting precision, recall and F1-Score, the Random Forest algorithm outperforms the other two algorithms. Except the MLP behaves better slightly after normalization. Besides, the Random Forest has the best training efficiency, with remarkably short training time. Therefore, as an ensemble learning method, the Random Forest is suitable for network intrusion detection in this paper. For future work, more intrusion detection algorithms and feature transformation techniques will be investigated.

Acknowledgement. This work was supported in part by the National Natural Science Foundation of China (No. 61571104), the Sichuan Science and Technology Program (No. 2018JY0539), the Key projects of the Sichuan Provincial Education Department (No. 18ZA0219), the Fundamental Research Funds for the Central Universities (No. ZYGX2017KYQD170), the CERNET Innovation Project (No. NGII20190111), the Fund Project (Nos. 61403110405, 315075802), and the Innovation Funding (No. 2018510007000134). The authors wish to thank the reviewers for their helpful comments.

References

1. Xie, J., Li, S., Zhang, Y., et al.: A method based on hierarchical spatiotemporal features for trojan traffic detection. In: 2019 IEEE 38th International Performance Computing and Communications Conference (IPCCC), pp. 1–8 (2019)

2. Li, Z., Batta, P., Trajkovic, L.: Comparison of machine learning algorithms for detection of network intrusions. In: 2018 IEEE International Conference on Systems, Man, and Cybernetics (SMC), pp. 4248–4253 (2018)

3. Qi, S., Jiang, D., Huo, L.: A prediction approach to end-to-end traffic in space information networks. Mob. Netw. Appl. (2019). https://doi.org/10.1007/s11036-019-01424-2, online available

4. Wang, Y., Jiang, D., Huo, L., Zhao, Y.: A new traffic prediction algorithm to software defined networking. Mob. Netw. Appl. (2019). https://doi.org/10.1007/s11036-019-01423-3. online available

5. Ahmad, I., Basheri, M., Iqbal, M.J., et al.: Performance comparison of support vector machine, random forest, and extreme learning machine for intrusion detection. IEEE Access **6**, 33789–33795 (2018)

6. Jiang, D., Huo, L., Li, Y.: Fine-granularity inference and estimations to network traffic for SDN. PLoS ONE **13**(5), 1–23 (2018)

7. Cosar, M., Kiran, H.E.: Performance comparison of open source IDSs via Raspberry Pi. In: 2018 International Conference on Artificial Intelligence and Data Processing (IDAP), pp. 1–5 (2018)

8. Jiang, D., Huo, L., Song, H.: Rethinking behaviors and activities of base stations in mobile cellular networks based on big data analysis. IEEE Trans. Netw. Sci. Eng. **7**(1), 80–90 (2020)

9. Sarvari, S., Sani, N.F.M., Hanapi, Z.M., et al.: An efficient anomaly intrusion detection method with feature selection and evolutionary neural network. IEEE Access **8**, 70651–70663 (2020)

10. Jiang, D., Wang, W., Shi, L., Song, H.: A compressive sensing-based approach to end-to-end network traffic reconstruction. IEEE Trans. Netw. Sci. Eng. **7**(1), 507–519 (2020)

11. Chiba, Z., Abghour, N., Moussaid, K., et al.: A hybrid optimization framework based on genetic algorithm and simulated annealing algorithm to enhance performance of anomaly network intrusion detection system based on BP neural network. In: 2018 International Symposium on Advanced Electrical and Communication Technologies (ISAECT), pp. 1–6 (2018)

12. Jiang, D., Li, W., Lv, H.: An energy-efficient cooperative multicast routing in multi-hop wireless networks for smart medical applications. Neurocomputing **2017**(220), 160–169 (2017)

13. Yang, H., Wang, F.: Wireless network intrusion detection based on improved convolutional neural network. IEEE Access **7**, 64366–64374 (2019)
14. Jiang, D., Zhang, P., Lv, Z., et al.: Energy-efficient multi-constraint routing algorithm with load balancing for smart city applications. IEEE Internet of Things J. **3**(6), 1437–1447 (2016)
15. Singh, K., Mathai, K.J.: Performance comparison of intrusion detection system between deep belief network (DBN) algorithm and state preserving extreme learning machine (SPELM) algorithm. In: 2019 IEEE International Conference on Electrical, Computer and Communication Technologies (ICECCT), pp. 1–7 (2019)
16. Jiang, D., Wang, Y., Lv, Z., Wang, W., Wang, H.: An energy-efficient networking approach in cloud services for IIoT networks. IEEE J. Sel. Areas Commun. **38**(5), 928–941 (2020)
17. Zhang, Y., Li, P., Wang, X.: Intrusion detection for IoT based on improved genetic algorithm and deep belief network. IEEE Access **7**, 31711–31722 (2019)
18. Wang, F., Jiang, D., Qi, S.: An adaptive routing algorithm for integrated information networks. China Commun. **7**(1), 196–207 (2019)
19. Liu, W., Liu, X., Di, X., et al.: A novel network intrusion detection algorithm based on fast fourier transformation. In: 2019 1st International Conference on Industrial Artificial Intelligence (IAI), pp. 1–6 (2019)
20. Jiang, D., Wang, Y., Lv, Z., Qi, S., Singh, S.: Big data analysis based network behavior insight of cellular networks for Industry 4.0 applications. IEEE Trans. Ind. Inf. **16**(2), 1310–1320 (2020)
21. Liang, W., Li, K., Long, J., et al.: An industrial network intrusion detection algorithm based on multifeature data clustering optimization model. IEEE Trans. Industr. Inf. **16**(3), 2063–2071 (2020)
22. Jiang, D., Huo, L., Lv, Z., Song, H., Qin, W.: A joint multi-criteria utility-based network selection approach for vehicle-to-infrastructure networking. IEEE Trans. Intell. Transp. Syst. **19**(10), 3305–3319 (2018)
23. Khan, R.U., Zhang, X., Alazab, M., et al.: An improved convolutional neural network model for intrusion detection in networks. In: 2019 Cybersecurity and Cyberforensics Conference (CCC), pp. 74–77 (2019)
24. Huo, L., Jiang, D., Qi, S., et al.: An AI-based adaptive cognitive modeling and measurement method of network traffic for EIS. Mob. Netw. Appl. (2019). https://doi.org/10.1007/s11036-019-01419-z. online available
25. Miehling, E., Rasouli, M., Teneketzis, D.: A POMDP approach to the dynamic defense of large-scale cyber networks. IEEE Trans. Inf. Forensics Secur. **13**(10), 2490–2505 (2018)

On Exponential Stability for Delayed Inertial BAM Neural Networks via Non-reduced Order Approach

Bingnan Tang[1], Bingjun Li[2(✉)] , Jianjun Jiao[3], and Fengjun Di[3]

[1] Business School, Jiangsu University of Technology, Changzhou, China
regales1988@sina.com
[2] School of Mathematics and Statistics, Guizhou University of Finance
and Economics, Guiyang, China
[3] School of Mathematics and Big Data, Anhui University of Science and Technology,
Huainan, China

Abstract. The present paper is studying a class of inertial BAM neural networks with general activations and delays. With the help of the non-reduced order method and designing some useful Lyapunov functions, criterions ensuring the exponential stability of the investigated network system are proposed, the obtained conditions are essentially new and complement previously stability results. Moreover, a simulated example is also presented in order to support the established fruits.

Keywords: General BAM neural network · Stability

1 Introduction

In recent decades, numerous neural networks (NNs) have attracted lots of attention of researchers in view of their wide applications in many engineering fields. As an significant kind of NNs, the known bidirectional associative memory (BAM) NNs, firstly introduced by Kosko [1,2], have a wide application prospect in all kinds of fields, for example, pattern recognition, intelligent information processing, optimization problem calculation and complex control, see [3–10]. It be universally known that the limited signal propagation time and switching time interval are inevitable in nature, the time delay is ubiquitous and inescapable in the real world applications. Thus, the kinetic study of delayed NNs has been extensively noticed and discussed during these years, particularly, dynamical behaviors including stability [11], periodic oscillation [12,13], synchronization

B. Li—This work was supported by Social science fund project of Jiangsu Institute of Technology (NO: KYY17504), Guizhou University of Finance and Economics (NO: 2018YJ19, 2019XYB21).

H. Song and D. Jiang (Eds.): SIMUtools 2020, LNICST 369, pp. 225–237, 2021.
https://doi.org/10.1007/978-3-030-72792-5_21

problem [14,15], and bifurcation [16,17], and so on, many kinds of delayed BAM NNs have been widely investigated.

It is worth highlighting that the aforementioned theoretical results are mainly with regard to neural networks modeling by first order DDEs (namely, delay differential equations). Actually, inertial effects are inescapable in many practical systems, for instance, power electronics, GRNs, NNs, etc., see such as [18–20]. Consequently, it is important and meaningful to research the dynamical behaviors of NNs with inertia characteristics. As a result of the existence of inertial factors, the model stemming from the real word is usually expressed by two order functional differential equations, which is having nothing in common with the traditional ones and brings many theoretical and technical obstacles when investigating their dynamical behaviors. In addition, in many existing literatures, many researchers applied the reduced-order technique to consider the inertial NNs, although it is an effective method but there are still some problems, for example, when by applying appropriate variable transformations, the two order DEs are equivalent to two sub-systems, and considering BAM neural networks are binary systems, which unquestionably raises the dimension of the system and tremendously causes difficulty on theoretical analysis and the computational complexity of the established outcomes. Consequently, it is badly in need of new approach to investigate the exponential stability of delayed inertial BAM NNs with general activations.

On account of the above discussions and some recent references [21–23], the exponential stability of delayed inertial BAM NNs with activations. By employing the non-reduced order methods, a up-to-date Lyapunov-Kraiiovskii function is constructed, efficient criterions are established for the investigated NNs. Distinct from existing theoretical results with regard to the exponential stability of delayed inertial neural network where the reduced-order methods is adopted, the obtained main results improve some of the latest research results.

This followings are the arrangements of this paper. Section 2 presents some preliminaries. In part 3, we concretely research the exponential stability. Section 4 provides a simulated example. Ultimately, a conclusion is obtained in Sect. 5.

2   Preliminaries

In this part, we will study the delayed inertial general BAM neural networks with general activations:

$$
\begin{cases}
m_i''(t) = -a_i m_i'(t) - d_i m_i(t) + \sum\limits_{j=1}^{n} p_{ji} f_j(m_j(t - \sigma_{ji}), z_j(t - \tau_{ji})) + I_i, \\
z_j''(t) = -b_j z_j'(t) - h_j z_j(t) + \sum\limits_{i=1}^{n} q_{ij} g_i(m_i(t - \delta_{ij}), z_i(t - \eta_{ij})) + J_j,
\end{cases}
\tag{1}
$$

the initial datas concerning (1) are equipped as

$$
\begin{cases}
m_i(t) = \vartheta_i(t), & s \in [-r_1, 0], \quad r_1 = \max\{\max_{1 \le i \le n, 1 \le j \le n} \sigma_{ji}, \ \max_{1 \le i \le n, 1 \le j \le n} \delta_{ij}\}, \\
z_j(t) = \psi_j(t), & s \in [-r_2, 0], \quad r_2 = \max\{\max_{1 \le i \le n, 1 \le j \le n} \tau_{ji}, \ \max_{1 \le i \le n, 1 \le j \le n} \eta_{ij}\},
\end{cases}
\tag{2}
$$

In system (1), the second derivative terms are the so-called inertial terms, m_i and z_j stand for the states of the ith neuron and the jth neuron, respectively; $f_j(\cdot, \cdot)$ and $g_i(\cdot, \cdot)$ on behalf of the activation functions of the jth and ith unit, respectively; d_i and h_j delegate the rate with which the i-th nerve cell and j-th nerve cell will reset its potential to the resting state in isolation when they are not related to the system and external input; a_i, b_j are positive constants, p_{ji} and q_{ij} mean the connection weights of the neuron i and j, and $i, j = 1, 2, ..., n$.

In order to establish the theoretical results, we impose the Lipschitz conditions on the activation functions.

($\mathbf{H_1}$) There are positive constants $\alpha_j, \beta_j, \omega_i, \gamma_i$, such that

$$
|f_j(p_1, q_1) - f_j(p_2, q_2)| \le \alpha_j |p_1 - p_2| + \beta_j |q_1 - q_2|,
$$

$$
|g_i(p_1, q_1) - g_i(p_2, q_2)| \le \omega_i |q_1 - q_2| + \gamma_i |q_1 - q_2|,
$$

for any $p_1, p_2, q_1, q_2 \in R$, $i, j = 1, 2, ..., n$.

3   Main Results

Theorem 1. *Let Hypothesis* ($\mathbf{H_1}$) *hold. Then system (1) is globally exponentially stable if the coefficients satisfy the following conditions:*

$$
\mathfrak{J}_i < 0, \quad \mathcal{J}_i < 0,
\tag{3}
$$

and

$$
4\mathfrak{J}_i \mathfrak{K}_i > (\mathcal{L}_i)^2, \quad 4\mathcal{J}_i \mathcal{K}_i > (\mathcal{L}_i)^2,
\tag{4}
$$

in which

$$
\begin{cases}
\mathfrak{J}_i = \xi_{1i}\zeta_{1i} - a_i \xi_{1i}^2 + \frac{1}{2} \sum_{j=1}^{n} \xi_{1i}^2 |p_{ji}|(\alpha_j + \beta_j), \\
\mathfrak{K}_i = \frac{1}{2} \sum_{j=1}^{n} |\xi_{1i}||\zeta_{1i}||p_{ji}|(\alpha_j + \beta_j) + \frac{1}{2} \sum_{j=1}^{n} \left(\xi_{1i}^2 |p_{ji}|\alpha_j + |\xi_{1i}||\zeta_{1i}||p_{ji}|\alpha_j \right) \\
\quad + \frac{1}{2} \sum_{j=1}^{n} \left(\xi_{2i}^2 |q_{ij}|\omega_i + |\xi_{2i}||\zeta_{2i}||q_{ij}|\omega_i \right) - d_i \xi_{1i}\zeta_{1i}, \\
\mathcal{L}_i = \lambda_{1i} + \zeta_{1i}^2 - d_i \xi_{1i}^2 - a_i \xi_{1i}\zeta_{1i},
\end{cases}
$$

and

$$
\begin{cases}
\mathcal{J}_i = \xi_{2i}\zeta_{2i} - b_j\xi_{2i}^2 + \frac{1}{2}\sum_{j=1}^{n}\xi_{2i}^2|q_{ij}|(\omega_i + \gamma_i), \\
\mathcal{K}_i = \frac{1}{2}\sum_{j=1}^{n}|\xi_{2i}||\zeta_{2i}||q_{ij}|(\omega_i + \gamma_i) + \frac{1}{2}\sum_{j=1}^{n}\left(\xi_{1i}^2|p_{ji}|\beta_j + |\xi_{1i}||\zeta_{1i}||p_{ji}|\beta_j\right) \\
\qquad + \frac{1}{2}\sum_{j=1}^{n}\left(\xi_{2i}^2|q_{ij}|\gamma_i + |\xi_{2i}||\zeta_{2i}||q_{ij}|\gamma_i\right) - h_j\xi_{2i}\zeta_{2i}, \\
\mathcal{L}_i = \lambda_{2i} + \zeta_{2i}^2 - h_j\xi_{2i}^2 - b_j\xi_{2i}\zeta_{2i}.
\end{cases}
$$

Proof. Let $\mathbf{m(t)} = (m_1(t), m_2(t), \cdots, m_n(t))$, $\mathbf{z(t)} = (z_1(t), z_2(t), \cdots, z_n(t))$ and $\mathbf{m^*(t)} = (m_1^*(t), m_2^*(t), \cdots, m_n^*(t))$, $\mathbf{z^*(t)} = (z_1^*(t), z_2^*(t), \cdots, z_n^*(t))$ be two different solutions of system (1). Denote $x_i(t) = m_i(t) - m_i^*(t)$, $y_j(t) = z_j(t) - z_j^*(t)$, then

$$
\begin{cases}
x_i''(t) = -a_i x_i'(t) - d_i x_i(t) + \sum_{j=1}^{n} p_{ji}\tilde{f}_j(x_j(t - \sigma_{ji}), y_j(t - \tau_{ji})), \\
y_j''(t) = -b_j y_j'(t) - h_j y_j(t) + \sum_{i=1}^{n} q_{ij}\tilde{g}_i(x_i(t - \delta_{ij}), y_i(t - \eta_{ij})),
\end{cases}
\tag{5}
$$

where

$$
\tilde{f}_j(x_j, y_j) = f_j(m_j, z_j) - f_j(m_j^*, z_j^*),
$$

and

$$
\tilde{g}_i(x_i(t), y_i(t)) = g_i(m_i(t), z_i(t)) - g_j(m_i^*(t), z_i^*(t)).
$$

We deduce from the continuity theory and (3)–(4) that there is a constant $\varepsilon > 0$ satisfying

$$
\mathfrak{I}_i^\varepsilon < 0, \quad \mathcal{J}_i^\varepsilon < 0,
$$

and

$$
4\mathfrak{I}_i^\varepsilon \mathfrak{K}_i^\varepsilon > (\mathfrak{L}_i^\varepsilon)^2, \quad 4\mathcal{J}_i^\varepsilon \mathcal{K}_i^\varepsilon > (\mathcal{L}_i^\varepsilon)^2,
$$

where

$$
\begin{cases}
\mathfrak{I}_i^\varepsilon = \xi_{1i}^2\varepsilon + \xi_{1i}\zeta_{1i} - a_i\xi_{1i}^2 + \frac{1}{2}\sum_{j=1}^{n}\xi_{1i}^2|p_{ji}|(\alpha_j + \beta_j), \\
\mathfrak{K}_i^\varepsilon = \lambda_{1i}\varepsilon + \zeta_{1i}^2\varepsilon + \frac{1}{2}\sum_{j=1}^{n}|\xi_{1i}||\zeta_{1i}||p_{ji}|(\alpha_j + \beta_j) \\
\qquad + \frac{1}{2}\sum_{j=1}^{n}\left(\xi_{1i}^2|p_{ji}|\alpha_j + |\xi_{1i}||\zeta_{1i}||p_{ji}|\alpha_j\right) \\
\qquad + \frac{1}{2}\sum_{j=1}^{n}\left(\xi_{2i}^2|q_{ij}|\omega_i + |\xi_{2i}||\zeta_{2i}||q_{ij}|\omega_i\right) - d_i\xi_{1i}\zeta_{1i}, \\
\mathfrak{L}_i^\varepsilon = \lambda_{1i} + \zeta_{1i}^2 + 2\varepsilon\xi_{1i}\zeta_{1i} - d_i\xi_{1i}^2 - a_i\xi_{1i}\zeta_{1i},
\end{cases}
\tag{6}
$$

and

$$
\begin{cases}
\mathcal{J}_i^\varepsilon = \xi_{2i}^2\varepsilon + \xi_{2i}\zeta_{2i} - b_j\xi_{2i}^2 + \frac{1}{2}\sum_{j=1}^n \xi_{2i}^2|q_{ij}|(\omega_i + \gamma_i), \\[2mm]
\mathcal{K}_i^\varepsilon = \lambda_{2i}\varepsilon + \zeta_{2i}^2\varepsilon + \frac{1}{2}\sum_{j=1}^n |\xi_{2i}||\zeta_{2i}||q_{ij}|(\omega_i + \gamma_i) \\[2mm]
\qquad + \frac{1}{2}\sum_{j=1}^n \left(\xi_{1i}^2|p_{ji}|\beta_j + |\xi_{1i}||\zeta_{1i}||p_{ji}|\beta_j\right) \\[2mm]
\qquad + \frac{1}{2}\sum_{j=1}^n \left(\xi_{2i}^2|q_{ij}|\gamma_i + |\xi_{2i}||\zeta_{2i}||q_{ij}|\gamma_i\right) - h_j\xi_{2i}\zeta_{2i}, \\[2mm]
\mathcal{L}_i^\varepsilon = \lambda_{2i} + \zeta_{2i}^2 + 2\varepsilon\xi_{2i}\zeta_{2i} - h_j\xi_{2i}^2 - b_j\xi_{2i}\zeta_{2i}.
\end{cases}
\tag{7}
$$

Designing Lyapunov function with integral term as follows:

$$
V(r) = \underbrace{\frac{1}{2}\sum_{i=1}^n \lambda_{1i}x_i^2(r)e^{2\varepsilon t} + \frac{1}{2}\sum_{i=1}^n (\xi_{1i}x_i'(r) + \zeta_{1i}x_i(r))^2 e^{2\varepsilon r}}_{V_1(r)}
$$

$$
+ \underbrace{\frac{1}{2}\sum_{i=1}^n \lambda_{2i}y_i^2(r)e^{2\varepsilon r} + \frac{1}{2}\sum_{i=1}^n (\xi_{2i}y_i'(r) + \zeta_{2i}y_i(r))^2 e^{2\varepsilon r}}_{V_2(r)}
$$

$$
+ \underbrace{\frac{1}{2}\sum_{i,j=1}^n [\xi_{1i}^2|p_{ji}|\alpha_j + |\xi_{1i}||\zeta_{1i}||p_{ji}|\alpha_j]\int_{r-\sigma_{ji}}^r e^{2\varepsilon(s+r_1)}(x_j(s))^2 ds}_{V_3(r)}
\tag{8}
$$

$$
+ \underbrace{\frac{1}{2}\sum_{i,j=1}^n [\xi_{1i}^2|p_{ji}|\beta_j + |\xi_{1i}||\zeta_{1i}||p_{ji}|\beta_j]\int_{r-\tau_{ji}}^r e^{2\varepsilon(s+r_2)}(y_j(s))^2 ds}_{V_3(r)}
$$

$$
+ \underbrace{\frac{1}{2}\sum_{i,j=1}^n [\xi_{2i}^2|q_{ij}|\omega_i + |\xi_{2i}||\zeta_{2i}||q_{ij}|\omega_i]\int_{r-\delta_{ij}}^r e^{2\varepsilon(s+r_1)}(x_i(s))^2 ds}_{V_4(r)}
$$

$$
+ \underbrace{\frac{1}{2}\sum_{i,j=1}^n [\xi_{2i}^2|q_{ij}|\gamma_i + |\xi_{2i}||\zeta_{2i}||q_{ij}|\gamma_i]\int_{r-\eta_{ij}}^t e^{2\varepsilon(s+r_2)}(y_i(s))^2 ds}_{V_4(r)}\,.
$$

Compute the derivatives of (8), we deduce

$$\frac{dV_1(r)}{dr} = 2\varepsilon\left[\frac{1}{2}\sum_{i=1}^n \lambda_{1i}x_i^2(r)e^{2\varepsilon r} + \frac{1}{2}\sum_{i=1}^n (\xi_{1i}x_i'(r) + \zeta_{1i}x_i(r))^2 e^{2\varepsilon r}\right]$$

$$+ \sum_{i=1}^n \lambda_{1i}x_i(r)x_i'(r)e^{2\varepsilon r} + \sum_{i=1}^n (\xi_{1i}x_i'(r) + \zeta_{1i}x_i(r))(\xi_{1i}x_i''(r) + \zeta_{1i}x_i'(r))e^{2\varepsilon r}$$

$$= 2\varepsilon\left[\frac{1}{2}\sum_{i=1}^n \lambda_{1i}x_i^2(r)e^{2\varepsilon r} + \frac{1}{2}\sum_{i=1}^n (\xi_{1i}x_i'(r) + \zeta_{1i}x_i(r))^2 e^{2\varepsilon r}\right]$$

$$+ \sum_{i=1}^n (\lambda_{1i} + \zeta_{1i}^2)x_i(r)x_i'(r)e^{2\varepsilon r} + \sum_{i=1}^n (\xi_{1i}\zeta_{1i})(x_i'(r))^2 e^{2\varepsilon r}$$

$$+ \sum_{i=1}^n \xi_{1i}(\xi_{1i}x_i'(r) + \zeta_{1i}x_i(r))e^{2\varepsilon r}\left[-a_ix_i'(r) - d_ix_i(r)\right.$$

$$\left. + \sum_{j=1}^n p_{ji}(\alpha_j|x_j(r - \sigma_{ji})| + \beta_j|y_j(r - \tau_{ji})|)\right]$$

$$\leq e^{2\varepsilon r}\left[\sum_{i=1}^n (\lambda_{1i} + \zeta_{1i}^2 + 2\varepsilon\xi_{1i}\zeta_{1i} - d_i\xi_{1i}^2 - a_i\xi_{1i}\zeta_{1i})x_i(r)x_i'(r)\right.$$

$$+ \sum_{i=1}^n (\lambda_{1i}\varepsilon + \zeta_{1i}^2\varepsilon - d_i\xi_{1i}\zeta_{1i})(x_i(r))^2$$

$$+ \sum_{i=1}^n (\xi_{1i}^2\varepsilon + \xi_{1i}\zeta_{1i} - a_i\xi_{1i}^2)(x_i'(r))^2$$

$$+ \left.\sum_{i=1}^n\sum_{j=1}^n (\xi_{1i}^2|x_i'(r)| + |\xi_{1i}||\zeta_{1i}||x_i(r)|)|p_{ji}|(\alpha_j|x_j(r - \sigma_{ji})| + \beta_j|y_j(r - \tau_{ji})|)\right].$$

$$(9)$$

By the elementary inequalities, we have that

$$\sum_{i,j=1}^{n} (\xi_{1i}^2 |x_i'(r)| + |\xi_{1i}||\zeta_{1i}||x_i(r)|)|p_{ji}|(\alpha_j |x_j(t - \sigma_{ji})| + \beta_j |y_j(r - \tau_{ji})|)$$

$$= \sum_{i,j=1}^{n} \xi_{1i}^2 |p_{ji}||x_i'(r)|(\alpha_j |x_j(r - \sigma_{ji})| + \beta_j |y_j(r - \tau_{ji})|)$$

$$+ \sum_{i,j=1}^{n} |\xi_{1i}||\zeta_{1i}||p_{ji}||x_i(r)|(\alpha_j |x_j(r - \sigma_{ji})| + \beta_j |y_j(r - \tau_{ji})|)$$

$$\leq \frac{1}{2} \sum_{i,j=1}^{n} \xi_{1i}^2 |p_{ji}|\alpha_j [(x_i'(r))^2 + (x_j(r - \sigma_{ji}))^2]$$

$$+ \frac{1}{2} \sum_{i,j=1}^{n} \xi_{1i}^2 |p_{ji}|\beta_j [(x_i'(r))^2 + (y_j(r - \tau_{ji}))^2]$$

$$+ \frac{1}{2} \sum_{i,j=1}^{n} |\xi_{1i}||\zeta_{1i}||p_{ji}|\alpha_j [(x_i(r))^2 + (x_j(r - \sigma_{ji}))^2] \tag{10}$$

$$+ \frac{1}{2} \sum_{i,j=1}^{n} |\xi_{1i}||\zeta_{1i}||p_{ji}|\beta_j [(x_i(r))^2 + (y_j(r - \tau_{ji}))^2]$$

$$= \frac{1}{2} \sum_{i,j=1}^{n} \xi_{1i}^2 |p_{ji}|(\alpha_j + \beta_j)(x_i'(r))^2 + \frac{1}{2} \sum_{i,j=1}^{n} |\xi_{1i}||\zeta_{1i}||p_{ji}|(\alpha_j + \beta_j)(x_i(r))^2$$

$$+ \frac{1}{2} \sum_{i,j=1}^{n} [\xi_{1i}^2 |p_{ji}|\alpha_j + |\xi_{1i}||\zeta_{1i}||p_{ji}|\alpha_j](x_j(r - \sigma_{ji}))^2$$

$$+ \frac{1}{2} \sum_{i,j-1}^{n} [\xi_{1i}^2 |p_{ji}|\beta_j + |\xi_{1i}||\zeta_{1i}||p_{ji}|\beta_j](y_j(r - \tau_{ji}))^2.$$

Putting (9) and (10) together, we have

$$\frac{dV_1(r)}{dr} \leq e^{2\varepsilon r} \Bigg[\sum_{i=1}^{n} (\lambda_{1i} + \zeta_{1i}^2 + 2\varepsilon \xi_{1i}\zeta_{1i} - d_i \xi_{1i}^2 - a_i \xi_{1i}\zeta_{1i})x_i(r)x_i'(r)$$

$$+ \sum_{i=1}^{n} \Big(\lambda_{1i}\varepsilon + \zeta_{1i}^2\varepsilon - d_i \xi_{1i}\zeta_{1i} + \frac{1}{2} \sum_{j=1}^{n} |\xi_{1i}||\zeta_{1i}||p_{ji}|(\alpha_j + \beta_j)\Big)(x_i(r))^2$$

$$+ \sum_{i=1}^{n} \Big(\xi_{1i}^2\varepsilon + \xi_{1i}\zeta_{1i} - a_i \xi_{1i}^2 + \frac{1}{2} \sum_{j=1}^{n} \xi_{1i}^2 |p_{ji}|(\alpha_j + \beta_j)\Big)(x_i'(t))^2 \tag{11}$$

$$+ \frac{1}{2} \sum_{i,j=1}^{n} [\xi_{1i}^2 |p_{ji}|\alpha_j + |\xi_{1i}||\zeta_{1i}||p_{ji}|\alpha_j](x_j(r - \sigma_{ji}))^2$$

$$+ \frac{1}{2} \sum_{i,j=1}^{n} [\xi_{1i}^2 |p_{ji}|\beta_j + |\xi_{1i}||\zeta_{1i}||p_{ji}|\beta_j](y_j(r - \tau_{ji}))^2 \Bigg].$$

Analogously, we have

$$
\begin{aligned}
\frac{dV_2(r)}{dr} \leq & e^{2\varepsilon r}\Bigg[\sum_{i=1}^{n}(\lambda_{2i} + \zeta_{2i}^2 + 2\varepsilon\xi_{2i}\zeta_{2i} - h_j\xi_{2i}^2 - b_j\xi_{2i}\zeta_{2i})y_i(r)y_i'(r) \\
& + \sum_{i=1}^{n}\Big(\lambda_{2i}\varepsilon + \zeta_{2i}^2\varepsilon - h_j\xi_{2i}\zeta_{2i} + \frac{1}{2}\sum_{j=1}^{n}|\xi_{2i}||\zeta_{2i}||q_{ij}|(\omega_i + \gamma_i)\Big)(y_i(r))^2 \\
& + \sum_{i=1}^{n}\Big(\xi_{2i}^2\varepsilon + \xi_{2i}\zeta_{2i} - b_j\xi_{2i}^2 + \frac{1}{2}\sum_{j=1}^{n}\xi_{2i}^2|q_{ij}|(\omega_i + \gamma_i)\Big)(y_i'(t))^2 \\
& + \frac{1}{2}\sum_{i,j=1}^{n}[\xi_{2i}^2|q_{ij}|\omega_i + |\xi_{2i}||\zeta_{2i}||q_{ij}|\omega_i](x_i(r - \delta_{ij}))^2 \\
& + \frac{1}{2}\sum_{i,j=1}^{n}[\xi_{2i}^2|q_{ij}|\gamma_i + |\xi_{2i}||\zeta_{2i}||q_{ij}|\gamma_i](y_i(r - \eta_{ij}))^2\Bigg].
\end{aligned}
\tag{12}
$$

Through a simple manipulation, one yields

$$
\begin{aligned}
\frac{dV_3(r)}{dt} \leq & \frac{1}{2}\sum_{i,j=1}^{n}[\xi_{1i}^2|p_{ji}|\alpha_j + |\xi_{1i}||\zeta_{1i}||p_{ji}|\alpha_j]e^{2\varepsilon r}(x_j(r))^2 \\
& - \frac{1}{2}\sum_{i,j=1}^{n}[\xi_{1i}^2|p_{ji}|\alpha_j + |\xi_{1i}||\zeta_{1i}||p_{ji}|\alpha_j]e^{2\varepsilon r}(x_j(r - \sigma_{ji}))^2 \\
& + \frac{1}{2}\sum_{i,j=1}^{n}[\xi_{1i}^2|p_{ji}|\beta_j + |\xi_{1i}||\zeta_{1i}||p_{ji}|\beta_j]e^{2\varepsilon r}(y_j(r))^2 \\
& - \frac{1}{2}\sum_{i,j=1}^{n}[\xi_{1i}^2|p_{ji}|\beta_j + |\xi_{1i}||\zeta_{1i}||p_{ji}|\beta_j]e^{2\varepsilon r}(y_j(r - \tau_{ji}))^2,
\end{aligned}
\tag{13}
$$

and

$$
\begin{aligned}
\frac{dV_4(r)}{dr} \leq & \frac{1}{2}\sum_{i,j=1}^{n}[\xi_{2i}^2|q_{ij}|\omega_i + |\xi_{2i}||\zeta_{2i}||q_{ij}|\omega_i]e^{2\varepsilon r}(x_i(r))^2 \\
& - \frac{1}{2}\sum_{i,j=1}^{n}[\xi_{2i}^2|q_{ij}|\omega_i + |\xi_{2i}||\zeta_{2i}||q_{ij}|\omega_i]e^{2\varepsilon r}(x_i(r - \delta_{ij}))^2 \\
& + \frac{1}{2}\sum_{i,j=1}^{n}[\xi_{2i}^2|q_{ij}|\gamma_i + |\xi_{2i}||\zeta_{2i}||q_{ij}|\gamma_i]e^{2\varepsilon r}(y_i(r))^2 \\
& - \frac{1}{2}\sum_{i,j=1}^{n}[\xi_{2i}^2|q_{ij}|\gamma_i + |\xi_{2i}||\zeta_{2i}||q_{ij}|\gamma_i]e^{2\varepsilon r}(y_i(r - \eta_{ij}))^2.
\end{aligned}
\tag{14}
$$

With the help of (11)–(14) and (8) produces

$$
\begin{aligned}
\frac{dV(r)}{dr} \leq & e^{2\varepsilon r}\bigg\{ \sum_{i=1}^{n} (\lambda_{1i} + \zeta_{1i}^2 + 2\varepsilon\xi_{1i}\zeta_{1i} - d_i\xi_{1i}^2 - a_i\xi_{1i}\zeta_{1i})x_i(r)x_i'(r) \\
& + \sum_{i=1}^{n}\bigg[\lambda_{1i}\varepsilon + \zeta_{1i}^2\varepsilon - d_i\xi_{1i}\zeta_{1i} + \frac{1}{2}\sum_{j=1}^{n}|\xi_{1i}||\zeta_{1i}||p_{ji}|(\alpha_j + \beta_j) \\
& + \frac{1}{2}\sum_{j=1}^{n}\left(\xi_{1i}^2|p_{ji}|\alpha_j + |\xi_{1i}||\zeta_{1i}||p_{ji}|\alpha_j\right) \\
& + \frac{1}{2}\sum_{j=1}^{n}\left(\xi_{2i}^2|q_{ij}|\omega_i + |\xi_{2i}||\zeta_{2i}||q_{ij}|\omega_i\right)\bigg](x_i(r))^2 \\
& + \sum_{i=1}^{n}\left(\xi_{1i}^2\varepsilon + \xi_{1i}\zeta_{1i} - a_i\xi_{1i}^2 + \frac{1}{2}\sum_{j=1}^{n}\xi_{1i}^2|p_{ji}|(\alpha_j + \beta_j)\right)(x_i'(r))^2\bigg\} \\
& + e^{2\varepsilon r}\bigg\{ \sum_{i=1}^{n}(\lambda_{2i} + \zeta_{2i}^2 + 2\varepsilon\xi_{2i}\zeta_{2i} - h_j\xi_{2i}^2 - b_j\xi_{2i}\zeta_{2i})y_i(r)y_i'(r) \\
& + \sum_{i=1}^{n}\bigg[\lambda_{2i}\varepsilon + \zeta_{2i}^2\varepsilon - h_j\xi_{2i}\zeta_{2i} + \frac{1}{2}\sum_{j=1}^{n}|\xi_{2i}||\zeta_{2i}||q_{ij}|(\omega_i + \gamma_i) \\
& + \frac{1}{2}\sum_{j=1}^{n}\left(\xi_{1i}^2|p_{ji}|\beta_j + |\xi_{1i}||\zeta_{1i}||p_{ji}|\beta_j\right) + \frac{1}{2}\sum_{i=1}^{n}\sum_{j=1}^{n}\left(\xi_{2i}^2|q_{ij}|\gamma_i\right. \\
& \left. + |\xi_{2i}||\zeta_{2i}||q_{ij}|\gamma_i\right)\bigg](y_i(t))^2 \\
& + \sum_{i=1}^{n}\left(\xi_{2i}^2\varepsilon + \xi_{2i}\zeta_{2i} - b_j\xi_{2i}^2 + \frac{1}{2}\sum_{j=1}^{n}\xi_{2i}^2|q_{ij}|(\omega_i + \gamma_i)\right)(y_i'(t))^2\bigg\} \\
= & e^{2\varepsilon t}\bigg\{ \sum_{i=1}^{n}\left[\mathfrak{J}_i^\varepsilon(x_i'(r))^2 + \mathfrak{K}_i^\varepsilon(x_i(r))^2 + \mathfrak{L}_i^\varepsilon x_i(r)x_i'(r)\right] \\
& + \sum_{i=1}^{n}\left[\mathcal{J}_i^\varepsilon(y_i'(r))^2 + \mathcal{K}_i^\varepsilon(y_i(r))^2 + \mathcal{L}_i^\varepsilon y_i(r)y_i'(r)\right]\bigg\} \\
= & e^{2\varepsilon r}\bigg\{ \sum_{i=1}^{n}\mathfrak{J}_i^\varepsilon\left(x_i'(r) + \frac{\mathfrak{L}_i^\varepsilon}{2\mathfrak{J}_i^\varepsilon}x_i(r)\right)^2 + \sum_{i=1}^{n}\left(\mathfrak{K}_i^\varepsilon - \frac{(\mathfrak{L}_i^\varepsilon)^2}{4\mathfrak{J}_i^\varepsilon}\right)(x_i(r))^2 \\
& + \sum_{i=1}^{n}\mathcal{J}_i^\varepsilon\left(y_i'(r) + \frac{\mathcal{L}_i^\varepsilon}{2\mathcal{J}_i^\varepsilon}y_i(r)\right)^2 + \sum_{i=1}^{n}\left(\mathcal{K}_i^\varepsilon - \frac{(\mathcal{L}_i^\varepsilon)^2}{4\mathcal{J}_i^\varepsilon}\right)(y_i(r))^2\bigg\} \\
\leq & 0, \quad \text{for all} \quad r \in [0, \infty).
\end{aligned}
\tag{15}
$$

Therefore,

$$V(r) \leq V(0), \quad \text{for all} \quad r \in [0, \infty),$$

we can deduce from (8) that

$$|x_i(r)| \leq Me^{-\varepsilon r}, \quad |y_i(r)| \leq Me^{-\varepsilon r},$$

where M is a constant, the above inequality means that $|x_i(r)|$, $|y_i(r)|$ exponentially converge to 0. The proof of Theorem 1 is ended.

4 Numerical Simulations

Example 1. Consider the inertial delayed general BAM NNs with a general binary activation function:

$$
\begin{cases}
m_i''(t) = -a_i m_i'(t) - d_i m_i(t) + \sum_{j=1}^{2} p_{ji} f_j(m_j(t-0.4), z_j(t-0.4)) + I_i, \\
z_j''(t) = -b_j z_j'(t) - h_j z_j(t) + \sum_{i=1}^{2} q_{ij} g_i(m_i(t-0.4), z_i(t-0.4)) + J_j,
\end{cases}
\tag{16}
$$

where
$$
f_j(u,v) = g_i(u,v) = 0.8|u| + 0.2|v|, \quad i,j = 1,2,
$$

where $a_1 = 4.21$, $a_2 = 3.15$, $b_1 = 4.15$, $b_2 = 3.9$, $p_{11} = q_{11} = 1.46$, $p_{12} = q_{12} = -1.28$, $p_{21} = q_{21} = -2.1$, $p_{22} = q_{22} = 1.9$, $I_1 = J_1 = 1.5$, $I_2 = J_2 = 1.2$, $d_1 = 10$, $d_2 = 9$, $h_1 = 5.2$, $h_2 = 7.1$. By a simple calculation, we have $\alpha_j = \omega_i = 0.8$, $\beta_j = \gamma_i = 0.2$, $\xi_{1i} = \xi_{2i} = \zeta_{1i} = \zeta_{2i} = 1$, $\lambda_{11} = 11.36$, $\lambda_{12} = 10.15$, $\lambda_{21} = 8.2$, $\lambda_{22} = 8.5$, and

$$
\mathfrak{J}_1 = -1.43, \mathfrak{K}_2 = -0.56, \mathfrak{K}_1 = -3.18, \mathfrak{K}_2 = -1.666, \mathfrak{L}_1 = -1.85, \mathfrak{L}_2 = -1,
$$

and

$$
\mathcal{J}_1 = -1.78, \mathcal{J}_2 = -0.9, \mathcal{K}_1 = -2.57, \mathcal{K}_2 = -3.664, \mathcal{L}_1 = -0.15, \mathcal{L}_2 = -1.5.
$$

It is easy to see that

$$
\mathfrak{J}_1 < 0, \quad 4\mathfrak{J}_1\mathfrak{K}_1 = 18.1896 > 3.4225 = \mathfrak{L}_1^2,
$$

$$
\mathfrak{J}_2 < 0, \quad 4\mathfrak{J}_2\mathfrak{K}_2 \approx 3.7318 > 1 = \mathfrak{L}_2^2,
$$

and

$$
\mathcal{J}_1 < 0, \quad 4\mathcal{J}_1\mathcal{K}_1 = 18.2984 > 0.0225 = \mathcal{L}_1^2,
$$

$$
\mathcal{J}_2 < 0, \quad 4\mathcal{J}_2\mathcal{K}_2 = 13.1904 > 2.25 = \mathcal{L}_2^2.
$$

that the system (16) is exponentially stable. The performed numerical simulations by Matlab to strongly verify this fact, see Figs. 1–2.

Remark 1. In recent years, many nice theoretical results concerning the dynamics of BAM NNs have been reported, see, e.g., [6,9,24–26], nevertheless, the models studied in the aforementioned references do not include the inertial effect, and therefore the established results effectively complement and extend existing ones. On the other hand, by choosing proper variable transformation and reduced-order approach, the authors in [27–30] studied the dynamical behaviors of inertial BAM NNs, clearly, the non reduced-order methods employed in this paper enrich the analysis method for studying inertial BAM NNs.

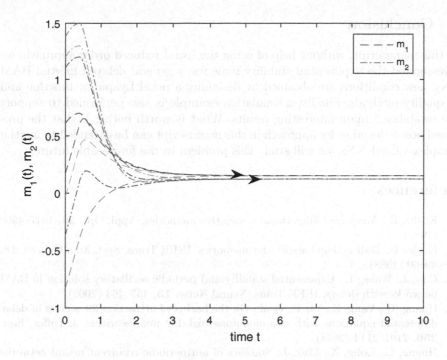

Fig. 1. The orbit graphics of variables $m_i(t)$ with distinct initial datas.

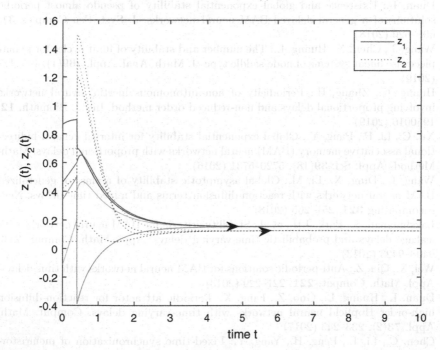

Fig. 2. The orbit graphics of variables $z_i(t)$ with distinct initial datas.

5   Conclusion

In this manuscript, without help of using the usual reduced order approach, we investigated the exponential stability issue for a general delayed inertial BAM NNs, new conditions are obtained by designing a novel Lyapunov function and inequality methods. Finally, a simulation example is also performed to support the established main interesting results. What is worth noting is that the proposed non-reduced order approach in this manuscript can be extended to inertial complex-valued NNs, we will study this problem in the foreseeable future.

References

1. Kosko, B.: Adaptive bidirectional associative memories. Appl. Opt. **26**, 4947–4960 (1987)
2. Kosko, B.: Bidirectional associative memories. IEEE Trans. Syst. Man Cybern. **18**, 49–60 (1988)
3. Cao, J., Wang, L.: Exponential stability and periodic oscillatory solution in BAM networks with delays. IEEE Trans. Neural Netw. **13**, 457–463 (2002)
4. Huang, C., Yang, Z., Yi, T., et al.: On the basins of attraction for a class of delay differential equations with non-monotone bistable nonlinearities. J. Differ. Equ. **256**, 2101–2114 (2014)
5. Huang, C., Long, X., Cao, J.: Stability of antiperiodic recurrent neural networks with multiproportional delays. Math. Methods Appl. Sci. **43**(9), 6093–6102 (2020)
6. Duan, L.: Existence and global exponential stability of pseudo almost periodic solutions of a general delayed BAM neural networks. J. Syst. Sci. Complex **31**, 608–620 (2018)
7. Wang, J., Chen, X., Huang, L.: The number and stability of limit cycles for planar piecewise linear systems of node-saddle type. J. Math. Anal. Appl. **469**(1), 405–427 (2019)
8. Huang, C., Zhang, H.: Periodicity of non-autonomous inertial neural networks involving proportional delays and non-reduced order method. Int. J. Biomath. **12**, 1950016 (2019)
9. Xu, C., Li, P., Pang, Y.: Global exponential stability for interval general bidirectional associative memory (BAM) neural networks with proportional delays. Math. Methods Appl. Sci. **39**(18), 5720–5731 (2016)
10. Wang, L., Ding, X., Li, M.: Global asymptotic stability of a class of generalized BAM neural networks with reaction-diffusion terms and mixed time delays. Neurocomputing **321**, 251–265 (2018)
11. Lakshmanan, S., Park, J.H., et al.: Stability criteria for BAM neural networks with leakage delays and probabilistic time-varying delays. Appl. Math. Comput. **219**, 9408–9423 (2013)
12. Wei, X., Qiu, Z.: Anti-periodic solutions for BAM neural networks with time delays. Appl. Math. Comput. **221**, 221–229 (2013)
13. Duan, L., Huang, L., Guo, Z., Fang, X.: Periodic attractor for reaction-diffusion high-order Hopfield neural networks with time-varying delays. Comput. Math. Appl. **73**(2), 233–245 (2017)
14. Chen, C., Li, L., Peng, H., Yang, Y.: Fixed-time synchronization of memristor-based BAM neural networks with time-varying discrete delay. Neural Netw. **96**, 47–54 (2017)

15. Duan, L., Shi, M., Huang, L.: New results on finite-/fixed-time synchronization of delayed diffusive fuzzy HNNs with discontinuous activations. Fuzzy Sets Syst. (2020). https://doi.org/10.1016/j.fss.2020.04.016

16. Gupta, P., Majee, N., Roy, A.: Stability and Hopf-bifurcation analysis of delayed BAM neural network under dynamic thresholds with distributed delay Nonlinear Anal. Model. Control 14, 435–461 (2009)

17. Huang, C., Zhang, H., Cao, J., Hu, H.: Stability and Hopf bifurcation of a delayed prey–predator model with disease in the predator. nt. J. Bifur. Chaos 29(07), 1950091 (2019)

18. Babcock, K.L., Westervelt, R.M.: Stability and dynamics of simple electronic neural networks with added inertia. Phys. D 23, 464–469 (1986)

19. Angelaki, D.E., Correia, M.J.: Models of membrane resonance in pigeon semicircular canal type II hair cells. Biol. Cybern. 65(1), 1–10 (1991)

20. Shi, M., Guo, J., Fang, X., Huang, C.: Global exponential stability of delayed inertial competitive neural networks. Adv. Differ. Equ. 2020(87), 1–12 (2020)

21. Li, X., Li, X., Hu, C.: Some new results on stability and synchronization for delayed inertial neural networks based on non-reduced order method. Neural Netw. 96, 91–100 (2017)

22. Huang, C., Liu, B.: New studies on dynamic analysis of inertial neural networks involving non-reduced order method. Neurocomputing 325, 283–287 (2019)

23. Hu, H., Zou, X.: Existence of an extinction wave in the Fisher equation with a shifting habitat. Proc. Amer. Math. Soc. 145(11), 4763–4771 (2017)

24. Abdurahman, A., Jiang, H.: Nonlinear control scheme for general decay projective synchronization of delayed memristor-based BAM neural networks. Neurocomputing 357, 282–291 (2019)

25. Zhang, J., Huang, C.: Dynamics analysis on a class of delayed neural networks involving inertial terms. Adv. Differ. Equ. 2020(1), 1–12 (2020)

26. Wang, J., Huang, C., Huang, L.: Discontinuity-induced limit cycles in a general planar piecewise linear system of saddle-focus type. Nonlinear Anal. Hybrid Syst. 33, 162–178 (2019)

27. Qi, J., Li, C., Huang, T.: Stability of inertial BAM neural network with time-varying delay via impulsive control. Neurocomputing 161, 162–167 (2015)

28. Zhang, Z., Quan, Z.: Global exponential stability via inequality technique for inertial BAM neural networks with time delays. Neurocomputing 151, 1316–1326 (2015)

29. Zhang, W., Huang, T., Li, C., Yang, J.: Robust stability of inertial BAM neural networks with time delays and uncertainties via impulsive effect. Neural Process. Lett. 48, 245–256 (2018)

30. Maharajan, C., Raja, R., Cao, J., Rajchakit, G.: Novel global robust exponential stability criterion for uncertain inertial-type BAM neural networks with discrete and distributed time-varying delays via Lagrange sense. J. Franklin Inst. 355, 4727–4754 (2018)

Simulation Study on Chinese Stock Market Development Based on System Dynamics Model

Chenggang Li[1,2] and Tao Lin[1(✉)]

[1] School of Big Data Application and Economics, Guizhou University
of Finance and Economics, Guiyang 550025, China
[2] Collaborative Innovation Center for Poverty Reduction and Development in Western China,
Guiyang 550025, China

Abstract. This paper selects money supply, interest rate and gross domestic product (GDP) as the key variables that affect the stock market value, and builds a system dynamics simulation model. The annual data from 2011 to 2018 are selected to simulate and analyze the impact of money supply, interest rate and GDP on the development of the stock market by adjusting the values of key variables. The simulation results show that money supply and GDP have a positive effect on stock market value, while interest rate has a negative effect on stock market value.

Keywords: Stock market development · System dynamics · Simulation

1 Introduction

Since the establishment of the Shanghai stock exchange in the 1990s, China's stock market has experienced 29 years of rapid development. By the end of 2018, China's A-share market value had reached 43.37 trillion yuan, with 3,570 listed companies. The stock market is the barometer of national economic development, and the sustained and stable development of the stock market is crucial to national economic development. On one hand, high-quality enterprises with good development status and capital needs can be listed on the stock market for financing, thus promoting the development of the real economy; On the other hand, the healthy and sustainable development of the stock market also provides investment channels for the idle funds of individual investors and enterprises, thus improving the utilization efficiency of social funds. Conversely, the sustained and healthy development of the national economy can also promote the development and improvement of the stock market.

China's stock market has a long history of "policy market", "bull short bear long" said. Compared with the US stock market, the Chinese stock market started late and developed relatively immaturely. The research on the development and fluctuation of stock market has always been the focus of scholars. In this paper, through the literature analysis method, we use system dynamics theory to build a simulation model, to simulate the stock market under the comprehensive effect of various factors. Based on the simulation results, it is expected to put forward relevant policy suggestions for promoting the development of the stock market and reducing the volatility of the stock market.

H. Song and D. Jiang (Eds.): SIMUtools 2020, LNICST 369, pp. 238–250, 2021.
https://doi.org/10.1007/978-3-030-72792-5_22

2 Literature Review

There are many factors influencing the development and volatility of the stock market. Domestic and foreign scholars mainly study the stock market from the following three aspects:

First, the impact of money supply on stock market volatility and stock market development. Ioannidis and Kontonika (2007) [1] studied the relationship between monetary policy changes and stock market returns in 13 OECD countries from 1972 to 2002. The results showed that monetary policy changes had a significant impact on stock market returns and the stock market transmission mechanism of monetary policy was effective. Jansen and Tsai (2010) [2] divided stock returns into bull market and bear market by using data from 1994 to 2005, and respectively studied the impact of monetary policy on stock market. The empirical results showed that monetary policy had a negative and significant impact on stock market in bear market. Xiao (2012) [3] by using Granger causality test and Vector Autoregressive model, analyzed of the interactions of the money supply and stock market. The empirical results found that changes in the money supply has a certain influence on stock price, but the effect was not significant. However money supply changes affect the stock price volatility to a certain extent. Bekaert et al. (2013) [4] decomposed the stock market volatility index VIX into two parts: risk aversion and stock market expectation risk, building the VAR model, and analyzed the correlation between them by impulse response analysis and variance decomposition. The research results showed that loose monetary policy reduced risk aversion and uncertainty. Xu et al. (2014) [5] took the data of China's money supply and stock market volatility from 1997 to 2013 and used wavelet analysis to study the correlation between money supply and SSE composite index volatility. The empirical results show that M1 change and SSE index volatility have significant interaction effect in the short and medium term, while M2 change and SSE index volatility have significant interaction effect in the short term. Liu et al. (2015) [6] divided Chinese stock market into three interval states by using data from 1997 to 2014 and SSE vector autoregressive model, and analyzed the influence of monetary policy on stock market return rate under different interval states. The results show that monetary policy has an asymmetric effect on stock market return. Fang and An (2019) [7] selected the monthly data of Shanghai composite index and money supply (M2) from 2001 to 2019 and conducted an empirical study on the relationship between money supply and stock market by using VAR model and BEKK-GARCH model. The empirical results showed that money supply had unilateral volatility spillover effect on the stock market.

Second, the impact of interest rate adjustment on stock market volatility. Roberto and Sack (2003) [8] conducted an empirical study on the relationship between interest rate adjustment and stock price volatility. The empirical results showed that when short-term interest rate was increased by 0.25%, the S&P index dropped by 1.9%. Rigobon and Brian (2004) [9] analyzed the relationship between monetary policy changes and stock market fluctuations in the United States, and the results showed that short-term interest rates were negatively correlated with stock prices. Bernanke and Kuttner (2005) [10] used event analysis to study the impact of unexpected changes in the funds rate on stock market returns. The results showed that when the federal funds target rate was unexpectedly lowered by 0.0025%, the stock market index rose by 1%. Stock market indexes move in the opposite direction of the federal funds rate. Hu (2016) [11] selected monthly data from 2005 to 2015 and empirically analyzed the dynamic time-varying correlation among interest rate, stock price and stock market volatility by using the TVP-VAR model. The empirical results showed that during the sample period, the relationship between China's interest rate change and stock market volatility successively showed positive correlation, non-correlation and negative correlation. This shows that the interest rate transmission channel of China's monetary policy is gradually improving. Yang et al. (2017) [12] used the RS-EGARCH model to study the impact of interest rate adjustment on stock market volatility after 2012. The research results showed that when the Shanghai stock market was on the rise, the reduction of interest rate would significantly increase volatility and yield, but when the Shanghai stock market was on the decline, the yield would be significantly reduced. Wang et al. (2019) [13] selected the monthly interest rate and SSE composite index volatility data from 2001 to 2018, and used the TVP-VAR model to empirically analyze the impact of China's central bank's monetary policy on the volatility of China's stock market. The analysis results showed that the impact of interest rate on stock market volatility should be classified into stages and short and long periods. After 2012, raising interest rates will increase stock market volatility in the short term and reduce stock market volatility in the medium and long term.

Third, the interaction between stock market development and economic growth. In the research on the relationship between stock market development and economic growth, most previous literatures have studied the one-way influence of stock market growth on economic development, but few have studied the influence of economic growth on stock market development. Gavin (2006) [14] believes that the rise in the price of financial assets represented by stocks has a wealth effect. The increase in asset prices will lead to the increase in household wealth. If the marginal propensity to consume remains unchanged, the increase in household wealth will lead to the increase in consumption expenditure, thus promoting economic growth. Saciet et al. (2009) [15] constructed the GMM dynamic panel model and empirically studied the relationship between stock market volatility and economic growth. The empirical results showed that stock market development had a significant impact on economic growth. Zalgiryte et al. (2014) [16] selected GDP as a proxy indicator of economic development and studied the relationship between economic growth and stock market development in the United States and France. The results showed that stock market development was a powerful indicator of economic growth. Lin and Cao (2014) [17] used the quarterly data of stock market and economic growth from 1992 to 2012 to test the relationship between stock market development and economic growth in China by using GMM method. The test results showed that stock market development had a significant negative effect on economic growth. Ding (2018) [18] tested the two-way causal relationship between China's stock market volatility and economic growth from both linear and non-linear perspectives. The test results show that there is no significant linear Granger causality between the two, but the nonlinear Granger causality between the two is significant. Wang and Xu (2019) [19] empirically analyzed the threshold effect of stock market development on economic growth by taking the size of China's stock market as the threshold variable. The empirical results showed that the size of stock market had a negative effect on economic growth on the whole, but showed an increasing trend of marginal effect.

To sum up, domestic and foreign scholars mainly analyze the influence of interest rate, money supply and economic growth on the development and fluctuation of stock market. In terms of methods, Vector Autoregression model and Granger causality test are mainly used to analyze the mutual dynamic influence of various factors and stock market volatility. The factors influencing the development of the stock market are complex and varied, and it is not complete to analyze the explanatory power of stock market volatility only by using a certain influencing factor. At present, there are few literatures studying the development of stock market from the perspective that multiple influencing factors constitute a whole system. Based on this, this paper USES the system dynamics theory to construct a simulation model of stock market development to simulate the development of stock market. By analyzing the simulation results, it is expected to put forward targeted policy Suggestions for the sustainable and healthy development of stock market.

3 Model Construction

3.1 Data Sources

Combined with the development cycle of China's stock market, this paper selects the annual data of relevant variables from 2011 to 2018. In this period, China's stock market experienced a complete bull - bear market. The market value of the stock market is selected from the market value of Shanghai stock market, the money supply is selected from the broad money supply (M2), the interest rate is selected from the seven-day interbank lending rate, and the economic development is selected from GDP as the proxy indicator. The data came from the wind database, the national bureau of statistics website and the people's bank of China website.

3.2 System Boundary Determination and Structure Analysis

According to the theory of system dynamics, the dynamic change and development of things over time is the result of the comprehensive action of internal variables rather than external variables. By constructing the system dynamics simulation model, three problems are mainly solved. Secondly, it systematically analyzes the influence of the changes of variables in each subsystem on the development of the stock market, and the influence of stock market fluctuations on each variable. Third, adjust various variables to simulate the development of the stock market in various economic and financial environments, and provide decision-making basis for relevant departments. In order to solve these three problems, this paper refers to the subsystems divided by Li et al. (2018) [20] when constructing the trust industry simulation system, and constructs the simulation system of stock market development, which consists of four subsystems: the economic subsystem, the financial subsystem, the stock market subsystem and the policy subsystem. The system framework is shown in Fig. 1.

3.3 Description of Variables in the System Model

Based on the development status of China's stock market, securities and Banks, this paper selects 44 indicators, including 10 level variables, 19 rate variables and 15 auxiliary

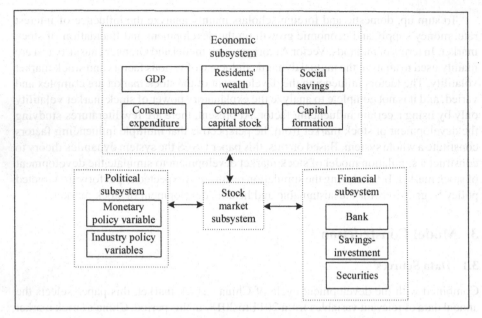

Fig. 1. Systematic framework of stock market development.

variables, to simulate the operation of the stock market by constructing a functional relationship between indicators. Among them, three key indicators of money supply, GDP and interest rate are selected to simulate the development of the stock market under different circumstances by adjusting the parameters of these three indicators. This paper ignores the impact of household income, savings-investment, government expenditure and other factors. The description of each variable is shown in Table 1.

3.4 Analysis of Main Feedback Loops

This paper divides the main body of stock purchase into three types: individual investors, institutional investors and industrial enterprises. Individual investors invest in stocks through asset allocation to obtain dividend income and capital income, thus increasing personal non-wage income, and then invest in stocks through asset allocation. Institutional investors through the analysis of market conditions, select the stock market investment targets, part of the capital into the stock market. Institutional investors continue to invest part of their money in the stock market after distributing investment income to shareholders and employees. After going public, industrial enterprises will hold part of the shares or carry out stock buybacks. With the development of enterprises, enterprises themselves can gain the benefits brought by the rising stock prices. In addition, the three major purchasers of the stock market obtain investment returns, which will increase savings, thus increasing social savings. Through the savings-investment effect, part of the capital flows into the stock market, promoting the growth of stock market value. In addition, enterprises go public through listing financing to obtain the capital needed for their own development. On the one hand, enterprises can promote the

Table 1. Main variables of the system dynamics model of China stock market development.

Level variable	Rate variable	Rate variable	Auxiliary variable	Auxiliary variable
Stockmarket value	Capital inflow	Annual household income	Money supply	Resident stock investment expenditure
Institutional holdings	Capital outflow	Annual household expenditure	GDP	Corporate capital income
Residents holdings	Institutional buy	Corporate capital inflow	interest rate	Corporate dividend income
Corporate holdings	Institutional sell	Corporate capital outflow	Investment profit	Labor compensation
Institutional assets	Residents buy	Savings increase	Resident capital income	Corporate deposits
Corporate assets	Residents sell	Absorb savings	Resident dividend income	
savings stock	Corporate buy	Savings allocation	Institutional stock investment expenditure	
Bank capital	Corporate sell	Bank loan	Other income	
Savings—investment	Institutional capital inflow	Interest expense	Wage income	
Resident wealth	Institutional capital outflow		Proportion of net capital	

increase of the gross national product, thus increasing the total social assets and increasing the stock market capital inflow; On the other hand, when the performance of listed enterprises improves, the stock price reflecting the company's operating conditions will also continue to increase.

The correlation among subsystems of the stock market development system is comprehensively studied. In this paper, Vensim PLE software is used to draw the causal circuit diagram of the stock market development system, as shown in Fig. 2. As can be seen from Fig. 2, the development of the stock market takes the market value as the core indicator. With the development and improvement of the stock market, the market value will gradually increase. In the causal loop diagram of the stock market development system, there are 23 positive loops involving the market value:

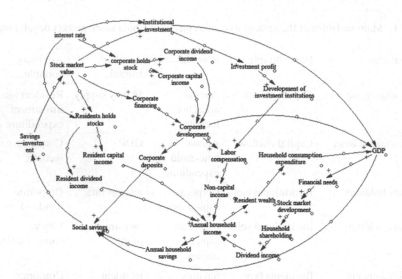

Fig. 2. Causal circuit diagram of stock market development system.

3.5 Establishment of Stock Market Development System Flow Chart

In this paper, according to the stock market development system module, the internal structure of each system and their mutual relations, the flow diagram of the stock market development system is established, as shown in Fig. 3.

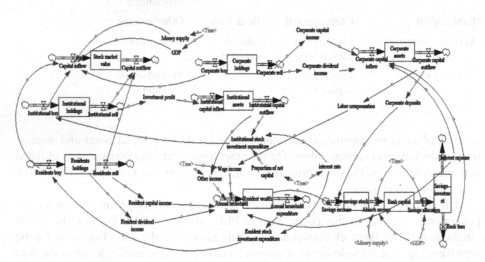

Fig. 3. Flow diagram of stock market development system.

The system flow diagram is based on the causal circuit diagram. The mathematical formulas between variables in the system flow diagram are established according to the internal relationship between variables, or the parameter values are obtained by regression based on historical data, or by referring to the parameter values obtained by relevant experts and scholars [21].

4   Model Verification and Simulation

4.1   Model Test

There are mainly three kinds of system dynamics simulation model test: (1) intuition test. Combined with the relevant professional knowledge of the research content and the requirements of the simulation model, the determination of the system boundary, variable type, variable definition, function relationship between variables and so on were tested. China's stock market is heavily influenced by external factors. In order to clarify the relationship between variables and improve the approximation between simulation model and actual data, this paper simplifies the model and ignores the impact of exchange rate volatility and foreign stock market volatility on China's stock market. (2) Running test. When Vensim PLE software is used for simulation, the software will automatically conduct repeated tests on the model structure, model equation and parameter rationality, etc. After repeated modifications, the model in this paper passes the internal test of the software system. (3) Historical test. The simulation results are compared with the historical data to verify the fitting degree of the model. This paper will measure the variable of stock market development – stock market value for simulation analysis. The simulation results are shown in Table 2 and Fig. 4. It can be found from Table 2 that the relative error between the simulation value and the historical actual value of the stock market value is controlled within 6%, which can better simulate the development of the stock market. Therefore, the simulation model established in this paper has passed the historical test.

Table 2. Simulation results of stock market development system dynamics model.

Year	Stock market value (RMB 100 million)		
	Simulation value	Actual value	Relative error
2011	148376	148376	0.00%
2012	152828	158698	−3.70%
2013	156003	151165	3.20%
2014	231196	243974	−5.24%
2015	292171	295194	−1.02%
2016	292317	284607	2.71%
2017	345351	331325	4.23%
2018	276256	269515	2.50%

Fig. 4. Simulation results of stock market value.

4.2 Scenic Setting and Policy Simulation

After testing, the simulation model of stock market development can better simulate the development of China's stock market. In the sensitivity analysis of system dynamics, the changes of the system are observed by setting different situations and changing the values of variables. In general, changing the value of a variable has little impact on the overall system development, that is, the system development has little response to the change of a single variable. When the change of a variable has a great impact on the system, the policy action point is generated. Policy makers adjust the parameter values of variables to promote better development of the system. By adjusting the value of money supply, interest rate and GDP, this paper simulates and analyzes the influence of these variables on the development of the stock market, so as to provide relevant policy Suggestions for policy makers.

(1) The influence of money supply on the development of stock market
    Money supply and demand directly affect the liquidity of funds in the market, thus affecting the volatility of stock prices. The money supply in the simulation model is increased by 2%, 4% and 6% respectively, and the changes of stock market value are shown in Fig. 5. As can be seen from Fig. 5, the market value of the stock market is positively correlated with the money supply. With the increase of the money supply, the market value of the stock market also increases gradually. Changes in the money supply have a direct impact on the market value of the stock market. The implementation of monetary policy and fiscal policy will change the money supply, thus affecting the development of the stock market.

(2) The impact of interest rate adjustment on the development of the stock market.
    The change of interest rate policy is an important factor affecting the fluctuation and development of the stock market, and adjusting the benchmark interest rate is a common monetary policy tool of the central bank. The central bank indirectly regulates the supply and demand of money in the market by adjusting the benchmark interest rate. The interest rates in the system were reduced by 0.25%, 0.5% and 0.75%, respectively. The changes in the market value of the stock market are shown

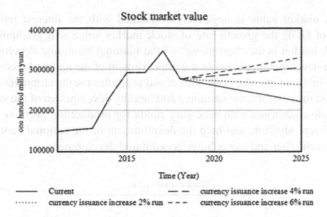

Fig. 5. Influence of money supply adjustment on stock market value.

in Fig. 6. With the increase of interest rate reduction, the increase of stock market value gradually increased. The central bank's cut in the benchmark interest rate has had a significant impact on the stock market. First, the yield of savings deposits decreases, and residents are unwilling to deposit their income in Banks. Residents tend to invest more in stocks, so capital flows into the stock market and the market value increases. Second, the larger the rate cut by the central bank, the smaller the financing cost of enterprises, which is conducive to the expansion of reproduction of enterprises, increase the value of enterprises, and the rise of stock prices. Third, the base rate cuts, the central bank to release the flow. When institutional investors issue funds in the securities market, they can integrate funds more quickly. However, stocks are one of the important targets of fund investment, and some funds flow into the stock market.

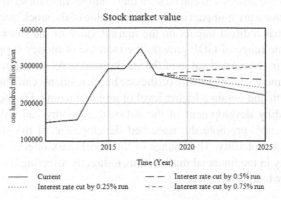

Fig. 6. Impact of interest rate adjustment on stock market value.

(3) The impact of economic growth on the stock market

By increasing the GDP in the system by 10%, 20% and 30% respectively, the changes in stock market value are shown in Fig. 7. As can be seen from Fig. 7, the stock market value is negatively correlated with the interest rate. With the increase of GDP, the growth rate of stock market value will gradually increase. The stock market is the "barometer" of the national economic development. The economic development promotes the improvement of the national income level, so more capital flows into the stock market and promotes the development of the stock market. On the contrary, the sustained and healthy development of the stock market can provide enterprises with necessary funds for production, promote enterprises to expand reproduction, and help the development of the national economy. They promote each other and can achieve coordinated development.

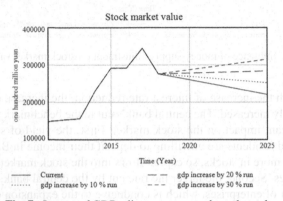

Fig. 7. Impact of GDP adjustment on stock market value.

4.3 Results Analysis

From the above scenic analysis, it can be seen that changes in money supply, interest rate and GDP can all have a great impact on the market value of the stock market. The change of money supply has a direct impact on the market value of the stock market. On the premise of the same range of GDP growth, the increase of money supply can promote a greater increase in the market value of the stock market. As an important indicator of economic development – GDP growth, on the one hand, residents can obtain the dividend of economic growth and obtain a higher level of annual income. On the other hand, the sustained and healthy development of the national economy can enhance investors' investment confidence, promote the sustained development of the stock market and reduce stock market volatility. The change of the benchmark interest rate can regulate the capital liquidity in the financial market, thus indirectly affecting the market value of the stock market, which is negative.

5 Conclusion

Based on the comprehensive analysis of the internal and external factors affecting the development of China's stock market and their impact on social and economic development, this paper constructs a system dynamics simulation model for the development of

China's stock market, and simulates the development of China's stock market. Based on literature analysis, it is concluded that money supply, interest rate and GDP are important factors influencing the development of stock market. Among them, the change of money supply has a direct impact on the stock market volatility, and the adjustment of interest rate affects the market capital liquidity by changing the money supply in the financial market, thus affecting the development of the stock market. When other financial market conditions remain unchanged, changes in money supply, interest rate and GDP will have a significant impact on the development of the stock market.

The system boundary determined in this paper is limited to the domestic financial market, and the effects of exchange rate fluctuations and foreign stock market fluctuations are not included in the stock market development simulation model. However, the error between the simulation data and the real data is small, which has strong explanatory power. In addition to money supply, interest rate and GDP, this paper does not consider other factors that affect the development of China's stock market. It is an important research direction to study the development status and future development trend of China's stock market by using complex system theory in the future.

References

1. Ioannidis, C., Kontonikas, A.: The impact of monetary policy on stock prices. J. Policy Model. **30**(1), 33–53 (2008)
2. Jansen, D.W., Tsai, C.L.: Monetary policy and stock return: financing constrains and asymmetries in bull and bear markets. J. Empirical Finance **32**(12), 2606–2616 (2010)
3. Xiao, Y., Ni, Y.J., Fang, Z.: Empirical study on the nexus among stock price, real economy and monetary policy: based on China's data from 1997 to 2011. Econ. Rev. **2**, 97–104 (2012)
4. Bekaert, G., Hoerova, M., Duca, M.L.: Risk, uncertainty and monetary policy. J. Ics **60**(7), 771–788 (2013)
5. Xu, X.G., Yu, B.W., Zheng, Z.X.: Research on the relationship between China's money supply and stock market price fluctuation. Price Theory Pract. **12**, 91–93 (2014)
6. Liu, W.J., Ding, Y., Sui, J.L.: An empirical research on the asymmetric effect of monetary policy on stock yield in China. J. Guangdong Univ. Bus. Stud. **30**(5), 69–77 (2015)
7. Fang, Y., An, X.Q.: Research on the Influence of money supply and interest rate on stock market——an empirical analysis based on quantitative and price monetary policies. Price Theory Pract. **5**, 96–99 (2019)
8. Roberto, R., Sack, B.P.: Measuring the reaction of monetary policy to the stock market. Finance Econ. Discuss. Ser. **118**(2), 639–669 (2001)
9. Rigobon, R., Brian, S.: The impact of monetary policy on asset prices. J. Monetary Econ. **51**(8), 1553–1575 (2004)
10. Bernanke, B.S., Kuttner, K.N.: What explains the stock market's reaction to federal reserve policy? J. Finance **60**(3), 1221–1257 (2005)
11. Hu, Y.B.: Study on the time-varying relationship between interest rate changes and stock market volatility based on TVP-VAR model. Modernization Manage. **36**(1), 7–9 (2016)
12. Yang, J.P., Feng, Y.J.: The impact of interest rate adjustment on the volatility of China's stock market with different regimes. J. Manage. Sci. China **20**(2), 63–75 (2017)
13. Wang, L., Chen, L.N., Jia, X.W.: An empirical study of the impact of Chinese monetary policy on stock market volatility. Rev. Investment Stud. **38**(1), 109–118 (2019)
14. Gavin, M.: The stock market and exchange rate dynamics. J. Int. Money Finance **2**, 181–200 (2006)

15. Saci, K., Giorgioni, G., Holden, K.: Does financial development affect growth? Appl. Econ. **13**, 1701–1707 (2009)
16. Lina, Z., Andrius, G., Vidas, T.: Stock market and economic growth in the US & France: evidence from stock market sector indices. Inzinerine Ekonomike-Engineering Economics **25**(1), 47–53 (2014)
17. Lin, J., Cao, Q.: An empirical analysis on bank, stock market and economic growth using China data in 1992–2012. Word Econ. Stud. **3**, 80–86+89 (2014)
18. Ding, Y.: Research on the relationship between China's stock market fluctuation and economic growth cycle——based on linear and nonlinear granger causality test. Jiangsu Soc. Sci. **3**, 175–182 (2018)
19. Wang, D.X., Xu, R.H.: The threshold effect of china's stock market development on economic growth——an empirical analysis based on provincial panel data. Dong yue Tribune **40**(8), 50–61+191–192 (2019)
20. Li, Z.M., Zhong, C.L., Liu, J.J.: A simulation study of the development of China's trust industry based on system dynamics. Manage. Rev. **30**(4), 3–11 (2018)
21. Jiang, D., Wang, Y., Lv, Z., Qi, S., Singh, S.: Big data analysis based network behavior insight of cellular networks for Industry 40 applications. IEEE Trans. Ind. Inform. **16**(2), 1310–1320 (2020)

Accelerating Method of Evolutionary Ensemble Learning Based on Gaussian Random Field

Guanghua Xu, Zifeng Dai, Zhihong Liu, Chen Zhang, Bin Zhang,
and Changsheng Zhang$^{(\boxtimes)}$

Northeastern University, Shenyang 110819, People's Republic of China
zhangchangsheng@mail.neu.edu.cn

Abstract. In recent years, research on ensemble learning of neural networks is very popular. As a research hotspot in the field of machine learning, ensemble learning methods can effectively improve the accuracy and generalization of deep network models, but not all neural networks are suitable for participating in the construction of ensemble model. Deep network ensemble learning requires a single neural network participating in the ensemble to have a high accuracy rate, and there is a large difference between the networks. In the initial stage of deep network ensemble learning, the generation process of the candidate deep network set is first required. In this article, a multi-objective evolutionary ensemble model is improved, and an evolutionary ensemble learning acceleration method based on Gaussian random field is added before the evaluation of fitness function which can screen individuals with great potential for improvement in the evaluation of fitness function during the generation of candidate deep network sets, thereby effectively improving the quality of the solution and reduce the time spent training neural networks. This pre-screening strategy is applied to the solution of the multi-objective differential evolution algorithm, which can conveniently obtain a large number of neural network models with high accuracy and large network differences. And this strategy speeds up the solution process of multi-target algorithm.

Keywords: Gaussian random field · Ensemble learning · Differential evolution algorithm · Neural network · Deep learning

1 Introduction

Ensemble learning [1] improved the prediction accuracy of the final model by building and combining multiple basic models. Almost all machine learning algorithms or models can improve the generalization performance by introducing the idea of ensemble learning, which makes it a research hotspot in the field of machine learning. With the development of modern science and technology and the improvement of productivity, major breakthroughs have been made in computer performance, and the acquisition of massive data is no longer a difficult task. As a synonym for artificial neural networks, deep learning [2] has suddenly become the hottest research direction in the field of

Published by Springer Nature Switzerland AG 2021. All Rights Reserved
H. Song and D. Jiang (Eds.): SIMUtools 2020, LNICST 369, pp. 251–262, 2021.
https://doi.org/10.1007/978-3-030-72792-5_23

machine learning, various algorithms for improving the training speed of neural networks have been proposed successively. Based on this, neural networks have achieved rapid development, and more and more deep network models [3–6] have been proposed and widely used in various fields such as face recognition, image classification, and natural language processing.

Because ensemble learning methods have significant advantages in improving generalization performance, many experts and scholars are committed to combining deep networks with ensemble learning to further improve the accuracy of neural network models in various application scenarios [7–9] and specific tasks. If the neural network is considered as an individual in ensemble learning, it is important to consider that not all neural networks are suitable for participating in the construction of the ensemble model. Deep network ensemble learning requires [10] that a single neural network participating in the ensemble has high accuracy rate, and there are large differences between networks.

In the initial stage of deep network ensemble learning, the process of generating candidate deep network sets needs to be performed first. In the candidate network generation stage, a multi-objective algorithm based on differential evolution is used to solve the problem of generating candidate deep network sets, and the targets to be optimized are the prediction accuracy of the deep network and the differences between the networks. However, since each individual in the population corresponds to a specific neural network, and the individual needs to train the corresponding neural network when evaluating the fitness function, this part will take a lot of time, so pre-screening is required. An existing pre-screening strategy is a guide model pre-screening strategy, which can accelerate the evolution rate of the population and find the optimal solution faster, but it is very expensive in terms of computational cost. This article proposes an evolutionary ensemble learning acceleration method based on Gaussian random fields, which can select individuals with great potential for evaluation during the generation of candidate deep network sets for fitness function evaluation, thereby effectively improving the quality of the solution and reducing time spent training a neural network.

The rest of this article is arranged as follows. The second part introduces an existing multi-objective deep belief networks sensitive (MODBNE) method [11]. The third part details the evolutionary ensemble learning acceleration method based on Gaussian random fields. The fourth part evaluates this method based on the existing two data sets, and its performance is analyzed. The fifth part summarizes the research results and future research plans of this article.

2   MODBNE Method

Differential Evolution algorithm [12] (Differential Evolution, DE) was originally proposed by Rainer Storn and Kenneth Price. The idea is derived from the Genetic Algorithm (GA) proposed earlier, and it is also a search and optimization strategy simulating biological evolution. The multi-objective differential evolution algorithm is often used to solve multi-objective optimization problems. The multi-objective optimization (MOP) problem [13] is a mutually exclusive relationship between the objective functions. The optimization of one goal will inevitably lead to the deterioration of other goals, which means that there is a trade-off between the various objective functions.

Zhang C et al.'s article proposes a multi-objective deep belief networks ensemble (MODBNE) method [11]. In the multi-objective evolutionary ensemble learning model, the MOEA/D algorithm [14] is integrated with traditional DBN training techniques, and multiple DBNs are evolved at the same time. Accuracy and diversity are used as two conflicting goals. The development of ensemble learning groups based on two goals effectively balances the accuracy and diversity of individuals in the ensemble learning group, and greatly optimizes the ensemble model. And the evaluation of this method on the NASA C-MAPSS aero engine data set shows that MODBNE has excellent performance.

In her article, metrics are established for accuracy and difference. In terms of accuracy metrics, the problem of maximizing accuracy is converted to the problem of minimizing error rate. The specific calculation method after converting it into an objective function is shown in formula (2.1)

$$minimize: Err_m = \frac{1}{N} \sum_{i=1}^{N} \left(p_m^i - REAL^i \right) \tag{2.1}$$

among them N represents the total number of samples in the data set, Err_m represents the m-th ($1 \leq m \leq M$) classification error rate (accuracy index) of each network, p_m^i represents the output result of the m-th neural network on the i-th sample, $REAL^i$ represents the true value corresponding to the i-th sample, and agreed to be used in the classification task when p_m^i is equal to $REAL^i$, the difference between the two is 0, otherwise it is 1.

In terms of difference metrics, the differences between the output of neural networks and other networks are used to characterize the differences between networks. By introducing the idea of negative correlation learning [15], it can subtly transform the problem of maximizing the difference between networks into the problem of minimizing the correlation between networks. Increasing the difference between networks is to reduce the correlation or similarity between networks. The specific calculation method after converting it into an objective function is shown in formula (2.2):

$$minimize: Div_m = \sum_{i=1}^{N} \left(p_m^i - P^i \right) \sum_{j=1, j \neq m}^{M} \left(p_j^i - P^i \right) \tag{2.2}$$

among them M represents the number of basic networks in the deep network set, N represents the total number of samples in the data set, Div_m represents the difference (correlation) value between the m-th ($1 \leq m \leq M$) network and other networks, P^i is the average of the prediction results of the M-th network on the i-th sample, p_j^i represents the output results of the j-th neural network on the i-th sample.

The article's way reduces the difficulty of solving effectively by decomposing the multi-objective optimization problem into N scalar sub problem. First, generate a distributed average weight vector for all sub problems, and the weight vector $\lambda_i = \{\lambda_1^i, \ldots \lambda_F^i\}$ corresponding to the i-th sub problem, and then by calculating the Euclidean distance between the weight vectors corresponding to the sub problems, we can get the closest T sub problems of each sub problem (called the neighborhood), the evolution of the multi-objective algorithm is realized through the information exchange between adjacent sub-problems.

After getting the corresponding neighborhood of each subproblem, two indexes j and k are randomly selected from the neighborhood of i-th subproblem. And then get the corresponding individuals x_g^i, x_g^j and x_g^k, get mutant individuals $x_g^{i'}$ according to the basic mutation formula of the differential evolution algorithm and add a Gaussian random variable to each dimensional value of the mutated individual according to the probability. The specific method is shown in formula (2.3):

$$x_{gx}^{i'} = \begin{cases} x_g^i + F \cdot \left(x_g^j - x_g^k \right) + rnd_G(0, \sigma) \ if \ rnd_U(0, 1) \le 0.5 \\ x_g^i + F \cdot \left(x_g^j - x_g^k \right) \qquad\qquad otherwise \end{cases} \quad (2.3)$$

among them $rnd_U(0, 1)$ represents the fraction obtained from uniform random sampling in range of [0, 1], scaling factor $F \in [0, 2]$, $rnd_G(0, \sigma)$ represents a Gaussian random vector with mean of 0 and standard deviation σ, and the value of σ is taken as one-twentieth of the value range of the corresponding dimensional element. In the mutation process of algorithm evolution, strict boundary control is required for each dimensional element of the mutant individual. Once the corresponding maximum or minimum boundary is exceeded, then it is mapped to a reasonable range through a specific operation.

The method mentioned in this article during the evaluation stage of the implementation of the multi-objective differential evolution algorithm requires the evaluation of fitness functions for all mutated new individuals one by one, which greatly wastes computing power and time. So this paper proposes to use an evolutionary ensemble learning acceleration method based on Gaussian random field before the fitness function evaluation. Calculate the increasable probability of all new mutant individuals by establishing a pre-screening model. The fitness function evaluation was performed on individuals with higher upgradeable probability, and Individuals with lower promotion probability are directly discarded. This pre-screening model can effectively reduce the number of fitness function evaluations and speed up the solution process of the multi-objective algorithm.

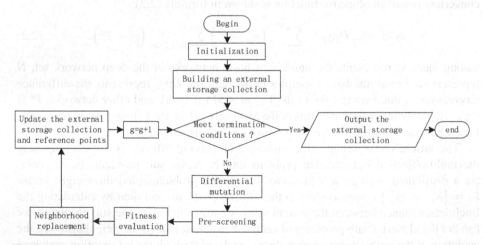

Fig. 1. The flow chart of multi-objective differential evolution algorithm based on Gaussian random field.

3 Multi-objective Differential Evolution Algorithm Based on Gaussian Random Field

As shown in Fig. 1, before the population initialization, the accuracy rate objective function is first measured and a single-objective evolutionary algorithm is used to initialize the population. The condition for stopping the iteration of this step is that the network accuracy of all individuals in a certain generation of population is greater than a certain threshold. Then all the individuals in the population are stored in the constructed external storage set, and the weight vectors and reference points are initialized to determine whether the population meets the termination conditions. If the termination conditions are not met, then the MOEA/D algorithm is used to make the difference mutation operation, and use Gaussian random field model to predict the fitness value of the mutated new individual, and use the predicted value of fitness to substitute into the sub problem corresponding to the individual to calculate the function value's *PoI* of the scalar sub problem (Possible boost value). If the value of *PoI* is greater than or equal to 0.5, it indicates that the mutant individual may be better, then it is evaluated using the true fitness function, and finally the neighborhood is replaced, and the reference point information and the external storage set are updated, while the evolution generation $g = g + 1$, then determine whether the population meets the termination conditions. If the termination conditions are met, the external storage set is directly output, and the algorithm ends.

3.1 Prediction of Fitness Value Using Gaussian Random Field Model

Michael TM et al. [16] proposed a meta-model method based on a Gaussian random field, which can effectively reduce the number of fitness function evaluations of the evolutionary algorithm in the optimization process. The basic principle is before performing the true fitness function evaluation, using the evaluated solution to build a Gaussian random field model, and then predicting the value of the function corresponding to the unknown solution. By setting a pre-screening rule, only those solutions with a large improvement space are retained, thereby achieving the purpose of reducing the true fitness function evaluation: Compared with other agent models, Gaussian random field models generally take more accurate results when making predictions because of the variance information.

The Gaussian random field model is mainly based on the following two assumptions:

(1) In terms of a time-consuming function $y = g(x)$, $x \in R^n$, the Gaussian random field model assumes that it obeys the normal distribution of mean value μ and variance δ^2.

(2) In any $x, x' \in R^n$, $c(x, x') = exp[-d(x, x')]$ is a correlation function, represents the correlation between $g(x)$ and $g(x')$. Among them, $d(x, x') = \sum_{i=1}^{n} \theta_i |x_i - x_i'|^{p_i}$, the value of the correlation function is only related to the size of $(x - x')$. The larger $(x - x')$ is, the less correlation is and vice versa.

If we know K points $x_1, x_2, \ldots, x_K \in R^n$ and their corresponding function values are $y_1, y_2, \ldots, y_K$, Super parameter $\mu, \delta, \theta_1, \ldots, \theta_n, p_1, \ldots, p_n$ can be given by the following maximum likelihood estimate:

$$PDF = \frac{1}{(2\pi\delta^2)\sqrt{det(C)}} exp\left[-\frac{(y-\mu 1)^T C^{-1}(y-\mu 1)}{2\delta^2}\right] \qquad (3.1)$$

among them C is an $K \times K$ Matrix of, and $C_{i,j} = c(x^i, x^j)$, $y = (y^1, y^2, \ldots y^K)$ as well as 1 is all K dimensional column vector. To maximize the likelihood function pdf, there must be $\mu = \frac{1^T C^{-1} y}{1^T C^{-1} 1}$, $\delta^2 = \frac{(y-1\mu)^T C^{-1}(y-1\mu)}{K}$.

The unbiased estimate of $g(x)$ is c, variance $\hat{s}^2(x) = \hat{\delta}^2\left[1 - r^T C^{-1}r + \frac{(1-1^T C^{-1}r)^2}{1^T C^{-1}1}\right]$.

Among them $r = (c(x, x^1), c(x, x^2), \ldots, c(x, x^K))^T$, it can be considered $g(x)$ obeys $N(\hat{y}(x), \hat{s}^2(x))$.

The Gaussian random field model can effectively reduce the number of evaluations of the fitness function of the optimization algorithm in the optimization process. Although it takes a lot of time to build a Gaussian random field model, for the problem of time-consuming fitness function evaluation, the method can effectively reduce the solution time of the optimization problem.

Each time the fitness function evaluation is performed on an individual in this article, the specific neural network corresponding to the individual needs to be trained, and the training of the neural network is time consuming. In order to reduce the number of fitness function evaluations in the multi-objective algorithm, this article uses Gaussian random field model to predict fitness values for mutated new individuals.

Suppose $f_i(x)$ obeys the mean value of $\hat{y}_i(x)$, the normal distribution of variance $\hat{s}_i^2(x)$, that is $f_i(x) \sim N(\hat{y}_i(x), \hat{s}_i^2(x))$ holds for any $i = 1, 2, \ldots m$, where m represents the number of objective functions. Therefore, each independent subproblem $g^{te}(x|\lambda, z^*) = \max_{1 \leq i \leq m} \{\lambda_i(f_i(x) - z_i^*)\}$ has $\lambda_i(f_i(x) - z_i^*) \sim N(\lambda_i(\hat{y}_i(x) - z_i^*), [\lambda_i\hat{s}_i^2(x)])$ after decomposing the multi-objective problem based on Chebyshev decomposition method, according to the research in the article [16] we can get the normal distribution that $g^{te}(x|\lambda, z^*)$ obeys the mean value $\hat{y}^{te}$ and the variance $(\hat{s}^{te})^2$, that is, the function value of $g^{te}(x|\lambda, z^*)$ can be estimated by $\hat{y}_i(x)$ and $\hat{s}_i^2(x)$, the specific calculation method of $\hat{y}^{te}$ is shown in formula (3.2):

$$\hat{y}^{te} = \mu_1 \Phi(\alpha) + \mu_2 \Phi(-\alpha) + \tau\phi(\alpha) \qquad (3.2)$$

Where $\mu_i = \lambda_i(\hat{y}_i(x) - z_i^*)$, reference point $z^* = (z_1^*, z_2^*, \ldots, z_m^*)$ for $\forall i = 1, \cdots, m$ has $z_i^* = min\{f_i(x)|x \in \Omega\}$, $\tau = \sqrt{[\lambda_1\hat{s}_1(x)]^2+[\lambda_2\hat{s}_2(x)]^2}$, $\alpha = (\mu_1 - \mu_2)/\tau$, $\phi(t) = (2\pi)^{-1/2}exp(-t^2/2)$ and $\Phi(t) = \int_{-\infty}^t \phi(\theta)d\theta$.

$$PoI(x) = \int_{-\infty}^{fmin} \varphi(y)dy = \Phi\left(\frac{I(x)}{\hat{s}(x)}\right) \qquad (3.3)$$

Where x represents a solution vector, $I(x) = f_{min} - \hat{y}(x)$, f_{min} represent the minimum value (unknown value) of the fitness function. This article the minimum function value obtained in the evolution process is used to replace f_{min}. $\hat{y}(x)$ as well as $\hat{s}(x)$ sees the specific definition above, $PoI(x)$ represents the possible improvement probability corresponding to the solution vector x, which is about 0.5.

First, record the individuals evaluated and their corresponding fitness function values in the set S_{eval} during the population initialization process and then each time a new mutant individual is obtained, first select $2d$ individuals from S_{eval} (d represents the dimension of the search space) during the evolution of the algorithm, and establish a Gaussian random field model, and then calculate the fitness prediction value of the mutated individual. Then use the predicted value of the fitness value to substitute into the sub-problem corresponding to the individual to calculate the function value's PoI of the sub quantum problem (Possible boost value), here PoI is defined as shown in formula (3.3), and finally predict the probability that an individual may be improved according to PoI.

3.2 Acceleration Algorithm Based on Gaussian Random Field

When the multi-objective differential evolution algorithm is executed, the final generation population obtained in advance is used as the initial population, and then the external storage set is constructed by the fitness function $outEP$, used to calculate the value of the difference objective function. After the algorithm is executed, all the individuals in the external storage set are the candidate network set. In addition, in order to prevent the individuals with lower accuracy generated during the mutation process from being excessively guided the algorithm searches in the direction of difference. Before updating the reference point, it is necessary to determine whether the accuracy of the network corresponding to the mutant individual is greater than the threshold r1. If the accuracy is greater than r1, the reference point is updated, otherwise the reference point is not updated. Where the reference point $z^* = \left(z_1^*, z_2^*, \ldots, z_m^*\right)$ has formula (3.4) for $\forall i = 1, \cdots, m$

$$z_i^* = min\{f_i(x)|x \in \Omega\} \tag{3.4}$$

When performing a neighborhood replacement operation, the i-th individual's (sub-problem)T neighboring individuals is judged, and when the formula (3.5) is satisfied, the corresponding domain individuals are replaced with mutant individuals.

$$\max_{n_f \in \{1,\ldots m\}} \lambda_{n_f}^i \cdot \left|z_{n_f}\left(x_g^i\right) - z_{n_f}^*\right| \leq \max_{n_f \in \{1,\ldots m\}} \lambda_{n_f}^{i_s} \cdot \left|z_{n_f}\left(x_g^{i_s}\right) - z_{n_f}^*\right| \tag{3.5}$$

Where i_s is the element of the neighborhood $B(i)$ corresponding to the i-th individual. It can be seen from the above, the accuracy of the mutant individuals is controlled here in this article, and only when the network accuracy of the mutant individuals is greater than the threshold r1 and the replacement condition shown in formula (3.5) is satisfied, perform neighborhood replacement operation. This is to avoid the situation where individuals with higher accuracy are replaced by individuals with lower accuracy. The specific operation of the multi-objective differential evolution algorithm based on Gaussian random field is as follows:

Input M (the number of basic networks in the deep network set), T (the number of weight vectors in the neighborhood of each weight vector), G (the maximum population number), r1 (the threshold for updating outEP).

The first step is to obtain the initial population through a single-objective evolution algorithm, calculate the fitness of all individuals, and add them to outEP and S_{eval}.

The second step is to generate uniformly distributed M weight vectors $\lambda^1, ..., \lambda^M$. For each i in {1, ..., M}, by calculating the Euclidean distance between the two vectors, find the T closest weight vectors, then add them to B(i). And initialize the reference point z^*.

In the third step, a mutant individual is generated according to formula (2.3) for each g in {1, ..., G} and each i in {1, ..., M}. If the elements of the mutant individuals exceed the boundary, then reset within boundary.

The fourth step is to construct a Gaussian random field model based on S_{eval} and predict $x_g^{i'}$'s fitness. Use the fitness function to predict the PoI of g^{te} according to formula (3.2) and formula (3.3). If the value of PoI is less than 0.5, it indicates that the individual is unlikely to achieve improvement, so it is abandoned to evaluate the fitness function. If the value of PoI is greater than or equal to 0.5, it indicates that the mutant individual may be better, and then it is evaluated using the true fitness function and added to the evaluated set S_{eval} for future use, the reference point z^* is then updated, and the neighborhood is updated with formula (3.5). On this basis, if the network accuracy is greater than r1, the mutation individual is recorded and the outEP is updated. The algorithm ends.

The pseudo code of the above steps is shown in Algorithm 3.2.

Algorithm 3.2. Pseudo code of evolutionary ensemble learning acceleration method based on Gaussian random field in candidate depth network set generation.

Algorithm MOEA/D-GRF

Input

M: the number of individuals/networks in a generation

T: the number of the weight vectors in the neighborhood of each weight vector.

G: the max generations

r_1: a threshold of updating *outEP*

Output

outEP: a set of deep neural networks

Begin

1. get the initial population;
2. calculate the fitness of all individuals, and add them into *outEP* and S_{eval};
3. generate uniformly distributed M weight vectors $\lambda^1,...,\lambda^M$;
4. **For each** i in $\{1,...,M\}$ **do**
5.   Find out T closest weight vectors by computing Euclidean distances between two vectors, and then add them into $B(i)$.
6. **End for**
7. initialize the reference point z^*;
8. **For each** g in $\{1,...,G\}$ **do**
9. **For each** i in $\{1,...,M\}$ **do**
10.   generate the mutant individual $x_g^{i'}$ according to formula (2.3);
11.   **If** an element of mutant individual is out of boundary **then**:
12.   reset it inside the boundary;
13.   **End if**
14.   construct Gaussian random field model based on S_{eval}, and predict the fitness of $x_g^{i'}$;
15.   compute *PoI* of g^{te} based on the predicted fitness with formula (3.2) and formula (3.3);
16.   **If** *PoI* is greater than 0.5 **then**:
17.   calculate the real fitness of the mutant individual;
18.   **End if**;
19.   update set S_{eval} and reference point z^*;
20.   update neighboring solutions with formula (3.4);
21.   record the mutant individual if the network's accuracy is greater than r_1;
22. **End for**
23. update *outEP*;
24. **End for**
25. **End**

When using the algorithm proposed in this article to solve a problem of d-dimensional search space, the main steps are generating mutant individuals, establishing the high random field model, replacing individual neighborhoods, and updating reference points. Among them, the most time-consuming is to build a Gaussian random field model, whose time complexity is $O(d^3)$. Therefore, the total time complexity of the entire multi-objective evolutionary algorithm is $O(G * N * d^3)$, among them G is the evolutionary generation of the multi-objective evolution algorithm, N represents population size.

4 Experiment

In the experiments of this article, the last-generation population of the single-objective evolutionary algorithm is used as the initial population of the multi-objective optimization algorithm, which not only ensures the accuracy of the deep network corresponding to each individual in the initial population is sufficiently high, but also makes the calculation of the difference between the netwks meaningful. In order to verify the effectiveness of the multi-objective differential evolution algorithm based on the Gaussian random field in reducing running time, while the overall algorithm setting remains unchanged, five experiments were carried out to test whether the accelerated evolutionary ensemble learning method based on Gaussian random field was set up or not to eliminate the chance of the experiment and ensure the accuracy of the experimental results as much as possible. Take the average of the experimental results and round up the running time. The performance of the ensemble model in MNIST test set and fashion MNIST test set and the running time of multi-objective part are obtained under the two conditions of whether the pre- screening strategy is set or not. The specific experimental data are shown in Table 1 and Table 2.

Table 1. The influence of pre-screening strategy based on Gaussian random field on the results (MNIST).

Pre-screening strategy	Training set accuracy (%)	Verification set accuracy (%)	Test set accuracy (%)	Multi-objective algorithm running time (s)
No	99.7453	99.5840	99.4390	22432
Yes	99.7592	99.6150	99.4750	19389

With the same population size and evolutionary generation, it can be seen from the experimental data in Tables 1 and 2 that the evolutionary ensemble learning acceleration method based on Gaussian random fields can effectively reduce the running time of multi-objective algorithms under the premise of ensuring high accuracy, which is because the pre-screening strategy can reduce the algorithm's evaluate of fitness function for those individuals who have no obvious improvement possibility, thereby reducing the time to train the corresponding neural network. However, the proportion of time improvement

Table 2. The influence of pre-screening strategy based on Gaussian random field on the results (Fashion-MNIST).

Pre-screening strategy	Training set accuracy (%)	Verification set accuracy (%)	Test set accuracy (%)	Multi-objective algorithm running time (s)
No	96.7853	92.9400	92.8300	23452
Yes	96.6764	93.4800	93.1200	19947

is limited, which may be related to the time consumption of establishing a Gaussian random field. And as the number of evaluated individuals increases, the time it takes to calculate the correlation between unrated individuals and evaluated individuals also increases.

It can be seen that the ensemble model obtained by the overall algorithm of the evolutionary ensemble learning acceleration method based on the Gaussian random field is only slightly improved in the accuracy index compared to the ensemble model obtained without the pre-screening strategy. During the experiment, it was found that this situation may be related to the less evolutionary algebra of the evolutionary algorithm. The reason is that when the evolutionary algebra is less, the amount of data in the set of evaluated individuals may not be very sufficient, so when building the Gauss random field model, because the correlation between the non-evaluated solution and the known solution is weak, the fitness prediction is not particularly accurate, which leads to the limited performance improvement of the final ensemble network. In the future, more complete experiments will be used to verify this problem.

To sum up, the pre-screening strategy based on the Gaussian random field model can effectively improve the generation efficiency of candidate deep network sets and effectively shorten the running time. And at the same time, the integrated model obtained by this strategy also guarantees a high accuracy rate when verified on the MNIST and Fashion-MNIST data sets.

5   Conclusion and Future Work

This article mainly proposes an acceleration method of evolutionary ensemble learning based on Gaussian random field. This method is applied to the solution process based on the multi-objective differential evolution algorithm, which effectively reduces the number of evaluations of the adaptation function and the running time of the multi-objective algorithm, thereby making obtain the appropriate network set accurately faster. The experimental results show that the method can effectively reduce the algorithm to evaluate the fitness function of those individuals without obvious improvement. And it can conveniently obtain a large number of neural network model with high accuracy and large network differences.

In future work, consider using other methods and models to improve the pre-screening strategy, as well as using more effective methods to optimize the two metrics of accuracy and disparity of the multi-objective differential evolution algorithm.

This paper is funded by the project 202010145225 supported by National Training Program of Innovation and Entrepreneurship for Undergraduates. And this paper is supported by "the Fundamental Research Funds for the Central Universities" (project approval number: N182410001).

References

1. Dietterich, T.G.: Ensemble methods in machine learning. In: Kittler, J., Roli, F. (eds.) MCS 2000. LNCS, vol. 1857, pp. 1–15. Springer, Heidelberg (2000). https://doi.org/10.1007/3-540-45014-9_1
2. Lecun, Y., Bengio, Y., Hinton, G.: Deep learning. Nature **521**(7553), 436 (2015)
3. He, K., Zhang, X., Ren, S., Sun, J.: Deep residual learning for image recognition. In: IEEE Conference on Computer Vision and Pattern Recognition. IEEE Computer Society (2016)
4. Ronneberger, O., Fischer, P., Brox, T.: U-net: convolutional networks for biomedical image segmentation. In: Navab, N., Hornegger, J., Wells, W.M., Frangi, A.F. (eds.) MICCAI 2015, Part III. LNCS, vol. 9351, pp. 234–241. Springer, Cham (2015). https://doi.org/10.1007/978-3-319-24574-4_28
5. Girshick, R.: Fast R-CNN. Computer Science (2015)
6. Kim, J., Lee, J.K., Lee, K.M.: Accurate image super-resolution using very deep convolutional networks (2016)
7. Peimankar, A., Puthusserypady, S.: An ensemble of deep recurrent neural networks for P-wave detection in electrocardiogram. In: ICASSP 2019 - 2019 IEEE International Conference on Acoustics, Speech and Signal Processing (ICASSP). IEEE (2019)
8. Yu, J.: A selective deep stacked denoising autoencoders ensemble with negative correlation learning for gearbox fault diagnosis. Comput. Ind. **108**, 62–72 (2019)
9. Li, J., Wu, S., Liu, C., Yu, Z., Wong, H.S.: Semi-supervised deep coupled ensemble learning with classification landmark exploration. IEEE Trans. Image Process. **29**, 538–550 (2019)
10. Jiang, W., Chen, Z., Xiang, Y., Shao, D., Zhang, J.: Ssem: a novel self-adaptive stacking ensemble model for classification. IEEE Access **7**, 120337–120349 (2019)
11. Zhang, C., Lim, P., Qin, A.K., Tan, K.C.: Multiobjective deep belief networks ensemble for remaining useful life estimation in prognostics. IEEE Trans. Neural Netw. Learn. Syst. **28**, 2306–2318 (2016)
12. Ali, I.M., Essam, D., Kasmarik, K.: A novel design of differential evolution for solving discrete traveling salesman problems. Swarm Evol. Comput. **52**, 100607 (2020)
13. Pan, L., He, C., Tian, Y., Wang, H., Zhang, X., Jin, Y.: A classification-based surrogate-assisted evolutionary algorithm for expensive many-objective optimization. IEEE Trans. Evol. Comput. **23**(1), 74–88 (2019)
14. Zhang, Q., Li, H.: MOEA/D: a multiobjective evolutionary algorithm based on decomposition. IEEE Trans. Evol. Comput. **11**(6), 712–731 (2007)
15. Liu, Y., Yao, X., Higuchi, T.: Evolutionary ensembles with negative correlation learning. IEEE Trans. Evol. Comput. **4**(4), 380–387 (2000)
16. Emmerich, M.T.M., Giannakoglou, K.C., Naujoks, B.: Single- and multiobjective evolutionary optimization assisted by gaussian random field metamodels. IEEE Trans. Evol. Comput. **10**(4), 421–439 (2006)

Approximation Algorithms for the Balanced Optimization Splicing Problem in Undirected Graph

Yongsong Wen[1,2](✉) (iD)

[1] School of Management, Wuhan University of Technology,
Wuhan 430070, People's Republic of China
[2] School of Mathematics and Statistics, GuiZhou University of Finance
and Economics, Guiyang 550025, People's Republic of China

Abstract. One-dimensional bin packing problem and balanced optimization problem are two classical problems in combinatorial optimization, inspired by this, we research a balanced optimization splicing problem: given a weight connected $G(V, E; w)$, a balanced spanning tree structure $\mathcal{A}$ and a specific material of fixed length ℓ, where $w : E \rightarrow Q^+$ (or $w : E \rightarrow Z^+$), each edge in the graph G is allowed to be greater than or equal to ℓ, we will use this specific material to splice a subgraph T from graph G with balanced spanning tree structure $\mathcal{A}$, and these edges spliced in such required structures are supposed to be cut from some pieces of a specific material of fixed length ℓ, the objective is to minimize the amount of special material used when splicing all the edges of the subgraph T with the given material. In this paper, we consider three kinds of balanced spanning tree structures for this problem and design three approximation algorithms.

Keywords: Balanced optimization · Balanced spanning tree · Approximation algorithms

1 Introduction and Problem Description

Consider the example of an area which wants to a signal stations network will be built to connect several towns, the construction period of the road linking any two towns is known, and all sections of the road commenced at the same time, we need design a signal station connected network to be finished at the same time as possible and meet the requirements to connect the signal station networks of cities and towns. In other words, the gap between maximum construction duration and minimum construction duration should be minimum. This example is a typical of the balanced optimization (BO) problem. Generally, the balanced optimization problem can be applied to the fair allocation of resources [1]. For further applications of BO problem and related problems we refer to [2] and [3]. We will give a brief introduction to the balanced optimization problem, let

© ICST Institute for Computer Sciences, Social Informatics and Telecommunications Engineering 2021
Published by Springer Nature Switzerland AG 2021. All Rights Reserved
H. Song and D. Jiang (Eds.): SIMUtools 2020, LNICST 369, pp. 263–273, 2021.
https://doi.org/10.1007/978-3-030-72792-5_24

$E = \{1, 2, \ldots, m\}$ be a finite set of m elements and F be a family of subsets of E, and $f : F \mapsto R$. Let w_e be a prescribed cost associated with each element e of E. For each $S \in F$, define $f(S) = \max_{e \in S} w_e - \min_{e \in S} w_e$. Then, the balanced optimization (BO)problem is to find $S \in F$ such that $f(S)$ is minimum. The balanced optimization problem was introduced by Martello et al., and they suggested a general algorithm, called the double threshold algorithm to solve the problem in polynomial time [3]. [4] considered balanced spanning tree problem and proposed an $\mathcal{O}(m^2)$ algorithm where m is the number of edges in the underlying graph. Later, Galil and Schieber [5] improved the algorithm presented in [4], the complexity of the Algorithm is $\mathcal{O}(mlogn)$, where n is the number of vertices considered in the graph. Wu [7] showed the balanced optimization problem with edge set restrictions$(BOP\text{-}ESR)$, they provided efficient algorithms to solve the problem in polynomial time $\mathcal{O}(mn)$. Punnen and Nair [6] consider the balanced optimization problem with an additional linear constraint under a general combinatorial optimization setting. It is shown that this constrained balanced optimization (CBO) problem can be solved in polynomial time whenever an associated minimum problem can be solved in polynomial time. Other related special cases of BO problem can be referred to [8–12].

1.1   Problem Definition

In this paper, let's consider the previous example of BO problem again, in order to ensure connectivity different signal stations, we not only require that the between the maximum construction period and the minimum construction period is minimal, but we also need to use some special materials to connect the various signal stations, where the use of these special materials is limited in length, we objective is to use the least amount of special materials. We can regard each signal station as the vertex in the network and the route between stations as the path connected by the edge in the graph, so this problem can be regarded as a balanced optimization problem. In reality, when we splice such a balanced spanning subgraph with a special material, we generally need to consider the limitations of the length of the special material. Our motivation for considering the constraints is that each piece of specific material has a fixed length, and one piece of specific material can not splice all the edges of a balanced spanning tree structure $\mathcal{A}$ in this paper.

Furthermore, When we intend to splice an edge of any length $w(u, v)$ into such a balanced spanning tree structure, this splicing process can be roughly divided into two steps: (1) if one edge $(u, v) < \ell$, we need to "cut" a part of specific material, using a specific material of length $w(u, v)$ to splice this edge (u, v);(2) if an edge (u, v) $w(u, v) \geq \ell$, we first use $r(u, v)$ whole pieces of such a specific material of length ℓ, and then "cut" a part of such a specific material with the length$w(u, v) - r(u, v) \cdot L$, splicing the edge (u, v), where $r(u, v) = \left\lceil \frac{w(u,v)}{L} \right\rceil - 1$.
Through the (1) and (2) splicing process, each edge (u, v) in this balanced spanning tree structure, the length of the remaining edges is less than ℓ, in addition to the other $r(u, v)$ as a whole for such a specific material in balanced span-

ning tree structure. Thus, we need to consider the minimum amount of material of length ℓ to be used in the splicing process. So we study a new problem of splicing some required balanced structures in undirected graph, that is formally defined as follows: given a weight connected $G(V, E; w)$, a balanced spanning tree structure $\mathcal{A}$ and a specific material of fixed length ℓ, where $w : E \rightarrow Q^+$ (or $w : E \rightarrow Z^+$), each edge in the graph G is allowed to be greater than or equal to ℓ, we will use this specific material to splice a subgraph T from graph G with balanced spanning tree structure $\mathcal{A}$, and these edges spliced in such required structures are supposed to be cut from some pieces of a specific material of fixed length ℓ, the objective is to minimize the amount of special material used when splicing all the edges of the subgraph T with the given material.

For the new objective mentioned above, we consider the following three different structures $\mathcal{A}$: (1)If the structure is a minimal balanced spanning tree, we may call it the a minimal balanced spanning tree splicing($MBSTS$, abbreviations) problem; (2)If the structure is a minimal balanced spanning tree with edge set restricted problem, we may call it the minimal balanced spanning tree splicing problem with edge set restricted ($MBSTS\text{-}ESR$, abbreviations); (3)When the structure is a constrained balanced tree problems, we may call it the constrained balanced trees splicing ($CBTS$, abbreviations)problems.

1.2 Main Results

In this paper, for problems of $MBSTS$, $MBSTS\text{-}ESR$ and $CBTS$, there is no approximation algorithm to solve these problems, nor is there a special version of polynomial time to solve them. Therefore, we design three kinds of approximation algorithms to solve these three problems. The organization of this paper is as follows. In Sect. 2, We give a general description of terminology and lemmas. In Sect. 3, when this is a $MBSTS$ problem, we design a $\frac{3}{2}$-approximation algorithm, and an asymptotic polynomial time approximation scheme($PTAS$). In Sect. 4, when this is a $MBSTS\text{-}ESR$ problem, we present a $\frac{3}{2}$-approximation algorithm. In Sect. 5, when this is a $CBTS$ problem, we present an asymptotic $\frac{3}{2}$-approximation algorithm.

2 Terminology and Lemmas

We will use the packing problem to solve the balanced optimization splicing problem, we need to introduce some notation and terminology can be found in reference [14–17]. For the sake of the clarity, we regard a particular material of length ℓ as the capacity of a bin ℓ. If we are given an edge about an edge in the undirected graph, we expressed this weight of edge (u, v) as "item" of size $w(u, v)$. We can assume that the length of the edge $w(u, v)$ is allowed to exceed the length of ℓ. For each edge (u, v) of length $w(u, v)$, we might first use the material length ℓ of $r(u, v)$ as a whole and then "cut" the part at the $w(u, v)$ length, from a piece of material length ℓ, to splice the edge (u, v) together, where $r(u, v) = \left\lceil \frac{w(u,v)}{L} \right\rceil - 1$ and $w'(u, v) = w(u, v) - r(u, v) \cdot L$. This process means that this item of size $w(u, v)$ is "packed" into a bin with capacity ℓ. Further, if we can use m pieces of a specific material to splice all edges needed in the balance spanning subgraph T, expressed this process as the one that it is sufficient to use m pieces of such a specific material with length ℓ to splice all edges needed in the balance spanning graph.

We use three notations, $G(V, E; w; \ell)$, $G(V, E; w; E_0; \ell)$ and $G(V, E; w; B; \ell)$ to respectively represent an instance of the $BSTS$ problem, the $MBSTS\text{-}ESR$ problem, the $CBTS$ problem, where E_0 is a set of required edges of an instance of the $MBSTS\text{-}ESR$ problem, and B is a positive integer constraint condition on $CBTS$ problem. The two graphs G and T may have the same structure, and this case that $w(e) = f(e)$ for every edge $e \in E$ may be considered viable. Other undefined notations and terminology can be found in papadimotriou and steiglitz (1998) [17], schrijver (2003) [18]. The lemma used in this paper is as follows.

Lemma 1 *[5]. The Galil and Schieber designed a polynomial time algorithm to solves the most uniform problem in $\mathcal{O}(m \log n)$ time, where n is the number of vertex in connected graph G, m is the amount of edges in connected graph G.*

Lemma 2 *[6]. The double threshold algorithm (DT-Algorithm) can correctly solved constrained balanced optimization problem in $\mathcal{O}(m f(m))$, $\mathcal{O}(f(m))$ is the complexity of solving $SUM(a, b)$, where $SUM(a, b) : min \sum_{e \in S} w(e)$, subject to $S \in F(a, b) = \{S \in F : e \in S, implies\ a \le w(e) \le b\}$.*

Lemma 3 *[7]. The Wu's improved algorithm correctly solves the minimum balanced spanning tree with edge restrictions and runs in $\mathcal{O}(mn)$ time.*

Lemma 4 *[16]. Suppose that m items $b_1, b_2, \ldots, b_m$ have sizes $w(b_1), w(b_2), \ldots, w(b_m)$, respectively, If we use the fist-fit-decreasing algorithm (FFD, abbreviations) to pack these mitems into some bins with capacity 1, the total size of each bin generated by the algorithm FFDis larger than $\frac{2}{3}$, with the exception of the last bin.*

Lemma 5 *[16]. Suppose that m items $b_1, b_2, \ldots, b_m$ have sizes $w(b_1), w(b_2), \ldots, w(b_m)$, respectively, where $0 < w(b_i) \le \frac{1}{2}$. When we use the fist-fit-decreasing algorithm (FFD, for short) to pack these m items into some bins with capacity 1, then the total size of items packed into each bin produced by the algorithm FFD is greater than $\frac{2}{3}$, except the last bin used.*

Lemma 6 *[18]. For any edge-weighted graph $G(V, E; w)$, $w : E \to Q^+$ is a weight function. If a minimum spanning tree T of G has the edge set $E_T = \{e_{i_1}, e_{i_2}, \ldots, e_{i_{n-1}}\}$ to satisfy: $w(e_{i_1}) \le w(e_{i_2}) \le \cdots \le w(e_{i_{n-1}})$, and if any spanning tree T' of G has the edge set $E_T = \{e_{j_1}, e_{j_2}, \ldots, e_{j_{n-1}}\}$ to satisfy: $w(e_{j_1}) \le w(e_{j_2}) \le \cdots \le w(e_{j_{n-1}})$, then $w(e_{i_k}) \le w(e_{j_1}), k = 1, 2, \ldots, n-1$.*

3   The Minimal Balanced Spanning Tree Splicing Problem

In this section, in the case of $MBSTS$ problem, given a balanced spanning tree $T = (V, E; w)$ as an instance, it can become the bin packing problem with the n items $w(e)$ as an input. In other word, the bin packing problem polynomial time can reduction to splice balanced spanning tree problem, due to bin packing problem is NP-hard, so the splicing balanced spanning tree problem is also NP-hard [15]. The approximate algorithm of $MBSTS$ problem is described as follows.

Algorithm 3.1: $MBSTS$

Input :	A simple connected weighted graph $G(V, E; w; \ell)$.

Output: A balanced spanning tree $T = G(V, E')$ and the number of bins used.

Step 1   A minimum balanced spanning tree $T = G(V, E')$ in simple connected weighted graph $G(V, E; w; \ell)$ is obtained by using the balanced spanning tree algorithm [5], where $E' = \{e_{i_1}, e_{i_2}, \ldots, e_{i_{n-1}}\}$;

Step 2   For $\forall e \in T$, let $insert(e) = \lceil \frac{w(e)}{\ell} \rceil - 1$, then we use $insert(e)$ pieces of whole material to splice part of edge e, and denote $m_0 = \sum_{e \in T} insert(e)$ as the number of special materials used in this step;

Step 3   For $\forall e \in T$, let $w'(e) = w(e) - insert(e) \cdot \ell$, $w'(e_{i_1}), w'(e_{i_1}), \ldots, w'(e_{i_{n-1}})$ are the length of remaining edge e in the balanced spanning tree T that are spliced with the whole special materials. We regard the weight of these edges of $w'(e_{i_1}), w'(e_{i_1}), \ldots, w'(e_{i_{n-1}})$ as the size of the items, then we use the FFD algorithm to pack $w'(e_{i_1}), w'(e_{i_1}), \ldots, w'(e_{i_{n-1}})$ into bins with capacity ℓ, and denote m_1 as the number of bins used this step;

Step 4   Output a balanced spanning tree T and the number of $m_0 + m_1$ bins used in this algorithm, i.e. $OUT = m_0 + m_1$.

Using the 3.1 algorithm, we get the result of the $BSTS$ problem as follows:

Theorem 1. *Algorithm 3.1 is a $\frac{3}{2}$-approximation algorithm to solve the BSTS problem, that is, the algorithm satisfies $OUT \leq \frac{3}{2} \cdot OPT$, where OUT refers to the numbers of special materials output by the algorithm 3.1, OPT refers to the numbers of optimization materials required for the BSTS problem, and its running time is $\mathcal{O}(n \log n)$.*

Proof. Suppose that $T = G(V, E')$ is a minimum balanced spanning tree produced by algorithm 3.1 with the value OUT, we assume that $T = G(V, E')$ has the edges set $E' = \{e_{i_1}, e_{i_2}, \ldots, e_{i_{n-1}}\}$, and satisfying $w(e_{i_1}) \leq w(e_{i_2}) \leq \cdots \leq w(e_{i_{n-1}})$, where $n = |V|$. We also assume that $T^* = G(V, E^*)$ is an optimal balanced spanning tree to the instance G for the $BSTS$ problem with the value OPT, and the corresponding edge set satisfies $w(e_{j_1}) \leq w(e_{j_2}) \leq \cdots \leq w(e_{j_{n-1}})$. By lemma 2.6, we can obtain this inequality $w(e_{i_k}) \leq w(e_{j_k})$ holds for each $k = 1, 2, \ldots, n - 1$.

Now let's think about the splicing scheme for tree T, follow the previous analysis in Sect. 2, we can divide the splicing of tree T into two stages for analysis:(1) let $insert(e) = \lceil \frac{w(e)}{\ell} \rceil - 1$, let's first cover the length of edges e with the whole special materials ℓ for all edges of length greater than or equal to ℓ in T, until the length of all edges is less than ℓ. (2) let $w'(e) = w(e) - insert(e) \cdot \ell$, we use the FFD algorithm to pack all the remaining edges of the tree T with length $w'(e_{i_k})(k = 1, 2, \ldots, n - 1)$ into bins, and denote m_1 as the number of bins used this step, but the theoretical optimal value is m^* in this step, so there is $m_1 \leq \frac{3}{2} \cdot m^*$. Then we obtain the fact $OUT = \sum_{e_{i_k} \in T} insert(e_{i_k}) + m_1 \leq \sum_{e_{i_k} \in T} insert(e_{i_k}) + \frac{3}{2} m^* \leq \frac{3}{2} (\sum_{e_{i_k} \in T} insert(e_{i_k}) + m^*) \leq \frac{3}{2} \cdot OPT_T$.

Since $T^* = G(V, E^*)$ is an optimal balanced spanning tree to the instance G for the $CBTS$ problem, and the items $w(e_{i_1}), w(e_{i_2}), \ldots, w(e_{i_{n-1}})$ are packed into OPT bins with capacity ℓ, we also can pack these items $w(e_{i_1}), w(e_{i_2}), \ldots, w(e_{i_{n-1}})$ of T into these OPT bins as follows:(1) if $insert(e_{i_k}) = insert(e_{j_k})$, we use the optimal packing method of T^* to find $insert(e_{j_k})$ bins that can be pack into the bin with $insert(e_{i_k})$ edges in T, and these edges of length $w(e_{i_k}) - insert(e_{i_k}) \cdot \ell$ can be packed into $w(e_{j_k}) - insert(e_{j_k}) \cdot \ell$ bins. (2) if $insert(e_{i_k}) \leq insert(e_{j_k})$, we can pack this part of $w(e_{i_k}) - insert(e_{i_k}) \cdot \ell$ into one of $insert(e_{j_k}) - insert(e_{i_k})$ bins. It implies that the minimum number OPT_T of bins for the items $w(e_{i_1}), w(e_{i_2}), \ldots, w(e_{i_{n-1}})$ of T is no more than OPT, so we have the inequality $OPT_T \leq OPT$. Thus, we finally obtain $OUT \leq \frac{3}{2} \cdot OPT$ by the fact $OPT_T \leq OPT$.

Runtime analysis of Algorithm 3.1: by Lemma 1, step 1 needs running time $\mathcal{O}(mlogn)$ to find a minimal balanced spanning tree $T = G(V, E')$; at step 2, it's most running time $\mathcal{O}(n)$ pack all items into bins; at step 3, FFD algorithm needs at most running time $\mathcal{O}(nlogn)$ to pack $n - 1$ items of lengths of T into bins with length ℓ. Hence, the whole algorithm needs the running time $\mathcal{O}(nlogn)$.

In step 4 of Algorithm 3.1, when we use the bin packing algorithm to solve the $MBSTS$ problem, we use an asymptotic polynomial time approximation scheme $(PTAS)\mathcal{A}_\varepsilon$ [15] instead of the FFD algorithm, that is, using an asymptotic $PTAS$ $\mathcal{A}_\varepsilon$ [15] to pack $w'(e_{i_1}), w'(e_{i_1}), \ldots, w'(e_{i_{n-1}})$ into m_1 bins with capacity ℓ in the step 3. Thus, we can get a improved algorithm for the $MBSTS$ problem, the conclusion is as follows.

Theorem 2. *For any $0 < \varepsilon \leq \frac{1}{2}$ and given an instance $G(V, E; w; \ell)$ of the $MBSTS$ problem, there is an algorithm $\mathcal{A}_\varepsilon$ that runs in time polynomial in n, and the improved algorithm 3.1 can get at most $(1 + 2\varepsilon)OPT + 1$ special materials of length ℓ to splice all edges in a balanced spanning tree T, where the improved algorithm 3.1 is an asymptotic $PTAS$ to solve the $MBSTS$ problem.*

Proof. In the third step of algorithm 3.1, use an asymptotic $PTAS$ $\mathcal{A}_\varepsilon$ [15] to pack $w'(e_{i_1}), w'(e_{i_1}), \ldots, w'(e_{i_{n-1}})$ into m_1 bins with capacity ℓ in a balanced spanning tree, and an asymptotic $PTAS$ $\mathcal{A}_\varepsilon$ can obtain the output value of a feasible solution m_1 to satisfy $m_1 \leq (1 + 2\varepsilon)(OPT_T - m_0) + 1$. The same proof is used for algorithm 3.1, we also have $OPT_T \leq OPT$. From what has been discussed above, for each value of ε, we get $OUT = m_0 + m_1 \leq m_0 + (1 + 2\varepsilon)(OPT_T - m_0) + 1 \leq (1 + 2\varepsilon)OPT - 2\varepsilon \cdot m_0 + 1 \leq (1 + 2\varepsilon)OPT + 1$.

4   The Balanced Spanning Tree Splicing Problem with Edge Set Restricted

In this section, we consider the splicing balanced spanning tree problem with edge set restricted ($MBSTS\text{-}ESR$). The argument for the $MBSTS\text{-}ESR$problem is similar to that for the $MBSTS$problem, the $MBSTS\text{-}ESR$ problem also can not be approximated within performance ration $\frac{3}{2} - \varepsilon$, $\forall \varepsilon > 0$, unless $P = NP$. We now can present an approximation algorithm to solve the $MBSTS\text{-}ESR$ problem as follows.

Algorithm 4.1: $MBSTS\text{-}ESR$

Input:	A simple connected weighted graph $G(V, E; w; E_0; \ell)$
Output:	A minimum balanced spanning tree $T = G(V, E')$ with edge set Restricted, and the number of m bins used.
step 1	A minimum balanced spanning tree $T = G(V, E')$ with edge set Restricted in graph $G(V, E; w; E_0; \ell)$ is obtained by using the balanced spanning tree algorithm with edge set restricted [7], where $E_0 \subset E' = \{e_{i_1}, e_{i_2}, \ldots, e_{i_{n-1}}\}$;
step 2	For $\forall e \in T$, let $insert(e) = \lceil \frac{w(e)}{\ell} \rceil - 1$, use complete special materials ℓ to splice part of edge e, and denote $m_0 = \sum_{e \in T} insert(e)$;
step 3	For $\forall e \in T$, let $w'(e) = w(e) - insert(e) \cdot \ell$, we denote the weight of these edges by $w'(e_{i_1}), w'(e_{i_1}), \ldots, w'(e_{i_{n-1}})$ as the size of the items, then we use the FFD algorithm to pack $w'(e_{i_1}), w'(e_{i_1}), \ldots, w'(e_{i_{n-1}})$ into bins with capacity ℓ, and denote m_1 as the number of bins used this step;
step 4	Output a balanced spanning tree T and the number of $OUT = m_0 + m_1$ bins used in this algorithm.

Using the Algorithm 4.1, we obtain the following result for the $MBSTS\text{-}ESR$ problem.

Theorem 3. *Algorithm 4.1 is a $\frac{3}{2}$-approximation algorithm to solve the $MBSTS\text{-}ESR$ problem, that is the algorithm satisfies $OUT \leq \frac{3}{2} \cdot OPT$, where OUT refers to the numbers of special materials output by the algorithm, OPT refers to the numbers of optimization materials required for the $MBSTS\text{-}ESR$ problem, and its running time is $\mathcal{O}(mn)$.*

Proof. Suppose that $T = G(V, E')$ is a minimum balanced spanning tree with edge set restricted produced by algorithm 4.1, having the output value $OUT = m_0 + m_1$, we assume that $T = G(V, E')$ has the edges set $E' = \{e_{i_1}, e_{i_2}, \ldots, e_{i_{n-1}}\}$, and satisfying $w(e_{i_1}) \leq w(e_{i_2}) \leq \cdots \leq w(e_{i_{n-1}})$, where $n = |V|, E_0 \subset E'$. We also assume that $T^* = G(V, E^*)$ is an optimal balanced spanning tree to the instance G for the $BSTS$ problem with the value OPT, and the corresponding edge set satisfies $w(e_{j_1}) \leq w(e_{j_2}) \leq \cdots \leq w(e_{j_{n-1}})$, $E_0 \subset E^*$. By Lemma 6, we can obtain this inequality $w(e_{i_k}) \leq w(e_{j_k})$ holds for each $k = 1, 2, \ldots, n-1$.

Now let's think about the splicing scheme for tree T with edge set restricted, the proof method of this algorithm is similar to Theorem 1, this splice process can be broadly broken into two steps:(1) let $insert(e) = \lceil \frac{w(e)}{\ell} \rceil - 1$, let's cover the length of edges e with the whole special materials ℓ for all edges of length greater than or equal to ℓ in T, until the length of all edges is less than ℓ. (2) let $w'(e) = w(e) - insert(e) \cdot \ell$, we use the FFD algorithm to pack all the remaining edges of the tree T with length $w'(e_{i_k})(k = 1, 2, \ldots, n-1)$ into bins, and denote m_1 as the number of bins used this step, but the theoretical optimal value is m^* in this step, so there is $m_1 \le \frac{3}{2} \cdot m^*$. Then we obtain the fact $OUT = \sum_{e_{i_k} \in T} insert(e_{i_k}) + m_1 \le \sum_{e_{i_k} \in T} insert(e_{i_k}) + \frac{3}{2}m^* \le \frac{3}{2}(\sum_{e_{i_k} \in T} insert(e_{i_k}) + m^*) \le \frac{3}{2} \cdot OPT_T$.

Due to $T^* = G(V, E^*)$ is an optimal balanced spanning tree with edge set restricted to the instance G of the $MBSTS$-ESR problem, and the items $w(e_{i_1}), w(e_{i_2}), \ldots, w(e_{i_{n-1}})$ are packed into OPT bins with capacity ℓ, we also can pack these items $w(e_{i_1}), w(e_{i_2}), \ldots, w(e_{i_{n-1}})$ of T into these OPT bins as follows:(1) if $insert(e_{i_k}) = insert(e_{j_k})$, we use the optimal packing method of T^* to find $insert(e_{j_k})$ bins that can be pack into the bin with $insert(e_{i_k})$ edges in T, and these edges of length $w(e_{i_k}) - insert(e_{i_k}) \cdot \ell$ can be packed into $w(e_{j_k}) - insert(e_{j_k}) \cdot \ell$ bins. (2) if $insert(e_{i_k}) \le insert(e_{j_k})$, we can pack this part of $w(e_{i_k}) - insert(e_{i_k}) \cdot \ell$ into one of $insert(e_{j_k}) - insert(e_{i_k})$ bins. It show that the minimum number OPT_T of bins for the items $w(e_{i_1}), w(e_{i_2}), \ldots, w(e_{i_{n-1}})$ of T is no more than OPT, so we have the inequality $OPT_T \le OPT$. Thus, we finally obtain $OUT \le \frac{3}{2} \cdot OPT$ by the fact $OPT_T \le OPT$.

Runtime analysis of Algorithm 4.1: in step 1 of Algorithm 4.1, by Lemma 3, we know that computing the running time of a balanced spanning tree $T = G(V, E')$ with edge set restricted is $\mathcal{O}(mn)$; in step 2 of algorithm 4.1, it's running time is $\mathcal{O}(n)$ is $\mathcal{O}(mn)$; in step 3 of Algorithm 4.1, it's most running time is $\mathcal{O}(nlogn)$. Hence, the algorithm 4.1 needs the running time $\mathcal{O}(mn)$.

This completes the proof of the Theorem 3 mentioned-above.

5   The Constrained Balanced Spanning Tree Splicing Problem

In this section, we consider the splicing problem of constrained balanced spanning tree($CBTS$), use a simple connected graph $G(V, E; w; B; \ell)$ as instance of the splicing constrained balanced spanning tree problem, where $w : E \to Z^+$ is a non-negative function, and B is positive integer. There are some special materials with length ℓ, we need find a balanced spanning tree $T \subset F$ from the undirected graph G, it satisfies $w(T) = \sum_{e \in T} w(e) \le B$, so that each edge in the balanced spanning graph T is spliced by a part of a piece (or some whole pieces)of a special material of length ℓ, where F be a family of subsets of E. The objective is to minimize the number of necessary pieces of such a specific material to splice all edges needed in constrained balanced spanning tree T.

For the instance of $G(V, E; w; B; \ell)$, if we can find a balanced spanning tree $T \subset F$ from the graph G, it satisfies $w(T) = \sum_{e \in T} w(e) \le B$, and the length of all edges e in the tree T does no longer than the length of the special material ℓ, then the $CBTS$ problem is the promotion form of the packing problem. According to the inapproximability of the packing problem, the $CBTS$ problem can not be approximated within performance ration $\frac{3}{2} - \varepsilon$, $\forall \varepsilon > 0$, unless $P = NP$. We need design an asymptotic approximation algorithm to solve the $CBTS$ problem, and the method of the algorithm is as follows:(1)for each edge e in graph G, we denote $insert(e) = \lceil \frac{w(e)}{\ell} \rceil - 1$, $w'(e) = insert(e) \cdot \ell$, $w''(e) = w(e) - w'(e)$, and if $\frac{\ell}{2} < w''(e) < \frac{2\ell}{3}$, then $\theta(e) = 1$, otherwise,$\theta(e) = 0$; (2) given a simple connected weighted graph $G(V, E; w; \ell; B)$, we used the double threshold algorithm (DT-algorithm) [6] to find a constrained minimum balanced spanning tree T in graph G. (3) use the FFD algorithm [16] for the bin packing problem to pack the items of lengths of edges in T into some bins with capacity ℓ.

Algorithm 5.1: $CBTS$

Input: a simple connected weighted graph $G(V, E; w; B; \ell)$

Output: the number of bins used, and a minimum balanced spanning tree $T = G(V, E')$, where $T \subset F$, $w(T) = \sum_{e \in T} w(e) \leq B$.

Step 1   Use the DT-algorithm to find a minimum balanced spanning tree $T = G(V, E')$ in $G(V, E; w; \ell; B)$, if $w(T) = \sum_{e \in T} w(e) > B$, then output "There is no feasible solution for this instance", the algorithm stopped; if $w(T) = \sum_{e \in T} w(e) \leq B$ and $T \subset F$, where $E'(T) = \{e_{i_1}, e_{i_2}, \ldots, e_{i_{n-1}}\}$, then go to the next step;

Step 2   For each edge e in graph G, we denote $insert(e) = \lceil \frac{w(e)}{\ell} \rceil - 1$, $w'(e) = insert(e) \cdot \ell$, $w''(e) = w(e) - w'(e)$, and if $\frac{\ell}{2} < w''(e) < \frac{2\ell}{3}$, then $\theta(e) = 1$, otherwise, $\theta(e) = 0$;

Step 3   For $\forall e \in E'$, the part of size $w'(e)$ on edge e is packed into $insert(e)$ bins with capacity ℓ, and denotes $m_0 = \sum_{e \in E'} insert(e)$ as the number of bins used in this step.

Step 4   For items of size $w''(e_{i_1}), w''(e_{i_1}), \ldots, w''(e_{i_l})$, use the FFD algorithm to pack $w''(e_{i_1}), w''(e_{i_1}), \ldots, w''(e_{i_{n-1}})$ into bins with capacity ℓ, and denote m_1 as the number of bins used this step;

Step 5   Output a minimum balanced spanning tree T and the number of $m_0 + m_1$ bins used in this algorithm, i.e. $OUT = m_0 + m_1$.

By the Algorithm 5.1, we obtain the following result for the $CBTS$ problem.

Theorem 4. *Algorithm 5.1 is an asymptotic $\frac{3}{2}$-approximation algorithm to solve the $CBTS$ problem, that is the algorithm satisfies $OUT \leq \frac{3}{2} \cdot OPT + \frac{1 + r_0}{4}$, where OUT refers to the numbers of special materials output by the algorithm, OPT refers to the numbers of optimization materials required for $CBTS$ problem, r_0 denote the number of edges on the tree T where the remaining length satisfies $\frac{\ell}{2} < w''(e) < \frac{2\ell}{3}$, and its running time is $\mathcal{O}(m f(m))$.*

Proof. Suppose that $T^* = G(V, E^*)$ is an optimal balanced spanning tree to the instance G for the $CBTS$ problem with the value OPT, where $T^* \subset F$, $w(T^*) = \sum_{e \in T} w(e) \leq B$. We also assume that $T = G(V, E')$ is a minimum balanced spanning tree produced by Algorithm 5.1 with the value $OUT = m_0 + m_1$.

Since T is a minimum balanced spanning tree for weight function $w(\cdot)$ in simple connected weighted undirected graph G, we get $\sum_{e \in T} w(e) \leq \sum_{e \in T^*} w(e) \leq \ell \cdot OPT$ by Lemma 6. For every edge e in a balanced spanning tree T, we first use $insert(e)$ pieces of whole special materials of length ℓ to splice them, and then the remaining length of the unspliced part of edge e in T is denoted as $w''(e)$, it indicates that m_0 pieces of whole special materials of length ℓ were used in the step 3. For items of size $w''(e_{i_1}), w''(e_{i_1}), \ldots, w''(e_{i_l})$ in the step 4, we use the following notation, let r_0 denote the number of remaining edges in the tree T that satisfy $\frac{\ell}{2} < w''(e) < \frac{2\ell}{3}$, use r_1 denote the number of remaining edges in the tree T should be $\frac{2\ell}{3} \leq w''(e)$. The m_1 bins used in the step 4 are listed as $B_1, B_2, \ldots, B_{m_1}$, respectively, and the sum of the items in each bin B_i is denoted as $f(B_i)(\ i = 1, 2, \ldots, m_1)$, so we can get the following facts.

(1) $f(B_i) \geq \frac{2\ell}{3}, i = 1, 2, \ldots, r_1$;
(2) $f(B_i) \geq \frac{\ell}{2}, i = 1 + r_1, 2 + r_1, \ldots, r_1 + r_0$; (by Lemma 4)
(3) $f(B_i) > \frac{2\ell}{3}, i = r_1 + r_0 + 1, r_1 + r_0 + 2, \ldots, m_1 - 1$; (by Lemma 5)
(4) $f(B_i) + f(B_{m_1}) > \ell, i = 1, 2, \ldots, m_1 - 1$.

Thus, we can get
$$w(T) = \sum_{e \in T} w(e) = \sum_{e \in T} w'(e) + \sum_{e \in T} w''(e) = \sum_{e \in T} insert(e) \cdot \ell + \sum_{i=1}^{m_1} f(B_i) = m_0 \cdot \ell + \sum_{i=1}^{r_1} f(B_i) + \sum_{i=r_1+1}^{r_1+r_0} f(B_i) + \sum_{i=r_1+r_0+1}^{m_1-1} f(B_i) + f(B_{m_1}) = m_0 \cdot \ell + \sum_{i=1}^{r_1} f(B_i) + \sum_{i=r_1+1}^{r_1+r_0} (f(B_i) + \frac{\ell}{6}) + \sum_{i=r_1+r_0+1}^{m_1-1} f(B_i) + f(B_{m_1}) - \frac{r_0}{6} \cdot \ell > m_0 \cdot \ell + \frac{2\ell}{3}(m_1 - 2) + \ell + \frac{r_0}{6} \cdot \ell \geq \frac{2\ell}{3} \cdot (m_0 + m_1) - \frac{r_0+2}{6} \cdot \ell = \frac{2\ell}{3} \cdot OUT - \frac{r_0+2}{6} \cdot \ell.$$

In summary, we know $\frac{2\ell}{3} \cdot OUT - \frac{r_0+2}{6} \cdot \ell < \sum_{e \in T} w(e) \leq \ell \cdot OPT$, implying $4OUT < 6OPT + r_0 + 2$. Hence, we obtain the fact $OUT \leq \frac{3}{2}OPT + \frac{r_0+1}{4}$ by the integral property.

Runtime analysis of Algorithm 5.1: at step 1, by Lemma 2, the running time of the DT-algorithm is $\mathcal{O}(mf(m))$; at step 3, it's needs most running time is $\mathcal{O}(n)$; at step 4, the FFD algorithm needs at most running time $\mathcal{O}(n log n)$. Hence, the whole algorithm needs the running time $\mathcal{O}(mf(m))$. The running time of the FFD algorithm is $\mathcal{O}(mf(m))$. Hence, the whole algorithm needs the running time $\mathcal{O}(mf(m))$.

6   Conclusions

In this paper, we proposed three kinds of algorithms, and obtain three main results:(1) for the $MBSTS$ problem, we obtain an $\frac{3}{2}$-approximation algorithm and an asymptotic $PTAS$, algorithm 3.1 running time is $\mathcal{O}(n log n)$; (2) for the $MBSTS$-ESR problem, we obtain an $\frac{3}{2}$-approximation algorithm, and algorithm 4.1 has its running time $\mathcal{O}(nm)$; (3)for the $CBTS$ problem, we get an asymptotic $\frac{3}{2}$-approximation algorithm, and Algorithm 5.1 has its running time $\mathcal{O}(mf(m))$. Further improvement requires deeper exploration. The most hardest work is to design approximation algorithms with lower constant approximation ratios to solve the $CBTS$(or$MBSTS$-ESR) problem.

References

1. Punnen, A.P., Taghipour, S., Karapetyan, D., Bhattacharyya, B.: The quadratic balanced optimization problem. Discret. Optim. **12**(2), 47–60 (2014). https://doi.org/10.1016/j.disopt.2014.01.001
2. Duin, C.W., Volgenant, A.: Minimum deviation and balanced optimization: a unifed approach. Oper. Res. Lett. **10**(1), 43–48 (1991). https://doi.org/10.1016/0167-6377(91)90085-4
3. Martello, S., Pulleyblank, W.R., Toth, P., Werra, D.: Balanced optimization problems. Oper. Res. Lett. **3**(5), 275–278 (1984). https://doi.org/10.1016/0167-6377(84)90061-0
4. Camerni, P.M., Maffioli, F., Martello, S., Toth, P.: Most and least uniform spanning trees. Discret. Appl. Math. **15**(2), 181–197 (1986). https://doi.org/10.1016/0166-218X(86)90041-7
5. Galil, Z., Schieber, B.: On finding most uniform spanning trees. Discret. Appl. Math. **20**(2), 173–175 (1988). https://doi.org/10.1016/0166-218X(88)90062-5
6. Punnen, A.P., Nair, K.P.K.: Constrained balanced optimization problems. Comput. Math. Appl. **37**, 157–163 (1999). https://doi.org/10.1016/S0898-1221(99)00119-4
7. Wu, L.: An efficient algorithm for the most balanced spanning tree problems. Adv. Sci. Lett. **11**, 776–778 (2012). https://doi.org/10.1166/asl.2012.3033
8. Punnen, A.P., Aneja, Y.P.: Lexicographic balanced optimization problems. Oper. Res. Lett. **32**(1), 27–30 (2004). https://doi.org/10.1016/S0167-6377(03)00065-8
9. Gupta, S.K., Punnen, A.P.: Minimum deviation problems. Oper. Res. Lett. **7**(4), 201–204 (1988). https://doi.org/10.1016/0167-6377(88)90029-6
10. Cappanera, P., Scutella, M.G.: Balanced paths in acyclic networks: Tractable cases and related approaches. Networks **45**(2), 104–111 (2005). https://doi.org/10.1002/net.20053
11. Ahuja, R.K.: The balanced linear programming problem. Eur. J. Oper. Res. **101**(1), 29–38 (1997). https://doi.org/10.1016/S0377-2217(96)00142-7
12. Eppstein, D.: Minimum range balanced cuts via dynamic subset sums. J. Algorithms **23**(2), 375–385 (1997). https://doi.org/10.1006/jagm.1996.0841
13. Li, J., Ge, Y., He, S., et al.: Approximation algorithms for constructing some required structures in digraphs. Eur. J. Oper. Res. **232**(2), 307–314 (2014). https://doi.org/10.1016/j.ejor.2013.07.033
14. LaRusic, J., Punnen, A.P.: The balanced traveling salesman problem. Comput. Oper. Res. **38**(5), 868–875 (2011)
15. Vazirani, Vijay V.: Approximation Algorithms. Springer, Heidelberg (2003). https://doi.org/10.1007/978-3-662-04565-7
16. Simchi-Levi, D.: New worst case results for the bin-packing problem. Nav. Res. Logist. **41**(4), 579–858 (1994). https://doi.org/10.1002/1520-6750(199406)41:4
17. Papadimitiou, C.H., Steiglitz, K.: Combinatorial Optimization: Algorithms and Complexity. Dover, New York (1988). https://doi.org/10.1109/TASSP.1984.1164450
18. Schrijver, A.: Combinatorial Optimization: Poluhedra and Efficiency. Springer, Dordrecht (2003)

The Influence of Employees' Financial Equity Perception on Organizational Effectiveness in NPOs

Xia Li[1](✉) and Xiaoxia Xie[2]

[1] Accounting College, Anhui University of Finance and Economics,
Bengbu 233000, People's Republic of China
[2] Institute of Social Development Research, Southwestern University of Finance
and Economics, Chengdu 611130, People's Republic of China

Abstract. The Employees' Financial Equity Perception in NPOs is the important content of NPO human resource management. It has an important influence on the efficiency of organization management by effecting on the organizational effectiveness. Through a questionnaire survey of employees of some NPOs, the structural equation analysis indicates the influence path of the employees' financial equity perception on organizational effectiveness in NPOs, the results show that the NPO employee job satisfaction is mainly positively affected by distributive equity and procedural equity; the degree of being approved of the staff is mainly positively influenced by the financial information fairness and financial result fairness; staff satisfaction affects organizational citizenship behavior and organizational commitment; organizational commitment has some negative effect on organizational failure behavior; normative commitment and continuance commitment have positive influence on organizational identity perception, while affective commitment has not obvious positive impact on organizational identification perception.

Keywords: Nonprofit organization · Financial justice · Organizational citizenship behavior · Organizational commitment · Job satisfaction

1 Introduction

In recent years, the enhancement of social functions, the rapid development of non-profit organizations (NPOs) and the complex and changeable environment together push the organizations themselves to strengthen their construction, improve their financial and human resource management level, so as to be able to flexibly respond to the changes of various internal and external conditions, and provide better products and services for customers. It is not only the important content of NPO human resource management, but also the important way to improve the efficiency and effect of NPO management.

The perceived organizational justice is the subjective perception of stakeholders to organizational justice, including four dimensions: distribution justice, procedural justice, interpersonal justice and information justice. The perceived financial justice is the

H. Song and D. Jiang (Eds.): SIMUtools 2020, LNICST 369, pp. 274–295, 2021.
https://doi.org/10.1007/978-3-030-72792-5_25

financial part of organizational justice perception. By analyzing the details of organizational justice, it is concluded that except interpersonal justice, the other three kinds of justice are closely related to the funds movement. Therefore, the perceived financial justice includes the perceived justice of financial procedures, outcomes and information, emphasizing the process of economic income distribution, the amount of economic income obtained by employees and the transmission of relevant information. The financial justice of NPO is the application of financial equity theory in NPO, including the justice of distributions, procedures and information.

Organizational citizenship behavior (OCB), as an extra role behavior, can improve organizational efficiency, although it is not included in the formal compensation system. As a subjective perception, job satisfaction affects the behavior of employees, and plays an important role in the mobilization and play of their work enthusiasm and initiative. As a psychological contract, organizational commitment reflects employees' loyalty to the organization and their sense of belonging. OCB, job satisfaction and organizational commitment are all important contents of organizational effectiveness, which can reflect the role of employees in promoting organizational efficiency. The perceived financial justice of employees in NPOs has a profound impact on their OCB, job satisfaction and organizational commitment.

At present, some scholars have done some research on the impact of financial justice on organizational effect, and think that the perceived financial justice of employees has a certain impact on organizational effect. However, few scholars have made a systematic analysis and discussion on the relationship between the perceived financial justice and organizational effectiveness of NPOs. From the existing research, the impact of financial justice is the main part of the impact of organizational effectiveness variables. Distributive justice and procedural justice can greatly influence employees' work attitude and OCBs (Colquitt et al. 2001). According to Tyler (1994), individual seeking justice is to achieve personal goals under the stimulation of economic interests. Perceived justice can promote more positive behaviors by comparing individual input-output ratio with others. Perceived organizational justice can well predict many main organizational effect variables (Liu et al. 2015). For NPOs, does the perceived financial justice of employees have an impact on the organizational effect? If so, how?

In this paper, based on the investigation of NPO employees in China, the impact of distribution, procedure and information justice on job satisfaction, organizational commitment and OCBs are analyzed. The contribution of this paper is mainly reflected in three aspects: Firstly, the effect of NPO is discussed from a new perspective of financial justice, and the influences of financial procedure, outcomes and information justice on organizational commitment, job satisfaction and OCB are investigated, which is conducive to the improvement of human resource management and financial management of NPO. Secondly, a scale of employee financial equity, job satisfaction, organizational commitment and OCB, which is in line with the reality of NPOs in China, has been developed, and the reliability and validity of the survey data have been tested. Eventually, a formal scale with high reliability and validity has been formed for NPOs in China, which provides an appropriate tool for the follow-up research. Thirdly, the influence path of employee perceived financial justice on the main organizational effect variables in NPOs has been clarified, and the impact of employee perceived financial justice on OCB in NPOs has been systematically analyzed, which provides a basis for organizations to motivate employees, improve employee satisfaction and enthusiasm, and formulate scientific reward and punishment systems.

2 Theoretical Basis and Research

Sufficient financial information disclosure helps the employees of non-profit organizations fully understand the organization's distribution process and outcomes. Moreover, they need to express their different opinions through unimpeded channels, which is a necessary condition for the fair realization of financial outcomes. The disclosure of financial information also makes the distribution process more transparent and reasonable. Reasonable financial procedures will also promote the outcomes of distribution to ensure the interests of more people. So the following hypotheses are made:

h1: Financial information justice of employees in NPOs has a significant positive impact on financial procedure justice.
h2: Financial information justice of employees in NPOs has a significant positive impact on distribution justice.
h3: Distribution justice of employees in NPOs has a significant positive impact on distribution justice.

The perceived justice has both direct and indirect influence on employee's job satisfaction in enterprises. Han and Zhang (2015) discovered that perceived justice has a positive impact on employee job satisfaction and organizational justice behavior, and moral leadership also has an indirect effect on OCB and subordinate job satisfaction through perceived justice. There is a strong correlation between perceived organizational justice and job satisfaction, and strongly perceived justice can bring high job satisfaction. On the contrary, a strong sense of injustice will lead to a low level of job satisfaction (Al-Zubi 2010). Job satisfaction includes job, promotion and pay. So the following hypotheses are made:

h4: Financial information justice of employees in NPOs has a significant positive impact on job satisfaction itself.
h5: Financial information justice of employees in NPOs has a significant positive impact on pay satisfaction.
h6: Financial information justice of employees in NPOs has a significant positive impact on chance of promotion.
h7: Financial procedural justice of employees in NPOs has a significant positive impact on job satisfaction itself.
h8: Financial procedural justice of employees in NPOs has a significant positive impact on pay satisfaction.
h9: Financial procedural justice of employees in NPOs has a significant positive impact on chance of promotion.
h10: Distribution justice of employees in NPOs has a significant positive impact on job satisfaction itself.

h11: Distribution justice of employees in NPOs has a significant positive impact on pay satisfaction.

h12: Distribution justice of employees in NPOs has a significant positive impact on chance of promotion.

Bateman and Organ (1983) discovered that OCB is composed of a series of informal cooperative behaviors, neither out of labor contract, nor informal role requirements, but a kind of behavior and posture outside the role that is beneficial to the organization, which can improve the organizational efficiency as a whole. OCB includes altruism toward colleagues, identification with the company, conscientiousness, interpersonal harmony and protection of natural resources. The sense of personal fairness will have a certain impact on employees OCB (Organ 1990) When employees feel unfair, they will reduce OCB, and when they feel fair, they will continue to show OCB in return for the organization (Zhang and Qi 2001). Perceived organizational justice has a positive impact on OCB.

Shen and Zhang (2016) discovered that job satisfaction of employees has a positive impact on organizational commitment and OCB, and organizational commitment has a positive impact on OCB. According to Wang (2010), employees' job satisfaction is significantly positively correlated with OCB. In NPOs, employees' sense of happiness, satisfaction and appreciation in their work will promote them to work harder and complete some informal contract behaviors, otherwise, it is the opposite. OCB may be an organizational identity behavior that has a beneficial impact on the organization, or it may be an organizational destruction that seeks personal interests by using positions and private use of the organization's shared resources. The higher the employee's job satisfaction is, the more positive the working mood is, and the easier it is to engage in organizational and altruism toward colleagues (Zhang and Qi 2001). So the following hypotheses are made:

h13: Pay satisfaction of employees in NPOs has a significant positive impact on identification with the company.

h14: Pay satisfaction of employees in NPOs has a significant positive impact on altruism toward colleagues.

h15: Pay satisfaction of employees in NPOs has a significant positive impact on conscientiousness.

h16: Pay satisfaction of employees in NPOs has a significant positive impact on interpersonal harmony.

h17: Pay satisfaction of employees in NPOs has a significant positive impact on protecting company resources.

h18: Chance of promotion of employees in NPOs has a significant positive impact on identification with the company.

h19: Chance of promotion of employees in NPOs has a significant positive impact on altruism toward colleagues.

h20: Chance of promotion of employees in NPOs has a significant positive impact on conscientiousness.

h21: Chance of promotion of employees in NPOs has a significant positive impact on interpersonal harmony.

h22: Chance of promotion of employees in NPOs has a significant positive impact on protecting company resources.

h23: job satisfaction of employees in NPOs has a significant positive impact on identification with the company.

h24: job satisfaction itself of employees in NPOs has a significant positive impact on altruism toward colleagues.

h25: job satisfaction itself of employees in NPOs has a significant positive impact on conscientiousness.

h26: job satisfaction itself of employees in NPOs has a significant positive impact on interpersonal harmony.

h27: job satisfaction itself of employees in NPOs has a significant positive impact on protecting company resources.

Organizational commitment, also known as organizational attachment and organizational loyalty, refers to the strength of individual identification and participation in an organization. As a psychological contract, rather than a written one, it stipulates the non-professional role behaviors that cannot be specified in a formal contract, including continuous commitment, affective commitment and normative commitment (Meyer and Allen 1991). According to Becker (1960), the organizational commitment is a psychological phenomenon that employees have to stay in the organization due to the increase of organizational input, including the loss of turnover and the lack of alternative jobs. Both procedural justice and distribution justice can lead to organizational support, which can mediate organizational commitment (Jiang 2007). Organizational justice also affects organizational commitment through job satisfaction, which is a major factor affecting and has a significant correlation with organizational commitment (Ling and Ling 2009; Kuang and Ling 2009). Employees with higher satisfaction will be more loyal to the organization, will not change jobs frequently, and will get more happiness from their work. They are more emotionally dependent on the existing organization, and think that once they leave, it will probably mean a lot of personal sacrifice and less selectivity. So the following hypotheses are made:

h28: job satisfaction itself of employees in NPOs has a positive impact on their continuous commitment.

h29: job satisfaction itself of employees in NPOs has a positive impact on their affective commitment.

h30: job satisfaction itself of employees in NPOs has a positive impact on their normative commitment.

h31: Pay satisfaction of employees in NPOs has a positive impact on their continuous commitment.

h32: Pay satisfaction of employees in NPOs has a positive impact on their affective commitment.

h33: Pay satisfaction of employees in NPOs has a positive impact on their normative commitment.

h34: Chance of promotion of employees in NPOs has a positive impact on their continuous commitment.

h35: Chance of promotion of employees in NPOs has a positive impact on their affective commitment.

h36: Chance of promotion of employees in NPOs has a positive impact on their normative commitment.

The impact of perceived justice on employees' citizenship behavior is realized by job satisfaction perception and organizational commitment. Organizational commitment has a significant impact on OCB (Wang and Zhang 2008). OCB is positively related to organizational justice and organization, and organizational commitment plays an intermediary role in organizational justice and OCB (Yan and Zhang 2010). As for the influence of organizational commitment on OCB, Johnson and Chang (2006) discovered that shared group orientation and focus, group goals and norms internalization make affective commitment significantly related to group shape self-image; continuous commitment is related to individual self-image, because employees pay attention to and maintain individual investment interests to avoid negative results; self-image is a buffer variable between organizational commitment and organizational citizenship behavior. The enhancement of emotional dependence on the organization and the recognition of loyalty to the organization in terms of values will increase employees' identification with the company, promote their altruism toward colleagues and conscientiousness, contribute to interpersonal harmony within the organization, and also reduce their organizational destruction. Shore and Wayne (1993) discovered that affective commitment, perceived organizational support and OCB are positively correlated, while continuous commitment is negatively correlated with OCB. So the following hypotheses are made:

h37: Continuous commitment of employees in NPOs has a positive impact on their identification with the company.

h38: Continuous commitment of employees in NPOs has a positive impact on their altruism toward colleagues.

h39: Continuous commitment of employees in NPOs has a positive impact on their conscientiousness.

h40: Continuous commitment of employees in NPOs has a positive impact on their interpersonal harmony.

h41: Continuous commitment of employees in NPOs has a positive impact on their protecting company resources.

h42: Affective commitment of employees in NPOs has a positive impact on their identification with the company.

h43: Affective commitment of employees in NPOs has a positive impact on their altruism toward colleagues.

h44: Affective commitment of employees in NPOs has a positive impact on their conscientiousness.

h45: Affective commitment of employees in NPOs has a positive impact on their interpersonal harmony.

h46: Affective commitment of employees in NPOs has a positive impact on their protecting company resources.

h47: Normative commitment of employees in NPOs has a positive impact on their identification with the company.

h48: Normative commitment of employees in NPOs has a positive impact on their altruism toward colleagues.

h49: Normative commitment of employees in NPOs has a positive impact on their conscientiousness.

h50: Normative commitment of employees in NPOs has a positive impact on their interpersonal harmony.

h51: Normative commitment of employees in NPOs has a positive impact on their protecting company resources.

3   Research Methods and Design

3.1   Scale Development

According to Colquitt's (2001), justice perception scale excluding the dimension of interpersonal justice is thus selected to study the perceived financial justice of employees in NPOs because it has nothing to do with finance, and the rest three dimensions in which are fitted with finance which are used to measure the financial justice by 16 items of three dimensions: procedural, distribution and information justice. The internal consistency coefficients of the subscale are 0.78, 0.85 and 0.83, respectively.

The three dimensions of organizational effectiveness, namely, citizenship behavior, organizational commitment and job satisfaction, are measured by using the appropriate scale according to the existing results and the actual situation. The five-level scale is used in the dimension of OCB (Farh et al. 1997), dividing organizational effectiveness into five dimensions: identification with the company, altruism toward colleagues, conscientiousness, interpersonal harmony and protecting company resources. Each dimension has 3–5 items, 20 items in total, and their internal consistency coefficients are 0.87, 0.87, 0.82, 0.86 and 0.81 respectively.

According to Allen (1990), the organizational commitment scale used by is selected, which has three dimensions: affective commitment scale (ACS), continuous commitment scale (CCS) and normative commitment scale (NCS). Each dimension has 8 questions, a total of 24 items, which measure the commitment of individual loyalty to the organization from the perspective of employee's emotion and dependence on the organization. The internal consistency coefficients of the three subscales are 0.87, 0.75 and 0.79.

According to Spector (1985), a 9-dimensional job satisfaction scale was developed. The 9 dimensions of the original scale are pay, promotion, supervision, pay, contingent rewards, operating procedures and co-workers, job satisfaction and communication. Each dimension has 4 items, 36 items in total. Yang et al. (2010) discovered that the overall structural validity of this scale is poor, especially the reliability of two subscales is lower, which are not suitable for job satisfaction survey on Chinese employees. Among them, the pay, chance of promotion, job satisfaction and supervision satisfaction are applicable to the measurement of job satisfaction of Chinese employees, but during the utilization, there are still some items in co-workers that need to be corrected due to the consideration of different cultural backgrounds. Therefore, the sub-scales that are not suitable for employees in China and the co-workers scale that needs to be revised are removed, and the sub-scale of supervision that has nothing to do with financial matters is removed, thus finally, a three-dimensional 12-item scale including pay, chance of promotion and job satisfaction is formed.

In addition, variables such as employee education, age, gender, and length of working hours also have different effects on organizational effect variables such as perceived organizational justice and organizational commitment (Tian 2014). Therefore, the relevant control variables are set.

3.2 Scale Pretest

A few questionnaires were sent out for pretest, and 260 valid ones were recovered. An exploratory factor analysis was carried out by using the prediction test data to form the final use scale.

OCB Scale. By exploratory factor analysis, two factors are extracted, and the items with factor load less than 0.6 and cross loading are eliminated, and two factors are obtained, respectively as organizational destruction (OD) and identification with the company (IC). The dimensions of organizational destruction include the following options: to seek personal interests by using improper strategies that are harmful to interpersonal harmony (IH1), to seek personal interests by using position power (IH2), to haggle over every detail for personal benefits (IH3), to often speak ill of colleagues or leaders behind their backs (IH4), to do private things during working hours, such as stock speculation, shopping, hairdressing, etc. (PR1), to use organizational resources for private affairs, such as private use of office computers, copiers, telephones, etc. (PR2), to use illness as the reason for asking for leave (PR3). The items in this dimension are the destruction of organizational interests by employees, while seeking personal interests or destroying unity in various ways that harm the interests of organization is the combination of interpersonal harmony and resource protection dimensions in the original scale. The dimensions of identification with the company include my willingness to stand up to maintain organizational reputation (IC1), my desire to clarify misunderstandings and deliver good news of organization (IC2), proposal of constructive suggestions for the operation of organization (IC3), and active participation in organizational meetings (IC4).

The new scale extracted after factor analysis is further analyzed, as shown in Table 1. The KOM value is 0.904, greater than 0.7, the explained total variance is 68.284%, the factor loads are all greater than 0.6, and the internal consistency coefficients of the two dimensions are 0.933 and 0.737, respectively, which have good reliability and validity.

Organizational Commitment Scale. After analyzing, the organizational commitment scale is extracted, including three dimensions, namely, continuous commitment scale (CCS), affective commitment scale (ACS) and normative commitment scale (NCS). The dimension of affective commitment includes two items: I am not part of the organization family (ACS6), and I am not attached to the organization emotionally (ACS7); the dimension of continuous commitment includes three items: If I leave the organization now, my life will fall into chaos (CCS2), the lack of selectivity is one of several serious consequences of leaving the organization (CCS5), and the main reason that I continue to work for the organization is that leaving means a lot of personal sacrifice - other organizations can't provide the current amount of revenue (CCS6); the dimension of

Table 1. Analysis on reliability and validity of OCB scale.

Dimensionality	Test item	KMO	Factor loading	Total variance of interpretation	Reliability
Organizational destruction (OD)	IH1	0.904	0.843	68.284%	0.933
	IH2		0.846		
	IH3		0.862		
	IH4		0.865		
	PR1		0.801		
	PR2		0.807		
	PR3		0.828		
Identification with the company (IC)	IC1		0.826		0.797
	IC2		0.785		
	IC3		0.788		
	IC4		0.721		

normative commitment includes three items: one of the main reasons that I continue to work for the organization is that loyalty is very important and I should fulfill moral responsibility (NCS2), I should hold the values of being loyal to the organization (NCS4), and it is better to spend most of my career in one organization (NCS5).

The new scale extracted after factor analysis is further analyzed, as shown in Table 2. The KOM value is 0.735, greater than 0.7, the explained total variance is 74.266%, the factor loads are all greater than 0.7, and the internal consistency coefficients of the three dimensions are 0.785, 0.761 and 0.773, respectively, which have good reliability and validity.

Table 2. Analysis on reliability and validity of organizational commitment scale.

Dimensionality	Test item	KMO	Factor loading	Total variance of interpretation	Reliabilit
Affective commitment scale (ACS)	ACS6	0.735	0.881	74.266%	0.785
	ACS7		0.902		
Continuous commitment scale (CCS)	CCS2		0.726		0.761
	CCS5		0.857		
	CCS6		0.823		
Normative commitment scale (NCS)	NCS2		0.821		0.773
	NCS4		0.820		
	NCS5		0.739		

Nature of Work Scale. The factors of job satisfaction scale are extracted and 5 items are eliminated. According to the re-integration of the test items, a new scale with two dimensions and seven items is obtained, which are job satisfaction self (NW) and work acceptance (WA). After further analysis, it is found that the KOM value is 0.849, greater than 0.7, the explained total variance is 74.869%, the factor loads are all greater than 0.7, and the internal consistency coefficients of the two dimensions are 0.757 and 0.914, respectively, which have good reliability and validity. See Table 3 for the detailed indexes.

Table 3. Analysis on reliability and validity of job satisfaction scale.

Dimensionality	Test item	KMO	Factor loading	Total variance of interpretation	Reliability
Job satisfaction self (NW)	NW1	0.849	0.880	74.869%	0.735
	NW2		0.848		
Work acceptance (WA)	PN3		0.833		0.907
	PN4		0.851		
	PY4		0.849		
	NW3		0.803		
	NW4		0.813		

Financial Justice Scale. By analyzing the scale of financial justice of employees, a three-dimensional 9-factor scale of distribution justice (DJ), procedural justice (PJ) and information justice (IJ) is obtained. After further analysis, it is found that the KOM value is 0.920, greater than 0.7, the explained total variance is 80.387%, the factor loads are all greater than 0.7, and the internal consistency coefficients of the two dimensions are 0.857, 0.836 and 0.909, respectively, which have good reliability and validity. See Table 4 for the detailed indexes.

Table 4. Analysis on reliability and validity of employees financial justice scale.

Dimensionality	Test item	KMO	Factor loading	Total variance of interpretation	Reliability
Distribution justice (DJ)	DJ4	0.920	0.771	80.387%	0.857
	DJ5		0.807		
	DJ6		0.819		
Procedural justice (PJ)	PJ2		0.825		0.836
	PJ3		0.747		
Information justice (IJ)	IJ1		0.840		0.909
	IJ2		0.805		
	IJ3		0.737		
	IJ4		0.738		

Model Confirmatory Factor Analysis. The results of confirmatory factor analysis are shown in Table 5, $\chi^2/df = 1.918$ (p < 0.001), TLI = 0.934, CFI = 0.943, RMSEA = 0.048, most of the indexes meet the requirements, and the model fit is good.

Table 5. Goodness of fit index of first-order model.

	χ^2/df	IFI	RMR	RMSEA	GFI	CFI	TLI
Standard values	≦3	>0.9	<0.05	<0.08	>0.9	>0.9	>0.9
Model	1.918	0.944	0.051	0.048	0.868	0.943	0.934
Fitting judgment	Reach standard	Reach standard	sub-standard	Reach standard	Sub-standard	Reach standard	Reach standard

3.3 Hypotheses for Formal Use

According to the pre-test results mentioned above, some dimensions or items of the scale are removed, and the dimensions of the scale are re-integrated to get new hypotheses for formal analysis. Among them, in OCB, the dimension of "organizational destruction" integrates the original two dimensions of "interpersonal harmony" and "resource protection". As these items are all reverse items, the assumed direction is adjusted during the assumption, and the rest are kept the original assumed direction. The hypotheses used in the formal analysis are as follows:

H1: Information justice of employees in NPOs has a significant positive impact on the procedural justice.

H2: Information justice of employees in NPOs has a significant positive impact on the distribution justice.

H3: Procedural justice of employees in NPOs has a significant positive impact on the distribution justice.

H4: Information justice of employees in NPOs has a significant positive impact on the job satisfaction.

H5: Information justice of employees in NPOs has a significant positive impact on the work acceptance.

H6: Procedural justice of employees in NPOs has a significant positive impact on the job satisfaction.

H7: Procedural justice of employees in NPOs has a significant positive impact on the work acceptance.

H8: Distribution justice of employees in NPOs has a significant positive impact on the job satisfaction.

H9: Distribution justice of employees in NPOs has a significant positive impact on the work acceptance.

H10: job satisfaction of employees in NPOs has a significant positive impact on the identification with the company.

H11: job satisfaction of employees in NPOs has a significant positive impact on the organizational destruction.

H12: Work acceptance of employees in NPOs has a significant positive impact on the identification with the company.

H13: Work acceptance of employees in NPOs has a significant positive impact on the organizational destruction.

H14: job satisfaction of employees in NPOs has a significant positive impact on the continuous commitment.

H15: job satisfaction of employees in NPOs has a significant positive impact on the affective commitment.

H16: job satisfaction of employees in NPOs has a significant positive impact on the normative commitment.

H17: Work acceptance of employees in NPOs has a significant positive impact on the continuous commitment.

H18: Work acceptance of employees in NPOs has a significant positive impact on the affective commitment.

H19: Work acceptance of employees in NPOs has a significant positive impact on the normative commitment.

H20: Continuous commitment of employees in NPOs has a significant positive impact on the identification with the company.

H21: Continuous commitment of employees in NPOs has a significant positive impact on the organizational destruction.

H22: Affective commitment of employees in NPOs has a significant positive impact on the identification with the company.

H23: Affective commitment of employees in NPOs has a significant positive impact on the organizational destruction.

H24: Normative commitment of employees in NPOs has a significant positive impact on the identification with the company.

H25: Normative commitment of employees in NPOs has a significant positive impact on the organizational destruction.

3.4 Object of Study

600 questionnaires were distributed to employees of NPOs for investigation, and 545 valid ones were collected. The statistical description results of valid samples are shown in Table 6. In the process of issuing the questionnaire, in order to make the identity of the respondents fit, Wenjuanxing as the professional platform of questionnaire service is entrusted to select the internal staff of NPO to answer, so as to ensure that the respondents meet the requirements of the role of questionnaire. The respondents are aged between 20 and 40, most of them are regular employees who have worked in NPOs for more than one year, and their education level is concentrated in high school or above. Among them, nearly 40% of the employees have not changed their working place, and nearly 50% of the employees have changed their working place once or twice, with few of them changing their work frequently.

Table 6. Statistics of basic characteristics of samples.

Items	State variable	Number of people (PCs)	Percentage (%)	Items	State variable	Number of people (PCs)	Percentage (%)
Gender	Male	310	56.88	Education degree	Master or above	24	4.4
	Female	235	43.12		Undergraduate	336	61.65
Age	≤ 20	7	1.28		Junior college student	97	17.8
	21–30	254	44.95		Vocational high school education	71	13.03
	31–40	197	36.15				
	41–50	73	13.39		Junior high school and below	17	3.12
	>50	23	4.22				
Years of working in the unit	≤ half	30	5.5	Job-hopping number	0	202	37.06
	half-1	27	4.95		1	147	26.97
	1–2	96	17.61		2	112	20.55
	2–5	155	28.44		3–4	71	13.03
	>5	237	43.49		≥5	13	2.39
Position	Intern	12	2.2	Marital status	Unmarried	140	25.69
	General staff	391	71.74		Married	391	71.74
	Boss	142	26.06		Divorced	13	2.39
Be religious or not	Yes	105	19.27		Remarried	1	0.18
	No	440	80.73		Widowed	0	0

3.5 Research Tools

According to the pretest results, the scales of financial justice, job satisfaction, organizational commitment and OCB are finally determined, which have 9, 7, 8 and 11 items respectively. As mentioned above, the reliability and validity of each scale are good. Then, the formal scale will be used as a tool for analysis.

It should be noted that in these scales, the three scales of work acceptance, affective commitment and organizational destruction are all reverse. In the above hypotheses, the impact of all dimensions on organizational destruction is assumed to be negative, reflecting the characteristics of negative indexes. However, the hypotheses related to work acceptance and affective commitment are all set as positive impact except for the impact on organizational destruction. Therefore, in the follow-up path analysis, when the work acceptance or affective commitment does not appear at the same time with other negative indicator dimensions, the correlation coefficient of negative value is positive correlation, and the correlation coefficient of positive value is negative correlation in the relationship between the work acceptance or affective commitment and the positive measurement dimension.

4 Data Analysis and Results

4.1 Model Fitting

Amos21.0 was used for the confirmatory factor analysis based on the first-order factor. The results are shown in Table 7, $\chi^2/df = 2.425$ (p < 0.001), TLI = 0.936, CFI = 0.945, RMSEA = 0.051, and the model has a good fit.

Table 7. Goodness of fit index of first-order model.

	X^2/df	IFI	RMR	RMSEA	GFI	CFI	TLI
Standard values	≤3	>0.9	<0.05	<0.08	>0.9	>0.9	>0.9
Model	2.425	0.945	0.051	0.051	0.881	0.945	0.936
Fitting judgment	Reach standard	Reach standard	Sub-standard	Reach standard	Sub-standard	Reach standard	Reach standard

4.2 Confirmatory Factor Analysis

Confirmatory factor analysis was used to test the reliability and validity of the model. The validity was tested by convergence validity and discriminant validity. Convergence validity was judged by factor composite reliability (CR) and average variation extraction (AVE). Discriminant validity was judged by the comparison between the square root of potential variable AVE and the correlation coefficient between potential variables. Results as shown in Table 8 and Table 9, the reliability and validity of each scale were good.

Table 8. Confirmatory factor analysis results.

Dimensionality	Test item	Factor loading	CR	Reliability
Organizational destruction (OD)	IH2	0.870^{***}	0.945	0.945
	IH3	0.875^{***}		
	IH4	0.871^{***}		
	PR1	0.804^{***}		
	PR2	0.793^{***}		
	PR3	0.826^{***}		

(continued)

Table 8. (*continued*)

Dimensionality	Test item	Factor loading	CR	Reliability
Identification with the company (IC)	IC1	0.821^a	0.831	0.829
	IC2	0.768^{***}		
	IC3	0.728^{***}		
	IC4	0.647^{***}		
Affective commitment scale (ACS)	ACS6	0.884^a	0.805	0.799
	ACS7	0.754^{***}		
Continuous commitment scale (CCS)	CCS2	0.662^a	0.772	0.765
	CCS5	0.758^{***}		
	CCS6	0.763^{***}		
Normative commitment scale (NCS)	NCS2	0.723^a	0.797	0.797
	NCS4	0.726^{***}		
	NCS5	0.807^{***}		
Job satisfaction self (NW)	NW1	0.728^a	0.7609	0.757
	NW2	0.837^{***}		
Work acceptance (WA)	PN3	0.873^a	0.9087	0.914
	PN4	0.879^{***}		
	PY4	0.890^{***}		
	NW3	0.711^{***}		
	NW4	0.712^{***}		
Distribution justice (DJ)	DJ4	0.771^a	0.8723	0.870
	DJ5	0.840^{***}		
	DJ6	0.887^{***}		
Procedural justice (PJ)	PJ2	0.841^a	0.8545	0.854
	PJ3	0.886^{***}		
Information justice (IJ)	IJ1	0.838^a	0.9223	0.923
	IJ2	0.844^{***}		
	IJ3	0.874^{***}		
	IJ4	0.863^{***}		

Note: a represents the measurement item with factor load of 1 by default, and *** represents that factor load is significant at the significance level of 0.001

4.3 Path Analysis

The impact path as shown in Fig. 1 can be obtained based on the above hypotheses and analysis. The financial justice of NPO employees influences OCB by influencing the job satisfaction. The job satisfaction has a direct impact on OCB, as well as an indirect impact through organizational commitment. Organizational commitment has a direct impact on OCB. Thus it is clear that the financial justice of NPO employees directly or indirectly affects the job satisfaction, organizational commitment and OCB.

Table 9. List of variable correlation coefficients, AVEs and mean values.

	Mean Value	AVE Square Root	IJ	DJ	PJ	NW	WA	CCS	ACS	NCS	OD	IC
IJ	3.5482	0.8649	**0.7481**									
DJ	3.5994	0.8340	0.764	**0.6956**								
PJ	3.6991	0.8638	0.841	0.779	**0.7461**							
NW	3.9037	0.7844	0.647	0.646	0.734	**0.6153**						
WA	2.6624	0.8173	−0.528	−0.517	−0.457	−0.508	**0.6679**					
CCS	3.3364	0.7292	0.379	0.334	0.303	0.331	−0.141	**0.5317**				
ACS	2.4046	0.8216	−0.330	−0.259	−0.291	−0.416	0.737	0.024	**0.675**			
NCS	3.9083	0.7530	0.532	0.453	0.517	0.687	−0.281	0.554	−0.307	**0.567**		
OD	1.8784	0.8433	−0.047	0.043	−0.035	−0.154	0.410	0.180	0.517	−0.155	**0.7112**	
IC	4.0252	0.7437	0.595	0.465	0.619	0.597	−0.311	0.268	−0.303	0.613	−0.206	**0.5531**

Note: The data in black diagonal font represents the AVE square root value of each factor

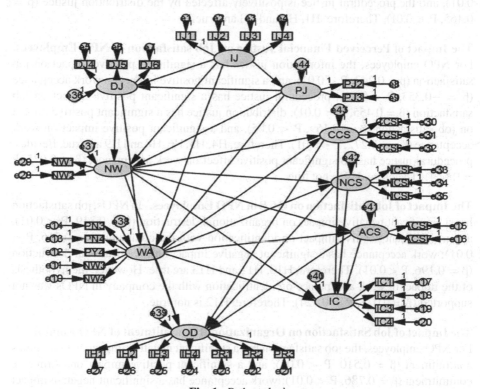

Fig. 1. Path analysis.

The parameter estimation and model fitting analysis of the model show that most of the indexes reach the standard level, with good fitting degree, which can be used to verify the hypothesis. The specific values are shown in Table 10 and Table 11.

Table 10. Goodness of fit index of the model.

	X^2/df	IFI	SRMR	RMSEA	GFI	CFI	TLI
Standard Values	≤3	>0.9	<0.05	<0.08	>0.9	>0.9	>0.9
Model	2.710	0.932	0.0623	0.056	0.865	0.931	0.924
Fitting Judgment	Reach standard	Reach standard	Sub-standard	Reach standard	Sub-standard	Reach standard	Reach standard

4.4 Hypotheses Testing

Internal Influence Relationship of Three Dimensions of Perceived Financial Justice of NPO Employees. As shown in the above table, the procedural justice of NPO employees is positively affected by the information justice ($\beta = 0.840$, P < 0.01), the distribution justice is positively affected by the information justice ($\beta = 0.374$, P < 0.01), and the procedural justice is positively affected by the distribution justice ($\beta = 0.465$, P < 0.01). Therefore, H1, H2 and H3 are true.

The Impact of Perceived Financial Justice on Job satisfaction of NPO Employees. For NPO employees, the information justice has a significant positive impact on job satisfaction ($\beta = 0.242$, P < 0.01), and a significant positive impact on work acceptance ($\beta = -0.353$, P < 0.01); procedural justice has a significant positive impact on job satisfaction ($\beta = 0.455$, P < 0.01); distribution justice has a significant positive impact on job satisfaction ($\beta = 0.159$, P < 0.05), and a significant positive impact on work acceptance ($\beta = -0.272$, P < 0.01). Therefore, H4, H5, H6, H8 and H9 are true. Besides, procedural justice has no significant positive effect on work acceptance, ($\beta = 0.045$, P = 0.664). Therefore, H7 is not true.

The Impact of Job Satisfaction on OCB of NPO Employees. In NPOs, job satisfaction has a significant negative impact on organizational destruction ($\beta = 0.319$, P < 0.01), and a significant positive impact on identification with the company ($\beta = 0.516$, P < 0.01); work acceptance has a significant negative impact on organizational destruction ($\beta = 0.196$, P < 0.01). Therefore, H10, H11 and H13 are true. However, the hypothesis of the impact of work acceptance on identification with the company in NPOs was not supported ($\beta = 0.071$, P = 0.324). Therefore, H12 is not true.

The Impact of Job Satisfaction on Organizational Commitment of NPO Employees. For NPO employees, the job satisfaction has a significant negative impact on continuous commitment ($\beta = 0.510$, P < 0.01), and a significant positive impact on normative commitment ($\beta = 0.786$, P < 0.01); work acceptance has a significant negative impact on affective commitment ($\beta = 0.725$, P < 0.01). H14, H16 and H18 are supported. Besides, the hypotheses of the impact of job satisfaction on affective commitment was not supported ($\beta = -0.018$, P = 0.679), the impact of work acceptance on continuous commitment was not supported ($\beta = 0.129$, P < 0.05) was not supported, and the positive effect of work acceptance on normative commitment is not significant ($\beta = 0.089$, P = 0.056). Therefore, H15, H17 and H19 are not supported.

Table 11. Model path coefficient estimation.

Unnormalized path coefficient estimation	S.E.	C.R.	Significance	Normalized path coefficient estimation
PJ<--- IJ	0.044	18.971	***	0.840
DJ<--- IJ	0.080	4.831	***	0.374
DJ<--- PJ	0.084	5.824	***	0.465
NW<--- IJ	0.065	2.807	***	0.242
WA<--- IJ	0.087	-3.696	***	-0.353
NW<--- DJ	0.052	2.207	**	0.159
WA<--- DJ	0.070	3.389	***	-0.272
WA<--- PJ	0.095	0.434	0.664	0.045
NW<--- PJ	0.075	4.656	***	0.455
ACS<--- NW	0.056	-0.389	0.697	-0.018
NCS<--- NW	0.061	11.737	***	0.786
CCS<--- NW	0.074	7.752	***	0.510
ACS<--- WA	0.057	12.812	***	0.725
NCS<--- WA	0.035	1.915	*	0.089
CCS<--- WA	0.051	2.378	**	0.129
OD<--- NW	0.120	3.204	***	0.319
IC<--- NW	0.090	5.266	***	0.516
OD<--- WA	0.074	2.643	***	0.196
IC<--- WA	0.055	0.987	0.324	0.071
IC<--- ACS	0.053	-1.451	0.147	-0.101
OD<--- ACS	0.074	5.231	***	0.389
IC<--- NCS	0.081	3.562	***	0.285
OD<--- NCS	0.114	-4.127	***	-0.355
IC<--- CCS	0.043	-2.058	**	-0.107
OD<--- CCS	0.057	4.375	***	0.233
IC	.055	.987	.324	par_41

Note: "*, * *, * *", respectively, means significant at the significance level of 0.1, 0.05, 0.01.

The Impact of Organizational Commitment on OCB of NPO Employees. For NPO employees, continuous commitment has a significant negative impact on organizational destruction ($\beta = 0.233$, P < 0.01), affective commitment has a significant negative impact on organizational destruction ($\beta = 0.389$, P < 0.01), normative commitment has a significant positive impact on identification with the company ($\beta = 0.285$, P < 0.01), normative commitment has a significant negative impact on organizational destruction ($\beta = -0.355$, P < 0.01). H21, H23, H24 and H25 are supported. Besides, the hypotheses of the impact of continuous commitment on the identification with the company was not supported ($\beta = -0.107$, P = 0.40), and the impact of affective commitment on the identification with the company was not supported ($\beta = -0.101$, P = 0.147). Therefore, H20 and H22 are not supported.

5 Conclusions and Enlightenment

5.1 Conclusions

In the perceived financial justice of employees in NPOs, distribution justice is affected by both information justice and procedural justice, and information justice also has a positive impact on procedural justice; the three dimensions of justice have a positive impact on the job satisfaction; the perceived recognition and good expectation of NPO employees in the work do not make them actively put forward constructive opinions for the organization and actively send positive information to the outside, while the job satisfaction can stimulate the employees' motivation to actively serve the organization. Both job satisfaction and work acceptance have the significant negative impacts on organizational destruction; if the employees are very satisfied with their work, they will be more loyal to the organization and have a stronger willingness to serve the existing organizations for life, and they believe that after leaving the existing organizations, they have less selectivity and their lives are easy to fall into chaos. However, employees' acceptance of work and their degree of being recognized in work will make them more emotionally dependent on the organization and regard themselves as a part of the organization family; NPO employees' organizational commitment as a kind of commitment, obligation and responsibility to the organization can promote them to safeguard the organizational rights and interests, and oppose the destruction behaviors of seeking personal interests at the expense of organizational interests. The three dimensions of organizational commitment have significant negative impacts on organizational destruction. However, identification with the company is affected by normative commitment and continuous commitment, while the positive impact of affective commitment on identification with the company is not significant. Employees' lack of confidence after leaving the existing organization will make them more dependent on the current organization.

5.2 Theoretical Enlightenment

Based on the above analysis process and research conclusions, this paper holds that the dimensions and specific contents of financial justice and organizational effectiveness of NPO employees are different from those of enterprises. It is clear from the selection of scale items that, the NPO employees compared with the employees from enterprises care less about whether they can participate in the formulation of salary distribution system and whether everyone is equal in front of the distribution system; NPO employees pay less attention to salary, and are more concerned about their happy experience in work and the embodiment of their own value; NPO employees pay less attention to the problem-solving of their colleagues and challenging work, and less take the initiative to invest more efforts in business research to improve and better complete the task.

Financial justice of NPO employees has different influence paths on organizational effectiveness variables, which has direct influence on the job satisfaction, and indirect influence on organizational commitment and OCB through job satisfaction. In the direct impact on the job satisfaction, except that the impact of financial procedures on work acceptance is not obvious, in other cases, the three dimensions of financial justice have significant impact on the job satisfaction. The identification with the company of employees mainly comes from the standardization of organizational management, less emotional. The higher the employee's job satisfaction is, the more willing they are to abide by the rules and regulations and work for the organization for a long time. When making employee incentive plan, NPOs should focus on the dimensions and specific contents of employees' financial justice, analyze the relationship between employees' financial justice and job satisfaction, organizational commitment and OCB, and formulate practical measures and systems to enable employees to play a greater potential and complete more work that is not stipulated in the formal contract but is beneficial to the organization.

5.3 Deficiency and Prospect

In this paper, the influence path of the subjectively perceived financial justice on the organizational effectiveness variables of NPOs is systematically analyzed from the perspective of financial justice, but there are still deficiencies. The influence of the perceived financial justice of NPO employees on the organizational effectiveness may also be affected by some control variables or adjustment variables, such as organizational culture, leader style, structure setting, etc., which will be included in the later research. In addition, when choosing organizational effectiveness variables, three aspects of job satisfaction, organizational commitment and OCB are used, which do not cover all variables, and a more detailed analysis will be made in the follow-up study.

The financial equity is an important part of financial topics of nonprofit organizations. During the research of this topic, information and data acquisition is very difficult. This is not related to the level of development of nonprofit organizations, but also related to researchers' information access technology. In future research, we will learn from other research fields about the analysis of the related activities under the condition of big data, such as network behavior analysis (Jiang 2020) and use some advanced technology such as network selection (Jiang 2018), and establish a big data system related to nonprofit organizations, so as to promote the financial research process of non-profit organizations.

Acknowledgment. This paper is supported by the following fund projects: social sciences research key-project of Anhui province "research on factors influencing the financial performance of non-profit organizations and their action mechanism from the perspective of interest conflict" (SK2019A0470).

References

Allen, N.J.: The measurement and antecedents of affective, continuance and normative commitment to the organization. J. Occup. Psychol. **63**, 1–18 (1990)

Al-Zubi, H.A.: A study of relationship between organizational justice and job satisfaction. Int. J. Bus. Manage. **5**(12), 102–109 (2010)

Bateman, T.S., Organ, D.W.: Job satisfaction and the good soldier: the relationship between affect and employee "citizenship." Acad. Manage. J. **26**, 587–595 (1983)

Becker, H.S.: Notes on the concept of commitment. Am. J. Sociol. **66**, 32–42 (1960)

Colquitt, J.A.: On the dimensionality of organizational justice: a construct validation of a measure. J. Appl. Psychol. **86**, 386–400 (2001)

Colquitt, J.A., Conlon, D.E., Wesson, M.J., Porter, C.O.L.H., Ng, K.Y.: Justice at the millennium: a meta-analytic review of 25 years of organizational justice research. J. Appl. Psychol. **86**, 425–455 (2001)

Farh, J.L., Earley, P.C., Lin, S.C.: Impetus for action: a cultural analysis of justice and organizational citizenship behavior in Chinese society. Adm. Sci. Q. **42**(9), 421–444 (1997)

Han, L.L., Zhang, C.Y.: The influence of moral influence on subordinates' working attitude and behavior. Soft Sci. **6**, 86–89 (2015)

Jiang, C.Y.: The relationship between employee equity perception and organizational commitment and turnover intention. Econ. Sci. **6**, 118–128 (2007)

Johnson, R.E., Chang, C.H.: "I" is to continuance as "We" is to affective: the relevance of the self concept for organizational commitment. J. Organ. Behav. **27**(5), 549–570 (2006)

Kuang, P.B., Ling, L.: Relationship between job satisfaction and organizational commitment in different organizational trust contexts. Econ. Manage. **4**, 93–98 (2009)

Liu, Y., Liu, L.R., Li, Y.: The influence of perceived organizational justice on organizational effect variables. Manage. World **3**, 126–132 (2003)

Tyler, T.: Psychological models of the justice motive: antecedents of distributive and procedural justice. J. Pers. Soc. Psychol. **67**, 850–863 (1994)

Ling, L., Ling, H.: Empirical research on the relationship among job satisfaction, organizational trust and organizational commitment. Bus. Econ. **1**, 43–45 (2009)

Meyer, J., Allen, J.: A Three-component conceptualization of organizational commitment. Hum. Resour. Manage. Rev. **91**(1), 61–89 (1991)

Organ, D.W.: The motivational basis of organizational citizenship behavior. Res. Organ. Behav. **12**, 43–72 (1990)

Shen, P.Y., Zhang, Y.: The influence of service orientation on organizational citizenship behavior and organizational performance. East China Econ. Manage. **1**, 142–149 (2016)

Shore, L.M., Wayne, S.J.: Commitment and employee behavior: comparison of affective commitment and continuance commitment with perceived organizational support. J. Appl. Psychol. **78**, 774–780 (1993)

Spector, P.E.: Measurement of human service staff satisfaction: development of the job satisfaction survey. Am. J. Community Psychol. **13**(6), 693–713 (1985)

Tian, H.: Research on the relationship between organizational equity, organizational commitment and turnover intention. Learn. Explor. **2**, 114–118 (2014)

Wang, L.: Employee accountability, job satisfaction, and organizational citizenship. Bus. Econ. Manage. **12**, 32–37 (2010)

Wang, Y.: Research on the influence of organizational commitment on individual behavior, performance and welfare. Sci. Res. Manage. **2**, 142–148 (2008)

Yan, D., Zhang, L.J.: Organizational equity affects organizational commitment and organizational citizenship behavior. Ind. Eng. Manage. **6**, 76–80 (2010)

Yang, Y.W., Li, H.M., Zhai, Q.G.: Study on the applicable dimension of job satisfaction scale in China. Stat. Decis. Making **5**, 160–162 (2010)

Zhang, X.J., Xi, A.L.: Research on the theory of organizational fair behavior and its application. Psychol. Dyn. **4**, 352–360 (2001)

Jiang, D., Huo, L., Song, H.: Rethinking behaviors and activities of base stations in mobile cellular networks based on big data analysis. IEEE Trans. Netw. Sci. Eng. **7**(1), 80–90 (2020a)

Jiang, D., Wang, Y., Lv, Z., Qi, S., Singh, S.: Big data analysis based network behavior insight of cellular networks for Industry 4.0 applications. IEEE Trans. Ind. Inform. **16**(2), 1310–1320 (2020b)

Jiang, D., Huo, L., Lv, Z., Song, H., Qin, W.: A joint multi-criteria utility-based network selection approach for vehicle-to-infrastructure networking. IEEE Trans. Intell. Transp. Syst. **19**(10), 3305–3319 (2018)

Empirical Analysis of Supply Chain Finance Innovation Model Based on Blockchain Technology

Jun Chen, Maoguo Wu[✉], Shiyan Xu, and Chenyang Zhao

SILC Business School, Shanghai University, Shanghai, China
wumaoguo@shu.edu.cn

Abstract. This paper attempts to establish a conceptual framework for the solution of blockchain-driven supply chain finance. This framework is designed to facilitate the coordination relationship between buyer and seller. Besides, it alleviates implementation inefficiency in discrete supply chain financial instruments, such as reverse factoring and dynamic discounting. In addition, this paper proposes the value drivers of blockchain technology and elaborates its unique characteristics in the application of supply chain finance. Although blockchain technology is considered a breakthrough financial technology, research on its impact on supply chain finance is scanty. Therefore, this paper contributes to the future development of supply chain finance based on the latest technological innovations.

Keywords: Blockchain technology · Supply chain finance · Reverse factoring · Dynamic discounting

1 Introduction

With the increasing application of supply chain financial instruments in various industries, working capital optimization and capital costs reduction is highly correlated. From the perspective of individual company, it is imperative to optimize the financing processes by adopting low-cost solutions (Klapper 2006). From the perspective of supply chain, supply chain finance could both benefit buyers and suppliers by facilitating the ease and capital allocation efficiency along the entire value chain (Popa 2013). Financial tools such as reverse factoring and dynamic discounting may enable companies to optimize the allocation of working capital and alleviate financial risks. Although supply chain finance possesses significant advantages in theory, the implementation of its component tools in practice is scanty. Although supply chain finance provides a wide range of technologies, blockchain technology in supply chain finance brings cutting-edge advancement for the development, deployment, and utilization of effective business applications.

In recent years, the digitization of the physical supply chain has attracted widespread interest. However, the logistics, information flow, and financial flow, more often than not, are regarded as independent flows across differential functional departments and

H. Song and D. Jiang (Eds.): SIMUtools 2020, LNICST 369, pp. 296–312, 2021.
https://doi.org/10.1007/978-3-030-72792-5_26

sections. As a result, the start of business application tends to rely on manual input and sequential confirmation (Zhang and Dhaliwal 2009). In addition, business transactions consist of numerous participants and intermediaries. The high expenditure and sophistication of complex information technology systems, security deficiencies, and lengthy processing time are typical disadvantages among others of nowadays' usual operations (Fellenz et al. 2009).

Accordingly, weak credit contract, taxes, legal enforcement, and regulations have intensified efficient interactions and standard processes among supply chain participants (Klappe 2006). In addition, the inconsistent governance structure complicates the gathering of key accounts receivables and the acquisition of archival data on default risk assessments. Pfohl and Gomm (2009) argued that buyers were not able to oversee associated account receivables. Subsequently, it would be sellers who implement the accounts receivable monitoring procedure, and buyers still could not observe this process. Therefore, in the traditional reverse factoring practice, intransigence and fraud are a major problem (Beck et al. 2003; Klapper 2006).

By adjusting all pertinent data flows utilizing digital process to build creditability and transparency, the transaction process can be significantly more functional while regulatory control can also be improved by eliminating as many unnecessary procedures as possible (Templar et al. 2016). A truly valuable digitalized, autonomous, decentralized, and distributed network will be applicable to numerous services and procedures (Raval 2016). Until now, there has been no method to show the function of supply chain finance by comprehensively examining its shortfalls and potentials. The initial concept provided a pathway to fill in the gap between opaque assumptions and actual implementation. If a foundational conceptual framework could be proposed, relevant orientation and tactics could be adopted. Additionally, it can identify plausible exploration in this field and address the scale of industry adaption and business application. Blockchain technology may offer such a technological advantage and serves as one of the most state-of-the-art technologies at the moment. In terms of the fact that operational barriers poses hurdles for key companies of widely adopting supply chain financial instruments, this paper examines the general benefits of blockchain technology and elaborates in detail its value in business practice along with supply chain finance. This paper attempts to answer the following research questions:

1. From a technical perspective, what are the inefficiencies of existing supply chain financial instruments?
2. In general, what are the potential and benefits of blockchain technology?
3. How can blockchain technology benefit supply chain financial solutions by mitigating technical deficiencies?

This paper first discusses how blockchain technology can improve the supply chain financial solution from the buyer's perspective. The concept study of Meredith (1993) is adopted. Following the design proposed in the research, the current situation of supply chain finance was studied, especially two specific methods of reverse factoring and dynamic discounting. Another goal is to determine the value drivers of blockchain technology. Based on literature review and desk research, this article highlights the main capabilities of blockchain technology to characterize its unique characteristics from a technical perspective. In addition, this article emphasizes problem awareness by explaining the need to improve existing supply chain financial instruments. This paper develops design propositions and requirements through an iterative approach. On this basis, the conceptual framework of two practical cases is designed. Finally, it evaluates and discusses its overall benefits from a theoretical and practical perspective. The remaining part of this paper is organized as follows: Sect. 2 provides relevant theories by summarizing the most essential parts of blockchain technology and related difficulties facing supply chain finance. The third section first discusses reverse factoring and dynamic discounting use cases by adding a technical dimension to handle analysis and key findings. The fourth section is summary and prospect.

2 Stylized Facts

2.1 Block Chain Technology

Blockchain has emerged as a technology breakthrough in the last decade. It has attracted wide attention in both academia and industry. Scientists and business practitioners have been avidly following the development of blockchain. (Kelly and William 2016). To be specific, blockchain can be regarded as a new form of decentralized data management. It is considered as a synonym for a publicly accessible distributed ledger that ensures the integrity of various transactions. It is usually referred to the major making-up component of operating cryptocurrency Bitcoin, and it has attracted increasing follow-up since it was invented in 2008. Blockchain technology, as an enabling technology, is gaining more and more attention because it can build creditability between agents in a decentralized network without calling for a third party (Swan 2015). In contrast, traditional transactions are usually processed on a centralized platform and monitored by an additional party. Therefore, the competent third party testifies whether the transaction has occurred and complied with all orders. General wealth, such as all kinds of assets, have complex security signals and therefore cannot display in two spots at the same time. However, data in digital form can be easily duplicated or intercepted. Therefore, intermediaries in the form of banks are required to perform digital payments. This process can also be applied to the produce digital products, such as keys to initiate software or downloadable music pieces. The same for our daily lives, the certification of a notary public or the registration of a public authority is necessary and often unavoidable. As a result, the inconvenient correlation between the two main participants is takes a lengthy time and costs a fortune, and it is a single point of failure for centralized systems (Bertino and Sandhu 2005). Meanwhile, a shared ledger can make a record of its content on thousands of nodes, rather than an authorized ledger with evidence that the transaction took place. If most ledgers can exceed the information that has been corrupted and manipulated, trust will shift to multiple copies. Therefore, centralized authentication of the ledger is no longer required. Although data dispersion is a viable option, an overwhelming section is required to decide which information should be processed and recorded in a timely manner. In terms of technical usage, to update the entire network, one must determine which system truth to choose (Mainelli and Milne 2016). It is acknowledged that replication serves as the main function of decentralization, the shared distributed ledger as mentioned above visualizes the conceptual framework of providing functioning prototype among equal-capacity agents. It was not until the 2008 Bitcoin white paper was released that a practical concept emerged that technically could build creditability between strangers in the trading system.

Blockchain poses one of the first innovations to achieve a completely shared, unlicensed distributed ledger. The system may function to establish creditability between strangers in the trading system basically is on one hand usually associated with the intactness of data, and is on the other hand related to the structure, generation, and distribution of information. Therefore, this technology integrates a great deal of research and consists of four major components (Antonopulus 2015):

- Peer-to-peer network: this topography offers a data ware system for the publicly shared ledger distribution
- Transaction logic: encryption and digital signatures are utilized to protect the transaction procedures among anonymous accounts
- Data immutability: the ledger consists of continuous data blocks that are individually protected and sealed in an encrypted manner, interconnected with previous data in the chain
- Consistency mechanism: an algorithm allows participants to agree on a authentic system state of the network, consequently performing synchronization of the shared ledger

Blockchain and distributed ledger, in practice, are referred to interchangeably. However, the shared ledger method is not necessarily technically reliant on the use of blockchain. Today, the development of blockchain technology has enabled many decentralized data ware houses to keep a record of an expanding volume of transaction records. All kinds of assets, physical or digital transactions, can be recorded in cyber space. People verify that the transaction has actually been carried out because the transactions records are always checked automatically according to the design. Therefore, no intermediary is needed. Although the blockchain contains information about all occured transactions, complete data integrity is also embedded in the blockchain framework (Swan 2015).

Due to the numerous application possibilities in different fields, this paper proposes three key features on the basis of its technical capacities. In terms of efficiency, we can improve processing in various aspects such as management, testification, approval, trading and settlement. As a matter of fact, in terms of hypervisors, blockchain technology can be applied to handle and replace any standard procedures that do not involve human thinking or accounting. This application saves tremendous time and minimizes errors, lowers expenditures, reducing waste, and optimizes resource allocation and cuts friction. The second prominent characteristic of blockchain is enhanced transparency thanks to the disclosure of complete records and the secure distributed public ledger. Due to insufficient information, regulations, cooperation, legal enforcement and disbelief of authorities, the operation of most firms are opaque. Blockchain technology improves the visibility of errors, misappropriation and misleading. Moreover, it provides information on business procedures and routines, strengthen business accountability, and facilitate more precise evaluation and enhanced monitoring. The third striking feature to mention is the realization of autonomy through decentralization and decentralization. These larger autonomous functions enable to reach anonymous consent and establish creditability among agents involved in the system. It can set up a more compliant, fair and feasible implementation. Despite incumbent technical difficulties and deficiencies, yet the overwhelming expansion of blockchain-based applications to all kinds of industries is a promising and growing area for future exploration (Swan 2015; Burgess 2015).

2.2 Supply Chain Finance and Its Challenges in the Supply Chain

Due to globalization, intense business competition, and ever-increasing levels of supply chain risk, a large number of companies are exposed to complication and economic uncertainty (De Boer et al. 2015). A potential outcome of this complication is that to properly handle basic supply chain procedures, risks, and capital flows, the supply chain needs to be transparent. To address these problems, companies that used to work independently now need to work together to reduce redundant costs and increase efficiency (Omran et al. 2016). In reality, the majority of companies have realized that it is necessary to optimize not only logistics and information flows, but also capital flows. In addition, companies realize that optimizing the capital flow and capital allocation in the supply chain can improve the overall outcome of the supply chain and reduce financial risks. In order to meet these challenges, supply chain finance has emerged as an integration of modern innovation, and continues to evolve, providing innovative financial solutions to participants along the supply chain. Therefore, supply chain finance are defined in many different ways in extant literature. Pfohl and Gomm (2009) define supply chain finance as inter-company optimization that optimizes financing by integrating financing processes with supply chain partners. Wuttke et al. (2013) regarded the supply chain financial management as the optimization, planning and control of cash flow in the value chain and promote the optimal control of logistics. In addition, Hofmann (2005) defines supply chain finance as an embedded approach of creating value by multiple organizations in the supply chain (including third-party service providers) by designing, executing, and allocating existing financial resources at the inner-organizational level.

Supply chain finance is a leading method adopted by prominent companies to optimize the flow and distribution of resources in the supply chain. Therefore, it contributes to increased corporate profit margins and reduced costs. Supply chain finance includes a variety of financial instruments and technologies to improve capital flows. More broadly, these solutions are designed to aid transactions among supply chain partners. By providing financing and payment options, these solutions may optimize the ease and financial position of all participants in the network. Reverse factoring and dynamic discounting are two methods of supply chain finance after delivery (after invoicing), which are aimed at alleviating the tight payment situation for buyers and suppliers.

Reverse factoring is regarded as a buyer-centric approach. Large buyers are closely associated with financial institutions and provide their suppliers with short-term financing at low costs. By implementing reverse factoring, both buyers and suppliers benefit in the process. The buyer compromised with the supplier so they can extend the payment period. By doing so can the supplier benefit from the advance payment. Due to the functioning of reverse factoring, by selling their receivables to financial institutions can suppliers increase their liquidity. The supplier receives a discount payment from the finance department with a charged interest rate deducted from the invoice value. The buyer eventually pays the bank on the due date (Seifert and Seifert 2011). Figure 1 shows the process of reverse factoring.

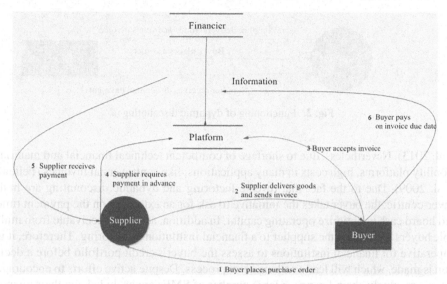

Fig. 1. Functioning of reverse factoring

During the process of reverse factoring, the buyer initiates the process and has to join the supplier one by one, which may take a lot of time and costs quite a fortune. In addition, financial institutions require "know your customers" and testify if suppliers as new participating agents. Dynamic discounting, similar to reverse factoring, is a buyer-driven approach. It enables companies to optimize cash flow by dynamically clearing invoices in a buyer-supplier relationship (Nienhuis et al. 2013). Dynamic discounting allows buyers to get discounts on dynamic payment behavior from suppliers. In addition, both suppliers and buyers are united on the same playground in dynamic discounting. Given this condition, involved parties optimize the timing of invoice payments by exchanging advance payment suggestions. The earlier the supplier receives payment, the higher the discount the buyer receives from the supplier. In addition, buyers with abundant cash started paying in advance in exchange for an agreed discount rate. As buyers and suppliers interact directly, non-financiers are also involved (Nienhuis et al. 2013). Figure 2 illustrates dynamic discounting. During the entire functioning of dynamic discounting, suppliers are able to obtain finance directly from buyers rather than borrowing from financiers. In addition, once the supplier has the funds, there is no need to "know your customer" check-in for dynamic discounting.

Reverse factoring, together with dynamic discounting, provides participants with the possibility of using supply chain finance and cooperation for efficient resource allocation and distribution (Popa 2013). As for reverse factoring, financial institutions purchase receivables from choice buyers and gather relevant information to assess the default risk of related buyers (Klapper 2006). On the contrary, dynamic discounting serves to optimize cash flow through dynamic invoices in a buying and selling relationship (Nienhuis

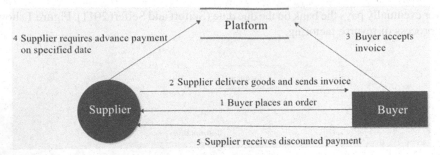

Fig. 2. Functioning of dynamic discounting

et al. 2013). Nevertheless, due to shortage of competent technical financial and material mobility platforms, high costs in many applications, like controversial invoices (Fellenz et al. 2009). Due to the fact that reverse factoring and dynamic discounting are both buyer-centric, the buyer takes the initiative to ask for an extension on the payment time and hoard cash to optimize operating capital. In addition, accounts receivable from multiple buyers are sold by the supplier to a financial institution or factoring. Therefore, it is imperative for financial institutions to assess the buyer's credit portfolio before a decision is made, which will lead to a long-term process. Despite active efforts to encourage the use of supply chain finance, a large number of SMEs are excluded and their financing options are limited. Due to the insufficiency in automation that discloses up-to-date financial information of SMEs with financing needs, banks and other types of financing institutions have always considered financing SMEs a risky business. This prevents smooth integration and cooperation. For example, conventional banking, mobile banking, and Internet-based services are not effectively delivered (Nienhuis et al. 2013). In addition, physical transactions and insufficient automation processing deteriorates total transaction costs of supply chain participants. As for now, in the supply chain financial environment, when a large buyer needs to integrate many suppliers, supplier entry is a complex activity. Implementation consists of numerous tasks and. In this stage, multiple parties can work effectively together. In the supplier entry process, there are still inefficiencies, like man-made operations, wrongful information, or lack of up-to-date data. In addition, the implementation process should be clear to all stakeholders so that they can overcome communication difficulties. Due to the fact that inefficient operations and high investments often deter companies from utilizing new supply chain financial solutions, blockchain may poses as an intangible benefit (Wuttke et al. 2016). Extant literature has found that information sharing, data distribution, creditability, transparency, and cooperation among supply chain participants are important conditions for the successful implementation of supply chain financial tools across the network. The lack of up-to-date information, like purchase information detail, order volumns, and order ID numbers, can also cause delays in cash flow evaluation and payment delivery (Gavirneni et al. 1999). Therefore, innovative technologies, like web-based cloud computing calculation, play a vital role in successful utilization. Novel hardware can to a larger extent access up-to-date data bypassing the boundaries of the physical supply chain.

As a result, transparency and automation will be key foundations of relationships and cooperation between buyers and sellers (Hofmann and Belin 2011).

Due to the nature official documents and sensitive information, digitalization stands a high chance of low authenticity. Contracts, licenses, and certificates possess the distinguished feature of security to display official identity. Digital property can be duplicated, so creditability has to be built up through centralized data management or authorized intermediaries. This consists of large information technology systems located in a single institution. Meanwhile, participants including traders, exchanges, clearing houses and other institutions responsible for legal information can conduct transactions. In particular, ledgers are major component part of business and are therefore centrally recorded and managed by credit entities. With the initiation of blockchain embedded in supply chain finance, the algorithm enables the coordinated establishment of a fully digital register. Blockchain technology has the ability to convert ledgers into tools for recording, enabling, and protecting large numbers of transactions. Working in a similar way like the Internet, blockchain is not centrally administered by a central system. Instead, it is a shared data ware house of information distributed across a large network of users (Raval 2016). Official documents in physical form are no longer the only way to build creditability among unacquainted entities. Given this set up, the fundamental blockchain function can be adapted to incorporate rules, smart contracts, digital signatures, and many more options.

3 Discussion and Main Findings

3.1 Overall Findings

Evolving technology development and increasing information accessibility in the supply chain have led to novel advancement in supply chain financial solutions. The negative impact of the economic situation has accelerated this trend, increasing the importance of liquidity and ease. In a complicated environment, obtaining financial resources might be challenging, while it gives certain advantages of full adoption among large and small companies. When each participant individually controls how supply chain finance is organized, dependence on financial institutions is reduced, such as onboarding and the "know your customer" process. This novel idea originates from digital trust infrastructure, like blockchain technology as a new form of license-free and collaborative platform. Based on the original inspiration, any participant can establish an ecosystem by providing new services. First, this paper analyzes post-shipment financing when the supplier receives financing after the invoice is approved by the buyer. However, financial institutions also face additional risks because the shipment has not been finalized yet. In addition, further development of technology on the basis of the full integration of all parties in the financial supply chain can enhance the transparency of the value chain. Building such an open platform allows financial institutions and companies to arrange supply chain finance under their own control. Therefore, it is not recommended to rely on new onboarding activities. Besides, the proposed solutions can provide active cooperation among companies, scientific institutions, and governments soon.

Blockchain technology is a destructive solution that can make the transaction process between supply chain partners more efficient, improve the relationship between buyers and sellers during the payment process, and eliminate inefficiency in the flow of funds. Working in the same fashion like the Internet, blockchain possesses the ability of making transaction secure, transparent, and efficient. With the digitization of the process, supply chain finance still has huge development potential. Nevertheless, with the aim of creating new solutions combining the new technology, a new conceptual framework is needed. To be specific, the digitization of the entire value chain calls upon all participants together on the scale of digitization and collaboration. This integrated approach unifies material flows, and at the same time takes into account of information flows and capital flows. Following extant literature, this paper develops a supply chain financial framework with blockchain technology (Fig. 3).

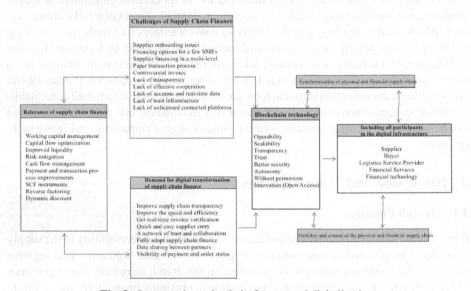

Fig. 3. Integrated supply chain finance and digitalization

Today, the supply chain finance has standardized procedures to optimize capital flows and operating capital through the supply chain. The complex process and low operating efficiency of incumbent financial services have brought significant risks to the effective management of working capital. In addition, insufficient transparency and visibility causes mistrust and certain degree of insecurity among supply chain participants. Technology is a key factor in making supply chain finance more efficient in process and information sharing. With the aid of digital technology, supply chain participants can be integrated into an ecosystem, which is fully effective and transparent. All involved parties, like suppliers, buyers, financial service providers, logistics service providers, and technology providers can benefit from it. Logistics service providers leads a vital role in the whole process, especially when they are in charge of most of the customer's supply chain. The financial supply chain is mainly utilized in the banking sector for the time being. With the continuous advancement of supply chain finance application, such as improved invoice management, logistics service providers can provide cross-functional quotations. Logistics service providers have a lot of data on the logistics process because they keep a close eye on the status of the goods. The risks are even more pronounced, allowing logistics service providers to work with partners (such as financial institutions) to initiate inaugural services in the field of supply chain finance. The buyer's rapid approval of the invoice is an indispensable for reverse factoring. Because of the inefficiency of logistics service providers in the process of invoicing, payment processing time may increase. Therefore, only through digitization and technology can automatically process transaction, invoice and payment status, and access to up-to-date information by all relevant participants. All participants can benefit from this comprehensive supply chain financing method in terms of transparency and reduced costs. Meanwhile, disputes and transaction costs are cut to the minimum.

The digitization of supply chain finance depends on both the technical level and the need for active collaboration. Digitalization enables to bring all participants together given the presence of an integrated supply chain financial ecosystem. As a matter of fact, a new generation of collaboration networks can facilitate companies smoothly process invoice and help supplier with onboarding and liquidity distribution. However, in an isolated and disconnected business network, these benefits cannot be realized. Blockchain technology, as an innovative revolution, has the capability of fundamentally modify business operations. By introducing this technology to incumbent networks, it can to a large extent increase supply chain financing and supply chain transparency.

3.2 The Case of Reverse Factoring

The business environment keeps changing. Supply chain finance and its practical tools still have great potential. Reverse factoring has become a short-term method for tier one supplier financing. This tool demonstrates a well-functioning advantage of unleashing cash in the supply chain and financing suppliers through advance payments. However, in the interests of suppliers, this tool still has considerable potential. In addition, regarding the upstream and downstream supply chain, supply chain finance has not been given full integration, as it is only utilized for the coordination of buyers with high credit ratings and their direct suppliers. Partner networks include a integrated end-to-end supply chain from start to finish. As a result, supply chain finance hardly affects indirect suppliers traditionally assigned to tier one supplier. When it comes to operation, for simplicity, reverse factoring does not receive timely information about accounts receivable and credit limits. For tactic usage, empowerment is an essential condition for building creditability. In order to organize the flow of funds and securely record ownership data, it will take several days to verify that the company actually received the goods. The conclusion is that there is a match between the inefficiency of supply chain financial practices and the value drivers of blockchain technology.

To elaborate on the impact on reverse factoring, this paper proposes a framework that combines supply chain finance with digitalization, as depicted in Fig. 3. This paper discusses the potential main value creation of blockchain technology to extend the reverse factoring tool and equip it with the advantages and unique characteristics of the technology. However, creating a new solution requires a perspective that involves all partners in a digital collaboration network. Therefore, Fig. 4 shows an integrated supply chain financial reverse factoring solution based on blockchain technology.

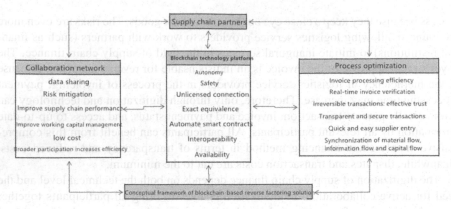

Fig. 4. Conceptual framework of a reverse factoring solution based on blockchain technology

This integrated method has to be implemented across partners' ecosystem of supply chain. This result will enable participants to obtain up-to-date information related to supplies, data and capital flows, gain a clearer understanding of the supply chain, and reduce potential risks of supply chain failures. Blockchain technology may trigger a new perspective on innovation in the field of supply chain finance, especially in the field of reverse factoring. Compared to other information technology infrastructures, blockchain technology has the capability of enabling databases, which are directly shared between trust barriers. Each party in the blockchain independently testifies and facilitates transactions. This works well as every participant in the system can view the functioning database, access status, and real-time verification of transactions through digital signatures and private keys.

By utilizing blockchain technology as the facility of the ecosystem of supply chain, buyers and suppliers can get connected in the upstream supply chain. At the same time, suppliers of financial institutions do not rely on new onboarding activities. Information on invoice status is transmitted securely, and financiers can offer high-efficiency financing services for any transaction type regardless of the value with lower risk. Similarly, suppliers can connect with customers in this digital system. Credit ratings and supplier assessments are recorded in the blockchain and protected with encryption. If the buyer fails to honor the payment on time or the supplier does not deliver in a timely manner, dynamic adjustments and automatic evaluations are performed. Each participant involved in reverse factoring will further see this information in order to set incentives and improve reliability for all partners. Consequently, all participants can benefit from simultaneous access to data related to transactions, invoices, and payments.

Blockchain technology can also enhance transparency in the supply chain and allow trading entities to coordinate more effectively and reach a new high level of efficiency and responsiveness. Blockchain provides an innovative technology for tracking inventory, overseeing product components, and tracking global footprints. It distributes the origin of the product to all relevant personnel, like the place of production to the end user. It eliminates the need to track projects manually. Blockchain can also set up a formal registry to identify individual products and keep a record on material ownership at different nodes in the supply chain.

Compared to other IT infrastructures, robustness is another advantage of blockchain technology. It ensures a higher availability of data, and ensures greater fault tolerance working under centralized systems. Blockchain technology enables participating entities to draft smart contracts, and it can automatically enforce contract terms. If participants in a smart contract meet a series of prerequisites, payment can be automatically initiated by the contract agreement in a transparent and efficient way. In addition, blockchain can create a listserv database that records all kinds of data that may be open to all participants in the system. Data can be accessed, shared, and added if appropriate in reverse factoring, but individuals cannot change or delete it at all. People can use a shared ledger and the only authentic information to increase transparency and creditability through a tamper-resistant and error-free system. These advantages play an essential role in blockchain technology as the preferred information technology topology in the context of supply chain finance.

3.3 Dynamic Discounting Use Cases

If effective cooperation among supply chain entities primarily relies on valuable information exchange. Effective integration of information and communication technologies is needed to automatically process business procedures and transactions (Pramatari 2007). Therefore, new financing tools in supply chain finance depend primarily on supply chain links. Blockchina utilizes electronic data interchange and integrated business solutions to optimize working capital and create financial value for relevant organizations (Gelsomino 2016). To elaborate on dynamic discount use cases, this paper proposes a broader concept framework of supply chain collaboration. This proposal can compare the generality of blockchain technology with conventional IT solutions, especially alternative supply chain financial applications.

According to the potential of supply chain cooperation, this paper defines supply chain cooperation as a business procedure in which supply chain participants undertake supply chain work together (Mentzer et al. 2001). Bowersox et al. (2003) extended this definition by incorporating information, resources, and risk sharing. By combining two concepts, this paper adds the first concept component to the conceptual framework. It is made up of six interconnected parts that achieve cooperative advantages by cutting expenditures, response time, distributing resources, and enhancing innovation (Cao and Zhang 2010). Regarding describing and evaluating the differential principles and mechanisms of blockchain technology, this paper adopts concepts of general system theory. Following Boulding (1956), the function, structure and dynamics of technology-based systems introduced a second dimension. Figure 5 shows the conceptual framework of a blockchain-based integrated solution in supply chain finance. Dynamic discounting uses the visibility of trade processes to initiate the dynamic processing of invoices in a buying and selling relation and therefore relies on available technology (Polak et al. 2012). The framework proposed in this paper is the starting point for discussing the premise of integrating blockchain technology in the practice of dynamic discounting.

According to Gelsomino et al. (2016), the procedure of dynamic discounting can be divided into four stages. To check and evaluate relevant value drivers, every stage

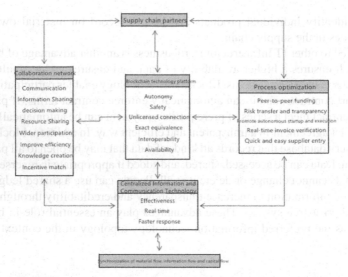

Fig. 5. Conceptual framework of a dynamic discount solution based on blockchain technology

applies elements of the conceptual framework. In this study, we further considered buyer-centric out-of-pocket payments and assumed that invoiced goods were pre-shipped. All procedures are usually performed through a single application, cloud solution, or a third-party supplement based on an incumbent enterprise resource planning system.

Generally, the buyer's size initiates the transaction by paying suppliers in advance under discounted conditions. Under the agreement, invoice processing occurs when suppliers create, upload, and exchange related documents electronically through electronic data interchange (EDI). This stage is completed when the electronic invoice is electronically delivered to the buyer. In the second phase, the buyer's size initiates the receipt, reconciliation, and final registration of the required payment to begin defining an repetitive approach to advance payment proposal (EPP). Therefore, the third phase aims to approve the date for payment settlement and discounting of the proposals for such advance payments. Therefore, after the buyer submits an advance payment proposal, the supplier can accept or reject it. If rejected, the buyer may modify the terms and conditions further. If an agreement is reached, this phase is finalized through archiving. With regard to the last step, the supplier and the buyer both store the invoices electronically or physically.

Compared with ordinary information and communication technology platforms, the blockchain technology exhibits valuable advantages in terms of structure. To be specific, in multi-level supply chains or supply networks, distributed databases and interoperability improve data sharing and resource distribution. Combined with its facilities, especially smart contracts, blockchain technology helps, or even speculates the launch of dynamic discount plans. Similar to the multi-standard approach in the process of supplier onboarding, the enhanced availability and auditability of trusted information automates decision making. Thanks to the interconnection of different blockchains, implementing autonomous methods through pegged sidechains becomes feasible. If the flow of funds across the value chain is built up on the same ledger that connects all components, the risk of early default and shrinking liquidity can be automatically eliminated. For more solvency participants in the downstream supply chain, the parameters of advance payment proposal will be calculated consistently. Regarding the dynamics of blockchain technology, a solution will be applicable to consider not only vertical structures but also horizontal structures. What is decisive is no longer the buyer's current financial situation, but more likely to be the anticipated demand for customer orders in the pulling supply chain. The multi-standard method can also be applied in other cases like transforming physical objects into intelligent attributes and overseeing the material flow on the blockchain.

In general, blockchain technology always represents a more accessible, secure and inexpensive solution. This is particularly the case if the ICT service provider provides funding to the buyer. Under this circumstance, blockchain technology can provide direct funding among parties completely based on a peer-to-peer network that does not rely on intermediary. Although there is no difference in the level of transparency between different techniques, insufficient of blockchain technology remains a major hurdle in the future. In a binary configuration, centralized ICT solutions enable simutaneous data faster. Blockchain technology is still restricted to its consensus mechanism. Therefore, it takes a short while to create a block, because as the time elapses, the security of the entire chain also increases. In addition to these technical features, user cases outline the aspects of supplier-buyer relation in a quantitative way based on autonomy and key characteristics of autonomy. As complexity increases, a solution is recognized that executes decisions within a well-established set of rules based on decentralized resources and group consensus. If the entire supply chain utilizes the same visible information and protocols, the all participants can benefit from it. As for traditional buyer-initiated dynamic discounting, business exhibits significant concentration on independent participants. To make good use of the solution based on blockchain technology, a paradigm switch must be undertaken to obtain a global rather than two single local optimizations between the buyer and the supplier. Therefore, it is assumed that the main value drivers of adoption are key aspects of quality, like transparency and autonomy, rather than efficiency. Finally, the adoption of blockchain technology solutions can largely depend on the supply chain configuration and the market environment per se. Once the technical limitations are overcome and a new consensus mechanism is established, blockchain technology can ultimately have the opportunity to gain significant adoption in a highly integrated supply chain.

4   Conclusion

With digital technologies such as blockchain, the flow of funds can be increasingly streamlined, and all relevant participants can share and oversee financing-related information, including the latest invoice status, check credit limits, and payments in a transparent manner. The new era of digitalization and mobility allows all entities to easily access synchronized supply chain financial information. Participants can continuously check detailed products and transactions digitally. This inclusive infrastructure calls for a shared ledger which provides any information related to the supply chain, while ensuring the global authenticity and security of data and information. This greatly reduces the cost and complexity of the incumbent systems.

By answering the first research problem and determining the inefficiency of existing supply chain financial instruments, this paper argues that existing challenges demand the digitization of supply chain finance. Emerging technologies can fill in the gap and achieve effective management. The flow of material, information, and funds that are considered to be independent flows can now be synchronized, and all partners can benefit from this new digital infrastructure. In addition to supply chain collaboration and traditional centralized technologies, blockchain technology is a technology that that simplifies the flow of information, goods and funds on a digital platform.

By analyzing the main potential of blockchain, this paper approaches the second research question. It proposes a conceptual approach and identify value drivers. The framework revealed the unique value proposition of blockchain technology to aid the implementation of supply chain finance practices. Based on this, supply chain participants benefit significantly from three key features: efficiency, transparency, and autonomy. This paper discusses how the value drivers mentioned above can improve supply chain finance solutions by elaborating on two practices in supply chain finance, namely reverse factoring and dynamic discounting.

Therefore, based on supply chain collaboration, this paper proposes a conceptual framework and defines the technical requirements of supply chain finance practices. Therefore, this paper shows how companies can benefit from blockchain technology, manage their capital flows in their supply chain, and identify how to improve the value drivers of reverse factoring and dynamic discounting services. Blockchain-based reverse factoring and dynamic discounting aid supply chain participants in making independent decisions and smoothing the flow of funds in the supply chain. In addition, it improves the security and service quality of reverse factoring, enabling the entire process to be supervised in a visual and credible manner. This paper argues that interoperability, trust, and robustness are the key drivers of blockchain technology's superiority over traditional information technology infrastructure. The research results also show that blockchain technology provides an open organization platform of supply chain financing for all participants. Discussion on dynamic discounting compares blockchain technology with traditional information and communication technology from the level of structure, function, and dynamic capabilities. Traditional and centralized technologies show higher efficiency in terms of quantitative aspects, such as responsiveness and speed, while blockchain technology offers more qualitative advantages like dynamic discounting. Due to the blockchain-based solution, the interoperability, availability, and trustworthiness of information make it possible to automatically process within a fully peer-to-peer information system. The results show that the choice of blockchain technology over traditional solutions largely depends on the configuration of a single supply chain and the initial trade-offs between quantity and quality aspects. Supply chain technology has been proved to be more suitable for responsive and multi-level supply chains, in which the reliability and availability of information and the automation of decision-making processes lead to less expenditure. While in a stable supply chain with a higher level of vertical integration and a focus on efficiency, centralized information and communication technology solutions may be preferred.

The research results of this paper show that, unlike other information technology architectures, blockchain technology is a technology platform that endeavors to create transparency, automation, and trust for supply chain financial tools. Based on this, a case-based practice study is proposed to investigate and provide useful applications. Although two solutions have been proposed, specific evaluations of their effectiveness are still yet to be tested. In addition to theoretical discussions, more practical research methods are necessary. Scenario analysis and even simulations can be used to measure both qualitative and quantitative aspects. This will facilitate the further development and widespread adoption of blockchain technology applications.

References

Antonopoulus, A.M.: Mastering Bitcoin: Unlocking Digital Cryptocurrencies. 1st Edition, O'Reilly Media: Sebastopol (2015)

Beck, T.H.L, Demirgüç-Kunt, A., Maksimovic, V.: Bank competition and access to finance. J. Money, Credit Bank (2004)

Bertino, E., Sandhu, R.: Database security: concepts, approaches, and challenges. IEEE Trans. Dependable Secure Comput. 1(1), 2–19 (2005)

Boulding, K.E.: General systems theory—the skeleton of science. Manage. Sci. 2(3), 197–208 (1956)

Bowersox, D.J., Closs, D.J., Stank, T.P.: How to master cross-enterprise collaboration. Supply Chain Manage. Rev. 7(4), 18–27 (2003)

Burgess, K.: The Promise of Bitcoin and the Blockchain. Bretton Woods 2015 Working Paper, Consumers Research (2015)

Cao, M., Qingyu, Z.: 2010 Supply chain collaboration: impact on collaborative advantage and firm performance. J. Oper. Manage. 29(3), 163–180 (2011)

Carter, R.C., Rogers, D.S., Choi, T.Y.: Toward the theory of the supply chain. J. Supply Chain Manage. 51(2), 2015 (2015)

De Boer, R., van Bergen, M., Steeman, M.A.: Supply Chain Finance, its Practical Relevance and Strategic Value. The Supply Chain Finance Essential Knowledge Series. Zwolle (2015)

Fairchild, A.: Intelligent matching: integrating efficiencies in the financial supply chain. Supply Chain Manage. 10(3/4), 244–249 (2005)

Fellenz, M.R., Augustenborg, C., Brady, M., Greene, J.: Requirements for an evolving model of supply chain finance: a technology and service providers perspective. Commun. IBIMA. 10(29), 227—235, (2009). ISSN: 1943-7765

Frankel, R., Bolumole, A.Y., Eltantawy R.A., Paulraj, A., Gundlach, G.: The domain and scope of SCM's foundational disciplines. Insights and Issues to advance research. J. Bus. Logistics 29(1), 1–30 (2008)

Gelsomino, M., Mangiaracina, R., Perego, A., Tumino, A.: Supply chain finance: modelling a dynamic discounting programme. J. Adv. Manage. Sci. 4(4) (2016)

Gupta, S., Dutta, K.: Modeling financial supply chain. Eur. J. Oper. Res. 211(1), 47–56 (2011)

Hofmann, E., Belin, O.: Supply Chain Finance Solutions: Relevance, Propositions, Market Value, 1st edn. Springer, Berlin (2011)

Hofmann, E., Kotzab, H.: A supply chain-oriented approach of working capital management. J. Bus. Logistics 31(2), 305–330 (2010)

Hofmann, E.: Supply chain finance: some conceptual insights, in Lasch, R., Janker, C.G. (Eds), Logistik Management. Innovative Logistikkonzepte, German Universitätsverlag, Wiesbaden, pp. 203–214 (2005)

Kelly, J., Williams, A.: Forty Big Banks Test Blockchain-Based Bond Trading System (2016)

Klapper, L.: The role of factoring for financing small and medium enterprises. J. Bank. Finance **30**(2006), 3111–3130 (2006)

Mainelli, M., Milne, A.: The impact and potential of Blockchain on the securities transaction lifecycle. In: SWIFT Institute Working Paper No. 2015–007 (2016)

Meredith, J.: Theory Building Through Conceptual Methods. Int. J. Oper. Product. Manage. **13**(5), 3–11 (1993)

Mentzer, J.T., DeWitt, W., Keebler, J.S., Min, S., Nix, N.W., Smith, C.D., Zacharia, Z.G.: Defining supply chain management. J. Bus. Logistics **22**(2), 1–25 (2001)

Nienhuis, J.J., Corte, M., Lycklama, D.: Real-time financing: extending e-invoicing to real-time SME financing. J. Payments Strat. Syst. **7**(3), 232–245 (2013)

Omran, Y.: Inclusive Supply Chain Finance Approach: Integrated Supply Chain Finance Solution With Digitalization. White paper, Fraunhofer IML (2016)

Popa, V.: The financial supply chain management: a new solution for supply chain resilience. Amfiteatru Econ. **15**(33), 140–153 (2013)

Palia, D., Sopranzetti, B.J.: Securitizing account receivable. Rev. Quant. Finance Account. **22**(29–38), 2004 (2004)

Seifert, R.W., Seifert, D.: Financing the chain. Int. Comm. Review **10**(1), 32–44 (2011)

Swan, M.: The Blockchain: Blueprint of a new economy. 1st Edition, O'Reilly Media: Sebastopol (2015)

Templar, S., Findlay, C., Hofmann, E.: Financing the End-to-end Supply Chain: A Reference Guide to Supply Chain Finance. First ed. Kogan Page (2016)

Wuttke, D.A., Blome, C., Heese, H.S., Protopappa-Sieke, M.: Supply chain finance: optimal introduction and adoption decisions. Int. J. Product. Econ. **178**, 72–81 (2016)

Wuttke, D., Blome, C., Henke, M.: Focusing the financial flow of supply chains: an empirical investigation of financial supply chain management. Int. J. Product. Econ. **145**(2), 773–789 (2013)

Zhang, C., Dhaliwal, J.: 2009. An investigation of resource-based and institutional theoretic factors in technology adoption for operations and supply chain management. Int. J. Product. Econ. **120**(1), 252–269 (2009)

Bayesian Analysis for Multivariate Skew-Normal Simplex Mixed-Effects Models with Heterogeneous Dispersion

Xingde Duan[1], Shi Zhang[1], Wenzhuan Zhang[1(✉)], and Xinli Miao[2]

[1] Guizhou University of Finance and Economics, Guiyang 550025, China
zhangwenzhuan@mail.gufe.edu.cn

[2] Chuxiong Normal University Chuxiong, Chuxiong 675000, China

Abstract. Continuous proportional data frequently appears in many areas of research, where proportional outcome are in the open interval $(0,1)$. Simplex mixed-effects model is a powerful tool for modeling longitudinal continuous proportional data; however, the normality assumption of random effects in classic simplex mixed-effects model may be questionable in the analysis of skewed data. In this paper, we relax the normality assumption of random effects by specifying the random-effect distribution with the multivariate skew-normal distribution in mixed-effect model and simultaneously model the dispersion parameter (heterogeneity) in mixed-effect model. An efficient Markov chain Monte Carlo algorithm that combines the block Gibbs sampler, the Metropolis-Hastings algorithm and the data-augmentation technique is proposed for producing the joint Bayesian estimates of unknown parameters and random effects. The Deviance Information Criterion (DIC), as a popular model comparison criterion, is employed to select better model. The proposed methodology is illustrated by several simulation studies and a real example.

Keywords: Simplex distribution · Gibbs sampler · Metropolis–Hastings algorithm · Proportional data · Model selection

1 Introduction

Various random-effects models and marginal models based on simplex distribution are two classes of popular tool for modeling longitudinal continuous proportional data; therefore, statistical inference on these complex simplex models have been drawing much attention in the last two decades. For example, Song and

This research was supported in part by grants from the National Natural Science Foundation of China (11501073), the Science and Technology Foundation of Guizhou Province ([2020]1Y009), the talents for scientific research project of Guizhou University of Finance and Economics (2018YJ104).

H. Song and D. Jiang (Eds.): SIMUtools 2020, LNICST 369, pp. 313–326, 2021.
https://doi.org/10.1007/978-3-030-72792-5_27

Tan [12] and Song et al. [11] proposed the simplex marginal model with the constant and varying dispersion parameter under the GEE framework, respectively; Qiu et al. [9] proposed a simplex generalized linear mixed model by using the PQL/REML inference; Zhang and Wei [16] developed the stochastic approximation (SA) algorithm for simplex distribution nonlinear mixed models; Zhao et al. [17] studied Bayesian analysis of simplex distribution nonlinear mixed models based on MCMC algorithm; Bandyopadhyay et al. [3] proposed the augmented general proportion density (GPD) random effects model for clustered proportion data; Bonat et al. [4] investigated a class of simplex mixed models based on likelihood analysis. However, the random effects in all the above mentioned mixed-effects models follow the multivariate normal distribution. It is difficult for the normality assumption of random effects to capture the features of skewed and heavy-tailed data.

Recently, the skew-normal distribution is widely incorporated into various mixed effects models to relax the normality assumption of random effects and response variables. For example, Sahu et al. [10] proposed the Bayesian version of the multivariate skew-normal (SN) distributions; Arellano-Valle et al. [2] presented skew-normal linear mixed models by assuming the random effects and response variables to be a multivariate SN; Michaelis et al. [8] proposed a new class of multivariate distributional regression with skewed responses and skewed random effects by introducing the skew-normal and skew-t distribution; Xing et al. [14] proposed a two-part mixed-effects model with logistic mixed-effects model on the occurrence of positive values and linear mixed-effects model with skew-t (ST) and skew-normal (SN) distributions on the continuous positive values; Han et al. [6] proposed a class of skew-normal nonlinear mixed-effects joint models in the presence of covariates measured with errors to analyze complex longitudinal data; Zhang et al. [15] proposed the quantile regression-based partially linear mixed-effects joint models for longitudinal data with multiple features. However, to the best of our knowledge, there is little work done for Bayesian analysis of simplex mixed-effects model with random effects following the multivariate skew-normal distribution. Therefore, a novel Bayesian approach to simplex mixed-effects model is developed by specifying the random-effect distribution with the multivariate skew-normal distribution.

On the other hand, modelling dispersion parameter has been considered by different authors using various heterogeneous dispersion model. For example, see Artes and Jørgensen [1], Song et al. [11], Duan et al. [5]. In particular, Duan et al. [5] recommended the usage of modeling heterogeneous dispersion in a semiparametric simplex regression model when the homogeneous dispersion assumption is uncertain. Therefore, we introduce a new model for longitudinal continuous proportional data by incorporating multivariate skew-normal random effects into simplex regression models with heterogeneous dispersion. Also, an efficient Markov chain Monte Carlo algorithm that combines the block Gibbs sampler, the Metropolis-Hastings algorithm and the data-augmentation technique is developed.

2 Model

2.1 The Multivariate Skew-Normal Distribution

In this section, we first introduce the following notations. Let $N_k(\mu, \Sigma)$ stand for a k-variate normal distribution with k-dimensional mean vector μ and $k \times k$ covariance matrix Σ. In what follows, the probability density function and cumulative distribution function of $N_k(\mu, \Sigma)$ valued at z will be denoted by $\phi_k(z|\mu, \Sigma)$ and $\Phi_k(z|\mu, \Sigma)$; respectively. For abbreviation, we let $\text{diag}(a_1, \ldots, a_k)$ denote a diagonal matrix with elements $a_1, \ldots, a_k$ and I_k denote a $k \times k$ identity matrix. In this work, we implement the Bayesian version of the multivariate SN distributions proposed by Sahu et al. [10], and the corresponding probability density function is given as follow.

Definition 1. A k-dimensional random vector $\mathbf{Z}$ is subject to a k-variate skew-normal distribution, if its probability density function can be expressed in the following form

$$\begin{aligned}
f(\mathbf{z}|\mu, \Sigma, \Delta) = {} & 2^k \phi_k(\mathbf{z}|\mu, \Sigma + \Delta\Delta^T) \\
& \times \Phi_k(\Delta^T(\Sigma + \Delta\Delta^T)^{-1}(\mathbf{z} - \mu)|0, (I_k + \Delta^T\Sigma^{-1}\Delta)^{-1}),
\end{aligned} \tag{1}$$

where $\mu \in \mathbb{R}^k$ is the location vector, Σ is the $k \times k$ scale positive-definite matrix, $\Delta = \text{diag}(\delta)$ with diagonal elements $\delta = (\delta_1, \ldots \delta_k)^T \in \mathbb{R}^k$ is the $k \times k$ diagonal skewness matrix, $\mathbf{z}$ is a real k-dimensional vector.

From now on, the aforementioned distribution can be denoted by $\mathbf{Z} \sim SN_k(\mu, \Sigma, \Delta)$. Clearly, the multivariate normal distribution is a special distribution of multivariate SN distribution, if $\Delta = \mathbf{0}$. Following Arellano-Valle et al. [2], we introduce the following propositions.

Proposition 1. If $\mathbf{Z} \sim SN_k(\mu, \Sigma, \Delta)$, then $\mathbf{Z} = \Delta|\mathbf{Z_0}| + \mathbf{Z_1}$, where $\mathbf{Z_0} \sim N_k(\mathbf{0}, I_k)$ and $\mathbf{Z_1} \sim N_k(\mu, \Sigma)$ and $\mathbf{Z_0}$ and $\mathbf{Z_1}$ are independent.

A proof of this proposition has been given in Sahu et al. [10] and Arellano-Valle et al. [2]. This proposition represents the stochastic representation which can readily generate the random variables from the multivariate SN distribution. In addition, this proposition has the following hierarchical structure: $\mathbf{Z}|\mathbf{Z_0} = \mathbf{z_0} \sim N_k(\mu + \Delta|\mathbf{z_0}|, \Sigma)$ and $\mathbf{Z_0} \sim N_k(\mathbf{0}, I_k)$. Under the Bayesian framework, this hierarchical structure readily facilitates the Markov chain Monte Carlo algorithm in the skew-normal distribution.

Proposition 2. If $\mathbf{Z} \sim SN_k(\mu, \Sigma, \Delta)$, then $E(\mathbf{Z}) = \mu + \sqrt{\frac{2}{\pi}}\delta$ and $\text{var}(\mathbf{Z}) = \Sigma + \left(1 - \frac{2}{\pi}\right)\Delta^2$.

Similarly, the proof of this proposition refer to Arellano-Valle et al. [2]. In this work, we assume the location parameter $\mu = -\sqrt{\frac{2}{\pi}}\delta$ in order to construct a zero mean vector with respect to multivariate skew-normal distribution on random effects in the following mixed-effect model.

2.2   Model Formulation

To study a longitudinal proportional data based on regression-type technique, we assume that y_{ij} is proportional outcome of the ith patient measured at time $t_{ij}(i = 1, 2, \ldots, n, j = 1, \ldots, n_i)$. For each ith patient, $y_{i1}, y_{i2}, \ldots, y_{in_i}$ given $\mathbf{b_i}$, which is a $k \times 1$ vector of random effects characterized by the ith patient, are conditionally independent and each $y_{ij}|\mathbf{b_i}$ is assumed to be a simplex distribution with conditional means $\mu_{ij} = \mathrm{E}(Y_{ij}|\mathbf{b_i}) \in (0, 1)$ and dispersion parameter $\sigma_{ij}^2 > 0$:

$$
\begin{cases}
p(y_{ij}|\mathbf{b_i}, \sigma_{ij}^2, \beta, \gamma) = \left[2\pi\sigma_{ij}^2\{y_{ij}(1 - y_{ij})\}^3\right]^{-1/2} \exp\left\{-\frac{1}{2\sigma_{ij}^2}d(y_{ij}; \mu_{ij})\right\} \\
\mathrm{logit}(\mu_{ij}) = \mathbf{x_{ij}^T}\beta + \mathbf{z_{ij}^T}\mathbf{b_i}, \\
\log(\sigma_{ij}^2) = \mathbf{w_{ij}^T}\gamma, \\
\mathbf{b_i} \sim SN_k\left(-\sqrt{2/\pi}\delta, \Sigma, \Delta\right)
\end{cases}
\tag{2}
$$

where $0 < y_{ij} < 1$, $d(y_{ij}; \mu_{ij}) = \frac{(y_{ij}-\mu_{ij})^2}{y_{ij}(1-y_{ij})\mu_{ij}^2(1-\mu_{ij})^2}$, $\mathrm{logit}(\mu_{ij}) = \log\left(\frac{\mu_{ij}}{1-\mu_{ij}}\right)$, β is a $p \times 1$ vector of unknown parameters for the fixed effects in the mean model, γ is a $q \times 1$ vector of unknown parameters to be estimated in the dispersion model, $\mathbf{x_{ij}}$, $\mathbf{z_{ij}}$ and $\mathbf{w_{ij}}$ are the $p \times 1$, $k \times 1$ and $q \times 1$ vector of design explanatory variables. Also, Σ, δ and Δ are given by the Definition 1. Here, $\mathbf{w_{ij}}$ may comprise some or all of the variables in $\mathbf{x_{ij}}$. Thus, the model defined in (2) is referred to as a multivariate skew-norml simplex mixed-effects models with heterogeneous dispersion. In what follows, we will denote by $y_{ij}|\mathbf{b_i} \sim \mathrm{S}^{-1}(\mu_{ij}, \sigma_{ij}^2)$, if $y_{ij}|\mathbf{b_i}$ follows a simplex distribution with conditional means μ_{ij} and dispersion parameter σ_{ij}^2. For the convenience of the implementation of the MCMC algorithms, it can be seen from Proposition 1 and Proposition 2 that $\mathbf{b_i} \sim SN_k\left(-\sqrt{2/\pi}\delta, \Sigma, \Delta\right)$ in model (2) can derived as the simple hierarchical structure:

$$
\mathbf{b_i}|\mathbf{u_i} \sim N_k(-\sqrt{2/\pi}\delta + \Delta\mathbf{u_i}, \Sigma), \mathbf{u_i} \sim N_k(0, I_k)\mathrm{I}\{\mathbf{u_i} > 0\},
\tag{3}
$$

where $\mathbf{u_i}$ is $k \times 1$ vector of unobserved latent variable, $\mathrm{I}\{\cdot\}$ represents an indicator function.

3   Bayesian Analysis of Mixed-Effects Model

Let $\mathbf{Y} = \{\mathbf{y_{ij}} : i = 1, \cdots, n, j = 1, \ldots, n_i\}$, $\mathbf{X} = \{\mathbf{x_{ij}} : i = 1, \cdots, n, j = 1, \ldots, n_i\}$, $\mathbf{Z} = \{\mathbf{z_{ij}} : i = 1, \cdots, n, j = 1, \ldots, n_i\}$, $\mathbf{W} = \{\mathbf{w_{ij}} : i = 1, \cdots, n, j = 1, \ldots, n_i\}$, $\mathbf{y_i} = \{y_{i1}, \ldots, y_{in_i}\}$, $\mathbf{x_i} = \{x_{i1}, \ldots, x_{in_i}\}$, $\mathbf{z_i} = \{z_{i1}, \ldots, z_{in_i}\}$, $\mathbf{w_i} = \{w_{i1}, \ldots, w_{in_i}\}$, $\mathbf{b} = \{\mathbf{b_i} : i = 1, \cdots, n\}$, $\mathbf{u} = \{\mathbf{u_i} : i = 1, \cdots, n\}$, $\mathbf{1_k} = (1, \ldots, 1)^T$ and $\theta = (\beta, \gamma, \Sigma, \delta)$. Clearly, it is difficult to generate the random sample from the marginal posterior distribution $p(\theta|\mathbf{Y}, \mathbf{X}, \mathbf{Z}, \mathbf{W})$ because of high-dimensional integral with respect of random effects $\mathbf{b}$ and latent variable $\mathbf{u}$ involved. To address this issue, we adopt the data-augmentation strategy to augment the observed data $(\mathbf{Y}, \mathbf{X}, \mathbf{Z}, \mathbf{W})$ with the unobserved data $\mathbf{b}$ and $\mathbf{u}$. Specifically, an efficient Markov chain Monte Carlo algorithm is used to generate random observations from the joint posterior distribution $p(\theta, \mathbf{b}, \mathbf{u} | \mathbf{Y}, \mathbf{X}, \mathbf{Z}, \mathbf{W})$, which is proportional to

$$\left\{ \prod_{i=1}^{n} [\prod_{j=1}^{n_i} p(y_{ij} | \mathbf{x_{ij}}, \mathbf{z_{ij}}, \mathbf{w_{ij}}, \mathbf{b_i}, \mathbf{u_i}, \theta)] p(\mathbf{b_i} | \mathbf{u_i}, \theta) p(\mathbf{u_i} | \mathbf{u_i} > 0) \right\} p(\theta), \quad (4)$$

where $p(\theta)$ is the prior distribution for unknown parameter θ. Furthermore, the prior distribution $p(\theta)$ is specified as follows:

$$p(\boldsymbol{\beta}) \overset{D}{=} N_p(\boldsymbol{\beta^0}, \mathbf{H_{\beta 0}}), p(\boldsymbol{\gamma}) \overset{D}{=} N_q(\boldsymbol{\gamma^0}, \mathbf{H_{\gamma 0}}), p(\boldsymbol{\delta}) \overset{D}{=} N_k(\boldsymbol{\delta^0}, \mathbf{H_{\delta 0}}),$$
$$p(\boldsymbol{\Sigma}) \overset{D}{=} IW_k(\rho_0, \mathbf{R_0}), \quad (5)$$

where $\boldsymbol{\beta^0}$, $\mathbf{H_{\beta 0}}$, $\boldsymbol{\gamma^0}$, $\mathbf{H_{\gamma 0}}$, $\boldsymbol{\delta^0}$, $\mathbf{H_{\delta 0}}$, ρ_0, $\mathbf{R_0}$ are hyperparameters whose values are given based on prior information; and IW_k denotes the k-dimensional inverse Wishart distribution.

3.1   Full Conditional Distributions

In this section, we derive the full conditional distributions of interest in the MCMC sampling procedures as follows.

A tedious calculation gives that the full conditional distribution for latent variable $\mathbf{u_i}$ can be written as

$$p(\mathbf{u_i} | \mathbf{y_i}, \mathbf{x_i}, \mathbf{z_i}, \mathbf{w_i}, \mathbf{b_i}, \theta) \propto$$
$$\exp\left\{ -\tfrac{1}{2} \mathbf{u_i^T} \mathbf{u_i} - \tfrac{1}{2} (\mathbf{b_i} - \boldsymbol{\Delta}(\mathbf{u_i} - \sqrt{2/\pi} \cdot \mathbf{1_k}))^T \boldsymbol{\Sigma}^{-1} (\mathbf{b_i} - \boldsymbol{\Delta}(\mathbf{u_i} - \sqrt{2/\pi} \cdot \mathbf{1_k})) \right\} \mathrm{I}(\mathbf{u_i} > 0),$$

which gives rise to

$$\mathbf{u_i} | \mathbf{y_i}, \mathbf{x_i}, \ \mathbf{z_i}, \mathbf{w_i}, \mathbf{b_i}, \theta \sim N_k(\mathbf{A}_{ui} \mathbf{a}_{ui}, \mathbf{A}_{ui}) \mathrm{I}(\mathbf{u_i} > 0), \ i = 1, 2, \ldots n \quad (6)$$

where $\mathbf{A}_{ui} = (I_k + \boldsymbol{\Delta} \boldsymbol{\Sigma}^{-1} \boldsymbol{\Delta})^{-1}$, $\mathbf{a}_{ui} = \sqrt{2/\pi} \boldsymbol{\Delta} \boldsymbol{\Sigma}^{-1} \boldsymbol{\delta} + \boldsymbol{\Delta} \boldsymbol{\Sigma}^{-1} \mathbf{b}_i$.

The full conditional distribution for random effect $\mathbf{b_i}$ is proportional to

$$p(\mathbf{b_i} | \mathbf{y_i}, \mathbf{x_i}, \mathbf{z_i}, \mathbf{w_i}, \mathbf{u_i}, \theta) \propto$$
$$\exp\left\{ -\tfrac{1}{2} [\sum_{j=1}^{n_i} \frac{d(y_{ij}; \mu_{ij})}{\sigma_{ij}^2} + (\mathbf{b}_i - \boldsymbol{\Delta}(\mathbf{u_i} - \sqrt{2/\pi} . \mathbf{1_k}))^T \boldsymbol{\Sigma}^{-1} (\mathbf{b_i} - \boldsymbol{\Delta}(\mathbf{u_i} - \sqrt{2/\pi} . \mathbf{1_k}))] \right\}. \quad (7)$$

The full conditional distribution for scale positive-definite matrix $\boldsymbol{\Sigma}$ is proportional to

$$p(\boldsymbol{\Sigma} | Y, X, Z, W, b, u, \theta) \propto |\boldsymbol{\Sigma}|^{-(n+k+\rho_0+1)/2}$$
$$\exp\left\{ -\tfrac{1}{2} \mathrm{tr} \left[\boldsymbol{\Sigma}^{-1} (\mathbf{R_0} + \sum_{i=1}^{n} (\mathbf{b}_i - \boldsymbol{\Delta}(\mathbf{u_i} - \sqrt{2/\pi} . \mathbf{1_k}))(\mathbf{b}_i - \boldsymbol{\Delta}(\mathbf{u_i} - \sqrt{2/\pi} . \mathbf{1_k}))^T) \right] \right\}$$

Clearly, the full conditional distribution for $\boldsymbol{\Sigma}$ has the following inverse Wishart distribution:

$$\boldsymbol{\Sigma}|\mathbf{Y}, \mathbf{X}, \mathbf{Z}, \mathbf{W}, \boldsymbol{b}, \boldsymbol{u}, \boldsymbol{\beta}, \boldsymbol{\gamma}, \boldsymbol{\delta} \sim$$
$$IW_k\left(\mathbf{R}_0 + \sum_{i=1}^{n}(\mathbf{b}_i - \boldsymbol{\Delta}(\mathbf{u}_i - \sqrt{2/\pi}.\mathbf{1}_k))(\mathbf{b}_i - \boldsymbol{\Delta}(\mathbf{u}_i - \sqrt{2/\pi}.\mathbf{1}_k))^T, n + \rho_0\right).$$
$$(8)$$

The full conditional distribution for parameters $\boldsymbol{\beta}$ in the mean model is proportional to

$$p(\boldsymbol{\beta}|\mathbf{Y}, \mathbf{X}, \mathbf{Z}, \mathbf{W}, \mathbf{b}, \mathbf{u}, \boldsymbol{\gamma}, \boldsymbol{\Sigma}, \boldsymbol{\delta}) \propto \exp\left\{-\frac{1}{2}\left[\sum_{i=1}^{n}\sum_{j=1}^{n_i}\frac{d(y_{ij}; \mu_{ij})}{\sigma_{ij}^2} + (\boldsymbol{\beta} - \boldsymbol{\beta}^0)^T \mathbf{H}_{\beta 0}^{-1}(\boldsymbol{\beta} - \boldsymbol{\beta}^0)\right]\right\}.$$
$$(9)$$

Clearly, the conditional distribution for skewness parameter $\boldsymbol{\delta}$ can be written as

$$p(\boldsymbol{\delta}|\mathbf{Y}, \mathbf{X}, \mathbf{Z}, \mathbf{W}, \mathbf{b}, \mathbf{u}, \boldsymbol{\gamma}, \boldsymbol{\Sigma}, \boldsymbol{\beta}) \propto$$
$$\exp\left\{-\frac{1}{2}\left[(\boldsymbol{\delta} - \boldsymbol{\delta}^0)^T \mathbf{H}_{\delta 0}^{-1}(\boldsymbol{\delta} - \boldsymbol{\delta}^0) + \sum_{i=1}^{n}(\mathbf{b}_i - \boldsymbol{\Delta}(\mathbf{u}_i - \sqrt{2/\pi}.\mathbf{1}_k))^T \boldsymbol{\Sigma}^{-1}(\mathbf{b}_i - \boldsymbol{\Delta}(\mathbf{u}_i - \sqrt{2/\pi}.\mathbf{1}_k))\right]\right\}$$

which yields the multivariate normal distribution as follows:

$$\boldsymbol{\delta}|\mathbf{Y}, \mathbf{X}, \mathbf{Z}, \mathbf{W}, \mathbf{b}, \mathbf{u}, \boldsymbol{\gamma}, \boldsymbol{\Sigma}, \boldsymbol{\beta} \sim N_k(\mathbf{A}_\delta \mathbf{a}_\delta, \mathbf{A}_\delta), \qquad (10)$$

where $\mathbf{A}_\delta = \left[\mathbf{H}_{\delta 0}^{-1} + \sum_{i=1}^{n}(\sqrt{2/\pi}\mathbf{I}_k - \mathrm{diag}(\mathbf{u}_i))^T \boldsymbol{\Sigma}^{-1}(\sqrt{2/\pi}\mathbf{I}_k - \mathrm{diag}(\mathbf{u}_i))\right]^{-1}$

and $\mathbf{a}_\delta = \mathbf{H}_{\delta 0}^{-1}\boldsymbol{\delta}_0 - \sum_{i=1}^{n}(\sqrt{2/\pi}\mathbf{I}_k - \mathrm{diag}(\mathbf{u}_i))^T \boldsymbol{\Sigma}^{-1}\mathbf{b}_i$.

The full conditional distribution for parameter $\boldsymbol{\gamma}$ in the dispersion model is proportional to

$$p(\boldsymbol{\gamma}|\mathbf{Y}, \mathbf{X}, \mathbf{Z}, \mathbf{W}, \mathbf{b}, \mathbf{u}, \boldsymbol{\beta}, \boldsymbol{\Sigma}, \boldsymbol{\delta}) \propto$$
$$\exp\left\{-\frac{1}{2}\left[\sum_{i=1}^{n}\sum_{j=1}^{n_i}\log\sigma_{ij}^2 + \sum_{i=1}^{n}\sum_{j=1}^{n_i}\frac{d(y_{ij}; \mu_{ij})}{\sigma_{ij}^2} + (\boldsymbol{\gamma} - \boldsymbol{\gamma}^0)^T \mathbf{H}_{\gamma 0}^{-1}(\boldsymbol{\gamma} - \boldsymbol{\gamma}^0)\right]\right\}. \qquad (11)$$

Clearly, it is straightforward to generate random observations from the standard and familiar conditional distributions given in (6), (8) and (10); however, it is rather difficult to draw random observations from the unfamiliar and complicated conditional distributions given in (7), (9) and (11). Therefore, we will implement the Metropolis-Hastings (MH) algorithm to deal with these sampling difficulties as follows.

3.2   MH Algorithm

For the full conditional distribution $p(\mathbf{b}_i|\mathbf{y}_i, \mathbf{x}_i, \mathbf{z}_i, \mathbf{w}_i, \mathbf{u}_i, \theta)$, $p(\boldsymbol{\beta}|\mathbf{Y}, \mathbf{X}, \mathbf{Z}, \mathbf{W}, \mathbf{b}, \mathbf{u}, \boldsymbol{\gamma}, \boldsymbol{\Sigma}, \boldsymbol{\delta})$ and $p(\boldsymbol{\gamma}|\mathbf{Y}, \mathbf{X}, \mathbf{Z}, \mathbf{W}, \mathbf{b}, \mathbf{u}, \boldsymbol{\beta}, \boldsymbol{\Sigma}, \boldsymbol{\delta})$, we choose the normal distribution and multivariate normal distribution as the proposal distribution.

The procedure for implementation of MH algorithm is presented as follows. Given the current value $\mathbf{b}_i^{(t)}$, $\boldsymbol{\beta}^{(t)}$ and $\boldsymbol{\gamma}^{(t)}$, some new candidates $\mathbf{b}_i^*$, $\boldsymbol{\beta}^*$ and $\boldsymbol{\gamma}^*$ generated from $N_k(\mathbf{b}_i^{(t)}, \sigma_{b_i}^2 \Omega_{b_i})$, $N\left(\boldsymbol{\beta}^{(t)}, \sigma_\beta^2 \Omega_\beta\right)$ and $N\left(\boldsymbol{\gamma}^{(t)}, \sigma_\gamma^2 \Omega_\gamma\right)$ can calculate the following accepted probability

$$\min\left\{1, \frac{p\left(\mathbf{b}_i^* | \mathbf{y_i}, \mathbf{x_i}, \mathbf{z_i}, \mathbf{w_i}, \mathbf{u_i}, \theta\right)}{p\left(\mathbf{b}_i^{(t)} | \mathbf{y_i}, \mathbf{x_i}, \mathbf{z_i}, \mathbf{w_i}, \mathbf{u_i}, \theta\right)}\right\},$$

$$\min\left\{1, \frac{p\left(\boldsymbol{\beta}^* | \mathbf{Y}, \mathbf{X}, \mathbf{Z}, \mathbf{W}, \mathbf{b}, \mathbf{u}, \boldsymbol{\gamma}, \boldsymbol{\Sigma}, \boldsymbol{\delta}\right)}{p\left(\boldsymbol{\beta}^{(t)} | \mathbf{Y}, \mathbf{X}, \mathbf{Z}, \mathbf{W}, \mathbf{b}, \mathbf{u}, \boldsymbol{\gamma}, \boldsymbol{\Sigma}, \boldsymbol{\delta}\right)}\right\},$$

$$\min\left\{1, \frac{p\left(\boldsymbol{\gamma}^* | \mathbf{Y}, \mathbf{X}, \mathbf{Z}, \mathbf{W}, \mathbf{b}, \mathbf{u}, \boldsymbol{\beta}, \boldsymbol{\Sigma}, \boldsymbol{\delta}\right)}{p\left(\boldsymbol{\gamma}^{(t)} | \mathbf{Y}, \mathbf{X}, \mathbf{Z}, \mathbf{W}, \mathbf{b}, \mathbf{u}, \boldsymbol{\beta}, \boldsymbol{\Sigma}, \boldsymbol{\delta}\right)}\right\},$$

where

$$\Omega_{b_i}^{-1} = \sum_{j=1}^{n_i}\left[3\mu_{ij}\left(1 - \mu_{ij}\right) + \frac{1}{\sigma_{ij}^2 \mu_{ij}\left(1 - \mu_{ij}\right)}\right] z_{ij} z_{ij}^T + \boldsymbol{\Sigma}^{-1},$$

$$\Omega_\beta^{-1} = \sum_{i=1}^{n}\sum_{j=1}^{n_i}\left[3\mu_{ij}\left(1 - \mu_{ij}\right) + \frac{1}{\sigma_{ij}^2 \mu_{ij}\left(1 - \mu_{ij}\right)}\right] x_{ij} x_{ij}^T + \mathbf{H}_{\beta 0}^{-1},$$

$$\Omega_\gamma^{-1} = \frac{1}{2}\sum_{i=1}^{n}\sum_{j=1}^{n_i} w_{ij} w_{ij}^T + \mathbf{H}_{\gamma 0}^{-1},$$

and $\sigma_{b_i}^2$, σ_β^2 and σ_γ^2 are referred to as the tuned variance coefficients.

3.3   Bayesian Model Selection

Deviance Information Criterion (DIC) proposed by Spiegelhalter et al. [13] is a popular criteria for model selection under the Bayesian framework. It is easily to calculate the estimator for DIC in the complex model by using MCMC algorithm . Thus, it follows from the idea of Spiegelhalter et al. [13] that the DIC under our proposed model is defined as

$$\text{DIC} = \overline{D(\theta)} + p_D$$

where $\overline{D(\theta)} = -2\mathbb{E}_{\theta,\mathbf{b},\mathbf{u}}\left\{\log p\left(\mathbf{Y}, \mathbf{b}, \mathbf{u}|\theta, \mathbf{X}, \mathbf{Z}, \mathbf{W}\right)|\mathbf{Y}, \mathbf{X}, \mathbf{Z}, \mathbf{W}\right\}$ is the posterior mean of deviance $D(\theta) = -2\mathbb{E}_{\mathbf{b},\mathbf{u}}\left\{\log p\left(\mathbf{Y}, \mathbf{b}, \mathbf{u}|\theta, \mathbf{X}, \mathbf{Z}, \mathbf{W}\right)|\mathbf{Y}, \mathbf{X}, \mathbf{Z}, \mathbf{W}\right\}$, $p_D = \overline{D(\theta)} - D\left(\widehat{\theta}\right)$ is a Bayesian measure of model complexity, $\widehat{\theta}$ is the posterior mean of θ . Then, DIC can be simplied as

$$\text{DIC} = 2\overline{D(\theta)} - D\left(\widehat{\theta}\right)$$

$$= -4\mathbb{E}_{\theta,\mathbf{b},\mathbf{u}}\left\{\log p\left(\mathbf{Y}, \mathbf{b}, \mathbf{u}|\theta, \mathbf{X}, \mathbf{Z}, \mathbf{W}\right)|\mathbf{Y}, \mathbf{X}, \mathbf{Z}, \mathbf{W}\right\}$$

$$+ 2\mathbb{E}_{\mathbf{b},\mathbf{u}}\left\{\log p\left(\mathbf{Y}, \mathbf{b}, \mathbf{u}|\widehat{\theta}, \mathbf{X}, \mathbf{Z}, \mathbf{W}\right)|\mathbf{Y}, \mathbf{X}, \mathbf{Z}, \mathbf{W}\right\}.$$

Clearly, the aforementioned expression for DIC involve the complicated expectation algorithm; therefore, we use Monte Carlo method to approximate the estimator for DIC as follows:

$$\widehat{DIC} = -\frac{4}{T}\sum_{t=1}^{T}\log p\left(\mathbf{Y},\mathbf{b}^{(t)},\mathbf{u}^{(t)}|\theta^{(t)},\mathbf{X},\mathbf{Z},\mathbf{W}\right)$$

$$+ \frac{2}{T}\sum_{t=1}^{T}\log p\left(\mathbf{Y},\mathbf{b}^{(t)},\mathbf{u}^{(t)}|\widehat{\theta},\mathbf{X},\mathbf{Z},\mathbf{W}\right).$$

4   Numerical Examples

4.1   Simulation Study

In this simulation study, we suppose that the longitudinal proportional data $y_{ij}(i = 1, 2, \ldots, n, j = 1, \ldots, n_i)$ given skew-normal random effect $\mathbf{b_i}$ follows the simplex distribution, $y_{ij}|\mathbf{b_i} \sim S^{-1}(\mu_{ij}, \sigma_{ij}^2)$. The structure of the mean model and the dispersion model are given by

$$\text{logit}(\mu_{ij}) = x_{1ij}\beta_1 + x_{2ij}\beta_2 + b_i$$

$$\log(\sigma_{ij}^2) = \gamma_1 + x_{2ij}\gamma_2,$$

where discrete covariate x_{1ij} is randomly drawn as $-1, 0, 1$, continuous covariate x_{2ij} is simulated from the uniform distribution $U[0, 1]$, the true values are set as $\beta = (\beta_1, \beta_2)^T = (0.5, 0.5)^T$ and $\gamma = (\gamma_1, \gamma_2)^T = (3, 2)^T$. Also, the random effect $\mathbf{b_i}$ is distributed as the skew-normal distribution, $\mathbf{b_i} \sim SN\left(-\sqrt{2/\pi}\delta, \Sigma, \Delta\right)$, where the true value of the skewness parameter δ is 3 and variance component Σ is 0.6.

In order to investigate the effect of different prior inputs on the Bayesian estimate for parameter, three types of prior information for β and γ are specified by

Type I: $\beta^0 = (0.5, 0.5)^T$, $\mathbf{H}_{\beta 0} = 0.25I_2$, $\gamma^0 = (3, 2)^T$, $\mathbf{H}_{\gamma 0} = 0.25I_2$, $\delta^0 \sim N(0, 1)$, $\mathbf{H}_{\delta 0} = 100$, $\mathbf{R_0} = 2$ and $\rho_0 = 5$, where I_2 stands for 2×2 identity matrix. This scenario represents a good prior information.

Type II: $\beta^0 = 1.5 \times (0.5, 0.5)^T$, $\mathbf{H}_{\beta 0} = 10I_2$, $\gamma^0 = 1.5 \times (3, 2)^T$, $\mathbf{H}_{\gamma 0} = 10I_2$; whilst the other hyperparameter were set to be the same as those given in Type I. This scenario shows an inaccurate prior information.

Type III: $\beta^0 = (0, 0)^T$, $\mathbf{H}_{\beta 0} = 100I_2$, $\gamma^0 = (0, 0)^T$, $\mathbf{H}_{\gamma 0} = 100I_2$. Similarly, the other hyperparameter were set to be the same as those given in Type I. This scenario regards a non-informative prior information.

For the above simulated data sets, we used the preceding proposed hybrid algorithm combining the Gibbs sampler and the Metropolis Hastings algorithm to evaluate the Bayesian estimates of unknown parameter and random effects based on different sample size $n = 50$ and $n = 100$. To monitor convergence of the proposed algorithm, we randomly chose and plotted a mixing process of three Markov chains for unknown parameters via three different starting values in a few test runs. Figure 1 indicated that the traces of three Markov chains for parameters β and γ with three different starting values mix well under type III prior input. Another useful tool for convergence diagnosis is the "estimated potential scale reduction (EPSR)" values obtained from three parallel chains of all the parameters generated with three different starting values in a few test replications. We observed that the EPSR values are less than 1.2 after about 1000 iterations in all test cases and plotted the EPSR values for all unknown parameters against iterations in a randomly selected case in Fig. 2. To be conservative, for each setting, 5000 observations collected after 5000 burn-ins in producing the Bayesian estimate based on 100 replications were reported in Table 1, where 'EST' denotes the mean of the estimates based on 100 replications, 'SD' is the standard deviation of the estimates based on 100 replications, 'RMS' is the root mean square between the estimates based on 100 replications and its true value. Table 1 showed that (i) Bayesian estimates for parameters β and γ are relatively close to the corresponding true values under various prior inputs with different sample size, which implies that the estimates are not sensitive to the prior inputs and sample size in our considered simulation studies; (ii) the skewness parameter δ gave some large deviation with small sample size; whereas the performance of Bayesian estimate for δ is satisfactory as the sample size goes larger; (iii) the values of 'SD' and 'RMS' are quite close, which implies that the estimated standard deviation is rather reliable when the Bias is small.

4.2 A Real Example

We reanalysed the longitudinal proportional data for a prospective ophthalmology study taken from Meyers et al. [7]. The prospective ophthalmology data were analyzed by different authors using various approaches. To compare our proposed approach with the existing approach, we simultaneously considered a normal simplex mixed-effects models with heterogeneous dispersion; that is, $b_i \sim N(0, \Sigma)$. Thus, we called $b_i \sim N(0, \Sigma)$ as the normal approach; whereas $b_i \sim SN_k \left(-\sqrt{2/\pi}\delta, \Sigma, \Delta\right)$ was called as the skewed normal approach in the remainder of this paper. This prospective ophthalmology study described that three gas concentration levels of C_3F_8 were injected into the 31 patients' eye before surgery and percentage of remained gas volume in all patients were recorded at followed-up three to eight times over a 3-month period. We considered the following several variables such as percentage of remained gas volume, gas concentration of C_3F_8, and time for 31 patients. Our scientific interest of this study is to link percentage of remained gas volume with three initial gas concentration levels of C_3F_8 and time while accounting for which covariates lead to heterogeneity. Therefore, following the work of Song et al. [11], the structure of the mean parameter and the dispersion parameter in simplex distribution are modeled by

Table 1. Summary statistics of the estimates in the simulation study.

Type	Parameters	n=50			n=100		
		EST	SD	RMS	EST	SD	RMS
I	β_1	0.4930	0.0938	0.0935	0.4906	0.0571	0.0576
	β_2	0.5011	0.1570	0.1562	0.4848	0.1277	0.1279
	γ_1	2.9988	0.1177	0.1171	3.0028	0.0741	0.0738
	γ_2	1.9618	0.1305	0.1354	1.9713	0.1054	0.1087
	Σ	0.6783	0.2686	0.2785	0.6103	0.2525	0.2515
	δ	2.8102	0.7924	0.8109	3.0093	0.3534	0.3517
II	β_1	0.4882	0.0877	0.0881	0.5024	0.0604	0.0602
	β_2	0.5024	0.2189	0.2178	0.5079	0.1404	0.1399
	γ_1	2.9982	0.1245	0.1239	3.0083	0.0763	0.0764
	γ_2	2.0013	0.1718	0.1709	2.0036	0.1237	0.1232
	Σ	0.6771	0.2645	0.2742	0.6391	0.3218	0.3225
	δ	2.6431	1.0444	1.0987	2.9275	0.4292	0.4332
III	β_1	0.5092	0.1015	0.1014	0.5006	0.0523	0.0520
	β_2	0.5039	0.2047	0.2037	0.4942	0.1534	0.1527
	γ_1	3.0077	0.1161	0.1158	3.0191	0.0803	0.0821
	γ_2	2.0232	0.1696	0.1703	1.9999	0.1165	0.1159
	Σ	0.6617	0.2704	0.2761	0.5838	0.2276	0.2270
	δ	2.7506	0.8660	0.8970	3.0025	0.3035	0.3020

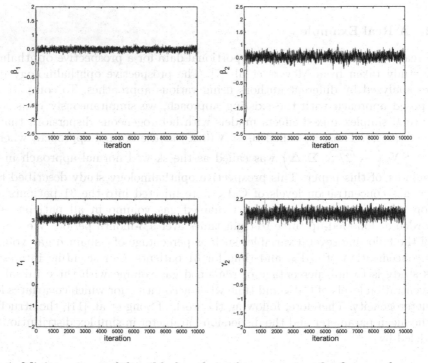

Fig. 1. Mixing process of three Markov chains for parameters β_1, β_2, γ_1 and γ_2 under prior III.

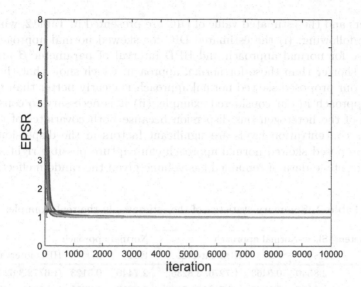

Fig. 2. EPSR values of all parameters against iterations in the simulation study.

$$\begin{cases} y_{ij}|\mathbf{b_i} \sim S^{-1}\left(\mu_{ij}, \sigma_{ij}^2\right) \\ \text{logit}(\mu_{ij}) = \beta_0 + \beta_1 \log(t_{ij}) + \beta_2 \log^2(t_{ij}) + \beta_3 x_{ij} + \mathbf{b_i}, \\ \log(\sigma_{ij}^2) = \gamma_0 + \gamma_1 \log(t_{ij}) + \gamma_2 x_{ij} \\ \mathbf{b_i} \sim SN_k\left(-\sqrt{2/\pi}\delta, \Sigma, \Delta\right) \end{cases} \quad (12)$$

where response y_{ij} denote the jth percentage of remained gas volume for the ith patient at follow-up day t_{ij}, the time covariate t_{ij} is the follow-up day after the C_3F_8 injection, and the discrete covariate x_{ij} are equal to -1, 0 and 1 by transforming the initial gas concentration levels of 15%, 20% and 25%, parameters δ, Σ and Δ involved random effect $\mathbf{b_i}$ are specified by the Definition 1.

The model in Eq. (12) under the skewed normal approach together with the proceeding proposed Bayesian hybrid algorithm was fitted to the data set. To implement the hybrid algorithm, we set the hyperparameters with non-informative prior information in Eq. (5) to be $\beta^0 = 0$, $\mathbf{H}_{\beta 0} = 100I_4$, $\gamma^0 = 0$, $\mathbf{H}_{\gamma 0} = 100I_3$, $\delta^0 \sim N(0,1)$, $\mathbf{H}_{\delta 0} = 100$, $\mathbf{R}_0 = 2$ and $\rho_0 = 5$. In the MH algorithm, we took the tuned variance parameters $\sigma_{b_i}^2 = 18$, $\sigma_\beta^2 = 2$ and $\sigma_\gamma^2 = 2$, which give rise to the average acceptance rates to be 31.8%, 30.5% and 30.7%, respectively. Also, we plotted the "estimated potential scale reduction (EPSR)" values against iterations in Fig. 3 to investigate the convergence of the proposed hybrid. It can be seen from Fig. 3 that the hybrid algorithm converges about 2500 iterations because EPSR values of all unknown parameters were less than 1.2 after about 2500 iterations. Thus, we collected 5000 observations after 5000 burn-ins in producing the Bayesian estimate under the normal approach and skewed normal approach. Bayesian estimates (EST), as well as their standard error (Stderr) and 95% highest posterior density interval (HPD) of the unknown parameters and the estimated value of DIC are presented in Table 2, which indicated the following: (i) the estimated DIC for skewed normal approach is less than those for normal approach and HPD interval of parameter β and γ are generally shorter than those for normal approach, which show that the performance of our proposed skewed normal approach is clearly better than those for normal approach in our considered example; (ii) it is necessary to consider the structure of the heterogeneous dispersion because both covariates of time and initial gas concentration levels are significant factors in the dispersion model; (iii) the proposed skewed normal approach can capture possible right-skewness of the percentage data of remained gas volume given the random effects.

Table 2. Summary statistics of the estimates in the real example.

Parameters	Skew-Normal approach			Normal approach		
	EST	SD	HPD interval	EST	SD	HPD interval
β_0	2.8540	0.5463	[1.7276, 3.8235]	2.7446	0.5123	[1.6772, 3.6224]
β_1	0.3106	0.5983	[−0.7124, 1.7133]	0.3813	0.9255	[−0.5841, 1.8754]
β_2	−0.4273	0.1429	[−0.7321, −0.1594]	−0.4372	0.1519	[−0.7896, −0.2046]
β_2	0.7158	0.3312	[0.0997, 1.3596]	0.5823	0.3107	[0.0187, 1.2538]
γ_0	5.7944	0.2759	[5.2541, 6.2945]	5.8476	0.2726	[5.3070, 6.3328]
γ_1	−0.4789	0.1066	[−0.6859, −0.2835]	−0.4936	0.1105	[−0.7127, −0.2770]
γ_2	−0.5229	0.1750	[−0.8773, −0.1829]	−0.5177	0.1772	[−0.8382, −0.1724]
Σ	0.6494	0.4498	[0.1112, 1.5479]	1.3485	0.5194	[0.5052, 2.3720]
δ	1.0002	1.3245	[−1.8292, 2.7875]	–	–	–
DIC	−4143.5	–	–	−4119.5	–	–

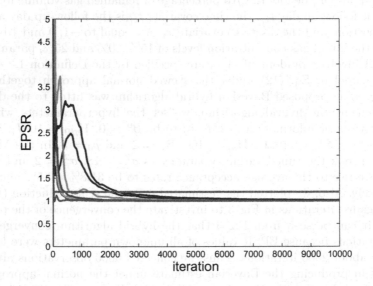

Fig. 3. EPSR values of all parameters against iterations in the real example.

5   Conclusion

This paper proposed a multivariate skew-norml simplex mixed-effects models with heterogeneous dispersion, obtained by incorporating skew-normal random effects into simplex regression model. To conduct Bayesian analysis for the proposed model, a hybrid algorithm combining the Gibbs sampler and the MH algorithm is used to simultaneously obtain Bayesian estimates of unknown parameters as well as their standard errors, random effect, model comparison criteria. Several simulation studies and a real example from a prospective ophthalmology study are used to illustrate the proposed methodologies. Empirical results show that our proposed skew-normal approach performs better than normal approach based on the estimate of HPD interval and DIC (see Table 2).

References

1. Artes, R., Jørgensen, B.: Longitudinal data estimating equations for dispersion models. Scand. J. Stat. **27**(2), 321–334 (2000)
2. Arellano-Valle, R.B., Bolfarine, H., Lachos, V.H.: Bayesian inference for skewnormal linear mixed models. J. Appl. Stat. **34**(6), 663–682 (2007)
3. Bandyopadhyay, D., Galvis, D.M., Lachos, V.H.: Augmented mixed models for clustered proportion data. Stat. Methods Med. Res. **26**(2), 880–897 (2017)
4. Bonat, W.H., Lopes, J.E., Shimakura, S.E., Ribeiro Jr, P.J.: Likelihood analysis for a class of simplex mixed models. Chil. J. Stat. **9**(2), 3–7 (2018)
5. Duan, X.D., Zhao, Y.Y., Tang, A.M.: A semiparametric Bayesian approach to simplex regression model with heterogeneous dispersion. Commun. Stat. Simul. Comput. **48**(8), 2487–2500 (2019)
6. Han, G., Huang, Y.X., Yuan, A.: Bayesian-frequentist hybrid approach for skewnormal nonlinear mixed-effects joint models in the presence of covariates measured with errors. Stat. Interface **11**(2), 223–236 (2018)
7. Meyers, S.M., Ambler, J.S., Tan, M., Werner, J.C., Huang, S.S.: Variation of perfluorpropane disapperance after vitrectomy. Retina **12**(4), 359–363 (1992)
8. Michaelis, P., Klein, N., Kneib, T.: Bayesian multivariate distributional regression with skewed responses and skewed random effects. J. Comput. Graph. Stat. **27**(3), 602–611 (2018)
9. Qiu, Z., Song, P.X.K., Tan, M.: Simplex mixed-effects models for longitudinal proportional data. Scand. J. Stat. **35**(4), 577–596 (2008)
10. Sahu, S.K., Dey, D.K., Branco, M.D.: A new class of multivariate skew distributions with applications to Bayesian regression models. Can. J. Stat. **31**(2), 129–150 (2003)
11. Song, P.X.K., Qiu, Z., Tan, M.: Modelling heterogeneous dispersion in marginal models for longitudinal proportional data. Biometrical J. **46**(5), 540–553 (2004)
12. Song, P.X.K., Tan, M.: Marginal models for longitudinal continuous proportional data. Biometrics **56**(2), 496–502 (2000)
13. Spiegelhalter, D.J., Best, N.G., Carlin, B.P., Van der Linde, A.: Bayesian measures of model complexity and fit. J. Royal Stat. Soc. Ser. B **64**(2), 583–639 (2002)
14. Xing, D.Y., Huang, Y.X., Chen, H.N., Zhu, Y.L., Dagne, G.A., Baldwin, J.: Bayesian inference for two-part mixed-effects model using skew distributions, with application to longitudinal semicontinuous alcohol data. Stat. Methods Med. Res. **26**(4), 1838–1853 (2017)

15. Zhang, H.Z., Huang, Y.X., Wang, W., Chen, H.N., Langland-Orban, B.: Bayesian quantile regression-based partially linear mixed-effects joint models for longitudinal data with multiple features. Stat. Methods Med. Res. **28**(2), 569–588 (2019)
16. Zhang, W.Z., Wei, H.J.: Maximum likelihood estimation for simplex distribution nonlinear mixed models via the stochastic approximation algorithm. Rocky Mountain J. Math. **38**(5), 1863–1875 (2008)
17. Zhao, Y.Y., Xu, D.K., Duan, X.D., Dai, L.: Bayesian estimation of simplex distribution nonlinear mixed models for longitudinal data. Int. J. Appl. Math. Stat. **52**(3), 1–10 (2014)

Multi-radio Relay Frequency Hopping Based on USRP Platforms

Luying Huang(✉), Yitao Xu, Xueqiang Chen, Dianxiong Liu, and Ximing Wang

College of Communications Engineering, Army Engineering University of PLA, Nanjing 210000, China
lgdxwxm@sina.com

Abstract. The wireless relay communication system can realize space diversity, expand the communication range, and increase capacity. The technology of frequency hopping communication helps the relay system randomly hop on multiple channels, which can improve system reliability. At present, most of the research related to relay communication and frequency hopping is based on theoretical analysis and numerical simulations, which can not precisely simulate the channel characteristics of the actual wireless communication environment. According to the decoding and forwarding (DF) relay transmission technology, this paper designs and implements the wireless multi-radio relay frequency hopping transmission system based on the software radio hardware platform USRP. The results show that the system realizes multimedia wireless data communication with a low packet loss rate through relay frequency hopping transmission.

Keywords: Relay communication · Frequency hopping · USRP · LabVIEW

1 Introduction

Complex wireless channel environment seriously affects the reliability and coverage of the signal transmission. Relay communication technologies can effectively increase the coverage, enhance reliability and availability of the communication system, which are widely used in wireless communication systems [1]. After Erlang put forward the basic principles of relay theory, relay technologies have been studied more and more extensively [2]. That is, the received wireless signal from the base station is processed through a series of relay stations and then forwarded. Microwave relay communication is the earliest communication system

This work was supported by the National Natural Science Foundation of China under Grant No. 61771488, No. 61671473 and No. 61631020.

using relay technology. Its carrier wave is microwave, and long-distance radio communication is realized by relay on the ground. If node A and node B are far apart, to achieve communication between them, several relay stations need to be added. After receiving the signal, the relay node amplifies and forwards it to the next relay, and finally realizes the communication between the two places [3]. The forwarding protocols of relay communication mainly include the amplify-and-forward (AF), compress-and-forward (CF) and decode-and-forward (DF) in [4]. The sending node sends the signal to the RN, and the RN simply amplifies the received signal and then forwards it, which is called amplified forwarding [5,6]. Differently, the RN in DF mode will decode and restore the original signal after receiving the signal from the previous node, and then encodes and modulates the signal and forwards it to the next node [7,8]. When the channel quality is poor, the RN with the AF protocol not only amplifies the received signal, but also accumulates noise, which ultimately affects the probability of correct decoding by the destination node. If DF protocol is used, the noise can be well controlled, ensuring the performance of the communication system. Therefore, the DF mode is employed in this paper.

The quality of information transmission is subject to harmful interference. To ensure the unimpeded transmission of information, the communication system needs to have a certain anti-interference ability. Frequency-hopping communication is a type of spread-spectrum communication [9], which is characterized by pseudo-random hopping of the carrier frequency at multiple frequencies and has a certain ability to resist interference.

Universal Software Radio Periphehal (USRP) [10–12] is a very nimble open source hardware device developed by Matt Ettus et al. The USRP works as a digital baseband, RF front-end, and digital intermediate frequency, and the remaining of the signal processing is done by software programming on the computer [13]. LabVIEW is a virtual instrument development software which can be used with USRP, with a flexible user interface and powerful interactivity. Combining USRP with LabVIEW can overcome the limitations of traditional communication experiment simulation methods, such as poor scalability of the curing test chamber and non-objective software simulation results.

In this paper, combining relay cooperative communication and frequency hopping communication, a wireless relay frequency hopping communication system based on USRP platform and LabVIEW software simulation is built. The main contribution of this paper is to achieve fixed sequence frequency hopping transmission from source node (SN) to relay node (RN) and relay node (RN) to destination node (DN), in addition, SN-RN link and R-D link do not interfere with each other. Through relay frequency hopping transmission, wireless communication can resist the attack of traditional interference, expand the scope of communication.

The remaining of the paper is arranged as follows. In Sect. 2, physical layer and data frame structure design are investigated. Section 3 is the system construction and the introduction of related functional modules. Section 4 introduces the design principles and system implementation of relay frequency hopping transmission. In Sect. 5, the experimental results are given. Finally, the paper is concluded in Sect. 6.

2 Related Works

The authors in [14] implemented a single relay wireless transmission system based on USRP and GNU Radio. The authors in [15] implemented a multi-relay wireless transmission system based on USRP and GNU Radio. However, the existing work [14,15] mainly focused on the construction of relay system, while communication protocol was not discussed, as well as the multi-channel model. In [18], a concept proof of LTE DF RN using two SDRs was proposed. In [19], a cooperative communication system experimental platform based on NI USRP2920 was proposed. The implemented experiments included voice communications and video streaming by GMSK modulation transmission to develop the cooperative advantages of multimedia communication. In [20], the authors used LabVIEW and USRP as the experimental platform. The three nodes cooperative communication based on amplifying and forwarding was simulated, and the system performance was analyzed by turning the system time slot settings by software.

Different from them, this paper combines wireless relay technology and frequency hopping technology to achieve picture transmission, based on the software radio platform USRP and software platform LabVIEW. The results show that the system can realize relay frequency hopping transmission with low packet loss rate.

3 General Design of Relay System

The designed wireless relay frequency hopping communication system is shown in Fig. 1. The system is mainly composed of one SN, one RN and one DN. The SN and DN are composed of a PC and a NI USRP2920, respectively. The RN is simulated by one PC, one switch and two NI USRP2920. The system consists of four transmission links, which are two data links and two ACK transmission links. Two data links include the data link f_{sr} from SN to RN, and the data link f_{rd} from RN to DN. Two ACK transmission links include an ACK link f_{ack}^{rs} from RN to SN and an ACK link f_{ack}^{dr} from DN to RN.

Before the experiment, the system framework of the experiment is introduced. The hardware of the experimental system in this paper mainly includes NI USRP 2920, supporting antenna, switch and computers. The software platform adopts LabVIEW visual simulation programming environment. LabVIEW is a virtual instrument development software that can be used with USRP, with flexible user interface and strong interactivity.

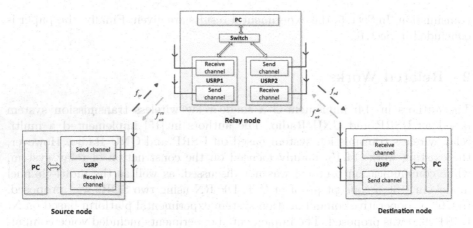

Fig. 1. USRP-based wireless relay frequency hopping system framework.

3.1   System Physical Layer Design

In the LabVIEW software platform, most modulation methods, such as FSK, BPSK, QAM, GMSK, etc., have corresponding modules and corresponding demodulation module. This experiment uses QPSK for modulation and demodulation to ensure transmission reliability.

3.2   Data Frame Structure Design

In order to make sure the accuracy of the received data, we need to design the frame format of the data. In this system, the sender performs equal-length splitting, framing, and encapsulation of the data bit stream to form a data bit packet for modulation transmission. The encapsulation frame format is shown in Table 1. The definition of each data field function is shown in Table 2.

Table 1. Encapsulated frame format.

Protection bit	Sync bit	Message type	Data frequency	ACK frequency	Package number	Data bit	Check bit	Padding

Frame synchronization is extremely important for the receiver correctly receiving data. Only when the sender and the receiver have achieved frame synchronization can they correctly distinguish the starting position of the data frame during reception and receive valid data. In a wireless communication system, data is inevitably subject to errors during transmission due to various adverse factors. Hence, data are detected and corrected, then the upper layers can transmit more reliably. Error detection codes do not correct transmission errors, but can increase transmission reliability and effectiveness. CRC (Cyclic

Table 2. Frame format function.

Data field	Number of bits	Function
Protection bit	30	Allows the automatic gain control module to reach a steady state quickly before processing useful data
Sync bit	30	Generate a 30-bit random sequence using a PN sequence generator for easy frame synchronization
Message type	8	0000 0000 represents data; 0000 0001 represents ACK
Data frequency	32	Data transmission channel
ACK frequency	32	ACK transmission channel
Package number	32	Received packet sequence number
Data bit	1024	Service data bit length in each frame, which can be set by the user
Check bit	16	CRC check the data
Padding	30	Used to eliminate filter effects

Redundancy Check) is an error check code that is often used in the field of data communications to detect or verify data transmission. The verification method used in this experiment is CRC-16 [16].

4   System Construction and Function Modules

4.1   System Construction

The NI USRP2920 has two antennas, TX/RX1 and RX2. TX/RX1 can be used to send and receive signals, and RX2 can only be used to receive signals. In the wireless relay frequency hopping transmission communication system, because the SN and the DN both need to send and receive information, the SN and the DN are composed of one PC and one NI USRP2920, respectively. The RN is relatively complicated which needs to receive the data information of the SN and forwards the data processing to the DN, at the same time initiates a frequency change request to the SN and receive the frequency change request initiated by the DN. It can be seen that the RN needs two transmissions and two receptions, so the RN needs to be composed of a PC, a switch, and two NI USRP2920. Figure 2 shows a schematic diagram of the experimental system in this paper.

4.2   Function Modules

The experimental system in this paper is composed of three nodes. In general, the design of RN is relatively complicated, two receptions and two transmissions

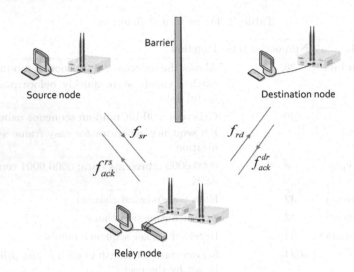

Fig. 2. Experimental system diagram.

are required. To improve the development efficiency of the system, the SN and the DN can be selected to implement the corresponding functions of the RN.

The RN can be divided into two major blocks, the receiving module and the sending module. Among them, the receiving module is further divided into data receiving and ACK receiving, the sending module is further divided into sending data module and sending ACK module. The design of sending and receiving data and ACK are different except for the frame structure design, the other designs are the same, hence the processing flow of the transmitting module and receiving module of the node are introduced here.

At the transmitting end of the node, the service to be transmitted is first converted into a binary bit stream. According to the designed data frame format, the binary data bit stream is grouped into several data packets of the same length. The digital baseband signals are obtained through raised cosine filtering and QPSK modulation, and finally written into USRP through the Ethernet port and transmitted through the antenna.

On the receiving end of the node, the USRP obtains the baseband signal through the receiving antenna and reads it into the PC. The data processing process is completed with LabVIEW program. First, the received baseband signal is separated according to the packet (remove DC component, the correspongding position of each packet is detected by correlation operation, and the data packet is separated), then the extracted data packet is resampled and QPSK demodulated to obtain a binary bit stream. After the serial validity check (CRC check and frame synchronization check), the correctly received data packets are reconstructed and converted into a format to restore the original data information [17].

5 Principle and Implementation of Relay Frequency Hopping Transmission System

5.1 Design Principles of Relay Frequency Hopping

In actual wireless communication, comprehensive coverage is sought. For remote areas, the coverage of the cell is limited and severely affected by shadow fading. Relay communication technology can effectively conquer the fading of wireless channels and increase spectrum efficiency and communication range. The basic concept of wireless relay technology is to add a RN between a SN and a DN. The RN receives the signal from the SN and forwards it to the DN after a certain processing. Generally, in a wireless single-relay network, there are three communication links, namely SN-DN, SN-RN, and RN-DN. In this experimental system, the SN-DN link is not considered.

The handling of the received signal by the RN is diverse. Wireless repeater technology is divided into two categories, AF and DF. AF: After receiving the signal from the SN, the RN simply amplifies the signal and forwards it. DF: The RN decodes and demodulates the received signal to recover the original signal, then encodes and modulates the recovered signal to the DN. In this experiment, the RN uses DF.

The interaction procedure among SN, RN and DN in wireless relay frequency hopping transmission communication system is shown in the Fig. 3. The steps of wireless relay frequency hopping transmission are analyzed as follows:

Step 1: The SN sends data to the RN on the channel f_{sr} and receives ACK signal sent by the RN on the channel f_{ack}^{rs}, and reconfigures the transmission carrier frequency f_{sr} after receipting the ACK signal.

Step 2: The RN receives data on the channel f_{sr}, decodes and forwards it, and sends the data to the DN on the channel f_{rd}; after a time interval Tr, initiates a frequency change request, sends an ACK to the SN on the channel f_{ack}^{rs}, and reconfigures the RN receive the carrier frequency f_{sr}. At the same time receive the ACK signal sent by the DN on the channel f_{uck}^{dr}, and reconfigure the transmit carrier frequency f_{rd} after receiving the ACK signal.

Step 3: The DN receives data information on the channel f_{rd}. After a time interval Td, initiates a frequency change request, sends an ACK to the RN on the channel f_{ack}^{dr}, and reconfigure the receive carrier frequency f_{rd} of the DN.

5.2 System Implementation

Based on the above design analysis, a physical simulation system was built based on the USRP software radio platform and LabVIEW software. The system consists of 3 computers, 4 NI USRP2920, and 1 switch. The computer and USRP are connected through a Gigabit Ethernet port, which simulates the SN, RN, and DN.

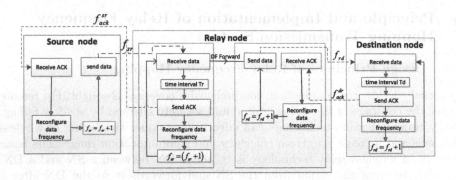

Fig. 3. Experimental flow chart.

The test steps of the system are as follows:

(1) Connect the USRP and the computer;
(2) Configure system related parameters (such as I/Q rate, carrier frequency, antenna, gain, modulation method, frequency hopping interval, frequency hopping range, frequency hopping time interval, etc.) on the front panel of the program, as shown in the Table 3;
(3) Power on the USRP and run the SN, RN, and DN programs at the same time for data transmission.

Table 3. Related parameter configuration.

Related parameters	Value
S-R Frequency range	800 MHz~845 MHz
R-D Frequency range	915 MHz~960 MHz
Frequency interval	5MHz
S-R frequency hopping interval	3s
R-D frequency hopping interval	3s
Number of channels	10
Antenna gain	10 dB
S-R data I/Q rate	1M Sample/s
R-D data I/Q rate	800K Sample/s
I/Q rate of R-S ACK	400K Sample/s
I/Q rate of D-R ACK	400K Sample/s
Modulation	QPSK
R-S ACK frequency	750 MHz
D-R ACK frequency	500 MHz

6 Physical Test Results

During the system test, the SN selects a 400k image and sends it to the RN. The front panel operation interface of the SN is shown in Fig. 4, where module 1 is a modulation transmission constellation diagram, module 2 is a time domain waveform diagram of a transmission signal; module 3 is an access frequency point of each time slot, and module 4 is a picture to be transmitted. The access frequency sequence is obtained by the ACK of the RN. The set of available frequencies is {800 MHz, 805 MHz, 810 MHz, 815 MHz, 820 MHz, 825 MHz, 830 MHz, 835 MHz, 840 MHz, 845 MHz}. It can be seen from the Fig. 4. that the modulation method is QPSK.

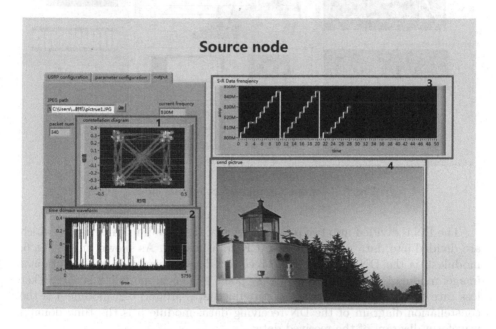

Fig. 4. User operation interface of source node.

The system RN uses the decoding and forwarding (DF) method to re-encode the received data information and send it to the DN. The RN is divided into four parts in terms of function realization, data reception and transmission, and ACK transmission and reception. The front panel operation interface of the RN is displaied in Fig. 5. In Fig. 5, module 1 is the frequency hopping sequence from the SN to the RN, module 2 is the packet loss rate of the RN receiving data, module 7 is the constellation diagram of the RN receiving data, module 8 is the time-domain waveform diagram of the RN receiving data, module 3 is the frequency hopping sequence from the RN to the DN, available frequency points are {915 MHz, 920 MHz, 925 MHz, 930 MHz, 935 MHz, 940 MHz, 945 MHz, 950 MHz, 955 MHz, 960 MHz}, module 5 is the constellation diagram and time domain waveform diagram of the RN sending data to the DN, module 6 is a constellation diagram for sending ACK to the SN and a time-domain waveform diagram for sending ACK information, module 4 is the original picture recovered by the RN. It can be seen from the picture that there is a packet loss phenomenon. There is a time lag between the SN and the RN during each frequency change, resulting in a small amount of packet loss during the frequency change, the packet loss rate floating around 0.1.

Fig. 5. User operation interface of relay node.

The DN is divided into two parts in terms of function implementation, which are divided into data reception and ACK transmission. As shown in the Fig. 6, module 3 is the DN to restore the received data information to the original image, module 1 is the access frequency point sequence, module 2 is the packet loss rate of the DN, the packet loss rate fluctuates around 0.2, module 4 is the constellation diagram of the DN receiving data, module 5 is the time domain waveform diagram of the received data.

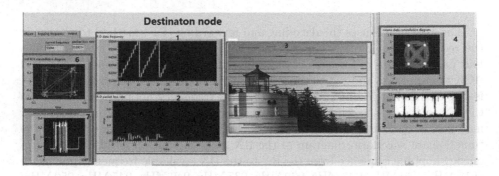

Fig. 6. User operation interface of destination node.

7 Conclusions

This paper makes full use of the reconfigurable, flexible and easy to operate characteristics of the NI USRP software radio platform to build a wireless relay frequency hopping communication transmission system. After many experiments, the system runs stably reliable, and packet loss rate is also within a certain range. On the basis of this article, the next step is to consider the existence of interference, and implement intelligent relay frequency hopping anti-interference combined with reinforcement learning.

References

1. Gouissem, A., Hasna, M.O., Hamila R., et al.: Outage performance of ofdm ad-hoc routing with and without subcarrier grouping in multihop network. In: IEEE Vehicular Technology Conference (VTC Fall) IEEE, vol. 2012, pp. 1–5 (2012)
2. Laneman, J.N., Tse, D.N.C., Wornell, G.W.: Cooperative diversity in wireless networks: efficient protocols and outage behavior. IEEE Trans. Inf. Theory **50**(12), 3062–3080 (2004)
3. Chau, Y.A., Huang, K.Y.: Channel statistics and performance of cooperative selection diversity with dual-hop amplify-and-forward relay over Rayleigh fading channels. IEEE Trans. Wireless Commun. **7**(5), 1779–1785 (2008)
4. Lee, D., Kim, S.I., Lee, J., et al.: Performance of multihop decode-and-forward relaying assisted device-to-device communication underlaying cellular networks. In: 2012 International Symposium on Information Theory and its Applications. IEEE, pp. 455–459 (2012)
5. Krikidis, I., Thompson, J., McLaughlin, S., et al.: Amplify-and-forward with partial relay selection. IEEE Commun. Lett. **12**(4), 235–237 (2008)
6. Hwang, K.S., Ko, Y.C., Alouini, M.S.: Performance analysis of two-way amplify and forward relaying with adaptive modulation over multiple relay network. IEEE Trans. Commun. **59**(2), 402–406 (2010)
7. Luo, J., Blum, R.S., Cimini, L.J., et al.: Decode-and-forward cooperative diversity with power allocation in wireless networks. IEEE Trans. Wireless Commun. **6**(3), 793–799 (2007)
8. Mills, D.G., Edelson, G.S., Egnor, D.E.: A multiple access differential frequency hopping system. In: IEEE Military Communications Conference, MILCOM 2003. IEEE 2003, vol. 2, pp. 1184–1189 (2003)
9. Sendonaris, A., Erkip, E., Aazhang, B.: Increasing uplink capacity via user cooperation diversity. In: Proceedings. 1998 IEEE International Symposium on Information Theory (Cat. No. 98CH36252). IEEE, p. 156 (1998)
10. Abirami, M., Hariharan, V., Sruthi, M.B, et al.: Exploiting GNU radio and USRP: an economical test bed for real time communication systems. In: 2013 fourth international conference on computing, communications and networking technologies (ICCCNT). IEEE, pp. 1–6 (2013)
11. Ettus, M.: Universal software radio peripheral (USRP). Ettus Research LLC http://www.ettus.com (2008)
12. Tong, Z., Arifianto, M.S, Liau, C.F.: Wireless transmission using universal software radio peripheral. In: 2009 International Conference on Space Science and Communication. IEEE, pp. 19–23 (2009)

13. Xin, X., Hui, Z.: Design of experimental platform for wireless communication based on LabVIEW and USRP. Experimental Technology and Management, vol. 33 (2016)
14. Bo, F.: Experimental Study of Wireless Relay Transmission Based on USRP Platform (2019)
15. Xiaofang, Y.: Experimental Study of Wireless Multi-relay Transmission Based on USRP Platform (2018)
16. Keller, R.B.: Fast cyclic redundancy check (CRC) generation: U.S. Patent 6,701,479[P]. 2004-3-2 (2004)
17. Lijun, K., Yuhua, X., Xueqiang, C., et al.: design and implementation of data transmission system based on USRP and selective retransmission protocol. Commun. Technol. **51**, 1259–1267 (2018)
18. MarGarc, J.A., Romero-Franco, C., Alonso, J.I.: A software defined radio platform for decode and forward relay nodes implementation. In: 2019 IEEE Conference on Standards for Communications and Networking (CSCN), pp. 1–4 (2019) https://doi.org/10.1109/CSCN.2019.8931410
19. Prince, A., Abdalla, A.E., Dahshan, H., Rohiem, A.E.D.: Multimedia SDR-based cooperative communication. In: 2018 13th International Conference on Computer Engineering and Systems (ICCES), Cairo, Egypt, pp. 381–386 (2018) https://doi.org/10.1109/ICCES.2018.8639312
20. Yu, Z., Luo, H., Li, L., Zhang, Y., Han, Z.: Research on the influence of system slot setting on the performance of three-node cooperative communication system. In: IEEE 3rd Information Technology, Networking, Electronic and Automation Control Conference (ITNEC). Chengdu, China, vol. 2019, pp. 368–371 (2019). https://doi.org/10.1109/ITNEC.2019.8729297

Progressive Iterative Approximation of SOR for Non-uniform Cubic B-spline Curve and Surface Interpolation

Liangchen Hu[1] (ID), Huahao Shou[1]([⊠]) (ID), and Shiaofen Fang[2] (ID)

[1] College of Science, Zhejiang University of Technology, Hangzhou, Zhejiang, China
shh@zjut.edu.cn

[2] Department of Computer and Information Science, Indiana University-Purdue University Indianapolis, Indianapolis, IN, USA

Abstract. Progressive iterative approximation (PIA) is an efficient data fitting technique which makes the initial curve or surface approximate the data points to be processed by successive iterations. However, since the spectral radius of iterative matrix in traditional PIA is relatively large, the iterative convergence rate is relatively slow, which results in poor efficiency of data fitting. In this paper, we develop a successive over-relaxation progressive iterative approximation (SOR-PIA) for non-uniform cubic B-splines to overcome the defect. Besides, we employ the equidistant search strategy to estimate the relaxation factor, which greatly accelerates the convergence speed of the iterative process. Experimental results show that SOR-PIA iterative interpolation can achieve a higher accuracy within the equivalent number of iterations compared with the standard PIA and weighted PIA (WPIA) iterative interpolation.

Keywords: B-spline interpolation · Progressive iterative approximation · Successive over-relaxation · Iterative acceleration

1 Introduction

Data fitting is a crucial basic task of modeling and forecasting, which is widely employed in various fields. In fact, there have been many innovations and improvements in data fitting technology, among which PIA plays an important role due to its many satisfactory features. As a geometrically intuitive approach, PIA takes given data points as initial control points and dynamically updates them in a certain direction. PIA method has a broad application prospect, and it is of great significance to find a new fast iterative method for its applications.

In 2004, Lin proved the property of profit-and-loss for non-uniform cubic B-spline curve and surface [1], and for blending curves and tensor product blending patches with normalized totally positive basis in 2005 [2]. The approach proposed in [2] is called progressive iterative approximation (PIA), which addresses

Supported by the National Science Foundation of China (No. 61572430).

H. Song and D. Jiang (Eds.): SIMUtools 2020, LNICST 369, pp. 339–349, 2021.
https://doi.org/10.1007/978-3-030-72792-5_29

both interpolation and approximation (including EPIA [3] and LSPIA [4,10,11]). On the problem of iterative acceleration of PIA, Lu [5] derived the optimal iteration weights for the best convergence speed, and named it as WPIA. For large scale data fitting problems, Lin proposed the LSPIA algorithm using T-splines [6]. PIA has also been applied for hexahedral mesh generation in finite element analysis [7]. Since the iteration speed is independent of the number of control points in LSPIA, it provides a robust and efficient solution for the equation system of a tetrahedral mesh for an ideal NURBS body[1][8]. In [9], the method of how to determine fewer control points in the least square fitting is also considered, which improves the fitting efficiency. PIA has also been used in satellite image processing, pattern recognition, hand drawn curve approximation, rational curve approximation, and tree trunk shape modeling. Recently, Lin et al. [12] provided an overview of the interpolatory and approximate geometric iteration methods, including PIA, geometric iteration and so on, and summarized that geometric iterative methods have wide applications in academic studies and engineering practices. The above improvements have a common property that the spectral radii of their iterative matrices are essentially at the same level, limiting their performance. Inspired by this, we proposed an efficient progressive iterative approximation algorithm based on HSS iteration in [13], whose spectral radius is much smaller than PIA. The contributions of our paper can be summarized as follows. Innovatively, we develop a SOR-PIA technique for non-uniform cubic B-spline curve and surface interpolation. Besides, we employ the equidistant search strategy to estimate the relaxation factor.

The rest of the paper is organized as follows. Section 2 reviews the standard iterative non-uniform B-spline curve and surface and presents a simple analysis of the relationship between the standard iterative format and directly solving equation system. The successive over-relaxation iteration method is introduced in Sect. 3 for solving the iterative interpolation problem, including the equidistant search strategy to make approximate computation for the best relaxation factor and to accelerate the convergence speed. The results of our numerical experiments are presented in Sect. 4. Section 5 concludes the paper with some additional summary.

2   Standard Iterative Interpolation and Its Analysis

2.1   Iterative Format of Curve

Given a set of data points list $\{Q_i\}_{i=1}^m$, the accumulative chord length parameterization method can be used to calculate the parameter values $\{u_i\}_{i=1}^m$ on the initial iteration curve corresponding to the data points. Cubic non-uniform B-spline basis function is defined by the knot vector $\{0\ 0\ 0\ 0\ u_2\ u_3\ \cdots\ u_{m-1}$ $1\ 1\ 1\ 1\}$, whose interior knots are the parameter values.

Let $P_i^0 = Q_i, i = 1, \cdots, m$, $P_0^0 = P_1^0$, $P_{m+1}^0 = P_m^0$, the initial iterative interpolation curve $C^0(u) = \sum_{i=0}^{m+1} P_i^0 N_{i,3}(u)$ can be constructed. Assuming

---

[1] The NURBS body, or NURBS solid, refers to a NURBS-based CAD model.

that the maximum number of iterations is N, the curve iterative formula is

$$\boldsymbol{P}_i^k = \boldsymbol{P}_i^{k-1} + \boldsymbol{\Delta}_i^{k-1}, i = 1, \cdots, m; k = 1, \cdots, N, \tag{1}$$

in which, the difference vector is calculated as

$$\boldsymbol{\Delta}_i^{k-1} = \boldsymbol{Q}_i - \boldsymbol{C}^{k-1}(u_i), i = 1, \cdots, m; k = 1, \cdots, N,$$

and $\boldsymbol{P}_0^k = \boldsymbol{P}_1^k$, $\boldsymbol{P}_{m+1}^k = \boldsymbol{P}_m^k$. The Eq. (1) can be rewritten in matrix form as follows

$$\boldsymbol{P}^k = (\boldsymbol{I} - \boldsymbol{N})\boldsymbol{P}^{k-1} + \boldsymbol{Q},$$

where $\boldsymbol{I}$ is unit matrix,

$$\boldsymbol{N} = \begin{pmatrix} \overset{1}{N_{1,3}(u_2)} & N_{2,3}(u_2) & N_{3,3}(u_2) & \\ & \ddots & & \ddots & \\ & & N_{m-2,3}(u_{m-1}) & N_{m-1,3}(u_{m-1}) & \underset{1}{N_{m,3}(u_{m-1})} \end{pmatrix},$$

and $\boldsymbol{P}^k = (\boldsymbol{P}_1^k, \boldsymbol{P}_2^k, \cdots, \boldsymbol{P}_m^k)^T$, $\boldsymbol{Q} = (\boldsymbol{Q}_1, \boldsymbol{Q}_2, \cdots, \boldsymbol{Q}_m)^T$.

2.2 Iterative Format of Surface

Given a set of data matrix $\{\boldsymbol{Q}_{i,j}\}_{i=1,j=1}^{m,n}$, the cumulative chord length parameterization method can be used to calculate the parameter values $\{u_i, v_j\}_{i=1,j=1}^{m,n}$ on the initial iteration surface corresponding to the data points. Bi-cubic non-uniform B-spline basis functions are defined respectively by the knot vectors $\{0\ 0\ 0\ 0\ u_2\ u_3\ \cdots\ u_{m-1}\ 1\ 1\ 1\ 1\}$ and $\{0\ 0\ 0\ 0\ v_2\ v_3\ \cdots\ v_{n-1}\ 1\ 1\ 1\ 1\}$, whose interior knots are the parameter values.

Let $\boldsymbol{P}_{i,j}^0 = \boldsymbol{Q}_{i,j}$, $\boldsymbol{P}_{i,0}^0 = \boldsymbol{P}_{i,1}^0$, $\boldsymbol{P}_{i,n+1}^0 = \boldsymbol{P}_{i,n}^0$, $\boldsymbol{P}_{0,j}^0 = \boldsymbol{P}_{1,j}^0$, $\boldsymbol{P}_{m+1,j}^0 = \boldsymbol{P}_{m,j}^0$, $i = 1, \cdots, m, j = 1, \cdots, n$; $\boldsymbol{P}_{0,0}^0 = \boldsymbol{P}_{1,1}^0$, $\boldsymbol{P}_{0,n+1}^0 = \boldsymbol{P}_{1,n}^0$, $\boldsymbol{P}_{m+1,0}^0 = \boldsymbol{P}_{m,1}^0$, $\boldsymbol{P}_{m+1,n+1}^0 = \boldsymbol{P}_{m,n}^0$, the bi-cubic initial iterative interpolation tensor product surface $\boldsymbol{C}^0(u, v) = \sum_{i=0}^{m+1} \sum_{j=0}^{n+1} \boldsymbol{P}_{i,j}^0 N_{i,3}(u) N_{j,3}(v)$ can be constructed. Suppose the maximum number of iterations is N, then the surface iterative formula is

$$\boldsymbol{P}_{i,j}^k = \boldsymbol{P}_{i,j}^{k-1} + \boldsymbol{\Delta}_{i,j}^{k-1}, i = 1, \cdots, m; j = 1, \cdots, n; k = 1, \cdots, N, \tag{2}$$

where the difference vector is calculated as

$$\boldsymbol{\Delta}_{i,j}^{k-1} = (\boldsymbol{Q}_{i,j} - \boldsymbol{C}^{k-1}(u_i, v_j)), i = 1, \cdots, m; j = 1, \cdots, n; k = 1, \cdots, N,$$

and $\boldsymbol{P}_{i,0}^k = \boldsymbol{P}_{i,1}^k$, $\boldsymbol{P}_{i,n+1}^k = \boldsymbol{P}_{i,n}^k$, $\boldsymbol{P}_{0,j}^k = \boldsymbol{P}_{1,j}^k$, $\boldsymbol{P}_{m+1,j}^k = \boldsymbol{P}_{m,j}^k$, $i = 1, \cdots, m, j = 1, \cdots, n$; $\boldsymbol{P}_{0,0}^k = \boldsymbol{P}_{1,1}^k$, $\boldsymbol{P}_{0,n+1}^k = \boldsymbol{P}_{1,n}^k$, $\boldsymbol{P}_{m+1,0}^k = \boldsymbol{P}_{m,1}^k$, $\boldsymbol{P}_{m+1,n+1}^k = \boldsymbol{P}_{m,n}^k$.

Similar to the case of curve iteration, the Eq. (2) can be rewritten in matrix form as follows

$$\boldsymbol{P}^k = (\boldsymbol{I} - \boldsymbol{N})\boldsymbol{P}^{k-1} + \boldsymbol{Q},$$

where I is unit matrix, $N = N_1 \otimes N_2$ is the Kronecker product between N_1 and N_2,

$$N_1 = \begin{pmatrix} \overset{1}{N_{1,3}(u_2)} & N_{2,3}(u_2) & N_{3,3}(u_2) & \\ & \ddots & \ddots & \\ & & N_{m-2,3}(u_{m-1}) & N_{m-1,3}(u_{m-1}) & \underset{1}{N_{m,3}(u_{m-1})} \end{pmatrix},$$

$$N_2 = \begin{pmatrix} \overset{1}{N_{1,3}(v_2)} & N_{2,3}(v_2) & N_{3,3}(v_2) & \\ & \ddots & \ddots & \\ & & N_{n-2,3}(v_{n-1}) & N_{n-1,3}(v_{n-1}) & \underset{1}{N_{n,3}(v_{n-1})} \end{pmatrix},$$

and

$$P^k = (P_{1,1}^k, P_{1,2}^k, \cdots, P_{1,n}^k, P_{2,1}^k, P_{2,2}^k, \cdots, P_{2,n}^k, \cdots, P_{m,1}^k, P_{m,2}^k, \cdots, P_{m,n}^k),$$
$$Q^k = (Q_{1,1}^k, Q_{1,2}^k, \cdots, Q_{1,n}^k, Q_{2,1}^k, Q_{2,2}^k, \cdots, Q_{2,n}^k, \cdots, Q_{m,1}^k, Q_{m,2}^k, \cdots, Q_{m,n}^k).$$

2.3 Analysis of Standard Iterative Interpolation

Remark 1. The standard iteration format of non-uniform B-spline curve and surface can be seen as an iterative matrix decomposition $N = I - (I - N)$ from N, so that

$$NP = (I - (I - N))P = Q$$
$$\Downarrow$$
$$P = (I - N)P + Q.$$

If an initial vector P^0 is substituted into the right-hand side of above formula, we can calculate a new vector $P^1 = (I - N)P^0 + Q$. When P^1 is substituted into the right-hand side of the formula, we will get P^2, and so on. As this process continues, we have $P^k = (I - N)P^{k-1} + Q, k = 1, 2, \cdots$. The coefficient matrix for this iterative process is: $(I - N)$.

Lemma 1. *Standard iterative format of the non-uniform B-spline curve and surface is convergent.*

Proof. Details are referred to Ref. [1].

Theorem 1. *The standard iterative interpolation for non-uniform B-spline curve and surface is an iterative method for solving linear equations system.*

Proof. For the iterative interpolation of curve or surface, we know from Remark 1 as follows

$$P^k = (I - N)P^{k-1} + Q, k = 1, 2, \cdots.$$

We take limit to the above formula on both sides, then

$$\lim_{k \to \infty} P^k = (I - N) \lim_{k \to \infty} P^{k-1} + Q. \tag{3}$$

By Lemma 1, we know the sequence of data points is convergent, suppose $\lim_{k\to\infty} \boldsymbol{P}^k = \boldsymbol{P}$, then Eq. (3) can be written as $\boldsymbol{NP} = \boldsymbol{Q}$, which is the equation system of non-uniform B-spline curve or surface interpolation. Thus, the standard iterative interpolation for non-uniform B-spline curve and surface is actually an iterative method for solving linear equations system.

3   The Derivation of SOR-PIA

In this section, we introduce the successive over-relaxation iteration for non-uniform B-spline curve and surface interpolation. Compared with the standard iteration interpolation method PIA [1,2], successive over-relaxation iteration has a significant reduction of iterative steps for the iteration process.

3.1   The Case of Curve

Maintain the same conditions as the standard iteration such as the size of the data points, the parameterization of the data points, the value of the knot vector, the initial values of the control vertices. Using $\boldsymbol{P}_1^k, \boldsymbol{P}_2^k, \cdots, \boldsymbol{P}_{i-1}^k$ that has been calculated before $\boldsymbol{P}_i^k$ to participate in the calculation of $\boldsymbol{P}_i^k$ in the standard iteration process for non-uniform B-spline curve interpolation, then the iteration curve $\boldsymbol{C}^{k-1}(u) = \sum_{p=0}^{m+1} \boldsymbol{P}_p^{k-1} N_{p,3}(u)$ can be replaced by $\boldsymbol{C}^{k,k-1}(u) = \sum_{p=0}^{i-1} \boldsymbol{P}_p^k N_{p,3}(u) + \sum_{p=i}^{m+1} \boldsymbol{P}_p^{k-1} N_{p,3}(u)$, and iterative format of curve can be written as follows

$$\boldsymbol{P}_i^k = \boldsymbol{P}_i^{k-1} + \boldsymbol{\Delta}_i^{k,k-1}, i = 1, \cdots, m; k = 1, 2, \cdots, \tag{4}$$

where the difference vector is calculated as

$$\boldsymbol{\Delta}_i^{k,k-1} = \boldsymbol{Q}_i - \boldsymbol{C}^{k,k-1}(u_i), i = 1, \cdots, m; k = 1, 2, \cdots.$$

Then we make an improvement on the Eq. (4) by adding a weight $\frac{\omega}{N_{i,3}(u_i)}$ to the iterative difference vector as follows

$$\boldsymbol{P}_i^k = \boldsymbol{P}_i^{k-1} + \frac{\omega}{N_{i,3}(u_i)} \boldsymbol{\Delta}_i^{k,k-1}, i = 1, \cdots, m; k = 1, 2, \cdots. \tag{5}$$

The iterative process expressed in Eq. (5) is progressive iterative approximation format of successive over-relaxation for non-uniform B-spline curve interpolation called SOR-PIA of curve. Its difference from the traditional PIA is that it uses $\boldsymbol{P}_1^k, \boldsymbol{P}_2^k, \cdots, \boldsymbol{P}_{i-1}^k$ that has been calculated before $\boldsymbol{P}_i^k$ to participate in the calculation of $\boldsymbol{P}_i^k$ and adds a weight $\frac{\omega}{N_{i,3}(u_i)}$ which includes a relaxation factor ω in iterative difference vector.

Rewrite the Eq. (5) as follows

$$\boldsymbol{P}_i^k = \boldsymbol{P}_i^{k-1} + \frac{\omega}{N_{i,3}(u_i)} \boldsymbol{\Delta}_i^{k,k-1} = \boldsymbol{P}_i^{k-1} + \frac{\omega(\boldsymbol{Q}_i - \boldsymbol{C}^{k,k-1}(u_i))}{N_{i,3}(u_i)}$$

$$= (1 - \omega)\boldsymbol{P}_i^{k-1} + \omega \frac{\boldsymbol{Q}_i - \boldsymbol{P}_{i-1}^k N_{i-1,3}(u_i) - \boldsymbol{P}_{i+1}^k N_{i+1,3}(u_i)}{N_{i,3}(u_i)},$$

therefore the Eq. (5) can be written in matrix form

$$P^k = (1 - \omega)P^{k-1} + \omega D^{-1}\left(Q - LP^k - UP^{k-1}\right), k = 1, 2, \cdots,$$

in which, $D + L + U = N$, where D is a diagonal matrix, L is a strictly lower triangular matrix, U is a strictly upper triangular matrix.

3.2 The Case of Surface

Similar to the case of curve. Using $P^k_{1,1}, \cdots, P^k_{1,j}, P^k_{2,1}, \cdots, P^k_{2,j}, \cdots, P^k_{i-1,1}, \cdots, P^k_{i-1,j}, P^k_{i,1}, \cdots, P^k_{i,j-1}$ that has been calculated before $P^k_{i,j}$ to participate in the calculation of $P^k_{i,j}$ in the standard iteration process for non-uniform B-spline surface interpolation, then the iteration surface $C^{k-1}(u,v) = \sum_{p=0}^{m+1}\sum_{q=0}^{n+1} P^{k-1}_{p,q} N_{p,3}(u)N_{q,3}(v)$ can be replaced by $C^{k,k-1}(u,v) = \sum_{p=0}^{i-1}\sum_{q=0}^{n+1} P^k_{p,q}N_{p,3}(u)N_{q,3}(v) + \sum_{q=0}^{j-1} P^k_{i,q}N_{i,3}(u)N_{q,3}(v) + \sum_{q=j}^{n+1} P^{k-1}_{i,q}N_{i,3}(u)N_{q,3}(v) + \sum_{p=i+1}^{m+1}\sum_{q=0}^{n+1} P^{k-1}_{p,q}N_{p,3}(u)N_{q,3}(v)$, and iterative format of surface can be written as follows

$$P^k_{i,j} = P^{k-1}_{i,j} + \Delta^{k,k-1}_{i,j}, i = 1, \cdots, m; j = 1, \cdots, n; k = 1, 2, \cdots, \tag{6}$$

in which, the difference vector is calculated as

$$\Delta^{k,k-1}_{i,j} = Q_{i,j} - C^{k,k-1}(u_i, v_j), i = 1, \cdots, m; j = 1, \cdots, n; k = 1, 2, \cdots.$$

Then we make an improvement on the Eq. (6) by adding a weight $\frac{\omega}{N_{i,3}(u_i)N_{j,3}(v_j)}$ to the iterative difference vector as follows

$$P^k_{i,j} = P^{k-1}_{i,j} + \frac{\omega}{N_{i,3}(u_i)N_{j,3}(v_j)}\Delta^{k,k-1}_{i,j}, i = 1, \cdots, m;$$
$$j = 1, \cdots, n; k = 1, 2, \cdots, \tag{7}$$

The iterative process expressed in Eq. (7) is progressive iterative approximation format of successive over-relaxation for non-uniform B-spline surface interpolation called SOR-PIA of surface. It possesses properties similar to that of curve iterative interpolation expressed in Eq. (5).

Similar to the case of curve, Eq. (7) can also be written as follows

$$P^k_{i,j} = P^{k-1}_{i,j} + \frac{\omega}{N_{i,3}(u_i)N_{j,3}(v_j)}\Delta^{k,k-1}_{i,j} = P^{k-1}_{i,j} + \frac{\omega(Q_i - C^{k,k-1}(u_i, v_j))}{N_{i,3}(u_i)N_{j,3}(v_j)}$$

$$= (1 - \omega)P^{k-1}_{i,j} + \omega\frac{\left(\begin{array}{c} Q_{i,j} - P^k_{i,j-1}N_{i,3}(u_i)N_{j-1,3}(v_j) - P^{k-1}_{i,j+1}N_{i,3}(u_i)N_{j+1,3}(v_j) - \\ \sum_{q=j-1}^{j+1}((P^k_{i-1,q}N_{i-1,3}(u_i) + P^{k-1}_{i+1,q}N_{i+1,3}(u_i))N_{q,3}(v_j)) \end{array}\right)}{N_{i,3}(u_i)N_{j,3}(v_j)}.$$

When $i = 1, 2, \cdots, m, j = 1, 2, \cdots, n$, Eq. (7) can also be written in matrix form

$$P^k = (1 - \omega)P^{k-1} + \omega D^{-1}\left(Q - LP^k - UP^{k-1}\right), k = 1, 2, \cdots,$$

in which, $D + L + U = N$, where D is a diagonal matrix, L is a strictly lower triangular matrix, U is a strictly upper triangular matrix, $N = N_1 \otimes N_2$.

3.3 Computing the Relaxation Factor

As described in Sects. 3.1 and 3.2, the matrix form of SOR-PIA for non-uniform B-spline curve and surface interpolation can be written as

$$
\begin{aligned}
\boldsymbol{P}^k &= (1 - \omega)\boldsymbol{P}^{k-1} + \omega \boldsymbol{D}^{-1}\left(\boldsymbol{Q} - L\boldsymbol{P}^k - U\boldsymbol{P}^{k-1}\right) \\
&= (\boldsymbol{D} + \omega \boldsymbol{L})^{-1}\left((1 - \omega)\boldsymbol{D} - \omega \boldsymbol{U}\right)\boldsymbol{P}^{k-1} + \omega(\boldsymbol{D} + \omega \boldsymbol{L})^{-1}\boldsymbol{Q}, k = 1, 2, \cdots.
\end{aligned}
\tag{8}
$$

Let $\boldsymbol{B}_\omega = (\boldsymbol{D} + \omega \boldsymbol{L})^{-1}\left((1 - \omega)\boldsymbol{D} - \omega \boldsymbol{U}\right)$, and $\boldsymbol{l}_\omega = \omega(\boldsymbol{D} + \omega \boldsymbol{L})^{-1}\boldsymbol{Q}$, the Eq. (8) can be written as

$$
\boldsymbol{P}^k = \boldsymbol{B}_\omega \boldsymbol{P}^{k-1} + \boldsymbol{l}_\omega, k = 1, 2, \cdots,
\tag{9}
$$

where $\boldsymbol{B}_\omega$ is the iteration matrix. It is obvious that $\rho(\boldsymbol{B}_\omega) \geq |\omega - 1|$. If Eq. (9) is convergent, then $|\omega - 1| \leq \rho(\boldsymbol{B}_\omega) < 1$, i.e. $0 < \omega < 2$.

The speed of over-relaxation iteration is closely related to the relaxation factor. There is currently no automatic method for the selection of the relaxation factor. A common practice is to select multiple different values within [0,2] and compare them. Here, we adopt an equidistant search strategy with an interval of 0.05.

4 Experiments

In this section, we employ two examples to illustrate the effectiveness of the proposed SOR-PIA method and compare it with methods of PIA [1,2] and WPIA [6]. First of all, we give two test examples, namely, an example of iterative curve interpolation and an example of iterative surface interpolation. The fitting curve and surface we used are all non-uniform cubic B-spline curve and surface. The parameterization of data points is determined by the cumulative chord length parameterization method, and the knot vector is determined by the parameters of data points. The fitting error is measured by the Euclidean distance between the data points to be interpolated and the points corresponding to the parameter values on the curve or surface.

Example 1. 19 data points are taken in plane to constitute a 19×1 sequence, and shown in Fig. 1(a): (40, 200); (50, 200); (50, 240); (100, 240); (100, 210); (80, 210); (80, 220); (70, 220); (70, 200); (100, 200); (100, 160); (150, 160); (150, 190); (130, 190); (130, 180); (120, 180); (120, 200); (150, 200); (150, 210).

Example 2. 40 data points are taken in space to constitute a 7×9 matrix, shown in Fig. 1(b): (0, 0, 0);(0, –8, –10), (8, –8, –10), (8, 0, –10), (8, 8, –10), (0, 8, –10), (–8, 8, –10), (–8, 0, –10), (–8, –8, –10), (0, –8, –10); (0, –10, 0), (10, –10, 0), (10, 0, 0), (10, 10, 0), (0, 10, 0), (–10, 10, 0), (–10, 0, 0), (–10, –10, 0), (0, –10, 0); (0, –15, 10), (15, –15, 10), (15, 0, 10), (15, 15, 10), (0, 15, 10), (–15, 15, 10), (–15, 0, 10), (–15, –15, 10), (0, –15, 10); (0, –6, 30), (6, –6, 30), (6, 0, 30), (6, 6, 30), (0, 6, 30), (–6, 6, 30), (–6, 0, 30), (–6, –6, 30), (0, –6, 30); (0, –6, 50), (6, –6, 50), (6, 0, 50), (6, 6, 50), (0, 6, 50), (–6, 6, 50), (–6, 0, 50), (–6, –6, 50), (0, –6, 50); (0, –8, –55), (8, –8, –55), (8, 0, –55), (8, 8, –55), (0, 8, –55), (–8, 8, –55), (–8, 0, –55), (–8, –8, –55), (0, –8, –55).

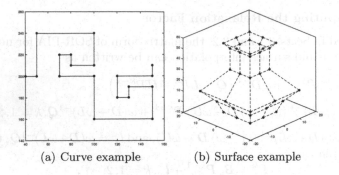

(a) Curve example   (b) Surface example

Fig. 1. Test examples.

The experimental results of the first 15 iteration levels are shown in Tables 1 and 2, where PIA is the standard iterative interpolation method, WPIA is the PIA method with a acceleration weight, SOR-PIA_1 is our method with an arbitrary relaxation factor, SOR-PIA_2 is our method with a relaxation factor calculated by using equidistant search strategy. In Table 1, the relaxation factor is 1.1 in SOR-PIA_1 and it is 1.05 in SOR-PIA_2. In Table 2, the relaxation factor is 1.2 in SOR-PIA_1 and it is 1.1 in SOR-PIA_2. Based on the nature of the iterative process, it is generally believed that the smaller the error, the faster the iteration speed. By comparison, we can find that the SOR_PIA proposed in this paper is much faster than PIA and WPIA, and it is effective to calculate the relaxation factor by using the equidistant search strategy.

To visually show the performance of the three methods, we compare the results after the first iteration, as shown in Fig. 2 and Fig. 3. The reason for choosing to compare the visual results of the first iteration is that with the increase of the number of iterations, the visual results of the subsequent iterations can hardly be distinguished by the naked eye. And the relaxation factor of SOR-PIA is 1.05 in Fig. 2. In Fig. 3, the relaxation factor is 1.1. As can be seen from these figures, the iterative interpolation effect of SOR-PIA is significant.

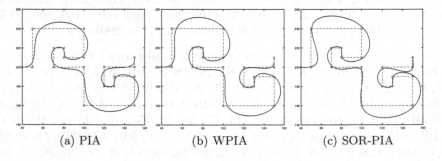

(a) PIA   (b) WPIA   (c) SOR-PIA

Fig. 2. Iterative interpolation in different methods of example 1.

Table 1. The iterative errors of Example 1

Level	PIA	WPIA	SOR-PIA_1	SOR-PIA_2
0	1.114 199e+02	1.114 199e+02	1.114 199e+02	1.114 199e+02
1	5.496 593e+01	3.267 479e+01	2.881 771e+01	2.745 255e+01
2	3.045 766e+01	1.312 380e+01	8.007 956e+00	7.344 945e+00
3	1.774 285e+01	6.003 406e+00	2.161 996e+00	2.020 399e+00
4	1.067 390e+01	2.843 402e+00	5.918 348e−01	5.670 205e−01
5	6.757 224e+00	1.412 444e+00	1.664 159e−01	1.432 362e−01
6	4.417 398e+00	7.102 530e−01	4.051 463e−02	3.272 078e−02
7	2.908 802e+00	3.617 117e−01	8.886 908e−03	6.845 107e−03
8	1.926 791e+00	1.851 538e−01	2.328 287e−03	1.383 686e−03
9	1.283 424e+00	9.518 904e−02	6.213 399e−04	2.749 991e−04
10	8.592 878e−01	4.899 593e−02	1.485 333e−04	6.815 204e−05
11	5.779 434e−01	2.528 939e−02	3.353 955e−05	1.988 929e−05
12	3.902 047e−01	1.305 820e−02	8.514 881e−06	5.739 107e−06
13	2.642 543e−01	6.756 562e−03	2.495 848e−06	1.405 999e−06
14	1.793 757e−01	3.495 290e−03	6.867 457e−07	2.930 517e−07
15	1.219 730e−01	1.811 265e−03	1.710 329e−07	5.940 200e−08

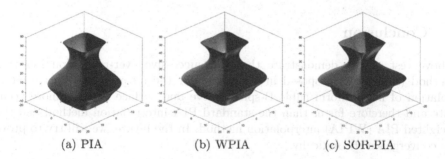

(a) PIA   (b) WPIA   (c) SOR-PIA

Fig. 3. Iterative interpolation in different methods of example 2.

Table 2. The iterative errors of Example 2

Level	PIA	WPIA	SOR-PIA_1	SOR-PIA_2
0	1.491 585e+02	1.491 585e+02	1.491 585e+02	1.491 585e+02
1	7.611 221e+01	4.922 341e+01	7.385 814e+01	6.129 211e+01
2	4.328 730e+01	2.795 687e+01	3.935 802e+01	2.789 917e+01
3	2.791 393e+01	1.486 221e+01	2.061 524e+01	1.217 103e+01
4	1.914 628e+01	9.058 060e+00	1.038 640e+01	5.080 306e+00
5	1.342 518e+01	5.846 255e+00	5.177 180e+00	2.045 256e+00
6	9.538 961e+00	3.848 654e+00	2.405 970e+00	7.489 668e-01
7	6.872 865e+00	2.644 782e+00	1.022 007e+00	2.500 636e-01
8	5.042 845e+00	1.833 794e+00	4.040 267e-01	7.804 021e-02
9	3.789 818e+00	1.283 230e+00	1.410 842e-01	1.974 009e-02
10	2.918 993e+00	9.107 264e-01	4.056 066e-02	4.886 369e-03
11	2.290 105e+00	6.444 096e-01	9.181 990e-03	1.281 902e-03
12	1.821 722e+00	4.623 262e-01	1.671 155e-03	5.012 722e-04
13	1.465 099e+00	3.298 248e-01	3.670 073e-04	1.940 344e-04
14	1.188 773e+00	2.379 626e-01	1.140 689e-04	6.683 711e-05
15	9.715 385e-01	1.708 819e-01	4.277 461e-05	2.057 718e-05

5 Conclusion

Above test results demonstrate that the successive over-relaxation iteration method (SOR-PIA) proposed in this paper for the purpose of iterative interpolation of non-uniform cubic B-spline curve and surface is much more accurate and therefore faster than the standard PIA interpolation method and the weighted PIA (WPIA) interpolation method. In the future, we will try to prove its convergence theoretically.

References

1. Lin, H., Wang, G., Dong, C.: Constructing iterative non-uniform B-spline curve and surface to fit data points. Sci. China Ser. F **47**(3), 315–331 (2004)
2. Lin, H., Bao, H., Wang, G.: Totally positive bases and progressive iteration approximation. Comput. Math. Appl **50**(3/4), 575–586 (2005)
3. Lin, H., Zhang, Z.: An extended iterative format for the progressive-iteration approximation. Comput. Graph. **35**(5), 967–975 (2011)
4. Deng, C., Lin, H.: Progressive and iterative approximation for least squares B-spline curve and surface fitting. Comput.-Aided Des. **47**(1), 32–44 (2014)
5. Lu, L.: Weighted progressive iteration approximation and convergence analysis. Comput. Aided Geom. Des. **27**(2), 129–137 (2010)
6. Lin, H., Zhang, Z.: An efficient method for fitting large data sets using T-splines. SIAM J. Sci. Comput. **35**(6), A3052–A3068 (2013)

7. Lin, H., Jin, S., Liao, H., et al.: Quality guaranteed all-hex mesh generation by a constrained volume iterative fitting algorithm. Comput.-Aided Des. **67–68**(C), 107–117 (2015)
8. Lin, H., Jin, S., Hu, Q., Liu, Z.: Constructing B-spline solids from tetrahedral meshes for isogeometric analysis. Comput. Aided Geom. Des. **35–36**, 109–120 (2015)
9. Galveza, A., Iglesiasa, A., Avilaa, A., Oteroc, C., Ariasc, R., Manchadoca, C.: Elitist clonal selection algorithm for optimal choice of free knots in B-spline data fitting. Appl. Soft Comput. **26**, 90–106 (2015)
10. Zhang, L., Ge, X., Tan, J.: Least square geometric iterative fitting method for generalized B-spline curves with two different kinds of weights. Visual Comput. **32**(9), 1109–1120 (2015). https://doi.org/10.1007/s00371-015-1170-3
11. Liu, M., Li, B., Guo, Q., Zhu, C., Hu, P., Shao, Y.: Progressive iterative approximation for regularized least square bivariate B-spline surface fitting. J. Comput. Appl. Math. **327**, 175–187 (2018)
12. Lin, H., Maekawa, T., Deng, C.: Survey on geometric iterative methods and their applications. Comput.-Aided Des. **95**, 40–51 (2018)
13. Hu, L., Shou, H., Dai, Z.: HSS-iteration-based iterative interpolation of curves and surfaces with NTP bases. Wirel. Netw., 1–13 (2020). https://doi.org/10.1007/s11276-019-02224-y

FLSim: An Extensible and Reusable Simulation Framework for Federated Learning

Li Li[1(✉)], Jun Wang[2], and ChengZhong Xu[3]

[1] ShenZhen Institutes of Advanced Technology, Chinese Academy of Sciences, Beijing, China
li.li@siat.ac.cn
[2] Futurewei Technologies, Santa Clara, US
[3] State Key Laboratory of IoTSC, University of Macau, Zhuhai, China

Abstract. Federated learning is designed for multiple mobile devices to collaboratively train an artificial intelligence model while preserving data privacy. Instead of collecting the raw training data from mobile devices to the central server, federated learning coordinates a group of devices to train a shared model in a distributed manner with their local data. However, prior to effectively deploying federated learning on resource-constrained mobile devices in large scale, different factors including the convergence rate, energy efficiency and model accuracy should be well studied. Thus, a flexible simulation framework that can be used to investigate a wide range of problems related to federated learning is urgently required.

In this paper, we propose FLSim, a framework for efficiently building simulators for federated learning. Unlike ad hoc simulators, FLSim is envisioned as an open repository of building blocks for creating simulators. To this end, FLSim consists of a set of software components organized in a well-structured software architecture that provides the foundation for maximizing flexibility and extensibility. With FLSim, creating a simulator generally involves only putting the selected components together, thus allowing users to focus on the problems being studied. We describe the design of the framework in detail and use a few use cases to demonstrate the ease with which various simulators can be constructed with FLSim.

1 Introduction

Mobile devices (e.g., smartphone and wearable devices), powered by batteries, intimately connect users and their environment. Equipped with various types of sensors (e.g., GPS, accelerometer, gyroscope), mobile devices can collect different kinds of data, ubiquitously [19,21]. These data are valuable resources for intelligent applications to efficiently understand user behavior and significantly improve user experience from different perspectives. Acquiring these data raises

© ICST Institute for Computer Sciences, Social Informatics and Telecommunications Engineering 2021
Published by Springer Nature Switzerland AG 2021. All Rights Reserved
H. Song and D. Jiang (Eds.): SIMUtools 2020, LNICST 369, pp. 350–369, 2021.
https://doi.org/10.1007/978-3-030-72792-5_30

a big question mark on preserving users' privacy with any service provided [4]. For example, the scandal swirling around the Facebook App and Cambridge Anaytica has begun to usher in a new era for this once-ignored community of privacy researchers and developers [14,23]. Thus, intelligently analyzing the data being generated from mobile devices while preserving data privacy is a critical challenge.

Federated learning [22] is proposed in order to effectively train the data ubiquitously from mobile devices while removing the concern of privacy. Unlike the cloud-based approach which collects the local training data in the data center, federated learning collaboratively trains a shared model with the data located on each mobile device [16]. Specifically, in a training round, each participating device computes the updates to the current global model based on its local training data. These updates are then sent to the central server. After receiving the updates, the central server aggregates them, updates the shared model and broadcasts the updated model to the mobile participants. This process iterates until the model converges. In this approach, the predictive model can be collaboratively learned while the data privacy is well preserved. This is because the privacy sensitive raw data never leaves the mobile device during the whole training process. Currently, federated learning has been adopted to support various kinds of applications such as human activity recognition, on-device item ranking, and next-word prediction [20].

Despite all the promising benefits, effectively deploying federated learning on mobile devices in large scale is challenging. The whole system can be severely impacted by different factors in a highly dynamic environment. For instance, the training data generated from different mobile devices can have highly different distributions due to different user interaction behaviors which can impact the model convergence in totally different ways. On the other side, the participating devices in a federated learning system usually possess different hardware configurations which lead to totally different training capability. Thus, the training progress of each device can be highly unbalanced which severely impacts the overall training progress of the whole system. Moreover, some uncertainty issues such as out of battery and poor network connection can further affect the convergence rate of a federated learning system in practice. In addition, energy consumption of the on-device learning process is another critical concern that determines whether a specific user is willing to participate in the training process. Prior to deploying a federated learning framework on real mobile devices in large scale, assessing the impacts of different factors is critical for developers and researchers to make corresponding strategies for efficient and effective deployment. *Thus, a framework that can efficiently create simulators to simulate different usage scenarios in federated learning and quickly obtain corresponding information (e.g., model accuracy, model convergence rate and energy consumption) is urgently required.*

In this paper, we propose FLSim, an extensible and reusable simulation framework for federated learning. FLSim adopts a layered software architecture. It supports commonly used deep learning frameworks such as PyTorch and Tensorflow. Thus developers familiar with any one of these frameworks can conveniently use FLSim to create corresponding simulators. FLSim can be easily ported to run on different hardware platforms. Moreover, FLSim adopts a highly modular design, allowing different simulators to be easily created through the integration of different components in FLSim. We use different case studies to evaluate the effectiveness of FLSim. The results show that FLSim can effectively simulate different scenarios in Federated Learning and obtain corresponding information accurately. To the best of our knowledge, FLSim is the *first* work that provides a flexible simulation framework that can be efficiently used to study a wide range of problems related to federated learning. Specifically, our major contributions are as follows:

- We propose FLSim, a simulation framework for federated learning, which intelligently helps developers create different simulators to simulate different scenarios in an efficient way.
- FLSim adopts a layered software architecture. Moreover, techniques such as inversion of control are used to make FLSim flexible and extendable.
- We implement the prototype of FLSim and use different use cases to demonstrate the effectiveness of FLSim.

The rest of the paper is organized as follows. Section 2 introduces the background about federated learning and the previous research closely related to our work. Section 3 introduces the system design and the implementation of different components. Section 4 discusses different case studies we adopt to evaluate the effectiveness of FLSim. Section 5 briefly evaluates the performance of FLSim. Finally, Sect. 6 concludes the paper.

2   Background and Related Work

In this section, we introduce the background of federated learning and previous work that is closely related with this paper.

2.1   Background About Federated Learning

Federated learning (FL) is proposed to effectively train the data being generated on mobile devices while protecting data privacy. A typical FL system mainly consists of a central server and multiple mobile devices with heterogeneous hardware configurations. The typical workflow of a federated learning procedure contains the following main steps:

1. **Initialization.** At the initialization step of each training round, the central server selects a set of mobile devices to participate in the training process.
2. **Model Download.** The selected participants download the current shared model state (e.g., current model parameters (w_t)).
3. **On-device Training.** Each mobile device conducts local training based on the shared model state and its local training dataset for a certain number of training epochs.

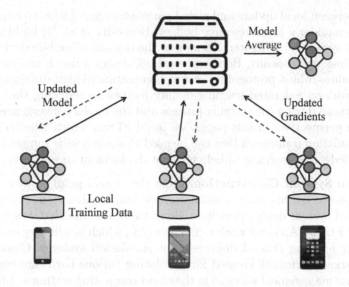

Fig. 1. Workflow of a typical federated learning system.

4. **Gradient Update.** After completing the local training process, each mobile device sends the updated gradients back to the central server.
5. **Model Fusion.** After receiving the updated gradients from all selected participants, the central server aggregates these gradient updates and comes up with the updated global model. Then, the system enters the next training round.
6. **Training Iterates.** The whole process iterates until the global model converges.

We can note that, the raw training data (e.g., raw data generated during user interaction with mobile devices) never leave the mobile device during the whole training process. Data privacy is therefore well preserved which is the key advantage of Federated Learning.

2.2 Related Work

Our work is closely related to the following research topics.

Federated Learning. Federated learning has raised a lot of attention as a machine learning paradigm that effectively trains the data being generated from mobile devices while guaranteeing the data privacy [7,8,11,15,17,22,24,25,28]. Sprague et al. [25] present a new asynchronous federated learning algorithm and study its convergence rate when distributed across many edge devices, with hard data constraints, relative to training the same model on a single device. Wang et al. [28] analyze the convergence bound of distributed gradient descent from a theoretical point of view and propose a control algorithm that determines the trade-off between local update and global parameter aggregation to minimize the loss function under a given resource budget. Bonawitz et al. [7] build a scalable production system for federated learning in the domain of mobile devices, based on Tensorflow. Additionally, Bonawitz et al. [8] design a novel, communication-efficient, failure-robust protocol for secure aggregation of high-dimensional data. Previous work on federated learning mainly focuses on reducing the communication overhead during the training process and the model convergence from the theoretical perspective. In this paper, we build FLSim which tries to provide a flexible simulation framework that can be used to study a wide range of problems related to federated learning to help efficient deployment in practice.

Simulation System Construction. From the system point of view, the most relevant concept to this work is simulation system construction. Previous work has explored system design principles along the same line that has guided the creation of FLSim. An early work is SimJava [13], which is a library of Java components for building general discrete-event simulation systems. CloudSim [10] is a simulation framework created for simulating various hardware components and software management services in the cloud computing settingss. Like FLSim its main design focus is to provide a toolkit that is highly extensible and customizable. Not surprisingly, it also adopts a layered software architecture. Wang et al. [27] discuss component-based design followed in creating the Manifold simulation framework [26] for multicore computer architectures. They particularly emphasize the importance of dependency management. Although targeting a different application domain, its design principles are similar to what we have adopted for FLSim.

3   FLSim System Design and Implementation

In designing FLSim, our goal is to provide a flexible simulation framework that can be used to study a wide range of problems related to federated learning, instead of an ad hoc simulator that limits itself to a single or a small number of use cases. This idea is captured in our fundamental design rule.

Fundamental Design Rule. FLSim is a simulation framework that provides building blocks for users to easily create simulators tailored for their own federated learning problems.

Another import question we face is whether the training of the neural networks should be simulated or literally carried out. It is obvious that any federated learning simulator will spend most of its time performing the training. If the training can be simulated, it will greatly reduce the simulation time. However, we suspect that in most cases the user would want for the neural networks to be actually trained. Therefore, in the current version of FLSim, training is literally performed.

With the Fundamental Design Rule in mind, we set the following design goals for FLSim.

- FLSim should support all the commonly used deep learning frameworks such as PyTorch [2] and TensorFlow [3], so that users familiar with any one of those frameworks should be able to use FLSim at the same level of ease.
- FLSim should, under the control of one or a few configuration parameters, be able to run on different underlying hardware platforms.
- FLSim should be highly modular such that different simulators can be created simply by choosing different components. On the other hand, if the system does not include a component that fully meets the user's needs, a new one can be easily created and incorporated into the system.

The following sections give a detailed description of the system design of FLSim.

3.1 Design Overview

In order to achieve the design goals outlined above, we adopt a layered software architecture [9]. This type of architectures allows complex systems to be decomposed into different levels of abstraction with cleanly defined interfaces and dependence relationships. To be more precise, our design is a relaxed layered system where components in a given layer can use the services from any layer below it, not just the one immediately below. However, no layer is allowed to use any functionality from any layer above it. Figure 2 shows the software architecture of FLSim.

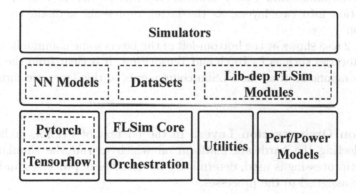

Fig. 2. System architecture.

From the user's standpoint, building a simulator is a simple two-step process. First, the user selects the essential components such as the neural network model, the dataset, and the hardware platform. The user can also create customized components by sub-classing existing classes to meet their requirements. For example, if one needs to select clients in each training round in a particular way, they can simply extend the FLClientSelector class.

Once the user has configured the system, in the second step the user instantiates a `Federation` object and starts running the simulator.

In order to realize the clean dependencies as required by the layered software architecture, we adopt a few design guidelines that center on dependency management.

First of all, we adopt the design technique known as inversion of control [12] whenever possible. When an object A directly uses an object B, A has a dependence on B. The coupling between A and B would become too tight if B is created by A. With inversion of control, the dependence of A on B is injected. That is to say, B is created elsewhere and passed to A, while A only requires an interface that B implements.

Another guideline is library-neutrality. Deep learning libraries such as PyTorch and TensorFlow are commonly used. A pitfall we want to avoid is tying the system to any particular library. Therefore, the components in general are designed in a library-neutral manner, with library-dependent extensions provided as a convenience. We next explain the layers individually.

3.2   Library-Independent Layer

At the bottom of the layered architecture is the Library Independent Layer. As the name indicates, components in this layer are independent of deep learning libraries such as PyTorch. This layer contains FLSim Core, Simulation Orchestration, common utilities, and, for studying system performance and energy efficiency, Performance and Power Models. We further divide FLSim Core and Orchestration into two layers, as the latter represents a distinctive layer of abstraction.

Figure 2 also shows at the bottom-left of the layers some commonly used deep learning libraries such as PyTorch and TensorFlow. It is clear from the positions of these components that the FLSim components in this layer are independent of them.

Simulation Orchestration Layer. In the context of FLSim, orchestration means selecting the hardware platform on which to run the simulator, and, when multiprocessing is used, determining the number of processes and how the clients are assigned to the processes.

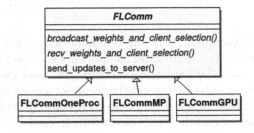

Fig. 3. Orchestration layer

At the core of the Orchestration Layer is the class hierarchy for client-server communications, as shown in Fig. 3. At present, we support using a single CPU process, multiple CPU processes, and GPU SIMT execution, which are respectively implemented in the sub-classes shown in Fig. 3.

These communication classes provide the abstraction for orchestration and insulate the users of these classes from such details as the underlying inter-process communication mechanism, or communication between CPU and GPU. Once a platform is selected, the clients and server simply use the interface functions such as those listed in Fig. 3 to communicate.

FLSim Core. This component includes the basic classes that implement a Federated Learning system, such as server and client. Major classes of this component are illustrated in Fig. 4.

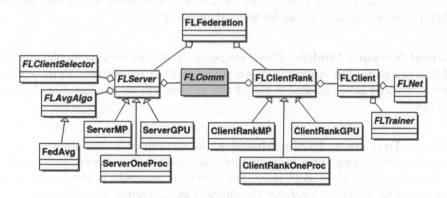

Fig. 4. FLSim Core class diagram.

Clearly the classes form two clusters centered on `FLServer` and `FLClientRank`, the latter representing a group of clients. The server has a few injected dependencies: `FLComm` for communications with the clients, `FLClientSelector` for client selection, and `FLAvgAlgo` for model averaging.

On the client side, injected dependencies include `FLNet` representing a neural network model, `FLTrainer` representing a local trainer that trains the model.

Finally, the class `FLFederation` represents the federation and wraps a server and one or more client ranks.

Utilities. The Utilities component contains utility functions that are independent of deep learning libraries. These include the following: dataset splitter, logging, visualization, and charting.

Performance and Power Models. A special feature of FLSim is its incorporation of performance and power models to support the study of system performance and energy efficiency. At present this is mainly provided in the form of device profiles represented by the `DevProfile` class. This class basically has a performance table and a power table. The former is an array of execution time required to finish one round of training using different CPU frequencies, and the latter is an array of the same size with the corresponding power consumption values.

3.3   Library-Dependent Layer

The library-dependent layer contains modules that rely on specific deep learning libraries such as PyTorch. At present this layer focuses on PyTorch.

Datasets. Strictly speaking, datasets should be independent of the deep learning libraries. However, libraries like PyTorch provides utilities for some common datasets, making it easier to deal with the datasets. Obviously we can also include library-neutral datasets in the library independent layer.

Neural Network Models. These are generally bound to a particular library. FLSim includes a few models from simple multi-layer perceptrons to more complex CNN and DNN models. Some of the models will be discussed in the case studies.

Library-Dependent FLSim Modules. As mentioned, to maintain the clean layered architecture, some functionalities are split into a library independent part and a library dependent part. The former is generally in the form of base classes, while the latter leverages the support of commonly used libraries.

An example is the `FLTrainer` class. This base class includes an interface for carrying out training of a neural network. The `PytorchTrainer` class extends the base class and is used to train PyTorch neural network models.

3.4   Simulators

At the top of the layered architecture we find simulators which are built with the components from the lower layers. Some of the FLSim simulators are discussed in the case study section. However, it is important to stress that the goal of FLSim is to provide well-structured components for constructing simulators efficiently.

3.5   Steps for Constructing a Simulator

Using the components provided by FLSim, we can construct a generic simulator for federated learning with the following steps:

- Step 1. Create a dataset partitioner and partition the dataset among the given number of clients.
- Step 2. Create a neural network model.

- Step 3. Create a local trainer object.
- Step 4. Create a client selector object.
- Step 5. Create an averaging algorithm object.
- Step 6. Create an `FLFederation` object with the following parameters:
  - The neural network model
  - The local trainer
  - The dataset and the partitioning
  - The client selector
  - The averaging algorithm object.
  - The platform. If CPU is selected, the number of processes as well.
- Step 7. In a loop call the `run_one_round()` method of the `FLFederation` object.

4 Case Studies

In this section we present a few use cases to demonstrate different types of federated learning simulation that can be realized with the FLSim framework. A brief description of the use cases is given below, followed by more details.

- **Basic case.** In this test case we try to repeat some of the experiments reported in [22] to prove the basic capabilities of FLSim.
- **Federated learning with non-IID data.** In this test case we try to repeat some of the experiments presented in [30], which focuses on the effects of non-IID data.
- **Real-time federated learning**: In this test case we build a simulator that is a simplified version of the work presented in [18] to study problems in real-time federated learning.

4.1 Basic Test Case

We start with a basic test case in which we try to duplicate some experiments reported in [22] in order to perform some basic validation of the implementation of FLSim. We use FLSim to build a neural network that is referred to as *2NN* in [22] for the task of classifying hand-written numerical digits from the MNIST dataset [29], which includes a training set of 60,000 images and a test set of 10,000.

The *2NN* model is a multilayer perceptron (MLP) [6] with 1 input layer, 2 hidden layers and 1 output layer, the sizes of which are respectively 768, 200, 200, and 10, for a total of 199,210 parameters.

Components required to create the simulator include theose listed in Table 1.

Note that all those components are readily available in FLSim. Therefore, building the simulator is a straightforward process.

In the first experiment, we modify a couple of training parameters and try to find the least number of training rounds required to achieve a test accuracy of 97.0%, and we compare the results with what are reported in [22]. Specifically, we fix the number of local training epochs to 20, and set the batch size to three

Table 1. FLSim components for the basic test case.

- The 2NN model based on PyTorch
- The MNIST dataset
- The default federation FLFederation
- The FLRandomClientSelector to randomly select 10 clients out of 100 in each training round
- The PytorchLocalTrainer, a PyTorch based local training module

Table 2. 2NN MNIST with epochs fixed at 20: best of 10 runs.

Epoch	BatchSize	#Batches	LearnRate	Rounds	Rounds [22]
20	10	60	0.1	31	32
20	50	12	0.3	38	39
20	50	12	0.1	88	
20	∞	1	0.95	94	92
20	∞	1	0.1	409	

different values (i.e., 10, 50, and all), and select different learning rates to see if we can obtain results similar to [22]. The test results are listed in Table 2.

The infinity symbol (∞) means including all the local training data in the batch, i.e., there is only one batch for each client. For the three batch sizes, the best learning rate are respectively 0.1, 0.3, and 0.95. The last column contains the results from [22]. Note that [22] did not state the learning rate used in obtaining the results. We can see that in all three cases our results are very close to those of [22], confirming the soundness of FLSim implementation. Additionally, we have found that the learning rate has a great impact on the number of training rounds required, and it is sensitive to the batch size. For example, while 0.1 is a good learning rate for batch size 10, it produces bad results when the batch size is much larger. Finally, Fig. 5a shows the evolution of the model accuracy with three different batch sizes.

Table 3. 2NN MNIST with fixed batch sizes: best of 10 runs.

Epoch	BatchSize	#Batches	LearnRate	Rounds	Rounds [22]
1	10	60	0.1	98	92
5	10	60	0.1	39	–
10	10	60	0.1	35	34
20	10	60	0.1	31	32
30	10	60	0.1	31	–
1	50	12	0.3	131	144
10	50	12	0.3	40	45
20	50	12	0.3	38	39

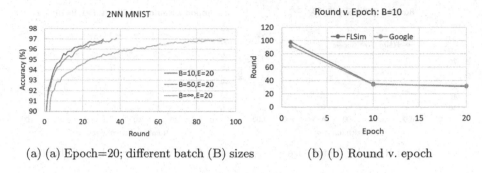

(a) (a) Epoch=20; different batch (B) sizes   (b) (b) Round v. epoch

Fig. 5. 2NN results: (a) Epoch (E) set to 20, numbers of rounds with different batch sizes (B). (b) Comparison with [22]: batch size set to 10, epoch set to 1, 10, and 20.

We next try to find the best numbers of rounds with different parameters and compare the results with [22]. Table 3 shows the results of fixing the batch size and changing the epoch. The last column contains results from [22]. It can be seen that in most cases the results are very close.

Table 4 shows the results of the best numbers of rounds obtained with different numbers of clients. In all the four cases here, our results differ from those in [22] by about 10 rounds. One possible reason for this difference is the learning rate. Unlike [22], we did not test a large set of different learning rates. Note that for the case E=1, B=10, two different results are reported in [22], namely 92 and 87, as listed in Tables 3 and 4.

Table 4. 2NN MNIST with different federation sizes; Batch = 10; Epoch = 1

#Clients	LearnRate	Rounds	Rounds [22]
10	0.1	98	87
20	0.1	85	77
50	0.1	83	75
100	0.1	81	70

The numbers of rounds with different epochs, batch sizes, and number of clients are graphically depicted in Figs. 5(b), 6(a), and 6(b), respectively.

4.2 Federated Learning with Non-IID Data

In a federated learning system, when the clients have IID (independent and identically distributed) data, high model accuracy can generally be achieved, as demonstrated in the Basic Case above (e.g., Fig. 5(a). Zhao et al. [30] studied the impact on model accuracy when clients have non-IID data instead. They demonstrate that the model accuracy is significantly reduced, especially in the

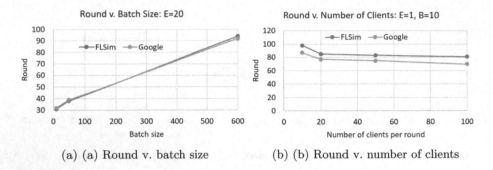

(a) (a) Round v. batch size   (b) (b) Round v. number of clients

Fig. 6. 2NN results in comparison with [22]: (a) Epoch (E) set to 20, batch size (B) set to 10, 50, 600. (b) Epoch set to 1, batch size set to 10, number of clients set to 10, 20, 50, 100.

extreme case where each client has data from only one class. To address this problem, they propose creating a common set of data and giving it to all the clients. It has been shown that even with a small amount of shared data, the model accuracy can be greatly improved.

In this case study, we show how this problem can be studied with FLSim. Two CNNs are used in this test case: one for MNIST and one for CIFAR-10 [5]. The CIFAR-10 is also an image dataset with 10 classes. It has a training set of 50,000 images and a test set of 10,000. The CNN for MNIST is the same as the one in [22], with 1,663,370 parameters. However, [30] does not provide the parameters of the CNN for CIFAR-10 in that work. Therefore we have created our own network using the PyTorch library. This CNN has three convolution layers with sizes 3×64, 64×128, and 128×256 respectively, and three fully connected layers with sizes 1024×128, 128×256, and 256×10 respectively. The total number of trainable parameters is 537,610.

Components for this test case are mostly available from the FLSim framework. The only extension required is to create two utility classes that create non-IID distributions for MNIST and CIFAR-10 respectively. We list the major components for this test case in Table 5.

Table 5. FLSim components for the non-IID test case.

- The CNN models for both MNIST and CIFAR-10 based on PyTorch
- The MNIST and CIFAR-10 datasets
- The default federation `FLFederation`
- The `FLRandomClientSelector` to randomly select 10 clients out of 100 in each training round
- The `PytorchLocalTrainer`, a PyTorch based local training module
- Two utility classes that respectively divide the MNIST and CIFAR-10 into non-IID distributions

In the first step of this test case, we run the training tasks for 500 rounds on the two data sets with three different distributions: IID, 2-class non-IID where each client has data from 2 classes, and 1-class non-IID where each client has data from only 1 class. Using the same parameters as in [30], we set the batch size B to 10, and epoch E to 1. Learning rates are respectively 0.01 and 0.1 for MNIST and CIFAR-10.

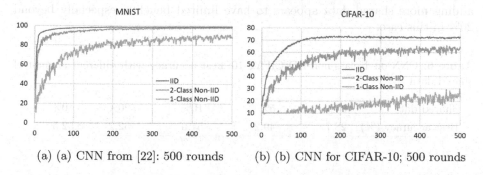

(a) (a) CNN from [22]: 500 rounds   (b) (b) CNN for CIFAR-10; 500 rounds

Fig. 7. Impact of training data distribution on model accuracy: (a) MNIST on CNN. (b) CIFAR-10 on CNN. Batch size = 10, epoch = 1.

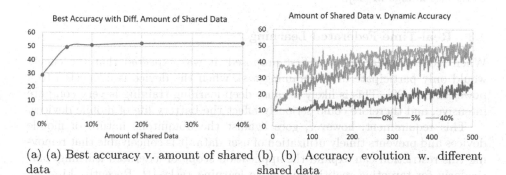

(a) (a) Best accuracy v. amount of shared   (b) (b) Accuracy evolution w. different
data   shared data

Fig. 8. CNN on CIFAR-10, 1-class non-IID data: impact of amount of shared data on model accuracy: (a) best accuracy (b) accuracy evolution

Figures 7 (a) and (b) show the evolution of test set accuracy for MINST and CIFAR-10 respectively. For MNIST, the trend is very similar to [30]. For CIFAR-10, because our CNN likely has fewer parameters than the one used in [30], the achieved accuracy level is lower, even in the IID case. However, the impact of data distribution is still clearly demonstrated.

In the second part of this test case we evaluate the effect of adding a set of shared data to all the clients. This is done with the CIFAR-10 dataset using the 1-class non-IID distribution.

In this test, each client has 500 images from 1 class only. We create a common set of data that includes images from all the 10 classes. The size of the common set range from 25 to 200, representing 5% to 40% of each client's data.

Table 6 lists the best accuracy obtained in 500-round runs using different sizes of shared data. The trend is graphically illustrated in Fig. 8(a) as well. Without the shared data, the best accuracy we have achieved is 28.7%. With only 5% of shared data, this is raised to 49.2%, a 71% improvement. However, adding more shared data appears to have limited benefits, especially beyond 20% in this case.

Table 6. CNN on 1-class non-IID CIFAT-10: best accuracy with different amount of shared data

Shared data	0%	5%	10%	20%	40%
Best accuracy (%)	28.7	49.2	51.0	52.2	52.5

Figure 8(b) shows the accuracy evolution of this test. We compare the original test case that includes no shared data with adding respectively 5% and 40% shared data. It is clear that, by adding just a small amount of shared data we can dramatically increase the accuracy level. These results conform very well with the findings in [30].

4.3 Real-Time Federated Learning

When federated learning was first proposed, it was expected that the clients would only participate in the training task when the device is connected to a power source [22]. This is likely because deep learning training is very compute intensive, and therefore could seriously affect the battery life of mobile devices.

This requirement, however, goes against the ubiquitous nature of mobile devices and prevents timely utilization of user data. It is conceivable that removing this restriction can expand the application scope of federated learning, particularly for targeting real-time machine learning tasks [1]. Recently, Li et al. [18] proposed SmartPC, a framework that allows on-device federated learning to take place when the device is not being charged. Among the key features of that work are the following:

- Instead of making the server wait for all clients to respond, SmartPC ends a training round when a certain proportion (e.g., 80%) of clients have responded.
- The server estimate a training deadline in each round. Based on the deadline, an on-device controller adjusts the device CPU frequency to meet the deadline and to minimize energy consumption of the training process.

In this case study, we use FLSim to create a simulator to study a simplified version of the main problems addressed in [18]. Specifically, we focus on two problems: 1) how it would impact model accuracy and training time if the server uses only a subset of client updates, and 2) how a device can meet the training time requirement while saving energy.

As presented previously, a special feature of FLSim is its incorporation of performance and power models for studying system performance and energy efficiency. This feature is key to this test case.

We make the following changes to FLSim in order to implement the simulator.

- We extend the orchestration layer shown in Fig. 3 to add two additional data items in the client-server communications. From the server to the clients, a training deadline is appended to the model parameters, and from the clients to the server, we add the simulated completion time.
- A new client type is created which includes a device profile for computing performance and energy consumption.
- A new server type is also created because now it has the additional job of selecting the subset of clients as well as determining the training deadline.

This real-time federated learning system works as follows:

- Step 1. The server broadcasts the model parameters and the training deadline to all clients. The deadline for the very first round is based on the device profiles.
- Step 2. Clients perform local training, and compute the associated time and energy using their device profiles. Clients then send model updates along with training time to the server.
- Step 3. The server selects the first $p\%$ of clients (p is predefined) based on their completion time and performs model averaging using their updates only. The deadline is updated using a mechanism such as exponential weighted moving average.
- Repeat the above steps for the next round.

The process for a client to compute its training time and energy is as follows. As explained, each client has a device profile which includes a performance table and a power table. The performance table is basically an array of training times under different CPU frequencies, $[t_1, t_2, ..., t_n]$, in ascending order, while the power table contains the corresponding power consumptions $[p_1, p_2, ..., p_n]$ in descending order. Given a deadline d, we first compute a base training time T and base energy E as follows. If $d < t_1$, set $T = t_1, E = p_1 * t_1$. If $d > t_n$, set $T = t_n, E = p_n * t_n$. Otherwise set $T = d$. Assuming $t_i < d < t_{i+1}$, we find α such that $d = \alpha * t_i + (1-\alpha) * t_{i+1}$. The corresponding power is $p = \alpha * p_i + (1-\alpha) * p_{i+1}$, and set $E = p * d$. Finally, to simulate random factors that affect the training time and energy, random values are added to T and E.

In this experiment, we use the CNN and MNIST dataset with 1-class non-IID distribution as described in Sect. 4.2. Two different device profiles are used in the federations with a 40–60 split. We summarize the components used in Table 7.

Test results for this use case are illustrated in Figs. 9 and 10. In Fig. 9 we show the accuracy in 500-round runs when the server uses a certain proportion

Table 7. FLSim components for the non-IID test case.

- The CNN model for MNIST
- The MNIST dataset
- The utility class that divides MNIST into non-IID distributions
- The real-time federation `FLFedRT`, including corresponding
server and client components
- Two device profiles representing two device models
- The `FLAllClientSelector` that selects all the clients in a given set
- The `PytorchLocalTrainer`, a PyTorch based local training module

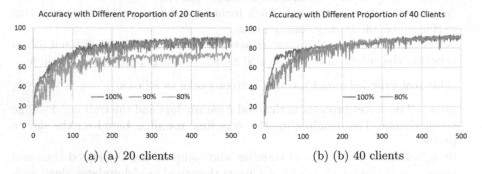

(a) (a) 20 clients   (b) (b) 40 clients

Fig. 9. Model accuracy in 500-round runs with different proportions of clients selected in each round: (a) 20 clients (b) 40 clients

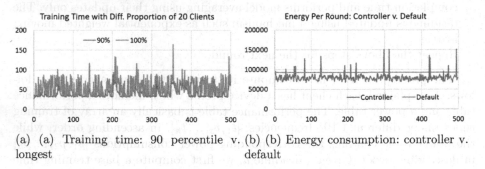

(a) (a) Training time: 90 percentile v. (b) (b) Energy consumption: controller v.
longest   default

Fig. 10. Training time and energy consumption.

of client updates to update the global model. Figure 9(a) shows the results from a small federation of 20 clients. Although setting the proportion to 80% has a clear gap of accuracy level compared with using all clients, increasing the proportion to 90% results in the same accuracy level as using all clients. This means that the server can ignore the 10% slowest clients in each round and will not lose model accuracy. Clearly this would reduce the overall training time. In Fig. 10(a) we compare the 90 percentile training time in each round with the longest time among the 20 clients. The corresponding energy results are shown in Fig. 10(b) for one particular client. Here we compare the case of dynamically adjusting CPU frequency against the default, which is to always use the highest frequency for the training task. It is important to point out that the time and energy results here are not really important. What we are demonstrating here is the capability of FLSim for this type of research. Quantified studies obviously require more accurate models.

Intuitively, as the size of the federation increases, the proportion of clients selected can be reduced to get the highest levels of accuracy. This indeed is the case. Figure 9(b) shows the results for the same test as in Fig. 9(a) except that the number of clients is increased to 40. Now we can see setting the proportion of clients to 80% can achieve the highest level of accuracy after about 200 rounds.

5   Evaluation of Using Multiple CPU Processes

In this section we briefly present some performance results of FLSim when it uses multiple CPU processes. That is to say, the federation is built with ServerMP and ClientRankMP. Experiments here are run on a server with a 16-core Intel Xeon E5-2620 CPU. The OS is Ubuntu 18.04.

Table 8. Multi-Process Performance: Time in Seconds for One Training Round.

Test Case	#Clients	1 Proc	2 Proc	5 Proc	10 Proc
CNN MINST E=1, B=10	10	27.8	18.8 (1.5×)	13.7 (2.0×)	13.3 (2.1×)
	20	46.0	28.0 (1.6×)	19.2 (2.4×)	17.9 (2.6×)
	40	83.0	47.0 (1.8×)	27.6 (3.0×)	23.4 (3.5×)
CNN CIFAR E=1, B=10	10	40.7	30.2 (1.3×)	23.9 (1.7×)	21.7 (1.9×)
	20	62.7	40.8 (1.5×)	28.7 (2.2×)	24.9 (2.5×)
	40	105.1	63.1 (1.7×)	38.1 (2.8×)	31.9 (3.3×)
2NN MINST E=10, B=10	10	26.7	13.1 (2.0×)	6.6 (4.0×)	4.8 (5.6×)
	20	45.1	24.1 (1.9×)	11.4 (4.0×)	7.1 (6.4×)
	40	94.7	45.6 (2.1×)	21.1 (4.5×)	12.1 (7.8×)

Table 8 shows the time in seconds to run one training round with three different models. For each model we tested three different federation sizes and four different numbers of CPU processes. Speedup numbers for the multi-process cases are also displayed. A couple of observations can be made. First, while the two CNN models have similar speedup trends, the simpler 2NN model has a very different trend. Second, as we increase the number of clients, the workload in a training round is increased, and this leads to higher speedup numbers. Third, for the CNN models, using more than five processes has limited effect on speedup.

6 Conclusions

In this paper, we propose FLSim, a simulation framework for federated learning in order to efficiently build different simulators to investigate different scenarios in federated learning. Different from the ad hoc simulators, FLSim can be envisioned as an open repository of building blocks for creating simulators. Specifically, FLSim consists of a set of software components organized in a well-structured software architecture that provides the foundation for maximizing flexibility and extensibility. Developers can create different simulators through easily putting the selected components together, thus allowing developers/researchers to focus on the problems being studied. In addition, we use different case studies to demonstrate the effectiveness of FLSim.

Acknowledgement. This work is supported by the National Key R&D Program of China (No. 2019YFB2102100), Science and Technology Development Fund of Macao S.A.R (FDCT) under number 0015/2019/AKP, Guangdong Key R&D Project (No. 2020B010164003), Shenzhen Discipline Construction Project for Urban Computing and Data Intelligence.

References

1. Real Time Applications of Machine Learning. https://www.redalkemi.com/blog/post/5-real-time-applications-of-machine-learning
2. Pytorch. https://pytorch.org
3. Tensorflow. https://www.tensorflow.org
4. Ram, A.: How smartphone apps track users and share data (2018). https://ig.ft.com/mobile-app-data-trackers/
5. Krizhevsky, A., Nair, V., Hinton, G.: The cifar-10 dataset. https://www.cs.toronto.edu/~kriz/cifar.html
6. Bishop, C.M., et al.: Neural Networks for Pattern Recognition. Oxford University Press, Oxford (1995)
7. Bonawitz, K., Eichner, H., Grieskamp, W., Huba, D., Ingerman, A., Lvanov, V.: Towards federated learning at scale: system design. arXiv preprint arXiv:1902.01046 (2019)
8. Bonawitz, K., et al.: Practical secure aggregation for privacy-preserving machine learning. In: Proceedings of the 2017 ACM SIGSAC Conference on Computer and Communications Security, pp. 1175–1191. ACM (2017)
9. Buschmann, F., Meunier, R., Hans, R., Peter, S., Michael, S.: Pattern-Oriented Software Architecture: A System of Patterns, vol. 1. Wiley, New Jersey (1996)
10. Calheiros, R.N., Ranjan, R., Beloglazov, A., De Rose, C.A., Buyya, R.: Cloudsim: a toolkit for modeling and simulation of cloud computing environments and evaluation of resource provisioning algorithms. Softw. Pract. Experience 41(1), 23–50 (2011)
11. Mo, F., Haddadi, H.: Efficient and private federated learning using tee. In: EuroSys (2019)
12. Fowler, M.: Inversion of control containers and the dependency injection pattern (2004). https://martinfowler.com/articles/injection.html

13. Howell, F., McNab, R.: Simjava: a discrete event simulation library for java. Simul. Ser. **30**, 51–56 (1998)
14. Wong, J.C.: The Cambirdge Analytica scandal changed the world, but it didn't change Facebook (2018). https://www.theguardian.com/technology
15. Konečnỳ, J., McMahan, H.B., Yu, F.X., Richtárik, P., Suresh, A.T., Bacon, D.: Federated learning: strategies for improving communication efficiency. arXiv preprint arXiv:1610.05492 (2016)
16. Hautala, L.: Google tool lets any AI app learn without taking all your data (2018). https://www.cnet.com/news/google-ai-tool-lets-outside-apps-get-smart-without-taking-all-your-data/
17. Lalitha, A., Shekhar, S., Javidi, T., Koushanfar, F.: Fully decentralized federated learning. In: Third Workshop on Bayesian Deep Learning (NeurIPS) (2018)
18. Li, L., Xiong, H., Guo, Z., Wang, J., Xu, C.: Smartpc: hierarchical pace control in real-time federated learning system. In: 2019 IEEE Real-Time Systems Symposium (RTSS) (2019)
19. Hamblen, M.: Mobile users prefer Wi-Fi over cellular for lower cost, speed, and reliability (2012). https://www.computerworld.com/article/2506011/
20. Hamblen, M.: Google AI Blog: Federated Learning: Collaborative Machine Learning for Mobile Devices (2017). https://ai.googleblog.com/2017/04/federated-learning-collaborative.html
21. Marketing-Schools: Marketing Mobile Phones (2018). http://www.marketing-schools.org/consumer-psychology
22. McMahan, H.B., Moore, E., Ramage, D., Hampson, S., Arcas, B.A.y.: Communication-efficient learning of deep networks from decentralized data. In: Proceedings of the 20th International Conference on Artificial Intelligence and Statistics (2017)
23. Halpern, S.: The champaign for mobile phone voting is getting a midterm test (2018). https://www.newyorker.com/tech/annals-of-technology/
24. Smith, V., Chiang, C.K., Sanjabi, M., Talwalkar, A.: Federated multi-task learning. In: Advances in Neural Information Processing Systems, pp. 4424–4434 (2017)
25. Sprague, M.R., et al.: Asynchronous federated learning for geospatial applications. In: Monreale, A., et al. (eds.) ECML PKDD 2018. CCIS, vol. 967, pp. 21–28. Springer, Cham (2019). https://doi.org/10.1007/978-3-030-14880-5_2
26. Wang, J., et al.: Manifold: a parallel simulation framework for multicore systems. In: 2014 IEEE International Symposium on Performance Analysis of Systems and Software (ISPASS), pp. 106–115 (2014)
27. Wang, J., Beu, J., Yalamanchili, S., Conte, T.: Designing configurable, modifiable and reusable components for simulation of multicore systems. In: 2012 SC Companion: High Performance Computing, Networking Storage and Analysis, pp. 472–476 (2012)
28. Wang, S., et al.: Adaptive federated learning in resource constrained edge computing systems. Learning, vol. 8, p. 9 (2018)
29. Lecun, Y., Cortes, C., Burges, J.C.: The mnist database of handwritten digits. http://yann.lecun.com/exdb/mnist/
30. Zhao, Y., Li, M., Lai, L., Suda, N., Civin, D., Chandra, V.: Federated learning with non-iid data. arXiv preprint arXiv:1806.00582 (2018)

Algorithm for Double-Layer Structure Multi-label Classification with Optimal Sequence Based on Attention Mechanism

Geqiao Liu[1,2](✉) and Mingjie Tan[1,2]

[1] College of Engineering and Technology, Sichuan Radio and Television University, Chengdu, China
liugq@scrtvu.net
[2] Research Center for Educational Information Management and Information Systems, Open University of China, Beijing, China

Abstract. A common approach to multi-label classification is to perform problem transformation, whereby a multi-label problem is transformed into one or more single-label problems. Problem transformation considers label correlations by extending the attributes, but ignores the importance of each feature attribute for different classification targets, weakens the sensitivity of the classifier, and reduces the classification accuracy. Attention mechanism is a model that simulates the mechanism of human brain attention. It mainly emphasizes the influence of some crucial inputs on the output by calculating the attention probability distribution, which has a good optimization effect on the traditional model. Based on this, this paper proposes a two-layer chain structure multi-label classification (ATDCC-OS) algorithm, which incorporates the attention mechanism. This algorithm constructs a two-layer multi-label classification model in order to realize the correlation between labels through inter-layer and intra-layer interaction. At the same time, the attention mechanism is introduced to focus selectively on the sample features, identify more important information for the current task, and further improve the classification performance of the algorithm. Furthermore, an optimal sequence selection algorithm (OSS) is proposed, seeking to label the pecking order, solving the problem of reduced classification accuracy caused by randomly selecting the class label sequence to train the binary classifier by the chain classification model. The OSS will be used to optimize the second-layer chain classification model of ATDCC-OS. Comparisons on seven benchmark data sets with related algorithms verify the effectiveness of ATDCC-OS.

Keywords: Multi-label classification · Double layer · Attention mechanism

1 Introduction

Classification is a popular branch of data mining techniques, it is aimed at training sample data set to construct a classification model, and use classification model to the measured

H. Song and D. Jiang (Eds.): SIMUtools 2020, LNICST 369, pp. 370–390, 2021.
https://doi.org/10.1007/978-3-030-72792-5_31

data to predict the category information. In traditional single label classification, a sample instance belongs to only one category. However, There are a lot of ambiguities examples in the real world, namely a sample instance might also belong to two different categories, the corresponding classification problems referred to as multi-label classification. Initially, multi-label learning originates from the document classified in the ambiguity problem. After decades of development, multi-label classification technology has been widely applied to medical diagnosis, recommender systems, information retrieval, image, video and other fields [1–8]. In recent years, the frequency of "multi-label" discussions have continued to increase from international conferences related to machine learning such as ACL, NIPS, CIKM, COLING, AAAI, INTERSPEECH, ICML, KDD, ICDM, and IJCAI. These make multi-label classification a popular research direction in machine learning, and it has also attracted the attention of the authoritative publication "Machine Learning" in the international machine learning community. Therefore, a large number of multi-label classification algorithms have been proposed.

The existing multi-label learning algorithms are mainly divided into two categories: problem transformation and algorithm adaptation. Problem transformation will transform a multi-label problem into one or more single-label problems. In this way, single-label classifiers are employed; and their single label predictions are transformed into multi-label predictions [9]. Algorithm adaptation is to modify an algorithm (such as AdaBoost, decision trees) directly to make multi-label predictions. This article will focus on the research of problem transformation.

After studying the problem transformation algorithm, it is found that many algorithms (such as BR [10], CC [9], MBR [11], and DLMC-OS [12]) often neglect the correlation between labels, and randomly select label sequences and redundant interactive label information in the design process, which results in the reduction of classification accuracy. At the same time, problem transformation mainly considers the correlation between labels by extending attributes, but ignores the importance of each feature attribute for different classification targets, thus weakening the sensitivity of classifiers and affecting the classification effect of each classifier. Attention Mechanism [13] is a model that simulates the human brain's attention mechanism. It highlights the effect of some key inputs on the output by calculating the probability distribution of attention, which has a better optimization effect on the traditional model. Based on this, this paper proposes a multi-label classification algorithm based on attention mechanism (ATDCC-OS), which combines attention mechanism and double-layer chain structure.

The ATDCC-OS algorithm integrates three classical problem transformation types of multi-label classification frameworks (BR, CC, and MBR), and constructs a multi-label classification model based on a double-layer chain structure. In the first layer of the model, a binary association classification framework is used to accomplish the first classification of unseen instances, and the label information interacts with the second layer. In the second layer of the model, a chain classification model with an "update process" is used to accomplish the final classification of unseen instances. On this basis, attention mechanism is introduced to calculate dynamically the weight of each feature attribute in the second layer, which can identify more important attributes for the current classification task and further improve the classification performance of the algorithm. In order to solve the random chain order problem of the chain model in ATDCC-OS, an optimal sequence selection algorithm (OSS) is proposed. The OSS combines mutual information, PageRank, Kruskal's algorithm, and hierarchical traversal algorithm to find a tag priority order, and uses this sequence to guide the construction of classifiers in the chain classification model and further optimize the ATDCC-OS.

The rest of the paper is organized as follows: Sect. 2describes related work, Sect. 3 describes the proposed ATDCC-OS model, Sect. 4 introduces experimental data, evaluation methods, experimental set up, and experimental results and discussion. This paper is concluded in Sect. 5.

2   Related Work

2.1   Multi-label Classification

At present, problem transformation and algorithm adaptation are two popular research directions in the field of multi-label classification. In the problem transformation method, the multi-label classification task transforms one or more single-label classification, regression, or sorting tasks [11]. The basic classification algorithms often used in problem transformation are supporting vector machine [14], naive Bayesian, and k-nearest neighbor algorithm. The algorithm adaptations often modify the single-label classification algorithm to adapt to multi-label classification data. Representative algorithms include ML-RBF [15, 16], ML-kNN [17, 18], Rank-SVM [19], associated classification algorithm LRwAR [20, 21], etc.

The most common problem transformation method is BR [10], which converts a multi-label problem into multiple binary problems, training a binary model for each label to determine whether it belongs to the class label. The classification prediction for a new instance will be the sum of all binary classifier results. Although the computational complexity of the BR algorithm is low and linearly related to the class label, the correlation between the class labels is not considered in the process of classification, which leads to a certain degree of information loss. S. Godbole et al. [11] proposed the MBR of the two-layer BR model. It considers label correlations by adding the output of the first layer as the sample attribute to the second layer. However, when performing the second-layer model training, there is a problem of redundant consideration of the label value.

J. Read et al. [9] introduced the "chain" to consider the correlation between labels, and proposed CC. It links all binary classifiers into a random chain, and the output of the previous classifier is added to its sample attributes as input to the next classifier. However, the random chain still has some disadvantages. First, when training the binary classifier, the CC only considers the output predictions of the previous classifiers, and ignores the back-end classifier, so that the correlation between labels cannot be fully considered. Secondly, the implicit directionality in the chain will also affect the classification accuracy. If there is a low-precision binary classifier at the head of the chain, the low-precision classification results will propagate backward along the chain, thus affecting the accuracy of the overall classification. Finally, CC is a random chain, and the randomness will increase with the number of labels, which will seriously affect the stability of the algorithm [22, 23].

G. Q. Liu and T. Guo [12] proposed a multi-label classification with optimal sequence based on double layers (DLMC-OS). The algorithm constructs a two-layer classification model. Each classifier in the second layer receives all the extended features transmitted from the first layer, and links the backward update to consider the correlations existing between labels. Although the algorithm effectively solves the randomness problem of the chain classification model, it does not solve the uniqueness of the sequence.

2.2 Attention Mechanism

The attention mechanism [24–26] was first applied to the field of computer vision to simulate human visual attention mechanism. It quickly scans the global image to obtain the target area that needs attention, and then puts more attention resources into the area to obtain more detailed information and suppress other useless information. This improves the efficiency and accuracy of visual information processing exceptionally. Attention mechanism in deep learning is essentially similar to human selective visual attention mechanism, and the core goal is to select more critical information for the current task goal from a large amount of information. D. Bahdanau et al. [27] applied attention mechanism to machine translation tasks for the first time and obtained good results. The Google Mind [28] team was inspired by the human attention mechanism and published an article in 2014 that introduced people not looking at the pixels of the entire image at once when viewing images. Instead, they focus on a specific part of the image according to their needs. Moreover, humans will obtain a position that needs to be focused on in the future based on the observation of the previous image. A. M. Rush et al. [29] proposed a completely data-driven abstract sentence summarization method based on the local attention model. H. Chen et al. [30] captured key components at different semantic levels by introducing user-product attention mechanism for emotional analysis. Z. Yang et al. [31] proposed a hierarchical attention network for document classification, enabling it to differentiate between unimportant content. R. He et al. [32] used attention mechanism to extract viewpoint entities from text. W. Yin et al. [33] combined the attention mechanism with CNN for machine translation, which is an early exploratory work of the attention mechanism in CNN. In "Attention is all you need" published by the Google Machine Translation Team [34], the self-attention mechanism is widely used to learn text representation. It is not only separated from traditional RNN/CNN, but also uses a novel multi-head mechanism.

3 ATDCC-OS

3.1 Preliminaries

Let $\chi \in \Re^d$ be the input domain of all possible d-dimensional attribute values. The set $\gamma = \{y_1, y_2, v, y_L\}$ is the output domain of L-dimensional label values. Each instance x is associated with a subset of these labels. This set is represented by a L-vector $Y = [y_1, y_2, v, y_L]$, where $y_j = 1$ if and only if label j is associated with instance x, and 0 otherwise. Given a multi-label training set $D = \{(x_i, Y_i) | 1 \leq i \leq m\}$, where $x_i \in \chi$ is the d-dimensional attribute vector $(x_{i1}, x_{i2}, v, x_{id})^T$ and $Y_i \subset \gamma$ is a set of labels corresponding to x_i. Learning multi-label classification is learning a multi-label classifier $H : \chi \rightarrow 2^y$. $H^f = \left(H_1^f, H_2^f, v, H_L^f \right)$ and $H^s = \left(H_1^s, H_2^s, v, H_L^s \right)$ are the classifiers constructed in the first and second layer, respectively. $c^f = \left(y_1^f, y_2^f, v, y_L^f \right)$ and $c^S = \left(y_1^S, y_2^S, v, y_L^S \right)$ are the classification results of the corresponding layer.

3.2 The ATDCC Framework

According to the design idea of the DLMC-OS algorithm, a Double-Layer Chain Classification Model Based on Attention Mechanism (ATDCC) is constructed. ATDCC sets two layers to decompose the multi-label classification problem into independent binary-classification problems. In the first layer, the ATDCC model involves L binary transformations one for each label and each binary model is trained to predict the relevance of one of the labels [12]. The first layer of ATDCC implements the first classification of the instance, and then the classification result is transmitted to the second layer by extending the attribute. In the second layer, ATDCC builds a chained classification model with an update process, which uses the chain to pass and update label information, achieves the second interaction of label information, and simultaneously accomplishes the final classification of the instance. ATDCC fully considers the correlation between labels through inter-layer label information interaction and intra-layer label information transfer.

ATDCC^First-layer. ATDCC^First-layer inherits the idea of the binary relevance classification model to construct a corresponding binary classifier for each label, and then combines the classification results of all binary classifiers as the first classification of unseen instances (see Fig. 1).

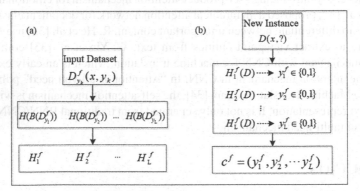

Fig. 1. a The procedure of ATDCC^First−layer in training stage. **b** The procedure of ATDCC^First−layer in training stage.

In the first step, for a dataset with L labels, ATDCC^First−layer constructs a corresponding data set for each class label according to Eq. (1):

$$D_{y_k}^f = \{ (x_i, y_k) | 1 \le i \le m \}$$

$$\text{Where} \quad y_k = \begin{cases} 1, & \text{if } y_k \in Y_k \\ 0, & \text{otherwise} \end{cases} \tag{1}$$

In the second step, for any multi-label training example, some binary algorithm B (such as SMO) is used to induce a binary classifier: $H_{y_k}^f \leftarrow B(D_{y_k}^f)$.

In the third step, the unseen instance X is classified and predicted using the constructed binary classifier.

$$H_{y_k}^f : X \rightarrow \{0, 1\}$$

$$y_k^f = \left\{ H_{y_k}^f(X) | 1 \le k \le L \right\} \tag{2}$$

Finally, ATDCC will combine the prediction value (i.e.$c^f = (y_1^f, y_2^f, \cdots, y_L^f)$) of each classifier as the first classification of the unseen instance, and add c^f to the original sample attribute to form a new sample attribute $x' = \{(x_i, c^f) | 1 \le i \le m\}.x'$ will be taken as the input of the next layer of ATDCC.

ATDCC$^{\text{AT-layer}}$. The attention mechanism has been successfully applied to sequence-to-sequence learning tasks. For classification tasks, the attention mechanism is able to learn the weight of each attribute in the sample to reflect its impact on the final classification result.

ATDCC$^{\text{AT-layer}}$ introduces the attention mechanism to calculate dynamically the weight value of the attribute values passed to the second layer model, discriminates the more important information for the current classification task for each classifier in the second layer, and enhances the sensitivity of each classifier.

In the first step, according to the dimension of the incoming data of the first layer, a weight matrix W is defined. ATDCC$^{\text{AT-layer}}$ will use the tanh function to quantize the correlation between the input data and the i-th label. In Eq. (3), W is the weight matrix that needs to be learned, and b is the bias of the model.

$$e_{ij} = \tanh(W_{ij}x_{ij}' + b)(1 \le i \le m) \tag{3}$$

In the second step, ATDCC$^{\text{AT-layer}}$ will convert the result of Eq. (3) into a probability value by the softmax function to obtain attention weights:

$$W_{ij}' = \text{softmax}(e_{ij}) = \frac{\exp(e_{ij})}{\sum_{j=1}^m \exp(e_{ij})} \tag{4}$$

Finally, the original input will be weighted using the attention weights from Eq. (4):

$$x'' = \sum_{i=1}^m x_{ij}' \omega_{ij}' \tag{5}$$

We update and optimize the parameters in the model by minimizing the loss function. The loss function used here is the cross-entropy loss function (Eq. 6), which is the negative log likelihood of the actual and predicted labels for each sample:

$$J(\theta) = -\frac{1}{l} \sum_{k=1}^l \log p(y_k | y_k') \tag{6}$$

ATDCC$^{\text{Second-layer}}$. ATDCC$^{\text{Second-layer}}$ (see Fig. 2) is the second layer of the ATDCC model, which uses the chained classification model with the update process to complete the second classification of the instances. The instance with attribute space for each binary model is extended with label relevance of all previous classifiers to form a classifier chain. The attribute space for each binary model is augmented with the 0/1 label prediction coming from first-layer classifiers and all prior binary relevance predictions from the second layer in which the classifier chain is built. The correlation between each label is fully considered after the procedure of the second layer. Each classifier in the chain is responsible for learning and predicting the binary association of the label, given the attribute space.

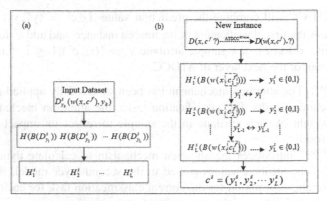

Fig. 2. a The procedure of ATDCC$^{\text{Second-layer}}$ in training stage. **b** The procedure of ATDCC$^{\text{Second-layer}}$ in training stage.

In the first step, ATDCC$^{\text{Second-layer}}$ constructs a corresponding data set $D^s_{y_k}$ ($1 \le k \le$ L) for each class label according to Eq. (7), where W is the attribute weight obtained from the ATDCC$^{\text{AT-layer}}$.

$$D^s_{y_k} = \left\{ \left(\left[w_i x_i, w_{i+1}y^f_1, \cdots, w_{i+k-1}y^f_{k-1}, w_{i+k+1}y^f_{k+1} \cdots, w_{i+L}y^f_L \right], y^f_k \right) | 1 \le i \le m \right\}$$
(7)

In the second step, a binary algorithm B (such as SMO)is used to train the corresponding binary classifier on the constructed data set, i.e. $H^s_{y_k} \leftarrow B(D^s_{y_k})$.

In the third step, the unseen instance X is classified and predicted using the constructed binary classifier.

$$H^s_{y_k} : X \rightarrow \{0, 1\}$$
$$y^s_k = \left\{ H^s_{y_k}(X) | 1 \le k \le L \right\}$$
(8)

During the classification process, the latest predicted label value is used to update the corresponding label value of the sample attribute space. For example, for the third classifier $H^s_{y_3}$ in the chain, the incoming sample attribute value is $\left[x, y^s_1, y^s_2, y^f_3, y^f_4, \cdots, y^f_L \right]$ instead of $\left[x, y^f_1, y^f_2, y^f_3, y^f_4, \cdots, y^f_L \right]$.

Finally, ATDCC will combine the classification prediction value c^s = $(y_1^s, y_2^s, \cdots, y_L^s)$ of each classifier as the final classification for the unseen instance.

3.3 OSS

Because the chain classification model has a random chain order problem, if there is a lower-precision binary classifier at the front of the chain, the low-precision classification result will propagate backward along the chain, affecting the classification accuracy of the subsequent classifier. It even affects the classification accuracy of the entire chain, and the randomness of the chain orders increases with the number of labels. Although the DLMC-OS algorithm alleviates the randomness problem of the chain classification model, it cannot find the optimal label sequence because it cannot fix the root node. Then the most straightforward solution is to sequence the random chain order, but the formation of the label sequence is not a simple arrangement, and needs to be combined with the characteristics of the chain classification model. To this end, the labeling order sought in this article needs to have the following points:

A. The label sequence is an ordered sequence containing all label information.
B. The label sequence is a sequence with the greatest correlation.
C. The label sequence is an optimal sequence.

Based on the above design principles, OSS is proposed. The algorithm combines mutual information, PageRank, Kruskal's algorithm, and hierarchical traversal algorithm to find a label with the most relevance. The sequence is used to guide the construction order for each classifier in the chain classification model, and the second layer of ATDCC is optimized using OSS.

Related Sub-algorithm of OSS. (1) *Mutual Information (MI).* In probability theory and information theory, the mutual information (MI) of two random variables is a measure of the mutual dependence between the two variables. More specifically, it quantifies the "amount of information" obtained about one random variable by observing the other random variable. The MI of the two variables is defined by Eq. (9). With the constant research of experts and scholars, the theory of MI has gradually infiltrated all walks of life. In machine learning, MI is applied to feature selection [35, 36]. In search engine technology, MI between phrases and contexts is used to discover semantic clusters [37]. In statistical mechanics, MI is combined with Loschmidt's paradox to solve mechanical problems [38, 39].
Based on the MI design idea and application, this work will measure the correlation between tags by calculating the MI between the two labels, and use it as the weight of the edges of the full connection graph.

(2) *PageRank.* PageRank (PR) [40] was proposed by Sergey Brin and Larry Page in 1998 to solve the problem of page ranking in link analysis. The core idea is that the importance of a page depends on the number and quality of other pages pointing to it. Reference [41] mentioned that Google's search engine uses the PageRank algorithm based on the importance (popularity) of Web pages. The importance of

a Webpage is discovered through the analysis of its link structure, and does not depend on the specific search request. Personalized PageRank is used by Twitter to present users with other accounts they may wish to follow [42].

Based on PageRank's design idea and priority search principle, this work will use the PageRank algorithm to find an important tag as a chain head node, which solves the problem of low-precision classifier in the chain.

Algorithm 1. Description of PageRank algorithm

Input: M, alpha, M: label matrix, alpha: damping factor (default value 0.85)
Output: root

---

1. V ← {}
2. N ← M. shape [1]
3. V ← random Matrix (n, 1)
4. Last_V ← Matrix (n, 1, 10)
5. M_hat ← (alpha * M) + (((1 - alpha) / N) * Matrix. ones ((N, N)))
6. While (Last_V -V > epsilon)
7.   Last_V ← V
8.   V ← M_hat * V
9. end while
10. root ← *MaxIndex*(V)
11. Return root

---

(3) *Edge-Weight Graph Algorithm.* A weighted graph [43] is a graph in which a number (the weight) is assigned to each edge. Such weights might represent, for example, costs, lengths, or capacities, depending on the problem at hand [44–47]. This work will use Edge-weight graph algorithm to construct a fully connected graph with the association with labels.

Algorithm 2. Description of Edge-weight graph algorithm

Input: $Y = \{y_1, y_2, \ldots, y_L\}$
Output: G

---

1. G ← {}
2. G. V ← Y
3. For each (u, v) in G.V:
4.   Calculate the mutual information of MI (u, v) according to definition 1.
5.   G. E ← MI (u, v)
6. G ← G(V, E)
7. Return G

---

(4) *Kruskal's algorithm.* Kruskal's algorithm [48] was proposed by Joseph Kruskal in 1956 to find the minimum spanning tree. This paper will introduce Kruskal's algorithm to find the largest-label spanning tree, which provides the basis of finding the sequence of the largest association with labels.

Algorithm 3. Description of Kruskal's algorithm

Input: G (V, E)
Output: MWT
1. MWT ← {}
2. For each v ∈ G.V:
3.   MAKE-SET(v)
4. For each (u, v) in G.E ordered by weight (u, v) increasing:
5.   If FIND-SET(u) ≠ FIND-SET(v):
6.   MST=MST∪ {(u, v)}
7.   UNION (u, v)
8. Return MWT ←MST

(5) *Breadth-First Search Algorithm.* Breadth-first search (BFS) and its application for finding connected components of graphs was invented in 1945 by Konrad Zuse. BFS is an algorithm for traversing or searching tree or graph data structures. In this paper, the BFS algorithm will take the tag node obtained by PageRank as the starting point, and traverse the largest-tag spanning tree to obtain the final tag order.

Algorithm 4. Description of Breadth-first search algorithm

Input: MWT (V, E)
Output: OS
1. Queue Q ← {}
2. For each v ∈ MWT.V:
3. $Q \leftarrow Q \cup (v)$
4.   *while(Q!=∅)*
5. $v \leftarrow Q.head$, $w \leftarrow Q.next$
6.   *while(w! = ∅)*
7. $Q \leftarrow Q \cup (w)$
8.   end while
9.   end while
10. end for
11. $OS \leftarrow Q$
12. Return OS

The OSS Framework. The design steps for the OSS algorithm are as follows (see Fig. 3):

In the first step, this work uses mutual information to measure the correlation between tags. If there are N labels $y_1, y_2 \cdots , y_n$, the mutual information on any two tags y_i and y_j is calculated by formula (9).

Definition 1: MI of two variables:

$$I(x_i, x_j) = \sum_{x_i x_j} p(x_i, x_j) \log\left(\frac{p(x_i, x_j)}{p(x_i)p(x_j)}\right) \text{ and must be non - negative.} \tag{9}$$

In the second step, a full-connection graph G representing the association with labels is constructed, the label is used as the vertex of the graph, and the mutual information value between the labels is used as the weight of the edge. In order to enable the

Kruskal algorithm to obtain the maximum weight label tree, it is necessary to reverse the mutual information value. In this way, the minimum-weight spanning tree obtained by the Kruskal algorithm is the maximum-weight spanning tree.

In the third step, the PageRank algorithm is used to perform "voting" sorting through each label in the data set to find the label node with the highest PR value. The selected node will be taken as the root node of the maximum weight tree and the starting node of the hierarchical traversal algorithm, which can solve the problem of reducing the overall classification accuracy caused by the existence of a low-precision classifier at the head of the label chain.

In the fourth step, the Kruskal's algorithm is used to generate a minimum-weight label tree (also MWT) for the full connection graph G. The label tree contains all the labels and edges connecting the label nodes, and the sum of weights is the largest.

In the fifth step, The BFS will use the label node obtained by PageRank as a starting node, and traverse MWT to obtain a label sequence. The sequence is used to guide the construction order for each classifier in the chain model to solve the randomness problem of the classification model.

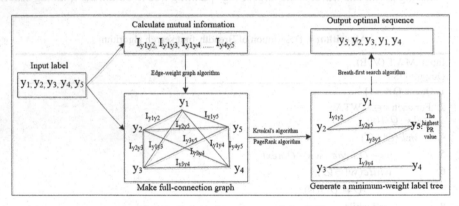

Fig. 3. Calculation process of the OSS

Algorithm 5. Description of OSS algorithm

Find the labels' optimized chain order.

Input: $D=(x_1,x_2,\cdots,x_n \,|\, y_1,y_2,\cdots,y_L)$

Output: $OS(y_1, y_2, \cdots, y_L)$

---

1. ▷ Calculate mutual information according to definition 1
2. for i = 1,2 ⋯ , L
3.   for j = i+1,2,⋯, L

4. $I_{ij} \leftarrow MI(y_i, y_j)$
5. $Array \; A \leftarrow \overline{I_{ij}}$

6.   End for
7. End for
8. ▷ Make a fully connected graph
9. $G \leftarrow Edge\text{-}weighted\ graph(L, A)$

10. ▷ Determine the root node by PageRank
11. $V \leftarrow PageRank(D)$

12. ▷ Get the maximum weight label Tree
13. $T \leftarrow Kruskal(G, V)$

14. ▷ Get the optimal sequence
15. $OS(y_1, y_2, \cdots, y_L) \leftarrow Breadth\text{-}first\ search(T)$

16. Return OS

3.4   The ATDCC-OS Framework

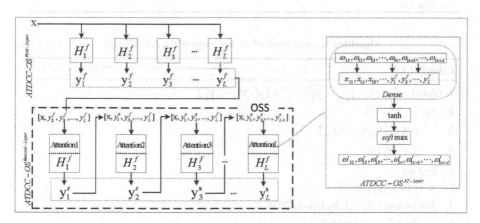

Fig. 4. Framework of the ATDCC-OS model

The ATDCC-OS framework is shown in Fig. 4, where ATDCC^First-layer and ATDCC^Second-layer are the first and second layers of the model, respectively. The OSS algorithm is used to optimize the second-layer chain model of ATDCC-OS, find a label optimal sequence in it, and use the optimal sequence as the training order for each classifier in the second-layer model. The ATDCC$^{\text{AT-layer}}$ is the attention mechanism layer in the second layer, which is used to identify more important attributes to current classification tasks for each classifier in the second layer.

Algorithm 6. Description of the train stage of the ATDCC-OS

D is training set, L is number of labels

TRAINING $D = \{(x_i, Y_i) \mid i = 1, 2, \cdots, m\}$

1. *for* j = 1,2,$\cdots$,L
2. $D_{y_j}^f \leftarrow \{\ \}$
3.   *do* x $\leftarrow [x_{i1}, x_{i2}, \cdots, x_{im}]$
4. $D_{y_j}^f \leftarrow x \cup y_j$
5. $H_j^f \leftarrow B(D_{y_j}^f)$
6. end for
7. for j=sort1,2,$\cdots$,LbyOSS(D)
8. $D_{y_j}^s \leftarrow \{\ \}$
9.   *do* x $\leftarrow [x_{i1}, x_{i2}, \cdots, x_{im}, y_1, \cdots, y_{j-1}, y_{j+1}, \cdots, y_L]$
10. $W \leftarrow \{W_{i1}, W_{i2}, \cdots, W_{im+L}\}$
11. $W \leftarrow attention\ (x)$
12. $x' \leftarrow x \times W$
13. $D_{y_j}^s \leftarrow x' \cup y_j$
14. $H_j^s \leftarrow B(D_{y_j}^s)$
15. $y_j = H_j^s(x')$
16. End for

Algorithm 7. Description of the test stage of the ATDCC-OS

Classify (x)

1. Global $c^f = (y_1^f, y_2^f, \cdots, y_L^f)$, $c^s = (y_1^s, y_2^s, \cdots, y_L^s)$
2. *for* j = 1,2,$\cdots$,L
3.   *do* x $\leftarrow [x_{i1}, x_{i2}, \cdots, x_{im}]$
4. $y_j^f \leftarrow H_{y_j}^f(x)$
5. End for
6. $x' \leftarrow [x, y_1^f, y_2^f, \cdots, y_L^f]$
7. *for* j = sort1,2,$\cdots$,L by OS-CC(D)
8.   *do* x'' $\leftarrow x' \times W_j'$
9. $y_j^s \leftarrow H_j^s(x'')$
10. End for
11. $c^s \leftarrow (y_1^s, y_2^s, \cdots, y_L^s)$
12. *Return* c^s

4   Experiments

In this section, we will compare ATDCC-OS with DLMC-OS, BR, CC, and MBR on the basis of five evaluation metrics on seven benchmark multi-label data sets. We will introduce the multi-label benchmark datasets, evaluation measurements, and experiment setup in turn, and finally show the experimental results and discuss them.

4.1   Data Sets

The multi-label benchmark datasets used in the experiments are derived from the standard dataset provided by the Mulan [49] platform. Table 1 displays multi-label datasets from a variety of domains, and their associated statistics. Here, N is the number of instances in the dataset. F is the number of attributes included in each instance of the dataset. L is the number of labels in the dataset. Label Cardinality (LCard) is a standard measure of "multi-labelled-ness," introduced in Tsoumaskas and Katakis [50]. It is simply the average number of labels associated with each example. This measure gives a good idea of label frequency, but gives no indication of the regularity or uniformity of the labelling scheme.

Table 1. Multi-label datasets

Dataset	N	F	L	LCard	Type
Flags	194	19	7	3.392	Images
Emotion	593	72	6	1.87	Music
Birds	654	300	21	1.104	Audio
Medical	978	1449	45	1.245	Text
Enron	1702	1001	53	3.38	Text
Yeast	2417	103	14	4.24	Biology
Bibtex	7395	1836	159	2.40	Text

4.2   Evaluation Methods

In multi-label classification experiments, it is important to evaluate the performance of each algorithm. In order to evaluate the algorithm better, we use Average Precision, Coverage, One-Error, Ranking Loss, and Micro-averaged AUC.

(1)   Average Precision: Average precision [12] is a measure that combines recall and precision for ranked retrieval results. It evaluates the average fraction of relevant labels ranked higher than a particular label $y \in y_i$. For this indicator, the bigger the value, the better. The formula for Average Precision is as follows:

$$avgprec_D(H) = \frac{1}{P} \sum_{i=1}^{P} \frac{1}{|Y_i|} \sum_{y \in Y_i} \frac{|\{y' | rank_C(x, y') \leq rank_C(x_i, y), y' \in Y_i\}|}{rank_C(x_i, y)}$$

Where $rank(.)$ is a sort function.

(2) Coverage [12]: the coverage measure is for assessing the performance of a system for all the possible labels of documents. That is, coverage measures how far we need, on average, to go down the list of labels in order to cover all the possible labels assigned to a document. Coverage is loosely related to precision at the level of perfect recall. For this indicator, the smaller value is better. The formula for Coverage is as follows:

$$coverage_D(H) = \frac{1}{P} \sum_{i=1}^{P} \max rank_f(x_i, y) - 1$$

Where $rank(.)$ is the sort function that matches the classifier $H(.)$.

(3) One-Error [51]: The one-error evaluates the fraction of examples whose top-ranked label is not in the relevant label set. For this indicator, the smaller value is better. The formula for One-Error is as follows:

$$one - error_D(H) = \frac{1}{P} \sum_{i=1}^{P} \left[\!\left[\arg\max_{y \in \gamma} f(x_i, y) \notin Y_i \right]\!\right]$$

Where $f(.)$ is a real-valued function corresponding to the multi-label classifier $H(.)$.

(4) Ranking Loss [12]: Ranking Loss is used in the case where the class label sorting of the response sample is out of order, that is, in the class label sorting queue, the class label unrelated to the instance is located before the related class label. For this indicator, the smaller value is better. The formula for Ranking Loss is as follows:

$$rloss_D(H) = \frac{1}{P} \sum_{i=1}^{P} \frac{1}{|Y_i||\overline{Y_i}|} \left|\{(y', y'')|f(x_i, y') \leq f(x_i, y''), (y', y'') \in Y_i \times \overline{Y_i}\}\right|$$

(5) Micro-averaged AUC [51]: This indicator is the area under the ROC curve, which is between 0.1 and 1. AUC as a numerical value can be used to evaluate the quality of the classifier intuitively. For this indicator, the bigger value is better. The formula for Micro-averaged AUC is as follows:

$$AUC_{micro} = \frac{\left|\{(x', x'', y', y'')|f(x', y') \geq f(x'', y''), (x', y') \in S^+, (x'', y'') \in S^-\}\right|}{|S^+||S^-|}$$

The right side of the equation follows from the close relation between AUC and the Wilcoxon-Mann-Whitney statistic [52], where $f(.)$ is a real-valued function, $S^+ = \{(x_i, y)|y \in Y_i, 1 \leq i \leq p\}$ and $S^- = \{(x_i, y)|y \notin Y_i, 1 \leq i \leq p\}$ is a set of related (unrelated) label pairs.

4.3   Experimental Set up

In this experiment, we evaluate all algorithms under a Mulan platform. Mulan [49] is a multi-label classification open source library developed based on Weka. SMO is used as the base classification algorithm. We have considered four classifiers to perform comparisons: DLMC-OS, MBR, CC, and BR. We set 80% of each complete dataset as training sets and the remaining part is used as testing sets. Because of its high computational efficiency, low memory requirements, and fast convergence, the Adam algorithm is very popular with the field of deep learning. Adam [53] is used to optimize the loss function. Adam's hyperparameters are set to the default parameters suggested in [53]: alpha = 0.001, beta1 = 0.9, beta2 = 0.999, and epslon = 10^{-8}.

4.4 Results and Discussion

Tables 2–6 give the comparisons of the performances of ATDCC-OS with DLMC, MBR, CC, and BR for Average Precision, Coverage, One-Error, Ranking Loss, and Micro-averaged AUC. The Fredman [54] test based on the method average ranking (Ave. Rank) is used to evaluate the difference between the algorithms.

From the overall analysis of Tables 2–6, it can be seen that ATDCC-OS has the best performance on all datasets, DLMC-OS ranks second, and other algorithms are relatively stable. From Ave. Rank's point of view, ATDCC-OS is far superior to other algorithms, and the highest gap is about four times.

Among the evaluation metrics, Average Precision and Micro-averaged AUC are mainly used to evaluate and reflect the classification performance of the classifier visually. The larger the metrics value, the better. According to Tables 2 and 3, ATDCC-OS and DLMC-OS are superior to other algorithms. This conclusion is not surprising; the main reason is that these two algorithms benefit from the design of their two-layer structure classification model and the interaction of tag information. On this basis, ATDCC-OS also introduces attention mechanism enhancing classifier sensitivity. The three types of indicators—Coverage, Ranking Loss, and One-Error—are mainly used to measure irrelevant labels before the relevant labels in the classification results. From Tables 4, 5, and 6, it can be found that ATDCC-OS and DLMC-OS are still superior to other algorithms, BR is centered, and MBR and CC are the worst. ATDCC-OS and DLMC-OS benefit from the optimization algorithm (such as OSS), so that the training of each classifier becomes orderly. The random sequence of CC and MBR is the cause of poor results. Instead, BR without considering the label sequence is better than them.

From the dataset point of view, ATDCC-OS performs better than other algorithms on most datasets, but it does not perform well on Yeast and Birds. As J. Read [9] stated, an algorithm cannot perform best on all types of datasets. The quality of the algorithm depends not only on the design of the structure, but also on the type and size of the data.

Table 2. Performance comparison of algorithms based on average precision

Dataset	BR	CC	MBR	DLMC-OS	ATDCC-OS
Flags	0.7952(2.5)	0.7950(4)	0.7308(5)	0.7952(2.5)	0.8315(1)
Emotion	0.7157(4)	0.7018(5)	0.7742(2)	0.7438(3)	0.8085(1)
Birds	0.4311(3.5)	0.4312(2)	0.4198(5)	0.4311(3.5)	0.4884(1)
Medical	0.8260(3)	0.8206(5)	0.8207(4)	0.8285(2)	0.8606(1)
Enron	0.3802(4)	0.3675(5)	0.3890(2)	0.3815(3)	0.4224(1)
Yeast	0.6669(2.5)	0.6618(4)	0.6671(1)	0.6669(2.5)	0.6533(4)
Bibtex	0.3938(5)	0.3961(2.5)	0.3961(2.5)	0.3949(4)	0.4307(1)
Ave. rank	3.5(4)	3.93(5)	3.07(3)	2.93(2)	1.43(1)

Table 3. Performance comparison of algorithms based on micro-averaged AUC

Dataset	BR	CC	MBR	DLMC-OS	ATDCC-OS
Flags	0.7671(3)	0.7544(4)	0.7010(5)	0.7710(2)	0.7941(1)
Emotion	0.7336(4)	0.7321(5)	0.7750(2)	0.7527(3)	0.8615(1)
Birds	0.6731(3.5)	0.6798(2)	0.6803(1)	0.6731(3.5)	0.6495(5)
Medical	0.9012(2.5)	0.8991(5)	0.8994(4)	0.9012(2.5)	0.9565(1)
Enron	0.7085(2)	0.7020(5)	0.7081(4)	0.7083(3)	0.7923(1)
Yeast	0.7363(4)	0.7303(5)	0.7364(2.5)	0.7364(2.5)	0.7681(1)
Bibtex	0.6925(2)	0.6896(4)	0.6838(5)	0.6922(3)	0.7165(1)
Ave. Rank	3(3)	4.29(5)	3.35(4)	2.79(2)	1.57(1)

Table 4. Performance comparison of algorithms based on coverage

Dataset	BR	CC	MBR	DLMC-OS	ATDCC-OS
Flags	4.5385(2.5)	4.6923(4)	4.8462(5)	4.5385(2.5)	3.8718(1)
Emotion	2.6639(5)	2.6471(4)	2.4202(2)	2.6218(3)	1.7815(1)
Birds	4.6406(3)	4.6406(3)	4.8438(5)	4.6406(3)	4.2656(1)
Medical	5.6939(3)	5.9745(5)	5.8367(4)	5.6888(2)	2.8367(1)
Enron	33.3588(4)	34.0000(5)	32.6206(2)	33.1647(3)	27.4676(1)
Yeast	9.0787(3.5)	8.6046(2)	9.0828(5)	9.0787(3.5)	7.0373(1)
Bibtex	68.9277(3)	68.6748(2)	70.4834(5)	69.0730(4)	61.5463(1)
Ave. rank	3.42(4)	3.57(3)	4(5)	3(2)	1(1)

Table 5. Performance comparison of algorithms based on one-error

Dataset	BR	CC	MBR	DLMC-OS	ATDCC-OS
Flags	0.2308(3)	0.2308(3)	0.3590(5)	0.2308(3)	0.2051(1)
Emotion	0.3277(4)	0.3782(5)	0.2521(1)	0.2773(3)	0.2689(2)
Birds	0.7813(2.5)	0.8125(5)	0.7969(4)	0.7813(2.5)	0.7500(1)
Medical	0.1582(3.5)	0.1582(3.5)	0.1582(3.5)	0.1531(1)	0.1582(3.5)
Enron	0.5882(2)	0.6235(5)	0.6118(4)	0.6088(3)	0.5676(1)
Yeast	0.2609(2.5)	0.2609(2.5)	0.2609(2.5)	0.2609(2.5)	0.4472(5)
Bibtex	0.5531(3)	0.5571(5)	0.5321(2)	0.5544(4)	0.4956(1)
Ave. rank	2.92(3)	3.71(5)	3.14(4)	2.71(2)	2.07(1)

Table 6. Performance comparison of algorithms based on ranking loss

Dataset	BR	CC	MBR	DLMC-OS	ATDCC-OS
Flags	0.2615(2.5)	0.2697(4)	0.4009(5)	0.2615(2.5)	0.1915(1)
Emotion	0.3141(4)	0.3147(5)	0.2444(2)	0.2780(3)	0.1579(1)
Birds	0.1832(2.5)	0.1836(4)	0.1894(5)	0.1832(2.5)	0.1556(1)
Medical	0.0956(3)	0.0984(5)	0.0967(4)	0.0954(2)	0.0424(1)
Enron	0.3258(4)	0.3350(5)	0.3159(2)	0.3242(3)	0.2435(1)
Yeast	0.3150(3.5)	0.3270(5)	0.3149(2)	0.3150(3.5)	0.2433(1)
Bibtex	0.2789(2)	0.2793(3)	0.2877(5)	0.2794(4)	0.2595(1)
Ave. rank	3.07(3)	4.43(5)	3.57(4)	2.93(2)	1(1)

5 Conclusions

Many problem-transformation multi-label classification algorithms consider the correlation between labels by extending attributes, but ignore the different importance of each attribute value of different classification tasks. Based on the wide application and good results from attention mechanism in various types of deep-learning tasks, such as natural language processing, image recognition, and speech recognition, this paper proposes the ATDCC-OS algorithm. This algorithm integrates the multi-label classification framework of three classic problem-conversion types, and combines their common advantages to solve the problem of ignoring the correlation between labels in the classification process. The algorithm also introduces the "update replacement" idea to solve the problem that the label information interaction is not real-time. At the same time, the algorithm also introduces the attention mechanism to calculate the weight of each feature attribute dynamically, and then distinguishes the more important attribute values to the current classification target for each classifier, enhances the sensitivity of each classifier, and improves the classification accuracy. The ATDCC-OS method solves the defect that the BR algorithm does not consider the correlation between labels, corrects the redundant interaction and information loss of the MBR algorithm, and optimizes the problem that the DLMC-OS does not find the optimal label sequence. It also solves the problem of neglecting the importance of different feature attributes to different classification targets by extending the attribute method to consider the correlation between labels. In order to verify the classification performance of the algorithm, we used five evaluation indicators to compare ATDCC-OS with DLMC-OS, MBR, CC, and BR on seven standard data sets. The experimental results show that ATDCC-OS achieves good results compared to other algorithms.

Acknowledgements. The authors gratefully acknowledge the financial support of the Planning Subject for the 13th Five Year Plan of National Education Sciences under Grant No. DCA160258 and the Key Research Project of Education Department of Sichuan Province of China under Grant No. 18ZA319.

References

1. Shao, H., Li, G., Liu, G., Wang, Y.: Symptom selection for multi-label data of inquiry diagnosis in traditional Chinese medicine. Sci. China Inf. Sci. **56**(5), 1–3 (2013)
2. Glinka, K., Wosiak, A., Zakrzewska, D.: Improving children diagnostics by efficient multi-label classification method. In: Piętka, E., Badura, P., Kawa, J., Wieclawek, W. (eds.) Information Technologies in Medicine. AISC, vol. 471, pp. 253–266. Springer, Cham (2016). https://doi.org/10.1007/978-3-319-39796-2_21
3. Yao, L., Poblenz, E., Dagunts, D., Covington, B., Bernard, D., Lyman, K.: Learning to diagnose from scratch by exploiting dependencies among labels. arXiv preprint arXiv:1710.10501 (2017)
4. Zhu, H., et al.: Learning tree-based deep model for recommender systems. In: The 2018 24th ACM SIGKDD International Conference on Knowledge Discovery and Data Mining (2018)
5. Son, J., Kim, S.B., Kim, H., Cho, S.: Review and analysis of recommender systems. J. Korean Inst. Ind. Eng. **41**(2), 185–208 (2015)
6. Bogaert, M., Lootens, J., Van den Poel, D., Ballings, M.: Evaluating multi-label classifiers and recommender systems in the financial service sector. Eur. J. Oper. Res. **279**(2), 620–634 (2019)
7. Ray, J., Heng Wang, D., Tran, Y.W., Feiszli, M., Torresani, L., Paluri, M.: Scenes-objects-actions: a multi-task, multi-label video dataset. In: Ferrari, V., Hebert, M., Sminchisescu, C., Weiss, Y. (eds.) Computer Vision – ECCV 2018: 15th European Conference, Munich, Germany, September 8–14, 2018, Proceedings, Part XIV, pp. 660–676. Springer International Publishing, Cham (2018). https://doi.org/10.1007/978-3-030-01264-9_39
8. Chen, Z.M., Wei, X.S., Wang, P., Guo, Y.: Multi-label image recognition with graph convolutional networks. In: CVPR (2019)
9. Read, J., Pfahringer, B., Holmes, G., Frank, E.: Classifier chains for multi-label classification. In: Buntine, W., Grobelnik, M., Mladenić, D., Shawe-Taylor, J. (eds.) ECML PKDD 2009. LNCS (LNAI), vol. 5782, pp. 254–269. Springer, Heidelberg (2009). https://doi.org/10.1007/978-3-642-04174-7_17
10. Boutell, M.R., Luo, J., Shen, X., Brown, C.M.: Learning multi-label scene classification. Patt. Recogn. **37**(9), 1757–1771 (2004)

11. Godbole, S., Sarawagi, S.: Discriminative methods for multi-labeled classification. In: Dai, H., Srikant, R., Zhang, C. (eds.) PAKDD 2004. LNCS (LNAI), vol. 3056, pp. 22–30. Springer, Heidelberg (2004). https://doi.org/10.1007/978-3-540-24775-3_5

12. Liu, G.Q., Guo, T.: Algorithm for multi-label classification with optimal sequence based on double layers. Comput. Eng. Des. **37**(4), 921-927+948 (2016)

13. Pan, C., Tan, J., Feng, D., Li, Y.: Very short-term solar generation forecasting based on LSTM with temporal attention mechanism. In: ICCC (2019)

14. Chen, W.J., Shao, Y.H., Li, C.N., Deng, N.Y.: MLTSVM: a novel twin support vector machine to multi-label learning. Patt. Recogn. **52**, 61–74 (2016)

15. Xu, X., Shan, D., Li, S., Sun, T., Xiao, P., Fan, J.: Multi-label learning method based on ML-RBF and laplacian ELM. Neurocomputing **331**, 213–219 (2019)

16. Zhang, N., Ding, S., Zhang, J.: Multi layer ELM-RBF for multi-label learning. Appl. Soft. Comput. **43**, 535–545 (2016)

17. Roseberry, M., Krawczyk, B., Cano, A.: Multi-label punitive kNN with self-adjusting memory for drifting data streams. ACM Trans. Knowl. Disc. Data **13**(6), 1–31 (2019). https://doi.org/10.1145/3363573

18. Yapu, D.: An Improved ML-KNN Approach for Weibo text classification. Chin. Comput. Commun. **7**, 18 (2018)

19. Wu, G., Zheng, R., Tian, Y., Liu, D.: Joint ranking SVM and binary relevance with robust Low-rank learning for multi-label classification. Neural Netw. **122**, 24–39 (2020)

20. Charte, F., Rivera, A., del Jesus, M.J., Herrera, F.: Improving multi-label classifiers via label reduction with association rules. In: Corchado, E., Snášel, V., Abraham, A., Woźniak, M., Graña, M., Cho, S.-B. (eds.) HAIS 2012. LNCS (LNAI), vol. 7209, pp. 188–199. Springer, Heidelberg (2012). https://doi.org/10.1007/978-3-642-28931-6_18

21. Luo, F., Guo, W., Yu, Y., Chen, G.: A multi-label classification algorithm based on kernel extreme learning machine. Neurocomputing **260**, 313–320 (2017)

22. Kulessa, M., Mencía, E.L.: Dynamic classifier chain with random decision trees. In: Soldatova, L., Vanschoren, J., Papadopoulos, G., Ceci, M. (eds.) DS 2018. LNCS (LNAI), vol. 11198, pp. 33–50. Springer, Cham (2018). https://doi.org/10.1007/978-3-030-01771-2_3

23. Ali, T., Asghar, S.: Efficient label ordering for improving multi-label classifier chain accuracy. J. Nat. Sci. Found. Sri Lanka **47**(2), 175 (2019). https://doi.org/10.4038/jnsfsr.v47i2.9159

24. Firat, O., Cho, K., Bengio, Y.: Multi-way, multilingual neural machine translation with a shared attention mechanism. arXiv preprint. arXiv:1601.0107 (2016)

25. Mnih, V., Heess, N., Graves, A.: Recurrent models of visual attention. In: NIPS, pp. 2204–2212. MIT Press, US (2014)

26. Borji, A., Itti, L.: State-of-the-art in visual attention modeling. IEEE Trans. Pattern Anal. Mach. Intell. **35**(1), 185–207 (2012)

27. Bahdanau, D., Cho, K., Bengio, Y.: Neural machine translation by jointly learning to align and translate. arXiv preprint. arXiv:1409.0473 (2014)

28. Mnih, V., Heess, N., Graves, A.: Recurrent models of visual attention. In:NIPS, pp. 2204–2212 (2014)

29. Rush, A.M., Chopra, S., Weston, J.: A neural attention model for abstractive sentence summarization. arXiv preprint. arXiv:1509.00685 (2015)

30. Chen, H., Sun, M., Tu, C., Lin, Y., Liu, Z.: Neural sentiment classification with user and product attention. In: EMNLP (2016)

31. Yang, Z., Yang, D., Dyer, C., He, X., Smola, A., Hovy, E.: Hierarchical attention networks for document classification. In:NAACL HLT, pp. 1480–1489. ACL, California (2016)

32. He, R., Lee, W. S., Ng, H. T., Dahlmeier, D.: An unsupervised neural attention model for aspect extraction. In: the 55th Annual Meeting of the Association for Computational Linguistics, pp. 388–397. ACL, Canada (2017)

33. Yin, W., Schütze, H., Xiang, B., Zhou, B.: Abcnn: Attention-based convolutional neural network for modeling sentence pairs. Trans. Assoc. Comput. Linguist. **4**, 259–272 (2016)
34. Vaswani, A., et al.: Attention is all you need. In: NIPS, pp. 5998–6008. MIT Press, US (2017)
35. Coelho, F., Braga, A.P., Verleysen, M.: A mutual information estimator for continuous and discrete variables applied to feature selection and classification problems. Int. J. Comput. Intell. Syst. **9**(4), 726–733 (2016)
36. Sefidian, A.M., Daneshpour, N.: Missing value imputation using a novel grey based fuzzy c-means, mutual information based feature selection, and regression model. Exp. Syst. Appl. **115**, 68–94 (2019)
37. Cao, X., Cong, G., Jensen, C.S.: Mining significant semantic locations from GPS data. Proc. VLDB Endow. **3**(1–2), 1009–1020 (2010)
38. Yanagisawa, T., et al.: Electrocorticographic control of a prosthetic arm in paralyzed patients. Ann. Neurol. **71**(3), 353–361 (2012)
39. Liu, X.S., et al.: High-resolution peripheral quantitative computed tomography can assess microstructural and mechanical properties of human distal tibial bone. J. Bone Miner. Res. **25**(4), 746–756 (2010)
40. Brin, S., Page, L.: The anatomy of a large-scale hypertextual web search engine. Comput. Netw. ISDN Syst. **30**(1–7), 107–117 (1998). https://doi.org/10.1016/S0169-7552(98)00110-X
41. Singhal, R., Srivastava, S.R.: Enhancing the page ranking for search engine optimization based on weightage of in-linked web pages. In: ICRAIE (2016)
42. Gupta, P., Goel, A., Lin, J., Sharma, A., Wang, D., Zadeh, R.: Wtf: the who to follow service at Twitter. In: IW3C2 (2013)
43. Fletcher, P., Hoyle, H., Patty, C.W.: Foundations of Discrete Mathematics. PWS-KENT Pub. Co., Boston (1991)
44. Jiang, D., Wang, Y., Lv, Z., Qi, S., Singh, S.: Big data analysis based network behavior insight of cellular networks for industry 4.0 applications. IEEE Trans. Ind. Inf. **16**(2), 1310–1320 (2020). https://doi.org/10.1109/TII.2019.2930226
45. Jiang, D., Huo, L., Lv, Z., Song, H., Qin, W.: A joint multi-criteria utility-based network selection approach for vehicle-to-infrastructure networking. IEEE Trans. Intell. Transp. Syst. **19**(10), 3305–3319 (2018)
46. Wang, Y., Jiang, D., Huo, L., Zhao, Y.: A new traffic prediction algorithm to software defined networking. Mob. Netw. Appl., 1–10 (2019).https://doi.org/10.1007/s11036-019-01423-3
47. Wang, F., Jiang, D., Qi, S.: An adaptive routing algorithm for integrated information networks. China Commun. **16**(7), 195–206 (2019)
48. Kruskal, J.B.: On the shortest spanning subtree of a graph and the traveling salesman problem. Proc. Am. Math. Soc. **7**(1), 48–50 (1956)
49. Tsoumakas, G., Spyromitros-Xioufis, E., Vilcek, J., Vlahavas, I.: Mulan: a java library for multi-label learning. J. Mach. Learn. Res. **12**, 2411–2414 (2011)
50. Tsoumakas, G., Katakis, I.: Multi-label classification: an overview. Int. J. Data Warehouse. Min. **3**(3), 1–3 (2007)
51. Zhang, M.L., Zhou, Z.H.: A review on multi-label learning algorithms. IEEE Trans. Knowl. Data Eng. **26**(8), 1819–1837 (2013)
52. Hanley, J.A., McNeil, B.J.: The meaning and use of the area under a receiver operating characteristic (ROC) curve. Radiology **143**(1), 29–36 (1982)
53. Da, K.: A method for stochastic optimization. arXiv preprint. arXiv:1412.6980 (2014)
54. DemšCar, J.: Statistical comparisons of classifiers over multiple data sets. J. Mach. Learn. Res. **7**(1), 30 (2006)

Optical Solitons and Their Numerical Simulations of Coupled Nonlinear Schrödinger's Equation in a Cascaded System

Dahe Feng(✉) ⓘD

School of Mathematics and Statistics, Guizhou University of Finance and Economics, Guiyang, Guizhou 550025, China

Abstract. This work focuses on the coupled nonlinear Schrödinger's equation which appears in a cascaded three-level atomic system. By using the trial solution technique and the symbolic computation method, the exact bright-dark soliton, dark-bright soliton and singular soliton solutions are obtained. The propagation properties of the above solitons are simulated.

Keywords: Coupled nonlinear Schrödinger's equation · Bright-dark soliton · Dark-bright soliton · Singular soliton · Numerical simulations

1 Introduction

Nonlinear phenomena, which widely exists in various scientific fields, are usually characterized by nonlinear partial differential equations called governing equations (GEs). It is a very important topic to study their exact analytical solutions of these GEs since these solutions can help one easily research the dynamical behaviors and nonlinear phenomena. The nonlinear Schrödinger equation, as one of the most famous governing equations, is a significant mathematical model in different areas such as nonlinear optics [1–8], finance [9], biophysics [10] and so on. Moreover the Schrödinger equation has many mathematical features and has been widely applied in nonlinear optical communications. Along with the growing interest in nonlinear phenomena, coupled nonlinear Schrödinger's (CNLS) equations have also attracted a lot of attentions [11–13]. The CNLS equations can be used to describe the interaction among the modes in the case of birefringent or other two-mode fibers [14,15] and the solitary waves in CNLS equations called

---

Supported by National Natural Science Foundation of China (No. 11761019), Project of High-level Innovative Talents of Guizhou Province, China ([2017]5658) and Foundation of Science and Technology of Guizhou Province, China ([2020]1Y001).

H. Song and D. Jiang (Eds.): SIMUtools 2020, LNICST 369, pp. 391–401, 2021.
https://doi.org/10.1007/978-3-030-72792-5_32

vector solitons have more rich phenomena and complex dynamics. In the past decades, the related research achievements on CNLS equations have emerged in endlessly [16–24].

In this paper, we focus on the propagation of two intense optical beam of different frequencies in a three-level atomic system in the cascade configuration. This cascade system is governed by a coupled nonlinear Schrödinger's equation. The coupled Schrödinger's equation is such an equation whose unknown functions are interrelated. We try to construct exact and explicit optical soliton solutions by means of the trial solution technique and the symbolic computation method [25, 26]. As a result, exact coupled bright-dark soliton, dark-bright soliton and singular soliton solutions are obtained and the propagation properties of these solitons are simulated.

2 Governing Equation

We consider two coupled optical beams of different frequencies propagating in the cascaded three-level atomic system governed by the following coupled nonlinear Schrödinger's equation [27]

$$ia_1 q_{1,t} + b_1 q_{1,xx} + c_1 |q_2|^2 q_1 = 0, \tag{1a}$$

$$ia_2 q_{2,t} + b_2 q_{2,xx} + (c_2 |q_1|^2 + d_2 |q_2|^2) q_2 = 0, \tag{1b}$$

where $q_1(x,t)$ and $q_2(x,t)$ are the dependent variables representing the complex-valued wave profile. Moreover a_j, b_j and c_j $(j = 1, 2)$ respectively are the temporal evolution coefficients, the group velocity dispersion coefficients and the cross-phase modulation while d_2 is the self-phase modulation [28]. Konar et al. [27] studied the existence and stability of soliton solutions to (1) and derived an existence curve of stable soliton pairs. Recently, Bhrawy et al. [28] obtained some bright-bright and dark-dark soliton solutions by applying the ansatz method.

The goal in this paper is to find the bright-dark soliton, dark-bright soliton and singular soliton to (1), which belong to different type solitons and have different dynamical behaviors from the results in [28].

To find the exact solutions of (1), we make the wave transformation

$$q_1(x,t) = Q_1(\xi) e^{i\eta_1}, \tag{2a}$$

$$q_2(x,t) = Q_2(\xi) e^{i\eta_2}, \tag{2b}$$

where $Q_1(\xi)$ and $Q_2(\xi)$ stand for amplitude components of the traveling waves. η_1 and η_2 in (2) are phase components of the traveling waves given by

$$\eta_j = -k_j x + \omega_j t + \phi_j, \ j = 1, 2, \tag{3}$$

where k_j, ω_j and ϕ_j $(j = 1, 2)$ are wave numbers, frequencies and phase constants. And ξ in (2) is the wave variable defined by

$$\xi = x - vt + \xi_0, \tag{4}$$

where v and ξ_0 respectively are wave velocity and mean positions of $Q_1(\xi)$ and $Q_2(\xi)$. From Eqs. (2)–(4), it is clear that

$$i\, q_{1,t} = -\left(\omega_1 Q_1 + i\, v Q_1'\right) e^{i\eta_1}, \tag{5a}$$

$$q_{1,xx} = \left(Q_1'' - k_1^2 Q_1 - 2i\, k_1 Q_1'\right) e^{i\eta_1}, \tag{5b}$$

$$i\, q_{2,t} = -\left(\omega_2 Q_2 + i\, v Q_2'\right) e^{i\eta_2}, \tag{5c}$$

$$q_{2,xx} = \left(Q_2'' - k_2^2 Q_2 - 2i\, k_2 Q_2'\right) e^{i\eta_2}, \tag{5d}$$

where the primes denote the derivatives with respect to ξ. Substituting (5) into (1) and decomposing it into real and imaginary parts, it follows from the real parts of the two components that

$$b_1 Q_1'' - \left(a_1\omega_1 + b_1 k_1^2\right) Q_1 + c_1 Q_2^2 Q_1 = 0, \tag{6a}$$

$$b_2 Q_2'' - \left(a_2\omega_2 + b_2 k_2^2\right) Q_2 + \left(c_2 Q_1^2 + d_2 Q_2^2\right) Q_2 = 0. \tag{6b}$$

From the imaginary parts of the two components, we can derive the wave velocity as

$$v = -\frac{2b_1 k_1}{a_1}, \tag{7}$$

and

$$v = -\frac{2b_2 k_2}{a_2}. \tag{8}$$

From (7) and (8), we obtain the following constraint relation

$$a_1 b_2 k_2 = a_2 b_1 k_1, \quad a_1 a_2 \neq 0. \tag{9}$$

From (9), we have

$$k_2 = \frac{a_2 b_1 k_1}{a_1 b_2}, \tag{10}$$

which shows that the ratio of the wave numbers k_1 and k_2 depend on the evolutions and the dispersions. To consider the exact solutions to (1), we must only discuss the real part equations given by (6) under the constraint relation (9).

3 Bright-Dark Soliton Solution and Its Numerical Simulations

3.1 Bright-Dark Soliton Solution

In this subsection, we will construct the bright-dark soliton solution of (1). By using the following transformations

$$Q_1(\xi) = A_1 \operatorname{sech}^{p_1}(B\xi), \tag{11a}$$

$$Q_2(\xi) = A_2 \tanh^{p_2}(B\xi), \tag{11b}$$

where A_1 and A_2 are the amplitudes of the solitons while B is the inverse width of the solitons. Substituting (11) into (6) and balancing the terms Q_1'' between

$Q_2^2 Q_1$ in (6a) along with Q_2'' between $Q_1^2 Q_2$ in (6b), we obtain that $p_1 = p_2 = 1$ and therefore yield the following equations:

$$\left(c_1 A_2^2 + b_1 B^2 - a_1 \omega_1 - b_1 k_1^2\right) - \left(c_1 A_2^2 + 2b_1 B^2\right) \operatorname{sech}^2(B\xi) = 0, \qquad (12a)$$

$$\left(d_2 A_2^2 - a_2 \omega_2 - b_2 k_2^2\right) + \left(c_2 A_1^2 - d_2 A_2^2 - 2b_2 B^2\right) \operatorname{sech}^2(B\xi) = 0. \qquad (12b)$$

Making all the constant terms and the coefficients of $\operatorname{sech}^2(B\xi)$ in (12) equal to zero, we get a series of algebraic equations

$$c_1 A_2^2 + b_1 B^2 - a_1 \omega_1 - b_1 k_1^2 = 0, \qquad (13a)$$

$$c_1 A_2^2 + 2b_1 B^2 = 0, \qquad (13b)$$

$$d_2 A_2^2 - a_2 \omega_2 - b_2 k_2^2 = 0, \qquad (13c)$$

$$c_2 A_1^2 - d_2 A_2^2 - 2b_2 B^2 = 0. \qquad (13d)$$

Solving (13) gives

$$A_1 = \sqrt{\frac{2(b_1 d_2 - b_2 c_1)}{-c_1 c_2}}\, B, \qquad (14a)$$

$$A_2 = \sqrt{\frac{2b_1}{-c_1}}\, B, \qquad (14b)$$

$$\omega_1 = -\frac{b_1}{a_1}\left(k_1^2 + B^2\right), \qquad (14c)$$

$$\omega_2 = -\frac{2b_1 d_2}{a_2 c_1} B^2 - \frac{b_2}{a_2} k_2^2, \qquad (14d)$$

with the constraint conditions $b_1 c_1 < 0$ and $c_1 c_2 (b_1 d_2 - b_2 c_1) < 0$.

Substituting (11) and (14) into (2), we get a bright-dark soliton solution for (1)

$$q_1(x,t) = \sqrt{\frac{2(b_1 d_2 - b_2 c_1)}{-c_1 c_2}}\, B \operatorname{sech}\left[B\left(x - vt + \xi_0\right)\right] e^{i\left(-k_1 x + \omega_1 t + \phi_1\right)}, \qquad (15a)$$

$$q_2(x,t) = \sqrt{\frac{2b_1}{-c_1}}\, B \tanh\left[B\left(x - vt + \xi_0\right)\right] e^{i\left(-k_2 x + \omega_2 t + \phi_2\right)}. \qquad (15b)$$

3.2 Numerical Simulations of Propagation Properties of the Bright-Dark Soliton

In this subsection, we will graphically discuss the numerical simulations of the propagation properties of the bright-dark soliton for (1). Based on (15), we have

$$\chi_1(x,t) = \sqrt{\frac{2(b_1 d_2 - b_2 c_1)}{-c_1 c_2}}\, B \operatorname{sech}\left[B\left(x - vt + \xi_0\right)\right], \qquad (16a)$$

$$\chi_2(x,t) = \sqrt{\frac{2b_1}{-c_1}}\, B \tanh\left[B\left(x - vt + \xi_0\right)\right], \qquad (16b)$$

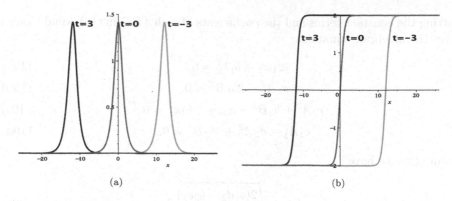

Fig. 1. The propagation of the bright-dark soliton wave (15) of (1) by choosing suitable parameters: $b_1 = 2$, $B = d_2 = c_2 = a_1 = k_1 = 1$, $c_1 = b_2 = -1$, $\xi_0 = 0$. (a) Wave propagation pattern of $\chi_1(x, t)$ along the x axis. (b) Wave propagation pattern of $\chi_2(x, t)$ along the x axis.

where χ_1 and χ_2 denote the amplitudes for the components q_1 and q_2 respectively. χ_1 achieves the maximum $\sqrt{\frac{2(b_1 d_2 - b_2 c_1)}{-c_1 c_2}} |B|$ if and only if $x - vt + \xi_0 = 0$ and tends to the minimum if $x - vt + \xi_0 \to \pm\infty$. And χ_2 tends to the maximum $\sqrt{\frac{2b_1}{-c_1}} |B|$ as $x - vt + \xi_0 \to +\infty$ and the minimum $-\sqrt{\frac{2b_1}{-c_1}} |B|$ as $x - vt + \xi_0 \to -\infty$. Thus q_1 is bright while q_2 is dark. The bright-dark soliton maintains its shape, velocity and amplitude during the propagation. The propagation of the bright-dark soliton is presented in Fig. 1.

4 Dark-Bright Soliton Solution and Its Numerical Simulations

4.1 Dark-Bright Soliton Solution

For dark-bright soliton, the hypothesis for Q_1 and Q_2 will be

$$Q_1(\xi) = A_1 \tanh^{p_1}(B\xi), \tag{17a}$$
$$Q_2(\xi) = A_2 \operatorname{sech}^{p_2}(B\xi). \tag{17b}$$

Substituting (17) into (6) and balancing the terms Q_1'' between $Q_2^2 Q_1$ in (6a) along with Q_2'' between $Q_1^2 Q_2$ in (6b), we get $p_1 = p_2 = 1$ and therefore obtain the equations

$$(a_1\omega_1 + b_1 k_1^2) - (c_1 A_2^2 - 2b_1 B^2)\operatorname{sech}^2(B\xi) = 0, \tag{18a}$$
$$(c_2 A_1^2 + b_2 B^2 - a_2\omega_2 - b_2 k_2^2) - (c_2 A_1^2 - d_2 A_2^2 + 2b_2 B^2)\operatorname{sech}^2(B\xi) = 0. \tag{18b}$$

Setting the constant terms and the coefficients of $\text{sech}^2(B\xi)$ in (18) equal to zero gives the algebraic equations

$$a_1\omega_1 + b_1k_1^2 = 0, \tag{19a}$$

$$c_1A_2^2 - 2b_1B^2 = 0, \tag{19b}$$

$$c_2A_1^2 + b_2B^2 - a_2\omega_2 - b_2k_2^2 = 0, \tag{19c}$$

$$c_2A_1^2 - d_2A_2^2 + 2b_2B^2 = 0. \tag{19d}$$

From (19), we have

$$A_1 = \sqrt{\frac{2(b_1d_2 - b_2c_1)}{c_1c_2}}\, B, \tag{20a}$$

$$A_2 = \sqrt{\frac{2b_1}{c_1}}\, B, \tag{20b}$$

$$\omega_1 = -\frac{b_1}{a_1}k_1^2, \tag{20c}$$

$$\omega_2 = \frac{2b_1d_2}{a_2c_1}B^2 - \frac{b_2}{a_2}(k_2^2 + B^2), \tag{20d}$$

with the constraint relations $b_1c_1 > 0$ and $c_1c_2(b_1d_2 - b_2c_1) > 0$.

Substituting (20) and (17) into (2), we get the dark-bright soliton solution for (1)

$$q_1(x,t) = \sqrt{\frac{2(b_1d_2 - b_2c_1)}{c_1c_2}}\, B\tanh\left[B\left(x - vt + \xi_0\right)\right]\, e^{i\,(-k_1x+\omega_1t+\phi_1)}, \tag{21a}$$

$$q_2(x,t) = \sqrt{\frac{2b_1}{c_1}}\, B\,\text{sech}\left[B\left(x - vt + \xi_0\right)\right]\, e^{i(-k_2x+\omega_2t+\phi_2)}. \tag{21b}$$

4.2   Numerical Simulations of Propagation Properties of the Dark-Bright Soliton

In this subsection, we discuss the numerical simulations of the propagation properties of the dark-bright soliton for (1). It follows from (21) that

$$\delta_1(x,t) = \sqrt{\frac{2(b_1d_2 - b_2c_1)}{c_1c_2}}\, B\tanh\left[B\left(x - vt + \xi_0\right)\right], \tag{22a}$$

$$\delta_2(x,t) = \sqrt{\frac{2b_1}{c_1}}\, B\,\text{sech}\left[B\left(x - vt + \xi_0\right)\right], \tag{22b}$$

where δ_1 and δ_2 denote the amplitudes for the components q_1 and q_2 in (21) respectively. δ_1 tends to the maximum $\sqrt{\frac{2(b_1d_2-b_2c_1)}{c_1c_2}}\,|B|$ as $x - vt + \xi_0 \to +\infty$ and the minimum $-\sqrt{\frac{2(b_1d_2-b_2c_1)}{c_1c_2}}\,|B|$ as $x - vt + \xi_0 \to -\infty$. And δ_2 achieves the maximum $\sqrt{\frac{2b_1}{c_1}}\,|B|$ if and only if $x - vt + \xi_0 = 0$ and tends to the minimum if $x - vt + \xi_0 \to \pm\infty$. Hence q_1 is dark and q_2 is bright. The dark-bright soliton maintains its shape, velocity and amplitude during the propagation. The propagation of the dark-bright soliton is shown in Fig. 2.

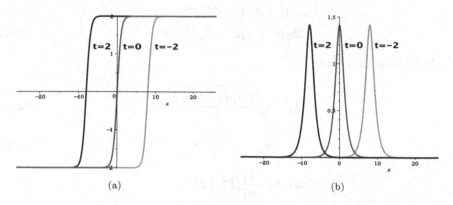

(a)   (b)

Fig. 2. The propagation of the dark-bright soliton wave (21) for (1) by choosing suitable parameters: $b_1 = 2$, $B = d_2 = c_1 = c_2 = b_2 = a_1 = k_1 = 1$, $\xi_0 = 0$. (a) Wave propagation pattern of $\delta_1(x, t)$ along the x axis. (b) Wave propagation pattern of $\delta_2(x, t)$ along the x axis.

5 Singular Soliton Solutioin and Its Numerical Simulations

5.1 Singular Soliton Solutioin

For singular soliton solutions, we assume that the solutions of (1) take the forms

$$Q_1 = A_1 \coth^{p_1}(B\xi), \tag{23a}$$
$$Q_2 = A_2 \coth^{p_2}(B\xi). \tag{23b}$$

Substituting (23) into (6) and balancing the terms Q_1'' between $Q_2^2 Q_1$ in (6a) along with Q_2'' between $Q_1^2 Q_2$ in (6b) gives $p_1 = p_2 = 1$. Substituting (23) with $p_1 = p_2 = 1$ into (6) again respectively yields

$$(c_1 A_2^2 + 2b_1 B^2) - (2b_1 B^2 + a_1\omega_1 + b_1 k_1^2)\tanh^2(B\xi) = 0, \tag{24a}$$
$$(c_2 A_1^2 + d_2 A_2^2 + 2b_2 B^2) - (2b_2 B^2 + a_2\omega_2 + b_2 k_2^2)\tanh^2(B\xi) = 0. \tag{24b}$$

Making all the constant terms and the coefficients of $\tanh^2(B\xi)$ in (24) equal to zero gives the following algebraic equations

$$c_1 A_2^2 + 2b_1 B^2 = 0, \tag{25a}$$

$$2b_1 B^2 + a_1\omega_1 + b_1 k_1^2 = 0, \tag{25b}$$

$$c_2 A_1^2 + d_2 A_2^2 + 2b_2 B^2 = 0, \tag{25c}$$

$$2b_2 B^2 + a_2\omega_2 + b_2 k_2^2 = 0. \tag{25d}$$

It follows from (25) that

$$A_1 = \sqrt{\frac{2(b_1 d_2 - b_2 c_1)}{c_1 c_2}}\, B, \tag{26a}$$

$$A_2 = \sqrt{\frac{2b_1}{-c_1}}\, B, \tag{26b}$$

$$\omega_1 = -\frac{b_1}{a_1}(k_1^2 + 2B^2), \tag{26c}$$

$$\omega_2 = -\frac{b_2}{a_2}(k_2^2 + 2B^2), \tag{26d}$$

with the constraint relations $b_1 c_1 < 0$ and $c_1 c_2 (b_1 d_2 - b_2 c_1) > 0$.

We thus obtain the singular soliton solution of (1)

$$q_1(x,t) = \sqrt{\frac{2(b_1 d_2 - b_2 c_1)}{c_1 c_2}}\, B \coth\left[B\left(x - vt + \xi_0\right)\right]\, e^{i\,(-k_1 x + \omega_1 t + \phi_1)}, \tag{27a}$$

$$q_2(x,t) = \sqrt{\frac{2b_1}{-c_1}}\, B \coth\left[B\left(x - vt + \xi_0\right)\right]\, e^{i(-k_2 x + \omega_2 t + \phi_2)}. \tag{27b}$$

5.2 Numerical Simulations of Propagation Properties of the Singular Soliton

In this subsection, we discuss the numerical simulations of the propagation properties of the singular soliton of (1). It follows from (27) that

$$\rho_1(x,t) = \sqrt{\frac{2(b_1 d_2 - b_2 c_1)}{c_1 c_2}}\, B \coth\left[B\left(x - vt + \xi_0\right)\right], \tag{28a}$$

$$\rho_2(x,t) = \sqrt{\frac{2b_1}{-c_1}}\, B \coth\left[B\left(x - vt + \xi_0\right)\right], \tag{28b}$$

where ρ_1 and ρ_2 denote the amplitudes for the components q_1 and q_2 in (27) respectively. Since $\rho_1 \to \infty$ and $\rho_2 \to \infty$ as $x - vt + \xi_0 \to 0$, namely, both ρ_1 and ρ_2 blow up in finite time. Therefore (27) is a singular soliton solution for (1) and also maintains its shape, velocity and amplitude during the propagation. The propagation of the singular soliton is presented in Fig. 3.

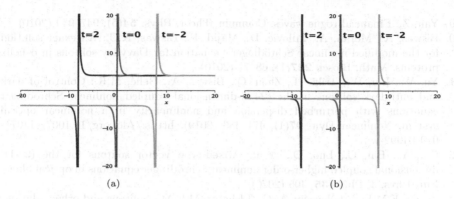

(a)   (b)

Fig. 3. The propagation of the singular soliton wave (27) for (1) by choosing suitable parameters: $b_1 = 2$, $B = d_2 = a_1 = k_1 = 1$, $c_1 = b_2 = -1$, $c_2 = -\frac{1}{8}$, $\xi_0 = 0$. (a) Wave propagation pattern of $\rho_1(x, t)$ along the x axis. (b) Wave propagation pattern of $\rho_2(x, t)$ along the x axis.

6 Conclusion

In this work, we investigate the coupled nonlinear Schrödinger equation and obtain the exact bright-dark soliton, dark-bright soliton and singular soliton solutions by employing the trial solution technique and the symbolic computation method. The propagation properties of these solutions are numerically simulated, which help one better understand their dynamical properties.

References

1. Inc, M., Ates, E., Tchier, F.: Optical solitons of the coupled nonlinear Schrödinger's equation with spatiotemporal dispersion. Nonlinear Dyn. **85**(2), 1319–1329 (2016)
2. Ghanbari, B., Nisar, K.S., Aldhaifallah, M.: Abundant solitary wave solutions to an extended nonlinear Schrödinger's equation with conformable derivative using an efficient integration method. Adv. Differ. Equ. **2020**, 328 (2020)
3. Plokhotnikov, K.E.: About One method of numerical solution of Schrödinger's equation. Math. Models Comput. Simul. **12**, 221–231 (2020)
4. He, Y., Lin, X.: Numerical analysis and simulations for coupled nonlinear Schrödinger equations based on lattice Boltzmann method. Appl. Math. Lett. **106**, 106391 (2020)
5. Zhou, Q., Liu, S.: Dark optical solitons in quadratic nonlinear media with spatiotemporal dispersion. Nonlinear Dyn. **81**(1-2), 733–738 (2015)
6. Huang, X., Ling, L.: Soliton solutions for the nonlocal nonlinear Schrödinger equation. Eur. Phys. J. Plus **131**(5), 1–11 (2016). https://doi.org/10.1140/epjp/i2016-16148-9
7. Chavanis, P.-H.: Derivation of a generalized Schrödinger equation from the theory of scale relativity. Eur. Phys. J. Plus **132**(6), 1–48 (2017). https://doi.org/10.1140/epjp/i2017-11528-3
8. Kruglov, V.I.: Solitary wave and periodic solutions of nonlinear Schrödinger equation including higher order dispersions. Opt. Commun. **472**, 125866 (2020)

9. Yan, Z.: Financial rogue waves. Commun. Theor. Phys. **54**(5), 947–949 (2010)
10. Biswas, A., Moran, A., Milovic, D., Majid, F., Biswas, K.C.: An exact solution for the modified nonlinear Schrödinger's equation for Davydov solitons in α-helix proteins. Math. Biosci. **227**(1), 68–71 (2010)
11. Yu, W., Liu, W., Triki, H., Zhou, Q., Biswas, A., Belić, M.R.: Control of dark and anti-dark solitons in the (2+1)-dimensional coupled nonlinear Schrödinger equations with perturbed dispersion and nonlinearity in a nonlinear optical system. Nonlinear Dyn. **97**(1), 471–483 (2019). https://doi.org/10.1007/s11071-019-04992-w
12. Cai, Y., Bai, C., Luo, Q., et al.: Mixed-type vector solitons for the (2+1)-dimensional coupled higher-order nonlinear Schrödinger equations in optical fibers. Eur. Phys. J. Plus **135**, 405 (2020)
13. Zayed, E.M.E., Al-Nowehy, A.-G., Elshater, M.E.M.: Solitons and other solutions for coupled nonlinear Schrödinger equations using three different techniques. Pramana **92**(6), 1–8 (2019). https://doi.org/10.1007/s12043-019-1762-y
14. Lan, Z.: Rogue wave solutions for a coupled nonlinear Schrödinger equation in the birefringent optical fiber. Appl. Math. Lett. **98**, 128–134 (2019)
15. Chen, J., Luan, Z., Zhou, Q., Alzahrani, A.K., Biswas, A., Liu, W.: Periodic soliton interactions for higher-order nonlinear Schrödinger equation in optical fibers. Nonlinear Dyn. **100**(3), 2817–2821 (2020). https://doi.org/10.1007/s11071-020-05649-9
16. Sweilam, N.H., Al-Barb, R.F.: Variational iteration method for coupled nonlinear Schrödinger equations. Comput. Math. Appl. **54**, 993–999 (2007)
17. Zhou, X., Wang, L.: A variational principle for coupled nonlinear Schrödinger equations with variable coefficients and high nonlinearity. Comput. Math. Appl. **61**(8), 2035–2038 (2011)
18. Wang, Y., Guo, B., Liu, N.: Optical rogue waves for the coherently coupled nonlinear Schrödinger equation with alternate signs of nonlinearities. Appl. Math. Lett. **82**, 38–42 (2018)
19. Du, Z., Tian, B., Chai, H., Sun, Y., Zhao, X.: Rogue waves for the coupled variable-coefficient fourth-order nonlinear Schrödinger equations in an inhomogeneous optical fiber. Chaos Solitons Fract. **109**, 90–98 (2018)
20. Feng, L., Zhang, T.: Breather wave, rogue wave and solitary wave solutions of a coupled nonlinear Schrödinger equation. Appl. Math. Lett. **78**, 133–140 (2018)
21. Guo, B., Liu, N., Wang, Y.: A Riemann-Hilbert approach for a new type coupled nonlinear Schrödinger equations. J. Math. Anal. Appl. **459**(1), 145–158 (2018)
22. Du, Z., Tian, B., Qu, Q.-X., Zhao, X.-H.: Characteristics of higher-order vector rogue waves to a coupled fourth-order nonlinear Schrödinger system in a two-mode optical fiber. Eur. Phys. J. Plus **135**(2), 1–9 (2020). https://doi.org/10.1140/epjp/s13360-020-00240-y
23. Yuan, Y., Tian, B., Chai, H., Wu, X., Du, Z.: Vector semirational rogue waves for a coupled nonlinear Schrödinger system in a birefringent fiber. Appl. Math. Lett. **87**, 50–56 (2019)
24. Yin, H., Tian, B., Zhao, X.: Chaotic breathers and breather fission/fusion for a vector nonlinear Schrödinger equation in a birefringent optical fiber or wavelength division multiplexed system. Appl. Math. Comput. **368**, 124768 (2020)
25. Chen, L., Chen, J., Chen, Q.: Mixed lump-soliton solutions to the two-dimensional Toda lattice equation via symbolic computation. Nonlinear Dyn. **96**, 1531–1539 (2019)

26. Wang, D., Yin, Y.: Symmetry analysis and reductions of the two-dimensional generalized Benney system via geometric approach. Comput. Math. Appl. **71**(3), 748–757 (2016)
27. Konara, S., Jovanoskic, Z., Towers, I.: Two-color bright solitons in a three-level atomic system in the cascade configuration. J. Mod. Optic. **58**, 1035–1040 (2011)
28. Bhrawy, A., Alshaery, A., Hilal, E., et al.: Bright and dark solitons in a cascaded system. Optik **125**, 6162–6165 (2014)

Design of a Novel T-Type Power Divider Feed Network

Ji Shen[1], Lulu Bei[1(✉)], Lei Chen[1], and Kai Huang[2]

[1] School of Information and Electrical Engineering,
Xuzhou Institute of Technology, Xuzhou, China
[2] JiangSu XCMG Information Technology Co., LTD., Xuzhou 221008, China

Abstract. A novel type of T-type Power Divider feed network is designed for the difficulty of meeting the needs of both the broadband and miniaturized applications of the existing circularly polarized antenna. At the center frequency, the input signal is transmitted through the active shift phase feed network, and the four-way signal is equitized at its output port, with a phase lag of 90° in turn. It is worth noting that the T-type node does not have an isolation resistor, so the matching and isolation of the output port is not considered. The test results list the echo loss of the internal functional feed network Input port, the insertion loss of the circuit, and the phase difference between the output ports. The network theory is applied in the antenna feed network, which can improve the performance of the antenna and is suitable for long-distance highly directional reading and writing applications.

Keywords: T-type power divider · Feed network · Antenna

1 Introduction

With the rapid development of modern wireless communication technology, wireless communication has played an increasingly important role in people's production and life. In recent years, 3G (3rd generation mobile communication technology), 4G (4th generation mobile communication technology), IEEE802.11 WLAN (Wireless Local Area Networks), WPAN (Wireless Personal Area Network), IEEE 802.16 WMAN (Wireless Metropolitan Area Networks) and a variety of communication technologies and standards have been rapidly developed and widely used. Wireless communication system is moving towards broadband, high speed and high quality [1–6].

In these communication systems, RF front-end and antenna, as an indispensable part of the communication system, play a key role in the quality of the whole communication system [7–10]. The RF front-end is mainly composed of microwave passive components such as filters, power splitters, directional couplers, phase shifters and microwave active components such as impedance converters, amplifiers, mixers [11–18]. Antenna is the key component of signal receiving and transmitting in wireless communication system. The performance of its feed network directly affects the quality of signal receiving and

H. Song and D. Jiang (Eds.): SIMUtools 2020, LNICST 369, pp. 402–408, 2021.
https://doi.org/10.1007/978-3-030-72792-5_33

transmitting. So, the feed network applied to circularly polarized antenna has a good theoretical significance and research value in the field of RF microwave communication.

Wilkinson power divider was first proposed by Ernest J. Wilkinson in document [19–25] in 1959. Based on the principle of quarter wavelength impedance conversion, this power divider realizes the matching of any port and the isolation between ports. The disadvantage is that the isolation resistance is located between each output port, which makes it difficult to add conveniently Load radiator, so it cannot be used in high-power occasions. To this end, Ulrich H. Gysel proposed an improved Wilkinson power divider [26–30], namely Gysel power divider, in 1975. The power divider successfully designs an eight-way combiner with 20% working bandwidth by grounding the isolation resistance. Because of the resistance grounding, it effectively conducts heat and is suitable for high-power occasions. However, no matter Wilkinson power divider or Gysel power divider, due to the use of isolation resistor, it has the disadvantage that it cannot be arbitrarily extended to any path in the plane. Therefore, a Bagley polygon power divider [31–35] is proposed. Because the isolation between output ports is not considered, only the matching of input ports and the transmission characteristics of the circuit are considered, the circuit structure can be extended to any odd number of paths Therefore, a lot of research has been done. In addition, as the feed network of microstrip antenna, power divider plays an important role in the design of antenna. Next, the power divider theory is applied to the antenna feed network to improve the performance of the antenna [36–40]. In this paper, a new design method of T-type power divider feed network is proposed, and its simulation and test are carried out.

2 Structure of T-Type Power Divider Based Feed Network

The T-type Power Divider proposed in this section, shown in Fig. 1(a). The input port is the standard 50 Ω, and the output port is 100 Ω. Based on this Power Divider and microband delay line shifter, a four-point power feed network is formed. Figure 1 (b) is a T-type Power Divider based feed network with the same structure for the internal and external branch, but the four output ports of the two feed networks have different characteristic impedances. The characteristic impedance of the internal feed network output port is the standard 50 Ω, and the characteristic of the external feed network output port is the input impedance of the rectangular radiation patch of 130 Ω. The microstrip with an electrical length of 180° and 90°, respectively, and a microstrip with a characteristic impedance of Z1 is a delay line for both feed networks, with an electrical length of 90°. The microstrip line with feature impedances of Z2 and Z3 acts as an impedance converter.

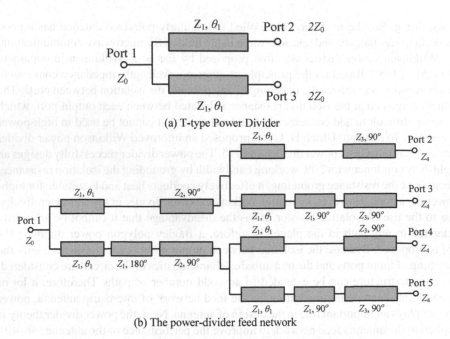

(a) T-type Power Divider

(b) The power-divider feed network

Fig. 1. T-type power divider and its power-divider feed network

3 The Working Principle of T-Type Power Divider Based Feed Network

The following analysis of the antenna internal function feed network works (external function feed network works the same): the input signal feeds from the input port. The first through the first stage of the machine and 180° delay line shifter, so that the input signal is divided into two signals with equal amplitude and opposite phase. Then the impedance is transformed to the standard 50 Ω via a quarter wavelength impedance converter. The two inverted signals are passed through the second stage of the machine and the 90° delay line shifter, respectively. The above two signals are further assigned to two orthogonal signals with an equal phase difference of 90°. Finally, the impedance is transformed again to the output port, i.e. 50 Ω, through a quarter-wavelength impedance converter. It can be seen that at the center frequency, after the input signal passes through the power division phase-shifting feed network, four signals with equal amplitude and phase lag of 90° can be obtained at the output port. It is worth noting that the T- type power divider has no isolation resistance, so the matching and isolation of the output port are not considered.

4 Simulation and Testing

Based on the theory of odd and even mode analysis and two-stage feed network analysis, the expression of the circuit electrical parameters of the internal power division feed

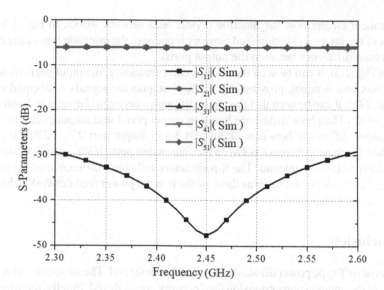

(a)The echo loss of the input port and the insertion loss of the circuit

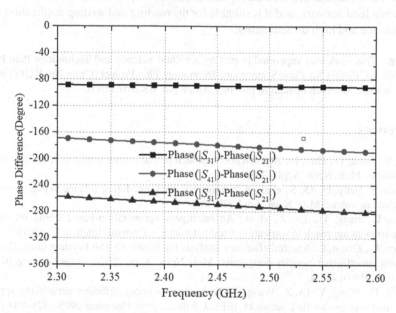

(b)Phase difference between output ports

Fig. 2. Scattering parameters and phase difference of the power divider feed network

network can be obtained: Z0 = 50 Ω, Z1 = 100 Ω, θ1 = 100°, Z2 = 71 Ω, Z3 = 71 Ω, Z4 = 50 Ω. The expression of the circuit electrical parameters of the external power division feeding network is: Z0 = 50 Ω, Z1 = 100 Ω, θ1 = 100°, Z2 = 71 Ω, Z3 = 114 Ω, Z4 = 130 Ω.

To make it clearer how the function divider feed network works, in Fig. 2 lists the echo loss of the internal function feed network input port, the insertion loss of the circuit, and the phase difference between the output ports.

From Fig. 2(a), it can be seen that at the center frequency, the input ports match and the insertion loss is equal, proving that the four outputs are signals with equal energy. From Fig. 2 (b), it can be seen that the phase difference between output port 3 and output port 2 is $-90°$. The phase difference between output port 4 and output port 2 is $-180°$, and the phase difference between output port 5 and output port 2 is $-270°$. It is fully proved that the phase difference between the four output ports is $90°$ in turn, which feeds the circularly polarized antenna. The S-parameters and phase difference of the external power feed network are the same as those of the internal power feed network, which will not be analyzed here.

5   Conclusion

A novel type of T-type power divider feed network is designed. The structure and working principle of the antenna power division feed network are analyzed. Finally, the simulation and test show that the network theory can improve the performance of the antenna in the antenna feed network, and it is suitable for the reading and writing application of the long-distance and high directionality.

Funding. This work was supported in part by Xu Zhou Science and Technology Plan Project (Grant No. KC19003) Xu Zhou Science and Technology Plan Project (Grant No. KC17140) and Natural Science Research of Jiangsu province (Grant No. BK20161165).

References

1. Qi, S., Jiang, D., Huo, L.: A prediction approach to end-to-end traffic in space information networks. Mob. Netw. Appl. (2019)
2. Wang, F., Jiang, D., Qi, S., et al.: A dynamic resource scheduling scheme in edge computing satellite networks. Mob. Netw. Appl. (2019)
3. Huo, L., Jiang, D., Lv, Z., et al.: An intelligent optimization-based traffic information acquirement approach to software-defined networking, Comput. Intell. 1–21 (2019)
4. Chen, L., Zhang, L.: Spectral efficiency analysis for massive MIMO system under QoS constraint: an effective capacity perspective. Mob. Netw. Appl. (2020). https://doi.org/10.1007/s11036-019-01414-4
5. Jiang, D., Wang, Y., Lv, Z., Wang, W., Wang, H.: An energy-efficient networking approach in cloud services for IIoT networks. IEEE J. Select. Areas Commun. **38**(5), 928–941 (2020)
6. Jiang, D., Wang, W., Shi, L., Song, H.: A compressive sensing-based approach to end-to-end network traffic reconstruction. IEEE Trans. Netw. Sci. Eng. **7**(1), 507–519 (2020)
7. Chen, L., Jiang, D., Bao, R., Xiong, J., Liu, F., Bei, L.: MIMO scheduling effectiveness analysis for bursty data service from view of QoE. Chin. J. Electron. **26**(5), 1079–1085 (2017)
8. Lulu, B., Bao, R., Chen, L., et al.: Out-of-phase power divider with complex impedance transformation based on miniaturized isolation network. Electromagnetics, **37**(3), 139–149 (2017)
9. Lulu, B., Chen, L., Zhao, W., et al.: Out-of-phase power divider with harmonic suppression. Progress Electromag. Res. **75**, 43–52 (2017)

10. Bei, L., Zhang, S., Huang, K.: Complex impedance-transforming out-of-phase power divider with high power-handling capability. Prog. Electromagn. Res. Lett. **53**, 13–19 (2015)
11. Jiang, D., Huo, L., Song, H.: Rethinking behaviors and activities of base stations in mobile cellular networks based on big data analysis. IEEE Trans. Netw. Sci. Eng. **7**(1), 80–90 (2020)
12. Jiang, D., Wang, Y., Lv, Z., Qi, S., Singh, S.: Big data analysis based network behavior insight of cellular networks for industry 4.0 applications. IEEE Trans. Ind. Inform. **16**(2), 1310–1320 (2020)
13. Jiang, D., Huo, L., Lv, Z., Song, H., Qin, W.: A joint multi-criteria utility-based network selection approach for vehicle-to-infrastructure networking. IEEE Trans. Intell. Transp. Syst. **19**(10), 3305–3319 (2018)
14. Wilkinson, E.J.: An N-way hybrid power divider. Microwave Theory Tech. IRE Trans. **8**(1), 116–118 (1960)
15. Jiang, D., Huo, L., Li, Y.: Fine-granularity inference and estimations to network traffic for SDN. PLoS ONE **13**(5), 1–23 (2018)
16. Wang, Y., Jiang, D., Huo, L., Zhao, Y.: A new traffic prediction algorithm to software defined networking. Mob. Netw. Appl. (2019)
17. Qi, S., Jiang, D., Huo, L.: A prediction approach to end-to-end traffic in space information networks. Mob. Netw. Appl. (2019)
18. Gysel, U.H.: A new N-way power divider/combiner suitable for high-power applications. In: 1975 IEEE-MTT-S International Microwave Symposium, pp. 116–118. IEEE (1975)
19. Elles, D.S., Yoon, Y.K.: Compact dual band three-way Bagley polygon power divider using composite right/left-handed (CRLH) transmission lines. In: 2009. IEEE MTT-S International Microwave Symposium Digest, 2009. MTT, pp. 485–488 (2009)
20. Liu, X., Yu, C., Liu, Y., et al.: Design of planar dual-band multi-way power dividers, pp. 722–725. IEEE (2010)
21. Jiang, D., Zhang, P., Lv, Z., et al.: Energy-efficient multi-constraint routing algorithm with load balancing for smart city applications. IEEE Internet Things J. **3**(6), 1437–1447 (2016)
22. Jiang, D., Li, W., Lv, H.: An energy-efficient cooperative multicast routing in multi-hop wireless networks for smart medical applications. Neurocomputing **2017**(220), 160–169 (2017)
23. Wang, F., Jiang, D., Qi, S.: An adaptive routing algorithm for integrated information networks. China Commun. **7**(1), 196–207 (2019)
24. Shamaileh, K.A., Dib, N., Abushamleh, S.: A dual-band 1:10 Wilkinson power divider based on multi-T-section characterization of high-impedance transmission lines. IEEE Microw. Compon. Lett. **27**(10), 897–899 (2017)
25. Abdelrahman, B.M., Ahmed, H.N., Nashed, A.I.: A novel tri-band Wilkinson power divider for multiband wireless applications. IEEE Microw. Compon. Lett. **27**(10), 891–893 (2017)
26. Moulay, A., Djerafi, T.: Wilkinson power divider with fixed width substrate-integrated waveguide line and a distributed isolation resistance. IEEE Microw. Compon. Lett. **28**(2), 114–116 (2018)
27. Huo, L., Jiang, D., Qi, S., et al.: An AI-based adaptive cognitive modeling and measurement method of network traffic for EIS, Mobile Networks and Applications (2019)
28. Huo, L., Jiang, D., Lv, Z., et al.: An intelligent optimization-based traffic information acquirement approach to software-defined networking. Comput. Intell. 1–21 (2019)
29. Alexiou, A., Martin, H.: Smart antenna technologies for future wireless systems: trends and challenges. IEEE Commun. Mag. [H.W. Wilson - AST], **42**(9), 90 (2004)
30. Liu, H., Gao, S., Loh, T.: Electrically small and low cost smart antenna for wireless communication. IEEE Trans. Antennas Propag. **60**(3), 1540–1549 (2012)
31. Nasimuddin, Z.C., Xianming, Q.: Asymmetric-circular shaped slotted microstrip antennas for circular polarization and RFID applications. Antennas Propag. IEEE Trans. **58**(12), 3821–3828 (2010)

32. Luo, B., Li, P., Luo, B., et al.: Design of circular polarization microstrip antenna in RFID reader for 5.8 GHz electronic toll collection application. In: 2009. ICMTCE. International Conference on Microwave Technology and Computational Electromagnetics, IET, pp. 84–87 (2009)

33. Jain, R.K., Katiyar, S., Agrawal, N.K.: Smart antenna for cellular mobile communication. 1(9), 530–541 (2012)

34. Sun, Z., Zhang, L., Yan, Y., et al.: Design of unequal dual-band Gysel power divider with arbitrary termination resistance. IEEE Trans. Microwave Theory Tech. 59(8), 1955–1962 (2011)

35. Wilkinson, E.J.: An N-way hybrid power divider. Microwave Theory Tech. IRE Trans. 8(1), 116–118 (1960)

36. Gysel, U.H.: A new N-way power divider/combiner suitable for high-power applications. In: 1975 IEEE-MTT-S International Microwave Symposium, pp. 116–118 (1975)

37. Elles, D.S., Yoon, Y.K.: Compact dual band three way Bagley polygon power divider using composite right/left handed (CRLH) transmission lines. In: IEEE MTT-S International Microwave Symposium Digest, 2009. MTT 2009, pp. 485–488 (2009)

38. Liu, X., Yu, C., Liu, Y., et al.: Design of planar dual-band multi-way power dividers, pp. 722 – 725. IEEE (2010)

39. Srisathit, S., Chongcheawchamnan, M., Worapishet, A.: Design and realisation of dual-band 3 dB power divider based on two-section transmission-line topology. Electron. Lett. 39(9), 723–724 (2003)

40. Gao, B., Liu, Y.: Novel design of dual-band unequal Wilkinson power divider with wide band-ratios and simple layout. In: 2012 10th International Symposium on Antennas, Propagation & EM Theory (ISAPE), pp. 121–123. IEEE (2012)

A Dynamic Acceleration Method for Remote Sensing Image Processing Based on CUDA

Xianyu Zuo[1,3], Zhe Zhang[1,3], Baojun Qiao[1,2], Junfeng Tian[2,3](✉), Liming Zhou[2,3], and Yunzhou Zhang[4]

[1] Henan Key Laboratory of Big Data Analysis and Processing, Henan University, Kaifeng 475004, People's Republic of China
[2] Henan Engineering Laboratory of Spatial Information Processing, Henan University, Kaifeng 475004, People's Republic of China
[3] College of Computer and Information Engineering, Henan University, Kaifeng 475004, China
[4] National Cultural Heritage Administration, Beijing 100010, People's Republic of China

Abstract. The incredible increase in the volume of remote sensing data has made the concept of Remote Sensing as Big Data reality with recent technological developments. Remote sensing image processing is characterized with features of massive data processing and intensive computation, which makes the processes difficult. To optimize the remote sensing image processing for GPU, compute unified device architecture (CUDA) is widely used to implement remote sensing algorithms. However, the usage of GPU in remote sensing image processing has been constrained by the complexity of its implementation and configuration. Therefore, how to take fully advantage of the parallel organization of GPU architecture is awfully challenging. In this paper, a dynamic adaptive acceleration (DAA) method is proposed to determine calculation parameters of GPU adaptively and preprocess the input remote sensing images on host dynamically. By this method, we determine calculation parameters according to the hardware parameters of GPU firstly. And then, the input remote sensing images are reconstructed based on the calculation parameters. Finally, the preprocessed image blocks are arranged to stream tasks and executed on GPU respectively. Effectiveness of the proposed DAA method in accelerate remote sensing algorithm with point operations were verified by experiments in this paper, and the experimental results indicated that the DAA method can obtain better performance than traditional methods.

Keywords: Remote sensing data · Image processing · CUDA stream · Dynamic acceleration

1 Introduction

With the rapid development of the modern remote sensing technology, remote sensing data having both spectral and spatial information are provided by hyperspectral sensors [1]. And with the increased spatial and spectral resolution of sensors, the amount of remote sensing data has dramatically increased. Remote sensing data has met the basic

H. Song and D. Jiang (Eds.): SIMUtools 2020, LNICST 369, pp. 409–426, 2021.
https://doi.org/10.1007/978-3-030-72792-5_34

characteristics of big data which defined as 3V: volume, velocity, and variety [2, 3]. Thus, remote sensing data reaching high dimensions is defined as remote sensing big data and analyzed in many studies [2, 4, 5]. While acquisition of remote sensing data is no longer the most significant issue, but the processing performance of remote sensing images. Remote sensing image processing is characterized with features of massive data processing, intensive computation, and complex processing algorithms which make the processing of remote sensing image difficult and inefficient [6]. In order to obtain a better performance, GPU (Graphics Processing Unit) is widely used in the field of remote sensing image processing.

GPU are successful accelerators as they show high data throughput with sustainable power budget and is well supported by the SIMT (Single Instructions, Multiple Threads) programming models such as CUDA and OpenCL [6]. In past studies, it has been proved that the time consumption of many remote sensing image processing algorithms can be significantly reduced when optimized for GPU. For example, Wu *et al.* [7] presented a computationally efficient parallel implementation for a spectral-spatial classification method that achieved significant acceleration factors higher than 70 times with NVIDIA GPU. Li *et al.* [8] focused on the most time-consuming part of the manifold learning algorithms designed for HIS data analysis, accelerated by GPU and obtained an excellent speedup performance. Ayomide yusuf *et al.*[7] had surveyed the studies about the usages of GPU in hyperspectral images, and concluded that the implementation of parallel algorithms on GPU has significantly improved the classification of hyperspectral images.

Moreover, CUDA stream have further improved the performance of GPU based programs. Without any synchronization and based on architectural capabilities, NVIDIA's CUDA stream allows some processes to run simultaneously [8]. Leonel Toledo *et al.* [9] illustrated that using dynamic parallelism and CUDA streams were able to achieve up to 30% speedups. HuiChao Hong *et al.* [10] implemented the method based on CUDA streams to compute the GLCM of an image and 50 times faster than ever before. However, in spite of the excellent performance that GPU based remote sensing applications have achieved, how to fully take advantage of CUDA streams in remote sensing processing and reduce the utilization complexity is awfully challenging. In order to take fully advantage of CDUA streams, Mohamad B R *et al.* [8] proposed a method to predict program parts which are able to be overlapped on CUDA streams. However, the parallel processes were carefully designed and optimized with the knowledge of a specific algorithm in most studies, but rarely consider to propose an adaptive and efficient method that can determine execution parameters of CUDA streams according to GPU hardware and features of the input data to be processed dynamically.

Concerning the advantages and shortcomings aforementioned of CUDA streams, this paper proposed a dynamic adaptive acceleration (DAA) method for remote sensing image processing to improve the performance of GPU based programs and reduce the utilization complexity of CUDA streams. The DAA method can determine the appropriate number of streams automatically and determine the suitable size of image blocks adaptively according to the GPU hardware parameters and the remote sensing images to be processed. With this method, developers can take advantages of CUDA streams more conveniently for remote sensing image processing. The main contributions of this paper are as following:

(1) Architecture of CUDA-enabled GPU was introduced, and theoretical analysis about the acceleration mode and execution characteristics of typical GPU parallel models, the multi-thread parallel model and the multi-stream parallel model, were performed respectively. Moreover, the advantage and disadvantage of multi-stream parallel model based on CUDA streams were explained straightly.

(2) According to the correlations between GPU hardware and CUDA programming model, an adaptive strategy which aim to determine the appropriate calculation parameters for CUDA based programs was proposed in this paper.

(3) This paper proposed an DAA method to maximize resource utilization of GPU and is effective to accelerate the remote sensing image processing based on the previous adaptive strategy and the characteristics of remote sensing images. The theoretical analysis and experimental results have verified the superiority of the DAA method compared to general methods.

The remainder of this paper is organized as follows. Section 2 provides the related works about architecture of CUDA-enabled GPU and the typical parallel models of CUDA. Section 3 presents the proposed DAA method for remote sensing image processing on GPU and Sect. 4 validates the method with experiments. Section 5 concludes this paper and describes the future works.

2 Related Work

2.1 Architecture of CUDA-Enabled GPU

Generally, A GPU is composed of massive parallel processors with high floating point performance and memory bandwidth, and has high data throughput [11, 12]. In terms of NVIDA GPUs, SP (Streaming Processor) is the basic unit for the execution of the GPU, and multiple SPs and memories make up the SM. And, multiple SMs, memories, and interconnection networks make up the whole GPU, as shown in Fig. 1. Moreover, GPU is specialized for highly parallel computation, which is exactly what image processing is about, and therefore designed such that more processors are devoted to data processing rather than data caching and flow control [13]. Furthermore, in order to apply GPU to the general purpose computing, CUDA was introduced by NVIDIA in November 2006, which is a general purpose parallel computing platform and programming model that leverages the parallel compute engine in NVIDIA GPUs to solve many complex computational problems in a more efficient way [13, 14]. Mapping images or data to be processed to the parallel processors, the burdensome tasks can be accelerated by GPU effectively. To take fully advantage of the parallel organization of GPU and obtain the best speedup, it is suggested to design and optimize the parallel process carefully with the knowledge of GPU hardware architecture and the features of image processing algorithms [6].

2.2 Parallel Models of CUDA

In this section, the two parallel models of CUDA are discussed and analyzed. In order to demonstrate the characteristics of the models clearly, the time consumption of data transfers between host (CPU) and device (GPU) is not considered.

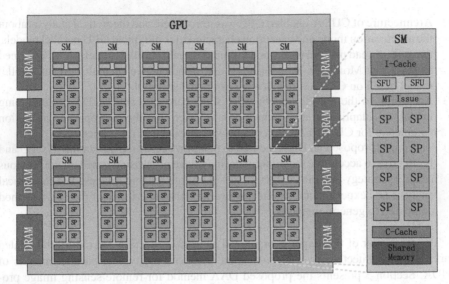

Fig. 1. The general hardware architecture of CUDA-enabled GPU produced by NVIDIA.

2.2.1 Multi-thread Parallel Model

The SIMT architecture of CUDA is akin to SIMD (Single Instruction, Multiple Data) vector organizations in that a single instruction controls multiple processing elements [13]. As described above, the CUDA-enabled GPU generally has a large number of processors compared to CPU. And therefore, the simplest implementation for applications which accelerated by CUDA is to divide tasks into subtasks and then executed by thread blocks. And this method which called multi-thread parallel model, as shown in Fig. 2, is widely used in order to take advantage of the abundant computing cores.

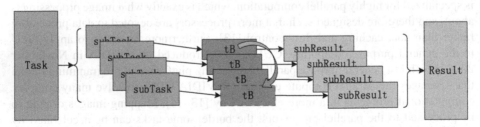

Fig. 2. Multi-thread parallel model of CUDA.

The Multi-thread parallel model divides the computing task into a set of subtasks on the granularity of threads. It should be noted that the computing task is not divided into subtasks spatially, but automatically divided by thread blocks logically. In other words, part of the whole computing task that executed by a single thread block is called subtask. Generally, a single thread block can handle one or more subtasks. When the current subtask is completed, the next subtask will be processed by the released thread block according to the predefined steps. Finally, when all subtasks are completed, the calculation sub-results will be combined to obtain the final result. The procedures can be presented as the following equation.

$$Rt(n, t) = \sum_{i=0}^{n} K_t(subT_i) \tag{1}$$

Where n is the total number of subtasks, $subT_i$ stands for the subtask i, t represents the thread block (according to the previous analysis, we can assume that the thread blocks and subtasks correspond to each other in this paper), and K_t represents the kernel function executed by thread block t. In addition, the sub-result of $subT_i$ is represented by $K_t(subT_i)$, and Rt represents the final result of the task. From the multi-thread parallel model, it can be easily known that the computing task is divided into multiple subtasks logically and executed concurrently by the thread blocks, which can obtain a better performance theoretically in most cases. And the total time consumption of the computing task executed by multi-thread parallel model is calculated as the maximum difference between the earliest start time and the latest end time of all these subtasks handled by thread blocks. The computing method can be simply presented as the following equation.

$$T_{total}(n, t) = max\{K_t(subT_i)\} - min\{K_t(subT_i)\} \tag{2}$$

Where, as demonstrated in Eq. (1), $i = (1,.....,n)$, n is the number of subtasks and $subT_i$ stands for the subtask i. $K_i(subT_i)$ represents the processing procedures and the corresponding sub-result of $subT_i$ executed by thread block t. Additionally, the latest end time of all thread blocks is obtained by function max, and the earliest one is obtained by function min.

However, although the multi-thread parallel model has effectively achieved acceleration effects, the time consumption of data transfers between the host and device cannot be hidden. And computing resources are in an idle state when performing the operations of data transfer. Therefore, the more the operations of data transfer, the lower the occupation ratio of computing resource will be. To address this issue, the multi-stream parallel model was utilized.

2.2.2 Multi-stream Parallel Model

A stream in CUDA is a sequence of operations execute on device in order which are issued by the host code [13, 15, 16]. Operations within a single stream are guaranteed to execute in the prescribed order, but operations in separate streams can be interleaved and, when possible, they can even execute concurrently [17]. In other words, CUDA streams act as independent work queues through which different kernels can be executed simultaneously [18]. And, CUDA streams is a technique that can overlap kernel execution with data transfers, and different kernel executions can even be overlapped through Hyper-Q [19–21]. With CUDA streams and the feature of Hyper-Q, the overall parallelism is increased due to the added granularity of streams on the basis of threads. In fact, the multi-stream parallel model contains the multi-thread parallel model and improves the degree of parallelism (as shown in Fig. 3). When there is only a default stream, the multi-stream parallel model is the same as the multi-thread parallel model.

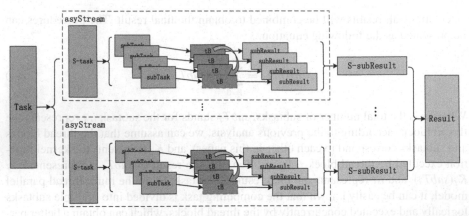

Fig. 3. Multi-stream parallel model of CUDA.

The process procedures of multi-stream parallel model can be concluded in three stages. Firstly, the multi-stream parallel model divides the computing task into subtasks (*S-task* in Fig. 3) spatially on the granularity of streams. For example, the processing task of a large size image can be divided into multiple image blocks spatially with regular size. Each of the blocks is a part of the task and then assigned to separate streams for execution. In terms of batch processing of multiple small size images, each image is generally viewed as a single *S-task* and executed on separate streams respectively. Secondly, separate *S-tasks* is executed through the multi-thread parallel model. But the difference is that the execution result of each *S-task* is only the result of its own stream (*asySresult* in Fig. 3), which is a sub-result of the whole task. Finally, in order to get the final result, sub-results will be combined in two steps: one for the multi-thread parallel model and the other for the multi-stream parallel model. The procedures can be presented as the following equation.

$$Rs(n, s, t) = \sum_{i=0}^{s} \left(\sum_{j=0}^{n} K_t(subS_i T_j) \right)$$ (3)

Where n is the number of subtasks on separate stream, and s is the number of streams. $SubS_i T_j$ stands for the subtask on the granularity of threads. K_t represents the kernel executed by thread block j on stream i, and $K_t(subS_i T_j)$ represents the processing procedures and the corresponding sub-result. Rs is the final result of the whole computing task. Additionally, the total time consumption of task executed by the multi-stream parallel model is calculated as the maximum difference between the earliest start time and the latest end time of all these subtasks. With reference to Eq. (2), the computing method can be formulated as Eq. (4).

$$T_{total}(n, s, t) = max\{K_t(subS_i T_j)\} - min\{K_t(subS_i T_j)\}$$ (4)

Although the multi-stream parallel model is commonly better than the multi-thread parallel model in terms of parallelism and performance under most cases, the complexity of designing and programming is relatively higher than that of the multi-thread parallel model. Therefore, how to take advantages of the multi-stream parallel model more conveniently and effectively is awfully challenging.

2.3 Problem Statement

As described in the section above, it's obvious that the multi-stream parallel model can indirectly hide partial time consumption of data transfers and obtain a higher performance than the multi-thread parallel model due to the characteristic of overlap. However, CUDA streams are a series of orders executed in sequence, but different stream can execute in their own order at the same time or not regardless of sequence [10]. Paper [22, 23] have effectively improved the performance using CUDA streams. Therefore, it seems that the larger the number of streams, the greater the performance improvement. But, unfortunately, due to the constraints of hardware resources, the larger number of streams does not necessarily mean the better performance. Only the supported streams which have enough computing resources can be executed simultaneously. And the more the streams are created, the more the intervals between operations of data transfer and kernel execution are generated. In other words, it is no use to simply create more streams, because the unsupported streams will still be executed serialized at hardware level partially, as illustrated in Fig. 4, and compromise the performance of processing.

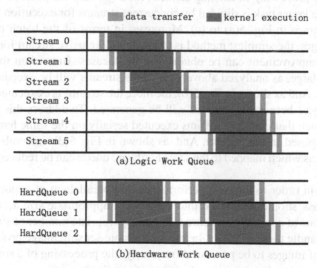

Fig. 4. Streams that executed serially partially.

The performance of device cannot be fully utilized when the number of CUDA streams is insufficient. However, the large amount of CUDA streams will cause additional time consumption that could have been avoided. Therefore, how to determine the appropriate number of CUDA streams and take fully advantage of GPU to accelerate the remote sensing image processing are awfully challenging. In order to obtain a better performance and simplify the configuration complexity of CUDA streams, this study proposes a dynamic method to overcome the problem above.

3 Algorithm Design of DAA Method

From those characteristics of GPU described above, it can be known that the GPU is effective in accelerating the remote sensing image processing and the performance can be improved significantly. To obtain the best speedup, it is suggested to design and optimize the parallel applications carefully with the basic knowledge of GPU hardware architecture and different features of the remote sensing image algorithms.

In order to obtain better performance and to use the multi-stream parallel model easily and efficiently, a dynamic acceleration method for remote sensing image processing is proposed in this section. With this method, the utilization of multi-stream parallel model can be more conveniently and efficiently applied to remote sensing image processing algorithms to a certain degree.

3.1 Adaptive Strategy of CUDA Streams

There are various means having been used to examine methods for improving concurrency and parallelism of algorithms implemented by CUDA [15, 20]. The commonly and effectively method is to optimize applications using the multi-stream parallel model on GPU. To obtain better performance, the larger size image was divided into blocks of regular size for processing in existing studies [10, 24]. From the point of view of computing task, the larger task is divided by concurrent streams for execution into multiple subtasks, as shown in Fig. 5(a) to (c). Moreover, in terms of the batch processing of small size images, the simplest method is to create an exclusive stream for each image, and effective improvement can be obtained in most cases. But, when the number of streams is too large, as analyzed above, part of the streams will be executed serially at hardware level. And as shown in Fig. 5(b), the more the streams are executed serially, the more the intervals between operations will be generated. To address this problem, the efficient approach that combine streams executed serially on the same hardware queue into one is proposed in this section. And, as shown in Fig. 5(d), intervals between the scattered streams which mapped to the same hardware queue can be reduced with stream combination.

Therefore, in order to improve performance and parallelism of applications based on GPU, the task should be divided into subtasks of appropriate size according to the various situations of computing resource, and the appropriate number of streams should be created to handle these subtasks. In terms of remote sensing image processing, there are two cases of images to be processed frequently: the processing of a single image of larger size and the batch processing of images of small size.

For the former case, in order to overlap data transfers with kernel execution, a larger size image is usually divided into blocks and optimized for the multi-stream parallel model. For the latter case, in order to avoid the situation shown as Fig. 5(b), a new method that combine input images partially before processing and creates streams adaptively, instead of creating a stream for each image, according to the hardware parameters is proposed. And, for the benefit of the adaptive method, an adaptive strategy for determining the appropriate number of streams and the size of image blocks adaptively is defined as follows:

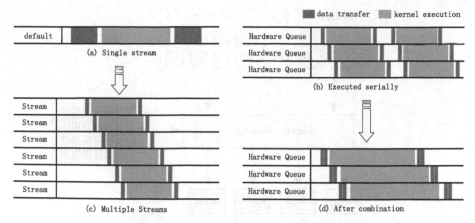

Fig. 5. Diagram of execution based on CUDA streams at hardware level.

1. The number of streams should be equal to or slightly bigger than the number of SMs, and the computing resources (i.e. threads and memories) occupied by separate stream should not exceed the resources owned by a single SM.
2. The number of image blocks should be equal to the number of streams or an integer times of the number, and the size of single image blocks should satisfy the following formula:

$$(B_s + R_s) * S_n \leq G_m \tag{5}$$

While B_s is the size of individual image block, R_s represents the size of the processing result of the image block. S_n represents the number of streams, and G_m is the total size of graphic memories.

3.2 Dynamic Adaptive Acceleration Method

Complying with these constraints defined in the previous section, an appropriate number of CUDA streams can be created, and the input images can be processed dynamically into regular-size blocks. And thus image blocks can be distributed evenly to each stream for execution, the intervals will be reduced, and the resources occupancy ratio of GPU will be increased. Furthermore, according to the analyses and strategies proposed above, a dynamic adaptive acceleration (DAA) method to divide or combine input images and to create streams dynamically for remote sensing image processing is proposed.

As shown in Fig. 6, the input images are automatically divided or combined into blocks of regular size according to the different types of them and GPU hardware parameters firstly. And then, the streams of appropriate number are created and the image blocks are loaded onto the corresponding streams for execution. Finally, execution results are combined to obtain the final result. With this method, the appropriate number of streams and image blocks can be determined automatically, and the complexity of using the multi-stream parallel model can be greatly reduced or even hidden without performance improvement declining.

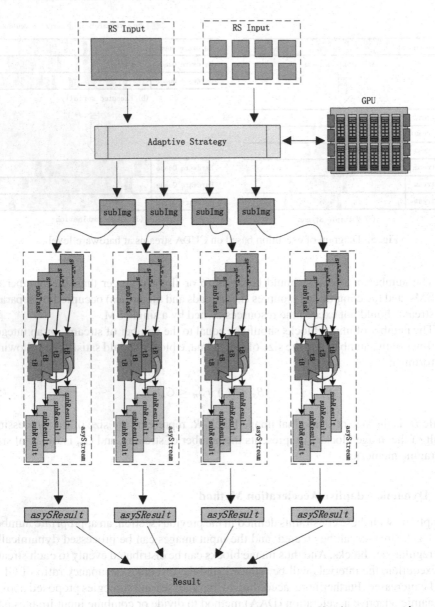

Fig. 6. Dynamic adaptive acceleration method for remote sensing image processing.

Given constraints as following, (1) the output data (remote sensing images in this paper) and the input data are roughly equal in size. (2) the time consumption of the kernel function with the same amount of data to be processed is fixed. The time consumption equations of the proposed DAA method and the general method based on multi-thread parallel model can be described as Eq. (6) and Eq. (7) respectively, in terms of the single large size image processing.

$$2(T_{\text{int}} + \frac{1}{n}T_{copy}) + KT_{init} + KT_{launch} + KT_{compute} \tag{6}$$

$$2(T_{init} + T_{copy}) + KT_{init} + KT_{launch} + KT_{compute} \tag{7}$$

Where n represents the number of CUDA streams which determined based on the adaptive strategy, T_{int} is the time consumption and of data engine initialization and T_{copy} is the time consumption of data transfer. KT_{init}, KT_{launch} and $KT_{compute}$ represents the time consumption of kernel function initialization, kernel launch and kernel execution respectively.

Moreover, the time consumption equations of the proposed DAA method and the general method based on multi-stream parallel model can be described as Eq. (8) and Eq. (9) respectively, in terms of the batch processing of small size images.

$$2(T_{\text{int}} + \frac{m}{n}T_{copy}) + m(KT_{init} + KT_{launch} + KT_{compute}) \tag{8}$$

$$2\lfloor \frac{m}{n} \rfloor (T_{\text{int}} + T_{copy}) + 2(m\,MOD\,n)(T_{\text{int}} + T_{copy}) + m(KT_{init} + KT_{launch} + KT_{compute}) + \lfloor \frac{m}{n} \rfloor \beta \tag{9}$$

Where m represents the number of images, the number of CUDA streams in general method as well, and the β in Eq. (9) is defined as below.

$$\beta = \begin{cases} 0, & m = n \\ \beta, & m \neq n \end{cases}$$

The proposed DAA method can take advantages of the CUDA streams to overlap data transfers and kernel executions, and reduce the calling intervals between operations on each stream by load tasks to appropriate number of streams. According to the analysis above, it can be easily concluded that the proposed DAA method can theoretically obtain a better performance than general methods that simply based on the multi-thread parallel model and multi-stream parallel model.

4 Experiment

In this section, experiments were conducted to demonstrate the performance and effectiveness of DAA method.

4.1 Discussion and Preparation

Operations of various remote sensing image processing algorithms can be classified roughly into three types: point operation, local operation and global operation. As shown in Fig. 7, the simplest type is the point operation that the output result only depends on the corresponding input image. For local operation, the output result are correlated with the neighborhood of the pixel in input image, such as convolution calculation and median filtering. And about global operation, the output result is associated with the whole input image which is the most complex calculation.

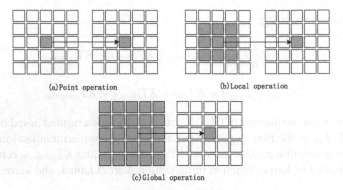

(a) Point operation   (b) Local operation

(c) Global operation

Fig. 7. Typical operation of remote sensing image processing algorithms.

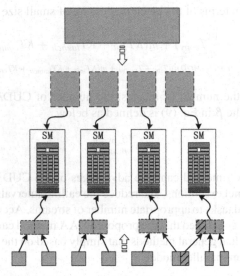

Fig. 8. Diagram of adaptive strategy for algorithms with point operations.

According to the three types of operations, it is obvious that DAA is more applicable for the algorithms with point operations because of the computational independence of point operations. Therefore, in terms of point operations, all the small-size images either of the same size or of different size can use the DAA, as shown Fig. 8.

However, when the DAA method is applied to algorithms with local operations, the adaptive strategy of DAA should be changed. In terms of large size image, the neighborhood data should be considered when DAA is applying to the algorithm of local operations. Changes should be made and vary with features of local operation algorithms, as shown in Fig. 9(a). In addition, integrity of small size images should be guaranteed, which means that small size images are required to have the same size, as shown in Fig. 9(b). Given that, design and implementation of algorithms with local or global operations accelerated by DAA method are still difficult, and the generality and performance of DAA method will be greatly compromised. It is obvious that the DAA method is not suitable enough for algorithms with local operations or global operations. Therefore, only experiments on the algorithms of point operations was carried out in this paper.

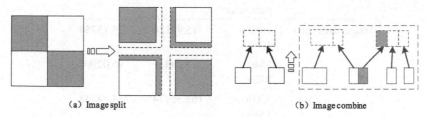

(a) Image split   (b) Image combine

Fig. 9. Changes and constraints of adaptive strategy in DAA for local operations.

The remote sensing images that produced by GF1 satellite were selected for experiments in this section, and the hardware parameters of experimental GPU is shown in Table 1. In order to evaluate the effectiveness of the proposed method better, the time consumption of applications in host was ignored.

Table 1. Experimental environment.

GPU	GeForce GTX 1060		
Cores	1280	SMs	10
Clock rate	1.67 GHz	CUDA Cores	1280
Global memory	6 GB	UVA Support	Yes
CUDA version	9.2	Warp Size	32

4.2 Experimental Result

In the first experiment, the NDVI calculation [25], a typical remote sensing image processing algorithm of point operations is selected. The processing of large size image accelerated by DAA and general purpose multi-thread parallel model (called G-MT in this paper) was respectively discussed. To illustrate the impact of different size images, the original remote sensing images of different sizes (8540 × 8520 and 12000 × 13400) were chosen, and remote sensing images of other regular sizes (4000 × 4000, 16000 × 16000 and 20000 × 20000) were obtained by splitting and stitching. Additionally, the total size of GPU computing resources used by the method of G-MT is equal to that used by DAA. Results and perform configuration of the first experiment are shown in Table 2.

In the first experiment, the time consumption of method G-MT and method DAA was compared, including all the operations of data transfer and kernel execution. It can be easily seen from Fig. 10 that DAA had achieved better performance compared

Table 2. Experimental result.

Specifications		DAA	G-MT
Configuration	Streams	10	1 (default)
	Execution parameter	<1, 128 >	<10, 128 >
Image sizes (ms)	4000 × 4000	15.99124	25.15754
	8540 × 8520	73.2981	96.02902
	12000 × 13400	162.36974	234.44748
	16000 × 16000	253.1896	389.38958
	20000 × 20000	468.82148	651.24778

to G-MT. And with the increasing size of image, the acceleration effect was further improved. As demonstrated in previous section, the multi-stream parallel model has achieved parallelism with a higher degree than the multi-thread parallel model does. Given that, the DAA divided large size image into regular size image blocks and created streams according to the hardware situations, and then loaded image blocks evenly onto the separate stream. Therefore, DAA has obtained a better performance improvement in the processing of large size remote sensing image than G-MT. And, as the image size increases, so did the performance improvement.

In the second experiment, the application of DAA in batch processing of small size images was evaluated. There are 9 groups of images were used in this experiment, from 20 to 180 images and with an interval of 20 images between each group. In terms of image data, remote sensing tile images of 1000 × 1000 size were chosen. In this experiment, the groups of images were processed using the general purpose multi-stream parallel model (G-MS) was implemented that streams were created for each image respectively. Besides, batch processing of image groups using DAA was implemented too. Results and perform configuration of the second experiment are shown in Table 3.

As shown in Fig. 11, DAA has achieved better performance improvement than G-MS. Reasons for this improvement was analyzed in previous sections that DAA has effectively reduced the calling intervals, which were generated by G-MS frequently and increased with the number of images in batch image processing.

Particularly, when the number of images in the group is 20, DAA took the same or even more time consumption compared to G-MS. The reason is that when the size and number of images are not large enough, more streams could achieve a higher parallelism and resources occupancy rate. This is also the case for group that contains 80 images. When the number of images was 80, only slight performance improvement was achieved. However, in general, DAA has achieved better acceleration effects than G-MS

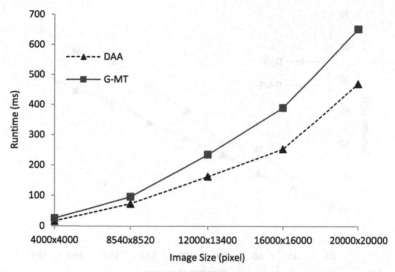

Fig. 10. Comparison of G-MT and DAA for processing of large size image.

Table 3. Experimental result.

Specifications		DAA	G-MS
Configuration	Streams	10	*Number of images*
	Execution parameter	<1, 128 >	<1, 128 >
Images	20	10.9963	10.27162
	40	16.55978	19.1056
	60	20.7585	28.35928
	80	26.70484	30.25702
	100	31.72824	39.98284
	120	36.57192	48.22432
	140	42.89492	55.39422
	160	46.34424	58.61586
	180	51.92558	65.094

in the experiment. And, as the the number of images increased, so did the performance improvement.

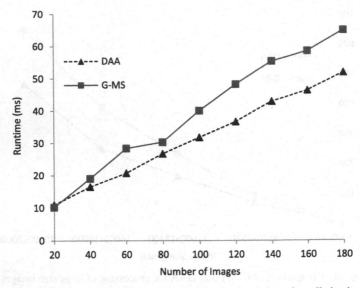

Fig. 11. Comparison of G-MS and DAA for batch processing of small size images.

5   Conclusion and Future Work

In this paper, a dynamic acceleration method for remote sensing image processing is proposed. The method can create streams and process the input images into blocks of appropriate size dynamically according to hardware parameters, and finally can load image blocks onto the corresponding streams evenly for execution. Moreover, the efficiency and performance of the proposed method in the typical remote sensing image processing algorithms of point operation is proved through experiments with different number and size of images. With this method, the two typical situations in remote sensing image processing algorithms of point operation have both obtained efficiently performance improvement, without the need to set calculation parameters of GPU and preprocess the input images manually. Therefore, it is concluded that the method proposed can be more convenient and obtain a better performance than traditional methods in accelerating remote sensing image processing.

According to the experimental results in this paper, it is obvious that the method proposed still has some deficiencies, and there was only its performance and generality in algorithms of point operation were proved. Therefore, the future study will focus on how to further improve the performance of the method proposed based on different hardware situations and computing modes [26–29]. Moreover, the application of the DAA method in other typical types of remote sensing image processing algorithms is taken into the agenda.

Acknowledgements. The authors would like to thank the referees and Editor for their helpful suggestions for revising this manuscript. The project is supported in partly by National Key Research and Development Program of China (2017YFD0301105), Natural Science Foundation of China (61202098, U1604145, U1704122), Science and Technological Research of Key

Projects of Henan Province (202102110121, 202102210352, 202102210368, 192102210096, 201400210300), and Excellent Youth Foundation of Science Technology Innovation of Henan Province (184100510004).

References

1. Giordano, R., Guccione, P.: ROI-based on-board compression for hyperspectral remote sensing images on GPU. Sensors **17**(5), 1160 (2017)
2. Gao, S., Li, L., Li, W., et al.: Constructing gazetteers from volunteered Big Geo-Data based on Hadoop. Comput. Environ. Urban Syst. **61**(b), 172–186 (2017)
3. Jiang, D., Wang, Y., Lv, Z., et al.: Big data analysis based network behavior insight of cellular networks for industry 4.0 applications. IEEE Trans. Ind. Inform. **16**(2), 1310–1320 (2020)
4. Pektürk, M.K., Ünal, M.: Performance-aware high-performance computing for remote sensing big data analytics. In: Data Mining, Chapter 5, pp. 69–90. BoD–Books on Demand (2018)
5. Levin, N., Ali, S., Crandall, D., et al.: World heritage in danger: big data and remote sensing can help protect sites in conflict zones. Glob. Environ. Chang. **55**, 97–104 (2019)
6. Ma, Y., Chen, L., Liu, P., et al.: Parallel programing templates for remote sensing image processing on GPU architectures: design and implementation. Computing **98**(1), 7–33 (2016)
7. Yusuf, A., Alawneh, S., et al.: A survey of GPU implementations for hyperspectral image classification in remote sensing **44**(5), 532–550 (2018)
8. Roui, M.B., Shekofteh, S.K., Noori, H., et al.: Efficient scheduling of streams on GPGPUs, pp. 1–33 (2020)
9. Toledo, L., Pena, A.J., Catalan, S., et al.: Tasking in Accelerators: Performance Evaluation. Parallel and Distributed Computing: Applications and Technologies (2019)
10. Hong, H., Zheng, L., Pan, S.: Computation of Gray level co-occurrence matrix based on CUDA and optimization for medical computer vision application. IEEE Access **6**, 67762–67770 (2018)
11. Xu, L., Ziedan, N.I., Niu, X., Guo, W.: Correlation acceleration in GNSS software receivers using a CUDA-enabled GPU. GPS Solutions **21**(1), 225–236 (2016). https://doi.org/10.1007/s10291-016-0516-2
12. Ikeda, K., Ino, F., Hagihara, K., et al.: An OpenACC optimizer for accelerating histogram computation on a GPU. In: 2016 24th Euromicro International Conference on Parallel, Distributed, and Network-Based Processing (2016)
13. NVIDIA: CUDA Programming Guide. https://docs.nvidia.com/cuda/archive/10.1/cuda-c-programming-guide/index.html. Accessed 28 Dec 2019
14. Wu, Z., Shi, L., Li, J., et al.: GPU parallel implementation of spatially adaptive hyperspectral image classification. IEEE J. Sel. Top. Appl. Earth Observations Remote Sens. **11**(4), 1131–1143 (2017)
15. Li, T., Narayana, V.K., El-Ghazawi, T.: Symbiotic scheduling of concurrent GPU kernels for performance and energy optimizations. In: Proceedings of the 11th ACM Conference on Computing Frontiers, p. 36. ACM, Cagliari, Italy (2014)
16. Li, W., Zhang, L., Zhang, L., et al.: GPU parallel implementation of isometric mapping for hyperspectral classification. IEEE Geosci. Remote Sens. Lett. **14**(9), 1532–1536 (2017)
17. Baca, H.A.H., Valdivia, F.D.L.P.: Efficient sparse matrix-vector multiplication on GPUs using the CSR format, pinned memory and overlap data transfer. In: 2019 IEEE XXVI International Conference on Electronics, Electrical Engineering and Computing (2019)
18. Kim, J., Cha, J., Park, J.J.K., et al.: Improving GPU multitasking efficiency using dynamic resource sharing. IEEE Comput. Archit. Lett. **18**(1), 1–5 (2019)

19. Adriaens, J.T., Compton, K., Kim, N.S., et al.: The case for GPGPU spatial multitasking. In: IEEE International Symposium on High-Performance Comp Architecture (2012)

20. Luley, R.S., Qiu, Q.: Effective utilization of CUDA Hyper-Q for improved power and performance efficiency. In: 2016 IEEE International Parallel and Distributed Processing Symposium Workshops, IPDPSW, pp. 1160–1169. IEEE, Chicago, IL (2016)

21. Dominguez, J.M., Crespo, A.J.C., Valdezbalderas, D., et al.: New multi-GPU implementation for smoothed particle hydrodynamics on heterogeneous clusters. Comput. Phys. Commun. 184(8), 1848–1860 (2013)

22. Czarnul, P.: Benchmarking overlapping communication and computations with multiple streams for modern GPUs. Ann. Comput. Sci. Inf. Syst. 17, 105–110 (2018)

23. Knap, M., Czarnul, P.: Performance evaluation of Unified Memory with prefetching and oversubscription for selected parallel CUDA applications on NVIDIA Pascal and Volta GPUs. J. Supercomput. 75(11), 7625–7645 (2019). https://doi.org/10.1007/s11227-019-02966-8

24. Yang, Z., Zhu, Y., Pu, Y.: Parallel image processing based on CUDA. In: 2008 International Conference on Computer Science and Software Engineering, pp. 198–201. IEEE, Hubei, China (2008)

25. Alvarez-Cedillo, J., Herrera-Lozada, J., Rivera-Zarate, I.: Implementation strategy of NDVI algorithm with Nvidia thrust. In: Pacific-Rim Symposium on Image and Video Technology, pp. 184–193. Springer, Berlin, Heidelberg (2013). https://doi.org/10.1007/978-3-642-53842-1_16

26. Kiani, A., Ansari, N., et al.: Edge Computing Aware NOMA for 5G Networks. IEEE Internet Things J. 5(2), 1299–1306 (2018)

27. Campostaberner, M., Morenomartínez, Á., Garcíaharo, F.J., et al.: Global estimation of biophysical variables from Google earth engine platform. Remote Sens. 10(8), 1167 (2018)

28. Kumar, L., Mutanga, O., et al.: Google earth engine applications since inception: usage, trends, and potential. Remote Sens. 10(10), 1509 (2018)

29. Gorelick, N., Hancher, M., Dixon, M., et al.: Google earth engine: planetary-scale geospatial analysis for everyone. Remote Sens. Environ. 202, 18–27 (2017)

Simulation Study on the Development of Chinese Bank Industry Based on System Dynamics

Cheng Gang Li[1,2] and Xin Tong Zuo[2(✉)]

[1] Guizhou Key Laboratory of Big Data Statistical Analysis, Guizhou University of Finance and Economics, Guiyang 550025, Guizhou, China
[2] School of Big Data Application and Economics, Guizhou University of Finance and Economics, Guiyang 550025, Guizhou, China

Abstract. There are many factors influencing the development of the bank indus-try, and scholars have paid much attention to the influence of these factors on the development of the bank industry. In order to better promoting the healthy and steady development of China's bank industry, studying the influence of the factors on the development of the bank industry, this paper uses Vensim PLE software to build a simulation model for the development of the bank industry. This paper simulates and analyzes the impact of the changes in money supply and supervision level on the profit level of the bank industry. The simulation results show that the profit level of the bank industry will increase when the money supply is reduced. Higher levels of regulation make banks less profitable. The simulation results also show that the change of money supply has no obvious effect on the nonperforming loan balance.

Keywords: Bank industry · System dynamics · Simulation analysis

1 Introduction

The bank industry has always played an important role in China's development. Lu and Zhou (2019) [1] believed that the development of China's bank industry played an important role in the high-quality economic development. The China central economic conference proposed to increase the proportion of direct financing, so as to solve the problem of the financing difficulty and high cost of private enterprises. However, com-pared with developed countries, the proportion of direct financing in China has always been relatively low. In 2001, the outline of the tenth five-year plan for national economic and social development proposed to gradually increase the proportion of direct financ-ing. Therefore, Shu and Cao (2018) [2] believed that the period from 2002 to 2012 was a period of vigorous development of financing reform in China. During this period of vigorous development, the scale of direct financing increased from 99.5 billion RMB in 2002 to 2.5006 trillion RMB in 2012, and the proportion of direct financing increased from 4.93% in 2002 to 21.52% in 2012. Meanwhile, the share of indirect financing decreased from 95.07% in 2002 to 78.48% in 2012. By 2019, the proportion of direct financing reached 14.71%, while indirect financing decreased to 85.29%.

H. Song and D. Jiang (Eds.): SIMUtools 2020, LNICST 369, pp. 427–441, 2021.
https://doi.org/10.1007/978-3-030-72792-5_35

With the continuous development of direct financing, the importance of indirect financing has decreased. However, it can be seen from data that the main financing channels in China are still indirect financing dominated by the bank industry. In the report on China's regional financial operation released by the People's Bank of China in 2016, it was pointed out that P2P online lending had had a positive impact in supporting financing of small and medium-sized enterprises. This report affirms the development of Internet finance from a policy perspective, stimulates the rapid development of Internet finance in China, and direct financing develops even more rapidly. However, in recent years, Internet financial "credit crisis" events keep happening, and financing platforms keep "running off the road". This is because the most essential difference between direct financing and indirect financing is that direct financing is subject to less supervision by financial regulators and is more prone to credit risk. Therefore, the bank industry has an indispensable position in the financing market.

However, banks have been fined and notified repeatedly. Due to the development of financial innovation, the deposit-taking capacity of the bank industry is limited, and the bank industry has been paying higher regulatory costs than other non-bank financial institutions. So the profit of the bank industry has been severely damaged. In view of the incompleteness of the current regulatory system, the scope of supervision often cannot cover all banking businesses. The bank industry will rely on regulatory loopholes to participate in high-risk investment projects and increase additional revenue through regulatory arbitrage. For example, under the policy environment of supporting the financing of "small and micro" and "agriculture, rural areas and farmers" enterprises, in order to stimulate the commercial banks to increase loans to these enterprises, the central bank will adopt monetary policy tools such as differential ratio, refinancing and rediscount monetary policy tools. While enjoying these preferential policies, commercial banks channel funds to high-risk projects to obtain high returns. Therefore, the central bank to strengthen the supervision of commercial banks.

Since there are many influencing factors for the development of China's bank industry, it is of great significance to systematically study the influencing factors of the development of the bank industry. Furthermore, we need to explore the influence of the changes of different factors on the profit of the bank industry. This will reduce the operational risk of the bank industry and promote the healthy and sustainable development of the bank industry.

The purpose of this paper is to explore the influence of changes in different factors on the profit of the bank industry. This paper simulates the real development environment of the bank industry by simulation analysis. Also, this paper simulates the influence of these factors on the profit of the bank industry in advance, so as to effectively maintain the stable development of the bank industry. The contribution of this paper lies in: starting from the realistic environment of the development of the banking industry, analyzing the subsystem of the development of the banking industry in China, constructing the system flow diagram of the development of the banking industry, and using the system dynamics model to carry out simulation analysis of the development of the banking industry in China.

The rest structure of this paper is organized as follows: the second part is the literature review. The third part is the construction of the system dynamics model, including the theoretical basis of system dynamics, the system boundary and main variables set by the model, the drawing of causal loop diagram and system flow diagram, and variable assignment and function relation determination. The fourth part is the model test and simulation analysis, including the test of model effectiveness, and the scenario simulation results analysis when changing money supply and supervision level. The fifth part is the conclusion and policy recommendations.

2 Literature Review

The development of China's bank industry has been fully discussed in the existing literature. Based on the dynamic panel model, Li et al. (2014) [3] found that Chinese Banks could reduce the credit risk and bankruptcy risk by developing non-interest business. Qiu et al. (2015) [4] thought that the administrative monopoly had a negative impact on the market structure of China's bank industry. Peng et al. (2016) [5] found that the interest rate liberalization had a significant impact on the interest margin of China's banking sector through the research results of the H-S model. Gu and Yang (2017) [6] used the threshold panel model to find that monetary policy was an important factor influencing the credit scale difference of Chinese Banks. Dong et al. (2017) [7] found that the development of China's direct financing market had a positive impact on the profitability and robustness of the bank industry. Meng and Yang (2017) [8] pointed out that the profit level of China's bank industry changed in the same direction due to the changes in GDP and CPI. Wang and Shi (2017) [9] believed that the technology finance had a heterogeneous impact on total factor productivity of China's regional banks. Jiang and Huang (2017) [10] argued that the increase of bank liabilities significantly increased the risk level. Jiang and Fei (2017) [11] concluded that the asset-backed bond business could mitigate the impact on banks' lending capacity during the crisis. Guo and Zhao (2017) [12] believed that the development of shadow banking stimulated the deposit competition and increased the systemic risk of the bank industry. Wang and Li (2017) [13] found that the role of price-based monetary instrument was stronger than that of quantitative-based monetary instrument, which increased the risk taking of the bank industry.

In recent two years, many scholars researched the influencing factors of the development of banking industry. Based on the empirical results of the panel data, Yao (2018) [14] found that the development of human resources could promote the positive development of bank industry. Zhu et al. (2018) [15] used the multi-directional efficiency analysis method to research the efficiency of China's bank industry, and found that the main reasons for the low efficiency of China's bank industry were the low level of non interest income and the high level of non-performing loan balance. Fang et al. (2018) [16] found that the risks of China's banking sector increased due to the risk changes in the real estate market and the stock market. Yang et al. (2018) [17] pointed out that there was heterogeneity impact of the final Basel III on China's banking sector. Wang (2018) [18] found that the deleveraging decision-making operation could reduce the bankruptcy probability of China's bank industry. Shen and Zhao (2018) [19] argued that non-interest income business had a positive impact on the income level of the bank industry. Li (2019) [20] thought that the strengthening of official supervision promoted the internal competition of bank industry. Gao et al. (2019) [21] believed that the scale of residential mortgage loans had a negative impact on the risk of China's bank industry. Based on the panel data of the bank industry from 2011 to 2017, Li (2019) [22] found that asset securitization had a positive effect on the credit risk of China's bank industry. Zhang and Zhang (2019) [23] pointed out that the excessive competition reduced the operating efficiency of regional commercial banks. Based on the inter-provincial panel data, Su and Meng (2019) [24] found that local government intervention could promote the competition of the bank industry. Wang et al. (2019) [25] showed that the deposit insurance system reduced the risk faced by the bank industry due to the change of net interest margin.

For the research of System Dynamics, since its birth in 1956, System Dynamics has been widely used. There are many studies on the application of system dynamics in supply chain in foreign literatures. Tian et al. (2014) [26] studied green supply chain management based on the system dynamics model. Sana et al. (2018) [27] used the system dynamics model to analyze the operational and financial relationships among channel members in the supply chain. Rebs et al. (2019) [28] analyzed the impact of stakeholders on sustainable supply chain management by establishing a system dynamics model. At present, there are many literature in China discussing economic correlation based on the system dynamics model. Liu et al. (2015) [29] studied the influence of the four operating tools of monetary policy on the broad money supply (M2) based on system dynamics model. Dong et al. (2016) [30] analyzed the development of China's financing structure by constructing the system dynamics model. Li et al. (2018) [31] studied the development of China's trust industry based on system dynamics model.

From the above literature, it can be seen that the existing studies focus on investigating the impact of one banking business on the development of the bank industry, but few literature systematically analyzes the development of the whole bank industry from the perspective of the multiple banking businesses. Moreover, there is a lack of literature on the development of China's bank industry based on system dynamics model. Based on system dynamics, this paper uses Vensim PLE software to build a simulation model for the development of China's bank industry, analyzes the impact of changes in different factors on the development of the bank industry by simulation analysis, and predicts the future development trend.

3   Model Construction

3.1   Theoretical Basis

System dynamics is an interdisciplinary subject that studies information feedback and system problems (Zhong, 2015) [32]. System dynamics is based on the close dependence between the system behavior and the internal mechanism, and is obtained through the establishment and manipulation of mathematical models, and gradually excavates the cause-effect relationship that produces the change form. The thought of using system dynamics method to analyze the research object is as follow: firstly, determine the boundaries of the research target. Secondly, according to the determined boundaries, divide the system hierarchy which lays the foundation for drawing causal loop diagram and system flow diagram owing to the relationship of variables. Thirdly, establish the model for the simulation operation and compare with historical data to test the validity of the analysis model. Fourthly, carry out scenario analysis of the model and obtain the results of the simulation analysis.

3.2 Determination of System Boundaries and Subsystems

Considering the complexity of the whole banking environment, this paper divides the model of the bank industry thought into three subsystems, namely the economic environment subsystem, the banking industry subsystem and the policy environment subsystem.

For the economic environment subsystem, Tan (1999) [33] believed that the development of China's financial institutions would promote economic growth. Sun and He (2015) [34] mentioned that Internet finance was a kind of financial innovation and had a great impact on China's bank industry. Therefore, in the subsystem of economic environment, the main influencing variables are defined as GDP and financial innovation.

For the the banking industry subsystem, Ge (2005) [35] believed that bank scale expansion had a positive impact on the development of China's bank industry. Zheng and Niu (2007) [36] pointed out that non-interest income played an increasingly important role in the income structure of China's bank industry. Li and Suo (2009) [37] pointed out that non-performing loans had a great impact on the credit supply of China's bank industry. Therefore, in the bank industry subsystem, the main influencing variables are defined as loan income, deposit reserve ratio, non-interest income, scale, non-performing loan balance and profit. Bank industry subsystem here only considers the basic business and non-interest income of "taking deposits and making loans". This paper sets the absorbed deposits by all banks are used to make loans.

For the policy environment subsystem, Rose and Hudgins (2002) [38] once mentioned that banking is one of the most heavily regulated industries in the world. Jin et al. (2014) [39] believed that the monetary policy would influence the credit and investment decisions of China's bank industry. Therefore, the subsystem of policy environment mainly considers the two variables of supervision cost and money supply.

The main variables of the three subsystems are shown in Table 1.

Table 1. Main variables of the system

Economic environment subsystem	GDP, financial innovation
Bank industry subsystem	Loan income, deposit reserve ratio, non-interest income, scale, non-performing loan balance and profit
Policy environment subsystem	Regulatory costs, the money supply

3.3 Establishment of Causal Loop Diagram and System Flow Diagram

The causal loop diagram refers to the loop diagram drawn according to the causal relationship between the selected main variables to be studied. The variables are connected by causal chains. The positive arrow represents positive feedback, indicating trend strengthening, while the negative arrow represents negative feedback, indicating trend weakening. The causal loop diagram of bank industry development is shown in Fig. 1. As can be seen from Fig. 1, non-interest income and loan income will have positive feedback to profits, regulatory costs and non-performing loan balance will have negative feedback to profits, while profits will eventually have positive feedback to GDP.

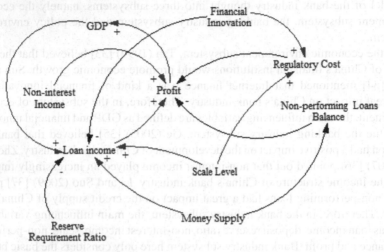

Fig. 1. Causal loop diagram of banking development

The system flow diagram is the stock flow diagram drawn on the basis of the causal loop diagram. By setting horizontal variables, rate variables and auxiliary variables, the structure of the flow diagram of the whole system is improved by adding functional relationships among the variables. In this paper, the development of the bank industry is mainly concerned with the changes in the profit variables. The changes in the income and expenditure are used to investigate the changes in the overall profit level, which will eventually have an impact on economic growth. The variables of banking income are considered as the impact of loan income, non-interest income and scale of banking business, while the variables of expenditure are considered as the impact of banking regulatory costs, deposit interest expense, loan loss provision and scale expansion. Therefore, referring to the system dynamics model for the development of China's trust industry designed by Li et al. (2018) [31], on the basis of the causal loop diagram, this paper constructs the system dynamics model for the development of the bank industry. The system flow diagram is shown in Fig. 2.

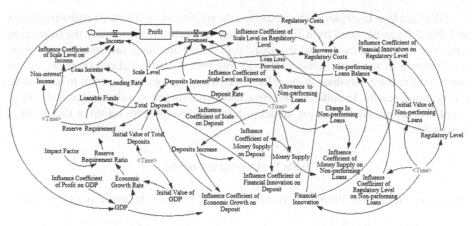

Fig. 2. System flow diagram of banking development

3.4 Variable Assignment and Function Relation Determination

The data in the whole model are selected from the annual data from 2011 to 2018, which are from the China Banking Regulatory Commission, the People's Bank of China, the National Bureau of Statistics and the World Bank. The functional relationship and assignment of some variables in the flow diagram are determined by setting up table functions and then determined by least square regression. Some variables are assigned by reference and historical data estimation results.

4 Test and Simulation

4.1 Model Test

The test methods of system dynamics are divided into intuitive test, operational test and historical test (Liu, 2011) [40]. Visual test means to check whether the bounds, main variables, causality and system equations of the model are appropriate. Running test refers to the test of units and equations in the system flow diagram by running Vensim PLE software. If the units of variables in the flow diagram or the functional relationship between variables are not suitable, the software will appear a warning interface, indicating that the units or equations need to be changed. During the operation test of this model, the unit setting was not appropriate, and all variables connected by causal chain were not included in the equation setting. After repeated modification and improvement, the final setting of the model was reasonable. Historical test means comparing the simulation results with the existing historical data to verify the validity of the model.

In this paper, the relative error test method is used for historical test. The test formula of relative error is shown in Formula (1).

$$e_i = (\hat{y}_i - y_i)/y_i \tag{1}$$

Where, $\hat{y}_i$ represents the simulation value of phase i, and y_i represents the actual value of phase i.

GDP and loan loss reserve are used to test the relative error. The test results are shown in Table 2. It can be found from Table 2 that there are some errors between the simulation values of the two indicators and the actual data. There are many factors influencing the development of the bank industry. Considering that the influencing factors set in this paper are the main variables in the selection of many factors, it is normal to have some errors in the results. In addition, the error between simulation value and actual data is small. Therefore, the simulation model of banking development set up in this paper is reasonable.

Table 2. Historical test results

Indicators	GDP (unit: 100 million Yuan)			Provision for loan losses (unit: RMB 100 million)		
Year	The actual value	The simulation value	The relative error	The actual value	The simulation value	The relative error
2011	487940.2	487932	−0.0017%	11898	11920.1	0.19%
2012	538580.0	538346	−0.0434%	14564	14717.5	1.05%
2013	592963.2	594425	0.2465%	16740	16850.6	0.66%
2014	641280.6	642107	0.1289%	19552	19487.2	−0.33%
2015	685992.9	686426	0.0631%	23089	23152.3	0.27%
2016	740060.8	741040	0.1323%	26676	26623.2	−0.20%
2017	820754.3	820533	−0.0270%	30944	31022.6	0.25%
2018	900309.5	900137	−0.0192%	37734	37711.9	−0.06%
The average error	0.08%			0.33%		

4.2 Scenario Simulation

(1) The Impact of Changes in Money Supply

The simulation result of the impact of a 5%, 10% and 15% reduction in the money supply on the non-performing loan balance is shown in Fig. 3. In Fig. 3, the solid line represents the non-performing loan balance at the current money supply level, the long dashed line represents the non-performing loan balance after reducing the money supply by 5%. The dotted line represents the non-performing loan balance after reducing the money supply by 10%. The short dashed line represents the non-performing loan balance after reducing the money supply by 15%. The Fig. 3 shows that the reduction in the money supply will increase the non-performing loans balance. However, as other conditions have not changed, the non-performing loan balance increases steadily after a period of time, so it is shown as a horizontal change in the Fig. 3. The increase of the non-performing loans balance is more obvious when reducing the money supply by 10% and 15% than that of educing the money supply by 5%.

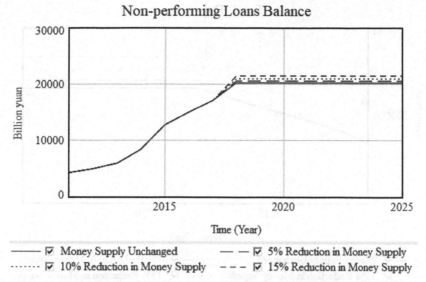

Fig. 3. The influence of money supply changes on non-performing loan balance

The simulation results of the impact of the reduction in money supply on the total deposits is shown in Fig. 4. In Fig. 4, the solid line represents the total deposits in the current money supply level. The long dashed line represents the total deposits after a 5% decrease in the money supply. The dotted line represents the total deposits after a 10% decrease in the money supply. The short dashed line represents the total deposits after a 15% decrease in the money supply. It can be seen from Fig. 4 that in the context of decreasing money supply, the total amount of deposits will continue to increase. The decrease of money supply will not only increase the non-performing loans balance, but also increase the total amount of deposits.

The impact of a 5%, 10% and 15% reduction in money supply on profit level is shown in Fig. 5. In Fig. 5, the solid line in the figure represents the profit level under the current money supply level. The long dashed line represents the profit level after the reduction of 5% money supply. The dotted line represents the profit level after the reduction of 10% money supply. The short dashed line represents the profit level after the reduction of 15% money supply. Figure 5 shows that with the decrease of money supply, the profit level of the bank industry will continue to rise. The larger the decrease of money supply, the higher the increase of profit level. As the increase of money supply leads to a large increase in the total amount of deposits and a small increase in the non-performing loans balance, the growth of the income side is higher than that of the expenditure side, so the profit level of the bank industry continues to increase.

(2) The Impact of the Changes in the Supervision Level

Because of its importance to the economy, the development of the bank industry has always been the focus of regulators. With the continuous development of financial innovation, the bank industry is faced with the business squeeze of internet finance. In

Total Deposits

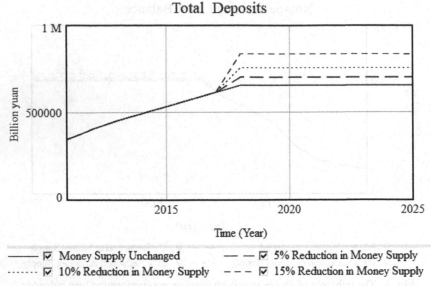

Fig. 4. The effect of changes in money supply on total deposits

Profit

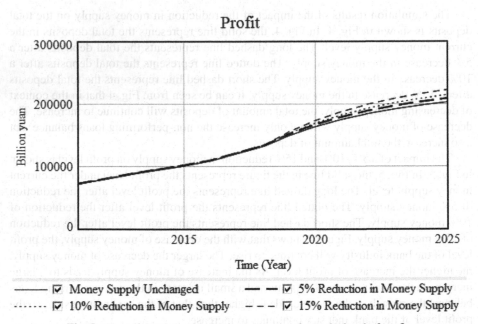

Fig. 5. The effect of changes in the money supply on the level of profits

order to seek more profits, the bank may pursue high-risk business, which forces the regulatory authorities to strengthen supervision. In 2016, the People's Bank of China established the macro-prudential assessment system (MPA). In 2017, financial products were included in the MPA index, and in 2018, interbank certificates of deposit were included in the MPA index. Wang (2019) [41] believes that the bank industry has entered a period of strict regulation. This paper sets the supervision level referring to the development simulation model of P2P network lending platform designed by Zhao and Gou (2015) [42]. This paper sets a series of constant values for the supervision level in the simulation model. Under the supervision level set in this paper, the scenario simulation is carried out to increase the regulation level by 5%, 10% and 15%, respectively.

The impact of the supervision level on the regulation cost is shown in Fig. 6. In Fig. 6, the solid line indicates the supervision cost under the supervision level set in this paper. The long dashed lines represents the change of the regulatory costs under the supervision level increased by 5%. The dotted line represents the change of regulatory costs under the supervision level increased by 10%. The short dashed line represents the change of the regulatory costs under the supervision level increased by 15%. As can be seen from Fig. 6, the greater the supervision level, the greater the supervision costs. If the supervision level is increased, the regulation cost will increase significantly in a short period of time.

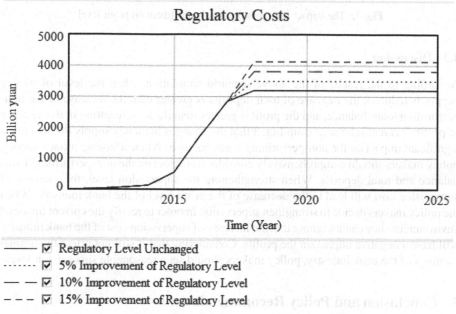

Regulatory Costs

Regulatory Level Unchanged
5% Improvement of Regulatory Level
10% Improvement of Regulatory Level
15% Improvement of Regulatory Level

Fig. 6. The influence of regulatory level adjustment on regulatory cost

The impact of the supervision level on the profit level is shown in Fig. 7. According to the system flow diagram set up in this paper, it can be seen that higher regulatory costs and higher expenses will lead to lower profits. In Fig. 7, we can see that the profit level gradually decreases over time with the increase of supervision level, and the more the supervision level increases, the more the profit level decreases.

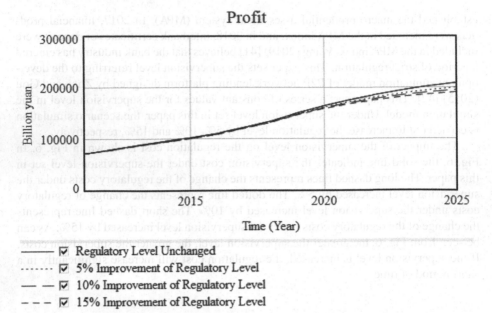

Fig. 7. The impact of regulatory level adjustment on profit level

4.3 Discussion

According to the results of the above scenario simulation, when the level of money supply is reduced, the increase of total deposits is greater than the increase of the non-performing loans balance, and the profit is greater than the loss, resulting in the increase of profit. It can also be seen from Fig. 3 that the changes in money supply do not have a significant impact on the non-performing loans balance. When adjusting money supply, policy makers should comprehensively consider its impact on the non-performing loans balance and total deposits. When strengthening the supervision level, the increase of supervision cost will lead to the decrease of the profit level of the bank industry. When the policy makers decide to strengthen supervision in order to rectify the current financial environment, they cannot ignore that the increase of supervision cost of the bank industry will have a negative impact on the profits. Considering that it will not affect the normal earnings of the bank industry, policy makers should set a reasonable supervision level.

5   Conclusion and Policy Recommendations

Based on the analysis of the main factors influencing the development of China's bank industry and the theory of system dynamics, this paper establishes a system dynamics simulation model for the development of China's bank industry. This paper analyzes the impact of the changes of money supply and supervision level on the bank industry. First, this paper simulates and analyzes the impact of the money supply changes on the non-performing loan balance, total deposits and profit level. Then, this paper simulates and analyzes the impact of regulatory level changes on banking regulatory costs and profit level. The simulation results show that the profit level of the bank industry will increase when the money supply is reduced. Higher levels of regulation make banks less profitable. The simulation results also show that the change of money supply has no obvious effect on the nonperforming loan balance.

Based on the above research conclusions, this paper puts forward the following three policy recommendations:

First, stabilize the money supply. Since the increase or decrease of the money supply is inversely related to the profit level of the bank industry, when the policy makers expand the money supply in order to promote economic development, they cannot ignore that this policy will restrict the profit increase of the bank industry.

Second, promote the marketization of interest rate. Policymakers should continue to actively promote the liberalization of interest rate, accelerate the transition from quantitative intermediary indicators to price intermediary indicators, and increase the means of adjusting the economy through price indicators, so as to reduce the impact of quantitative indicators adjusting the economy on the profit level of the bank industry.

Finally, maintain reasonable supervision. Due to the reverse relationship between the regulatory level and the profit level of the bank industry, policy makers should not blindly pursue the strong supervision of the financial environment and ignore the vitality creation of the bank industry. They should consider multiple factors and set a reasonable regulatory strength, so that the bank industry can retain certain innovation vitality and develop actively.

Under the background that there is a lack of literature on the development of China's bank industry by using the method of system dynamics, this paper constructs a system dynamics model of the development of bank industry. This paper simulates and analyzes the impact of the changes of money supply and supervision level on the development of the bank industry. The scenario simulation analysis provides policy makers with decision reference. It has important practical significance. However, the actual environment faced by the bank industry is more complex. This paper fails to comprehensively analyze some more influencing factors of the development of the bank industry. The established model has some shortcomings. In the future, more influencing factors of bank industry development will be included. A better system dynamics model of bank industry development will be built to simulate and analyze the influence of these factors on the development of bank industry.

Acknowledgments. This paper was supported by Guizhou Key Laboratory of Big Data Statistics Analysis (No. Guizhou Science and Technology Cooperation Platform Talent [2019] 5103).

References

1. Lu, M.F., Zhou, J.Y.: A review of the development footprint of Chinese banking industry over the past 70 years and a study of future trends. J. Univ. Jinan (Soc. Sci. Edn.) **29**(4), 5–19+157 (2019)
2. Shu, H.T., Cao, L.K.: An overview of the development and evolution of China's corporate financing policy – from the perspective of 40 years of reform and opening up. Enterp. Econ. **12**, 41–47 (2018)

3. Li, M.H., Liu, L.Y., Sun, S.: Is it good for banks to develop non-interest businesses? – Based on the empirical analysis of china's banking industry. Stud. Int. Finan. **11**, 11–22 (2014)
4. Qiu, Z.X., Liu, H., An, S.Y.: On the impact of administrative monopoly on Chinese banking market structure. J. Finan. Res. **2**, 175–191 (2015)
5. Peng, J.G., Wang, S.J., Guan, T.Y.: Does interest rate liberalization narrow interest margins of commercial bank? Empirical evidence based on Chinese banking industry. J. Finan. Res. **7**, 48–63 (2016)
6. Gu, H.F., Yang, L.X.: Monetary policy, bank size differences and credit transmission characteristics: evidence from China's banking industry in 2006–2015. Stud. Int. Finan. **12**, 53–64 (2017)
7. Dong, N., Fu, L., Xu, S.: The impact of direct financing on the franchise value of China's banking industry: an empirical study based on Panzar-Rosse model. Stud. Int. Finan. **6**, 65–74 (2017)
8. Meng, C., Yang, X.C.: Market concentration changes and performances of China's banking industry. Rev. Ind. Econ. **1**, 87–100 (2017)
9. Wang, Y., Shi, Y.D.: Heterogeneity of technological finance nurturing banks—empirical evidence from China's regional banks. Stud. Sci. Sci. **35**(12), 1821–1831 (2017)
10. Jiang, H., Huang, M.: The impact of debt structure on bank risk-taking: an empirical study based on China's listed banks. Stud. Int. Finan. **7**, 54–65 (2017)
11. Jiang, H.S., Fei, X.: The impact of asset securitization on bank credit channels—based on the panel data of European banking industry. Finan. Econ. **9**, 12–26 (2017)
12. Guo, Y., Zhao, J.: Deposit competition, shadow banking and bank systemic risk: evidence from the listed banks in China. J. Finan. Res. **6**, 81–94 (2017)
13. Wang, J.B., Li, B.: Empirical study on the effects of China's monetary policy on risk taking behaviors of commercial banks. J. World Econ. **40**(1), 25–43 (2017)
14. Yao, S.Ã.: Bank development and human development in WAEMU countries: evidence from panel data estimation. Int. J. World Policy Dev. Stud. **4**(6), 50–59 (2018)
15. Zhu, N., Liang, L., Shen, Z.Y., et al.: Endogenous efficiency of Chinese commercial banks and its decomposition under the China's new normal economy. J. Finan. Res. **7**, 108–123 (2018)
16. Fang, Y., Chen, M., Yang, P.P.: The spillover effect and channel identification of financial market to banking systemic risk. Nankai Econ. Stud. **5**, 58–75 (2018)
17. Yang, K.S., Liu, R.X., Feng, Q.: The impact and countermeasures of the finalisation of Basel III. J. Finan. Res. **2**, 30–44 (2018)
18. Wang, L.J.: A study on deleveraging and the stability of banking system – based on the empirical evidence of China's banking industry. Stud. Int. Finan. **10**, 55–64 (2018)
19. Shen, C., Zhao, S.M.: The study on the impact of market competition degree and non-interest income on bank returns. Nankai Econ. Stud. **1**, 50–66 (2018)
20. Li, S.F.: The impact of bank regulation and supervision on competition: evidence from emerging economies. Emerg. Mark. Finan. Trade **55**(10), 2334–2364 (2019)
21. Gao, B., Li, Y., Li, M.: Analysis of residential mortgage loan and bank risk: empirical evidence from China's commercial banks. Ind. Econ. Res. **4**, 101–112 (2019)
22. Li, J.: Can asset securitization ease bank credit risk? – Empirical evidence from China's banking sector. Stud. Int. Finan. **6**, 57–66 (2019)
23. Zhang, D.Y., Zhang, Z.W.: An empirical study based on regional commercial banks in China. J. Finan. Res. **4**, 111–129 (2019)
24. Su, Q., Meng, N.N.: How does local government intervention affect regional financial inclusion? – Spatial econometric analysis based on provincial panel data. Stud. Int. Finan. **8**, 14–24 (2019)
25. Wang, X.B., Xu, Q.Y., Xin, F.F.: Empirical study on the impact of deposit insurance system on commercial banks' interest rate risk. J. Manage. Sci. China **22**(5), 110–126 (2019)

26. Tian, Y.H., Govindan, K., Zhu, Q.H.: A system dynamics model based on evolutionary game theory for Green supply chain management diffusion among Chinese manufacturers. J. Clean. Prod. **80**(1), 96–105 (2014)
27. Sana, S.S., Ferro-Correa, J., Quintero, A., et al.: A system dynamics model of financial flow in supply chains: a case study. RAIRO-Oper. Res. **52**(1), 187–204 (2018)
28. Rebs, T., Thiel, D., Brandenburg, M., et al.: Impacts of stakeholder influences and dynamic capabilities on the sustainability performance of supply chains: a system dynamics model. J. Bus. Econ. **89**(7), 893–926 (2019)
29. Liu, C., Xu, F.H., Lu, Y.: Multi-target interactions of monetary policy based on system dynamics. Syst. Eng. **33**(4), 82–91 (2015)
30. Dong, Z., Li, X.T., Dong, J.C.: Simulation of financing structure based on system dynamics. Syst. Eng. Theor. Pract. **36**(5), 1109–1117 (2016)
31. Li, Z.M., Zhong, C.L., Liu, J.J., et al.: A simulation study of the development of China's trust industry based on system dynamics. Manage. Rev. **30**(4), 3–11 (2018)
32. Zhong, Y.G., Xia, X.J., Qian, Y., et al.: System Dynamics. 2th Edition. Science Press, Beijing (2015)
33. Tan, R.Y.: An empirical study on the relationship between financial development and economic growth in China. Econ. Res. J. **10**, 53–61 (1999)
34. Sun, J., He, C.: Internet finance innovation and traditional bank transformation based on big data. Finan. Econ. **1**, 11–16 (2015)
35. Ge, Z.Q.: Bank mergers and acquisitions, the growth of commercial banks and the development of China's banking industry. Stud. Int. Finan. **2**, 30–36 (2005)
36. Zheng, R.N., Niu, M.H.: A study on the relationship between non-interest business and bank characteristics in China's banking industry. J. Finan. Res. **9**, 129–137 (2007)
37. Li, L., Suo, Y.F.: Economic volatility, non-performing loans and systemic risks in the banking sector. Stud. Int. Finan. **6**, 55–63 (2009)
38. Rose, P.S., Hudgins, S.C.: ANK Management and Financial Services, 8th edn. China Machine Press, Beijing (2013)
39. Jin, P.H., Zhang, X., Gao, F.: The effect of monetary policy on bank risk taking: from the banking industry perspective. J. Finan. Res. **2**, 16–29 (2014)
40. Liu, W.J.: The Construction of System Dynamics Model of Financial Efficiency from the Perspective of Capital Running. Ocean University of China, Qingdao (2011)
41. Wang, G.G.: 70 years of banking in China: brief history, main features and historical experience. Manage. World **35**(7), 15–25 (2019)
42. Zhao, B.G., Gou, J.K.: Network hatred: obstruction and decomposition of order construction in virtual public domain. J. Beijing Univ. Posts Telecommun. (Soc. Sci. Edn.) **17**(4), 41–49 (2015)

A Many-Objective Squirrel Hybrid Optimization Algorithm: MaSHOA

Zhuoran Liu, Fanhao Zhang, Xinyuan Wang, Qidong Zhao, Changsheng Zhang, and Bin Zhang$^{(\boxtimes)}$

Northeastern University, Shenyang 110819, People's Republic of China
zhangchangsheng@mail.neu.edu.cn, paper820@sohu.com

Abstract. Many-objective optimization problems (MaOP) are important to the field of computing intelligence which leads to more requirements for the evolutionary many-objective Algorithms (EMaOA). Meanwhile, we consider that the evolution process also has some influence on the performance of results. And we present a many-objective squirrel hybrid optimization algorithm (MaSHOA) which takes an effective squirrel search algorithm (SSA) as the evolution framework and a reference-point-based many-objective evolutionary algorithm (NSGA-III) as the EMaOA framework. This paper applies the scalarizing evaluation to make sure the solution quality among the neighborhood and takes the reference point association achievement as the reference-point-based part. Taking iterations into account, we design a joint fitness function. For both the evolution and selection operations, a joint fitness function is applied to sort solutions to guide others and select them respectively. Besides, the distance penalization is introduced to prevent the local convergence. About useless reference points, this paper proposes an adjustable reference points strategy. The simulation experiment of the proposed algorithm is carried on different test problems with 3 to 15 objectives. Compared with other classic EMaOAs, the means, variances, box plots and parallel coordinate plots of the obtained results are utilized to analyze the convergence and diversity. And this proposed algorithm has good performance on solving MaOPs.

Keywords: Many-objective optimization · Squirrel search algorithm · Adjustable reference points strategy

1 Introduction

In recent years, with the development of computer technology and the prosperity of artificial intelligence, computing intelligence based on computer technology has developed rapidly [1]. As an important branch of computational intelligence, applying evolutionary computation to solve multi-objective optimization problems has become a research hotspot in the field of computational intelligence [2]. However, the calculations required for complicated projects no longer consider only one single indicator but consider multiple indicators that are mutually constrained. Optimization problems with two or more objectives are often referred to as Multi-objective Optimization Problems (MOPs) [3].

H. Song and D. Jiang (Eds.): SIMUtools 2020, LNICST 369, pp. 442–459, 2021.
https://doi.org/10.1007/978-3-030-72792-5_36

And we take the MOPs with four or more objectives into consideration as a special optimization problem known as the Many-objective Optimization Problem (MaOP) [4]. Algorithms based on Pareto domination are widely accepted in solving multi-objective optimization problems [3, 5]. But when it comes to MaOPs, the non-dominated solution set obtained by the traditional many-objective optimization algorithms based on Pareto domination is not of great quality. In recent years, with many relevant strategies proposed, difficulties [4, 6] in solving MaOPs are also exposed:

1) Most of the solutions in the population of evolutionary algorithms are non-dominated, which causes that the ascendancy of two different solutions becomes ambiguous.
2) The exponential growth of the number of non-dominated solutions is a huge challenge to the processing power of the algorithm.
3) Visualization of high-dimensional solutions becomes difficult. It's tough for decision makers to understand the distribution of the solution and how to evaluate it.

Based on the above reasons, some Evolutionary Many-objective Algorithms (EMaOA) using special environment selection strategies have attracted widespread attention in MaOP research due to their advantages of fast solution speed and wide application range [7]. Used to solve ultra-multi-objective optimization problems. These algorithms can be broadly classified as follows:

1) Algorithms based on Pareto-dominated [6–8] are proposed. NSGA-III [9, 10] is a typical example of a dominated many-objective algorithm that improves the ranking method, which also continues the attempt to use reference points in MONSGA-II [11]. Besides, θ-DEA [12] is a typical algorithm for improving Pareto domination rules.
2) Decomposition-based EMaOA [7, 13] decomposes MaOP into multiple single-objective subproblems which cover the decision space, and solves the subproblems independently, the algorithm uses the optimal solutions of all subproblems to fit the pareto front (PF), like MOEA/D [14]. And some algorithms presented some new concepts into the solving process. RVEA [15] introduces a scalar method called angle-penalized distance (APD) to evaluate the convergence and diversity of candidate solutions.
3) Select the subset with the best index value in the population [7, 16]. Performance indicators can usually evaluate the convergence and diversity of the population at the same time. For example, HypE [17] uses HV indicator, MOMBI-II [18] uses R2 indicator, and MaOEA/IGD [19] uses IGD indicator.

The method of evaluating many-objective optimization algorithms is to analyze their convergence and diversity. Convergence refers to finding a set of solutions closed to the true Pareto front. Meanwhile, diversity means finding a set of solutions that should be sufficient to represent the entire range of Pareto front. Algorithms are usually evaluated by these two types of indicators.

In addition, some scholars are committed to applying some classic and efficient single-objective optimization algorithms to more objects [5, 8, 9, 20–22], such as NSGA-III with genetic algorithm (GA) [23]. Among them, the squirrel search algorithm (SSA) [24], as a single-objective optimization algorithm [25], has the characteristics of strong robustness and fast convergence. To a certain extent, it avoids the dimensional catastrophe problem that exists in many-objective optimization problems.

Based on the many-objective optimization framework of NSGA-III and the evolution framework of SSA, this paper presents a many-objective optimization hybrid squirrel search algorithm (MaSHOA). The contributions are outlined as following:

- This algorithm proposes scalarizing evaluation to make sure the convergence of population members in the neighborhood. And the reference point association achievement presents the effect that associated reference points produce on the candidate solutions.
- The influence of the number of current generations on optimization focus is introduced to design a joint fitness function which combines scalarizing evaluation and reference point association achievement.
- In the evolutionary process, squirrels move forward the direction of best ones rated by the joint fitness function. And also, the distance penalization is applied in the winter detection to prevent the local convergence.
- For selection operator, the members of feasible solution set are selected following the sorting obtained by this joint fitness function.
- This algorithm also presents an adjustable reference points strategy to change some reference points without associated solutions into some solutions by considering the distance between solutions and reference points.

Finally, this paper designs a simulation experiment to compare the presented algorithm with NSGA-III and MOEA/D on the DTLZ test problems [26]. The inverse generational distance (IGD) metric [19, 27] is applied to analyze the results by numbers and box plots, and also the parallel coordinate plots of PF are presented to visualize the performance of algorithms. It turns out that the proposed algorithm has good performance on convergence and diversity.

2 Design of MaSHOA

2.1 Basic Concept of MaSHOA

This paper proposes a Many-Objective Optimization Hybrid Squirrel Search Algorithm (MaSHOA), which utilizes NSGA-III for reference of many-objective optimization framework and integrates SSA into it. The basic framework of MaSHOA is similar to the original NSGA-III, the selection and mutation operator is modified with some strategies.

The algorithm execution process is shown in Algorithm 1. Before starting the process, the reference points set is calculated. First, a population is initialized randomly named P. Before the stop criteria are achieved, the proposed algorithm runs the following actions.

Normalization of population members, the association operation and the niche-preservation operation according to the original NSGA-III is executed first (line 4–6).

And the number P_j of population members that are associated with the certain reference point that associates the individual is obtained for each member.

Based on the above results, the reference point association achievement and scalarizing evaluation is calculated (line 8). And after the number of current generations is affiliated, a joint fitness function is created according to Reference Point Association Achievement and Scalarizing Evaluation (line 9).

Algorithm 1. Procedure for MaSHOA

Input:
  Population number N, test problem, parameter definition
Output
  Feasible solution set
Begin
  1. Generate reference points;
  2. Initialized population randomly P;
  3. **do while** stop criteria==false
  4. Normalization of population members;
  5. Association operation;
  6. Niche-preservation operation;
  7. Calculate the number of population members that are associated with the certain reference point that associates the member p_j;
  8. Generate Scalarizing Evaluation and Reference Point Association Achievement according to Eq. 1& Eq. 3;
  9. Calculate joint fitness function according to Section 2.2;
  10. Squirrels evolutionary to new population set according to Section 2.3;
  11. Archive current population as set S;
  12. Merge two populations P and S into M;
  13. Non-dominated sorting;
  14. Choose individuals by the level of non-dominated sorting in turn until the current level L makes the size of population more than N, still choose all the members of level L into the current population P (size > N);
  15. Select N of the current population members by the sorting of the joint fitness function;
  16. Exchange reference points by an adjustable strategy according to Section 2.4;
  17. External archive current population as set P;
  18. **end while**
  19. **return** feasible solution set;
End

Then during population evolution, the original squirrel search algorithm is designed to solve single-objective optimization problems. For the MOPs, SSA is modified in this algorithm. For the migration operator, squirrels are evaluated by a joint fitness function to sort (line 10). Besides, the distance penalization is introduced into winter detection to avoid solutions from local convergence. And then the external archive is established to store the current population as S (line 11). And the current and previous population are merged to be applied to the next selection operator to maintain the elite information as M (line 12).

Next, the non-dominated sorting is applied to select current members in non-dominated level order into population P until members with the current level L are selected to make the size of P more than N. It is changed from the original process that the members with the current level L are also added into P (line 14).

For the selection of parent and offspring individuals, the original framework utilizes the number of population members that are associated with each reference point which associates each individual as the selection condition after non-dominated sorting. Then the joint fitness function is applied to sort and choose members into the current population (line 15).

In the original framework, the reference points without population members will be deleted. Besides, an adjustable reference points strategy is utilized to update reference points with none associated members which could be deleted in the original framework (line 16). And finally, the solution set is stored as P which is the output at the last generation (line 19).

2.2 A Joint Fitness Function

This section shows how the joint fitness function is comprised of Scalarizing Evaluation, Reference Point Association Achievement and the number of current generations.

Besides, in the original selection operator after the non-dominated sorting, only the P_j could be considered to assist the following selection operators. The joint fitness function is applied to sort and choose the candidate solutions. The solutions with the better joint fitness value could be selected into the new population first.

Scalarizing Evaluation. As we know, one important characteristic of MaOPs is that the number of objectives is large. Thus, the selection pressure would become lower if only the non-dominated levels are regarded as the measurement of convergence. Therefore, the proposed algorithm applies a method to represent the convergence during the selection opera-tion. After normalization, the gap between candidate solutions and extreme points in each dimension is calculated to be the parameter for measure the convergence of the solution set.

As the good performance that it has, the achievement scalarizing function (ASF) is utilized for reference with the measurement of the convergence. Based on ASF, MaSHOA proposes the Scalarizing Evaluation (SE) to make sure the convergence. It calculates the maximum difference between the value on each dimension of objective vectors with the preference vector w_i and the best value on each dimension as shown in Eq. 1.

$$SE(x) = maxF\left(x, z_i^{min}\right) = max_{i=1}^m \left(w_i \cdot f_i(x) - z_i^{min}\right) \tag{1}$$

$$w_i = \frac{f_i(x)}{\sum_{j=1}^m f_j(x)} \tag{2}$$

Where m is the number of objectives, $f_i(x)$ is the value of objective vector on the ith dimension, z_i^{min} is the value of extreme point on the ith dimension, w_i is the preference vector which is calculated as Eq. 2. We can see that the smaller value of $SE(x)$ is, the closer objective vector is near to the best value, the better convergence it is.

Reference Point Association Achievement. The relationship between reference points and population solutions is shown as the Reference Point Association Achievement (RPAA). It contains two parts to represent the diversity of solutions. One is the distance between current solution and the reference vector formed by the reference point associated with it, and another is the number of solutions associated with the reference point of the current solutions P_j. Thus, the distance (Eq. 4) between the current candidate solution and reference vector r_j and the scalarized current P_j (Eq. 5) is represented as RPAA shown in Eq. 3.

$$RPAA(x_i) = distance(x_i, r_j) \cdot \frac{P_j}{\bar{P}} \qquad (3)$$

$$distance(x_i, r_j) = |x_i| \times \sin(x_i, r_j) = |x_i| \times \frac{|x_i \times r_j|}{|x_i| \cdot |r_j|} \qquad (4)$$

$$\bar{P} = \frac{\sum_{j=1}^{s} P_j}{s} \qquad (5)$$

Where x_i represents the current candidate solution vector, r_j is the reference vector, P_j represents the number of solutions associated with the reference point of the current solution. We can see that the smaller the value of RPAA is, the better the diversity of solutions becomes.

Joint Fitness Function. It is believed that the feasible solution should focus on the convergence as much as possible in the early stage of the process, that is, making solutions forward better. And in the late stage of the process, the diversity of solution set is becoming more im-portant, that is, making distribution of the solution more spread and even. Therefore, the value of iterations is significant to the quality of solutions. The calculation con-siders the number of current generations as a variable. Combining SE and RPAA, the joint fitness function (JF) is presented as Eq. 6.

$$JF(x) = \frac{1}{g} \times SE(x) + g \times RPAA(x) \qquad (6)$$

Where g is the number of current generations. We can see that the smaller g is, the more important the convergence is, and the larger g is, the more important the diversity is.

2.3 Many-Objective Optimization Squirrels Evolution

The population p evolves and mutates through the method of this section into population S. In this part, the joint fitness function is treated as the sorting reference. And Algorithm 2 shows the procedure of the many-objective optimization squirrel evolution.

According to the rank, the first $n1(n1 = N/50)$ squirrels are the best squirrels which are considered to be on the hickory trees. And the following $n2$ ($n2 = 3N/50$) squirrels are the second-best squirrels which are considered to be on the acorn nuts trees. And the last $n3$ ($n3 = N - n1 - n2$) squirrels are normal squirrels which are considered to be on the normal trees.

As the living habits of squirrels, when there are no natural enemies of squirrels, squirrels begin to migrate. This paper sets the probability P_e of natural enemies existing as 0.1. The probability of squirrel migration is based on P_e. Besides, whether squirrels migrate is decided with the random number. A random number is generated between 0 and 1 in every condition. And if this number is more than 0.1, squirrels do the migration. The distance constant SC of squirrel moving is set as [0.5, 1.11] due to experience, and moving distance of every time is decided randomly in this range.

Algorithm 2. Procedure for many-objective optimization squirrel evolution

Input:
  Squirrels population
Output
  New squirrel population
Begin
  1. evaluate fitness value according to Section2.2;
  2. sorting squirrels with the fitness value;
  3. According to the rank, first n1 squirrels are the best squirrels, the following n2 squirrels are the second-best squirrels, and all the others are normal squirrels.;
  4. Random number of the range of [0,1] as r1, r2, r3;
  5. **While** r1 > P_e (for second-best squirrels)
  6.   **For** n = 1 to n2.;
  7.   squirrel migration according to Eq. 7;
  8. **While** r2 > P_e (for normal squirrels)
  9.   For n = 1 to n4;
  10.   squirrel migration according to Eq. 8;
  11. **While** r3 > P_e (for normal squirrels)
  9.   For n = 1 to n5;
  10.   squirrel migration according to Eq. 9;
  11. Calculate distance penalization constant according to Eq. 10;
  12. **While** (season != winter)
  13.   Normal squirrels levy flight according to Eq. 11;
End

Squirrels on acorn nuts trees are moving to one of the directions of hickory trees randomly according to Eq. 7.

$$ST'_{2nd} = ST_{2nd} + (ST_{best} - ST_{2nd}) \times SC \tag{7}$$

Where ST_{2nd} represents the current location of the second-best squirrel, ST'_{2nd} represents the new location of the moving second-best squirrel, $(ST_{best} - ST_{2nd})$ is the distance between the best squirrel and the current moving second-best squirrel.

Squirrels on the normal trees are moving to one of the directions of acorn nuts trees randomly according to Eq. 8. Some of normal squirrels have never been on the acorn nuts trees (the number of them is n4).

$$ST'_n = ST_n + (ST_{2nd} - ST_n) \times SC \tag{8}$$

Where ST_n represents the current location of the normal squirrel, ST'_n represents the new location of the moving normal squirrel, $(ST_{2nd} - ST_n)$ is the distance between the second-best squirrel and the current moving normal squirrel.

Besides, some of normal squirrels were on acorn nuts trees in the past generations (the number of them is n5 = n3 − n4). Thus, they are moving to one of the directions of hickory trees randomly according to Eq. 9.

$$ST_n' = ST_n + (ST_{best} - ST_n) \times SC \tag{9}$$

Where ST_n represents the current location of the normal squirrel, ST_n' represents the new location of the moving normal squirrel, $(ST_{best} - ST_n)$ is the distance between the second-best squirrel and the current moving normal squirrel.

Meanwhile, the winter detection is applied to prevent the algorithm from local convergence. The difference between the best squirrels of the current generation and the last generation is considered as the distance penalization constant. The minimum distance between best squirrels of the current and last generation is calculated to be the distance penalization constant (DPC) as Eq. 10. WDC is applied to evaluate the similarity of these two generations and judge whether the process is going into the local convergence.

$$DPC = min_{i,j=1}^{n1,n1'} \sqrt{\left(ST_i^g - ST_j^{g-1}\right)^2} \tag{10}$$

Where g is the current generation, n1 is the number of best squirrels in this generation, n1' is the number of best squirrels in last generation, ST_i^g is the vector of ith best squirrel in this generation, and ST_j^{g-1} is the vector of jth best squirrel in last generation. So DPC can represent the minimum distance between the best squirrels from two generations.

And a threshold value is fixed to compare with DPC to judge whether it is the end of winter (see Eq. 11). If the DPC is less than the fixed threshold, it is considered as the situation of local convergence.

$$WD^{min} = \frac{10E^{-6}}{(365)^{\frac{g}{g_m/2.5}}} \tag{11}$$

Where g is the number of the current generation, g_m is the maximum number of generations. So WD^{min} is the threshold of winter detection.

In addition, the best and second-best squirrels of the current generation should be preserved, and the normal squirrels should mutate using Levy flight according to Eq. 12.

$$ST_n' = ST_n + (ST_{max} - ST_{min})_2 \times Levy \tag{12}$$

$$Levy = \frac{0.01 \times r_a \times \sigma}{|r_b|^{\frac{1}{\beta}}} \tag{13}$$

$$\sigma = \left(\frac{\Gamma(1+\beta) \times \sin(\frac{\pi\beta}{2})}{\Gamma\left(\frac{1+\beta}{2}\right) \times \beta \times 2^{\left(\frac{\beta-1}{2}\right)}}\right)^{\frac{1}{\beta}} \tag{14}$$

$$\Gamma(x) = (x-1)! \tag{15}$$

Where ST_n' is the new location of moving normal squirrels, ST_{min} and ST_{max} are the squirrel location of the best and worst fitness value respectively. And Levy is shown in Eq. 13.

After the winter detection, the new squirrel population S is generated completely which can be utilized to merge with the previous population.

2.4   Adjustable Reference Points Strategy

In the original reference points set method, the reference point associated without any solutions will be deleted. And in this section, an adjustable reference point strategy is proposed to update the reference point.

After the reference point associated without any solutions is detected, the solution with the farthest distance between others and itself is chosen to be the new reference point based on the feasible solution set as shown in Fig. 1. The original reference points and their corresponding reference vectors are shown in Fig. 1(a). As is shown in Fig. 1(b), there are no solutions associated with R2, so x1 with the maximum distance is chosen to adjust R2 to X1. X1 becomes the new reference point. This strategy could make sure the diversity while making solution set evolve to the advantageous direction, instead of the original even reference point set. Meanwhile, in every adjustment process, the one reference point cannot be associated with more than one new reference point. This means the solution associated with the reference point with the previous new reference point could not be the new reference point. This constrain can prevent the solving process from evolutionary convergence forward one certain direction. And After the previous X1 in Fig. 1(b) is becoming the new reference point, we are assuming that the new solution with the maximum distance from its reference vector should be selected to be the new reference. But the new solution is also associated with the R1 (same as Fig. 1(b)), so this solution could not be employed to be the new reference set. In this case, the other solution with the second farthest distance should be selected to be the new reference point.

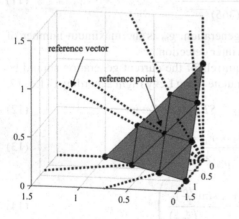

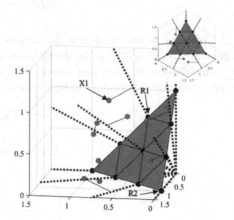

a. Reference points and vectors settings   b. An adjustable reference point strategy

Fig. 1. Based on the reference points set, an adjustable reference point strategy is designed shown in this figure.

3 Simulative Results Analysis

To analyze the performance of the proposed algorithm, this section designs the comparative simulation experiment. Based on the previous work, we choose NSGA-III and MOEA/D to contrast the MaSHOA. And all these three EMaOAs are simulated at five classic many-objective optimization test problems (DTLZ 7, DTLZi, i = 1 − 4) [26] as shown in Table 1. And the selected algorithms are tested on the 3-objective to 15-objective DTLZ test problems.

Both NSGA-III and MOEA/D apply the genetic algorithm as the mutation strategy. Table 2 shows the parameters of mutation operators used in the NSGA-III and MOEA/D.

Table 1. Test problems

Name	Dimensions of solutions	Feature of PF
DTLZ1	4 + N	Linear multi-modal
DTLZ2	9 + N	Concave
DTLZ3	9 + N	Concave multi-modal
DTLZ4	9 + N	Concave non uniform
DTLZ7	19 + N	Mixed, Disconnected multi-modal

Table 2. Parameters of variation operators

Parameters	NSGA-III	MOEA/D
SBX probability [28] p_c	1	1
Polynomial mutating probability [29] p_m	1/n	1/n
Crossover distribution index η_c	30	20
Mutation distribution index η_m	20	20

The number of reference points depends on both the simple-lattice design factor [10] D and the number M of objectives. D represents the number of points which are distributed evenly on one borderline of the solution space. We can calculate the number R of reference points or directions according to Eq. 16.

$$R = \binom{D + M - 1}{D} \tag{16}$$

When $M \geq 8$, the two layers of reference points are employed to generate the reference points. And the reference points are divided into the inside layer and the boundary layer. Table 3 presents the number of objectives, divisions, reference points

Table 3. Number of reference points/directions and population sizes used in this experiment

No. of objectives (M)	No. of divisions (D)	No. of reference p/d (R)	MaSHOA popsize (N)	NSGA-III popsize (N')	MOEA/D popsize (N'')
3	12	91	91	92	91
5	6	210	210	212	210
8	(3,2)	156	156	156	156
10	(3,2)	275	275	276	275
15	(2,1)	135	135	136	135

and population size of all the algorithms used in the experiments. To ensure the accuracy of the experiment results, these simulative experiments are carried out 30 times on each test problem respectively.

3.1 Analysis on IGD Metric

In general, the solution set of MaOPs is composed of many solutions, which leads to the difficulty of the evaluation of solutions of different algorithms. So, the evaluation method on EMaOAs is complicated to transfer the solution set to a mode easy to evaluate. The inverse generational distance (IGD) is widely applied to evaluate the convergence and the diversity of PF. The convergence describes the gap between the approximate PF and the ideal PF. And the diversity means that the solution set could represent the whole page of the ideal PF.

In this experiment, we take the IGD metric as the evaluation indicator. The IGD metric represents the average distance between each solution of the reference set and the solution closest to it of approximate PF. The IGD metric is defined as Eq. 17. Z_i is the ideal solution set, P is the approximate solution set obtained by all the EMaOAs, z_i and x_j is the solution of the ideal and approximate set respectively.

$$\text{IGD}(P, Z_i) = \frac{1}{|Z_i|} \sum_{i=1}^{Z_i} \min_{\substack{P \\ j=1}} d(z_i, x_j) \tag{17}$$

We can see that the smaller the IGD value, the closer the approximate solution to the real PF, the better the performance of the algorithm. Meanwhile, the lower IGD value could represent that there exist solutions around each solution of the ideal PF, which is the meaning of the diversity.

Table 4 shows all the means and variances (shown in the first and second line) of IGD values of all the results on the five DTLZ test problems and the maximum generations of each situation of different objectives.

On the DTLZ1 problems, MaSHOA has the best means on the 3-, 8-, 10-, 15-objective problems, and the best variances on the 5-, 8-, 15- objective problems. And the other two algorithms do not have better performance on all DTLZ1 problems. A similar measurement is made for DTLZ2 problems, MaSHOA has the best results on the 8-, 10-,

Table 4. The means and variances of IGD obtained by simulation results on DLTZ

Problems	No. of objectives	MaxGen	NSGA-III	MOEA/D	MaSHOA
DLTZ1	3	30000	**5.742E−4**	0.0408	2.626E−4
			6.847E−7	0.00305	**1.26E−11**
	5	30000	6.532E−4	0.184	**5.32E−4**
			1.124E−8	0.0356	**3.02E−11**
	8	50000	0.0447	0.292	**0.01765**
			2.910E−4	0.0641	**5.782E−5**
	10	50000	0.0199	0.116	**0.0196**
			1.510E−4	0.0072	1.612E-4
	15	50000	0.0114	0.0288	**0.00105**
			3.059E−5	0.00125	**4.952E–9**
DLTZ2	3	30000	**5.877E−4**	6.507E-4	6.735E-4
			4.50E−13	1.22E-11	2.825E-11
	5	30000	**0.00170**	0.00238	0.00175
			1.88E−12	8.95E-10	1.453E-10
	8	50000	0.0102	0.00924	**0.00823**
			6.606E−6	3.933E−7	**1.85E-12**
	10	50000	0.00816	0.00698	**0.00561**
			8.742E−7	3.206E-7	**4.22E-11**
	15	50000	0.00421	0.00363	**0.00306**
			2.047E−8	6.538E-8	**2.44E-13**
DLTZ3	3	30000	0.00403	0.187	**6.765E-4**
			9.444E−5	0.0416	**7.27E-11**
	5	30000	0.00181	0.421	**0.00172**
			8.798E−9	0.209	**5.51E-11**
	8	50000	0.107	0.597	**0.0410**
			0.00233	0.210	**8.399E-4**
	10	50000	**0.0418**	0.3178	0.0455
			0.00102	0.147	**1.28E-4**
	15	50000	0.01432	0.0216	**0.00307**
			8.19E-5	0.00233	**5.04E-11**
DLTZ4	3	30000	0.00522	**0.00147**	0.00369
			1.024E-5	**1.355E-6**	9.082E-6
	5	30000	**0.00170**	0.00367	0.00176
			2.22E-12	2.653E-8	1.954E-10
	8	50000	0.00851	0.0109	**0.00823**
			4.021E-7	3.39E-7	**2.947E-12**

(continued)

Table 4. (*continued*)

Problems	No. of objectives	MaxGen	NSGA-III	MOEA/D	MaSHOA
	10	50000	**0.00557** **5.19E-14**	0.00793 1.021E-7	0.00559 2.589E-11
	15	50000	0.00311 1.920E-9	0.00374 6.156E-9	**0.003062** **7.68E-14**
DLTZ7	3	30000	0.0322 3.720E-5	0.0473 1.539E-4	**0.0300** **3.02E-10**
	5	30000	0.104 9.885E-5	0.0870 7.121E-6	**0.0736** **3.59E-10**
	8	50000	0.265 2.410E-4	0.103 4.313E-5	**0.0961** **2.960E-8**
	10	50000	0.349 6.335E-4	0.124 6.965E-5	**0.110** **2.487E-8**
	15	50000	0.573 1.304E-4	0.216 3.599E-4	**0.146** **1.766E-7**

15-objective problems, while NSGA-III has good results on the 3-, 5- objective problems which have a little gap with MaSHOA. We can see that the proposed algorithm has better performance on a higher dimension of DTLZ2 problems. And for DTLZ3 problems, MaSHOA has the best results on the 3-, 5-, 8-, 10-, 15-objective problems except that NSGA-III has better means of the 10-objective problems. For problem DTLZ4, MaSHOA has the best performance on the 8-, 15-objective problems, and it still gets good results in other problems. MaSHOA has the best performance on the 3-, 5-, 8-, 10-, 15-objective DTLZ7 problems. From Table 4, MaSHOA has better stabilization and solving performance on these DTLZ problems than other algorithms.

Figure 2 shows the box plots of all the algorithms on 8-, 10- and 15-objective DTLZ problems. The box plots present minimum, maximum, median, first quartile and third quartile (sometimes outliers) of repetitious experiment results. The stability of results can be directly observed through the box plots.

For the 8-objective DTLZ problems (in Fig. 2a–e), MaSHOA has smaller boxes with lower values than the other two algorithms. MOEA/D has good results on the DTLZ2 and DTLZ7, and NSGA-III has good results on the DTLZ1 and DTLZ4, but the shape of MaSHOA is much flatter in these five figures and MaSHOA doesn't have outliers like other two algorithms. There is a similar survey made on the 10-objective DTLZ problems (in Fig. 2f–g) that MaSHOA has better performance on all the problems. And also, NSGA-III is good on the DTLZ1 and DTLZ4while MOEA/D is worse than others. For 15-objective DTLZ problems (in Fig. 2k–o), MaSHOA still has better results than others. And both NSGA-III and MOEA/D don't hold the second position on all the five problems.

It is shown that some of MaSHOA boxes are compressed into a line which means the proposed algorithm has great stability rather than others. And the boxes of MaSHOA are

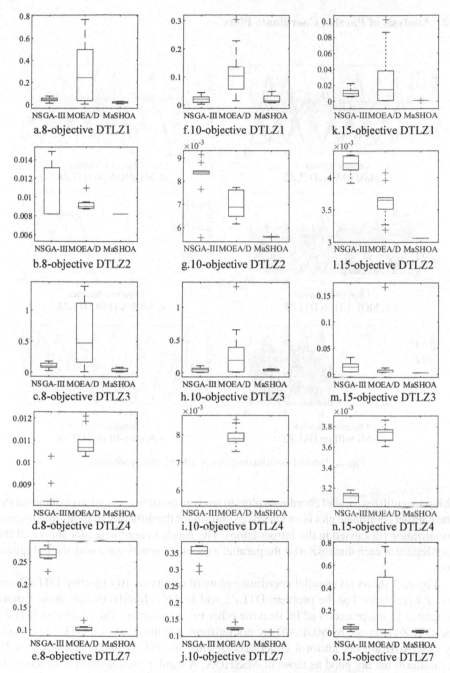

Fig. 2. Box plots of 8-, 10-, 15-objective DTLZ problems.

lower than others on the height in the figures which means the IGD values of MaSHOA are less than others. So MaSHOA has better convergence and diversity.

3.2   Analysis of Parallel Coordinate Plots

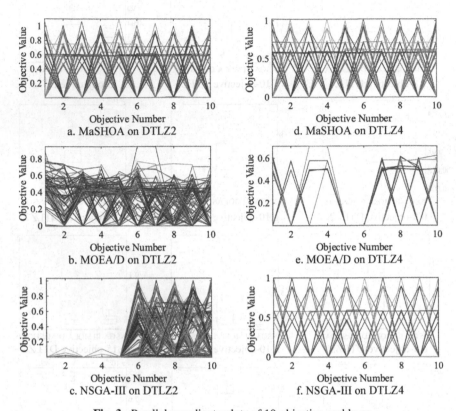

Fig. 3. Parallel coordinate plots of 10-objective problems

This paper utilizes parallel coordinate plots to analyze the fitting precision of obtained PF. The parallel coordinate plot is an effective solution for the difficulty of high-dimensional visualization (discussed in the introduction). The parallel coordinate plot shows all the coordinates of each dimension on the parallel axis and connects them with the polygonal lines.

Figure 3 shows six parallel coordinate plots of results on 10-objective DTLZ2 and DTLZ4 problems. For the problem DTLZ2 and DTLZ4, MaSHOA can show a more integrated fitting precision of PF than the other two algorithms. The results on DTLZ2 and DTLZ4 obtained by MOEA/D are not uniform, and the results on DTLZ2 obtained by NSGA-III are not uniform either. The results on DTLZ4 obtained by NSGA-III are uniform but not good as those of MaSHOA. A similar phenomenon is observed in Fig. 4 which presents six parallel coordinate plots of results on 15-objective DTLZ2 and DTLZ3 problems. The results of MaSHOA are better than others.

And it is shown that the performance of three algorithms is affected by increasing the number of objectives. And MOEA/D and NSGA-III could only present the part of ideal PF while the proposed algorithm could show integrally the PF relatively.

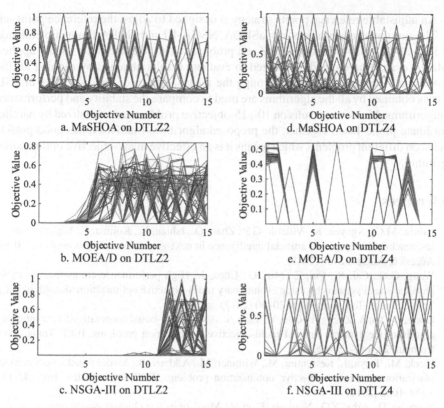

Fig. 4. Parallel coordinate plots of 15-objective problems

On the basis of the simulative experiment analysis, the proposed algorithm MaSHOA has good performance and stability on the DTLZ test set rather than MOEA/D and NSGA-III.

4 Conclusion

This paper presents a many-objective squirrel hybrid optimization algorithm (MaSHOA) which uses the framework of SSA and NSGA-III for reference and improves it on the evolution and selection operators.

A new joint fitness function combines the scalarizing evaluation which evaluates the convergence of the solution among the neighborhood and the reference point association achievement which shows the influence of the associated relationship between reference points and candidate solutions on the quality of solutions and considers the different preference of solving goals from early to late iterations. The new joint fitness function is applied to sort solutions in both evolution and selection operators. The better solutions are treated as the guide of others according to the sorting in the evolutionary process, and the candidate solutions are selected in terms of the sorting results. Besides, the distance penalization is proposed to prevent local convergence during the evolution.

An adjustable reference points strategy is designed to adjust the reference point set. The simulative experiments of MaSHOA, NSGA-III and MOEA/D are implemented on 3-, 5-, 8-, 10-, 15-objective DTLZ test problems. The IGD metric, a widely applied EMaOA evaluation method, is utilized to evaluate results obtained by running all the algorithms 30 times repeatedly. Through the means, variances and box plots of IGD metrics obtained by all the algorithms are used to compare the stability and performance of algorithms. Moreover, results on 10-, 15-objective problems are visualized by parallel coordinate plots. Taken together, the proposed algorithm, MaSHOA, has good performance on different problems which means it is an effective many-objective optimization algorithm.

References

1. Kibria, M.G., Nguyen, K., Villardi, G.P., Zhao, O., Ishizu, K., Kojima, F.: Big data analytics, machine learning, and artificial intelligence in next-generation wireless networks. IEEE Access **6**, 32328–32338 (2018)
2. Wang, G.G., Cai, X., Cui, Z., Min, G., Chen, J.: High performance computing for cyber physical social systems by using evolutionary multi-objective optimization algorithm. IEEE Trans. Emerg. Top. Comput. **8**, 20–30 (2017)
3. Gong, D., Xu, B., Zhang, Y., Guo, Y., Yang, S.: A similarity-based cooperative co-evolutionary algorithm for dynamic interval multi-objective optimization problems. IEEE Trans. Evol. Comput. **24**, 142–156 (2019)
4. Fleck, M., Troya, J., Kessentini, M., Wimmer, M., Alkhazi, B.: Model transformation modularization as a many-objective optimization problem. IEEE Trans. Softw. Eng. **43**(11), 1009–1032 (2017)
5. Zouache, D., Arby, Y.O., Nouioua, F., et al.: Multi-objective chicken swarm optimization: a novel algorithm for solving multi-objective optimization problems. Comput. Ind. Eng. **129**, 377–391 (2019)
6. Jiang, S., Yang, S.: A strength Pareto evolutionary algorithm based on reference direction for multiobjective and many-objective optimization. IEEE Trans. Evol. Comput. **21**(3), 329–346 (2017)
7. Ishibuchi, H., Sato, H.: Evolutionary many-objective optimization. In: Proceedings of the Genetic and Evolutionary Computation Conference Companion, pp. 614–661, July 2019
8. Luo, J., Liu, Q., Yang, Y., Li, X., Chen, M.R., Cao, W.: An artificial bee colony algorithm for multi-objective optimisation. Appl. Soft Comput. **50**, 235–251 (2017)
9. Cho, J.H., Wang, Y., Chen, R., et al.: A survey on modeling and optimizing multi-objective systems. IEEE Commun. Surv. Tutor. **19**(3), 1867–1901 (2017)
10. Jain, H., Deb, K.: An evolutionary many-objective optimization algorithm using reference-point based nondominated sorting approach, part II: handling constraints and extending to an adaptive approach. IEEE Trans. Evol. Comput. **18**(4), 602–622 (2013)
11. Gong, D., Sun, J., Miao, Z.: A set-based genetic algorithm for interval many-objective optimization problems. IEEE Trans. Evol. Comput. **22**(1), 47–60 (2016)
12. Yuan, Y., Xu, H., Wang, B., Yao, X.: A new dominance relation-based evolutionary algorithm for many-objective optimization. IEEE Trans. Evol. Comput. **20**(1), 16–37 (2015)
13. Zhao, H., Zhang, C., Zhang, B., Duan, P., Yang, Y.: Decomposition-based sub-problem optimal solution updating direction-guided evolutionary many-objective algorithm. Inf. Sci. **448**, 91–111 (2018)
14. Zhang, Q., Li, H.: MOEA/D: a multiobjective evolutionary algorithm based on decomposition. IEEE Trans. Evol. Comput. **11**(6), 712–731 (2007)

15. Cheng, R., Jin, Y., Olhofer, M., et al.: A reference vector guided evolutionary algorithm for many-objective optimization. IEEE Trans. Evol. Comput. **20**(5), 773–791 (2016)
16. Zhu, Y., Liang, J., Chen, J., Ming, Z.: An improved NSGA-III algorithm for feature selection used in intrusion detection. Knowl.-Based Syst. **116**, 74–85 (2017)
17. Shang, K., Ishibuchi, H.: A new hypervolume-based evolutionary algorithm for many-objective optimization. IEEE Trans. Evol. Comput. **24**, 839–852 (2020)
18. Du, Y., Xing, L., Zhang, J., et al.: MOEA based memetic algorithms for multi-objective satellite range scheduling problem. Swarm Evol. Comput. **50**, 100576 (2019)
19. Sun, Y., Yen, G.G., Yi, Z.: IGD indicator-based evolutionary algorithm for many-objective optimization problems. IEEE Trans. Evol. Comput. **23**(2), 173–187 (2018)
20. Liu, Z., Jiang, D., Zhang, C., et al.: A novel fireworks algorithm for the protein-ligand docking on the AutoDock. Mobile Netw. Appl. 1–12 (2019)
21. Mirjalili, S., Jangir, P., Saremi, S.: Multi-objective ant lion optimizer: a multi-objective optimization algorithm for solving engineering problems. Appl. Intell. **46**(1), 79–95 (2017)
22. Mirjalili, S.Z., Mirjalili, S., Saremi, S., et al.: Grasshopper optimization algorithm for multi-objective optimization problems. Appl. Intell. **48**(4), 805–820 (2018)
23. Kumar, M., Guria, C.: The elitist non-dominated sorting genetic algorithm with inheritance (i-NSGA-II) and its jumping gene adaptations for multi-objective optimization. Inf. Sci. **382**, 15–37 (2017)
24. Jain, M., Singh, V., Rani, A.: A novel nature-inspired algorithm for optimization: squirrel search algorithm. Swarm Evol. Comput. **44**, 148–175 (2019)
25. Liu, Z., Zhang, C., Zhao, Q., Zhang, B., Sun, W.: Comparative study of evolutionary algorithms for protein-ligand docking problem on the AutoDock. In: Song, H., Jiang, D. (eds.) SIMUtools. LNICSSITE, vol. 295, pp. 598–607. Springer, Cham (2019). https://doi.org/10.1007/978-3-030-32216-8_58
26. Ishibuchi, H., Setoguchi, Y., Masuda, H., et al.: Performance of decomposition-based many-objective algorithms strongly depends on Pareto front shapes. IEEE Trans. Evol. Comput. **21**(2), 169–190 (2016)
27. Ruiz, A.B., Saborido, R., Luque, M.: A preference-based evolutionary algorithm for multi-objective optimization: the weighting achievement scalarizing function genetic algorithm. J. Global Optim. **62**(1), 101–129 (2014). https://doi.org/10.1007/s10898-014-0214-y
28. Deb, K., Agrawal, R.B.: Simulated binary crossover for continuous search space. Complex Syst. **9**(2), 115–148 (1995)
29. Deb, K.: Multi-objective Optimization Using Evolutionary Algorithms, vol. 16. Wiley, Hoboken (2001)

Effective Handover Process for Reliable Video Streaming Over Software-Defined Wireless Networking

Kavyashree Puttaswami[1] and Chung-Horng Lung[2(✉)]

[1] Department of Electrical Engineering and Computer Science,
University of Ottawa, Ottawa, Canada
KavyashreePuttaswami@cmail.carleton.ca
[2] Department of Systems and Computer Engineering, Carleton University, Ottawa, ON, Canada
chlung@sce.carleton.ca

Abstract. Handover process plays a crucial role in a Wireless Local Area Network (WLAN) with multiple Access Points (APs). To meet Quality of Service (QoS) or Quality of Experience (QoE) requirements for end-users, especially during video transmissions, such as real-time multimedia streaming or VoIP, the time required for handovers from one AP to another AP should be highly efficient; otherwise, end users may likely experience packet losses or longer delay, which leads to loss of significant information and degraded QoS/QoE. This paper discusses handover mechanisms using Software Defined Networking (SDN) for AP selection in a WLAN. The proposed approach enhances the existing handover process by considering both the received signal strength and load balancing of APs in order to provide better QoS/QoE during video transmissions over a Software-defined WLAN with multiple APs. A number of experiments have been performed using the Mininet-WiFi environment and the Ryu SDN controller. The results show that the proposed method improves QoS/QoE with lower delay, higher transmitted bytes, and visually higher quality video images.

Keywords: Software-Defined Networking (SDN) · Wireless Local Area Network (WLAN) · Handover · Video streaming · Received Signal Strength Indicator (RSSI)

1 Introduction

Cisco has predicted that 82% percent of the Internet traffic would be IP video transmissions by 2021 in a recent survey [1], especially mobile devices such as smartphones would become most end-user devices or host stations for the Internet video traffic. Although 5G, 4G and 3G wireless technologies are in trend for mobile radio communications, Wi-Fi is still highly popular. Wi-Fi is standard IEEE 802.11x media access protocol that is widely used in Wireless Local Area Network (WLAN), especially in schools, universities, buildings, apartments, public transport stations and places where people gather.

H. Song and D. Jiang (Eds.): SIMUtools 2020, LNICST 369, pp. 460–476, 2021.
https://doi.org/10.1007/978-3-030-72792-5_37

Wi-Fi is more preferable for indoor communications compared to 3G or 4G technologies because of its download and upload speed, bandwidth usage and cost-effectiveness.

In a large WLAN environment where multiple Access Points (APs) exist, handovers of mobile terminals (MTs) from one AP to another AP are common for user mobility. A handoff is a process where a mobile terminal (MT) disassociates from currently connected AP and then associates to another AP whenever the MT moves away from the current AP or when the current AP highly congested. It is a standard and well-established technique that in normal conditions may require a few seconds to complete. For simple applications, such as web browsing and email, it works smoothly and as expected. However, for delay-sensitive applications, especially real-time video streaming and Voice over IP (VoIP), a few seconds may compromise Quality of Service (QoS) and/or Quality of Experience (QoE) by introducing undesirable delay, jitter and packet losses which is unreliable for the communication [2].

The AP from where the MT gets disassociated is known as Source Access Point (SAP) and the one with which it gets associated after handover is known as Target Access Point (TAP). The standard handover mechanism of IEEE 802.11x introduces handover delay of 2 to 6 s which is undesirable for video streaming applications [3]. Moreover, as a new MT is connected to an AP which is already to a number of MTs, throughput for each MT becomes even lower. Hence, it is important to distribute load among other APs, if possible, in order to achieve high throughput for each MT, especially for video transmissions [4].

The connection of MTs to a nearby AP typically is based on the Received Signal Strength Indicator (RSSI) value in Wi-Fi networks. However, as the number of MTs connected to AP increases, the may AP become overloaded and balancing of data throughput to each MT becomes difficult. One mitigation to this issue is that AP shares load with neighbor APs within the network through the handover process. The handover also happens when an MT exits one AP's radio range and enters the region of other's radio range. The crucial point in the handover process is how fast the handover process can occur so that mobile users or MTs can have low delay, i.e., in *msec*, particularly for Multimedia transmission, so that it can achieve reliable communications by providing high throughput, low delay, low contention on each AP. Moreover, it provides the opportunity to select multiple communication paths for data transmission.

Video streaming is one of the main services which could be affected by the handover transition and MTs encounter increased freeze time for the video which eventually distress the QoS/QoE [5]. The main challenge is to load balance among MTs by maintaining higher RSSI values, and less freeze time and delay.

The proposed method in the paper uses Software-defined Networking (SDN) solution. Since the SDN controller has full information for the entire network topology, it can control the flow of data through network switches based on the network configuration and traffic conditions. In the case of WLAN, SDN can assist and control the connection of MTs connected to APs during handover. The paper presents:

- An enhanced handover process by considering both RSSI and the load balancing of APs for handover decision with the SDN controller in order to improve QoS/QoE during video steaming for WLANs.
- A performance comparison using various algorithms, including IEEE 802.11 b.

We have conducted a number of experiments using Mininet-WiFi, Ryu SDN controller [24], and other related tools. The results show that our proposed handover mechanism reduces delay, increases the number of transmitted bytes, and higher visual quality.

The rest of the paper is organized as follows. Section 2 highlights the background information and related work. Section 3 presents the design and implementation of the proposed approach. Section 4 presents some experimental results using the SDN environment. Section 5 describes the conclusion and future directions.

2 Background and Related Work

2.1 Handovers in WLAN

Substantial research has been conducted to improve QoS and shorten low latency during the handover process in the field of wireless. However, some major challenge still exists for handover delay for live video streaming. Since the demand on live video streaming is increasing rapidly, handovers and load balancing among APs for WLAN becomes challenging to provide uninterrupted video streaming services to the end users. Specifically, there is a requirement to provide low handover delay and to perform load balancing among APs in order to provide better QoS/QoE to the end users.

Most of the current solutions to handover process improvement either lead to major change in the standardized wireless protocol during adaptation or focus on standalone changeover such as only in scanning, IP configuration, Authentication related to Association. (See Sect. 2.2 for a description on those tasks.) In order to reduce the scanning delay, various papers proposed algorithms to scan certain channels and avoid the entire set of channels to scan for selecting a best channel for the wireless connection hence scanning latency can be reduced [7–9]. In [7], the author proposed a method to inform the stations about the neighboring APs to scan before the handover process starts. The author in [8] proposed an adaptive algorithm in the scanning phase based on the use-case requirements. In [9], the author proposed a method to reduce the scanning time based on IEEE 802.11 standards by utilizing White-Fi channel space.

The above-mentioned methods lack concentrating on the other factors during handover, such as load balancing and distribution of stations. The authors in [10] explained a handover method to load balance among APs by utilizing SDN. However, the approach does not pinpoint the delay during scanning and authentication during the handover process.

The authors in [11] discussed multi-connectivity design with one or more APs in order to reduce handover cost because of network densification. However, the approach does not address challenges faced and latency introduced in handovers.

In [12], the authors discussed about optimizing the handover performance in 5G heterogeneous networks by utilizing cloud server to calculate the Congestion Window (CWND) values which is collected from wireless access networks. Chi et al. [13] presented a technique for fast handover which concentrates on the mobility of inter-area where MTs visit another domain which is monitored by its associated radius server. The researchers in [14] discussed about 5G wireless networks that co-exist with 4G networks by deploying small cells in large amount of ultra-dense networks. Due to the increased number of handovers, mobility management becomes difficult and the proposed approach mitigates the degradation of handover performance based on the fuzzy self-optimization algorithm for the enhancement of the handover control parameters.

The aforementioned approaches cover certain aspects of the handover process, but some parameters or the metrics are not in the consideration. Some methods are difficult to achieve in the real world, some are inconvenient for deployments and certain implementations are not open source. In order to cover wholesome from the AP selection to handover transition latency and complete load balancing of the adjacency APs, this paper proposes to implement a non-proprietary, non-vendor specific, standalone handover method which lessens the latency and improves the overall handover process in order to enhance the experience of high-speed video transmission.

2.2   IEEE 802.11 Wi-Fi and Handover Process

IEEE 802.11 protocols work under MAC and PHY. It was first released in 1997, but a number of subsequent amends have been released since then [15, 16]. Some have still been introduced recently, which reveals its popularity in practice. For instance, the following highlight some recent developments and key features:

- IEEE 802.11u (2011): support pre-association discovery of service
- IEEE 802.11v (2011): include additional wireless network management features
- IEEE 802.11aa (2012): support audio and video high-speed streaming
- IEEE 802.11ac (2013): contain multi-user MIMO (multiple input multiple output)
- IEEE 802.11ad (2012): include very high throughput, up to 7 Gbits/sec for short-range communications
- IEEE 802.11af (2014), also known as Super-WiFi/White-Fi: cover TV spectrum and supports up to 568.9 Mbits/sec.

In a multi-AP WLAN environment, when an MT reconnects from one AP to another AP due to mobility or another reason, the Source AP (SAP) must transfer the station active connectivity to Target AP (TAP) by following a series of four handoff procedures [3]:

- **Discovery:** SAP starts by scanning the suitable APs which are in the range to connect. There are two methods of scanning, active scanning and passive scanning. Active scanning is preferred over passive scanning since passive scanning station has to wait and listen for beacon frames from all the channels to get control and timing information of the TAP. For instance, new IEEE 802.11 standards have multiple channels, e.g., 11 channels.
  For active scanning, an MT sends a probe request and starts probe timer, it waits for probe response till *minChannelTime* then it moves onto the next channel. If it receives probe response within that time, it keeps on receiving it until *maxChannelTime* then it moves onto the next channel and repeats the procedure. Scanning time for each channel takes 8 ms [19]. However, further reduction is required to reduce the latency during video streaming to improve QoS/QoE.

- **Authentication:** Only legitimate users are allowed to establish a connection with the TAP. Latency in this phase depends on the security standards defined in IEEE 802.11 protocols. IEEE 802.11r introduced fast handover transition [22] which has lower authentication latency, but still the authentication latency is 30–60 ms [13].
- **Key exchange:** TAP and MT undergo several key exchange mechanisms using a four-way handshake and generate the cryptographic keys which are exchanged and placed on connecting TAP and station. Further, SAP and TAP exchange Inter Access Point Protocol (IAPP) security information block related to the station [21].
- **Association:** Association phase reconnects the MT to TAP based on the configured associate factors such as RSSI, etc. When the MT trying to associate with the TAP which sends a reassociation request to the SAP. SAP then initiates an IAPP-Move Request frame to TAP [20].

2.3 Software-Defined Networking and OpenFlow Protocol

SDN has been developed as the predominant programmable network architecture. SDN decouples the software control plane from the forwarding hardware nodes such as routers and switches and runs the control software either in a local server or using cloud which controls several devices [4]. SDN allows network administrators to manage their network equipment in a flexible and efficient manner using external server software as a controller to communicate with and manage network switches [6] using standard OpenFlow protocol.

OpenFlow allows the SDN controller to program all the configuration and flows to the devices [17]. OpenFlow supports network administrators to partition forwarding traffic and control flows according to their requirements which ultimately allow better performance of the system. SDN allows traffic based on the flow entry configuration on the switch and it can be modified by the controller. Figure 1 shows the key modifiable parameters.

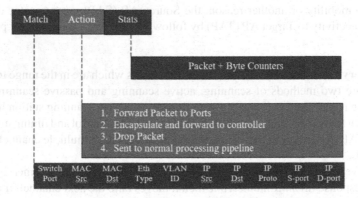

Fig. 1. OpenFlow protocol flow table entry [17]

Packets are forwarded by switches based on the entries in the flow table. The entries in the flow tables can be added, deleted and updated by the controller using OpenFlow messages [17]. OpenFlow switches keep a simple flow table than the ordinary switches. The OpenFlow switch flow table would consist of various flow entries and every flow entry includes six parameters. The Match fields include packet headers and ingress port that are used to match incoming packets to allow data. Priority in the Stats field is used for matching the preference of the flow entry. Counters in the Stats filed is used to count the matching packets. Instructions in the Stat filed provide a way to modify the action set and pipeline processing. The Stat Timeouts field sets the total time or idle time to live before the switch expires. The controller uses cookies to filter the flow statistics, change the flow and delete the flow [18]. The Match field supports 12 header fields and some of them are shown in Fig. 1. In this paper, programming the controller and APs has done based on the above parameters.

SDN can also be used to improve handover and load balancing in wireless networks [4, 10, 25]. It can retrieve workload information from APs and then make handover decisions based on the workload in the case of AP load balance-based handover. Accessing workload information inside APs would be difficult without SDN. Hence, it is considered as one of the main benefits of SDN in the handover process.

Hence, our proposed approach makes use of SDN and OpenFlow to program the controller and APs based on the RSSI information, traffic flow information and workload of APs for handover decision making with an aim to reduce the handover time.

3   Design and Implementation

This section describes the system design and experimental implementation. AP selection is a key step in handover. We have considered four different algorithms for AP selection based on RSSI, workload, and a pre-configured threshold value (see description in Sect. 3.1). Further, active scanning is adopted based on total interference factor [23] and IEEE802.11r for fast roaming is also adopted. The pre-authentication feature introduced in IEEE 802.11r together with the SDN controller are integrated for our proposed solution.

3.1   Proposed Design for AP Selection

Handover consists of four main phases: Discovery, Authentication, Key exchange and Association, as described in Sect. 2.2. Singh and Pandey [3] presented techniques in reducing the delay for the Discovery phase and the Authentication phase. The scanning feature used in the Discovery phase can impose high delay and is considered a performance bottleneck [7, 19]. The authors in [3] proposed to shorten the scanning delay by checking the scan cache associated with appropriate TAP, instead of scanning all the channels (14 channels for 2.4 GHz band and 40 channels for 5 GHz band). As a result, the number of channels needs to be scanned is reduced and hence the time it takes is reduced as well. The Authentication Latency can be reduced to eliminate re-authentication at the neighboring APs with the support of SDN controller [3].

This paper focuses on reduction of the Association latency and load balancing among APs to improve video streaming experience during mobility. Two main factors are considered in the design: RSSI and workload of APs. We investigated four algorithms for the Association mechanism for AP selection during the handover process [4, 10]:

- Algorithm 1: Strongest Signal First (SSF)
- Algorithm 2: Least Load First (LLF)
- Algorithm 3: Combination of LLF and SSF (LLF_SSF)
- Algorithm 4: LLF-SSF with a pre-configured workload threshold (LLF-SSF-T)

Algorithm 1 SST: RSSI is the most commonly used criterion for handover, which is also adopted in IEEE 802.11 standards. For this paper, SSF is still designed and implemented with SDN controller. The stronger RSSI value is, typically the higher the data rate is, if an AP is not overloaded. When an MT moves to overlapping coverage area of two or more APs, SSF considers all the APs that the MT can detect and chooses the one with the highest RSSI value. The method is conceptually simple, as shown in Fig. 2, since it is only related to the physical distance between an MT and an AP. Specifically, for our SSF, the Association phase occurs if a neighboring AP provides higher RSSI than the SAP by 0.1 dBm which is configurable value.

However, considering SSF only may cause congestion or unbalanced workload on some APs if many MTs are connected to those overloaded APs, which may still have neighboring APs that have low MTs connected. In other words, congestion may happen on some APs, but some neighboring APs may still be lightly loaded.

Algorithm 2 LLF: In SSF, an MT can get high-speed data rate by connecting to a nearby AP provided the AP is not overloaded. However, load distribution among APs in WLAN is also an important factor for the Association decision, as it may lead to data congestion and result in poor QoS/QoE if many MTs try to associate to the same AP which provides high RSSI value.

LLF considers only load balance situation, i.e., LLF emphases only on one association control parameter, that is the load of the APs, which is in the coverage area of a moving MT in AP selection decision. The AP load in this paper is defined as the number of MTs associated with an AP. More sophisticated calculation of workload can also be considered, e.g., CPU utilization and available bandwidth.

Since all APs are connected to the SDN controller. The controller makes the decision based on each AP's data path ID (DPID) table which is maintained in the control plane. The AP DPID tables in the controller provide the number of MTs connected to each AP. By looking at all the APs' DPID tables which are in the coverage area of requested re-association mobile station, the controller chooses a TAP that has the least load and changes the flow table in that AP for the requested MT and initiates re-association with the MT.

The flowchart for the proposed LLF algorithm is shown in the Fig. 3. As described in the flowchart, the SDN controller keeps track of the number of stations associated with each AP and identify the least loaded neighbor AP for handover decision making. If the SAP has higher number of connected MTs than the identified neighboring AP, then it dissociates a station from itself and the MT starts the association phase with the neighboring AP with a smaller number of associated MTs to achieve load balancing and ultimately avoid overloaded APs as much as possible.

Algorithm 3 LLF-SSF: LLF tries to achieve load balancing with the possible expense of weaker RSSI which affects the data rate and eventually maybe QoS/QoE for some

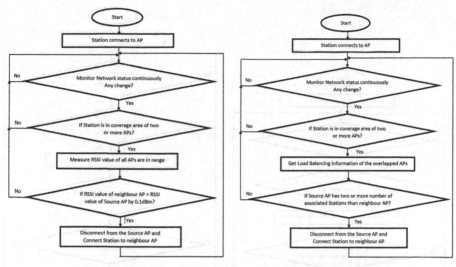

Fig. 2. SSF algorithm   **Fig. 3.** LLF algorithm

MTs. LLF-SSF integrates SSF and LLF by making the association decision based on both parameters: RSSI value with the moving MT and the load of each AP in the coverage range. This leads to higher RSSI values and higher date rate, while maintaining load distribution among APs.

The flowchart for this algorithm is depicted in Fig. 4. When an MT moves at a random direction, its behavior is observed at every *msec*. The controller selects the best AP according to the proposed algorithm when an MT moves to overlapping region of APs. The controller then updates the flow table of the selected TAP.

Algorithm 4 LLF-SSF-T: This algorithm extends LLF-SSF by adding a third parameter – a threshold indicating the maximum number of MTs that can be associated with an AP. The threshold is introduced to put a limit on the number of MTs to associate with certain APs by configuration. The motivation is to improve load balancing and higher RSSI values and QoS/QoE for MTs. The threshold value used in the experiment is only for feasibility study. In practice, the value needs to be supported by careful network monitoring and planning. The threshold value is examined after checking the load balance condition, but before testing the RSSI condition as to ensure the association decision based on load first. Such a design of choice can make the RSSI values of some MTs higher than those values that have been obtained with LLF-SSF. Figure 5 shows the flowchart of the proposed algorithm.

3.2 Implementation

The proposed framework was implemented using Mininet-Wifi which is an advancement of Mininet emulator software tool for wireless network environment. Ryu controller [24] is used as a remote SDN controller in the control plane to allow traffic based on the applied

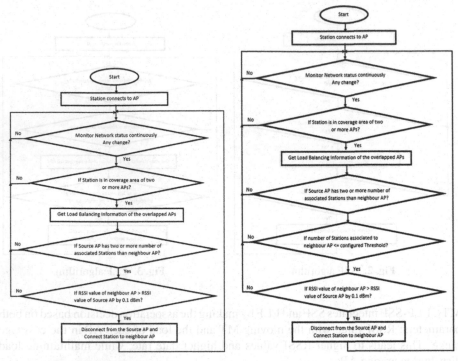

Fig. 4. LLF-SSF algorithm   **Fig. 5.** LLF-SSF-T algorithm

configuration rules on flows and to manage network topology. OpenFlow protocol is used between the control plane and the data plane. Figure 6 represents the high-level block diagram of implemented architecture. SDN mainly has three components, Data Plane at the bottom level, Control Plane at the middle level and Application Plane at the top level.

During the handover process, selection of AP is one of the critical decisions because if the stations are mobile and streaming live data (such as video), and if a poor-suited AP is chosen, for example weak signal strength, less bandwidth and low coverage area, then MTs experience poor QoS and congestion during roaming. Hence, AP Selection is one of the main design criteria.

Data Plane: All the configuration and flow control can be applied to the APs which is present in the forwarding plane so that APs allows MTs connectivity accordingly. MTs can move at random direction, hence the algorithm should be independent of the mobility.

Control Plane: The control plan contains the centralized SDN controller which monitors and retrieves the states of the network continuously such as MTs' positions, load status of each AP, radio-signal related data, i.e., RSSI of all MTs and then use such information to decide whether an MT needs to associate to another AP based on RSSI or load status.

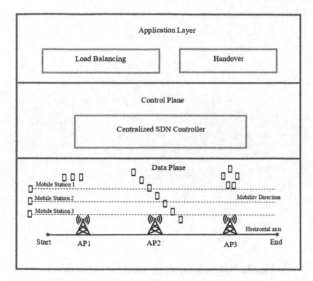

Fig. 6. High level block diagram of implemented architecture

Application Layer: The application layer contains load balancing and handoff services running above the SDN controller configured accordingly for the authentication server, neighbor list manager, topology service manager and IP mobility manager.

Experiments for handover mobility scenarios have been set up, which is described as follows:

- Figure 7 presents the emulated network topology where x and y axes indicate the distance in meters. There are three horizontally aligned APs with coverage areas: AP1 = 40, AP2 = 50 and AP3 = 90. These three APs are placed in such a way that their coverage areas overlap with a neighboring AP to observe handover as the MTs move through the ranges of the APs at the same speed.
- Eighteen stations are used, in which AP1 contains five stations that are stationary, fixed in one place. Seven stationary stations are associated to AP2 and five stations interact with AP3 which are stationary as well. Stations are distributed unequally to three APs to get more accurate results in wide range of load balancing scenarios which affects video streaming as well.
- All three APs are connected to a switch. A host in Mininet-WiFi is configured as the video server that is connected to the switch. The switch and the video server are not shown in Fig. 7.
- The remaining three stations S1, S2, and S3 are MTs which move simultaneously along the x-axis at the same speed starting at x = 0 m and ending at x = 290 m in order to compare four handover algorithms.
- Also, S1, S2 and S3 are data receivers from the video server across APs. APs send special notifications to the controller to associate and disassociate with those MTs.

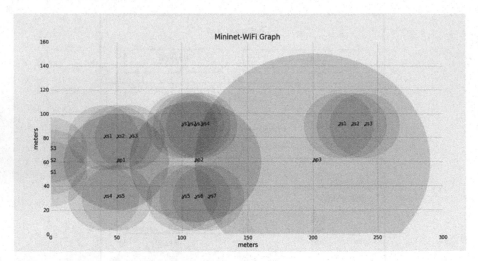

Fig. 7. Network topology used for experiments

IEEE 802.11ax was adopted for better results. Path loss was set to 5, the default value configured in Mininet-WiFi. Channels 36, 40 and 44 have chosen for different APs, i.e., a different channel has been selected for each AP to avoid interference between APs. Other important parameters used for experiments are listed in Table 1.

Table 1. Configuration parameters used in Mininet-WiFi

Access point	OVSKernelAP/UserAP
Mode	IEEE 802.11ax
Channel	1–6, 36–255 (varies for each mode)
Propagation Model	Logdistance/friis/twoRayGround logNormalShadowing/ITU
ac_method	ssl/llf
Authentication parameters Encrypt, passwd	WPA/WPA2
bgscanning parameters bgscan_threshold, s_inverval, l_interval	Threshold in dBm, interval in seconds

In addition, *bgscan* module and 802.11r are used to reduce scan and Authentication latency in Mininet-WiFi. IEEE 802.11r provides an equal amount of handover delay provided by LTE (i.e. 50 ms handover duration). Background scanning using *bgscan* module was utilized to roam within ESS in which all APs have the same SSID. *Bgscanning* is enabled for three moving stations in which *bgscan_threshold* represents whenever station reaches −60 dBm RSSI value AP starts scanning for the reassociation. *s_interval* indicates short time interval which was set to 5 s and *l_interval* indicates long time interval set to 10 s.

To reduce scanning latency, available channels are selected for data transmissions without scanning all the channels in every AP which is implemented in the code. To reduce authentication latency, WPA2 with 4-way handshake and IEEE 802.11r with background scanning is enabled. This was implemented during the handover process.

4 Experimental Results

Live video has been streamed using VLC media from the video server to moving stations or MTs which were emulated as data receiver just like smartphones/client using VLC media server by providing IP address and port of the video server. When the MTs start moving from AP1 to AP3, they receive live video continuously until the video transmission completes. During this time, handovers occur from AP1 to AP2 and AP2 to AP3 as expected. However, at which point handover happens depends on the proposed algorithms.

We have evaluated four aforementioned four algorithms for the Association phase for AP selection. The techniques used for the other three phases were identical for all experiments. Three performance metrics were used for evaluation:

- Signal Strength: The signal strength for the moving stations were measured.
- Delay: Delay is measured for the handovers. Higher the delay, lower the QoS/QoE.
- Transmitted bytes: Total transmitted bytes are captured. The values indicate the amount of data received at stations. This metric is highly related to packet delivery rate (PDR) that is often used for performance evaluation. The higher the number, the less packets have been discarded, which has direct impact on QoS/QoE.

As stated, three stations, S1, S2, and S3 were configured as MTs for evaluating handovers. Each experiment was repeated three times for each of the four algorithms. The average values obtained from the three runs were calculated for the final results. In addition, data have been collected for each of those three stations for video streaming from the server. Figure 8 depicts the results for signal strength for moving station S1 for all four algorithms, Fig. 9 shows the results for S2, and Fig. 10 presents the results for S3, respectively.

As shown in those figures, there are three peaks in each result, which indicates the RSSI value as a station moves along APs. RSSI increases when an MT is moving closer to another AP. As depicted in those figures, RSSI values are mostly higher for SSF for all three stations, S1, S2, and S3 compared to other three algorithms. In comparison of SSF and LLF, the average RSSI values are either similar between these two algorithms or higher for SSF, as RSSI is the sole consideration for SSF for handover decision. SSF mostly is used in IEEE 802.11 standards.

Unlike SSR, in LLF, handover happens when a station enters the overlapping region of two APs and chooses the least loaded AP for association. In the setup, AP1 has 5 stations, AP2 has 7 stations and AP3 has 3 stations. When these three mobile stations (S1, S2 and S3) move closer to the neighboring AP, e.g., in AP1–AP2 overlapping region, 3 stations are associated to AP1 as much as possible, because AP1 is less loaded compared to AP2. As a result, handovers from AP1 to AP2 occurred later for LLF. When MTs continue moving, they associate to AP3 as soon as they enter the AP2–AP3 overlapping region, since AP3 only has 3 stations. Hence, we can see in the figures that generally there is not steady increment and decrement of signal strength apart from AP1 due to immediate change in APs handover, as LLF is designed to equally distribute load among APs.

LLF-SSF is similar to LLF, since the load of APs has higher precedence over RSSI in the method. There is generally a smoother curve for LLF-SSF in the graphs after the first handover in comparison to that of LLF.

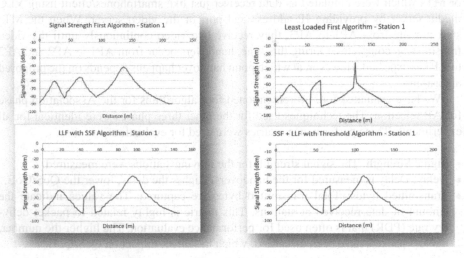

Fig. 8. Signal strength results for S1 for four algorithms

The result from LLF-SSF-T is similar to that of LLF-SSF. However, since a threshold is introduced on the allowable number of connected stations to AP, mobile stations when moving away from AP1 generally are associated with AP2 slower in time. Also, the effective coverage area of AP2 becomes smaller due to the fact that the handover from AP2 to AP3 happened earlier even though RSSI was considered because of the threshold condition. Hence the load in both APs becomes more balanced. From this method, video streaming quality would be better when there is a high number of video streaming stations, as it tries to maintain good signal strength and available bandwidth.

Moreover, we also evaluated the delay impact for the proposed LLF-SSF-T method and IEEE 802.11b that does not use the SDN controller. As stated earlier, the SSF presented in this paper is very similar to IEEE 802.11 standards, except SSF was still implemented with the SDN environment. Wireshark was used to capture data traffic. Figure 11 shows that there is lower latency (50–60 ms handover delay observed for the proposed LLF-SSF-T handover method compare to IEEE 802.11b experiment which has nearly 4–7 s handover delay, e.g., from ~43 s to 50 s for the handover process.

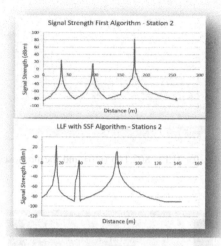

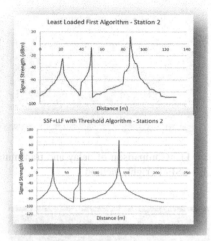

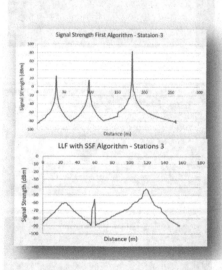

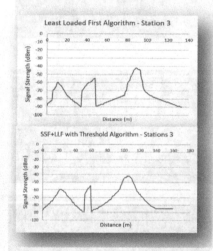

Fig. 9. Signal strength results for S2 for four algorithms

Fig. 10. Signal strength results for S3 for four algorithms

The number of transmitted bytes (y-axis) which is closely related to commonly used PDR, is much higher for LLF-SSF-T method than that of IEEE 802.11b for the entire experiment period. The higher delay for the handover periods is highly related to the result.

In addition, video quality has been observed and compared visually for both IEEE 802.11b and the proposed LLF-SSF-T. Fig. 12 illustrates three examples of results from two methods. The left column shows for results obtained from IEEE 802.11b and the right column shows images for the proposed LLF-SSF-T. As we can see visually, there is improved quality observed in the proposed method compared to that of IEEE 802.11b.

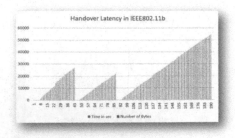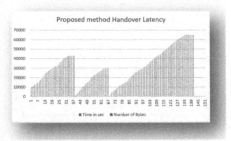

Fig. 11. Comparison of delay and transmitted bytes for IEEE 802.11b (left) and the proposed LLF-SSF-T (right) method.

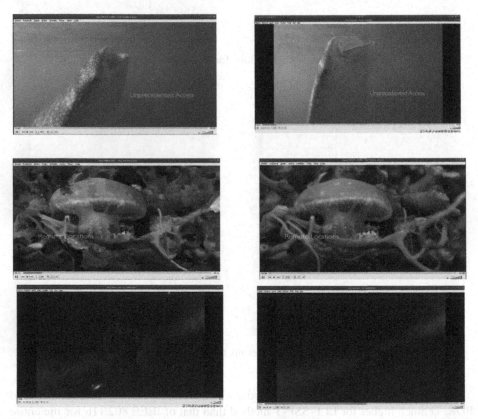

Fig. 12. Visual comparison of video quality for IEEE 802.11b (left) and the proposed LLF-SSF-T (right): an illustration.

5 Conclusions and Future Research

The paper presented SDN-based handover process for video streaming over SDN-based WiFi. The simulation was built with Mininet-WiFi, OpenFlow protocol, and the Ryu

SDN controller. The emphasis of the simulation evaluation was on the Association phase for handovers. We evaluated four SDN-based algorithms that could be used to improve QoS/QoE or the overall system performance. Further, all the algorithms are compared in terms of performance and quality of video streaming using VLC.

The results obtained from a number of experiments demonstrated that the proposed handover methods in WLAN with the use of SDN improves the performance of video streaming by reducing handover latency compared to standardized wireless protocol handover latency. This solution is also independent on external network elements such as modifying in APs or at the end MTs. SDN locally handles the changes which effect on mobility of the MTs to improve seamless video transmission.

Several research directions can be further investigated. Some areas include: (i) increase the number of stations, MTs and APs for performance evaluation; (ii) vary the speeds of MTs and switching rates for handovers; and (iii) consider network caching for the experiments and QoS/QoE evaluation.

References

1. Cisco Visual Networking Index: Forecast and Methodology, 2016–21. White Paper Cisco Publis, June 2017. https://www.reinvention.be/webhdfs/v1/docs/complete-white-paper-c11-481360.pdf. Accessed Mar 2020
2. Filho, J.Q., Cunha, N., Lima, R., Anjos, E., Matos, E.: A software defined wireless networking approach for managing handoff in IEEE 802.11 networks. Wireless Commun. Mob. Comput. **2018**, 11 (2018). Article ID 9246824
3. Singh, K., Pandey, M.: SDN-based fast handover approach to improve the QoS of video streaming over Wi-Fi networks. In: Peng, S.-L., Dey, Ni., Bundele, M. (eds.) Computing and Network Sustainability. LNNS, vol. 75, pp. 137–146. Springer, Singapore (2019). https://doi.org/10.1007/978-981-13-7150-9_14
4. Kiran, N., Yin, C., Akram, Z.: AP load balance based handover in software defined WiFi systems. In: 5th International Conference on Network Infrastructure and Digital Content, September 2016
5. Su, G., Su, X., Bai, Y., et al.: QoE in video streaming over wireless networks: perspectives and research challenges. Wireless Netw. **22**, 1571–1593 (2016)
6. Linthicum, D.S.: Software-defined networks meet cloud computing. IEEE Cloud Comput. **3**(3), 8–10 (2016)
7. Powar, Y.A., Apte, V.: Improving the IEEE 802.11 MAC layer handoff latency to support multimedia traffic. In: IEEE Wireless Communications and Networking Conference, April 2009, pp. 1–6 (2009)
8. Montavont, N., Arcia-Moret, A., Castignani, G.: On the selection of scanning parameters in IEEE 802.11 networks. In: IEEE 24th International Symposium on Personal, Indoor, and Mobile Radio Communications, September 2013, pp. 2137–2141 (2013)
9. Bawazeer, B., Akkari, N., Aldabbagh, G., Dimitriou, N.: Reducing scanning delay for WiFi-to-WhiteFi handovers. In: 5th International Conference on Digital Information and Communication Technology and Its Applications, May 2015, pp. 49–53 (2015)
10. Nahida, K., Yin, C., Hu, Y., Arain, Z.A., Pan, C.: Handover based on AP load in software defined Wi-Fi systems. J. Commun. Netw. **19**, 596–604 (2017)
11. Zhang, H., Huang, W., Liu, Y.: Handover probability analysis of anchor-based multi-connectivity in 5G user-centric network. IEEE Wirel. Commun. Lett. **8**(2), 396–399 (April 2019)

12. Ishikawa, R., Iida, K., Koga, H., Shimamura, M.: Improved handover using cloud control in heterogeneous wireless networks. In: IEEE 39th Annual Computer Software and Applications Conference (COMPSAC), July 2015
13. Chi, K.-H., Tseng, C.-C., Tsai, Y.-H.: Fast handoff among IEEE 802.11r mobility. J. Inf. Sci. Eng. **26**(4), 1345–1362 (2010)
14. Alhammadi, A., et al.: Advanced handover self-optimization approach for 4G/5G HetNets using weighted fuzzy logic control. In: 15th International Conference on Telecommunications, pp. 1–6, July 2019
15. IEEE 802.11. https://en.wikipedia.org/wiki/IEEE_802.11. Accessed Mar 2020
16. Shaw, K.: 802.11: Wi-Fi standards and speeds explained, October 2018. https://www.networkworld.com/article/3238664/80211-wi-fi-standards-and-speeds-explained.html. Accessed Mar 2020
17. SDxCentral Staff: What is OpenFlow?, SDxCentral, 26 August 2013. https://www.sdxcentral.com/networking/sdn/definitions/what-is-openflow/. Accessed Mar 2020
18. Farhady, H., Lee, H., Nakao, A.: Software-defined networking: a survey. Comput. Netw. **81**, 79–95 (2015)
19. Purushothaman, I., Roy, S.: FastScan: a handoff scheme for voice over IEEE 802.11 WLANs. Wirel. Netw. **16**, 2049–2063 (2010)
20. Virtual AP for 802.11 Seamless Handoff, IETF Tools. https://tools.ietf.org/html/draft-song-80211-seamless-handoff-00. Accessed Nov 2019
21. Mishra, A., Shin, A.M., Arbaugh, W.: An empirical analysis of the IEEE 80211 MAC layer. SIGCOMM Comput. Commun. Rev. **33**, 93–102 (2003)
22. Sanchez, M.I., Boukerche, A.: On IEEE 802.11K/R/V amendments: do they have a real impact? IEEE Wirel. Commun. **23**(1), 48–55 (Feb. 2016)
23. ACS (Automatic Channel Selection): Linux Wireless, en:users:documentation:acs [Linux Wireless]. https://wireless.wiki.kernel.org/en/users/Documentation/acs. Accessed Mar 2020
24. RYU SDN Framework. https://osrg.github.io/ryu/index.html. Accessed Mar 2020
25. Rangisetti, A.K., Baldaniya, H.B., Pradeep Kumar, B., Tamma, B.R.: Load-aware hand-offs in software defined wireless LANs. In: IEEE 10th International Conference on Wireless and Mobile Computing, Networking and Communications (WiMob), pp. 685–690 (2014)

Observation Period Length for Channel Selection

Yi Shi, Lei Chen[✉], Kailiang Zhang, Yuan An, and Ping Cui

Jiangsu Province Key Laboratory of Intelligent Industry Control Technology,
Xuzhou University of Technology, Xuzhou 221018, China
chenlei@xzit.edu.cn

Abstract. The transmitter needs to select optimal wireless channel from several available ones in mobile communication. Since the instantaneous channel rate is time-varying with unknown statistics, the channel selection is based on observation. As the packets arrive, controller need to observe channel state in observation period, and then transmit packets through optimal channel in transmission period. We investigate the trade-off between observation period and transmission period. Short observation period might lead to wrong decision while long observation period wastes time. The simulation results show that there is an optimal length of observation period. The total transmission time experience a sharp decreasing before the optimal point. The longer observation does not cause an obvious increasing of length. This implies that the observation could be set longer rather than shorter.

Keywords: Channel selection · Scheduling policy · Wireless communication

1 Introduction

To accommodate the requests from different application scenarios, mobile communication network needs special designing for vehicle, industry and so on [1–4]. Traffic analysis is important for these special designing, some new techniques are therefore adopted to investigate the characters of network traffic [5–8]. To evaluate these network scheduling schemes, some researches focus on the effectiveness [9–11] and energy cost [12–14]. It is found that the user behaviors and service activities affect the network traffic [15], and then affect the network performance indicators [16–18]. In the future application scenarios, the most concerned performance indicators include quality of service [19–22], quality of experience [23–26], spectral efficiency [27–30] and effective capacity of channel [31–35]. Based on these researches, transmitter could choose optimal policy. However, in mobile communication, a channel observation is essential before channel selection because of the time-varying channel state. Therefore, the regret is proposed to evaluate the effective of channel selection which actually affects the schedule scheme [36–39].

The system's regret index is defined to measure the system stability [36]. In mobile communication, the real statistics of state of time-varying channel is usually unknown.

H. Song and D. Jiang (Eds.): SIMUtools 2020, LNICST 369, pp. 477–484, 2021.
https://doi.org/10.1007/978-3-030-72792-5_38

The regret index compares the backlog with a controller select the policy based on observed statistics and the backlog under a controller that knows the best policy. This problem is known as a stochastic multi-armed bandit problem. The regret bound is drawn in [37]. Some practical policies have been studied for a long time to deal the multi-armed bandit problems [38]. Under fixed arrival rate and service rate, the boundary of regret is obtained in [39].

To reduce the regret, transmitter could evaluate the candidate channels during idle period. Through the channel estimation, transmitter can select optimal channel. The effect of channel estimations is affected by the length of idle period. In some situations, a controller begins to observe the channel state after a flow arrives in the queue. Therefore it also needs to estimate channel in busy period. A short observation period might lead to wrong decision while long observation period wastes time. In this paper, we design a simulation to explore how observation period affects the latency. In our simulation, the capacity of channel state is treated as service rate. Considering the different transmission rate between backbone network and edge network, we assume that all packets have arrived into the queue of edge network.

The paper is divided as six sections. In the second section, we give the system model. The algorithm and simulation results analysis is given in the third section. We conclude in the fourth section.

2 System Model

This channel observation problem is similar to the traditional bandit algorithms. The multi-armed bandit problem is a problem in which a fixed limited set of resources need to be allocated between alternative choices in a way that maximizes their expected gain [38]. The choice's stochastic properties are unknown at the time of allocation, and the allocation must be made under observation. As time passes, we can better evaluate the choices. However, lose time to treat the backlogged queue in transmitter. The good scheduling policy must make trade-off between observation time and dealing time. During the initial periods, we can select a candidate service to observe. When controller learns accurate channel state, we can select the optimal one. However, it is difficult to find the precise time point to stop observation. The main issue is that the it should be shorter or longer than the optimal observation time. Which policy cost more time?

In this problem, the total time T is the sum of time T_1 and time T_2. Time T_1 is the time of the test phase, which is used to count the time spent in the test period. Time T_2 means the service phase of processing packets. T can be used as the main criterion, can be written as:

$$T = T_1 + T_2 \tag{1}$$

During the period of T_1, $S_i(t)$ is the service rate of the i th server at the t th time slot which is treated as 1 with the probability u, otherwise as 0,

$$S_i(t) = \begin{cases} 1, & with\,probability \quad u \\ 0, & with\,probability \quad 1-u \end{cases}. \tag{2}$$

In this paper, the controller does not know the values of u and must therefore use observations of $S_i(t)$ to identify u_i^*. The $C_i(t)$ is defined as:

$$C_i(t) = \begin{cases} 1, \text{ the ith server is selected to test at tth time slots} \\ 0, \text{ otherwise} \end{cases} \tag{3}$$

We assume that the controller tests u_i^* through $S_i(T)$, and $C_i(t)$ means the total number of times the server is tested in time T_1, so that the test value that is infinitely close to the true service rate can be calculated.

$$u^* = \frac{\sum_{t=1}^{T_1} S_i(t)}{\sum_{t=1}^{T_1} C_i(t)} \tag{4}$$

Then, through the u_i^*, we can choose the best server to serve the packets.

3   Simulation and Analysis

3.1   Algorithm

The algorithm we adopt in simulation is shown in Fig. 1. The algorithm uses T_1 time slots to observe the service rates of channels. In T_2 period, the channel with best service rate u_i^* observed in T_1 time slots to proceed the packets in blogged queue. The algorithms are presented as followed (Fig. 2):

Step1	While (queue is not empty)
Step2	If (Time < T_1)
Step3	Select next channel to test;
Step4	Observe the selected channel;
Step5	Update the service rate of observed channel;
Step6	Time++;
Step7	else
Step8	Select randomly a channel from the set of servers with highest rate ;
Step9	Decide randomly whether deal with the packet according to real service rate;
Step10	If(the selected channel works at current time slot)
Step11	length of blogged queue --;
Step12	End if
Step13	Update the service rate of the selected channel;
Step14	End if
Step15	End while

Fig. 1. Simulation algorithm1

Step1   While (queue is not empty)
Step2   If (Time $< T_1$)
Step3   Select next channel to test;
Step4   Observe the selected channel and processing packets ;
Step5   Update the service rate of observed channel;
Step6   Time++
Step7   else
Step8   Select randomly a channel from the set of servers with highest rate ;
Step9   Decide whether transmit the packet according to real service rate;
Step10   If(the selected channel works at current time slot)
Step11   length of blogged queue --;
Step12   End if
Step13   Update the service rate;
Step14   End if
Step15   End while

Fig. 2. Simulation algorithm2

3.2 Simulation Parameters

We make two simulations, the simulation parameters are listed in Table 1.

In these two simulations, we have 5 candidate channels with a service rate range from 0.3 to 0.7 similarly. Both the T_1 time increase 5 at each test from 10 to 400. Therefore, there are 79 tests in each simulation. And each test last 100 times under the fixed T_1 time.

Table 1. Simulation parameters.

Parameter name	Value of parameter in simulation 1,2
Number of data packet in blogged queue at beginning	10000
T_1 range (time slots)	[10–400]
Increasing of time slots in T_1 time range for each test	5
Number of candidate channels	5
Service rates of channel 1	0.3
Service rates of channel 2	0.4
Service rates of channel 3	0.5
Service rates of channel 4	0.6
Service rates of channel 5	0.7

3.3 Simulation Results

The simulation1 results are shown in Fig. 3 where the transmitter does not deal with the packets of blogged queue at observation period.

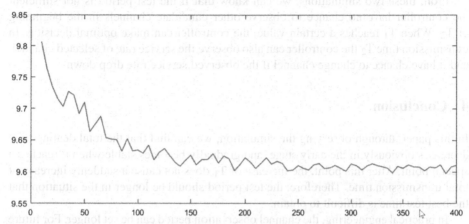

Fig. 3. Total transmission time in Simulation1 (horizontal axis unit is T1 time slot, vertical axis unit is $\ln(T_1 + T_2)$)

The simulation 2 results are shown in Fig. 4 where the transmitter send packets in blogged queue while it observes the channel state.

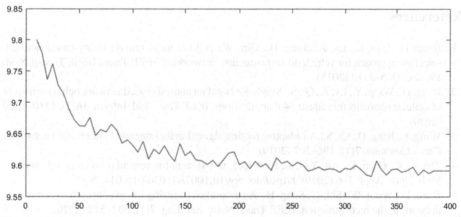

Fig. 4. Total transmission time in Simulation2 (horizontal axis unit is T1 time slot, vertical axis unit is $ln(T_1 + T_2)$)

In Fig. 3, with the increase of test period, the $ln(T_1 + T_2)$ drop down at first stage and the total transmission time gradually changes from fluctuation to stability at second stage. With the increase of T_1 time, the observed service rate becomes more accurate, so that the controller can make better decision to reduce the total time.

In Fig. 4, with the increase of period, the $ln(T_1 + T_2)$ experience a similar reducing in the test stage and the downward trend also disappear at the second stage. The total transmission time is shorter than simulation 1, because the packet processing is also carried out in T_1 time.

From these two simulations, we can know that if the test period is not sufficient the controller have no chance to observe other candidate channels in the beginning of T_2. When T_1 reaches a certain value, the controller can make optimal decision. In transmission time T_2 the controller can also observe the service rate of selected channel, and it have chance to change channel if the observed service rate drop down.

4 Conclusion

In this paper, through observing the simulation, we can find that the total dealing time decreases obviously in the early stage, and gradually becomes stable when it reaches a special point. After this point, the increase of T_1 does not cause a suddenly increase of total transmission time. Therefore, the test period should be longer in the situation that the best test time is difficult to obtain.

In practical engineering, the channel observation period can be set longer. For future research, the optimal observation should be investigated.

Acknowledgements. This work is partly supported by Jiangsu technology project of Housing and Urban-Rural Development (No. 2018ZD265) and Jiangsu major natural science research project of College and University (No. 19KJA470002).

References

1. Jiang, D., Huo, L., Lv, Z., Song, H., Qin, W.: A joint multi-criteria utility-based network selection approach for vehicle-to-infrastructure networking. IEEE Trans. Intell. Transp. Syst. **19**(10), 3305–3319 (2018)
2. Jiang, D., Wang, Y., Lv, Z., Qi, S., Singh, S.: Big data analysis based network behavior insight of cellular networks for industry 4.0 applications. IEEE Trans. Ind. Inform. **16**(2), 1310–1320 (2020)
3. Wang, F., Jiang, D., Qi, S.: An adaptive routing algorithm for integrated information networks. China Commun. **7**(1), 196–207 (2019)
4. Zhang, K., Chen, L., An, Y., Cui, P.: A QoE test system for vehicular voice cloud services. Mob. Netw. Appl. 1–6 (2019). https://doi.org/10.1007/s11036-019-01415-3
5. Jiang, D., Wang, W., Shi, L., Song, H.: A compressive sensing-based approach to end-to-end network traffic reconstruction. IEEE Trans. Netw. Sci. Eng. **7**(1), 507–519 (2020)
6. Wang, Y., Jiang, D., Huo, L., Zhao, Y.: A new traffic prediction algorithm to software defined networking. Mob. Netw. Appl. 1–10 (2019). https://doi.org/10.1007/s11036-019-01423-3
7. Qi, S., Jiang, D., Huo, L.: A prediction approach to end-to-end traffic in space information networks. Mob. Netw. Appl. 1–10 (2019). https://doi.org/10.1007/s11036-019-01424-2
8. Huo, L., Jiang, D., Lv, Z., et al.: An intelligent optimization-based traffic information acquirement approach to software-defined networking. Comput. Intell. **36**, 151–171 (2019)
9. Chen, L., et al.: A lightweight end-side user experience data collection system for quality evaluation of multimedia communications. IEEE Access **6**(1), 15408–15419 (2018)

10. Chen, L., Zhang, L.: Spectral efficiency analysis for massive MIMO system under QoS constraint: an effective capacity perspective. Mob. Netw. Appl. 1–9 (2020). https://doi.org/10.1007/s11036-019-01414-4

11. Chen, L., Jiang, D., Bao, R., Xiong, J., Liu, F., Bei, L.: MIMO scheduling effectiveness analysis for bursty data service from view of QoE. Chin. J. Electron. 26(5), 1079–1085 (2017)

12. Jiang, D., Wang, Y., Lv, Z., Wang, W., Wang, H.: An energy-efficient networking approach in cloud services for IIoT networks. IEEE J. Sel. Areas Commun. 38(5), 928–941 (2020)

13. Jiang, D., Zhang, P., Lv, Z., et al.: Energy-efficient multi-constraint routing algorithm with load balancing for smart city applications. IEEE Internet Things J. 3(6), 1437–1447 (2016)

14. Jiang, D., Li, W., Lv, H.: An energy-efficient cooperative multicast routing in multi-hop wireless networks for smart medical applications. Neurocomputing 220, 160–169 (2017)

15. Bao, R., Chen, L., Cui, P.: User behavior and user experience analysis for social network services. Wireless Netw. (2019). https://doi.org/10.1007/s11276-019-02233-x

16. Jiang, D., Huo, L., Song, H.: Rethinking behaviors and activities of base stations in mobile cellular networks based on big data analysis. IEEE Trans. Netw. Sci. Eng. 7(1), 80–90 (2020)

17. Jiang, D., Huo, L., Li, Y.: Fine-granularity inference and estimations to network traffic for SDN. PLoS ONE 13(5), 1–23 (2018)

18. Huo, L., Jiang, D., Qi, S., Song, H., Miao, L.: An AI-based adaptive cognitive modeling and measurement method of network traffic for EIS. Mob. Netw. Appl. 1–11 (2019). https://doi.org/10.1007/s11036-019-01419-z

19. Tan, J., Xiao, S., Han, S., Liang, Y., Leung, V.C.M.: QoS-aware user association and resource allocation in LAA-LTE/WiFi coexistence systems. IEEE Trans. Wireless Commun. 18(4), 2415–2430 (2019)

20. Wang, Y., Tang, X., Wang, T.: A unified QoS and security provisioning framework for wiretap cognitive radio networks: a statistical queueing analysis approach. IEEE Trans. Wireless Commun. 18(3), 1548–1565 (2019)

21. Hassan, M.Z., Hossain, M.J., Cheng, J., Leung, V.C.M.: Hybrid RF/FSO Backhaul networks with statistical-QoS-aware buffer-aided relaying. IEEE Trans. Wireless Commun. 19(3), 1464–1483 (2020)

22. Zhang, Z., Wang, R., Yu, F.R., Fu, F., Yan, Q.: QoS aware transcoding for live streaming in edge-clouds aided HetNets: an enhanced actor-critic approach. IEEE Trans. Veh. Technol. 68(11), 11295–11308 (2019)

23. Barakabitze, A.A., et al.: QoE management of multimedia streaming services in future networks: a tutorial and survey. IEEE Commun. Surv. Tutor. 22(1), 526–565 (2020)

24. Orsolic, I., Skorin-Kapov, L.: Framework for in-network QoE monitoring of encrypted video streaming. IEEE Access 8, 74691–74706 (2020)

25. Song, E., et al.: Threshold-oblivious on-line web QoE assessment using neural network-based regression model. IET Commun. 14(12), 2018–2026 (2020)

26. Seufert, M., Wassermann, S., Casas, P.: Considering user behavior in the quality of experience cycle: towards proactive QoE-aware traffic management. IEEE Commun. Lett. 23(7), 1145–1148 (2019)

27. Lee, Y., Kim, Y., Park, S.: A machine learning approach that meets axiomatic properties in probabilistic analysis of LTE spectral efficiency. In: 2019 International Conference on Information and Communication Technology Convergence (ICTC), Jeju Island, Korea (South), pp. 1451–1453 (2019)

28. Ji, H., Sun, C., Shieh, W.: Spectral efficiency comparison between analog and digital RoF for mobile Fronthaul transmission link. J. Lightwave Technol. 38, 5617–5623 (2020)

29. Hayati, M., Kalbkhani, H., Shayesteh, M.G.: Relay selection for spectral-efficient network-coded multi-source D2D communications. In: 2019 27th Iranian Conference on Electrical Engineering (ICEE), Yazd, Iran, pp. 1377–1381 (2019)

30. You, L., Xiong, J., Zappone, A., Wang, W., Gao, X.: Spectral efficiency and energy efficiency tradeoff in massive MIMO downlink transmission with statistical CSIT. IEEE Trans. Signal Process. **68**, 2645–2659 (2020)

31. Guo, C., Liang, L., Li, G.Y.: Resource allocation for low-latency vehicular communications: an effective capacity perspective. IEEE J. Sel. Areas Commun. **37**(4), 905–917 (2019)

32. Shehab, M., Alves, H., Latva-aho, M.: Effective capacity and power allocation for machine-type communication. IEEE Trans. Veh. Technol. **68**(4), 4098–4102 (2019)

33. Cui, Q., Gu, Y., Ni, W., Liu, R.P.: Effective capacity of licensed-assisted access in unlicensed spectrum for 5G: from theory to application. IEEE J. Sel. Areas Commun. **35**(8), 1754–1767 (2017)

34. Xiao, C., Zeng, J., Ni, W., Liu, R.P., Su, X., Wang, J.: Delay guarantee and effective capacity of downlink NOMA fading channels. IEEE J. Sel. Top. Sig. Process. **13**(3), 508–523 (2019)

35. Björnson, E., Larsson, E.G., Debbah, M.: Massive MIMO for maximal spectral efficiency: how many users and pilots should be allocated? IEEE Trans. Wireless Commun. **15**(2), 1293–1308 (2016)

36. Stahlbuhk, T., Shrader, B., Modiano, E.: Learning aloglrithms for mining queue length regret. In: 2018 IEEE International Symposium on Information (2018)

37. Bubeck, S., Cesa-Bianchi, N.: Regret analysis of stochastic and nonsochastic multi-armed bandit problems. Found. Trends Mach. Learn. **5**(1), 1–122 (2012)

38. Auer, P., Cesa-Bianchi, N., Fischer, P.: Finite-time analysis of the multiarmed Bandit problem. Mach. Learn. **47**(2–3), 235–256 (2002). https://doi.org/10.1023/A:1013689704352

39. Krishnasamy, S., et al.: Regret of queueing bandits. In: Proceedings of the Neural Information Processing Systems, pp. 1669–1677 (2016)

Learning Parameter Analysis for Machine Reading Comprehension

Xuekui Li, Lei Chen[✉], Yi Shi, and Ping Cui

Jiangsu Province Key Laboratory of Intelligent Industry Control Technology,
Xuzhou University of Technology, Xuzhou 221018, China
chenlei@xzit.edu.cn

Abstract. Machine reading comprehension is a classic issue artificial intelligence. It is a key technology in the next generation search engine and intelligent interactive service. The traditional methods usually work in a small scale of data sets. The traditional system cannot meet the emerging demand. Deep learning and cloud computation have ability to deal with the large scale data sets. In real scene, the parameters affect the performance of machine reading comprehension task. In this paper, we analyze how the parameters of deep neural network affect the machine reading comprehension. The experiment results show that the performance is only sensitive to a few parameters which should be key point for engineers.

Keywords: Machine reading comprehension · BiDAF · Bleu · Rouge-I · Parameter analysis · Deep learning

1 Introduction

The rapid development of 5G and artificial intelligent technologies lead to the possibility of complex human-machine interaction in mobile real-time environment. The current communication researches focus on improving some key performance, such as energy-efficiency [1–3], spectral-efficiency [4–7], traffic flow optimization [8–11], and QoS guarantee [12–15]. To meet the requirements of different services in a large number of fields, some special optimization strategies are proposed [16–18]. The new strategies can effectively improve the user experience [19–22] in the basis of user behavior analysis [23, 24] and traffic prediction [25, 26]. However, for some special human-machine communication services, the user experience is not like the traditional service that is affected by only the effective capacity of links [27–30]. The cloud computation capacity, data set quality, and interactive algorithm can also affect the end user experience [31]. With limited computation capacity, the algorithm efficiency is important for user experience improvement. And a lot of parameters might cause performance fluctuation [32–34].

In this paper, we investigate how the deep learning parameters affect the performance on DUREADER that is an open-access Chinese machine reading comprehension data

H. Song and D. Jiang (Eds.): SIMUtools 2020, LNICST 369, pp. 485–494, 2021.
https://doi.org/10.1007/978-3-030-72792-5_39

set. Compared with the previous MRC data set, DUREADER has the following characteristics. 1) All questions and original texts are actual data collected from the Baidu search engine data and Baidu community; 2) The data set contains both a large number of right and wrong samples that were rarely studied before; 3) Each question corresponds to multiple answers. As the largest Chinese MRC data at present, DUREADER set contains 200K questions, 1000K original texts and 420k answers.

2 BiDAF Model

In the process of machine reading comprehension, we will give a question (q) and one or more paragraphs (P) / document (d), and then use the machine to find the correct answer (a) in the given paragraphs, that is, $q + P \, or \, D = > A$. machine reading comprehension is one of the key tasks in natural language processing (NLP), which requires the machine to have a deep understanding of the language to find the correct answer. We adopt paddle-fluid as tools to implement the classic reading comprehension model – BiDAF [35] on DUREADER [36].

The model diagram is shown in Fig. 1.

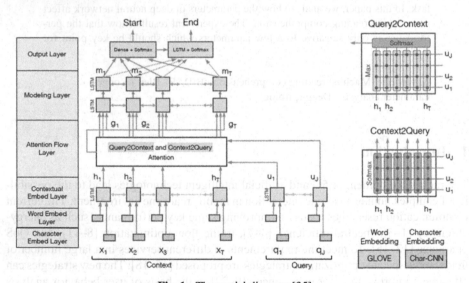

Fig. 1. The model diagram [35].

The model is a multi-layer process with six layers of network [35].

(1) Character embed layer: Mapping each word to vector space with character level CNN.
(2) Word embed layer: Using the pre-trained word embedding model, each word is mapped to a vector space. After embedding and splicing characters and words, input them to a double-layer highway network, and the output is two d-Dimension vectors [37]. Mark the output of the original as $X \in R^{d*t}$, and the output of the question as $Q \in R^{d*t}$ [35].

(3) Context embed layer: Use context clues of surrounding words to refine the embedding of words. The first three layers are applied to both the question and the original.

(4) Attention flow layer: The question vector is coupled with the original vector, and a set of feature vectors related to the question is generated for each word in the original. The above three layers are mainly used to extract information of different levels and granularity from text and query, and this layer is used to link and integrate text and query information [38].

(5) Modeling layer: Use RNN to scan the entire text. The input of this layer of network is the output G of attention flow layer (a text word representation of query aware). The whole network can capture the relationship between text words based on the query. This is different from the contextual embedding layer, which is not based on queries to capture the relationship between text words.

(6) Output layer: Output answers corresponding to questions. The output layer is a specific network structure. The BIDAF network allows you to modify the output layer according to specific tasks, but keep other layer structures. So we set up a specific output layer for QA tasks.

3   Experiment and Analysis

Through the experimental study of machine reading, the parameters (learning rate, weight decay, hidden size, embedded size) in the model are tested to see how the changes of parameters affect the running results and performance (bleu-4, rouge-1) [39, 40]. First, the following parameters are introduced:

(1) Learning rate: the size of learning rate. The type is float. The default value is 0.001.

(2) Weight decay: weight attenuation, type is float, default is 0.0001.

(3) Hidden_size: the size of running hidden units. The data type is int, and the default is 300.

(4) Embed_size: the dimension of the embedded table. The data type is int, and the default value is 300.

The following is the calculation formula and meaning of the result:

The full name of Bleu is bilingual evaluation understanding. The score range of Bleu is 0–1. The closer the score is to 1, the higher the quality of translation. Bleu is mainly based on precision. The following is the overall formula of Bleu [39]:

$$\text{BLEU} = BP \times \exp\left(\sum_{n=1}^{N} W_n \times \log P_n\right)$$

$$BP = \begin{cases} 1, & lc > lr \\ \exp(1 - lr/lc), & lc \le lr \end{cases}$$

(1)

Bleu needs to calculate the accuracy of translation 1-g, 2-g, …, n-gram. PN in the formula refers to the accuracy of n-gram. Wn refers to the weight of n-gram, which is generally set as uniform weight, that is, for any n, WN = 1/n [4]. BP is the penalty factor, if the length of the translation is less than the shortest reference translation, then BP is less than 1. LC is the length of machine translation, LR is the shortest length of reference translation sentence. Bleu's 1-g accuracy indicates the degree of faithfulness of the translation to the original, while other n-grams indicate the fluency of the translation.

The full name of the rouge indicator is "recall oriented under study for giving evaluation", which is mainly based on the recall rate. Rouge is a commonly used evaluation index of machine translation and abstracts of articles, which is proposed by Chin yew Lin. Four Rouge methods are proposed in this paper [40]: 1) Rouge-n: calculate the recall rate on n-gram. 2) Rouge-l: the longest common subsequence between machine translation and reference translation is considered. 3) Rouge-w: improved rouge-l to calculate the longest common subsequence by weighted method.

In this paper, we employ the rouge-l method. L in rouge-l refers to the longest common subsequence (LCS). The calculation formula is as follows:

$$R_{LCS} = \frac{LCS(C,S)}{len(S)}$$

$$P_{LCS} = \frac{LCS(C,S)}{len(C)} \tag{2}$$

$$F_{LCS} = \frac{(1+\beta^2)R_{LCS}P_{LCS}}{R_{LCS} + \beta^2 P_{LCS}}$$

RLCs in the formula represents the recall rate, while PLCs represents the accuracy rate, and FLCs is the rouge-l. Generally, beta is set to a large number, so FLCs only considers RLCs (recall rate) [5]. Note that if the beta is large, then f will pay more attention to r than P. see the formula below. If the beta is large, then PLCs is negligible [40].

$$\frac{1}{F_{LCS}} = \frac{1}{(1+\beta^2)P_{LCS}} + \frac{\beta^2}{(1+\beta2)R_{LCS}} \tag{3}$$

Next is the test chart of the experimental parameters:

The experimental parameters are listed in Table 1, 2, 3 and Table 4.

The test result are shown in Fig. 2.

It can be seen from the figure that different parameter changes cause different levels of fluctuation. It shows that the changes of learning_rate and Weight_decay cause a non-monotonous fluctuation. Engineers should pay more attention to adjust these parameters. And some parameters, such as hidean_size, does not cause acute performance fluctuation. The developer noly need to avoid the worst point.

Table 1. Learning_rate experimental parameters.

Learning_rate	Bleu-4	Rouge-L
0.00022	0.301159816	0.335547702
0.000222	0.327446346	0.349522438
0.000223	0.310633997	0.343745255
0.000224	0.309503916	0.345074965
0.00022425	0.314377135	0.3490552
0.0002245	0.300811443	0.341126438
0.000225	0.299887976	0.346905289
0.00023	0.275785047	0.325982007
0.00024	0.305897563	0.338380032
0.00025	0.260849998	0.326924794

Table 2. Weight_decay experimental parameters.

Weightdecay	Bleu-4	Rouge-L
0.0002	0.268626609	0.332181801
0.000225	0.254432416	0.332603854
0.00025	0.268450285	0.336462598
0.000275	0.301540809	0.355285356
0.0003	0.273552474	0.340523308
0.000325	0.253350986	0.333022634
0.00035	0.280247462	0.334507126
0.000375	0.272113977	0.337251798
0.0004	0.301491039	0.344305035
0.000425	0.318691688	0.355967577
0.00045	0.246738094	0.329907082
0.000475	0.285758484	0.346616667
0.0005	0.268979783	0.336884469

Table 3. Hidden_size experimental parameters.

Hiddensize	Bleu-4	Rouge-L
300	0.287737556	0.342004994
350	0.297440165	0.347887622
400	0.174288674	0.30164207
450	0.303693193	0.35553517
500	0.273745151	0.339456535
550	0.293851017	0.341371026
600	0.317234853	0.353995966
650	0.318028688	0.3578506
700	0.303053313	0.34409938
750	0.290282375	0.34627556

Table 4. Embed_size experimental parameters.

Embedsize	Bleu-4	Rouge-L
300	0.274609626	0.343514817
350	0.275633768	0.342759499
400	0.268605629	0.338488701
450	0.27385542	0.336640192
500	0.308942148	0.351445457
550	0.247504463	0.332083785
600	0.250511795	0.320621626
650	0.276932374	0.339581689
700	0.309809729	0.349099037
750	0.298543118	0.346263549

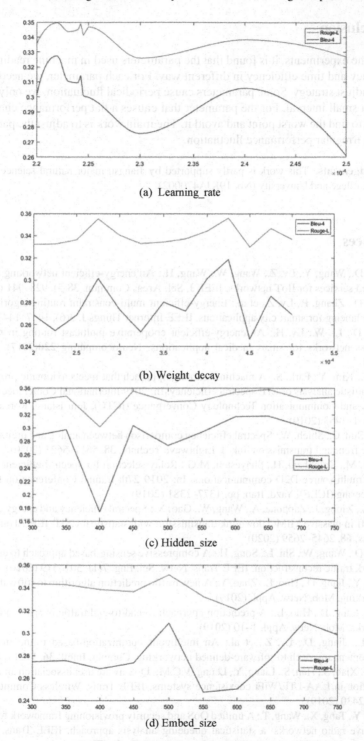

(a) Learning_rate

(b) Weight_decay

(c) Hidden_size

(d) Embed_size

Fig. 2. Parameters and performances.

4 Conclusion

Through the experiments, it is found that the parameters used in machine reading affect the accuracy and time efficiency in different way. For each parameter, we need to have different adjust strategy. Some parameters cause periodical fluctuation, we only need to adjust in a small interval. For the parameter that causes a flat performance change, we only need to find the worst point and avoid it. The main work is to adjust the parameters that cause irregular performance fluctuation.

Acknowledgements. This work is partly supported by Jiangsu major natural science research project of College and University (No. 19KJA470002).

References

1. Jiang, D., Wang, Y., Lv, Z., Wang, W., Wang, H.: An energy-efficient networking approach in cloud services for IIoT networks. IEEE J. Sel. Areas Commun. **38**(5), 928–941 (2020)
2. Jiang, D., Zhang, P., Lv, Z., et al.: Energy-efficient multi-constraint routing algorithm with load balancing for smart city applications. IEEE Internet Things J. **3**(6), 1437–1447 (2016)
3. Jiang, D., Li, W., Lv, H.: An energy-efficient cooperative multicast routing in multi-hop wireless networks for smart medical applications. Neurocomputing **220**(2017), 160–169 (2017)
4. Lee, Y., Kim, Y., Park, S.: A machine learning approach that meets axiomatic properties in probabilistic analysis of LTE spectral efficiency. In: 2019 International Conference on Information and Communication Technology Convergence (ICTC), Jeju Island, Korea (South), pp. 1451–1453 (2019)
5. Ji, H., Sun, C., Shieh, W.: Spectral efficiency comparison between analog and digital RoF for mobile fronthaul transmission link. J. Lightwave Technol. **38**, 5617–5623 (2020)
6. Hayati, M., Kalbkhani, H., Shayesteh, M.G.: Relay selection for spectral-efficient network-coded multi-source D2D communications. In: 2019 27th Iranian Conference on Electrical Engineering (ICEE), Yazd, Iran, pp. 1377–1381 (2019)
7. You, L., Xiong, J., Zappone, A., Wang, W., Gao, X.: Spectral efficiency and energy efficiency tradeoff in massive MIMO downlink transmission with statistical CSIT. IEEE Trans. Signal Process. **68**, 2645–2659 (2020)
8. Jiang, D., Wang, W., Shi, L., Song, H.: A compressive sensing-based approach to end-to-end network traffic reconstruction. IEEE Trans. Netw. Sci. Eng. **7**(1), 507–519 (2020)
9. Wang, Y., Jiang, D., Huo, L., Zhao, Y.: A new traffic prediction algorithm to software defined networking. Mob. Netw. Appl. (2019)
10. Qi, S., Jiang, D., Huo, L.: A prediction approach to end-to-end traffic in space information networks. Mob. Netw. Appl. 1–10 (2019)
11. Huo, L., Jiang, D., Lv, Z., et al.: An intelligent optimization-based traffic information acquirement approach to software-defined networking. Comput. Intell. **36**, 1–21 (2019)
12. Tan, J., Xiao, S., Han, S., Liang, Y., Leung, V.C.M.: QoS-aware user association and resource allocation in LAA-LTE/WiFi coexistence systems. IEEE Trans. Wireless Commun. **18**(4), 2415–2430 (2019)
13. Wang, Y., Tang, X., Wang, T.: A unified QoS and security provisioning framework for wiretap cognitive radio networks: a statistical queueing analysis approach. IEEE Trans. Wireless Commun. **18**(3), 1548–1565 (2019)

14. Hassan, M.Z., Hossain, M.J., Cheng, J., Leung, V.C.M.: Hybrid RF/FSO backhaul networks with statistical-QoS-aware buffer-aided relaying. IEEE Trans. Wireless Commun. **19**(3), 1464–1483 (2020)

15. Zhang, Z., Wang, R., Yu, F.R., Fu, F., Yan, Q.: QoS aware transcoding for live streaming in edge-clouds aided HetNets: an enhanced actor-critic approach. IEEE Trans. Veh. Technol. **68**(11), 11295–11308 (2019)

16. Jiang, D., Huo, L., Lv, Z., Song, H., Qin, W.: A joint multi-criteria utility-based network selection approach for vehicle-to-infrastructure networking. IEEE Trans. Intell. Transp. Syst. **19**(10), 3305–3319 (2018)

17. Jiang, D., Wang, Y., Lv, Z., Qi, S., Singh, S.: Big data analysis based network behavior insight of cellular networks for industry 4.0 applications. IEEE Trans. Industr. Inf. **16**(2), 1310–1320 (2020)

18. Wang, F., Jiang, D., Qi, S.: An adaptive routing algorithm for integrated information networks. China Commun. **7**(1), 196–207 (2019)

19. Barakabitze, A.A., et al.: QoE management of multimedia streaming services in future networks: a tutorial and survey. IEEE Commun. Surv. Tutor. **22**(1), 526–565 (2020)

20. Orsolic, I., Skorin-Kapov, L.: A framework for in-network QoE monitoring of encrypted video streaming. IEEE Access **8**, 74691–74706 (2020)

21. Song, E., et al.: Threshold-oblivious on-line web QoE assessment using neural network-based regression model. IET Commun. **14**(12), 2018–2026 (2020)

22. Seufert, M., Wassermann, S., Casas, P.: Considering user behavior in the quality of experience cycle: towards proactive QoE-aware traffic management. IEEE Commun. Lett. **23**(7), 1145–1148 (2019)

23. Jiang, D., Huo, L., Song, H.: Rethinking behaviors and activities of base stations in mobile cellular networks based on big data analysis. IEEE Trans. Netw. Sci. Eng. **7**(1), 80–90 (2020)

24. Bao, R., Chen, L., Cui, P.: User behavior and user experience analysis for social network services. Wireless Netw. (2020). https://doi.org/10.1007/s11276-019-02233-x

25. Jiang, D., Huo, L., Li, Y.: Fine-granularity inference and estimations to network traffic for SDN. PLoS ONE **13**(5), 1–23 (2018)

26. Huo, L., Jiang, D., Qi, S., et al.: An AI-based adaptive cognitive modeling and measurement method of network traffic for EIS. Mob. Netw. Appl. (2019).

27. Guo, C., Liang, L., Li, G.Y.: Resource allocation for low-latency vehicular communications: an effective capacity perspective. IEEE J. Sel. Areas Commun. **37**(4), 905–917 (2019)

28. Shehab, M., Alves, H., Latva-aho, M.: Effective capacity and power allocation for machine-type communication. IEEE Trans. Veh. Technol. **68**(4), 4098–4102 (2019)

29. Cui, Q., Gu, Y., Ni, W., Liu, R.P.: Effective capacity of licensed-assisted access in unlicensed spectrum for 5G: from theory to application. IEEE J. Sel. Areas Commun. **35**(8), 1754–1767 (2017)

30. Xiao, C., Zeng, J., Ni, W., Liu, R.P., Su, X., Wang, J.: Delay guarantee and effective capacity of downlink NOMA fading channels. IEEE J. Sel. Top. Sign. Process. **13**(3), 508–523 (2019)

31. Zhang, K., Chen, L., An, Y. et al.: A QoE test system for vehicular voice cloud services. Mobile Netw. Appl. (2019). https://doi.org/10.1007/s11036-019-01415-3

32. Farooq, H., Kaushik, B.: Review of deep learning techniques for improving the performance of machine reading comprehension problem. In: 2020 4th International Conference on Intelligent Computing and Control Systems (ICICCS), Madurai, India, pp. 928–935 (2020)

33. Guo, J., Liu, G., Xiong, C.: Multiple attention networks with temporal convolution for machine reading comprehension. In: 2019 IEEE 9th International Conference on Electronics Information and Emergency Communication (ICEIEC), Beijing, China, pp. 546–549 (2019)

34. Jin, W., Yang, G., Zhu, H.: An efficient machine reading comprehension method based on attention mechanism. In: 2019 IEEE International Conference on Parallel & Distributed Processing with Applications, Big Data & Cloud Computing, Sustainable Computing & Communications, Social Computing & Networking (ISPA/BDCloud/SocialCom/SustainCom), Xiamen, China, pp. 1297–1302 (2019)

35. Seo, M., Kembhavi. A., Farhadi. A., et al.: Bidirectional attention flow for machine comprehension. arXiv preprint arXiv:1611.01603 (2016)

36. He, W., Liu. K., Liu, J., et al.: DuReader: a Chinese machine reading comprehension dataset from real-world applications. In: Association for Computational Linguistics, Special Issue: Proceedings of the Workshop on Machine Reading for Question Answering, pp. 37–46 (2018)

37. Etzioni, O., Banko, M., Cafarella, M.J.: Machine reading. In: AAAI Spring Symposium: Machine Reading, Technical Report, Stanford, California, USA, DBLP, pp. 1–5 (2007)

38. Shen, Y., Huang, P.S., Gao, J., et al. ReasoNet: learning to stop reading in machine comprehension. In: Proceedings of the 23rd ACM SIGKDD International Conference. ACM (2017)

39. Papineni, K., Roukos, S., Ward, T., Zhu, W.-J.: BLEU: a method for automatic evaluation of machine translation. In: Proceedings of 40th Annual Meeting of the Association for Computational Linguistics(ACL), Philadelphia, pp. 311–318 (2002). https://doi.org/10.3115/107 3083.1073135

40. Lin, C.Y.: ROUGE: a package for automatic evaluation of summaries. In: Proceedings of the Workshop on Text Summarization Branches Out, Post-Conference Workshop of ACL 2004, Barcelona, Spain, pp. 74–81 (2004). https://www.aclweb.org/anthology/W04-1013

Research on the Path to Brand-Building of Characteristic Agricultural Products
An Empirical Analysis Based on Southwest China

Dayou Xu[1], Yanping Lin[1], Chenggang Li[2,3($\boxtimes$)], and Tiantian Tong[1]

[1] School of Business Management, Guizhou University of Finance and Economics, Guiyang 550025, People's Republic of China
[2] School of Big Data Application and Economics, Guizhou University of Finance and Economics, Guiyang 550025, People's Republic of China
[3] Guizhou Key Laboratory of Big Data Statistics Analysis, Guizhou University of Finance and Economics, Guiyang, Guizhou, People's Republic of China

Abstract. The brands associated with characteristic agricultural products reflect the quality, advantages, and culture of regional products; these brands affirm the regional characteristics and advantages of specific agricultural products. Exploring the path to building the brands of characteristic agricultural products helps provide a reference for transforming the advantages of existing resources into competitive advantages for the southwest region. This can further enhance the level of brand development of characteristic agricultural products. This study investigated the factors influencing characteristic agricultural product brands, constructed a theoretical model for brand building for characteristic agricultural products, and conducted an empirical study on the mechanism forming of the brands of characteristic agricultural products in southwestern China using a structural equation model (SEM). The empirical results show that in descending order of importance, the factors influencing the regional brand reputation are: geographical resource endowment, management, regional culture, and government support. The geographical resource endowment and regional culture factors influence regional brand reputation through management. The intermediary effect of management is significant in the corresponding path, and serves as the core driving force to advance the reputation of the regional brand. The intermediary effect of government support is not significant in the corresponding path.

Keywords: Brand building · Characteristic agricultural products · Regional brands of agricultural products · Reputation of regional brands

1 Introduction

By 2019, Document No. 1 of the CPC Central Committee had focused on "agriculture, rural areas and farmers" for 16 consecutive years. In the context of a new era of development, a new development direction has been proposed to develop characteristic rural industries and agricultural product brands. Brand building for characteristic agricultural

H. Song and D. Jiang (Eds.): SIMUtools 2020, LNICST 369, pp. 495–512, 2021.
https://doi.org/10.1007/978-3-030-72792-5_40

products is a driving force for agricultural industry development, and is an important way to realize the sustainable agriculture development. Building brands for characteristic agricultural products supports improvements in agricultural efficiency, farmer income, and rural development. All of these are of great significance to the development of the agricultural economy in southwest China.

Researchers have investigated the influencing factors associated with the brand building of agricultural products from the perspectives of competitiveness, building strategy, and the value chain. Some researchers have focused on the brand competitiveness of agricultural products. Using geographic indicators and collective trademarks supports the standardization of regional brands, and the comprehensive use of marketing strategy supports improvements in regional brand competitiveness [1]. Six factors influence evaluations of brand competitiveness with respect to agricultural products: resource-based capacity, industrial development capacity, organization and management ability, brand innovation ability, marketing ability, and brand equity ability [2]. Brand resources, brand foundation, brand support, and brand development are several important factors influencing the regional brand competitiveness of agricultural products [3]. Some scholars have highlighted research about brand building strategies related to agricultural products. As an example, brand building strategies related to agricultural products can be specific to tea industry. The product and brand personality promote the brand building of the tea; the brand culture improves the brand reputation; and the level of management plays an important role in advancing the brand building of tea [4]. Relevant factors include the brand strategy concept for the agricultural product brand, the innovative brand marketing strategy on the Internet, the material basis of industrial thinking for the agricultural product brand, and government functions. All of these factors support improvements in the core competitiveness of agricultural products, and promoting the strategic management of agricultural brands [5]. Other scholars have researched the brand building of agricultural products from a value chain perspective. Internal brand building and external communication create a joint brand building framework of characteristic agricultural products. Establishing the brand value chain for characteristic agricultural products helps build a platform for stakeholders inside and outside the enterprise. This provides consumers with a unique psychologically-based added value through interaction, enhancing the long-term core competitiveness of characteristic agricultural enterprises, and promoting sustainable development [6]. From the perspective of the industrial value chain, the three aspects of brand value components, brand value innovation, and advertising, serve as a point of action. This strengthens the brand image building of agricultural products and the exploration and analysis of a brand building strategy for agricultural products [7].

In summary, researchers have conducted wide and fruitful investigations on the brand building of agricultural products, with a range of research results. Previous studies on the brand building of agricultural products have laid a foundation for this study, providing a basis for measuring the effect of relevant factors on the formation of regional brand reputations in China. Few studies have addressed characteristic agricultural products in southwest China, and the relevant existing studies are mostly qualitative, with fewer empirical studies focusing on brand building paths. Based on this, this study focused on the characteristic agricultural products in Southwest China, establishing a structural equation model (SEM) to conduct an empirical analyses of the region's or products' brand building path to apply the research results to practice. This also provides a useful reference for the development of characteristic agriculture in China.

The structure of the remaining part of this article is as follows: The second part is a literature review and research hypothesis. It mainly elaborates five latent variables such as geographic resource endowment, regional culture, government support advantages, management advantages and regional brand reputation.to provide the basis for the theoretical model; the third part is the research design, which mainly introduces the sample source and data collection, as well as the measurement of variables; the fourth part conducts empirical analysis of the article, first conducts the reliability and validity test, and then analyzes and discusses the empirical results; The fifth part is the conclusion and enlightenment, summarizes the results of the previous research, and puts forward corresponding countermeasures and suggestions on this basis.

2 Literature Review and Research Hypotheses

2.1 Geographical Resource Endowment, Regional Culture, and Regional Brand Reputation

Producing agricultural products is characterized by regionalism and resource dependence. Product quality is closely related to a region's environment and resources. The close relationship between the products and regions, unique geographical features, competitive resource advantages, and the origin effect form a connection with the humanities. The regional brand of agricultural products formed based on this is regionally specific with distinctive geographical characteristics [8, 9]. Under different geographical environments and natural conditions, a cultural characteristic is formed with a significant geographical location correlation. This is known as regional culture [10]. Due to the different geographical environments in different regions, the resulting regional culture also has its own characteristics and is relatively independent. Thus, geographical resource endowment can advance the formation of regional culture. Based on this, this study proposed the following hypothesis:

H1: Geographical resource endowment has a positive influence on regional culture.

Regional factors influence the regional brand of characteristic agricultural products; this involves the factors of regional natural resources and regional culture. The production of agricultural products depends highly on the condition of the regional natural geography resources [11]. Agricultural development is the outcome of the integrated development of nature and economy. This is because biological resources and natural resources form the foundations of a region, and natural resource endowments can strengthen the regional characteristics of agricultural product brands [12]. The development and expansion of many agricultural product brands with geographical indicators are closely related to the endowed factors in a region, including the superior ecological environment, abundant natural resources, and sound humanistic conditions. The "geographical" conditions of locations play a positive role in advancing characteristic agricultural products. Specifically, geographical resource endowment advances the quality of characteristic agricultural products, and enhances brand reputation and attraction [13]. Based on this, the study proposed the following hypothesis:

H2: Geographical resource endowment advances the formation of regional brand reputation.

One of the main factors influencing the local characteristic development of regional agricultural product brands is the humanistic environment in a region [14]. A region's agricultural product brand and the regional culture are inseparable. As such, developing regional agricultural product brands should be based on the region's characteristic culture. To better advance brand development, the local government and regional media should attach importance to expanding the influence of a characteristic culture in a region. This should strengthen people's understanding and good feelings about the regional culture. This in turn builds the brands of agricultural products [15]. The inheritance and accumulation of regional culture and history is the basis for the regional brand formation of agricultural products. This deepens the connotation of the regional brand, shapes the unique brand culture, strengthens the regional brand image of agricultural products, and advances the popularity and reputation of agricultural products. On this basis, the following hypothesis is proposed:

H3: The regional culture promotes the formation of regional brand reputation.

2.2 Geographical Resources, Regional Culture, and Government Support

Geographical resources are an important material basis for the government to support regional agriculture. Resource endowment affects the development of family farms and serves as an important factor influencing government intervention and support strategies [16]. The brands of local characteristic agricultural products are formed by relying on natural resources, with the subsequent comprehensive application of social resources, such as government support, labor force, capital, and technical progress [17]. While cultivating and developing industries in regions with abundant resources, the central government should consciously guide the process by implementing targeted financial subsidy policies and other mechanisms [18]. Conducting in-depth investigations on local geographical factors, resource factors, industrial basis, and other factors is important for planning support. Determining the advantages and disadvantages of geographical locations helps maximize the advantages of local resources and strengthens the support and cultivation of key industrial clusters by relying on the advantages associated with local industries [19]. Government support is based on natural resources, which in turn influence the implementation of government policies. That is, the more abundant the resources are, the more the government should strengthen policy guidance and support. Based on this, the study proposed the following hypothesis:

H4: Geographical resource endowment positively influences the advantages of government support.

Regional culture supports the distinctive differential positioning of regional brands of characteristic agricultural products. A more prosperous cultural industry indicates better economic benefits, attracting larger investments. The development of cultural industry is an important factor attracting investment, and its stable development mainly benefits from government support [20]. Regional culture positively impacts regional development, affecting government policymaking and the provision of public services. This provides "rooted soil" for the development of cluster brands. Culture is a spiritual force that can stimulate the internal cohesion of cluster enterprises, realizing a better division of labor and coordination between upstream and downstream enterprises, promoting the development mode of enterprise brands [21]. Based on this, the study proposed the following hypothesis:

H5: Regional culture positively influences the advantages of government support.

2.3 Government Support and Regional Brand Reputation

Motivating regional brand development mainly comes from resource factors and system-related factors. The key to developing regional brands lies in attention and strong support from regional administrative leaders [22, 23]. Developing regional brands is the result of joint efforts made by many stakeholders. Government management and coordination are essential for the joint efforts that support regional objectives, convey consensus information, and form regional identification in a bid to restrain opportunistic behaviors of enterprises and stakeholders [24]. The government is the main body leading the development of regional agricultural product brands. As such, the government should strengthen its macro-control, and optimize regional planning of famous agricultural products. In the process of integrating unique agricultural product into regional brands, regional brands can influence the government's behavior. The government's behavior can gradually strengthen regional brand development. Government behavior leads to different new brand values for regional brand development at different stages. The increased brand value benefiting from the government behavior will gradually accumulate with brand development [25]. Local governments advance the formation and development of regional brands by formulating brand strategy, policy guidance, and normative constraint [26]. Based on this, the study proposed the following hypothesis:

H6: The advantage of government support promotes the formation of regional brand reputation.

2.4 Geographical Resource, Regional Culture, and Business Management

Geographical resource endowment is a necessary condition and material basis for the formation of agricultural industry clusters. These directly impact the formation and development of agricultural industrial clusters. Effective management is an essential part of characteristic agriculture, relying on abundant natural resources. Characteristic agriculture is a large chain involving the natural environment, infrastructure, raw material, marketing, logistics distribution, and business management. Conducting unified management and scientific planning can effectively avoid disordered production. Therefore, the scientific planning and distribution of characteristic agriculture in regions where ethnic groups have a small population should be strengthened, and the development of characteristic agriculture should be under the unified management of the regional agricultural sector [27]. A scientific management mode plays a crucial role in building agricultural product brands in regions with relatively abundant resources. Based on this, the study proposed the following hypothesis:

H7: Geographical resource endowment positively influences the advantages of business management.

Regional brands often have profound regional culture connections, and this culture may be strongly independent. In many ways, this means that the regional branding strategy is based on the individuals' and organizations' cultural cognition of regional branding [28]. Integrating natural resources and regional culture, and conducting intensive joint management of regional agricultural product brands can support the formation of effective mechanisms for managing agricultural regional brands. In addition, they lay foundations for gathering and optimizing high-quality regional agricultural resources, and advance regional agricultural product brands to gradually develop into a better system design, with higher a popularity and reputation [29]. Based on this, the study proposed the following hypothesis:

H8: Regional culture positively influences the advantages of business management.

2.5 Management and Reputation of Regional Brands

Innovating the operating mechanism and expanding leading enterprises can help advance the development of characteristic agriculture in the ethnic areas of southeast Chongqing [30]. Enterprises can optimize the allocation of regional resources in the process of building regional brands, and can play an important role in enhancing the regional competitive advantages and advancing improvements in regional brand performance [31]. Moreover, one side cannot complete the building and management of agricultural product brands; it must be a systematic project. Building a coordinated "four-in-one" management mechanism, with clear responsibilities among the main bodies of regional agricultural product brands, supports the formation of an overall joint force to promote regional brand development [32]. Based on this, the study proposed the following hypothesis:

H9: The advantage of business management advances the formation of regional brand reputation.

Based on the hypotheses above, Fig. 1 presents the theoretical model studied in this paper:

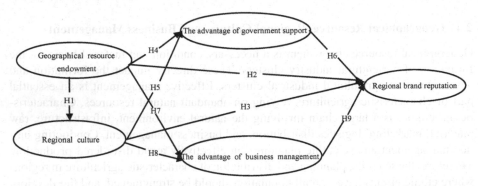

Fig. 1. A theoretical model for the brand building of characteristic agricultural products

3 Study Design

3.1 Sample Source and Data Collection

The subjects for this study were from southwest China, including Yunnan, Guangxi, Guizhou, Sichuan, and Chongqing. The characteristic agricultural products in southwest

China were selected as the research object; the specific investigation subjects included staff from the government, agricultural enterprises, agricultural industry associations, and other departments and units, farmers and consumers. This fully represented the relevant personnel using and managing characteristic agricultural products in the region. A total of 354 questionnaires were collected in this investigation; 270 questionnaires were considered valid through screening and verification, reflecting a recovery efficiency of 76.3%.

3.2 Variable Measurement

To ensure the reliability and validity of the measurement scales, related studies by foreign researchers were used for reference. In the specific operational process, the scales were translated from the foreign language and then back-translated by professionals, and then their Chinese versions were provided to guarantee the reliability and validity of the scales. The complete questionnaire for this study consisted of two parts. These parts included variable and item designs, as well as 5 identification items and necessary text descriptions. The questionnaire involved 5 constructs: geographical resource endowment, regional culture, government support advantages, business management advantages, and regional brand reputation. A 7-level Likert scale was adopted for the item design. The numbers from 1 to 7 indicated an increase of the degree of agreement, with "1" denoting "strongly disagree," and "7" denoting "strongly agree."

Geographical Resource Endowment. A study by Zhou Xinde, Li Deli, and Song Liying was used as a reference for this scale. The measurement scale had 5 items developed by Yu Yan et al. [33], including items such as "the local climate, soil, water and soil, geography and other conditions for the growth of the agricultural products are advantageous" and "clusters help optimize variety structures and develop the varieties of high value-added products." The Cronbach's α coefficient for the internal consistency of the variables was 0.893.

Regional Culture. This measurement scale included 4 items developed by Yu Yan et al. [33] The scale included items such as "unique cultural customs, lifestyles, and national culture have been formed in the cultivation, processing, and consumption of agricultural products in the region" and "the government has developed a series of traditional and characteristic cultural activities focused on the local agricultural product culture to enhance the reputation." The Cronbach's α coefficient for the internal consistency of variables was 0.897.

The Advantage of Government Support. This study adopted the measurement scale developed by Zhang Chuantong. [29] The scale included 15 test items from three dimensions: policy support service, development design, and regional marketing. Items included the items "actively improving the layout and planning of agricultural industry," "implementing a famous-brand strategy and making a development plan for regional brands of agricultural products," and "actively promoting evaluation, publicity and recommendation of regional brands of agricultural products." The Cronbach's α coefficient for the internal consistency of the variables was 0.925.

The Advantage of Business Management. The measurement scale developed by Zhang Chuantong [29] was adopted, including 16 test items from four dimensions: brand licensing, oversight standard, service guidance, and marketing promotion. These includes items such as "actively promoting management certification, quality certification, product certification, etc.," "establishing a relatively perfect brand application authorization system," "actively providing services such as technical rights protection, packaging anti-counterfeiting, logo management, etc.," and "actively carrying out the application for regional famous brand and well-known brand certification of agricultural products." Cronbach's α coefficient for the internal consistency of the variables was 0.937.

The Regional Brand Reputation. Regional brand formation was denoted by a variable index for regional brand reputation [21]. The measurement scale revised by Chhaudhuri [34] was adopted, including 5 items, including "this brand is influential" and "this brand has a good reputation." Cronbach's α coefficient for the internal consistency of the variables was 0.936.

4 Empirical Analysis

4.1 Reliability and Validity Test

The software package SPSS22.0 was used to assess the relationship between the variables reflected in questionnaire data. A reliability test on the questionnaires was conducted using the coefficient method; Table 1 shows the test results. The KMO and Bartlett spherical test value was 0.929; this shows that the correlation between variables was good, and the data were suitable for factor analysis [35]. The Cronbach's α coefficient for the overall questionnaires was 0.941, indicating the variables had high reliability. The values for the average variance extracted (AVE) of each variable all exceeded 0.5, indicating the measurement model had good convergence validity. The square root of AVE of each variable was consistently greater than the correlation coefficient between this variable and the other variables. This indicated there were significant differences between different potential variables. The measurement variables in this study had better discriminant validity (as shown in Table 2).

Table 1. KMO and Bartlett spherical test.

KMO		0.929
Bartlett sphericity test	Chi-square	3763.034
	Degree of freedom	210
	Significance	0.000

Table 2. Correlation coefficient of each variable and AVE square root.

	AVE	Geographical resource endowment	Regional culture	The advantage of government support	The advantage of business management	Regional brand reputation
Geographical resource endowment	0.632	0.795				
Regional culture	0.686	0.513**	0.828			
The advantage of government support	0.740	0.498**	0 .561**	0.860		
The advantage of business management	0.792	0.509**	0.554**	0.665**	0.890	
Regional brand reputation	0.745	0.556**	0.544**	0.546**	0.638**	0.863

Note: The diagonal line denotes the square root of AVE; and ** denotes that the correlation is significant at 0.01 (bilateral test)

4.2 Analysis and Discussion on Empirical Results

Structural Model Test

In this study, the software package SPSS 22.0 and the software package Mplus 7.4 were used to conduct the statistical analysis. When the sample size is relatively small, but there are too many measurement items, the original items cannot be used for modelling. Therefore, before using software Mplus 7.4 for analysis, the measurement items were packaged using the balance method to avoid larger parameter estimation bias [36]. After processing, the advantage of government support included three items, and the variable for the advantage of operation and management included four items. In combination with the conceptual framework and research hypothesis proposed above, software Mplus 7.4 was used to conduct a model fitting test on the brand building path of characteristic agricultural products in southwest China. Figure 2 shows the resulting structural equation model.

Table 3 shows the test results of structural equation model M. The corresponding model adaptation indices are as follows: the value for $\chi2/df$ is 2.29; RMSEA $= 0.069$; SRMR $= 0.053$; CFI $= 0.937$; and TLI $= 0.926$. Each index shows a good model fit. The results in Table 3 show that model M effectively explains the data. This can be used to research the brand building path associated with characteristic agricultural products in southwest China inhabited by ethnic groups.

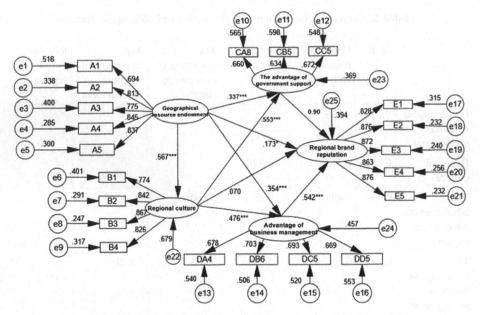

Fig. 2. Standardized structural equation model M.

Table 3. Test results of standardized structural equation model M.

Fitting coefficient	χ^2	df	χ^2/df	TLI	SRMR	CFI	RMSEA
Statistic	411.889	180	2.29	0.926	0.053	0.937	0.069
Preliminary fit criteria	n/a	n/a	0–5	>0.90	<0.08	>0.90	<0.08

Table 4 shows the test results from the standardized structural equation model M. The p-value for the relationship between regional culture and regional brand reputation is 0.440 (p-value of > 0.05), leading to the rejection of H3. The p-value for the relationship between the advantage of government support and regional brand reputation is 0.469 (p-value of > 0.05), leading to the rejection of H6. Hypothesis H1 was supported, with a ß-value between geographical resource endowment and regional culture of ß = 0.567, and a p-value of < 0.001. Hypothesis H2 was also supported; the ß-value for the relationship between geographical resource endowment and regional brand reputation was ß = 0.173, with a p-value of < 0.05. Hypothesis H4 was supported with a ß-value for the relationship between geographical resource endowment and the advantage of government support of ß = 0.354, and a p-value of < 0.001. Hypothesis H5 was also supported, with a ß-value for the relationship between regional culture and government support of ß = 0.337, and a p-value of < 0.001. Hypothesis H7 was also supported, with a ß-value for the relationship between geographical resource endowment and the advantage of business management of ß = 0.476, with a p-value of < 0.001. Hypothesis H8 was also supported, with the ß-value for the relationship between regional culture and the advantage of business management of ß = 0.553, and a p-value of < 0.001. Finally, H9 was supported, with a ß-value for the relationship between the advantage of business management and regional brand reputation of ß = 0.542, and a p-value of < 0.001. Therefore, H1, H2, H4, H5, H7, H8, and H9 were supported and H3 and H6 were not.

Table 4. Estimate and test results on the path of Model M.

Path	Estimate	S.E.	C.R.	P
Geographical resource endowment → Regional culture	0.567	0.048	11.736	***
Geographical resource endowment → Regional brand reputation	0.173	0.074	2.360	*
Regional culture → Regional brand reputation	0.070	0.091	0.773	0.440
Geographical resource endowment → The advantage of government support	0.337	0.075	4.506	***
Regional culture → The advantage of government support	0.553	0.071	7.761	***
The advantage of government support → Regional brand reputation	0.090	0.124	0.724	0.469
Geographical resource endowment → The advantage of business management	0.354	0.071	4.978	***
Regional culture → The advantage of business management	0.476	0.069	6.926	***
The advantage of business management → Regional brand reputation	0.542	0.094	5.762	***

Note: * denotes $p < 0.05$; ** denotes $p < 0.01$; and *** denotes $p < 0.001$

Effect Analysis

Geographical resource endowment and regional culture affected regional brand reputation through government support and business management. Business management and government support directly affected regional brand reputation. Table 5 shows the values associated with the effect of each potential variable on regional brand reputation. The total values of the effects of geographical resource and regional culture on regional brand reputation were 0.610 and 0.467, respectively. Business management and government support directly affected regional brand reputation, with total effect values of 0.090 and 0.542, respectively. As such, the four factors affecting regional brand reputation, in increasing order of influence, were geographical resource endowment, business management, regional culture, and government support.

The model's path analysis results shows that geographical resource endowment and regional culture enhanced regional brand reputation through the advantage of government support and the advantage of business management, respectively. To further verify the intermediary effect of government support and business management, the Bootstrap

Table 5. Direct effects of each potential variable on regional brand reputation.

Path	Direct effect	Indirect effect	Total effect
Geographical resource endowment - Regional brand reputation	0.173	0.436	0.610
Regional culture- Regional brand reputation	0.034	0.433	0.467
The advantage of business management - Regional brand reputation	0.542	–	0.542
The advantage of government support - Regional brand reputation	0.090	–	0.090

program within the software package Mplus7.4 was used to test the statistical significance of the intermediary effects. Given the sample count of N = 270, the confidence interval was set at 95%. There were 5,000 samples used to conduct the Bootstrap operation; Table 6 shows the results. The confidence interval for the paths including government support contained 0. This indicated that the intermediary effect of government support did not significantly impact the corresponding path. The confidence interval for the paths including the advantage of business management did not contain 0. This indicated that the intermediary effect of business management significantly impacted the corresponding path. Further, the value for the geographical resource endowment-the advantage of business management-regional brand reputation effect path was 0.192 (p-value of < 0.01). The value for the geographical resource endowment-regional culture-the advantage of business management-regional brand reputation effect path was 0.146 (p-value of < 0.01). The value for the regional culture-the advantage of business management-regional brand reputation effect path was 0.376 (p-value of < 0.001). These three paths indicate that the advantage of business management had a significant intermediary effect. Turning to effect paths involving government support, the value of the geographical resource endowment-the advantage of government support-regional brand reputation effect path was 0.030, with a p-value of 0.685 (exceeding a p-value of 0.05). The value of the geographical resource endowment-regional culture-the advantage of government support-regional brand reputation effect path was 0.028, with a p-value of 0.723 (also exceeding a p-value of 0.05). Finally, the value of the regional culture-the advantage of government support-regional brand reputation effect path was 0.057, with p-value of 0.717 (also exceeding a p-value of 0.05). The three paths above indicate that the advantage of government support did not have a significant intermediary effect.

Analysis of Results
Table 7 shows the results of the testing against the original hypotheses with respect to the brand building conceptual model for characteristic agricultural products. Of the nine hypotheses proposed in the previous section, all hypotheses passed the test except H3 and H6 (p < 0.05). H3 did not pass the test, indicating that regional culture had no significantly direct effect on regional brand reputation. To increase the role of regional culture on regional brand reputation, agricultural enterprises should conduct better business management. Together with government support, the two can be more closely combined,

Table 6. Bootstrap test effects on intermediary effect.

Indirect effect path	Standardized effect		Proportion of the total effect (%)	95% confidence interval	
	Indirect effect	Total effect		Upper limit	Lower limit
Geographical resource endowment-the advantage of business management-regional brand reputation	0.192		44.04	0.052	0.334
Geographical resource endowment-the advantage of government support-regional brand reputation	0.030		6.88	−0.205	0.152
Geographical resource endowment-regional culture-regional brand reputation	0.040	0.436	9.17	−0.307	0.193
Geographical resource endowment-regional culture-the advantage of business management-regional brand reputation	0.146		33.49	0.048	0.254
Geographical resource endowment-regional culture-the advantage of government support-regional brand reputation	0.028		6.42	−0.163	0.149
Regional culture-the advantage of business management-regional brand reputation	0.376		86.84	0.132	0.540
Regional culture-the advantage of government support-regional brand reputation	0.057	0.433	13.16	−0.341	0.288

rooting regional culture in regional agricultural products and maximizing the inner value of regional culture. Hypothesis H6 also did not pass the test, indicating that government support had no significantly direct effect on the formation of regional agricultural product brands. This shows that government support had no significant intermediary effect. The government provides strong support for regional brands; however, the influence and reputation of regional brands experienced little improvement. This is mainly because market mechanisms are the fundamental driver for the formation and development of regional brands. In the process of formulating and implementing policies supporting regional brands, the government had a relatively weak awareness related to advancing regional brand development through market mechanisms. As a result, government support did not significantly affect regional brand reputation.

Table 7. Summary of empirical results on regional brand reputation.

Hypothesis	Content	Result
H1	Geographical resource endowment had a positive influence on regional culture	Pass
H2	Geographical resource endowment promoted the formation of regional brand reputation	Pass
H3	Regional culture promoted the formation of regional brand reputation	Unsupported
H4	Geographical resource endowment positively influenced the advantages of government support	Pass
H5	Regional culture positively influenced the advantages of government support	Pass
H6	The advantage of government support advanced the formation of regional brand reputation	Unsupported
H7	Geographical resource endowment positively influenced the advantages of business management	Pass
H8	Regional culture positively influenced the advantages of business management	Pass
H9	The advantage of business management advanced the formation of regional brand reputation	Pass

5 Discussion

5.1 Conclusions

This study developed a new theoretical model to investigate the mechanisms involved in the formation of characteristic agricultural product brands in southwest China. Questionnaire data and a structural equation model were used to measure the effects of relevant factors on the formation of regional brand reputations in China. An empirical analysis was conducted to describe the brand building path of characteristic agricultural products in southwest China. The empirical results led to the following key findings.

1) The main factors influencing the brand reputation of characteristic agricultural products in southwest China include, in descending order of importance: geographical resource endowment, business management, regional culture, and government support. This indicates that in forming regional brands of characteristic agricultural products in southwest China, natural geographical resource endowment plays a basic and core role, and business management plays a decisive role in developing a regional brand reputation.

2) Business management had a significant intermediary effect on the corresponding path. As the core driver, it advanced improvements in regional brand reputation. Government support had no significant intermediary effect on the corresponding path, and it had insufficient advancement effects and influence on regional brands. This indicates that market mechanism was the fundamental driver for the formation and development of regional brands, and that although government support is strong, it had no significant effect on improving the influence and reputation of regional brands.

3) Geographical resource endowment and regional culture influenced regional brand reputation through business management. The two factors significantly impacted regional brand reputation through the following paths: "geographical resource endowment - the advantage of business management - regional brand reputation;" "geographical resource endowment - regional culture - the advantage of business management - regional brand reputation," and "regional culture - the advantage of business management - regional brand reputation." Of these, the path of "regional culture - the advantage of business management - regional brand reputation" had the most significant effect.

5.2 Theoretical Contributions

First of all, the current research on branding of agricultural products is relatively rich, but there are few specific researches on branding of agricultural products in Southwest China. In addition, most of the research methods for shaping the path of characteristic agricultural products are theoretical narratives, and empirical tests are rarely used to study the branding of characteristic agricultural products. The research in this article has not only improved the relevant theories of branding, but also deepened the research method system.

Secondly, through the research on the development status of characteristic agricultural products brand in southwest, construct the brand modeling model of characteristic agricultural products and conduct empirical test, research and put forward the development strategy of characteristic agricultural products regional brand. Through the research on the development strategy of regional brand of characteristic agricultural products, it has further enriched the practical guiding value of the mountain characteristic agricultural product brand theory, and provided valuable theoretical reference for the brand development of my country's traditional regional famous and special agricultural product resources.

5.3 Managerial Implications

The research conclusions above lead to the following recommendations for advancing the brand building of characteristic agricultural products.

1) In developing characteristic agricultural products, it is important to follow the principle of taking local materials and adopting measures appropriate for local conditions. Based on marketing requirements, regional comparative advantages should be leveraged to support the adaptation of agricultural product development to the current status of regional economic development. By developing agricultural products with regional characteristics, regions can realize the transformation from "resource advantage" to "brand advantage."

2) Some characteristic agricultural products in southwest China mainly grow in areas with ethnic minorities. Agricultural management should focus on showing the distinctive regional characteristics and cultural connotation of these agricultural products. This lays the foundation for building the brands of national cultural agricultural products, improving their popularity and influence.

3) Scientific management of regional agricultural product brands is crucial to brand building for characteristic agricultural products. Applying the principle of "supporting the advantageous, the strong, the special and the large," the focus should be on building leading backbone enterprises for characteristic agriculture. This involves enhancing their innovative ability, extending the product development chain, and improving the level of deep processing. These support the establishment of scientific management for regional agricultural product brands.

4) Government support creates a good development environment for characteristic agriculture. Guidance and support advance the establishment of characteristic agricultural industry system in ethnic areas. Based on this, regional planning and layouts can be conducted on industrial chains of characteristic agriculture. In turn, characteristic agriculture can be included in the scope of economic development and county planning. This facilitates the establishment of demonstration counties for characteristic agriculture, creating a typical model for development. These may accelerate the formation of a good pattern of competitive development, complementary advantages, and echelon improvement of characteristic agriculture in southwest China.

Acknowledgement. This work was supported in part by the Jointly Funded Project of the Ministry of Commerce of Guizhou Province under Grant [2015] SWBZD20, in part by the Humanities and Social Sciences in Colleges and Universities of Guizhou Education Department Project under Grant 2019dxs008,and in part by the Soft Science Plan Project of Guizhou under Grant Guizhou branch basis [2016] 1530-3.

References

1. Shi, R., Liu, X.: Analysis of regional brand building in the process of enterprise cluster upgrading. J. Enterp. Econ. **30**(5), 40–43 (2011)

2. Shen, P.: Evaluation of regional brand competitiveness of agricultural products based on fuzzy comprehensive evaluation. Stat. Decis. **28**(1), 40–43 (2012)
3. Li, D., Song, L.: Analysis on influential factors of agricultural products regional brand competitiveness. World Agric. **35**(5), 85–90+155 (2013)
4. Tang, K.: Discussion on the methods of tea brand building. J. Tea Fujian **38**(12), 169–170 (2016)
5. Yu, F.: Strategic brand management of agricultural products in China under the new normal. Reformation Strategy **33**(6), 64–66 (2017)
6. Wei, W., Fang, S.: Brand building theory of agricultural products based on life cycle theory. Agric. Econ. **33**(3), 32–34 (2011)
7. Huang, B., Wang, Q.: Countermeasures for brand building of agricultural products-based on the perspective of industrial value chain. Commer. Econ. **38**(3), 62–65 (2019)
8. Hu, Z., Jiang, T.: Analysis on the essential attribute of regional brand. Rural Econ. **28**(5), 89–92 (2010)
9. Jin, M., Zhou, L.: Analysis on country of origin effect of green agri-food and brand strategy. Collected Essays Financ. Econ. **22**(4), 84–90 (2006)
10. Zhang, L., Cai, Q.: Elementary analysis on the influence of regional culture on regional economic development. People's Tribune **22**(2), 88–89 (2013)
11. Xue, G.: Analysis on construction of Chinese agricultural products' regional brand. Res. Agric. Modernization **31**(6), 88–691 (2010)
12. Dong, X.: Regional brand image building and communication strategy of natural resource endowment dependent agricultural products. Commer. Econ. **34**(23), 56–57 (2015)
13. Liu, Y., Song, J.: Brand development strategy of characteristic agricultural products with geographical indication based on the perspective of resources endowment. Northern Hortic. **39**(14), 191–196 (2017)
14. Xu, J., Li, J.: An analysis of regional brand image structure of featured agricultural products based on consumer's perception. Contemp. Financ. Econ. **31**(7), 71–78 (2010)
15. Chen, L.: Discuss on how to use regional characteristic culture to promote the brand construction of regional agricultural products. J.Commer. Econ. **34**(31), 76–77 (2015)
16. Xiao, H., Zhou, Q.: Foreign experience of support system to family farms and its references. Hunan Agric. Univ. (Soc. Sci.) **18**(2), 82–87 (2017)
17. Hu, Z., Wang, Y.: The study on the regional brand formation of agricultural products and its growth pattern. Jiangxi Univ. Financ. Econ. **12**(6), 64–68 (2010)
18. Hu, J., Dong, C.: Government financial subsidies and natural resources industry cluster: an extension for Krugman CP model. Mod. Econ. Sci. **34**(4), 43–48+125 (2012)
19. Li, W., Li, C.: A theoretical model of industrial clusters development and case study in an underdeveloped region-based on the perspective of government support. East China Econ. Manag. **28**(1), 80–84 (2014)
20. Gao, J.: The measurement and empirical analysis of the fluctuation factors of cultural industry investment. Seeker **33**(2), 0233–0235 (2013)
21. Yu, Y., Li, Y.: Research on the formation mechanism of Chinese agricultural cluster of regional brand with traditional characteristic: theoretical construction and empirical analysis—taking Turpan grape clusters as an example. Collected Essays Financ. Econ. **28**(4), 11–18 (2015)
22. Xiong, A., Xing, X.: Place branding and resource endowment: an empirical study. China Popul. Resour. Environ. **28**(4), 167–176 (2017)
23. Allen, G.: Place branding: new tools for economic development. Des. Manag. Rev. **18**(2), 60–68 (2011)
24. Andersson, M.: Region branding: the case of the Baltic Sea Region. Place Branding Public Diplomacy **3**(2), 120–130 (2007)

25. Wang, J., Li, X.: A study on the government behavior of brand integration of regional special agricultural products-take Changbai Mountain Ginseng brand as an example. Issues Agric. Econ. **35**(5), 21–26 (2014)
26. Wang, Y., Hu, N.: Research on the influence channel and function of local government in regional brand development. Theory J. **34**(1), 72–77 (2017)
27. Liu, S., Sun, L.: Current situation of the characteristic agriculture in the minority national ties regions with less population-Taking GongShan county, YunNan as an example. Chin. J. Agric. Resour. Reg. Plan. **36**(6), 136–138+168 (2015)
28. Campelo, A., Aitken, R., Thyne, M., Gnoth, J.: Sense of place: the importance for destination branding. J. Travel Res. **53**(2), 154–166 (2014)
29. Zhang, C.: Research on the development of regional brand of agricultural products. Ph.D dissertation, CAU, Beijing, China (2015)
30. Yuan, C., Li, L., Luo, R., Hu, X.: Research on characteristic agriculture development in SouthEast minority areas of ChongQing. Chin. J. Agric. Resour. Reg. Plan. **31**(3), 70–75 (2010)
31. Klijn, E.H., Eshuis, J., Braun, E.: The influence of stakeholder involvement on the effectiveness of place branding. Public Manag. Rev. **14**(4), 499–519 (2012)
32. Guan, C.: Research on the coordinated management of regional agricultural products brand. Acad. Res. **47**(6), 74–79 (2012)
33. Yan, Y.Yu.: The investigation on the formation mechanism, effect and promotion strategies of regional brand of agriculture products in XinJiang-a case study of Turpan grape brands. Ph.D dissertation, Huzhong Agricultural University Wuhan, China (2015)
34. Chaudhuri, A.: How brand reputation affects the advertising brand equity link. J. Advert. Res. **42**(3), 33–43 (2012)
35. Kaiser, H.F., Rice, J.: Little jiffy, mark IV. Educ. Psychol. Measur. **34**(1), 111–117 (1974)
36. Wu, Y., Wen, Z.: Item parceling strategies in structural equation modeling. Adv. Psychol. Sci. **19**(12), 1859–1867 (2011)

A Simulation-Based Optimization Framework for Online Adaptation of Networks

Stefan Herrnleben[1]([✉])(iD), Johannes Grohmann[1](iD), Piotr Rygielski[2],
Veronika Lesch[1](iD), Christian Krupitzer[1](iD), and Samuel Kounev[1](iD)

[1] University of Würzburg, Würzburg, Germany
{stefan.herrnleben,johannes.grohmann,veronika.lesch,
christian.krupitzer,samuel.lounev}@uni-wuerzburg.de
[2] D4L data4life gGmbH, Potsdam, Germany
piotr.rygielski@data4life.care

Abstract. Today's data centers face continuous changes, including deployed services, growing complexity, and increasing performance requirements. Customers expect not only round-the-clock availability of the hosted services but also high responsiveness. Besides optimizing software architectures and deployments, networks have to be adapted to handle the changing and volatile demands. Approaches from self-adaptive systems can optimize data center networks to continuously meet Service Level Agreements (SLAs) between data center operators and customers. However, existing approaches focus only on specific objectives like topology design, power optimization, or traffic engineering.

In this paper, we present an extensible framework that analyzes networks using different types of simulation and adapts them subject to multiple objectives using various adaptation techniques. Analyzing each suggested adaptation ensures that the network continuously meets the performance requirements and SLAs. We evaluate our framework w.r.t. finding Pareto-optimal solutions considering a multi-dimensional cost model, and scalability on a typical data center network. The evaluation shows that our approach detects the bottlenecks and the violated SLAs correctly, outputs valid and cost-optimal adaptations, and keeps the runtime for the adaptation process constant even with increasing network size and an increasing number of alternative configurations.

Keywords: Network · Modeling · Simulation · Self-adaptation · Optimization

1 Introduction

Modern technologies like cloud computing enable dynamic and flexible allocation of computing and storage resources without requiring the cumbersome booking of dedicated resources in advance [36]. Such technologies enable the dynamic

H. Song and D. Jiang (Eds.): SIMUtools 2020, LNICST 369, pp. 513–532, 2021.
https://doi.org/10.1007/978-3-030-72792-5_41

instantiation of new services and create new opportunities for novel applications. It also supports flexible on-demand scaling of services depending on the workload intensity.

In addition to computing and storage resources, networks also have to be adapted and scaled accordingly to handle the variation of traffic. The performance requirements of a network, like bandwidth or latency, are usually specified in Service Level Agreements (SLAs). Different approaches exist to manage resources and traffic flows in network infrastructures. Examples include Virtual Local Area Networks (VLANs) that support isolation and prioritization of traffic, dynamic routing protocols for determining shortest paths, and Software-defined Networking (SDN) [25] that enables fine granular control of data traffic on a per traffic flow basis. Besides these techniques, sophisticated Quality of Service (QoS) configuration parameters, license upgrades, or hardware changes are valid adaptation approaches for network infrastructures. Configuration of these comprehensive configuration options could be a challenging task with increasing network size and complexity.

Network designers and performance experts can make an educated guess for network optimizations to meet the QoS criteria, but this raises several issues. First, with increasing size and complexity of networks, it is challenging to suggest SLA compliant and cost-optimal solutions, even for experts, and especially to validate them before applying them to a real network. Second, educated guesses might also require hypothetical what-if analyses, which require dedicated measurements or monitoring data. Third, relying on human intervention is generally undesirable due to limitations on availability and time-to-result. Existing recommendation tools for network optimizations either only support a limited set of adaptation operations, cover only specific objectives, or do not verify the adaptations, resulting in a trial and error approach [3,14,44].

In this paper, we propose a framework for network optimization that integrates a network simulation for bottleneck and SLA violation detection and suggests verified network adaptations. A network model is analyzed under a specified workload to obtain information about the performance characteristics of links, interfaces, switches, and nodes. Based on the analysis results, our framework detects bottlenecks and the resulting SLA violations. An iterative MAPE-K adaptation control loop [2] resolves these bottlenecks using objective-oriented strategies and adaptation tactics that ensure that the network complies with current SLAs under given technical constraints. Multiple adaptation tactics are triggered in parallel by a Branch & Bound algorithm [31] to determine the diversity of possible solutions, leveraging different types of adaptations like configuration changes, hardware replacements, or rerouting of flows. Before applying a solution to a real-world network, a simulation verifies the suggested adaptations on the modeled system. The returned solutions all lie on the Pareto-front, i.e., they are all cost-optimal.

The proposed approach enables data center networks to autonomically react and adapt to environmental changes for compliance with a given set of predefined SLAs. The approach furthermore considers costs in multiple dimensions and autonomically selects the cost-optimal solutions. Software-based adaptations, e.g., configuration changes or traffic rerouting, can be applied automatically, without the need for human intervention and before the actual SLA violation occurs.

The remainder of this work is structured as follows. Section 2 discusses related work. Section 3 presents an overview of our framework, the workflow of the used models. Section 4 describes our multi-objective MAPE-K-based adaptation process, which our adaptation framework uses. Section 5 presents and discusses the evaluation results, including two data center network scenarios for effectiveness and scalability investigation. Section 6 addresses aspects of future work. Lastly, Sect. 7 concludes this paper.

2   Related Work

For single-objective problems, a system can be optimized towards the single best solution, but for multi-objective problems (MOPs), the optimization has to deal with several potentially conflicting goals. Consequently, the optimization ends with no clear optimal solution, but the Pareto-front [7] represents a multitude of so-called Pareto-optimal solutions. To handle the optimization of MOPs, several generic approaches exist, such as evolutionary algorithms [13] (e.g., NSGA-II [16] or SPEA2 [27]), scatter search [34], particle swarm optimizers [40], or ant colony optimization [18]. Several frameworks provide generic applicable implementations of optimization techniques, e.g., jMetal [19], Opt4J [32], and ECJ [33] to mention only a few. A recent study on optimization in the field of self-adaptive systems [21] found that self-adaptive systems often integrate generic optimization techniques by customizing the representation of the required information for specific modeling of a specific application, cf. Rainbow [22], hence, reducing the applicability of such an approach. As MOP modeling is an integral part of the optimization, we also pursue domain-specific modeling.

Consequently, the remainder of this section focuses on related work in the two areas of (i) network performance modeling and simulation and (ii) network optimization.

2.1   Network Performance Modeling and Simulation

Existing approaches for network modeling and network performance simulation do not completely integrate both aspects of modeling and simulation. They can be categorized as (i) approaches that focus on simulating the network performance directly and (ii) approaches that generate a model of the network and apply simulation-based evaluation.

Tools from the first category, focusing on simulation, are amongst others, OPNET [12], OpenWNS [8], Georgia Tech Network Simulator (GTNetS) [41], and IKR SimLib [45]. The scope of these tools is simulating large-scale topologies and more complex systems. The widely used approaches OMNeT++ [48], ns-3 [11], CloudSim [10], and DNI [42] belong to the second category and support modeling and simulation.

We chose the Descartes Network Infrastructures modeling language (DNI) [42] as a basis for our work as it provides a fine-grained description of networks, including a detailed performance specification of network interfaces [24]. The generic modeling approach allows the definition of custom protocol stacks and an autonomous traffic pattern extraction from real networks. The modular design of DNI supports multiple exchangeable simulation tools like OMNeT++ or SimQPN [29]. SimQPN is a discrete event simulator based on stochastic modeling and analysis of Queueing Petri Nets (QPNs) [4] and is already used in other modeling languages for self-adaptive software systems, for modeling of Java EE applications [28] , and message-oriented event-driven systems [43]. We use and extend DNI to specify the network structure, its configuration, the traffic patterns, and the adaptation points.

2.2   Network Optimization

In the literature, several network optimization approaches focus on the design-time optimization of network topology [1,14,38], energy efficiency [44], or network virtualization [39]. However, as our approach deals with the optimization of networks at runtime, we focus on runtime approaches. The identified related approaches can be classified into three categories: (i) service placement, (ii) power optimization, and (iii) traffic optimization.

The service placement approach optimizes the number of deployed services, for example, by using linear programming [9]. Approaches optimizing power consumption, for example, by turning off as many unneeded network components as possible, use greedy bin packing algorithms or linear programming for rerouting and placement optimization [20,46,50]. The third category of traffic optimization enhances the bandwidth, traffic flow distribution, or link utilization by using Markov Chain approximations [26], bin packing heuristics [6], CPLEX [47], or linear programming [5].

Although many of the approaches validate their suggested changes, these validations are often based on simple analytical models that are only suitable for a small range of applications. Existing simulative approaches are often too complex, which might violate runtime constraints for complex scenarios. However, a validation of the adaptation on the model level is useful; otherwise, the changes would have to be applied to a real network to obtain further information about additional bottlenecks and to determine whether all objectives are fulfilled. Our approach uses a feedback loop combined with network simulation to evaluate and improve the optimization plan without the need to execute the changes on a running network. Furthermore, existing approaches focus on specific objectives while our approach provides multiple adaptation tactics to cover possible alternative approaches for ensuring the fulfillment of multiple objectives. These tactics, as well as further objectives, can be easily extended.

3   Approach

This section provides an overview of our network adaptation approach, including the input models, the applied concepts MAPE-K and Branch & Bound, the underlying adaptation techniques, and the output models. Our adaptation approach pursues the following objectives and quality criteria:

- Bottleneck detection: Bottlenecks are identified and localized through network analysis.
- Model-based: The adaptation process integrates a model of the network, which enables analysis without influencing the real network.
- Online network adaptation: A network and its current state can be monitored and adapted in an autonomic manner at runtime.
- Validation: The suggested solutions are validated based on an analysis for each adaptation.
- Multi-objective: The adaptation considers multiple objectives and executes different adaptation tactics with various solution approaches (such as rerouting, reconfiguration, or hardware change).
- Efficient: Bounding mechanisms filter non-optimal branches to reduce the number of analyses.
- Extendable: New adaptation tactics can be easily added.
- Multiple solutions: Pareto-optimal solutions taking into account the multi-dimensional costs model.

The network optimization requires a *network modeling language* to define the network structure, the network configuration, and the workload. To analyze the network, i.e., to determine the utilization and detect the bottlenecks, a *network analysis* is used, which has to support the chosen network modeling language. Replacing the network modeling language and the analysis is easy due to the design of our network optimization approach. Depending on the selected network modeling language, both simulative and analytical methods can be used.

3.1   Input Models

The adaptation process requires several input models, which are depicted on top of Fig. 1 and are introduced in the following. We refer the interested reader to [23] for a detailed specification of the respective meta-models.

The *network model* describes the network structure, its configuration, and the current workload. The *structure* captures the topology of the network, which includes physical and virtual nodes, the connections between them, the network interfaces, and the performance descriptions of all entities. The *configuration* defines the initial routes for the traffic flows as well as the used protocols and protocol stacks. The *workload* describes all flows between the nodes and specifies the type of flow as well as their source, destination, size, and temporal behavior. For the network model, we chose the *Descartes Network Infrastructures Modeling Language* (DNI) [42]. Existing adapters allow simulating a DNI network

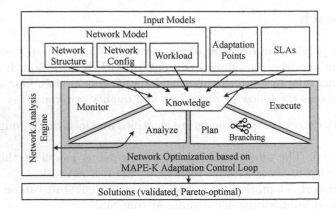

Fig. 1. Abstract illustration of network optimization algorithm.

model by OMNeT++ [49] or SimQPN [29]. Although our current implementation bases on DNI, the framework's modularly design allows integrating other network modeling languages. The interchangeability also applies to the analysis component, i.e., simulation or analytical method.

The *adaptation points* define the valid alternative components such as nodes, links, and components within the network model. This model also specifies the alternative configuration parameters, performance specifications and settings for the components. The adaptation points further describe the costs for component replacement or configuration changes. The multi-dimensional cost model can capture several cost aspects like downtime, handling time, or the total cost of ownership (TCO).

The *Service Level Agreements (SLAs)* contain the agreed performance characteristics (e.g., minimum bandwidth guarantees) between the customers and the network operator. The SLAs' objectives are bound to a specific link, switch, network interface, flow, or combination of them. The goal of network optimization is to fulfill all objectives.

3.2   Adaptation Process: MAPE-K

There are two challenges when eliminating a bottleneck in a network: On the one hand, the effect of a configuration change or a replacement cannot be fully predicted. On the other hand, eliminating a bottleneck can result in an additional bottleneck at another location, so-called bottleneck shifting. Through the integration of a *MAPE-K control loop*, the effects of changes can already be detected on the model, without being applied to the real network, and if necessary improved in further iterations. Therefore, the proposed control loop in Fig. 1 solves the aforementioned challenges.

The four phases of the MAPE-K adaptation control loop **M**onitor, **A**nalyze, **P**lan, and **E**xecute as well as the **K**nowledge base are integrated by our approach as follows: The *monitoring phase* uses the network model as an input parameter to capture the current network structure, configuration, and workload. These data are passed to the *analysis phase*, which triggers the network analysis, depicted on the left side of Fig. 1. The analysis determines the used bandwidth, utilization, latency, and packet loss of nodes, including their components such as backplanes and interfaces, as well as links. These performance characteristics are used to localize the bottlenecks and to identify the violated objectives. The analysis result and the violated objectives are passed to the subsequent *planning phase* to determine operations that could eliminate the bottlenecks. The possible adaptation operations are derived from the domain knowledge and the provided adaptation points. If there are several, more performant options available for one parameter, e.g., alternative backplane speeds, the cost-optimal solution is chosen first. Branching supports the exploration of several solutions. The suggested adaptation operations are integrated into an adaptation plan, which is passed to the execution phase. The *execution phase* applies the scheduled adaptation operations to the network model so that the changed network can be analyzed again by the loop in the next iteration. If all bottlenecks have been eliminated by the scheduled operations, the proposed adapted network model is valid and is output. Otherwise, further adaptations will be applied in subsequent iterations. The *knowledge base* contains the defined SLAs and the adaptation points, as well as other user constraints and configuration parameters. As depicted in Fig. 1, the knowledge base is accessible from all MAPE phases.

After one or several possible solutions are found, these proposed operations can be executed on a real-world network. If the adaptation operations can be executed in an automatic manner, such as changing configuration parameters or rerouting, they can be passed to a network management software API or, in case of *Software-defined Network (SDN)* to an SDN controller [25]. Manual changes can be forwarded to network operators.

The whole adaption process can be triggered continuously or event-based to react to changes in workloads, network structure, or configuration. Using forecasted workloads [51] allows a proactive adaptation or what-if analysis.

3.3   Adaptation Process: Branch and Bound

Sometimes it cannot be predicted if a particular operation will eliminate the bottleneck. Due to the multiple cost dimensions, there may be several cost-optimal solutions. To address this challenge, our adaptation framework employs a *Branch & Bound* algorithm to track different adaptation operations in parallel [37]. This algorithm explores different solution candidates if it is unclear which solution strategy will be most cost-optimal. For example, to increase the bandwidth, the algorithm will explore a branch of upgrading a network interface and explore another branch to replace the whole switch. Solutions that do not improve the system or violate constraints are bounded to limit the number of tracked branches.

3.4   Output Models

Adaptation plan models are used to describe the required adaptation on a network. Depending on the number of valid solutions, one or a set of adaptation plans are output. They represent the delta between the original network state and the desired one. An adaptation plan defines the replacement of entities like entire nodes or just individual components, the change of configuration parameters, or the modification of routes in a descriptive manner.

Depending on the validation status, different terminologies are used for the solutions identified in our network optimization algorithm:

– *Solution candidates* are network models that have not yet been validated w.r.t. SLA compliance. Further adaptations may be necessary on the model or it may be discarded later.
– *Solutions* are network models for resolving the SLA violations. The solutions are validated by analysis while at the same time ensuring that they do not violate filter criteria (bounding).
– *Cost optimal solutions* are solutions that are cost-optimal in terms of representing the Pareto-front.

The adaptation framework outputs a set of solutions with the following properties. First, the solution resolves all SLA violations, even if created by bottleneck shifting (verified by analysis). Second, they are cost-optimal and represent the Pareto-front concerning the multi-dimensional cost model.

4   Adaptation Process

This section describes the adaptation process of the multi-objective network optimization, based on the MAPE-K adaptation control loop with Branch & Bound (cf. Sect. 3.3). The process of the adaptation is separated into multiple modules (see Fig. 2). This section describes each of these modules.

4.1   Analysis

The purpose of the analysis module is to analyze the network model, including the workload to determine, among other things, the utilization and throughput of components as well as packet loss and waiting times. To take the previously scheduled adaptations into account, the adaptation plan, which is empty in the first iteration, is applied to the network model. This adapted network model is analyzed through simulative or analytical methods, depending on the used network modeling language. The analysis is invoked as an external module, as depicted in Fig. 2, which is not in the scope of our network optimization. Instead of the current workload, predicted workloads can be used for proactive adaptation of the network for adjusting to future demands. Customized network models for what-if analysis, e.g., changes in the network structure or additional customers, are also supported. The result of the analysis is passed to the underlying SLA violation detection.

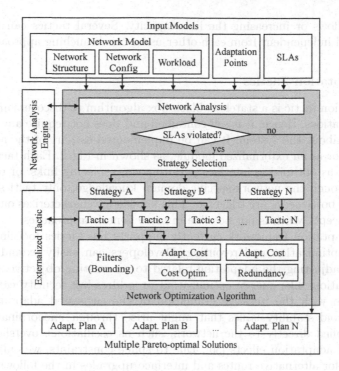

Fig. 2. Network optimization algorithm with the steps analysis, SLA violation detection, branching, and bounding.

4.2 SLA Violation Detection

The SLA violation detection module receives the results from the network analysis and uses the provided SLAs to determine if objectives are violated. If all objectives are fulfilled, the process outputs the current adaptation plan as no further adaptations are necessary. If all objectives are already fulfilled in the first iteration, this represents the trivial case in which the adaptation plan is empty, and the network complies with all SLAs without the need for adaptations. If the module detects an SLA violation, the objective, and the associated bottleneck are marked for adaptation and are passed to the next module, the strategy selection (cf. Fig. 2).

4.3 Branching Through Strategies and Tactics

The strategy selector chooses a high-level goal, i.e., an adaptation strategy, by evaluating the violated objectives identified in the SLA violation detection. If multiple strategies can resolve a bottleneck, all of them are started independently by branching, as shown in Fig. 2. For each of these strategies, several adaptation tactics exist. Those are specific algorithms to reach the goal. For example, a bottleneck on an overloaded link can be handled either by rerouting one of the respective flows or increasing the link capacity. Several tactics can be run in parallel and independent from each other using our branching approach.

4.4 Adaptation Tactics

An adaptation tactic is a stateless, black-box algorithm to discover suitable network adaptations. Hence, it is self-contained and does not require any historical knowledge about the system. It can be implemented as part of the adaptation framework or as an externalized module, as shown in Fig. 2. Each tactic has its scope, such as optimizing interface performance, replacing links, or optimizing routes. Through the network-specific domain knowledge, only tactics that can remedy the bottlenecks are triggered. This knowledge characterizes our domain-specific concept, which is not possible in more generic approaches.

Our adaptation framework currently supports ten tactics focusing on performance optimization and rerouting. Developers can easily extend them by improving/adjusting the adaptation-related to an existing objective, or adding new adaptations like energy optimization or addressing security concerns. In combination with the iterative evaluation of the suggested adaptations, this helps to avoid stability issues that might arise through uncoordinated adaptations applied directly to the network, such as oscillations, overshooting, or damping of adaptation effects [30]. Due to space constraints, we only describe the tactics for alternative routes and interface upgrades in the following. Other tactics can be found in the implementation given in our Git repository[1].

Alternative Routes. Rerouting is particularly useful in data centers where alternative paths exist that are intended for load-balancing purposes. In contrast to existing flow optimization algorithms, our approach tries to minimize the number of changed routes. We use the Dijkstra algorithm to search for alternative routes [17]. The Dijkstra algorithm is a greedy algorithm and searches in its native version the shortest path between two nodes. Although a network is already a graph with nodes and edges, the Dijkstra algorithm cannot be applied directly on the network, as it does not consider the capacities of interfaces and nodes. To take this into account, each entity is transformed into one input and one output graph node in a preprocessing step. The algorithm of the rerouting tactic removes flows that should not be rerouted from the graph, and the capacities of the other links are reduced by the bandwidths of these flows to avoid a bottleneck shifting. The Dijkstra shortest-path algorithm is then executed for every flow on the overloaded link, and one or multiple candidate solutions are passed to the next module.

Interface Upgrade. This tactic addresses the replacement of network interfaces. The upgrade of an interface can either be hardware-based for physical nodes or software-based for virtual machines or SDN. Examples for physical replacements are *small form-factor pluggables (SFPs)*, which are frequently used

---

[1] https://gitlab2.informatik.uni-wuerzburg.de/descartes/dni-adaptation.

in network devices to connect fiber optic cables. This tactic leverages the bottleneck determined by the SLA violation detection, to identify the interface, which should be upgraded. A separate adaptation process is initiated for each interface representing a bottleneck, identified by the SLA violation detection. The adaptation points model defines the valid alternative interfaces and configuration parameters that are compatible with the containing device. As a replacement, the most cost-effective, performance-optimizing interface is selected first. If the performance optimization is not sufficient yet, further optimization occurs in the next iteration of the MAPE-K adaptation control loop. Additionally, if there is no uniquely cost-optimal or performance-optimal solution, the tactic creates a branch for each possibility and returns all potential solutions.

4.5 Bounding Through Filters

The filter module receives the adaptation plans from the tactics, which are all tracked in independent branches. Sometimes branches are generated which are redundant, exceed cost limitations, are not cost-optimal, or violate user constraints. To save computation time and increase the efficiency of the adaptation process, the filter module bounds (i.e., cuts) such branches, as intended by the Branch & Bound algorithm. Figure 2 shows the four stages of this module. In the following, this section briefly describes them.

Adaptation Count Bounding. To avoid a complete redesign of the network which usually increases downtime and risk of errors, this filter removes branches that exceed the specified limit of adaptation operations to ensure that network optimization is applied with manageable effort.

Cost Constraint Bounding. This filter removes branches that exceed a specified limit for at least one cost dimension. Since the tactics select the most cost-effective adaptations, a branch that exceeds the cost limit can be safely removed, as the costs of this branch can only increase in subsequent iterations.

Cost Optimization Bounding. If multiple branches are tracked in parallel, some branches can become irrelevant once cost-optimal solutions are found on other branches. This filter module bounds branches exceeding the costs in all dimensions compared to an already found solution.

Redundancy Eliminator. By branching several times in repeated iterations, different branches can result in the same adaptation operations. Since identical branches lead to the same results in further iterations, this filter discards branches with redundant adaptation plans.

Adaptation plans, which are not bounded in the filter module, are passed to the next iteration of the adaptation process, as shown in Fig. 2. This is repeated until a valid solution is discovered, no further possible adaptations are found, or the solution is bounded later.

4.6   Solutions

The adaptation process discovers all cost-optimal (Pareto-optimal) solutions. To apply the computed adaptations, these solutions do not represent an adapted network model; instead, solutions simply consist of adaptation plans, i.e., a list of adaptation operations to be performed on the network. This makes it easier to interpret and to apply in practice. By applying these adaptation operations on the network model, the resulting network model can be generated. The solutions have the following three characteristics: (i) Every solution is validated through analysis and fulfills the SLA. (ii) Every solution is cost-optimal, and the set of all solutions represents the Pareto-front. (iii) Every solution does not exceed the specified amount of adaptation operations and does not exceed the defined cost limits in any dimension.

5   Evaluation

We evaluated our framework w.r.t. different qualitative and quantitative aspects. Section 5.1 validates our network adaptation process that the found *Pareto-optimal* solutions resolve the bottlenecks, i.e., no further SLA violations exist, and are cost-optimal. Section 5.2 presents an analysis of the scalability of our approach within an example network model with cascaded adaptation operations. Section 5.3 summarizes the results of the evaluation and discusses their applicability.

All experiments are executed on a notebook with an Intel i7-7500U CPU with 2.7 GHz and 16 GB RAM. The used operating system is Windows 10 64-Bit, running an OpenJDK 11.0.2.

5.1   Pareto-Optimality and Performance

The adaptation framework outputs cost-optimal solutions representing the Pareto-front [15,19]. This is particularly important since the multi-dimensional cost model can provide several most favorable solutions for different cost dimensions. Depending on a weighting function, the most appropriate solution is selected for applying it to the respective real-world network. Our framework focuses only on cost-optimized solutions through our objective-oriented approach, the sophisticated bounding mechanism, and several filters. This is especially important since every further solution candidate is analyzed and leads to a longer duration for the overall process.

In this evaluation, we investigate the aspects of: (i) finding all Pareto-optimal solutions and (ii) the performance gain of our optimized algorithm compared to a brute-force approach. For this experiment, we use a small network consisting of 9 nodes, 8 links, and 20 alternative configurations. They possible adaptations are annotated by costs that are partly specified in opposite ways, which means that some are preferred for a low investment and others for short handling time. This leads to several best solutions, depending on the weights of the cost dimensions.

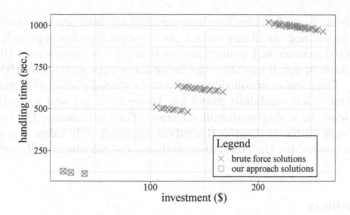

Fig. 3. Pareto front generated by the optimized adaptation process compared to solutions, generated by a brute-force approach. The results of the brute-force approach are depicted as red crosses and the results of our optimized adaptation are depicted as blue squares. (Color figure online)

Table 1. Comparison between brute-force and our approach regarding solutions, solution candidates, and runtime.

Observed metric	Brute-force	Optimized approach
Cost-optimal solutions	3	3
Solutions	231	3
Solution candidates	3190	10
Overall duration (sec.)	6379	24

We executed the experiment in two different setups. In the first setup, the network is adapted by our optimized approach with objective-oriented strategies, smart selection of alternative configurations, and bounding after introducing the artificial bottleneck. A second setup uses a brute-force approach to explore all possible adaptations and find all valid solutions as a baseline. The use of the brute-force algorithm ensures that all solutions are found, therefore especially including all cost-optimal ones.

Figure 3 depicts all returned solutions from both setups. The x-axis presents the cost dimension of the investment, while the y-axis shows the cost dimension of handling time. As the brute-force algorithm outputs all found solutions – which is a significantly higher number than the number of solutions that our optimization approach outputs – it also contains all cost-optimal solutions. Our approach only returns three solutions. However, it can be concluded from Fig. 3 that these are the three cost-optimal solutions.

Table 1 shows a comparison between the brute-force and our optimized approach. We validated in Fig. 3 that both approaches return all three cost-optimal solutions. The brute-force approach identified 231 solutions. However, taking the focus on of our cost objective into account, 228 of them are non-optimal solutions, and hence, not useful in practice. As our optimization approach works in a goal-oriented manner and bounds useless branches, it creates only 10 solution candidate models, much less than the brute-force approach with 3190 solution candidates. The number of solution candidates especially affects the algorithm's run-time, since each candidate model has to be analyzed and a small number of models leads to a shorter overall duration. For that reason, the brute-force approach takes 6379 s, and our optimization approach only takes 24 s, including the time necessary for the simulative analysis, for calculating all cost-optimal solutions.

5.2   Scalability

Data center networks typically consist of a vast amount of nodes and links. While Sect. 5.1 only considers a small network topology due to the execution of the time-intensive brute-force run, this section focuses on the scalability aspect of our adaptation algorithm. An addition to the previous section, the selected scenario requires multiple subsequent adaptations to remedy the violated SLAs.

The considered network, depicted in Fig. 4, represents a fat-tree topology commonly used in data centers. It consists of two core switches on the top, access and edge switches on the subsequent layers, and at least some servers with VMs. We consider each pair of access and edge switches and two servers with VMs as one block. The core switches are independent of the number of blocks. The initial setup contains one block; more blocks will be added later during the evaluation. As each block consists of 6 nodes and the number of core switches is independent, the number of overall nodes can be derived from the number of blocks as follows:

$$|nodes| = 2 + 6 \cdot |blocks| \tag{1}$$

The notation $|x|$ is taken from graph theory and describes the number of elements x, e.g., $|nodes|$ means the amount of *nodes*. Each block adds 10 links to the network, 6 within the block, and 4 links to the core switches. Therefore the number of links can be derived from the number of blocks as follows:

$$|links| = 10 \cdot |blocks| \tag{2}$$

For each link, six alternative bandwidths are specified in the adaptation points by replacing the cable or reconfiguration. Furthermore, each switch can be replaced by three alternatives. As the number of nodes and links increases with the network size, the number of adaptation points also increases, which can be determined by the following formula:

$$|adaptationpoints| = 6 \cdot |links| + 4 \cdot (|nodes| - 2 \cdot |blocks|) \tag{3}$$

The relationship between the number of blocks, nodes, links, and adaptation points is depicted in the first four columns of Table 2.

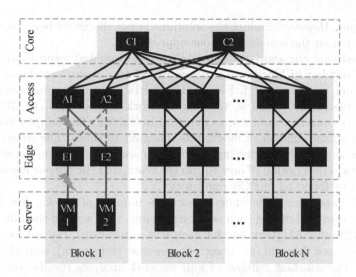

Fig. 4. Network used for the scalability evaluation.

Table 2. Runtime of our adaptation process considering increasing network sizes.

Blocks	Nodes	Links	Adap.points	Bran.	Anal.	Bound.bran.	Sol.	Adaptation (mean)	Process (sd)
1	8	10	84	5	4	2	2	0.693 s	0.108 s
5	32	50	388	5	4	2	2	0.695 s	0.120 s
10	62	100	768	5	4	2	2	0.715 s	0.130 s
20	122	200	1528	5	4	2	2	0.547 s	0.145 s
30	182	300	2288	5	4	2	2	0.690 s	0.105 s
40	242	400	3048	5	4	2	2	0.547 s	0.256 s
50	302	500	3808	5	4	2	2	0.792 s	0.446 s

Adap. points = number of adaptation points; Bran. = number of generated branches; Anal. = number of executed analysis, i.e., simulations; Sol. = number of returned solutions

Figure 4 illustrates the scenario for the scalability evaluation: VM1 initiates a transmission of a 20 GB file to VM2. Initially the flow is routed over the red path, from VM1 over E1-A1-E2 to VM2. In the network, the links between VM1 and E1 as well as between E1 and A1 represent bottlenecks, denoted by the lightning symbol in Fig. 4. These bottlenecks may be caused either by links with insufficient bandwidth or through the impacts of other flows. To remedy the bottleneck between VM1 and E1, a link upgrade is the only feasible adaptation operation defined in the adaptation points. The second bottleneck between E1 and A1 can either be resolved by another link upgrade or by bypassing the insufficient link using the blue dashed path from E1 over A2 to E2. The resulting two possible solutions are: (i) link upgrades from VM1 to E1 and from E1 to A1, or (ii) one link upgrade from VM1 to E1 and rerouting the flow over the blue dashed path (E1-A2-E2). The adaptation framework correctly determines the two solutions. However, finding the solutions is not discussed here, as we focus in this section on the scalability of our approach.

To investigate our approach's scalability, the presented setup is adjusted by a variable number of blocks, each consisting of two access switches, two edge switches, and two servers (cf. Fig. 4). The initial network contains one block, and more blocks are added so that the network sizes of 1, 5, 10, 20, 30, 40, and 50 blocks can be examined, as depicted in Table 2. The adaptation of each setup with a fixed number of blocks was repeated 10 times. The source code of our adaptation framework, the input models, a script for running the scalability experiments, a description of how to run the tests, and the output measurement results can be found on our Git repository[2].

Table 2 shows that independent from the number of blocks, five branches have been generated during each adaptation runs, representing the link upgrade between VM1 and E1 (two; one for each cost dimension), the subsequent link upgrade between E1 and A1 (two; one per cost dimension), and the parallel rerouting. The constant number of four network analyses results from the initial analysis, the analysis after the first link upgrade between VM1 and E1, and the final analysis of the two solutions. In each of the runs, two branches are bounded by the redundancy eliminator. This number results from the parallel tracked cost-efficient solutions, which finished in identical adaptation plans and therefore, could be eliminated. Table 2 shows that the required time for the adaptation process is constant, independent from the network size and the number of adaptation points, and varies between 0.547 and 0.792 s.

5.3 Discussion

In Sect. 5.1, our adaptation process was compared to an approach determining all solutions via brute-force. We purposefully chose a small example network for this experiment, as the time-consuming brute force approach made the evaluation of bigger networks infeasible. Even with this network size, it becomes clear how important the reduction to the relevant solutions is. Although the chosen brute force solution represents a lower baseline, it shows clearly the applicability of our adaptation approach as it finds all cost-optimal solutions only within a few iterations by objective orientation and domain knowledge.

The evaluation of scalability in Sect. 5.2 shows that our approach performs well, even on increasing network sizes and an increasing number of adaptation points. Due to the target-oriented approach, the size of the network beyond the bottleneck does not matter, so that the number of branches, analyses, and truncated branches remains constant. This also applies to the adaptation time, which remains constant on a wide-scaled network. The required time for the adaptation process is below 0.8 s for all investigated network sizes. In cases of physical changes, which require human hands-on, this time is negligible. Given a self-adaptive autonomic environment, the time for the adaptation is acceptable compared to, e.g., flow rule installation time in SDN switches [35].

---

[2] https://gitlab2.informatik.uni-wuerzburg.de/descartes/dni-adaptation.

The evaluation does not consider the time required to analyze the network. This depends on the used method (simulative or analytical) and the chosen network modeling language. Our ongoing research includes comparing the experiments presented in this paper with results using different network modeling approaches and a variety of different network analysis approaches. These results can be utilized to analyze different modeling approaches and/or to compare the performance of different analysis methods.

6 Future Work

As future work, we aim to extend our framework with tactics concerning the placement and movement of virtual network functions (VNFs) and virtual machines (VMs) of data centers. This enables our framework to actively organize the flow of network traffic in order to optimize network performance. A further direction could be to develop an adapter to connect our optimization framework to a real data center network. This enables the fully autonomous management of the network concerning software changes (e.g., SDN flow rerouting, reconfigurations) using our approach. Our multi-dimensional cost-model will become useful as we can associate different changes with different types of costs (e.g., investment cost, required working hours, expected downtime, network stability). In combination with other advanced monitoring and forecasting techniques, our approach will also be able to warn and possibly even proactively react to performance issues before they appear in the network.

7 Conclusion

To continuously meet the requirements in changing environments with frequently changing demands, networks have to be adapted at runtime. Several approaches exist for the adaptation and optimization of networks, however, these either focus on design-time or are limited to a single objective. In this paper, we present a multi-objective adaptation framework for the online adaptation of networks through different adaptation techniques. A MAPE-K adaptation control loop enables iterative adaptations until all SLAs are met. Branch & Bound tracks different solutions and filters useless solution candidates at an early stage.

The strategies and tactics consider the objectives to only trigger meaningful adaptation operations w.r.t. to the violated SLA. Adaptation tactics use network-specific domain knowledge for choosing alternative configurations. Additional adaptation tactics can be easily added. Each solution candidate is analyzed to provide only SLA compliant solutions. The resulting solutions are all cost-optimal and represent the Pareto-front.

A comparison to a brute force approach shows that all cost-optimal solutions are found, where the simulation ensures the correctness. An additional scenario demonstrates the subsequent execution of adaptation operations and identifies a constant adaptation time even on large networks and an increasing number of adaptation points.

Acknowledgements. This work was funded by the German Research Foundation (DFG) under grant No. (KO 3445/18-1). Special thanks to our student Pascal Fries, who assisted us with the implementation and evaluation of the alternative route adaptation tactic.

References

1. Ahn, J.H., Binkert, N., Davis, A., McLaren, M., Schreiber, R.S.: HyperX: Topology, Routing, and Packaging of Efficient Large-Scale Networks. In: Proceedings of the Conference on High Performance Computing Networking, Storage and Analysis, pp. 1–11 (November 2009)
2. Arcaini, P., Riccobene, E., Scandurra, P.: Modeling and analyzing MAPE-K feedback loops for self-adaptation. In: 2015 IEEE/ACM 10th International Symposium on Software Engineering for Adaptive and Self-Managing Systems, pp. 13–23. IEEE (2015)
3. Bari, M.F., et al.: Data center network virtualization: a survey. IEEE Commun. Surv. Tutorials **15**(2), 909–928 (2013)
4. Bause, F.: Queueing Petri Nets-A formalism for the combined qualitative and quantitative analysis of systems. In: Proceedings of 5th international workshop on Petri nets and performance models, pp. 14–23. IEEE (1993)
5. Benson, T., Anand, A., Akella, A., Zhang, M.: The Case for Fine-Grained Traffic Engineering in Data Centers. In: INM/WREN (2010)
6. Benson, T., Anand, A., Akella, A., Zhang, M.: MicroTE: fine grained traffic engineering for data centers. In: 7th CoNEXT. ACM (2011)
7. Buchanan, J.M.: The relevance of pareto optimality. J. Conflict Resolut. **6**(4), 341–354 (1962)
8. Bültmann, D., Mühleisen, M., Klagges, K., Schinnenburg, M.: OpenWNS-open Wireless Network Simulator. In: European Wireless Conference, EW. IEEE (2009)
9. Farooq Butt, N., Chowdhury, M., Boutaba, R.: Topology-awareness and Reoptimization Mechanism for Virtual Network Embedding. In: Crovella, M., Feeney, L.M., Rubenstein, D., Raghavan, S.V. (eds.) NETWORKING 2010. LNCS, vol. 6091, pp. 27–39. Springer, Heidelberg (2010). https://doi.org/10.1007/978-3-642-12963-6_3
10. Calheiros, R.N., Ranjan, R., Beloglazov, A., De Rose, C.A., Buyya, R.: CloudSim: a toolkit for modeling and simulation of cloud computing environments and evaluation of resource provisioning algorithms. Softw. Pract. Exp. **41**(1), 23-50 (2011)
11. Campanile, L., Gribaudo, M., Iacono, M., Marulli, F., Mastroianni, M.: Computer network simulation with ns-3: a systematic literature review. Electronics **9**(2), 272 (2020)
12. Chen, M., Miao, Y., Humar, I.: OPNET IoT Simulation. Springer Nature, Singapore (2019)
13. Coello, C.A.C., Lamont, G.B., Van Veldhuizen, D.A., et al.: Evolutionary Algorithms for Solving Multi-objective Problems, vol. 5. Springer, New York (2007)
14. Curtis, A.R., Carpenter, T., Elsheikh, M., López-Ortiz, A., Keshav, S.: Rewire: An Optimization-based Framework for Unstructured Data Center Network Design. In: INFOCOM. IEEE (2012)
15. Datta, S., Das, S.: Multiobjective support vector machines: handling class imbalance with pareto optimality. IEEE Trans. Neural Netw. Learn. Syst. **30**(5), 1602–1608 (2018)

16. Deb, K., Pratap, A., Agarwal, S., Meyarivan, T.: A fast and elitist multiobjective genetic algorithm: NSGA-II. IEEE Trans. Evol. Comput. **6**(2), 182–197 (2002)
17. Dijkstra, E.W.: A note on two problems in connexion with graphs. Numerische Mathematik **1**(1), 269–271 (1959)
18. Dorigo, M., Di Caro, G.: Ant colony optimization: a new meta-heuristic. In: Proceedings of the 1999 Congress on Evolutionary Computation-CEC99 (Cat. No. 99TH8406), vol. 2, pp. 1470–1477. IEEE (1999)
19. Durillo, J.J., Nebro, A.J., Alba, E.: The jMetal framework for multi-objective optimization: Design and architecture. In: IEEE Congress on Evolutionary Computation, pp. 1–8. IEEE (2010)
20. Fang, W., Liang, X., Li, S., Chiaraviglio, L., Xiong, N.: VMPlanner: optimizing virtual machine placement and traffic flow routing to reduce network power costs in cloud data centers. Comput. Netw. **57**(1), 179–196 (2013)
21. Fredericks, E.M., Gerostathopoulos, I., Krupitzer, C., Vogel, T.: Planning as optimization: dynamically discovering optimal configurations for runtime situations. In: Proceedings of the 13th IEEE International Conference on Self-Adaptive and Self-Organizing Systems, SASO 2019, IEEE (June 2019)
22. Garlan, D., Cheng, S.W., Huang, A.C., Schmerl, B., Steenkiste, P.: Rainbow: architecture-based self-adaptation with reusable infrastructure. Computer **37**(10), 46–54 (2004)
23. Herrnleben, S.: Model-Based Network Analysis and Optimization. Master Thesis, University of Wuerzburg (2017)
24. Herrnleben, S., Rygielski, P., Grohmann, J., Eismann, S., Hossfeld, T., Kounev, S.: Model-based performance predictions for SDN-based networks: a case study. In: Proceedings of the 20th International GI/ITG Conference on Measurement, Modelling and Evaluation of Computing Systems. MMB 2020 (March 2020)
25. Jarschel, M., Zinner, T., Hoßfeld, T., Tran-Gia, P., Kellerer, W.: Interfaces, attributes, and use cases: a compass for SDN. IEEE Commun. Mag. **52**(6), 210–217 (2014)
26. Jiang, J.W., Lan, T., Ha, S., Chen, M., Chiang, M.: Joint VM placement and routing for data center traffic engineering. In: INFOCOM, vol. 12 (2012)
27. Kim, M., Hiroyasu, T., Miki, M., Watanabe, S.: SPEA2+: improving the performance of the strength pareto evolutionary algorithm 2. In: Yao, X. (ed.) PPSN 2004. LNCS, vol. 3242, pp. 742–751. Springer, Heidelberg (2004). https://doi.org/10.1007/978-3-540 30217-9_75
28. Kounev, S.: Performance modeling and evaluation of distributed component-based systems using queueing petri nets. IEEE Trans. Software Eng. **32**(7), 486–502 (2006)
29. Kounev, S., Buchmann, A.: SimQPN–a tool and methodology for analyzing queueing Petri net models by means of simulation. Perform. Eval. **63**(4–5), 364–394 (2006)
30. Lalanda, P., McCann, J.A., Diaconescu, A.: Autonomic Computing. Springer, New York (2013)
31. Lawler, E.L., Wood, D.E.: Branch-and-bound methods: a survey. Oper. Res. **14**(4), 699–719 (1966)
32. Lukasiewycz, M., Glaß, M., Reimann, F., Teich, J.: Opt4J - a modular framework for meta-heuristic optimization. In: Proceedings of the Genetic and Evolutionary Computing Conference (GECCO 2011), pp. 1723–1730. Dublin, Ireland (2011)
33. Luke, S.: Ecj then and now. In: GECCO (Companion), pp. 1223–1230 (2017)
34. Martí, R., Laguna, M., Glover, F.: Principles of scatter search. Eur. J. Oper. Res. **169**(2), 359–372 (2006)

35. Nguyen-Ngoc, A., Lange, S., Geissler, S., Zinner, T., Tran-Gia, P.: Estimating the flow rule installation time of SDN switches when facing control plane delay. In: 19th International GI/ITG MMB Conference. Erlangen (2 2018)
36. Pawar, C.S., Wagh, R.: A review of resource allocation policies in cloud computing. World J. Sci. Technol. **2**(3), 165–167 (2012)
37. Przybylski, A., Gandibleux, X.: Multi-objective branch and bound. Eur. J. Oper. Res. **260**(3), 856–872 (2017)
38. Qiu, T., Li, B., Qu, W., Ahmed, E., Wang, X.: TOSG: A topology optimization scheme with global small world for industrial heterogeneous Internet of Things. IEEE Trans. Industr. Inf. **15**(6), 3174–3184 (2018)
39. Qu, L., Assi, C., Shaban, K.: Delay-aware scheduling and resource optimization with network function virtualization. IEEE Trans. Commun. **64**(9), 3746–3758 (2016)
40. Reyes-Sierra, M., Coello, C.C., et al.: Multi-objective particle swarm optimizers: a survey of the state-of-the-art. Int. J. Comput. Intell. Res. **2**(3), 287–308 (2006)
41. Riley, G.F.: Simulation of large scale networks II: large-scale network simulations with GTNetS. In: Proceedings of the 35th Conference on Winter Simulation: Driving Innovation. Winter Simulation Conference (2003)
42. Rygielski, P., Seliuchenko, M., Kounev, S.: Modeling and prediction of software-defined networks performance using queueing petri nets. In: Proceedings of the Ninth International Conference on Simulation Tools and Techniques (SIMUTools 2016) (August 2016). http://dl.acm.org/citation.cfm?id=3021426.3021437
43. Sachs, K., Kounev, S., Buchmann, A.: Performance modeling and analysis of message-oriented event-driven systems. Soft. Syst. Model. **12**(4), 705–729 (2013)
44. Sofi, I.B., Gupta, A., Jha, R.K.: Power and energy optimization with reduced complexity in different deployment scenarios of massive MIMO network. Int. J. Commun. Syst. **32**(6), e3907 (2019)
45. Sommer, J., Scharf, J.: IKR Simulation Library. In: Wehrle, K., Güneş, M., Gross, J. (eds.) Modeling and Tools for Network Simulation. Springer, Berlin https://doi.org/10.1007/978-3-642-12331-3_4 (2010)
46. Tajiki, M.M., Salsano, S., Chiaraviglio, L., Shojafar, M., Akbari, B.: Joint Energy Efficient and QoS-aware Path Allocation and VNF Placement for Service Function Chaining. In: IEEE TNSM (2018)
47. Tso, F.P., Pezaros, D.P.: Improving data center network utilization using near-optimal traffic engineering. IEEE Trans. Parallel Distrib. Syst. **24**(6), 1139–1148 (2013)
48. Varga, A.: A practical introduction to the OMNeT++ simulation framework. In: Virdis, A., Kirsche, M. (eds.) Recent Advances in Network Simulation. Varga, A.: A practical introduction to the OMNeT++ simulation framework. In: Recent Advances in Network Simulation, pp. 3–51. Springer (2019), pp. 3–51. Springer, Cham (2019). https://doi.org/10.1007/978-3-030-12842-5_1
49. Varga, A., Hornig, R.: An Overview of the OMNeT++ Simulation Environment. In: SIMUtools 2008. ICST (Institute for Computer Sciences, Social-Informatics and Telecommunications Engineering), ICST, Brussels, Belgium, Belgium (2008). http://dl.acm.org/citation.cfm?id=1416222.1416290
50. Wang, L., Zhang, F., Vasilakos, A.V., Hou, C., Liu, Z.: Joint virtual machine assignment and traffic engineering for green data center networks. SIGMETRICS Perform. Eval. Rev. **41**(3), 107–112 (2014)
51. Züfle, M., et al.: Autonomic Forecasting Method Selection: Examination and Ways Ahead. In: Proceedings of the International Conference on Autonomic Computing (ICAC), pp. 167–176 (2019)

Accelerating Spectrum Sharing Algorithms for Cognitive Radio Transmitters in a Momentum Q-Learning Approach

Lianghui Zhu, Zhanke Zhou, Zhaochuan Peng, and Xiaojun Hei[✉]

Huazhong University of Science and Technology, Wuhan 430074, China
{unrealluver,zhankezhou,pengzc,heixj}@hust.edu.cn

Abstract. The radio frequency spectrum is a scarce resource and cognitive radio has been under heavy research to improve the utilization of spectrum in the past thirty years. It is crucial to optimize the performance of cognitive radio for high values for practical applications while it has turned out to be very technically challenging. The conventional cognitive radio methods have strong pertinence and coupling because they are generally designed for a specific application environment. To address the problem of spectrum sharing with collision avoidance mechanisms in cognitive radio, in this paper we propose a new momentum-based Q-learning algorithm to accelerate reinforcement learning based spectrum sharing algorithms for cognitive radio transmitters. We conduct a performance evaluation study based on a simulation toolkit for the reinforcement learning research and the ns-3 network simulator "ns3-gym". As a demonstrating case study, the proposed algorithm is able to capture the learnable patterns from a periodic channel occupation in a wireless environment and avoid channel collision effectively, finally improving channel efficiency and reducing the end-to-end time delay. The simulation results demonstrated that our proposed momentum Q-learning algorithm achieves a lower collision rate, faster convergence as well as stronger generalization capacity compared with two conventional algorithms including a greedy algorithm and a deep Q-learning network algorithm.

Keywords: Reinforcement learning · Cognitive radio · Spectrum sharing

1 Introduction

In the past decades, wireless communication technologies have been rapidly developed and widely applied, and various wireless communication devices compete for spectrum resources. However, spectrum resources have not been fully

L. Zhu, Z. Zhou and Z. Peng—These authors contributed equally to this work.

© ICST Institute for Computer Sciences, Social Informatics and Telecommunications Engineering 2021
Published by Springer Nature Switzerland AG 2021. All Rights Reserved
H. Song and D. Jiang (Eds.): SIMUtools 2020, LNICST 369, pp. 533–547, 2021.
https://doi.org/10.1007/978-3-030-72792-5_42

utilized, and only a small part of them are frequently used [6]. Cognitive radio has been proposed as one of the effective approaches to improve the utilization of spectrum resources, which utilizes the idle spectrum for dynamic network access and data transmission, to achieve transmission in a crowded spectrum space and improve the spectrum utilization [10]. Nevertheless, it is very technically challenging and has high values for practical applications to optimize the performance of cognitive radio. The traditional network access methods (e.g. carrier-sense multiple access (CSMA)) are not able to obtain the wireless environment information and effectively adapt to the changing channels, which are prone to collisions, and finally, increase the end-to-end time delay.

In the cognitive wireless network system proposed by [13], based on the cognitive characteristics, through information processing and artificial intelligence, the perception, decision-making, resource allocation and network reconstruction of the network can be enabled. A close internal logical relationship that exists between the four parts. In this architecture, cognitive wireless networks can sense, perceive and learn the states of network environments, make intelligent decisions, fine-tune the configurations and change the behaviors of nodes and network adaptively, to achieve intelligent optimizations of the network performance.

Reinforcement learning (RL) enables software agents take actions for a changing network environment in order to maximize the cumulative reward. With the rapid development of artificial intelligence algorithms, reinforcement learning has been playing an increasingly important role in computer networking and outperforming traditional control schemes in terms of performance and efficiency. In this paper, we study the optimization issues of Q-learning algorithms for spectrum sharing in cognitive radio networks. Our main contributions are summarized as follows:

(1) We propose a new momentum Q-learning based spectrum sharing algorithm for cognitive radio transmitters to accelerate the convergence and accuracy.
(2) We conduct a simulation study to evaluate the performance of the spectrum sharing algorithms based on ns3-gym [4] which utilizes the OpenAI Gym in the ns3 simulator in various wireless scenarios.

The rest of the paper is organized as follows: we the briefly review the related work in industry and academia in Sect. 2, followed by our algorithm design in Sect. 3. We present the simulation-based performance evaluation results in Sect. 4. Finally, we conclude the paper in Sect. 5.

2   Related Work

In this section, we review the representative work on spectrum sharing and reinforcement learning.

2.1   Spectrum Sharing

Wireless networks have become increasingly crowded [3]. Cognitive radio provides a promising technical approach to relieve the channel deficiency with frequency reuse [2] to improve spectrum utilization. The nonorthogonal multiple access (NOMA) has been proposed to improve transmission efficiency and minimize the overall delay with jointly optimizing computation offloading and communication [15]. An analytical study has shown that that, whether the connection-based access outperforms the packet-based access in spectrum utilization, crucially depends on the sensing capability of nodes [1]. Deep learning algorithms have been studied to improve spectrum efficiency in recent years. Deepika Rajpoot [11] proposed to optimize the frequency search algorithm for secondary users accessing to primary users in the NOMA cognitive radio networks, and finally to obtain the optimal detection time and maximum throughput to improve spectrum efficiency. In the dynamic channel access (DSA), Kassab et al. proposed a multi-agent deep deterministic policy gradient (MADDPG) learning algorithm based on the channel access event [5]. These algorithms are designed to avoid collisions and transmit redundant information, and adequately utilize the time and device-level correlation of monitored events and devices, respectively.

2.2   Reinforcement Learning

Wu et al. proposed a cognitive radio based on a reinforcement learning algorithm to divide channel users into main users and cognitive users [14]. Lo et al. proposed a collaborative awareness method, reinforcement learning cooperative sensing (RLCS), based on reinforcement learning to reduce the collaboration cost in cognitive radio ad-hoc networks and improve the collaboration gain [7].

In recent years, reinforcement learning has attracted extensive research attention. In WiFi networks, the traditional CSMA protocol may cause serious performance degradation due to the inconsistent protocols used by different nodes. Yu et al. proposed an efficient and fair channel sharing protocol (CS-DLMA) based on reinforcement learning [17]. The experiments show that CS-DLMA can effectively improve various performance metrics such as throughput. Especially in WiFi scenarios, CS-DLMA achieves higher Pareto than CSMA. The standardization of telecommunication protocols may take a long time. With more devices entering the network, a unified and efficient protocol framework becomes a major trend in the future. Valcarce and Hoydis introduced reinforcement learning into the formulation and standardization of communication protocols [12], by using the signals transmitted between devices as an incentive channel, so that the model may effectively deploy the best channel access strategy in cellular networks, and saves costs of the manual formulation and the protocol standardization. In addition, the reinforcement learning has shown portability in more unknown scenarios [12,17].

In addition to the theoretical feasibility, simulation frameworks have been proposed to foster reinforcement learning algorithms in ns-3 [4,16]. A large number of research studies have aimed at the fairness of spectrum sharing. In this paper, we study the optimization issues of reinforcement learning algorithms for spectrum sharing based on an ns-3 based simulation study.

3   Algorithm Design

In this section, we first illustrate the spectrum sharing problem between primary users and secondary users in cognitive radio networks. Then, we present a greedy algorithm and a deep Q-learning network algorithm as benchmark algorithms for addressing the spectrum sharing problem. To accelerate reinforcement learning based spectrum sharing algorithms for cognitive radio transmitters, we propose a new momentum-based Q-learning algorithm. We present the algorithm implementations and the ns3-gym simulation framework. Based on the ns3-gym framework, we instrument the network environment of the reinforcement learning agents and the ns-3 simulator.

3.1   Problem Statement

For the sake of simplicity, we assume that a cognitive radio network consists of 4 primary users (PU), 1 secondary user (SU), and 1 base station. PUs and SUs are able to share the same spectrum and communicate with the base station. Nevertheless, cognitive radio ensures that PUs are allocated to the available channels with preemptive priorities over SUs in that if there are idle channels in the wireless link, SUs can still utilize the spectrum for their data transmission. We consider special cases in that these 4 PUs periodically 4 channels, and the SU aims to utilize idle channel resources for transmission. As illustrated in Fig. 1, an intelligent agent is deployed to sense the entire channel utilization and then select the idle channel time slots for the SU to transmit its data.

We propose how to sense the idle channel time slots and design RL algorithms to learn the periodic patterns by PUs and evaluate the proposed algorithms based on ns-3 simulation experiments, so as to reduce the probability of collisions, improve the channel utilization, and finally achieve a better spectrum sharing strategy in cognitive radio. To compare the performance of RL algorithms, we deploy a greedy algorithm and a deep Q-learning network algorithm as benchmark.

3.2   Greedy Algorithm

In the greedy algorithm, a centralized channel intelligent assembles all information from the network. The occupied channel at the $(N-1)$th time step is defined as the state of Nth time step, and the transmitter takes the action in selecting an idle channel for its data transmission at the Nth time step. In our experiment settings, the greedy algorithm transmitter will be given a specific state-action table for that scene, in which we preset values for the transmitter to choose the best channel. Then, based on the principle of maximizing the value, the transmitter selects the best channel from the highest value to the lowest value

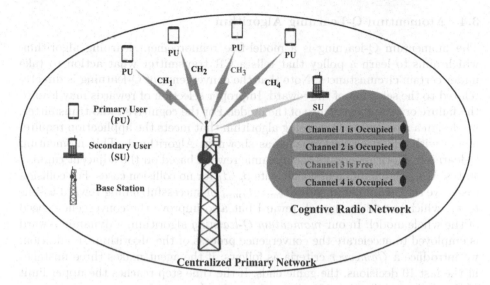

Fig. 1. Spectrum sharing between primary users and secondary users in cognitive radio networks

following the state-action corresponding table, to determine the final channel selection. The channel selection decision is determined based on the prepared state-action corresponding table. The advantages of the greedy algorithm are fast speed and low computational complexity, but the channel selection may not be optimal. The disadvantage of this greedy algorithm is that it relies heavily on the state-action table tailored for specific network environments.

3.3 Deep Q-Learning Network Algorithm

Q-learning is a representative reinforcement learning method which is to construct a control strategy to optimize the algorithm performance. For a cognitive radio transmitter, the Q-learning agent perceives and processes collision information from the network environment. The Q-learning transmitter agent can tune its parameters and change its behaviors by learning, to produce the transmit choice of cognitive radio. The transmit choice makes the agent choose a channel, and then impact the environment.

We intuitively apply a deep Q-learning network (DQN) algorithm for a cognitive radio transmitter [4] with the following parameter mapping from reinforcement learning to cognitive radio application scenarios. For a fair performance comparison, we assign the same set of parameters of our proposed momentum Q-learning algorithm as presented in Sect. 3.4.

The *Observation* represents the occupied channel corresponding to the previous time step which reflects the holistic state of the network, while the *Action* denotes selecting the channel for the next time step to transmit data. The *Reward* is defined as a positive reward that is given if there is no collision; otherwise, a negative reward.

3.4   Momentum Q-Learning Algorithm

The momentum Q-learning is a model-free reinforcement learning algorithm, which aims to learn a policy that tells a CR transmitter what action to take under certain circumstances. Note that the convergence of Q-learning is directly related to the selection of the reward. Improper selection of rewards may lead to the failure or slow convergence of the model. For the cognitive radio transmitter, we design a momentum Q-learning algorithm that meets the application requirements with enhanced performance as shown in Algorithm 1. This momentum Q-learning algorithm adopts the dynamic reward based on the adjacent running states. We assign 2 different coefficients β_s/β_f for no collision cases. For collision cases, we set the minimum value t_{smin}/t_{fmin} of successful/failing reward tokens t_s/t_f, which provide a smooth reward but also improve the convergence speed of the whole model. In our *momentum Q-learning* algorithm, a dynamic reward is employed to accelerate the convergence process of the algorithm. In addition, we introduce a *Gameover* criteria as follows: if the agent makes three mistakes in the last 10 decisions, the game ends. If the time step reaches the upper limit of simulation verification 100 times, the game also ends.

The algorithm details are stated as follows: Q-learning needs to rely on the Q-table to judge when selecting channels. If the number of channels is M, then Q-table is a $M \times M$ matrix. The corresponding values in the Q-table characterize the probability of selecting the corresponding action based on a specific observation. For example, $Q(2,3)$ is the probability that Channel 2 is occupied at the $(n-1)$th time step, and the transmitter selects Channel 3 at the nth time step. First, the Q-table is initialized to 0. In each episode, the network environment states are sensed, and the successful token and failed token are set to 0. At the beginning of each step, the action with the largest value in the Q-table is selected as the channel selected by the transmitter according to the greedy strategy, and the corresponding channel is selected and the feedback from the network environment is received. Then, the successful token and failed token are updated based on this feedback. If there is no collision, the successful token t_s is multiplied by the coefficient $\beta_s \in (t_{smin}, t_{smax})$; the failed token t_f is multiplied by the coefficient $\beta_f \in (t_{fmin}, t_{fmax})$. If the collision occurs, the successful token is reset to $t_s = t_{smin}$ and the failed token is reset to $t_f = t_{fmin}$. Then, the sum of the above two tokens is regarded as the reward r, and the state s' is predicted. Then, the Q-table is updated with $Q(s,a) \leftarrow Q(s,a) + \alpha[r + \gamma max_{a'}Q(s',a') - Q(s,a)]$, and s is updated to s'. If the step reaches the default value of 100 for the maximum number of steps in the experiments or there are at least 3 collisions in the last 10 time steps, the episode is regarded as the end. We configure the experiment duration to last for 200 episodes if not explicitly specified.

3.5   Simulation Framework

We deploy an ns-3 layer to simulate the interaction between the RL agents and the network environment. The *timestep* represents the incremental change in time. We study two cases of the periodic channel usage patterns by the primary

---

Algorithm 1. The momentum Q-learning algorithm for the cognitive radio transmitter.

Input: State(s): The occupied channel in the $(N-1)$th time step.

Input: Channel collision status: if the channel which the transmitter selects at the $(N-1)$th time step occurs collision.

Output: Action(a): The channel the transmitter selects in the Nth time step.

1: Initialize $Q(s,a)$ by zero.
2: **repeat**(for each episode):
3:    Get initial state(s) from the network environment.
4:    Initialize successful token $t_s \leftarrow 0$ and failed token $t_f \leftarrow 0$.
5:    **repeat**(for each step of episode):
6:       Choose action(a) from state using ϵ-greedy policy from Q.
7:       Take actions, and pass it to the network environment:
8:       **if** no collision **then**
9:          $t_s \leftarrow min(t_s * \beta_s, t_{smax})$.
10:          $t_f \leftarrow min(t_f * \beta_f, t_{fmax})$.
11:       **else**
12:          $t_s \leftarrow t_{smin}$.
13:          $t_f \leftarrow t_{fmin}$.
14:       **end if**
15:       Get reward $r \leftarrow (t_s + t_f)$, and predict state s'.
16:       $Q(s,a) \leftarrow Q(s,a) + \alpha[r + \gamma max_{a'}Q(s',a') - Q(s,a)]$.
17:       $s \leftarrow s'$.
18:    **until** The time steps equal to 100 or 3 collisions occur in the latest 10 time steps.
19: **until** through each episode

---

users in the cognitive radio network as shown in Fig. 2. With the progress of time steps, 4 PUs occupied the channels periodically in order from Channel 1 to 4. The brown blocks represent the occupied channel time slots by the primary users at this time point and the white blocks indicate the idle time slots.

Figure 3 is depicted to illustrate a sample path of the channel usage of the CR transmitter. After the reinforcement learning agent makes a decision in selecting a channel, the SU uses this channel for data transmission in the current time step. We use the blue block to mark the selected idle channel time slot by the RL agent. If the RL agent selects occupied channel time slots by the primary users, those time slots are marked as red in Fig. 3(a), which is plotted as a demonstrating case for the periodic channel usage pattern by the primary users in case 1. In this example, among the total 60 time slots the SU utilizes, 14 time slots experience collisions for case 1. Given the same sample path of the 60 time slots selected by the SU, 17 time slots experience collisions for case 2 as shown in Fig. 3(b). The RL agent aims to minimize the probability of red blocks by learning the periodic pattern by PUs and selecting those idle time slots in this example.

As shown in Fig. 4, the ns3-gym simulation framework consists of three parts: the ns-3 network model, OpenAI Gym, and the reinforcement learning agent. The ns-3 network model provides us a basic network simulation environment that builds the cognitive radio network and statistic functions. The middle layer,

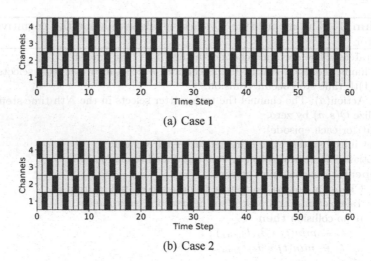

(a) Case 1

(b) Case 2

Fig. 2. Periodic channel usage patterns by the primary users in the cognitive radio network

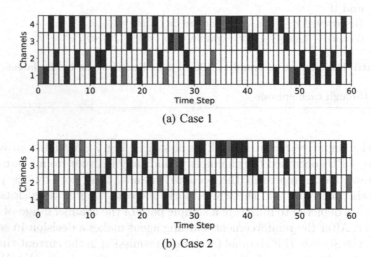

(a) Case 1

(b) Case 2

Fig. 3. A sample path of the channel usage of the CR transmitter with collisions

OpenAI Gym, plays an important role in the middle-ware to integrate the reinforcement learning agent and the simulated network environment. This layer passes the actions that the RL agent launches to the network environment and return the reactions of the network to the reinforcement learning layer. In this way, we are capable to deploy the reinforcement learning agent at the top layer to implement decision-making on the low layer. Exactly in this layer, we deploy the deep Q-learning network algorithm and the proposed momentum-based Q-learning algorithm.

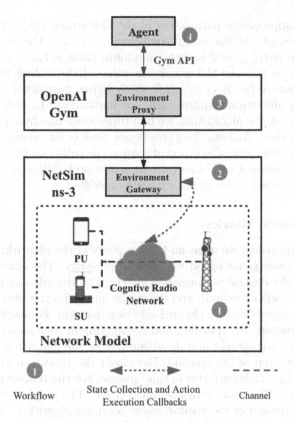

Fig. 4. The ns3-gym simulation framework for spectrum sharing by the cognitive radio transmitter

4   Performance Evaluation

We conduct a simulation study of the proposed momentum Q-learning based channel sharing algorithm for the cognitive radio transmitters. In this section, we present the simulation results to evaluate the performance of the proposed momentum Q-learning algorithm against a greedy algorithm and a deep Q-learning network algorithm.

4.1   Simulation Setup

With the manual tuning of the hyper parameters of the proposed MQL algorithm, we recommend the following parameters utilizing ns3-gym in our simulation. We control the wireless network environment following the suggested settings in ns3-gym. The stochastic gradient descent (SGD) is used as the optimizer of the deep reinforcement learning algorithm. We find that the deep Q-learning rate may lead to reliable performance while it is set as 0.001. For the proposed momentum Q-learning algorithm, we set the exploration rate to 0.3 to keep the ability to seek appropriate parameters in the Q-learning table. To improve the performance, we set the successful coefficient $\beta_s = 1.1$, the maximum of the successful token is $t_{smax} = 2$ and the minimum value is $t_{smin} = 0$. The failing coefficient is $\beta_f = 0.9$ and the maximum value of the failing token is $t_f = 0$ and the minimum value is $t_f = -2.5$. Each hyper parameter of the momentum Q-learning algorithm requires skills for fine-tuning. In order to maximize the performance of the algorithms, we fine-tuned only one hyper parameter via debugging each time. At last, the *Disturbance Bias* is introduced in our experiments to simulate the potential errors of sensing the collisions in that the network channel will be assigned with a certain deviation probability at other channels. This probability is set as 5% if not explicitly specified.

4.2   Performance Metrics

In our simulation study, we focus on three aspects of the algorithms: generalization capacity, convergence speed and time complexity. The convergence of the algorithms are the central performance metric. The default x-axis in the result figures is the episode by default, and the y-axis quantifies the time step, in which the transmitter agents make a channel selection decision. For each algorithm, we continuously simulate 200 episodes, and the maximum time step of each episode is 100 steps. The advantages and disadvantages of the algorithm are characterized by the time step of the episode. The closer the time step approaches 100, the better the algorithm performs in this episode. For the reinforcement learning algorithm, there will be an extra backward curve. The reward curve represents the cumulative reward of the reinforcement learning algorithm in each episode. It captures the learning performance that the reinforcement learning algorithm achieves for multiple episodes.

4.3   Simulation Results

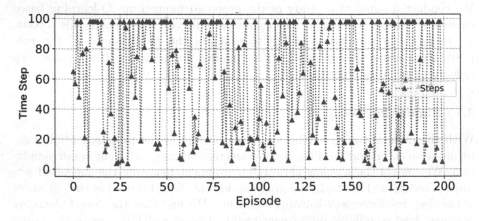

Fig. 5. The performance of the greedy algorithm with disturbance bias in case 1

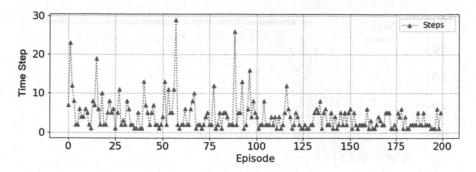

Fig. 6. The performance of the greedy algorithm with disturbance bias in case 2

Algorithm Generalization. As shown in Fig. 5, the greedy method has lots of episodes with over 100 steps, indicating that the greedy algorithm made the transmitter could achieve the whole transmit process well. We use different cases to perform different application environments. We assume the situation showed in Fig. 2 is case 1, and case 2 adopt a totally different periodic channel usage pattern by primary users. Given a state-action corresponding table designed for the case 1 in advance, the transmitter will make a corresponding greedy selection through the value given in the table. It has strong pertinence because it is generally designed for a specific application environment which brings strong coupling to its system. Although it is easy for the greedy algorithm to achieve considerable results for a specific networking environment, such as case 1, it will end up with a poor effect (see Fig. 6) when the environment fluctuates or changes to case 2 as shown in Fig. 2(b). However, for both case 1 and case 2, reinforcement learning is able to construct the most appropriate state-action table from the current environment because it does not need to set the state-action table in advance. We select the most representative case 1 environment to conduct more experiments to evaluate DQN and MQL. The representative experimental results are depicted in Fig. 7 and Fig. 8. From the time step curves, we observe that the adaptive trend of the reinforcement learning algorithm for the changing network environment gradually improves.

Convergence Speed. Following the experiments in ns3-gym [4], we adopt a deep Q-learning network algorithm with a one-hidden-layer neural network for training. Obtaining the training effect as shown in Fig. 7. In the meantime, we design a momentum Q-learning algorithm as presented in Sect. 3.4. The adaptive reward helps us learn the features more quickly in Fig. 8. From both time and reward curves, we observe that the DQN algorithm converges at about 70-th episodes but the momentum Q-learning algorithm convergence much faster in the 20-th episode and achieves better performance. After convergence, the steep curve of sustains at 100 steps, and the reward curve also maintains at a high level. The performance of the momentum Q-learning algorithm is stable, and finally, we can harvest the highest reward.

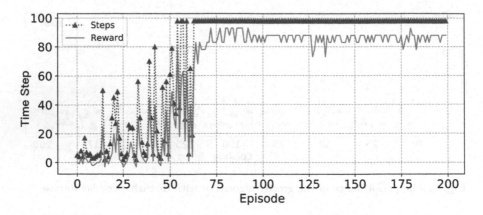

Fig. 7. The performance of the deep Q-learning network algorithm with disturbance bias

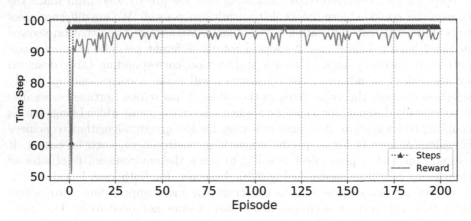

Fig. 8. The performance of the momentum Q-learning algorithm with disturbance bias

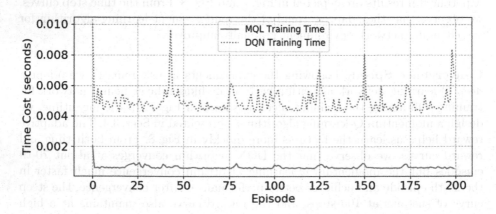

Fig. 9. Training time: momentum Q-learning v.s. DQN

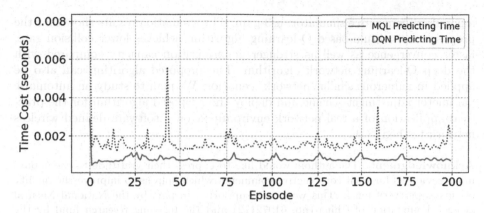

Fig. 10. Predicting time: momentum Q-learning v.s. DQN

Time Complexity. As shown in Fig. 9 and Fig. 10, we apply "MQL Training/Predicting Time" to represent the training average time-cost of training step of each episode with the momentum Q-learning algorithm, and "DQN Training/Predicting Time" for the deep Q-learning network algorithm. The x-axis depicts each episode of the algorithm episode, and the y-axis indicates the time consumed in seconds. The momentum Q-learning average predicting time is only half of deep Q-learning, the average training time of each step is only 1/5 of that of DQN and the curves' fluctuation range of MQL will be smaller, more stable, and there will be no significant fluctuation changes. The training time and the predicting time of the momentum Q-learning is far less than that of deep Q-learning, and more stable too. In summary, in the actual application scenarios, we recommend the momentum Q-learning algorithm for the cognitive radio transmitter to achieve lower judgment delay and training time cost in this way.

Discussions. The reason for the difference in convergence speed and time is mainly due to the backward update mode and the parameter number of DQN and MQL. For DQN, the number of parameters includes the parameters in the neural network, which makes the total number of parameters required is the number of network parameters. If we want to improve the effectiveness of the model and increase the depth of the network, these parameters will increase. MQL only needs the number of M^2 Q-table parameters. Assume we have M channels in the environment, plus a constant number of momentum reward control parameters. The number of parameters is fewer, and the reward with momentum ensures that MQL requires less training time and achieves faster convergence speed.

5   Conclusion

In this paper, we presented a momentum-based Q-learning based spectrum sharing algorithm for cognitive radio transmitters to ensure effectiveness and applicability. We conducted a simulation based performance evaluation study based on a popular open-source simulator, ns3-gym. The simulation results show that the proposed momentum-based Q-learning algorithm achieves lower collision rate, faster convergence as well as stronger generalization capacity compared with the deep Q-learning network algorithm. The proposed algorithm can also be applied in numerous similar network scenarios. We plan to study an automatic parameter adjustment scheme and deploy the proposed algorithm for the practical application of a real network environment on a software defined wireless network testbed [8,9].

Acknowledgment. The authors would like to express their gratitude to the anonymous reviewers for their constructive comments which help us to improve the quality of this paper very much. This work was supported in part by the National Natural Science Foundation of China (no. 61972172) and the teaching research fund by the Huazhong University of Science and Technology (no. 2018077).

References

1. Gao, Y., Dai, L.: Random access: packet-based or connection-based? IEEE Trans. Wirel. Commun. **18**(5), 2664–2678 (2019)
2. Gao, Y., Roy, S.: Achieving proportional fairness for LTE-LAA and Wi-Fi coexistence in unlicensed spectrum. IEEE Trans. Wirel. Commun **19**(5), 3390–3404 (2020)
3. Gao, Y., Dai, L., Hei, X.: Throughput optimization of multi-BSS IEEE 802.11 networks with universal frequency reuse. IEEE Trans. Commun. **65**(8), 3399–3414 (2017)
4. Gawłowicz, P., Zubow, A.: Ns-3 meets OpenAI Gym: the playground for machine learning in networking research. In: Proceedings of the 22nd International ACM Conference on Modeling, Analysis and Simulation of Wireless and Mobile Systems, pp. 113–120 (2019)
5. Kassab, R., Destounis, A., Tsilimantos, D., Debbah, M.: Multi-agent deep stochastic policy gradient for event based dynamic spectrum access (2020). arXiv
6. Leibovitz, J.S.: The great spectrum debate: a commentary on the FCC spectrum policy task force's report on spectrum rights and responsibilities. Yale J. Law Technol. **6**, 390–414 (2003)
7. Lo, B., Akyildiz, I.: Reinforcement learning for cooperative sensing gain in cognitive radio ad hoc networks. Wirel. Netw. **19**, 1237–1250 (2012)
8. Manzoor, S., Chen, Z., Gao, Y., Hei, X., Cheng, W.: Towards QoS-aware load balancing for high density software defined Wi-Fi networks. IEEE Access **8**, 117623–117638 (2020)
9. Manzoor, S., Yin, Y., Gao, Y., Hei, X., Cheng, W.: A systematic study of IEEE 802.11 DCF network optimization from theory to testbed. IEEE Access **8**, 154114–154132 (2020)
10. Mitola, J., Maguire, G.Q.: Cognitive radio: making software radios more personal. IEEE Pers. Commun. **6**(4), 13–18 (1999)
11. Rajpoot, D.: Sensing-throughput analysis in NOMA-based CR network (2020). arXiv
12. Valcarce, A., Hoydis, J.: Towards joint learning of optimal signaling and wireless channel access (2020) arXiv

13. Wei, J.B., Wang, S., Zhao, H.T.: Cognitive wireless networks: key techniques and sate of the art. Tongxin Xuebao/J. Commun **32**, 147–158 (2011)
14. Wu, C., Chowdhury, K., Di Felice, M., Meleis, W.: Spectrum management of cognitive radio using multi-agent reinforcement learning. In: Proceedings of the 9th International Conference on Autonomous Agents and Multiagent Systems: Industry Track, pp. 1705–1712. International Foundation for Autonomous Agents and Multiagent Systems, Richland (2010)
15. Wu, Y., Qian, L.P., Ni, K., Zhang, C., Shen, X.: Delay-minimization nonorthogonal multiple access enabled multi-user mobile edge computation offloading. IEEE J. Sel. Topics Signal Process. **13**(3), 392–407 (2019)
16. Yin, H., et al.: NS3-AI: fostering artificial intelligence algorithms for networking research. In: Proceedings of the 2020 Workshop on Ns-3, pp. 57–64 (2020)
17. Yu, Y., Liew, S.C., Wang, T.: Non-uniform time-step deep Q-network for carrier-sense multiple access in heterogeneous wireless networks. IEEE Trans. Mob. Comput. (2020)

Artificial Fish Swarm Algorithm-Based Sparse System Estimation

Si Zhang, Dan Li$^{(\boxtimes)}$, Lulu Bei, Kailiang Zhang, and Ping Cui

Xuzhou University of Technology, Xuzhou 221000, Jiangsu, China

Abstract. In this paper, the estimation of Doppler-distorted underwater acoustic (UWA) channels is investigated. The UWA channels are characterized by severe multipath spread and significant Doppler effects, and can be well modeled as a multi-scale multi-lag (MSML) channel. Furthermore, exploiting the sparsity of UWA channels, MSML channel estimation can be transformed into the estimation of parameter sets (Doppler scale factor, delay, amplitude). Based on this, orthogonal matching pursuit (OMP) algorithm has been widely used. But the estimation accuracy of OMP depends on the size of the dictionary and finer resolution requires higher computational complexity. Thus, this paper proposes a new method called improved artificial fish swarm algorithm (IAFSA), for the UWA channel estimation. Different from basic AFSA, IAFSA proceeds in an iterative manner to separate multipath and will adaptively adjust fish's positions and step during each sub-iteration, thus can achieve fine resolution and fast convergence. The performance of the IAFSA is evaluated by various numerical simulations, including channels generated by BELLHOP. The simulation results show that IAFSA outperforms OMP algorithm in both estimation accuracy and computational complexity.

Keywords: Sparse system estimation · Artificial fish swarm algorithm · Underwater acoustic channel · Doppler spread

1 Introduction

Underwater acoustic (UWA) channels [1–3] pose grand challenges for reliable high data-rate communications, due to significant Doppler effects [4, 5] and severe multipath spread. In underwater communications [6–8], acoustic waves propagate at 1500 m/s, much lower than 3×10^8 m/s, the speed of electromagnetic wave in terrestrial wireless systems. Thus, the motion of platform will cause more significant Doppler effects, which is expressed as signal compressing or dilating in time domain and can be treated as Doppler scale [9]. And the multipath spread is formed by exhaustive reflections in underwater environment. For the low propagation speed of acoustic waves, multipath spread results in long time delay and severe inter-symbol interference (ISI). To fully understand the channel characteristics and overcome challenges it poses, accurate channel models and estimation methods are essential to investigate.

As observed in many experiments [10–12], signals from different paths will experience different Doppler scale, arrive at different time and have different energy, and

H. Song and D. Jiang (Eds.): SIMUtools 2020, LNICST 369, pp. 548–561, 2021.
https://doi.org/10.1007/978-3-030-72792-5_43

the received signal will be a superposition of these signals. So the multi-scale multi-lag (MSML) channel, denoted in [13] can well model acoustic channel and has been adopted in many researches [11, 14–16]. In MSML channel model [17, 18], each path can be parameterized by Doppler scale factor, time delay and amplitude. However, for severe multipath spread, this model will be too complex to estimate. To overcome such difficulty, many researchers investigated the sparsity of UWA channel [19–21], that is, most of the energy is concentrated in some small regions. So only a few channel taps in MSML channel [22] model are nonzero and need to be tracked. As a result, the computational complexity has been reduced and many sparse channel estimation algorithms based on compressed-sensing (CS) have been proposed [11, 23–28].

These algorithms can be generally grouped in two categories: dynamic programming like matching pursuit (MP), and linear programming like basis pursuit (BP) [11, 29, 30]. BP aims at the minimization which needs high computational complexity, thus is less attractive for practical large-scale applications. Therefore, we will mainly focus on MP algorithm and its successors.

In [23], MP algorithm is applied to estimated Doppler scale factors of different paths. It iteratively selects one column from the dictionary that is most relevant with the residual signal, and subtract the estimated path component to update the residual signal. Compared with MP, it's orthogonal version, orthogonal matching pursuit (OMP) algorithm [24, 31–33] makes the residual signal be orthogonal with all the selected columns, thus has better convergence speed and accuracy. [11, 25, 26] compares the traditional subspace methods and CS-based methods for channel estimation, and concludes that CS- based methods have better performance. Meanwhile, some improved algorithms, which focus on adaptively estimating path numbers, like sparsity adaptive matching pursuit (SaMP) [27]and adaptive step size SaMP (AS-SaMP) [28] have been applied to sparse channel estimation. Furthermore, some references propose methods to reduce computation: [34, 35] proposes a two-stage OMP algorithm, which estimates the Doppler scale factor and time delay respectively, rather than simultaneously as OMP does. But it requires some preprocessing before channel estimation. [36] analyzes that fast Fourier transform (FFT) [37, 38] can be utilized in OMP to simplify calculation. But the reduction is limited as it only focuses on the computing process rather than on the reducing of column dimensions in the dictionary.

Therefore, the main limitation of MP algorithm and its successor is that the estimation accuracy depends on the size of the dictionary. To guarantee a fine resolution, the number of columns in the dictionary could be extremely large [39]. Thus, calculating inner product of received signal and each column sequentially as MP algorithm does leads to extensive calculation, especially for UWA channel, where the delay-scale spread is large. To overcome this difficulty, this paper proposes a novel algorithm called IAFSA for UWA channel estimation.

AFSA is one of the intelligent algorithms which can find the optimal solution quickly with the help of each fish's individual competition and swarm cooperation [40]. Based on AFSA, the proposed method, IAFSA, proceeds in an iterative manner and will adjust step and fish's positions during the sub-iteration. Then it will update the residual signal at the end of each iteration and return the parameters of one path. The proposed method can effectively reduce computational complexity while has a good estimation performance.

The rest of this paper is organized as follows. Section 2 gives a brief introduction of the channel model. In Sect. 3, we present the basic AFSA and the process of the proposed IAFSA in detail. Section IV focuses on the simulation results and section V concludes the paper.

2 Channel Model

UWA channel features large multipath spread for the interaction with ocean surface, bottom medium, as well as inhomogeneous particles of water column. MSML channel model can well describe the UWA multipath channel, that is:

$$h(\tau, t) = \sum_{l=1}^{L} A_l(t)\delta(\tau - (\tau_l - (a_l - 1)t)) \tag{1}$$

where L is the number of channel taps. $A_l(t)$ is the time- varying amplitude of the lth path and can be assumed to be constant during a short period of time, for example, the transmission duration of one data frame. τ_l and a_l are the time delay and Doppler scale factor of the lth path, respectively. And $\delta(\cdot)$ is a delta function defined as following:

$$\delta(t) = \begin{cases} 1 & t = 0 \\ 0 & otherwise \end{cases} \tag{2}$$

Let $s(t)$ be the transmitted signal and the corresponding received signal $r(t)$ can be written as:

$$r(t) = \sum_{l=1}^{L} A_l(t)s(a_l t - \tau_l) + w(t) \tag{3}$$

where $w(t)$ is the additive noise.

Given the sparsity of UWA channel, only some channel taps are nonzero in (1), which means that $r(t)$ is a superposition of only a few delay-scaled versions of $s(t)$. Therefore, the calculation complexity for channel estimation is significantly reduced.

3 IAFSA-Based Sparse Channel Estimation

3.1 Basic AFSA

AFSA (artificial fish swarm algorithm)is an optimization method which imitates the behaviors of fish, including preying, swarming and following. In underwater world, fish can find areas with higher food density based on their individual competition and swarm cooperation. Similarly, AFSA can get the optimal solution in the problem space by imitating fish behaviors. Before introducing these behaviors, we will give some definitions first.

Denoting Xp as the position of an artificial fish(AF):

$$X_p = \left(x_1^p, x_2^p, \ldots, x_N^p\right) \qquad (p = 1, \ldots, P) \tag{4}$$

where P is the population size and N is the dimension of the position. The fitness value of position Xp can be calculated by

$$y_p = f(X_p) \tag{5}$$

And the distance between two individuals Xp and Xq is defined as

$$d(X_p, X_q) = \sqrt{\sum_{n=1}^{N} (X_p(n) - X_q(n))^2} \tag{6}$$

There are three basic behaviors of AF:

1) Preying: Suppose the current position of AF p is Xp, then it randomly selects a position Xv within its visual range. If $yv > yp$, the AF will move a step toward Xv, that is

$$X_{pnext} = X_p + \frac{X_v - X_p}{||X_v - X_p||} \cdot \Delta \tag{7}$$

where Δ is the step size. This process will repeat I times until one Xv meets the requirement, or the AF will choose a position randomly within visual.

2) Swarming: Let Xp be the current position of AF p and Q be the number of its partners within its visual range. If $Q > 0$, calculating the center position of these Q partners:

$$X_c = \frac{1}{Q} \sum_{q=1}^{Q} X_q \tag{8}$$

Define λ as the crowd factor, if $yc/Q > \lambda yp$, which means that the food density at Xc is high and the surrounding is not crowded, so AF p will move toward Xc as in (7); otherwise, it will execute the behavior of preying. If $Q = 0$, AF will also execute the behavior of preying.

3) Following: AF p finds Q partners within its visual range. If $Q > 0$, finds the partner Xq which has the maximum yq. Then if $yq/Q > \lambda yp$, AF p will move toward Xq as in (7). If $yq/Q \leq \lambda yp$ or $Q = 0$, AF p will execute the behavior of preying.

At each iteration, each AF calculates the fitness values of swarming and following, then selects one behavior with better fitness value. The optimal position and corresponding fitness value among all AFs will be recorded on the call-board. The algorithm will stop when reaching maximum iterations or the error meets the requirement. Then we can get the optimal solution from the call-board.

3.2 Improved AFSA (IAFSA) and Channel Parameters Estimation

Let one fish position represent one path's Doppler and delay parameters, $\{a_l, \tau_l\}_{l=1}^{L}$. And let $r(t)$ be the received signal, $s(t)$ be the preamble, then signal from path Xp can be represented as $s^{X_p}(t)$. So the fitness value can be calculated by

$$f(X_p) = \frac{\int_{-\infty}^{+\infty} r(t)s^{X_p}(t)dt}{\int_{-\infty}^{+\infty} \|s^{X_p}(t)\|^2 dt} \tag{9}$$

This is just the estimated path amplitude: $f(X_p) = \hat{A}_{X_p}$. Thus AFSA can be applied to channel estimation for one-path case. However, for MSML channels, the received signal is a superposition of several different multipath components, parameter estimation is more complicated and some modifications are necessary when applying AFSA to MSML channel estimation.

Inspired by MP algorithm, we propose an improved artificial fish swarm algorithm (IAFSA) in this paper, which proceeds in an iterative manner and estimates parameters for one path at each iteration. Specifically, during one iteration, basic AFSA, with some modifications, will be applied as a sub-iteration. The modifications include step adjustment and part of fish's position adjustment. Then the estimated path component will be eliminated from the received signal by subtracting the delay-scaled version of the known preamble.

The process of IAFSA is given as Algorithm 1.

Algorithm 1: Doppler-distorted UWA channel estimation based on IAFSA

Input:

Transmitted signal vector s; received signal vector r; path numbers L; threshold ε.

Initialization:

Set the residual signal $r_e = r$, the crowd factor λ, the visual range D, the step Δ ,the number of trying I, the maximum sub-iterations k_{max}, set $l=1$;

Iterate:

1: Initialize a population of AF with random positions $X_p (p = 1, \cdots, P)$ in the problem space and calcu late corresponding fitness values $y_p (p = 1, \cdots, P)$. Record the maximum fitness value y_{opt} and corresponding X_{opt} on call-board.

2: Set counters $k = 1$.

3: Do swarming and following within visual range D, then select one behavior with better fitness value, and update X_p.

4: Calculate fitness value for each fish and update call- board.

5: When $k > k_{max}/2$, if call-board keeps unchanged and $y_{opt} > \varepsilon$, change half of AFs positions to be X_{opt}.

6: Set $k = k + 1$, step $\Delta' = (1 - \dfrac{k}{2k_{max}})\Delta$, and loop to step 3 until $k > k_{max}$.

7: Select the position from call-board and get the delay-scaled training signal as s_l , and corresponding fitness value y_{opt} is $\hat{A}_l$. Then update the residual signal as:

$$r_e = r_e - \hat{A}_l s_l \qquad (10)$$

8: If $l = L$, stop the iteration; else, set $l = l + 1$ and go to step 1.

Output:

The estimated channel parameters: $\{\hat{A}_i, \hat{a}_i, \hat{\tau}_i\}_{i=1}^{L}$.

Path number L can be got from the process of signal synchronization before channel estimation; and the threshold ε is set according to the energy of the signal from one path which can be detected at the receiver.

4 Experiment and Analysis

In this part, we use various computer simulations to evaluate the performance of IAFSA, and compared with OMP algorithm will also be included.

4.1 Channel 1

We consult [11]to set the path parameters in our simulation, that is, the number of discrete paths L from transmitter to receiver is 10 in total, and the inter-arrival time is distributed randomly within 25 ms with the minimal delay synchronized to zero. The path amplitudes are uniformly distributed and the strongest path is normalized to 1. The Doppler scale factors are randomly distributed within [1,1.02], with an accuracy to four decimal places. And we use a pseudo-random noise (PN) signal of 511 symbol length as the training sequence, which is binary phase-shift keying (BPSK) modulated onto the carrier. The carrier frequency is 10 kHz and the sampling rate is 20 kHz.

At the receiver, both IAFSA and OMP will be applied to channel estimation. The initialization parameters of IAFSA are listed in Table 1, while for OMP algorithm, we build a dictionary with a resolution of 1×10^{-4} in the Doppler rate and 0.1 ms in the tap delay. The dictionary covers a Doppler rate variation of 0.02 and a delay spread of 25 ms, which is also the position space of AFSA.

Table 1. Parameter of IAFSA.

Parameter	Value
Population size (P)	50
Crowd factor (λ)	0.3
Visual range (D)	[0.005;1.0 ms]
Step (Δ)	0.2
Maximum iterations ($k$max)	10
Trying number (I)	10
Threshold (ε)	0.2

Figure 1 displays the normalized mean squared error (NMSE) of the estimated scale factor versus signal to noise ratio (SNR), as defined in the following:

$$NMSE = \frac{\sum_{l=1}^{L} \left| \hat{\alpha}_l - \alpha_l \right|^2}{\sum_{l=1}^{L} |\alpha_l|^2} \tag{11}$$

From Fig. 1, it is clearly that the IAFSA outperforms OMP in Doppler scale estimating. The accuracy of OMP depends on the resolution of the columns in the dictionary, thus it is limited by the dictionary size. While IAFSA can get a better resolution by step adjusting in the sub-iteration, as well as that at the last stage of iteration, many fish will search around the optimal solution to achieve better accuracy.

The estimating error of time delay, $\frac{1}{L} \sum_{l=1}^{L} \left| \hat{\tau}_l - \tau_l \right|$ is plotted in Fig. 2. The IAFSA is slightly better than OMP in low SNR, with a gain about 2 dB. When SNR exceeds 8 dB, both algorithms become stable and IAFSA gets a lower delay estimating error, for it's search range is smaller at the last stage of sub-iteration and can get better resolution.

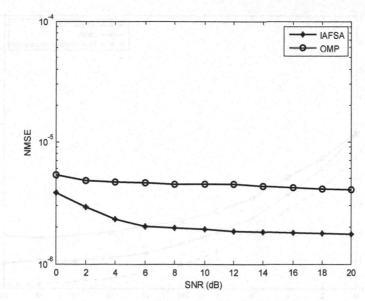

Fig. 1. NMSE of the estimating scale factor versus SNR

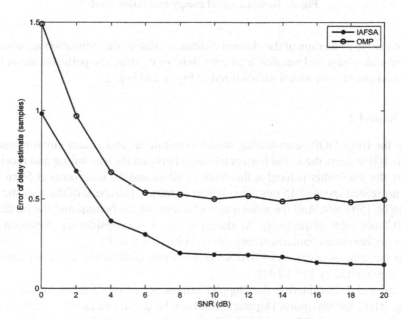

Fig. 2. Errors of the estimating delay versus SNR

Figure 3 illustrates the residual signal energy rates, $||r_e||^2/||r||^2$ versus SNR of both estimation algorithms. And a reference which uses the true channel information is also included. It can be seen that IAFSA performs better than OMP, gaining about 2 dB when SNR exceeds 2 dB and is closer to the ideal values. Residual signal energy rate is a

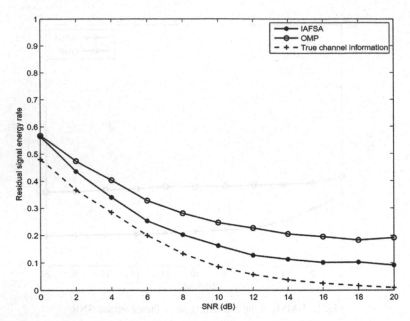

Fig. 3. Residual signal energy rate versus SNR

comprehensive evaluation of the channel estimation, that is, the estimation accuracies of Doppler scale, delay and amplitude all contribute to it. Thus, the performance in Fig. 3 is also coincident with which we analyzed in Fig. 1 and Fig. 2.

4.2 Channel 2

We use the BELLHOP beam-tracing model to mimic an underwater environment: the water is 100 m deep, the initial horizontal range between the transmitter and receiver is 2000 m. the transmitter is fixed at the depth of 80 m, and the receiver is at 50 m depth with a horizontal speed of 15 m/s toward the transmitter. The speed of the acoustic wave is set to be 1500 m/s. And the reflection coefficients of the bottom and the surface are set to 0.7 and −0.9, respectively. As shown in Fig. 4, we consider ten dominant paths and the performance comparisons are shown in Figs. 5, 6 and 7.

It is the same as in channel 1, IAFSA outperforms OMP when testing by channel 2 which is generated by BELLHOP.

In channel 2, considering the Doppler effects are mainly caused by the receiver moving. Thus, the maximum Doppler spread can be calculated as $v/c = 0.01$. And ten paths all arrive within 25 ms with the delay of the first arrival path synchronized to zero. So the difference between two channels for OMP is the column numbers in the dictionary. The dictionary size in channel 1 is twice as in channel 2 for the Doppler spread is 0.02 in channel 1. However, for IAFSA, the only adjustment is to change the position space when initializing fish positions. So it is more convenient when channel changes and does not need additional computation.

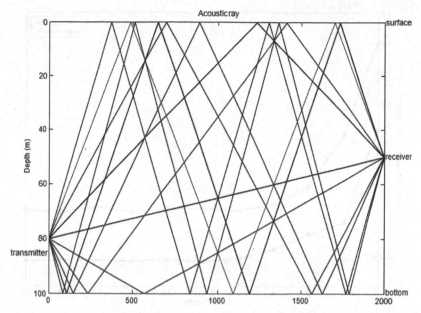

Fig. 4. Acoustic ray paths of UWA channel

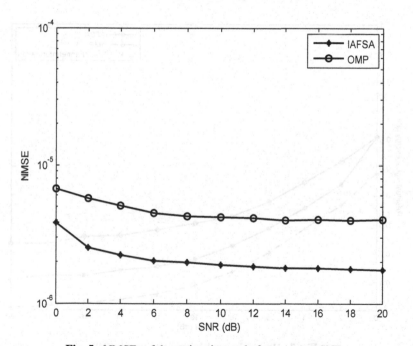

Fig. 5. NMSEs of the estimating scale factor versus SNR

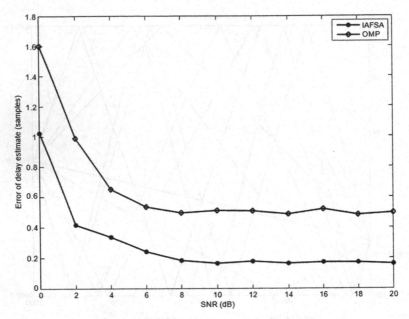

Fig. 6. Errors of the estimating delay versus SNR

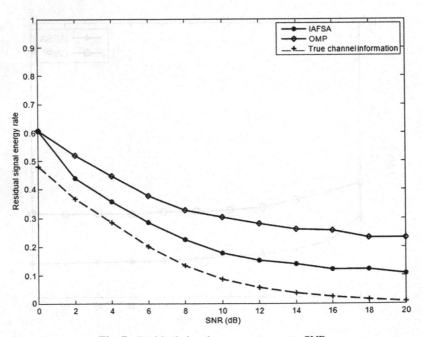

Fig. 7. Residual signal energy rate versus SNR

4.3 Complexity Analysis

As both OMP and IAFSA will iterate L times to estimate parameters for all paths, the mainly difference of computation lies in the process of one iteration. So we will focus on the computation of one iteration.

For OMP algorithm, let K_L be the length of the preamble, $N = N\tau\, Na$ be the total number of delay-scaled versions of preamble, that is, the column dimensions of the dictionary. Thus, the inner products of the received signal and columns in the dictionary requires $\rho = NK_L$ complex multiplications. For channel 1, $N\tau = 250$, $Na = 200$, thus $N = 5 \times 10^4$, while for channel 2, $Na = 100$, and $N = 2.5 \times 10^4$.

For IAFSA, each iteration includes $k$max sub-iterations, and during each sub-iteration, P fish will be involved and each fish will do swarming and following. For the worst case, that is, both swarming and following fail to find a better position, fish will turn to preying, and this requires to calculate inner products of the received signal and the delay-scaled version $2I$ times. Thus, the whole computation is $\rho = K_L P k_{\max} 2I$. For both channel 1 and 2, $P = 50$, $k$max $= 10$ and $I = 10$. So, $\rho = 1 \times 10^4$.

From the above analysis, the computational complexity of IAFSA is much lower than OMP algorithm, especially when the delay spread and Doppler spread are large, which is the case of UWA channel.

5 Conclusion

We have invested the problem of Doppler-distorted UWA channels estimation in this paper and propose the IAFSA method. In particular, during each iteration, a sub-iteration is included and we propose to adjust the step and fish's positions during the sub-iteration to search more carefully around the optimal solution. And the estimated signal component will be eliminated from the received signal for next iteration. The new method has the advantages of faster convergence and finer resolution compared with OMP algorithm. The simulation results show that IAFSA outperforms OMP in estimation accuracy as well as has a lower computational complexity.

Acknowledgement. This work is partly supported by the Xuzhou Science and Technology Plan Projects (KC19003), Science and Technology Project of Jiangsu Provincial Department of Housing and Construction(2019ZD039,2019ZD041).

References

1. Hao, Y., Chi, C., Liang, G.: Sparsity-driven adaptive enhancement of underwater acoustic tonals for passive sonars. J. Acoust. Soc. Am. **147**(4), 2192–2204 (2020)
2. Cui, H., Sun, D., Hong, X., Liu, L.: Iterative multi-channel FH-MFSK reception in mobile shallow underwater acoustic channels. IET Commun. **14**(5) (2020)
3. Padala, S.K., D'Souza, J.: Performance of spatially coupled LDPC codes over underwater acoustic communication channel. In: 2020 National Conference on Communications (NCC) (2020)

4. Drgowski, M., Wodarczyk, M.: The Doppler effect and the anisotropy of the speed of light. Found. Phys. (2020)
5. Zhang, F., Zhang, Z., Yu, W., Truong, T.K.: Joint range and velocity estimation with intrapulse and intersubcarrier Doppler effects for OFDM-based RadCom systems. IEEE Trans. Sig. Process. **68**(99), 662–675 (2020)
6. Xi, J., Yan, S., Xu, L., Zhang, Z., Zeng, D.: Frequency–time domain turbo equalization for underwater acoustic communications. IEEE J. Oceanic Eng. 1–15 (2020)
7. Jing, L., He, C., Wang, H., Zhang, Q., Yin, H.: A new IDMA system based on CSK modulation for multiuser underwater acoustic communications. IEEE Trans. Veh. Technol. **69**(3), 3080–3092 (2020)
8. Jiang, D., Wang, Y., Lv, Z., Wang, W., Wang, H.: An energy-efficient networking approach in cloud services for IIoT networks. IEEE J. Sel. Areas in Commun. **38**(5), 928–941 (2020)
9. Qu, F., Wang, Z., Yang, L., Wu, Z.: A journey toward modeling and resolving Doppler in underwater acoustic communications. IEEE Commun. Mag. **54**(2), 49–55 (2016)
10. Mason, S., Berger, C.R., Zhou, S. and et al.: Receiver comparisons on an OFDM design for Doppler spread channels. In: Proceedings of IEEE OCEANS Conference, Europe, pp. 2201–2208, May 2009
11. Berger, C.R., Zhou, S., Preisig, J., Willet, P.: Sparse channel estimation for multicarrier underwater acoustic communication: from subspace methods to compressed sensing. IEEE Trans. Sig. Process. **58**(3), 1708–1721 (2010)
12. Jiang, D., Wang, Y., Lv, Z., Qi, S., Singh, S.: Big data analysis based network behavior insight of cellular networks for industry 4.0 applications. IEEE Trans. Ind. Inf. **16**(2), 1310–1320 (2020)
13. Xu, T., Tang, Z., Leus, G., Mitra, U.: Multi-rate block transmission over wideband multi-scale multi-lag channels. IEEE Trans. Sig. Process. **61**(4), 964–979 (2013)
14. Daoud, S., Ghrayeb, A.: Using resampling to combat Doppler scaling in UWA channels with single-carrier modualtion and frequency-domain equalization. IEEE Trans. Veh. Technol. **65**(3), 1261–1270 (2016)
15. Huo, L., Jiang, D., Qi, S., et al.: An AI-based adaptive cognitive modeling and measurement method of network traffic for EIS. Mob. Netw. Appl. (2019)
16. Jiang, D., Zhang, P., Lv, Z., et al.: Energy-efficient multi-constraint ligent optimization-brouting algorithm with load balancing for smart city applications. IEEE Internet Things J. **3**(6), 1437–1447 (2016)
17. Beygi, S., Mitra, U.: Multi-scale multi-lag channel estimation using low rank approximation for OFDM. IEEE Trans. Sig. Process. **63**(18), 4744–4755 (2015)
18. Beygi, S., Mitra, U.: Optimal Bayesian resampling for OFDM signaling over multi-scale multi-lag channels. IEEE Sig. Process. Lett. **20**(11), 1118–1121 (2013)
19. Aman, W., Haider, Z., Shah, S.W.H., Rahman, M.M.U., Dobre, O.A.: On the effective capacity of an underwater acoustic channel under impersonation attack (2020)
20. Jiang, D., Wang, W., Shi, L., Song, H.: A compressive sensing-based approach to end-to-end network traffic reconstruction. IEEE Trans. Netw. Sci. Eng. **7**(1), 507–519 (2020)
21. Qi, S., Jiang, D., Huo, L.: A prediction approach to end-to-end traffic in space information networks, Mob. Netw. Appl. (2019). https://doi.org/10.1007/s11036-019-01424-2
22. Dunn, S., Saleem, A.: MSML package for the media control channel framework. Lymphatic Res. Biol. **13**(1), 3563–3563 (2015)
23. Cotter, S., Rao, B.: Sparse channel estimation via matching pursuit with application to equalization. IEEE Trans. Commun. **50**(3), 374–377 (2002)
24. Tropp, J.A., Gilbert, A.C.: Signal recovery from random measurements via orthogonal matching pursuit. IEEE Trans. Inf. Theory. **53**(12), 4655–4666 (2007)

25. Do, T.T., Lu, G., Nam, N., Tran, T.D. : Sparsity adaptive matching pursuit algorithm for practical compressed sensing. In: Proceedings of 42nd Asilomar Conference on Signals Systems and Computers, Pacific Grove, CA, pp. 581–587, October 2008
26. Jiang, D., Huo, L., Song, H.: Rethinking behaviors and activities of base stations in mobile cellular networks based on big data analysis. IEEE Trans. Netw. Sci. Eng. 1(1), 1–2 (2018)
27. Wang, F., Jiang, D., Qi, S.: An adaptive routing algorithm for integrated information networks. China Commun. 7(1), 196–207 (2019)
28. Zhang, Y., Venkatesan, R., Dobre, O.A., Li, C.: An adaptive matching pursuit algorithm for sparse channel estimation. In: Proceedings of IEEE Wireless Communications Networking Conference (WCNC), New Orleans, LA, USA, pp. 626–630, March 2015
29. Jiang, D., Huo, L., Li, Y.: Fine-granularity inference and estimations to network traffic for SDN. PLoS ONE 13(5), 1–23 (2018)
30. Wang, Y. Jiang., D., Huo, L., Zhao, Y.: A new traffic prediction algorithm to software defined networking. Mob. Netw. Appl. (2019). https://doi.org/10.1007/s11036-019-01423-3.pdf
31. Lü, S.S., Jiang, M.S., Su, C.H., Zhang, L., Jia, L.: Novel phase difference extraction method of FPP system based on DWT and OMP algorithm. Optoelectron. Lett. 16(2), 131–136 (2020)
32. Panayirci, E., Altabbaa, M.T., Uysal, M., Poor, H.V.: Sparse channel estimation for OFDM-based underwater acoustic systems in Rician fading with a new OMP-map algorithm. IEEE Trans. Sig. Process. 67(6), 1550–1565 (2019)
33. Jiang, D., Li, W., Lv, H.: An energy-efficient cooperative multicast routing in multi-hop wireless networks for smart medical applications. Neurocomputing 220, 160–169 (2017)
34. Qu, F., Nie, X., Xu, W., et al.: A two-stage approach for the estimation of doubly spread acoustic channels. IEEE J. Ocean Eng. 40(1), 131–143 (2015)
35. Huo, L. , Jiang, D. , Lv, Z. , et al. :An intelligent optimization-based traffic information acquirement approach to software-defined networking. Comput. Intell. 1–21(2019)
36. Yu, F., Li, D., Guo, Q., et al.: Block-FFT based OMP for compressed channel estimation in underwater acoustic communications. IEEE Com- mun. Lett. 19(11), 1937–1940 (2015)
37. Liu, W., Liao, Q., Qiao, F., Xia, W., Lombardi, F.: Approximate designs for fast Fourier transform (FFT) with application to speech recognition. IEEE Trans. Circ. Syst. I: Regular Papers (99), 1–13 (2019)
38. Buzachis, A., Galletta, A., Celesti, A., Fazio, M., Villari, M.: Development of a smart metering microservice based on fast Fourier transform (FFT) for edge/internet of things environments. In: 2019 IEEE 3rd International Conference on Fog and Edge Computing (ICFEC) (2019)
39. Jiang, D., Huo, L., Lv, Z., et al.: A joint multi-criteria utility-based network selection approach for vehicle-to-infrastructure networking. IEEE Trans. Intell. Transp. Syst. 19(10), 3305–3319 (2018)
40. Jiang, M., Li, C., Yuan, D., Lagunas, M.A.: Multiuser detection based on wavelet packet modulation and artificial fish swarm algorithm. Wireless, Mob. Sen. Netw. IET. 117–120 (2007)

Dynamic Adaptive Search Strategy Based Incremental Extreme Learning Machine Based on

Zuozhi Liu[1]($\boxtimes$)(iD), Jianjun Jiao[1], and Quan Yuan[2]

[1] School of Mathematics and Statistics, Guizhou University of Finance and Economics, Guiyang, Guizhou, People's Republic of China
[2] Finance Department, Guizhou University of Finance and Economics, Guiyang, Guizhou, People's Republic of China

Abstract. Extreme learning machine (ELM) is a promising method for the learning of single-hidden layer feedforward network (SLFN) which is attractive for its simplicity and high efficiency. However, during the rapid development of ELM algorithm, the determination of suitable network architecture is still a challenging work. To deal with this issue, this work develops a modified ELM algorithm based on a novel adaptive optimization method. Specifically, we use the growth structure strategy to design the network architecture. During the learning process of the proposed algorithm, the grey wolf optimization (GWO) technique is then introduced to seek the optimal parameters for hidden nodes instead of random selection. In addition, to improve the convergence speed, we further ameliorate the traditional GWO approach. Experiment results over some benchmark applications indicate that our AI-ELM algorithm can dramatically reduce the scale of network and obtains the better generalization performance than other classical ELM algorithms.

Keywords: Single-hidden layer feedforward network · Incremental extreme learning machine · Enhanced grey wolf optimization · Universal approximation

1 Introduction

Artificial neural network (ANN) is one of the important research branches of machine learning and computational intelligence. Simple speaking, the purpose of this bionic network is to simulate the information processing function of the brain nervous system. In the past decades, ANN has been widely studied and has become a powerful information processing technique because of its self-learning, self-adapting, and fault-tolerant. Single-hidden-layer feedforward

This work was supported by the Fund of Guizhou University of Finance and Economics (No. 2019XYB02) and the Science and Technology Project of Guizhou Province (No. [2020]1Y253).

network (SLFN) is a special kind of ANN which only contains a single hidden layer. Due to its simplicity and good generalization performance (GP), SLFN has attracted great interest and has been applied to various fields ranging from scientific research to engineering application [1, 2]. However, the most of existing learning algorithms for SLFN are usually designed based on gradient optimization strategy, which are proven to be complex and slow in computation. As a result, it is urgent to develop a learning algorithm which can satisfy the need of the rapid development of SLFN. To this end, Huang et al. developed a novel learning algorithm for SLFN called extreme learning machines (ELM) [3]. Generally speaking, the key idea of ELM is to take advantage of the random mechanism to select the parameters of hidden nodes and use the least-mean square method to resolve the output weights. Compared with traditional gradient-based learning algorithms, ELM not only learns faster but also shows better GP, especially in some practical applications [4, 5].

Although ELM learns faster than the traditional learning algorithms, the scale of network architecture (NA) is still determined by trial and error. Therefore, how to build a suitable NA is a prerequisite for the successful application of ELM. To deal with this problem, various construction methods were currently proposed with their own advantages and drawbacks. Among these methods, incremental ELMs are the most famous and representative. I-ELM uses the incremental mechanism to obtain the optimal NA. In this algorithm, the hidden nodes are recruited one by one with randomly selected parameters [6]. In order to improve the convergence rate of I-ELM, CI-ELM referred in [7] proposes to constantly update the output weights of the added hidden nodes rather than unchanged. In addition, EI-ELM was developed to reduce the network complexity of I-ELM. Different from I-ELM, EI-ELM takes several randomly hidden nodes into consideration at each learning step and only recruits the one with the maximum error decreasing into the network [8]. In addition, a large number of experiments have shown that these algorithms can reduce the network scale to a great extent. However, during the learning procedure of all the above-mentioned algorithms, the parameters of hidden nodes are randomly assigned. Although this random mechanism can simplify the learning procedure, it also brings some redundant hidden nodes into the network, which will increase the network scale.

In order to obtain a more compact NA for specific problem, we propose a new ELM algorithm based on a novel adaptive optimization method (referred as AI-ELM). Similar to I-ELM, in this work, we take advantage of the growth structure strategy to design the network architecture. In other words, we recruit one hidden node into network at each learning step. Differently, during the learning process of AI-ELM, a novel adaptive optimization method is introduced to seek the optimal parameters for hidden nodes instead of random selection. Considering the simplicity and great search capacity, the hot grey wolf optimization (GWO) method is taken as the optimizer. In addition, to improve the convergence speed, we further ameliorate the traditional GWO algorithm. Finally, we compare AI-ELM with the existing algorithms on some benchmark problems.

The corresponding experimental results indicate that our AI-ELM can obtain a more compact NA with the better GP.

2   Brief on I-ELM and GWO

2.1   I-ELM Algorithm

In terms of structure, SLFN is composed of three main parts: input layer, hidden layer and output layer. Mathematically, the SLFN as shown in Fig. 1 can be represented as

$$f_l(\mathbf{x}) = \sum_{i=1}^{l} \beta_i g_i(\mathbf{x}) = \sum_{i=1}^{l} \beta_i G(\mathbf{a}_i, b_i, \mathbf{x}) \qquad (1)$$

where $\mathbf{x} \in R^d$ is the input sample, l is the number of the hidden nodes, $(\mathbf{a}_i, b_i)$ are the parameters of the ith hidden node, β_i is the ith output weight, and $g_i(\mathbf{x})$ or $G(\mathbf{a}_i, b_i, \mathbf{x})$ denotes the output of the ith hidden node [6].

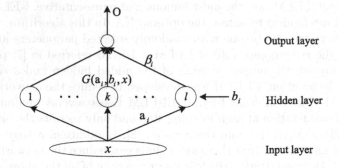

Fig. 1. Single-hidden layer feedforward network architecture.

I-ELM is an incremental constructive approach where the hidden nodes are recruited into network one after one with randomly selected parameters. Specifically, at each learning step of I-ELM, only one node is added to the hidden layer of the current network. The parameters of new added nodes are selected in a fixed interval at random. When lth hidden node is added to the network, the output of I-ELM can be expressed as

$$f_l(\mathbf{x}) = f_{l-1}(\mathbf{x}) + \beta_l g_l(\mathbf{x}). \qquad (2)$$

It is worth noting that although I-ELM adopts random mechanism to seek the parameters of hidden nodes, it has been proven that I-ELM can accurately approximate the objective function. That is

Theorem 1. *Given a SLFN with any nonconstant piecewise continuous function $g : R \to R$, if $span\{G(\mathbf{a}, b, \mathbf{x}) : (\mathbf{a}, b) \in R^d \times R\}$ is dense in L^2, then for any continuous target function f and any randomly generated function sequence $\{g_l(\mathbf{x}) = G(\mathbf{a}_l, b_l, \mathbf{x})\}$, $\lim_{l \to \infty} \| f - f_{l-1} - \beta_l g_l \| = 0$ holds with probability one if*

$$\beta_l = \frac{< e_{l-1}, g_l >}{\| g_l \|^2}, \tag{3}$$

where $e_{l-1} = f - f_{l-1}$.

2.2   GWO Algorithm

Grey wolf optimization (GWO) is an emerging intelligent optimization algorithm developed by Mirjalili et al. in 2014 [9]. Due to its great search capacity, GWO has attracted increasing interest and has been successfully used to solve many real-world problems [10]. In addition, this technique only has few uncertain parameters to be adjusted and can be easy to implement.

The core idea of GWO algorithm can be generally summarized as two parts: social pyramid and hunting strategy. Firstly, grey wolves are grouped into four types, namely $\alpha, \beta, \delta, \omega$, where α, β, δ denote three levels of solutions from good to inferior, and ω is the solutions except for α, β, δ. As shown in Fig. 2, four types of grey wolves constitute a strict social hierarchy.

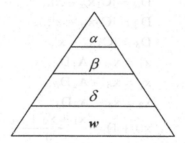

Fig. 2. Social pyramid of grey wolves.

Figure 3 gives an intuitive illustration of how grey wolves hunt the prey. In general, the hunting strategy consists of the following two steps:

(1) *Encircling prey.* Before the hunting, grey wolves firstly move towards the prey and surround it. Mathematically, this phase can be modeled as

$$\mathbf{D} = |\mathbf{C}\mathbf{x}_p(t) - \mathbf{x}(t)|, \tag{3}$$
$$\mathbf{x}(t+1) = \mathbf{x}_p(t) - \mathbf{A}\mathbf{D}, \tag{4}$$
$$\mathbf{A} = 2a\mathbf{r}_1 - \mathbf{a}, \tag{5}$$
$$\mathbf{C} = 2\mathbf{r}_2. \tag{6}$$

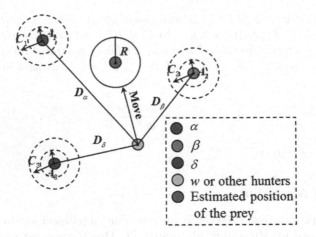

Fig. 3. Hunting strategy of grey wolves.

where $\mathbf{r}_1, \mathbf{r}_2$ are two random vectors, $\mathbf{a} = 2 - 2t/Iter_{\max}$, and $\mathbf{x}_p(t), \mathbf{x}(t)$ denote the current locations of prey and wolves, respectively.

(2) *Hunting prey.* During the hunting phase, grey wolves α usually conducts β, δ to attack the prey. Meanwhile, the rest of grey wolves ω adjust their locations according to α, β and δ. This phase can be expressed as follows,

$$\mathbf{D}_\alpha = |\mathbf{C}_1\mathbf{x}_\alpha - \mathbf{x}|, \tag{7}$$

$$\mathbf{D}_\beta = |\mathbf{C}_2\mathbf{x}_\beta - \mathbf{x}|, \tag{8}$$

$$\mathbf{D}_\delta = |\mathbf{C}_3\mathbf{x}_\delta - \mathbf{x}|, \tag{9}$$

$$\mathbf{x}_1 = \mathbf{x}_\alpha - \mathbf{A}_1\mathbf{D}_\alpha, \tag{10}$$

$$\mathbf{x}_2 = \mathbf{x}_\beta - \mathbf{A}_2\mathbf{D}_\beta, \tag{11}$$

$$\mathbf{x}_3 = \mathbf{x}_\delta - \mathbf{A}_3\mathbf{D}_\delta, \tag{12}$$

$$\mathbf{x}(t+1) = \frac{\mathbf{x}_1 + \mathbf{x}_2 + \mathbf{x}_3}{3} \tag{13}$$

where $\mathbf{C}_1, \mathbf{C}_2, \mathbf{C}_3, \mathbf{A}_1, \mathbf{A}_2,$ and $\mathbf{A}_3$ are six random vectors, $\mathbf{x}_\alpha, \mathbf{x}_\beta, \mathbf{x}_\delta$ denote the locations of α, β and δ, respectively.

3   Proposed AI-ELM

As described earlier, the original I-ELM adopts random mechanism to seek the parameters for hidden nodes. Although this random mechanism can simplify learning process, it also brings some unnecessary hidden nodes into network. In other words, some randomly added hidden nodes may play a small part in the whole network. It means that I-ELM usually needs more hidden nodes to approximate target function.

In order to achieve a more compact network, this work proposes an improved I-ELM based on a novel adaptive optimization method, named adaptive incremental extreme learning machine (AI-ELM). Similar to traditional I-ELM, in this work, the growth structure strategy is also employed to design the network architecture. During the learning process, we recruit hidden nodes into current network one after another. Differently, during the learning process of AI-ELM, we introduce a novel adaptive optimization method to seek the optimal parameters for hidden nodes instead of random selection. Considering the simplicity and great search capacity, the hot grey wolf optimization (GWO) method is taken as optimizer. The clear schematic of our AI-ELM is shown in Fig. 4.

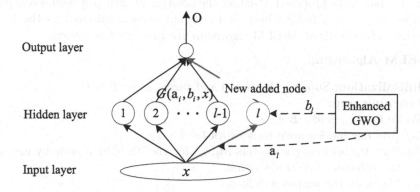

Fig. 4. Block diagram of the proposed AI-ELM.

However, researches have demonstrated that similar to other optimization algorithms, the traditional GWO may fall into local minima in practical applications. To address this issue, we make the following two improvements to ameliorate the traditional GWO algorithm. Firstly, we further modify the convergence factor **a** to enhance the nonlinear dynamic capability of it, that is

$$\mathbf{a} = \frac{2}{1 + e^{\gamma(\frac{2t}{Iter_{\max}} - 1)}},\tag{14}$$

where γ is a generalized coefficient that is used to restrict **a** to the interval $[0, 2]$. Here, we set $\gamma = 8$. With the help of the modified convergence factor, it can effectively balance the global search and local exploration.

Considering the fact that the traditional GWO may fall into local minima, we introduce the dynamic learning rates to update the position information. That is

$$\mathbf{x}(t+1) = \begin{cases} \frac{x_1 + x_2 + x_3}{3} & |\frac{x_1 + x_2 + x_3}{3}| \leq |\frac{w_1 x_1 + w_2 x_2 + w_3 x_3}{3}| \\ \frac{w_1 x_1 + w_2 x_2 + w_3 x_3}{3} & \text{other} \end{cases}\tag{15}$$

where

$$w_1 = \frac{|\mathbf{x}_1|}{|\mathbf{x}_1| + |\mathbf{x}_2| + |\mathbf{x}_3|}, \tag{16}$$

$$w_2 = \frac{|\mathbf{x}_2|}{|\mathbf{x}_1| + |\mathbf{x}_2| + |\mathbf{x}_3|}, \tag{17}$$

$$w_3 = \frac{|\mathbf{x}_3|}{|\mathbf{x}_1| + |\mathbf{x}_2| + |\mathbf{x}_3|}. \tag{18}$$

By doing so, the search ability of GWO algorithm can be further enhanced so as to avoid falling into local minima.

Note that in the proposed AI-ELM, the position of each grey wolf is composed of input weight and hidden bias, and residual error is adopted as the fitness function. The details of AI-ELM algorithm are presented as follows.

AI-ELM Algorithm:

1. **Initialization:** Suppose that $l = 0$ and target error $E = t$;
2. **Learning step:**
   While $l < l_{\max}$ and $\| E \| > \epsilon$
   (a) Add one hidden node to network $l = l + 1$;
   (b) Seek the optimal parameters $(\mathbf{a}_i, b_i)$ for the lth hidden node by means of the enhanced GWO algorithm;
   (c) Compute the output weight β_l :

$$\beta_l = \frac{E \cdot H_l^T}{H_l \cdot H_l^T}; \tag{19}$$

   (d) Update the target error E when the lth hidden node is added:

$$E = E - \beta_l \cdot H_l. \tag{20}$$

   Endwhile

As stated above, each hidden node recruited by the proposed AI-ELM plays an important part in the whole network, which means that AI-ELM needs less hidden nodes to complete the learning task. Therefore, it can be concluded that AI-ELM achieves a better NA than the traditional I-ELM in real applications.

4   Experimental Verification

In this section, we test our method in terms of NA and GP. Specifically, the proposed AI-ELM is compared with three classical ELM algorithms (I-ELM [6], EI-ELM [8], and D-ELM [11]) on some benchmark problems. Table 1 gives a detailed description of these eight UCI benchmark problems. For the fairness, all the tests are conducted in the same environment.

Table 1. Specification of regression problems.

Data sets	Attributes	Cases	Training data	Testing data
Abalone	8	4177	2000	2177
Boston Housing	13	506	250	256
California Housing	8	20640	8000	12640
Census (House8L)	8	22784	10000	12784
Delta Ailerons	6	7129	3000	4129
Delta Elevators	6	9517	4000	5517
Japanese Vowels	12	9961	4275	5686
Kin8nm	9	8192	4000	4192

In order to compare the NA and GP of each algorithm, for each problem, we first set the same expected accuracy (stopping RMSE) for all four algorithms, and the specification of expected accuracy is presented in Tables 2 and 3. In addition, the maximum learning step is set to 200 for all eight problems. Note that the less hidden nodes a method needs, the more compact NA it has. Meanwhile, the smaller the error a method achieves, the better GP it has. Therefore, a better algorithm must has less hidden nodes and residual error at the same time. In order to reduce the instability of the results, for each algorithm, the average result over fifty trails are taken as the final comparison results. Note that the better results in tables are emphasized in bold to facilitate the intuitive analysis.

The performance of four ELM algorithms on eight real-world problems is shown in Tables 2, 3, 4, and 5. Tables 2 and 3 show the NA comparison of four different algorithms with sigmoid nodes and sine nodes, respectively. It can be seen that the number of hidden nodes needed by the proposed AI-ELM is much less than those of other three algorithms for all cases. In view of this fact, we

Table 2. NA comparison of different algorithms with sigmoid nodes.

Datasets	Stop	I-ELM		EI-ELM		D-ELM		AI-ELM	
	RMSE	Nodes	Dev	Nodes	Dev	Nodes	Dev	Nodes	Dev
Abalone	0.09	177.78	52.84	66.80	40.65	4.75	1.41	**3.82**	0.61
Boston Housing	0.11	183.48	30.14	68.12	41.57	11.84	3.50	**8.44**	2.62
California Housing	0.16	197.98	12.60	48.96	14.52	5.74	1.37	**3.66**	1.12
Census (House8L)	0.09	194.34	21.04	48.12	19.04	5.80	1.34	**4.52**	0.94
Delta Ailerons	0.05	182.08	35.12	26.16	17.21	4.02	0.88	**3.12**	0.08
Delta Elevators	0.06	189.72	21.43	30.88	11.10	5.26	0.96	**3.36**	0.07
Japanese Vowels	0.11	199.10	6.36	74.94	31.10	7.52	1.31	**5.14**	1.92
Kin8nm	0.14	194.16	18.88	137.96	66.16	12.34	3.53	**8.68**	3.13

can find that our AI-ELM achieves a more compact NA. Tables 4 and 5 show the GP comparison of four different ELM algorithms. Apparently, AI-ELM performs better than the other three algorithms. Therefore, it can be concluded that the proposed AI-ELM achieves a more compact NA with better GP.

Table 3. NA comparison of different algorithms with sine nodes.

Datasets	Stop	I-ELM		EI-ELM		D-ELM		AI-ELM	
	RMSE	Nodes	Dev	Nodes	Dev	Nodes	Dev	Nodes	Dev
Abalone	0.09	139.88	59.65	20.54	12.97	6.20	1.50	**4.24**	0.19
Boston Housing	0.11	189.68	26.75	53.58	17.58	21.56	3.45	**13.44**	1.52
California Housing	0.16	111.24	55.60	18.04	13.41	6.74	1.42	**3.92**	1.32
Census (House8L)	0.09	78.44	24.30	13.80	4.33	6.70	1.65	**4.56**	0.25
Delta Ailerons	0.05	148.22	63.90	53.42	72.23	5.80	1.12	**3.40**	0.07
Delta Elevators	0.06	194.84	25.56	134.38	69.80	8.68	1.50	**5.10**	0.07
Japanese Vowels	0.11	198.46	10.89	89.24	55.09	11.46	2.05	**7.86**	0.32
Kin8nm	0.14	200.00	0.00	100.38	22.94	26.68	5.15	**16.76**	0.78

Table 4. GP comparison of different algorithms with sigmoid nodes.

Datasets	I-ELM		EI-ELM		D-ELM		AI-ELM	
	Mean	Dev	Mean	Dev	Mean	Dev	Mean	Dev
Abalone	0.0943	0.0045	0.0903	0.0032	0.0873	0.0043	**0.0851**	0.0020
Boston Housing	0.1256	0.0119	0.1200	0.0131	0.1170	0.0115	**0.1142**	0.0124
California Housing	0.1711	0.0081	0.1607	0.0022	**0.1556**	0.0043	0.1564	0.0027
Census (House8L)	0.0927	0.0024	0.0901	0.0030	0.0883	0.0035	**0.0877**	0.0016
Delta Ailerons	0.0527	0.0042	0.0492	0.0019	0.0462	0.0029	**0.0411**	0.0006
Delta Elevators	0.0641	0.0054	0.0596	0.0011	0.0572	0.0020	**0.0543**	0.0005
Japanese Vowels	0.1234	0.0089	0.1102	0.0013	0.1158	0.0044	**0.1118**	0.0010
Kin8nm	0.1445	0.0027	0.1413	0.0023	_0.1398_	0.0023	_0.1396_	0.0026

Table 5. GP comparison of different algorithms with sine nodes.

Datasets	I-ELM		EI-ELM		D-ELM		AI-ELM	
	Mean	Dev	Mean	Dev	Mean	Dev	Mean	Dev
Abalone	0.0915	0.0040	0.0898	0.0032	0.0888	0.0034	**0.0846**	0.0031
Boston Housing	0.1435	0.0146	0.1360	0.0183	0.1302	0.0150	**0.1228**	0.0124
California Housing	0.1553	0.0040	0.1542	0.0028	0.1547	0.0039	**0.1512**	0.0034
Census (House8L)	0.0896	0.0029	0.0892	0.0027	0.0882	0.0032	**0.0858**	0.0018
Delta Ailerons	0.0528	0.0045	0.0498	0.0024	0.0466	0.0028	**0.0414**	0.0012
Delta Elevators	0.0727	0.0115	0.0634	0.0046	0.0587	0.0017	**0.0554**	0.0015
Japanese Vowels	0.1301	0.0140	0.1108	0.0016	0.1079	0.0030	**0.1038**	0.0036
Kin8nm	0.1862	0.0159	0.1418	0.0025	0.1408	0.0029	**0.1377**	0.0029

5   Conclusion

In this work, an modified I-ELM called AI-ELM is developed, which automatically determines the optimal network architecture. In AI-ELM, the hidden nodes are recruited one after one, but the parameters of each hidden node are sought based on the enhanced GWO algorithm instead of random selection. Compared with the other ELMs, AI-ELM achieves a more compact NA with better GP. This fact has been further verified by a performance comparison on some real-world applications.

References

1. Bishop, C.-M.: Neural Networks for Pattern Recognition. Oxford University Press, New York (1995)
2. Li, T.-S., et al.: A spintronic memristor-based neural network with radial basis function for robotic manipulator control implementation. IEEE Trans. Syst. Man Cybern. Syst. **46**(4), 582–588 (2017)
3. Huang, G.-B., et al.: Extreme learning machine: theory and applications. Neurocomputing **70**(1–3), 489–501 (2006)
4. Duan, M., et al.: A parallel multiclassification algorithm for big data using an extreme learning machine. IEEE Trans. Neural Netw. Learn. Syst. **29**(6), 2337–2351 (2018)
5. Chen, K., Laghrouche, S., Djerdir, A.: Proton exchange membrane fuel cell prognostics using genetic algorithm and extreme learning machine. Fuel Cells **20**(3), 263–271 (2020)
6. Huang, G.-B., Chen, L., Siew, C.-K.: Universal approximation using incremental constructive feedforward networks with random hidden nodes. IEEE Trans. Neural Netw. **17**(4), 879–892 (2006)
7. Huang, G.-B., Chen, L.: Convex incremental extreme learning machine. Neurocomputing **70**(16), 3056–3062 (2007)
8. Huang, G.-B., Chen, L.: Enhanced random search based incremental extreme learning machine. Neurocomputing **71**(16), 460–468 (2008)
9. Mirjalili, S., et al.: Grey wolf optimizer. Adv. Eng. Soft. **69**, 46–61 (2014)
10. Martin, B., Marot, J., Bourennane, S.: Mixed grey wolf optimizer for the joint denoising and unmixing of multispectral images. Appl. Soft. Comput. **74**, 385–410 (2019)
11. Zhang, R., et al.: Dynamic extreme learning machine and its approximation capability. IEEE Trans. Cybern. **43**(6), 2054–2065 (2013)

Block-Diagonal and Anti-block-Diagonal Splitting Iteration Method for Absolute Value Equation

Cui-Xia Li and Shi-Liang Wu[✉]

School of Mathematics, Yunnan Normal University, Kunming 650500, Yunnan, People's Republic of China

Abstract. In this paper, the absolute value equation (AVE) is equivalently reformulated as a nonlinear equation in the form of 2 times 2 blocks. A block diagonal inverse block diagonal iteration method based on block-diagonal and anti-block-diagonal splitting (BAS) is proposed. Theoretical analysis shows that BAS is convergent, and numerical experiments show that the method is effective.

Keywords: Absolute value equation · Block-diagonal and anti-block-diagonal splitting · Convergence

1 Introduction

For the given matrix $A \in \mathbb{R}^{n \times n}$ and the given vector $b \in \mathbb{R}^n$, we consider the iterative solution of the absolute value equation (AVE)

$$Ax - |x| = b, \tag{1}$$

where $|\cdot|$ is the absolute value. Like linear programming, quadratic programming, bimatrix games and quasi complementarity problems [1–5]), AVE has been widely concerned as a practical optimization tool. AVE (1) is a NP hard problem, because there is a nonlinear and non differentiable term $|x|$, which makes AVE (1) nonlinear and non differentiable. When the $|x|$ in (1) disappears, the AVE (1) will be reduced to a linear system, see [13,14,16,18,24–29].

In recent years, the numerical solutions of AVE can be obtained by iterative methods, including the successful linearization algorithm [2], Picard and Picard-HSS algorithm [7,8], sign accord algorithm [6] and hybrid algorithm [12], interval algorithm [19], preconditioned AOR iterative algorithm [22], the generalized Newton algorithm [9,20,21], and so on.

This research was supported by National Natural Science Foundation of China (No.11961082).

H. Song and D. Jiang (Eds.): SIMUtools 2020, LNICST 369, pp. 572–581, 2021.
https://doi.org/10.1007/978-3-030-72792-5_45

For solving the AVE (1), the generalized Newton (GN) method in [9] works below

$$x^{k+1} = (A - D(x^k))^{-1}b, k = 0, 1, \ldots, \tag{2}$$

where $D(x^k) = diag(sign(x^k))$. Here, the $sign(x)$ is a vector composed of $1, 0, -1$, which determines whether the value of x is greater than zero, equal to zero or less than zero.

In [9], the convergence of the GN method is given by Mangasarian under appropriate conditions. In numerical experiments, the GN method is superior to the successive linearization method in [2]. After that, the GN method is extended to solve the GAVE [10,11] related to the second-order cone.

On the basis of the previous work in [14], in [15], on the basis of Hermitian and skew Hermitian splitting (HSS in [13]) of matrix A in (1), a nonlinear HSS (NHSS) method for ave (1) is proposed.

The NHSS method. Let $\alpha > 0$ and $x^{(0)} \in \mathbb{R}^n$ be an arbitrary initial value. For $k = 0, 1, 2, \ldots$ until the iterative sequences $\{x^{(k)}\}_{k=0}^{\infty}$ is convergent, calculate $x^{(k+1)}$ by the following procedure:

$$\begin{cases} (\alpha I + H)x^{(k+\frac{1}{2})} = (\alpha I - S)x^{(k)} + |x^k| + b, \\ (\alpha I + S)x^{(k+1)} = (\alpha I - H)x^{(k+\frac{1}{2})} + |x^{(k+\frac{1}{2})}| + b, \end{cases} \tag{3}$$

where $H = \frac{1}{2}(A + A^T)$ and $S = \frac{1}{2}(A - A^T)$, A^* stands for the transpose of the matrix A.

Compared with GN method, NHSS method can avoid variable coefficient matrix $A - D(x^k)$, which is an advantage of this method. However, it is worth noting that in each iteration step using the NHSS iterative method, both matrices $\alpha I + H$ and $\alpha I + S$ need to be calculated. It is well known that the coefficient matrix of a linear system $\alpha I + S$ is skew-Hermitian, and generally it is difficult to obtain its solution. See [16] for more details.

It is well known that different iterative methods are suitable for different matrix splittings. On this basis, based on the block-diagonal and anti-block-diagonal splitting (BAS) of linear term coefficient matrix in AVE, the block-diagonal and anti-block-diagonal splitting (BAS) iterative methods for AVE (1) are designed. Theoretical analysis shows that BAS method is convergent under mild conditions.

The remainder of the paper lays out below. In Sect. 2, for solving the AVE (1), the BAS iteration method is established and its convergence properties are studied in detail. In Sect. 3, numerical experiments are given to confirm the effectiveness and feasibility of the proposed method. In Sect. 4, some conclusions are given to end the paper.

2   The BAS Method

In this section, to solve the AVE (1), the BAS iteration method is introduced. To this end, we reformulate equivalently AVE (1) as a nonlinear equation with two-by-two block form. That is to say, let $y = |x|$, then the AVE is equal to

$$\begin{cases} Ax - y = b, \\ -|x| + y = 0, \end{cases}$$

that is,

$$\mathcal{A}z \equiv \begin{bmatrix} A & -I \\ -\hat{D} & I \end{bmatrix} \begin{bmatrix} x \\ y \end{bmatrix} = \begin{bmatrix} b \\ 0 \end{bmatrix}, \tag{4}$$

where $\hat{D} = D(x) = diag(sign(x)), x \in \mathbb{R}^n$.

A block-diagonal and anti-block-diagonal splitting (BAS) of matrix $\mathcal{A}$ can be constructed as follows

$$\mathcal{A} = \begin{bmatrix} A & -I \\ -\hat{D} & I \end{bmatrix} = \begin{bmatrix} A & 0 \\ 0 & I \end{bmatrix} + \begin{bmatrix} & -I \\ -\hat{D} & 0 \end{bmatrix}.$$

Further, matrix $\mathcal{A}$ can be expressed as

$$\mathcal{A} = \begin{bmatrix} A & -I \\ -\hat{D} & I \end{bmatrix} = \begin{bmatrix} \alpha I + A & 0 \\ 0 & \alpha I + I \end{bmatrix} - \begin{bmatrix} \alpha I & I \\ \hat{D} & \alpha I \end{bmatrix},$$

where α is a given appropriate constant. This splitting naturally leads to the BAS iteration method for solving the nonlinear equation (4).

The BAS iteration method: Let $b \in \mathbb{R}^n$ and $A \in \mathbb{R}^{n \times n}$ be a nonsingular. Given an initial pair vector $(x^{(0)} y^{(0)})$, for $k = 0, 1, 2, ...$, until the iteration sequence $\{x^{(k)}, y^{(k)}\}_{k=0}^{+\infty}$ is convergent, compute

$$\begin{bmatrix} \alpha I + A & 0 \\ 0 & \alpha I + I \end{bmatrix} \begin{bmatrix} x^{(k+1)} \\ y^{(k+1)} \end{bmatrix} = \begin{bmatrix} \alpha I & I \\ \hat{D} & \alpha I \end{bmatrix} \begin{bmatrix} x^{(k)} \\ y^{(k)} \end{bmatrix} + \begin{bmatrix} b \\ 0 \end{bmatrix}, \tag{5}$$

or

$$\begin{cases} x^{(k+1)} = (\alpha I + A)^{-1}(\alpha x^{(k)} + y^{(k)} + b), \\ y^{(k+1)} = \dfrac{1}{1+\alpha}(\hat{D}x^{(k)} + \alpha y^{(k)}), \end{cases} \tag{6}$$

where α is a given appropriate constant.

Lemma 1. [18] *Let λ be any root of the quadratic equation $x^2 - bx + d = 0$ with $b, d \in \mathbb{R}$. Then $|\lambda| < 1$ if and only if $|d| < 1$ and $|b| < 1 + d$.*

Let (x^*, y^*) be the solution pair of the Eq. (4) and the iteration errors

$$e_k^x = x^* - x^{(k)}, e_k^y = y^* - y^{(k)},$$

where $(x^{(k)}, y^{(k)})$ is generated by the iteration method (5) or (6). Then we give the following main result with respect to the BAS iteration method (5) or (6).

Theorem 1. *Let $b \in \mathbb{R}^n$ and $A \in \mathbb{R}^{n \times n}$ be nonsingular. Denote*

$$\beta = \|(\alpha I + A)^{-1}\|,$$

where $\| \cdot \|$ denotes the Euclid norm.

If

$$\beta(1 + \alpha) < 1, \tag{7}$$

then

$$|||(e_{k+1}^x, e_{k+1}^y)||| < |||(e_k^x, e_k^y)|||, k = 0, 1, \ldots,$$

where

$$|||(e_k^x, e_k^y)||| = \sqrt{\|e_k^x\|^2 + \|e_k^y\|^2}.$$

This implies that the BAS iteration method is convergent.

Proof. Based on (5) and (6),

$$\begin{cases} e_{k+1}^x = \alpha(\alpha I + A)^{-1}e_k^x + (\alpha I + A)^{-1}e_k^y, \\ e_{k+1}^y = \dfrac{1}{1+\alpha}(\hat{D}e_k^x + \alpha e_k^y). \end{cases} \tag{8}$$

From (8), we can get

$$\begin{aligned} \|e_{k+1}^x\| &= \|\alpha(\alpha I + A)^{-1}e_k^x + (\alpha I + A)^{-1}e_k^y\| \\ &\le \alpha\|(\alpha I + A)^{-1}e_k^x\| + \|(\alpha I + A)^{-1}e_k^y\| \\ &\le \alpha\|(\alpha I + A)^{-1}\| \cdot \|e_k^x\| + \|(\alpha I + A)^{-1}\| \cdot \|e_k^y\| \\ &= \alpha\beta\|e_k^x\| + \beta\|e_k^y\|. \end{aligned}$$

and

$$\begin{aligned} \|e_{k+1}^y\| &= \|\frac{1}{1+\alpha}(\hat{D}e_k^x + \alpha e_k^y)\| \\ &\le \|\frac{1}{1+\alpha}\hat{D}e_k^x\| + \|\frac{\alpha}{1+\alpha}e_k^y\| \\ &= \frac{1}{1+\alpha}\|\hat{D}e_k^x\| + \frac{\alpha}{1+\alpha}\|e_k^y\| \\ &\le \frac{1}{1+\alpha}\|\hat{D}\| \cdot \|e_k^x\| + \frac{\alpha}{1+\alpha}\|e_k^y\| \\ &\le \frac{1}{1+\alpha}\|e_K^x\| + \frac{\alpha}{1+\alpha}\|e_k^y\|. \end{aligned}$$

Further,

$$\begin{aligned} \begin{pmatrix} \|e_{k+1}^x\| \\ \|e_{k+1}^y\| \end{pmatrix} &\le \begin{pmatrix} \alpha\beta & \beta \\ \frac{1}{1+\alpha} & \frac{\alpha}{1+\alpha} \end{pmatrix} \begin{pmatrix} \|e_k^x\| \\ \|e_k^y\| \end{pmatrix} \\ &\le \begin{pmatrix} \alpha\beta & \beta \\ \frac{1}{1+\alpha} & \frac{\alpha}{1+\alpha} \end{pmatrix}^2 \begin{pmatrix} \|e_{k-1}^x\| \\ \|e_{k-1}^y\| \end{pmatrix} \\ &\cdots \\ &\le \begin{pmatrix} \alpha\beta & \beta \\ \frac{1}{1+\alpha} & \frac{\alpha}{1+\alpha} \end{pmatrix}^k \begin{pmatrix} \|e_0^x\| \\ \|e_0^y\| \end{pmatrix} \end{aligned}$$

Let

$$T = \begin{pmatrix} \alpha\beta & \beta \\ \frac{1}{1+\alpha} & \frac{\alpha}{1+\alpha} \end{pmatrix}$$

Clearly, if $\rho(T) < 1$, then $\lim_{k\to\infty} T^k = 0$. This implies

$$\lim_{k\to\infty} \|e_k^x\| = 0 \text{ and } \lim_{k\to\infty} \|e_k^y\| = 0.$$

In this way, the iteration sequence $\{x^{(k)}\}$ produced by the BAS iteration method (5) or (6) can achieve to the unique solution of the AVE (1).

Next, we just need to get the sufficient conditions for $\rho(T) < 1$. Let λ represent an eigenvalue of the matrix T. Then λ satisfies

$$(\lambda - \alpha\beta)(\lambda - \frac{\alpha}{1+\alpha}) - \frac{\beta}{1+\alpha} = 0,$$

which is equal to

$$\lambda^2 - (\alpha\beta + \frac{\alpha}{1+\alpha})\lambda - (1-\alpha)\beta = 0. \tag{9}$$

Applying Lemma 1 to Eq. (9), $|\lambda| < 1$ if and only if

$$|(1-\alpha)\beta| < 1$$

and

$$|\alpha\beta + \frac{\alpha}{1+\alpha}| < 1 - (1-\alpha)\beta.$$

Therefore, if the condition (7) holds, then $\rho(T) < 1$. This completes the proof. $\qquad\square$

Theorem 2. *Let $\lambda_{\min}$ denote the smallest eigenvalue of matrix A, where $A \in \mathbb{R}^{n\times n}$ is symmetric positive definite. If*

$$\alpha < \lambda_{\min},$$

then

$$|||(e_{k+1}^x, e_{k+1}^y)||| < |||(e_k^x, e_k^y)|||, k = 0, 1, \dots,$$

where

$$|||(e_k^x, e_k^y)||| = \sqrt{\|e_k^x\|^2 + \|e_k^y\|^2}.$$

This implies that the BAS method is convergent.

Proof. By simple calculation, we have

$$\begin{aligned} \beta(1+\alpha) &= (1+\alpha)\|(\alpha I + A)^{-1}\| \\ &= (1+\alpha)\|(\alpha I + A)^{-1}\| \\ &= \frac{1+\alpha}{1+\lambda_{\min}}. \end{aligned}$$

Obviously, when $\alpha < \lambda_{\min}$, $\beta(1+\alpha) < 1$. This complete the proof. $\qquad\square$

Corollary 1. *Let $A \in \mathbb{R}^{n \times n}$ be nonsingular and $b \in \mathbb{R}^n$. If*

$$\|A^{-1}\| \leq \frac{1}{1 + 2\alpha},$$

then

$$|||(e_{k+1}^x, e_{k+1}^y)||| < |||(e_k^x, e_k^y)|||, k = 0, 1, \ldots,$$

where

$$|||(e_k^x, e_k^y)||| = \sqrt{\|e_k^x\|^2 + \|e_k^y\|^2}.$$

This implies that the BAS iteration method is convergent.

Proof. Based on the Banach perturbation lemma in [23], we obtain

$$\beta(1 + \alpha) \leq \frac{(1 + \alpha)\|A^{-1}\|}{1 - \alpha\|A^{-1}\|}.$$

Obviously, when

$$\|A^{-1}\| \leq \frac{1}{1 + 2\alpha},$$

$\beta(1 + \alpha) < 1$. This complete the proof. □

3   Numerical Experiments

In this section, to demonstrate the performance of the BAS method for solving the AVE (1), some numerical experiments are given. To this end, we compare the BAS method with the GN method [9] and the NHSS method in [14, 15].

In our computations, we chose zero vector as all initial vectors and all iterations are stopped once the relative residual error meets

$$\frac{\|Ax^{(k)} - |x^{(k)}| - b\|_2}{\|b\|_2} \leq 10^{-6}$$

or if the prescribed iteration number 500 is exceeded. The vector b in (1) is properly chosen such that the vector $x = (x_1, x_2, \ldots, x_n)^T$ with

$$x_i = (-1)^i i, i = 1, 2, \ldots, n,$$

is the exact solution of the AVE (1). The coefficient matrix $\alpha I + H$ of the first subsystems in the NHSS method is symmetric positive definite and can be solved by the Cholesky factorization, and the coefficient matrix $\alpha I + S$ of the second subsystems in the NHSS method can be solved by the LU factorization. All tests were completed in MATLAB 7.0.

In our numerical experiments, the experimentally found optimal parameters α_{exp} are employed, which result in the least numbers of the BAS and NHSS iterations. Therefore, the optimal parameters employed in the BAS and NHSS iteration methods are used experimentally. As mentioned in [14] the computation of the optimal parameter is generally difficult to be gained and often problem-dependent.

In our numerical experiments, we consider the two-dimensional convection-diffusion equation

$$\begin{cases} -(u_{xx} + u_{yy}) + q(u_x + u_y) + pu = f(x,y), \ (x,y) \in \Omega, \\ u(x,y) = 0, \ (x,y) \in \partial\Omega, \end{cases} \tag{10}$$

where $p \in \mathbb{R}$ and $q \in \mathbb{R}$ is used to measure the magnitude of the diffusive term, $\Omega = (0,1) \times (0,1)$, and $\partial\Omega$ is its boundary, see [15]. On the unit square Ω, using the five-point finite difference technique for the diffusive terms and the central difference technique for the convective terms with the mesh-size $h = 1/(m+1)$, we obtain the linear equations $Cx = d$, where C is of the form

$$C = T_x \otimes I_m + I_m \otimes T_y + pI_n,$$

and its order is $n = m^2$, $\otimes$ stands for the Kronecker product, I_m and I_n are the identity matrices of order m and n, respectively,

$$T_x = \text{tridiag}(-1 - R_e, 4, -1 + R_e), T_y = \text{tridiag}(-1 - R_e, 0, -1 + R_e)$$

and $R_e = \frac{qh}{2}$ is the mesh Reynolds number. In our numerical experiments, we define the matrix A in AVE (1) by

$$A = C + 2(L - L^T)$$

with L being the strictly lower part of C. In Tables 1, 2 and 3, for different values of n, p and q, the numerical results are listed.

Table 1. Numerical results of $(q,p) = (0,-1)$

		n	400	900	1600	2500	3600
BAS	IT		41	53	69	87	107
	RES		1.8048e−7	2.7662e−7	3.1273e−7	6.2514e−7	3.0472e−7
	α_{exp}		0	0	0	0	0
NHSS	IT		51	70	89	111	137
	RES		9.2033e−7	8.8056e−7	9.9765e−7	9.9698e−7	8.4863e−7
	α_{exp}		7	7	6.9	6.8	7
GN	IT		−	−	−	−	−
	RES		−	−	−	−	−

In Tables 1, 2 and 3, it is easy to find that the number steps of the BAS and NHSS methods increase with the mesh size n increasing. When the GN method is used to solve the AVE, we find that it does not converge in 500 iterations

Table 2. Numerical results of $(q, p) = (0, -0.5)$

	n	400	900	1600	2500	3600
BAS	IT	35	45	55	67	83
	RES	8.7387e–7	4.5606e–7	4.7165e–7	8.1872e–7	7.8321e–7
	α_{exp}	0	0	0	0	0
NHSS	IT	38	51	64	78	92
	RES	6.0528e–7	7.2623e–7	8.9910e–7	8.1588e–7	8.5619e–7
	α_{exp}	5	5.2	4.9	5.4	5.5
GN	IT	–	–	–	–	–
	RES	–	–	–	–	–

Table 3. Numerical results of $(q, p) = (1, -1)$

	n	400	900	1600	2500	3600
BAS	IT	39	51	67	85	105
	RES	4.9489e–7	5.6453e–7	4.3071e–7	8.6319e–7	4.0652e–7
	α_{exp}	0	0	0	0	0
NHSS	IT	51	69	88	110	136
	RES	6.8367e–7	9.7396e–7	9.6429e–7	8.3406e–7	5.8932e–7
	α_{exp}	6.8	6.7	6.8	6.6	7.3
GN	IT	–	–	–	–	–
	RES	–	–	–	–	–

(denoted by '–' in tables). Compared the BAS method with the NHSS method, the number of iterations of the former are less than that of the latter. This implies that when the BAS and NHSS iteration methods are employed, the BAS method overmatches the NHSS method in terms of the number of iterations. From the numerical results in Tables 1, 2 and 3, the BAS method has better computing efficiency, compared with the GN and NHSS methods.

4   Conclusions

In this paper, based on the block-diagonal and anti-block-diagonal splitting (BAS) of the coefficient matrix of the equal two-by-two block nonlinear equation of the AVE, a block-diagonal and anti-block-diagonal splitting (BAS) iteration method is introduced. Some convergence conditions are obtained. Numerical experiments confirm that the BAS method is feasible, robust and efficient for the AVE.

Acknowledgments. The authors thank the anonymous referees for their constructive suggestions and helpful comments, which lead to significant improvement of the original manuscript of this paper.

References

1. Rohn, J.: A theorem of the alternatives for the equation $Ax + B|x| = b$. Linear Multilinear A. **52**, 421–426 (2004)
2. Mangasarian, O.L.: Absolute value programming. Comput. Optim. Appl. **36**, 43–53 (2007)
3. Mangasarian, O.L., Meyer, R.R.: Absolute value equations. Linear Algebra Appl. **419**, 359–367 (2006)
4. Wu, S.-L., Guo, P.: Modulus-based matrix splitting algorithms for the quasi-complementarity problems. Appl. Numer. Math. **132**, 127–137 (2018)
5. Cottle, R.W., Pang, J.-S., Stone, R.E.: The Linear Complementarity Problem. Academic, San Diego (1992)
6. Rohn, J.: An algorithm for solving the absolute value equations. Electron. J. Linear Algebra. **18**, 589–599 (2009)
7. Rohn, J., Hooshyarbakhsh, V., Farhadsefat, R.: An iterative method for solving absolute value equations and sufficient conditions for unique solvability. Optimization Letters **8**(1), 35–44 (2012). https://doi.org/10.1007/s11590-012-0560-y
8. Salkuyeh, D.K.: The Picard-HSS iteration method for absolute value equations. Optim. Lett. **8**, 2191–2202 (2014)
9. Mangasarian, O.L.: A generalized Newton method for absolute value equations. Optim. Lett. **3**, 101–108 (2009)
10. Hu, S.-L., Huang, Z.-H., Zhang, Q.: A generalized Newton method for absolute value equations associated with second order cones. J. Comput. Appl. Math. **235**, 1490–1501 (2011)
11. Nguyena, C.T., Saheyab, B., Chang, Y.-L., Chen, J.-S.: Unified smoothing functions for absolute value equation associated with second-order cone. Appl. Numer. Math. **135**, 206–227 (2019)
12. Mangasarian, O.L.: A hybrid algorithm for solving the absolute value equation. Optimization Letters **9**(7), 1469–1474 (2015). https://doi.org/10.1007/s11590-015-0893-4
13. Bai, Z.-Z., Golub, G.H., Ng, M.K.: Hermitian and skew-Hermitian splitting methods for non-Hermitian positive definite linear systems. SIAM J. Matrix Anal. Appl. **24**, 603–626 (2003)
14. Bai, Z.-Z., Yang, X.: On HSS-based iteration methods for weakly nonlinear systems. Appl. Numer. Math. **59**, 2923–2936 (2009)
15. Zhu, M.-Z., Zhang, G.-F., Liang, Z.-Z.: The nonlinear HSS-like iteration method for absolute value equations, arXiv.org:1403.7013v2 [math.NA] Jan 2, 2018
16. Benzi, M.: A generalization of the Hermitian and skew-Hermitian splitting iteration. SIAM J. Matrix Anal. Appl. **31**, 360–374 (2009)
17. Wu, S.-L., Li, C.-X.: The unique solution of the absolute value equations. Appl. Math. Lett. **76**, 195–200 (2018)
18. Wu, S.-L., Huang, T.-Z., Zhao, X.-L.: A modified SSOR iterative method for augmented systems. J. Comput. Appl. Math. **228**, 424–433 (2009)
19. Wang, A.-X., Wang, H.-J., Deng, Y.-K.: Interval algorithm for absolute value equations. Centr. Eur. J. Math. **9**, 1171–1184 (2011)
20. Ketabchi, S., Moosaei, H.: An efficient method for optimal correcting of absolute value equations by minimal changes in the right hand side. Comput. Math. Appl. **64**, 1882–1885 (2012)
21. Zhang, C., Wei, Q.-J.: Global and finite convergence of a generalized newton method for absolute value equations. J. Optim. Theory. Appl. **143**, 391–403 (2009)

22. Li, C.-X.: A preconditioned AOR iterative method for the absolute value equations. Int. J. Comput. Meth. (2017) https://doi.org/10.1142/S0219876217500165

23. Ortega, J.M., Rheinboldt, W.C.: Iterative Solution of Nonlinear Equations in Several Variables. Academic Press, New York (1970)

24. Jiang, D.-D., Wang, Y.-Q., Lv, Z.-H., Wang, W.-J., Wang, H.-H.: An energy-efficient networking approach in cloud services for IIoT networks. IEEE J. Sel. Area. Comn. **38**(5), 928–941 (2020)

25. Jiang, D.-D., Wang, W.-J., Shi, L., Song, H.-B.: A compressive sensing-based approach to end-to-end network traffic reconstruction. IEEE T. Netw. Sci. Eng. **7**(1), 507–519 (2020)

26. Jiang, D.-D., Huo, L.-W., Song, H.-B.: Rethinking behaviors and activities of base stations in mobile cellular networks based on big data analysis. IEEE T. Netw. Sci. Eng. **7**(1), 80–90 (2020)

27. Jiang D.-D., Wang Y.-Q., Lv Z.-H., Qi S., Singh S.: Big data analysis based network behavior insight of cellular networks for industry 4.0 applications. IEEE T. Ind. Inform. **16**(2), 1310–1320 (2020)

28. Jiang, D.-D., Huo, L.-W., Lv, Z.-H., Song, H.-B., Qin, W.-D.: A joint multi-criteria utility-based network selection approach for vehicle-to-infrastructure networking. IEEE T Intell. Transp. **19**(10), 3305–3319 (2018)

29. Jiang, D.-D., Huo, L.-W., Li, Y.: Fine-granularity inference and estimations to network traffic for SDN. Plos One. **13**(5), 1–23 (2018)

Engineering Semantic Composability Based on Ontological Metamodeling

Zhi Zhu[1]($\boxtimes$) (iD), Ning Zhu[2], Yongling Lei[1], Qun Li[1], and Huabing Wang[2]

[1] National University of Defense Technology, Changsha 410073, China
zhuzhi@nudt.edu.cn

[2] State Key Laboratory of Complex Electromagnetic Environment Effects on Electronics and Information System, Luoyang 471003, China

Abstract. Combat system modeling generally includes two aspects: structure and behavior. Structural modeling is to build the structure of entities and their internal and external static relationships. Behavioral modeling aims at the typical working processes. The simulation modeling definition language (SMDL) of Simulation Modeling Platform (SMP2) can describe system structure well, but it is difficult to support behavioral modeling. The modeling and simulation tool named Ptolemy is able to support the description of system behavior, but it lacks effective support for structural modeling. For this reason, the goal of the paper is to explore a mechanism to combine structural and behavioral modeling, which can not only effectively support the architecture design but also support the expression of system behaviors. As a proof of concept, we extend the SMDL by adding the synchronous data flow (SDF) elements, and use this new language, namely, the extended Simulation Model Definition Language (ESMDL), to specify a radar system for both of structural and behavioral modeling.

Keywords: Metamodeling · Semantic composability · SMP2

1 Introduction

Combat system presents the characteristics of large-scale and multiple subsystems. It have reached a complexity that requires inevitably the combined use of different formalisms to ensure correct domain descriptions and good model specifications [1]. Traditionally, pure theoretical analysis and experimental observation are not able to answer these complex questions because it is very difficult to observe the real operation process of an actual system, or the cost may be too expensive and restricted by various external factors [2]. Therefore, many researchers have paid attentions to simulation as an effective alternative method. Using the advantages that simulation brings, system experiment and analysis can acquire many benefits that theoretical analysis and experimental observation have not. In addition, in the face of new system or novel functional requirements, it is a real challenge that how to standardize the representation of simulation model, with the objective of maximizing the reuse of existing model and simulation resources, to achieve rapid and high-quality development of simulation applications.

H. Song and D. Jiang (Eds.): SIMUtools 2020, LNICST 369, pp. 582–592, 2021.
https://doi.org/10.1007/978-3-030-72792-5_46

Specifically, along the development of simulation application, this problem needs to address the following three aspects, which are also the long-term attention in the modeling and simulation community. Firstly, simulation model lacks the unified reusable model specification. Consequently, as a valuable knowledge-intensive asset, simulation model lacks reusability, which makes it difficult to support the rapid and high-quality development of simulation applications. Secondly, combat system modeling includes structure and behavior in general. The structural domain integrate behaviors tightly, which will lead to many issues such as unnecessary repetitive processes and a set of modeling and simulation resources of waste. Thirdly, a simulation model is traditionally viewed as an ordinary software and it lacks the support of a standardized simulation modeling language which can describe its structure and behavior simultaneously.

For above problems, the goal of the paper is to design a new simulation modeling language called ESMDL (Extended Simulation Model Definition Language). This language is established by extending the SMP2, which can support typical behavioral modeling paradigm like synchronous data stream (SDF). Furtherly, the simulation scheduling operation mechanism is designed to seek a simulation modeling method with high efficiency, strong reusability and easy expansion, which can effectively support the radar system construction in various environments. Finally, taking a certain radar system as an example, this paper uses ESMDL to model and simulate the radar target scene, echo simulation, signal processing, data processing, display and evaluation subsystem, and verifies the method proposed in the paper.

2 Related Works

Since 1960s, the research on radar system simulation modeling technology has been started and a large number of excellent simulation model specifications, modeling paradigms and simulation protocols have been formed, as well as a series of radar simulation models. However, the theory and method of simulation modeling have not yet formed a unified standard and specification, nor a general radar simulation application system [3]. Therefore, it is difficult to reuse the radar simulation model, and the combination and interoperability is not strong. Aiming at the problems of high level architecture (HLA) [4] such as complex architecture, difficult model granularity control and system maintenance, SISO (Simulation Interoperability Standards Organization) proposed the base object model (BOM). In the early 1990s, ESA (European Space Agent) recognized the problems of simulation reuse and model transplantation in different development stages and projects during the development of many spacecraft. In the mid-1990s, ESA initiated the formulation plan of simulation model portability standards (SMP) [5], with the goal of realizing the exchange of models among the simulation platforms.

Some research work has also done a lot of research work in radar system simulation modeling, and achieved many outstanding results. In the early 1990s, the National University of Defense Technology has begun to organize forces to develop distributed simulation support software. In 1996, DIS-Link, the first distributed simulation support software in China that met the DIS standard, solved the time synchronization and management problems of large-scale DIS, and surpassed VR link in terms of function and performance. In 1999, KD-RTI software, the first HLA compliant software in China, was developed. A system method for large-scale combat simulation system integration based on shared resource library and general simulation environment was proposed. The HLA simulation environment and platform software have been successfully used in hundreds of distributed simulation systems inside and outside the army.

In fact, the above-mentioned simulation modeling technologies fall into standards and specifications based and specific domain oriented. The former focuses on the syntactic heterogeneity of simulation models, while the latter focuses on the differences in semantic expression [6]. These two types of simulation modeling methods complement with each other, and build reusable simulation model library from syntax and semantic levels respectively to achieve simulation resource reuse, save simulation development cost and improve efficiency of simulation application development. The first mock exam is to attempt to unify the formal representation and formal definition of models from the technical or grammatical level, such as unified model specification and simulation protocol like HLA and SMP. Such as unified modeling methods and platforms like discrete event system specification (DEVS) [7, 8]. The second type is from domain or semantics. For example, the application system based on specific domain, including extended air defense system (EADSIM) [9], system effectiveness analysis simulation of air force (SEAS) [10], etc.

The above two kinds of simulation modeling technologies solve the problem of combination reuse of simulation models to a great extent from the perspective of standard specification and specific domain oriented, and have achieved good results, which also lay a solid foundation for current and future modeling and simulation research [11]. However, the following problems still exist in the field of radar simulation modeling. Firstly, most of the above simulation modeling standards and simulation systems are commercial, and their application fields are relatively sensitive. There is no effective model sharing mechanism among various units, and there is not enough support for new requirements in the new system radar and the expansion and development of new models. Secondly, most simulation systems have adopted relatively high performance. However, the radar models in these simulation systems either pay attention to the radar composition structure and external static interface relationship, or pay attention to the single representation of radar behavior. There is no effective and flexible integration mechanism between the two aspects. Thirdly, many radar simulation systems support a single electronic warfare style and lack of rapid combination of multiple scenarios in complex system combat environment. A set of integrated simulation software tools, including scenario editing, model development, experiment design, decision modeling, two-dimensional and three-dimensional situation display are not able to accurately and effectively evaluate the performance of radar in complex combat system [12].

3   Engineering Semantic Composability of Simulation Models

3.1   The Proposed Framework

The overall technical scheme of the paper is based on the system modeling and simulation platform, integrating ESMDL simulation operation scheduling mechanism, ESMDL simulation modeling language, and system application, as shown in Fig. 1.

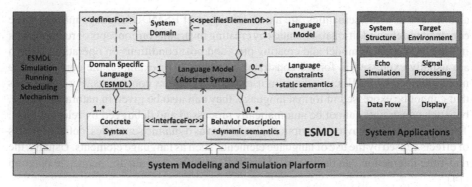

Fig. 1. The proposed framework.

Firstly, system modeling and simulation platform provides the operation environment and related tools for radar system simulation, including the whole process of equipment design and demonstration from the integrated development of simulation model, data preparation, scenario editing, experimental design, etc.

Secondly, the core of the project is the design of ESMDL. It is combination of SDF and SMP2. Like the new domain specific language (DSL), it mainly involves the definition of syntax and semantics [13]. The core language model, language model constraint and behavior description are aggregated together to form the core of ESMDL, namely language model. In addition, the concrete syntax is separated and is used to create a friendly human-computer interaction form of ESMDL.

Thirdly, the research of ESMDL simulation running scheduling mechanism supports the simulation execution algorithm of ESMDL model. It mainly extends the execution part of SDF based on the original basic model execution algorithm of SMP2, such as pipelined serial and parallel simulation scheduling algorithms, so as to improve the simulation execution efficiency of ESMDL model. Finally, taking a certain radar system application as an example, the new ESMDL simulation modeling language is used to design the radar model, including structure and behavior, to verify the feasibility and effectiveness of the project research content.

3.2 ESMDL Metamodeling

ESMDL is a new domain specific language based on SMP2 for behavioral computing models such as SDF. The key of this technology is to find out the extension points for SDF based on the deep understanding of SMP2 metamodel, and straighten out which elements need to be extended and which elements need mapping. Generally, domain specific language consists of language model and concrete grammar. Language model, also known as abstract grammar model, abstracts domain knowledge by defining elements of the target domain. It is composed of three parts: core language model, language model constraint and behavior description.

Firstly, the core language model defines the concepts related to a specific target domain and the relationship between them, which is usually described by appropriate modeling language, such as UML class diagram. Secondly, language model constraints, also known as static semantics, are a necessary part of ESMDL language model. These constraints define additional semantics by creating invariants on concepts or relationships in the core language model and creating pre - and post conditions on operations, which are usually expressed in formal constraint languages. For example, the core language model defined by UML class diagram uses OCL to express constraints. For constraints that cannot be expressed in formal language, they can also be given in natural language, but such constraints cannot be automatically processed and debugged by relevant tools. Thirdly, ESMDL behavior description, also known as dynamic semantics, defines a series of effects caused by the use of language elements, such as language elements. Usually, the real-time interaction can be expressed by UML activity diagram and sequence diagram [14].

The Synchronous Data Flow Metamodel. It is known as static data flow, is a special form of data flow model. In the data flow model, as long as the input data of the role meets the requirements. SDF is a simpler data flow, whose role execution order is static and does not depend on the data.

As shown in Fig. 2, the root node is schedule, which is composed of one or more nodes and transitions. One node can be connected to multiple transitions; on the contrary, a transition can only be connected to one node. A node can contain multiple input/output ports, and each port is associated with at least one token (It is an abstract class of all data, which is divided into two types required before and after the role is executed. The data transferred between roles are instances of token, making the real data invisible. The specific type of token is declared by the user in the role definition). A transition can have a buffer buffer (data transfer between nodes in a data flow graph can be implemented by using a FIFO queue buffer, and the size of this buffer will vary with the execution of the graph).

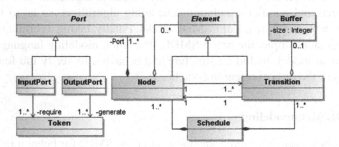

Fig. 2. The SDF metamodel.

The SMP Metamodel. It consists of three parts: catalog, assembly and schedule. The extension points related to SDF exist in the latter two parts, assembly (as shown in Fig. 3) and schedule (as shown in Fig. 4). In the assembly metamodel, links allows you to connect all model instances to the assembly itself.

1. Interface chain. It is responsible for connecting references and provided interfaces, used for interface based design and component-based design.

2. Event chain. It connects event slot with event source of the same type. For event based design.
3. Field chain. It connects input and output fields of the same type.

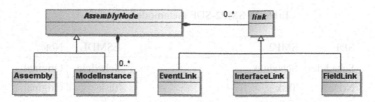

Fig. 3. SMP2-Assembly metamodel (part).

In the schedule metamodel, tasks are containers for activities. The order of activities defines the calling order of the entry points referenced by the activity element. Events are elements in a schedule that trigger tasks that themselves refer to entry points for model instances. Events can be timed events or periodic events. The timed event and timed event belong to the trigger that is called only once by the scheduler. The deltatime element is a relative time, which specifies when the event is executed; the kind attribute specifies the time type and supports the following four time formats.

1. Simulation time: start from 0 moment of simulation start, and advance in the execution mode of simulation.
2. Epochal time: it is an absolute time, which is typically advanced with simulation time. And simulation time offset may change during simulation.
3. Mission time: it is a relative time, expressed as the duration from a certain beginning, which is typically advanced together with epoch time.
4. Zulu time: is the computer clock time, also known as the wall clock time, regardless of the simulation stage will advance forward.

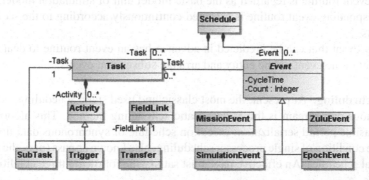

Fig. 4. SMP2-Schedule metamodel (part).

SMP2-SDF Metamodel Mapping. Based on the analysis of the above SMP2 and SDF meta models, the extended points for SDF in SMP2 metamodel are found out, and the mapping relationship of smp2-sdf meta model is defined, which elements need to be used, which elements need to be extended or added, as shown in Table 1.

Table 1. SMP2-SDF metamodel mapping.

SDF	SMP2	ESMDL	Note
Schedule	Schedule	Schedule	Original
Node	Task	Task	Original
Port	FieldLink/EventLink/InterfaceLink	Port	extended
Transition	Sink/Source, output/input	Transition	extended
Token	None	Token	Added
Buffer	None	Buffer	Added

3.3 ESMDL Scheduling Strategy

In SMP2, schedule is a document, which contains any number of tasks (task elements) and the events that trigger these tasks. It is necessary to specify the event triggering strategies to get the execution order of tasks. These tasks refer to the entry points of model instances. In SDF, role triggering requires multiple input tokens and does not necessarily produce a single token, which is called multi rate SDF. In this case, it is necessary to define the execution order of roles and the execution times of each role, that is, the model execution scheduling problem.

Event Scheduling. The event scheduling method first appeared in the early version of SIMSCRIPT language, which was introduced in 1963. Its basic idea includes:

1. The event routine is regarded as the basic model unit of simulation model, and the corresponding event routine is executed continuously according to the sequence of events.
2. Every event that can be predicted in advance has an event routine to deal with the impact of the event on the entity and arrange subsequent events.

Serial Scheduling. At present, the most classic and used static scheduling method for synchronous data stream is the S-class static scheduling method. This algorithm can find a feasible period serialization execution schedule of synchronous data flow graph under the condition of single processor scheduling, also known as pass (periodic adaptive sequential schedule). An effective pass must satisfy the following three conditions:

1. Full participation. This ensures that each node is executed, that is, each node in pass appears at least once.

2. No deadlock. When there is delay unit, deadlock will not occur.
3. Buffer bounded. The output data generated by each node can be consumed equally by other nodes without causing buffer accumulation.

Parallel Scheduling. As shown in Fig. 5, in the parallel scheduling method, it is not necessary to wait for the completion of one iteration to start the next iteration, but it can be executed in parallel with the nodes in other iterations after the execution of one node in one iteration. Compared with the serial scheduling method, especially for the radar system which needs many Monte Carlo simulation experiments, the time utilization is greatly improved.

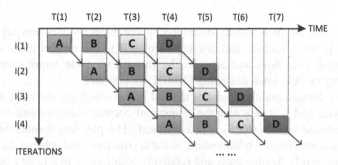

Fig. 5. Parallel scheduling.

4   Case Study

The system model framework based on ESMDL is divided into different domains and levels, which generally includes static structure, physical domain behavior and cognitive domain behavior horizontally, and system layer, subsystem layer, business component layer, algorithm support layer and computing model layer vertically [15, 16], as shown in Fig. 6. In this way, the flexibility, reusability and expansibility of radar system model are enhanced both vertically and horizontally, which supports the rapid development of radar system models with different functional characteristics and meets different radar system simulation requirements.

As can be seen from the above figure, the knowledge structure of model framework is divided into three parts: static structure, physical domain behavior and cognitive domain behavior.

1. Static structure mainly describes the related concepts and relationships in the domain, which is the most stable part and does not change with the change of human will or environment [17].
2. Physical domain behavior describes the concepts such as data flow, state change, event migration in the domain, which is the inherent behavior mode of an entity, and its flexibility is between the static organizational structure and the behavior of

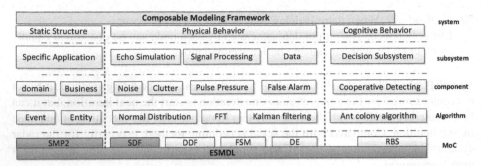

Fig. 6. CESS onto CMFs.

cognitive domain. It is usually described by synchronous data flow, dynamic data flow, finite state machine and discrete event (DE). The project plans to focus on synchronous data flow, and consider the future expansion requirements of other computing models when designing ESMDL metamodel.

3. Cognitive domain mainly describes tactical rules, which are the most flexible part of the three, and will vary with the changes of combat scenarios and commanders, and rule-based system (RBS) is usually used. The physical domain behavior can flexibly use entities and relationships in static structure, and achieve the purpose of reusing relatively flexible parts and relatively stable parts to a large extent without completely rewriting the model.

Vertically, the model framework is divided into five levels from top to bottom: system layer, subsystem layer, component layer, algorithm layer and computing model layer. When defining the upper layer, the appropriate concepts are selected from the next layer according to different applications to be specialized and extended to realize the reuse of concepts and relationships. This model can ensure high standards and quality.

1. The system layer is mainly for application, and users can easily build radar simulation system according to their needs by customizing various subsystems.
2. The subsystem is similar to the system layer, but with finer granularity, it can also customize and combine the lower level components to build subsystems with different functions freely.
3. The component layer is the module with specific functions. It can be an atomic module or a composite module assembled by lower level algorithms.
4. The algorithm layer is a composite function that encapsulates different mature algorithms into functions or a composite function constructed by simple algorithms, which is usually used to construct upper level components.
5. The computational model layer is mainly used to provide running environment and model semantics and control different levels of simulation model, and organize the running of simulation system.

5   Conclusions

The behavioral modeling technology based on SMP2 combines the advantages of SMP2 and SDF. It explores a system simulation modeling method which can support the description of system structure and behavior at the same time. Thus, this method can acquire high efficiency, strong reusability and easy expansion, so as to improve the development efficiency and construction quality of simulation system, and save the development cost. Furthermore, this technology provides an important reference for SMP2 to provide more behavioral computing models. It can further consider the expansion of dynamic data flow, state machine, discrete event and other behavioral computing models, so as to solve the development needs of large-scale, multi system and complex functions of current and future radar systems. In the face of new combat system or demand, it can realize the modeling and simulation of new simulation system comprehensively, rapidly and high quality, provide support for the system demonstration, development, test identification, use training and comprehensive support of radar equipment, and improve the scientific level of radar equipment development. However, as a drawback more simulations about different scenarios are necessarily required as further illustrations.

Acknowledgement. We are grateful to the anonymous referees for their helpful reviews, and all the volunteers who wrote and provided helpful comments on previous versions of this document. We gratefully acknowledge the State Key Laboratory of Complex Electromagnetic Environment Effects on Electronics and Information System (CEMEE) (NO. CEMEE2020K0302A) for supporting this research.

References

1. Taylor, S.J.E., Khan, A., Morse K.L., et al.: Grand challenges on the theory of modeling and simulation. In: Proceedings of the Symposium on Theory of Modeling & Simulation - DEVS Integrative M&S Symposium, pp. 1–8. Society for Computer Simulation International, San Diego (2013)
2. Lei, Y.L., Zhu, Z., Li, Q.: An ontological metamodeling framework for semantic simulation model engineering. J. Syst. Eng. Electron. **31**(3), 527–538 (2020)
3. Tolk, A.: The next generation of modeling & simulation: integrating big data and deep learning. In: Proceedings of the Conference on Summer Computer Simulation, pp. 1–8. Society for Computer Simulation International, San Diego (2015)
4. IEEE Computer Society. https://standards.ieee.org/standard/1516-2010.html. Accessed 25 Aug 2020
5. ESA. https://www.eurosim.nl/support/manuals/manual_4_2/pdf/SMP_2.0_Metamodel-1.2. pdf. Accessed 28 Aug 2020
6. Kim, B.S., Kang, B.G., Choi, S.H., et al.: Data modeling versus simulation modeling in the big data era: case study of a greenhouse control system. SIMULATION **93**(7), 579–594 (2017)
7. Zeigler, B.P., Praehofer, H., Kim, T.G.: Theory of Modeling and Simulation: Integrating Discrete Event and Continuous Complex Dynamic Systems, 2nd edn. Academic Press, New York (2000)

8. Tendeloo, Y.V., Vangheluwe, H.S.: Classic DEVS modelling and simulation. In: Winter Simulation Conference, Las Vegas, Nevadam, pp. 644–658. Society of International Modeling and Simulation (2017)

9. Azar, M.C.: Assessing the Treatment of Airborne Tactical High Energy Lasers in Combat Simulations. M.S. Thesis, Air Force Institute of Technology, Dayton, OH (2003)

10. Miller, J.O., Jason, L., Honabarger, B.: Modeling and measuring network centric warfare (NCW) with the system effectiveness analysis simulation (SEAS). In: 11th International Command and Control Research and Technology Symposium, pp.1–12 (2006)

11. Pidd, M.: Tools for Thinking-Modeling in Management Science. Wiley, New York (2009)

12. Antoine-Santoni, T., Poggi, B., Vittori, E., Van Hieux, H., Delhom, M., Aiello, A.: "Smart Entity" – how to build DEVS models from large amount of data and small amount of knowledge? In: Song, H., Jiang, D. (eds.) SIMUtools 2019. LNICSSITE, vol. 295, pp. 615–626. Springer, Cham (2019). https://doi.org/10.1007/978-3-030-32216-8_60

13. Grieves, M.W.: Product lifecycle management: the new paradigm for enterprises. Int. J. Prod. Dev. 2(1–2), 71–84 (2005)

14. Deist, T., Patti, A., Wang, Z., et al.: Simulation assisted machine learning. Bioinformatics 35(20), 1–1 (2018)

15. Atkinson, C., Kuhne, T.: Model-driven development: a metamodeling foundation. IEEE Softw. 20(5), 36–41 (2003)

16. Zhu, Z., Lei, Y.L., Zhu, N., Zhu, Y.F.: Composable modeling frameworks for networked air & missile defense systems. J. Nat. Univ. Defense Technol. 36(5), 186–190 (2014)

17. Zhu, Z., Lei, Y.L., Zhu, Y.F.: Model-driven combat effectiveness simulation systems engineering. Def. Sci. J. 70(1), 54–59 (2020)

An Empirical Study on the Impact of Scientific and Technological Innovation on New Urbanization

In Case of Guangdong Province

Hu Ping[1]([✉]), Xie Qun[2], and Hu Zhong Ping[3]

[1] Guangdong University of Foreign Studies South China Business College, Guangzhou 510545, Guangdong, China
[2] Guangzhou College of Commerce, Guangzhou 510545, Guangdong, China
[3] Changde Municipal Party School of CPC, Changde 415000, Hunan, China

Abstract. Based on the data of new urbanization and scientific and scientific and technological innovation in Guangdong Province from 2006 to 2018, the regression model and typical correlation coefficient analysis method are used to study the impact of scientific and technological innovation level on new urbanization in Guangdong Province. The results show that the scientific and technological innovation level and the new urbanization level are fluctuating, and the scientific and technological innovation has a positive and significant impact on the new urbanization in Guangdong. When the scientific and technological innovation factor changes by 1%, the new urbanization rate changes by 0.524%. And technology innovation and population urbanization, economic urbanization and social urbanization related to a higher degree, but with infrastructure and resources environment urbanization slightly inadequate. Therefore, in the process of accelerating the construction of new urbanization in Guangdong Province, we need to change the development mode of "factor-driven" to "innovation-driven".

Keywords: Scientific and technological innovation · New urbanization · Canonical correlation coefficient

1 Foreword

China has entered the decisive stage of building a well-to-do society in an all-round way. It is in an important period of economic transformation and upgrading and speeding up the socialist modernization, as well as in a key period of new-type urbanization construction. It is of great significance to deeply understand the urbanization and urban development to the economic and social development, grasp the great opportunity of urbanization, accurately study and judge the new trend and new characteristics of urbanization development, and properly deal with the risk challenge of urbanization. With the economic development entering into the "new normal", the dynamic mechanism of urban development and urbanization will undergo structural changes in China.

H. Song and D. Jiang (Eds.): SIMUtools 2020, LNICST 369, pp. 593–610, 2021.
https://doi.org/10.1007/978-3-030-72792-5_47

The mode of development has shifted from intensive factor input and extensive development to innovative activities and production services, which will lead to changes in urban employment structure, functional division, spatial layout and even adjustment of urbanization patterns. Scientifically analyze and accurately grasp the new law of urban development and urbanization under the "new normal" and enhance the forward-looking nature of urban and town group planning, which is not only related to the general direction of china's urban construction in the next few decades, but also related to further enhance the comprehensive competitiveness of our cities. Due to the continuous growth of population and the improvement of urbanization level, Chinese cities have experienced unprecedented rapid expansion. China is faced with prominent urban diseases and great resource pressure, which restrict the sustainable and healthy development of cities. How to improve the quality of urban development and urban service functions through scientific and technological innovation, and further realize the balanced development of urban and rural areas, and build a beautiful China, is a major and urgent practical problem during the 14th five-year Plan period. In order to clarify the development ideas, overall objectives, key tasks and safeguard measures of scientific and technological innovation in the field of urbanization and urban development during the 13th Five Year Plan period, a series of documents were formulated for overall deployment. For example "The "13th Five-Year" Urbanization and Urban Development Science and Technology Innovation Special Plan", "National Innovation-driven Development Strategy Outline", "13th Five-Year" National Science and Technology Innovation Plan, "National Medium and Long-term Science and Technology Development Plan Outline (2006–2020)", "National New Urbanization Plan (2014–2020)". It is the first time that the field of urbanization and urban development has been independently deployed as a key area, highlighting the important position and strategic significance of urbanization and urban development in China's economic and social development. The innovation of science and technology is the strong support of the new-type urbanization, which accelerates the process of urbanization and promotes the industrial transformation and upgrading. In the new socialist era, we should further clarify the laws of scientific and technological innovation and the development of new urbanization, clarify the technological needs of the development of new urbanization and the strategic path of relying on scientific and technological innovation to promote the development of new urbanization. It is of great significance to actively and steadily promote the construction of new-type urbanization.

2 Literature Review

Through an overview of domestic and foreign research trends, scientific and technological innovation and urbanization have always been one of the hot topics for scholars to study, and have made abundant achievements. By the end of 2020, a total of 52,939 literatures were searched on CNKI with "urbanization" as the key word. A total of 169,320 literatures were searched with "scientific and technological innovation" as the key word. However, there are only 877 literatures on the relationship between scientific and technological innovation and urbanization, among which only one was published in 1991. During the five years from 2013 to 2017, the research results were the most, with about 100 articles per year. It can be seen that the relationship between scientific and technological innovation and urbanization has attracted more and more attention from scholars. However, compared with the research results of "urbanization" and "scientific and technological innovation", it can be seen that the research in relevant fields is slightly insufficient. From the current literature, it can be concluded as the following three aspects:

First, It is theoretical research British economist K. J. Button (1986) thought that "the development of industrialization promoted the development of urbanization and the development of urbanization reacted on the development of industrialization because of the agglomeration effect and promotes the further development of the scale of cities. And pointed out that scientific and technological innovation is the basis of urbanization, driving the development of urbanization. Grossman believed that "endogenous technological progress can promote the development of urbanization" [1]. Chen Qiang yuan and Liang Qi used the framework of spatial economics research, simulation, derivation and numerical methods that found under the assumption of heterogeneous labor force and knowledge spillover. It is considered that high productivity and high technology industries support the development of urbanization. The local government should attach importance to the technological progress and industrial upgrading of the city, and cultivate the comparative advantage of the technology of the city, so as to improve the comprehensive strength of its own city [2].

Second, It is empirical research. Lu JiTong used VAR model to study the dynamic relationship between scientific and technological innovation, direct investment and urbanization in the Beijing-Tianjin-Hebei region from 1998 to 2013. He believed that scientific and technological innovation and the evolution trend of urbanization level are similar, and scientific and technological innovation has a strong driving effect on the development of urbanization [3]. Wang WanYin applied the structural equation model analysis method, and the result showed that the innovation ability of science and technology in Shanxi Province has the support function to the new urbanization development, and the science and technology investment and the environment have the biggest promotion function to the new type urbanization [4]. Tian Yi-piao, Xu Xiuchuan and others used inter-provincial panel data to analyze the dynamic correlation between scientific and technological innovation in 30 provinces and cities and the development of newly opened urbanization. The results show that there is a two-way positive relationship between scientific and technological innovation and new urbanization. However, the impact of science and technology on urbanization has some lag, and science and technology show the characteristics of "inverted U" type [5]. Zhang Jian Qing used PVAR model to analyze the correlation between new urbanization and scientific and technological innovation in the middle and lower reaches of the Yangtze River. The results show that the dynamic correlation between scientific and technological innovation and new urbanization is time-delay, and the interaction effect between the two is negative. The influence between the two changes from negative to positive over time. Moreover, the effect of new urbanization on scientific and technological innovation is stronger than that on new urbanization, and there is a strong regional difference in the interaction between the two [6]. Zheng Qiang's method of building the panel threshold model systematically analyzes the impact of China's scientific and technological innovation on new-type urbanization. The results show that: "in the sample period, the level of China's new-type urbanization presented a fluctuating upward trend and had the spatial pattern characteristics of decreasing gradient in coastal, inland and border regions; The impact of scientific and technological innovation on new-type urbanization is significantly based on the positive double-threshold effect of scientific and technological innovation level and time" [7]. The positive effect of scientific and technological innovation on new-type urbanization will gradually weaken with the improvement of scientific and technological innovation level and the passage of time.

Third, the study of the relationship between the scientific and technological innovation and urbanization. The research on the relationship between scientific and technological innovation and urbanization mainly includes two aspects: on the one hand, it is about the impact of scientific and technological innovation on urbanization. Grossman believes that "endogenous technology innovation can improve the development level of urbanization" to promote a country's long-term economic development [1]; Wang Jiwu believes that the key to breaking through the bottleneck of urbanization lies in scientific and technological innovation [8]; Liu Weiwei believes that "scientific and technological innovation to promote and promote the development of new urbanization" [9]; Yu Lian (2016) thought that "scientific and technological innovation is the strong support of new urbanization" [10]. On the other hand, the research on the interactive relationship between scientific and technological innovation and urbanization. Cheng Kaiming et al. found that urbanization has a strong influence on scientific and technological innovation, and vice versa [11]. Through empirical studies, Tian Yiqian proved that there was a bidirectional positive relationship between S&T innovation and new urbanization, but the effect of mutual influence was lagging [12].

A comprehensive review of the literature, although there is a considerable amount of research on urbanization and scientific and technological innovation materials. However, the research on the interaction between technology innovation and urbanization is relatively insufficient, which mainly shows two points. First, the focus of the study is to replace urbanization with population urbanization and the research on new urbanization is slightly deficient because the new urbanization emphasizes the urbanization of people and the connotation of all-round development. Second, there are more qualitative studies on the relationship between scientific and technological innovation and new urbanization and fewer articles use quantitative analysis with more analysis of national or provincial data. Due to the natural environment, geographical location, resource endowment, economic base and policy inclination, the level of scientific and technological innovation in each region may also be different so the impact on new urbanization may also be different. From the current literature, there is little research on the correlation analysis of scientific and technological innovation and new urbanization in Guangdong. Therefore, it is necessary to explore the impact of scientific and technological innovation on the new urbanization in Guangdong Province.

Based on this, this study attempts to make a comparative and systematic study of Guangdong Province from the following two aspects. First, based on the connotation of new urbanization, 18 indicators were selected from the five aspects of population, economy, society, resources and environment and infrastructure urbanization to build a comprehensive evaluation index system for the new urbanization level. Based on the connotation of scientific and technological innovation, a comprehensive evaluation index system of scientific and technological innovation is constructed from the four aspects of input of scientific and technological innovation, output capacity of scientific and technological innovation, environment of scientific and technological innovation and transformation capacity of scientific and technological innovation. Second, it carries out non-dimensionless quantification of the two index systems. Then the standard deviation, mean value and coefficient of variation of each indicator are calculated, and the weight of each indicator, the level of scientific and technological innovation and the level of new urbanization are calculated. Finally, the regression analysis is carried out.

3 Construction of Evaluation Index System of Scientific and Technological Innovation and New Urbanization

3.1 Selection of Indicators

The scientific and technological innovation ability and the new urbanization appraisal index system follow the principle: first, the comprehensive principle. According to the existing research results, try to reflect the connotation of comprehensive scientific and technological innovation and new urbanization; The second is the principle of brevity, which requires the reflection of essential or important problems in the design of indicators. For those special, secondary, non-essential issues are not considered; Third, the availability of data. The availability of data is an important condition for measurement. Starting from the connotation of science and technology innovation ability and new urbanization development, this paper designs the evaluation level index of science and technology innovation development and new urbanization development, and selects 11 and 18 indexes for data collection, and then makes statistics and analysis on them. The indicators are shown in Tables 1 and 2:

3.2 Methods of Research

The measurement of scientific and scientific and technological innovation ability and new urbanization is a comprehensive measure. We first determine the weight of 15 indicators of scientific and scientific and technological innovation ability by using the coefficient of variation method, and then determine the annual comprehensive score through the efficiency coefficient method. The new urbanization is calculated by the same method. The calculation process of variation coefficient method and efficacy coefficient method is as follows:

1. Normalization of data

Since there are 15 indicators in the evaluation of scientific and scientific and technological innovation capability, the order of magnitude and units of each index are quite different. Therefore, we first normalize the data, that is, dimensionless quantitative method. There are two common methods for data normalization, one is maximum and minimum normalization, and the other is standard coefficient normalization. Since the normalization of standard coefficient requires the number of samples to be compared Therefore, this paper uses simple normalization. The calculation formula is as follows:

Table 1. Indicator system of STI capability

Level indicators	The secondary indicators	Level 3 indicators
Index of scientific and technological innovation ability (X)	Scientific and technological innovation input (X1)	R&D Investment status (billion) (X01)
		R&D Activity growth rate (%) (X02)
		R&D Full-time personnel equivalent (Ten thousand person years) (X03)
		R&D Intensity of investment (%) (X04)
	Output capacity of scientific and technological innovation (X2)	Number of applications for invention patents accepted (piece) (X05)
		Power of attorney for patent application for invention (piece) (X06)
		Number of scientific papers published(sheet) (X07)
		Number of technological activities (nape) (X08)
	Scientific and technological innovation environment (X3)	Number of college graduates(people) (X09)
		The share of Science Education in GDP (%) (X10)
		The share of Government Science and Technology Appropriations in Local Fiscal Expenditure (%) (X11)
		Number of libraries per 10,000 people (individual) (X12)
	Ability to transform scientific and technological innovation (X4)	Number of contracts in the technical market (nape) (X13)
		Technology market turnover (billion) (X14)
		Output value of high-tech industry (billion) (X15)

Dimensionless quantification:

$$z_{ij} = \frac{x_{ij} - \min(x_{ij})}{\max(x_{ij}) - \min(x_{ij})} \quad i = 1, 2, ..., 13; \quad j = 01, 02, ..., 15 \qquad \text{(formula1)}$$

Table 2. New urbanization indicator system

Level indicators	The secondary indicators	Level 3 indicators
New type urbanization comprehensive development level (Y)	Population urbanization (Y1)	Proportion of non-agricultural population (%) (Y01)
		Population density (person/km^2) (Y02)
		Second and third industry personnel accounted for the total population proportion (%) (Y03)
	Economic urbanization (Y2)	Per capita gross domestic product (Yuan/person) (Y04)
		Per capita retail sales of consumer goods (yuan) (Y05)
		Per capita disposable income of urban residents (yuan) (Y06)
		The second and third industries' output value as a proportion of GDP (%) (Y07)
		Per capita investment in fixed assets (Yuan/person) (Y08)
	Social urbanization (Y3)	Passenger vehicles (thousands) (Y09)
		Number of students in colleges and universities per 10,000 population (people) (Y10)
		Number of hospital beds per 10,000 persons (sheet) (Y11)
	Infrastructure urbanization (Y4)	Total urban water supply (10,000 cubic metres) (Y12)
		Urban water penetration rate (%) (Y13)
		Urban construction land area (km^2) (Y14)
	Resources and environment urbanization (Y5)	Green coverage (%) (Y15)

(*continued*)

Table 2. (*continued*)

Level indicators	The secondary indicators	Level 3 indicators
		Per capita park green area (m^2/person) (Y16)
		Per capita forest area (ha) (Y17)
		Water resources per capita (m^3/person) (Y18)

Among them, i represents the years from 2006 to 2018, 2006 is 1, and 2008 is 13; j represents the number of indicators, a total of 15 indicators; X_{ij} represents the number of indicators 15 for raw data; X_{ij} represents the dimensionless value.

2. Calculate the coefficient of variation of each index

Firstly, the standard deviation and mean value of each index are calculated, and then the coefficient of variation is calculated by using the formula of coefficient of variation. Finally, the weight of each index, the level of scientific and scientific and technological innovation and the level of new urbanization are calculated.

$$\text{mean value} : \overline{z_j} = \sum_{i=1}^{n} z_{ij} \ (i = 1, 2, ..., 13; \ j = 01, 02, ...15)$$

$$\text{standard deviation} : \sigma_j = \sqrt{\sum_{i=1}^{n} \frac{(z_{ij} - \overline{z_j})^2}{n}} \ (i = 1, 2, ..., 13; \ j = 01, 02, ..., 15)$$

$$\text{Coefficient of variation} : v_j = \frac{\sigma_j}{\overline{z_j}} \ (j = 01, 02, ..., 15) \qquad \text{(formula2)}$$

Among them, σ_j represents the standard deviation of each index, $\overline{z_j}$ represents the average value of each index, and v_j represents the coefficient of variation of the index.

3. Calculate the weight of each index

$$\text{The weight of each index} : w_j = \frac{v_j}{\sum_{j=1}^{n} v_j} \ (j = 01, 02, ..., 15) \qquad \text{(formula3)}$$

4. Comprehensive score of scientific and scientific and technological innovation development level

Development level of scientific and scientific and technological innovation:

$$c_i = \sum_{j=y}^{n} z_{ij} * (w_j)^T \ (i = 1, 2, ..., 13; \ j = 01, 02, ..., 15) \qquad \text{(formula4)}$$

Among them, c_i represents the annual comprehensive score of the development level of scientific and scientific and technological innovation, $(w_j)^T$ represents the transposition of the weight matrix. According to the same calculation method, the weight and comprehensive score of the development level of new urbanization are calculated.

3.3 Sources of Data

According to the index system established above, the original data of scientific and scientific and technological innovation indicators and new urbanization development indicators can be found in the statistical yearbook of Guangdong Province, science and Technology Yearbook of Guangdong Province, China Science and Technology Yearbook, wind database and Government Gazette from 2006 to 2019.

4 An Empirical Study on the Impact of Scientific and Technological Innovation on the Development of New Urbanization

4.1 The Measurement of Technology Innovation Ability

According to the index system of scientific and scientific and technological innovation ability constructed above, the weights of 15 indicators of scientific and scientific and technological innovation ability are obtained through coefficient of variation method from 2006 to 2018 in Guangdong statistical yearbook, Guangdong science and Technology Yearbook, China Science and Technology Yearbook, wind database and Government Gazette.

Table 3. Weight of STI capability indicators

Index	Code name	Weight
Scientific and technological innovation investment	X1	0.318992033
Investment in R&D (a hundred million of yuan)	X01	0.063883841
Growth rate of R&D activists (%)	X02	0.1524177
R&D hourly equivalent (10,000 person-years)	X03	0.0513548
Investment intensity of R&D (%)	X04	0.051335692
Technology innovation output ability	X2	0.284985464
Number of applications for patent for invention (piece)	X05	0.089058722
Patent Application Authorization letter for Invention (piece)	X06	0.076175194
Number of scientific papers published (article)	X07	0.046925845
Number of topics on technological activities (item)	X08	0.072825702
Scientific and technological innovation environment	X3	0.200313548
Number of graduates of higher education (persons)	X09	0.047001536
The share of science education in GDP (%)	X10	0.037332483
Share of government science and technology appropriations in local fiscal expenditure (%)	X11	0.071862958
Number of libraries per 10,000 people (units)	X12	0.044116572

(*continued*)

Table 3. (*continued*)

Index	Code name	Weight
Transformation ability of science and technology innovation	X4	0.195708955
Number of contracts in technology market (item)	X13	0.05514667
Turnover in Technology Market (one hundred million)	X14	0.078427355
Output value of high-tech industries (one hundred million)	X15	0.062134929

According to the weight of Table 3 and formula 2, 3 and 4, the level of scientific and scientific and technological innovation ability is measured. Table 4 shows the level of scientific and scientific and technological innovation of Guangdong Province from 2006 to 2018.

Table 4. Level of technology innovation in Guangdong Province 2006–2017

Year	2006	2007	2008	2009	2010	2011	2012
Level of scientific and technological innovation	6.9	12.2	13.8	19.5	26.3	28.9	35.5
Year	2013	2014	2015	2016	2017	2018	
Level of scientific and technological innovation	42.2	40.8	48.5	63.5	73.6	93.4	

4.2 The Measurement of Technology Innovation Ability

According to the index system of new urbanization level constructed above, the weight of new urbanization level is calculated by coefficient of variation method based on the data found in Guangdong statistical yearbook, Guangdong science and Technology Yearbook, China Science and Technology Yearbook, wind database and Government Gazette from 2006 to 2019, as shown in Table 5.

Table 5. Weights of indicators for new urbanization capacity

Index	Code name	Weight
Urbanization of population	Y1	0.163961149
Proportion of non-agricultural population (%) [proportion of urban population]	Y01	0.067815278
Population density (person/km^2)	Y02	0.050513224
Proportion of second and third industry personnel in total population (%)	Y03	0.045632647

(*continued*)

Table 5. (*continued*)

Index	Code name	Weight
Economic urbanization	Y2	0.307369052
GDP per capita (yuan/person)	Y04	0.078117884
Total retail sales of consumer goods per capita (yuan)	Y05	0.059112076
Per capita disposable income of urban residents (yuan)	Y06	0.065515644
Second, third industry output value as a proportion of GDP (%)	Y07	0.039726222
Per capita fixed asset investment (yuan/person)	Y08	0.064897226
Social urbanization	Y3	0.17763937
Passenger cars (ten thousand)	Y09	0.070780826
Number of students in colleges and universities per 10,000 population (number of students)	Y10	0.048480027
Number of hospital beds per 10,000 persons (sheet)	Y11	0.058378517
Infrastructure urbanization	Y4	0.147219444
Total urban water supply ($10,000/m^3$)	Y12	0.052441346
Urban water penetration rate (%)	Y13	0.02970857
Urban construction land area (square kilometers)	Y14	0.065069529
Urbanization of resources and environment	Y5	0.203810984
Completion green coverage rate (%)	Y15	0.036360052
Park green area per capita (square meters/person)	Y16	0.050569134
Forest area per capita (ha)	Y17	0.056369138
Per capita water resources (m^3/person)	Y18	0.060512659

According to the weight and formula 2, 3 and 4 obtained in Table 5, the capacity level of new-type urbanization was measured and the comprehensive development level of new-type urbanization in Guangdong province from 2006 to 2018 was obtained in Table 6.

Table 6. Comprehensive development level of new urbanization in Guangdong province from 2006 to 2017.

Year	2006	2007	2008	2009	2010	2011	2012
New urbanization level (%)	23.4	25.4	36.2	39.4	50.8	48.9	56.2
Year	2013	2014	2015	2016	2017	2018	
New urbanization level (%)	60.7	61.2	72.2	74.1	79.2	77.9	

4.3 Empirical Analysis of the Impact of Scientific and Technological Innovation on the Development of New Urbanization

Scientific and technological innovation influences the urbanization of population, economy, society, resources, environment and infrastructure, and then affects the whole process of new urbanization. The rate of scientific and technological innovation and the rate of new urbanization are both time series data. Through the unit root test, it is found that the rate of scientific and scientific and technological innovation and the rate of new urbanization are both unstable time series, and the logarithm of the two variables tends to be stable and the scatter plot of lnx and lny can be seen that the correlation between the two is very strong (Table 7).

Table 7. Stationary test for each variable

Variable	ADF Inspection value	Critical value (5%)	Prob*	Conclusion	Smoothness
X	2.89667	−6.605269	1.0000	Unit root exists	Unsmooth
lnX	−6.265369	−1.974028	0.0000	No unit root	Steady
Y	2.446107	−1.974028	0.9923	Unit root exists	Unsmooth
lnY	−8.424613	−1.977738	0.0000	No unit root	Steady

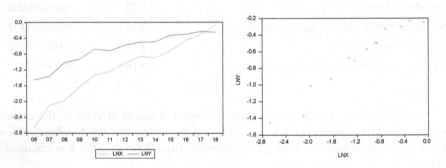

After unit root test, in order to avoid pseudo regression, we use LNY and LNX as our dependent variables and independent variables. First of all, In this paper, there are assumptions about scientific and scientific and technological innovation and new urbanization.

$$\ln(UR_t) = \alpha_1 + \alpha_2 \ln(KT_t) + \varepsilon$$

Among them, UR_t stands for the level of urbanization and KT_t stands for the level of scientific and technological innovation.

Secondly, OLS regression analysis was used. According to the above hypothesis, regression analysis is carried out on the level of scientific and scientific and technological innovation (Table 4) and new urbanization level (Table 6) through Eviews 10.0 (Table 8).

Table 8. OLS Regression Results of New Urbanization in technology innovation

Variable	Coefficient	Std. Error	t-Statistic	Prob
C	−0.063253	0.049318	−1.282575	0.2260
LNX	0.523536	0.035616	14.69926	0.0000
R-squared	0.951557	Durbin-Watson stat		2.056871

The regression results showed that: $R^2 = 0.951557$, the equation fitted well, and the significance P = 0.0000. It passed the 0.05 significance test. The results showed that the innovation of science and technology has a positive effect on the new urbanization in Guangdong. According to the parameters of the double-to-analog model, the elastic coefficient of the urbanization rate of the two new cities on the innovation rate of science and technology is reflected. When the change of the innovation coefficient of science and technology is 1%, the change of the new urbanization rate is 0.524%.

Finally, the paper used R language and canonical correlation coefficient analysis method to analyze the scientific and scientific and technological innovation, and to test the correlation between the mechanism of new urbanization. From 2006 to 2018, both scientific and technological innovation and new urbanization in Guangdong Province developed rapidly, and scientific and technological innovation played a role in promoting the development of new urbanization in Guangdong Province. Based on this basis, this paper examines the relevance of scientific and technological innovation to the indicators of new urbanization, as shown in Table 9:

Table 9. The correlation between scientific and technological innovation and the development of new urbanization

Index	Code name	Pearson correlation
Proportion of non-agricultural population (%) [proportion of urban population]	Y01	0.921
Population density (person/km^2)	Y02	0.914
Proportion of second and third industry personnel in total population (%)	Y03	0.54
Per capita GDP (yuan/person)	Y04	0.987
Total retail sales of consumer goods per capita (yuan)	Y05	0.885
Per capita disposable income of urban residents (yuan)	Y06	0.978
Ratio of output value of the second and third industries to GDP (%)	Y07	−0.555
Per capita fixed asset investment (yuan/person)	Y08	0.94

(*continued*)

Table 9. (*continued*)

Index	Code name	Pearson correlation
Passenger cars (ten thousand)	Y09	0.444
Number of college students per 10,000 population (person)	Y10	0.869
Number of hospital beds per 10,000 persons (sheet)	Y11	−0.094
Total urban water supply (10,000/m³)	Y12	0.776
Urban water penetration rate (%)	Y13	0.356
Urban construction land area (square kilometers)	Y14	0.812
Completion green coverage rate (%)	Y15	0.857
Park green area per capita (square meters/person)	Y16	0.899
Forest area per capita (ha)	Y17	−0.726
Per capita water resources (m³/person)	Y18	−0.263

Note: according to experience, the correlation coefficient is divided into: $0.8 \leq P < 1$ was highly correlated; $0.5 \leq P < 0.8$, was moderately correlated; $0.3 \leq P < 0.5$, was low correlated; $0.3 \leq P < 0.5$ was weakly correlated; $P < 0$ was negatively correlated.

According to Table 3 and Table 4, the scientific and technological innovation level of Guangdong Province has been significantly improved in the observation period. However, the weight of "input in science and technology innovation" is much greater than that of "output of science and technology". This shows that the level of scientific and technological innovation in this region mainly depends on "science and technology investment". Although it is obvious advantages in economic development, and easier to attract innovative talents and capital agglomeration, but it needs to be improved about the transformation ability of scientific and technological innovation and technological innovation environment.

As can be seen from Table 5 and Table 6, the urbanization level of Guangdong province has been significantly improved in the observation period, reaching a peak of 79.2% in 2017, while in 2018, the urbanization level has declined. This may be related to the return of population. According to the data in recent years, the urbanization rate of Guangdong Province is mainly manifested in economic urbanization, while population urbanization and infrastructure urbanization are relatively weak.

As shown in Table 9, The relationship between the level of technological innovation and specific indicators of urbanization. Non-agricultural population proportion, population density, per capita GDP, per capita disposable income of urban residents, per capita investment in fixed assets, the correlation coefficients of the five indicators are all greater than 0.9, all of them have strong correlations. The correlation coefficient of the total retail sales of social consumer goods per capita (yuan), the number of students in Colleges and universities per 10000 population, the area of urban construction land, the coverage rate of built-up green space and the per capita green area of parks are also above 0.8, which has a strong correlation.

The correlation coefficient of the proportion of secondary and tertiary industry personnel in the total population is between 0.5 and 0.8, which belongs to moderate correlation. However, the output value of the secondary and tertiary industries accounted for the proportion of GDP, the number of hospital beds per 10,000 people, the per capita forest area, and the per capita water resources, the four indicators have negative correlation coefficients.

5 Conclusions and Recommendations

5.1 The Main Conclusion

This paper estimates the level of scientific and technological innovation and urbanization rate in Guangdong Province from 2006 to 2018, and simulates the role of scientific and technological innovation level in promoting urbanization. The results show that: first, during the observation period, the level of scientific and technological innovation and the level of new urbanization in Guangdong Province showed an upward trend. At present, the level of scientific and technological innovation is mainly based on scientific and technological input, while the ability of scientific and technological output and transformation is relatively weak. The new urbanization level of Guangdong Province is mainly manifested in population urbanization and economic urbanization, infrastructure urbanization, resource and environment urbanization development is not enough. But in 2018, the urbanization rate declined for the first time, which may be related to the return of population.

Second, the level of scientific and technological innovation has a positive role in promoting the change of new urbanization in Guangdong Province. Every 1% change of science and technology innovation coefficient will bring about 0.524% change of new urbanization rate. Scientific and technological innovation can promote the new urbanization in Guangdong Province, but its role is not particularly obvious. The possible reason is that science and technology innovation in Guangdong Province mainly relies on a large amount of investment, and forms a "crowding out" effect on the development of urbanization. It should be noted that the correlation coefficient between scientific and technological innovation and the proportion of the output value of the secondary and tertiary industries in GDP, the number of hospital beds per 10000 people, the per capita forest area and the per capita water resources are negative. On the one hand, it reflects that the driving force of the development of the secondary and tertiary industries in Guangdong Province mainly comes from the input of labor, land and capital elements and the high cost of environmental resources. On the other hand, it shows that the urban public infrastructure in Guangdong Province is relatively weak.

5.2 Suggestions and Countermeasures

First, Guangdong provincial government should maintain investment in scientific and scientific and technological innovation and build a better environment for scientific and scientific and technological innovation. Although the development of economic urbanization and social urbanization in Guangdong Province is good, there is a situation of unbalanced development structure, and the development of infrastructure urbanization and population towns is still relatively backward, and there is a big gap with other urbanization processes.

At present, there are still some problems in Guangdong Province, such as the lack of basic research and original innovation ability, the lack of close integration of science and technology resources with local economy, the weak technical support of leading industries, the shortage of high-level innovation and entrepreneurship talents, and the relatively insufficient intensity of science and technology investment.

In the new normalization of the economy, although the growth rate of Guangdong's GDP is relatively stable in recent years, and the investment in scientific and technological innovation is also in a relatively high growth rate. However, in order to see the current problems, Guangdong should aim at the general trend and direction of future scientific and technological innovation, prepare early and plan early, dare to "empty the cage and replace the bird" for the backward production capacity, and boldly innovate the traditional industries. It is necessary to continue to increase technological investment, improve the joint mechanism between schools and enterprises, seize the strategic opportunity of the new normal economy, increase the transformation of technological achievements, build a better scientific and technological innovation environment, enhance the technological content of manufacturing industry, and promote industry upgrade, and improve the environment of scientific and technological innovation in Guangdong Province.

Second, China is stepping into an aging society, and the population will reach its peak soon. Over the past three decades, due to the continuous growth of population and the continuous improvement of urbanization level, Guangdong Province has promoted urban development from focusing on quantity expansion to focusing on quality improvement. Cities in Guangdong Province have experienced unprecedented high-speed expansion. At the same time, these cities are facing prominent urban diseases and great pressure of resources and environment, which restrict the sustainable and healthy development of cities. Urban environmental pollution, water shortage, traffic congestion, urban garbage and other issues need to play the core role of scientific and technological innovation. How to improve the development quality and service function of the city through scientific and technological innovation, and further realize the coordinated development of urban and rural areas, and build a beautiful Guangdong Province, is a major and urgent practical problem during the "14th five year plan".

At the same time, China's social development has entered the "new normal", which puts forward new requirements for urban functions and management system. On the one hand, China's urban aging population is growing, which puts forward new requirements for urban functions and facilities. On the other hand, the population flow between urban and rural areas and between cities is becoming more and more complex. It is urgent to realize the reconstruction of urban functions and the improvement of service management level through scientific and technological innovation, accelerate the citizenization of migrant population, promote local urbanization nearby, and optimize the spatial layout and structure of urban and rural areas. Therefore, to lead and adapt to the "new normal" of social development through scientific and technological innovation is a new major task for the scientific and technological circles.

Therefore, it is a new major task for the scientific and technological circles to lead and adapt to the "new normal" of social development through scientific and technological innovation. Urban construction and operation need to pay more attention to people-oriented, and the concept of scientific research also needs to be changed. Therefore, Guangdong Province should rely on scientific and technological progress to optimize the development of urban construction, strengthen the scientificity of urban planning, improve the construction of municipal public facilities, and constantly improve the application of science and technology in urbanization construction.

Third, we need to strengthen our capacity for scientific and technological innovation in combination with the development of new urbanization.

The government should follow the laws of urban development and enhance the forward-looking and scientific nature of urban and regional planning; Strengthen key technology integration research and improve urban infrastructure support capacity and spatial efficiency; Strengthen the research of new technology application, improve the construction quality and construction level. The government should strengthen the construction of big data platforms, improve urban smart management and social governance capacity, strengthen the construction of technology transformation platforms, and upgrade the industrialization of technological achievements. The government should increase the capacity of science and technology to support urbanization, resolve difficulties in urbanization development, and release new drivers of economic development. Therefore, the local government needs to strengthen the investment of scientific and technological innovation ability and the research of urban science and technology. For example, strengthen the construction of a strong data platform to improve the ability of urban intelligent management and social governance. Research and develop the provincial urban and rural planning management information platform, focus on social organizations, floating population and poor people, employment and entrepreneurship, social security and other fields, establish urban operation, social governance and public service platform, standards, systems and equipment, promote the promotion and application and demonstration in the whole country, improve the social governance ability and fine level of public service, and realize social governance and public service refinement The intellectualization and modernization of public services provide strong scientific and technological support.

We will build a team of scientific and technological innovation talents, innovative enterprises and scientific research platforms. Through various forms such as independent training and active introduction, we will cultivate and form leading talents in science and technology, high skilled talents, entrepreneurs, specialists in science and technology benefiting the people and innovation service personnel. We will also train a number of key enterprises in scientific and technological innovation in the field of urbanization and backbone enterprises in the application and demonstration of the whole industrial chain, and promote the construction of science and technology innovation base, innovation team and industrial technology innovation strategic alliance in Guangdong Province.

Fourth, we can accelerate the transformation of the economy driven by scientific and technological innovation.

We will accelerate the transformation of the economy driven by scientific and technological innovation, establish a mechanism for regular assessment and structural analysis of technological progress and promote the coordinated development of population urbanization and ecological urbanization. We will strengthen our capacity for scientific and technological innovation and promote the concentration of resources, technologies and talents in technological enterprises through technological progress. Finally, the goal of driving new urbanization development in Guangdong province with scientific and technological innovation is achieved. At the same time, the local government fully mobilize the enthusiasm, initiative and creativity of universities, scientific research institutes, enterprises and other aspects through the combination of regulation and optimization of service. We should build an open and efficient innovation resource sharing network, promote the organic combination of scientific and technological innovation with mass entrepreneurship and innovation, expand the space for public participation, enrich the public participation carrier, and promote the development of urban science and technology through collaborative innovation.

References

1. Grossman, J.: The evolution of inhaler technology. J. Asthma **1**, 55–64 (1994)
2. Chen, Q., Qi, L.: Technical comparative advantage, Knowledge spillover of Labor Force and urbanization of economies in transition. Managing World **11**, 47–59 (2017)
3. Lu, J.: The dynamic relationship between technological innovation, FDI and urbanization in Beijing-Tianjin-Hebei—an empirical analysis based on the VAR model. J. Guangdong Inst. Adm. **4**, 67–74 (2015)
4. Wenyin, L.J., Li, Y.: The influence of technology innovation ability on the new urbanization level-taking Shanxi province as an example. Econ. Issue **11**, 121–124 (2016)
5. Tian, Y., Xu, X.C., et al.: The dynamic relationship between scientific and technological innovation and the development of new urbanization and its regional differences-PVAR analysis of interprovincial panel data. Technological progress and countermeasures **9**, 42–50 (2016)
6. Zhang, J., Bianna: Research on the relationship between new urbanization and scientific and technological innovation in the urban agglomeration of the middle reaches of the Yangtze River based on PVAR model. Sci. Technol. Manag. Res. **16**, 103–108 (2017)
7. Zheng, Q.: The influence of technology innovation on new urbanization-empirical analysis based on panel threshold model. Urban Issues **6**, 25–35 (2017)
8. Wang, J.: The key to break through the bottleneck of urbanization is scientific and technological innovation. China Business Times, 17 April 2013
9. Liu, W.: The internal mechanism of technology innovation to promote the development of new urbanization in China. Sci. Technol. Innov. Prod. **2**, 6–8 (2017)
10. Yu, L.: The correlation between technology innovation and New urbanization. Chongqing Soc. Sci. **2**, 23–28 (2016)
11. Cheng, K.: The mechanism and evidence of urbanization promoting scientific and technological innovation. Manage. Res. Develop. **2**, 26–34 (2010)
12. Tian, Y., Xu, X., et al.: The dynamic relationship between scientific and technological innovation and the development of new urbanization and its regional differences-PVAR analysis of interprovincial panel data. Technol. Prog. Countermeasures **9**(42), 50 (2016)
13. Shan, L., Xiang, S.: The dynamic Impact analysis of scientific and technological innovation and new urbanization in Xingjing. J. Bingtuan Educ. Inst. **2**, 5–12 (2020)

Developing an Interactive Web-Based Programming Platform for Learning Computer Networking Protocols

Dewei Zeng, Zhiyu Zhang, Jiye Chen, and Xiaojun Hei[✉]

Huazhong University of Science and Technology, Wuhan 430074, China
{zengdewei,zhiyuzhang,youtiao,heixj}@hust.edu.cn

Abstract. Computer networking protocols have become important domain knowledge for electrical engineering professionals. The learning-by-doing approach has shown its effectiveness to learn these complex protocols by reproducing research results. In this paper, we design a web-based ns-3 lab platform by integrating various open-source modules for beginners to get hands on network simulations to learn networking protocols with a smoothed learning curve. This platform consists of a vue-based front-end and a docker-based back-end to support elastic on-demand capacity expansion. We implement a simulator scheduling module based on Node.js and restify to achieve load balancing for reducing the simulation waiting time. We conduct a measurement study to evaluate the performance of this prototype system. The measurement results demonstrate the technical feasibility of the prototype design to develop a scalable but user-friendly computer network simulation platform for massive open online lab courses.

Keywords: ns-3 · Online learning · Networking protocols · Engineering education

1 Introduction

In recent years, engineering courses have shown strong tendency toward science courses, lacking of sufficient practical lab platforms. Engineering students are required to accomplish systematically-designed theory and practice modules in order to develop their system capabilities progressively in a pipeline fashion [8–10]. The "computer networking" course is an important professional fundamental course for undergraduate programs on electrical engineering with both theoretical and practical characteristics. It is an effective learning approach to reproduce research results to learn computer networking protocols [1,12]. Nevertheless, it is prerequisite to provision network facilities to support the reproduction of

---

D. Zeng, Z. Zhang and J. Chen—These authors contributed equally to this work.

H. Song and D. Jiang (Eds.): SIMUtools 2020, LNICST 369, pp. 611–625, 2021.
https://doi.org/10.1007/978-3-030-72792-5_48

research results. With the rapid development of the network, the complexity and customization of the network hardware equipments have been increasing significantly in recent years. Therefore, computer networking educators have been increasingly adopting network simulation labs instead of hardware-based networking labs [3–5,14].

Ns-3 is a popular open-source network simulation tool [7] which has been widely used in the networking research and teaching communities. Many third-party modules have been developed to enhance ns-3, such as ns3-gym [6] and ns3-AI [13] to foster artificial intelligence algorithms in networking research.

When beginners learn to conduct ns-3 network simulations, it is common that they find it difficult and time consuming to get started due to the complicated installation steps and largely scattered learning resources. In this paper, we are motivated to design an online ns-3 learning platform with potential easy capacity expansion, which provides the ns-3 tutorial labs for beginners with a convenient user interface but without any required system configuration. The learners are able to catch up with the latest networking protocols in a low-cost, repeatable virtual experiment environment, and potentially large-scale network simulation experiments. Our platform integrates the ns-3 tutorial guidelines, reference source codes and various programming functions, which forms a smooth learning flow of from theory learning, source coding to lab practice. In this research-oriented learning of network simulation experiments, beginners are able to concentrate on their learning without being distracted by the simulator configuration and maintenance and are motivated to explore more learning experiences independently. In summary, our contributions are listed as follows.

- We design and implement this web-based ns-3 learning platform, so that a beginner is able to study the ns-3 tutorial lab guidelines step-by-step in a learning-by-doing approach. The back-end of the platform is constructed based on the open-source ns-3 network simulator; hence, the development cost of the platform is effectively reduced but harness the progress of the active ns-3 development.
- In order to increase the scalability of the proposed learning system, we create a ns-3 docker image to generate potentially a large number of isolated ns-3 running containers, which enable the elastic on-demand capacity expansion to support users as needed. The proposed architecture implements a scheduling mechanism to balance the simulation jobs to these ns-3 running containers to minimize the waiting time for learners to receive simulation results.

The rest of the paper is organized as follows. First, we review the related work in Sect. 2. Then, we present the platform design in Sect. 3, and present the implementation details in Sect. 4. Next, we present the performance evaluation results in Sect. 5. Finally, we conclude the paper in Sect. 6.

2   Related Work

In this section, we review the representative work on the online simulation platform in engineering education for communication and networking. Derr et al.

developed a web-based simulation tool, PGCPMT, for power grid communication network simulation. PGCPMT provides a GUI interface for the network topology, allowing users to define a network by dragging and dropping network elements [2]. Zou et al. proposed a teaching platform, EasyHPC, deployed on the supercomputer Milkyway-2 [15]. The front-end of EasyHPC provides an experimental tutorial, and the back-end of EasyHPC provides the environmental support for online programming. This is a feasible case of combining an online programming platform with tutorials. Gao et al. designed a set of ns-3 labs on the EasyHPC online platform such as learning the IEEE 802.11 Wi-Fi protocol, and positive feedback was reported from the students [4]. Sljivo et al. developed an interactive web simulation tool for the IEEE 802.11ah protocol [11]. The tool provides visual results for ns-3 simulation through PyViz, and provides a monitoring view of nodes status. Gao et al. re-designed an ns-3 simulation based networking lab course by reproducing research results aiming to teach both engineering rigor and critical thinking for undergraduate students, which are crucial for their future career or research [5].

Motivated by these previous works, our platform integrates the ns-3 tutorial guidelines, relevant experimental designs and programming functions, which creates a smooth learning curve from the theory learning, lab design and coding practice. In this learning-by-doing approach, this network simulation learning platform effectively reduces the additional time and efforts for beginners to quickly get hands on the ns-3 labs.

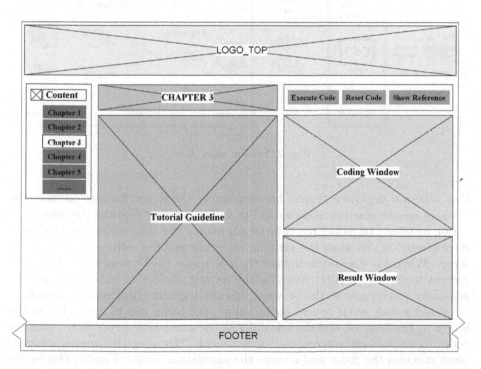

Fig. 1. User interface design

3 System Design

In this section, we first examine the requirements of an online platform in that we should provide learners with a user-friendly web-based interface, an online program execution environment, learning materials and reference codes, etc. Then, we present the system architecture design in details.

3.1 User Interface

As shown in Fig. 1, a learner edit the ns-3 source codes online with a code editor; with a single click on the execute button, the ns-3 source codes can be uploaded to the back-end ns-3 simulator compiler; the simulation experiments are conducted by the ns-3 simulator; finally, the simulation results are returned and displayed on the result page before the learner. Hence, ns-3 learners are able to enhance the comprehension in a learning-by-doing approach with minimum configuration efforts.

3.2 System Architecture

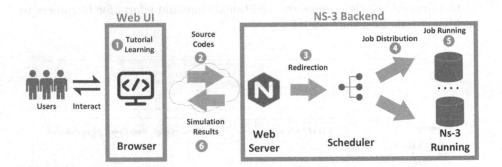

Fig. 2. System work flow

Our platform deploys a typical browser/server (B/S) architecture to meet the needs of user interaction as shown in Fig. 2. The browser provides the user interaction interface, including the tutorial guidelines, the code editor and the result display window. We store the learning materials and the reference codes on the server. When a learner needs to view the web pages, the browser sends an HTTP request to the server. After receiving the request, the server will return the corresponding web pages to the browser, and the pages are displayed on screen.

When a user needs to run codes online, the codes will be uploaded to the server by the browser, and the scheduler in the simulation server distributes the codes to an independent running environment. This selected running environment executes the codes and returns the simulation results. Finally, the results are displayed in the browser.

4 Implementation

In this section, we present the web framework to implement our system prototype. Then, we present the architecture implementation details.

4.1 Web UI

We use a popular frameworks, Vue, to build the front-end. This framework has ready-made component libraries, and we can use well-designed UI libraries to build web sites quickly. We implement the buttons and menu bar based on the antd-vue component library. Then, we download the ns-3 official web site tutorial guidelines and render them on the pages. Additionally, we integrate the code-mirror open source code editor to edit the source codes [11].

4.2 System Architecture

In order to implement the function of the online execution of the simulation experiments, we set up the ns-3 simulation environment on the server. When a learner executes the simulation codes, the browser uploads the codes to the server via HTTP, and the server process the received codes, including compilation, execution, and returning the simulation results and the execution information to the learner.

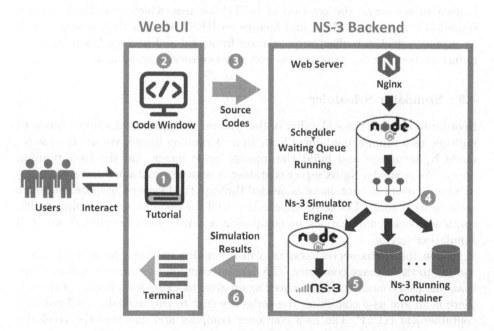

Fig. 3. System architecture

Our system implements the modules as shown in Fig. 3. In this B/S architecture, the server is composed of 3 modules: the Nginx server, the manager container and the ns-3 running container. The Nginx server is a HTTP server, which can display the web files (such as HTML, pictures) on the server to the clients through the HTTP protocol, instead of requesting resources through the server, which could reduce server pressure. It also provides a reverse proxy function to forward the HTTP request of the browser to the manager container. Note that a ns-3 process compiles its source codes in a default folder. In order to maximize the utilization of computing resources, we instrument multiple containers deployed with duplicated ns-3 environments. When the manager container receives the codes, it just forwards the codes to an idle ns-3 running container via HTTP; then, the ns-3 running container compiles the codes and executes the simulations, and returns the results to the manage container. Afterwards, the manage container returns the simulation results to the browser, and the browser displays the results in the output console for learners.

We select the Node.js and restify framework to implement our system. Node.js is used to provide the HTTP service, which is a JavaScript runtime built on Chrome's V8 JavaScript engine. Node.js is a single-threaded language. It treats the received request as a task and schedules work in a single thread through a task queue, which reduces the overhead caused by thread switching, which will show a significant performance advantage when the service is mainly IO service. Our service is mainly based on IO requests that distribute tasks through HTTP, so Node.js has a great performance advantage. Restify is used to accelerate the creation of HTTP services, which is a REST service framework based on Node.js, and focuses on REST services than modules such as express, which can effectively separate front-end and back-end development, reduce project development cycles, and improve service scalability.

4.3 Simulator Scheduler

In order to increase the scalability of the system, we apply the docker to generate multiple ns-3 running containers from an ns-3 running image. We use the ready-made Nginx image and build the manage node image and the ns-3 running image. We created a Nginx server container, a manager container and a changing number of ns-3 run containers as needed through the Docker-Compose container orchestration tool[1]. Docker-Compose is a tool for defining and running multi-container docker applications by composing a YAML file to configure our ns-3 simulation service.

When the Nginx server receives a ns-3 running request, the request is forwarded to the manage container. The manage container examines whether there is an idle ns-3 container. If not, check again after blocking for a period of time. If there is an idle ns-3 container, the codes are sent to this available ns-3 running container via HTTP. The ns-3 container compiles and executes the receiving

---

[1] https://github.com/docker/compose.

codes, harvests the simulation results and returns the results to the management container. Finally, the management container returns the results to the learner's browser for display.

5   Performance Evaluation

5.1   Web UI

Interface Outlook. The Web UI of our platform is shown in Fig. 4. The tutorial window is on the left side and the code window on the right side.

The tutorial guidelines are transformed from the official web site of the ns-3 tutorial. We have selected 5 basic chapters, and the chapter switching can be performed by the switch button at the upper left corner.

As shown in Fig. 5, the platform includes 5 basic chapters of ns-3 tutorials for learners to start with as a use-case, including the conceptual overview, tweaking, building topologies, tracing and data collection. A learner can click the directory button in the upper left corner of the Web UI to switch chapters. In addition, the tutorial labs are also extensible, and instructors can customized tutorial labs as needed.

Code Editing. In order to allow learning to have enhanced learning experiences, our platform provides the function of online programming, allowing learners to immediately perform relevant coding training after reading relevant chapters, so as to understand ns-3 programming and network protocols in a learning-by-doing approach with immediate feedback.

As shown in Fig. 6, we integrate an online code editor on the right side of the Web UI, and a learner can edit the ns-3 codes in the code window. After a

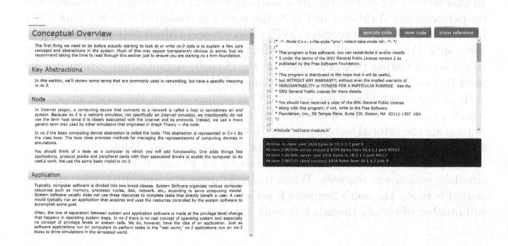

Fig. 4. Web UI overview

learner finishes the coding, he or she clicks the *Execute Code* button to submit the codes to the back-end, which will compiles the codes by the back-end ns-3 engines. The learner can also click the *Reset Code* to reset the code editor to its initial version.

As shown in Fig. 7, the simulation results are returned to the command line of the code window, which are consistent with the real ns-3 console output as well.

Interactivity. In order to enhance interactive user experience, our platform implement the interactive design. After a learner submit the codes, the platform returns the simulation results as soon as the back-end simulator accomplishes the simulation job. Therefore, the learner can correct the errors in the codes based on the output log. If the learner still has troubles in coding correctly, she or he can click the *See Answer* button at the upper right corner of the Web UI to find out how the reference codes work.

Platform Comparison. In summary, our platform integrates three important features of learning, online programming and interactivity. We compare our platform qualitatively with several related platforms as shown in Table 1. Our platform is customized to the need of ns-3 beginners with careful design. Second, our platform instruments several necessary features for most online programming platforms. Though our platform does not yet have the full functions of graphical programming, we have been considering to upgrade the system along this direction in the future development.

5.2   Testbed Setup

In this section, we deploy this ns-3 learning system in a testbed to evaluate the its performance. As shown in Fig. 8, the server is equipped with a 1-core CPU Intel Xeon E5-2682 v4 processor, 2 GB memory, and 1 Mbps network bandwidth. We apply JMeter to conduct the loading test on the server. JMeter is a Java-based stress testing tool developed by the Apache organization, which can be used to measure the system response time of the static and dynamic resources, such as static web files, Java servlets, CGI scripts etc. on the server under different loading levels. We adopt JMeter to simulate different user behaviors by requesting the tutorial web pages, and downloading the reference codes, submitting the simulation codes for experiments. Round by round, JMeter continuously initiates simulation testing circles until lasting for 10 min. We also use JMeter to simulate concurrent requests. When multiple users are simulated, the ramp-up period between the user's requests is set at 1 s. JMeter gradually adds up to the full number of testing threads following the ramp-up period.

...

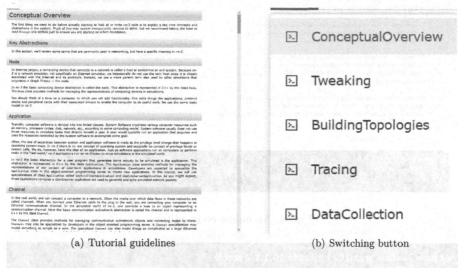

(a) Tutorial guidelines   (b) Switching button

Fig. 5. Web UI details

Table 1. Platform comparison

Functions	EasyHPC [15]	PGCPMT [2]	Our Platform
Programmability	Yes	Yes	Yes
Results visibility	No	No	Yes
Graphic programming	No	Yes	No
NS-3 tutorial	**no**	**no**	**yes**

5.3 System Performance

Performance Metrics. We measure several important performance metrics of the ns-3 simulation services, including the response time, throughput, and CPU & Memory. The response time is defined as the time duration (second) for a user to download the tutorial pages, fetch reference source codes, execute the codes and retrieve the simulation results. The throughput is defined as the traffic volume per unit of time sent and received by a user (bps). We configure the number of threads of JMeter to simulate different number of users who request the ns-3 simulation services at the same time. We are interested to examine the CPU utilization and the memory consumption (such as swap memory, free memory, buffer size and cache size) of the back end system when the system is stressed with different loads.

Fig. 6. An online code editor

At time 2s client sent 1024 bytes to 10.1.1.2 port 9
At time 2.00369s server received 1024 bytes from 10.1.1.1 port 49153
At time 2.00369s server sent 1024 bytes to 10.1.1.1 port 49153
At time 2.00737s client received 1024 bytes from 10.1.1.2 port 9

Fig. 7. Simulation results

Table 2. Average response time with different loads and containers (second)

User concurrency	1	2	4
Single container	5.21	5.51	15.01
Double containers	5.27	10.68	11.57
Triple containers	5.24	11.02	11.64

Response Time. As shown in Table 2, the average response time is 5.21 s for the case of the single user and the single ns-3 container. Additionally, the response time of the case of 4 users and the single ns-3 container is 15.01 s, which demonstrates the queueing effect of the simulator scheduler in our platform. If the number of the ns-3 running containers is not sufficient, the response time increases and impacts learning experiences significantly. When the server is lightly loaded with the 1–2 concurrent users, single ns-3 container achieves the least response time. When the concurrent users increase to 4, more ns-3 containers are required to maintain a small response time. The deployment of the container mechanism in our platform enable an elastic capacity expansion to serve an increasing number of concurrent users while maintaining a low response time.

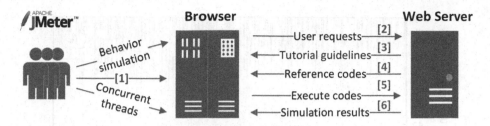

Fig. 8. Stress tests with JMeter

Table 3. Average throughput in different loads and containers (kbps)

User concurrency	1	2	4
Single container	41.28	80.72	100.48
Double containers	40.96	62.24	118.4
Triple containers	41.04	59.76	117.92

Throughput. As is illustrated in Table 3, the average throughput of a single user and four users are around 41 kbps and 112 kbps, respectively, where the network bandwidth of our server is throttled by 1 Mbps. It shows that a local area network is able to serve the need of ns-3 lab course based on this platform. Thus, network bandwidth may not be the bottleneck of a high-load ns-3 lab platform while CPU and memory may bring forth the major resource bottlenecks.

CPU and Memory. We examine the utilization of CPU and memory of the sever to analyze the resource utilization when deploying different numbers of containers when the concurrent users are simulated up to 4.

In Fig. 9, the green line depicts the percentage of the time the CPU runs user-level codes. The dark blue line depicts the percentage of the time the CPU runs system-level codes. The purple blue line depicts the percentage of the time the CPU is idle. The light blue line depicts the CPU usage for waiting I/O devices. When the concurrent user number is 4, the CPU idle time with single ns-3 container is expectedly larger than the double-container case. Because when a process executes a task, it will not completely exhaust the computing resources of the CPU, which means that the computing resources are not fully utilized. While if there are two processes compile, CPU computing resources will be more fully utilized. For triple-container, the concurrent user number is 4 means that there will be 3 task being executed together, which takes about 3 times the time to execute a single task, and the last one will be executed separately. This results in about 3/4 of the time that the CPU idle is extremely low, and the remaining 1/4 of the time CPU idle is slightly higher, just like what shown in Fig. 9. When the concurrent user number is 4, the total user-level and system-level CPU usage is beyond 80% most of the time. It shows that the performance bottleneck of the platform lies in the computing power of the CPU.

As shown in Fig. 10, with 4 concurrent users, we compare the memory consumption with different ns-3 running containers. "Swapped" depicts the amount

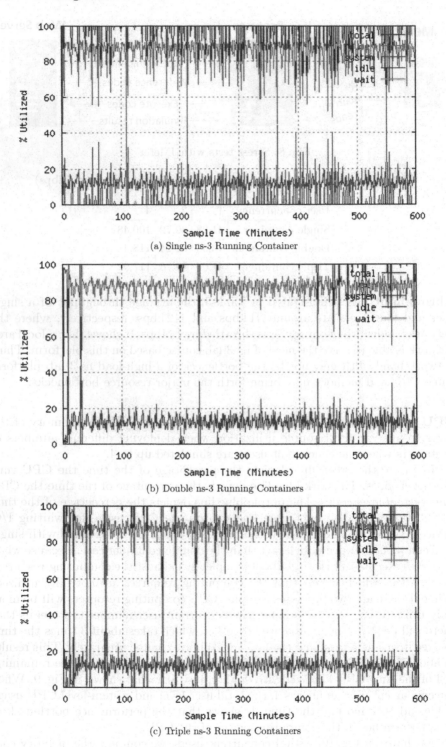

(a) Single ns-3 Running Container

(b) Double ns-3 Running Containers

(c) Triple ns-3 Running Containers

Fig. 9. CPU utilization 4 concurrent users

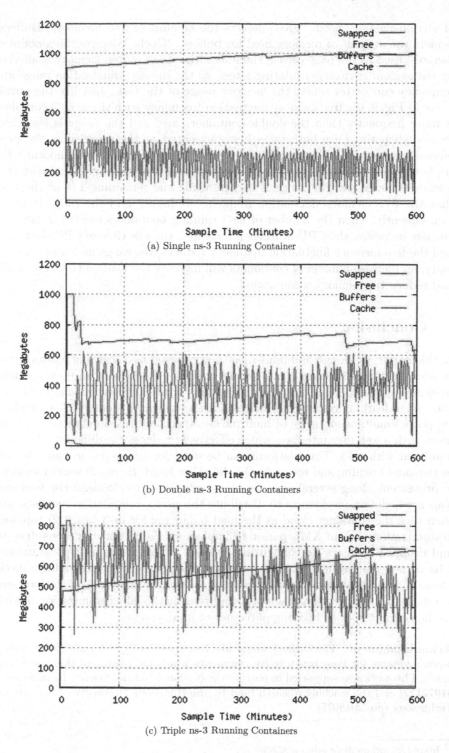

(a) Single ns-3 Running Container

(b) Double ns-3 Running Containers

(c) Triple ns-3 Running Containers

Fig. 10. Memory consumption with 4 concurrent users

of virtual memory used. "Free" depicts the amount of free memory. "Buffers" depicts the amount of memory used for buffers. "Cache" depicts the amount of memory used as the page cache. The fluctuating base of free memory is affected by the system environment during a test, so the memory fluctuation range and frequency can better reflect the memory usage of the task. Just like the purple curve in Fig. 9, the free memory fluctuation frequency with single ns-3 container is more frequently than the double-container case, and the range is less. This means when there are both tasks being executed at the same time, the peak memory usage will be higher and the free memory changes more smoothly. For triple-container, about 3/4 of the time that the free memory fluctuation frequency is lower and the range is higher, while the remaining 1/4 of the time that the free memory fluctuation frequency is higher and the range is lower. Consequently, when the number of ns-3 running containers executing Simultaneously increases, the CPU utilization increases, the idle time of CPU decreases, and the free memory fluctuation frequency reduces, the range increases. In summary, an increase number of containers will increase the load on the server CPU and reduce the memory consumption.

6   Conclusion

In this paper, we design and implement a web-based ns-3 learning platform [2] to provide beginners to learn computer networking protocols in an easy learning-by-doing approach. Our platform integrates various tutorial lab modules with convenient learning resources, which smoothes the learning curves. The platform supports simultaneous usage by multiple users, and returns simulation results for users with a web user interface, which effectively reduces the difficulty of getting hands on with ns-3. This platform can be used for lab course learning as well as personal learning and research. On the other hand, there are some rooms for improvement along several aspects: 1) asynchronous mechanism: the back-end uses a scheduling mechanism to distribute the user's compilation requests, and then uses the container cloud as the load balancing for ns-3 tasks; 2) topology customization: use an XML parser to implement visual network icons dragged and dropped by users for configuring network topologies in ns-3 programming labs; 3) user management: for student users, the platform provides a login mechanism so that the student users are able to code and submit labs in the back-end database; for teacher users, the platform provides the lab customization module to the support specific learning outcomes of a lab course.

Acknowledgment. The authors would like to express their gratitude to the anonymous reviewers for their constructive comments which the quality of this paper very much. This work was supported in part by the National Natural Science Foundation of 61972172) and the teaching research fund by the Huazhong University of Science and Technology (no. 2018077).

---

[2] http://cloud.eic.hust.edu.cn:8585.

References

1. David, A., et al.: Reproducible computer network experiments: a case study using popper. In: Proceedings of the 2nd International Workshop on Practical Reproducible Evaluation of Computer Systems, pp. 29–34 (2019)
2. Derr, K.: Ns-3 web-based user interface: power grid communications planning and modeling tool. In: Proceedings of the Workshop on Ns-3, pp. 93–100 (2016)
3. Gao, Y., Peng, J., Yin, Y., Hei, X., Wang, X.: Improving a software/hardware integrated computer networking laboratory course. In: IEEE International Conference on Teaching, Assessment, and Learning for Engineering (TALE), pp. 1189–1192 (2018)
4. Gao, Y., Peng, J., Yin, Y., Hei, X., Wu, D.: Developing wireless networking labs for MOOC learners on an online programming platform. In: IEEE International Conference on Teaching, Assessment, and Learning for Engineering (TALE), pp. 1154–1157 (2018)
5. Gao, Y., Zhang, C., Zhong, G., Hei, X.: Learning networking by reproducing research results in an ns-3 simulation networking laboratory course. In: IEEE International Conference on Teaching, Assessment, and Learning for Engineering (TALE) (2019)
6. Gawłowicz, P., Zubow, A.: Ns-3 meets OpenAI Gym: the playground for machine learning in networking research. In: Proceedings of the 22nd International ACM Conference on Modeling, Analysis and Simulation of Wireless and Mobile Systems, pp. 113–120 (2019)
7. Gupta, S., et al.: Open-source network simulation tools: an overview. Int. J. Adv. Res. Comput. Eng. Technol. (IJARCET) **2**(4), 1629 (2013)
8. Hei, X., Cheng, W.: Work in progress: fostering a telecommunication engineering pipeline: a curriculum design. In: IEEE International Conference on Teaching, Assessment, and Learning for Engineering (TALE), pp. 258–261 (2015)
9. Hei, X., Cheng, W.: Developing a telecommunication engineering pipeline of communication networks. In: IEEE International Conference on Teaching, Assessment, and Learning for Engineering (TALE), pp. 185–189 (2016)
10. Hei, X., Wen, H., Cheng, W., Huang, X.: Boosting computer-assisted telecommunication engineering education in internet thinking. In: Proceedings of ACM Turing Celebration Conference - China, pp. 123–124 (2018)
11. Šljivo, A., Kerkhove, D., Moerman, I., De Poorter, E., Hoebeke, J.: Interactive web visualizer for IEEE 802.11ah ns-3 module. In: Proceedings of the 10th Workshop on Ns-3, pp. 23–29 (2018)
12. Yan, L., McKeown, N.: Learning networking by reproducing research results. SIGCOMM Comput. Commun. Rev. **47**(2), 19–26 (2017)
13. Yin, H., et al.: NS3-AI: Fostering artificial intelligence algorithms for networking research. In: Proceedings of the 2020 Workshop on Ns-3, pp. 57–64 (2020)
14. Yin, Y., Gao, Y., Hei, X.: Performance evaluation of a unified IEEE 802.11 DCF model in ns-3. In: Song, H., Jiang, D. (eds.) Simulation Tools and Techniques, pp. 395–406 (2019)
15. Zou, Z., Zhang, Y., Li, J., Hei, X., Du, Y., Wu, D.: EasyHPC: an online programming platform for learning high performance computing. In: IEEE International Conference on Teaching, Assessment, and Learning for Engineering (TALE), pp. 432–435 (2017)

Weights Optimization Method of Differential Evolution Based on Artificial Bee Colony Algorithm

Ying Wu[1], Zibo Qi[1], Ling Jiang[1], Zifeng Dai[2], Chen Zhang[2], Changsheng Zhang[2(✉)], and Jian Xu[2]

[1] Shenyang Fire Science and Technology Research Institute of MEM, Shenyang 110034, People's Republic of China
[2] Software College of Northeastern University, Shenyang 110819, People's Republic of China
paper820@sohu.com, zhangchangsheng@mail.neu.edu.cn

Abstract. Differential evolution algorithm is a search and optimization strategy that simulates the process of biological evolution. In the initial stage of the algorithm, it is necessary to generate a series of deep neural networks with sufficient accuracy as the initial population of subsequent algorithms. In this article, an artificial bee colony search strategy is added to the cross-operation of the differential evolution algorithm to optimize the weight value. The artificial bee colony algorithm search operator is introduced to guide the search of the population to avoid individuals in the population from falling into a local optimal situation. The experiments in this article verify the validity of the method through the handwritten digit recognition data set. The final results show that in the process of obtaining the initial population, using the differential evolution weight optimization method of the artificial bee colony search strategy optimizes the process of the fitness calculation in the model. It significantly improves the accuracy of the first-generation population and speeds up the overall process of the algorithm.

Keywords: Artificial bee colony algorithm · Differential evolution · Neural network · Ensemble learning · Deep learning

1 Introduction

In recent years, the research of ensemble learning algorithm has developed vigorously. For almost any kind of machine learning algorithm, the idea of ensemble learning can be used to improve the accuracy and generalization of the algorithm. The ensemble learning model completes the learning task and improves the prediction accuracy of the final model by constructing and combining multiple learners. It is an excellent idea and method in the field of machine learning [1–4].

The differential evolution algorithm DE [5] is a stochastic model that simulates biological evolution. Through repeated iterations, those individuals who adapt to the environment are preserved. Because the algorithm has a simple structure, is easy to

H. Song and D. Jiang (Eds.): SIMUtools 2020, LNICST 369, pp. 626–635, 2021.
https://doi.org/10.1007/978-3-030-72792-5_49

implement, does not require gradient information, and has fewer parameters, it has attracted the attention and research of many scholars as soon as it was proposed. Similar to other intelligent algorithms, DE also has the problems of being easily trapped into a local optimum, slow convergence in the later stages of evolution, may not be able to search for optimal solutions for problems that are too complicated, and the calculation accuracy is not high.

The artificial bee colony algorithm [6] uses the communication, transformation and cooperation between bees of different roles to achieve swarm intelligence optimization by researching the behavior of bees during honey collection. Compared with the classic optimization methods, the artificial bee colony algorithm has simple operation, less control parameters, high search accuracy and strong robustness.

The artificial bee colony search strategy has strong exploration ability, and shows excellent optimization performance when optimizing complex multimodal problems. Therefore it is very suitable for combining it with differential evolution algorithms to improve the performance of the model. Lingling Huang et al. [7] proposed a differential evolution algorithm with artificial bee colony search strategy to solve the problems of premature phenomenon and slow convergence speed of differential evolution algorithm. The artificial bee colony search strategy was used to guide the population to help the algorithm jump out of the local best with its strong exploration ability. In addition, in order to improve the global convergence speed of the algorithm, an initialization method based on anti-learning is used. Through simulation experiments on 12 standard test functions and comparison with other algorithms, it shows that the proposed algorithm has a faster convergence speed and strong ability to jump out of local optimum. However, the accuracy of the generalization ability of this model is not high enough, the generalization ability is limited, and it only obtains good results by testing in some functions. In this article, an artificial bee colony search strategy is added to the cross-operation of the differential evolution algorithm based on the ensemble learning model to optimize the weight value. The artificial bee colony algorithm search operator is introduced to guide the search of the population to avoid individuals in the population falling into a local optimal situation and improve the generalization ability of the neural network model.

The other parts of this article are as follows: Section 2 introduces a specific differential evolution weight optimization method based on artificial bee colony algorithm; Section 3 uses the method and model described in this article to perform experiments on the data set, and the results show the accuracy of the final output is higher, which proves the effectiveness of the method in this paper; Section 4 summarizes the method in this paper and briefly proposes future research content.

2 Evolutionary Ensemble Learning Model Based on Artificial Bee Colony Algorithm

In the existing models built based on the differential evolution algorithm, the algorithm often falls into a local optimum at the later stage of the execution, which leads to the final convergence rate being too slow. And it is often unable to solve complex multimodal problems or the accuracy of the results is low. These disadvantages limit the scope of the differential evolution algorithm. This article proposes that the hyper parameters that need to be determined in advance in the neural network are used as individuals of the evolutionary algorithm, the evolutionary algorithm is optimized by the artificial bee colony algorithm, and then the neural network with higher accuracy is obtained through the optimized evolutionary algorithm. The specific process of optimizing the evolutionary algorithm is shown in Fig. 1.

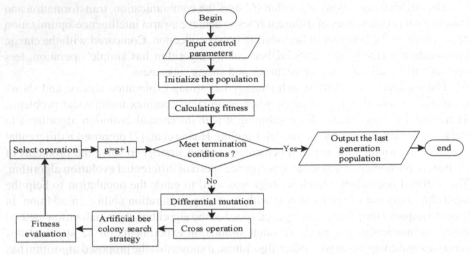

Fig. 1. Flow chart differential evolution algorithm based on artificial bee colony search strategy.

First, enter the preset control parameters, perform population initialization, calculate the initial fitness and use it as the evaluation standard for subsequent fitness. Then when the existing population size is smaller than the control value of the offspring, new offspring are generated cyclically. The cyclic process first differentiates and then crosses to get the new individuals, and then uses the artificial bee colony search strategy to search for more excellent individuals around the new individuals. Finally, the optimal individual is selected as a new individual to generate a new offspring individual. When the population size reaches the threshold, it exits the cycle and outputs the final generation population of the process, which is used as the initial population to input into the subsequent algorithm process.

2.1 Fitness Calculation Method Based on Artificial Bee Colony Search Strategy

Artificial bee colony (ABC) was proposed by Turkish scholar Karaboga in 2005. Its basic idea is to inspire the bee colony to cooperate with each other to complete the honey collection task through individual division of labor and information exchange. Although a single bee's own ability is limited, without a unified command, the entire bee colony can always find high-quality nectar sources more easily. Artificial bee colony algorithm is a new type of intelligent optimization algorithm by simulating the honey collecting process of bees. It consists of three parts: food source, hired bee and non-employed bee. The core of the algorithm includes 3 parts: leading bees searching for honey source; leading bees share honey source information and follow the bees to select a honey source to search with a certain probability; the scout bees randomly search in the search space.

In this paper, an artificial bee colony algorithm is added between the cross operation and the selection operation of the differential evolution algorithm to optimize the combined weight value in the process of fitness calculation. With the evolution of the population of the differential evolution algorithm, when the accuracy of the corresponding network output results of all individuals in the population is high enough, the last generation of the population at this time is regarded as the initial type of the subsequent algorithm Group, so as to ensure the accuracy of each network in the follow-up algorithm can be high enough.

Firstly, the initialization operation is carried out, and m individuals are randomly and uniformly generated in the corresponding decision space (each individual is the real number code of the super parameter to be optimized). Each individual is composed of n-dimensional vector (assuming that there are n parameters to be optimized), see formula (2.1).

$$X_i(0) = \left(x_{i,1}(0), x_{i,2}(0), \ldots, x_{i,n}(0)\right), \ i = 1, 2, 3 \ldots, M \tag{2.1}$$

The initialization method of the j-th dimension vector of the i-th individual is shown in formula (2.2).

$$X_{i,j}(0) = L_{j\_min} + rand(0, 1)\left(L_{j\_max} - L_{j\_min}\right)$$
$$i = 1, 2, 3 \ldots, M, \ j = 1, 2, 3, \ldots, n \tag{2.2}$$

L_{j_min} and L_{j_max} represent the upper and lower boundaries of the value of the j-th dimension vector and X represents every individual.

Then the mutation operation is started. The classic differential strategy of differential evolution algorithm is used to implement individual mutation. That is to say, two different individuals in the population are randomly selected, and their vector differences are scaled to synthesize vectors with the individuals to be mutated, as shown in formula (2.3).

$$X_i'(g) = X_{r1}(g) + F \cdot (X_{r2}(g) - X_{r3}(g)) \, F \in [0, 2], \ i \neq r_1 \neq r_2 \neq r_3 \tag{2.3}$$

At the same time, we need to strictly control the boundary of each element of the new individual. If it goes beyond its corresponding range, it is different from the initial random generation method. In this paper, we map it to the appropriate range by some operations. Then the crossover operation is started. According to the crossover probability cr $\in$ [0,1], the elements of each dimension are selected from the variation individual and the original individual, and the crossover individual is obtained. See formula (2.4).

$$V_{i,j} = \begin{cases} X_{i,j}'(g + 1), \ rand(0, 1) \leq cr \\ X_{i,j}(g), \quad else \end{cases} \tag{2.4}$$

At this time, according to the search rules of artificial bee colony, search for the individual with the lowest adaptive value around the crossed individual, and select as a new individual. See (2.5) for the formula.

$$z_{i,j} = x_{i,j} + \phi_{i,j}(x_{i,j} + x_{k,j}) \tag{2.5}$$

In the next selection operation, according to the greedy rule, cross individuals and original individuals are selected based on the fitness function value to build a new generation of population, as shown in formula (2.6).

$$X_i(g+1) = \begin{cases} V_i(g), f(V_i(g)) < f(X_i(g)) \\ X_i(g), else \end{cases} \tag{2.6}$$

$$k \in \{1, 2, \cdots M\}, \ j \in \{1, 2, \cdots D\}, k \neq i, \ \phi_{i,j} \in [-1, 1]$$

The fitness function here is an objective function constructed by using the gap between the output result of the network corresponding to the specific parameter vector and the real result, which is used to evaluate the merits and demerits of individuals. See formula (2.7) for the calculation method.

$$minimize : f(x) = \frac{1}{N} \sum_{i=1}^{N} \left(NET_x^i - REAL^i \right) \tag{2.7}$$

$NET_{(x)}^i$ represents the output of the depth neural network constructed by the parameter vector x in the ith training sample. $REAL^i$ represents the real result of the ith training sample.

Finally, through the above steps, the operations of crossover, mutation and selection are carried out repeatedly, and the population is continuously updated. When certain conditions are met, the single objective optimization part is completed. The condition here is set as: when the accuracy of network output results corresponding to all individuals in a generation population meets a threshold, the cycle will be terminated.

2.2 Weight Optimization Method Based on Artificial Bee Colony Algorithm

In the artificial bee colony algorithm, the artificial bee colony is divided into three categories: leading bee, following bee, and investigating bee. During each search process, the leading bee and following bee are mining food sources in succession, that is for finding the optimal solution, and the investigating bee observes whether it is trapped in a local optimum, if it is trapped in a local optimum, it randomly searches for other possible food sources. Each food source represents a possible solution to the problem, and the amount of nectar from the food source corresponds to the quality of the corresponding solution (fitness value fit_i). The detailed steps of weight optimization method based on artificial bee colony algorithm proposed in this paper are as follows.

Step 1: Initialize the population: Initialize each parameter, the total number of bee colonies S_n, the number of the food source is collected(the maximum number of iterations MCN), and the control parameter limit. Each solution x_i is a D-dimensional vector. D is the dimension of the problem. Determine the problem search range, and an initial solution $x_i(i = 1,2,...S_n)$ is randomly generated within the search range;

Step 2: Calculate and evaluate the fitness of each initial solution;

Step 3: Set cycling conditions and start cycling;

Step 4: Leading bee to perform a neighborhood search on the solution xi according to formula (2.5) to generate a new solution (food source) v_i, and calculate its fitness value fit_i;

Step 5: Perform greedy selection according to formula (2.8): if the fitness value of v_i is better than x_i, replace x_i with v_i, otherwise leave x_i unchanged;

$$v_i = \begin{cases} v_i \left(fit_{v_i} > fit_{x_i}\right) \\ x_i \left(fit_{x_i} \le fit_{v_i}\right) \end{cases} \tag{2.8}$$

Step 6: Calculate the probability x_i of the food source according to formula (2.9);

$$p_i = fit_i \Big/ \sum_{k=1}^{S_n} fit_k \tag{2.9}$$

Step 7: The following bee selects a solution or a food source according to the probability p_i, searches for a new solution (food source)v_i according to formula (2.5), and calculates its fitness;

Step 8: Perform greedy selection according to formula (2.8): if the fitness value of v_i is better than x_i, replace x_i with v_i, otherwise leave x_i unchanged;

Step 9: judge whether there is a solution to give up. If there is, the detection bee will randomly generate a new solution to replace it according to formula (2.10);

$$x_{i,j} = x_{min,j} + rand\,(0,\,1) \times \left(x_{max,j} - x_{min,j}\right) j \in \{1, 2...., D\} \tag{2.10}$$

Step 10: record the optimal solution so far;

Step 11: judge whether the cycle termination condition is met. If it is, the cycle ends and the optimal solution is output. Otherwise, return to step 4 to continue searching.

The pseudo code for the above procedure is shown below.

Algorithm 2.2. The process of artificial bee colony.

Algorithm Single-objective differential evolution algorithm
Input
Cross: the crossed individual
Iter_max: population number
nPop:the number of honey source
nLooker:the number of max search times
Output
The best value of fitness and the best individual
Begin
Initializing honey source location and calculating initial fitness accroding to eq.(2.7);
for iter **in** Iter_max:
for i in nPop:
Find next honey source according to eq.(2.5);
Greedily choose the individual according to eq.(2.8);
End for;
Calculating the selection probability matrix;
For k in nLooker:
Find next honey source according to eq.(2.5);
Greedily choose the individual according to eq.(2.8);
End for;
For k in nPop:
If the times of source reaching the nLooker:
Find next honey source according to eq.(2.5);
End if;
End for;
End for
Record the best individual and the best value of fitness;
End

In this process, the main advantage of the artificial bee colony algorithm is that it has a strong randomness when selecting. That is to say, in the process of exploring the best fitness of chromosomes, the probability of selecting individuals with good fitness and those with poor fitness is the same. It can be seen from the above pseudo code that for each generation of individuals, the time complexity of the artificial bee colony search strategy is $T_n = O(m * n)$, where m represents the number of populations and n represents the number of initial honey sources.

3 Experiment

In the experimental part of this paper, firstly, we use the differential evolution method based on the artificial bee colony algorithm to get the model with high accuracy. Then we use the multi-objective differential evolution algorithm to weigh the accuracy and difference of the network, and construct many networks with both accuracy and difference. Finally, we use the idea of integrated learning to combine these networks into the model. The experiment is carried out on MNIST dataset, and the results of the model with artificial bee colony search strategy and the model without it are compared and analyzed. Experimental results show that the proposed method can improve the accuracy of the model.

In order to reduce the interference of other factors, in the comparative test, other parameters are set to the same value. The specific parameter settings of the network collection stage obtained in the experiment are shown in Table 1.

Table 1. Parameter settings for the part of generating candidate deep networks.

Algorithm name	Parameter name	Specific value
Single-objective differential evolution algorithm	Population size	10
	Variation control parameters	0.5
	Cross control parameters	0.8
Multi-objective differential evolution algorithm	Population size	20
	Neighborhood number	6
	Evolutionary algebra	10

In the model, for the part of differential evolution weight optimization method based on artificial swarm search strategy proposed in this paper, the initial parameters of artificial swarm set in the experiment are shown in Table 2.

Table 2. Parameter setting of artificial bee colony search strategy.

Algorithm name	Parameter name	Specific value
Artificial bee colony search strategy	Population number	50
	Initial honey sources number	100
	Maximum number of iterations	100

Under the premise that the overall algorithm remains unchanged, the experiment compares and analyzes the experimental results with or without the artificial bee colony search strategy model. In order to avoid the influence of random chance on the experimental results, repeat each experiment ten times, take the average value of the results as the final result, and the specific data is shown in Table 3.

Table 3. The influence of differential evolution algorithm based on artificial swarm search strategy on experimental results.

Artificial bee colony search strategy	Training set accuracy (%)	Validation set accuracy (%)	Test set accuracy (%)
No	99.6485	99.4870	99.2430
Yes	99.7589	99.6140	99.4740

It can be seen from the above table that the accuracy of the model has been improved by combining the artificial bee colony search strategy, which shows that the method proposed in this paper can improve the performance of the model and achieve the purpose of optimizing the model.

As many existing models have achieved good results [8] on the MNIST data set, the model obtained in this paper is compared with the existing model. The results are shown in Table 4.

Table 4. The performance of other models on MNIST dataset.

Classifier	Test error rate (%)
K-Nearest neighbors	
K-NN with non-linear deformation (IDM)	0.54
K-NN with non-linear deformation (P2DHMDM)	0.52
K-NN, shape context matching	0.63
Convolutional nets	
Committee of 7 conv. Net, 1-20-P-40-P-150-10 [elastic distortions]	0.27 ± 0.02
Committee of 35 conv. Net, 1-20-P-40-P-150-10 [elastic distortions]	0.23
Large/deep conv. Net, 1-20-40-60-80-100-120-120-10 [elastic distortions]	0.35

As shown in Table 4, considering that the convolution neural network used in this paper has a small number of layers, the results show that it basically achieves the performance of some networks with deep layers. Therefore, the model proposed in this paper can exceed some networks with many layers, but it can not catch up with those models with deep convolution layers as a whole.

4 Summary

In the process of building the deep integration network model, this paper proposes a differential evolutionary weight optimization method based on the artificial bee colony algorithm. In general, the general differential evolution algorithm has insufficient search ability for the best fitness individuals, which greatly restricts the performance of the model, while the artificial bee colony algorithm has a strong search ability, which can be used in the process of cross selection to explore the best fitness individuals and improve the overall performance of the model. In the experimental part of this paper, an integrated learning model is constructed by using this method, which can effectively improve the generalization ability and make up for the shortcomings of the existing differential evolution algorithm. The integrated learning model and the single neural network model are tested repeatedly on the handwritten digit recognition data set. By comparing the experimental results on the training set, the verification set and the test set, the method has achieved good results.

Combined with the research content of this paper, there is still room for improvement in the following aspects in the future: (1) How to set the initial parameters of the artificial bee colony algorithm can get the required individuals more accurately and quickly. (2) In terms of network differences, more indicators can be considered to judge the differences between networks in multiple dimensions, such as the number of network layers and other factors. (3) This method will be applied to the identification scenes of fire-prone devices to improve identification efficiency.

References

1. Zhou, Z.H., Wu, J., Tang, W.: Ensembling neural networks: many could be better than all. Artif. Intell. 137(1–2), 239–263 (2002)
2. Partalas, I., Tsoumakas, G., Hatzikos, E.V., et al.: Greedy regression ensemble selection: theory and an application to water quality prediction. Inf. Sci. 178(20), 3867–3879 (2008)
3. Martín, I., de Diego, Á., Serrano, C.C., Cabello, E.: Face verification with a kernel fusion method. Pattern Recogn. Lett. 31(9), 837–844 (2010). https://doi.org/10.1016/j.patrec.2009.12.030
4. Takemura, A., Shimizu, A., Hamamoto, K.: Discrimination of breast tumors in ultrasonic images using an ensemble classifier based on the AdaBoost algorithm with feature selection. IEEE Trans. Med. Imaging 29(3), 598–609 (2010)
5. Storn, R., Price, K.: Differential evolution – a simple and efficient heuristic for global optimization over continuous spaces. J. Glob. Optim. 11(4), 341–359 (1997). https://doi.org/10.1023/A:1008202821328
6. Karaboga, D., Basturk, B.: A powerful and efficient algorithm for numerical function optimization: artificial bee colony (ABC) algorithm. J. Glob. Optim. 39, 459–471 (2007)
7. Huang, L., Liu, S., Gao, W.: Differential evolution with the search strategy of an artificial bee colony algorithm. Control Decis. 27(11), 1644–1648 (2012)
8. MNIST Homepage. https://yann.lecun.com/exdb/mnist/. Accessed 12 Feb 2020

The Heterogeneous Effects of Internet Finance on the Profits of Commercial Banks in China

Wanping Bai[1], Xinyuan Su[2(✉)], and Ge Bai[1]

[1] Guizhou University of Finance and Economic, Guiyang, Guizhou Province, China
[2] Xinxiang Technology Service Center, Xinxiang, Henan Province, China

Abstract. Since 2012, the Internet finance (ITFIN), as a rising star in the financial industry, has impacted the traditional finance with its unique operating model and market transmission path. Our work explores the role of ITFIN on the profit structure and profitability of commercial banks from a new perspective of market structure. Based on the research on the mechanism of action, we construct an econometric model and conduct an empirical analysis: our panel data model contains the main indicators disclosed by 16 representative commercial banks from 2010 to 2018, including the total asset profit rate and the three major business development data (asset, liability, and intermediary business), and tests the specific impact of ITFIN on the profitability of commercial banks. Our work draws the following conclusions and implications: First, the development of ITFIN will promote the profitability of commercial banks, and it will promote the diversified development of commercial banks' profit structure. Therefore, in the development process, the commercial banks should pay attention to win-win cooperation and develop financial technology, while optimizing market structure and integrating financial resources to promote the optimization of the market economy system. Second, the impacts of ITFIN on the profitability of different types of commercial banks are heterogeneous. The effects on the profitability of state-owned are more significant, while the effects on the diversified development of the municipals are more favorable. Therefore, when developing, the commercial banks should actively change their business philosophy, deepen the financial market, reasonably make market positioning and behavioural decisions based on their development, and improve the market competitiveness.

Keywords: Internet finance · Commercial banks · Heterogeneous effects

1 Introduction

Internet finance (ITFIN), as an innovation from the Internet to the financial industry in the concept of "the Internet plus", accelerates the interpretation of the theory of evolution of the new financial system, and brings profound effects on the financial field. Nowadays, Internet finance has become an important part of the financial industry. Based on Internet technology, Internet enterprises can achieve a higher degree of financing, online payment and information transmission channels than traditional financial enterprises, and

H. Song and D. Jiang (Eds.): SIMUtools 2020, LNICST 369, pp. 636–650, 2021.
https://doi.org/10.1007/978-3-030-72792-5_50

gradually formed an Internet financial format represented by Internet payment, Internet financial management and network lending. Chinese economy is in a critical period of structural adjustment and transformation. as a rising star of the financial industry, ITFIN affects the traditional finance, which is mainly commercial banking business, with its unique operation mode and market transmission path. It has an impact on the profits of commercial banks that can not be ignored. So, how to measure the impact of ITFIN on the profits of commercial banks? Does the development of ITFIN change the profitability and its structure of commercial banks? Is there heterogeneity among different types of commercial banks (such as state-owned, joint-stock and municipal ones)? The answers to these questions are of great significance to how to maximize the role of ITFIN, how to integrate traditional commercial banks with emerging Internet technologies, and how regulators formulate policies to maintain the orderly and stable development of the financial market.

1.1 Related Literature

In essence, ITFIN is a financial model based on Internet technology (IETF) and information communication technology (ICT) [1]. Scholars' theoretical and empirical research on its definition, development, and its impact on the profitability of commercial banks are still being enriched.

The Internet finance definition first appeared in the literature written by N. Richard [2]. Since the emergence of ITFIN, scholars have studied the impact of ITFIN on the profitability of commercial banks from various angles, but have not reached a unified conclusion. According to the international mainstream, the impact of the ITFIN on bank profits is not negative, such as Chande [3], Momparler [4] and so on. According to Strategic Treasurer and Kyriba [5], the innovation of financial technology is changing the asset allocation structure of commercial banks, and has gradually approached the banking enterprises in terms of market share, which has become the biggest resistance and threat to their business development and profitability. As for Chinese studies, represented by Ba [6], Liang and Shen [7], Gong [8], Guo and Shen [9], the ITFIN and commercial banks can achieve win-win cooperation. They assume that financial enterprises use the Internet financial platform to develop customer resources, improve the efficiency of resource allocation and reduce operating costs; On the other hand, the cooperation between Internet enterprises and financial institutions can also enhance the cross-domain operation ability of enterprises. Studies represented by Qiu [10] and Zheng [11] believe that ITFIN has a negative impact on the commercial banks' earning. They holds that TPC, online financial products and other forms divert a large amount of demand deposits from commercial banks and push down the banks' earning of intermediary business. And the disintermediation of ITFIN also causes the loss of profit sources for commercial banks.

Most of these studies consider that different ITFIN models bring variety impacts on the business model, financial function and operating risk of commercial banks. However, they have not done a systematic analysis on banking structure under the trend of economic and social development, nor formed a complete market transmission path in the discussion on the impact of the development of Internet finance on the profitability of commercial banks. In recent years, although panel model has been used in empirical researches, they mostly based on individual indicators such as assets, liabilities, or intermediary business of commercial banks from different forms of ITFIN. It is not based on the complete profit market transmission path of commercial banks yet.

1.2 Our Work

It can be seen that there are still various contradictions in empirical evidences, and studies have not reached a consensus on whether the impact is positive or negative. The existing literatures show that both sides are reasonable: the development of ITFIN has both positive and negative effects on the profits of commercial banks. It can be considered that the Catfish Effect and Cherry Picking Effect [12] of ITFIN on the profits of commercial banks exist at the same time, and the degree of this influence is related to the characteristics of the banks. Directly, the impact of ITFIN on the banking industry will be reflected in the profitability of commercial banks. Our study differs from the last mentioned studies in two ways following:

First, we start with the perspective of market structure in terms of theoretical analysis. We analyze the influence of ITFIN on the internal product pricing mechanism and product decision mechanism, the external market competitive environment and regulatory environment of commercial banks, and explore a complete path of this influence from a new perspective of market structure.

Second, we consider the influence of ITFIN in terms of empirical analysis. We establish a panel data model not only includes macro-economy, industry features and banks' characters, but also contains the Internet financial index, which is published by Wind. Our samples contain 16 commercial banks listed in China before the first year of Chinese Internet Finance era (2013). We focus particularly on different type of the banks, and give a factual evidence that the impact of ITFIN on them are heterogeneous. In general, the results show that the ITFIN has promoted the profitability of commercial banks and promoted the diversified development of commercial banks' profit structure. Respectively, it has greater effects on the profitability of the state-owneds while greater effects on the diversified development of the municipals.

2 Effects and Mechanism

"The first year of Chinese Internet Finance era" brought by Yu'ebao in 2013, and it marks the beginning of the rapid development of ITFIN in China. The traditional concept of "high-end" financial industry will be redefined by Internet technology and close to ordinary users infinitely [13]. In 2016, ITFIN was included in the outline of Chinese 13th five-year Plan, it mark the start of the recognition as a new economic form by Chinese Officials. As the "counterattack innovation" from the Internet to the financial industry in the concept of "Internet +". ITFIN accelerates the evolution of the financial system in the new era, and its profound impact on finance can never be ignored. By 2017, the scale of financial management in Chinese Internet financial industry was 3.15 trillion RMB, an increase of 52.39% over the same period last year, which only reached 10% of the remaining balance of 29.54 trillion RMB of banking wealth management products at same time. However, with professionalization, micromanagement and facilitation, the financial management scale is expected to reach 15.5 trillion RMB in 2020, thus it will reach the 70% level of the existing balance of 22 trillion RMB of banking financial products at same time.

With the development of ITFIN, it has formed a financial model represented by Internet payment, Internet financial management and network lending, and it has penetrated into every involving economic life. Compared with the traditional financial market, ITFIN, which is innovative in multi-dimension and multi-level, can reduce the degree of information asymmetry between investors and financiers through big data, cloud computation and variety technologies. It changed the market environments of commercial banks and prompt them to change their behaviour to adapt to the volatile external environment.

2.1 Two-Sides Effects

On the positive side, the development of ITFIN will have a certain Catfish Effect on commercial banks. ITFIN activates the innovation and development momentum of commercial banks in product upgrading, customer service and the financial technology application, and improve the banks' ability of financial efficiency, service quality and risk management. Thus they can improve their own market competitiveness, and promote the profitability. According to Li [14], the Internet economy is born to satisfy the Long-tailed of Chinese demand market. The development of ITFIN in China has made full use of Blue Ocean Strategy to create new value and open up incremental market of the Long-tailed. The emergence of ITFIN makes the commercial banks have more diversified business models, more reasonable asset allocation and more accurate service concepts.

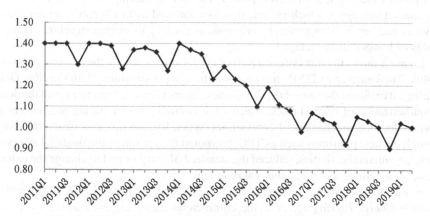

Fig. 1. ROA of Chinese commercial banks from 2011 to 2019 (%).

On the negative side, the impacts from ITFIN to banks are called Cherry Picking Effect, which make the Internet companies considering higher profits and lower risk when choosing products and cooperative banks. Through the way of investment and cooperation on high-quality assets, the financial magnates can achieve market monopoly, reduce competition, lower the barriers to entry or exit. Furthermore, the profits of commercial banks can be encroached. Figure 1 describes the return on assets (ROA) of Chinese commercial banks from 2011 to 2019 (data from the China Banking Regulatory Commission), It is shown that ROA had drawn a downtrend line during 2011 and 2019. Especially during 2014 and 2017, it reduced by nearly 30% while ITFIN mushrooming. The most prominent negative impact is the occupation of the banks' asset, liability and intermediary business.

2.2 Transmission Paths

Because of the system transfer, the economy shunt and the structure adjustment of China in recent years, a multi-level and multi-channel mode has been formed in the way of financial development, which is dominated by the banking industry and supports the development of the real economy. However, commercial banks still have deficiencies in asset structure and asset quality. In recent years, the rapid development of ITFIN has brought a great challenge to the future of commercial banks [15]. According to the traditional industrial organization theory (TIO), market power is the inevitable result of enterprise monopoly, which is an important factor to transmit the loss of social welfare and lead to rent-seeking behavior. According to Xiao and Su [16], the key to the structure adjustment of China is to establish a competitive market structure, break the long-term monopoly pattern of state-owned banks, and set up an efficient resource structure that adapts to the market mechanism. With a unique market structure, ITFIN in China has a distinctive mechanism for the profits of commercial banks. With big data, cloud computation and mobile network technology, ITFIN has developed. It has change the internal and external market structure of commercial banks, which is the hypostatic transmission path of the impacts on banks' profits. The key to making this effect come true is that market strategies, which include development and asset allocation strategies, and services and supervision concepts, are made according to market structure. Thus, the profits of banks will be changed.

Figure 2 shows the transmission path of ITFIN's influence on the commercial banks' profits. The entrance of ITFIN has changed the market structure. With the *Blue Ocean Strategy*, it explored the *Long-tailed* of Chinese financial market and improved the degree of marketization of interest rates, affected the internal product pricing mechanism and product decision mechanism of commercial banks, formed financial disintermediation through the new platforms such as TPC, promoted the reform of the financial system by doing commercial activities, reduced the standard of entry or exit to change the external market competitive and regulatory environment.

In the process of the development of ITFIN, the positive *Catfish Effect* and the negative *Cherry Picking Effect* to the commercial banks are exist at the same time, and are closely related to its degree of development. On one hand, it stimulate banks to take more efficient strategies, Such as improving the resource allocation ability by improving the pricing mechanism of products, form a market-oriented exploitation of products by changing the traditional demands, improve the efficiency of their services and operating by intensifying the competition, and promote the formulation of market regulation policies that supporting their merger and acquisition to let the construction more rational.

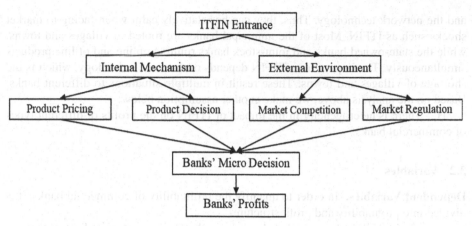

Fig. 2. Transmission paths of ITFIN's effects on the commercial banks' profits.

3 Data and Empirical Results

3.1 Basic Assumptions

Recent researches indicate that the factors that affect the profits of commercial banks include three aspects: macro-economy, industry features and banks' characters. In addition to them, the development of ITFIN is also an undeniable factor. Based on the theoretical analysis outlined above, we can build a panel data model to quantify and analyse the influence of ITFIN on the profits of commercial banks. To answer the question about how does the profitability and profit structure of commercial banks be affected, we make an assumption below:

H1: With the higher development of ITFIN, commercial banks have stronger profitability and more diversified profits structure.

In 2018, the total assets of Industrial & Commercial Bank of China (ICBC) have exceeded 27 trillion RMB, while those of small commercial banks generally do not exceed 100 billion RMB. So the differences among the scale of Chinese commercial banks are obvious. Relative to the scale, different commercial banks face to different external environment and make their own strategies in financial market. Relatively speaking, the large-scale banks have complex structures, and there will be a lag in decision-making when they face to the impact of ITFIN. While the small-scale banks are easy to adjust strategies in time to avoid the impact at the same time. According to Ma and Li [17], the large-scale banks are faced with the rigid constraint of national economic environment, and make strategy decisions highly consistent with the governmental policy guidance. On one hand, China is actively promoting the Internet + plan currently, what makes the enterprises choosing state-owned banks and joint-stock commercial banks with large scale. It brings not only the expansion of profit but also the promotion of risk to those banks. On the other hand, in response to changes, large-scale banks could design diversified products based on the scale advantages to avoid the impact of ITFIN. Compared with the small-scale banks, the large-scales have reached the higher level in the stability of the profit system, the ability of operation management and the network technology. Thus, they can be relatively calm when facing to market shocks such as ITFIN. Most of the municipal banks are rooted in villages and towns, while the state-owned banks and joint-stock banks running online and offline products simultaneously. The impact from ITFIN depends on Internet technology, which is the shortage of villages and towns. These result in multiple situations to different banks. Based on the analysis above, we make another assumption below:

H2: There is heterogeneity in the impact of ITFIN on the profits of different types of commercial banks.

3.2 Variables

Dependent Variables. In order to quantify the profitability of commercial banks, it is divided into profitability and profit structure.

As for profitability, theoretical analysis shows that there are many indicators that can be selected. According to the research of DeYoung and Rice [18], we choose the return on assets as the evaluation index of the profitability of commercial banks.

As for profits structure, non-interest income ratio is mostly used in the literature. But nowadays, the calculation and analysis based on it are not representative enough. Therefore, we build the profit structure index symbolled by *prostr* calculated as formula (1), considering the situation of assets, liabilities and intermediary business of commercial banks. Thus we can make an in-depth calculation and analysis of the profit structure of banks.

$$prostr = \left(\frac{NI}{Businc}\right)^2 + \left(1 - \frac{NI}{Businc}\right)^2 \tag{1}$$

Noted that *NI* is the non-interest income, and *Businc* is the total operating income.

Independent Variables. The development degree of ITFIN, symbolled by *intfi*, is the core independent variable of the model. ITFIN is still a new industry in the stage of rapid development, so the academic circles have not reached a unified consensus on the measurement indicators of its level. Considering the representativeness of indicators and the availability of datum, we select the Internet financial index published by *Wind* database.

Control Variables. According to the research method of Xing [19] on the profitability of commercial banks, we select control variables both external and internal facts.

The external control variables include two parts: one is the macroeconomic level; the other is the banking level. At the macroeconomic level, we choose the year-over-year growth of GDP to reflect the economic level, and the consumer price index to reflect the degree of stability of economic system. At the banking level, we divide Herfindahl Index by 10000 to reflect the market structure of banking. Referring the viewpoint from Yidirim and Philippatos [20] on the degree of direct financing, we choose indicators to measure the development of the stock market and the insurance market. The former is expressed by the ratio of stock market value to GDP, while the latter is expressed by the ratio of insurance premium income to GDP. As for the internal control variables, they mainly describe the operating conditions of commercial banks, including five variables:

the logarithm of total assets reflect assets scale, the capital adequacy, the cost-income ratio of bank reflect operating efficiency, the loan-to-deposit ratio of bank reflect assets structure and the non-performing loan ratio of bank reflect capital risk level (Table 1).

Table 1. List of variables.

Name	Symbol	Interpretation
Profitability of banks	roa^1	The return on assets
Profit structure of banks	$prostr^1$	Calculated by formula (1)
ITFIN's degree	$intfi^2$	Internet financial index
Economic development level	$gdpg^3$	Year-over-year growth of GDP
The stability of economic system	cpi^3	Consumer price index
Market structure of banking	hhi^3	Dividing Herfindahl Index by 10000
The degree of direct financing in stock market	$stock^3$	Ratio of stock market value to CDP
Assets scale	cta^3	Logarithm of total assets
Capital adequacy	car^3	Capital adequacy
Operating efficiency	cir^3	Cost-income ratio of bank
Assets structure	cdr^3	Loan-to-deposit ratio of bank
Capital risk level	npl^3	Non-performing loan ratio of bank

Noted that [1] marks of dependent variables, [2] marks of independent variables, [3] marks of control variables

3.3 Data Source

Our sample contains 16 commercial banks listed in China before the first year of Chinese Internet Finance era (2013), Table 2 shows the samples include 5 state-owned commercial banks (Industrial and Commercial Bank, China Construction Bank, Agricultural Bank of China, Bank of China, Bank of Communications) and 8 joint-stock commercial banks (China Merchants Bank, China Industrial Bank, Shanghai Pudong Development Bank, China CITIC Bank, China Minsheng bank, China Everbright Bank, Ping An Bank, Huaxia Bank) and 3 municipal commercial banks (Beijing, Nanjing, Ningbo). The datum period is from 2010 to 2018, based on quarterly datum. Deleting some missing samples, 548 valid samples were obtained.

The financial datum of commercial banks and ITFIN's degree are derived from the Wind and Resset database, while the GDP and CPI are derived from the National Statistics Bureau.

Through descriptive statistical and correlation analysis of variables, it can be found that the gap between the maximum and minimum of *prostr* and *roa* is obvious, which preliminarily shows that there are differences in profitability and profit structure of different commercial banks. In addition, because the gap between the maximum value and the minimum value of the *intfi* variable is too large, the natural logarithm of *intfi*, the *lnintfi*, is taken in the empirical analysis.

Table 2. List of sample banks description.

No.	Symbol	Name	Listing date
1	000001.SZ	Ping An Bank	1991-04-03
2	002142.SZ	Ningbo Bank	2007-07-19
3	600000.SH	Shanghai Pudong Development Bank	1999-11-10
4	600015.SH	Huaxia Bank	2003-09-12
5	600016.SH	China Minsheng bank	2000-12-19
6	600036.SH	China Merchants Bank	2002-04-09
7	601009.SH	Nanjing Bank	2007-07-19
8	601166.SH	China Industrial Bank	2007-02-05
9	601169.SH	Beijing	2007-09-19
10	601288.SH	Agricultural Bank of China	2010-07-15
11	601328.SH	Bank of Communications	2007-05-15
12	601398.SH	Industrial and Commercial Bank	2006-10-27
13	601818.SH	China Everbright Bank	2010-08-18
14	601939.SH	China Construction Bank	2007-09-25
15	601988.SH	Bank of China	2006-07-05
16	601998.SH	China CITIC Bank	2007-04-27

3.4 Econometric Model and Results

Based on the analysis above, a Panel Data Model was applied to analyse the impact of ITFIN on the profitability and profits structure if commercial banks. The following formula (2) and (3) are used to analyse both the whole datum and the heterogeneity of banks in different subgroups.

$$roa_{i,t} = \beta_0 + \beta_1 lnintfi_{i,t} + \sum\nolimits_{k=2}^{10} \beta_k X_{ikt} + \varepsilon_{it} \tag{2}$$

$$prostr_{i,t} = \beta_0' + \beta_1' lnintfi_{i,t} + \sum\nolimits_{k=2}^{10} \beta_k' X_{ikt} + \varepsilon_{it}' \tag{3}$$

Where i and k are the counter items, t represents time, ε is an error term, and β is the coefficient. Dependent variables are *roa* and *prostr*. Independent variable is *lnintfi*. X are control variables.

Full Samples' Regression Analysis. First, we need to verify the assumption that with the higher development of ITFIN, commercial banks have stronger profitability and more diversified profits structure. We use the least square method, fixed effect and random effect to regression respectively. *F*-test and *Hausman* test were present the setting form of the model was the fixed effect model.

Table 3. Regression results of full samples.

Roa				Prostr			
lnintfi	0.00366***	cta	−0.000974	lnintfi	0.0180**	cta	−0.0404***
	(7.843)		(−01.144)		(2.392)		(−06.700)
gdpg	−0.0806***	car	0.0611***	gdpg	0.0512	car	1.121***
	(−03.927)		(4.925)		(0.150)		(5.981)
cpi	0.0332***	cdr	−0.00256	cpi	−0.349*	cdr	−0.0756**
	(3.063)		(−01.266)		(−01.926)		(−02.431)
hhi	0.0530***	cir	0.0411***	hhi	1.120***	cir	0.278***
	(2.987)		(10.75)		(5.086)		(4.568)
stock	−0.00449***	npl	0.122**	stock	−0.0150**	npl	−05.276***
	(−011.49)		(2.330)		(−02.348)		(−06.201)
		Constant	−0.0416			Constant	1.711***
			(−01.375)				(6.152)
R-squared	0.820			R-squared	0.772		
Number of id	16			Number of id	16		

Noted that ***, **, * refer to significant correlations at significance levels of 1%, 5%, and 10%, respectively

Table 3 reports the regression results of full samples. It shows that the development of ITFIN has a significant positive effect on the profitability of commercial banks, and a significant negative decentralized effect on the profits structure. This shows that the development of Internet finance in China has brought diversified changes to the profit structure of commercial banks, as well as a high level of profitability.

Regression Analysis of Subgroups. By means of subgroup regression of state-owned, joint-stock and municipal banks, we analyse the heterogeneity of the impacts on different types of commercial banks.

Table 4. Regression results of full subgroups.

Variables	Roa		
Subgroup	State-owned	Joint-stock	Municipal
lnintfi	0.00231***	0.00320***	0.000686
	(3.885)	(4.286)	(1.100)
gdpg	−0.0525**	−0.0850**	−0.140***
	(−2.100)	(−2.360)	(−5.517)
cpi	0.0364***	0.0416***	0.0174
	(2.698)	(2.612)	(0.704)

(continued)

Table 4. (*continued*)

hhi	−0.126***	−0.0326	−0.123*
	(−4.084)	(−0.965)	(−1.815)
stock	−0.00235***	−0.00429***	−0.00388***
	(−4.286)	(−7.381)	(−4.415)
cta	−0.0206***	−0.00652***	−0.0109***
	(−6.875)	(−3.439)	(−3.405)
car	0.110***	0.0567***	0.0620***
	(4.522)	(3.148)	(2.892)
cdr	−0.000947	−0.00510	0.00174
	(−0.243)	(−1.554)	(0.440)
cir	0.0757***	0.0271***	0.0312***
	(14.47)	(4.848)	(3.044)
npl	−0.284***	0.0599	−0.607**
	(−3.285)	(0.579)	(−2.496)
Constant	0.581***	0.139**	0.281***
	(5.944)	(2.196)	(2.768)
Observations	177	277	92
R-squared	0.756	0.397	0.538
Number of id	5	8	3

Variables	*prostr*		
Subgroup	State-owned	Joint-stock	Municipal
lnintfi	0.00561	−0.00908	0.0489*
	(0.566)	(−1.009)	(1.974)
gdpg	0.370	0.0369	−3.805***
	(0.888)	(0.0851)	(−3.554)
cpi	−0.242	−0.104	−0.814
	(−1.075)	(−0.544)	(−1.404)
hhi	−1.351***	0.888**	9.646***
	(−2.623)	(2.184)	(6.080)
stock	−0.00871	0.00208	−0.0622***
	(−0.953)	(0.297)	(−3.026)

(*continued*)

Table 4. (*continued*)

cta	−0.279***		−0.0756***	0.330***
	(−5.591)		(−3.310)	(4.409)
car	1.651***		0.854***	0.387
	(4.061)		(3.941)	(0.771)
cdr	−0.133**		−0.111***	0.0824
	(−2.049)		(−2.808)	(0.889)
cir	0.248***		0.142**	0.482**
	(2.846)		(2.100)	(2.014)
npl	−3.443**		−2.172*	16.01***
	(−2.389)		(−1.743)	(2.814)
Constant	9.391***		2.754***	−9.905***
	(5.763)		(3.619)	(−4.168)
Observations	177		277	92
R-squared	0.600		0.906	0.710
Number of id	5		8	3

Noted that ***, **, * refer to significant correlations at significance levels of 1%, 5%, and 10%, respectively

Table 4 reports the regression results of subgroups. We can find that the impacts of ITFIN on different banks are heterogeneous, and the ITFIN has greater effects on the profitability of the state-owneds while greater effects on the diversified development of the municipals than others.

The empirical results present that the profits of commercial banks will be affected by ITFIN, and the positive effects are greater than the negative impacts. Due to the differences in market positioning and marketing strategies among the state-owned, joint-stock and municipal banks, the changes in profitability and profits structure are heterogeneous when they faced to the effects from ITFIN. The effects on the profitability of state-owneds are more significant, while the effects on the diversified development of the municipals are more favorable.

Robustness Check. In order to check for the validity of the aforementioned findings, we conducted a robustness check. We estimate the alternative profit frontier model. This specification uses the same explanatory variables as the function above and *roe* as the explained variable. Table 5 reports the regression results of re-estimation. The results are generally consistent with the aforementioned findings, and indicate that the results of this model are reliable.

Table 5. Regression results of full samples.

Variables	roe			
Subgroup	Full samples	State-owned	Joint-stock	Municipal
lnintfi	0.0531***	0.0268***	0.0420***	0.0743***
	(6.961)	(3.072)	(3.296)	(4.168)
gdpg	−1.109***	−0.868**	−1.481**	−0.783
	(−3.307)	(−2.361)	(−2.409)	(−1.018)
cpi	0.464***	0.570***	0.649**	−0.0792
	(2.619)	(2.878)	(2.390)	(−0.190)
dls	0.979***	−1.733***	−0.625	−0.708
	(3.375)	(−3.815)	(−1.085)	(−0.621)
hhi	−0.0661***	−0.0285***	−0.0633***	−0.0704***
	(−10.34)	(−3.539)	(−6.372)	(−4.767)
stock	8.67e−05	−0.299***	−0.126***	−0.106*
	(0.00622)	(−6.791)	(−3.882)	(−1.966)
cta	0.473**	1.097***	0.417	0.613*
	(2.334)	(3.063)	(1.359)	(1.700)
car	−0.0694**	−0.00552	−0.122**	−0.00212
	(−2.097)	(−0.0962)	(−2.175)	(−0.0318)
cdr	0.661***	1.151***	0.455***	0.565***
	(10.58)	(14.98)	(4.761)	(3.285)
cir	1.155	−4.416***	1.759	−10.13**
	(1.352)	(−3.477)	(0.996)	(−2.476)
npl	−0.976**	8.466***	3.016***	2.722
	(−1.972)	(5.895)	(2.798)	(1.593)
Constant	546	177	277	92
	0.437	0.771	0.410	0.464
Observations	548	178	277	93
R-squared	0.8331	0.8575	0.8293	0.8420
Number of id	16	5	8	3

Noted that ***, **, * refer to significant correlations at significance levels of 1%, 5%, and 10%, respectively

4   Conclusion and Implication

Chinese economy is in a critical period of structural adjustment and transformation, as a rising star of the financial industry, ITFIN affects the traditional finance, which is mainly commercial banking business. Our work started with the perspective of market structure in terms of theoretical analysis. We analysed the influences of ITFIN on the internal product pricing mechanism and product decision mechanism, the external market competitive and regulatory environment of commercial banks, and explored a complete path of this influence from a new perspective of market structure. Our work considered the influence of ITFIN in terms of empirical analysis, established a panel data model not only includes macro-economy, banking features and banks' characters, but also contains the Internet financial index.

Our empirical analysis has produced some findings. First, the development of ITFIN has both positive and negative effects on the profits of commercial banks, which generally promotes the profitability and the diversification of their profits structure. Although the profit margins of banks have declined in recent years, the decline is not mainly due to ITFIN. Through improving product pricing mechanism, the resource allocation capacity of commercial banks has been improved. By changing the traditional decision-making mechanism, banks can develop into a user-oriented mode. What's more, ITFIN has changed the competition and supervision mechanism of financial market, which makes banks improving their efficiency significantly. Banks should pay more attention to the cooperation with non-bank institutions and enhance their market competitiveness. Second, ITFIN impacts the profits of commercial banks through the hypostatic transmission path, and there is heterogeneity in the degree of different types. We found that there are greater effects on the profitability of the state-owneds and greater effects on the diversified development of the municipals. This is owing to the reasons following: with large scales, the state-owned commercial banks pay more attention to the risk avoidance of investment decisions, and have higher level of operation management ability and network technology. Compared with municipal banks, the large-scales have reached the higher level in the stability of the profit system. Conversely, the businesses of municipal banks are mainly existed in villages and towns, where has more rapidly promoting web, which is the backward region before. And in the increasingly fierce market competition, their external cooperation ability and product innovation ability grow faster.

We also draw some implications about the development of the commercial banks in China. First, it requires the enterprise to classify the financial market. Shareholders and management should improve the ability of asset allocation, classify the financial market, and refine product positioning to meet the multiple demands of customers. Second, it requires the FinTech to achieve a win-win condition. Shareholders and management better do follow the high-tech in decision making, cooperate with Internet firms to elevate the level of financial science and technology, and provide customers with more efficient, safe and convenient financial services. Finally, it requires marshalling resources to optimize the banking structure. Companies can promote the formulation of market regulation policies to get the rational construction and improve the mechanism for transmitting monetary policy.

References

1. Guidance on promoting the healthy Development of Internet Finance. https://www.pbc.gov. cn/goutongjiaoliu/113456/113469/2813898/index.html. Accessed 14 Dec 2015
2. Richard Werthamer, N., Raymond, S.U.: Technology and finance: the electronic markets. Technol. Forecast. Soc. Chang. **55**(1), 39–53 (1997). https://doi.org/10.1016/S0040-162 5(96)00144-8
3. Chande, N.: A Survey and Risk Analysis of Selected Non-bank Retail Payments Systems. Bank of Canada 2008–17 (2008)
4. Momparler, A., Lassala, C., Ribeiro, D.: Efficiency in banking services: a comparative analysis of Internet-primary and branching banks in the US. Serv. Bus. **7**(4), 641–663 (2012). https:// doi.org/10.1007/s11628-012-0179-1
5. Kyriba, S.T.: Fintech Providers are Disrupting the Bank-Led Supply Chain Finance Industry, New Survey Shows. PRNewswire (2019)
6. Shusong, B., Peng, S.: Interaction and integration: a new pattern of competition in the era of internet finance. Rural Credit Coop. Chin. **24**, 15–17 (2012)
7. Zhang, L., Fan, S.: How state-owned commercial banks deal with the challenge of internet financial model. New Financ. **07**, 47–51 (2013)
8. Xiaolin, G.: Internet financial model and the influence on traditional banking industry. South China Financ. **05**, 86–88 (2013)
9. Pin, G., Yue, S.: The impact of internet finance on commercial banks' risk-taking: theoretical interpretation and empirical test. Financ. Trade Econ. **10**, 102–116 (2015)
10. Xun, Q.: Internet based fund: challenges and enlightenments to commercial banks: a case study of YueBao. J. Shanghai Financ. Univ. **04**, 75–83 (2013)
11. Zhilai, Z.: Structural reform of commercial banks from the perspective of supply side and internet financial innovation. Reform Econ. Syst. **01**, 130–135 (2018)
12. Detragiache, E., Tressel, T., Gupta, P.: Foreign banks in poor countries: theory and evidence. J. Financ. **63**(5), 2123–2160 (2008)
13. Xie, P., Zou, C.: How A-Share Listed Industrial Companies Launch Internet Finance Business: 2013–2016, pp. 4–6. Economy & Management Publishing House (2017)
14. Li, Y., Li, J.: Internet Finance, pp. 147–275. Publishing House of Electronics Industry (2014)
15. Fan, D., Fu, C., Fan, S., Wu, A.: New Changes, pp. 119–136. China Economic Publishing House (2016)
16. Xiao, J., Su, Q.: Will the breaking of the banking monopoly ease the financing constraints of small and medium-sized enterprises? NanKai Econ. Stud. **05**, 19–35 (2016)
17. Ma, C., Li, C.: The efficiency of state-owned economy, economic growth target constraint and monetary policy overshoot. Econ. Res. J. **48**(07), 76–89+160 (2013)
18. De Young, R., Rice, T.: Erratum: noninterest income and financial performance at U.S. commercial banks. Financ. Rev. **41**(3), 449–450 (2006)
19. Tiancai, X., Jin, S., Lili, Y.: The influence of economic cycle strategy on the profitability of commercial banks. Stud. Int. Finan. **05**, 88–96 (2013)
20. Yildirim, H.S., Philippatos, G.C.: Restructuring, consolidation and competition in latin American Banking markets. J. Bank. Financ. **31**, 629–639 (2007)

Level Set Segmentation Based on the Prior Shape of Biological Feature

Ji Zhao[✉], Dongxu Ji, and Yuxiang Feng

School of Computer Science and Software Engineering, University of Science and Technology, Anshan 114051, Liaoning, China

Abstract. The identification of user's identity which is based on the analysis and measurement of the biological characteristics has become a research hotspot. The precise location and segmentation of the target is the basis for accurate biometric recognition. In view of the similarity of the external shape of human biological characteristics, the prior shape knowledge is introduced into active contour model based on level set. First, the training data of the shape function, which is expressed by the level set, are projected onto a lower dimensional subspace and achieved the primary attribute reduction on approximately Gaussian distribution of the training set using PCA method. Second, the further optimized properties are obtained by minimization class attribute interdependence minimization (CAIM) algorithm. Finally, under the constraints of the prior shape and object personality traits, level set curve based on the border and region can accurately evolve into the target boundary. Experiments demonstrate that our model can cope with image noise and clutter, as well as partial occlusions.

Keywords: Pattern recognition · Image processing technology · Image segmentation · Level set method · Prior shape

1 Introduction

In the field of computer science and technology, the biometric identification technology [1, 2] by analyzing and measuring the physiological characteristics of the human body has become a research hotspot. Compared with the traditional identification method, the biometric identification technology has the advantages of safety, reliability, not easy to forget, good security performance, not easy to be stolen and portability, and can be used at anytime and anywhere. The technology can be widely used in government, military, banking, social security, electronic commerce, security and defense [3]. Currently, the biometric features used for identification include fingerptints, iris, face, voice, palm, hand shape, retina, ear shape, etc.

The foundation of biometric identification is the segmentation and localization of the features. Due to the complexity of the background, the blurred edge and the defect of target, the segmentation method can not get the desired segmentation results. The main reason is that the low level gray information of the image can not fully express

© ICST Institute for Computer Sciences, Social Informatics and Telecommunications Engineering 2021
Published by Springer Nature Switzerland AG 2021. All Rights Reserved
H. Song and D. Jiang (Eds.): SIMUtools 2020, LNICST 369, pp. 651–666, 2021.
https://doi.org/10.1007/978-3-030-72792-5_51

the characteristics of the target [4]. The method of solving this problem is to introduce the prior information of object such as color and shape into the evolution of the curve in the segmentation model. We can use curve evolution global geometric features and the local shape features of object to effectively deal with occlusion, noise and target shape changes in image segmentation. The parametric shape modeling methods include distance mapping [5], snake line model with elastic properties [6], template method [7], and skeleton method [8]. Although these methods can effectively describe local deformation, but a large number of parameters is required and they can not handle topological shape change. So we use the level set method to overcome the parametric shape model shortcomings [10]. First, a shape model, which is constructed by using a set of samples in the level set space, is used to describe the change of a priori shape by variational framework. And then, the prior shape term is introduced into the level set energy model.

At present, the research of level set segmentation model based on shape a priori information has made some progress. Leventon M E, Grimson W E L and Faugeras O [9] established shape prior statistical model by using linear principal component analysis (PCA) method in shape training set. Rousson M and Pragios N [10] put forward the implicit expression of the level set model by integrating shape prior information into the regional information. Pan B, Wang W, Yan J, et al. [11] propose a level set model, which incorporates shape priors and the gradient information of the image into C-V model for prostate MRI segmentation, and can segment the prostate contour in MRI with high precision. Cremers D, Tischhauser E, Weickert J [12] combined the geodesic active contour model and the prior shape with kernal to guide curve evolution. Cremers D, Sochen N and Schnorr C [13] proposed tag function to make a fixed template and priori shape integrated with pose information. Karantzalos K and Paragios N [14] can automatically analyze the number and angle of target objects by integrating a priori information of different shapes, and then they proposes a 3D automatic reconstruction method of remote sensing data based on variational farmework [15], which solves the segmentation problem of optical images and digital elevation maps, and determines their positions and 3D geometric shapes based on prior knowledge.

2   Related Work

In terms of shape description, the level set model is used to present the shape features. First, it is an implicit and intrinsic measure of expression and can automatically deal with the changes in the topology. Secondly, it provides a natural way to estimate shape geometric properties such as curvature and normal vector. Typically, the level set function is often defined by the distance function in the image space. This form of expression is consistent with the level set model of curve evolution, therefore it can be naturally fused to the active contour segmentation framework.

Each curve in the training set is regarded as the zero level set on the high dimensional surface. It is the goal that shape modeling is to find the probability distribution of these surfaces. Since they all describe the shape of the same kind of object, the curves of the training set are dependent on each other. So it is inevitable to leads to more redundancy in the training set. It can be considered that the object shape approximately obeys mul-tidimensional Gauss distribution and the shape changes are mainly concentrated in the vicinity of the mean shape. Firstly, the new algorithm applys principal component analysis method to training set for rough extraction, which can get the data mainly affecting the shape modeling. After the PCA process the class attribute interdependency minimum (CAIM) method is used for data optimal reduction. In the image feature descriptor dimensionality reduction the combination plays an effective role, which removes the contents of the original descriptor redundancy, and also fully retains the important data.

Since CAIM algorithm is mainly related to attribute combination entropy and the attribute dependence entropy of the sample set, it can extract data with the more typical contribution and reduces the data with no typical contribution to improve the expression of prior shape.

2.1 Primary Feature Extraction Using PCA Method

Cootes T and Taylor C [16] proposed PCA to set up the parameters contour model to segment the different objects. Leventon M E, Grimson W E L and Faugeras O [9] applied the PCA to symbols distance function (SDF) in geometry contour model. In comparison, SDF has a greater tolerance than the parameterized contour and improves the robustness, accuracy and speed. The signed distance function of sample set is $\phi = \{\phi_1, \phi_2, \cdots, \phi_n\}$, where n is the number of training samples, can be calculated as:

$$\overline{\phi} = \frac{1}{n} \sum_{i=l}^{n} \phi_i \tag{1}$$

The mean shift is obtained by subtracting the mean value from each sample.

$$\hat{\phi}_i = \phi_i - \overline{\phi}, \quad i = 1, 2, 3, \cdots, n \tag{2}$$

The adjustment of the data structure is carried out to each mean shift. First, the mean shift is adjusted to the column vector of $(m \times l) \times 1$ from the original $(m \times l)$ matrix, and each column vector is combined together to form a new matrix $X (n(m \times l))$, where m, l are the sample image column width and row height. Secondly, we calculate the covariance between two columns of the X to form a covariance matrix $M (n \times n)$. Finally, the singular value decomposition of M is defined as:

$$M = U \Sigma \Lambda \tag{3}$$

where U is the feature vectors matrix of M, Σ is a diagonal matrix whose diagonal elements are eigenvalue $\Lambda = \{\lambda_1, \lambda_2, \cdots, \lambda_n\}$ of M. Then, the feature vectors are sorted according to the corresponding eigenvalues. Finally, the eigenvalue E of X is

$$E = XU = (e_1, e_2, \cdots, e_n) \tag{4}$$

After getting the feature vector of X, the regularization is needed. Thus the number of feature vectors is determined as follows:

$$Fd = \frac{SUM_k}{SUM_n} \tag{5}$$

where the symbol SUM_i is the sum of the former i eigenvalues and $k < n$. The final step in the principal component analysis is the reconstruction of the data. Given characteristic coefficient λ^k_{pca}, the new signed distance function is calculated.

$$\hat{\phi} = Ek\lambda^k_{pca} + \overline{\phi} \tag{6}$$

where the characteristic coefficient λ^k_{pca} is the weight coefficient of k change mode. Obviously, when λ^k_{pca} is zero, the mean value of the sample is obtained.

2.2 Attribute Reduction Based on Clustering Theory

Class Attribute Dependency Minimization Algorithm. Class attribute dependency minimization algorithm is mainly about the feature combination property and mutual interdependence relationship of feature patterns as well as formulation of the concept of typicality and diversity for data set [17]. Its targets are as follows:

- Through statistical filtering and feature being reattached weight value, we get the limited possible solutions in feature combination property and mutual interdependence relationship.
- Based on the estimation of the set entropy and mutual entropy, the model of feature combination property and mutual interdependence relationship is defined.
- An algorithm, which can be used to improve the inherent patterns and simplify the sample data, is proposed to reduce the uncertain sample data with deviation from the set Class attribute dependency minimization algorithm.

Ensemble Entropy Estimation. Given a finite set of n samples X, $Xi(i = 1, 2, \cdots, n)$ is a discrete random set $a_{i1}, a_{i2}, \cdots, a_{im}$ and a_{ij} is the jth observation variables of the ith sample. Matrix $A = aij|i = 1, \cdots, n; j = 1, \cdots, m$ is called the observation matrix of the set X. Therefore, the row vector $Xi = [a_{i1}, a_{i2}, \cdots, a_{im}]$ is a collectionof m observation variables about the first i samples, and the column vector $Y_{j'} = [a_{1j}, a_{2j}, \cdots, a_{nj}]$ is the collection of n samples for the first j observation variables. Some definitions are as follows:

- Definition 1: $\omega = \omega_1, \omega_2, \cdots, \omega_n$ is defined as weights of a n-dimensional vector set, in which ωi corresponds to the weight of the first i vector, and $\sum_{i=1}^n \omega_i = 1$.
- Definition 2: Based on ω, the estimated probability on Y is defined as:

$$p^k_j(\omega) = \sum_{i=1}^n \delta^k_{ij}\omega_i \tag{7}$$

where

$$\delta^k_{ij}(\omega) = \begin{cases} 1, |a_{ij} - a_{kj}| < \varepsilon \\ 0, |a_{ij} - a_{kj}| \geq \varepsilon \end{cases} \tag{8}$$

where, $k = 1, 2, \cdots, L_j, j = 1, 2, \cdots, m$. $\varepsilon(\varepsilon \geq 0)$ is a very small number relative to attribute values. L_j is the length of the j observation variable, the $p^k_j(\omega)$ is the p^k_j in the case of a given ω.

- Definition 3: The combination entropy of an observed variable Yj is:

$$H(j) = -\sum_{k=1}^{L} p_j^k \log p_j^k \qquad (9)$$

- Definition 4: The $\begin{pmatrix} m \\ 2 \end{pmatrix}$ finite schemes for all events in X is defined as:

$$\left\{ p_{ij}^{kl} \middle| k = 1, 2, \cdots, L_j; \quad l = 1, 2, \cdots, L_{j'}; \quad j, j' = 1, 2, \cdots, m; \quad j' > j \right\} \qquad (10)$$

- Definition 5: The mutual interdependence entropy between Y_j and $Y_{j'}$ is defined as:

$$H(j, j') = -\sum_{k=1}^{L_j} \sum_{l=1}^{L_j} q_{jj'}^{kl} \log q_{jj'}^{kl} \qquad (11)$$

- Definition 6: The $\begin{pmatrix} m \\ 2 \end{pmatrix}$ finite schemes for all events in X is defined as:

$$R_{jj'}^{(2)} = \frac{I(j, j')}{H(j, j')} \qquad (12)$$

where, $I(j, j') = H(j) + H(j') - H(j, j')$, and $0 \le R_{jj'}^{(2)} \le 1$, if $R_{jj'}^{(2)} = 0$, the Y_j and $Y_{j'}$ are completely independent, if $R_{jj'}^{(2)} = 1$, the two features are completely dependent. And if

$$R_{jj'}^{(2)} \ge \frac{X^2 (L_j - 1)(L_{j'} - 1)}{2nH(j, j')} \qquad (13)$$

it is showed that there is some dependencies between features Y_j and $Y_{j'}$.

3 A Variational Level Set Segmentation Model Based on Prior Shape Information

The energy functional for the variational level set model for image segmentation is

$$E(u) = \mu E_c + \alpha E_e + \beta E_R + \lambda E_S \qquad (14)$$

where E_c is the energy functional corresponding to the constraint term of the signed distance function, E_e is an energy functional based on edge, E_R is an energy functional based on region, and E_s is an energy functional of priori shape. E_c, E_e, E_R and E_S are defined as respectively:

$$Ec = \frac{1}{2} \int_{\Omega} (|\nabla u| - 1)^2 dxdy \qquad (15)$$

$$Ee = \int_{\Omega} g\delta(u)|\nabla u|dxdy \tag{16}$$

$$E_R = \int_{\Omega} \lambda_1 H(u)dxdy + \int_{\Omega} \lambda_2(1 - H(u))dxdy \tag{17}$$

$$ES(u) = \int_{\Omega} \rho(r(X))H(u)dxdy \tag{18}$$

where

$$r(X) = Su(x) - uG\left(\hat{X}\right) \tag{19}$$

$$\hat{X} = SRX + T \tag{20}$$

The final energy functional can be written as:

$$E(u) = \tfrac{1}{2}\mu \int_{\Omega} (|\nabla u| - 1)^2 dxdy + \alpha \int_{\Omega} g\delta(u)|\nabla u|dxdy + \beta_1 \int_{\Omega} \lambda_1 H(u)dxdy$$
$$+\beta_2 \int_{\Omega} \lambda_2(1 - H(u))dxdy + \lambda \int_{\Omega} H(u)\left(ku(X) - uG\left(\hat{X}\right)\right)^2 dxdy \tag{21}$$

The optimal solution of the energy function $E(u)$ is the stable solution of PDEs as follows:

$$\begin{cases} \dfrac{\partial u}{\partial t} = u\left(\Delta u - div\left(\dfrac{\partial u}{|\nabla u|}\right)\right) + \delta\varepsilon(u)\left[\begin{array}{c} \beta div\left(g\dfrac{\nabla u}{|\nabla u|}\right) - \beta_1\lambda_1(I - c_1) \\ +\beta_2\lambda_2(I - c_2) - \lambda(Su - uG)^2 \end{array}\right] \\ -\gamma H(u)S(Su - uG) \quad in \ (0, \infty) \times \Omega \\ \dfrac{\partial u}{\partial n} = 0 \quad on \ \partial\Omega \\ u(0, x, y) = u0(x, y) \quad in \ \Omega \end{cases} \tag{22}$$

$$\frac{\partial S}{\partial t} = -\int_{\Omega} H(u)\left(Su - uG\left(\hat{X}\right)\right)\left(u - \nabla_{\hat{X}}uG\nabla_S\hat{X}\right)dxdy \tag{23}$$

$$\frac{\partial(\theta, T)}{\partial t} = \int_{\Omega} H(u)\left(Su - uG\left(\hat{X}\right)\right)\left(\nabla_{\hat{X}}uG\nabla_{(\theta,T)}\hat{X}\right)dxdy \tag{24}$$

Through introducing parameter robust estimation model function $\rho(r)$ and $\phi(r)$, the corresponding equation is rewritten as

$$\frac{\partial u}{\partial t} = u\left(\Delta u - div\left(\frac{\nabla u}{|\nabla u|}\right)\right) + \delta_\varepsilon(u)\left[\alpha div\left(g\frac{\nabla u}{|\nabla u|}\right) - \beta_1\lambda_1(I - c_1) + \beta_2\lambda_2(I - c_2) - \lambda\rho(r(X))\right]$$
$$-\gamma H(u)\phi(r)S \tag{25}$$

$$\frac{\partial S}{\partial t} = -\int_{\Omega} H(u)\phi(r)\left(u - \nabla_{\hat{X}}uG\nabla_S\hat{X}\right)dxdy \tag{26}$$

$$\frac{\partial(\theta, T)}{\partial t} = \int_{\Omega} H(u)\phi(r)\left(\nabla_{\hat{X}}uG\nabla_{(\theta,T)}\right)dxdy \tag{27}$$

where respectively S, θ, T is the scaling factor, the rotation factor and the translation.

4 Experimental Results and Analysis

4.1 Segmentation of Human Body Contour

The Acquisition and Expression of Shape Training Set. The shape of body is segmented from 100 representative human images, which constitute a initial training set for priori shape. The eigenvalues of each training data are shown in Table 1. After PCA with fitting coefficient 0.98 attribute reduction, the remaining 27 items are the data of main factor in shape training set, and the eigenvalues of the remaining 27 data are shown in Table 2. And then the optimization of CAIM ($\varepsilon = 0.0008$)is carried out, as shown in Table 3, the 9 feature data are the main contribution to the expression of human body shape, which are selected to construct the priori shape.

Table 1. Eigenvalues of the training set's eigenvectors.

No.	Eigenvalue	No.	Eigenvalue	No.	Eigenvalue	No.	Eigenvalue	No.	Eigenvalue
1	170423.7500	2	138281.4844	3	63030.2813	4	51409.2266	5	39550.5977
6	25377.2617	7	22697.7891	8	15312.2451	9	11525.0322	10	8051.1055
11	6576.4102	12	4771.3081	13	4237.4751	14	3910.4451	15	3238.6929
16	2523.8118	17	2492.7739	18	1826.8881	19	1783.8018	20	1402.3051
21	1498.5015	22	1320.5691	23	1145.8143	24	992.4016	25	960.4662
26	863.5479	27	799.8417	28	682.5350	29	652.1017	30	598.7137
31	567.9088	32	525.1431	33	464.2548	34	460.5003	35	430.3991
36	409.0725	37	369.0485	38	359.8156	39	344.1356	40	337.6111
41	276.9188	42	271.2017	43	249.0898	44	234.0920	45	224.4437
46	210.7977	47	202.8804	48	198.6955	49	177.0910	50	171.4283
51	161.3509	52	151.3801	53	145.2543	54	137.7306	55	135.2908
56	127.0296	57	114.8879	58	111.2170	59	107.5084	60	104.4107
61	99.6913	62	93.6221	63	92.1430	64	84.7209	65	82.2678
66	80.8714	67	75.4714	68	70.7329	69	65.9291	70	63.9189
71	61.1338	72	58.2500	73	56.4961	74	52.8481	75	49.7694
76	48.3934	77	46.5804	78	44.9886	79	43.9146	80	42.1723
81	40.8940	82	0.0330	83	39.5448	84	38.2734	85	36.1238
86	34.7594	87	33.1616	88	31.2365	89	29.0265	90	12.4005
91	27.0900	92	14.1955	93	15.4931	94	16.7723	95	17.5104
96	19.2162	97	23.7321	98	22.9521	99	21.9240	100	19.9770

In order to illustrate the process of establishing training set, we selected a training subset which contains 14 images from the training set to elect binary image of the samples, the results are shown in Fig. 1.

Table 2. Eigenvalues after PCA reduction

No.	Eigenvalue	No.	Eigenvalue	No.	Eigenvalue	No.	Eigenvalue	No.	Eigenvalue
1	170,423.7500	2	138281.4844	3	63030.2813	4	51,409.2266	5	39550.5977
6	25,377.2617	7	22697.7891	8	15312.2451	9	11,525.0322	10	8051.1055
11	6,576.4102	12	4771.3081	13	4237.4751	14	3,910.4451	15	3238.6929
16	2,523.8118	17	2492.7739	18	1826.8881	19	1,783.8018	20	1402.3051
21	1,498.5015	22	1320.5691	23	1145.8143	24	992.4016	25	960.4662
26	863.5479	27	799.8417							

Table 3. Eigenvalues after CAIM optimization

No.	Eigenvalue	No.	Eigenvalue	No.	Eigenvalue	No.	Eigenvalue	No.	Eigenvalue
2	138281.4844	6	25377.2617	7	22697.7891	9	11525.0322	12	4771.3081
12	2492.7739	21	1498.5015	23	1145.8143	24	992.4016		

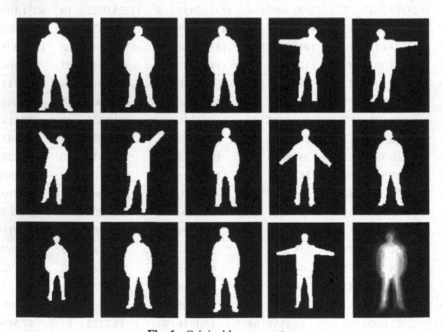

Fig. 1. Original human contour

In Fig. 1, the last image is a superposition of 14 images. As we can see, the overlapped area is relatively small, and the surrounding is fuzzy, which shows that the distribution of information in the image is dispersed.

Registration of Shape Training Set. Binary image registration operation includes three parts: translation, scaling and rotation.

Translation: The translation parameters is determined by object centroid coordinates, the centroid coordinates of binary image Ik can be calculated as

$$x^k = \frac{\sum_{i=1}^{m} \sum_{j=1}^{n} x_i I_k(x_i, y_i)}{\sum_{i=1}^{m} \sum_{j=1}^{n} I_k(x_i, y_i)}, \; y^k = \frac{\sum_{i=1}^{m} \sum_{j=1}^{n} x_i I_k(x_i, y_i)}{\sum_{i=1}^{m} \sum_{j=1}^{n} I_k(x_i, y_i)} \tag{28}$$

where $k = 1, 2, \cdots, 14$, m and n, respectively, is the number of rows and columns, (x_i, y_i) is the coordinates of the pixel.

Scaling: The zoom scale is measured by the average distance from the edge point of image to centroid. Assume that the edge point coordinate is $\left(x_i^k, y_i^k\right), i = 1, 2, \cdots, M^k$, M^k is the length of the target contour of the k image, the mean distance is defined as:

$$S^k = \frac{1}{M^k} \sum_{i=1}^{M^k} D\left(\left(x_i^k, y_i^k\right), \left(x^k, y^k\right)\right) \tag{29}$$

where $D\left(\left(x_i^k, y_i^k\right), \left(x^k, y^k\right)\right)$ is the Euclidean distance between points $\left(x_i^k, y_i^k\right)$ and point $\left(x^k, y^k\right)$.

Rotation: The rotation angle can be defined as:

$$\theta = \tan^{-1} \frac{\Delta x_i - x_{ti} - x_{si}}{\Delta y_i - y_{ti} - y_{si}} - \tan^{-1} \frac{\Delta x_i}{\Delta y_i} \tag{30}$$

where $(\Delta x_i, \Delta y_i)$ is the displacement vector, (x_{ti}, y_{ti}) is the translation vector, and (x_{si}, y_{si}) is the zoom vector.

In this work, the zoom scale is set to -7.4175, translation vector is $(-0.6266, -0.6335)$ and rotation angle is 0.7952.

Figure 2 shows the sample image after translation, scaling and rotation. The last image is a superimposed image of each sample. It can be seen that the overlap area is increased in comparison with Fig. 1.

The Level Set Expression of Training Samples. Figure 3 is the zero level set expression of the signed distance function of the contour of each target in the final sample training set.

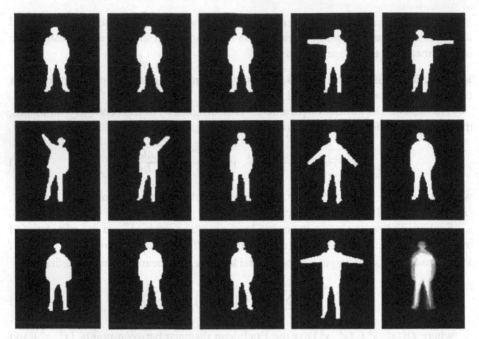

Fig. 2. Human contour's pan and zoom images

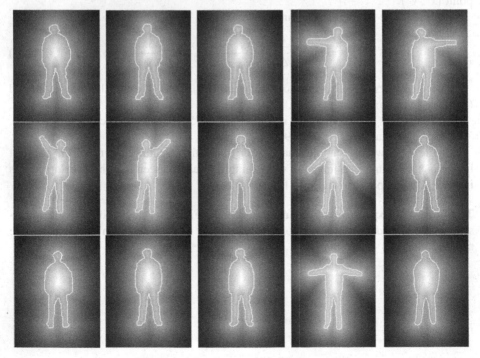

Fig. 3. Level set expression of body contour

Experimental Result. The segmentation process and results of the body using the proposed algorithm is shown in Fig. 4, among which Fig. 4(a) is a 110×140 original image. Figure 4(b) is the edge of Fig. 4(a). Figure 4(c) is the initial contour of the level set. Figure 4(d) is the zero level set of the initial contour. Figure 4(f) is the signed distance function of the zero level set. Figure 4(f)–(g) are the process and results of the evolution of the segmentation curve. The red line is the evolution curve, the green line is a priori shape contour curve, and the evolution curve is successfully stopped at the edge of the target after 45 iterations. The model parameters in the Formula (25) are $\mu = 25$, $\alpha = 0.1$, $\beta_1 = \beta_2 = 100$, $\lambda_1 = \lambda_2 = 1.2$, $\lambda = 1.7$, $\gamma = 5$, $\varepsilon = 1$, time step $t = 0.05$.

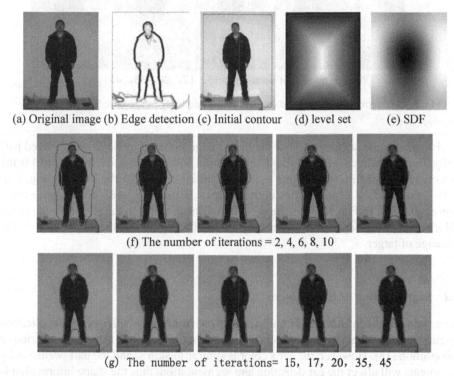

(a) Original image (b) Edge detection (c) Initial contour   (d) level set   (e) SDF

(f) The number of iterations = 2, 4, 6, 8, 10

(g) The number of iterations= 15, 17, 20, 35, 45

Fig. 4. Segmentation process and results for human body based on a prior shape

The right lower limb of the segmented object is partially occluded as shown in Fig. 5. Although there is occlusion, the curve after 45 iterations is still successful segmentation, which ensures the integrity of the body.

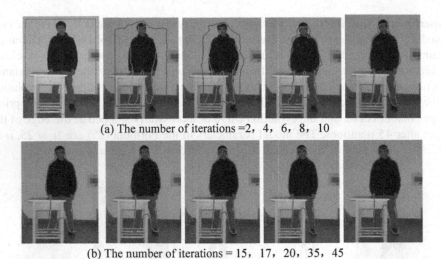

(a) The number of iterations =2, 4, 6, 8, 10

(b) The number of iterations = 15, 17, 20, 35, 45

Fig. 5. Segmentation process and results for blocked body image based on a prior shape

Figure 6 is the segmentation of the body image polluted by noise and covered partially. Figure 6(a) is a 110×140 picture with 0.4 salt pepper noise. Figure 6(b) is the detection edge of Fig. 6(a). Figure 6(c) is the initial contour of the level set, Fig. 6(d) is the zero level set expression of initial contour. Figure 6(e) is signed distance function expression. In Fig. 6(f)–(g), the second row corresponds to the segmentation curve (black) and prior shape curve (green), the curve after 55 iterations successfully stop in the edge of target.

4.2 Segmentation of Ear Contour

As a biometric identification technology, the ear recognition's theory and application research has been paid more attention. The segmentation of ear is also the foundation of recognition [18]. However, the ear's color is similar to skin's, and the part occlusion by ornaments will affect the ear detection and segmentation, thus the shape information is introduced into the level set segmentation model in order to extract the external contour of the ear.

Figure 7 is the segmentation process and results of the blurred image of ear. Figure 7(a) is a 110×140 right ear image, the photography equipment jitter leads to ambiguous. As we can see, the white line is the initial contour, and green line is prior shape curve. Although the ear edge is blured in image, prior shape curve can accurately locate near the edge, and the black curve under the guidance of the shape prior reaches the ideal edge.

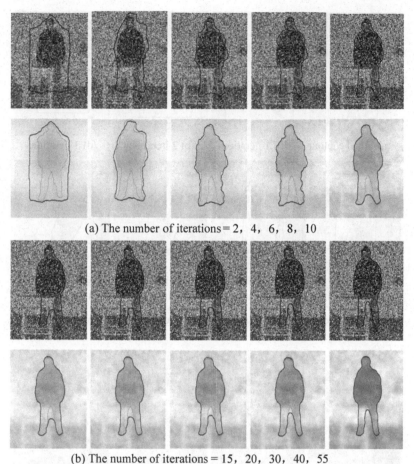

(a) The number of iterations = 2, 4, 6, 8, 10

(b) The number of iterations = 15, 20, 30, 40, 55

Fig. 6. Segmentation process and results for blocked and noisy body

4.3 Facial Contour Segmentation

Face segmentation has always been a hot topic in the field of image processing. Accurate facial contour segmentation plays a key role in face recognition, facial expression analysis and emotion understanding. Although the scholars have done a lot of research on human face segmentation, the influence of location, light, occlusion and complex background are still the difficulties of solving the problem.

In the first row of Fig. 8, Fig. 8(a) is a 150 × 120 color face image, and Fig. 8(b), Fig. 8(c) and Fig. 8(d) are the results of segmentation using the GAC, model C-V model and the proposed method respectively. Compared with the GAC model and C-V model, the proposed method is better. In the second row, the face is added obstacles as shown in Fig. 8(a), Fig. 8(b) is the segmentation result by the GAC model in 300 iterations, Fig. 8(c) is the result of the 100 iteration by the C-V model, Fig. 8(d) is iterative 5 times results by the proposed method. As we can see, the face can be segmented correctly by the new method.

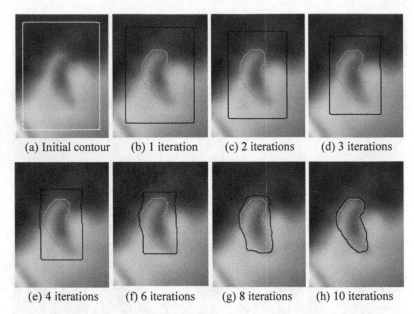

(a) Initial contour   (b) 1 iteration   (c) 2 iterations   (d) 3 iterations

(e) 4 iterations   (f) 6 iterations   (g) 8 iterations   (h) 10 iterations

Fig. 7. Segmentation process and results for fuzzy ear based on a prior shape

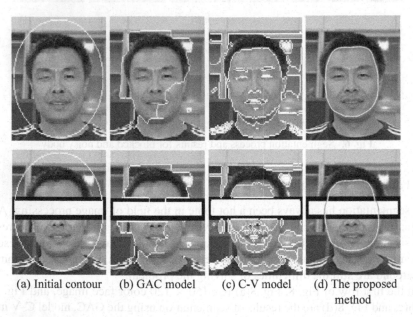

(a) Initial contour   (b) GAC model   (c) C-V model   (d) The proposed
                                                              method

Fig. 8. The results comparison between C-V, GAC and the proposed method

We use the Misclassified Error (ME) as the evaluation method of the experimental results. ME is ratio of number of misclassified pixel and number the object pixel. The smaller value of ME indicates, the better segmentation results is. The ME = 0 shows that the algorithm is consistent with the manual segmentation results. Through the segmentation of 275 personal face images, experiments show that the segmentation results of C-V model and GAC model are not good, and the ME is 17.3912 and 6.4136 respectively. In contrast, the proposed method can get the ideal segmentation results, the ME is 0.2315 and lower than that of the C-V and GAC model as shown in Table 4.

Table 4. The MEs for the different methods

Segmentation method	Mean error rate
C-V model	17.3912
GAC model	6.4136
The proposed method	0.2315

5 Conclusion

We introduce statistical shape prior information into segmentation model based on level set to improve the robustness of segmentation on biological characteristics. Theoretical analysis and experimental results prove that the proposed method is effective and workable. However, the improved method has some defects to be improved, especially if the background is complex and there are few differences between background and foreground. In addition, the time consuming of the algorithm is increased due to prior shape. Thus future research should focus on improving the robustness, accuracy and efficiency of the algorithm.

Acknowledgments. This Research is funded by the Education Department of Liaoning Province Foundation Grant Number LJQ2014033, the Natural Science Foundation of Liaoning Province Grant Number 20180551048 and the Doctoral Start-up Foundation of Liaoning Province Grant Number 20170520248.

References

1. Afifi, M.: 11K Hands: Gender recognition and biometric identification using a large dataset of hand images. Multimed. Tools Appl. **78**, 20835–20854 (2019). https://doi.org/10.1007/s11 042-019-7424-8
2. Sepas-Moghaddam, A., Pereira, F., Correia, P.L.: Ear recognition in a light field imaging framework: a new perspective. IET Biometrics **7**(3), 224–231 (2018)
3. Jain, A.K., Ross, A., Prabhakar, S.: An introduction to biometric recognition. IEEE Trans. Circ. Syst. Video Technol. Spec. Issue Image Video Based Biometrics **14**(1), 4–20 (2004)
4. Eriksson, E., Dan, G., Fodor, V.: Predictive distributed visual analysis for video in wireless sensor networks. IEEE Trans. Mob. Comput. **15**(7), 1743–1756 (2016)
5. Hajdu, A., Kormos, J., Nagy, B., et al.: Choosing appropriate distance measurement in digital image segmentation. Annales Univ. Sci. Budapest. Sec. Comp. **24**, 193–208 (2004)

6. Paragios, N., Chen, Y., Faugeras, O. (eds.): Handbook of Mathematical Models in Computer Vision. Springer, New York (2006). https://doi.org/10.1007/0-387-28831-7
7. Dockins, K.: Template method. In: Design Patterns in PHP and Laravel (2017)
8. Kuang, H., Cai, S., Ma, X., et al.: An effective skeleton extraction method based on kinect depth image. In: International Conference on Measuring Technology & Mechatronics Automation (2018)
9. Leventon, M.E., Grimson, W.E.L., Faugeras, O.: Statistical shape influence in geodesic active contours. In: Proceedings of the IEEE Conference on Compute Vision Pattern Recognition, vol. 1, pp. 316–323 (2000)
10. Rousson, M., Paragios, N.: Shape priors for level set representations. In: Heyden, A., Sparr, G., Nielsen, M., Johansen, P. (eds.) ECCV 2002. LNCS, vol. 2351, pp. 78–92. Springer, Heidelberg (2002). https://doi.org/10.1007/3-540-47967-8_6
11. Pan, B., Wang, W., Yan, J., et al.: For prostate MRI segmentation: a prior-shape-based level set model combined with gradient and regional information. In: 2018 IEEE International Conference on Mechatronics and Automation (ICMA) (2018)
12. Cremers, D., Tischhauser, E., Weickert, J., Schnorr, C.: Diffusion snakes: introducing statistical shape knowledge into the Mumford-Shah functional. Int. J. Comput. Vis. 50(3), 295–3133 (2002)
13. Cremers, D., Sochen, N., Schnorr, C.: A multiphase dynamic labeling model for variational recognition-driven image segmentation. Int. J. Comput. Vis. 66(1), 67–81 (2006)
14. Karantzalos, K., Paragios, N.: Recognition-driven two-dimensional competing priors toward automatic and accurate building detection. IEEE Trans. Geosci. Remote Sens. 47(1), 133-144 (2009)
15. Karantzalos, K., Paragios, N.: Large-scale building reconstruction through information fusion and 3-D priors. IEEE Trans. Geosci. Remote Sens. 48(5), 2283–2296 (2010)
16. Cootes, T.F., Taylor, C.J., Cooper, D.H., Grahan, J.: Active shape models their training and application. Comput. Vis. Image Underst. 61(1), 38–59 (1995)
17. Wong, A.K.C., Liu, T.S.: Typicality, diversity, and feature pattern of an ensemble. IEEE Trans. Comput. 24(2), 158–181 (1975)
18. Emersic, Z., Gabriel, L.L., Struc, V., et al.: Convolutional encoder-decoder networks for pixel-wise ear detection and segmentation. IET Biometrics 7(3), 175–184 (2018)

A Programmable Routing System
for Semi-physical Simulation

Yuan An[✉], Lei Chen, Ping Cui, and Kailiang Zhang

Jiangsu Province Key Laboratory of Intelligent Industry Control Technology, Xuzhou University
of Technology, Xuzhou 221018, China
anyuan@xzit.edu.cn

Abstract. The paper designs a programmable routing system, which can be used
for semi-physical and network testing. The system adopts the low-cost multi-
network card host as the router, and uses the operating system's own security policy
to block the connection between the network card and the operating system. The
system can prevent the operating system from automatically processing the data
frames. The sharpcap is used to capture and send data frames to process network
data frames. The transport protocol and routing algorithm are user-defined. During
the transmission process, the platform records the changes of routing table and
data frame, and comprehensively shows the transmission process of data frame
to the user, so that the user can have a more comprehensive understanding of the
principle of computer network, and better complete the test and simulation.

Keywords: Routing · Programmable · Computer network · Simulation

1 Introduction

Some new approaches are proposed to improve network routing and measurement [1–3].
Based on analysis on user behavior and traffic, researchers focus on resources utilization
[4], energy-efficiency [5] and traffic reconstruction [6]. To test these new technologies,
a cheap test platform is essential. Computer network is the product of the fusion of
computer and communication technology after a long time of development [7]. Computer network uses communication equipment and lines to connect computer systems
with different geographical locations and independent functions [8], so as to improve
network software, network communication protocol, information exchange mode and
network operating system [9, 10]. The computer network can realize the resource sharing
and information transmission in the network better [11]. The local area network(LAN)
generally uses a broadcast channel, which can easily access the entire network from a
site [12]. The connection between the computer and the external local area network is
through a network adapter (Adapter) [13], and the communication between the adapter
and the local area network is carried out in a serial transmission mode through cables
or twisted pairs [14]. The so-called broadcast communication is when a computer sends
data, all computers on the bus can detect this data [15]. In order to realize one-to-one

H. Song and D. Jiang (Eds.): SIMUtools 2020, LNICST 369, pp. 667–680, 2021.
https://doi.org/10.1007/978-3-030-72792-5_52

communication on the bus, each computer is equipped with a globally unique MAC address [16]. When sending a data frame, the address of the receiving station is written to the head of the frame. When each computer on the bus detects the data frame, the adapter will match the address of the data frame with its MAC address. If it is consistent, it will be received, otherwise it will be discarded. But in order to manage the network, the adapter has a special working mode: promiscuous mode, in which the adapter will receive all data frames on the bus [17].

The computer network experiment platform generally adopts the sending, capturing and parsing of network data frames to show users the processing process of the data frames by the computer network, and reveals the working principle of the computer network [18–20]. In the existing computer network platform, data frame forwarding and routing information changes are automatically handled by the operating system. Most users can only carry out Socket-based user space network programming and use the network as a transparent transmission channel [21]. Because the IP layer functions and processing mechanisms are mainly reflected in network devices such as routers [22], so it is difficult for users to touch the essence of network technologies, such as IP routing and forwarding during network experiment teaching and network testing, and they cannot intervene in routing information [23, 24]. It is impossible to try custom protocols and algorithms without processing the data frame. Therefore, it restricts the user's understanding of the computer network and limits the teaching and testing effects.

Routers and switches are important components of computer networks, and their internal implementation mechanism is the key to determining the multi-dimensional expansion capabilities of computer networks, such as performance, function, and security [25, 26]. Therefore, this article takes routing design as the entry point of computing network system design and designs a programmable routing system. The system transforms a multi-network card computer into a router, which can process network data frames. The protocol and routing algorithm are defined by the user, and the changes in the routing table and data frame are recorded process. The platform can enhance users' in-depth understanding of computer networks in order to achieve better simulation and testing results.

2 Routing Structure and Implementation Principle

In order to realize the design of the programmable routing system, this research group transform the multi-network card computer into a router to realize the processing of network data frames. The system includes more than two single network card hosts and one multi-network card host, in which the number of network adapters of the multi-network card host is more than the single-network card host. The network adapter of the single network card host and the network adapter of the multi network card host are connected through a network communication device to transfer data frames, and the star network connection is formed between the single network card host and the multi network card host.

The routing structure is divided into a hardware structure and a software structure [3, 27]. The hardware structure extracts data from the bottom layer of the hardware [28]. The software structure is the processing layer, which is responsible for processing the data extracted from the hardware to write its own forwarding strategy [29]. The combination of hardware and software, through the processing of the CPU, to achieve the routing function.

The hardware structure diagram is shown in Fig. 1:

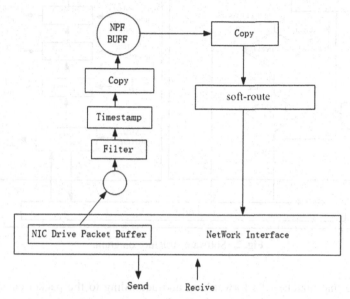

Fig. 1. Routing hardware structure diagram.

NIC Drive Packet Buffer: Network driver, responsible for copying the data on the network card.

Filter: Filter the data captured by the user at the kernel layer.

Timestamp: The time interval returned after each acquisition.

Copy: Copy the data of the kernel layer to the user memory.

NPF BUFF: Parallel and serial buffer.

NPF BUFF Copy: Take out the data and put it into the soft route for processing. The processed structure is sent directly from the network card through the soft route.

The software structure is shown in Fig. 2:

Packet_callback: routing function for soft routing to process packets.

DLL extension: the interface reserved for users to use for processing.

Ordinary PC computers only have the function of local routing, that is, they can only forward their own IP data packets, and cannot forward any other data packets [30, 31]. The core of the realization of soft routing is that compared with commercial routers on the market, the forwarding process and the principle of forwarding must be considered [32, 33]. When soft routing receives data from a certain network card, it first decrements the TTL time of its IP packet header. If the TTL time is found to be 0, the data packet is discarded, otherwise the routing table encapsulates it and replaces the Ethernet header. At the same time, the soft route checks the destination address and performs an AND operation with the destination address of the routing table [34, 35]. The longest match

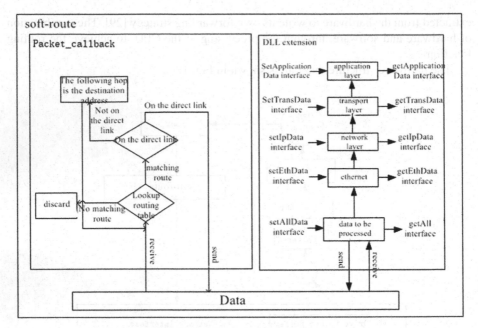

Fig. 2. Software structure diagram.

is the route that matches the forwarding, and according to the packet encapsulation, the checksum of the IP packet is recalculated and sent out from the network interface. Capturing and sending packets are implemented using winpcap. The route forwarding process is shown in Fig. 3.

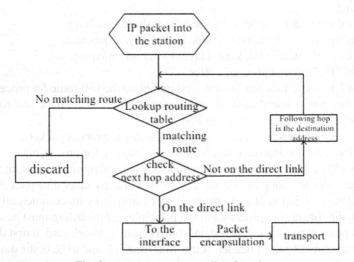

Fig. 3. Routing and forwarding flowchart.

3 Implementation Process

The programmable routing system designed in this paper can be used for computer network experiment teaching and network testing. Users can design protocols and routing algorithms by themselves and observe the routing process to deepen their understanding of the working principle of computer networks.

According to the system implementation technical solution, the system architecture diagram is shown in Fig. 4.

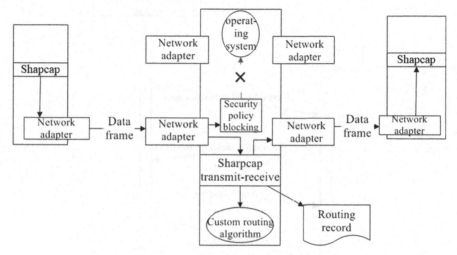

Fig. 4. System architecture diagram.

It can be seen from Fig. 4 that the system includes more than two single network card hosts and one multi-network card host. The number of network adapters of the multi-network card host is greater than that of the single network card host. The network adapter of the single network card host and the network adapter of the multi-network card host are connected through a network communication device to transfer data frames. A single network card host and a multi-network card host form a star connection. A single network card host is provided with a sharpcap interface for information exchange with its internal network adapter. It is blocked by the security policy between the network adapter of the multi-NIC host and its own operating system. The sharpcap interface is set in the multi-NIC host, and the packet capture, transmission and processing are carried out through the sharpcap interface between the multiple network adapters in the multi-NIC host. During the transmission of data packets between the network adapters of multiple network card hosts, the data packets are captured and processed according to the custom routing algorithm, and the transmitted data information is recorded at the same time.

The programmable routing system uses sharpcap and winpcap to capture and send network data frames, and uses security policies to prevent the operating system from accepting data frames. The experimental software processes the data frames, thereby transforming the multi-network card computer into a router. Users can design protocols and write their own routing algorithms freely. The system can record the changes of routing tables and data frames, and show the transmission process of data frames to user.

The sharpcap interface in this system is a direct interface for monitoring software to call Winpcap. It has the functions of packet capture, injection, analysis and construction to form a packet capture framework [29]. This framework is a perfect combination of Winpcap components and Windows network core functions. The framework set inherits

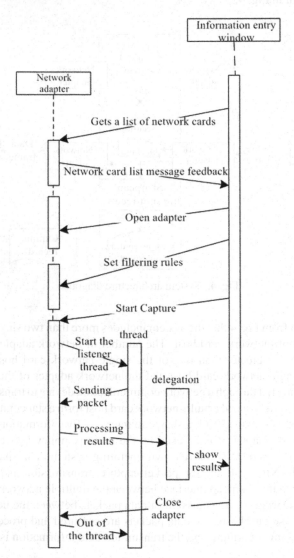

Fig. 5. System implementation process diagram.

Winpcap and surpasses Winpcap. It uses a message mechanism to maximize the superiority of object-oriented performance [36]. It also integrates some network API functions and API functions for reading the registry [37].

The process of the system using Sharpcap to capture packets is shown in Fig. 5. First, get the adapter list, get the MAC address and gateway address of the adapter, then open the corresponding adapter according to the operation selection, and then specify the corresponding filtering criteriafor the adapter, and start capturing information passed by the adapter. While capturing, you need to receive the captured data packets, process the data, and display the data, and finally close the adapter. In the process of data packet reception, the design of the reception affects the efficiency and accuracy of this capture, and even determines the success or failure of the captured data packet. During the capture process, sharpcap needs to start a new thread in the host memory, which is specifically responsible for listening to the adapter for the arrival of data packets. The meaning of this thread is to be separated from the main form thread, to avoid the main thread from blocking when a packet arrives, and to prevent the program from "dead".

The security strategy adopted in the system refers to the access protocol for the operating system to process the data packets in the network adapter. Security policy blocking refers to using the operating system's own security policy to block the connection between the network card and the operating system, preventing the operating system from automatically processing data frames.

The flow chart of the system using sharpcap for data packet capture is shown in Fig. 6:

The specific implementation steps of the above programmable routing platform are as follows:

1) Edit the link layer data frame

The data link layer is responsible for combining bits into bytes and combining bytes into frames. Frames are used at the data link layer, and the data packets passed from the network layer are encapsulated into frames for transmission according to the type of media access. The 802.3 frame is encapsulated on the network adapter, and its structure includes the preamble, destination address, original address, length, data and frame check sequence. The learner uses the interface software to edit each part of the frame as needed, and writes it into the encapsulation package to form a data package to be used.

2) Use sharpcap to send the edited data frame on the single NIC host side

The core technology in the network adapter is the random contention-based media access method, that is, the CSMA/CD method. The process of sending the edited data frame using sharpcap is as follows: a. Carrier sense, because Ethernet data uses Manchester side coding, it can determine whether the bus level jumps to determine whether the bus is idle; b. Conflict detection, both hosts hear that the bus is idle, both will send data, there may be conflicts, so conflict detection should be performed, and conflicts should stop sending data; Random delay retransmission, after stopping, the node performs a random delay retransmission. If the retransmission is still unsuccessful after 16 times, the transmission failure is declared.

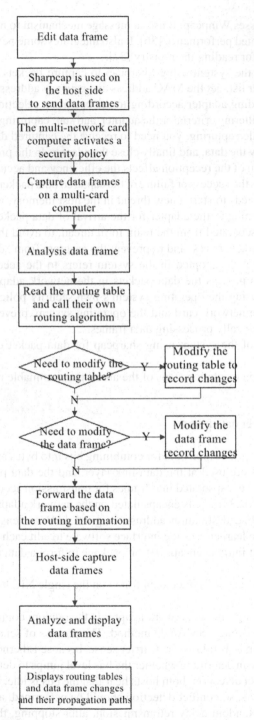

Fig. 6. Flow chart of packet capture using sharpcap.

3) Use multiple network card hosts as routers to receive data frames

In the process of receiving data frames mainly using network adapters, first check whether there is a collision or whether a frame is dropped, otherwise go to the next step; check the destination address of the frame to see if the frame can be accepted, if it can, then go to the next step; Check the CRC checksum and LLC data length. If both are correct, accept the frame, otherwise discard it.

4) Using security policies to prevent the operating system from automatically processing data frames

The use of the operating system's own security strategy blocks the connection between the network card and the operating system, and prevents the operating system from automatically processing the data frames. This prevents the loss of data frames and provides important protection for subsequent users.

5) Capture data frames on multiple network card hosts and analyze the data frames

In the packet parsing thread, it is necessary to analyze the content of the actual packet. The packet data captured by Sharpcap is stored in an instance of the RowPacket class. This instance provides a byte-type indexer to read the actual packet data. The indexer can be used as a byte-type read-only array. The packet information is stored in bytes. The data packet is generally a standard Ethernet frame, that is, the first 14 bits are MAC information; if it is a TCP/IP protocol frame, the 15–34 bytes are IP information, and the 35–55 bytes are TCP information; If it further connotes HTTP data packets, the bytes that follow are HTTP request and response information.

6) Read the routing table and call to write routing rules

According to the requirements of capturing data frames, the user writes the corresponding routing rules and stores them in the form of routing tables, and finally captures the corresponding data frames through custom routing rules.

7) Modify the data frame and routing table according to the algorithm;

After reading the captured data frame, it can be modified to make it familiar to the user to manipulate the format of the data frame and the construction of the routing table.

8) Forward and record data frame and routing table changes;
9) The host side of the single network card captures the message and identifies the data frame;

Data packet capture is used to intercept the data packets sent by users in the LAN at the transport layer and put the captured data packets into the program buffer; After receiving the captured data packet, the packet analysis module reads the data packet from the buffer, filters the junk data packet through the set filtering rules, and analyzes the packet after decomposing it to analyze the packet and improve The efficiency of capturing and parsing data packets; The decoding module automatically selects the appropriate decoding method to decode the search string according to the encoding rules, and is used to restore the search data string encoded by the browser.

10) Display data frame changes and propagation path, routing table changes

The display data frame is the analysis result of the data packet of the user's retrieval information in the current local area network, including the capture time of the data packet, source IP, source MAC, destination IP, search engine host name, use protocol, search string, original message and other related information, display data frame changes and propagation path, routing table changes.

4 Experimental Test

The router in the system is a special PC, which is equivalent to a forwarding station. When two PCs are communicating, it can decide whether to forward the data packet based on whether the destination network address is in the destination network segment.

Both hardware routers and software routers are classified as routers. The hardware devices in the hardware router are specially designed for the router to forward data. The software router does not have special hardware to handle forwarding. It uses a CPU, which can be said to be a process of the user's PC.

The "Routing Remote Access" service is manually turned on for the user. When it is turned on, it indicates that this PC can perform routing and forwarding, and when it is turned off, it indicates that this PC cannot perform routing and forwarding.

The steps of configuring routing and remote access in the experimental test are as follows:

Click "Administrative Tools" in "Start", and select "Routing and Remote Access" function in the administrative tools, then you will see the configuration wizard; select the local server, click "Operation"-"Configure and enable routing and remote access"; click "Next", select "Custom Configuration"-"Next"; select "LAN Routing" and then click "Next" and finally click Finish to start routing and remote access.

Create a new batch of processing file myroute.bat, and place it in the directory folder that starts automatically at boot, and edit the content of myroute.bat as follows:

Route add 192.168.1.0 mask 255.255.255.0 192.168.32.1

Double-click the bat batch to change the routing table.

The routing table before running is shown in Fig. 7:

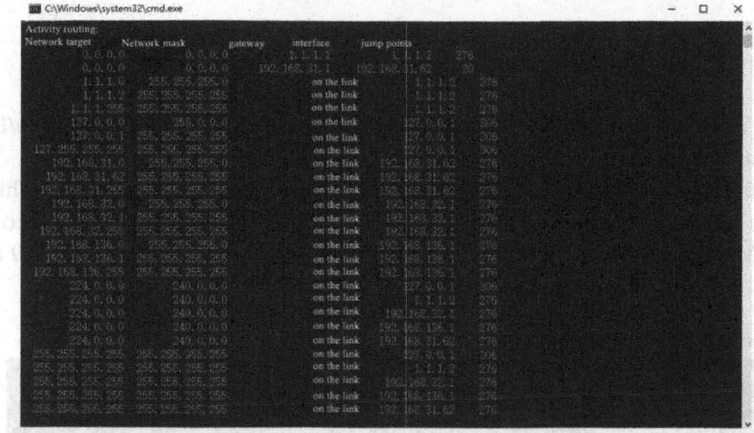

Fig. 7. Before adding the local routing table.

After adding the route, the routing table is shown in Fig. 8 below:

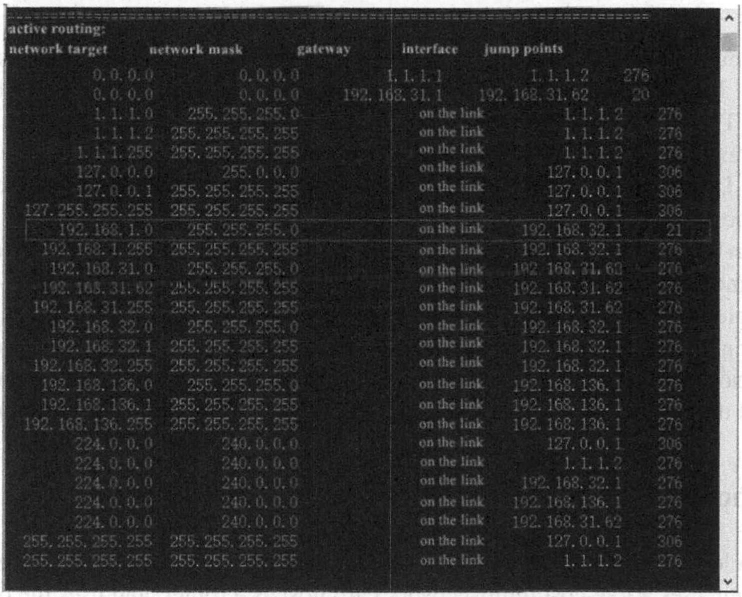

Fig. 8. After adding the local routing table.

Can complete the 192.168.1.0/24 destination network forwarding.
WIN7, WIN10 open routing and remote access modification

1) Open the registry editor.
2) Open the registry editor and find the following entries:

HKEY_LOCAL_MACHINE/SYSTEM/CurrentControlSet/Services/Tcpip/Parameters.
Select the following item: IPEnableRouter: REG_DWORD: 0 × 0.

To enable IP forwarding for all network connections installed and used on this computer, the value is 1 and off is 0. After the modification is complete, enter ipconfig/all on the CMD command line to view the opening information as shown in Fig. 9 below:

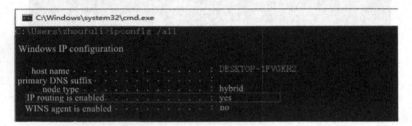

Fig. 9. NIC information.

In order to enable a process to call code that does not belong to it, we need a way to call it. Dynamic linking provides a way to make the process dynamically load and execute. The code of the function is encapsulated in a DLL file, the DLL contains one or more executable functions. And DLL also helps to share data and resources. When multiple DLLs are loaded, the shared resources can be accessed and modified at the same time.

When a program needs to be expanded, in order not to affect the operation of its normal modules, the method of dynamic link library can be used to make it easier and simpler to complete the expansion of the program. The system uses the method of displaying and calling the dynamic link library. Nothing needs to be operated during compilation. When the functions in the DLL need to be used, the DLL can be loaded and used through the two API functions LoadLibrary () and FindProcAdress ().

5   Conclusion

This article details the design and implementation of the programmable routing system. The system uses a low-cost multi-network card host as a router, and uses the operating system's own security strategy to block the connection between the network card and the operating system, preventing the operating system from automatically data frames deal with. The system simultaneously uses sharpcap to capture and send data frames. Experimental test results show that the system can realize functions such as routing and forwarding, remote access, recording data frames and routing table information.

Therefore, experimenters can use the system interface to design routing strategies and network protocols, and use the system to record information to understand the routing process. Therefore, the system helps experimenters to deepen their understanding of the working principle of computer networks, and better complete semi-physical simulation work.

Acknowledgements. This work is partly supported by Jiangsu technology project of Housing and Urban-Rural Development (No.2018ZD265, No.2019ZD039, No.2019ZD040, No.2019ZD041).

References

1. Zhang, K., Chen, L., An, Y., et al.: A QoE test system for vehicular voice cloud services. Mobile Network Application (2019). https://doi.org/10.1007/s11036-019-01415-3
2. Wang, F., Jiang, D., Qi, S.: An adaptive routing algorithm for integrated information networks. Chin. Commun. **7**(1), 196–207 (2019)
3. Hu, G., Xu, K., et al.: Research and development on programmable router. Chin. Educ. Netw. **65**(7), 40–43 (2010)
4. Huo, L., Jiang, D., Zhu, X., et al.: An SDN-based fine-grained measurement and modeling approach to vehicular communication network traffic. International Journal of Communication Systems, Online Available, pp. 1–12 (2019)
5. Huo, L., Jiang, D., Lv, Z., et al.: An intelligent optimization-based traffic information acquirement approach to software-defined networking. Computational Intelligence, pp. 1–21 (2019)
6. Chen, L., Jiang, D., Bao, R., Xiong, J., Liu, F., Bei, L.: MIMO scheduling effectiveness analysis for bursty data service from view of QoE. Chin. J. Electron. **26**(5), 1079–1085 (2017)
7. Lu, G., Shi, Y., Guo, C., et al.: A configurable packet forwarding engine for data center networks. In: Proceedings of the 2nd Workshop on ACM SIGCOMM, pp. 25–30 (2009)
8. Sommers, J., Barford, P., Cmvella, M.: Router primitives for programmable active measurement. In: The 2nd Workshop on ACM SIGCOMM, pp. 13–18 (2009)
9. Jiang, D., Wang, Y., Lv, Z., et al.: Big data analysis-based network behavior insight of cellular networks for industry 4.0 applications. IEEE Trans. Ind. Inform. **16**(2), 1310–1320 (2020)
10. Bolla, R., Bmsch, R.: PC-based software routers:high performance and application service support. In: The 1st Workshop on ACM SIGCOMM, pp. 27–32 (2008)
11. Spalink, T., Kariin, S., Peterson, L., et al.: Building a robust software based muter using network processors. In: The 18th ACM Symposium on Operating Systems Principles(SOSP), pp. 216–229 (2001)
12. Jiang, D., Huo, L., Song, H.: Rethinking behaviors and activities of base stations in mobile cellular networks based on big data analysis. IEEE Trans. Netw. Sci. Eng. **1**(1), 1–12 (2018)
13. Chen, L., et al.: A lightweight end-side user experience data collection system for quality evaluation of multimedia communications. IEEE Access **6**(1), 15408–15419 (2018)
14. Jiang, D., Huo, L., Li, Y.: Fine-granularity inference and estimations to network traffic for SDN. Plos One **13**(5), 1–23 (2018)
15. Chen, L., Zhang, L.: Spectral efficiency analysis for massive MIMO system under QoS constraint: an effective capacity perspective. Mobile Network Application (2020). https://doi.org/10.1007/s11036-019-01414-4
16. Wang, F., Jiang, D., Qi, S., et al.: A dynamic resource scheduling scheme in edge computing satellite networks. Mobile Networks and Applications, Online Available (2019)

17. Yu, M., Thottan, M., Li, L.: Latency equalization: a programmable muting service primitive. In: The 1st Workshop on ACM SIGCOMM, pp. 39–44 (2008)
18. Lam, C.F.: Passive Optical Networks: Principles and Practice. Academic Press, San Diego (2007)
19. Jiang, D., Wang, Y., Lv, Z., et al.: A joint multi-criteria utility-based network selection approach for vehicle-to-infrastructure networking. IEEE Trans. Intell. Transp. Syst. **19**(10), 3305–3319 (2018)
20. Jiang, D., Zhang, P., Lv, Z., et al.: Energy-efficient multi-constraint routing algorithm with load balancing for smart city applications. IEEE Internet Things J. **3**(6), 1437–1447 (2016)
21. Yang, Y., Yang, J., Qin, D.: Data center network multi-path routing algorithm. J. Tsinghua Univ. (Nat. Sci. Edn.) **3**, 262–268 (2016)
22. Jorgensen, B.: Guide to Network Programming (2008)
23. Jiang, D., Wang, Y., Lv, Z., Wang, W., Wang, H.: An energy-efficient networking approach in cloud services for IIoT networks. IEEE J. Sel. Areas Commun. **38**(5), 928–941 (2020)
24. Ibrahim, A., Alfa, A.: Optimization techniques for routing design problems over wireless sensor networks: a short tutorial. In: SENSORNETS 2017 - Proceedings of the 6th International Conference on Sensor Networks, pp. 156–167 (2017)
25. Jiang, D., Wang, Y., Lv, Z., Qi, S., Singh, S.: Big data analysis based network behavior insight of cellular networks for industry 4.0 applications. IEEE Trans. Ind. Inform. **16**(2), 1310–1320 (2020)
26. Huo, L., Jiang, D., Qi, S., et al.: An AI-based adaptive cognitive modeling and measurement method of network traffic for EIS. Mobile Networks and Applications, Online Available (2019)
27. Zhang, X., Liu, Z., Zhao, Y., et al.: Scalable router. J. Softw. **19**(6), 1452–1464 (2008)
28. Jiang, D., Li, W., Lv, H.: An energy-efficient cooperative multicast routing in multi-hop wireless networks for smart medical applications. Neurocomputing **220**(2017), 160–169 (2017)
29. Wu, D., Yin, Y.F., Lawphongpanich, S., Yang, H.: Design of more equitable congestion pricing and tradable credit schemes for multimodal transportation networks. Transp. Res. Part B Methodol. **46**(9), 1273–1287 (2012)
30. Jiang, D., Wang, Y., Lv, Z., et al.: Intelligent optimization-based reliable energy-efficient networking in cloud services for IIoT networks. IEEE Journal on Selected Areas in Communications, Online Available (2019)
31. Zhang, L.H., Yang, H., Wu, D., Wang, D.H.: Solving a discrete multimodal transportation network design problem. Transp. Res. Part C Emerg. Technol. **49**, 73–86 (2014)
32. Qi, S., Jiang, D., Huo, L.: A prediction approach to end-to-end traffic in space information networks. Mobile Networks and Applications, Online Available (2019)
33. Jiang, D., Wang, W., Shi, L., et al.: A compressive sensing-based approach to end-to-end network traffic reconstruction. IEEE Trans. Netw. Sci. Eng. **5**(3), 1–12 (2018)
34. Wang, Y., Jiang, D., Huo, L., et al.: A new traffic prediction algorithm to software defined networking. Mobile Networks and Applications, Online Available (2019)
35. Cheng, P., Xu, C.W., Lebreton, P., Yang, Z.D., Chen, J.M.: TERP: time-event-dependent route planning in stochastic multimodal transportation networks with bike sharing system. IEEE Internet of Things J. **6**(3), 4991–5000 (2019)
36. Peng, Y., Wang, W.Y., Guo, Z.J., Song, X.Q., Zhang, Q.: A stochastic seaport network retrofit management problem considering shipping routing design. Ocean Coast. Manag. **119**, 169–176 (2016)
37. Murata, H.: A new routing design methodology for multi-chip IC packages. Midwest symposium on circuits and systems. In: The 2004 47th Midwest Symposium on Circuits and Systems - Conference Procceedings, pp. 1473–1476 (2004)

Hyperparameter Analysis of Temporal Graph Convolutional Network Model Applied to Traffic Prediction

Jing Huang, Lei Chen[✉], Yuan An, Kailiang Zhang, and Ping Cui

Jiangsu Province Key Laboratory of Intelligent Industry Control Technology,
Xuzhou University of Technology, Xuzhou 221018, China
chenlei@xzit.edu.cn

Abstract. GCN based on time and space is an essential part of smart city construction because it can capture the spatiotemporal dynamics and effectively analyze the traffic data to get the best prediction results. In the specific operation of the model, the adjustment and optimal selection of super parameters can make the model provide the best results, thus saving time, cost and computing power. When it comes to the prediction scenarios with low computational power and urgent demand, the existing super parameter search methods and optimization models lack efficiency and accuracy. Therefore, this paper proposes a super parameter search and optimization method based on cross validation, which can efficiently and accurately optimize the parameters, and select the best parameters by using the similarity between the learning and training errors corresponding to each super parameter To improve the prediction ability of the model. Through the verification of the actual data set, the model runs well, and can provide the best prediction results for the traffic flow and other scenarios dominated by spatiotemporal state.

Keywords: GCN · Machine learning · Hyperparameters optimization · Traffic prediction

1 Introduction

Accurate traffic forecast can help travelers to arrange their travel reasonably, improve the operation efficiency of traffic network, alleviate traffic congestion, improve other related service functions of the city, improve the utilization rate of road network and energy utilization rate, and reduce the emission of various traffic pollutants, which is an essential part of smart city construction. In 5g era, some new methods are proposed to improve network routing and measurement [1–3]. Based on an effective user behavior and traffic analysis method [4–7], a new scheduling strategy is proposed to improve resource utilization [8–11] and efficiency [12, 13]. A new traffic reconstruction method is proposed to approve the service quality of end users [14–19]. However, the traffic speed is ahead of time. Network communication is very important to improve the virtual communication oriented to time-varying network structure. Traffic flow prediction is a

H. Song and D. Jiang (Eds.): SIMUtools 2020, LNICST 369, pp. 681–693, 2021.
https://doi.org/10.1007/978-3-030-72792-5_53

typical spatiotemporal data prediction problem. How to mine the hidden spatiotemporal patterns from these complex and nonlinear spatiotemporal data and analyze these patterns to extract valuable information, In recent years, with the rapid development of deep learning [20–22], the deep learning network model has attracted people's attention because it can capture the dynamic. The traffic data are analyzed and the best results are obtained, among which the representative model is t-gcn. In the aspect of deep neural network model, the adjustment of super parameters is a necessary technology Yes, the so-called hyperparameters are the framework parameters in the deep neural network model. These super parameters act as knobs and can be tuned during model training, In order to make our model provide the best results, we can judge what kind of training state the current model is by observing the monitoring indicators such as loss and accuracy in the training process, and timely adjust the super parameters to train the model more scientifically, which can improve the resource utilization rate. In essence, hyperparametric search is an iterative process constrained by computational power, money and time. In the case of limited computing power, money and time resources, everyone wants to get the best model. However, in the spatiotemporal model represented by t-gcn, due to the special needs of spatiotemporal state and demand urgency, there is still a lack of effective super parameter search and optimization model to achieve this goal.

Therefore, based on the deep neural network learning model represented by t-gcn model, this paper proposes a super parameter search and optimization method. By studying the RMSE, ACC and loss results of the learning and training model, the relationship among the two important optimization parameters (learning rate, batch size) is analyzed, and the performance of the model in the actual operation process is analyzed Finally, the influence of these three parameters on the traffic prediction performance is analyzed. The proposed search and optimization method can effectively and accurately optimize the parameters, and provide the best prediction results for traffic flow and other scenarios dominated by spatiotemporal state.

2   Related Work

In recent years, with the rapid development of deep learning [20–22], the deep neural network model has attracted people's attention because it can capture the dynamic characteristics of traffic data and obtain the best results. Rilett et al. [23] used feedforward neural networks to perform traffic prediction tasks. Huang et al. [24] proposed a network structure composed of deep belief network (DBN) and regression model, and verified that the network could capture random features from traffic data of multiple data sets, which improved the accuracy of traffic prediction. In addition, because the recursive neural network (RNN) and its variant LSTM and gated recursive unit (GRU) can effectively utilize the self-cycling mechanism, they can learn the time dependence relationship well and obtain good prediction results [25, 26]. Considering the spatiotemporal dependence of urban traffic, a time-based graph convolutional neural network (T-GCN) model is proposed [27], which combines graph convolutional network and gated recursive unit. The graph convolutional network is used to capture the topological structure of the road network for modeling spatial dependence. The gated recurrent unit is used to capture the dynamic change of traffific data on the roads for modeling temporal dependence. As a new deep neural network model [28–30], T-GCN contains multiple hyperparameters that need to be selected and set in advance. Hyperparameter optimization problem can be defined as: for the hyperparameters to be set in the model, find the optimal hyperparameters setting, so that the deep learning model based on hyperparameter setting training has the optimal performance evaluation index.

The performance of deep neural networks is well known to be sensitive to the setting of their hyperparameters. Hyperparameter optimization is a very difficult problem in developing deep learning algorithms. Optimization of the hyperparameters in each algorithm are necessary to obtain the highest accuracy. Among the hyperparameters of deep neural network, the most important parameters are learning rate, batch size, optimizer and training epoch. Among them, batch size and learning rate directly determine the weight update of the model, and from the perspective of optimization, they are the most important parameters affecting the performance of the model. Many experts and scholars have done some research on the optimization method of super parameters in deep learning model. Deep learning models are typically trained using stochastic gradient descent or one of its variants. It has been observed that when using large batch sizes there is a persistent degradation in generalization performance - known as the "generalization gap" phenomena. To solve the problem that the traditional optimization algorithm cannot converge to the optimal solution (or the critical point in the non-convex setting), Sashank J. Reddi et al. [31] propose new variants of the ADAM algorithm which not only fix the convergence issues but often also lead to improved empirical performance. In order to improve the defects of the traditional super parameter self-optimization method, Nitish Shirish Keskar and Richard Socher [32] propose the SWATS units, a simple strategy which Switches from Adam to SGD The when a triggering condition is satisfied. The results show that the strategy is capable of closing the generalization on a gap between SGD and Adam Majority of the tasks and does not increase the number of hyperparameters in the optimizer. Hoffer et al. [33] studied the method of optimizing the hyperparameter batch size in deep learning. This method can achieve the effect of eliminating generalization and improving model performance, but this method is only for traditional deep learning models and has a single application object. Whether it is suitable for hyperparameter optimization in the temporal graph convolutional neural network model applied in traffic prediction needs further study. Goyal et al. [34] studied the optimization method of the superparameter batch size and learning rate by using the stochastic gradient descent method, and the research results showed that the superparameter optimization improved the accuracy and expansion rate of the visual discrimination model. Due to the essential difference between the urban traffic data and the Image Net data set, whether the optimization method can be directly migrated to the T-GCN model remains to be further studied. In literature [35, 36], the parameter optimization method of Adam, which is a common optimizer, is discussed in detail, including the characteristics of superparameter optimizer and the methods to improve performance. Literatures [37, 38] studied and analyzed the trend of learning rate curve and established an optimization model of super parameter learning rate, which reduced the learning time on the premise of maintaining the accuracy. However, the model has a single super parameter and a high limitation, which cannot be directly used in the new traffic flow prediction analysis related to T-GCN. Cardona-Escobar et al. [39] present an automatic framework for hyperparameter selection in Convolutional Neural Networks. In order to achieve fast evaluation of several hyperparameter combinations, prediction of learning curves using non-parametric regression models is applied. Results show that this forecasting method is able to catch a complete behavior offuture iterations in the learning process. The optimal combination of superparameters in the deep network learning model is a research direction worthy of our reference.

As a new deep neural network learning model, the optimal setting of its super parameters directly determines the traffic prediction performance of the model. In this paper, we studied and discussed in detail the influence of super parameter learning rate and batch size on the performance of T-GCN model, and provided the optimal super parameter selection.

3 Principle of T-GCN Model

The traffific information is a general concept which can be traffific speed, traffific flow, or traffific density. Without loss of generality, T-GCN model use traffific speed as an example of traffific information in experiment section. The T-GCN model establishes a traffic prediction model based on spatial dependence and spatial dependence:

3.1 Spatial Dependency Modeling

The T-GCN model use the GCN model [40–45] to learn spatial features from traffific data. The calculation process is shown in Eq. 1, $X(t)$ represents the traffic condition matrix at time t. We need to train a function $h(\cdot)$, which operates on the matrix of T times in the past, outputs the matrix of T times in the future, and makes traffic prediction.

$$\left[X^{(t-T+1)}, \cdots X^{(t)}; G\right] \underset{\rightarrow}{h(\cdot)} \left[X^{(t+1)}, \cdots X^{(t+T)}\right] \tag{1}$$

The T-GCN model use an unweighted graph $G = (V, E)$ to describe the topological structure of the road network, and we treat each road as a node, where V is a set of road nodes, $V = \{v_1, v_2, \cdots v_N,\}$, N is the number of the nodes, and E is a set of edges. The edge relation between nodes is represented by the adjacency matrix $A \in R^{N \times N}$. The adjacency matrix contains only elements of 0 and 1. The element is 0 if there is no link between two roads and 1 denotes there is a link.

In this research, the 2-layer GCN model [41] is chosen to obtain spatial dependence, which can be expressed as:

$$f(X, A) = \sigma(\hat{A}ReLU(\hat{A}XW_0)W_1) \tag{2}$$

where $\hat{A} = \tilde{D}^{-\frac{1}{2}}\tilde{A}\tilde{D}^{-\frac{1}{2}}$ denotes pre-processing step, $W_0 \in R^{P \times H}$ represents the weight matrix from input to hidden layer, P is the length of feature matrix, and H is the number of hidden unit, $W_1 \in R^{N \times T}$ represents the weight matrix from hidden to output layer. $f(X, A) \in R^{N \times T}$ represents the output with the prediction length T, and $ReLU()$ standing for REctified Linear Unit, which is a frequently used activation layer in modern deep neural networks, $\sigma(\cdot)$ represents the sigmoid function for a nonlinear model.

3.2 Time Dependent Modeling

Obtaining time dependence is another key problem in traffic forecasting. In the T-GCN model, the GRU model is selected to obtain the time dependence of traffic data [46, 47]. As shown in Fig. 1, h^{t-1} denotes the hidden state at time $t-1$, x^t denotes the traffific information at time t,r is the reset gate, z is the update gate, and h^t is output state at time t. The GRU obtains the traffific information at time t by taking the hidden status at time $t-1$ and the current traffific information as inputs. While capturing the traffific information at the current moment, the model still retains the changing trend of historical traffific information and has the ability to capture temporal dependence.

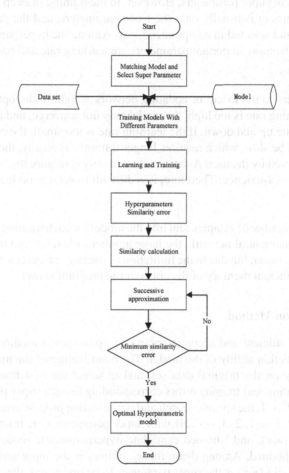

Fig. 1. Process optimization.

4 Deep Neural Network Hyperparameter and Performance Evaluation Model

4.1 Hyperparameter

In the deep neural network model, there are two sets of parameters: one is called elementary parameter, such as the weight and bias of the convolution layer or the full connection layer; the other is hyperparameter, such as the learning rate during network training and the coefficient of the L2 regularization item in the loss function. In practical application, to achieve good performance of deep neural network, it is very dependent on the selection of a good set of super parameters. However, in the training of deep neural network, the automatic learning is usually only the basic parameters, and the super parameters are mostly tried and selected in an optimized way. Among the hyperparameters of deep neural network, the most important parameters are learning rate and batch size.

Learning Rate

Learning raterefers to the extent of updating network weight in the optimization algorithm. If the learning rate is too high, the model may not converge, and the loss and loss constantly oscillate up and down. If the learning rate is too small, the convergence rate of the model will be slow, which requires longer training. Typically, the learning rate is randomly configured by the user. At best, users can only configure the best learning rate based on previous experience. Therefore, it is difficult to get a good learning rate.

Batch Size

Batch size is the number of samples sent into the model for each training neural network. In the convolutional neural network, the large number of batches can usually make the network converge faster, but due to the limitation of memory resources, too large a batch may lead to insufficient memory or the crash of the program kernel.

4.2 Optimization Method

In this paper, an efficient and accurate parameter optimization method is proposed to improve the prediction ability of the model. The main feature of the method is to learn and train directly on the original data set, and to select the best result by using the similarity of learning and training errors corresponding to each super parameter.

As shown in Fig. 1, the specific search and optimization process is as follows: model $\{(input_i, output_i), i = 1, 2, 3, \cdots, N\}$ with super parameter x_l is trained successively on all data set $k(\bullet|x)$, and l trained candidate hyperparametric model $\{ k(\bullet|x_l), l = 1, 2, \cdots, L\}$ is obtained, Among them, $input_i$, $output_i$ is the input and output of the i data set, x in model $k(\bullet|x)$ is the super parameter to be optimized, the candidate super-parameter set is $X = \{x_l, l = 1, 2, \cdots, L\}$, and l is the number of super parameters; Through the model $k(\bullet|x_1)$ of each super parameter x_l in $X = \{x_l, l = 1, 2, \cdots, L\}$, the error in each data set $(input_i, output_i)$ is obtained: the difference between the predicted value $k(input_i|x_1)$ of the model and the real result $output_i$ is recorded as $w^{(x_1)}$; Calculate the variance similarity matrix $T = (t_{mn})_{L \times L}$, where m, $n \in \{1, 2, \cdots, L\}$, t_{mn} in the matrix is $t_{mn} = \frac{1}{N} \sum\limits_{i=1}^{N} Q(w^{(x_m)} \cdot w^{(x_n)} > 0)$, where e s $Q(\bullet)$ the indicator function; The symmetric similarity of the first parameter is the average value of all rows P and $2l - p$ in the directional similarity matrix. Row P number needs to satisfy $1 \leq p \leq l$, and the symmetric similarity degree $TT(x_l)$ of x_l is calculated according to $\frac{1}{\min(1, L-l+1)} \sum\limits_{\substack{m+n=2l \\ m \leq n}} t_{mn}$.

The hyperparameter with minimum symmetric similarity is regarded as the optimal hyperparameter x^* and returned.

4.3 Performance Evaluation Model

We selected three indexes of Root Mean Squared Error (RMSE), Accuracy (ACC) and loss function (loss) to intuitively evaluate the influence of superparameters in the model on the prediction performance. In model evaluation, accuracy is the most commonly used measurement. Its advantage is the classification of data samples, but the disadvantage is that it can only conduct surface analysis and can not identify deception. Therefore, we introduce rmse and loss degree to further assist the evaluation. Among them, variance refers to the statistical limit of the model. If the model is over trained or too complex for the given training data set, it will cause high rmse (over fitting), and the prediction performance of the model will be very poor. In the standard state, the loss of accuracy is the lowest. Our goal is to maximize the similarity between the model predictions and the results shown in the training data.

Among them, RMSE measurement and prediction error, loss function represents the error between the actual traffic speed and the predicted value. The larger the RMSE and loss value is, the worse the prediction effect is, while the smaller the value is, the better the prediction effect is. Accuracy means the accuracy of the prediction. The specific calculation formula is:

$$\text{RMSE} = \sqrt{\frac{1}{MN} \sum_{j=1}^{M} \sum_{i=1}^{N} (y_i^j - \hat{y}_i^j)^2} \tag{3}$$

$$\text{ACC} = 1 - \frac{\|Y - \hat{Y}\|F}{\|Y\|F} \tag{4}$$

$$\text{loss} = \left\| Y_t - \hat{Y}_t \right\| + \lambda L_{reg} \tag{5}$$

Where y_i^j and $\hat{y}_i^j$ represent the real traffific information and predicted one of the jth time sample in the ith road. is M the number of time samples; N is the number of roads; Y and $\hat{Y}$ represent the set of y_i^j and $\hat{y}_i^j$ respectively. L_{reg} is the L2 regularization term that helps to avoid an overfifitting problem and λ is a hyperparameter.

5 Experiments

In order to verify the influence of parameter optimization on the prediction performance in the GCN model, this paper conducts experiments on one real dataset (SZ—taxi dataset), takes the road network traffic speed as the input parameter of the model, and obtains the parameter optimization scheme through comparison experiments and analysis of experimental results. Data set SZ-taxi is the track of shenzhen taxi on January 31, 2015. 156 main roads in luohu district were selected as the research area. The experimental data mainly include two parts: one is the adjacency matrix of 156 * 156, which describes the spatial relationship between roads. The other is the eigenmatrix, which describes the change of speed on each road with time. Each row represents a road, and each column represents the speed of traffic on the road at different time periods. In the experiments, the input data is normalized to the interval [0, 1].

5.1 The Influence of Learning Rate on Prediction Performance

In the experiment, we manually adjusted and set the batch_size to 20, the training epoch to 550, the hidden units to 100, the time length of inputs to 12, the time length of prediction to 3 and the rate of training set to 0.8. In previous studies, the learning rate was usually set to 0.001, and the influence of the change of learning rate on the prediction performance was not studied. In this paper, we studied how the change of learning rate affected the prediction performance of the model on the premise of other parameters being fixed. Referring to the range of learning rates in deep learning, in this paper, the parameter range of the Initial learning rate was [0.001, 0.03], and the parameters were successively increasing by 0.001. The influence of learning rate on the loss function is shown in Fig. 2.

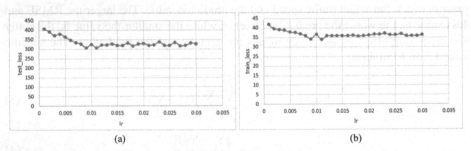

(a)   (b)

Fig. 2. The trend of the loss function under different learning rate in the training and test set based on SZ-taxi dataset. (a) Changes in loss function in the test set. (b) Changes in loss function in the training set.

The results show that in the initial stage, train_loss and test_loss decrease slightly with the increase of learning rate, then tend to be stable, and then overall tend to be stable with small fluctuations. A relatively stable and rational loss function value can be obtained by setting the learning rate as 0.015. The variation trend of RMSE with learning rate is shown in Fig. 3.

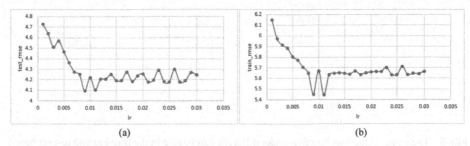

(a)   (b)

Fig. 3. The trend of the RMSE under different learning rate in the training and test set based on SZ-taxi dataset. (a) Changes in RMSE in the test set. (b) Changes in RMSE in the training set.

The results show that RMSE decreases significantly with the increase of learning rate in the initial stage, and then tends to be stable despite of fluctuations. When the learning rate is set to 0.015, the best root-mean-square error can be obtained. The trend of the prediction accuracy of the GCN model with the learning rate is shown in Fig. 4.

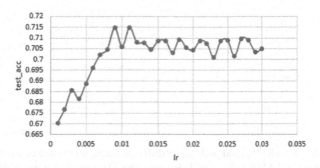

Fig. 4. The trend of the ACC under different learning rate based on SZ-taxi dataset.

The results show that with the increase of the learning rate, ACC presents an increasing trend, and when the learning rate is greater than 0.0125, ACC tends to be stable. At the learning rate of 0.015, a more rational prediction accuracy can be obtained. To sum up, in the GCN traffic prediction model, setting the learning rate as 0.015 can obtain better prediction performance.

5.2 The Influence of Batch_Size on Prediction Performance

In the process of studying the prediction performance of batch_size on model, we manually adjusted and set learning rate to 0.015, the training epoch to 500, the hidden units to 100, the time length of inputs to 12, the time length of prwediction to 3 and the rate of training set to 0.8. According to the principle of batch size Settings in depth study, in this experiment, the batch_size parameter range is [20, 30, 40, 50, 60, 70, 80, 90, 100, 110]. The influence trend of batch_size on the loss function is shown in Fig. 5.

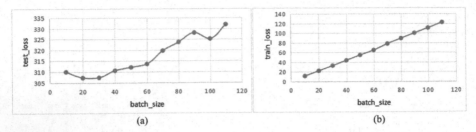

Fig. 5. The trend of the loss function under different batch_size in the training and test set based on SZ-taxi dataset. (a) Changes in loss function in the text set. (b) Changes in loss function in the training set.

And it turns out, with the increase of batch_size, the loss function shows an upward trend. When the value of batch_size is 32, a smaller loss function value can be obtained. The variation trend of RMSE value and ACC value with the learning batch size is shown in Fig. 6.

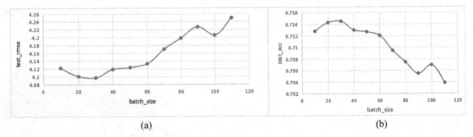

Fig. 6. The trend of the RMSE and ACC under different batch_size based on SZ-taxi dataset. (a) The variation trend of RMSE value with batch size. (b) The variation trend of ACC value with batch size.

The results show that RMSE value shows an upward trend with the increase of learning batch size, while ACC value shows a downward trend with the increase of learning batch size. When the learning batch size is 32, the minimum RMSE value and the maximum ACC value can be obtained, that is, the best prediction performance can be obtained. To sum up, in the GCN traffic prediction model, setting the batch_size as 32 can obtain better prediction performance.

6   Conclusion

This paper mainly studies the influence of super parameters on the prediction performance of traffic prediction model. Through a super parameter search and optimization method based on cross validation, the influence of three important factors, such as learning rate, learning batch size and training period, on traffic prediction performance is analyzed and discussed in detail. In the aspect of model evaluation, rmse, acc and loss function are used to evaluate the optimization degree of model performance. The results show that the super parameter search and optimization method can effectively and accurately optimize and select parameters, the model runs well, and can provide the best prediction results for traffic flow and other scenarios dominated by spatiotemporal state.

Acknowledgements. This work is partly supported by Jiangsu technology project of Housing and Urban-Rural Development (No. 2018ZD265, No. 2019ZD039, No. 2019ZD040, No. 2019ZD041).

References

1. Zhang, K., Chen, L., An, Y., et al.: A QoE test system for vehicular voice cloud services. Mob. Netw. Appl. (2019). https://doi.org/10.1007/s11036-019-01415-3
2. Wang, F., Jiang, D., Qi, S.: An adaptive routing algorithm for integrated information networks. China Commun. **7**(1), 196–207 (2019)
3. Huo, L., Jiang, D., Lv, Z., et al.: An intelligent optimization-based traffic information acquirement approach to software-defined networking. Comput. Intell. 1–21 (2019)
4. Chen, L., Jiang, D., Bao, R., Xiong, J., Liu, F., Bei, L.: MIMO Scheduling effectiveness analysis for bursty data service from view of QoE. Chin. J. Electron. **26**(5), 1079–1085 (2017)
5. Jiang, D., Wang, Y., Lv, Z., et al.: Big data analysis-based network behavior insight of cellular networks for industry 4.0 applications. IEEE Trans. Ind. Inform. **16**(2), 1310–1320 (2020)
6. Jiang, D., Huo, L., Song, H.: Rethinking behaviors and activities of base stations in mobile cellular networks based on big data analysis. IEEE Trans. Netw. Sci. Eng. **1**(1), 1–12 (2018)
7. Chen, L., et al.: A lightweight end-side user experience data collection system for quality evaluation of multimedia communications. IEEE Access **6**(1), 15408–15419 (2018)
8. Chen, L., Zhang, L.: Spectral efficiency analysis for massive MIMO system under QoS constraint: an effective capacity perspective. Mob. Netw. Appl. (2020). https://doi.org/10.1007/s11036-019-01414-4
9. Wang, F., Jiang, D., Qi, S., et al.: A dynamic resource scheduling scheme in edge computing satellite networks. Mob. Netw. Appl. 1–12 (2019)
10. Jiang, D., Huo, L., Lv, Z., et al.: A joint multi-criteria utility-based network selection approach for vehicle to infrastructure networking. IEEE Trans. Intell. Transp. Syst. **19**(10), 3305–3319 (2018)
11. Jiang, D., Zhang, P., Lv, Z., et al.: Energy-efficient multi-constraint routing algorithm with load balancing for smart city applications. IEEE Internet Things J. **3**(6), 1437–1447 (2016)
12. Jiang, D., Li, W., Lv, H.: An energy-efficient cooperative multicast routing in multi-hop wireless networks for smart medical applications. Neurocomputing **220**, 160–169 (2017)
13. Jiang, D., Wang, Y., Lv, Z., et al.: Intelligent optimization-based reliable energy-efficient networking in cloud services for IIoT networks. IEEE J. Select. Areas Commun. 1–6 (2019)
14. Jiang, D., Wang, W., Shi, L., et al.: A compressive sensing-based approach to end-to-end network traffic reconstruction. IEEE Trans. Netw. Sci. Eng. **5**(3), 1–12 (2018)
15. Jiang, D., Huo, L., Li, Y.: Fine-granularity inference and estimations to network traffic for SDN. PLoS ONE **13**(5), 1–23 (2018)
16. Wang, Y., Jiang, D., Huo, L., et al.: A new traffic prediction algorithm to software defined networking. Mob. Netw. Appl. 1–10 (2019)
17. Qi, S., Jiang, D., Huo, L.: A prediction approach to end-to-end traffic in space information networks. Mob. Netw. Appl. 1–10 (2019)
18. Huo, L., Jiang, D., Qi, S., et al.: An AI-based adaptive cognitive modeling and measurement method of network traffic for EIS. Mob. Netw. Appl. 1–11 (2019)

19. Huo, L., Jiang, D., Zhu, X., et al.: An SDN-based fine-grained measurement and modeling approach to vehicular communication network traffic. Int. J. Commun. Syst. 1–12, (2019)
20. Silver, D., et al.: Mastering the game of Go with deep neural networks and tree search. Nature **529**(7587), 484–489 (2016)
21. Silver, D., et al.: Mastering the game of go without human knowledge. Nature **550**(7676), 354–359 (2017)
22. Morav̌cik, M., et al.: DeepStack: Expert-level artifificial intelligence in heads-up no-limit poker. Science **356**(6337), 508–513 (2017)
23. Park, D., Rilett, L.R.: Forecasting freeway link travel times with a multilayer feedforward neural network. Comput.-Aided Civil Infrastruct. Eng. **14**(5), 357–367 (1999)
24. Huang, W., Song, G., Hong, H., Xie, K.: Deep architecture for traffific flow prediction: Deep belief networks with multitask learning. IEEE Trans. Intell. Transp. Syst. **15**(5), 2191–2201 (2014)
25. Fu, R., Zhang, Z., Li, L.: Using LSTM and GRU neural network methods for traffific flow prediction. In: 31st Youth Academic Annual Conference China Association Automation (YAC), Wuhan, China, pp. 324–328 (2016)
26. Van Lint, J.W.C., Hoogendoorn, S.P., van Zuylen, H.J.: Freeway travel time prediction with state-space neural networks: modeling statespace dynamics with recurrent neural networks. Transp. Res. Rec. **1811**(1), 30–39 (2002)
27. Zhao, L., Song, Y., Zhang, C., et al.: T-GCN: a temporal graph convolutional network for traffic prediction. IEEE Trans. Intell. Transp. Syst. **21**(9), 3848–3858 (2018)
28. Ding, L., Huang, Z., Chen, G.: An FPGA implementation of GCN with sparse adjacency matrix. In: 2019 IEEE 13th International Conference on ASIC (ASICON) (2019)
29. Zheng, J., Li, D.: GCN-TC: combining trace graph with statistical features for network traffic classification. In: 2019 IEEE International Conference on Communications (ICC) (2019)
30. Li, Z., Xiong, G., Chen, Y.: A hybrid deep learning approach with GCN and LSTM for traffic flow prediction. In: 2019 IEEE Intelligent Transportation Systems Conference (ITSC) (2019)
31. Reddi, S.J., Kale, S., Kumar, S.: On the Convergence of Adam and Beyond (2019)
32. Keskar, N.S., Socher, R.: Improving Generalization Performance by Switching from Adam to SGD (2017)
33. Hoffer, E., Hubara, I., Soudrym D.: Train longer, generalize better: closing the generalization gap in large batch training of neural networks. In: Advances in Neural Information Processing Systems, pp. 1731–1741 (2017)
34. Goyal, P., Dollar, P., Girshick, R.B., et al.: Accurate, Large Minibatch SGD: Training ImageNet in 1 Hour. arXiv: Computer Vision and Pattern Recognition (2017)
35. Keskar, N.S., Socher, R.: Improving generalization performance by switching from adam to sgd. arXiv preprint arXiv:1712.07628 (2017)
36. Reddi, S.J., Kale, S., Kumar, S.: On the convergence of adam and beyond (2018)
37. Smith, L.N.: Cyclical learning rates for training neural networks. In: 2017 IEEE Winter Conference on Applications of Computer Vision (WACV), pp. 464–472, IEEE (2017)
38. Smith, S.L., Kindermans, P.J., Ying, C., et al.: Don't decay the learning rate, increase the batch size. arXiv preprint arXiv:1711.00489 (2017)
39. Cardona-Escobar, A.F., Giraldo-Forero, A.F., Castro-Ospina, A.E., Jaramillo-Garzón, F.A.: Efficient hyperparameter optimization in convolutional neural networks by learning curves prediction. In: Mendoza, M., Velastín, S. (eds.) CIARP 2017. LNCS, vol. 10657, pp. 143–151. Springer, Cham (2018). https://doi.org/10.1007/978-3-319-75193-1_18
40. Defferrard, M., Bresson, X., Vandergheynst, P.: Convolutional neural networks on graphs with fast localized spectral fifiltering. Proc. Adv. Neural Inf. Process. Syst., 3844–3852 (2016)
41. Kipf, T.N., Welling, M.: Semi-supervised classifification with graph convolutional networks (2016). https://arxiv.org/abs/1609.02907

42. Bruna, J., Zaremba, W., Szlam, A., Lecun, Y.: Spectral networks and locally connected networks on graphs. https://arxiv.org/abs/1312.6203 (2013)
43. Ma, Y., et al: High performance graph convolutional networks with applications in testability Analysis. In: ACM/IEEE Design Automation Conference (DAC), Las Vegas, NV, pp. 18:1–18:6 (2019)
44. Forecasting road traffic speeds by considering area-wide spatio temporal dependencies based on a graph convolutional neural network (GCN). In: 2019 Chinese Control Conference (CCC) (2019)
45. Wu, C., Chai, L., Yang, J., Sheng, Y.: Facial expression recognition using convolutional neural network on graphs. In: The 38th China Control Conference, pp. 90–94 (2019)
46. Cho, K., van Merrienboer, B., Bahdanau, D., Bengio, Y.: On the properties of neural machine translation: Encoder-decoder approaches. https://arxiv.org/abs/1409.1259 (2014)
47. Chung, J., Gulcehre, C., Cho, K.H., Bengio, Y.: Empirical evaluation of gated recurrent neural networks on sequence modeling. https://arxiv.org/abs/1412.3555 (2014)

Research on User Experience Quality Evaluation Method of Internet of Vehicles Based on sEMG Signal

Jiamin Cheng, Yuan An[✉], Ping Cui, and Kailiang Zhang

Jiangsu Province Key Laboratory of Intelligent Industry Control Technology, Xuzhou University of Technology, Xuzhou 221018, China
anyuan@xzit.edu.cn

Abstract. In recent years, with the rapid development of Internet of vehicles, service providers and operators need to constantly upgrade and optimize their related services (communication nodes, terminal driving safety monitoring, intelligent vehicle), and the evaluation of end-user experience quality is the core of improving business. From the above point of view, this paper proposes an effective method to evaluate the psychological perception of end users by using the SEMG (Surface electromyograph) of end users. The method uses time domain features to represent the changing trend of users in different emotional states, and maps the relationship between psychological perception, so as to effectively evaluate the experience quality of end users. The results show that the method can adapt to the evaluation of experience quality of end users in the Internet of vehicles, obtain the psychological experience quality of current users, and provide strong support for service providers and operators to improve their core business of vehicle network.

Keywords: SEMG · RMG · The Internet of vehicles · QoE

1 Introduction

The Internet of things is regarded as the third wave of the world information industry after the computer Internet and mobile communication [1–3]. The application of the Internet of things in the field of intelligent transportation, namely the Internet of vehicles, has a very broad prospect and a high technical and economic feasibility. The Internet of vehicles is a concentrated embodiment of the application of the Internet of things technology in the field of intelligent transportation, and also a key area where the Internet of things technology has great potential [4–7]. The Internet of vehicles is expected to completely solve some existing traffic problems, such as traffic accidents, traffic congestion, etc. Internet of vehicles is a new application technology [6]. How to achieve high quality human-computer interaction in the vehicle network environment, that is to achieve seamless communication between people and vehicles, has attracted more and more attention [8]. Human physiological electrical signals are the direct response

H. Song and D. Jiang (Eds.): SIMUtools 2020, LNICST 369, pp. 694–703, 2021.
https://doi.org/10.1007/978-3-030-72792-5_54

of human behavioral consciousness and sensory experience. By extracting certain characteristics of human physiological signals, the recognition of human emotional state can be used as an effective bridge to realize seamless human-computer interaction [9–11]. Emotion recognition can remove the barriers between people and vehicles, make human-computer interaction more harmonious, and effectively improve the quality of human-computer interaction and user experience in the context of the Internet of vehicles [12–14]. Emotion recognition is the behavior that the computer analyzes and processes the signal collected from the sensor to obtain the psychological and emotional state the user is in. From the point of view of physiological psychology, emotional state is a kind of compound state of organism, which involves both experience and physiological reaction as well as behavior [15]. Its composition includes at least three factors: emotional experience, emotional expression and emotional physiology. At present, there are two ways for emotion recognition. One is to detect physiological signals such as respiration, heart rate and body temperature, and the other is to detect emotional behaviors such as facial feature expression recognition, voice emotion recognition and posture recognition. Among them, facial expression and speech emotion recognition system is relatively mature [16]. However, both of these methods are non-physiological signals and cannot directly reflect the inner psychological state of humans. Compared with facial images and speech sounds, physiological signals can express people's emotions more directly [17]. For example, GSR (galvanic skin response) can be used to analyze and judge people's mental stress level [18]. Surface electromyograph (SEMG), as the sum of the muscle motor potential, can quantitatively determine the internal load state of human muscles and evaluate the muscle stress state. Because sEMG signals can be obtained non-invasively, sEMG signals have been used in many fields, including motion analysis, muscle system analysis, muscle disease diagnosis and prosthesis control. SEMG signal has relatively mature analysis methods and acquisition technology, which is suitable for evaluating the user's forelimb muscle state in the on-board environment, so as to obtain the user's psychological and emotional state, determine the quality of user experience, and improve the human-computer interaction environment [19].

In view of this, from the perspective of end-user experience quality, this paper proposes an evaluation method of end-user experience quality based on the characteristics of SEMG. The mapping system is constructed by using the time-domain characteristics, and the parameters of user's psychological and emotional state are collected to evaluate the change trend of physiological signals in different emotional states, so as to obtain the end-user experience quality, and provide strong support for their core business and operators.

2 Related Work

In the context of Internet of vehicles, users' physiological signals show certain regularity as the quality of user experience changes. The quality of user experience can be directly or indirectly reflected by the changes in the characteristic parameters of human physiological signals. By analyzing the relationship between user physiological signal characteristic parameters and user experience quality, we can regard the evaluation system as an open-loop system, taking human physiological signal characteristic parameters as the input of the system and user experience quality as the output of the system, as shown in Fig. 1 [20, 21].

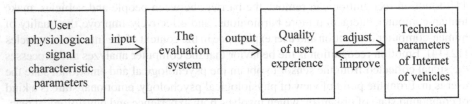

Fig. 1. User experience quality open-loop evaluation system.

In the Internet of vehicles environment, the quality evaluation standard of network protocol design and measurement is the quality of user experience. The preliminary study of our team shows that the differences in network protocols and communication capacity in the vehicle network environment can lead to different quality of user experience [22–25]. In order to improve the quality of user experience as the ultimate design goal, this paper intends to start with human physiological signals and studies the relationship between human physiological signals and users' emotional state, so as to further adjust the parameters such as network protocol or communication mode in real time through human physiological signals in the later research, and achieve the optimal user experience state [26, 27]. Human physiological signal contains a lot of information in human emotion, which is of great research significance. Physiological signals are modulated by the person's nervous system and endocrine system, and can directly reflect the true feelings of mankind, and the emotional signal associated with physiological signal process can largely reduce the interference of other factors [28, 29]. Therefore, the preliminary establishment of the relationship between users' physiological signals and their emotional states is conducive to the design of various parameters in the later Internet of vehicles environment.

The team's research on the technical parameters of the network architecture of the Internet of vehicles shows that the ultimate goal of the design of the technical parameters of the vehicle network is to achieve a higher quality of user experience. According to the quality of user experience represented by physiological signal parameters, it is more targeted to adjust and improve various technical parameters of the Internet of vehicles. SEMG signal is a comprehensive superposition of the action potential generated by the excitation of multiple motor units in the muscle at the detection electrode, which can be obtained by non-invasive measurement. In the field of biomedicine, the peak value of muscle potential in surface electromyography is often used as an indicator to evaluate the degree of muscle contraction [30–33]. The peak value is considered to be the most direct indicator to observe the degree of muscle activity. Experiments have proved that the conduction velocity of muscle fibers is directly related to the state of local muscles, and the characteristic parameters of sEMG signal can reflect the conduction velocity of muscle fibers and the state of muscle load. The characteristic parameters of sEMG signal are mainly obtained through time domain and frequency domain analysis. The time domain characteristic is a function of time, which is used to describe the amplitude characteristics of time series signal, and the time domain characteristic value is easy to extract and stable. In the experiment, the characteristic parameters of sEMG signals under different emotional states were extracted and analyzed in the time domain [34, 35].

Root mean square (RMS) is the most reliable characteristic parameter in time domain analysis, and is a traditional method to characterize EMG signals [25, 36]. RMS describe the average variation characteristics of sEMG signals over a period of time, showing a significant correlation with muscle tone, reflecting muscle activity, and is used to detect muscle motor unit recruitment and the size of action potential. RMS is defined as the square root of the sum of squares of all data points divided by the number of data points, which is defined as:

$$RMS = \sqrt{1/T \int_t^{t+T} sEMG^2(t)dt} \tag{1}$$

Where, T is the observation time length of sEMG signal.

Relevant studies have shown that the RMS of sEMG signals are in direct proportion to muscle tension, which is the basis for maintaining different positions and normal movements of the body [37, 38]. The greater the muscle tension, the more likely the user is to feel tired, and the less comfortable the human body is. The smaller the muscle tension, the better the comfort of the human body.

3 Assessment Process

The end user experience quality evaluation process based on sEMG is shown in Fig. 2.

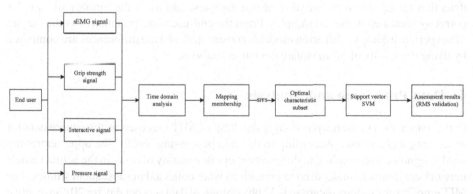

Fig. 2. Assessment process.

As shown in the figure, the preprocessing terminal user obtains the parameters and establishes sEMG signal $p(t)$, grip strength signal $q(t)$, interaction signal $r(t)$ and pressure signal $s(t)$. The characteristics of grip strength signal are time-domain and time-frequency-domain features. The mean value $\bar{y}$, variance $Var(\bar{y})$, maximum value $\max(y)$ and minimum value $\min(y)$ of the signal are extracted in time domain. The square sum m_i

of wavelet coefficients in layer I, the proportion of positive coefficients in wavelet coefficients mr_i, and the logarithm of the ratio of the sum of positive coefficients and the absolute sum of negative coefficients in wavelet coefficients are extracted in time-frequency domain.

The characteristic of the interaction signal is the duration t of the abnormal shift center pressure point, and the characteristic of the pressure signal is the absolute mean value. The dimension of different terminal parameters is different, and there is a big difference in the order of magnitude. When solving the optimal classification surface, the feature parameters with small order of magnitude will be dominated by the feature parameters with large order of magnitude, which weakens the feature parameters of small order of magnitude. Therefore, it is necessary to unify the magnitude of feature parameters to eliminate the differences. The formula (2) is used.

$$y_i' = \frac{2y_i - y_{max} - y_{min}}{y_{max} - y_{min}}, i = 1, 2, \cdots n \tag{2}$$

Where y_i is the original feature parameter component, y_i' is the normalized feature parameter component, and its range is between -1 and $+1$; y_{max} and y_{min} are the maximum and minimum values of the original feature parameters in the training samples, and N is the total number of training samples). Taking the optimal feature subset as the input of support vector machine, the features in the feature set are filtered based on SFFS selection and elimination criteria, and the criterion function (3) is established:

$$\max_Y G(Y) = \frac{n_Y}{N_Y}, Y \in X \tag{3}$$

Where x is the complete set of fatigue characteristic parameters, y is the non empty subset of X, G (y) is the criterion function, that is, the detection accuracy rate of fatigue detection model, N_Y is the number of test samples, and n_Y is the number of samples correctly identified in the test samples. From the end-user state parameters as the output, the experience quality evaluation model is constructed, and the differences are compared by using the results of mean square deviation analysis.

4   Data Processing and Analysis

In this paper, the emotional physiology database of MIT was used as the source data for processing and analysis. According to the data processing results, the upper extremity sEMG signals corresponding to different experience quality of users in the actual vehicle network environment under driving conditions were collected in subsequent studies. The MIT emotion physiology database is 32 physiological data sets per day for 20 consecutive days. The DataSet I consists of four physiological signals and eight emotional state measurements. The experimenter sat in a quiet space at the same time every day and tried to experience eight emotional states under the guidance of the computer prompt system, and recorded the physiological signals of the experimenter in real time. The sampling frequency of all data was 20 Hz and the sampling time was 100s. Participants were asked to experience eight emotional states: No emotion, Anger, Hate, Grief, Platonic love, Romantic love, Joy and Reverence.

The root mean square value (RMS) of the sEMG signal of the subjects in 8 different emotional states within 20 days was calculated and plotted as a change curve, as shown in Fig. 3.

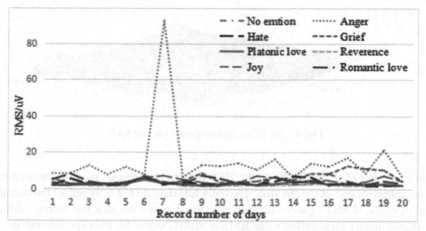

Fig. 3. The variation curve of RMS under eight emotions.

As can be seen from Fig. 3, the RMS value of sEMG signal varied greatly under Anger, Grief and Joy, indicating that the physiological signal of the experimenter was highly sensitive to the three emotions and was prone to fluctuations. Under Platonic love, Reverence, and No emotion, RMS of sEMG signal changed less, indicating that physiological signals of the subjects were less sensitive to the three emotions.

In this paper, RMS values of sEMG signals in eight emotional states during the 20-day test were comprehensively drawn into a three-dimensional diagram, as shown in Fig. 4. Figure 4 can comprehensively reflect the relationship between RMS value of sEMG signal, test time and users' emotional state. When the user enters a set emotional state for a certain period of time, a series of original emg signals will be generated to change with the emotional state. The three-dimensional diagram of the change of RMS value of sEMG signal characteristic value with the test time and the user's emotional state showed that, during the specific test time, the user's RMS value in Anger, Grief, Romantic Love and Joy emotional state was large, and the user's RMS value in the four states fluctuated greatly with the test time, indicating that the user's overall muscle load was large and it was easy to enter the fatigue state. In the state of No emotion, emotion and Platonic love, the sMEG signal characteristic value RMS amplitude is small, and the fluctuation is small in different test time, that is, the user's overall muscle load is small.

Figure 4 can reflect the changing relationship between the time-domain characteristic value RMS of user sEMG signal and the test time and the user's emotional state as a whole. The RMS amplitude of the EMG signal is averaged under eight emotional states during the 20-day test, which can reflect the relationship between the user's muscle load intensity and emotional state as a whole. At the same time, since the experimental data are 2000 data of subjects in different emotional states, the duration of each emotion

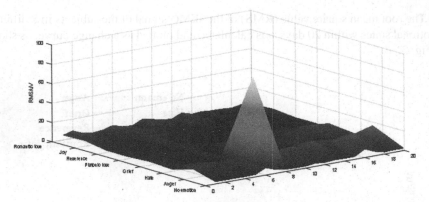

Fig. 4. The three-dimensional figure of RMS.

cannot be controlled absolutely, so the 2000 data in the data set may be intercepted at the beginning or end of the emotion. The daily test data do not fully reflect the changing trend of users' sEMG signals with their emotional states. We took the average value of the time-domain characteristic value RMS of sEMG signal for the experimenter in each emotional state for 20 days, and observed the overall change trend of the characteristic value RMS of sEMG signal for the experimenter under different emotions, as shown in Fig. 5.

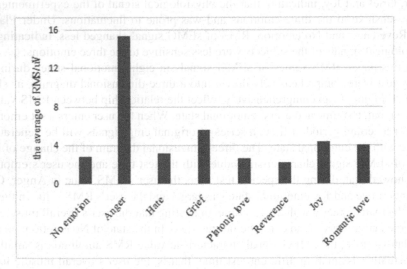

Fig. 5. Mean value of RMS under different emotions.

As can be seen from the results in Fig. 5, compared with other emotional states, the mean value of sEMG signal RMS was larger under Anger, Grief and Joy, indicating that the muscle tension of the subjects was larger under the corresponding emotional state, and it was easier to reach the fatigue state. However, the mean value of RMS of sEMG signal was lower under Platonic love, Reverence, and No emotion indicating that the muscle tone of the experimenter was lower and the comfort level was higher.

Data analysis results show that the user's physiological signal and there were some correlations between the emotional state, so in the networked environment, when the sensor technology, network communication technology, and other parameters of the corresponding change, user experience quality change, then lead to involuntary change user's physiological signal sEMG signal, and the trend of change trend in normal human cognition. In the context of the Internet of vehicles, the quality of user experience can be obtained through real-time detection of users' physiological signals, so as to make corresponding adjustments to various technical parameters of the Internet of vehicles and achieve seamless human-machine interaction.

5 Conclusion

In recent years, with the rapid development of vehicle Internet, service providers and operators need to constantly upgrade and optimize their related services (communication nodes, terminal driven security monitoring, intelligent vehicles) and end-user experience quality evaluation is the core of improving business level. From the above point of view, this paper proposes an effective method to evaluate the psychological perception of end users by sEMG (surface electromyography). This method uses time domain features to represent the changing trend and emotional state of different users, and maps the relationship between psychological perception, so as to effectively evaluate the experience quality of end users. The results show that the method can adapt to EVA to evaluate the experience quality of vehicle Internet end users, obtain the psychological experience quality of current users, provide strong support for service providers and operators, and improve their vehicle network core business.

Acknowledgements. This work is partly supported by Jiangsu technology project of Housing and Urban-Rural Development (No. 2018ZD265, No. 2019ZD039, No. 2019ZD040, No. 2019ZD041).

References

1. Jiang, D., Wang, Y., Lv, Z., et al.: Big data analysis-based network behavior insight of cellular networks for industry 4.0 applications. IEEE Trans. Ind. Inf. **16**(2), 1310–1320 (2020)
2. Xiong, A.B., Ding, Q.C., Zhao, X.G., Han, J.D., Liu, G.J.: Classification of hand gestures based on single-channel sEMG decomposition. Jixie Gongcheng Xuebao/J. Mech. Eng. **52**(7), 6–13 (2016)
3. Jiang, D., Wang, Y., Lv, Z., et al.: Intelligent optimization-based reliable energy-efficient networking in cloud services for IIoT networks. IEEE J. Selected Areas Commun. (2019)
4. Li, Y., Tian, Y.T., Xu, Z.J., Yang, Z.M.: Multi-channel sEMG detection and pattern recognition. In: Proceedings of the 2014 9th IEEE Conference on Industrial Electronics and Applications, ICIEA 2014, pp. 845–850,(2014)
5. Jiang, D., Wang, Y., Lv, Z., et al.: A joint multi-criteria utility-based network selection approach for vehicle-to-infrastructure networking. IEEE Trans. Intell. Transp. Syst. **19**(10), 3305–3319 (2018)

6. Herrera, E.V., et al.: SEMG onset detection caused by temperature variation. In: 2019 6th International Conference on Control, Decision and Information Technologies, CoDIT, pp. 1539–1543 (2019)
7. Jiang, D., Huo, L., Song, H.: Rethinking behaviors and activities of base stations in mobile cellular networks based on big data analysis. IEEE Trans. Netw. Sci. Eng. 1(1), 1–2 (2018)
8. Jiang, D., Wang, W., Shi, L., et al.: A compressive sensing-based approach to end-to-end network traffic reconstruction. IEEE Trans. Netw. Sci. Eng. 5(3), 1–12 (2018)
9. de Melo, W.C., de Lima Filho, E.B., da Silva Júnior, W.S.: SEMG signal compression based on two-dimensional techniques. BioMed. Eng. Online 15(1), 1–31 (2016)
10. Jiang, D., Huo, L., Li, Y.: Fine-granularity inference and estimations to network traffic for SDN. PLoS ONE 13(5), 1–23 (2018)
11. Li, L., Wang, J.H.: An improved method for sEMG segmentation. In: Proceedings of the 2012 24th Chinese Control and Decision Conference, CCDC 2012, pp. 1308–1311 (2012)
12. Jiang, D., Zhang, P., Lv, Z., et al.: Energy-efficient multi-constraint routing algorithm with load balancing for smart city applications. IEEE Internet Things J. 3(6), 1437–1447 (2016)
13. Kushwah, K., Narvey, R., Singhal, A.: Head posture analysis using sEMG signal. In: 2018 International Conference on Advanced Computation and Telecommunication, ICACAT (2018)
14. Jiang, D., Li, W., Lv, H.: An energy-efficient cooperative multicast routing in multi-hop wireless networks for smart medical applications. Neurocomputing 220(2017), 160–169 (2017)
15. Wang, Y., Jiang, D., Huo, L., et al.: A new traffic prediction algorithm to software defined networking. Mob. Netw. Appl. (2019)
16. Wang, X., Zhang, Y., Zhao, D.C., Wan, X.P., Peng, C.L.: Design and experimental study of wireless multichannel sEMG acquisition system. Yi Qi Yi Biao Xue Bao/Chin. J. Sci. Instrum. 33(11), 2460–2465 (2012)
17. Qi, S., Jiang, D., Huo, L.: A prediction approach to end-to-end traffic in space information networks. Mob. Netw. Appl. (2019)
18. Wang, F., Jiang, D., Qi, S., et al.: A dynamic resource scheduling scheme in edge computing satellite networks. Mob. Netw. Appl. (2019)
19. Wang, F., Jiang, D., Qi, S.: An adaptive routing algorithm for integrated information networks. China Commun. 7(1), 196–207 (2019)
20. Huo, L., Jiang, D., Qi, S., et al.: An AI-based adaptive cognitive modeling and measurement method of network traffic for EIS. Mob. Netw. Appl. (2019)
21. Gao, Y.S., Bai, J., Wang, S.X., Zhao, J., Li, X.Y.: A sEMG recording system. Key Eng. Mater. 620, 465–470 (2014)
22. Huo, L., Jiang, D., Lv, Z., et al.: An intelligent optimization-based traffic information acquirement approach to software-defined networking. Comput. Intell. 36, 1–21 (2019)
23. Huo, L., Jiang, D., Zhu, X., et al.: An SDN-based fine-grained measurement and modeling approach to vehicular communication network traffic. Int. J. Commun. Syst., 1–12 (2019)
24. Kim, M., Gu, G., Lee, W., Chung, W.K.: Pneumatic sleeve-assisted stable sEMG measurement for microneedle array electrode. In: 2018 15th International Conference on Ubiquitous Robots, pp. 1–4 (2018)
25. Zhang, K., Chen, L., An, Y., Cui, P.: A QoE test system for vehicular voice cloud services. Mob. Netw. Appl. (2019). https://doi.org/10.1007/s11036-019-01415-3
26. Kim, J., André, E.: Emotion recognition based on physio-logical changes in music listening. IEEE Trans. Pattern Anal. Mach. Intell. 30(12), 2067–2083 (2008)
27. Alja'afreh, M., Al Maadeed, S., Alja'am, J.M., El Saddik, A.: Towards a comprehensive study of fatigue deducing techniques for evaluating the quality of experience of haptic-visual applications. In: 2020 IEEE International Conference on Informatics, IoT, and Enabling Technologies (ICIoT), Doha, Qatar, pp. 339–344 (2020)

28. Song, T., Zheng, W., Cheng, L., Zong, Y., Zhang, X., Cui, Z.: MPED: a multi-modal physiological emotion database for discrete emotion recognition. IEEE Access **7**, 12177–12191 (2019)

29. Wang, K., An, N., Li, B.N., et al.: Speech emotion recognition using fourier parameters. IEEE Trans. Affect. Comput. **6**(1), 69–75 (2015)

30. Zhang, T., Zheng, W., Cui, Z., et al.: A deep neural network driven feature learning method for multi-view facial expression recognition. IEEE Trans. Multimedia **18**(12), 1 (2016)

31. Kurniawan, H., Maslov, A., V., Pechenizkiy, M.: Stress detection from speech and galvanic skin response signals. In: IEEE International Symposium on Computer-Based Medical Systems. IEEE (2013)

32. Picard, R., Vyzas, E., Healey, J.: Toward machine emotional intelligence: analysis of affective physiological state. IEEE Trans. Pattern Anal. Mach. Intell. **23**(10), 1175–1191 (2001)

33. Chen, L., Zhang, L.: Spectral efficiency analysis for massive MIMO system under QoS constraint: an effective capacity perspective. Mob. Netw. Appl. (2020). https://doi.org/10.1007/s11036-019-01414-4

34. Chen, L., Jiang, D., Bao, R., Xiong, J., Liu, F., Bei, L.: MIMO Scheduling effectiveness analysis for bursty data service from view of QoE. Chin. J. Electron. **26**(5), 1079–1085 (2017)

35. Chen, L., et al.: A lightweight end-side user experience data collection system for quality evaluation of multimedia communications. IEEE Access **6**(1), 15408–15419 (2018)

36. Rahimian, E., Zabihi, S., Atashzar, S.F., Asif, A., Mohammadi, A.: Semg-based hand gesture recognition via dilated convolutional neural networks. In: 2019 IEEE Global Conference on Signal and Information Processing (GlobalSIP), Ottawa, ON, Canada, pp. 1–5 (2019)

37. Wu, C., et al.: sEMG measurement position and feature optimization strategy for gesture recognition based on ANOVA and neural networks. IEEE Access **8**, 56290–56299 (2020)

38. Chaiyaroj, A., Sri-Iesaranusorn, P., Buekban, C., Dumnin, S., Thanawattano, C., Surangsrirat, D.: Deep neural network approach for hand, wrist, grasping and functional movements classification using low-cost sEMG sensors. In: 2019 IEEE International Conference on Bioinformatics and Biomedicine (BIBM), San Diego, CA, USA, pp. 1443–1448 (2019)

Research on Quantitative Models and Correlation of QoE Testing for Vehiclar Voice Cloud Services

Yuxin Li, Kailiang Zhang, Lei Chen[✉], Yuan An, and Ping Cui

Jiangsu Province Key Laboratory of Intelligent Industry Control Technology, Xuzhou University of Technology, Xuzhou 221018, China
chenlei@xzit.edu.cn

Abstract. Vehicle voice cloud service can help drivers reduce the dependence on vehicle operation and improve driving safety. In the related test of automobile voice cloud service quality evaluation, the research of quantitative model is an important part. The research and analysis of quantitative index correlation can effectively optimize and improve the test system, provide strong objective evaluation support for operators and service providers, and enhance the core competitiveness. Voice cloud service is composed of many modules and involves many fields. The user's business experience is closely related to the end-to-end transmission elements such as business category, terminal capability and occurrence scene. The traditional QoE (quality of experience) evaluation can not meet the evaluation requirements. Therefore, this paper uses the hierarchical method to build the key index system of automobile voice cloud service, puts forward the quantitative model of QoE test, and gives the key points The results show that the model has a high accuracy and can provide strong support for the evaluation and testing of related services for automobile voice cloud operators and service providers.

Keywords: QoE · FAHP · MoS · Vehicular unit

1 Introduction

With the development of Internet technology, the application of automobile voice cloud service is more and more widely. Its main business includes TSP (telematics service provider) business and intelligent safe driving. The former mainly includes remote information services (such as vehicle management, traffic information, high-precision maps, etc.) and life and entertainment services (games, video, car smart home, etc.); the latter mainly focuses on safety and auxiliary driving and formation driving. In order to improve user satisfaction, operators and service providers usually adopt the QoS (quality of experience) guarantee mechanism to optimize the KPI (key performance indicator) indicators. However, QoS can not reflect the characteristics of subjective perception on

H. Song and D. Jiang (Eds.): SIMUtools 2020, LNICST 369, pp. 704–715, 2021.
https://doi.org/10.1007/978-3-030-72792-5_55

voice cloud services. Ultimately, users do not care how these KPI indicators affect product quality, they just focus on the feeling of using the current service. Therefore, operators and service providers have shifted their service testing and evaluation from QoS to QoE. Vehicle voice cloud service is a complex overall system. Due to the characteristics of wireless channel conversion and mobile interconnection in vehicle environment, the related voice cloud service is composed of multiple modules and involves multiple fields. The user's business experience is closely related to the end-to-end transmission elements such as business category, terminal capability and occurrence scene. The traditional QoE evaluation cannot meet the evaluation requirements.

From the above point of view, this paper makes a detailed study on the indicators and correlation Related to the experience quality of vehicle voice cloud service, constructs a relatively comprehensive index mapping system, and forms an effective QoE evaluation model mechanism, which provides strong support for operators and service providers in the evaluation and testing of related services, thus improving user satisfaction and user stickiness, It reduces the rate of users leaving the network and improves the core competitiveness of enterprises.

2 Related Work

With the development of 5g technology, people have proposed some new methods to improve network routing and experience quality measurement [1–3]. Many scholars have also proposed new scheduling strategies and models based on effective user behavior and traffic analysis methods [4, 5] to improve resource utilization, optimize the structure of quality of experience model [6–8], and improve the performance of wireless communication related service products [9]. Some scholars have also carried out new research on QoE [10–13]. In previous studies, many traditional speech quality assessment models have been proposed for limited speech quality evaluation in communication services [14]. In the field of cloud services, most voice cloud services transmit data through TCP (transmission control protocol), resulting in high latency. In the aspect of environmental factor assessment, many scholars have developed some new methods for speech quality assessment in noisy environment [15, 16]. However, the evaluation result is single and does not have the objective definition ability of end users.

ETSI (European Telecommunications Standards Institute) and ITU (International Telecommunication Union) have successively issued a series of new standards. These standards usually focus on the quality of user experience, and fully consider the user's feelings from the end-to-end point of view, which changes the limitation of only focusing on the operators and network performance itself. As a traditional quality of service parameter, QoS (latency, jitter, packet loss and bandwidth) is widely used in the objective evaluation of network quality [17]. However, QoS can not reflect the overall perceived quality of users, so it is narrow-minded [18]. Therefore, the research on QoS focuses on mapping user metrics to defining QoE related factors. QoS measurement mainly describes the measurement of traditional network performance, so as to reflect the quality of some end-users' choice [19]. However, QoE fully considers more factors, including cognitive and contextual metrics, to generate an objective score, so as to define the real experience quality of users. Some scholars have proposed some new methods to predict the impact index in the end-to-end network [20–22], and thus confirm the QoE of the terminal [23]. This is helpful for the construction of test cases related to QoE evaluation. At the same time, on the premise of meeting QoE, a new communication architecture scheme is proposed to improve energy efficiency [24]. However, due to the rapid changes of network topology and complex service influencing factors, these methods can not be used to define the key metrics in vehicle voice cloud services. In addition, some existing simulation platforms and evaluation methods can not evaluate the key quality indicators of on-board voice cloud services. Some scholars have tried to apply various traditional mathematical methods to establish the connection model of user's subjective perception [25–27]. In recent years, many studies have proposed new QoE perception methods and evaluation models [28–30]. Although these methods and models have certain value, their forms are single and the actual evaluation efficiency remains to be investigated. Reference [31–38] proposed a test platform and evaluation model for on-board voice cloud service based on QoE. Through the QoE simulation of the terminal, it can truly reflect the QoE score in the live road network test. However, the evaluation model is still relatively simple, and the QoE impact level and factors of vehicle voice cloud service are not comprehensive, and need to be further expanded.

Through the above research, it is found that in the user experience quality test of vehicle voice cloud service, the user experience evaluation standard and method based on perception classification in the original voice service can not be directly applied to the service, and some existing achievements are relatively simple and lack of comprehensiveness. Therefore, this paper studies the acquisition system of vehicle voice cloud user experience indicators, and puts forward a more comprehensive and objective quantitative model, which helps to reduce enterprise costs and enhance core competitiveness, which is of great significance.

3 Analysis of Key Indicators

3.1 Influencing Factors of Vehiclar Voice Cloud Services

With the application of artificial intelligence, the voice cloud service for vehicle environment is personified as a voice assistant. The human-computer interaction design is also a transition from GUI (Graphical User Interface) based to the combination of VUI (Voice User Interface)and GUI. The technology based on cloud server provides better speech recognition ability of non fixed commands. The voice cloud service for the vehicle environment has an up and down relationship in the operation process, as shown in Fig. 1.

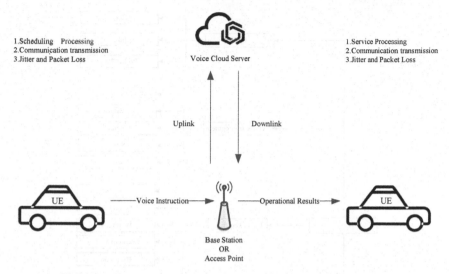

1.Scheduling Processing
2.Communication transmission
3.Jitter and Packet Loss

Voice Cloud Server

1.Service Processing
2.Communication transmission
3.Jitter and Packet Loss

Uplink   Downlink

UE   ——————Voice Instruction——►   ——————Operational Results——►   UE

Base Station
OR
Access Point

Fig. 1. Uplink and downlink diagram of vehicle voice cloud service.

As shown in Fig. 1, the uplink voice is mainly used for the user to provide an operational command that is uploaded to the cloud server through a wireless transmission. Therefore, the quality of the uplink voice, the data scheduling speed, the wireless transmission effect, etc. are important factors. The downlink voice is mainly used to provide the recognition result and an operational response. The speech recognition accuracy, cloud server performance, latency jitter and service latency are important factors influencing the user experience quality.

3.2 Construct Indicator System

Vehicular voice cloud service is a new hybrid service, including traditional voice class, data class of cloud communication, intelligent interaction class and other services. All these KPI can be divided into two levels: network level (latency, packet loss, jitter,, transmission bit rate, etc.) and application level (buffer, interactive perception, signal-to-noise ratio (PSNR), blur, motion, etc.). TMF (telemanagement Forum) has done a lot of research on the construction of QoE indicators. Its representative achievements analyze and define the mapping structure of performance indicator systems such as communication interaction. Through its definition, the QoE indicator system is divided into three levels from the bottom up, namely KPI (key performance indicator), KQI (key quality Indicators), QoE, and the overall indicator mapping architecture is shown in Fig. 2.

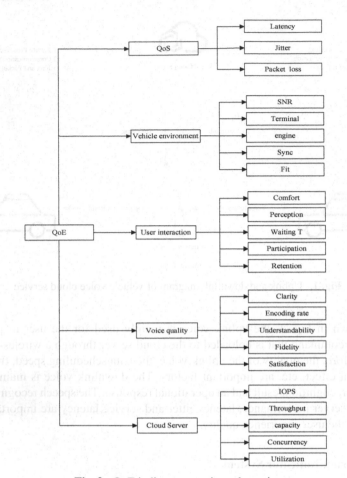

Fig. 2. QoE indicator mapping schematic.

As shown in Fig. 2, on the basis of fully studying the working process of vehicle voice cloud service, the system is constructed by using FAHP. The five levels that affect wireless video quality are QoS, quality of service vehicle-mounted environment, quality of user interaction, quality of voice, and quality of cloud. These five levels are the first level, which are KQI layer. Each KQI layer has its own secondary weight layer, namely KPI layer. Besides latency, jitter and packet loss, each index of the first layer and the second layer has its own weight proportion. The construction of appropriate QoE evaluation system can improve the ability of suppliers and operators to analyze and forecast business in a consultative manner.

4 Modeling

4.1 Quantitative Analysis

Subjective factors gradually turn to measurable quality system, which leads to the evaluation results gradually tend to the real QoE. Full research on the relationship between QoE and its influencing factors makes us need to quantify QoE and construct the relationship between QoE and real numbers from the perspective of mapping. In this paper, QoE index is divided into two aspects (subjective factors and measurable objective indicators). With the accumulation of knowledge and the progress of technology, there are more and more measurable systems that transform subjective factors into objective indicators. We find a more accurate relationship between QoE and its influencing factors. As a subjective indicator of QoE, it is very necessary to establish an appropriate objective model for quantitative evaluation, which is helpful for service providers and operators to analyze the acceptability of business, predict the real QoE, and find out the service defects, so as to improve continuously.

Generally speaking, evaluation methods can be divided into two categories (with reference value and without reference value). In terms of subjective and corresponding objective evaluation methods, the method based on MOS (average opinion score) recommended by ITU (International Telecommunication Union), as a method based on machine scoring, has been applied more and more widely. This paper uses MOS, which defines the specific criteria in ITU-T p.800 [39] recommended by ITU. The evaluation methods are divided into five levels: excellent, good, medium, poor and bad. As shown in Table 1, MOS has a fractional definition of 1 to 5.

Table 1. ITU-T Recommendation P.800 MOS scales.

MOS	Quality	Influence
5	Excellent	No damage can be observed
4	Good	Damage can be observed but is ok
3	Medium	Slightly dislike
2	Poor	Dislike
1	Bad	Extremely dislike

4.2 Layer Model

Our hierarchical model can be divided into three levels: QoE, KQI and KPI. Through the model of FAHP, the weight value of KQI and KPI layers is realized. Through the weight value of each level, the overall evaluation index of QoE can be obtained. The specific content is Represented by Formula (1).

$$QoE = \omega_1 \times QoS + \omega_2 \times QoCar + \omega_3 \times QoI + \omega_4 \times QoV + \omega_5 \times QoCloud \quad (1)$$

In Formula 1, QoS, qocar, qoi, qov and qocloud correspond to QoS, vehicle environment, user interaction, voice quality and cloud server in KQI layer respectively. Meanwhile,

ω_1, ω_2, ω_3, ω_4 and ω_5 are the weight values of each index in the KQI layer. The weight value of each KQI layer can be obtained by formula (2).

$$QoX = \sum_{i=1}^{n} \omega_1 KPI, X = S, Car, I, V, Cloud \tag{2}$$

In formula (2), QoX represents the index of each KQI layer. Then, QoE can be obtained by formula (3).

$$QoE = \sum_{i=1}^{m} \sum_{j=1}^{n} \omega_{ij} KPI_{ij} \tag{3}$$

In our hierarchical system, the indicators of each KPI can be obtained through subjective or objective tests, which is conducive to get the value of KQI and obtain the final QoE results. Taking qoi as an example, the weight value is obtained through matrix calculation, as shown in formula (4).

$$W_{QoI} = (0.2112, 0.2069, 0.1950, 0.1921, 0.2107) \tag{4}$$

Through FAHP, similar calculation can be carried out to obtain the index weight values of all KQI and KPI layers.

In this paper, FAHP (fuzzy analytic hierarchy process) is used to calculate the weight value of each layer's index to QoE effect, and establish the evaluation system. We use the nine scale method to obtain the relative values of any two indexes. The nine scales are shown in Table 2.

Table 2. The number of scales.

Scale	Influence
0.5	Both elements are equally important
0.6	One element is a little more important than the other
0.7	One element is more important than the other
0.8	One element is much more important than the other
0.9	One element is extremely more important than the other

4.3 Bivariate Model

QoE is the subjective feeling of customers. It is very important to establish an appropriate objective model and make quantitative evaluation, which can help service providers and operators to analyze and predict the acceptability of business in a consultative manner. The on-board voice cloud service is a complex overall system, involving multiple fields, and the user's business experience is closely related to the end-to-end transmission elements. In our hierarchical evaluation system, the KPI corresponding to QoS layer does not exist alone, and its effect is not independent, so we can not get their respective weights. Since the extended KPI corresponding to packet loss and jitter is the recognition accuracy, this paper designs a double independent variable function F (Latency, Recognition), as shown in formula (5).

$$F(\text{Recognition}, \text{Latency}) = P * \frac{4(\ln(ST) - \ln(0.003\text{Max} + 0.12))}{\ln((0.003\text{Max} + 0.12)/\text{Max})} + 5 \quad (5)$$

In formula (5), $P = \frac{S+D+I}{N}$, S is the number of replaced strings and the original strings, D is the number of recognized strings and deleted characters in the original strings, I is the number of recognized strings and inserted characters in the original strings, n represents the length of the original strings; ST is the latency correlation function, and Max is the maximum latency.

5 Model Testing and Indicator Analysis

In this paper, the model is tested in the commercial network scenario, the purpose is to verify the effectiveness and reliability of the model in real scenarios. This platform can be used as a real-time test platform. The car is the mobile carrying platform for the test, and the vehicle brand is Rongwei 350. IFLYTEK is the service target under test, and the mobile terminal in its data service is only used for network access. In addition, the mobile platform uses oppo R9m. The PC system selects Shenzhou Xuanlong series, model prot1, 4G graphics card storage, 8g memory, Intel i7 processor and windows 10 operating system. According to the design standard, ffmpeg is used to edit audio in the format of PCM, the sampling rate is 16000, and the bit rate is 16bit; the sentence "today's weather in Beijing" is selected for recording, and the adult male voice has medium speech speed. In the functional verification of recognition success rate, we can use the advantages of the road test platform to edit the case file, add background noise and selected noise. It is the background sound of typical vehicle running, and the format conforms to the design standard.

Firstly, the delay and recognition accuracy indicators of the test model are set by using the vehicle road test platform. At the same time, 10 men and 10 women are selected to score the MOS of each index gradient test model, and the relationship among MOS, latency and recognition is obtained as shown in Fig. 3.

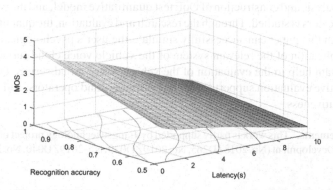

Fig. 3. MOS'-latency-recognition accuracy relationship graph.

As shown in the Fig. 3, as the latency and the corresponding recognition accuracy decrease, the user's psychological feelings tend to decline, and the MOS score gradually decreases. When the latency is 10 S, the user reaches the psychological tolerance limit and the recognition accuracy. When they are 0.85 and 0.7 respectively, the optimal values of the corresponding MOS scores are 4 and 3. It can be seen that when the recognition accuracy is 0.85 and above, the user feels good. When the recognition accuracy is 0.7 to 0.85, the user can accept, And below 0.7 is basically unbearable.

Next, the typical time and place of commercial test are determined and evaluated. According to the environmental factors of wireless channel, the mobile road network test under real vehicle environment is carried out near residential, residential, street, Internet cafe, underground parking, tunnel, suburbs and market, and the MOS value is obtained as shown in Fig. 4.

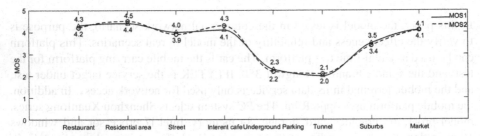

Fig. 4. MOS in typical scenarios.

As shown in Fig. 4, different wireless channel environments in each location result in significant differences in MOS. In underground parking and tunnel, the experience quality of end users is the worst.

6   Conclusions

In this paper, the characteristics of vehicle voice cloud service are studied, and the key index system is constructed by using FAHP. The validity of the model is verified by data sampling, analysis and construction of QoE test quantitative model, and the correlation of relevant indicators is studied. Through the research and evaluation, the quantitative model of QoE test in this paper can successfully simulate the user's psychological perception, meet the application of the relevant system of the vehicle voice cloud service QoE test, bring important help to the evaluation of the vehicle voice cloud service QoE, provide strong objective evaluation support for service providers and operators, and improve the core competitiveness.

Acknowledgements. This work is partly supported by Jiangsu technology project of Housing and Urban-Rural Development (No. 2018ZD265, No. 2019ZD039, No. 2019ZD040, No. 2019ZD041).

References

1. Montero, R., Agraz, F., Pagès, A., Spadaro, S.: End-to-End 5G service deployment and orchestration in optical networks with QoE guarantees. In: 2018 20th International Conference on Transparent Optical Networks (ICTON), Bucharest, pp. 1–4 (2018)
2. Wang, F., Jiang, D., Qi, S.: An adaptive routing algorithm for integrated information networks. China Commun. **7**(1), 196–207 (2019)
3. Huo, L., Jiang, D., Lv, Z., et al.: An intelligent optimization-based traffic information acquirement approach to software-defined networking. Comput. Intell. **36**, 1–21 (2019)
4. Jiang, D., Wang, Y., Lv, Z., et al.: Big data analysis based network behavior insight of cellular networks for industry 4.0 applications. IEEE Trans. Ind. Inf. **16**(2), 1310–1320 (2020)
5. Chen, L., Jiang, D., Song, H., Wang, P., Bao, R., Zhang, K., Li, Y.: A lightweight endside user experience data collection system for quality evaluation of multimedia communications. IEEE Access **6**(1), 15408–15419 (2018)
6. Chen, L., Zhang, L.: Spectral efficiency analysis for massive MIMO system under QoS constraint: an effective capacity perspective. Mob. Netw. Appl. (2020). https://doi.org/10.1007/s11036-019-01414-4
7. Wang, F., Jiang, D., Qi, S., et al.: A dynamic resource scheduling scheme in edge computing satellite networks. Mob. Netw. Appl. (2019)
8. Jiang, D., Huo, L., Lv, Z., et al.: A joint multi-criteria utility-based network selection approach for vehicle-to-infrastructure networking. IEEE Trans. Intell. Transp. Syst. **19**(10), 3305–3319 (2018)
9. Jiang, D., Wang, Y., Lv, Z., et al.: Intelligent optimization-based reliable energy-efficient networking in cloud services for IIoT networks. IEEE J. Sel. Areas Commun. (2019)
10. Jiang, D., Huo, L., Li, Y.: Fine-granularity inference and estimations to network traffic for SDN. Plos One **13**(5), 1–23 (2018)
11. Wang, Y., Jiang, D., Huo, L., et al.: A new traffic prediction algorithm to software defined networking. Mob. Netw. Appl. (2019)
12. Qi, S., Jiang, D., Huo, L.: A prediction approach to end-to-end traffic in space information networks. Mob. Netw. Appl. (2019)
13. Huo, L., Jiang, D., Qi, S., et al.: An AI-based adaptive cognitive modeling and measurement method of network traffic for EIS. Mob. Netw. Appl. (2019)
14. Mittag, G., Möller, S.: Non-intrusive speech quality assessment for super-wideband speech communication networks. In: ICASSP 2019 - 2019 IEEE International Conference on Acoustics, Speech and Signal Processing (ICASSP), Brighton, United Kingdom, pp. 7125–7129 (2019)
15. Huo, L., Jiang, D., Zhu, X., et al.: An SDN-based fine-grained measurement and modeling approach to vehicular communication network traffic. Int. J. Commun. Syst., 1–12 (2019)
16. Uhrig, S., Möller, S., Behne, D.M., Svensson, U.P., Perkis, A.: Testing a quality of experience (QoE) model of loudspeaker-based spatial speech reproduction. In: 2020 Twelfth International Conference on Quality of Multimedia Experience (QoMEX), Athlone, Ireland, pp. 1–6 (2020)
17. Kim, T., Nguyen-Duc, T.: OQR: on-demand QoS routing without traffic engineering in software defined networks. In: 2018 4th IEEE Conference on Network Softwarization and Workshops (NetSoft), Montreal, QC, pp. 362–365 (2018)
18. Jaiswal, K., Anand, V.: An optimal QoS-aware multipath routing protocol for IoT based wireless sensor networks. In: 2019 3rd International conference on Electronics, Communication and Aerospace Technology (ICECA), Coimbatore, India, pp. 857–860 (2019)
19. Skorin-Kapov, L., et al.: A survey of emerging concepts and challenges for QoE management of multimedia services. ACM Trans. Multimedia Comput. Commun. Appl. **14**(2), 29 (2018)

20. Jiang, D., Wang, W., Shi, L., Song, H.: A compressive sensing-based approach to end-to-end network traffic reconstruction. IEEE Trans. Netw. Sci. Eng. **5**(3), 1–2 (2018)
21. Jiang, D., Zhang, P., Lv, Z., Song, H.: Energy-efficient multiconstraint routing algorithm with load balancing for smart city applications. IEEE Internet Things J **3**(6), 1437–1447 (2018)
22. Peng, X., Duan, Y., Geng, B., Liu, X., Tao, X., Ge, N.: A QoE-based alarm model for terminal video quality. In: 2019 IEEE Global Conference on Signal and Information Processing (GlobalSIP), Ottawa, ON, Canada, pp. 1–5 (2019)
23. Dias, A., Reis, A.B., Sargento, S.: Improving the QoE of OTT multimedia services in wireless scenarios. In: 2019 IEEE Symposium on Computers and Communications (ISCC), Barcelona, Spain, pp. 1–6 (2019)
24. Chen, L., Jiang, D., Bao, R., Xiong, J., Liu, F., Bei, L.: MIMO scheduling effectiveness analysis for bursty data service from view of QoE. Chin. J. Electron. **26**(5), 1079–1085 (2017)
25. Jiang, D., Li, W., Lv, H.: An energy-efficient cooperative multicast routing in multi-hop wireless networks for smart medical applications. Neurocomputing **220**(2017), 160–169 (2017)
26. Reyes, J., López, J., Kushik, N., Zeghlache, D.: On the assessment and debugging of QoE in SDN: work in progress. In: 2019 IEEE 18th International Symposium on Network Computing and Applications (NCA), Cambridge, MA, USA, pp. 1–3 (2019)
27. Nightingale, J., Salva-Garcia, P., Calero, J.M.A., Wang, Q.: 5G-QoE: QoE Modelling for ultra-HD video streaming in 5G networks. IEEE Trans Broadcasting **64**(2), 621–634 (2018)
28. JiangD, H.: Song H: rethinking behaviors and activities of base stations in mobile cellular networks based on big data analysis. IEEE Trans Netw Sci Eng **1**(2), 1–2 (2018)
29. Raiyn, J.: Using intelligent cooperative system for travel flow management in autonomous vehicle networks. In: 2018 UKSim-AMSS 20th International Conference on Computer Modelling and Simulation (UKSim), Cambridge, pp. 38–42 (2018)
30. BritoI, V.S., Figueiredo, G.B.: Improving QoS and QoE through seamless handoff in software-defined IEEE 802.11 mesh networks. IEEE Commun. Lett. **21**(11), 2484–2487 (2017)
31. Zhang, K., Chen, L., An, Y., Cui, P.: A QoE test system for vehicular voice cloud services. Mob. Netw. Appl. (2019). https://doi.org/10.1007/s11036-019-01415-3
32. Belmoukadam, O., Spetebroot, T., Barakat, C.: ACQUA: a user friendly platform for lightweight network monitoring and QoE forecasting. In: 2019 22nd Conference on Innovation in Clouds, Internet and Networks and Workshops (ICIN), Paris, France, pp. 88–93 (2019)
33. Gomes, G.D., Flynn, R., Murray, N.: A QoE evaluation of an immersive virtual reality autonomous driving experience. In: 2020 Twelfth International Conference on Quality of Multimedia Experience (QoMEX), Athlone, Ireland, pp. 1–4 (2020)
34. Wang, L., Yang, J., Song, X.: A QoE-driven spectrum decision scheme for multimedia transmissions over cognitive radio networks. In: 2017 26th International Conference on Computer Communication and Networks (ICCCN), Vancouver, BC, pp. 1–5 (2017)
35. Gringoli, F., Serrano, P., Ucar, I., Facchi, N., Azcorra, A.: Experimental QoE evaluation of multicast video delivery over IEEE 802.11aa WLANs. IEEE Trans. Mob. Comput. **18**(11), 2549–2561 (2019)
36. Ciambrone, D., Tennina, S., Tsolkas, D., Pomante, L.: A QoE performance evaluation framework for LTE networks. In: 2018 IEEE 19th International Symposium on "A World of Wireless, Mobile and Multimedia Networks" (WoWMoM), Chania, pp. 14–19 (2018)
37. Ning, Z., Liu, Y., Wang, X., Feng, Y., Kong, X.: A novel QoS-Based QoE evaluation method for streaming video service. In: 2017 IEEE International Conference on Internet of Things (iThings) and IEEE Green Computing and Communications (GreenCom) and IEEE Cyber, Physical and Social Computing (CPSCom) and IEEE Smart Data (SmartData), Exeter, pp. 956–961 (2017)

38. Gao, Y., Wu, W., Zhou, T., Na, J., Li, M., Sun, Y.: QoE-aware access node selection considering mobile edge computing. In: 2018 IEEE 4th International Conference on Computer and Communications (ICCC), Chengdu, China, pp. 1914–1918 (2018)
39. ITU-T.P800.1. Mean Opinion Score (MOS) terminology, Geneva (2003)

User Experience Quality Analysis Method Based on Frequency Domain Characteristics of Physiological Signal

Ke Sun, Yuan An[(✉)], Kailiang Zhang, and Ping Cui

Jiangsu Province Key Laboratory of Intelligent Industry Control Technology,
Xuzhou University of Technology, Xuzhou 221018, China
anyuan@xzit.edu.cn

Abstract. In recent years, the development of intelligent driving is rapid, the related business is constantly upgrading, and the end-user service is becoming more and more perfect. From the perspective of end users, obtaining the evaluation results of experience quality is an effective way to enhance the core competitiveness of business. In this paper, the mapping method of user experience quality is established based on the frequency domain characteristics of SEMG signal, so as to obtain the current real experience quality of intelligent driving terminal users. Data analysis shows that this method can effectively obtain the quality of real user experience. This study can be used as reference data to improve the business experience of intelligent driving terminal users, improve the relevant technical parameters, and enhance the core competitiveness.

Keywords: Physiological signals · Frequency · Domain characteristics · QoE

1 Introduction

As a research hotspot in the field of intelligent transportation, vehicle network is a typical application of Internet of things technology in the field of transportation system [1, 2]. It is the only way for mobile Internet and Internet of things to develop into business essence and depth [3]. The Intelligent driving refers to the car and the car, car and road, cars and people, cars and sensing devices [4], such as interaction, realize vehicle dynamic system for mobile communications network communication with the public, including car and car, car and road, and sensing equipment through the established sensing technology and network communication technology for vehicle [5], road and environment information, and between cars and people, namely the human-computer interaction [6], how to realize the seamless docking is key to the current research [7, 8]. In the vehicle network environment, the quality of all sensor technology and network communication technology is measured by the experience quality of the driving user [9–11].

Emotion recognition is a research hotspot in artificial intelligence [12], human-computer interaction, pattern recognition and digital signal processing [13], as well as

H. Song and D. Jiang (Eds.): SIMUtools 2020, LNICST 369, pp. 716–726, 2021.
https://doi.org/10.1007/978-3-030-72792-5_56

an important branch of emotion based computing [14]. In 1997, professor Picard of MIT media lab proposed that affective computing is one of the research methods for emotion [15]. Its purpose is to build a harmonious human-computer environment by giving computers the ability to recognize, understand, express and adapt to human emotions, and to make computers have higher and comprehensive intelligence. With the development of science and technology, people have higher and higher requirements for artificial intelligence, and how to make seamless communication between people and computers is also getting more and more attention [16–18]. As the basis of communication, emotion plays a more and more important role in human-computer interaction. Facial expression and voice emotion recognition systems will mature, however, both of these are non-physiological signals that do not directly reflect the inner psychological state of humans [18, 19]. Physiological signals (EMG, ECG, EGG) can more directly express people's current emotions. For example, EMG signal analysis can be used to judge the mental stress level and muscle fatigue state [20–24].

In the vehicle-net environment, the electromyographic signals of the driving user are easier to detect and can reflect the real experience quality of the driving user in real time. So this article uses the eight different emotional states (No emotion, Anger, Hate, Grief, Platonic love, Romantic love, Joy and Reverence) under electromyographic signal, and analyzes the relationship between their frequency characteristics and emotional state, in order to get through the electromyographic signal parameters to evaluate the quality of the vehicle under the network environment the user experience.

2   Related Work

Physiological signal refers to the signal spontaneously produced by human body in the physiological process, which contains a lot of information in human emotion and has great research significance. Physiological signals are regulated by the human nervous system and endocrine system, which can directly reflect the real emotions of human beings, and can greatly reduce the interference of other factors in the process of emotion recognition [25]. In the context of Intelligent driving, physiological signals change with the change of driving users' experience results of sensing technology and network communication technology, and the quality of user experience can be directly or indirectly reflected by the changes of human physiological signals [26]. By analyzing the relationship between driving user physiological signal characteristic parameters and user experience quality, we can regard the evaluation system as an open-loop system, taking human physiological signal changes as the input of the system and user experience quality as the output of the system [27]. The open-loop system can objectively represent the driving users' experience quality of various sensor technologies and network communication technologies of the Intelligent driving, so as to facilitate technicians to adjust relevant technical parameters in real time.

The electromyographic signal is the bioelectrical signal produced by the muscle activity and is the synthesis of the single action potential produced by the motor unit. SEMG signals are recorded from the skin surface and reflect the functional state of nerves and muscles. Because EMG signals can be recorded noninvasively, EMG signals have been used in a variety of fields, including motion analysis, neuromuscular system analysis, neuromuscular disease diagnosis, and prosthesis control. Because of SEMG signal can overcome the problems existing in the subjective psychological evaluation, quantitative analysis of the working load and muscle function status and high correlation exists between the indexes and subjective fatigue, so its in human computer interaction and ergonomics application has a unique advantage, for the improvement of man-machine environment provides a more objective and effective theory basis [28, 29].

In terms of human-computer interaction, facial expression and speech emotion recognition system [30, 31] is relatively mature. However, these methods are non physiological signals, which can not directly reflect the internal psychological state of human beings. Compared with facial images and speech, physiological signals can express people's emotions more directly [32–34]. For example, GSR (galvanic skin reaction) can be used to analyze and judge people's psychological stress level [33]. As the sum of muscle motor potential, SEMG can quantitatively determine the internal load state of human body and evaluate the muscle stress state. Since SEMG signal can be obtained noninvasively, SEMG signal has been used in many fields, including motion analysis, muscle system analysis, muscle disease diagnosis and prosthesis control. SEMG signal has a relatively mature analysis method and acquisition technology, which is suitable for the evaluation of user's forelimb muscle state. In order to obtain the user's psychological and emotional state, determine the quality of user experience, and improve the human-computer interaction environment [27, 36].

Studies show that when the human body for a long time in a less or more excited emotional psychological state, the system remains tense muscles, it will produce a certain amount of load, the load build-up can cause muscle changes in physical properties of excitability and conductivity and reduced contractility, muscle physical exhibition staying power and flexibility is abate, the muscle will not be able to produce, the force needed for this phenomenon is called muscle fatigue. When fatigue occurs, the conduction velocity of muscle fibers decreases, and local muscles will produce such sensations as soreness, numbness and weakness. Therefore, it is an effective experimental method to extract surface EMG signals and find out the frequency characteristic parameters reflecting the change of conduction velocity [37, 38].

3   Assessment Process and Data Analysis

The end user experience quality evaluation process based on SEMG is shown in Fig. 1.

As shown in the figure, physiological comfort index includes human body pressure distribution data and EMG signal data. According to the data characteristics of physiological signal indicators and five levels of comfort evaluation level, the evaluation data set $K = \{k_1, k_2, \cdots, k_n\}$ is defined by maximum value and minimum value method, As shown in formula (1):

$$z = \frac{\max(x) - \min(x)}{n} \tag{1}$$

Among them, $\max(x)$ and $\min(x)$ represent the maximum and minimum values of a class of physiological data, $n \sim x_{ij}$ values are graded, and $z \sim n$ values are the mean difference between the grades. In this paper, trapezoidal fuzzy method is used to reflect

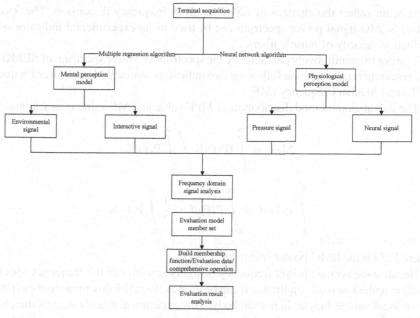

Fig. 1. Assessment process.

the subjectivity of the end-users, and the correlation between the evaluation indexes and the evaluation data set is studied. As shown in formula (2).

$$
\alpha_{ij} = \begin{cases}
\frac{x - \alpha_{ij}^{L}}{\alpha_{ij}^{ML} - \alpha_{ij}^{L}}, x \in \left(\alpha_{ij}^{L}, \alpha_{ij}^{ML} \right) \\
1, x \in \left(\alpha_{ij}^{ML}, \alpha_{ij}^{MR} \right) \\
\frac{x - \alpha_{ij}^{R}}{\alpha_{ij}^{MR} - \alpha_{ij}^{R}}, x \in \left(\alpha_{ij}^{MR}, \alpha_{ij}^{R} \right) \\
0, x \in \left(-\infty, \alpha_{ij}^{L} \right) \cup \left(\alpha_{ij}^{R}, 0 \right)
\end{cases}
\tag{2}
$$

Among them, a_{ij} is the membership degree of the u_{ij} index to the evaluation set $K = \{k_1, k_2, \cdots, k_n\}$, $\alpha_{ij}^{L}, \alpha_{ij}^{ML}, \alpha_{ij}^{MR}, \alpha_{ij}^{R}$ is the coordinate value of the trapezoidal membership function respectively, and there is $\alpha_{ij}^{L} < \alpha_{ij}^{ML} < \alpha_{ij}^{MR} < \alpha_{ij}^{R}$. If $\alpha_{ij}^{L} < \alpha_{ij}^{ML} = \alpha_{ij}^{MR} < \alpha_{ij}^{R}$, the trapezoidal membership function is transformed into a triangular membership function.

The experimental results show that the conduction velocity of muscle fibers is directly related to local muscle fatigue. Surface emg signals are extracted and converted into frequency characteristic parameters that can reflect the change of conduction velocity, thus reflecting the fatigue degree of muscles. These characteristic parameters are mainly obtained through time-domain and frequency-domain analysis.

In frequency domain analysis, the main analysis method is to conduct fast Fourier transform on EMG signal to obtain the spectrum or power spectrum of EMG signal, which can reflect the changes of EMG signal in different frequency components, so it can better reflect the changes of EMG signal in frequency dimension. The spectral shift of SEMG signal power spectrum can be used as an experimental indicator of the conduction velocity of muscle fibers.

In order to quantitatively characterize the spectrum or Power spectrum of SEMG signals, researchers often use the following two indicators, namely Mean Power Frequency (MPF) and Median Frequency (MF).

The calculation method distribution of MPF value and MF value is as follows:

$$\mathrm{MPF} = \int_{0}^{\infty} f P(f) df \bigg/ \int_{0}^{\infty} P(f) df \tag{3}$$

$$\int_{0}^{\mathrm{MF}} P(f) df = \int_{\mathrm{MF}}^{\infty} P(f) df = \frac{1}{2} \int_{0}^{\infty} P(f) df \tag{4}$$

Where $P(f)$ is the EMG power spectrum.

Because the average power frequency is highly sensitive to the frequency spectrum variation under low load conditions, it can be used as the reliability measurement parameter of local muscle fatigue in human body. This experiment mainly detects the change of SEMG signal spectrum under different psychological and emotional states of users. There is no obvious muscle activity. However, due to the long-term load accumulation process, frequency-domain parameters are adopted for analysis.

4   The Experimental Results

In this paper, the emotional physiology database of MIT was used as the source data for processing and analysis. According to the data processing results, the upper extremity SEMG signals corresponding to different experience quality of users in the actual vehicle network environment under driving conditions were collected in subsequent studies.

The MIT emotion physiology database is 32 physiological data sets per day for 20 consecutive days. The DataSet I consists of four physiological signals and eight emotional state measurements. The experimenter sat in a quiet space at the same time every day and tried to experience eight emotional states under the guidance of the computer prompt system, and recorded the physiological signals of the experimenter in real time. The sampling frequency of all data was 20 Hz and the sampling time was 100 s. Participants were asked to experience eight emotional states: No emotion, Anger, Hate, Grief, Platonic love, Romantic love, Joy and Reverence.

The average power frequency (MPF) of SEMG signals in eight different emotional states of the subjects within 20 days was calculated and plotted as the corresponding histogram, as shown in Fig. 2. Since the experimental data are 2000 data of subjects in different emotional states, the duration of each emotion cannot be controlled absolutely, so the 2000 data in the data set may be intercepted at the beginning or end of the emotion. We took the average value of the 20-day measurement data and observed the mean value of MPF value of the experimenter's SEMG signal under different emotions, as shown in Fig. 3.

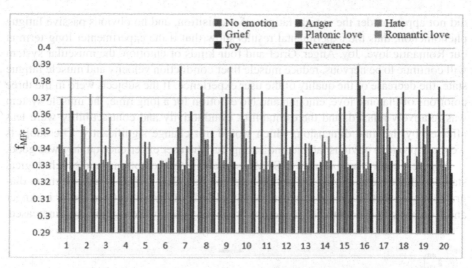

Fig. 2. Histogram of MPF value of SEMG signal in eight states.

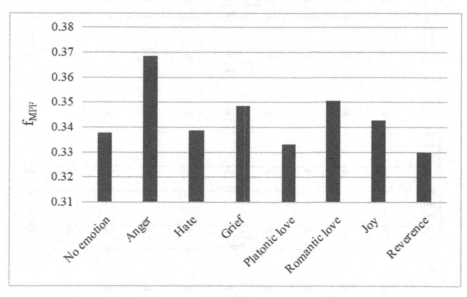

Fig. 3. Mean MPF value of SEMG signal in 8 states within 20 days.

According to the results in Fig. 1 and Fig. 3, under Anger, Grief, Romantic love and Joy, SEMG signal MPF value had a larger amplitude, It indicates that the conduction velocity of muscle fibers is faster. The MPF value of SEMG signal was smaller under Platonic love, emotion and No emotion, and the results indicate that the conduction velocity of muscle fibers is slow.

Previous studies showed that the average power frequency MPF decreased with the gradual fatigue of muscles under static load. This experimental data for the subjects did not appear under the muscle fatigue of acquisition, and no obvious passive fatigue phenomenon, thus the experimental results show that if the experimenter long-term at our Romantic love, Joy, Anger, Grief and four kinds of emotion, the muscular system will continue to be nervous, reduce muscle fiber conduction velocity and muscle fatigue state, the decrease of the quality of the user experience. If the subjects were in the three emotions of Platonic love, emotion and No emotion for a long time, the muscle system was relatively relaxed, and the excitability, conductivity and contractibility were less affected by the time dimension, which would not change significantly. The subjects were not prone to obvious fatigue, indicating that the user experience quality was good.

Figure 4 shows the spectrum of SEMG signals in eight emotional and psychological states of the subjects during the test on a certain day. The SEMG signal spectrum diagram showed that the frequency spectrum amplitude of the subject was larger in Anger and Romantic love, and the high and low frequency parts were significantly increased,

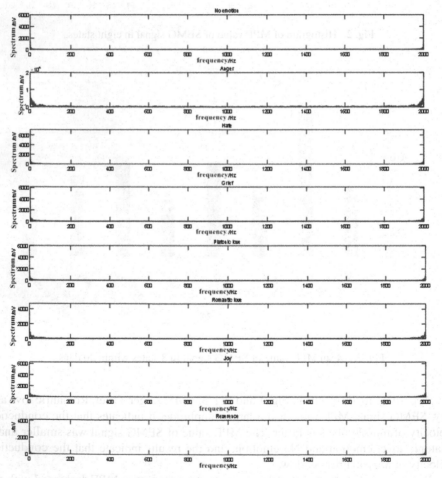

Fig. 4. SEMG spectrum diagram.

indicating that the muscle system of the subject was prone to fatigue in a certain period of time under these two emotions. Under emotion and No emotion, the amplitude of SEMG signal spectrum was small, and the distribution of high and low frequency was less, indicating that the muscle system of the subjects was not prone to fatigue in a certain period of time under these two emotions, and the quality of user experience was better than other psychological and emotional states.

Experiment found that the short-time Fourier transform of MPF, to some extent can well represent changes of muscle fatigue, but because of the Fourier transform is only applicable to smooth the mutations in the signal, so when change the SEMG signal, based on Fourier transform of frequency domain feature is not difficult to fully reflect the changes of muscle fatigue. Due to the experimental data for the subjects in the corresponding part of the SEMG signal with emotional state, likely in the mood or end the beginning of the end, there may be a jump, the results can only qualitative analysis to get the user psychological emotional state and there were some correlation between physiological signal characteristic parameters, can be used to get the user experience as a quality reference data. Later research can obtain corresponding user SEMG signals by changing various technical parameters in the Intelligent driving environment, and use more characteristic parameters to represent the user experience quality under different technical parameters, so as to provide guiding data for a more harmonious human-computer interaction environment.

5 Conclusion

In this paper, the mapping method of user experience quality is established based on the frequency domain characteristics of SEMG signal, so as to obtain the current real experience quality of intelligent driving terminal users. Data analysis shows that this method can effectively obtain the quality of real user experience. The relationship between MPF, the characteristic parameter of SEMG signal in frequency domain of No emotion, Anger, Hate, Grief, Platonic love, Romantic love, Joy and mood state of subjects was analyzed to provide reference data for judging the quality of user experience. The experimental results showed that in the state of Anger, Hate and other psychological mood swings, users had a large MPF amplitude and a large frequency spectrum in the low and high frequency bands, indicating that in this emotional state, the muscle system would be continuously tense, resulting in decreased muscle fiber conduction velocity, relatively easy muscle fatigue and decreased user experience quality. When users experience less disturbance of emotion such as agitation and No emotion, the muscle system is relatively relaxed, the excitability, conductivity and contractility are less affected by time dimension, and No significant change will occur. Users are not prone to obvious fatigue, indicating that the user experience quality is good.

The research results of this paper show that SEMG signals can be used as physiological signals to directly obtain user experience quality in the context of the Intelligent driving, and the characteristic parameters of user SEMG signals can be acquired in real time. The influence of technical parameters of the Intelligent driving on user experience quality can be analyzed, so as to create a more harmonious and integrated human-computer interaction environment.

Acknowledgements. This work is partly supported by Jiangsu technology project of Housing and Urban-Rural Development (No. 2018ZD265, No. 2019ZD039, No. 2019ZD040, No. 2019ZD041).

References

1. Jiang, D., Wang, Y., Lv, Z., et al.: Big data analysis-based network behavior insight of cellular networks for industry 4.0 applications. IEEE Trans. Ind. Inf. **16**(2), 1310–1320 (2020)
2. Jiang, D., Wang, Y., Lv, Z., et al.: Intelligent optimization-based reliable energy-efficient networking in cloud services for IIoT networks. IEEE J. Selected Areas Communi. (2019)
3. Jiang, D., Wang, Y., Lv, Z., et al.: A joint multi-criteria utility-based network selection approach for vehicle-to-infrastructure networking. IEEE Trans. Intell. Transp. Syst. **19**(10), 3305–3319 (2018)
4. Jiang, D., Huo, L., Song, H.: Rethinking behaviors and activities of base stations in mobile cellular networks based on big data analysis. IEEE Trans. Netw. Sci. Eng. **1**(1), 1–2 (2018)
5. Jiang, D., Wang, W., Shi, L., et al.: A compressive sensing-based approach to end-to-end network traffic reconstruction. IEEE Trans. Netw. Sci. Eng. **5**(3), 1–12 (2018)
6. Jiang, D., Huo, L., Li, Y.: Fine-granularity inference and estimations to network traffic for SDN. PLoS ONE **13**(5), 1–23 (2018)
7. Jiang, D., Zhang, P., Lv, Z., et al.: Energy-efficient multi-constraint routing algorithm with load balancing for smart city applications. IEEE Internet Things J. **3**(6), 1437–1447 (2016)
8. Jiang, D., Li, W., Lv, H.: An energy-efficient cooperative multicast routing in multi-hop wireless networks for smart medical applications. Neurocomputing **220**(2017), 160–169 (2017)
9. Wang, Y., Jiang, D., Huo, L., et al.: A new traffic prediction algorithm to software defined networking. Mob. Netw. Appl. (2019)
10. Qi, S., Jiang, D., Huo, L.: A prediction approach to end-to-end traffic in space information networks. Mob. Netw. Appl. (2019)
11. Wang, F., Jiang, D., Qi, S., et al.: A dynamic resource scheduling scheme in edge computing satellite networks. Mob. Netw. Appl. (2019)
12. Wang, F., Jiang, D., Qi, S.: An adaptive routing algorithm for integrated information networks. China Commun. **7**(1), 196–207 (2019)
13. Huo, L., Jiang, D., Qi, S., et al.: An AI-based adaptive cognitive modeling and measurement method of network traffic for EIS. Mob. Netw. Appl. (2019)
14. Huo, L., Jiang, D., Lv, Z., et al.: An intelligent optimization-based traffic information acquirement approach to software-defined networking. Computat. Intell. **36**, 1–21 (2019)
15. Huo, L., Jiang, D., Zhu, X., et al.: An SDN-based fine-grained measurement and modeling approach to vehicular communication network traffic. Int. J. Commun. Syst. **33**, 1–12 (2019)
16. Song, H.Y., Zhang, J.G., Wang, J., et al.: Study on muscle fatigue property of human body in shoulder loaded walking based on surface electromyogram. J. Biomed. Eng. **33**(3), 426–430 (2016)
17. Wu, Q., Chen, X., Ding, L., et al.: Classification of EMG signals by BFA-optimized GSVCM for diagnosis of fatigue statu. IEEE Trans. Autom. Sci. Eng. **14**(2), 915–930 (2017)
18. Liu, J., Zou, R.L., Zhang, D.H., et al.: Analysis of the muscle fatigue based on band spectrum entropy of multi-channel surface electromyography. J. Biomed. Eng. **33**(3), 431–435 (2016)
19. Wang, K.: Conventional time-frequency method of SEMG and strategy used for dynamic muscle fatigue analysis. Chin. J. Sports Med. **29**(1), 104–108 (2010)

20. Naeem, U.J., Xiong, C.H.: FFM: a muscle fatigue index extraction by utilizing fuzzy network and mean power frequency. Int. J. Eng. Bus. Enterp. Appl. **3**(1), 25–35 (2013)
21. Chowdhury, R., Reaz, B.M.I., Islam, M.T.: Wavelet transform to recognize muscle fatigue. In: Proceedings of the 2012 Third Asian Himalayas International Conference on Internet, pp. 1–5. IEEE, Piscataway (2012)
22. Li, Z., Wang, B., Yang, C., et al.: Boosting-based EMG patterns classification scheme for robustness enhancement. IEEE J. Biomed. Health Inf. **17**(3), 545–552 (2013)
23. Chen, L., Zhang, L.: spectral efficiency analysis for massive MIMO system under QoS constraint: an effective capacity perspective. Mob. Netw. Appl. (2020). https://doi.org/10.1007/s11036-019-01414-4
24. Chen, L., Jiang, D., Bao, R., Xiong, J., Liu, F., Bei, L.: MIMO Scheduling effectiveness analysis for bursty data service from view of QoE. Chin. J. Electron. **26**(5), 1079–1085 (2017)
25. Husič, J.B., Baraković, S., Muminović, S.: Is there any impact of human influence factors on quality of experience? In: 2017 40th International Convention on Information and Communication Technology, Electronics and Microelectronics (MIPRO), Opatija, pp. 434–439 (2017)
26. De Moor, K., Arndt, S., Ammar, D., Voigt-Antons, J., Perkis, A., Heegaard, P.E.: Exploring diverse measures for evaluating QoE in the context of WebRTC. In: 2017 Ninth International Conference on Quality of Multimedia Experience (QoMEX), Erfurt, pp. 1–3 (2017)
27. Alja'afreh, M., Al Maadeed, S., Alja'am, J.M., El Saddik, A.: Towards a comprehensive study of fatigue deducing techniques for evaluating the quality of experience of haptic-visual applications. In: 2020 IEEE International Conference on Informatics, IoT, and Enabling Technologies (ICIoT), Doha, Qatar, pp. 339–344 (2020)
28. Fall, C.L., et al.: Wireless SEMG-based body-machine interface for assistive technology devices. IEEE J. Biomed. Health Inf. **21**(4), 967–977 (2017)
29. Zhang, M., Zhang, W., Zhang, B., Wang, Y., Li, G.: Feature selection of mime speech recognition using surface electromyography data. In: 2019 Chinese Automation Congress (CAC), Hangzhou, China, pp. 3173–3178 (2019)
30. Hulliyah, K., Bakar, N.S.A.A., Ismail, A.R.: Emotion recognition and brain mapping for sentiment analysis: a review. In: 2017 Second International Conference on Informatics and Computing (ICIC), Jayapura, pp. 1–5 (2017)
31. Tzirakis, P., Zhang, J., Schuller, B.W.: End-to-end speech emotion recognition using deep neural networks. In: 2018 IEEE International Conference on Acoustics, Speech and Signal Processing (ICASSP), Calgary, AB, pp. 5089–5093 (2018)
32. Zhao, W., Zhao, Z., Li, C.: Discriminative-CCA promoted By EEG signals for physiological-based emotion recognition. In: 2018 First Asian Conference on Affective Computing and Intelligent Interaction (ACII Asia), Beijing, pp. 1–6 (2018)
33. Chettupuzhakkaran, P., Sindhu, N.: Emotion recognition from physiological signals using time-frequency analysis methods. In: 2018 International Conference on Emerging Trends and Innovations in Engineering And Technological Research (ICETIETR), Ernakulam, pp. 1–5 (2018)
34. Işik, Ü., Güven, A.: Classification of emotion from physiological signals via artificial intelligence techniques. In: 2019 Medical Technologies Congress (TIPTEKNO), Izmir, Turkey, pp. 1–4 (2019)
35. Widanti, N., Sumanto, B., Rosa, P., Miftahudin, M.F.: Stress level detection using heart rate, blood pressure, and GSR and stress therapy by utilizing infrared. In: 2015 International Conference on Industrial Instrumentation and Control (ICIC), Pune, pp. 275–279 (2015)
36. Al Jaafreh, M., Hamam, A., El Saddik, A.: A framework to analyze fatigue for haptic-based tactile internet applications. In: 2017 IEEE International Symposium on Haptic, Audio and Visual Environments and Games (HAVE), Abu Dhabi, pp. 1–6 (2017)

37. Chen, L., et al.: A lightweight end-side user experience data collection system for quality evaluation of multimedia communications. IEEE Access **6**(1), 15408–15419 (2018)

38. Zhang, K., Chen, L., An, Y., et al.: A QoE test system for vehicular voice cloud services. Mob. Netw. Appl. (2020). https://doi.org/10.1007/s11036-019-01415-3

Load-Balanced Delivery Strategy for Linear Wireless Sensor Networks

Xuecheng Liu, Chuangeng Tian[✉], and Lei Chen

School of Information and Electrical Engineering,
Xuzhou University of Technology, Xuzhou 221004, China

Abstract. Linear Wireless Sensor Networks (LWSN) play an important role in bridge healthy monitoring, such as vibration, deformation, stress and so on. It is basically based on the observation that energy balance and delivery rate directly determine the running time of the networks. So, we proposed an energy balance aggregate model. Specially, we first compute the energy consumption and data delivery of each node in the network according to LWSN network model. The calculation conditions of energy balancing and delivery rate are then obtained. Finally, we have tested the performance of the proposed model. Simulation experimental results demonstrate that the proposed method can produce reliable performance, which is suitable for bridge healthy monitoring.

Keywords: Linear Wireless Sensor Networks · Bridge healthy monitoring · Energy balance · Delivery rate

1 Introduction

Bridge real-time online monitoring and state evaluation can ensure the safety of the bridge and extend its service life. Wireless sensor network (WSN) plays an important role in bridge health monitoring, such as vibration, deformation, stress and so on. WSN is generally characterized by a set of sensor nodes deployed in resource constrained fixed area [1, 2]. The collection nodes sense a specific characteristic phenomenon in bridge health monitoring and route the collected data to a relatively small number of sink nodes for processing and analyzing. The bridge health monitoring based on WSN is a time-consuming process, the speed and balance of energy consumption directly determine the running time of the networks [3–5].

Up to now, many energy balancing approaches have been presented to pursue the best trade-off between the different energy-consuming activities. Such as, Kacimi et al. [6] used lifetime maximizing for optimization of nodes energy consumption to improve network performance. To eliminate collisions and obtain a bound on the time required to complete converge-cast, TDMA scheduling algorithms has widely concerned, which are introduced under WSN-based framework [7–10]. Liu et al. [11] used TDMA scheduling algorithm for general k-hop networks, which aim to maximize network lifetime through optimal and selecting hop-count, and the number of timeslots. These methods

H. Song and D. Jiang (Eds.): SIMUtools 2020, LNICST 369, pp. 727–731, 2021.
https://doi.org/10.1007/978-3-030-72792-5_57

were exploited on the basis of energy balancing strategies and thus achieve fairly high performance. However, in most cases, delivery rate is ignored. We proposed a model which considering both delivery rate and energy balancing based on LWSN for bridge health monitoring.

2 Method

In the simplified LWSN, there are several standard nodes and one sink node, the standard nodes deliver the data to the sink node through the wireless link, which is shown in Fig. 1. In the process of data delivery, the standard node forwards the data to the sink node through any node. Suppose that in LSWN, node i needs to deliver N packets to the sink node in unit time, where the location of the sink node is denoted as s, and the probability of sending packets to neighbor node j is represented by p_{ij}, the probability of successful delivery is q_{ij}. Each node needs to receive and forward in the whole LWSN is denoted as follows:

The number of packets sent by node j is denoted and computed by,

$$N_{Tj} = N + \sum_{i=1}^{j} p_{ij} N_{Ti} \tag{1}$$

The number of packets received is calculated and indicated by,

$$N_{Rj} = \sum_{i=1}^{j} p_{ij} N_{Ti} \tag{2}$$

The total number of packets sent and received by node j is represented by,

$$N_j = N_{Tj} + N_{Rj} = N + 2\sum_{i=1}^{j} p_{ij} N_{Ti} \tag{3}$$

The number delivered by the ith node to the sink node is as,

$$N_{Di} = N\left(p_{is} q_{is} + \sum_{j=i+1}^{s-1} p_{ij} Q_{js} \right) \tag{4}$$

where $Q_{(s-1)s} = p_{(s-1)s} q_{(s-1)s}$.

In order to achieve energy balance, lower total energy consumption and higher delivery rate, the following relationships need to be met:

(1) $max(|N_i - N_j|) < \alpha$, where $i \neq j$ and $j = 1, 2, 3 \cdots s - 1$.
(2) $\sum_{i=1}^{s} N_i < \beta$
(3) $\sum_{i=1}^{s} N_{Di} > \gamma$

In general, the smaller the values of α and β show better, the larger the values of γ denotes better quality. When the total amount of node delivery is as small as possible, the smaller the difference in energy consumption between each node show the better. Due to the delivery rate of data decreases exponentially according to the distance between nodes, the farther the transmission distance, the lower the delivery success rate of data. We need to consider the delivery rate of data as well as the node delivery rate.

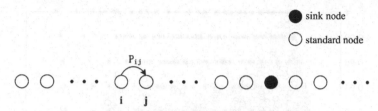

Fig. 1. LWSN network topology

3 Experimental Results and Analysis

3.1 Subjective Evaluation Analysis

The experimental network topology is shown in the Fig. 2. We present a network with four acquisition nodes and one sink node. Each acquisition node can communicate with two neighbour nodes. We set each standard node to transmit 1000 packets to the sink node, and the delivery rates of the two neighbour nodes are 1 and 0.8 respectively. At the interval of 0.1, the transmission probability of each acquisition node to the neighbour node is traversed, and the final delivery rate and energy consumption of the node are counted, so as to find the optimal link aggregation process.

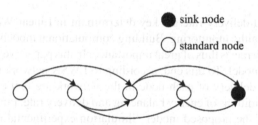

Fig. 2. Experiment topology.

3.2 Performance Evaluation

The simulation results are shown in Fig. 3. The abscissa represents the normalized variance of node energy consumption, which is used to represent the energy balance between nodes, "o" represents the delivery rate value of nodes, and "*" represents the total normalized energy consumption. It can be seen from the figure that the minimum total energy consumption is directly proportional to the delivery rate under the condition that the energy consumption difference of the whole node is small.

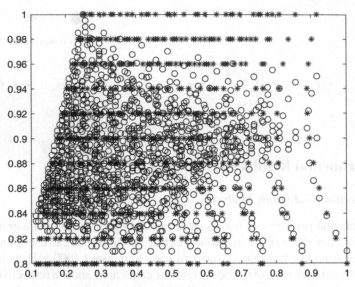

Fig. 3. Simulation results.

4 Conclusion

Energy balance and delivery rate are key determinant in Linear Wireless Sensor Networks for bridge healthy monitoring. Building computational models to estimate energy balance and delivery rate is thus of great importance. In this paper, we proposed an energy balance aggregate model. To this end, according to LWSN network model, energy consumption and data delivery of each node in the network are first computed. Then we give calculation conditions of energy balancing and delivery rate. Finally, we have tested the performance of the proposed model. Simulation experimental results demonstrate that the proposed method can produce reliable performance, which is suitable for bridge healthy monitoring.

Acknowledgment. This research was financially supported by the Xu Zhou Science and technology Program (KC17140).

References

1. Raghunathan, V., Schurgers, C., Park, S., Srivastava, M.B.: Energy-aware wireless microsensor networks. IEEE Signal Process. Mag. **19**(2), 40–50 (2002)
2. Shih, E., et al.: Physical layer driven protocol and algorithm design for energy-efficient wireless sensor networks. In: Proceedings of the 7th Annual International Conference on Mobile Computing and Networking (MobiCom 2001), pp. 272–287, ACM, New York (2001)
3. Daniele, T., Riccardo, S.: Microwave architectures for wireless mobile monitoring networks inside water distribution conduits. IEEE Trans. Microw. Theory Tech. **57**(12), 3298–3306 (2009)

4. Dong, W., Chen, C., Liu, X., Zheng, K., Chu, R., Bu, J.: FIT: a flexible, lightweight, and real-time scheduling system for wireless sensor platforms. IEEE Trans. Parallel Distrib. Syst. **21**(1), 126–138 (2010)
5. Gandham, S., Zhang, Y., Huang, Q.: Distributed minimal time converge-cast scheduling in wireless sensor networks. In: The 26th International Conference on Distributed Computing Systems (ICDCS06), Lisboan (2006)
6. Kacimi, R., Dhaou, R., Beylot, A.L.: Load balancing techniques for lifetime maximizing in wireless sensor networks. Ad Hoc Netw. **11**(8), 2172–2186 (2013)
7. Florens, C., McEliece, R.: Packets distribution algorithms for sensor networks. In: IEEE INFOCOM, San Diego, pp. 1063–1072 (2003)
8. Tao, S., Marwan, K.: Energy-efficient power/rate control and scheduling in hybrid TDMA/CDMA wireless sensor networks. Comput. Netw. **53**(9), 1395–1408 (2009)
9. Hossain, A., Radhika, T., Chakrabarti, S., Biswas, P.K.: Approach to increase the lifetime of a linear array of wireless sensor nodes. Int. J. Wirel. Inf. Netw. **15**, 72–81 (2008)
10. Powell, O., Leone, P., Rolim, J.: Energy optimal data propagation in wireless sensor networks. J. Parallel Distrib. Comput. **67**, 302–317 (2007)
11. Liu, A.F., Wu, X.Y., Chen, Z.G., Gui, W.H.: An Energy-Balanced data gathering algorithm for linear wireless sensor networks. Int. J. Wirel. Inf. Netw. **17**, 42–53 (2010)

Ecological Administration Contract Design for Enterprise and Local Government Based on Bottom-Line Thinking

Hongwei Lin[1] ⓘ, Chenggang Li[2(✉)] ⓘ, and Yihong Luo[3] ⓘ

[1] School of Public Health and Management, Hubei University of Medicine, Shiyan, China
[2] School of Economics, GuiZhou University of Finance and Economics,
Guiyang, Guizhou, China
[3] Guizhou Academy of Social Sciences, Guiyang, Guizhou, China

Abstract. Based on the perspective of ecological bottom-line thinking, government administration and corporate manufacturing are a new kind of cooperation instead of the relationship between cat and mouse. The corporate and the government are committed to sustainable economic development in the context of ecological and environmental protection. The ecological value preference parameters are introduced in the classic incentive contract model, and the improved incentive contract is constructed in the framework of ecological bottom-line and economic sustainable development thinking of government administration and corporate social responsibility, and the model equilibrium is analyzed. Finally, a numerical example is constructed to verify the correctness of the conclusion. The research results show that the introduction of ecological value preference parameters can effectively coordinate the interests of government and corporate, and control incentive costs; the ecological value preference of government and corporate, the marginal output of corporate and risk aversion will affect the change of incentive contracts.

Keywords: Bottom-line thinking · Government administration · Contract design

1 Introduction

Since the reform and opening up, with GDP as the main economic assessment indicator and the values of pollution before treatment, the demand for natural ecology far exceeds its carrying capacity. In some areas, local resources are being developed arbitrarily, and the relationship between economic development and ecological environmental protection has not been handled properly. Economic development has been traded at the expense of unrestrained consumption of resources and environmental damage, result in increasingly prominent energy resources and ecological environmental problems. Some areas do not hesitate to touch the ecological bottom line and have achieved short-term high-speed economic growth at the expense of the natural environment. However, due

H. Song and D. Jiang (Eds.): SIMUtools 2020, LNICST 369, pp. 732–747, 2021.
https://doi.org/10.1007/978-3-030-72792-5_58

to high resource consumption and heavy environmental pollution, which caused serious pollution of water bodies, the atmosphere or soil, urban haze weather has become the norm. The serious imbalance of natural ecosystems has become a serious problem for sustainable economic development. Facing the severe situation of intensified resource and environmental constraints, ecological environment pollution and ecosystem degradation, we must re-examine and coordinate the relationship between ecology and development.

Under the environmental governance system, it must emphasize and establish the ecological development concept of Lucid waters and lush mountains are invaluable assets, building an environmental administration system in which the government dominates, enterprises as the main body, social organizations and the public participate together, and improving the ecological environment Management system to resolutely stop and punish acts that damage the ecological environment. The economic development model based on development and ecological bottom line thinking reflects the value orientation and ecological ethics of ecological civilization construction. The economic development mode based on the bottom-line thinking means controlling economic construction activities within the range that the natural environment can bear, advocating the construction of ecological civilization, promoting the trans-formation of economic development pattern, and combine ecological environmental protection with the optimization of the spatial distribution of productivity to form a spatial structure of resource-saving and protecting environment. We will insist on building an environmentally-friendly economy and sustainable development with low cost, high efficiency, low emissions.

Under circumstance of the new normal of economic development, the government should not only ensure sustained and rapid development of economic construction in accordance with the established goals, but also enable enterprises to obtain considerable economic benefits, While achieving economic benefits, enterprises do not sacrifice the eco-logical environment at the expense of the ecological environment, but also promote the restoration and protection of the ecological environment system. We intend to introduce preference parameters of corporate social responsibility, and discuss the long-term mechanism design of sustainable economic development in the context of corporate social responsibility and government governance from the perspective of keeping the bottom-line of economic development and ecological protection. On the one hand, enterprises should bear the corporate social responsibility to protect the environment, and can obtain considerable economic benefits without touching the ecological bottom-line. On the other hand, the government should strengthen the ecological environment management, which not only can protect the ecological environment system, but also ensure the economy runs smoothly, safely and sustainable.

The paper is organized as follows. In Sect. 2, we review the literature regarding bottom-line thinking involving development and conservation of ecosystem between enterprise and government. We not only discuss the difference of ecological bottom-line and ecological bottom red line but also the game between enterprise and government. We have built contract model and assumption in Sect. 3. We analyzed the model and discuss influence on parameters in Sect. 4. The validity of model is verified with a numerical example and simulation in Sect. 5, and we conclude in Sect. 6.

2 Literature Review

Bottom-line thinking is a kind of strategic thinking, a thinking method and mentality bottom-line-oriented. It is an insurmountable critical line, critical point or critical area that the main body set according to his own interests, emotions, morals, and laws. It will lead to qualitative changes in attitudes, positions and decisions once the main body crosses the bottom-line (Louwei 2015). Bottom-line thinking points out possible risks and worst-case scenarios, and makes scientific judgments through systematic thinking, then keeps the bottom-line and pursues the best results of the system. It not only warns people to take precautions, carefully evaluate development risks, but also guides people to be mentally prepared to turn challenges into opportunities and passive to active, pursues the best results from the worst, and pursue the most optimized results while keeping the bottom-line, in order to achieve the best results and better established goals (Zou et al. 2015).

The bottom-line thinking is applied to the construction of ecological civilization, that is, the ecological bottom-line. It refers to the ecological security line that cannot be broken out. It is the minimum standard for maintaining basic regional ecosystem and ecological security. It is not only including a synthetic system that maintaining basic ecosystem services, the security pattern of hydrological regulation, climate regulation, water supply, and biodiversity protection, but also including the bottom-line of ecological function, environmental quality and safety, and natural re-source use, etc. (Liu 2015) Similar to the ecological bottom-line, there is also the ecological red line. Whether it is the ecological bottom line or the ecological red line in the perspective of connotation, it is the lifeline of ecological security, public health, sustainable development, and the ecological environment. Ecological red-line is a legal or institutional management tool with legally binding protection for the ecological bottom-line and restricts acts that damage ecosystems. Therefore, the ecological bottom-line more reflects the load-carrying limit of the natural system itself, and the ecological red-line is a kind of protection line set by the law and helping to keep the ecological bottom-line, it is the legal basis for investigating the legal responsibility for destroying the ecological environment (Wenzhi 2016).

Many scholars have studied the relationship between ecological environmental protection and economic development from different perspectives. For example, Peter Vandergeest et al. (2012) believe that transnational ecological certification can strengthen global ecological protection. The education policy of sustainable ecological-centered proposed by Gorobets A (2014) that can shape people's mentality and behavior, rather than dominate the current Economic growth model to avoid systemic global environmental problems. Zhang Wei et al. (2011) believe that a platform for government-business cooperation should be established to provide a green technical support system and financial services, support the construction of ecological civilization, incorporate ecological civilization indicators into the performance evaluation of government, and strengthen ecological civilization legislation. DeCanio S J et al. (2013) applied game theory to study the issue of climate diplomacy, discusses the prisoner's dilemma, the cock-fighting game and so on by constructing the 2 x 2 game model, intergovernmental negotiations depended on the severity of climate change risks. Shaoqing Chen et al. (2013) Proposed a comprehensive ecosystem-oriented risk assessment, which is helpful for environmental management. Korhonen J (2004) studied strategic decisions for sustainable development from the perspective of industrial ecology, and promoted industrial ecological integration through ecological economics and environmental management. Boland A et al. (2012) Studied the public participa-tion of community-based environmental protection activities, and discussed the incentive structure of project organizers and participants for China's green community activities.

However, Chinese scholars research the strategic games among government, enterprises and environmental protection departments from the perspective of game theory. Chuanjiang Liu (2014) believes that the essence of the environmental pollution problem in the new urbanization construction is the result of a game of the four main interests of the central government, local governments, enterprises and farmers. Like Wang (2016) believes that the primary task of the local government's environmental pollution prevention and control policy reform is to break through the complex interest entanglements. Xu Lin (2016) used dynamic game theories to establish the game models of government and polluting companies, polluting companies and insurance companies, respectively, Research conclusions show that to break through the plight of environmental pollution responsibility, the government should improve environ-mental legislation as soon as possible, strictly enforce the law, and provide insurance companies and insurance companies with Appropriate subsidies. Li Bin's (2015) research shows that the expansion of land finance scale has exacerbated environmental pollution, and economic growth, urbanization and energy efficiency are reasons of environ-mental pollution. Sunzhe Wong (2018) believes that the distortion of incentives will lead to poor government supervision, and setting strict responsibilities can reduce incentives. Wenbing Luo et al. (2015) believed that the establishment of a total emission control and distribution mechanism for pollutants in river valleys could strengthen the prevention and control of water pollution. Sun han's (2015) research shows that the government's environmental super-vision and related policy support is an important means to promote water pollution control in the western minority areas. Studies such as Fengxia Han et al. (2017) believe that the government should increase penalties for non-environmental protection behaviors, and enterprises should carry out green design and production, change production mode and protect the ecological environment through the support of green finance. Tong Yan (2016) believes that reasonable rules and technological innovation should be established to reduce pollution costs. Wang Xianjia (2018) used the evolutionary game to coordinate the path of environmental governance by considering the benefit coefficient, cost and vision level. Liao Qi et al. (2019) Proceeded from the protection of the ecological barrier in Hu-bei, which believed that the battle against pollution prevention and control should be done well and the ecological environment safety should be continuously improved. Zheng Jianxia et al. (2017) Studied the planning innovation and institutional break-throughs in the transition from ecological priority to ecological control from the aspects of ecological protection red line planning, concept definition, red line delineation, and policy control in Ningbo.

Based on the above comprehensive analysis, there are many studies on ecological environment issues, there still exist some problems: some scholars mainly focus on ecological environmental protection, industrial ecology and global ecological issues from a perspective of macro level, while the others scholars research eco-environment issues from a perspective of micro-level, for example, mainly focus on game theory between government and enterprises. Which protects the ecological environment through environmental policies, environmental legislation and punitive measures.

None of the above studies think about bottom-thinking from the perspectives of development, ecology and corporate social responsibility. We intend to establish a contract based on corporate social responsibility (CSR) and government management from the framework of development and ecological bottom-line thinking and corporate social responsibility, the assay introduce CSR value preference parameters into the contract, to discuss impacts of contract resulted from value preference parameter of the government, marginal output of enterprise unit effort based on CSR and risk aversion attitude of the enterprise. The government and enterprises will change the traditional game "cat chases for mice" through cooperation and creation, they are no longer conflicting. The government supports enterprises with technological reforms and industrial upgrading. Based on the corporate social responsibility, applying bottom-line thinking, the enterprise obtains economic benefit through developing green economy, recycling economy and other ecological economy methods, the government achieves good political performance through green GDP.

3 Model Assumption and Establishment

Within the framework of development and ecological bottom-line thinking, both governments and enterprises will consider their own benefits in long run, the government requires enterprises to fulfill their corporate social responsibilities and create more economic value and social value without touching the ecological bottom-line or ecological red-line. In order to obtain long-term benefits, enterprises generally also perform corporate social responsibilities and carry out production in the conditions of protecting the ecological environment system in accordance with the requirements of the government to govern the environment. When enterprises transform from destructive production to ecological economy or implement environmental protection measures, it is generally necessary to experience technological reform & industrial structure upgrading and input manpower and financial & material resources of large quantity, which increases production and management costs with reduced operation profit, and so, enterprises have no motivation to perform actively their corporate social responsibilities and participate in ecological environment construction. Therefore, in order to the government will take measures to curb environmental pollution. Therefore, government will provide political and fund supports for enterprises, stimulating them to input on environmental protection and ecological civilization construction, so as to ensure the normal operation and sustainable development of the economic and social development as well as to protect the ecological environment system from damage.

To explain game behavior between government (G) and enterprise (E), assumptions are hereby made as follows:

Assumption 1. To make convenience for problem discussion without loss of generality, it is assumed that enterprise should transform from destructive production to sustainable ecological economic production based on bottom-line thinking, the benefits created through ecological economic construction or transformation as $w = re + \varepsilon$. Where, e

refers to effort level made by enterprises to meet requirement of ecological economic transformation (including the input of manpower, financial resources, material resources, technical reform and structure upgrading, etc., For the convenience of the discussion, the following efforts are the same as those expressed here) based on corporate social responsibilities. $e \in [0, +\infty)$;r refers to marginal output made by enterprises working on ecological economy, which subject to effort level of enterprise, ε refers to exogenous and independent random variable. It is assumed that random variable should comply with $N(0, \sigma^2)$ distribution.

Assumption 2. It is assumed that in order to stimulate enterprise to undertake corporate social responsibilities and engage in ecological economic construction, the government should provide enterprise with linear mixed incentive contract $s = \alpha + \beta w$. Where:α refers to fixed compensation provided by government to compensate enterprise for eco-logical economic construction investment and carry out corporate social responsibilities; $\beta \in [0, 1]$ refers to distribution coefficient provided by government for enterprises work-ing on ecological economic construction and creating value (it is assumed hereof that government should distribute earnings with enterprises through fiscal taxation); larger β indicates less tax collected by government from enterprises and more support of govern-ment for enterprise, and vice versa. When α is 0, it indicates that government provides performance contract; when β is 0, it is fixed contract. Meanwhile, effort cost function of enterprise is assumed as $C = be^2/2$, where b refers to effort cost coefficient of enter-prise. Effort cost of enterprise is related to effort level e,with $C'(e) > 0, C''(e) > 0$. Namely, C is the strictly convex function of e. With effort level e increasing, effort cost C increases more rapidly.

Assumption 3. Assuming the government is risk-neutral and enterprise is risk-averse; the absolute risk- aversion measurement of $\rho > 0$, risk cost should be $\rho\beta^2\sigma^2/2$.

According to the above assumption, certain equivalence income of enterprise is

$$CE_E = \alpha + \beta re - be^2/2 - \rho\beta^2\sigma^2/2$$

Assumption 4. As the regulator, government shall consider both long-term interest of ecological environmental protection & sustainable development and value creation of enterprise interest during the process of decision making, ensuring economic and social sustainable development. Furthermore, without loss of generality, reservation utility of enterprise is assumed as $\tilde{u} = 0$.

Based on the above assumptions, the decision-making behavior of government can be expressed as:

$$\max_{\alpha,\beta,e} EU_G = (1 - \lambda)[(1 - \beta)re - \alpha] + \lambda re \tag{1}$$

$$s.t. \quad (IR)\alpha + \beta re - be^2/2 - \rho\beta^2\sigma^2/2 > \tilde{u} \tag{2}$$

$$(IC)e \in \arg\max \alpha + \beta re - be^2/2 - \rho\beta^2\sigma^2/2 \tag{3}$$

Where, $\lambda \in [0, 1]$ is the ecological value preference parameter of government; when $\lambda \to$ 1, government pays more attention to GDP that creation of enterprise for the government and allows the enterprise to destroy the ecological environment for production. When $\lambda \to 0$, it means that government prefers to focus on the protection of the ecosystem and sustainable development of economic construction considering ecological bottom-line thinking. Promoting the upgrading of industrial structure, industrial transformation to protect the environment with incentive measurement.

4 Model Equilibrium and Analysis

4.1 Model Equilibrium

Backward induction is applied to solve game equilibrium between government and enterprise based on development and ecological bottom-line thinking underneath. Since incentives and constraints cannot be constrained under complete information conditions, government governance can force companies to execute contracts. Therefore, for the optimal problem (1), in the equilibrium state, the constraints in formula (2) are tight. Namely, the following formula comes into existence:

$$\alpha + \beta re = be^2/2 + \rho\beta^2\sigma^2/2 + \tilde{u}$$

Substituting the above formula into the objective function (1):

$$\max_{\alpha,\beta} re - (1 - \lambda)(be^2/2 + \rho\beta^2\sigma^2/2 + \tilde{u}) \tag{4}$$

Furthermore, calculate the first-order optimal condition of the effort level in formula (3):

$$e = \beta r/b \tag{5}$$

Substituting formula (5) into formula (4), and calculate β the first derivative, we get the optimal benefit distribution coefficient of government and enterprises based on bottom-line thinking to encourage enterprises to protect the ecological environment and implement industrial structure upgrade and transformation:

$$\beta^* = r^2/(1 - \lambda)(r^2 + b\rho\sigma^2). \tag{6}$$

Substituting formula (6) into formula (5), we can get the optimal effort level of the enterprise:

$$e^* = r^3/(1 - \lambda)b(r^2 + b\rho\sigma^2). \tag{7}$$

According to the conditions of β^*, e^* and formula (2), the optimal incentive compensation given by the government can be calculated as:

$$\alpha^* = \left[r^4(b\rho\sigma^2 - r^2)/2(1 - \lambda)^2 b(r^2 + b\rho\sigma^2)^2\right] + \tilde{u} \tag{8}$$

Where, when $\alpha^* < 0$ at $b\rho\sigma^2 \leq r^2$ indicates the enterprise would be required to pay the government the protection costs caused by environmental damage for production, and the government would pay the funds for ecological environmental protection;

when $\alpha^* \geq 0$ at $bp\sigma^2 \geq r^2$ indicates the government will compensate the enterprise amount of expenses to support technological transformation, upgrading and other investment, encouraging enterprises protect the ecological environment which is conducive to sustainable economic development based on development and ecological bottom-line thinking.

4.2 Model Analysis

To discuss the win-win cooperation mechanism between the government and enterprise from the perspective of bottom-line thinking, the other exogenous parameters involved in the fixed standard model remain the same. Now analyzing ecological value preference parameters of government's, marginal output of efforts and risk aversion attitudes, discussing the impact of these variables on contract parameters, performance, optimal effort levels, and costs.

4.2.1 Analysis of Contract Parameters

Proposition 1. Given that the model and other parameters are invariable:

1) With λ increasing, the government will provide enterprise with higher income distribution coefficients and compensation for transformation and upgrading. Affected by the contract adjustment, the optimal effort level of enterprise will improve and the total revenue w will increase.
2) With r increasing, for $0 < r^2 \leq 0.5616bp\sigma^2$, the government will enlarge the distribution coefficient and compensation of enterprises to ensure that enterprises protect the ecological environment based on bottom-line thinking. When enterprise marginal output meets $0.5616bp\sigma^2 < r^2 \leq bp\sigma^2$, government will further increase distribution coefficient of enterprise and reduce fixed compensation α to regulate enterprise income. Under the influence of contract modification, the optimal effort level of enterprise will increase with marginal output r increasing.
3) With ρ increasing, the income distribution coefficient of the enterprise will decrease. Affected by contract modification, the effort level of enterprise will decrease too. When $\rho \in (0, 3r^2/b\sigma^2)$ condition is satisfied, the government will only reduce the distribution coefficient of enterprises, but does not reduce fixed compensation for enterprises. When $\rho \in (3r^2/b\sigma^2, +\infty)$ condition is satisfied, government will decrease both enterprise distribution coefficient and fixed compensation.

Proof. Let's prove the conclusion (1) in proposition 1. Fix other parameters invariable and calculate first-order derivative of λ in formula (6)~formula (8):

$$\partial\beta^*/\partial\lambda = r^2/(1-\lambda)^2(r^2 + bp\sigma^2) > 0$$

$$\partial e^*/\partial\lambda = r^3/(1-\lambda)^2 b(r^2 + bp\sigma^2) > 0$$

$$\partial\alpha^*/\partial\lambda = r^4/(1-\lambda)^3 b(r^2 + bp\sigma^2)^2 > 0$$

It can be inferred from the derivation result that β^*, e^* and α^* increase with λ increasing. It is obviously knowable in combination with formula $w = re + \varepsilon$ that total revenue w will increase with effort level e increasing.

Let's prove the conclusion (2) in Proposition 1, and similarly, calculate first-order derivative r in formula (6)~formula (7):

$$\frac{\partial \beta^*}{\partial r} = \frac{2rb\rho\sigma^2}{(1-\lambda)(r^2 + b\rho\sigma^2)^2} > 0, \quad \frac{\partial e^*}{\partial r} = \frac{r^2(r^2 + 3b\rho\sigma^2)}{(1-\lambda)b(r^2 + b\rho\sigma^2)^2} > 0$$

The result of derivation indicates that β^* and e^* increase with marginal output r increasing.

Formula (8) calculates first-order derivative for r

$$\frac{\partial \alpha^*}{\partial r} = -\frac{\lambda^2 r^3 [r^4 + 3b\rho\sigma^2 r^2 - 2b^2\rho^2\sigma^4]}{(1-\lambda)^4 b(r^2 + b\rho\sigma^2)^3}$$

Obviously, symbol of $\partial a^*/\partial r$ is subject to $\varphi(r) = r^4 + 3b\rho\sigma^2 r^2 - 2b^2\rho^2\sigma^4$. Solve $\varphi(r)$ and reach the following conclusion:

$\partial a^*/\partial r > 0$ at $r^2 \in (0, 0.5616b\rho\sigma^2]$, it can be known through $\partial\beta^*/\partial r > 0$ that government will increase enterprise distribution coefficient and fixed compensation to ensure that enterprises protect ecological and cleaner production; $\partial a^*/\partial r < 0$ at $r^2 \in (0.5616b\rho\sigma^2, b\rho\sigma^2]$, it can be known through $\partial\beta^*/\partial r > 0$ that government will further increase enterprise distribution coefficient, and will reduce fixed compensation α to regulate enterprise income; conclusion (2) in proposition 1 comes into existence according to $\partial e^*/\partial r > 0$.

For the conclusion (3) in Proposition 1, calculate first-order derivation for formula (6)~formula (7):

$$\frac{\partial \beta^*}{\partial \rho} = -\frac{r^2}{(1-\lambda)} \cdot \frac{b\rho^2}{(r^2 + b\rho\sigma^2)^2} < 0$$

$$\frac{\partial e^*}{\partial \rho} = -\frac{r^3}{(1-\lambda)b} \cdot \frac{b\rho^2}{(r^2 + b\rho\sigma^2)^2} < 0$$

$$\frac{\partial \alpha^*}{\partial \rho} = \frac{\sigma^2 r^4}{2(1-\lambda)^2} \cdot \frac{(3r^2 - b\rho\sigma^2)}{(r^2 + b\rho\sigma^2)^3}$$

$\partial\alpha^*/\partial\rho > 0$ at $3r^2 - b\rho\sigma^2 > 0$, namely: $0 < \rho < 3r^2/b\sigma^2$; $\partial\alpha^*/\partial\rho < 0$ at $3r^2 - b\rho\sigma^2 < 0$. Conclusion (3) shows that there is a certain interval for the risk aversion measures of enterprises. Within the interval, the government will only reduce the distribution coefficient, but will not reduce the level of fixed compensation. When outside the interval, the government will reduce both the distribution coefficient and fixed compensation, and even levies environmental protection costs on the enterprise.

Proposition 1 illustrates that the optimal effort level, distribution coefficient, and fixed compensation provided of the government for the enterprise based on bottom-line thinking for ecological civilization production are functions of the government's ecological value preference parameters, the enterprise's marginal output, and risk aversion parameters. When the government encourages enterprises to transform and upgrade to engage in ecological economic construction ($\lambda \to 1$) based on bottom-line thinking, they will provide enterprises with a higher income distribution coefficient and fixed compensation. Affected by government incentives, enterprise will improve their level of effort in upgrading and transformation, and at the same time, their total revenue will increase. When the marginal output of unit effort increases, the government will simultaneously by transforming incentive method of increasing distribution coefficient and fixed compensation to the method of enterprise performance level. At the same time, the enterprise will improve and maintain higher level of effort. When the enterprise risk aversion attitude increases, namely to reduce investment in environmental protection and ecological economic construction, the government will reduce the performance income of the enterprise, and levy more taxes on environmental protection expenses. When enterprise risk aversion level is within the expectation of government, it will only decrease distribution coefficient, and will not reduce fixed compensation for enterprise; if it exceeds expectation of government, it will reduce both distribution coefficient and fixed compensation of enterprise. Enterprise is enforced to carry out technological transformation and industrial upgrading based on bottom-line thinking through reverse incentives.

4.2.2 Economic Benefit Analysis

Proposition 2. Given the model and other parameters are invariant, and the following conclusions may be drawn:

1) As the value preference parameter λ increases, the economic output of enterprises will increase while revenue (mainly tax) of government will decrease. When $\lambda \in (0, 1/2)$, income of government is positive with per unit increasing income of enterprise greater than that of government. When $\lambda \in (1/2, 1)$, income of government is negative with per unit increasing income of enterprise less than that of government.

2) As the marginal output r increases, the economic output of the enterprise will increase. When $0 < \lambda < 1/2$, the government's certainty income will increase as r increases; when $1/2 \leq \lambda < 1$, certain income of government will decrease as r increases.

3) As risk measurement ρ increases, the economic output of the enterprise will decrease. When $\lambda \in (0, 1/2)$, certain income of government will decrease as ρ increases; when $\lambda \in [1/2, 1)$, certain income of government will increase as ρ increases.

Prove. Proving conclusion (1) Firstly. Based on formula (6)~formula (8), calculating the economic output of enterprise and certain income of government respectively as following:

$$Ew = re^* = r^4/(1 - \lambda)b(r^2 + b\rho\sigma^2) \tag{9}$$

$$CE_G = (1 - \beta^*)re^* - \alpha^* = \left[r^4(1 - 2\lambda)/2(1 - \lambda)^2 b(r^2 + b\rho\sigma^2)\right] - \tilde{u} \tag{10}$$

Calculating first derivative for formula (9) and formula (10) concerning λ:

$$\partial Ew/\partial \lambda = r^4/(1-\lambda)^2 b(r^2 + b\rho\sigma^2) > 0,$$

The results show that Ew will increases with λ increasing and decrease with λ increasing. in other words, the economic output of enterprises will increase while the government's certainty revenue will decrease. If set $\tilde{u} = 0$ and $CE_G = 0$ then $\lambda = 1/2$. Since $|\partial Ew/\partial \lambda/\partial CE_G/\partial \lambda| = 1 - \lambda/\lambda$, for any $0 < \lambda < 1/2$, $CE_G > 0$, $1 - \lambda/\lambda > 1$ indicates that income of government is positive but per unit increasing income of enterprise is greater than that of government. For any $1/2 < \lambda < 1, CE_G < 0$ $1 - \lambda/\lambda < 1$ indicates that income of government is negative and per unit increasing income of enterprise is less than that of government. At this moment, government not only obtains no tax revenues from enterprise but gives funding to ecological economic construction of enterprise which are used for upgrading and technological transformation for environmental protection construction.

Next proving the conclusion (2). Calculating first derivative for formula (9) and formula (10) concerning r respectively:

$$\frac{\partial Ew}{\partial r} = \frac{2r^3(r^2 + 2b\rho\sigma^2)}{(1-\lambda)b(r^2 + b\rho\sigma^2)^2} > 0,$$

$$\frac{\partial CE_G}{\partial r} = \frac{(1-2\lambda)r^3(r^2 + 2b\rho\sigma^2)}{(1-\lambda)^2 b(r^2 + 2b\rho\sigma^2)^2}.$$

According to $\partial Ew/\partial r > 0$, as r increases, economic outcome of enterprise will increase.

According to the sigh of $\partial CE_G/\partial r$, conclusions can be drawn: when $\lambda \in (0, 1/2)$, it has $\partial CE_G/\partial r \geq 0$ which shows that income of government will increase as r increases. When $1/2 \leq \lambda < 1$, there is $\partial CE_G/\partial r < 0$ which shows that income of government will decrease as r increases.

For the conclusion (3) in the proposition, calculating first derivative for formula (9) and formula (10) concerning ρ respectively:

$$\frac{\partial Ew}{\partial \rho} = -\frac{r^4}{(1-\lambda)b} \cdot \frac{b\sigma^2}{(r^2 + b\rho\sigma^2)^2} < 0, \quad \frac{\partial CE_G}{\partial \rho} = -\frac{r^4(1-2\lambda)}{2(1-\lambda)^2 b} \cdot \frac{b\sigma^2}{(r^2 + b\rho\sigma^2)^2}$$

According to $\partial Ew/\partial \rho < 0$, It is known that risk aversion is enhancing, the economic returns of enterprise will decrease. When $\lambda \in (0, 1/2), \partial CE_G/\partial \rho > 0$ which indicates that as ρ increases income of government will decrease. When $\lambda \in [1/2, 1), \partial CE_G/\partial \rho > 0$ which shows that as ρ increases income of government will increase.

Proposition 2 shows that in the process of the government governing the environment and motivating enterprises, if the government pays more attention to ecological values and supports the upgrading of enterprises ($\lambda \to 1$), the economic income both government and enterprises will be increasing. When $\lambda \in (0, 1/2)$, revenue of government is positive while revenue of government itself will decrease and increasing income of enterprise will be greater than decreasing income of government. When $\lambda \in (1/2, 1)$, income of government is negative while increasing income of enterprise will be less than decreasing income of government. During the process of actual distribution, government will adjust distribution coefficient β and fixed compensation α to adjust income of enterprise and result in income of government more reasonable. Therefore, when value preference of government prefers to mutual benefits, namely, the government focus on long-term interests with the bottom-line thinking, the revenue of both government and enterprises will increase to achieve win-win. When risk aversion of enterprise is enhanced and only short-term benefits are considered, the overall benefits will decrease as well as income of government.

4.2.3 Cost Analysis

Proposition 3. Given the model and other parameters are invariant, and the following conclusions may be drawn:

(1) With the increasing of λ, the incentive costs and the general agency costs of enterprises due to information asymmetry will decrease. When $\lambda \in [0, b\rho\sigma^2/2(r^2 + b\rho\sigma^2))$, both incentive cost and the general agency cost are positive. When $\lambda \in (b\rho\sigma^2/2(r^2 + b\rho\sigma^2), 1/2)$, incentive cost is negative while general agency cost of enterprise is positive. When $\lambda \in (1/2, 1]$, both incentive cost and general agency cost of enterprise are negative.

(2) When $\lambda \in (0, 1/2)$, general agency cost of enterprise caused by information asymmetry will increase with r increasing. When $\lambda \in (1/2, 1)$, general agency cost of enterprise caused by information asymmetry will decrease with r increasing. With increasing r, government will control general agency cost with choosing value preference parameter which is close to $1/2$.

Proof. The relation between government and the enterprise is actually principal-agent. For conclusion (1), when the information is symmetrical, the government can observe the effort level that enterprise protects the ecological environment, and then the incentive compatibility constraint *IC* is invalidated. The objective function of the government is as following:

$$\max_{\beta, e} u' = re - \frac{1}{2}(1 - \lambda)be^2 - \frac{1}{2}(1 - \lambda)\rho\beta^2\sigma^2 \tag{11}$$

Calculating first derivative for formula (11) concerning β and e respectively, the distribution coefficient and optimal effort level of the enterprise are as following:

$$\beta^{**} = 0, \ e^{**} = r/(1 - \lambda)b.$$

$\beta^{**} = 0$ shows that government only provides fixed compensation to the enterprises when the information is symmetric. $e^{**} - e^* < 0$ shows that the effort level of enterprise that protect the environment will decrease when the information changes from symmetric to asymmetric. The net loss of economic income due to the deceasing in the effort level of enterprise is:

$$\Delta Ew = re^{**} - re^* = \rho r^2\sigma^2/(1 - \lambda)(r^2 + b\rho\sigma^2). \tag{12}$$

While corresponding cost savings of effort is as following:

$$\Delta C = \frac{be^{**2} - be^{*2}}{2} = \frac{(2r^2 + b\rho\sigma^2)\rho\sigma^2 r^2}{2(1-\lambda)^2(r^2 + b\rho\sigma^2)^2} \tag{13}$$

The incentive costs incurred by the government is:

$$\Delta IC = \Delta Ew - \Delta C = \frac{-2\lambda\rho\sigma^2 r^4 + (1-2\lambda)br^2\rho^2\sigma^4}{2(1-\lambda)^2(r^2 + b\rho\sigma^2)^2} \tag{14}$$

Meantime, the risk cost due to asymmetric information is

$$\Delta RC = \frac{\rho\sigma^2 r^4}{2(1-\lambda)^2(r^2 + b\rho\sigma^2)^2} \tag{15}$$

Add incentive cost to risk cost to get the general agency cost:

$$TC = \frac{(1-2\lambda)\rho r^2\sigma^2}{2(1-\lambda)^2(r^2 + b\rho\sigma^2)} \tag{16}$$

Calculating first derivative for ΔIC and TC concerning λ respectively:

$$\frac{\partial \Delta IC}{\partial \lambda} = -\frac{(1+\lambda)\rho\sigma^2 r^4 + \lambda br^2\rho^2\sigma^4}{(1-\lambda)^3(r^2 + b\rho\sigma^2)} < 0, \quad \frac{\partial TC}{\partial \lambda} = -\frac{\lambda\rho r^2\sigma^2}{(1-\lambda)^3(r^2 + b\rho\sigma^2)} < 0$$

According to $\partial\Delta IC/\partial\lambda < 0$ and $\partial TC/\partial\lambda < 0$, incentive cost of enterprise and general agency cost due to the information asymmetry will decrease with λ increasing.

There is $\Delta IC > 0$ and $TC > 0$ in the condition of $\lambda \in [0, b\rho\sigma^2/2(r^2 + b\rho\sigma^2))$, namely, the incentive cost and general cost of the information due to changes from symmetric to asymmetric are both positive; there is $\Delta IC < 0$ and $TC > 0$ in the condition of $\lambda \in (b\rho\sigma^2/2(r^2 + b\rho\sigma^2), 1/2)$, which means incentive cost is negative and general agency cost is positive caused by the information changes from symmetric to asymmetric; there is $\Delta IC < 0, TC < 0$ in the condition of $\lambda \in (1/2, 1]$, in other words, both the incentive cost and the general cost of the information from symmetric to asymmetric are negative.

For the conclusion (2), $\partial TC/\partial r = (1-2\lambda)rb\rho^2\sigma^4/(1-\lambda)^2(r^2 + b\rho\sigma^2)^2 > 0$ in the condition of $0 < \lambda < 1/2$, which shows that when value preference parameter $\lambda \in (0, 1/2)$, TC will increase as r increases.

When $\lambda \in (1/2, 1)$, $\partial TC/\partial r = (1-2\lambda)rb\rho^2\sigma^4/(1-\lambda)^2(r^2 + b\rho\sigma^2)^2 < 0$, which shows that when value preference parameter $\lambda > 1/2$, TC will decrease as r increases. Because of monotonically decreases that $(1-2\lambda)/(1-\lambda)^2$ in the condition of $\lambda \in (0, 1)$, concerning TC with r increasing, government will choose value preference parameter that is close to $1/2$ controlling general agency cost.

Proposition 3 shows that under state of uncertain information, government will prefer to ecological value. Based on development and ecological bottom-line thinking, government will adopt measures of incentives, encouraging enterprise invests in costs to promote technological reform and upgrading result in win-win, ecosystem and enterprise development can operate well. In order to sustain this economic operation mode for a long term, government may decrease the pressure of information asymmetry, incentive cost, agency cost and increase economic output efficiency of enterprise. When marginal output of enterprise increases, government shall choose greater value preference parameter to control cost and achieve win-win cooperation.

5 Numerical Examples and Simulation

Assuming a local government G to encourage enterprise E to protect the ecological environment from the mode of traditional production to technological transformation and upgrading based on bottom-line of development and ecological. Assuming marginal output of the enterprise's efforts is r and the ecological value preference parameter of government governance is λ. Assuming enterprise's absolute risk aversion measure is ρ, the effort cost coefficient is b, and the standard deviation is σ. Assuming α, β, e are the fixed compensation, distribution coefficient and effort level of the enterprise respectively. Assuming w is income that enterprise engaged in ecological economic construction, CE_G is the government revenue, ΔIC, TC are the incentive cost and the general agency cost, respectively. And it is assumed that the retention utility of the enterprise is 0. Assumed numerical examples of each parameter and other specific numerical changes are shown in Table 1.

Table 1. Comparison of changes in government and enterprise parameters

r	λ	ρ	b	σ	α	β	e	w	CE_G	ΔIC	TC
2.00*	0.30	0.75	0.80	35.00	0.03	0.02	0.02	0.04	0.01	2.00	2.03
4.00*	0.30	0.75	0.80	35.00	0.42	0.05	0.15	0.61	0.16	7.56	7.99
6.00*	0.30	0.75	0.80	35.00	1.94	0.10	0.50	3.00	0.76	15.47	17.51
7.00*	0.30	0.75	0.80	35.00	3.42	0.13	0.78	5.47	1.34	19.78	23.44
8.00*	0.30	0.75	0.80	35.00	5.49	0.16	1.14	9.15	2.20	24 02	30.04
10.00	0.20*	0.75	0.80	45.00	6.30	0.10	1.19	11.88	4.40	47.28	54.14
10.00	0.30*	0.75	0.80	45.00	8.22	0.10	1.36	13.58	4.00	38.18	47.14
10.00	0.60*	0.75	0.80	45.00	25.19	0.15	2.38	23.76	− 4.99	− 99.63	− 72.18
10.00	0.70*	0.75	0.80	45.00	44.78	0.31	3.17	31.69	− 22.91	− 305.45	− 256.65
10.00	0.80*	0.75	0.80	45.00	100.75	0.38	4.75	47.53	− 71.28	− 975.99	− 866.21
6.00	0.25	0.50*	0.80	15.00	4.90	0.44	2.86	17.14	4.70	6.12	14.29
6.00	0.25	0.75*	0.80	15.00	4.88	0.33	2.11	12.63	3.59	9.14	15.79
6.00	0.25	1.00*	0.80	15.00	4.44	0.27	1.67	10.00	2.86	11.11	16.67
6.00	0.25	1.25*	0.80	15.00	4.00	0.22	1.38	8.28	2.46	12.49	17.24
6.00	0.25	1.50*	0.80	15.00	3.60	0.19	1.18	7.06	2.12	13.49	17.65

Note: *Indicates that the parameters are changed while other parameters are fixed.

From Table 1, the influence of change in value preference parameter λ, marginal output r and risk avoidance measurement ρ on incentive structure can be seen. As λ

increases, α, β, e, w will increase. When $1/2 \leq \lambda < 1$, $\Delta IC < 0$, $TC < 0$; When $0 < \lambda \leq 1/2$, $CE_G > 0$; when $1/2 < \lambda < 1$, $CE_G < 0$. As r increases, α, β, CE_G, w, etc. each value will increase. With the increase of enterprise risk avoidance measurement, enterprise partition coefficient will decrease and its profit will transform from performance distribution to fixed compensation.

6 Conclusions

Based on the view of two bottom-line thinking on development and ecology, in order to ensure the sustainable development and high-quality operation of the economy, the government and enterprises have changed the traditional environmental governance, supervision and punishment mechanism. Government administration and enterprises are new type of cooperation instead of the relationship between cat and mouse. The incentive contract model of government governance and enterprises is established based on the two bottom-line thinking of development and ecology. The traditional incentive contract model introduces ecological value preference parameters, and the model equilibrium changes due to the influence of ecological value preference parameters. After the equilibrium analysis of the model, the main conclusion reached is as follows: (1) Ecological value preference parameters can effectively coordinate the interest between government and enterprises. Governments with ecological value preferences can sacrifice part of their own interests at the cost of contract design to incentive enterprises to exert the best level of effort in ecological environmental protection based on development and ecological bottom-line thinking, and effectively control agency costs due to asymmetric information improve efficiency via ecological value preferences. (2) With the increase of marginal output, the government will change the incentive structure. Via modification of fixed compensation benefit and partition coefficient, government can stimulate enterprise to transform more fixed compensation benefit to incentive structure of distribution association with enterprise performance, and then raise the effort level of enterprise. To release the pressure of incentive cost increase, government will choose a mutual method to protect ecosystem from damage and promote the economic efficiency of enterprise. (3) With difference in risk avoidance extent of enterprise, change in risk preference may lead to change in incentive structure.

Under the framework of keeping the bottom-line of development and ecology, it should build environmental governance system that government-led and enterprises as the main body. Enterprises must perform their enterprise social responsibilities and establish the concept of Lucid waters and lush mountains are invaluable assets, keep to the basic national policy of saving resources and protecting the environment, and promoting comprehensive conservation and recycling of resource. Government should encourage enterprises to implement transformation, upgrading and green development, and give enterprises a series of incentive measures such as capital, tax exemption and policy preferences, in order to further stimulate the enthusiasm of enterprises. At the same time, the government should accelerate the establishment of a legal system and policy guidance for green production and consumption, build sound industrial system for the development of green and low-carbon cycle, and form a spatial pattern, industrial structure, and mode of production that can save resources and protect the environment.

References

Louwei, J.P.: The concept of ecological red line and ecological bottom line. People's Tribune **36**, 31–33 (2015)

Zou, C., Mengjia, X., Lin, N., et al.: Application of bottom line thinking in ecological protection. China Popul. Resour. Environ. **25**(S1), 159–161 (2015)

Liu, X.: Discuss on the bottom-line and bottom-line thinking in the construction of ecological civilization. J. Southwest Univ. (Soc. Sci. Ed.) **41**(02), 5–11 (2015)

Wenzhi, X.: Making the ecological red line an insurmountable bottom line for sustainable development. Resour. Habitant Environ. **08**, 34–36 (2016)

Vandergeest, P., Unno, A.: A new extra territoriality? aquaculture certification, sovereignty, and empire. Polit. Geogr. **31**(6), 358–367 (2012)

Gorobets, A.: Eco-centric policy for sustainable development. J. Clean. Prod. **64**(1), 654–655 (2014)

Wei, Z., Hulin, L., Xuebing, A.: Ecological civilization construction is the fundamental way to develop low-carbon economy. Energy Procedia **5**, 839–843 (2011)

DeCanio, S.J., Fremstad, A.: Game theory and climate diplomacy. Ecol. Econ. **85**, 177–187 (2013)

Chen, S., Chen, B., Fath, B.D.: Ecological risk assessment on the system scale: a review of state-of-the-art models and future perspectives. Ecol. Model. **250**(10), 25–33 (2013)

Korhonen, J.: Industrial ecology in the strategic sustainable development model: strategic applications of industrial ecology. J. Clean. Prod. **12**(8), 809–823 (2004)

Boland, A., Zhu, J.: Public participation in China's green communities: Mobilizing memories and structuring incentives. Geo Forum **43**(1), 147–157 (2012)

Liu, C.-J., Zhao, X.-M.: A game analysis on environmental pollution under the background of new urbanization. On Econ. Probl. **07**, 1–5 (2014)

Like, W.: Action logic of the local government pollution control and the public environmental struggle: based on game theory framework. J. Beijing Univ. Technol. **16**(03), 24–28 (2016)

Xu, L.L., Zhao, J.-X.: Break the plight of environmental pollution liability insurance development under government promotion—based on the dynamic game analysis among the government, the polluting corporations, and insurance companies. Hebei Academic J. **36**(03), 134–138 (2016)

Bin, L.I., Tuo, L.I.: Environmental regulation, land finance and pollution—based on a game model analysis and an empirical study on Chinese-style decentralization. Collect. Essays Finance Econ. **01**, 99–106 (2015)

Sun-zhe, W.: Research on game, incentive and ecological damage relief. Theory Monthly **11**, 97–105 (2018)

Wen-bing, L., Wang, Y., Wang, L.: Game analysis of water pollution control stakeholders. J. Hohai Univ. (Philos. Soc. Sci.) **17**(06), 72–77+99–100 (2015)

Han, S.: Game analysis of water pollution governance supervision of enterprises in western China minority regions. Guizhou Ethn. Stud. **36**(06), 38–41 (2015)

Fengxia, H., Hanjie, X., Dinghong, P., et al.: Development motive investigation of green finance under the new normal economy—based on a three-party game among the government, bank and enterprise. Rev. Econ. Manage. **33**(05), 88–94 (2017)

Yan, T., Lipan, J.: Analysis of game behavior between local governments and enterprises under environmental regulation. Enterp. Econ. **06**, 33–36 (2016)

Xianjia, W., Ke, X.: Vision-driven, evolutionary games and approaches to environmental pollution control. Jianghan Tribune **07**, 37–43 (2018)

Qi, L., Chuan, Y., Chaoqun, Z.: Build a strong ecological security barrier in Hubei Province with bottom-line thinking. Environ. Prot. **47**(08), 24–26 (2019)

Zheng, J., Zhou, Y., Gong, K.: From bottom-line thinking to bottom-line planning: planning of ecological protection red line in Ningbo. City Plan. Rev. **41**(04), 86–91 (2017)

Stability Analysis of Communication System Under Certain Session Arrival Rate

Jiamin Cheng, Lei Chen[✉], Ping Cui, Kailiang Zhang, and Yuan An

Jiangsu Province Key Laboratory of Intelligent Industry Control Technology,
Xuzhou University of Technology, Xuzhou 221018, China
chenlei@xzit.edu.cn

Abstract. The transmit rate of backbone network is much more fast than that of the edge network. In the edge wireless communication, transmitter often need select one channel from time-varying ones. Due to unknown statistics of time-varying channel, the channel, selection is based on observation. Evaluating the lost of scheduling based on observation is an important for design scheduling policy. By adopting the concept of queue regret fact, we can evaluate the effectiveness of scheduling policy. However, because the different arrival rates of backbone network and edge network in real commercial network, the traffic model affects the measurement in different way. In this paper, considering the difference between backbone networks transmit rate and edge network transmit rate, we adopt session arrival model to observe the relationship between arrival rate, channel service rate, queue length and queue regret is analyzed in the simulation.

Keywords: Queue regret · Scheduling policy · Wireless communication

1 Introduction

The transmit rate of edge wireless network has been significantly improved. However, the capacity of backbone network is still far more than that of access network. To let the edge network works in a more efficient way, some new approaches are proposed to improve network routing and measurement [1–3]. Based on effective user behavior and traffic analysis methods [4–7], new scheduling strategies are designed to raise resources utilization [8–11] and energy-efficiency [12–14]. To evaluate these new scheduling strategies, traffic reconstruction is important. Many researches focus on the edge network traffic [15–17] and core network traffic [18–20]. The traffic models are different for different network area [21]. Because of the traffic complexity caused by mobile users' behavior some AI-based approaches are designed to build the traffic model [3, 22, 23]. The traffic models have been used to improve the quality of service [24–27], quality of end user experience [28–31] and spectral efficiency [32–34]. However, most researches only concern about the short term performance index. The system's regret index is defined to measure the system stability [35]. In this paper, we investigate how the network traffic affects the regret index. The regret compares the backlog of real learning controller

H. Song and D. Jiang (Eds.): SIMUtools 2020, LNICST 369, pp. 748–758, 2021.
https://doi.org/10.1007/978-3-030-72792-5_59

which select policy based on statistics and the backlog under a controller that knows the best policy. As a stochastic multi-armed bandit problem, the regret bound is drawn in [36]. Some practical policies have been studied for a long time to deal these problems [37]. To project a perfect service rate observation in busy time under fixed arrival rate, the boundary of regret is obtained [38].

For most wireless communication situations, the channel state is stable in short term. Therefore, transmitter could observe these channels during idle period. By the channel estimation information, transmitter is able to select optimal channel. The effect of channel estimations is affected by the length of idle period. Some policies suggest that observe the candidate channels in busy period. This might raise the observation cost, but is help to do decision.

In this paper, we consider a more real environment. In the simulation, we consider the session arrival rate. Because the backbone network transmit packets far faster than that of edge network, when a session arrives the edge network at a time slot it contains several packets. For edge network, if the channel is available it only treat one packet each time slot. Through analyzing the record of queue length and queue regret, the relationship between arrival rate, service rate, queue length and queue regret is explored in our simulation.

The paper is divided as six sections. In the second section, we give the related work about queue regret problem. The system model based on session arrival rate is given in the third section. An analysis on queue regret facts is presented in the fourth section. The algorithm and simulation results analysis is given in the fifth section. We conclude in the sixth section.

2   Related Work

The queue regret problem belongs to the traditional bandit problem. In the multi-armed bandit problem, a fixed limited set of resources need to be allocated between alternative choices in a way that maximizes their expected gain [37]. For each choice, the stochastic properties are unknown at the time of allocation and the allocation must be made under observation. As time passes, we can better understand the choices. In this classic reinforcement learning problem the solution must deal with the exploration-exploitation tradeoff dilemma. Therefore, this multi-armed bandit problem also falls into a lot of stochastic scheduling.

A good scheduling policy is proven to be able to maximize the rate of offered service to the queue in a queuing system. During the idle time periods, the offered service is unused, and therefore we can select a candidate service to observe. However, most researches only focus on the relationship between queue regret and the length of passed time [35]. Those researches mainly consider the packet arrival rate. The main issue in this research is to observe how the session arrival rate affects the regret.

3   System Model

In this regret problem, the capacity of channel is referred to as service rate of server, and the system consists of a single queue and N servers. Controller schedules the servers over discrete time slots $t = 0, 1, 2\ldots$ Sessions arrive to the queue as a Bernoulli process, $A(t)$, with rate $\lambda \in (0, 1]$. We set one session contains L packets. Therefore the packet arrival rate should be $\lambda \cdot L$. The service rate is defined as the amount of packets that server $i \in [N]$ can provide follows a Bernoulli process $D^i(t)$ with rate μ_i, and the transmitter treats at most one packet in a time slot. The arrival process and server processes are arbitrarily assumed to be independent. In L time scale, if $\mu_i > \lambda \cdot L$ the system is referred to as stabilizing; otherwise, it is referred to as non-stabilizing.

The controller must select one of the N servers to provide service at the time slot when the queue is non-empty. We set the controller's choice at time t as $u(t) \in [N]$ and the service offered to the queue as $D(t)$ which is equal to $D^{u(t)}(t)$. The queue length $Q(t)$ can be written as [20]:

$$Q(t+1) = (Q(t) - D(t))^+ + L \cdot A(t), \text{ for } t = 0, 1, 2, \tag{1}$$

where $(x)^+$ denote the maximum value of x and 0. The queue length is assumed as 0 initially. The controller do not know the values of $D^i(t)$ prior to making its decision $u(t)$. The controller need to select the channel based on observed maximum expected throughout

$$i^* \triangleq \arg\max_{i \in [N]} \mu_i \tag{2}$$

to provide transmit service. In this paper, the controller does not a priori know the values of μ_i and must therefore use observations of $D(t)$ to obtain i^*. We assume that the controller can observe $D(t)$ at all time slots, even when the queue is empty. Define $Q^*(t)$ to be the queue length under the controller that always schedules i^* and $Q^\pi(t)$ the backlog under a policy that must learn the service rates. The performance of policy π is measured by queue length regret [35]:

$$R^\pi(T) \triangleq E\left[\sum_{t=0}^{T-1} Q^\pi(t) - \sum_{t=0}^{T-1} Q^*(t)\right]. \tag{3}$$

The π is scheduling policy; the assumption implies that $R^\pi(T)$ is monotonically with a high probability. Note that the service rate is a probability; the best channel might perform worse than other channel.

4   Queue Regret Analysis

In the stabilizing scenarios, the controller has enough idle periods to observe the service rate of each channel, especially in this session scenario. Based on plenty of observations the controller can select the best channel whose service rate is higher than packet arrival rate that is product of session arrival rate and the number of packets in sessions, the queue regret is expected to stop increasing after initial phase. In the non-stabilizing scenarios, the queue length is expected to increase sharply. Because many packets arrive at same time slot, the queue will keep a backlogged situation for a long time. We concern the relationship between the blogged queue length, the regret, the session arrival and the service rate.

For instance, the controller selects a channel with service rate μ_i. With a long busy period, the observation value of μ_i will approach the real value. If another channel with service rate μ_j with $\mu_j > \mu_i$, the controller only keep use ith channel while the observation value of μ_j is less than μ_i. This possibility can be written as:

$$P\{X \le n \cdot \mu_i\} = \sum_{k=0}^{n \cdot \mu_i} \binom{n}{k} \mu_j^k \mu_j^{n-k}, \qquad (4)$$

where the n is the number of controller observing the jth channel in initial phase. We know that the Eq. (4) increase fast when $n \cdot \mu_i$ approaching μ_j. Therefore, the possibility of controller changing channel would increase as the value of $\mu_j - \mu_i$ increase. This implies the queue regret has still chance to keep a low value within a long time busy period. The session arrival model means the longer continue idle time and the longer continue busy time. We would investigate how the size of session affects the performance of controller.

5 Simulation and Results

5.1 Algorithm

The simulation algorithm is shown in Fig. 1. The algorithm observes the service rates of candidate channels uses in idle period. In the busy period, the controller only observes the service rate of selected channel. The algorithm is presented as followed:

Step1	While (number of time slots > 0)
Step2	If (the queue is empty)
Step3	Select a random channel
Step4	Observe the selected channel
Step5	Update the service rate of observed channel
Step6	else
Step7	Select randomly a channel from the set of servers with highest rate
Step8	Decide whether transmit the packet according to real service rate
Step9	If (the channel works)
Step10	Queue's length --;
Step11	End if
Step12	Update service rate of the selected server
Step13	End if
Step14	Decide whether new session arrive according to arrival rate
Step15	If (new session arrives)
Step16	Queue's length += number of packets in session
Step17	End if
Step18	Number of time slots --
Step19	End while

Fig. 1. Simulation algorithm.

Table 1. Simulation parameters.

Parameter name	Value of parameter in small session	Value of parameter in big session
Number of slots	15000 for each test	15000 for each test
Service rates	0.3, 0.325, 0.35, 0.375, 0.4	0.3, 0.325, 0.35, 0.375, 0.4
Arrival rates	0.02–0.05, increase 0.01 each test	0.002–0.005, increase 0.01 each test
Packets in session	10	100

5.2 Simulation Parameters

Two simulations are carried out. The simulation parameters are listed in Table 1.

In these two simulations, we have 5 candidate channels with a service rate range from 0.3 to 0.4 respectively. The arrival rates increase 0.001 and 0.0001 for each test from 0.02 to 0.05 and 0.002 to 0.005 for the two simulations respectively. Therefore, there are 31 tests in each simulation. And each test last 15000 time slots under the fixed session rates. The queue length and queue regret is recorded for each time slot.

5.3 Simulation Results

The simulation results are shown in Fig. 2 and Fig. 3.

Figure 2 shows the simulation results while the system changes from stable to non-stable. The results shows that the queue lengths and queue regrets are stable while the stable situation in which the arrival rate is lower than all service rates. As expected, the queue regrets increase as the queue length increase while the packet arrival rate is approach the lowest service rate. In Fig. 3, the average queue lengths have an increasing trend while the arrival rate surpasses the service rate despite of some fluctuation. However, the queue regrets have no an obviously increasing trend as the arrival rate increases. The fluctuation is caused by randomly channel selection in initial phase when the controller lacks of observation. And the fluctuation is high in this session model since the queue length increase sharply at one time slot.

In another simulation, we let the session consist of more packets. The simulation results are shown in Fig. 4 and Fig. 5.

In Fig. 4, the simulation results shows that the queue lengths and queue regrets are stable even if the arrival rate is higher than some low service rates of candidate channels. And the queue regrets also increase as the queue length increase while the arrival rate is approach the lowest service rate. In Fig. 5, the average queue lengths have a more obviously increasing trend than that of simulation 1 while the arrival rate surpasses the service rate despite of some fluctuation. However, the queue regrets is very stable as the arrival rate increases. The fluctuation is also caused by randomly channel selection in initial phase when the controller lacks of observation. In these two simulations, the small session has higher arrival rate and the big session has lower arrival rate. Therefore, for a long term, the numbers of arrival packets of these two simulations are more likely same. Although these two simulations' packet arrival rates are same, this big session regret fluctuation is higher than that of small session regret, since the queue suddenly increases within big session model.

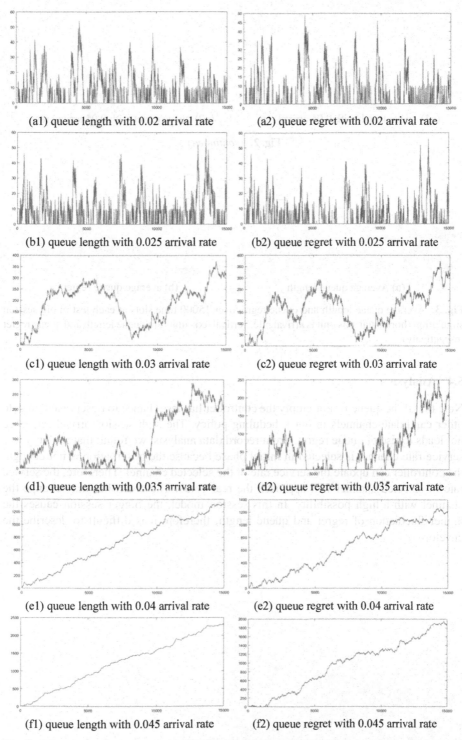

(a1) queue length with 0.02 arrival rate   (a2) queue regret with 0.02 arrival rate

(b1) queue length with 0.025 arrival rate   (b2) queue regret with 0.025 arrival rate

(c1) queue length with 0.03 arrival rate   (c2) queue regret with 0.03 arrival rate

(d1) queue length with 0.035 arrival rate   (d2) queue regret with 0.035 arrival rate

(e1) queue length with 0.04 arrival rate   (e2) queue regret with 0.04 arrival rate

(f1) queue length with 0.045 arrival rate   (f2) queue regret with 0.045 arrival rate

Fig. 2. Slices in small session simulation (horizontal axis unit is time slot, vertical axis units are queue length and queue regret respectively)

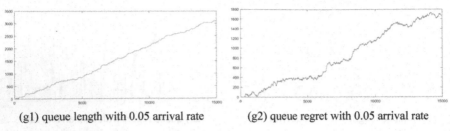

(g1) queue length with 0.05 arrival rate   (g2) queue regret with 0.05 arrival rate

Fig. 2. (*continued*)

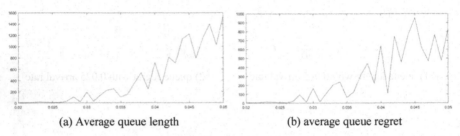

(a) Average queue length   (b) average queue regret

Fig. 3. Average queue length and queue regret over 15000 time slots at each test in big session simulation (horizontal axis unit is arrival rate, vertical axis units are queue length and queue regret respectively)

5.4 Analysis

Note that if the queue is non-empty the controller has less chance to observe and update other candidate channels in our scheduling policy. The high session arrival rate dose not leads to rise of queue regret. From record data analysis, we found that if a very low service rate channel is selected in initial phase because the observation is not enough, the controller can update the service rate of the selected channel. Therefore, the service rate of selected channel will approach the real value. The controller may change the channel with a high possibility. In this session model, the bigger session causes the higher fluctuation of regret and queue length, therefore it is difficult to describe the envelop.

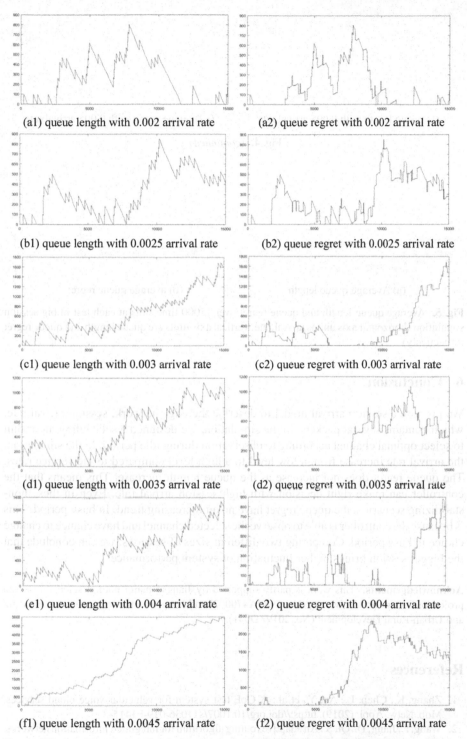

(a1) queue length with 0.002 arrival rate   (a2) queue regret with 0.002 arrival rate

(b1) queue length with 0.0025 arrival rate   (b2) queue regret with 0.0025 arrival rate

(c1) queue length with 0.003 arrival rate   (c2) queue regret with 0.003 arrival rate

(d1) queue length with 0.0035 arrival rate   (d2) queue regret with 0.0035 arrival rate

(e1) queue length with 0.004 arrival rate   (e2) queue regret with 0.004 arrival rate

(f1) queue length with 0.0045 arrival rate   (f2) queue regret with 0.0045 arrival rate

Fig. 4. Slices in big session simulation (horizontal axis unit is time slot, vertical axis units are queue length and queue regret respectively)

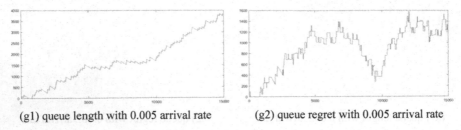

(g1) queue length with 0.005 arrival rate   (g2) queue regret with 0.005 arrival rate

Fig. 4. (*continued*)

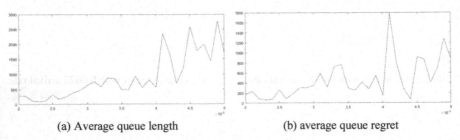

(a) Average queue length   (b) average queue regret

Fig. 5. Average queue length and queue regret over 15000 time slots at each test in big session simulation (horizontal axis unit is arrival rate, vertical axis units are queue length and queue regret respectively)

6 Conclusion

We propose a session arrival model to describe the edge network, session arrival rate, which contains several packets. In the simulation, we designed a scheduling algorithm to select optimal channel according to observation during idle period. In the simulation, the arrival rate increase from a low level to a high level compared to the service rates. The queue regret does not increase as the queue length increase. This means that the controller can make right decision with high session arrival rate. Even in these non-stabilizing scenarios, the queue regret have no an increasing trend. In busy period. This is because the controller is able to observe the selected channel and have chance to change choice in busy period. Comparing two different sizes of sessions, we can conclude that the bigger session brings higher fluctuation of system performance.

Acknowledgements. This work is partly supported by Jiangsu major natural science research project of College and University (No. 19KJA470002) and Jiangsu technology project of Housing and Urban-Rural Development (No. 2019ZD041).

References

1. Zhang, K., Chen, L., An, Y., et al.: A QoE test system for vehicular voice cloud services. Mob. Netw. Appl. (2019). https://doi.org/10.1007/s11036-019-01415-3
2. Wang, F., Jiang, D., Qi, S.: An adaptive routing algorithm for integrated information networks. China Commun. **7**(1), 196–207 (2019)

3. Huo, L., Jiang, D., Lv, Z., et al.: An intelligent optimization-based traffic information acquirement approach to software-defined networking. Comput. Intell. **36**, 1–21 (2019)
4. Chen, L., Jiang, D., Bao, R., Xiong, J., Liu, F., Bei, L.: MIMO scheduling effectiveness analysis for bursty data service from view of QoE. Chin. J. Electron. **26**(5), 1079–1085 (2017)
5. Jiang, D., Wang, Y., Lv, Z., et al.: Big data analysis-based network behavior insight of cellular networks for industry 4.0 applications. IEEE Trans. Ind. Inf. **16**(2), 1310–1320 (2020)
6. Jiang, D., Huo, L., Song, H.: Rethinking behaviors and activities of base stations in mobile cellular networks based on big data analysis. IEEE Trans. Netw. Sci. Eng. **1**(1), 1–12 (2018)
7. Chen, L., et al.: A lightweight end-side user experience data collection system for quality evaluation of multimedia communications. IEEE Access **6**(1), 15408–15419 (2018)
8. Chen, L., Zhang, L.: Spectral efficiency analysis for massive MIMO system under QoS constraint: an effective capacity perspective. Mob. Netw. Appl. (2020). https://doi.org/10.1007/s11036-019-01414-4
9. Wang, F., Jiang, D., Qi, S., et al.: A dynamic resource scheduling scheme in edge computing satellite networks. Mob. Netw. Appl. (2019)
10. Jiang, D., Huo, L., Lv, Z., et al.: A joint multi-criteria utility-based network selection approach for vehicle-to-infrastructure networking. IEEE Trans. Intell. Transp. Syst. **19**(10), 3305–3319 (2018)
11. Jiang, D., Zhang, P., Lv, Z., et al.: Energy-efficient multi-constraint routing algorithm with load balancing for smart city applications. IEEE Internet Things J. **3**(6), 1437–1447 (2016)
12. Jiang, D., Li, W., Lv, H.: An energy-efficient cooperative multicast routing in multi-hop wireless networks for smart medical applications. Neurocomputing **220**(2017), 160–169 (2017)
13. Jiang, D., Wang, Y., Lv, Z., et al.: Intelligent optimization-based reliable energy-efficient networking in cloud services for IIoT networks. IEEE J. Selected Areas Commun. (2019)
14. Shahini, A., Kiani, A., Ansari, N.: Energy efficient resource allocation in EH-Enabled CR networks for IoT. IEEE Internet Things J. **6**(2), 3186–3193 (2019)
15. Jiang, D., Wang, W., Shi, L., et al.: A compressive sensing-based approach to end-to-end network traffic reconstruction. IEEE Trans. Netw. Sci. Eng. **5**(3), 1–2 (2018)
16. Zeng, Y., Qi, Z., Chen, W. Huang, Y.: TEST: an end-to-end network traffic classification system with spatio-temporal features extraction. In: 2019 IEEE International Conference on Smart Cloud (SmartCloud), Tokyo, Japan, pp. 131–136 (2019)
17. Qi, S., Jiang, D., Huo, L.: A prediction approach to end-to-end traffic in space information networks. Mob. Netw. Appl. (2019)
18. Kim, E., Choi, Y.: Traffic monitoring system for 5G core network. In: 2019 Eleventh International Conference on Ubiquitous and Future Networks (ICUFN), Zagreb, Croatia, pp. 671–673 (2019).
19. Wang, Y., Jiang, D., Huo, L., et al.: A new traffic prediction algorithm to software defined networking. Mob. Netw. Appl. (2019)
20. Jiang, D., Huo, L., Li, Y.: Fine-granularity inference and estimations to network traffic for SDN. Plos One **13**(5), 1–23 (2018)
21. Wang, X., et al.: The joint optimization of online traffic matrix measurement and traffic engineering for software-defined networks. IEEE/ACM Trans. Netw. **28**(1), 234–247 (2020)
22. Gu, Y., Lu, W., Xu, X., Qin, L., Shao, Z., Zhang, H.: An improved bayesian combination model for short-term traffic prediction with deep learning. IEEE Trans. Intell. Transp. Syst. **21**(3), 1332–1342 (2020)
23. Huo, L., Jiang, D., Qi, S., et al.: An AI-based adaptive cognitive modeling and measurement method of network traffic for EIS. Mob. Netw. Appl. (2019)
24. Aung, S.T., Thein, T.: Internet traffic categories demand prediction to support dynamic QoS. In: 2020 5th International Conference on Computer and Communication Systems (ICCCS), Shanghai, China, pp. 650–654 (2020)

25. Attia, M.B., Nguyen, K.K., Cheriet, M.: Dynamic QoS-aware scheduling for concurrent traffic in smart home. IEEE Internet Things J. **7**(6), 5412–5425 (2020)
26. Lemeshko, O., Yeremenko, O., Yevdokymenko, M., Hailan, A.M.: Tensor based load balancing under self-similar traffic properties with guaranteed QoS. In: 2020 IEEE 15th International Conference on Advanced Trends in Radioelectronics, Telecommunications and Computer Engineering (TCSET), Lviv-Slavske, Ukraine, pp. 293–297 (2020)
27. Ren, S., Tang, G.: A reactive traffic flow estimation in software defined networks. In: 2020 5th International Conference on Computer and Communication Systems (ICCCS), Shanghai, China, pp. 585–588 (2020)
28. Mangla, T., Halepovic, E., Ammar, M., Zegura, E.: Using session modeling to estimate HTTP-based video QoE metrics from encrypted network traffic. IEEE Trans. Netw. Serv. Manage. **16**(3), 1086–1099 (2019)
29. Tian, F., Yu, Y., Li, D., Cui, J., Dong, Y.: QoE optimization for traffic offloading from LTE to WiFi. In: 2019 IEEE 8th Global Conference on Consumer Electronics (GCCE), Osaka, Japan, pp. 115–116 (2019)
30. Tang, S., Li, C., Qin, X., Wei, G.: Traffic classification for mobile video streaming using dynamic warping network. In: 2019 28th Wireless and Optical Communications Conference (WOCC), Beijing, China, pp. 1–5 (2019)
31. Bao, R., Chen, L., Cui, P.: User behavior and user experience analysis for social network services. Wirel. Netw. (2020). https://doi.org/10.1007/s11276-019-02233-x
32. Oszmianski, J., Safjan, K., Dottling, M., Bohdanowicz, A.: Impact of traffic modeling and scheduling on delay and spectral efficiency of the WINNER system. In: VTC Spring 2008 - IEEE Vehicular Technology Conference, Singapore, pp. 2661–2665 (2008)
33. Zhao, G., Chen, S., Zhao, L., Hanzo, L.: Energy-spectral-efficiency analysis and optimization of heterogeneous cellular networks: a large-scale user-behavior perspective. IEEE Trans. Veh. Technol. **67**(5), 4098–4112 (2018)
34. Zhao, G., Chen, S., Qi, L., Zhao, L., Hanzo, L.: Mobile-traffic-aware offloading for energy- and spectral-efficient large-scale D2D-enabled cellular networks. IEEE Trans. Wirel. Commun. **18**(6), 3251–3264 (2019)
35. Stahlbuhk, T., Shrader, B., Modiano, E.: Learning aloglrithms for mining queue length regret. In: 2018 IEEE International Symposium on Information (2018)
36. Bubeck, S., Cesa-Bianchi, N.: Regret analysis of stochastic and nonstochastic multi-armed bandit problems. Found. Trends Mach. Learn. **5**(1), 1–122 (2012)
37. Auer, P., Cesa-Bianchi, N., Fischer, P.: Finite-time analysis of the multiarmed bandit problem. Mach. Learn. **47**(2–3), 235–256 (2002)
38. Krishnasamy, S., et al.: Regret of queueing bandits. In: Proceedings of Neural Information Processing Systems, pp. 1669–1677 (2016)

On the Pricing Decision of Monopoly Online Car-Hailing Platform Considering Network Externality and Commission Rate

Yu Xiao-Jun[⊠]

School of Mathematics and Statistics, Guizhou University of Finance and Economics,
Guiyang 550025, China
xjyu-myu@163.com

Abstract. With the development of mobile internet, the online car-hailing (OCH) services have become one of the in urban transportation modes available. Accordingly, the OCH services pricing decision surfaces as a new transportation management problem that should be properly addressed. This paper analyzes the pricing and cooperation revenue sharing issues between the platform and the group of drivers by means of the dynamic game theory and the two-sided market theory. In order to reflect the characteristic of the practical situation of OCH industry, the network externality and the driver commission rate are considered in this model. The formula of the user payment, the driver commission rate, the user registration fee, the user and driver scale, and the platform profit at the equilibrium state as well as the relationship between them and network externality are analyzed. The simulation results validate the correctness of our analytical results.

Keywords: Online car-hailing platform · Pricing decision · Network externality · Commission rate · Two-sided market

1 Introduction

Over the last decades, with the rapid development and popularization of mobile internet, the OCH services have become one of the urban transportation modes available and the OCH companies such as Uber and Didi have obtained huge success and transformed the way we travel in cities. These companies connect users and drivers in real time by internet-based platforms to operate car-hailing services. Some achievements have been made in the research of OCH service mode selection behavior. Rayle et al. [1] find that the users of OCH display the characteristics of younger age and higher education level. At the same time, compared with taxi travel mode, the OCH services are more convenient and take a shorter waiting time. Dias et al. [2] study the choice behaviors of car-sharing and OCH services based on bivariate ordered probit model, and analyze the influence of basic characteristics of users such as whether they have children and the built environment on mobile travel choice. By observing the differences between users and non-users of OCH services, Dawes [3] finds that Uber and/or Lyft users are more likely

H. Song and D. Jiang (Eds.): SIMUtools 2020, LNICST 369, pp. 759–770, 2021.
https://doi.org/10.1007/978-3-030-72792-5_60

to hold a positive attitude towards OCH service. Dawes also learns that participating in social and leisure activities and avoiding alcohol driving are the main reasons for travelers to choose Uber or Lyft. Contreras and Paz [4] estimate the effects of OCH platform on the taxicab industry by using multinomial linear regression analysis, and find that OCH services had a negative and significant effect on taxicab ridership. Nelson and Sadowsky [5] find that the emergence of the first OCH platform is an important supplement to the public transport system, but with the entry of the second OCH company, the utilization rate of public transport would decline.

The matching problem of OCH is also investigated by researchers. Thaithatkul et al. [6] obtain a matching model by considering user preference and study the relationship between user preference and OCH system's performance. Fahnenschreiber et al. [7] study the matching problem combining dynamic OCH and existing public transport systems. Masoud and Jayakrishnan [8] discuss the randomness of the flexible OCH system and propose an algorithm to solve this problem in real-time. Thaithatkul et al. [9] investigate the characteristics of dynamics of passenger matching problem in smart OCH systems by the simulation approach. Cheikh et al. [10] obtain a novel approach to solving the dynamic multihop ridematching problem. As for the pricing problem of OCH, Yang and Yang [11] analyze the equilibrium properties of three specific issues for taxi market by using general bilateral searching and meeting function. Wang et al. [12] obtain a game model of the taxi market with a single taxi hailing app by using an aggregate and static approach, and conduct the existence, stability and sensitivity analysis of pricing strategies at the equilibrium state. Zha et al. [13] analyze the economic output of OCH platform under different scenarios by using an aggregate model, and deduce the pricing structure from monopoly, the first-best and the second-best perspectives. Further, Zha et al. [14] propose the equilibrium models in OCH market under dynamic scenario and investigate the impact of surge pricing by using bi-level programming method. He et al. [15] propose an equilibrium framework to depict the operations of a regulated taxi market, formulate an optimal design problem of the taxi-hailing platform's pricing and penalty/compensation strategies and get the solving algorithm.

With the emergence of OCH platform enterprises, competition between different platform enterprises seems inevitable. Hall et al. [16] consider the emergence of Uber is a complement for public transit. Specifically, Uber is a complement for buses and rail transit. Alley [17] argues that Uber breaks the monopoly position of taxi industry in New York City, reduces the average price level of taxi industry and provides more economical and faster travel services. Chen [18] studies the behavior of taxi drivers in the case of widespread OCH services. This study finds that Didi's technical strength poses challenge to the survival and development of traditional taxi drivers, and thus taxi drivers are compelled to gradually adapt themselves to new technologies in order to obtain higher income, and Uber does not significantly worsen the traffic congestion in urban areas. In order to promote the healthy development of OCH industry, scholars have also carried out research on policy and regulation strategy of OCH Market. Dudley [19] considers that regulation should be carried out under the condition of ensuring the positive role of OCH. Schneider [20] thinks that the traditional taxi market regulation policy is not suitable for the online car-hailing platform. Edelman and Geradin [21] discuss the specific regulatory measures of OCH platform. Beer et al. [22] take a qualitative comparative analysis on the regulation policies of OCH in major American cities through the driver and platform perspectives. Lee [23] discusses the government's regulatory framework from the perspective of government regulation. The empirical study of OCH is also conducted by researchers. For instance, Bengtsson [24] reveals that sidestepping the regulations increases cost efficiency and informal bargaining leads to Pareto improvement through studying the Cape Town taxi market. Jiao [25] evaluates the characteristic of OCH platform Uber's surge pricing by using collected data in Austin, and reveals the obscurity of the price surge mechanisms. Shaheen and Cohen [26] review the shared ride service models and the impact studies for North American, and explore the convergence of shared mobility, electrification and automation, offering some advice to improve the management of the shared ride services. Yang and Yu [27] compare and analyze the traditional and present management modes and measures taken by the government with the Shanghai taxi management model as a case.

The OCH platforms are a meeting place for drivers and users. The drivers find users via the platforms and transport them to their designated destinations. When the driver scale is large, the platform can provide more potential driver candidates for users, and the average waiting time for users is relatively small and the utility increases accordingly. Similarly, the utility of drivers providing travel services through the platform is also related to the size of users. Therefore, the OCH market is a typical two-sided market. The two-sided market theory was first proposed by Rochet and Tirole [28] and Armstrong [29], and has become the basic framework of two-sided market research. Hagiu and Halaburda [30] investigate the effect of levels of information on two-sided platform profits. Roger [31] studies the duopoly problem of two-sided platforms competing in differentiated products at the two-sided market. Nourinejad and Ramezani [32] obtain a dynamic non-equilibrium ride-sourcing model by the two-sided market theory, and a controller based on the model predictive control approach. Kung and Zhong [33] study the profit maximization problem of two-sided platform under three pricing strategies by considering network externality in order to understand pricing in the sharing economy. Malavolti [34] considers that the airport is a platform for shops and passengers by using two-sided market theory, and obtains the influence factors of retailing activity and aeronautical tax. Djavadian and Chow [35] investigate the flexible transport services and day-to-day adjustment process by the two-sided market approach, and assume that a perfectly matched state is equivalent to a social optimum by using the Ramsey pricing criterion.

The network externality is a core feature of platform economy, and meanwhile the waiting time and the driver commission rate are important factors of OCH services. In this paper, the network externality means the inter-group network externality which consists of marginal utility and waiting time. We establish a two-stage price game model based on the game theory and two-sided theory, analyzing the cooperatition game between monopoly platform and drivers, and conduct an equilibrium analysis under the monopoly platform optimum. We prove that the marginal utility of the drivers to the platform users and the marginal utility of the platform users to the drivers together determine the user payment, the driver commission rate, the user registration fee, the user and driver scale, and the platform profit at the equilibrium state. We also test the conclusion of the model through simulation.

Next, the basic model for a hypothetical OCH market is presented in the second section. The third section explores the properties of the monopoly OCH service at the equilibrium state. In the fourth section, the simulation is given to test the results in the third section.

2 Basic Model

2.1 Problem Description

Researchers have investigated the influence factor of the two-sided platform profit. Hagiu and Halaburda [30] show that the monopoly platform has higher profits when users are more informed while the competition platform prefers facing less informed users. Nourinejad and Ramezani [32] indicate that the overall profit may be higher when the user demand increases and the driver demand decreases simultaneously. Kung and Zhong [33] study the two-sided platform profit maximization problem by considering network externality. It is well known that the OCH market is a typical two-sided market, and the core feature of OCH services are not only the network externality in the general platform economy, but also the waiting time of two-sided user and the driver commission rate. In this paper, we assume a hypothetical OCH market with a monopoly platform, a group of drivers and a group of users and the market is mature such that the platform will gain profit from providing the services. The OCH platform adopts unilateral charge, that is, the user registration fee and the driver commission fee, while the driver decides the user payment at transaction. Suppose there is a line city of length 1, and the users and drivers are evenly distributed in the linear city. This paper assumes that the waiting time of users is negatively related to the driver scale, that is, when the number of drivers increases, the waiting time of users traveling through the OCH platform decreases; similarly, the waiting time of drivers is negatively related to the user scale, that is, when the number of users increases, the waiting time for drivers to provide travel services through the OCH platform decreases.

2.2 Game Model of the Problem

Suppose the user registration fee is r. Since the users are evenly distributed in the interval $[0, 1]$, then, the location of user i satisfying $x_i \in [0, 1]$, t is the unit cost of users joining the OCH platform, v is the basic utility of users, n is the number of drivers joining the platform, a is the marginal utility of the platform drivers to the users, i.e., the marginal utility brought by adding a driver to the monopoly platform for the users who join the platform, β_1 is the value of time of uses, $\gamma_1 n$ is the waiting time of users, $\gamma_1 < 0$ is the scale sensitive parameter of users, thus $a - \beta_1 \gamma_1$ is the network externality of users. p is the user payment at transaction. For balanced calling pattern, the user payment is pn, then, the utility of user i is

$$u_i = v + an - \beta_1 \gamma_1 n - r - tx_i - pn. \tag{1}$$

Similarly, for the location of driver j satisfying $y_j \in [0, 1]$, f is the unit cost of drivers joining the OCH platform, m is the number of users joining the platform, b is the marginal utility of the platform users to the drivers, that is, the marginal utility brought by adding a user to the monopoly platform for the drivers who join the platform, β_2 is the value of time of drivers, $\gamma_2 m$ is the waiting time of drivers, $\gamma_2 < 0$ is the scale sensitive parameter of drivers, thus $b - \beta_2\gamma_2$ is the network externality of drivers. λ is the commission rate of user's payment obtained by driver. For balanced calling pattern, the received of drivers is λpm, then, the profit of driver j is

$$L_j = bm - \beta_2\gamma_2 m + \lambda pm - fy_j. \tag{2}$$

From Eq. (1) and Eq. (2), we can obtain

$$x_i = (v - r + an - \beta_1\gamma_1 n - pn)/t, \quad y_j = (bm - \beta_2\gamma_2 m + \lambda pm)/f. \tag{3}$$

Then, the user and driver scale at the equilibrium state is described as follows, respectively,

$$m_e = [f(v - r)]/[ft - (a - \beta_1\gamma_1 - p)(b - \beta_2\gamma_2 + \lambda p)]. \tag{4}$$

$$n_e = [(v - r)(b - \beta_2\gamma_2 + \lambda p)]/[ft - (a - \beta_1\gamma_1 - p)(b - \beta_2\gamma_2 + \lambda p)]. \tag{5}$$

Assuming the marginal cost of platform is c, thus, the profit function of monopoly OCH platform can be written as follows:

$$
\begin{aligned}
L_1(r, p, \lambda) &= rm_e + [(1 - \lambda)p - c]n_e m_e \\
&= \{f(v - r)^2[(1 - \lambda)p - c](b - \beta_2\gamma_2 + \lambda p)\}/[ft - (a - \beta_1\gamma_1 - p)(b - \beta_2\gamma_2 + \lambda p)]^2. \\
&+ [fr(v - r)]/[ft - (a - \beta_1\gamma_1 - p)(b - \beta_2\gamma_2 + \lambda p)]
\end{aligned}
\tag{6}
$$

The drivers profit is calculated in the manner as follows:

$$L_2(r, p, \lambda) = [f(v - r)^2(b - \beta_2\gamma_2 + \lambda p)^2]/2[ft - (a - \beta_1\gamma_1 - p)(b - \beta_2\gamma_2 + \lambda p)]^2. \tag{7}$$

The consumer surplus is determined as follows:

$$CS(r, p, \lambda) = [f^2 t(v - r)^2]/2[ft - (a - \beta_1\gamma_1 - p)(b - \beta_2\gamma_2 + \lambda p)]^2. \tag{8}$$

The total social benefit is shown as follows:

$$
\begin{aligned}
TS(r, p, \lambda) &= L_1(r, p, \lambda) + L_2(r, p, \lambda) + CS(r, p, \lambda) \\
&= \frac{f(v-r)[ft(v+r) + 2(b-\beta_2\gamma_2+\lambda p)((a-\beta_1\gamma_1)r - rc + cv - pv) + (v-r)(\lambda^2 p^2 - (b-\beta_2\gamma)^2)]}{2[ft - (a-\beta_1\gamma_1-p)(b-\beta_2\gamma_2+\lambda p)]^2}.
\end{aligned}
\tag{9}
$$

3 Equilibrium Analysis

Now, we have established a two-stage price game model for equilibrium analysis. In the first stage, the platform decides the driver commission fee to maximize the platform profit, and in the second stage, the platform decides the user registration fee to maximize the platform profit, and the driver decides the user payment to maximize the drivers profit. This is a typical perfect information dynamic game. The Nash equilibrium can be solved according to the backward induction approach.

According to the backward induction approach, in the second stage the platform decides the user registration fee to maximize the platform profit, and the driver decides the user payment to maximize the drivers profit. Let $\partial L_1 / \partial r = 0$ and $\partial L_2 / \partial p = 0$, we can obtain

$$
\begin{aligned}
p &= \frac{\sqrt{ft\lambda} - (b - \beta_2\gamma_2)}{\lambda}, \\
r &= \frac{\left[(b - \beta_2\gamma_2) - 2(a - \beta_1\gamma_1 + b - \beta_2\gamma_2 - c)\lambda + (a - \beta_1\gamma_1 + 2\sqrt{ft\lambda})\lambda\right]v}{2\left[-(a - \beta_1\gamma_1 + b - \beta_2\gamma_2 - c)\lambda + \sqrt{ft\lambda}(1 + \lambda)\right]}.
\end{aligned}
\tag{10}
$$

In the first stage, the platform decides the driver commission fee to maximize the platform profit. In view of Eq. (10), we can show that Eq. (6) can be rewritten as follows:

$$
L_1 = \sqrt{f}v^2 / \left\{4\sqrt{t}[\sqrt{ft}(1 + \lambda) - (a - \beta_1\gamma_1 + b - \beta_2\gamma_2 - c)\sqrt{\lambda}]\right\}.
\tag{11}
$$

Then, let $\partial L_1 / \partial \lambda = 0$. Thus, the driver commission rate is

$$
\lambda^* = (a - \beta_1\gamma_1 + b - \beta_2\gamma_2 - c)^2 / 4ft.
\tag{12}
$$

Substituting Eq. (12) into Eq. (10) yields

$$
p^* = 2ft(a - \beta_1\gamma_1 - b + \beta_2\gamma_2 - c) / (a - \beta_1\gamma_1 + b - \beta_2\gamma_2 - c)^2.
\tag{13}
$$

$$
r^* = v \frac{4ft(b - \beta_2\gamma_2) + (a - \beta_1\gamma_1)(a - \beta_1\gamma_1 + b - \beta_2\gamma_2 - c)^2 - (a - \beta_1\gamma_1 + b - \beta_2\gamma_2 - c)^3}{(a - \beta_1\gamma_1 + b - \beta_2\gamma_2 - c)[4ft - (a - \beta_1\gamma_1 + b - \beta_2\gamma_2 - c)^2]}.
\tag{14}
$$

Substituting Eq. (13) and Eq. (14) into Eq. (4)-Eq. (9) yields

$$
m^* = 2fv / [4ft - (a - \beta_1\gamma_1 + b - \beta_2\gamma_2 - c)^2],
$$
$$
n^* = (a - \beta_1\gamma_1 + b - \beta_2\gamma_2 - c)v / [4ft - (a - \beta_1\gamma_1 + b - \beta_2\gamma_2 - c)^2].
$$

$$
L_1^* = fv^2 / [4ft - (a - \beta_1\gamma_1 + b - \beta_2\gamma_2 - c)^2].
$$

$$
L_2^* = (a - \beta_1\gamma_1 + b - \beta_2\gamma_2 - c)^2 fv^2 / \{2[4ft - (a - \beta_1\gamma_1 + b - \beta_2\gamma_2 - c)^2]^2\}.
$$

$$
CS^* = 2f^2v^2t / [4ft - (a - \beta_1\gamma_1 + b - \beta_2\gamma_2 - c)^2]^2.
$$

$$
TS^* = fv^2[12ft - (a - \beta_1\gamma_1 + b - \beta_2\gamma_2 - c)^2] / \{2[4ft - (a - \beta_1\gamma_1 + b - \beta_2\gamma_2 - c)^2]^2\}.
$$

Before equilibrium analysis, we first undertake the following assumption:

Assumption 1. $a - \beta_1\gamma_1 > b - \beta_2\gamma_2 \gg c$. This means the network externality of users is larger than the network externality of driver.

Assumption 2. $4ft - (a - \beta_1\gamma_1 + b - \beta_2\gamma_2 - c)^2 \geq 0$. This means there are obvious differences between users and drivers in the market, and it can also ensure the driver commission rate $\lambda^* = (a - \beta_1\gamma_1 + b - \beta_2\gamma_2 - c)^2/4ft \leq 1$.

Proposition 1. The driver commission rate at the equilibrium state is a strictly monotone increasing function of marginal utility a, b, a strictly increasing function of the value of time β_1, β_2, and a strictly decreasing function of the unit cost t, f.

Proof: from Eq. (12), it is easy to obtain

$$\partial\lambda^*/\partial a = \partial\lambda^*/\partial b = (a - \beta_1\gamma_1 + b - \beta_2\gamma_2 - c)/2ft > 0,$$

$$\partial\lambda^*/\partial\beta_1 = -\gamma_1(a - \beta_1\gamma_1 + b - \beta_2\gamma_2 - c)/2ft > 0,$$
$$\partial\lambda^*/\partial\beta_2 = -\gamma_2(a - \beta_1\gamma_1 + b - \beta_2\gamma_2 - c)/2ft > 0,$$

$$\partial\lambda^*/\partial t = -(a - \beta_1\gamma_1 + b - \beta_2\gamma_2 - c)^2/4ft^2 < 0,$$
$$\partial\lambda^*/\partial f = -(a - \beta_1\gamma_1 + b - \beta_2\gamma_2 - c)^2/4f^2t < 0.$$

This proposition obtains the relationship among the driver commission rate and marginal utility, value of time and the unit cost of two-sided user joining the OCH platform. When the marginal utility and value of time of two-sided user is higher, the driver can get higher commission from each transaction. When the unit cost of two-sided user joining the OCH platform is higher, the driver can get lower commission from each transaction.

Proposition 2. The user payment at equilibrium state is a strictly decreasing function of marginal utility b, a strictly decreasing function of the value of time β_2, and a strictly increasing function of the unit cost t, f. The monotone of function p^* with of a, β_1 depends on the relationship between $a - \beta_1\gamma_1$ and $3(b - \beta_2\gamma_2)$.

Proof: from Eq. (13), it is easy to obtain.

$$\partial p^*/\partial a = 2ft[3(b - \beta_2\gamma_2) - (a - \beta_1\gamma_1) + c]/(a - \beta_1\gamma_1 + b - \beta_2\gamma_2 \quad c)^3,$$

$$\partial p^*/\partial b = 2ft[(b - \beta_2\gamma_2) - 3(a - \beta_1\gamma_1) + 3c]/(a - \beta_1\gamma_1 + b - \beta_2\gamma_2 - c)^3 < 0,$$

$$\partial p^*/\partial\beta_1 = -\gamma_1\partial p^*/\partial a, \quad \partial p^*/\partial\beta_2 = -\gamma_2\partial p^*/\partial b < 0,$$

$$\partial p^*/\partial t = 2f(a - \beta_1\gamma_1 - b + \beta_2\gamma_2 - c)/(a - \beta_1\gamma_1 + b - \beta_2\gamma_2 - c)^2 > 0,$$

$$\partial p^*/\partial f = 2t(a - \beta_1\gamma_1 - b + \beta_2\gamma_2 - c)/(a - \beta_1\gamma_1 + b - \beta_2\gamma_2 - c)^2 > 0.$$

This proposition obtains the relationship between the user payment and other parameters. When the marginal utility and value of time of drivers is higher, the user needs to pay litter for transaction. When the unit cost of two-sided user joining the OCH platform is higher, the user has to pay more for transaction.

The monotone of function r^*, m^*, n^*, L_1^*, L_2^*, TS^* of a, b, β_1, β_2, t, f can be obtained in the manner as stated above.

4 Simulation Analysis

In this section, we only consider the relationship of functions λ^*, p^*, r^*, TS^*, m^*, n^*, L_1^*, L_2^* of marginal utility a, b, while the other parameters are constant. The condition of simulation diagram is listed in Table 1.

Table 1. The condition of simulation diagram

Figure Number	Function	a	b	c	f	t	v	β_1	β_2	γ_1	γ_2
Fig. 1	λ^*	[8, 14]	[3, 4]	0.001	10	10	–	3	1	−0.2	−0.1
Fig. 2	p^*	[8, 14]	[3, 4]	0.001	10	10	–	3	1	−0.2	−0.1
Fig. 3	r^*	[8, 14]	[3, 4]	0.001	10	10	0.01	3	1	−0.2	−0.1
Fig. 4	TS^*	[8, 14]	[3, 4]	0.001	10	10	0.01	3	1	−0.2	−0.1
Fig. 5	m^*	[8, 14]	[3, 4]	0.001	10	10	0.01	3	1	−0.2	−0.1
Fig. 6	n^*	[8, 14]	[3, 4]	0.001	10	10	0.01	3	1	−0.2	−0.1
Fig. 7	L_1^*	[8, 14]	[3, 4]	0.001	10	10	0.01	3	1	−0.2	−0.1
Fig. 8	L_2^*	[8, 14]	[3, 4]	0.001	10	10	0.01	3	1	−0.2	−0.1

The function in Table 1 is defined in Sect. 3. Then, the simulation diagram is indicated as follows:

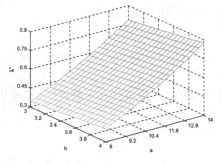   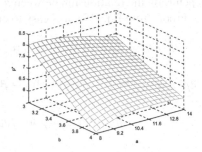

Fig. 1. The relationship among λ^* and a, b **Fig. 2.** The relationship among p^* and a, b

From Fig. 1, we can show that the driver commission rate at equilibrium state is a strictly monotone increasing function of the marginal utility a and b. This means that with the increase of marginal utility, drivers can get higher commission from each transaction. Figure 2 shows that the user payment at the equilibrium state is a strictly monotone decreasing function of marginal utility b and a strictly monotone increasing and then strictly monotone decreasing function of marginal utility a.

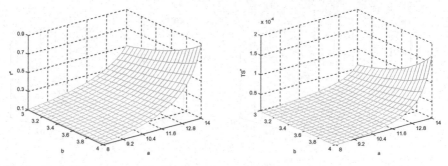

Fig. 3. The relationship among r^* and a, b **Fig. 4.** The relationship among TS^* and a, b

From Fig. 3 and Fig. 4, we can find that the user registration fee and the total social benefit are a strictly monotone increasing function of the marginal utility a and b, respectively. If the marginal utility a (b) is fixed, the increment of the user registration fee (the total social benefit) changes more obviously with the increase of b (a).

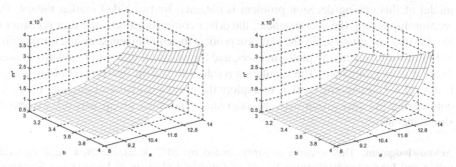

Fig. 5. The relationship among m^* and a, b **Fig. 6.** The relationship among n^* and a, b

From Fig. 5 and Fig. 6, we can see that the user and driver scale is a strictly monotone increasing function of the marginal utility a and b, respectively. If the marginal utility a (b) is fixed, the increment of the user scale (the drive scale) changes more obviously with the increase of b (a). If the marginal utility a and b is fixed at the same time, we can find that the user scale is larger than the driver scale.

From Fig. 7 and Fig. 8, we can find that the platform profit and driver profit is a strictly monotone increasing function of the marginal utility a and b, respectively. If the marginal utility a (b) is fixed, the increment of the platform profit (the drive profit) changes more obviously with the increase of b (a). When the marginal utility a and b is relatively smaller, the platform profit is larger than the drive profit. Otherwise, the platform profit is less than the driver profit fixed at the same time. We can find that the user scale is larger than the driver scale.

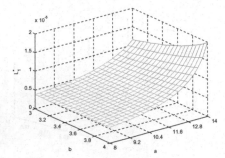 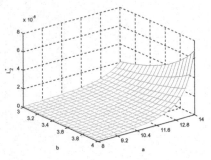

Fig. 7. The relationship among L_1^* and $a,\ b$ **Fig. 8.** The relationship among L_2^* and $a,\ b$

5 Conclusion

In this paper, we study the pricing decision of monopoly OCH platform considering network externality and commission rate. The network externality is inter-group externality which consists of marginal utility and the waiting time, and the dynamic game theory model of this pricing decision problem is obtained by two-sided market theory. The relationship among the user payment, the driver commission rate, the user registration fee, the user and driver scale, the platform profit at the equilibrium state and the marginal utility of the drivers to the platform users, and the marginal utility of the platform users to the drivers is obtained. The simulation results validate the correctness of our analytical results. Our ongoing work is to explore the pricing decision of duopoly platforms considering the inter-group network externality and inner-group network externality simultaneously.

Acknowledgment. This research is partly funded by 2017 Academic New Seedling Cultivation and Innovation Exploration Project of Guizhou University of Finance and Economics ([2017]5736–002), the National Natural Science Foundation of China (71761005).

References

1. Rayle, L., Dai, D., Chan, N., Cervero, R., Shaheen, S.: Just a better taxi? A survey-based comparison of taxis, transit, and ridesourcing services in San Francisco. Transp. Policy **45**, 168–178 (2016)
2. Dias, F.F., Lavieri, P.S., Garikapati, V.M., et al.: A behavioral choice model of the use of car-sharing and ride-sourcing services. Transportation **44**(6), 1307–1323 (2017)
3. Dawes, M.: Perspectives on the Ridesourcing Revolution: Surveying Individual Attitudes Toward Uber and Lyft to Inform Urban Transportation Policymarking. Massachusetts Institute of Technology, Cambridge (2016)
4. Contreras, S.D., Paz, A.: The effects of ride-hailing companies on the taxicab industry in Las Vegas, Nevada. Transpo. Res. Part A Policy Pract. **115**, 63–70 (2018)
5. Nelson, E., Sadowsky, N.: Estimating the impact of ride-hailing app company entry on public transportation use in major US urban areas. BE J. Econ. Anal. Policy **19**(1), 1–21 (2019)

6. Thaithatkul, P., Seo, T., Kusakabe, T., et al.: A passengers matching problem in ridesharing systems by considering user preference. J. Eastern Asia Soc. Transp. Stud. **11**, 1416–1432 (2015)
7. Fahnenschreiber, S., Giindling, F., Keyhani, M.H., et al.: A multi-modal routing approach combining dynamic ride-sharing and public transport. Transp. Res. Procedia **13**, 176–183 (2016)
8. Masoud, N., Jayakrishnan, R.: A real-time algorithm to solve the peer-to-peer ride-matching problem in a flexible ridesharing system. Transp. Res. Part B Methodol. **106**, 218–236 (2017)
9. Thaithatkul, P., Seo, T., Kusakabe, T., et al.: Simulation approach for investigating dynamics of passenger matching problem in smart ridesharing system. Transp. Res. Procedia **21**, 29–41 (2017)
10. Cheikh, S.B., Tahon, C., Hammadi, S.: An evolutionary approach to solve the dynamic multihop ridematching problem. Simulation **93**(1), 3–19 (2017)
11. Yang, H., Yang, T.: Equilibrium properties of taxi markets with search frictions. Transp. Res. Part B Methodol. **45**(4), 696–713 (2011)
12. Wang, X., He, F., Yang, H., et al.: Pricing strategies for a taxi-hailing platform. Transp. Res. Part E Logist. Transp. Rev. **93**, 212–231 (2016)
13. Zha, L., Yin, Y., Yang, H.: Economic analysis of ride-sourcing markets. Transp. Res. Part C Emerg. Technol. **71**, 249–266 (2016)
14. Zha, L., Yin, Y., Du, Y.: Surge pricing and labor supply in the ride-sourcing market. Transp. Res. Procedia **23**, 2–21 (2017)
15. He, F., Wang, X., Lin, X., et al.: Pricing and penalty/compensation strategies of a taxi-hailing platform. Transp. Res. Part C Emerg. Technol. **86**, 263–279 (2018)
16. Hall, J.D., Palsson, C., Price, J.: Is Uber a substitute or complement for public transit? J. Urban Econ. **108**, 36–50 (2018)
17. Alley, J.K.: The Impact of Uber Technologies on the New York city Transportation Industry. University of Arkansas, Arkansas (2016)
18. Chen, J.Y.: Thrown under the bus and outrunning it! The logic of Didi and taxi drivers' labour and activism in the on-demand economy. New Media Soc. **20**(6), 1–21 (2017)
19. Dudley, G., Banister, D., Schwanen, T.: The rise of Uber and regulating the disruptive innovator. Political Q. **88**(3), 492–499 (2017)
20. Schneider, A.: Uber takes the passing lane disruptive competition and taxi-livery service regulations. Elements **11**(2), 11–23 (2015)
21. Edelman, B.G., Geradin, D.: Efficiencies and regulatory shortcuts: how should we regulate companies like Airbnb and Uber? Stanford Technol. Law Rev. **19**, 293–328 (2016)
22. Beer, R., Brakewood, C., Rahman, S., et al.: Qualitative analysis of ride-hailing regulations in major American cities. Transp. Res. Rec. **2650**, 84–91 (2017)
23. Lee, C.: To uberize or not to uberize? opportunities and challenges in Southeast Asia's sharing economy. ISEAS Perspect. **33**, 1–6 (2016)
24. Bengtsson, N.: Efficient informal trade: theory and experimental evidence from the Cape Town taxi market. J. Dev. Econ. **115**, 85–98 (2015)
25. Jiao, J.F.: Investigating Uber price surges during a special event in Austin, TX. Res. Transp. Bus. Manag. **29**, 101–107 (2018)
26. Shaheen, S., Cohen, A.: Shared ride services in North America: definitions impacts, and the future of pooling. Transp. Rev. **39**(4), 427–442 (2019)
27. Yang, D., Yu, K.: "'Internet+'" epoch social management innovation: challenge and response to the case of Shanghai taxi operations management. Int. J. Social Sci. Stud. **3**(6), 197–201 (2015)
28. Rochet, J.C., Tirole, J.: Platform competition in two-sided markets. J. Eur. Econ. Assoc. **1**(4), 990–1029 (2003)

29. Armstrong, M.: Competition in two-sided markets. Rand J. Econ. **37**(3), 668–691 (2006)
30. Hagiu, A., Halaburda, H.: Information and two-sided platform profit. Int. J. Ind. Organ. **34**, 25–35 (2014)
31. Roger, G.: Two-sided competition with vertical differentiation. J. Econ. **120**(3), 193–217 (2016). https://doi.org/10.1007/s00712-016-0507-3
32. Nourinejad, M., Ramezani, M.: Ride-sourcing modeling and pricing in non-equilibrium two-sided market. Transp. Res. Procedia **38**, 833–852 (2019)
33. Kung, L.C., Zhong, G.Y.: The optimal pricing strategy for two-sided platform delivery in the sharing economy. Transp. Res. Part E Logist. Transp. Rev. **101**, 1–2 (2017)
34. Malavolti, E.: Single till or dual till at airports: A two-sided market analysis. Transp. Res. Procedia **14**, 3696–3703 (2016)
35. Djavadian, S., Chow, J.Y.: An agent-based day-to-day adjustment process for modeling 'mobility as a service' with a two-sided flexible transport market. Transp. Res. Part B Methodol. **104**, 36–57 (2017)

GTRS Based Joint Time Synchronization and Localization in Wireless Sensor Networks

Wei Liu, Qiqi Zhang, and Zhiqiang Dun$^{(\boxtimes)}$

State Key Labs of ISN, Xidian University,
Xi'an 710071, Shaanxi, People's Republic of China
liuweixd@mail.xidian.edu.cn, {qqzhang_7,Zhiqiangdun}@stu.xidian.edu.cn

Abstract. In this paper, we investigate the joint time synchronization and localization in wireless sensor networks. Specially, based on time-of-arrival (TOA), we consider a squared-range-based least squares formulation problem and propose a generalized trust region subproblem (GTRS) algorithm based joint time synchronization and localization, which can guarantee an optimal solution to the joint time synchronization and localization problem. Sufficient experiments results show that the estimation accuracy of the proposed algorithm outperforms the traditionalunconstraint linear least squares (ULLS) and nearly coincides with the Cramer-Rao lower bound (CRLB).

Keywords: Optimal solution · Joint time synchronization and localization · Generalized trust region sub-problems (GTRS)

1 Introduction

Source localization with wireless sensor networks has attracted significant attentions owing to the enormous number of applications and services, including vehicle navigation, target detection and indoor positioning, etc. [1]. Hence high accuracy localization methods have been widely investigated. Traditionally, source localization methods include time of arrival (TOA), time difference of arrival (TDOA), received signal strength (RSS) and angle of arrival (AOA) [2,3]. Among them, TOA based localization methods have attracted intensive interests [4–12]. In [4] TOA based localization was formulated as a maximum likelihood (ML) problem. As it is difficult to solve this ML problem directly, suboptimal methods such as the Taylor search method [4], and the Gauss-Newton search method [5] were proposed. [6] translated nonlinear constraints of an ML solution into a set of linear constraint equations and obtained an approximate solution to

The financial support of the program of Key Industry Innovation Chain of Shaanxi Province, China (2017ZDCXL-GY-04-02) and of the program of Xi'an Science and Technology Plan (201805029YD7CG13(5)), Shaanxi, China are gratefully acknowledged.

H. Song and D. Jiang (Eds.): SIMUtools 2020, LNICST 369, pp. 771–780, 2021.
https://doi.org/10.1007/978-3-030-72792-5_61

the ML problem. In addition, [7] and [8] relaxed the ML problem to a semi-definite programming (SDP) problem, which cannot guarantee an optimal solution. Another kind of localization methods extensively used formulate the localization problem into a nonlinear least squares (NLS) problem, for example the squared-range-based least square (SR-LS) [9]. In order to solve the SR-LS problem, [10] proposed a constrained weighted least squares (CWLS) algorithm using the Lagrange multiplier method to obtain a suboptimal solution to the SR-LS problem. Besides, a weighted linear least squares algorithm (WLS) only for a linear anchor node distribution was proposed in [11], which provided a suboptimal solution to the SR-LS problem. Furthermore, [12] proposed a generalized trust region subproblem (GTRS) based algorithm, which guaranteed an optimal solution to the SR-LS problem.

However, all works above assumed perfect synchronization among various sensors. Traditionally, synchronization and localization have been treated separately. In practice, sensors are asynchronous in time with clock bias [13]. In this case, even there is a small error in the synchronization, it can propagate into the localization step and be amplified, which may significantly degrade localization accuracy. Consequently, joint time synchronization and localization has aroused wide interests recently [14–16]. The author in [14] formulated the joint time synchronization and localization as an ML problem, and proposed an unconstraint linear least squares (ULLS) algorithm, which provided a suboptimal solution to the ML problem. A suboptimal WLS algorithm for joint time synchronization and localization was proposed in [15]. The authors in [16] relaxed the ML problem into a SDP problem, which can not always guarantee to obtain the optimal solution.

Against this background, we investigate the joint time synchronization and localization problem. Specially, we formulate it as a SR-LS problem and propose a novel GTRS based algorithm, which can guarantee to the optimal solution to the SR-LS problem.

Notation: The lower case represents a scalar, while the upper and the lower boldface represent a matrix and a vector, respectively. I_n represents the unit matrix of $n \times n$, and $0_{n \times k}$ represents the all-zero matrix of $n \times k$. $\| x \|$ denotes the 2-norm of the vector x. Denote $\nabla_x^n y(x)$ as the n order derivative of function $y(x)$ on vector x and denote $y'(z)$ as the first order derivative of function $y(z)$ on scalar z. $A \succ 0$ ($A \succeq 0$) indicates that A is a positive definite matrix (a semi-definite matrix).

2   System Model

The system considered in this paper is showed in Fig. 1, where there are m anchor nodes and one source node. For the ith anchor node, location vector $p^i \in \mathbb{R}^n$ and clock bias τ_i [15] ($i = 1, 2 \cdots m$) are known. For source node, location vector $p^i \in \mathbb{R}^n$ and clock bias τ are unknown. The ith TOA measurement is given by [15]

$$T_i = \tau - \tau_i + \frac{\| p - p_i \|}{c} + n_i \quad (i = 1, 2 \cdots m) \tag{1}$$

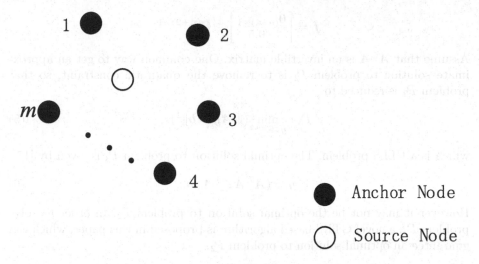

Fig. 1. Localization system

where n_i is the measurement noise at the ith anchor node, which is independent and identically distributed (i.i.d.) Gaussian random variables with zero mean and variance σ^2, while c is the propagation speed of electromagnetic waves. In this paper, for simplicity we assume $c = 1$, then the Eq. (1) can be written as [15]

$$T_i = \tau - \tau_i + \| \boldsymbol{p} - \boldsymbol{p}_i \| + n_i \quad (i = 1, 2 \cdots m). \tag{2}$$

Based on the Eq. (2), we want to find optimal $\boldsymbol{p}^*$ and τ^* to the following problem P_1.

$$P_1 : \min_{\tau \in \mathbb{R}, p \in \mathbb{R}^n} \sum_{i=1}^{m} ((T_i - \tau + \tau_i)^2 - \| \boldsymbol{p} - \boldsymbol{p}_i \|^2)^2, \tag{3}$$

which is a SR-LS problem. Denote $\alpha = \| \boldsymbol{p} \|^2 - \tau^2$, problem P_1 can be equivalently transformed into

$$P_2 : \min_{\boldsymbol{y} \in \mathbb{R}^{n+2}} \left\{ \| \boldsymbol{A}\boldsymbol{y} - \boldsymbol{b} \|^2 : \boldsymbol{y}^T \boldsymbol{D} \boldsymbol{y} + 2\boldsymbol{f}^T \boldsymbol{y} = 0 \right\}, \tag{4}$$

which is a constrained optimization problem, where

$$\boldsymbol{A} = \begin{bmatrix} -2\boldsymbol{p}_1{}^T & 2(\tau_1 + T_1) & 1 \\ \vdots & \vdots & \vdots \\ -2\boldsymbol{p}_m{}^T & 2(\tau_m + T_m) & 1 \end{bmatrix} \in \mathbb{C}^{m \times (n+2)}, \boldsymbol{y} = \begin{bmatrix} \boldsymbol{p}^T & \tau & \alpha \end{bmatrix}^T \in \mathbb{C}^{(n+2) \times 1}$$

$$\boldsymbol{b} = \begin{bmatrix} (\tau_1 + T_1)^2 - \| \boldsymbol{p}_1 \|^2 \\ \vdots \\ (\tau_m + T_m)^2 - \| \boldsymbol{p}_m \|^2 \end{bmatrix} \in \mathbb{C}^{m \times 1}, \boldsymbol{D} = \begin{bmatrix} \boldsymbol{I}_n & & \\ & -1 & \\ & & 0 \end{bmatrix} \in \mathbb{C}^{(n+2) \times (n+2)}$$

$$f = \begin{bmatrix} \mathbf{0}_{(n+1)\times 1} \\ -0.5 \end{bmatrix} \in \mathbb{C}^{(n+2)\times 1}$$

Assume that $A^T A$ is an invertible matrix. One common way to get an approximate solution to problem P_2 is to remove the quadratic constraint, so that problem P_2 is reduced to

$$P_3: \min_{y \in \mathbb{R}^{n+2}} (\| Ay - b \|^2). \tag{5}$$

which is a ULLS problem. The optimal solution to problem P_3 is given by [17]

$$\hat{y} = (A^T A)^{-1} A^T b. \tag{6}$$

However it may not be the optimal solution to problem P_2. In order to solve problem P_2, a novel GTRS based algorithm is proposed in this paper, which can guarantee an optimal solution to problem P_2.

3 GTRS Based Joint Time Synchronization and Localization

Denote

$$c(y) = y^T D y + 2 f^T y, \tag{7}$$

$$q(y) = \| Ay - b \|^2, \tag{8}$$

Problem P_2 can be equivalently expressed as

$$P_4: \min_{y \in \mathbb{R}^{n+2}} \{ q(y) : c(y) = 0 \}. \tag{9}$$

Theorem 1: If $c(y)$ and $q(y)$ are quadratic and continuous functions on $\mathbb{R}^{n+2}$ and $\min\{c(y)\} < 0 < \max\{c(y)\}$, y is an optimal solution for problem P_4 if and only if there is a λ that satisfies the following equations

$$(A^T A + \lambda D)y = A^T b - \lambda f, \tag{10}$$

$$y^T D y + 2 f^T y = 0, \tag{11}$$

$$A^T A + \lambda D \succeq 0. \tag{12}$$

Proof. As $c(y)$ is a quadratic and continuous function and $\min\{c(y)\} < 0 < \max\{c(y)\}$, based on [18, Theorem 3.2], y is an optimal solution for problem P_4, if and only if there is a λ satisfying the following equations

$$\nabla_y q(y) + \lambda \nabla_y c(y) = 0, \tag{13}$$

$$c(y) = 0, \tag{14}$$

$$\nabla_y^2 q(y) + \lambda \nabla_y^2 c(y) \succeq 0. \tag{15}$$

Following the rule of derivatives of vector [19, Chapter 2.4], we have

$$\nabla_y q(y) = 2A^T(Ay - b), \quad \nabla_y^2 q(y) = 2A^T A,$$
$$\nabla_y c(y) = 2Dy + 2f, \qquad \nabla_y^2 c(y) = 2D. \tag{16}$$

Based on Eqs. (16), Eqs. (13), (14) and (15) can be reduced to (10), (11) and (12), respectively.

Remark 1: $c(y)$ is a continuous and quadratic function.

Proof. Obviously, $c(y)$ is a continuous function on $\mathbb{R}^{n+2}$. Furthermore, as D is a nonzero matrix, $\nabla_y^2 c(y) \neq 0$ holds. Thus $c(y)$ is a quadratic function.

Remark 2: The inequality $\min\{c(y)\} < 0 < \max\{c(y)\}$ is always satisfied.

Proof. We can chose $y_1 = \begin{bmatrix} 0_{1\times(n+1)} & 1 \end{bmatrix}^T$ and $y_2 = \begin{bmatrix} 0_{1\times(n+1)} & -1 \end{bmatrix}^T$. Hence, $c(y_1) = -1 < 0$ while $c(y_2) = 1 > 0$. Consequently, $\min\{c(y)\} \leq c(y_1) = -1 < 0$ and $\max\{c(y)\} \geq c(y_2) = 1 > 0$. Hence $\min\{c(y)\} < 0 < \max\{c(y)\}$.

Remark 3: In order to satisfy the constraint $A^T A$ is an invertible matrix, m must satisfy $m \geq 4$.

Proof. As $A \in \mathbb{C}^{m\times(n+2)}$, $\text{Rank}(A^T A) \leq \min(m, n+2)$. As $n \geq 2$, $n+2 \geq 4$, in order to satisfy the constraint $A^T A$ is an invertible matrix, m must satisfy $m \geq 4$.

Theorem 2: If there exists a λ^* satisfying (10), (11) and (12), λ^* is the unique solution of

$$\varphi(\lambda) = 0, \lambda \in I, \tag{17}$$

where

$$\varphi(\lambda) = \tilde{y}(\lambda)^T D\tilde{y}(\lambda) + 2f^T \tilde{y}(\lambda), \tag{18}$$

where $\tilde{y}(\lambda)$ is the optimal solution of problem P_4 and $I = \left[-\frac{1}{\lambda_1}, -\frac{1}{\lambda_{n+2}} \right]$.

Proof. Denote $\phi(i), (i = 1, 2 \cdots n+2)$ as the ith eigenvalue of matrix $A^T A + \lambda D$. In order to satisfy (12), $\phi(i) \geq 0$ must hold.

As

$$A^T A + \lambda D = ((A^T A)^{\frac{1}{2}})^T (I_{n+2} + \lambda(A^T A)^{-\frac{1}{2}} D(A^T A)^{-\frac{1}{2}})(A^T A)^{\frac{1}{2}} \tag{19}$$

matrices $A^T A + \lambda D$ and $I_{n+2} + \lambda(A^T A)^{-\frac{1}{2}} D(A^T A)^{-\frac{1}{2}}$ are congruent [20]. Hence these two matrices have the same inertial index [20], i.e. they have same number of positive, zero and negative eigenvalues. Denote $\psi_i, (i = 1, 2 \cdots n+2)$ as the ith eigenvalue of $I_{n+2} + \lambda(A^T A)^{-\frac{1}{2}} D(A^T A)^{-\frac{1}{2}}$. Hence in order to satisfy $\phi(i) \geq 0$, $\psi(i) \geq 0$ must hold. Denote $\lambda_i, (i = 1, 2 \cdots n+2)$, arranged in the non-increasing order, as the ith eigenvalue of matrix $(A^T A)^{-\frac{1}{2}} D(A^T A)^{-\frac{1}{2}}$. Clearly, $\psi_i = 1 + \lambda\lambda_i, (i = 1, 2 \cdots n+2)$. Furthermore, as matrices $(A^T A)^{\frac{1}{2}} D(A^T A)^{-\frac{1}{2}}$ and D are congruent, these two matrices have the same inertial index as well. As the matrix D has n positive eigenvalues, one zero eigenvalue and one negative eigenvalue, λ_i satisfies following inequality.

$$\lambda_1 \geq \lambda_2 \geq \cdots \geq \lambda_n > \lambda_{n+1} = 0 > \lambda_{n+2}. \tag{20}$$

In order to satisfy $\psi(i) \geq 0, (i = 1, 2 \cdots n+2)$, there are three different scenarios to consider.

1. For $i \in [1, n]$, according to (20), $\lambda_i > 0$. Hence we have

$$\psi_i \geq 0 \Rightarrow \lambda \geq -\frac{1}{\lambda_i} \Rightarrow \lambda \geq -\frac{1}{\lambda_1}, i \in [1, n]; \tag{21}$$

2. For $i = n + 1$, according to (20), $\lambda_{n+1} = 0$. Hence we have

$$\psi_{n+1} = 1 > 0 \Rightarrow \lambda \in R; \tag{22}$$

3. For $i = n + 2$, according to (20), $\lambda_{n+2} < 0$. Hence we have

$$\psi_{n+2} \geq 0 \Rightarrow \lambda \leq -\frac{1}{\lambda_{n+2}}. \tag{23}$$

Denote I is the interval of λ. Consequently, if λ satisfies (12), $I = \left[-\frac{1}{\lambda_1}, -\frac{1}{\lambda_{n+2}} \right]$.

As λ satisfies (10), (11) and (12), according to Theorem 1, there exists an optimal solution y denoted as $\tilde{y}(\lambda)$ for problem P_4. Next, we will show that $\varphi(\lambda) = 0$ has a unique solution within the interval I. As $\tilde{y}(\lambda)$ satisfies (10), we have

$$(A^T A + \lambda D)\tilde{y}(\lambda) = A^T b - \lambda f \tag{24}$$

Following the rule of derivatives of scalars [19, Chapter 2.4], taking the derivative of (24) on λ at both sides, we have

$$-(D\tilde{y}(\lambda) + f) = (A^T A + \lambda D)\tilde{y}'(\lambda). \tag{25}$$

As $\tilde{y}(\lambda)$ satisfies (11), we have

$$\tilde{y}(\lambda)^T D\tilde{y}(\lambda) + 2f^T \tilde{y}(\lambda) = 0. \tag{26}$$

Denote

$$\varphi(\lambda) = \tilde{y}(\lambda)^T D\tilde{y}(\lambda) + 2f^T \tilde{y}(\lambda). \tag{27}$$

Obviously, $\varphi(\lambda)$ is a continuous function of λ. Taking the derivative of (27) on λ at both sides, we have

$$\varphi'(\lambda) = (\nabla_{\tilde{y}(\lambda)} \varphi(\lambda))^T \tilde{y}'(\lambda). \tag{28}$$

Following the rule of derivatives of vectors [19, Chapter 2.4], we can obtain

$$\nabla_{\tilde{y}(\lambda)} \varphi(\lambda) = 2D\tilde{y}(\lambda) + 2f = -2(A^T A + \lambda D)\tilde{y}'(\lambda), \tag{29}$$

where the second equality is based on (25). Upon substituting (29) into (28), we can obtain

$$\varphi'(\lambda) = -2\tilde{\boldsymbol{y}}'(\lambda)^T (\boldsymbol{A}^T \boldsymbol{A} + \lambda \boldsymbol{D})\tilde{\boldsymbol{y}}'(\lambda). \tag{30}$$

Furthermore, for

$$\lambda \in \left(-\frac{1}{\lambda_1}, -\frac{1}{\lambda_{n+2}}\right), \tag{31}$$

$\boldsymbol{A}^T \boldsymbol{A} + \lambda \boldsymbol{D}$ is a positive definite matrix, hence $\varphi'(\lambda) < 0$ and $\varphi(\lambda)$ is strictly monotonically decreasing. Note that here we strictly limit $\boldsymbol{A}^T \boldsymbol{A} + \lambda \boldsymbol{D}$ to be a positive definite matrix. The reason is that for tens of thousands of experiments, the unique solution to $\varphi(\lambda) = 0$ has never been the endpoints of interval I, so we assume $\boldsymbol{A}^T \boldsymbol{A} + \lambda \boldsymbol{D} \succ \boldsymbol{0}$. The same phenomenon is also observed in [12].

Moreover, it is very difficult to theoretically prove there exist two points λ_a and λ_b, which satisfy $\varphi(\lambda_a) < 0$ and $\varphi(\lambda_b) > 0$. However during our experimental simulations, we can always find two points λ_a and λ_b in interval I satisfying $\varphi(\lambda_a) < 0$ and $\varphi(\lambda_b) > 0$. Therefore, we can use bisection method to find the unique solution λ^* to $\varphi(\lambda) = 0$ [12].

In summary, the GTRS based joint time synchronization and localization is presented in Table 1.

Table 1. The GTRS based joint time synchronization and localization

1)	Calculate the interval I
2)	Find two points λ_a and λ_b in interval I to satisfy $\varphi(\lambda_a) < 0$ and $\varphi(\lambda_b) > 0$
3)	Use bisection method to find the unique solution λ^* of $\varphi(\lambda) = 0$
4)	Substitute the unique solution λ^* into $\tilde{\boldsymbol{y}}(\lambda^*) = (\boldsymbol{A}^T \boldsymbol{A} + \lambda^* \boldsymbol{D})^{-1}(\boldsymbol{A}^T \boldsymbol{b} - \lambda^* \boldsymbol{f})$ and get the optimal $\boldsymbol{p}^*$ and τ^*

4   Simulation Results

In this section, we demonstrate the performance of the proposed GTRS based joint time synchronization and localization. We simulate a localization system consisting of five anchor nodes and one source node. As showed in Fig. 2, the coordinate $\boldsymbol{p}_i$ of the ith anchor node is generated randomly following a uniform distribution in the region of $[-100, -50] \times [-100, -50]$ and the coordinate $\boldsymbol{p}$ of the source node is randomly placed following a uniform distribution in the region of $[10, 20] \times [10, 20]$. The clock bias τ_i and τ are drawn from one-dimensional uniform distribution in the region of $[0, 1]$. Besides, σ^2 is set to be $10^{-6}, 10^{-5}, 10^{-4}, 10^{-3}, 10^{-2}, 10^{-1}$ and 1, respectively.

In this simulation, our proposed GTRS based joint time synchronization and localization are compared with both ULLS algorithm in (6) and Cramer-Rao

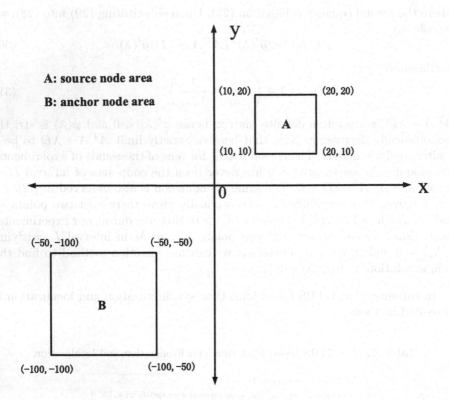

Fig. 2. Localization geometry

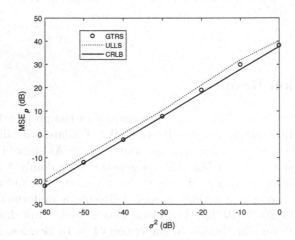

Fig. 3. MSE against σ^2 for source localization of the GTRS, ULLS and CRLB

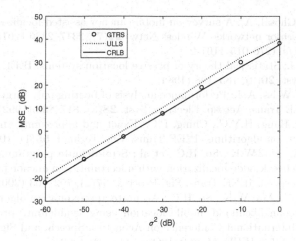

Fig. 4. MSE against σ^2 for clock bias of the GTRS, ULLS and CRLB

lower bound (CRLB) [21]. The metric of estimation performance for source node location and clock bias is mean square error (MSE). The MSE of source node coordinate is denoted as $\text{MSE}_{p} = \frac{1}{L} \sum\limits_{l=1}^{L} \| \bar{p}^l - p^l \|^2$ and the MSE of source node clock bias is denoted as $\text{MSE}_{\tau} = \frac{1}{L} \sum\limits_{l=1}^{L} \| \bar{\tau}^l - \tau^l \|^2$, where L is the total number of independent simulations for each value of σ^2. Furthermore p^l and τ^l are denoted as actual values at the lth simulation of L, while $\bar{p}^l$ and $\bar{\tau}^l$ denote the estimation values of p^l and τ^l, respectively. Specifically, in our simulation, $L = 10000$. The simulation results are presented in Fig. 3 and Fig. 4 respectively.

In Fig. 3, it can be seen the proposed GTRS based algorithm outperforms ULLS and nearly coincides with the CRLB. Similar phenomenon can be observed in Fig. 4, the estimation accuracy of clock bias of our proposed algorithm outperforms ULLS and nearly coincides with CRLB.

5   Conclusion

In this paper, we investigated the joint time synchronization and localization in wireless sensor networks. We proposed an optimal GTRS based joint time synchronization and localization algorithm by using TOA measurements, which can outperform traditional ULLS algorithm and nearly coincide with the CRLB.

References

1. Win, M.Z., Conti, A., Mazuelas, S., et al.: Network localization and navigation via cooperation. IEEE Commun. Mag. **49**(5), 56–62 (2011)
2. Mao, G., Fidan, B., Anderson, B.D.O.: Wireless sensor network localization techniques. Comput. Netw. **51**(10), 2529–2553 (2007)

3. Halder, S., Ghosal, A.: A survey on mobile anchor assisted localization techniques in wireless sensor networks. Wireless Netw. **22**(7), 2317–2336 (2015). https://doi.org/10.1007/s11276-015-1101-2

4. Torrieri, D.J.: Statistical theory of passive location systems. IEEE Trans. Aerosp. Electron. Syst. **20**(2), 183–198 (1984)

5. Gavish, M., Weiss, A.J.: Performance analysis of bearing-only target location algorithms. IEEE Trans. Aerosp. Electron. Syst. **28**(3), 817–828 (1992)

6. Chan, Y.T., Hang, H.Y.C., Ching, P.C.: Exact and approximate maximum likelihood localization algorithms. IEEE Trans. Veh. Technol. **55**(1), 10–16 (2006)

7. Lui, K.W.K., Ma, W.K., So, H.C., et al.: Semi-definite programming algorithms for sensor network node localization with uncertainties in anchor positions and/or propagation speed. IEEE Trans. Sig. Process. **57**(2), 752–763 (2009)

8. Cheung, K.W., Ma, W.K., So, H.C.: Accurate approximation algorithm for TOA-based maximum likelihood mobile location using semidefinite programming. In: 2004 IEEE International Conference on Acoustics, Speech, and Signal Processing, vol. 2, pp. ii–145-8 IEEE, Montreal, Que., Canada (2004)

9. Li, D., Hu, Y.: Least square solutions of energy based acoustic source localization problem. In: Proceeding of International Conference on Parallel Processing Workshops, pp. 443–446. IEEE, Montreal, QC, Canada (2004)

10. Cheung, K.W., So, H.C., Ma, W.K., et al.: Least squares algorithms for time-of-arrival-based mobile location. IEEE Trans. Signal Process. **52**(4), 1121–1130 (2004)

11. Kim, E., Kim, K.: Distance estimation with weighted least squares for mobile beacon-based localization in wireless sensor networks. IEEE Signal Process. Lett. **17**(6), 559–562 (2010)

12. Beck, A., Stoica, P., Li, J.: Exact and approximate solutions of source localization problems. IEEE Trans. Signal Process. **56**(5), 1770–1778 (2008)

13. Wu, Y.C., Chaudhari, Q., Serpedin, E.: Clock synchronization of wireless sensor networks. IEEE Sig. Process. Mag. **28**(1), 124–138 (2011)

14. Zheng, J., Wu, Y.-C.: Joint time synchronization and localization of an unknown node in wireless sensor networks. IEEE Trans. Sig. Process. **58**(3), 1309–1320 (2010)

15. Zhu, S., Ding, Z.: Joint synchronization and localization using TOAs: a linearization based WLS solution. IEEE J. Sel. Areas Commun. **28**(7), 1017–1025 (2010)

16. Vaghefi, R.M., Buehrer, R.M.: Cooperative joint synchronization and localization in wireless sensor networks. IEEE Trans. Sig. Process. **63**(14), 3615–3627 (2015)

17. Stoica, P., Li, J.: Lecture notes - source localization from range-difference measurements. IEEE Sig. Process. Mag. **23**(6), 63–66 (2006)

18. Moré, J.J.: Generalizations of the trust region problem. Optim. Meth. Softw. **2**(3–4), 189–209 (1993)

19. Petersen, K.B., Pedersen, M.S.: The matrix cookbook, 2nd edn. Technical University of Denmark, Denmark (2012)

20. Leon, S.J., Bica, I., Hohn, T.: Linear Algebra with Applications, 1st edn. Macmillan, New York (1980)

21. Larsson, G.: Cramer-Rao bound analysis of distributed positioning in sensor networks. IEEE Sig. Process. Lett. **11**(3), 334–337 (2004)

Neural Network Algorithm of Multi-team Game and Its Application in Parallel-Link Communication Networks Flow Control

Zixin Liu[1,2]([✉]) [ID], Huawei Yang[3], and Lianglin Xiong[4] [ID]

[1] School of Mathematics and Statistics, Guizhou University of Finance and Economics, Guiyang, People's Republic of China
[2] Guizhou Key Laboratory of Big Data Statistics Analysis, Guizhou University of Finance and Economics, Guiyang, People's Republic of China
[3] School of Big Data Application and Economics, Guizhou University of Finance and Economics, Guiyang, People's Republic of China
[4] School of Mathematics and Computer Science, Yunnan Minzu University, Kunming, People's Republic of China

Abstract. This paper investigates the approximate calculation problem of noninferior Nash equilibrium (NNE) in multi-team game. Combined with variational inequalities theory, Nash equilibrium theory, and dynamic system theory, a projection neural network (PNN) algorithm for computing NNE of multi-team game with smooth payoff functions is derived. Utilizing stable theory, stability criteria of NNE in multi-team game are further given. As an application, a flow control model of parallel-link communication networks based on multi-team game and neural network algorithm is elaborated. Finally, a simulation result for two teams, two communication links, and two users in each team parallel-linkcommunication network is also given to illustrate the effectiveness of the PNN algorithm proposed in this paper.

Keywords: Projection neural network · Multi-team game · Noninferior Nash equilibrium · Variational inequalities · Flow control · Parallel-link communication networks

This work is supported by National Nature Science Foundation of China under Grants 62062018, 61472093, 11461082, 11761018, Guizhou Province University Science and Technology Top Talents Project KY2018047, Guizhou University of Finance and Economics 2018XZD01, Science and Technology Planning Project of Guizhou Province of China under Grants [2017] 1016, the Innovation Exploration and Academic New Seedling Project of Guizhou University of Finance and Economics (No. Qian Ke He Ping Tai Ren Cai [2017] 5736-025), and Guizhou Key Laboratory of Big Data Statistics Analysis (No.: Guizhou Science and Technology Cooperation Platform Talent [2019] 5103).

H. Song and D. Jiang (Eds.): SIMUtools 2020, LNICST 369, pp. 781–795, 2021.
https://doi.org/10.1007/978-3-030-72792-5_62

1   Introduction

In essence, game theory is a mathematical model, which mainly studies the conflict and cooperation between players in a rational situation [1]. It is widely used in computer science, psychology, politics, economics, radio resource allocation and so on [2–7], and has been recognized as one of the most useful tool to deal with all kinds of science problems.

Recently, considering that the large collections of small agents make strategically interdependent decisions in many economic, social, and technological environments, convex static multi-team was first introduced in [8,9]. This work is very important because this game model can find specific application scenarios in economic management, biological evolution, wireless network and other real systems. Different from conventional noncooperative games and cooperative games, multi-team games not only have the characteristics of noncooperative games, but also the characteristics of cooperative games. In multi-team games, there is a non cooperative relationship among decision makers among groups, but it is a cooperative relationship among decision makers within a group. The characteristic of multi-team games lies in that they merge the concepts of team theory and game theory. And the equilibrium strategy introduced in [8] and [9] is called noninferior Nash strategy (NNS). This new equilibrium strategy provides a new framework for the analysis of the master-slave group game to solve the complex coordination and competeing problem between decision-makers. In [10], E. Ahmed et al. generalized the static multi-team game derived in [8,9] into dynamical case with bounded rationality. And they pointed out that the NNS is Pareto optimal if the players belong to different teams.

As is well known that, in game theory, computation problems, existence and stability analysis problems for Nash equilibrium are very important. In recent decades, there are many existence theorems and stability criteria for Nash equilibrium [11–13]. For existence problem, utilizing Brouwer fixed point theorem, Schauder fixed point theorem, and Ky fan inequality, J. Yu in [11] deeply researched the existence problems of all kinds of different game models, and derived many existence results. Additional, for set-valued case, applying Kukutani fixed point theorem, set-valued existence results are also given in [11]. For stability problem, by introducing a Hausdorff distance on a complete metric space, J. Yu also established some profound and significant stability results under Baire classification. It is worth pointing out that most of these previous existence and stability results are theoretical perfection but lack of practicality, since they are too abstract. They are theoretical significance instead of practice. In economic and engineering problems, people often care about the calculation of Nash equilibrium, it is a key step in the practical application of game theory. Recently, optimal algorithm, neural network algorithm, and experiment methods for Nash equilibrium have been derived in [14–16]. However, these previous work did not mention the noninferior Nash equilibrium computation problem on multi-team game. In [17] and [18], the authors only researched the noninferior Nash equilibrium computation problem on multi-team Cournot game in a simple case. For general case, how to establish a more practice algorithm is worth discussing, which motivates this study.

Combined with variational inequalities theory, Nash equilibrium theory, and dynamic system theory, a projection neural network (PNN) algorithm for computing NNE of multi-team game with smooth payoff functions is derived. Utilizing stable theory, stability criteria of NNE in multi-team game are further given. As an application, a flow control model of parallel-link communication networks based on multi-team game and neural network algorithm is elaborated. Finally, a simulation result for two teams, two communication links, and two users in each team parallel-link communication network is also given to illustrate the effectiveness of the PNN algorithm proposed in this paper.

This paper is organized as follows. The basic problem of multi-team game is given in Sect. 2. The equivalence between multi-team game with projection neural network is given in Sect. 3. Stability analysis is given in Sect. 4. In Sect. 5, an application of flow control model of wireless ad hoc network based on multi-team game is given. And its related simulation is also performed, while the conclusions are drawn in Sect. 6.

2   Continuous Static Multi-team Games

Considering a n-team continuous static multi-team games: Let team $N \in \mathbb{N}, \mathbb{N} = \{1, 2, \cdots, n\}$ have m_N members of decision makers, and let the control variable of the ith member x_i^N be a vector of dimension m_i^N. Let $x^N = (x_1^N, x_2^N, \cdots, x_{m_N}^N)$ denote the overall control vector for team N; matric space X_i^N be the strategy set of the ith player in team N, $X^N = \prod_{i=1}^{m_N} X_i^N$ denotes the strategy space for the overall control vector x^N of team N. For each $i \in \mathbb{N}$, denote $\hat{i} = \mathbb{N}\backslash\{i\}$, $X = \prod_{i=1}^{n} X^i$. $f_i^N : X \to R$ denotes the ith player's payoff function in team N, respectively.

For n-team noncooperative game, if there exists $x_* = (x_*^1, x_*^2, \cdots, x_*^n) \in X$ such that

$$f^i(x_*^i, x_*^{\hat{i}}) = \max_{u^i \in X^i} \sum_{j=1}^{m_i} \lambda_j^i f_j^i(u^i, x_*^{\hat{i}}), \forall i \in \mathbb{N},$$

then x_* is called the noninferior Nash equilibrium (NNE), where $\lambda^i = (\lambda_1^i, \lambda_2^i, \cdots, \lambda_{m_i}^i) \in W^i, i \in \mathbb{N}$, and W^i is given by

$$W^i = \{\lambda^i \in R^{m_i} | \sum_{j=1}^{m_i} \lambda_j^i = 1, 0 \leq \lambda_j^i \leq 1\}, i \in \mathbb{N}.$$

Assumptions.

(1) $\forall j \in \{1, 2, \cdots, m_i\}, i \in \mathbb{N}$, strategy set $X_j^i \in R^{m_i}$ is nonempty, convex, and compact.

(2) $\forall j \in \{1, 2, \cdots, m_i\}, i \in \mathbb{N}$, payoff function $f^i : X \to R$ is continuously differentiable, and $\forall x^{\hat{i}} \in X^{\hat{i}}, u^i \to f_j^i(u^i, x^{\hat{i}})$ is concave on X^i.

Remark 1. If function f satisfies assumptions (1) and (2), then our concerned n-team continuous static multi-team game at least has one NNE. See Lemma 4 for details.

Lemma 1. *Set* $\nabla f(x) = (\frac{\partial f}{\partial x_1}, \frac{\partial f}{\partial x_2}, \frac{\partial f}{\partial x_n})$, *if payoff function* f *satisfies assumptions (1) and (2), then*

$$f(y) \leq f(x) + \langle \nabla f(x), y - x \rangle,$$

Remark 2. In [8–10], the authors deeply researched the noninferior Nash strategies problem for multi-team system. However, they only gave out the algorithm of the noninferior Nash equilibrium for two-team system instead of multi-team system. In this paper, we will give out a general neural network algorithm for the noninferior Nash equilibrium of multi-team system.

Remark 3. By utilizing Kakutani fixed point theorem, Y. Liu and M.A. Simaan in [9] gave out the noninferior Nash equilibrium's existence theorem for two-team system, when the payoff function f is jointly continuous and strictly convex. In this paper, we will show that for two-team or multi-team system, the existence result only requires the payoff function f satisfying assumption (2).

3   Equivalent Relation Between Variational Inequality and Multi-team Game

Under assumptions (1) and (2), we will prove that a continuous static multi-team game problem can also uniquely correspond to a variational inequality problem.

Lemma 2. *Let* $f : X \to R$ *be a continuous differentiable and concave function defined on a nonempty closed convex set* X, *then* $f(x^*) = \max\limits_{x \in X} f(x)$ *if and only if*

$$\langle \nabla f(x^*), x - x^* \rangle \leq 0, \forall x \in X.$$

This result can be obviously obtained from Lemma 1, thus the proof is omitted here.

Remark 4. N-team non-cooperative game is called a concave one, if $\forall j \in m_i, i \in N$, payoff function f^i satisfies assumption (2). Reference [19] has proved that there is a special equivalence relationship between Nash equilibrium of non cooperative concave game and Brouwer fixed point theorem, as well as the solution of variational inequality. Moreover, the solution of variational inequality can be transformed into a dynamic system equilibrium point problem, which provides a solution for the neural network algorithm of Nash equilibrium.

Remark 5. In [8,9], and [17,18], the used opposite payoff functions can be regarded as special case of this paper. Thus the considered opposite payoff functions in this paper are more general.

Theorem 1. $\forall j \in m_i, i \in \mathbb{N}$, strategy set $X_j^i \in R^{m_i}$ satisfying assumption (1); payoff function $f^i : X \to R$ satisfying assumption (2); then, $x_* = (x_*^1, x_*^2, \cdots, x_*^n) \in X$ is a noninferior Nash strategies of N-team continuous static multi-team concave game if and only if x_* satisfies

$$\langle \nabla f(x_*), x - x_* \rangle \leq 0, \forall x \in X,$$

where

$$\nabla f(x_*) = (\nabla_{x_*^1} f^1, \nabla_{x_*^2} f^2, \nabla_{x_*^n} f^n) \in R^m, m = \sum_{i=1}^{n} m_{m^i}.$$

$$m_{m^l} = \sum_{k=1}^{m^l} m_k^l, l \in \mathbb{N}.$$

Proof: $\forall i \in \mathbb{N}, \forall x^i \in X^i$, Set $\bar{x} = (x^i, x_*^{\hat{i}})$, then $\bar{x} \in X$, since $\forall x \in X, \langle \nabla f(x_*), x - x_* \rangle \leq 0$, from Lemma 2, we have $f^i(x_*^i, x_*^{\hat{i}}) = \max\limits_{u^i \in X^i} f^i(u^i, x_*^{\hat{i}})$. Thus, $x_* = (x_*^1, x_*^2, \cdots, x_*^n) \in X$ is a noninferior Nash strategies of N-team concave game.

Conversely, if $x_* = (x_*^1, x_*^2, \cdots, x_*^n) \in X$ is a noninferior Nash strategies of N-team concave game, then $\forall i \in \mathbb{N}, f^i(x_*^i, x_*^{\hat{i}}) = \max\limits_{u^i \in X^i} f^i(u^i, x_*^{\hat{i}})$, from Lemma 2, $\forall x \in X, \langle \nabla f(x_*), x - x_* \rangle \leq 0$. This completes the proof.

Remark 6. It is difficult to calculate the NNEs of N-team continuous static multi-team game directly, especially when there are many players in the game. However, the conclusion of Theorem 1 provides an indirect calculation method of NNEs. The approximate calculation of NNEs can be realized by solving a special variational inequality.

4 Neural Network Model for Multi-team Non-cooperative Concave Game

4.1 Neural Network Model Construction

To give out neural network algorithm for above N-team non-cooperative concave game, an important lemma is needed

Lemma 3. For arbitrary $\alpha > 0$, x_* is a fixed point of equation $x = P_\Omega(x - \alpha f(x))$, if and only if it satisfies $\langle f(x_*), x - x_* \rangle \geq 0$ for all $x \in R^n$, where $f : R^n \to R^n$ is continuous on R^n, Ω is a subset of R^n, $P_\Omega(x - \alpha f(x))$ is a conventional projection operator.

By Theorem 1 and Lemma 3, NNE's computation problem of N-team continuous static multi-team game can be further transformed into an equilibrium point's approximate calculation problem of the following neural network model.

$$\frac{dx(t)}{dt} = -x(t) + P_X(x(t) + \alpha \nabla f(x(t))), \tag{1}$$

where
$$P_X(y) = arg \min_{x \in X} \|y - x\|.$$

$\nabla f(x(t)) = (\nabla_{x^1(t)} f^1(x(t)), \nabla_{x^2(t)} f^2(x(t)), \cdots, \nabla_{x^n(t)} f^n(x(t))), X = \Pi_{i=1}^n X^i$,
$f^i : X \to R$ is the payoff function of the i-th team.

4.2 Equilibrium's Existence Analysis

From Theorem 1 and Lemma 3, through a series of equivalent changes, NNE x_* of a N-team multi-game is finally proved to be equivalent to the equilibrium point of a special neural network and the solution of a special variational inequality. Therefore, to give out the existence conditions of NNE and the equilibrium of neural network, we only need to research the solution's existence conditions of concerned variational inequalities.

Lemma 4. *[19] There exists at least one $x_* \in X$ such that*

$$\langle \beta(x_*), y - x_* \rangle \leq 0, \forall y \in X.$$

where $\beta(.)$ is continuous, and X is a subset of R^n satisfying nonempty bounded closed convex property.

From Lemma 4, and assumptions (1) and (2), the following follows existence theorem is obviously.

Theorem 2. *The neural network model (1) established in this paper has at least one equilibrium point.*

Proof: By assumption (1), $\forall j \in m_i, i \in \mathbb{N}$, strategy set $X_j^i \in R^{m_i}$ is nonempty, convex, and compact, thus X is a nonempty, convex, bounded, and closed set. By assumption (2), since $\forall j \in m_i, i \in \mathbb{N}$, payoff function $f^i : X \to R$ is continuously differentiable, thus $\nabla f(x)$ is continuous on X. From Lemma 4, variational inequality $\langle \nabla f(x_*), x - x_* \rangle \leq 0$ at least exists one solution x_*. Namely, The neural network model (1) established in this paper has at least one equilibrium point, which completes the proof.

Remark 7. If assumptions (1) and (2) hold, and $\forall x^i \in X^i, u^i \to f_j^i(u^i, x^{\hat{i}})$ is strong concave on X^i, similar to the proof in [13], the uniqueness property of the equilibrium point of system (1) can also be obtained.

4.3 Stability Analysis

let $y(t) = x(t) - x_*$, where x_* is a NNE of n-team multi-game, substitute $y(t)$ into system (1), through simple equivalent deformation operation, system (1) is rewritten as

$$\frac{dy(t)}{dt} = -y(t) + P_X(y(t) + x_* + \alpha \nabla f(y(t) + x_*))$$
$$- P_X(x_* + \alpha \nabla f(x_*)), t > 0. \tag{2}$$

Lemma 5. *[20] For arbitrary closed convex set $\Theta \subseteq R^n$, $\xi, \eta, x \in R^n$, $y \in \Theta$, projection operator satisfies*

$$\|P_\Theta(\xi) - P_\Theta(\eta)\| \leq \|\xi - \eta\|,$$

$$(x - P_\Theta(x))^T (P_\Theta(x) - y) \geq 0, x \in R^n, y \in \Theta,$$

where $\|\cdot\|$ denotes $L^2(R^n)$ norm.

Lemma 6. *[21] If $\forall x \in R^n$, $F(x) : R^n \to R^n$ is continuous, and there exist nonnegative functions $M(t), N(t)$ such that*

$$\|F(x)\| \leq M(t)\|x\| + N(t),$$

then the solution existence interval of $\dot{x}(t) = F(x)$ with initial value $x(t_0)$ is $[t_0, +\infty)$.

Lemma 7. *[22] Let function $V : R^n \to R$ be positive definite local Lipschitz normal satisfying*

$$\frac{dV(x(t))}{dt} \leq 0.$$

If there exists a constant $l > 0$ such that $L_l = \{x \in R^n | V(x) \leq l\}$ is bounded, then for every solution $x(t)$ of $\dot{x}(t) = F(x)$ with initial value x_0, when $t \to +\infty$, we have

$$dist(x(t), M) \to 0,$$

here M is the maximum invariant set of $\bar{Z}_V \cap L_l$,

$$\bar{Z}_V = \{x \in R^n | 0 = \dot{V}(x)\}.$$

By using Lemma 5 and Lemma 6, the solution's existence result for system (1) can be derived as follows

Theorem 3. *For pre given initial value $x(t_0)$, the solution's existence interval of system (1) is $[t_0, +\infty)$.*

Proof: Set $F(x(t)) = -x(t) + P_X(x(t) + \alpha \nabla f(x(t)))$. Notice that if $f(x(t))$ is a convex function, then $f(x(t))$ is local Lipschitz continuous with Lipschitz constant $L(t)$, namely, $\|\nabla f(x(t))\| \leq L(t)$. From assumptions (1)–(2), and Lemma 5, we have

$$
\begin{aligned}
\|F(x(t))\| &= \| - x(t) + P_X(x(t) + \alpha \nabla f(x(t)))\| \\
&\leq \|P_X(x(t) + \alpha \nabla f(x(t))) - P_X(x(t))\| \\
&\quad + \|P_X(x(t)) - P_X(x_*)\| + \|P_X(x_*) - x(t)\|, \qquad (3) \\
&\leq \|\alpha \nabla f(x(t))\| + 2\|x(t)\| + \|x_*\| + \|P_X(x_*)\| \\
&\leq 2\|x(t)\| + \alpha L(t) + \|x_*\| + \|P_X(x_*)\|.
\end{aligned}
$$

From Lemma 6, it follows that, for pre given initial value $x(t_0)$, the solution's existence interval of system (1) is $[t_0, +\infty)$.

Using the proof method in reference [23], for system (1), the following invariant-set property can be obtained.

Theorem 4. *For any initial value $x_0 \in X$, the state vector $x(t)$ of system (1) is still in X, namely X is a invariant set of the solutions of system (1).*

Theorem 5. *Under hypothesis (1), (2), state vector $x(t)$ of neural network (1) with initial value $x(t_0) \in X$ converges to the NNE x_* of the multi-team noncooperative concave game asymptotically, if*

$$\langle \nabla_{y^i} f^i(y^i(t) + x_*^i, x_*^{\hat{i}}), \dot{y}^i(t) \rangle \leq \langle \nabla_{y^i} f^i(y^i(t) + x_*^i, x^{\hat{i}}(t)), \dot{y}^i(t) \rangle, i = 1, 2, \cdots, n,$$

where $y^i(t) + x_*^i = x^i(t)$.

Proof: From Theorem 4, since X is an invariable set, thus $\forall x(t_0) \in X$, $x(t) \in X$. Let x^* denote an equilibrium point of system (1), here $x^* \in X$. From Theorem 1 and Lemma 3, it follows that x^* is a NNE of multi-game. By the definition of non-inferior Nash equilibrium, it follows that $f^i(x_*^i, x_*^{\hat{i}}) = \max_{x^i(t) \in X^i} f^i(x^i(t), x_*^{\hat{i}})$. Using this relationship, a simple Lyapunov function can be constructed.

$$V(y(t)) = \alpha \sum_{i=1}^{n} [f^i(x_*^i, x_*^{\hat{i}}) - f^i(y^i(t) + x_*^i, x_*^{\hat{i}})], \tag{4}$$

where $y(t) + x_* = x(t) \in X$. It follows that $V(0) = 0$ and $V(y(t)) \geq 0$. By direct derivation operation, one can obtain

$$\dot{V}(y(t)) = \langle \nabla V(y(t)), \dot{y}(t) \rangle. \tag{5}$$

where

$$\nabla V(y(t)) = (-\alpha \nabla_{y^1} f^1(y^1(t) + x_*^1, x_*^{\hat{1}}), \cdots, -\alpha \nabla_{y^n} f^n(y^n(t) + x_*^n, x_*^{\hat{n}})).$$

Since

$$\langle \nabla_{y^i} f^i(y^i(t) + x_*^i, x_*^{\hat{i}}), \dot{y}^i(t) \rangle \leq \langle \nabla_{y^i} f^i(y^i(t) + x_*^i, x^{\hat{i}}(t)), \dot{y}^i(t) \rangle,$$

one can obtain that

$$\langle \nabla V(y(t)), \dot{y}(t) \rangle \leq \langle \nabla \overline{V}(y(t)), \dot{y}(t) \rangle,$$

where

$$\overline{V}(y(t)) = (-\alpha \nabla_{y^1} f^1(y^1(t) + x_*^1, x^{\hat{1}}(t)), \cdots, -\alpha \nabla_{y^n} f^n(y^n(t) + x_*^n, x^{\hat{n}}(t))).$$

This means that

$$\dot{V}(y(t)) = \langle \dot{y}(t), \nabla V(y(t)) \rangle \tag{6}$$
$$= \langle -\alpha\gamma, \psi \rangle,$$

where $\psi = -y(t) - x_* + P_X(y(t) + x_* + \alpha\gamma)$, $\gamma = \nabla f(y(t) + x_*)$. Denote $\omega = y(t) + x_* + \alpha\gamma$, notice that $x(t) = y(t) + x_*$, from (6), we have

$$\dot{V}(y(t)) = \langle \dot{y}(t), \nabla V(y(t)) \rangle$$
$$= \langle -\alpha\gamma, \psi \rangle$$
$$= \langle P_X(\omega) - x(t), -\omega + x(t), \rangle \tag{7}$$
$$\leq -\langle P_X(\omega) - x(t), \omega - P_X(\omega), \rangle$$
$$- \langle P_X(\omega) - x(t), P_X(\omega) - x(t) \rangle.$$

From Lemma 5, one can get $\dot{V}(y(t)) \leq 0$. Denote $L_l = \{y(t) \in R^n | V(y(t)) \leq l\}$, where $l = \max_{y(t)+x_* \in X} f(y(t) + x_*)$. Next, we will show that L_l is bounded. Denote $\gamma^* = \nabla f(x_*)$, by system (2), it follows that

$$y(t) = e^{-(t-t_0)} y(t_0) - \int_{t_0}^{t} e^{-(t-s)} [P_X(x^* + \alpha\gamma^*) \\ - P_X(y(s) + x^* + \alpha\nabla f(y(s) + x^*))] ds. \tag{8}$$

Then

$$\|y(t)\| \leq e^{-(t-t_0)} \|y(t_0)\|$$

$$+ \int_{t_0}^{t} e^{-(t-s)} \|P_X(x^* + \alpha\nabla f(x(s)))$$

$$- P_X(x(s) + \alpha\nabla f(x(s)))\| ds$$

$$+ \int_{t_0}^{t} e^{-(t-s)} \|P_X(x^* + \alpha\nabla f(x(s))) \tag{9}$$

$$- P_X(x^* + \alpha\gamma^*)\| ds$$

$$\leq e^{-(t-t_0)} \|y(t_0)\| + \alpha(L + \|\gamma^*\|)$$

$$+ \int_{t_0}^{t} e^{-(t-s)} \|y(s)\| ds.$$

where $L = \max_{x(t) \in X} \nabla f(x(t))$. Notice that $X \in R^m$ is an invariant set for arbitrary $x(t_0) \in X$, $\nabla f(x(t))$ is continuous on X, and $X \in R^m$ is convex and compact, thus L exists. By Gronwall-Bellman inequality, one can obtain

$$\|y(t)\| \leq e^{-(t-t_0)} \|y(t_0)\| e + e\alpha(L + \|\gamma^*\|) \\ \leq e[\|y(t_0)\| + \alpha(L + \|\gamma^*\|)]. \tag{10}$$

This means that L_l is bounded. Denote $M = \{x^*\}$, from Lemma 7, when $t \to +\infty$, it follows dist$(x(t), M) \to 0$, which complete the proof.

Remark 8. From Theorem 5, it follows that if the initial value $x(t_0)$ is in strategy set X, and $\langle \nabla_{y^i} f^i(y^i(t) + x_*^i, x_*^{\hat{i}}), \dot{y}^i(t) \rangle \leq \langle \nabla_{y^i} f^i(y^i(t) + x_*^i, x^{\hat{i}}(t)), \dot{y}^i(t) \rangle$, then the state vector of neural network (1) converges asymptotically to the equilibrium state. In order to get the convergence property and the convergence rate when $x(t_0)$ is not in X, we need more stronger condition for payoff function f.

Theorem 6. *Under assumptions (1) and (2), if there exists $\beta > 0$ such that $\|\nabla f(x(t)) - \nabla f(y(t))\| \leq \beta \|x(t) - y(t)\|$, then, the state vector $x(t)$ of system (1) with any initial value $x(t_0)$ exponentially globally converges to the Nash equilibrium point of system (1).*

Proof: If $\|\nabla f(x(t)) - \nabla f(y(t))\| \leq \beta\|x(t) - y(t)\|$, where constant $\beta > 0$, from (8), it follows that

$$
\begin{aligned}
\|y(t)\| &\leq e^{-(t-t_0)}\|y(t_0)\| \\
&+ \int_{t_0}^t e^{-(t-s)}\|P_X(x^* + \alpha\nabla f(x(s))) \\
&- P_X(x(s) + \alpha\nabla f(x(s)))\|ds \\
&+ \int_{t_0}^t e^{-(t-s)}\|P_X(x^* + \alpha\nabla f(x(s))) \\
&- P_X(x^* + \alpha\gamma^*)\|ds \\
&\leq e^{-(t-t_0)}\|y(t_0)\| \\
&+ \int_{t_0}^t e^{-(t-s)}\|P_X(x^* + \alpha\nabla f(x(s))) \\
&- P_X(x(s) + \alpha\nabla f(x(s)))\|ds \\
&+ \int_{t_0}^t e^{-(t-s)}\|P_X(x^* + \alpha\nabla f(x(s))) \\
&- P_X(x^* + \alpha\nabla f(x^*))\|ds \\
&\leq e^{-(t-t_0)}\|y(t_0)\| \\
&+ \int_{t_0}^t e^{-(t-s)}(1 + \alpha\beta)\|y(s)\|ds.
\end{aligned}
\tag{11}
$$

By Gronwall-Bellman inequality, one can obtain

$$
\|y(t)\| \leq e^{-(t-t_0)}\|y(t_0)\|e^{(1+\alpha\beta)} \tag{12}
$$

This means that, for any initial value $x(t_0)$, the state vector $x(t)$ of system (1) exponentially globally converges to the NNE. From (12), one can see the exponential convergence rate is equal to 1.

Remark 9. Since the stable state x_* of system (1) is equivalence to the NNE of mutil-team noncooperative concave game, thus Theorem 5 and Theorem 6 give out a neural network algorithm to approximatly calculate NNE of mutil-team game.

Remark 10. In [8–10], the payoff functions are all quadratic functions, obviously, any quadratic functions satisfy the constraint condition in Theorem 6, from Theorem 6, our neural network algorithm converges at the exponential convergence rate 1. Thus it is more advantageous that the methods used in [8–10].

5 Application of Multi-team Game in Flow Control of Parallel-Link Communication Networks

5.1 Model Analysis

Let $\mathbb{N} = \{1, 2, \cdots, n\}$ denote the set of team leaders. In each team, there exists several types of users. All users in the same team share a set $\mathbb{L} = \{1, 2, \cdots, L\}$ of communication links. And all users in the same team are connected to a common destination node and source node. If the capacity of communication link l is denoted by c_l, then $c = (c_1, c_2, \cdots, c_L)$ means the capacity configuration. Let M_N denote team leader $N \in \mathbb{N}$ who servers m_N users. We assume that the ith user's throughput demand in team N is a typical Poisson process, and the average rate is denoted as $x_i^N = (x_{i,1}^N, x_{i,2}^N, \cdots, x_{i,L}^N)$, where $x_{i,l}^N, l \in \mathbb{L}$ denotes average rate of the ith user in team N across link l. Namely, x_i^N is the strategy of the ith user in team N. Assumption the queuing model of the users' flow across every link l is $M/M/1$, $u_i^N(X)$ demote the utility function of the ith user in team N, similar to the analysis in [24], $u_i^N(X)$ can be defined as

$$u_i^N(X) = \alpha_i^N \sum_{l \in \mathbb{L}} \log(x_{i,l}^N + 1) - \beta_i^N \sum_{l \in \mathbb{L}} \frac{1}{c_l - \overline{x}_l}, N \in \mathbb{N},$$

$$\overline{x}_l = \sum_{i \in \mathbb{N}} \sum_{j \in M} x_{j,l}^i, M = \{1, 2, \cdots, \sum_{k=1}^N m_k\},$$

where $\alpha_i^N (0 < \alpha_i^N < 1)$ is sensitive parameter of the ith user in team N to the flow average rate. $\sum_{l \in \mathbb{L}} \log(x_{i,l}^N + 1)$ denotes link cumulative gain of the ith user in team N with strategy x_i^N. $0 < \beta_i^N < 1$ is sensitive parameter of the ith user in team N to the network delay, $\sum_{l \in \mathbb{L}} \frac{1}{c_l - \overline{x}_l}$ denotes link cumulative delay of the ith user in team N with strategy x_i^N.

For the Nth-team, team utility function is defined as all users' utility convex combination in N^{th}-team

$$f^N(X) = \sum_{j=1}^{m_N} \lambda_j^N u_j^N(X), \forall N \in \mathbb{N},$$

where $0 \leq \lambda_j^N \leq 1, \sum_{j=1}^{m_N} \lambda_j^N = 1$. The aim of every user in the same team is to select their flow average rate strategies such that the team utility to reach the maximum which they are belonged to. Obviously, this problem is a typical multi-team game model, and the noninferior Nash equilibrium strategy is $x_* = (x_*^1, x_*^2, \cdots, x_*^n) \in X$ satisfying

$$f^N(x_*^N, x_*^{\hat{N}}) = \max_{y^N \in X^N} \sum_{j=1}^{m_N} \lambda_j^N u_j^N(y^N, x_*^{\hat{N}}), \forall N \in \mathbb{N}.$$

The topological structure of parallel-link communication networks with multi-team is shown in Fig. 1.

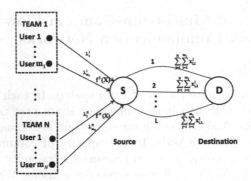

Fig. 1. The topological structure of parallel-link communication networks with multi-teams.

Theorem 7. $\forall j \in m_N, N \in \mathbb{N}, \forall x_{\hat{i}}^{\hat{N}} \in X_{\hat{i}}^{\hat{N}}, x_i^N \to f^N(x_i^N, x_{\hat{i}}^{\hat{N}})$ *is concave on* X_i^N, *and* f^N *is continuously and differentiable.*

Proof. Since $\forall x_{i,l}^N, \frac{\partial^2 f^N(X)}{\partial (x_{i,l}^N)^2} = -\frac{\lambda_i^N \alpha_i^N}{(x_{i,l}^N+1)^2} - \sum_{i=1}^{m_N} \frac{2\lambda_i^N \beta_i^N}{(c_l - \overline{x}_l)^3}$, notice that $0 \le \lambda_j^N \le 1, \sum_{j=1}^{m_N} \lambda_j^N = 1, 0 < \alpha_i^N < 1, 0 < \alpha_i^N < 1$, thus, $\forall x_{i,l}^N, \frac{\partial^2 f^N(X)}{\partial (x_{i,l}^N)^2} < 0$, which means that $f^N : X \to R$ is continuously differentiable, and $\forall x_{\hat{i}}^{\hat{N}} \in X_{\hat{i}}^{\hat{N}}, x_i^N \to f^N(x_i^N, x_{\hat{i}}^{\hat{N}})$ is concave on X_i^N. This completes the proof.

Remark 11. Since the ith user's average rate $x_{i,l}^N$ in team N across link l is not exceed the minimum capacity configuration $\min\{c_l, l \in \mathbb{L}\}$ of all links. Thus, X is a convex compact set. By Theorem 7, one can get that flow control of parallel-link communication networks based on multi-team game is a typical concave game, which means that there exists at least one NNE of this multi-team game.

By Theorem 1 and Lemma 3, following neural network model can be constructed to numerically calculate the NNE of our concerned multi-team concave game.

$$\frac{dx(t)}{dt} = -x(t) + P_X(x(t) + \alpha \nabla f(x(t))), \qquad (13)$$

5.2   Numerical Simulation

In this subsection, a simulation example will be given to illustrate the validity of neural network algorithm derived in subsection A of Sect. 5. For the convenience of simulation, suppose there are two team leaders, each team leader includes two user, they all share two communication links. The topological structure of communication network with $N = 2, m^N = 2, L = 2$ is shown in Fig. 2. Let $\lambda_j^N = 0.5, j, N = 1, 2; \alpha_i^N = 0.6; \beta_i^N = 0.1, i, N = 1, 2; c_1 = 5, c_2 = 9$. In this case, since $0 \le x_{i,l}^N \le \min\{c_l, l \in \mathbb{L}\}$, it yields that $0 \le x_{i,l}^N \le 5$. Denote $\alpha > 0$

to be an arbitrary positive constant, from (13), by simple calculation, it follows that $x(t) = (x_{1,1}^1, x_{1,2}^1, x_{2,1}^1, x_{2,2}^1, x_{1,1}^2, x_{1,2}^2, x_{2,1}^2, x_{2,2}^2)$,

$$\nabla_{x_{i,l}^1} f^1(x(t)) = \frac{1}{2}\sum_{i=1}^{2}[\sum_{l=1}^{2}\frac{3}{5(x_{i,l}^1 + 1)} - \sum_{l=1}^{2}\frac{1}{10(5 - \overline{x}_l)^2}],$$

$$\nabla_{x_{i,l}^2} f^2(x(t)) = \frac{1}{2}\sum_{i=1}^{2}[\sum_{l=1}^{2}\frac{3}{5(x_{i,l}^2 + 1)} - \sum_{l=1}^{2}\frac{1}{10(9 - \overline{x}_l)^2}],$$

$$P_X(x_{i,l}^N) = \frac{|x_{i,l}^N| + |x_{i,l}^N - 5|}{2} + \frac{5}{2}, i, j, n = 1, 2.$$

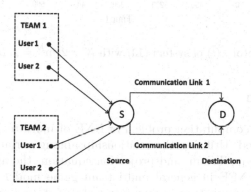

Fig. 2. The topological structure of parallel-link communication network with $N = 2, m^N = 2, L = 2$.

Utilizing MATLAB Simulink tool box, when $\alpha = 0.01, N = 2, m^N = 2, L = 2$, the simulation result with initial value $x(t) = (0.5, 1.6, 1.4, 2.3, 1.8, 0.9, 3.2, 2.7)$ for system (13) is shown in Fig. 3. From Fig. 3, one can see that the state vector of system (13) is asymptotically convergent to NNE x^*. From the result obtained in Theorem 5, this equilibrium point x^* is just a noninferior Nash equilibrium point of the multi-team noncooperative concave game.

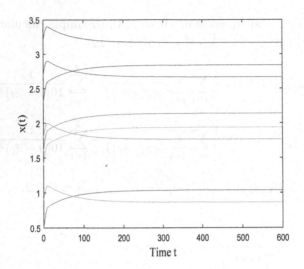

Fig. 3. State vector $x(t)$ of system (13) with $N = 2, m^N = 2, L = 2, \alpha = 0.01$.

6   Conclusion

In this paper, the computation problem of NNE of multi-team noncooperative game is investigated. Utilizing the relationship among variational inequalities, noninferior Nash equilibrium, and projection equation, the approximate calculation problem of NEE in general multi team game model with smooth and concave payoff function is transformed into a stable state numerical calculation problem by using projection neural network method. Finally, as an application, a flow control model of parallel-link communication networks based on multi-team game and neural network algorithm is also given. Simulation result shows that neural network algorithm for solving noninferior Nash equilibrium of multi-team noncooperative concave game is valid. In most cases, the payoff functions of communication network only satisfy concave condition, they are frequently nonsmooth. Thus, neural network algorithm for solving noninferior Nash equilibrium of multi-team with nonsmooth payoff functions is worth researching, and this will be our further work.

References

1. Myerson, R.B.: Game Theory: Analysis of Conflict. Harvard University Press, London (1991)
2. Aubin, J.P.: Mathematical methods of game and economic theory. Stud. Math. Appl. **235**(1), 19–30 (2007)
3. Glötzl, E.: Continuous time, continuous decision space prisoner's dilemma- a bridge between game theory and economic GCD-models. MPRA Paper (2016)
4. Morrow, J.D.: Game Theory for Political Scientists. Princeton University Press, New Jersey (1994)

5. Shoham, Y.: Computer science and game theory. Commun. ACM **51**(8), 74–79 (2008)
6. Abramsky, S., Mavronicolas, M.: Game theory meets theoretical computer science. Theoret. Comput. Sci. **343**(1–2), 1–3 (2005)
7. Salem, A.A., et al.: Profit of price with supermodular game for spectrum sharing in cognitive radio using genetic algorithm. Wireless Pers. Commun. **82**(4), 2601–2609 (2015)
8. Liu, Y., Simaan, M.: Noninferior Nash strategies for multi-team systems. J. Optim. Theory Appl. **120**(1), 29–51 (2004)
9. Liu, Y., Simaan, M.: Non-inferior Nash strategies for routing control in parallel-link communication networks. Int. J. Commun Syst **18**(4), 347–361 (2005)
10. Ahmed, E., et al.: On multi-team games. Physica A Stat. Mech. Appl. **369**(2), 809–816 (2006)
11. Yu, J.: Game Theory and Nonlinear Analysis Ekthesis. Science Press, Beijing (2011)
12. Yu, J.: Slightly altruistic equilibria of N-Person non-cooperative games. J. Syst. Sci. Math. Sci. **31**(5), 534–539 (2011)
13. Yu, J., Wang, N.-F., Yang, Z.: Equivalence results between Nash equilibrium theorem and some fixed point theorems. Fixed Point Theory Appl. **2016**(1), 1–10 (2016). https://doi.org/10.1186/s13663-016-0562-z
14. He, B.S., Yuan, X.M.: Convergence analysis of primal-dual algorithms for a saddle-point problem: from contraction perspective. SIAM J. Imag. Sci. **5**, 119–149 (2012)
15. Liu, Z.X., Wang, N.F.: Neural network to solve concave games. Int. J. Comput. Games Technol. **2014**, 1–10 (2014)
16. Herings, P.J.J., van den Elzen, A.: Computation of the Nash equilibrium selected by the tracing procedure in-person games. Games Econ. Behav. **38**(1), 89–117 (1998)
17. Askar, S.S., et al.: Dynamic Cournot duopoly games with nonlinear demand function. Appl. Math. Comput. **259**, 427–437 (2015)
18. Askar, S.S.: Complex dynamic properties of Cournot duopoly games with convex and log-concave demand function. Oper. Res. Lett. **42**(1), 85–90 (2014)
19. Yu, J.: Game Theory and Nonlinear Analysis. Science Press, Beijing (2008)
20. Li, J.H., Michel, A.N., Porod, W.: Analysis and synthesis of a class of neural networks Linear systems operating on a closed hypercube. IEEE Trans. Circ. Syst. **36**, 1405–1422 (1989)
21. Naito, T., et al.: Differential Equations with Time Lag-Introduction to Functional Differential Equations. Makino Shoten, Tokyo (2002)
22. Liao, X.X.: Theory Methods and Application of Stability. Huazhong University of Science and Technology Press, Wuhan (2005)
23. Liu, Q.S., Wang, J.: A projection neural network for constrained quadratic Minimax optimization. IEEE Trans. Neural Netw. Learn. Syst. **26**(11), 2891–2900 (2015)
24. Feng, H.B., et al.: Wireless Ad hoc network flow control model based on non-coopertative game theory. J. Electron. Inf. Technol. **31**(44), 925–928 (2009)

Workload Evaluation Tool for Metadata Distribution Method

Éloïse Billa[1,2]([✉]), Philippe Deniel[1], and Soraya Zertal[2]

[1] CEA/DAM, Arpajon, France
[2] Li-PaRAD, UVSQ, Paris Saclay, France

Abstract. In the *High Performance Computing* field (HPC), metadata server cluster is a critical aspect of a storage system performance and with object storage growth, systems must now be able to distribute metadata across servers thanks to distributed metadata servers. Storage systems reach better performances if the workload remains balanced over time. Indeed, an unbalanced distribution can lead to frequent requests to a subset of servers while other servers are completely idle. To avoid this issue, different metadata distribution methods exist and each one has its best use cases. Moreover, each system has different usages and different workloads, which means that one distribution method could fit to a specific kind of storage system and not to another one. To this end, we propose a tool to evaluate metadata distribution methods with different workloads. In this paper, we describe this tool and we use it to compare state-of-the-art methods and one method we developed. We also show how outputs generated by our tool enable us to deduce distribution weakness and chose the most adapted method.

Keywords: Metadata distribution · Load-balancing · Evaluation tool

1 Introduction

To reach the highest accuracy as possible, scientific applications and numerical simulations continuously look for more resources. It means huge data storage capacities since a high level of accuracy is mainly achieved by resolving more and more complex models. Dealing with larger datasets induce to get better computation units in order to run simulation codes in a human-admissible time. The High Performance Computing (HPC) field is permanently evolving to provide larger supercomputers and having a better computation power. As data sets rapidly grow in volume, the need for an efficient storage system becomes critical. Indeed, the well-known File System paradigm is not expected to handle the number of access requests related to massive data incoming in a near future [1]. This scalability limitation is due to the hierarchical organization of files in POSIX norms [2]. Hence, clusters need storage systems based on structures that are independent of POSIX norms and provide a higher level of parallelism. Object storage systems [3] have emerged in response to these issues. They distinguish

© ICST Institute for Computer Sciences, Social Informatics and Telecommunications Engineering 2021
Published by Springer Nature Switzerland AG 2021. All Rights Reserved
H. Song and D. Jiang (Eds.): SIMUtools 2020, LNICST 369, pp. 796–810, 2021.
https://doi.org/10.1007/978-3-030-72792-5_63

data flows from metadata flows, enabling parallel access and higher throughput. To reach another step in the requests parallelization, they also detach themselves from the hierarchical tree constraints by using a flat namespace to store data and metadata.

This kind of storage opens new opportunities to scalability challenges such as a highly distributed metadata service. A distributed and dedicated metadata service represents an important factor in the performance of a storage system [4] and the ability to manage distributed metadata is an arduous point to solve [5]. Managing several metadata servers (MDS) induces to know which is the server to ask for any metadata. For this purpose, the metadata namespace is split and distributed across all metadata servers using a namespace distribution method.

In this paper, we focus on the evaluation of those distribution methods. Each metadata distribution method has weaknesses and strengths and is adapted to different request flows. In the same manner, each storage system has its own requests flow depending on the system usage. A distribution method could be adapted to a particular storage system while being unable to cope with another system's workload. Finding the metadata distribution method which fits with a specific storage system workflow is not easy: It is necessary to evaluate the method with the system workload before choosing it.

Main Contribution: In order to choose a method adapted to a particular workflow, we provide a tool to evaluate metadata distribution methods and to test their robustness with representative HPC application traces. This tool provides a unified context of evaluation for all methods and allows to analyse and compare their behavior on different workflows. We propose also the implementation of three distribution methods to show the comparison process.

The structure of the paper is the following: In Sect. 2, we discuss current state-of-the-art and related works. Section 3 introduces the tool we developed and Sect. 4 presents the environment we have used to evaluate distribution methods. Using this ecosystem, Sect. 5 describes the evaluated methods. Section 6 compares them and presents the outputs our tool generates. Finally, we conclude in Sect. 7.

2 Related Work

Distributing metadata across all metadata servers in an efficient way is mandatory to make the global system scalable and efficient [4]. Indeed, distributing the metadata namespace to the MDS set in an unsuitable manner generates hot spots. In practice, these hot spots will be massively accessed and servers in charge of them will be overloaded, causing bottlenecks and slowing down the whole system. Well known metadata distribution methods are proposed such as the Dynamic Subtree Partitionning [6], hashing techniques used in Dynamo [7] or DROP [8] or table-based methods as the Dynamic Hashing method [9] or in Someta system [10].

Each new proposed method induces performance evaluation and usually comparisons with previous distribution methods. Benchmarking tools such as

MDtest [11] or *PostMark* [12] enables to evaluate performance for File Systems operations. They are used if the method is POSIX compliant as for Xing et al. in their adaptive method [13] and Yang et al. in PPMS [14], or for Tang et al. [10] which use *MDtest* to compare with Lustre File System [15]. However, lots of distribution methods are detached from POSIX norms and hence these tools are not suitable. Some tools exist for object storage systems, such as *COSBENCH* [16] and enable to evaluate overall system performance, but they do not specialize in metadata evaluation and could not provide a distribution specific analysis with for example a per-server workload.

The lack of specific comparison tools bring authors to implement their own method in their system and evaluate performance with a process they themselves design, as done in Landstore [17]. Each evaluated method has so its own metrics or measurements and does not follow one standard evaluation process. Then, to compare these methods to previous ones, most of the state-of-the-art authors choose to reimplement algorithms [6,18,19] to integrate them in their own evaluation process. Indeed, there are different parameters which affect evaluations such as workflow or number of servers, and to have a fair performance comparison, they have to reimplement state-of-the-art methods in the same system as the one which evaluates their own method. That means for each new method, previous ones had to be reimplemented to fit with their own evaluation processes, which is a real waste of time. Moreover, some reimplemented methods fit not well with the system in which they are integrated and adaptations are needed. It can generate performance variations with the original algorithm and so alters the comparison.

3   Framework

In order to fairly compare the different distribution methods, we decided to develop a complete framework that allows us to instrument and compare methods on many various ways. This framework allows us to run and evaluate distribution methods for various types of traces in the same context.

3.1   Architecture Overview

The distribution method choice depends on the storage system: each system has its particular workflow with different ratios of metadata creations/old metadata accesses or period of burst / period of low workload, or even different object naming policies. Similarly, every method has its main strengths and troublesome use cases. In order to select the namespace distribution method the most suitable for a particular workflow, it is mandatory to define an evaluation process based on practical experiments. We propose a framework to evaluate distribution policies on a same workload and so compare them on equal terms.

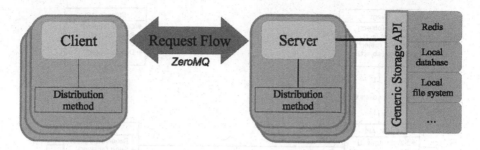

Fig. 1. Overview of framework architechture

Our framework allows to simulate a metadata service with a user-defined number of servers. It is a C-implemented project with 7000 lines of code in 80 files, which will be open-source [20]. An overview of the framework structure is shown on Fig. 1. There is a client-server interaction which is achieved through a *TCP* connection using the ZeroMQ library [21]. This interaction enables clients to establish requests to servers and servers to reply. The main specificity of our client-server interaction is the genericity: Each client and server have generic calls to the distribution method, allowing to switch methods without a whole reimplementation. The behavior of the distribution method on the client side is independent of the one on the server side. This allows us to mix the client behavior from one distribution policy and the server behavior of another one. The generic storage API we can see in Fig. 1 is another generic part of the proposed system which is associated with each server. This storage backend enables to easily adapt the framework to different storage systems.

3.2   Specific Features

We will now describe in more details some specific characteristics of our tool. To better understand these features, we should go deeper into the tool explanation. A more detailed view of the architecture is given in Fig. 2 with a class diagram.

Switching Namespace Distribution: Our tool allows to switch transparently the distribution method and to measure the impact of different policies on the server workload and the overall performances. The flexibility in the choice of the distribution method enables to highlight the hot spots in systems and to compare how different methods handle them. It is also possible to create new policies and to easily integrate them into our framework for evaluation.

As we can see in Fig. 2, there are two classes dedicated to the distribution method: the *Client Distribution* and the *Server Distribution*. The *Server Distribution* has an extra function named **end_epoch** which defines the behavior of the distribution when time is passing (this will be more detailled below). Both distributions have functions named **pre_send** and **post_receive**, which allows to perform distribution specific operations before sending the request (or the

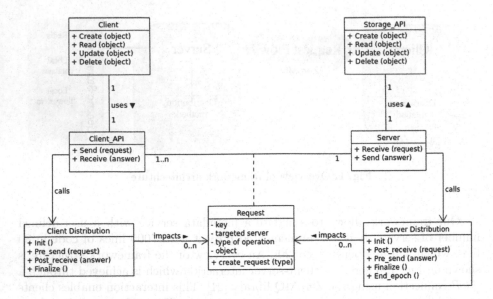

Fig. 2. Class diagram for the framework architechture

answer) and after receiving the answer (or the request). The complete request-ing process is the following:

1. *Client* class (which represents users which need to request metadata) gives information about the request to the *Client_API*. As all our requests follow the CRUD semantic [22], *Client* only needs to provide the requested metadata key and the operation to execute.
2. The *Client_API* creates an object of type *Request* and ask to the *Client Distribution* class for filling in the targeted server field, i.e. to compute the distribution method algorithm to find the server to request.
3. Before sending the *Request*, the *Client Distribution* can add information that is specific to the distribution method using the **pre_send** function.
4. Once the *Server* class receives the *Request*, it calls the **post_receive** function in the *Server Distribution* class to check distribution specific information. For example, it could check if the client cache is up-to-date and if it asks for the real server in charge of the metadata.
5. The *Server* executes the operation using the *Storage_API*.
6. Before sending the answer to the client, the *Server Distribution* is allowed to add other distribution specific information. For example, it could inform the client that the distribution has changed and it is no longer in charge of this metadata.
7. The *Client_API* receives the answer and the *Client Distribution* collects dis-tribution specific information provided by the server distribution with the **post_receive** function
8. *Client_API* returns an acknowledgment for the request execution to the *Client* class.

Federating Storage Devices: The Storage-API, shown in Fig. 2, could be connected to any storage media as long as it accepts CRUD semantic too. It enables to use our tool without taking care of the storage media type, but also to federate different media types such as magnetic tapes, databases or local file systems in the same storage system. We can for example have a heterogenous system with some servers linked to a local disk on POSIX [2] and others accessing to a *REDIS* cloud [23]. The API is a wrapper for access functions of each type of media linked to the server.

Input Traces: Our simulator framework accepts different input traces in a simple format: all operations are gathered in a CSV formatted file following the {*timestamp, operation, key, jobid*} pattern. A simple format enables for each user to artificially create workflow that is characteristic of the targeted storage system. If user has no input traces available, one default trace is proposed. It is a real trace extracted from 24h of a supercalculator (further explanation in Subsect. 4.2). Our framework also provides an embedded tool to generate traces representative of a particular workflow depending on user-defined parameters. Synthetic workflow used in the evaluation part (again, see Subsect. 4.2) is generated using this feature.

Controlling Time Passing: We designed a simulation process which controls and simulates time passing in order to run the operations of a trace in an accelerate fashion. Compressing a run and playing it in a limited time enables to limit potential failures during the execution. As our workload measures are not impacted by time, our simulator can play operations in an accelerated mode without any care. Moreover, our time control process ensures load metrics reproducibility: For one distribution method and one particular trace file, each run of these traces will provide same load values. It allows us to avoid noise in load comparison of two distribution methods.

To control time passing, we use a configurable time step mechanism: we play operations of a time step in concurrency and we take measures at the end of the step. It is possible to configure time steps small enough to run the traces in real time: a small time step enables to consider that operations are executed at the timestamp, allowing to measure other metrics influenced by time compression. A small time step takes more time and increase failures probabilities during the run whereas a big time step enables a faster run but could induce approximations.

In the first step of our simulation process, we split the trace file according to the time step. For each step, we spread requests across a user-defined number of clients and then each client executes its operation list concurrently. Once all clients finished, we take measurements for each server, and then we let the distribution method the possibility to make time-depending actions with the end-epoch function. Some distribution methods could have periodic checks or rebalancing processes. After this action, we can finally process the next step.

3.3   Metrics and Outputs

We choose as a principal metric of comparison the load of each server: each 5 min, we measure the number of requests received by each server and compute the percentage of load of each server at each step. We also recorded various information during the run such as information which belongs to the distribution method. At the end of the run of traces, the framework generates gnuplot curves such as the display of the received requests over time for the whole metadata service or per server. It also provides per server workload evolution in percentages and some statistics such as the maximum and the average distance between the load on a server and the ideal load it should receive.

4   Evaluation Environnement

4.1   Test Environnement and Experimentals Assumptions

All our tests have been conducted on a cluster composed of Intel Xeon Platinium 8167 processors and 187 GB memory. Nodes are interconnected by Infiniband EDR. Each server and client process runs on independent virtual machines coordinated by a VM-manager named *PCOCC* [24], which enables to host clusters of VMs on compute nodes, alongside regular job allocation. Each virtual machine in the cluster runs on 48 cores with *Centos 7.4* as operating system. Each test represents a new start of the system and storage disks are initially empty.

For evaluated dynamic methods, we assume the redistribution is immediate and does not influence the workload. We measure the load without taking the redistribution computation into account. The load evaluation of each server is negligible (4 arithmetic operations) and the redistribution algorithm needs few computations that can be neglected too. The most expensive part of the rebalancing stage corresponds to the metadata transfers. We choose to ignore this cost because our implementation is not optimized, and it is not the research purpose.

4.2   Workload Specification

To fairly compare methods, we have to evaluate them on different kinds of workloads. We choose on the first hand real traces, recorded on a cluster, that model typical HPC needs, and on the other hand, synthetic traces generated with our tool from a particular I/O pattern to challenge the methods.

Real Traces: We work with real traces extracted from a run of the industrial and academic supercalculator *Joliot Curie* [25]. With 1 656 *Skylake* nodes (Intel Xeon 8168 bi-processors nodes) and 828 *Knight Landing* nodes (many cores Intel Xeon Phi 7250 nodes), the supercalculator has a computational power of 9,4 Pflops. The dedicated storage system of 5 PB is a Lustre system with 2 MDS and 42 OST. Our traces reflect 24h of daily usage on this cluster and are representative of a wide set of HPC applications. Indeed, the usage of this cluster gathers different scientific fields including machine learning, chemistry, physics and climatology with well-known simulation code such as abinit, cp2k, gromacs or tensorflow. Initially, traces were recorded on the Lustre File System, then tree-specific operations (*mkdir, rmdir, unlink...*) have been adapted into object operations (*Create, Read, Update, Delete*). Figure 3 shows some requests extracted from the traces file.

```
1534555546.812093123,update,15,7
1534555546.812093123,delete,16,0
1534555546.812093124,update,13,1
1534555546.812093129,update,17,3
1534555546.812093131,create,18,4
```

Fig. 3. requests extracted from real traces

Synthetic Traces: The workload we generate follows the temporal pattern given in Fig. 4: on the first 15 min, it has a low level, which represents less than 50% that servers could handle. The workload intensifies linearly during 45 min to achieve a high level, which is 90% that servers could handle. It remains at the high level during 1 h. The number of accessed keys during the run is 10% of the total requests. To simulate a less favorable case, we artificially forced the repartition of the requests across servers in order to have one server overloaded in comparison with the others. The distribution across servers is computed with the initial distribution for the whole traces. So, we set the percentage distribution across our 4 servers at [70,10,10,10].

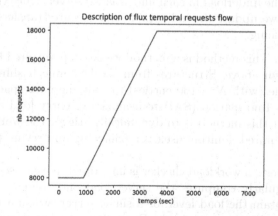

Fig. 4. Temporal request flow created for the metadata service in synthetic traces

5   Evaluated Methods

To have a base of comparison in our tool, we have implemented two state-of-the-art methods: the Static hashing method, which is a basic method and a dynamic version of hashing, to observe evolving behavior. The last described method is an adaptation of the Dynamic Hashing method [9].

Static Hashing: We implement the Static hashing method to distribute metadata across MDS. To know which server request, clients have to calculate hash modulo the number of available servers. To have a better balanced workload, we choose the Murmur3 hash function [26] because of the randomness of the distribution. The hash computation is performed by clients, so servers are fully engaged to process requests. Servers accept all the requests they receive as the spreading policy is done on the client side and the distribution does not change with time.

Dynamic Hashing: To assess the benefit of a dynamic distribution, we choose to implement a dynamic version of the already implemented hashing distribution. We implement a version of the Dynamic hashing first presented by Li et al. [9].

To distribute the namespace, metadata are first computed with a hash function (MurMur3 as said above), split between N entries of an index table (here we take $N = 100$) and each entry is spread across all the MDS. Every new client or server build an index table once and could then refer to the table for all the following requests. Periodically, a workload rebalancing algorithm named RElative LoAd Balancing (RELAB) is performed (we choose every hour). Between each rebalancing, servers compute for every entry a Synthetically Access Information (SAI), which are then summed to obtain the server load. With the complete set of workloads, the RELAB algorithm find a subset of entries from overloaded servers to fill in the underload in each underloaded server. Once these load transfers are defined, we update the index table and execute transfers to achieve the workload rebalancing.

Load-Adaptive: This method is a method we develop, inspired by the Dynamic hashing [9], shown above. Structures from the Dynamic hashing method such as the index table (with $N = 100$ entries) to split the namespace and the Synthetically Access Information (SAI) to evaluate an entry load are reused here. The main idea of this method is to dynamically trigger the workload rebalancing when it is required, limiting useless rebalancing and trying to better fit the overall workload.

For this purpose, a workload checker is integrated in every server. This workload checker regularly computes the server load and compare it to a critical threshold. To obtain the load level for a single server, we sum the SAI of each entry assigned to this server, as in the Dynamic hashing method. The threshold for rebalancing is initially set to 0 and is updated at each rebalancing, allowing to better fit to the current workflow. It is defined by the redistribution algorithm, and is the mean load each server should handle ideally with a margin of 15%. The margin is configurable and enables to rebalance in an aggressive way or not.

When a server reaches the load threshold, a rebalancing phase with a new redistribution algorithm inspired by the RELAB one [9] is requested. In this new algorithm, we try to spread overload across all underloaded servers. If the overload is too big, it is split before spreading. Once the index table is updated, we execute the transfers and the new ideal load threshold is also updated. Having a dynamic period to rebalance enables to have a system more tolerant to heavy workload changes, rebalancing the workload before a server become overloaded.

6 Evaluations and Outputs

We evaluate these three methods with our tool and we take as input the two workflows described in Subsect. 4.2: the real traces and the generated one. We present here outputs curves and an example of how we can analyse them. With real traces, loads are globally balanced with curves oscillating between 20 and 30 % for every method. With 4 servers, the ideal load value that every curve should approach is 25%. Even if it seems to be negligible, a tiny difference of load could lead to heavy imbalance of load if a high burst occurs.

Figure 5 shows the total workflow of requests over time with a measure each 5 min. This curve is about the metadata service in its entirety and not per server, that means it does not change depending on the distribution method: all methods are evaluated with this same request flow. This curve enables us to see the temporal profile of the input traces and see periods with few requests and other periods with high burst. It is easier to evaluate a method's behavior if we can know periods which could be problematic, i.e. periods of burst, or significative load changes.

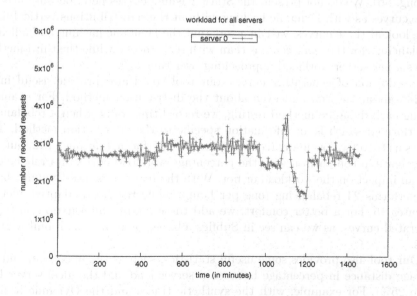

Fig. 5. Total number of requests received with real traces

In Fig. 6, we present how requests are distributed across the four servers with a percentage of received requests during 5 min, according respectively to the Static hashing (Subfig. 6a), the Dynamic hashing (Subfig. 6b) and the Load-adaptive method (Subfig. 6c). This enables us to spot imbalance period and see which server is in difficulty. We can use these curves in correlation with the first one, for example to see if a potential unbalanced period matches with a high requesting period, which highlight a big distribution method failing. In the current case, Subfig. 6a shows, during the first 450 min, an imbalance between all servers, while the workflow remain stable (in Fig. 5). This imbalance is fixed with the Dynamic hashing, as we can see in Subfig. 6b: after the first redistribution, illustrated by pink vertical lines, the percentages of workload of each server become nearer.

Again in the Fig. 6, we can see that from 450 min to 1000 min, a real imbalance happens: the server one (in yellow) is really more loaded than the three others. The metadata workflow during this time (in Fig. 5) is bigger than during the other periods, which means Dynamic hashing has difficulties to keep the workload balanced. Indeed, even if rebalancing are performed, the gap remains the same because of the RELAB algorithm: the server one overload could not fit in one idle server, hence there is no metadata transfer due to these redistributions. If we check how the third method behaves in Subfig. 6c, we can see that two rebalancing are performed around 500 min (again illustrated by pink vertical lines) and after these redistributions, the imbalance becomes significantly smaller, which means redistributions were effectives.

We also generate this kind of curves with the synthetic workload: Fig. 7 shows the requests workflows and Fig. 8 presents the percentage of loads per servers for the Dynamic hashing method (Subfig. 8a) and the Load-adaptive method (Subfig. 8b). We do not present the Static hashing curves here, because it is the same curves as with Dynamic hashing without the redistributions vertical lines. If we look at these curves, we can assert that the Dynamic hashing had failed its rebalancing (for the same reasons than with real traces), while the third method shows a per server workload approaching over time 25%.

In addition of generating curves, our tool could also provide useful information about the run and even about the distribution method. For example, during each dynamic method testing, we record time value when a rebalancing is performed which is an information specific to the distribution method. This allows us to know how many redistributions are performed during a run, but also to evaluate in comparison with the percentage workload curves if a rebalancing had an impact on the workload or not. With the real traces, the Dynamic hashing performs 24 rebalancing (one per hour), while the Load-adaptive method executes 15. For a better comfort, we add these kind of information on top of generated curves, as we can see in Subfigs. 6b, 6c, 8a and 8b with pink vertical lines.

Our tool also provides some useful statistics, such as the maximum and the average distance in percentage between a server load and the ideal server load (here 25%). For example, with the synthetic traces and the Dynamic hashing

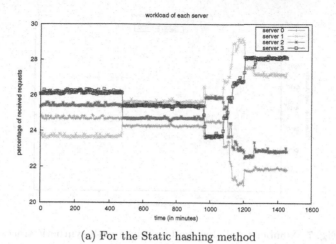

(a) For the Static hashing method

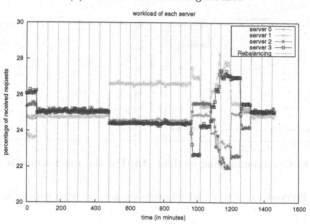

(b) For the Dynamic hashing method

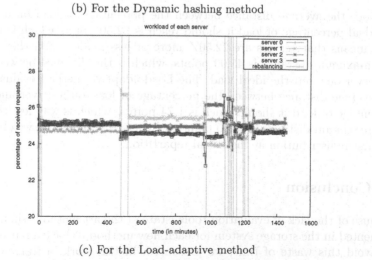

(c) For the Load-adaptive method

Fig. 6. Percentage of received requests by servers with real traces

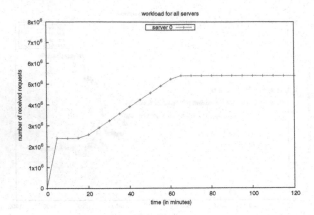

Fig. 7. Number total of requests received with synthetic traces

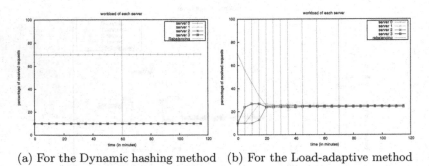

(a) For the Dynamic hashing method   (b) For the Load-adaptive method

Fig. 8. Percentage of received requests by servers with synthetic traces

method, the average distance between the percentage of load on a server and the ideal percentage of load it should reach is 22.50 points which is really high. This means that servers are 22.50% more or less loaded than they should be. The maximum distance is 45.00 points, which is the distance between the load on server one and the ideal load. The Load-adaptive method evaluation shows the average distance between the percentage of load on a server and the ideal percentage of load it should reach is 1.74 points, which is way less than before. The maximum distance is 45.00 points, which is the imbalance we obtain before the first redistribution at the initial repartition.

7   Conclusion

Because of the lack of evaluation tools, state of the art methods should be reimplemented in the storage system for each new method to have a fair comparison. To avoid this waste of time, we presented, in this work, a framework, which allows to evaluate and compare fairly various distribution methods on any kind of workflows. We proposed an evaluation by our tool of three distribution methods on two specific workflows: first with a real execution case and then with a synthetic unfavorable use case, generated by our tool. We have shown that curves and statistics generated by our tool enable to highlight imbalance points over time. We saw which server was overloaded in comparison of the others, or how many rebalancing was performed during the run. This kind of analyse allows to deduce which kind of workflows puts in trouble a distribution method and so which distribution method better fit to a storage system.

For now, our tool enables to measure workload metrics and highlight overloads due to metadata distribution method. It could be improved in different ways: first we plan to add more metrics to evaluate, as the response time of a request for a client or the cost in time of a redistribution. These metrics could help to better measure the impact of a distribution method which not fit to the workflow. Secondly, we could extend our model to simulate in a more realistic way a storage system: for example, we could add replication or fault tolerance protocols. This would allow us to evaluate distribution method behaviors more completely and even in other unfavorable use cases. Finally, it is also possible to adapt our tool to use it in other research field. The nearest example field is data distribution.

References

1. Raicu, I., Foster, I.T., Beckman, P.: Making a case for distributed file systems at exascale. In: Proceedings of the Third International Workshop on Large-Scale System and Application Performance (2011)
2. IEEE. IEEE 1003 - IEEE Standard for Information Technology - Portable Operating System Interface (POSIX(R)) (1988)
3. Mesnier, M., Ganger, G.R., Riedel, E.: Object-based storage. IEEE Commun. Mag. **41**(8), 84–90 (2003)
4. Meshram, V., Besseron, X., Ouyang, X., Rajachandrasekar, R., Darbha, R.P., Panda, D.K.: Can a decentralized metadata service layer benefit parallel filesystems? In: 2011 IEEE International Conference on Cluster Computing (2011)
5. Singh, H.J., Bawa, S.: Scalable metadata management techniques for ultra-large distributed storage systems-a systematic review. ACM Comput. Surv. (CSUR) **51**(4), 1–37 (2018)
6. Weil, S.J., Pollack, K.T., Brandt, S.A., Miller, E.L.: Dynamic metadata management for petabyte-scale file systems. In: Proceedings of the 2004 ACM/IEEE Conference on Supercomputing (2004)
7. DeCandia, G., et al.: Dynamo: amazon's highly available key-value store. ACM SIGOPS Oper. Syst. Rev. **41**(6), 205–220 (2007)
8. Xu, Q., Arumugam, R.V., Yong, K.L., Mahadevan, S.: Efficient and scalable metadata management in eb-scale file systems. IEEE Transactions on Parallel and Distributed Systems (2014)
9. Li, W., Xue, W., Shu, J., Zheng, W.: Dynamic hashing: adaptive metadata management for petabyte-scale file systems. In: 23rd IEEE/14th NASA Goddard Conference on Mass Storage System and Technologies (2006)

10. Tang, H., Byna, S., Dong, B., Liu, J., Koziol, Q.: Someta: scalable object-centric metadata management for high performance computing. In: Cluster Computing (CLUSTER), 2017 IEEE International Conference on (2017)
11. Morrone, C.J., Loewe, B., McLarty, T., Kroiss, R.: Hpc io benchmark repository (2011). https://github.com/hpc/ior
12. Katcher, J.: Postmark: a new file system benchmark. Technical report TR3022, Network Appliance (1997)
13. Xing, J., Xiong, J., Sun, N., Ma, J.: Adaptive and scalable metadata management to support a trillion files. In: Proceedings of the Conference on High Performance Computing Networking, Storage and Analysis (2009)
14. Yang, D., Wu, W., Li, Z., Yu, J., Li, Y.: PPMS: a peer to peer metadata management strategy for distributed file systems. In: Hsu, C.-H., Shi, X., Salapura, V. (eds.) NPC 2014. LNCS, vol. 8707, pp. 435–445. Springer, Heidelberg (2014). https://doi.org/10.1007/978-3-662-44917-2_36
15. Braam, P.: The lustre storage architecture. arXiv preprint arXiv:1903.01955 (2019)
16. Zheng, Q., Chen, H., Wang, Y., Duan, J., Huang, Z.: Cosbench: a benchmark tool for cloud object storage services. In: 2012 IEEE Fifth International Conference on Cloud Computing (2012)
17. Xue, W., Zhu, M.: Efficient dynamic management of distributed metadata. In: Zhu, R., Ma, Y. (eds.) Information Engineering and Applications. LNEE, vol. 154, pp. 354–362. Springer, London (2012). https://doi.org/10.1007/978-1-4471-2386-6_46
18. Xiong, J., Hu, Y., Li, G., Tang, R., Fan, Z.: Metadata distribution and consistency techniques for large-scalecluster file systems. IEEE Trans. Parallel Distrib. Syst. **22**(5), 803–816 (2010)
19. Wang, J., Feng, D., Wang, F., Lu, C.: MHS: a distributed metadata management strategy. J. Syst. Softw. **82**(12), 2004–2011 (2009)
20. Billa, B.: Medie: a metadata distribution evaluator for object storage systems (2020). https://github.com/Billae/MeDiE
21. Hintjens, P.: ZeroMQ, Messaging for Many Applications. O'Reilly Media, Sebastopol (2013)
22. Battle, R., Benson, E.: Bridging the semantic web and web 2.0 with representational state transfer (rest). J. Web Semant. **6**(1), 61–69 (2008)
23. Sanfilippo, S., Noordhuis, P., Stancliff, M.: Redis, an in-memory data structure store, used as a database, cache and message broker (2009). https://github.com/antirez/redis
24. Diakhate, F., Besnard, J.-B.: Pcocc: Run vms on an hpc cluster (2016). https://github.com/cea-hpc/pcocc
25. CEA. Inauguration of joliot-curie, the french supercomputer dedicated to french and european research (2019). http://www.cea.fr/english/Pages/News/Inauguration-of-Joliot-Curie,-the-French-supercomputer-dedicated-to-French-and-European-research.aspx
26. Scott, P.: C port of murmur3 hash (2011). https://github.com/PeterScott/murmur3

Understanding the Psychological Mechanisms of Impulse Buying in Live Streaming: A Shopping Motivations Perspective

Xiaolin Li[1], You Li[1(✉)], Jiali Cai[1], Yunzhong Cao[2], and Liangqiang Li[1]

[1] Business School, Sichuan Agricultural University, Chengdu 611830, China
[2] College of Architecture and Urban-Rural Planning, Sichuan Agricultural University, Chengdu 611830, China

Abstract. Live streaming is an effective tool to increase products sales, which has become a new social commerce. However, few studies have explored the psychological mechanisms of individuals' impulse buying, although live streaming has transformed behaviors of customers. In this study, ground on S-O-R paradigm and motivation theory, we developed a research model to explore how customers develop shopping motivations in live streaming shopping. The results from 318 actual customers in China showed that three situational factors: visibility, parasocial interaction, and social presence of others differently affect form utilitarian and hedonic motivation of consumers. The motivations of both utilitarian and hedonic drive customers' impulse buying decisions. Specifically, utilitarian motivation plays a less significant role in driving customers' purchase intention than hedonic motivation. In conclusion, these findings increase one's comprehension of customers' psychological mechanisms of impulse buying development in live streaming context and spread the range of motivation theory. The findings also supply perceptions to both sellers and platforms in developing strategies.

Keywords: Social commerce · Live streaming · Impulse buying · Parasocial interaction · S-O-R paradigm

1 Introduction

The emergence and development of live streaming have brought substantial transformations for both businesses and consumers' behaviors. The live streaming services are also incorporated into some popular social media platforms such as YouTube to draw more consumers' attention to get involved [1]. Further, some e-commerce websites including Amazon.com/live, Taobao.com provide live streaming services. Within the live streaming shopping, consumers can watch the product more realistically, and thus, live content possesses a high recreational value and stickiness [2]. An increasing number of consumers are immersed in live streaming shopping.

Under the background of big data era, artificial intelligence has gradually penetrated into all walks of life, especially in the field of new media. As an important direction

H. Song and D. Jiang (Eds.): SIMUtools 2020, LNICST 369, pp. 811–820, 2021.
https://doi.org/10.1007/978-3-030-72792-5_64

of simulation technology, virtual reality technology (VR) has been widely used in live streaming in recent years. High-tech VR live streaming enables the audience to enjoy a completely immersive live experience [3], which highlights the situational stimulation of live streaming. Mu Zhang (2019) pointed out that live streaming based on virtual simulation technology is widely used in social and commercial activities. As a theoretical guide of virtual simulation technology, motion-sensing interaction design can effectively improve users' sense of immersion and experience, so the author believed that it will become a new way of live streaming in the future [3]. Mengjuan Fan et al. (2016) proposed that virtual simulation technology provides a brand new display platform and communication channel for sports programs, and better excavates the commercial value of sports programs [4]. Virtual simulation technology can also be applied in the field of medical education, which can help doctors get rid of time and space constraints, learn surgery from the first perspective, and experience the feeling of being in the operating room in person [5]. In live streaming shopping, the application of virtual simulation technology has effectively improved the live streaming technical means, and better guides consumers to conduct live streaming shopping, thereby ultimately increasing the revenue of merchants' live streaming marketing.

Although the live streaming shopping is a new social commerce and has become more and more popular [6], especially in China, most studies focus on gifting behaviors, and only a few studies have inquired into how customers' purchase intention is influenced by live streaming. An understanding of consumers' motivations behind live streaming shopping is important for researchers and sellers. Therefore, this study inquires into the roles of situational factors to develop consumers' motivations. Specifically, we try to explore how to increase value of live streaming measured by visibility, parasocial interaction and social presence of others; then we investigate how the value of live streaming translates into two click motivations (hedonic motivation and utilitarian motivation), and then increase consumers' impulsive buying intentions on live streaming platforms. Our study provides vendors with significant practical enlightenments on how to understand and motivate consumers' shopping behavior in live streaming.

A number of researchers have employed the motivation theory to understand consumers' motivations by using different stimuli to watch their responses [7]. They found that both utilitarian and hedonic motivations have effects on people making behavior to a certain extent like shopping. Hedonic motivation and utilitarian motivation are two critical factors to drive impulse buying behavior [8]. This research extends motivation theory in the live streaming shopping and adopts utilitarian motivation and hedonic motivation as two motivational values to probe into consumers' behavior.

In this study, we use motivation theory and S-O-R paradigm to investigate consumers' impulse buying behavior. Specifically, we would like to answer two questions: (1) Do both utilitarian and hedonic motivations affect impulse buying when watching live streaming shopping? (2) Which factors that drive consumers to form motivations of utilitarian and hedonic respectively?

2   Literature Review

2.1   Live Streaming Shopping

Live streaming initially began as a social media for online video gaming individuals, but has diversified into other areas and has grown into a broader social commerce trend. With the rapid development and progress of science and technology, the form of live streaming has been constantly improved. The live streaming based on virtual simulation technology has gradually become a new development trend of live streaming in the future. Virtual simulation technology is based on computer technology, supplemented by other related science and technology, to generate a digital environment highly similar to the real environment, in which users can have a sense of reality and experience in person [4]. The application of virtual simulation technology has brought technical reform to live streaming, which has greatly improved the marketing effect of live streaming and induced more and more consumers to live streaming shopping. Although the sudden growth in live streaming shopping has driven online sellers and researchers to better understand and adapt to consumer purchase behavior, only a few researches have been reported on consumer purchase behavior.

2.2   Consumers' Motivations

Consumers can get information about products through watching live streaming, which is the first stage of information acquiring and motivations developing. Clicking the product page is the next stage to seek more information. We argue that some values created by live streaming motivate consumers' motivations to click through the product page and assure more about it. Therefore, we used utilitarian click (utilitarian motivation) and hedonic click (hedonic motivation) as motivation cues [9], which influence impulse buying.

2.3   The Stimulus-Organism-Response Paradigm

The S-O-R (stimulus-organism-response) paradigm is a feasible theoretical framework to explain consumers' behavior in online shopping [10]. Stimulus (situational factors) include the shopping environment, the products themselves and the people who shop with you. Organism state refers to an internal status of humans, which is represented by cognitive and emotional status. In this paper, we use utilitarian click and hedonic click, utilitarian and hedonic motivation respectively, as the organism factors, which is supported by some previous studies. Reaction refers to the response to individual's perceptions by some situational factors, such as purchase intention [11]. In this study, we focus on consumers' impulse buying in live streaming, so we just discuss purchase intention.

3   Theoretical Model and Hypotheses Development

In this paper, we began to investigate the drivers and development of consumers' motivations form from three dimensions: visibility, parasocial interaction, and social presence of others. We also subdivide the two types of motivations in the model to obtain an in-depth understanding of the role of live streaming value. We present the research model in Fig. 1.

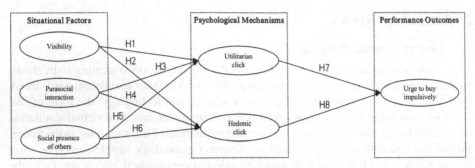

Fig. 1. Research model.

3.1 Visibility and Consumers' Click Motivation

In e-commerce, consumers are dependent mostly on product images or text descriptions to make purchase decision [12]. Unfortunately, there is a shortage of comprehensive understanding of the product itself which makes consumers hesitant to move to the next step in purchasing the product. In addition, consumers also cannot see the sellers, which also impacts on decision-making ability by the consumer. Visibility, and thus, interaction via online streaming shopping between user audience and online sellers can help decrease the uncertainty. The vividness can attract customers easyly [13], which is more likely to stimulate purchasing for consumers than traditional platforms. We hypothesize:

H1. Visibility has a positive impact on utilitarian click.
H2. Visibility has a positive impact on hedonic click.

3.2 Parasocial Interaction and Consumers' Click Motivation

Parasocial interaction refers to the relationship between a fan and a famous performer, which is a semblance of intimacy. This is a self-established relationship and others, especially the performer, may be unaware of this relationship and be influenced by them. Such a relationship and its features exist in live streaming platforms.

In live streaming, the interaction between the audience and a streamer can be exposed in a one-to-many or monodirectional mode, especially when attendance is in excess of a certain amount [14]. Therefore, this study tries to show interaction between viewers and streamers by using parasocial interaction. Parasocial interaction may exist on live streaming platforms [14]. If consumers establish an intimate illusory relationship with the streamers, they will be more willing to interact with the streamers and more likely to trust the streamers. Hence, we can hypothesize:

H3. Parasocial interaction has a positive impact on utilitarian click.
H4. Parasocial interaction has a positive impact on hedonic click.

3.3 Social Presence of Others and Consumers' Click Motivation

The presence of others directly influences user's arousal level [15]. Gefen and Straub (2004) suggest that perceived social presence has a mediating effect on consumers' purchase intention [16]. The presence of others can increase the likelihood of urge to buy impulsively. The presence of others can make online consumers feel more like in a real world. Hence, we suggest that the social presence of others will induce consumers to gain utilitarian or hedonic value through clicking the product page.

H5. Social presence of others has a positive impact on utilitarian click.
H6. Social presence of others has a positive impact on hedonic click.

3.4 Consumers' Click Motivation and Urge to Buy Impulsively

Many researchers adopted the S-O-R paradigm to study impulsive buying because it highlights the role of environmental cues [17]. Previous studies have found that hedonic motivation is a key determinant in the buying behavior [18]. When consumers explore a product page on a live streaming platform, regardless of whether there is any utilitarian or hedonic motivation, they can get more information about the products or services. This not only exposes the consumer to external stimuli, but also creates a positive influence, which are all additives factor forming "urge to buy impulsively" phenomenon [19]. Thus, we propose:

H7. Utilitarian click has a positive impact on the urge to buy impulsively.
H8. Hedonic click has a positive impact on the urge to buy impulsively.

4 Methodology

4.1 Scale Design

Visibility was measured according to Sun et al. (2019) [13]. Parasocial interaction was measured according to Hu et al. (2017) [14]. Social presence of others was measured according to Lu, Fan & Zhou (2016) [20]. Utilitarian click, hedonic click and urge to buy impulsively were measured according to Setyani et al. (2019) [21]. Instruments for all the constructs were adopted seven-point Likert scales, ranges from "1 = strongly disagree" to "7 = strongly agree".

4.2 Data Collection

An online survey was conducted by using sojump.com, which is a well-known survey website adopted in China. In total, 318 effective responses were gathered. We asked the respondents to complete the questionnaire according to their recent experience of watching live streaming shopping.

5 Data Analysis and Results

5.1 Measurement Model

Confirmatory Factor Analysis (CFA) is applied to inspect measurement model. Hair, Black, Babin & Anderson (2010) pointed out that using the indicators such as incremental fit index (IFI), goodness-of-fit index (GFI), adjusted goodness-of-fit index (AGFI), normed fit index (NFI), and relative fit index (RFI) to assess goodness-of-fit may change with sample size [22]. It was also suggested that researches use the relatively stable comparative fit index (CFI) and non-normed fit index (NNFI) to assess the model fit. The NNFI in this study was 0.954 and CFI was 0.960, which were both greater than 0.9, indicating that this study had good explanatory power. Chi-square ($\chi^{2)}$ test was also conducted to evaluate the goodness-of-fit. Root mean squared error of approximation (RMSEA) is applied to evaluate the divergence. RMSEA value of below 0.08 represents a good fit. In this study, $\chi^2 = 505.70$, $p < 0.01$, df $= 241$, $\chi^2/df = 2.098$, NNFI (TLI) $= 0.954$, IFI $= 0.960$, CFI $= 0.960$, RMSEA $= 0.059$, which point that the measurement model fits significantly well.

We also examined measurement model to look further into reliability, convergent validity, and discriminant validity. Dependability was accessed, and the values of all constructs' Cronbach's alpha and composite reliability transcend the recommended threshold 0.7 (see in Table 1). The factor loadings of all items exceed 0.7, showing adequate convergent validity. The item loadings on their allocation factors were greater than their cross-loading on other constructions, which shows well-pleasing discriminant validity. The square root of the AVE of each constructs was greater than its relationship with all other constructions (see in Table 2) showing sufficient discriminant validity.

5.2 Structural Model

The evaluation results of the structural model are shown in Fig. 2. The effects of the visibility on the utilitarian click ($\beta = 0.334$, $p < 0.001$) and on the hedonic click ($\beta = 0.198$, $p < 0.01$) were significant. Hence, H1 and H2 are supported. Parasocial interaction had an active impact on utilitarian click ($\beta = 0.283$, $p < 0.001$) and hedonic click ($\beta = 0.122$, $p < 0.05$). So H3 and H4 are supported. The Social presence of others was importantly associated with utilitarian click ($\beta = 0.296$, $p < 0.001$) and hedonic click ($\beta = 0.378$, $p < 0.001$), thereby supporting H5 and H6. Utilitarian click ($\beta = 0.279$, $p < 0.001$) and hedonic click ($\beta = 0.445$, $p < 0.001$) were discovered to be actively linked with urge to buy impulsively, which supported H7 and H8.

6 Discussion and Implications

6.1 Main Findings and Contributions

The results showed that the research model had powerful psychometric attributes and explicated most of the variances of consumers' urge to buy impulsively in live streaming context. This study have a few interesting findings.

Table 1. Construct reliability and validity.

Construct	Items	Factor loadings	CR	AVE	Cronbach's α	Mean	SD
Visibility(VI)	VI1	0.887	0.890	0.729	0.889	5.092	1.122
	VI2	0.825					
	VI3	0.846					
Parasocial interaction(PSI)	PSI1	0.833	0.891	0.732	0.887	3.940	1.360
	PSI2	0.936					
	PSI3	0.789					
Social presence of others(SPO)	SPO1	0.872	0.829	0.620	0.826	4.582	1.033
	SPO2	0.722					
	SPO3	0.756					
Utilitarian motivation(UM)	UM1	0.924	0.942	0.767	0.938	4.864	1.054
	UM2	0.945					
	UM3	0.905					
	UM4	0.894					
	UM5	0.682					
Hedonic motivation(HM)	HM1	0.809	0.940	0.757	0.939	4.610	1.038
	HM2	0.873					
	HM3	0.920					
	HM4	0.900					
	HM5	0.843					
Urge to buy impulsively(UB)	UB1	0.817	0.939	0.755	0.936	4.347	1.336
	UB2	0.884					
	UB3	0.908					
	UB4	0.926					
	UB5	0.790					

First, in this study, we support that hedonic motivation can promote impulsive buying. This indicates that most customers in live streaming are irrational. As shown in the results, utilitarian click impacts the impulsive buying. It's consistent with previous studies, which found utilitarian motivation can increase consumers' impulsive buying. Hedonic motivation is the pivotal driver of impulsive buying, but its role can be supplemented by utilitarian click.

Second, visibility significantly affects consumers' motivations in both utilitarian and hedonic dimensions. However, it influences utilitarian click more than hedonic click. Therefore, we assume that live streaming can reflect consumers' deeper needs, for example, consumers can get more information to know products like in the real world.

Table 2. Latent variable correlations.

	VI	PSI	SPO	UM	HM	UB
VI	**0.854**					
PSI	0.487	**0.855**				
SPO	0.529	0.517	**0.787**			
UM	0.682	0.720	0.617	**0.876**		
HM	0.470	0.452	0.508	0.591	**0.870**	
UB	0.436	0.504	0.557	0.661	0.716	**0.869**

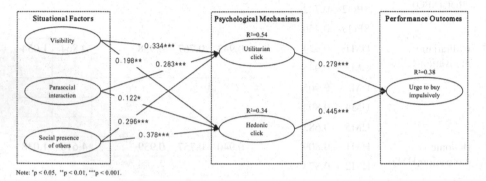

Note: *p < 0.05, **p < 0.01, ***p < 0.001.

Fig. 2. Structural model results.

Third, the social presence of others significantly affects customers' motivations in both utilitarian and hedonic dimensions, while its effects on hedonic click is powerful than that on utilitarian click. This is because the social presence of others is mainly related to other consumers' purchase behavior, interestes and sharings which can be presented on the screen.

6.2 Theoretical Implications

This research investigated impulse buying behavior in live streaming environment from consumers' psychological mechanism perspective. Based on S-O-R paradigm and motivation theory, we build a model to analyze the effect of motivations on consumers' impulse buying in live streaming.

First, this paper provides us with an integrated understanding of customers' impulse decision-making process surrounding live streaming shopping. The model reveals how situational factors influence customers' motivations, which in turn, promotes customers' impulse buying decision. The results provides a helpful framework for future studies in live streaming shopping. The results demonstrate that utilitarian click and hedonic click drive customers' impulse buying decisions.

Second, this research spreads the application range of motivation theory. It is appropriate to use utilitarian click and hedonic click to examine consumers' motivations in live streaming context because of its particular characteristics. Therefore, seen in this light, this study developed the motivation theory in live streaming.

Third, this research incorporates three main situational factors in live streaming and gives us an integrated understanding on customers' impulse purchase decision-making process. Few studies examined the influence of live streaming shopping on customers' impulse buying behavior. However, the existence of live streaming helps consumers to make impulsive decisions more easily. The results intensify our understanding of the impact of live shopping.

6.3 Practical Implications

There are some practical implications in this research. First, in order to triger customers' impulse buying decision, live streaming platforms should concentrate more on characteristics that trigger customers' hedonic, rather than utilitarian. Therefore, live streaming platforms should supply precise and thorough information to enhance users' watching experience.

Second, this study also supplies significances on how streamers stimulate consumers' shopping motivations. Watching live streaming is time-consuming compared to browsing static pictures on e-commerce websites. Therefore, in order to make consumers keep watching live streaming, streamers should reduce consumers' boredom and keep their engaged by entertaining activities (e.g., product demonstration) or incentives (e.g., promotion sale). These measures can bring some positive emotions for consumers and make it easier for them to form hedonic shopping motivation.

6.4 Limitations

This study also has some limitations. First, while the overall model explains the 38% of the variance in impulse buying, other relevant factors are not fully taken into account. Future research should consider a broader range of impulsive buying predictors. Second, this study merely focuses on exploring the influence of situational factors on customers' motivations and impulse buying behavior. Live streaming shopping is toujours a black box. Prospective study can investigate into the live streaming shopping patterns in detail and analyze which streamers' features influence customers' impulse buying behavior. Finally, this study only adopts the questionnaire survey method and the structural equation model for empirical analysis. The research method is relatively single, and future studies can combine the simulation technology to simulate the live streaming situation for more in-depth research.

References

1. Hilvert-Bruce, Z., Neill, J.T., Sj.blom, M., Hamari, J.: Social motivations of live-streaming viewer engagement on twitch. Comput. Hum. Behav. **84**, 58–67 (2018)
2. Zhou, F., Chen, L., Su, Q.: Understanding the impact of social distance on users broadcasting intention on live streaming platforms: a lens of the challenge-hindrance stress perspective. Telematics Inform. **41**, 46–54 (2019)

820   X. Li et al.

3. Zhang, Mu: Application of motion-sensing interaction design in new media live broadcast. Young J. **000**(014), 89–90 (2019)
4. Fan, M., Yan, Y., Zhong, Y.: Application of virtual reality technology in sports program production: opportunities and challenges. J. Wuhan Inst. Phys. Educ. **12**(5), 18–22, (2016)
5. Anonymous. Virtual reality operation live broadcast in Ruijin Hospital affiliated to Shanghai Jiao Tong university medical college. J. Shanghai Jiao Tong Univ. Med. Ed. **6**, 925 (2016)
6. Zhao, Q., Chen, C.-D., Cheng, H.-W., Wang, J.-L.: Determinants of live streamers continuance broadcasting intentions on twitch: a selfdetermination theory perspective. Telematics Inform. **35**, 406–420 (2018)
7. Lin, K.-Y., Lu, H.-P.: Why people use social networking sites: an empirical study integrating network externalities and motivation theory. Comput. Hum. Behav. **27**, 1152–1161 (2011)
8. Zheng, X., Men, J., Yang, F., Gong, X.: Understanding impulse buying in mobile commerce: an investigation into hedonic and utilitarian browsing. Int. J. Inf. Manage. **48**, 151–160 (2019)
9. Setyani, V., Zhu, Y.Q., Hidayanto, A.N., Sandhyaduhita, P.I., Hsiao, B.: Exploring the psychological mechanisms from personalized advertisements to urge to buy impulsively on social media. Int. J. Inf. Manage. **48**, 96–107 (2019)
10. Oh, J., Fiorito, S.S., Cho, H., Hofacker, C.F.: Effects of design factors on store image and expectation of merchandise quality in webbased stores. J. Retail. Consum. Serv. **15**, 237–249 (2008)
11. Hsin Chang, H., Wen Chen, S.: The impact of online store environment cues on purchase intention: trust and perceived risk as a mediator. Online Inf. Rev. **32**, 818–841 (2008)
12. Bai, Y., Yao, Z., Dou, Y.-F.: Effect of social commerce factors on user purchase behavior: an empirical investigation from renren. com. Int. J. Inf. Manage. **35**(5), 538–550 (2015)
13. Sun, Y., Shao, X., Li, X., Guo, Y., Nie, K.: How live streaming influences purchase intentions in social commerce: an it affordance perspective. Electron. Comm. Res. Appl. **37**, (2019)
14. Hu, M., Zhang, M., Wang, Y.: Why do audiences choose to keep watching on live video streaming platforms? an explanation of dual identification framework. Comput. Hum. Behav. **75**, 594–606 (2017)
15. Zhou, J., Zhou, J., Ding, Y., Wang, H.: The magic of danmaku: a social interaction perspective of gift sending on live streaming platforms. Electron. Comm. Res. Appl. **34**, (2019)
16. Gefen, D., Straub, D.W.: Consumer trust in b2c e-commerce and the importance of social presence: experiments in e-products and e-services. Omega **32**, 407–424 (2004)
17. Chan, T.K., Cheung, C.M., Lee, Z.W.: The state of online impulse-buying research: a literature analysis. Inf. Manage. **54**, 204–217 (2017)
18. Kukar-Kinney, M., Close, A.G.: The determinants of consumers online shopping cart abandonment. J. Acad. Mark. Sci. **38**, 240–250 (2010)
19. Huang, L.-T.: Flow and social capital theory in online impulse buying. J. Bus. Res. **69**, 2277–2283 (2016)
20. Lu, B., Fan, W., Zhou, M.: Social presence, trust, and social commerce purchase intention: an empirical research. Comput. Hum. Behav. **56**, 225–237 (2016)
21. Setyani, V., Zhu, Y.Q., Hidayanto, A.N., Sandhyaduhita, P.I., Hsiao, B.: Exploring the psychological mechanisms from personalized advertisements to urge to buy impulsively on social media. Int. J. Inf. Manage. **48**, 96–107 (2019)
22. Hair, J., Black, W., Babin, B., Anderson, R.: Multivariate data analysis 7th edth ed (2010)

Author Index